# I WAS BORN A SLAVE

**The Library of**
**Black America**

# *I Was Born a Slave*

## AN ANTHOLOGY OF CLASSIC SLAVE NARRATIVES

### VOLUME ONE
### 1770–1849

EDITED BY
## Yuval Taylor

FOREWORD BY
## Charles Johnson

Lawrence Hill Books

Library of Congress Cataloging-in-Publication Data

I was born a slave : an anthology of classic slave narratives / edited
  by Yuval Taylor ; foreword by Charles Johnson.
      p.      cm.
    Contents: v. 1. 1772–1849 — v. 2. 1849–1866.
    Includes bibliographical references.
    ISBN 1-55652-334-3 (cloth, v. 1) — ISBN 1-55652-335-1 (cloth, v. 2) —
  ISBN 1-55652-331-9 (paper, v. 1) — ISBN 1-55652-332-7 (paper, v. 2)
    1. Slaves—United States—Biography.   2. Afro-Americans—Biography.   3. Slaves'
  writings, American.   I. Taylor, Yuval.
  E444.I18   1999
  920'.009296073—dc21
[b]                                                                                                      98-42790
                                                                                                              CIP

In thinking of America, I sometimes find myself admiring her bright blue sky—her grand old woods—her fertile fields—her beautiful rivers—her mighty lakes, and star-crowned mountains. But my rapture is soon checked, my joy is soon turned to mourning. When I remember that all is cursed with the infernal spirit of slaveholding, robbery and wrong,—when I remember that with the waters of her noblest rivers, the tears of my brethren are borne to the ocean, disregarded and forgotten, and that her most fertile fields drink daily of the warm blood of my outraged sisters, I am filled with unutterable loathing, and led to reproach myself that any thing could fall from my lips in praise of such a land. America will not allow her children to love her. She seems bent on compelling those who would be her warmest friends, to be her worst enemies. May God give her repentance, before it is too late, is the ardent prayer of my heart. I will continue to pray, labor and wait, believing that she cannot always be insensible to the dictates of justice, or deaf to the voice of humanity.

FREDERICK DOUGLASS, letter to William Lloyd Garrison, January 1, 1846

If it were not for the stripes on my back which were made while I was a slave, I would in my will, leave my skin a legacy to the government, desiring that it might be taken off and made into parchment, and then bind the constitution of glorious happy *and free* America. Let the skin of an American slave, bind the charter of American Liberty.

WILLIAM GRIMES, *Life of William Grimes, the Runaway Slave,* 1824

The author . . . sends out this history—presenting as it were his *own body,* with the marks and scars of the tender mercies of slave drivers upon it . . .

AUSTIN STEWARD, *Twenty-Two Years a Slave, and Forty Years a Freeman,* 1857

Hot weather brings out snakes and slaveholders, and I like one class of the venomous creatures as little as I do the other. What a comfort it is, to be free to *say* so!

HARRIET JACOBS, *Incidents in the Life of a Slave Girl,* 1861

# CONTENTS

VOLUME ONE: 1770–1849

Foreword    ix

Introduction    xv

## James Albert Ukawsaw Gronniosaw

A NARRATIVE OF THE MOST REMARKABLE PARTICULARS IN THE LIFE OF JAMES
ALBERT UKAWSAW GRONNIOSAW, AN AFRICAN PRINCE    1

## Olaudah Equiano (Gustavus Vassa)

THE INTERESTING NARRATIVE OF THE LIFE OF OLAUDAH EQUIANO, OR
GUSTAVUS VASSA, THE AFRICAN    29

## William Grimes

LIFE OF WILLIAM GRIMES, THE RUNAWAY SLAVE    181

## Nat Turner

THE CONFESSIONS OF NAT TURNER, THE LEADER OF THE LATE INSURRECTION IN
SOUTHAMPTON, VA.    235

## Charles Ball

SLAVERY IN THE UNITED STATES: A NARRATIVE OF THE LIFE AND ADVENTURES
OF CHARLES BALL, A BLACK MAN, WHO LIVED FORTY YEARS IN MARYLAND,
SOUTH CAROLINA AND GEORGIA AS A SLAVE    259

## Moses Roper

A NARRATIVE OF THE ADVENTURES AND ESCAPE OF MOSES ROPER, FROM
AMERICAN SLAVERY    487

## Frederick Douglass

NARRATIVE OF THE LIFE OF FREDERICK DOUGLASS, AN AMERICAN SLAVE    523

## Lewis & Milton Clarke

Narratives of the Sufferings of Lewis and Milton Clarke, Sons of a
Soldier of the Revolution, During a Captivity of More than Twenty
Years Among the Slaveholders of Kentucky    601


## William Wells Brown

Narrative of William W. Brown, a Fugitive Slave    673


## Josiah Henson

The Life of Josiah Henson, Formerly a Slave, Now an Inhabitant of
Canada    719


Bibliography    757

I S slavery America's original sin? Despite the end of legal bondage 135 years ago, we are reminded of this national tragedy, and rightly, nearly every day through President Clinton's oft-stated feelings of shame about slavery, or black demands for reparations (or at least an apology), or countless books and magazine and newspaper articles that ground their interpretation of every aspect of contemporary black American life on the complexities of the Peculiar Institution. Adjoa Aiyetoro, director of the National Conference of Black Lawyers, reminds us of its lingering effects in a *Seattle Post-Intelligencer* article (June 29, 1997) when he says, "One of the issues we deal with every day is the vestiges of our enslavement, and our post-enslavement treatment in this country has been such that it has beat us down as a people in so many ways."

Perhaps those "vestiges" might have disappeared if Congress had passed after the Civil War a famous bit of legislation known as Senate Bill No. 60, which not only would have provided emergency relief for black freemen, but also "three million acres of good land" in Florida, Mississippi, and Arkansas for their settlement. In a January 18, 1866, edition of the *Congressional Globe*, Senator Lyman Trumball, a Republican from Connecticut, argued that "A homestead is worth more to these people than almost anything else. . . . I think that if it were in our power to secure a homestead to every family that has been made free by the constitutional amendment, we would do more for the colored race than by any other act we could do." This "forty acres and a mule" bill put America's racial future, one might say, squarely at a crossroads. If approved, it might have done much to heal the devastating wounds of slavery and assist an impoverished, landless people in their transition from bondage to a fuller participation in American life, particularly in the area of economic development. But the bill was vetoed by President Andrew Johnson, who argued that "it was never intended that they [ex-slaves] should thenceforth be fed, clothed, educated and sheltered by the United States. The idea on which the slaves were assisted to freedom was that, on becoming free, they would be a self-sustaining population. Any legislation that shall imply that they are not expected to attain a self-sustaining condition must have a tendency injurious alike to their character and their prospects."

With that veto an opportunity was forever lost for both newly freed bondsmen, many of whom would feel slavery was restored after the end of Reconstruction, and for whites, who for the next hundred years were able to sweep under the rug the question of racial justice. Not until the 1960s does the Peculiar Institution become the major premise, the algorithm, the single governing principle for *any* and *all* discussions about white dominance and the condition of blacks in this country. This monistic shift that made slavery the primary causal explanation behind everything black people are and are not, do and don't do, came about because the forgetfulness of whites, we might say, was studied. Since its rediscovery, first by academics in the 1960s, then by popular culture in the 1970s (remember the popularity of Alex Haley's *Roots*), slavery has been—and will continue to be—our obsession, partly because from the period of Reconstruction forward the Plantation School of writers, films like *Gone With the Wind,* and insouciant white Americans in general deliberately denied or downplayed the monstrous practices in the slaughterhouse of slavery. (Blacks often soft-pedaled them too before the 1960s, hoping to put the past behind them and keep moving forward, as when Martin Luther King, Jr., proclaimed, "The Negro understands and forgives and is ready to forget the past.") No event in American history—from the appearance of the first twenty black indentured servants sold off a Dutch ship at Jamestown in 1619 to the present debate on the future of affirmative action—can be properly understood without referencing the agony blacks endured as human chattel.

Everyone is stained, directly or indirectly, by those three hundred years of systematic oppression, including immigrants who arrived from Europe well after Abraham Lincoln's 1863 Emancipation Proclamation. Yet many Americans, blacks among them, sometimes feel weary from being reminded of events that ended so long ago, weary of being accused, weary of being called co-conspirators in crimes that took place before they were born. But they can object to our obsession with American slavery no more than one can object to our equally passionate interest in the hows and whys of the Holocaust. Still, I believe we should clarify a point or two, if only for the sake of fidelity to the enormous complexity of the three-thousand-year-old historical record on human bondage.

First of all, slavery is *humanity's* original sin.

It is safe to say that every country and culture, Eastern and Western, has at some benighted hour in its history enslaved other human beings. This execrable institution was not widely questioned as wrong until the eighteenth century, and then only in a Europe that had experienced the Enlightenment, and by Quaker abolitionists. As Thomas Sowell points out in *Race and Culture*, we owe the word "slave" itself to the *Slavs,* who were forced into bondage in Europe and the Ottoman Empire. Africa has its own long history of black-on-black slavery, one that includes the Ashanti tribe, which prospered by selling Africans to the Europeans. And even today Australia's Anti-Slavery Society suggests that this most evil of human practices is inexpugnable. The Society estimates there are 35,000 religious slaves in West Africa, girls as young as eight years old, who are sexually exploited by so-called holy men. Recently two *Baltimore Sun* reporters went to war-torn Sudan and bought the freedom of two boys, Garang Deng Kuot (age ten) and his brother Akok (twelve), from an Arab trader in Manyiel, a village in the southern province of Bahr el Ghazal; they purchased the brothers for five hundred dollars apiece, the cash equivalent of five cows. Adding to this evidence of slavery's interminable presence among our species, more than three hundred slaves in 1997 were returned to their families in southern Sudan with money raised by a Canadian evangelical television program called "100 Huntley Street" and the Swiss-based Christian Solidarity International. "It was women and children," explained Cal Bombay, vice president of Crossroads

Christian Communications, in an article in *The Seattle Times* (April 2, 1997). "Some of the boys were up to 13 years old, and some of the women had been forcibly circumcised. . . . Some had been mutilated. One girl had her lip cut off."

Although we, as Americans, condemn slavery on our shores as the worst crime against humankind, it remains a firm and healthy institution, as hideous as ever, half a world away. There is little if any Yankee anger, outrage, or activism aimed at ending it. Sadly—and ironically—we seem less concerned about slavery present than we are with slavery past, and I suspect the reason for this can be found in one of the uncomfortable, messy conundrums of human nature, made even more conflicted when we factor in the phenomena of color, white guilt, and black accusation. African societies are *different* from our own. There, we have nonwhites enslaving nonwhites, and many Americans (white and black) shrug helplessly and hypocritically, kvetching, "Who are *we* to condemn the practices of a foreign people?" But in America two centuries ago the barbarism of bondage fused with the profound, primal, emblematic masks of White and Black—a Manichean division between Self and racial Other, thereby casting this social evil in stark, even apocalyptically theatrical figures.

By now we know—or *should* know—that Race is an illusion, a construct of culture. "Race has no basic biological reality," reported Jonathan Marks, a Yale University biologist, in a recent Knight-Ridder newspaper article. "The human species simply doesn't come packaged that way." Other scientists in that same 1996 article agreed with Marks, among them Stanford geneticist Luigi Cavalli-Sforza, who said, "The characteristics that we see with the naked eye that help us distinguish individuals from different continents are, in reality, skin-deep. Whenever we look under the veneer we find that the differences that seem so conspicuous to us are really trivial."

Those differences were not trivial, of course, to white slaveholders who in the early nineteenth century needed "natural" (to their way of thinking) justifications—or biblical ones—for the profitable institution of slavery. We know the history of race theory. We know when this effort to "categorize" human lives began, and how ludicrous its early attempts were. Whites identified a score of "races," even among those now considered white. For example, Italians were not accepted as "white" until the mid-nineteenth century; the Irish were perceived as a separate race until the mid-1800s; and it is not until the end of that century that Jews slowly began to be accepted into the exclusive club of "whiteness" (obviously by the 1930s their inclusion was still not widely accepted in Europe). Many of these racial categories were based on geographic regions, not genetic differences. Even the critical intellect of a W. E. B. Du Bois was taken in by the lie of racial essentialism as late as the twentieth century when, in his essay "The Conservation of Races," he claims that each race has its own unique "message" for civilization. My point, if it isn't clear yet, is that Race is *maya*. Illusion. A chimera constructed for reasons of social, political, and economic domination. Yet it is this illusion that distinguished slavery in the American South from all other histories of bondage and led to its being called "The *Peculiar* Institution."

Peculiar, indeed.

Unlike slavery among the Greeks and Romans, in Africa or the Far East, the existence of this institution in America from 1619 through 1865 is tempered by not only the volatile factor of race but also, in 1776, by the ideals of freedom that fueled the revolt of the colonists against King George. Thomas Jefferson wrote, then struck from an early draft of the Declaration of Independence, a paragraph condemning slavery. The Founders, who were slaveholders, time and again framed their outrage at England by comparing themselves to slaves. In a word, from the beginning of the Republic to the Civil War, the American soul was schizophrenically divided between desiring the profits that came from this ancient social arrangement and its own belief that "We hold these truths to be self-evident, that all men are created equal, that they are endowed by their Creator with certain unalienable Rights, that among these are Life, Liberty and the pursuit of Happiness." Could any slaveholding state be *more* "peculiar" and at odds with itself than this? Historian Gordon Woods observes, "Before the revolution, Americans like every other people took slavery for granted. But slavery came under indictment as a result of the same principles that produced the American founding. In a sense, the prospect of the Civil War is implicitly contained in the Declaration of Independence."

Before that final conflict in the 1860s, America was a crazy quilt of blacks who were free and unfree. Given its principles, the nation's future *hinged* on the status of the Negro, whose presence in this republic, whose slave revolts, slave narratives, and relentless resistance to bondage forced a fledgling nation to confront the implicit universality of its most cherished ideals—indeed, to better understand its own soul. Such a conflict could only produce a maddeningly complex, even Kafkaesque social world. There were Negroes born free in the North, who devoted their lives to agitating for the cause of abolition. There were others who were freed by their masters, only to be kidnapped back into bondage, especially after the passage of the Fugitive Slave Act. There were still others, like Anthony Johnson, a seventeenth-century black Virginia planter, who after his manumission from indentured servitude began accumulating property and owned a black slave, John Casor. And of course there were ex-slaves who escaped from slavery—with and without the help of the Abolitionists—and lived to tell the daring tale of their adventures in thrilling narratives that comprise one of the truly indigenous genres of literature produced in America: a body of works that, like a tree, provides the roots from which spring in the late nineteenth century branches leading to the rich traditions of black autobiography and the black novel.

In this outstanding two-volume collection, *I Was Born a Slave,* editor Yuval Taylor places before us slave narratives that captured the complexities of this very Peculiar Institution and created a powerful literary tradition. These are seminal texts for understanding slavery. And ourselves. As a novelist, teacher, storyteller, and screenwriter, I have worked with many of these classic narratives, particularly for my second novel, *Oxherding Tale* (1982), which used the form common to all these stories as the springboard for a philosophical tale that explored bondage on several levels—physical, political, psychological, metaphysical, and spiritual. Then, as now, I find this literary form—with its structural similarities to the Puritan narrative, which place the slave narrative in a tradition stretching back to St. Augustine's *Confessions*—*more* than fascinating. I revisit them frequently, and I'm happy to admit their crucial influence on PBS dramas I've written, such as "Booker" (Wonderworks, 1985).

No American's education can be called complete if these works are missing from his understanding—specifically the narratives of Olaudah Equiano, whose declaration, "When you make men slaves you compel them to live with you in a state of war," rings as true for our time as it did for his; and that of Frederick Douglass, of whom James Russell Lowell said, "The very *look* of Douglass was an irresistible logic against the oppression of his race" (italics mine); as well as the stirring stories of William Wells Brown, Josiah Henson, Nat Turner, and Charles Ball.

We owe Yuval Taylor our thanks for bringing together so many of these intriguing documents—some long out of print, others appearing here for the first time since their original publication. On these pages you will find firsthand witnesses—many unique voices—to the shame that was slavery. But you will find as well adventure, ingenious escapes, humor (yes, that is here too), and the full, ambiguous range of the human spirit, its darkness and breathtaking triumphs.

You will find, in a word, our collective stories as Americans.

CHARLES JOHNSON
SEATTLE, 1998

No matter how many years may pass, the stigma of slavery will remain ineradicably imprinted on our country. It was an established fact long before our birth as a nation; it caused our greatest war; it has shadowed every struggle, defeat, and victory of our land. Whites still apologize for it; blacks still resent it; and we are all oppressed by its legacy.

The slaves whose narratives are collected here tried to redeem the burden of that oppression. They transformed themselves from victims into agents of resistance just by telling their stories and protesting the vast injustice that was being done to them. Together, they established a popular literary genre, sold hundreds of thousands of books, and inflamed antislavery sentiment. On the whole, they did not write for posterity—they intended a more immediate impact—yet they produced works of lasting literary and historical value. In doing so, they performed an act of liberation.

I hope this anthology can further this act by making these invaluable documents available once again in a compact, affordable edition. I hope it can liberate these works from their isolation in libraries, used-book stores, and difficult-to-read microfilms. I hope it will prove, once and for all, that the contribution of the slaves to our literature was not only two or three works of uncommon power, but a whole body of inventive, lucid, thoughtful, and passionate works of art.

---

Between the importation of the first documented shipload of Africans to Virginia in 1619 to the death of the last former slave in the 1970s, some six thousand North American slaves told their own stories in writing or in written interviews.[1] The majority of these accounts are brief (many were included in periodicals, collections, or other books), but approximately 150 of them were separately published as books or pamphlets ranging from eight pages to two volumes.[2]

These separately published narratives fall into three relatively distinct periods. From the 1770s to the 1820s, the narrators for the most part conceived of their lives as adventures or spiritual journeys, rather than as illustrations of a pernicious institution; in the titles of their books they called themselves Africans, not slaves.

But beginning in 1824, with the publication of the *Life of William Grimes, the Runaway Slave,* the reverse became the case. The slave narrative began to show distinct signs of being a cohesive genre that used the autobiographical form to enlighten the world about the facts of slavery. Over the years the narratives also became increasingly novelistic—those published after 1852, the date of Harriet Beecher Stowe's *Uncle Tom's Cabin,* were far more likely to employ fictionalized dialogue.

The abolitionist slave narratives written during the genre's heyday—over eighty were published between 1836 and the end of the Civil War in 1865—exhibit a large number of common elements. The typical narrative includes a preface describing it as a "plain, unvarnished tale";[3] the first sentence begins, "I was born . . . "; the plot includes, among other events, a slave auction, the separation of the narrator from his family, an exceptionally strong and proud slave who refuses to be whipped, and at least two escapes, one of them successful; and the narrative concludes with an appendix of some kind.[4] Yet because the experience and voice of each slave was unique, most of the narratives avoid being formulaic.[5]

After the Civil War, the narratives underwent a fundamental shift in tone. The righteousness and anger of the classic narratives were muted; the plots ended with the narrator adjusting to newfound freedoms, rather than calling for them from exile; and certain aspects of slave life began to seem quaint, in keeping with the imagery of the Sambo tales and minstrel shows then popular. This loss of urgency can be to some degree attributed to a change in the purpose of the narratives: rather than trying to convince their audience of slavery's evils, the writers attempted to present a balanced picture of their lives for the edification of readers. And thematically, the emphasis on *freedom* in the classic narratives was replaced by a corresponding emphasis on *progress*.[6]

Whether before or after emancipation, the slave narrative, with very few exceptions, was written or dictated by a *former* slave. Especially before the end of the Civil War, these narrators by no means represented a cross section of the slave population. In the history of the institution in the United States, probably between 1 and 2 percent of the slave population managed to escape. The narrators thus tended to be unusually brave, physically strong, resourceful, and imaginative individuals. Most of them hailed from near the Mason-Dixon line. They were often literate; a large number had served as "house slaves" and had thus acquired some of their masters' knowledge of the world; most had excellent memories and superb analytic skills. In addition, a disproportionate number of narrators were mulattos, who constituted only between 7 and 12 percent of the slave population—mulattos were not only more likely to be house slaves, but it was easier for them to pass as white when escaping.[7] The narrators varied in age from their early twenties (Moses Roper) to their mid-seventies (James Mars). Between 10 and 12 percent of them were women (however, only one self-penned narrative of a female American slave was published before 1865—Harriet Jacobs's 1861 *Incidents in the Life of a Slave Girl*).

More than half of the separately published slave narratives were penned by the slaves themselves,[8] and many were also self-published. A large number, however, were dictated by the slave to an amanuensis or editor, usually a white man. In many cases, as John W. Blassingame has shown, there is good reason to believe that the amanuensis hewed carefully to the words of the slave.[9] Sometimes editors added passages based on their own research. And occasionally the slave's story was more or less rewritten. For example, the *Narrative of Henry Box Brown* (1849) features the following words on the title page: "Written from a Statement of Facts Made by Himself. With remarks upon the remedy for slavery by Charles Stearns";[10] and the *Narrative of Sojourner Truth* (1850) is a third-person biography written by Olive Gilbert.

"The function of the slave narrative," writes Crispin Sartwell, "is apparently straightforward: resistance to oppression by speaking the truth"[11]—or, to quote a current catchphrase, "speaking truth to power." But this is the *central* goal, not the only one. Considering the great variety of narratives, one might name seven distinct functions: to document the conditions of slavery; to persuade the reader of its evils; to impart religious inspiration; to affirm the narrator's personhood; to redefine what it means to be black; to earn money; and, last but not least, to delight or fascinate the reader.

Although in the first half of this century slave narratives were disparaged as biased or fictionalized, in the 1970s scholars began to recognize that they are the richest firsthand source for information about plantation life.[12] The goal of documentation is evident in the titles of certain narratives, such as *Slavery in the United States* (Charles Ball, 1836), or *Slave Life in Georgia* (John Brown, 1855); in many of the appendices to the narratives, which draw from a wide variety of documentary material; and in sections of the narratives that spell out in detail the daily regimen of the slave, the method of growing crops, what and when the slaves ate, the different kinds of whips, and so on. Later narratives are especially explicit about this purpose: in his introduction, James Mars says his reason for publishing his narrative (1864) is that "many of the people now on the stage of life do not know that slavery ever lived in Connecticut"; in his preface, Louis Hughes (1897) asks, "To what purpose is the story which follows?" and responds, "the narrator presents his story . . . in the hope that it may add something of accurate information regarding the character and influence of an institution which for two hundred years dominated the country."[13]

Many narratives constituted political appeals; publishing a narrative could be as political an act as giving an abolitionist speech. Some—for example, Samuel Ringgold Ward's *Autobiography of a Fugitive Negro* (1855) or the first half of the *Narrative of Henry Box Brown*—are little more than abolitionist rhetoric in a narrative frame. Although many a narrative called itself a "plain, unvarnished tale," few were without some kind of exhortation or apostrophe on the evils of slavery and its conflict with Christian principles or those upon which this country was founded.

While edifying or inspirational matter was at times linked with political persuasion, the narratives were often fundamentally religious in character. For example, in the quasi-mystical *Incidents in the Life of Solomon Bayley* (1820) the narrator, a fugitive slave, is tendered divine protection by a circle of birds in the woods; and the *Life of John Thompson* (1856) concludes with a sermon that allegorizes the narrator's experiences aboard a whaling vessel. Some of the narratives are explicit about their religious or inspirational aims: near the beginning of his narrative, Bayley exclaims, "O! that all people would come to admire him [God] for his goodness and declare his wonders which he doth for the children of men";[14] and in his preface to *The Fugitive Blacksmith (1849)*, James W. C. Pennington declares, "Especially have I felt anxious to save professing Christians, and my brethren in the ministry, from falling into a great mistake."

The slave not only identified writing with his newfound freedom, but his book with his newfound selfhood. Austin Steward (1857) goes so far as to say, "The author . . . sends out this history—presenting as it were his *own body,* with the marks and scars of the tender mercies of slave drivers upon it."[15] Slaves were, of course, property, and therefore did not own themselves; they were also forbidden to read and write. Self-expression, then, was one of the greatest boons of freedom—witness the joy of Harriet Jacobs's exclamation, "What a comfort it is, to be free to *say* so!" Even if they did not put it into words, many a fugitive slave may have easily concluded that the mere act of writing was the ultimate act of self-affirmation, the ultimate denial of enslavement. As Annette Niemtzow puts it, "I write, therefore I am, says the slave autobiographer."[16]

The literature of the slavery era is replete with stereotypes of docile, idiotic, or savage Negroes, and one of the functions of slave narratives was to counteract such racist views. The very appearance of a book written by a black man could well confound white readers; as Sartwell notes, "the notion of black authorship, particularly early on, was vexed: it appeared to many people to be *a priori* impossible; it was as if we had discovered a book by a baboon." Beyond that, slaves needed to redefine themselves against the prevailing notion, broadcast by Southern slaveholders and accepted by many in the North, that slaves were "happy darkies gratefully accept[ing] the protection of fatherly masters."[17] The narratives are notable for their complete lack of, as Kenny J. Williams puts it, "lush green fields with singing slaves working hard but happily [near] the big plantation house staffed by authoritarian house slaves and beautiful women in billowing gowns."[18]

Naturally, the act of publication was usually influenced by pecuniary motives. Moses Grandy (1844) is one of several narrators who made this explicit: "Whatever profit may be obtained by the sale of this book . . . will be faithfully employed in redeeming my remaining children and relatives from the dreadful condition of slavery."[19] Another was William Grimes, who said at the end of his narrative, "I hope some will buy my books from charity; but I am no beggar. I am now entirely destitute of property; where and how I shall live I don't know." James Mars concluded the second edition of his narrative with these words: "I am now in my seventy-sixth year of life, and as my joints are stiff with old age and hard labor, finding so ready a sale for my pamphlets, I am induced to take this method to get a living, as I can walk about from house to house." The "Advertisement to the Second Edition" (1838) of Moses Roper's narrative states that its sale will help the author "create a fund which may enable him to qualify himself to instruct the heathen"; six years later Roper wrote, "by the sale of my book . . . [I] have paid for my education and supported myself."[20] As Williams points out, the words "written by himself" on the title pages of so many slave narratives "were used not only to assure the reader of reliability but also make certain that the reader was aware that the author would receive any monetary value from the sale of the book."[21]

The most explicitly denied function, yet the one to which slave narratives most owe their success, was their capacity to delight or fascinate the reader. To "delight and instruct" were the two standard aims of many eighteenth- and nineteenth-century narrative works, whether fiction or factual. Daniel Defoe, for example, writes in his preface to *Moll Flanders* (1722), "There is in this Story abundance of delightful Incidents, and all of them usefully apply'd. There is an agreeable turn Artfully given them in the relating, that naturally Instructs the Reader either one way or other." The slave narratives, however, very rarely make explicit any such aim to delight the reader, or make any claims for their artfulness. For example, Olaudah Equiano, whose masterful narrative (1789) appears to owe a good deal to Defoe,[22] implicitly denies the fact that his narrative "abound[s] in great or striking events." He spells out the goals of his narrative as follows: "If it affords satisfaction to my numerous friends . . . or in the smallest degree promotes the interests of humanity, the ends for which it was undertaken will be fully attained." In his dedication to Great Britain's Parliament, he states that "the chief design" of his narrative "is to excite in your august assemblies a sense of compassion for the miseries which the Slave-Trade has entailed on my unfortunate countrymen." However, large portions of his narrative have no relation whatever to the slave trade. Lastly, he admits,

> I am sensible I ought to entreat your pardon for addressing to you a work so wholly devoid of literary merit; but, as the production of an unlettered African, who is actuated by the hope of becoming an instrument towards the relief of his suffering countrymen, I trust that *such a man,* pleading to *such a cause,* will be acquitted of boldness and presumption.

Of course this kind of statement can be attributed to literary modesty, which is as old as literature itself; it is nevertheless striking how many narratives similarly insist upon their lack of literary merit, and that almost none of them purport to delight as well as instruct.[23] The *Narrative of the Life of J. D. Green* (1864), for example, clearly aims to amuse the reader with the many farcical incidents it describes; but one would never guess that from the prefatory material, which simply invokes the "horrors" of slavery.

The method of storytelling in the narratives—often reminiscent of adventure stories or sentimental novels—implies that delighting the audience was indeed one of their goals. While this goal may constitute a primary claim on readers' attention, however, it may have been seen at the time as detracting from their *central* goal (speaking truth to power). In the eighteenth and nineteenth centuries, when the conventions used to distinguish fiction from nonfiction were not as clear as those of today, it was important that the narratives deny being even remotely fictional—especially since a number of fictional slave narratives were published in the period as well.[24] As William L. Andrews writes:

> As a class, no group of American autobiographers has been received with more skepticism and resistance than the ex-slave. . . . Black autobiographers [were forced] to invent devices and strategies that would endow their stories with the appearance of authenticity. . . . The reception of [the black autobiographer's] narrative as truth depended on the degree to which his artfulness could hide his art.[25]

But their power to fascinate, delight, and thrill is a primary reason the slave narratives were so widely read. It seems that they were popular among both men and women, young and old, black and white, Northerners, Southerners (as evidenced by the scores of proslavery Confederate romances published to rebut slave narratives),[26] British, and, considering the number of translations into a host of languages, practically all literate people. In short, their appeal was universal. An 1855 issue of *Putnam's Monthly* explained:

> Our English literature has recorded many an example of genius struggling against adversity, . . . yet none of these are so impressive as the case of the solitary slave, in a remote district, surrounded by none but enemies, conceiving the project of his escape, teaching himself to read and write to facilitate it, accomplishing it at last, and subsequently raising himself to a leadership in a great movement in behalf of his brethren.[27]

Other readers remarked on the narratives' romantic nature. The transcendentalist minister Theodore Parker, in his oration on "The American Scholar," said, "there is one portion of our permanent literature . . . which is wholly indigenous and original. . . . I mean the Lives of Fugitive Slaves. . . . All the original romance of Americans is in them, not in the white man's novel."[28] Angelina Grimké wrote to Theodore Dwight Weld, "We rejoiced to hear of the fugitives' escape from bondage, tho' some of the pleasure was abridged by the caution to keep these things close. . . . Many and many a tale of romantic horror can the slaves tell."[29] And Senator Charles Sumner called the fugitive slaves "among the heroes of our age. Romance has no storms of more thrilling interest than theirs. Classical antiquity has preserved no examples of adventurous trial more worthy of renown."[30] Part trickster, part pilgrim, the fugitive slave—wandering the wilderness and defying death on a quasi-religious quest for freedom—proved indeed to be the ideal American hero. And his narrative was just what readers were thirsting for.

The first slave narrative, that of James Gronniosaw,[31] went through twelve editions between 1772 and 1800. Olaudah Equiano's went through thirteen editions between 1789 and 1794—including translations into Dutch, German, and Russian—and twenty-two editions by 1837. *The Confessions of Nat Turner* (1831) is said to have sold between forty and fifty thousand copies. Charles Ball's narrative went through at least ten editions in twenty-five years. Moses Roper's went through eleven editions, selling thirty thousand copies between 1837 and 1844. Frederick Douglass's 1845 *Narrative* went through seven U.S. and nine British editions in five years, selling over thirty thousand copies by 1860; his 1855 *My Bondage and My Freedom* sold five thousand copies in two days, and his 1881 *Life and Times* went through another dozen editions. William Wells Brown's went through four American editions between 1847 and 1849, selling ten thousand copies; it sold another eleven thousand in England. The first version of Josiah Henson's narrative (1849) sold six thousand copies in three years, well before his name became associated with that of Stowe's Uncle Tom; publishers estimated that one hundred thousand copies of the various versions of his narrative had been sold by the century's end, and it was translated into Welsh, French, Swedish, Dutch, and German. Solomon Northup's sold twenty-seven thousand copies in 1853 and 1854. And James Mars's 1864 narrative went into a thirteenth edition in 1876.[32] (For purposes of comparison, here are a few other sales figures from the 1850s: the most popular novel of the nineteenth century, *Uncle Tom's Cabin*, sold three hundred thousand copies in its first year; Longfellow's *Hiawatha* sold fifty thousand copies in five months; Hawthorne's *The Scarlet Letter* sold between thirteen and fourteen thousand copies in thirteen years; and *Walden, Moby Dick,* and *Leaves of Grass* sold fewer than two thousand copies each.)

Judging solely from these numbers, these ten slave narrators (all represented in this anthology) were probably the most popular. (If we consider *Up from Slavery* [1901] a slave narrative—although only its first chapter discusses slavery[33]—Booker T. Washington would share that status.) However, the number of editions is a problematic indication of popularity. In the case of James Mars, for example, this number can probably be attributed more to the persistence of the author in hand-selling what were no doubt small print runs than to a truly widespread popularity. At any rate, a score of other narratives went through between three and five editions each—including those of Venture Smith (1798), Thomas Cooper (1832), James Williams (*A Narrative of Events,* 1837), James Williams (*Narrative of James Williams,* 1838),[34] Elleanor Eldridge (1838), Lunsford Lane (1842), Moses Grandy (1843), Lewis and Milton Clarke (1845–46), Henry Bibb (1849), James W. C. Pennington (1849), Thomas H. Jones (1849), Sojourner Truth (1850), John Brown (1855), Peter Randolph (1855), Austin Steward (1856), and Jacob Stroyer (1879).

In the first half of this century slave narratives fell out of print and, because they were products of African American consciousness, were largely ignored by scholars of American history. But black writers have always appreciated them for their striking originality, complexity, and power. Nineteenth-century works influenced by slave narratives include Stowe's *Uncle Tom's Cabin* (1852); William Wells Brown's *Clotel* (1853); Harriet Wilson's *Our Nig* (1859); Martin R. Delaney's *Blake* (1861); and Mark Twain's *The Adventures of Huckleberry Finn* (1884); the number of twentieth-century works is too large to count, but some of the more prominent titles include James Weldon Johnson's *Autobiography of an Ex-Colored Man* (1912); Claude McKay's *Home to Harlem* (1928); Arna Bontemps's *Black Thunder* (1936); Zora Neale Hurston's *Their Eyes Were Watching God* (1937); W. E. B. Du Bois's *Dusk of Dawn* (1940); Richard Wright's *Black Boy* (1945); Ralph Ellison's *Invisible Man* (1952); James Baldwin's *Go Tell It on the Mountain* (1953); *The Autobiography of Malcolm X* (1965); Margaret Walker's *Jubilee* (1966); Maya Angelou's *I Know Why the Caged Bird Sings* (1970); Ernest Gaines's *The Autobiography of Miss Jane Pittman* (1971); Alex Haley's *Roots* (1976); Ishmael Reed's *Flight to Canada* (1976); Charles Johnson's *Oxherding Tale* (1982); Sherley Anne Williams's *Dessa Rose* (1986); Toni Morrison's *Beloved* (1987); and Caryl Philips's *Cambridge* (1991). Indeed, most if not all postbellum African American prose works are descended from the slave narrative, not only because it was the first distinctive African American literary genre, but because of its potent mixture of storytelling, racial awareness, social critique, and self-reflection—elements characteristic of the greatest black literary achievements.

———

While the narratives describe well the social, economic, legal, and labor conditions of the slaves, they also frequently refer to larger political matters. Their reading can thus be enhanced by a concise look at the major personalities,

events, and trends relating to the development of the institution of slavery and
the rise of abolitionism in the United States and Great Britain.[35]

If the United States was "conceived in Liberty," as Lincoln's Gettysburg
Address would have it, it was no less conceived in *slavery,* which had stained the
New World from the moment of its discovery. Christopher Columbus wrote of
the Caribbean natives that "there are no better people. . . . They love their neighbors as themselves, and they have the sweetest speech in the world; and are gentle and always laughing";[36] but he did not hesitate to impress them for service
on his ships, thus more or less enslaving them. John Smith, the leader of the early
British colonists, had been enslaved himself, in Turkey; as if establishing a pattern for the distant future, he killed his master and fled northward. In Jamestown,
Virginia, frustrated by the unwillingness of the colonists to endure hard labor,
he was dismissed from the governorship; his replacement, Sir Thomas Dale, as
Frederick Law Olmsted later wrote, "ordered them all, gentle and simple, to
work in gangs under overseers, and threatened to shoot the first man who refused to labor, or was disobedient."[37]

Shortly thereafter Africans were introduced to the British settlements—the
first documented shipload arrived in Virginia in 1619, but some may have been
landed even earlier.[38] Numerous black slaves were in Spanish Florida by that
time, and tens of thousands in the West Indies; but only small numbers of
Africans were shipped to the British colonies prior to the 1680s. Not until 1661
were these legally called slaves, and indeed many of them were only indentured
servants. At first, mulatto children followed the condition of the father, just as
in the French, Dutch, Danish, German, Spanish, and Portuguese colonies; however, in 1662 Virginia enacted a law that the children of slaves should follow the
condition of the mother, thus essentially licensing the rape of female slaves by
their masters. Soon thereafter, it was lawful in Virginia to do almost anything to
one's slaves—even kill them.[39]

It took little time for these and other pernicious effects of the institution to
be noticed, especially with the massive importation of Africans between 1680
and 1750. For example, when the colony of Georgia was founded in 1733, slavery was prohibited within its borders. William Byrd II, a prominent Virginia
farmer and slaveholder, perceptively predicted the future of Southern slavery in
a 1736 letter to John Perceval, Earl of Egmont:

> I am sensible of many bad consequences of multiplying these Ethiopians amongst us.
> They blow up the pride, & ruin the industry of our white people, who seing a rank
> of poor creatures below them, detest work for fear it shoud make them look like
> slaves. . . .
>    Another unhappy effect of many Negros, is, the necessity of being severe. Num-
> bers make them insolent, & then foul means must do, what fair will not. . . . Yet even
> this is terrible to a good naturd man, who must submit to be either a fool or a fury.
> And this will be more our unhappy case, the more Negros are increast amongst us.[40]

But the institution of slavery was not widely questioned until the late eighteenth century. After all, it predates recorded history. Slave labor was used in
building the Egyptian pyramids, and the Bible includes laws concerning the treatment—and manumission—of slaves. Modern slavery had its origins in the fif-

teenth century, when the Portuguese—followed by the British, Dutch, French, and Spanish—began to exploit Africans as slaves. And while it was in the Americas that their use was most widespread, it was in Europe that Enlightenment ideas led to the rise of abolitionism.

It was under the influence of those ideas that Thomas Jefferson, a slaveholder himself, wrote, in a subsequently stricken section of his Declaration of Independence, that King George III had "waged cruel war against human nature itself, violating its most sacred rights of life and liberty in the persons of a distant people who never offended him, captivating and carrying them into slavery in another hemisphere." But despite protestations such as these, and despite the tens of thousands of slaves who ran away during the American Revolution, slaves numbered 20 percent of the U.S. population by 1790, and the next two decades would witness the largest importation of Africans yet.

In 1787 the U.S. constitution declared a slave to count as three-fifths of a person in calculating representation for the states, thus granting a vastly disproportionate share of power to slaveholders. Ninety percent of the slaves lived in the South, where slavery had become an integral part of the plantation system of agriculture; and by 1804, in large part due to the influence of Quakers, all except one of the Northern states (Delaware) had at least begun to abolish slavery. It had become abundantly clear by this time that slavery was the great factor dividing the northern from the southern states. By 1808 the African slave trade had been outlawed by both the British Empire and the United States (though the illegal slave trade flourished for a long time thereafter), and in 1833, slavery itself, which had been abolished in England in 1772, was abolished throughout the British Empire. But in the United States, slavery was not only seemingly irrevocable, but had come to be seen as the overriding political, economic, and social issue of the age.

In the North, the 1830s witnessed the rise of the abolitionist movement, which grew out of the evangelical religious revivals of the 1820s. In 1829 David Walker, a free black man, published his seminal *Appeal,* one of the most vigorous denunciations of slavery ever written. The first issue of William Lloyd Garrison's *The Liberator,* a radical abolitionist journal, followed in 1831. The American Anti-Slavery Society, which grew out of Garrison's New England Anti-Slavery Society, was organized two years later in Philadelphia, primarily by Garrison and Arthur and Lewis Tappan, a few months after the abolition of slavery in the British Empire. Arthur Tappan, who had made a fortune in the dry-goods business, was the first president of the society; but Garrison, who was already famous for his intemperate language, dominated it. He would become president of the society in 1843, and retain that position—while continuing to publish his paper—until the end of the Civil War. The society integrated its black and white members, advocated nonviolence, and included in its goals equal rights for free blacks. In 1835 it launched a massive propaganda campaign, flooding the slave states with abolitionist literature, sending agents throughout the North to organize antislavery societies, and petitioning Congress to abolish slavery in the District of Columbia.

The mood quickly turned violent. Mobs attacked the abolitionists in the North; in the South their pamphlets were suppressed; the House of Representatives enacted a gag rule that prevented the discussion of antislavery proposals; and in 1837 the abolitionist editor Elijah P. Lovejoy was murdered while a mob destroyed his press for the fourth time. Despite these setbacks, by 1838 almost a quarter-million Americans belonged to antislavery societies.

In the South the suppression of freedoms was fed by fear. In 1831 Nat Turner had led the Southampton Insurrection in Virginia, killing between fifty-seven and sixty-five whites in the most deadly slave revolt in U.S. history. This uprising, like earlier ones led by Gabriel Prosser and Denmark Vesey, sparked violent reprisals and the passage of more oppressive laws throughout the South. In Virginia, for example, black ministers were forbidden to preach, education for free blacks was denied, and free blacks who had left the state could not return. Similarly, after the Denmark Vesey insurrection, black sailors landing in South Carolina were locked up in jail until their vessels put out to sea.

The North-South divide was further encouraged by the passage of a series of federal laws supposedly designed to delimit slavery. The Missouri Compromise, passed by Congress in 1820 and 1821, included a provision prohibiting slavery in the remainder of the Louisiana Purchase north of 36° 30′ (the southern boundary of Missouri); the Compromise of 1850 included the admission of California as a free state, the prohibition of the slave trade in the District of Columbia, and a more stringent fugitive slave law; and the Kansas-Nebraska Act of 1854, in contravention to the Missouri Compromise, allowed Kansas and Nebraska, both of which were north of the line, to decide themselves the question of slavery in their respective territories. While all of these laws purported to be compromises between Northern and Southern congressmen, they all favored the South, and did little to calm the conflict between the regions, instead entrenching each side more adamantly in its respective position. The key figures in enacting these compromises were Henry Clay, Daniel Webster, John C. Calhoun, and Stephen Douglas.

Henry Clay was at various times Speaker of the Senate, Speaker of the House, and secretary of state; he has been called the Great Pacificator and the Great Compromiser. Although he grew up in Virginia and Kentucky and represented the latter state in Congress, he was no apologist for slavery, denouncing extremists in both North and South. If there was one man most responsible for the Missouri Compromise and the Compromise of 1850, it was Clay.

Daniel Webster represented Massachusetts in Congress, both as representative and senator, through four decades; his speeches in Congress and his eloquent public addresses brought him acclaim as the greatest orator of his time, and he served as secretary of state under William Henry Harrison, John Tyler, and Millard Fillmore. His overriding concern was the preservation of the Union in the face of increasing sectionalism; when he backed the Compromise of 1850, which included the worst of the fugitive slave laws, he was reviled by antislavery groups in the North.

John C. Calhoun was a South Carolina congressman, secretary of war under President Monroe, vice president under John Quincy Adams and Andrew Jackson, and the preeminent spokesman for the South. It was Calhoun who directed the passage of the ordinance of nullification in South Carolina in 1832, declaring that the state had the power to nullify a Federal tariff. He was the most eloquent—and most extreme—defender of the doctrine of states' rights, proclaiming a position of absolute state sovereignty in dramatic debates with Daniel Webster; and he was equally eloquent in defending slavery. His theories later served as the foundation of the Confederate constitution.

Stephen Douglas served fourteen years as Illinois senator and originated the doctrine of popular sovereignty embodied in the Kansas-Nebraska Act, in which each state would decide for itself the question of slavery. Also a great orator, he found himself caught between the demands of his state and those of his party; he won the 1860 Democratic presidential nomination only after Southern delegates withdrew to nominate their own candidate, John C. Breckenridge.

Legislative compromises were not the only ways that Americans tried to resolve the slavery issue. The American Colonization Society was set up to deal with the problem of free blacks, who did not enjoy the same freedoms as whites anywhere in the United States, by resettling them in Africa. The society received support from Henry Clay, and in 1819 Congress appropriated one hundred thousand dollars for returning blacks to Africa. The result was the founding of Liberia in 1821. Abraham Lincoln would later profess to be in favor of colonization. But the movement was savagely attacked by abolitionists, who argued that it strengthened slavery in the South by removing free blacks; and blacks themselves were unenthusiastic about the project, maintaining that they were Americans, not Africans.[41]

In contrast to the compromisers and colonizationists, the abolitionists were largely unconcerned about making peace or preserving the Union. They boasted such national figures as Theodore Dwight Weld, James Birney, John Greenleaf Whittier, Wendell Phillips, Frederick Douglass, Charles Sumner, and William Henry Seward. Weld, who with Garrison was perhaps the most important abolitionist, organized agents for the American Anti-Slavery Society, edited its paper (the *Emancipator*), directed the national campaign to send antislavery petitions to Congress, and wrote the widely popular *American Slavery As It Is* (1839), a seminal influence on *Uncle Tom's Cabin*. Birney, a Kentuckian, freed his slaves in 1834, helped organize the Kentucky Anti-Slavery Society, became executive secretary of the American Anti-Slavery Society, and was nominated for the presidency by the abolitionist Liberty Party in 1840 and 1844. Whittier, a Massachusetts Quaker, was, along with Longfellow, one of the most popular American poets of the nineteenth century; he was also an active abolitionist, running for Congress on the Liberty ticket in 1842, helping to found the Republican Party, and serving as the amanuensis for the 1838 *Narrative of James Williams, An American Slave*. Phillips was a dynamic abolitionist lecturer, advocating not only an end to slavery, but the dissolution of the Union and the granting to blacks of land, education, and full civil rights. Douglass wrote three important slave narratives; edited his own abolitionist newspaper, *The North Star*, for seventeen years; lectured widely; was elected president of the New England Anti-Slavery Society; and organized Massachusetts blacks to fight in the Civil War. Sumner was a U.S. senator from Massachusetts for twenty-three years, during which time he attacked the fugitive slave laws, denounced the Kansas-Nebraska act, delivered notable antislavery speeches, and helped organize the Republican Party. Seward served two terms as governor of New York State, two terms as U.S. senator, and became secretary of state under Abraham Lincoln—during most of which he vociferously opposed slavery.

The 1850s witnessed a huge rise in the popularity of abolitionism. The 1793 fugitive slave law, providing for the return between states of escaped slaves, had been loosely enforced, with some Northern states allowing fugitives trials before their return and others forbidding state officials to capture them. So, as part of the Compromise of 1850, a new fugitive slave law was passed, commanding "all good citizens" to "aid and assist" Federal marshals in recapturing fugitive slaves, and imposing extraordinarily heavy penalties upon anyone who assisted a slave to escape. When captured, any black could be taken before a special commissioner, where he would be denied a jury trial, his testimony would not be admitted, and the affidavit of anyone claiming ownership would be sufficient to establish it in the eyes of the law. Thus all free blacks, whether fugitives or not, were put in danger of being enslaved. The result was an increase in kidnappings, in active resistance to the law, and in antislavery feeling in the North. Abolitionists, who had been widely considered extremists, finally started to gain widespread popularity.

Meanwhile the cotton the slaves produced had become not only the United States' leading export, but exceeded in value all other exports combined. After the slave trade was outlawed in 1807 approximately one million slaves were moved from the states that produced less cotton (Maryland, Virginia, the Carolinas) to those that produced more (Georgia, Alabama, Mississippi, Louisiana, Texas)—a migration almost twice as large as that from Africa to the British colonies and the United States. With the increase in cotton production, the price of slaves went up,[42] to such an extent that by 1860 capital investment in slaves in the South—who now numbered close to four million, or one-third of the population—exceeded the value of all other capital worth, including land.

Due to the increased economic importance of slavery, and in reaction to the North's ever more ardent condemnations of it, between 1830 and 1860 manumission was increasingly prohibited in Southern states, freed blacks were expelled, black churches were eliminated, and penalties for hurting or killing blacks were largely ignored. Proslavery literature was vigorously disseminated, the possession of abolitionist literature was made a serious crime, freedom of speech regarding slavery was effectively curtailed, and prices were even put on the heads of Garrison, Arthur Tappan, and other leading abolitionists. The large majority of slaves were still owned by a small minority of landowners—only one quarter of Southern whites owned slaves, and only 12 percent of those owned more than twenty. But whether slaveholders or not, whites now wielded absolute power over blacks.

In the dozen years before the Civil War, three important factors exacerbated the conflict over slavery and made secession inevitable: the increasing appeal of abolitionism; legal changes; and armed conflict between pro- and antislavery factions.

The rising popularity of slave narratives in the fifteen years before the Civil War is only one example of the power of abolitionist literature. *Uncle Tom's Cabin,* based in part on slave narratives, cannot be underestimated as a factor in turning Northerners against slavery. It sold over three hundred thousand copies in one year and helped bring respect to the antislavery movement worldwide. Its influence was so strong that upon meeting the author Lincoln is said to have commented, "So this is the little lady who made this great war."

The Underground Railroad is another potent instance of the success of abolitionists in altering public perceptions of slavery. As even a cursory reading of the narratives of fugitive slaves will indicate, the major factor in their escapes was their own resourcefulness, although the assistance of free blacks, Quakers, and sympathetic Northern sailors certainly helped. The stories of the Underground Railroad, on the contrary, created the impression that a highly systematic and secret organization, run mostly by white abolitionists, conducted a majority of the fugitive slaves along secret routes from the South to the North. No such nationally coordinated organization existed; and regional Underground Railroads were responsible for a relatively small number of successful escapes. The Underground Railroad was partially a propaganda device to dramatize abolitionist heroism, thereby attracting followers in the North and increasing alarm in the South.

The most important change in the legal status of blacks was the decision by the Supreme Court in the 1857 Dred Scott case that Congress had no power to prohibit slavery in the territories, that the Missouri Compromise was unconstitutional, and that a black "whose ancestors were . . . sold as slaves" was not entitled to the rights of a Federal citizen and therefore had no standing in court. According to Chief Justice Roger B. Taney, who gave the majority decision, blacks had not been citizens at the time of the adoption of the Constitution and had not become citizens of the nation since. By coming down strongly on the side of the South in the question of slavery in the territories, the decision caused a decisive split in the Democratic Party.

The Kansas-Nebraska Act of 1854 had already caused considerable violence in "bleeding Kansas." Both proslavery and antislavery groups pushed settlers into Kansas, hoping to influence elections. Each camp founded its own towns, Lawrence and Topeka being antislavery and Leavenworth and Atchison proslavery. The first elections were won by the proslavery group, but armed Missourians had intimidated voters and stuffed ballot boxes. Then the legislature ousted all free-state members, removed the governor, and adopted proslavery statutes. In retaliation, the abolitionists set up a rival government, and a bloody local war ensued—all despite the fact that slaves in Kansas in 1856 probably numbered only four hundred at most.

One of the most active abolitionists in Kansas was John Brown, who killed five proslavery men in the Pottawatomie massacre in 1856. Three years later, with twenty-one followers, he captured the U.S. arsenal at Harper's Ferry, Virginia (now West Virginia), imprisoned the inhabitants, and took possession of the town, intending to liberate the slaves by setting up an armed stronghold to which they could flee and from which revolts could be initiated. The U.S. Marines assaulted the arsenal, however, killing ten of Brown's men and wounding Brown himself. Brown, who was hanged after a spectacular trial, became a martyr of the abolitionist cause, galvanizing the North with his boldness; his raid so alarmed slaveholders that the whole South began to ready itself for war.

Lincoln's election, the Civil War, and the emancipation of the slaves need not be addressed here, since they are largely immaterial to the narratives included in this anthology, and since the basic facts are widely known. Suffice it to note that slavery in the United States by no means ended at the close of the Civil War in 1865. Although they were not called *slavery*, the post-Reconstruction Southern practices of peonage, forced convict labor, and to a lesser degree sharecropping essentially continued the institution of slavery well into the twentieth century, and were in some ways even worse. (Peonage, for example, was a complex system in which a black man would be arrested for "vagrancy," another word for unemployment, ordered to pay a fine he could not afford, and incarcerated. A plantation owner would pay his fine and "hire" him until he could afford to pay off the fine himself. The peon was then forced to work, locked up at night, and, if he ran away, chased by bloodhounds until recaptured. One important difference between peonage and slavery was that while slaves had considerable monetary value for the plantation owner, peons had almost none, and could therefore be mistreated—and even murdered—without monetary loss.) However, these practices were ignored by post-emancipation slave narratives, which aimed to emphasize the progress blacks had made since emancipation and to minimize their status as victims.

———

This anthology collects into two volumes the twenty most important and interesting separately published English-language slave narratives. They are unabridged from their first editions and supplemented with introductions and annotations. As a whole, the collection represents the most comprehensive attempt ever undertaken to make this body of literature widely available.

The anthology's title, *I Was Born a Slave,* is taken from the heartbreaking first sentence of Harriet Jacobs's narrative: "I was born a slave; but I never knew it until six years of happy childhood had passed away." *The Experiences of Thomas H. Jones, who was a Slave for Forty-Three Years* also begins, "I was born a slave. My recollections of early life are associated with poverty, suffering and shame."[43] Washington's *Up From Slavery* begins with these five words as well; and, as previously noted, most of the narratives begin with the words "I was born." As James Olney points out, "Escaped slaves . . . in the face of an imposed non-identity and non-existence were impelled to assert over and over, 'I *was* born.'"[44] (It should be noted that three of the narrators included here—Gronniosaw, Equiano, and Northup—were *not* born slaves.)

The selection of the narratives is necessarily a personal one. A number of factors went into it; in order of importance, they are: readability, literary quality, historical importance, authenticity, relevance, uniqueness, length, and scarcity. A few words are in order about each of these criteria.

The first, readability, is no doubt the most subjective. Some of the narratives, I felt, might prove difficult for today's reader to get through. I have excluded the extremely polemic narratives, such as those of Samuel Ringgold Ward and Peter Randolph, for this reason, as well as those by narrators, such as Richard Allen, who put little emphasis on the development of character, setting, or the overall shape of their work.

Literary quality, as a criterion, is closely allied to readability. However, it also takes into account other important questions. Are the meanings of the narrative on or below the surface? Are the characters one-, two-, or three-dimensional? Does the narrative have emotional impact? Is the author's style original or cliché ridden? Is his perspective obvious or thought provoking? Is the narrative monotonous or does it offer variety?

Although there have been a number of books written on slave narratives, few of them subject the individual narratives to the kind of close and rigorous literary analysis that scholars have long performed on the works of other writers of the era.[45] Until the middle of this century, in fact, slave narratives were commonly considered unreliable, tendentious, and subliterate. Most treatments of the last fifty years examine slave narratives either as historical documents—straightforward, uncomplicated texts with little merit as literature—or as a more-or-less homogeneous literary genre rather than one that encompasses a wide range of works. And there have been few claims made for their status as "literature," except, of course, for individual narratives: those of Olaudah Equiano, Frederick Douglass, and Harriet Jacobs have often been acknowledged as masterpieces of their kind. In my opinion, a number of others merit similar approbation. Certainly not all of the narratives collected here are works of genius. But more than a few deserve the same standing in the canon of American literature as certain contemporary narrative works by Cooper, Hawthorne, Melville, Poe, and Stowe.[46]

I determined the historical importance of a work by considering both its popularity at the time of its publication (see p. xx) and how often it has been cited by later historians and scholars of the slave narrative tradition. The ten most cited and discussed narratives appear to be those of Equiano, Douglass, William Wells Brown, Bibb, Henson, Pennington, Northup, William and Ellen Craft, Jacobs, and Washington; all but the last are included herein.

When I set out to compile this volume I had no intention of excluding post–Civil War narratives; and if this collection had been three volumes rather than two, I would have certainly included several.[47] However, in neither quality nor importance did these narratives measure up to the twenty I have decided to include, for they lack the urgency of the narratives written between 1820 and 1861. Frances Smith Foster describes them as "cheerleading exercises to urge continued opportunites for integration of blacks into American society or to depict black contributions to the Horatio Alger tradition. Their descriptions of slavery were mild and offered as 'historical' evidence only."[48] And William Andrews writes, "The postbellum slave narrator treat[s] slavery more as an economic proving ground than an existential battleground. . . . The agenda of the postbellum slave narrative thus emphasizes unabashedly the tangible contribution that blacks made to the South, in and after slavery."[49] The narrative of James Mars, although written before the end of the Civil War, may give the reader a hint of the tone of some of the postbellum narratives—rather than looking forward to a time of freedom, it looks back to a now-vanished past.

A narrative written by the slave himself was more likely to be included in this collection than one dictated to an amanuensis; I excluded narratives whose authenticity is even more problematic, such as the U.S. edition of Henry Box Brown's narrative and *The Narrative of Sojourner Truth,* for although these books were written with the cooperation of the subject, large portions of them are not autobiographical. (Nat Turner's *Confessions,* which I did include, presents a similar problem, but to a lesser degree.) As a result, thirteen out of these twenty narratives were written by the slaves themselves rather than in collaboration with white editors.

I believe, however, that the question of authorship has little bearing on literary quality. It has long been traditional among literary critics to exclude "as-told-to's" from the canon. Andrews, for example, argues:

> Should an autobiography whose written composition was literally out of the hands of its black narrator be discussed on an equal footing with those autobiographies that were autonomously authored by the black subject himself or herself? Many so-called edited narratives of ex-slaves ought to be treated as ghostwritten accounts insofar as literary analysis is concerned. . . . It was the editor who controlled the manuscript and thus decided how a "statement of facts" became a "fiction of factual representation," a readable, convincing, and moving autobiography. . . . It would be naive to accord dictated oral narratives the same discursive status as autobiographies composed and written by the subjects of the stories themselves. . . . Would not ex-slaves have been inhibited . . . when talking to whites, particularly when the latter's confidence and favor were so necessary to a narrative's publication?[50]

While a collaborative effort, however, might compromise the authenticity or "blackness" of a text, in many cases it can enrich it considerably. After all, every black cultural product in our history has been necessarily mediated to some degree by white culture and its institutions, making claims of authenticity somewhat problematic. Furthermore, why should a jointly authored book be any less subject to literary analysis than one written by a single author? As for "inhibitions," I cannot believe that a slave would be any more inhibited telling his story to a white editor—especially one who had expressed considerable interest in him, his story, and his future—than writing his story for an anonymous white audience; and a comparison between edited and single-authored slave narratives will, I believe, bear this out. Can one characterize Solomon Northup, for example—whose narrative affirms that "the oppressors of my people are a pitiless and unrelenting race"—as inhibited? One need not go as far as Foster to find her comments on this matter worth repeating:

> Why, I wondered, should I refrain from serious consideration of these works until I could verify who wrote what word at what time and under what circumstances? . . . Why the overwhelming need to verify that the author of record did in fact insert each comma and comment? . . . I decided that I did not have to delay a consideration of the text and social context of slave narratives until I had first answered the riddle of who really wrote them. As far as I was concerned, such questions needed to be pursued by those who considered them important. For me, they had the same relevance as trying to establish the exact date of John Keats's death when it was the "Ode to a Grecian Urn" that engaged my imagination and stimulated my curiosity.[51]

Many of the richest and most compelling twentieth-century black autobiographies, from Ethel Waters's *His Eye Is on the Sparrow* to *The Autobiography of Malcolm X,* have been as-told-to's. Without these, and without the narratives of

Gronniosaw, Turner, Ball, the Clarke brothers, Henson, Northup, and John Brown, the world of black literature would be a significantly poorer place.[52]

Also problematic to my selection were those autobiographical works by former slaves that had little relevance to the questions of slavery. For example, although the first chapter of Booker T. Washington's *Up from Slavery*, "A Slave Among Slaves," is an extraordinary piece of writing, the rest of the book says next to nothing about the matter.

Because slave narratives, as a genre, have so many elements in common, I tried to select only narratives that were in some way truly outstanding. I therefore excluded some slightly less interesting narratives, such as Austin Steward's or Isaac Mason's, although they certainly have unique qualities. Length was also a factor—which again mitigated against the inclusion of Austin Steward—as was the amount of prefatory and appended material: the less, the better. I was more inclined to include narratives that are scarce than those that are readily available, such as those of Venture Smith, Sojourner Truth, Elizabeth Keckley, or Booker T. Washington. The anthology includes two narratives—those of J. D. Green and William Parker—that have never been reprinted in full, and close to half of them are currently out of print elsewhere.

I read and reread dozens of narratives before making the final selection, and I regret that for reasons of space I was unable to include the narratives of Venture Smith, Solomon Bayley, Mary Prince, James Williams (1838), Lunsford Lane, Sojourner Truth, Frederick Douglass (*My Bondage and My Freedom*, 1855), Austin Steward, Elizabeth Keckley, and Louis Hughes. All of these are well worth reading, and all are either in print or available on-line; complete citations and short descriptions of each will be found in part I of the bibliography. I also regret that more women are not represented in these pages; the sex of the narrator was not a factor in my selection.

Lastly, I was influenced in my selection by certain ideals shared by many contemporary black thinkers. All too often slaves have been portrayed as victims—by writers stretching from Olmsted, Stowe, and Twain in the nineteenth century[53] to Stanley Elkins and William Styron in our own recent past. Typical of this view is the recent debate about whether the U.S. government should "apologize" for slavery. The narratives in this anthology present the testimony of slaves who saw themselves less as victims than as members of a resistance movement. In my selection, I favored those slaves who actively resisted the fate the white man had decreed for them—rebellious slaves such as Frederick Douglass and Harriet Jacobs, even killers such as Nat Turner and William Parker. (Instead of apologizing, shouldn't the government *honor* slaves such as these?) This is another reason postbellum narratives did not make the cut. Before emancipation, for a slave to tell his own story was an act of resistance, not reflection. And perhaps that explains why these narratives still possess so much power over a century after their initial publication.

---

In presenting the narratives I have followed some simple rules. First, each narrative is absolutely unabridged. From cover to cover, every word and illustration is presented intact (with two minor exceptions: to save space, I have left out half-title pages and copyright pages, unless they contain material of special interest); only the most obvious typographical errors have been corrected. Second, the text is usually that of the first edition.[54] Later editions almost always contained additional material, much of which seems superfluous, especially considering space constraints. Where material added in later editions might more fully explain some portion of the earlier edition, it is noted in the annotations. Douglass, William Wells Brown, and Henson each published several substantially different narratives; because the first of these is invariably the most succinct and immediate, it is the one included here.

Each narrative is introduced with a few words of biographical detail, publication history, and interpretation. All footnotes in the text appeared in the original edition; all endnotes are mine. In the endnotes, citations are brief; full citations are given in the bibliography at the end of each volume. Sources for the endnotes are cited at the close of each note, unless the source is a general reference work.

I have annotated with dates (where available) and a brief biography all persons mentioned whom contemporaneous readers might have been expected to know, except for the most obvious (Shakespeare, Lincoln, Frederick Douglass, etc.). Also annotated are geographical details and eighteenth- and nineteenth-century words that may have vanished from today's dictionaries. Where the narrator quotes a poem, address, or literary phrase I have done my best to locate and annotate its source, although in some cases I have not succeeded. Where the author misspelled names or made factual errors, I have annotated corrections. Lastly, the annotations often contain historical details about events discussed in the narrative that for one reason or another the author did not fully elucidate.

---

A reader who attempts to read all twenty of these narratives in a short time may become frustrated by a certain amount of repetition (most pronounced in the first quarter or so of each narrative). In order to help the reader plan which narratives to read in which order, I have given brief descriptions of each below.

- The 1772 autobiography of **James Albert Ukawsaw Gronniosaw** was the first slave narrative, and was both popular and influential. Gronniosaw's experience in slavery was benign, but as a free man he was taken advantage of and ill treated. A profound Calvinist, he imbues with religious significance his adventures in Africa, New York, Amsterdam, England, and with a Caribbean privateer.
- **Olaudah Equiano** published one of the most famous and influential black autobiographies, a conversion/captivity/slave narrative that functions as a travel book, adventure tale, and apologia as well. It includes an extraordinarily wide range of experiences and accomplishments, from his abduction from an idyllic African land to his assimilation into British high society, all unified by his sense of black pride.
- **William Grimes** suffered under ten different owners, was haunted by ghosts and ridden by a witch, went on a hunger strike, tried to break his own leg, and was accused of thievery, pimping, and rape. His may be the most complex and

disconsolate of the narratives, for Grimes did not heroically triumph over adversity, but instead succumbed to it.

- **Nat Turner,** believing himself a divinely guided prophet, led the deadliest slave revolt in U.S. history. His *Confessions* were taken down by a slaveowner who tried to paint Turner as the devil incarnate. Turner's graphic account of his religious visions and the systematic murder of scores of white men, women, and children is disturbing, audacious, and revolutionary in its implications.
- **Charles Ball**'s is the longest and most detailed antebellum slave narrative: no other source more fully describes plantation life from the slave's point of view. But it reads like an exceptionally well written adventure novel. It includes hair-raising escapes, kidnapping attempts, wild animals, military action, an unusual and chilling tale of black-on-white crime and its consequences, and a surprising twist at the end.
- **Moses Roper** was the first fugitive slave to widely publicize his experiences to British audiences. His horrifyingly vivid and popular self-penned narrative is notable for the nightmarish and ingenious tortures practiced upon him by his master Mr. Gooch, whose name soon became a popular symbol for the worst kind of slaveholder.
- **Frederick Douglass**'s *Narrative,* the first of his three autobiographies, is the most widely studied slave narrative. In it, Douglass equates identity, freedom, and literacy; displays unparalleled rhetorical skills; presents a stirring and persuasive abolitionist argument; and transforms himself into the embodiment of the fugitive slave and a potent symbol of liberty.
- **Lewis and Milton Clarke** were two of the most engaging slave storytellers. With their unique blend of biting sarcasm, self-deprecation, a colloquial manner, and an ability to see the comic side of things, their vivid narratives inspire both sympathy and laughter.
- **William Wells Brown,** who later became the first African American novelist and playwright, traveled up and down the Mississippi River as the manservant of a slave trader, witnessing horrific abuses of power and gaining an unparalleled education into the modus operandi of slavery. In his masterfully understated and quietly subversive book he presents himself as a signifying trickster rather than an epic hero.
- Although **Josiah Henson** later became known as "the original Uncle Tom," he was not at all obsequious—he just had a misplaced sense of duty. His narrative is straightforward, well constructed, and consistently surprising; in its various versions, it proved to be the most popular slave narrative of the nineteenth century.
- After **Henry Bibb** escaped from slavery, he kept going back—to try to rescue his wife and child. His affecting memoir, full of trickery, bravery, idealism, and pathos, doubles as a love story and a frontier adventure narrative.
- **James W. C. Pennington** was a well-known abolitionist minister and one of the most educated and literate black men of his time. His narrative, which is concerned primarily with questions of property and ownership, eloquently relates a thrilling and at times droll escape from bondage that shows he was as resourceful and inventive as any trickster-slave.

- **Solomon Northup** was a free black man of New York who was kidnapped, sold, and held as a slave in one of the remotest regions of the South for a period of twelve years. His book combines a mastery of detail with an unusual richness and strength of language; it was one of the fastest-selling and most popular narratives.
- **John Brown**'s is the most brutal of these narratives. Not for the faint of heart, it reads in parts like a litany of horrors—he was even experimented upon by a doctor who wanted to see how deep his black skin went.
- **John Thompson** was one of several slave narrators who professed to have had direct experience of God. His self-published story details a remarkable spiritual adventure, involving violent resistance to slavery, divine visitations, and an unforgettable sea voyage to Africa aboard a whaling vessel.
- **William and Ellen Craft** perpetrated one of the most ingenious and unusual methods of escape in the history of slavery. The pair became heroes, about whom speeches were made and poems written. William Craft proved to be a masterful writer—persuasive, erudite, and witty; his narrative successfully blurs distinctions between white and black, master and slave, man and woman.
- **Harriet Jacobs** was the first female slave to write her own autobiography— perhaps the most intimate and emotionally compelling slave narrative of all. In it she gives the lie to previous depictions of female slaves as sexual victims, redefining traditional roles and using her sexuality to avenge herself upon her lustful master. The result is a slave narrative that reads like a novel, heart-breaking yet inspiring.
- **Jacob D. Green** was the only slave narrator to make full use of the trickster tradition. A Brer Rabbit–like figure, he exposes both blacks and whites to his often cruel and usually hilarious pranks. His narrative is full of reversals, of sudden shifts between humor and horror, laughter and violence.
- **James Mars** was probably the only slave narrator to spend his entire life north of the Mason-Dixon line. Although he recollects his early life with tranquility, it was full of strong action: Mars escaped from one master, defied another, and insisted on his equality with whites. His is a coming-of-age story in which maturity arrives with the act of resistance.
- **William Parker** led an armed group of ex-slaves in battling would-be kidnappers; in 1851 they struck what many then considered the first blow of the Civil War. Among slave narratives, Parker's is perhaps the strongest example of black self-determination and quasi-revolutionary activity. Whether engaging in verbal braggadocio or physical battle, Parker never backed down, and his bravado made him an irresistible force.

---

For those interested in further reading, I highly recommend the following studies, to which I am greatly indebted: William L. Andrews's *To Tell a Free Story,* by far the best literary analysis of early black autobiography; Charles T. Davis and Henry Louis Gates, Jr.'s *The Slave's Narrative,* a collection of insightful essays; Francis Smith Foster's *Witnessing Slavery,* a consideration of the literary genre of the slave narrative; Marion Wilson Starling's *The Slave Narrative,* the pioneering and invaluable 1946 study that initiated serious attention to the genre; Blyden Jackson's *A History of Afro-American Literature, Volume I,* an elegantly written survey covering 1746–1895; Charles H. Nichols's *Many Thousands Gone,* John W. Blassingame's *The Slave Community,* and Eugene D. Genovese's *Roll, Jordan, Roll,* which all explore what slave narratives tell us about slavery; and *The Oxford Companion to African American Literature,* edited by Andrews, Foster, and Trudier Harris. In addition, three superlative anthologies should be read as companions to this one: John W. Blassingame's *Slave Testimony,* a collection of briefer narratives, letters, interviews, and speeches; Dorothy Porter's *Early Negro Writing, 1760–1837,* which includes almost every important short text of the period; and Vincent Carretta's *Unchained Voices,* which collects the work of black authors of the eighteenth century. The bibliography at the end of this volume gives a complete list of sources.

In closing, I would like to acknowledge and thank: Samuel Baker, who advised me about academic standards, provided me with background information about eighteenth- and nineteenth-century English literature, and went over much of my writing herein; Vincent Carretta, who helped with questions concerning the eighteenth-century narratives; Charles Johnson, who graciously provided both encouragement and a foreword that serves as a post hoc foundation for this book; Curt Matthews, who enabled me to embark on this project and has been tremendously supportive; Linda Matthews, my publisher and copyeditor, who has helped to organize my time and keep me sane when faced with deadlines; Jerry Morreale, who scanned the majority of the narratives; the folks at www.mudcat.org, who helped with questions about slave songs; Joan Sommers, who designed the anthology; my brother, Jonathan Taylor, and Katherine Wolff, who helped me access some of the scarcer narratives; the University of Chicago Library, which has been my primary resource; my wife, Kathryn Anne Duys, whose sustenance, advice, and inspiration have been invaluable; and my daughter, Thalia, whose cheerfulness helped me see that these pages contain not only the woes of oppression but the joys of being alive.

---

1. Starling, in *Slave Narrative,* provides "a bibliographic guide to the location of 6006 narrative records" (xviii, 337–356).

2. William Andrews writes that "approximately sixty-five American slave narratives were published in book or pamphlet form before 1865. Between the Civil War and the onset of the depression, at least fifty more ex-slaves saw their autobiographies in print" (Andrews, "Representation," 78). On the other hand, the reliable scholar John Blassingame writes, "Between 1760 and 1947 more than two hundred book-length autobiographies of southern former slaves were published in the United States and England" (Blassingame, *Slave Testimony,* 681). I find Andrews's estimate of 115 narratives quite low, given the number of pre-1865 slave narratives he lists in the bibliography of *To Tell a Free Story,* and given Blassingame's count of sixty-seven post-1860 narratives (Ibid., xli). Blassingame's figure of two hundred, however, seems quite high, even if one includes "book-length" autobiographies published in periodicals. A truly comprehensive bibliography of all known separately published slave narratives—one that would exclude autobiographies of blacks who were not slaves, fictional narratives, and biographies—has yet to be compiled.

3. This phrase, however often it appears in the narratives, was never written by the slave

himself, but always by a white editor or writer of appended material. It derives from Shakespeare's *Othello.* Olney, "'I Was Born,'" 166.

4. Ibid., 152–154.

5. James Olney, an eminent theorist of autobiography, scholar of slave narratives, and author of *Metaphors of Self* and *Tell Me Africa,* claims otherwise, calling slave narratives invariant and repetitive, and maintaining that "the slave narrative, with very few exceptions, tends to exhibit a highly conventional, rigidly fixed form that bears much the same relationship to autobiography in a full sense as painting by numbers bears to painting as a creative act. . . . The slave narratives do not qualify as either autobiography or literature, . . . and they have no real place in American Literature" (Ibid., 148–150, 168). One of the primary purposes of this anthology is to present evidence that Olney is gravely mistaken.

6. The best discussion of postbellum narratives is probably William Andrews's "The Representation of Slavery and the Rise of Afro-American Literary Realism, 1865–1920."

7. Foster, *Witnessing Slavery,* 128–131.

8. To be more precise, slightly less than half of the antebellum narratives, and almost all of the postbellum narratives, were self-penned.

9. Blassingame, *Slave Testimony,* xviii–xlii.

10. However, Brown also published a substantially different narrative in England in 1851, whose title page features the words, "Written by Himself."

11. Sartwell, *Act Like You Know,* 21.

12. Probably the most important step in this recognition was the publication of John W. Blassingame's *The Slave Community* in 1972, which defended slave narratives in the following words: "If historians seek to provide some understanding of the past experiences of slaves, then the autobiography must be their point of departure" (367).

13. Hughes, *Thirty Years a Slave,* 3.

14. Bayley, *Narrative,* 591.

15. Steward, *Twenty-Two Years,* xii.

16. Niemtzow, "Problematic of Self," 98.

17. Sartwell, *Act Like You Know,* 21, 22.

18. Williams, *They Also Spoke,* 89.

19. Grandy, *Narrative,* 42.

20. Roper, *Narrative* [2d British ed.], iii; Roper, "Anti-Slavery Society," 134.

21. Williams, *They Also Spoke,* 88.

22. Costanzo, *Surprizing Narrative,* 49.

23. The later versions of Josiah Henson's narrative constitute something of an exception to this rule, at least according to one reading of the opening of the 1858 edition (see Doyle, "Rhetorical Art," 89); the fact that Henson's was also the most popular slave narrative of all is probably not entirely coincidental.

24. The most prominent of these are probably *The Slave; or Memoirs of Archy Moore* (Richard Hildreth, 1836) and *Autobiography of a Female Slave* (Mattie Griffith, 1857); there were at least five others. On the other hand, some nonfiction slave narratives, such as those of Charles Ball and Harriet Jacobs, were long suspected of being fiction.

25. Andrews, *Free Story,* 2–3.

26. Davis and Gates, *Slave's Narrative,* xvii.

27. "Life and Bondage," 30–31.

28. Davis and Gates, *Slave's Narrative,* xxi.

29. Cited in Goldsby, "'I Disguised My Hand,'" 30.

30. Davis and Gates, *Slave's Narrative,* xxii.

31. The 1760 *Narrative of the Uncommon Sufferings and Surprizing Deliverance of Briton Hammon, a Negro Man,* a fourteen-page pamphlet, has been frequently cited as the first slave narrative; however, as several scholars have pointed out, Hammon may well have been a free man—he refers to himself as a servant, not a slave. His narrative begins, "On Monday, 25th day of December, 1747, with the leave of my Master, I went from Marshfield, with an Intention to go a Voyage to Sea . . ." This use of the word *master* may have confused historians of the genre—an employer was also usually called *master* in the eighteenth century. Hammon's

supposed status as a slave is difficult to reconcile with his obtaining leave to go to sea, his receipt of wages for his work aboard ship, or his failure to mention his slave status in his narrative. Of course, more research remains to be done. See Carretta, *Unchained Voices*, 20, 24–25; Dziwas, "Hammon, Briton," 1178–1179; Davis, "Hammon, Briton," 281. If Hammon was not a slave, then Gronniosaw's narrative, which has usually been considered the second slave narrative, becomes the first.

32. Many of these figures are cited in Bontemps, *Great Slave Narratives*, xviii; Davis and Gates, *Slave's Narrative*, xvii; Foster, *Witnessing Slavery*, 22; Gates, *Classic Slave Narratives*, xi; and Nichols, *Many Thousand Gone*, xiv–xv. Others are from Andrews, *Free Story*, 97; Carretta, *Unchained Voices*, 54; Jackson, *History*, 117; Low and Clift, *Encyclopedia of Black America*, 793; Potkay and Burr, *Black Atlantic Writers*, 162–163; Starling, *Slave Narrative*, 278; or are based on cards in the National Union Catalog.

33. "Many critics and historians regard [*Up from Slavery*] as the last great slave narrative authored in the United States" (Andrews, "Slave Narrative," 667). Frances Smith Foster, on the other hand, emphatically states, "Washington was encouraging his readers to place his work in the slave narrative tradition. It was not a slave narrative, however. Washington was born about five years before the Emancipation Proclamation and admits little personal knowledge about slavery" (Foster, *Witnessing Slavery*, 151).

34. There were at least four different narratives by slaves named James Williams.

35. Most of the information in the history that follows was gleaned from Chernow and Vallasi, *Columbia Encyclopedia*; Franklin and Moss, *From Slavery to Freedom*; Johnson et al., *Africans in America*; Kolchin, *American Slavery*; Low and Clift, *Encyclopedia of Black America*; and Salzman et al., *Encyclopedia*, unless otherwise noted.

36. *Diario*, Folio 47r, December 25, 1492.

37. Olmsted, *Seaboard Slave States*, I:241–246.

38. Davis, "A Big Business," 50.

39. Olmsted, *Seaboard Slave States*, I:259–261.

40. Byrd, *Correspondence*, 487–488.

41. On this last point, see Quarles, *Black Abolitionists*.

42. This was not a slow and steady increase—just prior to the panic of 1837, the average price of a prime field hand went up to $1,300 in New Orleans; it then fell to $800 in 1843 and gradually escalated again to $1,800 by 1860.

43. Jones, *Experiences*, 5.

44. Olney, "'I Was Born,'" 172.

45. The best treatment of the slave narratives as literature is doubtless William L. Andrews's *To Tell a Free Story: The First Century of Afro-American Autobiography, 1760–1865*.

46. As Kenny J. Williams writes, "The uniqueness of the slave narrative is to be found in its ability to combine various motifs of American literature and American ideology into a new and different form. Much of the prose in the America of the seventeenth and eighteenth centuries as well as that of the early years of the nineteenth century had emphasized not only religious but also political freedom. . . . These concepts were combined with the elements of the sentimental and adventure stories of the early years of the nineteenth century and the melodramatic works of the latter part of the century. Hence the link between the two periods is found not in the work of Emerson, Thoreau, Hawthorne, or Melville but rather in the work of a group of Negro writers . . ." Williams, *They Also Spoke*, 83.

47. William Parker's narrative might be considered postbellum since it was first published in 1866; it is also the only narrative included in this anthology that was published in a journal—*The Atlantic Monthly*—rather than as a book or pamphlet. However, Parker's narrative was clearly written prior to the Civil War, and, considering its length, he may have intended it to be published separately.

48. Foster, *Witnessing Slavery*, 150.

49. Andrews, "Representation," 85.

50. Andrews goes so far as to refrain from analyzing certain coauthored texts: "Lacking a way of distilling an authorial essence from the clouded stream of edited and dictated Afro-American autobiographies, I shall reserve close analytic readings for autonomously authored

black texts." *Free Story,* 19–22. In his bibliography, Andrews even lists the narratives of John Brown, Charles Ball, and Solomon Northup under the names of the amanuenses rather than the narrator (he does not, however, list Gronniosaw's, Turner's, Henson's, or Lewis and Milton Clarke's narratives in this way), despite ample internal evidence that the slaves participated heavily in their creation.

51. Foster, *Witnessing Slavery,* xix.

52. I may be somewhat defensive on this point because, like the nineteenth-century amanuenses, I am a white person responsible for publishing black autobiographies. Sartwell claims that the amanuensis "at once frees the slave to speak for himself and reasserts white power over that expression" (Sartwell, *Act Like You Know,* 23). But because these narratives were all previously published, I empower these black authors *without* a corresponding assertion of "white power" over their expression.

53. For a contrasting nineteenth-century view, see Thomas Wentworth Higginson's *Black Rebellion.* Higginson was practically unique among writers of his time in focussing on rebellious, rather than victimized, slaves.

54. Certain first editions were difficult to locate, and later editions were used instead in the following instances. The edition of Moses Roper's narrative included here is the first *American* edition, although the first *British* edition preceded it; I have not been able to ascertain the extent of the differences between them, but the differences between the first American and *second* British are extensive. Due to limited access to the first editions of Charles Ball's, Henry Bibb's, James W. C. Pennington's, John Brown's, and James Mars's narratives, I have based my text on the second editions, deleting material that was not in the first. The edition of Lewis and Milton Clarke's joint narrative included here is indeed the first, but Lewis Clarke had published an earlier edition on his own.

JAMES ALBERT UKAWSAW GRONNIOSAW

JAMES ALBERT UKAWSAW GRONNIOSAW (c.1712–?), an "African Prince," as the title page of his narrative informs us, dictated his life story to an anonymous *"young* LADY *of the town of* LEOMINSTER."[1] When published in 1772 with the aim of easing his desperate pecuniary situation, it became the first slave narrative.[2]

Prior to 1798 (the publication date of Venture Smith's narrative), almost all prose writings in English by blacks, as Vincent Carretta observes, "took the form of spiritual autobiographies that trace the transition from pagan beliefs to the Christianity shared with the authors' British readers."[3] The spiritual narrative had a long history, and followed a traditional pattern of sin, conversion, and subsequent rebirth. Gronniosaw, like most spiritual autobiographers, recast his life story so that almost every event had a religious significance. But, as Henry Louis Gates, Jr. has observed, Gronniosaw's narrative not only continues the tradition of "the Christian confession," but "inaugurates the genre of the slave narrative, from its 'I was born' opening sentence to the use of literacy training as a repeated figure that functions to unify the structure of his tale."[4]

Gronniosaw's treatment as a slave in the New World was relatively benign; it was only as a free man that he suffered ill treatment at the hands of those who took advantage of his ignorance of "the evils of this present world." Although he went through a variety of fascinating experiences in Africa, New York, Amsterdam, England, and with a Caribbean privateer, he recounts his misadventures with detachment and stoicism. In contrast with the self-affirmation of later slave narrators, Gronniosaw writes, "I am willing, and even desirous to be counted as nothing, a stranger in the world, and a pilgrim here; . . . and I'm thankful for every trial and trouble that I've met with, as I am not without hope that they have all been sanctified to me."

This statement shows how profoundly Calvinist doctrine had influenced Gronniosaw. Like most other black autobiographers of the eighteenth century, he was a follower of the teachings of George Whitefield, one of the original Methodists (along with John and Charles Wesley) and a friend of Gronniosaw's master Theodorus Frelinghuysen ("Mr. Freelandhouse"). Methodists remained part of the Church of England until 1791; but since they were often barred from churches, they preached in barns, fields, and houses, evangelizing as itinerants. Embracing all races and classes of people, they were fully accepting of blacks in their societies, eager to unite with them in an experience of rebirth in Jesus Christ. This rebirth was characterized by a sudden burst of illumination, similar to that which overcame Paul on the road to Damascus (*Acts* 9). While Wesley taught that redemption was available to all, Whitefield took the more traditional line that not everyone was able to attain to it: some people were "elect," destined for eternal salvation, and others were "reprobate," damned. This Calvinist belief in predestination, which was also part of the articles of faith of the Anglican church, caused a split between Whitefield and the Wesleys. The Countess of Huntingdon, to whom Gronniosaw's narrative is dedicated, was a patron to a large number of Methodist preachers and free blacks; she took Whitefield under her wing and helped introduce Calvinistic Methodism to the upper classes. As Adam Potkay and Sandra Burr put it,

> Whitefield hoped that the state of not knowing where one stood in the divine dispensation would inspire his listeners with salutary fear and trembling, a painstaking self-examination, and, ideally, the self-renunciation requisite to an acceptance of God's amazing grace. . . . Am I or am I not of the elect? This is the question that haunts all Puritan spiritual autobiographies. The basic drama we find in the spiritual lives of Gronniosaw, [John] Marrant, and [Olaudah] Equiano—uncertainty, despair, quickening, and regeneration—reflects not only Whitefield's influence, but that of the Puritan world of letters that Whitefield inherited, [including Richard] Baxter's *A Call to the Unconverted* (1658) [and John] Bunyan's *Holy War* (1682) [both of which Gronniosaw read].[5]

Gronniosaw's narrative was advertised in 1772 with the following words: "N.B. The whole Profits arising from the Sale are for the sole Benefit of James Albert and his distress'd Family." It went through at least twelve editions before the end of the century, including three in North America and two in Ireland,[6] and several more by 1840, the date of the last British edition. Its popularity was matched by its influence: Phillis Wheatley, the first English-language black poet, mentions it in a 1773 letter to Countess Huntingdon; and Ottobah Cugoano refers to it in his 1787 *Thoughts and Sentiments on the Evil and Wicked Traffic of the Slavery and Commerce of the Human Species.*[7] Moreover, Olaudah Equiano, who was doubtless familiar with the narrative, includes in his own 1789 *Interesting Narrative* an unattributed paraphrase of Gronniosaw's famous "talking book" passage. Gates calls the talking book "the ur-trope of the Anglo-African tradition," for it also appears in widely differing forms in later writings by John Marrant (1785), Cugoano, and John Jea (1815)[8]—providing yet another indication of how widely Gronniosaw's narrative was read.

A

# NARRATIVE

OF THE

## Most Remarkable Particulars

In the L I F E of

## James Albert Ukawsaw Gronniosaw,

An AFRICAN PRINCE,

As related by H I M S E L F .

———

*I will bring the Blind by a Way that they know not, I will lead them in Paths that they have not known: I will make Darkness Light before them and crooked Things straight. These Things will I do unto them and not forsake them.* Isa. xlii. 16.

———

## BATH:

Printed by W. GYE in Westgate-Street; and sold by T. MILLS,

Bookseller, in King's-Mead-Square.

Price SIX-PENCE.

TO THE

RIGHT HONOURABLE

The *Countess* of HUNTINGDON,[9]

THIS

# NARRATIVE

Of my *LIFE*,

And of GOD'S Wonderful Dealings

with me, is,

*(Through Her LADYSHIP's Permission)*

*Most Humbly Dedicated,*

*By her LADYSHIP's*

*Most obliged*

*And obedient Servant,*

**JAMES ALBERT.**

# THE PREFACE TO THE READER.

THIS *Account of the Life and spiritual Experience of* JAMES ALBERT, *was taken from his own Mouth and committed to Paper by the elegant Pen of a young* LADY *of the Town of* LEOMINSTER,[10] *for her own private Satisfaction, and without any Intention at first that it should be made public. But she has now been prevail'd on to commit it to the Press, both with a view to serve* ALBERT *and his distressed Family, who have the sole Profits arising from the Sale of it; and likewise as it is apprehended, this little History contains Matter well worthy the Notice and Attention of every Christian Reader.*

*Perhaps we have here in some Degree a Solution of that Question that has perplex'd the Minds of so many serious Persons, viz. In what Manner will God deal with those benighted Parts of the World where the Gospel of Jesus Christ hath never reach'd? Now it appears from the Experience of this remarkable Person, that God does not save without the Knowledge of the Truth; but, with Respect to those whom he hath fore-known, though born under every outward Disadvantage, and in Regions of the grossest Darkness and Ignorance, he most amazingly acts upon and influences their Minds, and in the Course of wisely and most wonderfully appointed Providences, he brings them to the Means of spiritual Information, gradually opens to their View the Light of his Truth, and gives them full Possession and Enjoyment of the inestimable Blessings of his Gospel. Who can doubt but that the Suggestion so forcibly press'd upon the mind of* ALBERT *(when a Boy) that there was a Being superior to the Sun, Moon, and Stars (the Objects of African Idolatry) came from the Father of Lights, and was, with Respect to him, the First-Fruit of the Display of Gospel-Glory? His long and perilous Journey to the Coast of Guinea,[11] where he was sold for a Slave, and so brought into a Christian Land; shall we consider this as the alone Effect of a curious and inquisitive Disposition? Shall we in accounting for it refer to nothing higher than mere Chance and accidental Circumstances? Whatever Infidels and Deists may think; I trust the Christian Reader will easily discern an All-wise and Omnipotent Appointment and Direction in these Movements. He belong'd to the Redeemer of lost Sinners; he was the Purchase of his Cross; and therefore the Lord undertook to bring him by a Way he knew not, out of Darkness into his marvellous Light, that he might lead him to a saving Heart-Acquaintance and Union with the triune God in Christ reconciling the World unto himself; and not imputing their Trespasses. As his Call was very extraordinary, so there are certain Particulars exceedingly remarkable in his Experience. God has put singular Honour upon him in the Exercise of his Faith and Patience, which in the most distressing and pitiable Trials and Calamities have been found to the Praise and Glory of God. How deeply must it affect a tender Heart, not only to be reduc'd to the last Extremity himself, but to have his Wife and Children perishing for Want before his Eyes! Yet his Faith did not fail him; he put his Trust in the Lord, and he was delivered. And at this Instant, though born in an exalted Station of Life, and now under the Pressure of various afflicting Providences, I am persuaded (for I know the Man) he would rather embrace the Dung-hill, having Christ in his Heart, than give up his spiritual Possessions and Enjoyment, to fill the Throne of Princes. It perhaps may not be amiss to observe that* JAMES ALBERT *left his native Country, (as near as I can guess from certain Circumstances) when he was about* 15 *Years old. He now appears to be turn'd of Sixty; has a good natural Understanding; is well acquainted with the Scriptures, and the Things of God, has an amiable and tender Disposition, and his Character can be well attested not only at Kidderminster,[12] the Place of his Residence but likewise by many creditable Persons in London and other Places. Reader, recommending this Narrative to your perusal, and him who is the Subject of it to your charitable Regard,*

I am your faithful and obedient Servant,

For Christ's Sake,

W. SHIRLEY.[13]

# AN ACCOUNT OF *James Albert, &c.*

---

I WAS born in the city BOURNOU; my mother was the eldest daughter of the reigning King there, of which BOURNOU is the chief city.[14] I was the youngest of six children, and particularly loved by my mother, and my grand-father almost doated on me.

I had, from my infancy, a curious turn of mind; was more grave and re-served in my disposition than either of my brothers and sisters. I often teazed them with questions they could not answer: for which reason they disliked me, as they supposed that I was either foolish, or insane. 'Twas certain that I was, at times, very unhappy in myself: it being strongly impressed on my mind that there was some GREAT MAN of power which resided above the sun, moon and stars, the objects of our worship. My dear indulgent mother would bear more with me than any of my friends beside.—I often raised my hand to heaven, and asked her who lived there? was much dissatisfied when she told me the sun, moon and stars, being persuaded, in my own mind, that there must be some SUPERIOR POWER.—I was frequently lost in wonder at the works of the Cre-ation: was afraid and uneasy and restless, but could not tell for what. I wanted to be informed of things that no person could tell me; and was always dissat-isfied.—These wonderful impressions begun in my childhood, and followed me continually 'till I left my parents, which affords me matter of admiration and thankfulness.

To this moment I grew more and more uneasy every day, in so much that one saturday, (which is the day on which we kept our sabbath) I laboured under anxieties and fears that cannot be expressed; and, what is more extraordinary, I could not give a reason for it.—I rose, as our custom is, about three o'clock, (as we are oblig'd to be at our place of worship an hour before the sun rise) we say nothing in our worship, but continue on our knees with our hands held up, ob-serving a strict silence 'till the sun is at a certain height, which I suppose to be about 10 or 11 o'clock in England: when, at a certain sign made by the priest, we get up (our duty being over) and disperse to our different houses.—Our place of meeting is under a large palm tree; we divide ourselves into many congrega-tions; as it is impossible for the same tree to cover the inhabitants of the whole City, though they are extremely large, high and majestic; the beauty and useful-ness of them are not to be described; they supply the inhabitants of the country with meat, drink and clothes;* the body of the palm tree is very large; at a cer-

---

*It is a generally received opinion, in *England,* that the natives of *Africa* go entirely unclothed; but this supposition is very unjust: they have a kind of dress so as to appear decent, though it is very slight and thin.

tain season of the year they tap it, and bring vessels to receive the wine, of which they draw great quantities, the quality of which is very delicious: the leaves of this tree are of a silky nature; they are large and soft; when they are dried and pulled to pieces it has much the same appearance as the English flax, and the inhabitants of BOURNOU manufacture it for cloathing &c. This tree likewise produces a plant or substance which has the appearance of a cabbage, and very like it, in taste almost the same: it grows between the branches. Also the palm tree produces a nut, something like a cocoa, which contains a kernel, in which is a large quantity of milk, very pleasant to the taste: the shell is of a hard substance, and of a very beautiful appearance, and serves for basons, bowls, &c.

I hope this digression will be forgiven.—I was going to observe that after the duty of our sabbath was over (on the day in which I was more distressed and afflicted than ever) we were all on our way home as usual, when a remarkable black cloud arose and covered the sun; then followed very heavy rain and thunder more dreadful than ever I had heard: the heav'ns roared, and the earth trembled at it: I was highly affected and cast down; in so much that I wept sadly, and could not follow my relations and friends home.—I was obliged to stop and felt as if my legs were tied, they seemed to shake under me: so I stood still, being in great fear of the MAN of POWER that I was persuaded in myself, lived above. One of my young companions (who entertained a particular friendship for me and I for him) came back to see for me: he asked me why I stood still in such very hard rain? I only said to him that my legs were weak, and I could not come faster: he was much affected to see me cry, and took me by the hand, and said he would lead me home, which he did. My mother was greatly alarmed at my tarrying out in such terrible weather; she asked me many questions, such as what I did so for, and if I was well? My dear mother says I, pray tell me who is the great MAN of POWER that makes the thunder? She said, there was no power but the sun, moon and stars; that they made all our country.—I then enquired how all our people came? She answered me, from one another; and so carried me to many generations back.—Then says I, who made the *First Man?* and who made the first Cow, and the first Lyon, and where does the fly come from, as no one can make him? My mother seemed in great trouble; she was apprehensive that my senses were impaired, or that I was foolish. My father came in, and seeing her in grief asked the cause, but when she related our conversation to him, he was exceedingly angry with me, and told me he would punish me severely if ever I was so troublesome again; so that I resolved never to say any thing more to him. But I grew very unhappy in myself; my relations and acquaintance endeavoured by all the means they could think on, to divert me, by taking me to ride upon goats, (which is much the custom of our country) and to shoot with a bow and arrow; but I experienced no satisfaction at all in any of these things; nor could I be easy by any means whatever: my parents were very unhappy to see me so dejected and melancholy.

About this time there came a merchant from the *Gold Coast*[15] (the third city in GUINEA) he traded with the inhabitants of our country in ivory &c. he took great notice of my unhappy situation, and enquired into the cause; he expressed vast concern for me, and said, if my parents would part with me for a little while, and let him take me home with him, it would be of more service to me than any thing they could do for me.—He told me that if I would go with him I should see houses with wings to them walk upon the water, and should also see the white folks; and that he had many sons of my age, which should be my companions; and he added to all this that he would bring me safe back again soon.—I was highly pleased with the account of this strange place, and was very desirous of going.—I seemed sensible of a secret impulse upon my mind which I could not resist that seemed to tell me I must go. When my dear mother saw that I was willing to leave them, she spoke to my father and grandfather and the rest of my relations, who all agreed that I should accompany the merchant to the Gold Coast. I was the more willing as my brothers and sisters despised me, and looked on me with contempt on the account of my unhappy disposition; and even my servants slighted me, and disregarded all I said to them. I had one sister who was always exceeding fond of me, and I loved her entirely; her name was LOGWY, she was quite white, and fair, with fine light hair though my father and mother were black.—I was truly concerned to leave my beloved sister, and she cry'd most sadly to part with me, wringing her hands, and discovered every sign of grief that can be imagined. Indeed if I could have known when I left my friends and country that I should never return to them again my misery on that occasion would have been inexpressible. All my relations were sorry to part with me; my dear mother came with me upon a camel more than three hundred miles, the first of our journey lay chiefly through woods: at night we secured ourselves from the wild beasts by making fires all around us; we and our camels kept within the circle, or we must have been torn to pieces by the Lyons, and other wild creatures, that roared terribly as soon as night came on, and continued to do so 'till morning.—There can be little said in favour of the country through which we passed; only a valley of marble that we came through which is unspeakably beautiful.— On each side of this valley are exceedingly high and almost inaccessible mountains—Some of these pieces of marble are of prodigious length and breadth but of different sizes and colour, and shaped in a variety of forms, in a wonderful manner.—It is most of it veined with gold mixed with striking and beautiful colours; so that when the sun darts upon it, it is as pleasing a sight as can be imagined.—The merchant that brought me from BOURNOU, was in partnership with another gentleman who accompanied us; he was very unwilling that he should take me from home, as, he said, he foresaw many difficulties that would attend my going with them.—He endeavoured to prevail on the merchant to throw me into a very deep pit that was in the valley, but he refused to listen to him, and said, he was resolved to take care of me: but the other was greatly dissatisfied; and when we came to a river, which we were obliged to pass through, he purpos'd throwing me in and drowning me; but the Merchant would not consent to it, so that I was preserv'd.

We travel'd 'till about four o'clock every day, and then began to make preparations for night, by cutting down large quantities of wood, to make fires to preserve us from the wild beasts.—I had a very unhappy and discontented journey, being in continual fear that the people I was with would murder me. I often reflected with extreme regret on the kind friends I had left, and the idea of my dear mother frequently drew tears from my eyes.—I cannot recollect how long we were in going from BOURNOU to the GOLD COAST; but as there is no shipping nearer to BOURNOU than that City, it was tedious in travelling so far by land, being upwards of a thousand miles.—I was heartily rejoic'd when we ar-riv'd at the end of our journey: I now vainly imagin'd that all my troubles and inquietudes would terminate here; but could I have looked into futurity, I should have perceiv'd that I had much more to suffer than I had before experienc'd, and that they had as yet but barely commenc'd.

I was now more than a thousand miles from home, without a friend or any means to procure one. Soon after I came to the merchant's house I heard the drums beat remarkably loud, and the trumpets blow—the persons accustom'd to this employ, are oblig'd to go upon a very high structure appointed for that purpose, that the sound might be heard at a great distance: They are higher than the steeples are in England. I was mightily pleas'd with sounds so entirely new to me, and was very inquisitive to know the cause of this rejoicing, and ask'd many questions concerning it: I was answer'd that it was meant as a compliment to me, because I was Grandson to the King of BOURNOU.

This account gave me a secret pleasure; but I was not suffer'd long to enjoy this satisfaction, for in the evening of the same day, two of the merchant's sons (boys about my own age) came running to me, and told me, that the next day I was to die, for the King intended to behead me.—I reply'd that I was sure it could not be true, for that I came there to play with them, and to see houses walk upon the water with wings to them, and the white folks; but I was soon inform'd that their King imag-ined I was sent by my father as a spy, and would make such discoveries at my return home that would enable them to make war with the greater advantage to ourselves; and for these reasons he had resolved I should never return to my native country.—When I heard this I suffered misery that cannot be described.—I wished a thousand times that I had never left my friends and country.—But still the ALMIGHTY was pleased to work miracles for me.

The morning I was to die, I was washed and all my gold ornaments made bright and shining, and then carried to the palace, where the King was to behead me himself (as is the custom of the place).—He was seated upon a throne at the top of an exceeding large yard, or court, which you must go through to enter the palace, it is as wide and spacious as a large field in England.—I had a lane of life-guards to go through.—I guessed it to be about three hundred paces.

I was conducted by my friend, the merchant, about half way up; then he durst proceed no further: I went up to the KING alone—I went with an undaunted courage, and it pleased GOD to melt the heart of the King, who sat with his scymi-tar in his hand ready to behead me; yet, being himself so affected, he dropped it out of his hand, and took me upon his knee and wept over me. I put my right hand round his neck, and prest him to my heart.—He sat me down and blest me; and added that he would not kill me, and that I should not go home, but be sold for a slave, so then I was conducted back again to the merchant's house.

The next day he took me on board a French brig; but the Captain did not chuse to buy me: he said I was too small; so the merchant took me home with him again.

The partner, whom I have spoken of as my enemy, was very angry to see me return, and again purposed putting an end to my life; for he represented to the other, that I should bring them into troubles and difficulties, and that I was so little that no person would buy me.

The merchant's resolution began to waver, and I was indeed afraid that I should be put to death: but however he said he would try me once more.

A few days after a Dutch ship came into the harbour, and they carried me on board, in hopes that the Captain would purchase me.—As they went, I heard them agree, that, if they could not sell me *then,* they would throw me overboard.—I was in extreme agonies when I heard this; and as soon as ever I saw the Dutch Captain, I ran to him, and put my arms round him, and said, "father, save me." (for I knew that if he did not buy me, I should be treated very ill, or, possibly, murdered) And though he did not understand my language, yet it pleased the ALMIGHTY to influence him in my behalf, and he bought me *for two yards of check,* which is of more value *there,* than in England.

When I left my dear mother I had a large quantity of gold about me, as is the custom of our country, it was made into rings, and they were linked into one another, and formed into a kind of chain, and so put round my neck, and arms and legs, and a large piece hanging at one ear almost in the shape of a pear. I found all this troublesome, and was glad when my new Master took it from me— I was now washed, and clothed in the Dutch or English manner.—My master grew very fond of me, and I loved him exceedingly. I watched every look, was always ready when he wanted me, and endeavoured to convince him, by every action, that my only pleasure was to serve him well.—I have since thought that he must have been a serious man. His actions corresponded very well with such a character.—He used to read prayers in public to the ship's crew every Sabbath day; and when first I saw him read, I was never so surprised in my whole life as when I saw the book talk to my master; for I thought it did, as I observed him to look upon it, and move his lips.—I wished it would do so to me.—As soon as my master had done reading I follow'd him to the place where he put the book, being mightily delighted with it, and when nobody saw me, I open'd it and put my ear down close upon it, in great hope that it wou'd say something to me; but was very sorry and greatly disappointed when I found it would not speak, this thought immediately presented itself to me, that every body and every thing despis'd me because I was black.

I was exceedingly sea-sick at first; but when I became more accustom'd to the sea, it wore off.—My master's ship was bound for Barbadoes. When we came there, he thought fit to speak of me to several gentlemen of his acquaintance, and one of them exprest a particular desire to see me.—He had a great mind to buy me; but the Captain could not immediately be prevail'd on to part with me; but however, as the gentleman seem'd very solicitous, he at length let me go, and I was sold for fifty dollars (*four and sixpenny-pieces in English.*) My new master's name was Vanhorn, a young Gentleman; his home was in New-England, in the City of New-York; to which place he took me with him. He dress'd me in his livery, and was very good to me. My chief business was to wait at table, and tea, and clean knives, and I had a very easy place; but the servants us'd to curse and swear surprizingly; which I learnt faster than any thing, 'twas almost the first English I could speak. If any of them affronted me, I was sure to call upon God to damn them immediately; but I was broke of it all at once, occasioned by the correction of an old black servant that liv'd in the family.—One day I had just clean'd the knives for dinner, when one of the maids took one to cut bread and butter with; I was very angry with her, and called upon God to damn her; when this old black man told me I must not say so. I ask'd him why? He replied there was a wicked man call'd the Devil, that liv'd in hell, and would take all that said these words, and put them in the fire and burn them.—This terrified me greatly, and I was entirely broke of swearing.—Soon after this, as I was placing the china for tea, my mistress came into the room just as the maid had been cleaning it; the girl had unfortunately sprinkled the wainscot with the mop; at which my mistress was angry; the girl very foolishly answer'd her again, which made her worse, and she call'd upon God to damn her.—I was vastly concern'd to hear this, as she was a fine young lady, and very good to me, insomuch that I could not help speaking to her, "Madam, says I, you must not say so," Why, says she? Because there is a black man call'd the Devil that lives in hell, and he will put you in the fire and burn you, and I shall be very sorry for that. Who told you this replied my lady? Old Ned, says I. Very well was all her answer; but she told my master of it, and he order'd that old Ned should be tyed up and whipp'd, and was never suffer'd to come into the kitchen with the rest of the servants afterwards.—My mistress was not angry with me, but rather diverted with my simplicity and, by way of talk, She repeated what I had said, to many of her acquaintance that visited her; among the rest, Mr. Freelandhouse,[16] a very gracious, good Minister, heard it, and he took a great deal of notice of me, and desired my master to part with me to him. He would not hear of it at first, but, being greatly persuaded, he let me go, and Mr. Freelandhouse gave £50. for me.—He took me home with him, and made me kneel down, and put my two hands together, and pray'd for me, and every night and morning he did the same.—I could not make out what it was for, nor the meaning of it, nor what they spoke to when they talk'd—I thought it comical, but I lik'd it very well.— After I had been a little while with my new master I grew more familiar, and ask'd him the meaning of prayer: (I could hardly speak english to be understood) he took great pains with me, and made me understand that he pray'd to God, who liv'd in Heaven; that He was my Father and BEST Friend.—I told him that this must be a mistake; that *my* father liv'd at BOURNOU, and I wanted very much to see him, and likewise my dear mother, and sister, and I wish'd he would be so good as to send me home to them; and I added, all I could think of to induce him to convey me back. I appeared in great trouble, and my good master was so much affected that the tears ran down his face. He told me that God was a GREAT and GOOD SPIRIT, that He created all the world, and every person and thing in it, in Ethiopia, Africa, and America, and every where. I was delighted when I heard this: There, says I, I always thought so when I liv'd at home! Now if I had wings like an Eagle I would fly to tell my dear mother that God is greater than the sun, moon, and stars; and that they were made by Him.

I was exceedingly pleas'd with this information of my master's, because it corresponded so well with my own opinion; I thought now if I could but get home, I should be wiser than all my country-folks, my grandfather, or father, or mother, or any of them.—But though I was somewhat enlighten'd by this information of my master's, yet, I had no other knowledge of God but that He was a Good Spirit, and created every body, and every thing—I never was sensible, in myself, nor had any one ever told me, that He would punish the wicked, and love the just. I was only glad that I had been told there was a God because I had always thought so.

My dear kind master grew very fond of me, as was his Lady; she put me to School, but I was uneasy at that, and did not like to go; but my master and mistress requested me to learn in the gentlest terms, and persuaded me to attend my school without any anger at all; that, at last, I came to like it better, and learnt to read pretty well. My schoolmaster was a good man, his name was Vanosdore,[17] and very indulgent to me.—I was in this state when, one sunday, I heard my master preach from these words out of the Revelations, chap. i. v. 7. *"Behold, He cometh in the clouds and every eye shall see him and they that pierc'd Him."* These words affected me excessively; I was in great agonies because I thought my master directed them to me only; and, I fancied, that he observ'd me with unusual earnestness—I was farther confirm'd in this belief as I look'd round the church, and could see no one person beside myself in such grief and distress as I was; I began to think that my master hated me, and was very desirous to go home, to my own country; for I thought that if God did come (as he said) He would be sure to be most angry with *me,* as I did not know what He was, nor had ever heard of him before.

I went home in great trouble, but said nothing to any body.—I was somewhat afraid of my master; I thought he disliked me.—The next text I heard him preach from was, Heb. xii. 14. *"follow peace with all men, and holiness, without which no man shall see the LORD."* he preached the law so severely, that it made me tremble.—he said, that GOD would judge the whole world; Ethiopia, Asia, and Africa, and every where.—I was now excessively perplexed, and undetermined what to do; as I had now reason to believe that my situation would be equally bad to go, as to stay.—I kept these thoughts to myself, and said nothing to any person whatever.

I should have complained to my good mistress of this great trouble of mind, but she had been a little strange to me for several days before this happened, occasioned by a story told of me by one of the maids. The servants were all jealous, and envied me the regard, and favour shewn me by my master and mistress; and the Devil being always ready, and diligent in wickedness, had influenced this girl, to make a lye on me.—This happened about hay-harvest, and one day when I was unloading the waggon to put the hay into the barn, she watched an opportunity, in my absence, to take the fork out of the stick, and hide it: when I came again to my work, and could not find it, I was a good deal vexed, but I concluded it was dropt somewhere among the hay; so I went and bought another with my own money: when the girl saw that I had another, she was so malicious that she told my mistress I was very unfaithful, and not the person she took me for; and that she knew, I had, without my master's permission, order'd many things in his name, that he must pay for; and as a proof of my carelessness produc'd the fork she had taken out of the stick, and said, she had found it out of doors—My Lady, not knowing the truth of these things, was a little shy to me, till she mention'd it, and then I soon cleared myself, and convinc'd her that these accusations were false.

I continued in a most unhappy state for many days. My good mistress insisted on knowing what was the matter. When I made known my situation, she gave me John Bunyan on the holy war,[18] to read; I found his experience similar to my own, which gave me reason to suppose he must be a bad man; as I was convinc'd of my own corrupt nature, and the misery of my own heart: and as he acknowledg'd that he was likewise in the same condition, I experienc'd no relief at all in reading his work, but rather the reverse.—I took the book to my lady, and inform'd her I did not like it at all, it was concerning a wicked man as bad as myself; and I did not chuse to read it, and I desir'd her to give me another, wrote by a better man that was holy and without sin.—She assur'd me that John Bunyan was a good man, but she could not convince me; I thought him to be too much like myself to be upright, as his experience seem'd to answer with my own.

I am very sensible that nothing but the great power and unspeakable mercies of the Lord could relieve my soul from the heavy burden it laboured under at that time.—A few days after my master gave me Baxter's *Call to the unconverted*.[19] This was no relief to me neither; on the contrary it occasioned as much distress in me as the other had before done, *as it* invited all to come to *Christ* and I found myself so wicked and miserable that I could not come—This consideration threw me into agonies that cannot be described; insomuch that I even attempted to put an end to my life—I took one of the large case-knives, and went into the stable with an intent to destroy myself; and as I endeavoured with all my strength to force the knife into my side, it bent double. I was instantly struck with horror at the thought of my own rashness, and my conscience told me that had I succeeded in this attempt I should probably have gone to hell.

I could find no relief, nor the least shadow of comfort; the extreme distress of my mind so affected my health that I continued very ill for three Days, and Nights; and would admit of no means to be taken for my recovery, though my lady was very kind, and sent many things to me; but I rejected every means of relief and wished to die—I would not go into my own bed, but lay in the stable upon straw—I felt all the horrors of a troubled conscience, so hard to be born, and saw all the vengeance of God ready to overtake me—I was sensible that there was no way for me to be saved unless I came to *Christ*, and I could not come to Him: I thought that it was impossible He should receive such a sinner as me.

The last night that I continued in this place, in the midst of my distress these words were brought home upon my mind, *"Behold the Lamb of God."*[20] I was something comforted at this, and began to grow easier and wished for day that I might find these words in my bible—I rose very early the following morning, and went to my school-master, Mr. Vanosdore, and communicated the situation of my mind to him; he was greatly rejoiced to find me enquiring the way to Zion, and blessed the Lord who had worked so wonderfully for me a poor heathen.—I was more familiar with this good gentleman than with my master,

or any other person; and found myself more at liberty to talk to him: he encouraged me greatly, and prayed with me frequently, and I was always bene-
fited by his discourse.

About a quarter of a mile from my Master's house stood a large remarkably fine Oak-tree, in the midst of a wood; I often used to be employed there in
cutting down trees, (a work I was very fond of) I seldom failed going to this place
every day; sometimes twice a day if I could be spared. It was the highest pleasure
I ever experienced to set under this Oak; for there I used to pour out all my complaints to the LORD: and when I had any particular grievance I used to go there,
and talk to the tree, and tell my sorrows, as if it had been to a friend.

Here I often lamented my own wicked heart, and undone state; and found
more comfort and consolation than I ever was sensible of before.—Whenever I
was treated with ridicule or contempt, I used to come here and find peace. I now
began to relish the book my Master gave me, Baxter's *Call to the unconverted,*
and took great delight in it. I was always glad to be employ'd in cutting wood,
'twas a great part of my business, and I follow'd it with delight, as I was then
quite alone and my heart lifted up to GOD, and I was enabled to pray continually; and blessed for ever be his Holy Name, he faithfully answer'd my prayers.
I can never be thankful enough to Almighty GOD for the many comfortable opportunities I experienced there.

It is possible the circumstance I am going to relate will not gain credit with
many; but this I know, that the joy and comfort it conveyed to me, cannot be expressed and only conceived by those who have experienced the like.

I was one day in a most delightful frame of mind; my heart so overflowed
with love and gratitude to the Author of all my comforts.—I was so drawn out
of myself, and so fill'd and awed by the Presence of God that I saw (or thought
I saw) light inexpressible dart down from heaven upon me, and shone around
me for the space of a minute.—I continued on my knees, and joy unspeakable
took possession of my soul.—The peace and serenity which filled my mind after
this was wonderful, and cannot be told.—I would not have changed situations,
or been any one but myself for the whole world. I blest God for my poverty, that
I had no worldly riches or grandeur to draw my heart from Him. I wish'd at that
time, if it had been possible for me, to have continued on that spot for ever. I felt
an unwillingness in myself to have any thing more to do with the world, or to
mix with society again. I seemed to possess a full assurance that my sins were
forgiven me. I went home all my way rejoicing, and this text of scripture came
full upon my mind. *"And I will make an everlasting covenant with them, that I
will not turn away from them, to do them good; but I will put my fear in their
hearts that they shall not depart from me."*[21] The first opportunity that presented
itself, I went to my old school-master, and made known to him the happy state
of my soul who joined with me in praise to God for his mercy to me the vilest of
sinners.—I was now perfectly easy, and had hardly a wish to make beyond what
I possess'd, when my temporal comforts were all blasted by the death of my dear
and worthy Master Mr. Freelandhouse, who was taken from this world rather
suddenly: he had but a short illness, and died of a fever. I held his hand in mine
when he departed; he told me he had given me my freedom. I was at liberty to

go where I would.—He added that he had always pray'd for me and hop'd I should be kept unto the end. My master left me by his will ten pounds, and my freedom.

I found that if he had lived 'twas his intention to take me with him to Holland, as he had often mentioned me to some friends of his there that were desirous to see me; but I chose to continue with my Mistress who was as good to me as if she had been my mother.

The loss of Mr. Freelandhouse distress'd me greatly, but I was render'd still more unhappy by the clouded and perplex'd situation of my mind; the great enemy of my soul being ready to torment me, would present my own misery to me in such striking light, and distress me with doubts, fears, and such a deep sense of my own unworthiness, that after all the comfort and encouragement I had received, I was often tempted to believe I should be a Cast-away at last.—The more I saw of the Beauty and Glory of God, the more I was humbled under a sense of my own vileness. I often repair'd to my old place of prayer; I seldom came away without consolation. One day this Scripture was wonderfully apply'd to my mind, *"And ye are compleat in Him which is the Head of all principalities and power."*22—The Lord was pleas'd to comfort me by the application of many gracious promises at times when I was ready to sink under my troubles. *"Wherefore He is able also to save them to the uttermost that come unto God by Him seeing He ever liveth to make intercession for them.*23 Hebrews x. ver. 14. *For by one offering He hath perfected forever them that are sanctified."*

My kind, indulgent Mistress liv'd but two years after my Master. Her death was a great affliction to me. She left five sons, all gracious young men, and Ministers of the Gospel.—I continued with them all, one after another, till they died; they liv'd but four years after their parents. When it pleased God to take them to Himself. I was left quite destitute, without a friend in the world, but I who had so often experienced the Goodness of GOD, trusted in Him to do what He pleased with me.—In this helpless condition I went in the wood to prayer as usual; and tho' the snow was a considerable height, I was not sensible of cold, or any other inconveniency.—At times indeed when I saw the world frowning round me, I was tempted to think that the LORD had forsaken me. I found great relief from the contemplation of these words in Isaiah xlix. v. 16. *"Behold I have graven thee on the palms of my hands; thy walls are continually before me."* And very many comfortable promises were sweetly applied to me. The lxxxix. Psalm and 34th verse, *"My covenant will I not break nor alter the thing that is gone out of my lips."* Hebrews, chap. vi. v. 17, 18. Phillipians, chap. i. v. 6; and several more.

As I had now lost all my dear and valued friends every place in the world was alike to me. I had for a great while entertain'd a desire to come to ENGLAND.—I imagined that all the Inhabitants of this Island were *Holy;* because all those that had visited my Master from thence were good, (Mr. Whitefield24 was his particular friend) and the authors of the books that had been given me were all English. But above all places in the world I wish'd to see Kidderminster, for I could not but think that on the spot where Mr. Baxter had liv'd, and preach'd, the people must be all *Righteous.*

The situation of my affairs requir'd that I should tarry a little longer in NEW-YORK, as I was something in debt, and was embarrass'd how to pay it.— About this time a young Gentleman that was a particular acquaintance of one of my young Master's, pretended to be a friend to me, and promis'd to pay my debts, which was three pounds; and he assur'd me he would never expect the money again.—But, in less than a month, he came and demanded it; and when I assur'd him I had nothing to pay, he threatened to sell me.—Though I knew he had no right to do that, yet as I had no friend in the world to go to, it alarm'd me greatly.—At length he purpos'd my going a Privateering, that I might by these means, be enabled to pay him, to which I agreed.—Our Captain's name was ———— ————. I went in Character of Cook to him.—Near St. Domingo²⁵ we came up to five French ships, Merchant-men.—We had a very smart engagement that continued from eight in the morning till three in the afternoon; when victory declar'd on our side.—Soon after this we were met by three English ships which join'd us, and that encourag'd us to attack a fleet of 36 Ships.—We boarded the three first and then follow'd the others; and had the same success with twelve; but the rest escap'd us.—There was a great deal of blood shed, and I was near death several times, but the LORD preserv'd me.

I met with many enemies, and much persecution, among the sailors; one of them was particularly unkind to me, and studied ways to vex and teaze me.—I can't help mentioning one circumstance that hurt me more than all the rest, which was, that he snatched a book out of my hand that I was very fond of, and used frequently to amuse myself with, and threw it into the sea.—But what is remarkable he was the first that was killed in our engagement.—I don't pretend to say that this happen'd because he was not my friend; but I thought 'twas a very awful Providence to see how the enemies of the LORD are cut off.

Our Captain was a cruel hard-hearted man. I was excessively sorry for the prisoners we took in general; but the pitiable case of one young Gentleman grieved me to the heart.—He appear'd very amiable; was strikingly handsome. Our Captain took four thousand pounds from him; but that did not satisfy him, as he imagin'd he was possess'd of more, and had somewhere conceal'd it, so that the Captain threatened him with death, at which he appear'd in the deepest distress, and took the buckles out of his shoes, and untied his hair, which was very fine, and long; and in which several very valuable rings were fasten'd. He came into the Cabbin to me, and in the most obliging terms imaginable ask'd for something to eat and drink; which when I gave him, he was so thankful and pretty in his manner that my heart bled for him; and I heartily wish'd that I could have spoken in any language in which the ship's crew would not have understood me; that I might have let him know his danger; for I heard the Captain say he was resolv'd upon his death; and he put his barbarous design into execution, for he took him on shore with one of the sailors, and there they shot him.

This circumstance affected me exceedingly, I could not put him out of my mind a long while.—When we return'd to NEW-YORK the Captain divided the prize-money among us, that we had taken. When I was call'd upon to receive my part, I waited upon Mr. ————, (the Gentleman that paid my debt and was the occasion of my going abroad) to know if he chose to go with me to receive my money, or if I should bring him what I owed.—He chose to go with me; and when the Captain laid my money on the table ('twas an hundred and thirty-five pounds) I desired Mr. —— to take what I was indebted to him; and he swept it all into his handkerchief, and would never be prevail'd on to give a farthing of money, nor any thing at all beside.—And he likewise secur'd a hogshead of sugar which was my due from the same ship. The Captain was very angry with him for this piece of cruelty to me, as was every other person that heard it.—But I have reason to believe (as he was one of the Principal Merchants in the city) that he transacted business for him and on that account did not chuse to quarrel with him.

At this time a very worthy Gentleman, a Wine Merchant, his name Dunscum, took me under his protection, and would have recovered my money for me if I had chose it; but I told him to let it alone; that I wou'd rather be quiet.—I believed that it would not prosper with him, and so it happen'd, for by a series of losses and misfortunes he became poor, and was soon after drowned, as he was on a party of pleasure.—The vessel was driven out to sea, and struck against a rock by which means every soul perished.

I was very much distress'd when I heard it, and felt greatly for his family who were reduc'd to very low circumstances.—I never knew how to set a proper value on money. If I had but a little meat and drink to supply the present necessaries of life, I never wish'd for more; and when I had any I always gave it if ever I saw an object in distress. If it was not for my dear Wife and Children I should pay as little regard to money now as I did at that time.—I continu'd some time with Mr. Dunscum as his servant; he was very kind to me.—But I had a vast inclination to visit ENGLAND, and wish'd continually that it would please Providence to make a clear way for me to see this Island. I entertain'd a notion that if I could get to ENGLAND I should never more experience either cruelty or ingratitude, so that I was very desirous to get among Christians. I knew Mr. Whitefield very well.—I had heard him preach often at NEW-YORK. In this disposition I listed in the twenty-eighth Regiment of Foot, who were design'd for Martinico in the late war.[26]—We went in Admiral Pocock's fleet from New-York to Barbadoes; from thence to Martinico.—When that was taken we proceeded to the Havannah, and took that place likewise.—There I got discharged.

I was then worth about thirty pounds, but I never regarded money in the least, nor would I tarry to receive my prize-money least I should lose my chance of going to England.—I went with the Spanish prisoners to Spain; and came to Old-England with the English prisoners.—I cannot describe my joy when we were within sight of Portsmouth. But I was astonished when we landed to hear the inhabitants of that place curse and swear, and otherwise profane. I expected to find nothing but goodness, gentleness and meekness in this Christian Land, I then suffer'd great perplexities of mind.

I enquir'd if any serious Christian people resided there, the woman I made this enquiry of, answer'd me in the affirmative; and added that she was one of them.—I was heartily glad to hear her say so. I thought I could give her my whole heart: she kept a Public-House. I deposited with her all the money that I had not an immediate occasion for; as I thought it would be safer with her.—It was 25 guineas but 6 of them I desired her to lay out to the best advantage, to buy me some shirts, hat and some other necessaries. I made her a present of a very handsome large looking glass that I brought with me from Martinico, in order to recompence her for the trouble I had given her. I must do this woman the justice to acknowledge that she did lay out some little for my use, but the 19 guineas and part of the 6, with my watch, she would not return, but denied that I ever gave it her.

I soon perceived that I was got among bad people, who defrauded me of my money and watch; and that all my promis'd happiness was blasted, I had no friend but GOD and I pray'd to Him earnestly. I could scarcely believe it possible that the place where so many eminent Christians had lived and preached could abound with so much wickedness and deceit. I thought it worse than *Sodom* (considering the great advantages they have) I cryed like a child and that almost continually: at length GOD heard my prayers and rais'd me a friend indeed.

This publican had a brother who lived on Portsmouth-common, his wife was a very serious good woman.—When she heard of the treatment I had met with, she came and enquired into my real situation, and was greatly troubled at the ill usage I had received, and took me home to her own house.—I began now to rejoice, and my prayer was turned into praise. She made use of all the arguments in her power to prevail on her who had wronged me, to return my watch and money, but it was to no purpose, as she had given me no receipt and I had nothing to show for it, I could not demand it.—My good friend was excessively angry with her and obliged her to give me back four guineas, which she said she gave me out of charity: Though in fact it was my own, and much more. She would have employed some rougher means to oblige her to give up my money, but I would not suffer her. let it go says I "My GOD is in heaven." Still I did not mind my loss in the least; all that grieved me was, that I had been disappointed in finding some Christian friends, with whom I hoped to enjoy a little sweet and comfortable society.

I thought the best method that I could take now, was to go to London, and find out Mr. Whitefield, who was the only living soul I knew in England, and get him to direct me to some way or other to procure a living without being troublesome to any Person.—I took leave of my christian friend at Portsmouth, and went in the stage to London.—A creditable tradesman in the City, who went up with me in the stage, offer'd to show me the way to Mr. Whitefield's Tabernacle. Knowing that I was a perfect stranger, I thought it very kind, and accepted his offer; but he obliged me to give him half-a-crown for going with me, and likewise insisted on my giving him five shillings more for conducting me to Dr. Gifford's[27] Meeting.

I began now to entertain a very different idea of the inhabitants of England than what I had figur'd to myself before I came amongst them.—Mr. Whitefield receiv'd me very friendly, was heartily glad to see me, and directed me to a proper place to board and lodge in Petticoat-Lane, till he could think of some way to settle me in, and paid for my lodging, and all my expences. The morning after I came to my new lodging, as I was at breakfast with the gentlewoman of the house, I heard the noise of some looms over our heads: I enquir'd what it was; she told me a person was weaving silk.—I expressed a great desire to see it, and ask'd if I might: She told me she would go up with me; she was sure I should be very welcome. She was as good as her word, and as soon as we enter'd the room, the person that was weaving look'd about, and smiled upon us, and I loved her from that moment.—She ask'd me many questions, and I in turn talk'd a great deal to her. I found she was a member of Mr. Allen's[28] Meeting, and I begun to entertain a good opinion of her, though I was almost afraid to indulge this inclination, least she should prove like all the rest I had met with at Portsmouth, &c. and which had almost given me a dislike to all white women.—But after a short acquaintance I had the happiness to find she was very different, and quite sincere, and I was not without hope that she entertain'd some esteem for me. We often went together to hear Dr. Gifford, and as I had always a propensity to relieve every object in distress as far as I was able, I used to give to all that complain'd to me; sometimes half a guinea at a time, as I did not understand the real value of it.—This gracious, good woman took great pains to correct and advise me in that and many other respects.

After I had been in London about six weeks I was recommended to the notice of some of my late Master Mr. Freelandhouse's acquaintance, who had heard him speak frequently of me. I was much persuaded by them to go to Holland.—My Master lived there before he bought me, and used to speak of me so respectfully among his friends there, that it raised in them a curiosity to see me; particularly the Gentlemen engaged in the Ministry, who expressed a desire to hear my experience and examine me. I found that it was my good old Master's design that I should have gone if he had lived; for which reason I resolved upon going to Holland, and informed my dear friend Mr. Whitefield of my intention; he was much averse to my going at first, but after I gave him my reasons appeared very well satisfied. I likewise informed my Betty (the good woman that I have mentioned above) of my determination to go to Holland, and I told her that I believed she was to be my Wife: that if it was the LORD's Will I desired it, but not else.—She made me very little answer, but has since told me, she did not think it at that time.

I embarked at Tower-wharf at four o'clock in the morning, and arriv'd at Amsterdam the next day by three o'clock in the afternoon. I had several letters of recommendation to my old master's friends, who receiv'd me very graciously. Indeed, one of the chief Ministers was particularly good to me; he kept me at his house a long while, and took great pleasure in asking questions, which I answer'd with delight, being always ready to say, *"Come unto me all ye that fear GOD, and I will tell what he hath done for my Soul."*[29] I cannot but admire the footsteps of Providence; astonished that I should be so wonderfully preserved! Though the Grandson of a King, I have wanted bread, and should have been glad of the hardest crust I ever saw. I who, at home, was surrounded and guarded by slaves, so that no indifferent person might approach me, and clothed with gold, have been inhumanly threatened with death; and frequently wanted clothing to defend me from the inclemency of the weather; yet I never murmured, nor was I discontented.—I am willing, and even desirous, to be counted as nothing, a stranger in the world, and a pilgrim here; for *"I know that my REDEEMER liveth,"*[30] and I'm thankful for every trial and trouble that I've met with, as I am not without hope that they have been all sanctified to me.

The Calvinist Ministers desired to hear my Experience from myself, which proposal I was very well pleased with: So I stood before 38 Ministers every Thursday for seven weeks together, and they were all very well satisfied, and persuaded I was what I pretended to be.—They wrote down my experience as I spoke it; and the LORD ALMIGHTY was with me at that time in a remarkable manner, and gave me words and enabled me to answer them; so great was his mercy to take me in hand a poor blind heathen.

At this time a very rich Merchant at AMSTERDAM offered to take me into his family in the capacity of his Butler, and I very willingly accepted it.—He was gracious worthy Gentleman and very good to me.—He treated me more like a friend than a servant.—I tarried there a twelvemonth but was not thoroughly contented, I wanted to see my wife; (that is now) and for that reason I wished to return to ENGLAND, I wrote to her once in my absence, but she did not answer my letter; and I must acknowledge if she had, it would have given me a less opinion of her.[31]— My Master and Mistress persuaded me much not to leave them and likewise their two Sons who entertained a good opinion of me; and if I had found my Betty married on my arrival in ENGLAND, I should have returned to them again immediately.

My Lady purposed my marrying her maid; she was an agreeable young woman, had saved a good deal of money, but I could not fancy her, though she was willing to accept of me, but I told her my inclinations were engaged in ENGLAND, and I could think of no other Person.—On my return home, I found my Betty disengaged.—She had refused several offers in my absence, and told her sister that, she thought, if ever she married I was to be her husband.

Soon after I came home, I waited on Doctor Gifford who took me into his family and was exceedingly good to me. The character of this pious worthy Gentleman is well known; my praise can be of no use or signification at all.—I hope I shall ever gratefully remember the many favours I have received from him.— Soon after I came to Doctor Gifford I expressed a desire to be admitted into their Church, and set down with them; they told me I must first be baptized; so I gave in my experience before the Church, with which they were very well satisfied, and I was baptized by Doctor Gifford with some others. I then made known my intentions of being married; but I found there were many objections against it because the person I had fixed on was poor. She was a widow, her husband had left her in debt, and with a child, so that they persuaded me against it out of real regard to me.—But I had promised and was resolved to have her; as I knew her to be a gracious woman, her poverty was no objection to me, as they had nothing else to say against her. When my friends found that they could not alter my opinion respecting her, they wrote to Mr. Allen, the Minister she attended, to persuade her to leave me; but he replied that he would not interfere at all, that we might do as we would. I was resolved that all my wife's little debt should be paid before we were married; so that I sold almost every thing I had and with all the money I could raise cleared all that she owed, and I never did any thing with a better will in all my Life, because I firmly believed that we should be very happy together, and so it prov'd, for she was given me from the LORD. And I have found her a blessed partner, and we have never repented, tho' we have gone through many great troubles and difficulties.

My wife got a very good living by weaving, and could do extremely well; but just at that time there was great disturbance among the weavers; so that I was afraid to let my wife work, least they should insist on my joining the rioters which I could not think of, and, possibly, if I had refused to do so they would have knock'd me on the head.—So that by these means my wife could get no employ, neither had I work enough to maintain my family. We had not yet been married a year before all these misfortunes overtook us.

Just at this time a gentleman, that seemed much concerned for us, advised me to go into *Essex* with him and promised to get me employed.—I accepted his kind proposal, and he spoke to a friend of his, a Quaker, a gentleman of large fortune, who resided a little way out of the town of *Colchester;* his name was *Handbarar;* he ordered his steward to set me to work.

There were several employed in the same way with myself. I was very thankful and contented though my wages were but small.—I was allowed but eight pence a day, and found myself; but after I had been in this situation for a fortnight, my Master, being told that a Black was at work for him, had an inclination to see me. He was pleased to talk to me for some time, and at last enquired what wages I had; when I told him he declared, it was too little, and immediately ordered his Steward to let me have eighteen pence a day, which he constantly gave me after; and I then did extremely well.

I did not bring my wife with me: I came first alone and it was my design, if things answered according to our wishes, to send for her—I was now thinking to desire her to come to me when I receiv'd a letter to inform me she was just brought to bed and in want of many necessaries.—This news was a great trial to me and a fresh affliction: but my GOD, *faithful and abundant in mercy,* forsook me not in this trouble.—As I could not read *English,*[32] I was obliged to apply to some one to read the letter I received, relative to my wife. I was directed by the good Providence of GOD to a worthy young gentleman, a Quaker, and friend of my Master.—I desired he would take the trouble to read my letter for me, which he readily comply'd with and was greatly moved and affected at the contents; insomuch that he said he would undertake to make a gathering for me, which he did and was the first to contribute to it himself. The money was sent that evening to LONDON by a person who happen'd to be going there; nor was this All the goodness that I experienced from these kind friends, for, as soon as my wife came about and was fit to travel, they sent for her to me, and were at the whole expence of her coming; so evedently has the love and mercy of GOD appeared through every trouble that ever I experienced. We went on very comfortably all the summer.—We lived in a little cottage near Mr. *Handbarrar's* House; but when the winter came on I was discharged, as he had no further occasion for me. And now the prospect began to darken upon us again. We thought it most adviseable to move our habitation a little nearer to the Town, as the house we lived in was very cold, and wet, and ready to tumble down.

The boundless goodness of GOD to me has been so very great, that with the most humble gratitude I desire to prostrate myself before Him; for I have been wonderfully supported in every affliction. My GOD never left me. I perceived light *still* through the thickest darkness.

My dear wife and I were now both unemployed, we could get nothing to do. The winter prov'd remarkably severe, and we were reduc'd to the greatest distress imaginable.—I was always very shy of asking for any thing; I could never beg; neither did I chuse to make known our wants to any person, for fear of offending as we were entire strangers; but our last bit of bread was gone, and I was obliged to think of something to do for our support. I did not mind for myself at all; but to see my dear wife and children in want pierc'd me to the heart.—I now blam'd myself for bringing her from London, as doubtless had we continued there we might have found friends to keep us from starving. The snow was at this season remarkably deep; so that we could see no prospect of being relieved. In this melancholy situation, not knowing what step to pursue, I resolved to make my case known to a Gentleman's Gardiner that lived near us, and entreat him to employ me: but when I came to him, my courage failed me, and I was ashamed to make known our real situation.—I endeavoured all I could to prevail on him to set me to work, but to no purpose: he assur'd me it was not in his power: but just as I was about to leave him, he asked me if I would accept of some Carrots? I took them with great thankfulness and carried them home; he gave me four, they were very large and fine.—We had nothing to make fire with, so consequently could not boil them: But was glad to have them to eat *raw*. Our youngest child was quite an infant; so that my wife was obliged to chew it, and fed her in that manner for several days. —We allowed ourselves but one every day, least they should not last 'till we could get some other supply. I was unwilling to eat at all myself; nor would I take any the last day that we continued in this situation, as I could not bear the thought that my dear wife and children would be in want of every means of support. We lived in this manner, 'till our carrots were all gone: then my Wife began to lament because of our poor babies: but I comforted her all I could; still hoping, and believing that *my* GOD would not let us die: but that it would please Him to relieve us, which *He* did by almost a Miracle.

We went to bed, as usual, before it was quite dark, (as we had neither fire nor candle) but had not been there long before some person knocked at the door & enquir'd if *James Albert* lived there? I answer'd in the affirmative, and rose immediately; as soon as I open'd the door I found it was the servant of an eminent Attorney who resided at *Colchester*.—He ask'd me how it was with me? if I was not almost starv'd? I burst out a crying, and told him I was indeed. He said his master suppos'd so, and that he wanted to speak with me, and I must return with him. This Gentleman's name was *Danniel*, he was a sincere, good christian. He used to stand and talk with me frequently when I work'd in the road for Mr. *Handbarrar*, and would have employed me himself, if I had wanted work.— When I came to his house he told me that he had thought a good deal about me of late, and was apprehensive that I must be in want, and could not be satisfied till he sent to enquire after me. I made known my distress to him, at which he was greatly affected; and generously gave me a guinea; and promis'd to be kind to me in future. I could not help exclaiming. *O the boundless mercies of my God!* I pray'd unto Him, and He has heard me; I trusted in Him, and He has preserv'd me: where shall I begin to praise Him, or how shall I love him enough?

I went immediately and bought some bread and cheese and coal and carried it home. My dear wife was rejoiced to see me return with something to eat. She instantly got up and dressed our Babies, while I made a fire, and the first Nobility in the land never made a more comfortable meal.—We did not forget to thank the LORD for all his goodness to us.—Soon after this, as the spring came on, Mr. Peter *Daniel* employed me in helping to pull down a house, and rebuilding it. I had then very good work, and full employ: he sent for my wife, and children to *Colchester,* and provided us a house where we lived very comfortably.—I hope I shall always gratefully acknowledge his kindness to myself and family. I worked at this house for more than a year, till it was finished; and after that I was employed by several successively, and was never so happy as when I had something to do; but perceiving the winter coming on, and work rather slack, I was apprehensive that we should again be in want or become troublesome to our friends.

I had at this time an offer made me of going to *Norwich* and having constant employ.—My wife seemed pleased with this proposal, as she supposed she might get work there in the weaving-manufactory, being the business she was brought up to, and more likely to succeed there than any other place; and we thought as we had an opportunity of moving to a Town where we could both be employ'd it was most adviseable to do so; and that probably we might settle there for our lives.—When this step was resolv'd on, I went first alone to see how it would answer; which I very much repented after, for it was not in my power immediately to send my wife any supply, as I fell into the hands of a Master that was neither kind nor considerate; and she was reduced to great distress, so that she was oblig'd to sell the few goods that we had, and when I sent for her was under the disagreeable necessity of parting with our bed.

When she came to *Norwich* I hired a room ready furnished.—I experienced a great deal of difference in the carriage of my Master from what I had been accustomed to from some of my other Masters. He was very irregular in his payments to me.—My wife hired a loom and wove all the leisure time she had and we began to do very well, till we were overtaken by fresh misfortunes. Our three poor children fell ill of the small pox; this was a great trial to us; but still I was persuaded in myself we should not be forsaken.—And I did all in my power to keep my dear partner's spirits from sinking. Her whole attention now was taken up with the children as she could mind nothing else, and all I could get was but little to support a family in such a situation, beside paying for the hire of our room, which I was obliged to omit doing for several weeks: but the woman to whom we were indebted would not excuse us, tho' I promised she should have the very first money we could get after my children came about, but she would not be satisfied and had the cruelty to threaten us that if we did not pay her immediately she would turn us all into the street.

The apprehension of this plunged me in the deepest distress, considering the situation of my poor babies: if they had been in health I should have been less sensible of this misfortune. But My GOD, *still faithful to his promise,* raised me a friend. Mr. Henry Gurdney,[33] a Quaker, a gracious gentleman heard of our distress, he sent a servant of his own to the woman we hired the room of, paid our rent, and bought all the goods with my wife's loom and gave it us all.

Some other gentlemen, hearing of his design, were pleased to assist him in these generous acts, for which we never can be thankful enough; after this my children soon came about; we began to do pretty well again; my dear wife work'd hard and constant when she could get work, but it was upon a disagreeable footing as her employ was so uncertain, sometimes she could get nothing to do and at other times when the weavers of *Norwich* had orders from LONDON they were so excessively hurried, that the people they employ'd were often oblig'd to work on the *Sabbath-day;* but this my wife would never do, and it was matter of uneasiness to us that we could not get our living in a regular manner, though we were both diligent, industrious, and willing to work. I was far from being happy in my Master, he did not use me well. I could scarcely ever get my money from him; but I continued patient 'till it pleased GOD to alter my situation.

My worthy friend Mr. Gurdney advised me to follow the employ of chopping chaff, and bought me an instrument for that purpose. There were but few people in the town that made this their business beside myself; so that I did very well indeed and we became easy and happy.—But we did not continue long in this comfortable state: Many of the inferior people were envious and ill-natur'd and set up the same employ and work'd under price on purpose to get my business from me, and they succeeded so well that I could hardly get any thing to do, and became again unfortunate: Nor did this misfortune come alone, for just at this time we lost one of our little girls who died of a fever; this circumstance occasion'd us new troubles, for the Baptist Minister refused to bury her because we were not their members. The Parson of the parish denied us because she had never been baptized. I applied to the Quakers, but met with no success; this was one of the greatest trials I ever met with, as we did not know what to do with our poor baby.—At length I resolv'd to dig a grave in the garden behind the house, and bury her there; when the Parson of the parish sent for me to tell me he would bury the child, but did not chuse to read the burial service over her. I told him I did not mind whether he would or not, as the child could not hear it.

We met with a great deal of ill treatment after this, and found it very difficult to live.—We could scarcely get work to do, and were obliged to pawn our cloaths. We were ready to sink under our troubles.—When I proposed to my wife to go to *Kidderminster* and try if we could do there. I had always an inclination for that place, and now more than ever as I had heard *Mr. Fawcet*[34] mentioned in the most respectful manner, as a pious worthy Gentleman, and I had seen his name in a favourite book of mine, Baxter's *Saints everlasting rest;* and as the Manufactory of *Kidderminster* seemed to promise my wife some employment, she readily came into my way of thinking.

I left her once more, and set out for *Kidderminster* in order to judge if the situation would suit us.—As soon as I came there I waited immediately on *Mr. Fawcet,* who was pleased to receive me very kindly and recommended me to *Mr. Watson* who employed me in twisting silk and worsted together. I continued here about a fortnight, and when I thought it would answer our expectation, I returned to *Norwich* to fetch my wife; she was then near her time, and too much indisposed. So we were obliged to tarry until she was brought to bed, and as soon as she could conveniently travel we came to *Kidderminster,* but we brought nothing with us as we were obliged to sell all we had to pay our debts, and the expences of my wife's illness, &c.

Such is our situation at present.—My wife, by hard labor at the loom, does every thing that can be expected from her towards the maintenance of our family; and GOD is pleased to incline the hearts of his People at times to yield us their charitable assistance; being myself through age and infirmity able to contribute but little to their support. As Pilgrims, and very poor Pilgrims, we are travelling through many difficulties towards our HEAVENLY HOME, and waiting patiently for his gracious call, when the LORD shall deliver us out of the evils of this present world and bring us to the EVERLASTING GLORIES of the world to come.—To HIM be PRAISE for EVER and EVER, AMEN.


FINIS.


1. An 1809 American version of Gronniosaw's narrative identifies this "young lady" in a footnote that reads: "Supposed to be Miss Hannah More" (Potkay and Burr, *Black Atlantic Writers,* 53). More (1745–1833) was a well-known British writer and reformer. But this identification is not replicated in any of More's own voluminous writings, nor in any memoirs by her contemporaries; if true, it would make Gronniosaw's narrative More's first published book. Moreover, More was not a resident of Leominster; she resided in Bristol at the time of the narrative's composition. The idealistic abolitionist fervor and high, quasi-romantic style of More's writing seems utterly at odds with the tenor, tone, and rhetoric of Gronniosaw's narrative. Dodd & Rumsey, who published the 1809 version, also made other major changes to the text, which they retitled *The Black Prince;* they may have wished to raise the esteem of the narrative by ascribing it, thirty-seven years after its initial publication, to a popular writer with a strong interest in both religion and the abolition of slavery.

2. See note 31 in the introduction, pp. xxxvi–xxxvii.

3. Carretta, *Unchained Voices,* 9.

4. Gates, "James Gronniosaw," 14.

5. Potkay and Burr, *Black Atlantic Writers,* 5–8.

6. Carretta, *Unchained Voices,* 54.

7. Ibid., 5, 55, 154.

8. Gates, "James Gronniosaw," 11.

9. Selina Hastings, Countess of Huntingdon (1707–91), was one of the most important Methodist leaders of her day. She was close to John and Charles Wesley and George Whitefield, the founders of Methodism, and when they split, took the part of Whitefield. The patron and protector of dozens of prominent clergymen, she was largely responsible for introducing Methodism to the upper classes. In addition, she was the patron of many Africans, including Gronniosaw, Phillis Wheatley, John Marrant, and Olaudah Equiano.

10. A small town twelve miles north of Hereford, England.

11. *Guinea* designated the West African shore stretching from Senegal all the way to Angola.

12. A town fifteen miles north of Worcester, England.

13. Walter Shirley (1725–86) was a clergyman, writer, publisher of hymns, and cousin and right-hand man of the Countess of Huntingdon. Carretta, *Unchained Voices,* 55; Potkay and Burr, *Black Atlantic Writers,* 53.

14. Bornu was a powerful Mohammedan state extending from 11°N to 15°N and from 10°E to 15°E, centered around Lake Chad, and including parts of the present-day countries of

Nigeria, Niger, Chad, and Cameroon. However, Bornu is not a city; and in later British, Scottish, and Irish editions of Gronniosaw's narrative, "Bournou" is specified as the chief city of "Zaara." (This may refer to Zaria, a province of Nigeria over a hundred miles west of Bornu.)

15. Ghana.

16. Theodorus Jacobus Frelinghuysen (1691–c. 1748) was a Dutch clergyman in New Jersey and a seminal figure of the Great Awakening, an important religious revival of the period. Carretta, *Unchained Voices*, 55; Potkay and Burr, *Black Atlantic Writers*, 8, 56.

17. Probably Peter Van Arsdalen, one of Frelinghuysen's "helpers" in the ministry. Carretta, *Unchained Voices*, 55; Potkay and Burr, *Black Atlantic Writers*, 56.

18. John Bunyan (1628–88), a celebrated English Puritan preacher and writer, wrote *The Holy War, Made by Shaddai upon Diabolus, for the Reigning of the Metropolis of the World*, an allegory, in 1682.

19. Richard Baxter (1615–91) was a Puritan minister at Kidderminster who wrote over two hundred works, including *A Call to the Unconverted to Turn and Live* (1658), perhaps the most popular seventeenth-century conversion treatise; he also preached against slavery and the slave trade.

20. *John* 1:29, 36.

21. *Jeremiah* 32:40.

22. *Colossians* 2:10.

23. *Hebrews* 7:25.

24. George Whitefield (1714–70) was an evangelist and the leader of the Calvinistic Methodist Church. An extraordinarily popular preacher, he gave open-air sermons throughout England and the American colonies, was an influential figure in the Great Awakening, and kept a house in Savannah, where he had established a home for orphans. Whitefield broke with John and Charles Wesley in 1741, which resulted in the establishment of two branches of Methodism. Although he welcomed blacks into Methodism, in 1747 he bought a plantation and slaves in South Carolina, and defended slavery on biblical grounds.

25. The island of Hispaniola, now the Dominican Republic and Haiti.

26. The Seven Years' War, 1756–63. Martinique and Cuba were captured by the British fleet, under Admiral George Pocock (1706–92), in 1762, but the Treaty of Paris the following year restored Martinique to France and Cuba to Spain.

27. Andrew Gifford (1700–84) was the Baptist minister of the Eagle Street meeting in London. Potkay and Burr, *Black Atlantic Writers*, 61.

28. John Allen was a Calvinist pastor of a Baptist church in Petticoat Lane, Spitalfields. Carretta, *Unchained Voices*, 57.

29. *Psalms* 66:16.

30. *Job* 19:25

31. "For an unmarried woman to write to a man to whom she was not formally betrothed was considered immodest." Carretta, *Unchained Voices*, 57.

32. Carretta suggests that Gronniosaw's prior reading had been in Dutch (*Unchained Voices*, 57); it is also quite possible, however, that he could only read the printed word, and not the handwritten, and that his amanuensis misunderstood him.

33. Henry Gurney (1721–77) was a worsted manufacturer and banker. Ibid., 58.

34. Benjamin Fawcett (1715–80) was a popular dissenting minister of Kidderminster, friend of the Countess of Huntingdon, publisher of many of Baxter's works, and author of *A Compassionate Address to the Christian Negroes in Virginia* (1756) and *The Religious Weaver: or, Pious Meditations on the Trade of Weaving* (1773). The Countess of Huntingdon opened a chapel in Kidderminster at his invitation. Ibid.; Potkay and Burr, *Black Atlantic Writers*, 53, 63.

OLAUDAH EQUIANO (GUSTAVUS VASSA)

OLAUDAH EQUIANO (a.k.a. Gustavus Vassa; c. 1745–97) published, in 1789, a sort of adventure story that "became the prototype of the nineteenth-century slave narrative"(Henry Louis Gates, Jr.).[1] It was clearly "the most famous and influential black autobiography of its time" (William Andrews);[2] and through it Equiano "did more than any other Negro before Frederick Douglass to stir up antislavery feeling"(Vernon Loggins).[3] But to characterize Equiano's *Interesting Narrative* is by no means easy. Vincent Carretta rightly calls it a "spiritual autobiography, captivity narrative, travel book, adventure tale, narrative of slavery, economic treatise, and apologia, among other things."[4] In fact, one of the hallmarks of Equiano's genius was his production of a work of literature that defies classification.

For its scope is almost encyclopedic, as if Equiano had tried to encompass in his narrative virtually every experience that a black man of his day could have had. If we can believe all he tells us, Equiano grew up in remotest Africa; was sold as a slave; was transported across the Atlantic in a slave ship; was cheated out of his freedom by an unscrupulous master; witnessed the worst aspects of slavery in the West Indies; made close friends with whites of both sexes; became a successful businessman; managed a slave estate; saved the crew of a shipwreck; captained a ship; officiated as a pastor at a funeral; made war under Wolfe in Canada and Boscawen in the Mediterranean; went on a voyage to the North Pole; worked as a hairdresser; became an accomplished French horn player; stayed with Turks in Smyrna and Miskito Indians in Central America; was employed by the British government to help resettle free blacks in Africa; wrote letters, poetry, and memoirs; cut a handsome figure in "superfine clothes"; gave evidence before a parliamentary committee on the slave trade; petitioned the queen for its abolition; knew many of the most famous personages of his day; and was visited by the Lord himself.

The *Interesting Narrative* was not the first of Equiano's writings; he was already prominent as the leading black abolitionist in England, as a number of his public letters had appeared in the press.[5] It was, however, his *chef d'oeuvre*. When published, it received favorable reviews from *The Monthly Review* and *The General Magazine and Impartial Review,* and Mary Wollstonecraft wrote an extensive, influential, and somewhat critical review of it for *The Analytical Review*.[6] It quickly became the most popular book to date written by a black author. Nine British editions were published over the next five years, with Equiano making minor changes to each; during the same period an edition was published in the United States and translations were published in Dutch, German, and Russian. Considering that the Dublin fourth edition, according to a letter Equiano wrote in 1792, numbered nineteen hundred copies, one may reasonably estimate that twenty thousand copies were sold during Equiano's lifetime. The work's popularity was not abated by Equiano's death: a total of twenty-two editions were published through 1837, including several in the United States.[7]

As Angelo Costanzo points out, among Equiano's devoted readers was John Wesley, the founder of Methodism, who read the narrative several days before he died and asked his friends to read passages to him on his deathbed. Wesley had "encouraged his brethren to write their autobiographies as means to moral self-evaluation and spiritual improvement. As a result, Methodists wrote thousands of conversion narratives";[8] this tradition clearly influenced Equiano. (For information on Methodism that may help the reader to more fully understand Equiano's milieu and conversion experience, see the introduction to Gronniosaw's narrative in this volume.) Other literary influences probably included Ottobah Cugoano, whose *Thoughts and Sentiments on the Evil and Wicked Traffic of the Slavery and Commerce of the Human Species, Calmly Submitted to the Inhabitants of Great-Britain* (1787) was the first extensive antislavery work written by a black man; James Albert Ukawsaw Gronniosaw, whose 1772 conversion narrative included a passage about a talking book that Equiano paraphrased in his narrative; Anthony Benezet, whose accounts of Africa Equiano frequently cited; John Marrant, a free black who, in 1785, published an extraordinarily imaginative conversion-cum-Indian-captivity narrative; and Daniel Defoe and John Bunyan, whose very different heroes Equiano may have wished to emulate to some degree.

The wide variety of these influences helps to explain the multiplicity of voices in Equiano's narrative. They enabled him to be, as Andrews puts it,

> outsider and insider and somewhere on the margin in between, with the self-appointed freedom to move from pole to pole on the axis of African-Western concepts of self. It was this intellectual and aesthetic freedom of the imagination that was Equiano's special triumph as an ex-slave narrator. . . . It was this exploration of first-person writing as the grounds on which discourse between two cultures could take place that made Equiano the prophet, if not the father, of Afro-American autobiography.[9]

Equiano's reading helped him appropriate certain aspects of the noble savage mythology while repudiating others, see both the blessings and curses of assimilation into British society, and balance his antislavery arguments with acutely perceptive self-revelations and vividly described adventures. Although, indeed, Equiano's narrative can be said to be "all over the map," his skill imposes coherence on a book that might otherwise veer too wildly between comic self-deprecation and earnest self-congratulation, between his vulnerability as an ignorant African and his pride as an accomplished British citizen. As Gates notes, "rarely would a slave narrator match Equiano's mastery of self-representation."[10]

Several documents illuminate Equiano's life subsequent to the initial publication of his narrative. In a letter dated February 27, 1792, he wrote:

> I went to Ireland & was there 8½ months—& sold 1900 copies of my narrative. I came here on the 10th inst.—& I now mean as it seem Pleasing to my Good God!—to leave London in about 8—or, 10 Days more, & take me a Wife—(one Miss Cullen—) of Soham in Cambridge shire—and when I have given her about 8 or 10

Days Comfort, I mean Directly to go Scotland—and sell my 5th. Editions—I Trust that my going about has been of much use to the Cause of the abolition of the accu[r]sed Slave Trade. . . .[11]

In the sixth and subsequent editions of his narrative, the following paragraph appears:

Since the first publication of my Narrative, I have been in a great variety of scenes in many parts of Great Britain, Ireland and Scotland, an account of which might well be added here; but this would swell the volume too much, I shall only observe in general, that, in May 1791, I sailed from Liverpool to Dublin where I was very kindly received, and from thence to Cork, and then travelled over many counties in Ireland. I was every where exceedingly well treated, by persons of all ranks. . . . I remained in London till I heard the debate in the House of Commons on the Slave Trade, April the 2d and 3d [1792]. I then went to Soham in Cambridgeshire, and was married on the 7th of April to Miss Cullen, daughter of James and Ann Cullen, late of Ely.[12]

Equiano died on March 31, 1797. In his will, he left half the residue of his estate, should his daughters not survive him, for the foundation of schools in Sierra Leone; but one of his two daughters, Joanna Vassa, did survive her father, and was given a substantial amount of money when she came of age in 1816. Equiano had apparently amassed a great deal of wealth—in his will, he speaks of the "Estates and property I have dearly earned by the sweat of my Brow in some of the most remote and adverse corners of the whole world to solace those I leave behind."[13] His written legacy was even more valuable.

*Olaudah Equiano*

or

GUSTAVUS VASSA,

*the African*

THE

# INTERESTING NARRATIVE

OF

# THE LIFE

OF

# OLAUDAH EQUIANO,

OR

# GUSTAVUS VASSA,

THE AFRICAN.

*WRITTEN BY HIMSELF.*

VOL. I.

———

*Behold, God is my salvation; I will trust and not be afraid, for*
*the Lord Jehovah is my strength and my song; he also is become*
*my salvation.*
*And in that day shall ye say, Praise the Lord, call upon his name,*
*declare his doings among the people.*      Isaiah xii. 2, 4.

———

## LONDON:
Printed for and sold by the AUTHOR,
No. 10, Union-Street, Middlesex Hospital;

Sold also by Mr. Johnson, St. Paul's Church-Yard; Mr. Murray, Fleet-Street; Messrs. Robson and Clark, Bond-Street; Mr. Davis, opposite Gray's Inn, Holborn; Messrs. Shepperson and Reynolds, and Mr. Jackson, Oxford-Street; Mr. Lackington, Chiswell-Street; Mr. Mathews, Strand; Mr. Murray, Prince's-Street, Soho; Mess. Taylor and Co. South Arch, Royal Exchange; Mr. Button, Newington-Causeway; Mr. Parsons, Paternoster-Row; and may be had of all the Booksellers in Town and Country.

[Entered at Stationer's Hall.]

## To the Lords Spiritual and Temporal,[14] and the Commons of the Parliament of Great Britain.

*My Lords and Gentlemen,*

PERMIT me, with the greatest deference and respect, to lay at your feet the following genuine Narrative; the chief design of which is to excite in your august assemblies a sense of compassion for the miseries which the Slave-Trade has entailed on my unfortunate countrymen. By the horrors of that trade was I first torn away from all the tender connexions that were naturally dear to my heart; but these, through the mysterious ways of Providence, I ought to regard as infinitely more than compensated by the introduction I have thence obtained to the knowledge of the Christian religion, and of a nation which, by its liberal sentiments, its humanity, the glorious freedom of its government, and its proficiency in arts and sciences, has exalted the dignity of human nature.

I am sensible I ought to entreat your pardon for addressing to you a work so wholly devoid of literary merit; but, as the production of an unlettered African, who is actuated by the hope of becoming an instrument towards the relief of his suffering countrymen, I trust that *such a man,* pleading in *such a cause,* will be acquitted of boldness and presumption.

May the God of heaven inspire your hearts with peculiar benevolence on that important day when the question of Abolition is to be discussed, when thousands, in consequence of your Determination, are to look for Happiness or Misery!

I am,
MY LORDS AND GENTLEMEN,
Your most obedient
And devoted humble Servant,

OLAUDAH EQUIANO,
OR
GUSTAVUS VASSA.

Union-Street, Mary-le-bone,
    March 24, 1789.

His Royal Highness the Prince of
    Wales.[16]
His Royal Highness the Duke of York.[17]

A

The Right Hon. the Earl of Ailesbury
Admiral Affleck
Mr. William Abington, 2 copies
Mr. John Abraham
James Adair, Esq.[18]
Reverend Mr. Aldridge[19]
Mr. John Almon[20]
Mrs. Arnot
Mr. Joseph Armitage
Mr. Joseph Ashpinshaw
Mr. Samuel Atkins[21]
Mr. John Atwood
Mr. Thomas Atwood[22]
Mr. Ashwell
J. C. Ashworth, Esq.

B

His Grace the Duke of Bedford[23]
Her Grace the Duchess of Buccleugh
The Right Rev. the Lord Bishop of Bangor[24]
The Right Hon. Lord Belgrave
The Rev. Doctor Baker
Mrs. Baker
Matthew Baillie, M.D.[25]
Mrs. Baillie
Miss Baillie
Miss J. Baillie[26]
David Barclay, Esq.
Mr. Robert Barrett
Mr. William Barrett
Mr. John Barnes
Mr. John Basnett
Mr. Bateman
Mrs. Baynes, 2 copies
Mr. Thomas Bellamy[27]
Mr. J. Benjafield
Mr. William Bennett
Mr. Bensley
Mr. Samuel Benson
Mrs. Benton
Reverend Mr. Bentley
Mr. Thomas Bently
Sir John Berney, Bart.[28]
Alexander Blair, Esq.
James Bocock, Esq.

Mrs. Bond
Miss Bond
Mrs. Borckhardt
Mrs. E. Bouverie
———— Brand, Esq.
Mr. Martin Brander
F. J. Brown, Esq. M. P. 2 copies
W. Buttall, Esq.
Mr. Buxton
Mr. R. L. B.
Mr. Thomas Burton, 6 copies
Mr. W. Button

C

The Right Hon. Lord Cathcart[29]
The Right Hon. H. S. Conway[30]
Lady Almiria Carpenter
James Carr, Esq.
Charles Carter, Esq.
Mr. James Chalmers
Captain John Clarkson, of the Royal Navy
The Rev. Mr. Thomas Clarkson,[31] 2 copies
Mr. R. Clay
Mr. William Clout
Mr. George Club
Mr. John Cobb
Miss Calwell
Mr. Thomas Cooper
Richard Cosway, Esq.[32]
Mr. James Coxe
Mr. J. C.
Mr. Croucher
Mr. Cruickshanks
Ottobah Cugoano, or John Stewart[33]

D

The Right Hon. the Earl of Dartmouth[34]
The Right Hon. the Earl of Derby
Sir William Dolben, Bart.
The Reverend C. E. De Coetlogon[35]
John Delamain, Esq.
Mrs. Delamain
Mr. Davis
Mr. William Denton
Mr. T. Dickie
Mr. William Dickson
Mr. Charles Dilly,[36] 2 copies
Andrew Drummond, Esq.
Mr. George Durant

E

The Right Hon. the Earl of Essex
The Right Hon. the Countess of Essex
Sir Gilbert Elliot, Bart.[37] 2 copies
Lady Ann Erskine
G. Noel Edwards, Esq. M. P. 2 copies
Mr. Durs Egg
Mr. Ebenezer Evans
The Reverend Mr. John Eyre[38]
Mr. William Eyre

F

Mr. George Fallowdown
Mr. John Fell[39]
F. W. Foster, Esq.
The Reverend Mr. Foster
Mr. J. Frith
W. Fuller, Esq.

G

The Right Hon. the Earl of Gainsborough
The Right Hon. the Earl of Grosvenor[40]
The Right Hon. Viscount of Gallway
The Right Hon. Viscountess Gallway
—— Gardner, Esq.[41]
Mrs. Garrick
Mrs. John Gates
Mr. Samuel Gear
Sir Philip Gibbes, Bart. 6 copies
Miss Gibbes
Mr. Edward Gilbert
Mr. Jonathan Gillett
W. P. Gilliess, Esq.
Mrs. Gordon
Mr. Grange
Mr. William Grant
Mr. John Grant
Mr. R. Greening
S. Griffiths
John Grove, Esq.
Mrs. Guerin
Reverend Mr. Gwinep

H

The Right Hon. the Earl of Hopetoun[42]
The Right Hon. Lord Hawke
Right Hon. Dowager Countess of
   Huntingdon[43]
Thomas Hall, Esq.
Mr. Haley
Hugh Josiah Hansard, Esq.
Mr. Moses Hart
Mrs. Hawkins
Mr. Haysom

Mr. Hearne
Mr. William Hepburn
Mr. J. Hibbert
Mr. Jacob Higman
Sir Richard Hill, Bart.[44]
Reverend Rowland Hill[45]
Miss Hill
Captain John Hills, Royal Navy
Edmund Hill, Esq.
The Reverend Mr. Edward Hoare
William Hodges, Esq.[46]
Reverend Mr. John Holmes, 3 copies
Mr. Martin Hopkins
Mr. Thomas Howell
Mr. R. Huntley
Mr. J. Hunt
Mr. Philip Hurlock, jun.
Mr. Hutson

J

Mr. T. W. J. Esq.
Mr. James Jackson
Mr. John Jackson[47]
Reverend Mr. James
Mrs. Anne Jennings
Mr. Johnson
Mrs. Johnson
Mr. William Jones
Thomas Irving, Esq. 2 copies
Mr. William Justins

K

The Right Hon. Lord Kinnaird
William Kendall, Esq.
Mr. William Ketland
Mr. Edward King[48]
Mr. Thomas Kingston
Reverend Dr. Kippis[49]
Mr. William Kitchener
Mr. John Knight[50]

L

The Right Reverend the Lord Bishop of
   London[51]
Mr. John Laisne
Mr. Lackington, 6 copies[52]
Mr. John Lamb
Bennett Langton, Esq.[53]
Mr. S. Lee
Mr. Walter Lewis
Mr. J. Lewis
Mr. J. Lindsey
Mr. T. Litchfield
Edward Loveden Loveden, Esq. M.P.

Charles Lloyd, Esq.[54]
Mr. William Lloyd
Mr. J. B. Lucas
Mr. James Luken
Henry Lyte, Esq.
Mrs. Lyon

### M

His Grace the Duke of Marlborough[55]
His Grace the Duke of Montague[56]
The Right Hon. Lord Mulgrave[57]
Sir Herbert Mackworth, Bart.
Sir Charles Middleton, Bart.
Lady Middleton
Mr. Thomas Macklane
Mr. George Markett
James Martin, Esq. M. P.
Master Martin, Hayes-Grove, Kent
Mr. William Massey
Mr. Joseph Massingham
John McIntosh, Esq.
Paul Le Mesurier, Esq. M. P.
Mr. James Mewburn
Mr. N. Middleton
T. Mitchell, Esq.[58]
Mrs. Montague,[59] 2 copies
Miss Hannah More[60]
Mr. George Morrison
Thomas Morris, Esq.[61]
Miss Morris
Morris Morgann, Esq.[62]

### N

His Grace the Duke of Northumberland[63]
Captain Nurse

### O

Edward Ogle, Esq.
James Ogle, Esq.
Robert Oliver, Esq.

### P

Mr. D. Parker,
Mr. W. Parker,
Mr. Richard Packer, jun.
Mr. Parsons, 6 copies
Mr. James Pearse
Mr. J. Pearson
J. Penn, Esq.
George Peters, Esq.
Mr. W. Phillips
J. Philips, Esq.
Mrs. Pickard
Mr. Charles Pilgrim

The Hon. George Pitt, M. P.
Mr. Thomas Pooley
Patrick Power, Esq.
Mr. Michael Power
Joseph Pratt, Esq.

### Q

Robert Quarme, Esq.

### R

The Right Hon. Lord Rawdon
The Right Hon. Lord Rivers,[64] 2 copies
Lieutenant General Rainsford
Reverend James Ramsay,[65] 3 copies
Mr. S. Remnant, jun.
Mr. William Richards, 2 copies
Mr. J. C. Robarts
Mr James Roberts
Dr. Robinson
Mr. Robinson
Mr. C. Robinson
George Rose, Esq. M. P.[66]
Mr. W. Ross
Mr. William Rouse
Mr. Walter Row

### S

His Grace the Duke of St. Albans
Her Grace the Duchess of St. Albans
The Right Reverend the Lord Bishop of St.
    David's[67]
The Right Hon. Earl Stanhope,[68] 3 copies
The Right Hon. the Earl of Scarbrough
William, the Son of Ignatius Sancho[69]
Mrs. Mary Ann Sandiford
Mr. William Sawyer
Mr. Thomas Seddon[70]
W. Seward, Esq.[71]
Reverend Mr. Thomas Scott[72]
Granville Sharp, Esq.[73] 2 copies
Captain Sidney Smith, of the Royal Navy[74]
Colonel Simcoe[75]
Mr. John Simco
General Smith
John Smith, Esq.
Mr. George Smith[76]
Mr. William Smith[77]
Reverend Mr. Southgate[78]
Mr. William Starkey
Thomas Steel, Esq. M. P.
Mr. Staples Steare
Mr. Joseph Stewardson
Mr. Henry Stone, jun. 2 copies
John Symmons, Esq.

T
Henry Thornton, Esq. M. P.[79]
Mr. Alexander Thomson, M. D.
Reverend John Till
Mr. Samuel Townly
Mr. Daniel Trinder
Reverend Mr. C. La Trobe[80]
Clement Tudway, Esq.
Mrs. Twisden

U
Mr. M. Underwood

V
Mr. John Vaughan[81]
Mrs. Vendt

W
The Right Hon. Earl of Warwick
The Right Reverend the Lord Bishop of
    Worcester[82]
The Hon. William Windham, Esq. M. P.[83]
Mr. C. B. Wadstrom

Mr. George Walne
Reverend Mr. Ward
Mr. S. Warren
Mr. J. Waugh
Josiah Wedgwood, Esq.[84]
Reverend Mr. John Wesley[85]
Mr. J. Wheble
Samuel Whitbread, Esq. M. P.
Reverend Thomas Wigzell
Mr. W. Wilson
Reverend Mr. Wills
Mr. Thomas Wimsett
Mr. William Winchester
John Wollaston, Esq.
Mr. Charles Wood
Mr. Joseph Woods
Mr. John Wood
J. Wright, Esq.[86]

Y
Mr. Thomas Young
Mr. Samuel Yockney

# CONTENTS of VOLUME I.

---

### CHAP. I.
The author's account of his country, their manners and customs, &c. . . . . . . . 41

### CHAP. II.
The author's birth and parentage—His being kidnapped with his sister—Horrors of a slave ship . . . . . . . . . . . . . . . . . . . . . . . . . . . . . . . . . . . . . . . . . . . . . 51

### CHAP. III.
The author is carried to Virginia—Arrives in England—His wonder at a fall of snow . . . . . . . . . . . . . . . . . . . . . . . . . . . . . . . . . . . . . . . . . . . . . . . . . . 61

### CHAP. IV.
A particular account of the celebrated engagement between Admiral Boscawen and Monsieur Le Clue . . . . . . . . . . . . . . . . . . . . . . . . . . . . . . . . . . . . . . . 70

### CHAP. V.
Various interesting instances of oppression, cruelty, and extortion . . . . . . . . . 82

### CHAP. VI.
Favorable change in the author's situation—He commences merchant with three-pence . . . . . . . . . . . . . . . . . . . . . . . . . . . . . . . . . . . . . . . . . . . . . . . . . . 94

# THE LIFE, &c.

## CHAPTER I.

*The author's account of his country, and their manners and customs—Administration of justice—Embrenche—Marriage ceremony, and public entertainments— Mode of living—Dress—Manufactures Buildings—Commerce—Agriculture— War and religion—Superstition of the natives—Funeral ceremonies of the priests or magicians—Curious mode of discovering poison—Some hints concerning the origin of the author's countrymen, with the opinions of different writers on that subject.*

I Believe it is difficult for those who publish their own memoirs to escape the imputation of vanity; nor is this the only disadvantage under which they labour: it is also for their misfortune, that what is uncommon is rarely, if ever, believed, and what is obvious we are apt to turn from with disgust, and to charge the writer with impertinence. People generally think those memoirs only worthy to be read or remembered which abound in great or striking events, those, in short, which in a high degree excite either admiration or pity: all others they consign to contempt and oblivion. It is therefore, I confess, not a little hazardous in a private and obscure individual, and a stranger too, thus to solicit the indulgent attention of the public; especially when I own I offer here the history of neither a saint, a hero, nor a tyrant. I believe there are few events in my life, which have not happened to many: it is true the incidents of it are numerous; and, did I consider myself an European, I might say my sufferings were great: but when I compare my lot with that of most of my countrymen, I regard myself as a *particular favourite of Heaven,* and acknowledge the mercies of Providence in every occurrence of my life. If then the following narrative does not appear sufficiently interesting to engage general attention, let my motive be some excuse for its publication. I am not so foolishly vain as to expect from it either immortality or literary reputation. If it affords any satisfaction to my numerous friends, at whose request it has been written, or in the smallest degree promotes the interests of humanity, the ends for which it was undertaken will be fully attained, and every wish of my heart gratified. Let it therefore be remembered, that, in wishing to avoid censure, I do not aspire to praise.

That part of Africa, known by the name of Guinea, to which the trade for slaves is carried on, extends along the coast above 3400 miles, from the Senegal to Angola, and includes a variety of kingdoms. Of these the most considerable is the kingdom of Benen, both as to extent and wealth, the richness and cultivation of the soil, the power of its king, and the number and warlike disposition of the inhabitants. It is situated nearly under the line,[87] and extends along the coast about 170 miles, but runs back into the interior part of Africa to a distance hitherto I believe unexplored by any traveller; and seems only ter-

minated at length by the empire of Abyssinia,[88] near 1500 miles from its beginning.[89] This kingdom is divided into many provinces or districts: in one of
the most remote and fertile of which, called Eboe,[90] I was born, in the year
1745, in a charming fruitful vale, named Essaka.[91] The distance of this province
from the capital of Benin and the sea coast must be very considerable; for I had
never heard of white men or Europeans, nor of the sea: and our subjection to
the king of Benin was little more than nominal; for every transaction of the government, as far as my slender observation extended, was conducted by the chiefs
or elders of the place. The manners and government of a people who have little
commerce with other countries are generally very simple; and the history of
what passes in one family or village may serve as a specimen of a nation. My father was one of those elders or chiefs I have spoken of, and was styled Embrenche; a term, as I remember, importing the highest distinction, and signifying in our language a *mark* of grandeur. This mark is conferred on the person
entitled to it, by cutting the skin across at the top of the forehead, and drawing
it down to the eye-brows; and while it is in this situation applying a warm hand,
and rubbing it until it shrinks up into a thick *weal* across the lower part of the
forehead. Most of the judges and senators were thus marked; my father had long
born it: I had seen it conferred on one of my brothers, and I was also *destined*
to receive it by my parents. Those Embrence, or chief men, decided disputes and
punished crimes; for which purpose they always assembled together. The proceedings were generally short; and in most cases the law of retaliation prevailed.
I remember a man was brought before my father, and the other judges, for kidnapping a boy; and, although he was the son of a chief or senator, he was condemned to make recompense by a man or woman slave. Adultery, however, was
sometimes punished with slavery or death; a punishment which I believe is inflicted on it throughout most of the nations of Africa*:[92] so sacred among them
is the honour of the marriage bed, and so jealous are they of the fidelity of their
wives. Of this I recollect an instance:—a woman was convicted before the judges
of adultery, and delivered over, as the custom was, to her husband to be punished. Accordingly he determined to put her to death: but it being found, just
before her execution, that she had an infant at her breast; and no woman being
prevailed on to perform the part of a nurse, she was spared on account of the
child. The men, however, do not preserve the same constancy to their wives,
which they expect from them; for they indulge in a plurality, though seldom in
more than two. Their mode of marriage is thus:—both parties are usually betrothed when young by their parents, (though I have known the males to be-
troth themselves). On this occasion a feast is prepared, and the bride and bridegroom stand up in the midst of all their friends, who are assembled for the
purpose, while he declares she is thenceforth to be looked upon as his wife, and
that no other person is to pay any addresses to her. This is also immediately proclaimed in the vicinity, on which the bride retires from the assembly. Sometime
after she is brought home to her husband, and then another feast is made, to

*See Benezet's "Account of Guinea" throughout.

which the relations of both parties are invited: her parents then deliver her to the bridegroom, accompanied with a number of blessings, and at the same time they tie round her waist a cotton string of the thickness of a goose-quill, which none but married women are permitted to wear: she is now considered as completely his wife; and at this time the dowry is given to the new married pair, which generally consists of portions of land, slaves, and cattle, household goods, and implements of husbandry. These are offered by the friends of both parties; besides which the parents of the bridegroom present gifts to those of the bride, whose property she is looked upon before marriage; but after it she is esteemed the sole property of her husband. The ceremony being now ended the festival begins, which is celebrated with bonefires, and loud acclamations of joy, accompanied with music and dancing.

We are almost a nation of dancers, musicians, and poets. Thus every great event, such as a triumphant return from battle, or other cause of public rejoicing is celebrated in public dances, which are accompanied with songs and music suited to the occasion. The assembly is separated into four divisions, which dance either apart or in succession, and each with a character peculiar to itself. The first division contains the married men, who in their dances frequently exhibit feats of arms, and the representation of a battle. To these succeed the married women, who dance in the second division. The young men occupy the third; and the maidens the fourth. Each represents some interesting scene of real life, such as a great achievement, domestic employment, a pathetic story, or some rural sport; and as the subject is generally founded on some recent event, it is therefore ever new. This gives our dances a spirit and variety which I have scarcely seen elsewhere*. We have many musical instruments, particularly drums of different kinds, a piece of music which resembles a guitar, and another much like a stickado.[93] These last are chiefly used by betrothed virgins, who play on them on all grand festivals.

As our manners are simple, our luxuries are few. The dress of both sexes is nearly the same. It generally consists of a long piece of callico, or muslin, wrapped loosely round the body, somewhat in the form of a highland plaid. This is usually dyed blue, which is our favourite colour. It is extracted from a berry, and is brighter and richer than any I have seen in Europe. Besides this, our women of distinction wear golden ornaments; which they dispose with some profusion on their arms and legs. When our women are not employed with the men in tillage, their usual occupation is spinning and weaving cotton, which they afterwards dye, and make it into garments. They also manufacture earthen vessels, of which we have many kinds. Among the rest tobacco pipes, made after the same fashion, and used in the same manner, as those in Turkey†.

Our manner of living is entirely plain; for as yet the natives are unacquainted with those refinements in cookery which debauch the taste: bullocks,

---

*When I was in Smyrna I have frequently seen the Greeks dance after this manner.
†The bowl is earthern, curiously figured, to which a long reed is fixed as a tube. This tube is sometimes so long as to be born by one, and frequently out of grandeur by two boys.

goats, and poultry, supply the greatest part of their food. These constitute likewise the principal wealth of the country, and the chief articles of its commerce. The flesh is usually stewed in a pan; to make it savoury we sometimes use also pepper, and other spices, and we have salt made of wood ashes. Our vegetables are mostly plantains, eadas,[94] yams, beans, and Indian corn. The head of the family usually eats alone; his wives and slaves have also their separate tables. Before we taste food we always wash our hands: indeed our cleanliness on all occasions is extreme; but on this it is an indispensable ceremony. After washing, libation is made, by pouring out a small portion of the food,[95] in a certain place, for the spirits of departed relations, which the natives suppose to preside over their conduct, and guard them from evil. They are totally unacquainted with strong or spirituous liquours; and their principal beverage is palm wine. This is gotten from a tree of that name by tapping it at the top, and fastening a large gourd to it; and sometimes one tree will yield three or four gallons in a night. When just drawn it is of a most delicious sweetness; but in a few days it acquires a tartish and more spirituous flavour: though I never saw any one intoxicated by it. The same tree also produces nuts and oil. Our principal luxury is in perfumes; one sort of these is an odoriferous wood of delicious fragrance: the other a kind of earth; a small portion of which thrown into the fire diffuses a most powerful odour*. We beat this wood into powder, and mix it with palm oil; with which both men and woman perfume themselves.

In our buildings we study convenience rather than ornament. Each master of a family has a large square piece of ground, surrounded with a moat or fence, or enclosed with a wall made of red earth tempered; which, when dry, is as hard as brick. Within this are his houses to accommodate his family and slaves; which, if numerous, frequently present the appearance of a village. In the middle stands the principal building, appropriated to the sole use of the master, and consisting of two apartments; in one of which he sits in the day with his family, the other is left apart for the reception of his friends. He has besides these a distinct apartment in which he sleeps, together with his male children. On each side are the apartments of his wives, who have also their separate day and night houses. The habitations of the slaves and their families are distributed throughout the rest of the enclosure. These houses never exceed one story in height: they are always built of wood, or stakes driven into the ground, crossed with wattles, and neatly plastered within, and without. The roof is thatched with reeds. Our day-houses are left open at the sides; but those in which we sleep are always covered, and plastered in the inside, with a composition mixed with cow-dung, to keep off different insects, which annoy us during the night. The walls and floors also of these are generally covered with mats. Our beds consist of a platform, raised three or four feet from the ground, on which are laid skins, and different parts of a spungy

---

*When I was in Smyrna I saw the same kind of earth, and brought some of it with me to England; it resembles musk in strength, but is more delicious in scent, and is not unlike the smell of a rose.

tree called plaintain. Our covering is calico or muslin, the same as our dress. The usual seats are a few logs of wood; but we have benches, which are generally perfumed, to accommodate strangers: these compose the greater part of our household furniture. Houses so constructed and furnished require but little skill to erect them. Every man is a sufficient architect for the purpose. The whole neighbourhood afford their unanimous assistance in building them and in return receive, and expect no other recompense than a feast.

As we live in a country where nature is prodigal of her favours, our wants are few and easily supplied; of course we have few manufactures. They consist for the most part of calicoes, earthern ware, ornaments, and instruments of war and husbandry. But these make no part of our commerce, the principal articles of which, as I have observed, are provisions. In such a state money is of little use; however we have some small pieces of coin, if I may call them such. They are made something like an anchor; but I do not remember either their value or denomination. We have also markets, at which I have been frequently with my mother. These are sometimes visited by stout mahogany-coloured men from the south west of us: we call them Oye-Eboe, which term signifies red men living at a distance. They generally bring us fire-arms, gunpowder, hats, beats and dried fish. The last we esteemed a great rarity, as our waters were only brooks and springs. These articles they barter with us for odoriferous woods and earth, and our salt of wood ashes. They always carry slaves through our land; but the strictest account is exacted of their manner of procuring them before they are suffered to pass. Sometimes indeed we sold slaves to them, but they were only prisoners of war, or such among us as had been convicted of kidnapping, or adultery, and some other crimes, which we esteemed heinous. This practice of kidnapping induces me to think, that, notwithstanding all our strictness, their principal business among us was to trepan[96] our people. I remember too they carried great sacks along with them, which not long after I had an opportunity of fatally seeing applied to that infamous purpose.

Our land is uncommonly rich and fruitful, and produces all kinds of vegetables in great abundance. We have plenty of Indian corn, and vast quantities of cotton and tobacco. Our pine apples grow without culture; they are about the size of the largest sugar-loaf, and finely flavoured. We have also spices of different kinds, particularly pepper; and a variety of delicious fruits which I have never seen in Europe; together with gums of various kinds, and honey in abundance. All our industry is exerted to improve those blessings of nature. Agriculture is our chief employment; and every one, even the children and women, are engaged in it. Thus we are all habituated to labour from our earliest years. Every one contributes something to the common flock; and as we are unacquainted with idleness, we have no beggars. The benefits of such a mode of living are obvious. The West India planters prefer the slaves of Benin or Eboe to those of any other part of Guinea, for their hardiness, intelligence, integrity, and zeal. Those benefits are felt by us in the general healthiness of the people, and their vigour and activity; I might have added too in their comeliness. Deformity is indeed unknown almost us, I mean that of shape. Numbers of the natives of Eboe now in London might be brought in support of this assertion: for, in regard to complexion, ideas of beauty are wholly relative. I remember while in Africa to have seen three negro children, who were tawny, and another quite white, who were universally regarded by myself, and the natives in general, as far as related to their complexions, as deformed. Our women too were in my eyes at least uncommonly graceful, alert, and modest to a degree of bashfulness; nor do I remember to have ever heard of an instance of incontinence amongst them before marriage. They are also remarkably cheerful. Indeed cheerfulness and affability are two of the leading characteristics of our nation.

Our tillage is exercised in a large plain or common, some hours walk from our dwellings, and all the neighbors resort thither in a body. They use no beasts of husbandry; and their only instruments are hoes, axes, shovels, and beaks, or pointed iron to dig with. Sometimes we are visited by locusts, which come in large clouds, so as to darken the air, and destroy our harvest. This however happens rarely, but when it does, a famine is produced by it. I remember an instance or two wherein this happened. This common is often the theatre of war; and therefore when our people go out to till their land, they not only go in a body, but generally take their arms with them for fear of a surprise; and when they apprehend an invasion they guard the avenues to their dwellings, by driving sticks into the ground, which are so sharp at one end as to pierce the foot, and are generally dipt in poison. From what I can recollect of these battles, they appear to have been irruptions of one little state or district on the other, to obtain prisoners or booty. Perhaps they were incited to this by those traders who brought the European goods I mentioned amongst us. Such a mode of obtaining slaves in Africa is common; and I believe more are procured this way, and by kidnapping, than any other*.[97] When a trader wants slaves, he applies to a chief for them, and tempts him with his wares. It is not extraordinary, if on this occasion he yields to the temptation with as little firmness, and accepts the price of his fellow creatures liberty with as little reluctance as the enlightened merchant. Accordingly he falls on his neighbours, and a desperate battle ensures. If he prevails and takes prisoners, he gratifies his avarice by selling them; but, if his party be vanquished, and he falls into the hands of the enemy, he is put to death: for, as he has been known to foment their quarrels, it is thought dangerous to let him survive, and no ransom can save him, though all other prisoners may be redeemed. We have firearms, bows and arrows, broad two-edged swords and javelins; we have shields also which cover a man from head to foot. All are taught the use of these weapons; even our women are warriors, and march boldly out to fight along with the men. Our whole district is a kind of militia; on a certain signal given, such as the firing of a gun at night, they all rise in arms and rush upon their enemy. It is perhaps something remarkable, that when our people march to the field a red flag or banner is borne before them. I was once a witness to a battle in our common. We had been all at work in it one day as usual, when our people were suddenly attacked. I climbed a tree at some distance, from which I beheld the fight. There were many women

---

*See Benezet's "Account of Africa" throughout.

as well as men on both sides; among others my mother was there, and armed with a broad sword. After fighting for a considerable time with great fury, and after many had been killed our people obtained the victory, and took their enemy's Chief prisoner. He was carried off in great triumph, and, though he offered a large ransom for his life, he was put to death. A virgin of note among our enemies had been slain in the battle, and her arm was exposed in our market-place, where our trophies were always exhibited. The spoils were divided according to the merit of the warriors. Those prisoners which were not sold or redeemed we kept as slaves: but how different was their condition from that of the slaves in the West Indies! With us they do no more work than other members of the community, even their masters; their food, clothing and lodging were nearly the same as theirs, (except that they were not permitted to eat with those who were free-born); and there was scarce any other difference between them, than a superior degree of importance which the head of a family possesses in our state, and that authority which, as such, he exercises over every part of his household. Some of these slaves have even slaves under them as their own property, and for their own use.

As to religion, the natives believe that there is one Creator of all things, and that he lives in the sun, and is girted round with a belt that he may never eat or drink; but, according to some, he smokes a pipe, which is our own favourite luxury. They believe he governs events, especially our deaths or captivity; but, as for the doctrine of eternity, I do not remember to have ever heard of it; some however believe in the transmigration of souls in a certain degree. Those spirits, which are not transmigrated, such as our dear friends or relations, they believe always attend them, and guard them from the bad spirits or their foes. For this reason they always before eating, as I have observed, put some small portion of the meat, and pour some of their drink, on the ground for them; and they often make oblations of the blood of beasts or fowls at their graves. I was very fond of my mother, and almost constantly with her. When she went to make these oblations at her mother's tomb, which was a kind of small solitary thatched house, I sometimes attended her. There she made her libations, and spent most of the night in cries and lamentations. I have been often extremely terrified on these occasions. The loneliness of the place, the darkness of the night, and the ceremony of libation, naturally awful and gloomy, were heightened by my mother's lamentations; and these, concurring with the cries of doleful birds, by which these places were frequented, gave an inexpressible terror to the scene.

We compute the year from the day on which the sun crosses the line, and on its setting that evening there is a general shout throughout the land; at least I can speak from my own knowledge throughout our vicinity. The people at the same time make a great noise with rattles, not unlike the basket rattles used by children here, though much larger, and hold up their hands to heaven for a blessing. It is then the greatest offerings are made; and those children whom our wise men foretel will be fortunate are then presented to different people. I remember many used to come to see me, and I was carried about to others for that purpose. They have many offerings, particularly at full moons; generally two at harvest before the fruits are taken out of the ground: and when any young animals are killed, sometimes they offer up part of them as a sacrifice. These offerings, when made by one of the heads of a family, serve for the whole. I remember we often had them at my father's and my uncle's, and their families have been present. Some of our offerings are eaten with bitter herbs. We had a saying among us to any one of a cross temper, 'That if they were to be eaten, they should be eaten with bitter herbs.'

We practised circumcision like the Jews, and made offerings and feasts on that occasion in the same manner as they did. Like them also, our children were named from some event some circumstance, or fancied foreboding at the time of their birth. I was named *Olaudah*,[98] which, in our language, signifies vicissitude or fortune also, one favoured, and having a loud voice and well spoken. I remember we never polluted the name of the object of our adoration; on the contrary, it was always mentioned with the greatest reverence; and we were totally unacquainted with swearing, and all those terms of abuse and reproach which find their way so readily and copiously into the languages of more civilized people. The only expressions of that kind I remember were 'May you rot, or may you swell, or may a beast take you.'

I have before remarked that the natives of this part of Africa are extremely cleanly. This necessary habit of decency was with us a part of religion, and therefore we had many purifications and washings, indeed almost as many, and used on the same occasions, if my recollection does not fail me, as the Jews. Those that touched the dead at any time were obliged to wash and purify themselves before they could enter a dwelling-house. Every woman too, at certain times, was forbidden to come into a dwelling-house, or touch any person, or any thing we ate. I was so fond of my mother I could not keep from her, or avoid touching her at some of those periods, in consequence of which I was obliged to be kept out with her, in a little house made for that purpose, till offering was made, and then we were purified.

Though we had no places of public worship, we had priests and magicians, or wise men. I do not remember whether they had different offices, or whether they were united in the same persons, but they were held in great reverence by the people. They calculated our time, and foretold events, as their name imported, for we called them Ah-affoe-way-cah, which signifies calculators or yearly men, our year being called Ah-affoe. They wore their beards, and when they died they were succeeded by their sons. Most of their implements and things of value were interred along with them. Pipes and tobacco were also put into the grave with the corpse, which was always perfumed and ornamented, and animals were offered in sacrifice to them. None accompanied their funerals but those of the same profession or tribe. These buried them after sunset, and always returned from the grave by a different way from that which they went.

These magicians were also our doctors or physicians. They practiced bleeding by cupping; and were very successful in healing wounds and expelling poisons. They had likewise some extraordinary method of discovering jealousy, theft, and poisoning; the success of which no doubt they derived from their unbounded influence over the credulity and superstition of the people. I do not remember what those methods were, except that as to poisoning: I recollect an instance or two, which I hope it will not be deemed impertinent here to insert, as it may serve as a kind of specimen of the rest, and is still used by the negroes in the West Indies. A virgin had been poisoned, but it was not known by whom: the doctors ordered the corpse to be taken up by some persons, and carried to the grave. As soon as the bearers had raised it on their shoulders, they seemed seized with some*[99] sudden impulse, and ran to and fro unable to stop themselves. At last, after having passed through a number of thorns and prickly bushes unhurt, the corpse fell from them close to a house, and defaced it in the fall; and, the owner being taken up, he immediately confessed the poisoning[†].

The natives are extremely cautious about poison. When they buy any eatable the seller kisses it all round before the buyer, to shew him it is not poisoned; and the same is done when any meat or drink is presented, particularly to a stranger. We have serpents of different kinds, some of which are esteemed ominous when they appear in our houses, and these we never molest. I remember two of those ominous snakes, each of which was as thick as the calf of a man's leg, and in colour resembling a dolphin in the water, crept at different times into my mother's night-house, where I always lay with her, and coiled themselves into folds, and each time they crowed like a cock. I was desired by some of our wise men to touch these, that I might be interested in the good omens, which I did, for they were quite harmless, and would tamely suffer themselves to be handled; and then they were put into a large open earthen pan, and set on one side of the highway. Some of our snakes, however, were poisonous: one of them crossed the road one day when I was standing on it, and passed between my feet without offering to touch me, to the great surprise of many who saw it; and these incidents were accounted by the wise men, and therefore by my mother and the rest of the people, as remarkable omens in my favour.

Such is the imperfect sketch my memory has furnished me with of the manners and customs of a people among whom I first drew my breath. And here I cannot forbear suggesting what has long struck me very forcibly, namely, the strong analogy which even by this sketch, imperfect as it is, appears to prevail in

---

*See also Leut. Matthew's *Voyage*, p. 123.

[†]An instance of this kind happened at Montserrat in the West Indies in the year 1763. I then belonged to the Charming Sally, Capt. Doran.—The chief mate, Mr. Mansfield, and some of the crew being one day on shore, were present at the burying of a poisoned negro girl. Though they had often heard of the circumstance of the running in such cases, and had even seen it, they imagined it to be a trick of the corpse-bearers. The mate therefore desired two of the sailors to take up the coffin, and carry it to the grave. The sailors, who were all of the same opinion, readily obeyed; but they had scarcely raised it to their shoulders, before they began to run furiously about, quite unable to direct themselves, till, at last, without intention, they came to the hut of him who had poisoned the girl. The coffin then immediately fell from their shoulders against the hut, and damaged part of the wall. The owner of the hut was taken into custody on this, and confessed the poisoning.—I give this story as it was related by the mate and crew on their return to the ship. The credit which is due to it I leave with the reader.

the manners and customs of my countrymen and those of the Jews, before they reached the Land of Promise, and particularly the patriarchs while they were yet in that pastoral state which is described in Genesis—an analogy, which alone would induce me to think that the one people had sprung from the other. Indeed this is the opinion of Dr. Gill, who, in his commentary on Genesis,[100] very ably deduces the pedigree of the Africans from Afer and Afra, the descendants of Abraham by Keturah his wife and concubine (for both these titles are applied to her). It is also conformable to the sentiments of Dr. John Clarke, formerly Dean of Sarum, in his Truth of the Christian Religion:[101] both these authors concur in ascribing to us this original. The reasonings of these gentlemen are still further confirmed by the scripture chronology;[102] and if any further corroboration were required, this resemblance in so many respects is a strong evidence in support of the opinion. Like the Israelites in their primitive state, our government was conducted by our chiefs or judges, our wise men and elders; and the head of a family with us enjoyed a similar authority over his household with that which is ascribed to Abraham and the other patriarchs. The law of retaliation obtained almost universally with us as with them: and even their religion appeared to have shed upon us a ray of its glory, though broken and spent in its passage, or eclipsed by the cloud with which time, tradition, and ignorance might have enveloped it; for we had our circumcision (a rule I believe peculiar to that people:) we had also our sacrifices and burnt-offerings, our washings and purifications, on the same occasions as they had.

As to the difference of colour between the Eboan Africans and the modern Jews, I shall not presume to account for it. It is a subject which has engaged the pens of men of both genius and learning, and is far above my strength. The most able and Reverend Mr. T. Clarkson, however, in his much admired Essay on the Slavery and Commerce of the Human Species,[103] has ascertained the cause, in a manner that at once solves every objection on that account, and, on my mind at least, has produced the fullest conviction. I shall therefore refer to that performance for the theory*, contenting myself with extracting a fact as related by Dr. Mitchel†.[104] "The Spaniards, who have inhabited America, under the torrid zone, for any time, are become as dark coloured as our native Indians of Virginia; of which I myself have been a witness." There is also another instance‡ of a Portuguese settlement at Mitomba, a river in Sierra Leona; where the inhabitants are bred from a mixture of the first Portuguese discoverers with the natives, and are now become in their complexion, and in the wooly quality of their hair, perfect negroes, retaining however a smattering of the Portuguese language.

These instances, and a great many more which might be adduced, while they shew how the complexions of the same persons vary in different climates, it is hoped may tend also to remove the prejudice that some conceive against the natives of Africa on account of colour. Surely the minds of the Spaniards did not

---

*Page 178 to 216.
†Philos. Trans. N° 476, Sect. 4, cited by Mr. Clarkson, p. 205.
‡Same page.

change with their complexions! Are there not causes enough to which the apparent inferiority of an African may be ascribed, without limiting the goodness of God, and supposing he forbore to stamp understanding on certainly his own image, because "carved in ebony." Might it not naturally be ascribed to their situation? When they come among Europeans, they are ignorant of their language, religion, manners, and customs. Are any pains taken to teach them these? Are they treated as men? Does not slavery itself depress the mind, and extinguish all its fire and every noble sentiment? But, above all, what advantages do not a refined people possess over those who are rude and uncultivated. Let the polished and haughty European recollect that his ancestors were once, like the Africans, uncivilized, and even barbarous. Did Nature make *them* inferior to their sons? and should *they too* have been made slaves? Every rational mind answers, No. Let such reflections as these melt the pride of their superiority into sympathy for the wants and miseries of their sable brethren, and compel them to acknowledge, that understanding is not confined to feature or colour. If, when they look round the world, they feel exultation, let it be tempered with benevolence to others, and gratitude to God, "who hath made of one blood all nations of men for to dwell on all the face of the earth* and whose wisdom is not our wisdom, neither are our ways his ways."[105]

## CHAP. II.

*The author's birth and parentage—His being kidnapped with his sister—Their separation—Surprise at meeting again—Are finally separated—Account of the different places and incidents the author met with till his arrival on the coast—The effect the sight of a slave ship had on him—He sails for the West Indies—Horrors of a slave ship—Arrives at Barbadoes, where the cargo is sold and dispersed.*

I HOPE the reader will not think I have trespassed on his patience in introducing myself to him with some account of the manners and customs of my country. They had been implanted in me with great care, and made an impression on my mind, which time could not erase, and which all the adversity and variety of fortune I have since experienced served only to rivet and record; for, whether the love of one's country be real or imaginary, or a lesson of reason, or an instinct of nature, I still look back with pleasure on the first scenes of my life, though that pleasure has been for the most part mingled with sorrow.

I have already acquainted the reader with the time and place of my birth. My father, besides many slaves, had a numerous family, of which seven lived to grow up, including myself and a sister, who was the only daughter. As I was the youngest of the sons, I became, of course, the greatest favourite with my mother,

---

*Acts, c. xvii, v. 26.

and was always with her; and she used to take particular pains to form my mind. I was trained up from my earliest years in the art of war; my daily exercise was shooting and throwing javelins; and my mother adorned me with emblems, after the manner of our greatest warriors. In this way I grew up till I was turned the age of eleven, when an end was put to my happiness in the following manner:—Generally when the grown people in the neighbourhood were gone far in the fields to labour, the children assembled together in some of the neighbours' premises to play; and commonly some of us used to get up a tree to look out for any assailant, or kidnapper, that might come upon us; for they sometimes took those opportunities of our parents' absence to attack and carry off as many as they could seize. One day, as I was watching at the top of a tree in our yard, I saw one of those people come into the yard of our next neighbour but one, to kidnap, there being many stout young people in it. Immediately on this I gave the alarm of the rogue, and he was surrounded by the stoutest of them, who entangled him with cords, so that he could not escape till some of the grown people came and secured him. But alas! ere long it was my fate to be thus attacked, and to be carried off, when none of the grown people were nigh. One day, when all our people were gone out to their works as usual, and only I and my dear sister were left to mind the house, two men and a woman got over our walls, and in a moment seized us both, and, without giving us time to cry out, or make resistance, they stopped our mouths, and ran off with us into the nearest wood. Here they tied our hands, and continued to carry us as far as they could, till night came on, when we reached a small house, where the robbers halted for refreshment, and spent the night. We were then unbound, but were unable to take any food; and, being quite overpowered by fatigue and grief, our only relief was some sleep, which allayed our misfortune for a short time. The next morning we left the house, and continued travelling all the day. For a long time we had kept the woods, but at last we came into a road which I believed I knew. I had now some hopes of being delivered; for we had advanced but a little way before I discovered some people at a distance, on which I began to cry out for their assistance: but my cries had no other effect than to make them tie me faster and stop my mouth, and then they put me into a large sack. They also stopped my sister's mouth, and tied her hands; and in this manner we proceeded till we were out of the sight of these people. When we went to rest the following night they offered us some victuals; but we refused it; and the only comfort we had was in being in one another's arms all that night, and bathing each other with our tears. But alas! we were soon deprived of even the small comfort of weeping together. The next day proved a day of greater sorrow than I had yet experienced; for my sister and I were then separated, while we lay clasped in each other's arms. It was in vain that we besought them not to part us; she was torn from me, and immediately carried away, while I was left in a state of distraction not to be described. I cried and grieved continually; and for several days I did not eat any thing but what they forced into my mouth. At length, after many days travelling, during which I had often changed masters, I got into the hands of a chieftain, in a very pleasant country. This man had two wives and some children, and they all used me extremely well, and did all they could to comfort me; particularly the first wife,

who was something like my mother. Although I was a great many days journey
from my father's house, yet these people spoke exactly the same language with
us. This first master of mine, as I may call him, was a smith, and my principal
employment was working his bellows, which were the same kind as I had seen
in my vicinity. They were in some respects not unlike the stoves here in gentlemen's kitchens; and were covered over with leather, and in the middle of that
leather a stick was fixed, and a person stood up, and worked it, in the same manner as is done to pump water out of a cask with a hand pump. I believe it was
gold he worked, for it was of a lovely bright yellow colour, and was worn by the
women on their wrists and ancles. I was there I suppose about a month, and they
at last used to trust me some little distance from the house. This liberty I used in
embracing every opportunity to inquire the way to my own home: and I also
sometimes, for the same purpose, went with the maidens, in the cool of the
evenings, to bring pitchers of water from the springs for the use of the house. I
had also remarked where the sun rose in the morning, and set in the evening, as
I had travelled along; and I had observed that my father's house was towards the
rising of the sun. I therefore determined to seize the first opportunity of making
my escape, and to shape my course for that quarter; for I was quite oppressed
and weighed down by grief after my mother and friends; and my love of liberty,
ever great, was strengthened by the mortifying circumstance of not daring to eat
with the free-born children, although I was mostly their companion. While I was
projecting my escape, one day an unlucky event happened, which quite disconcerted my plan, and put an end to my hopes. I used to be sometimes employed
in assisting an elderly woman slave to cook and take care of the poultry; and one
morning, while I was feeding some chickens, I happened to toss a small pebble
at one of them, which hit it on the middle and directly killed it. The old slave,
having soon after missed the chicken, inquired after it; and on my relating the
accident (for I told her the truth, because my mother would never suffer me to
tell a lie) she flew into a violent passion, threatened that I should suffer for it;
and, my master being out, she immediately went and told her mistress what I had
done. This alarmed me very much, and I expected an instant flogging, which to
me was uncommon dreadful; for I had seldom been beaten at home. I therefore
resolved to fly; and accordingly I ran into a thicket that was hard by, and hid myself in the bushes. Soon afterwards my mistress and the slave returned, and, not
seeing me, they searched all the house, but not finding me, and I not making answer when they called to me, they thought I had run away, and the whole neighbourhood was raised in the pursuit of me. In that part of the country (as in ours)
the houses and villages were skirted with woods, or shrubberies, and the bushes
were so thick that a man could readily conceal himself in them, so as to elude the
strictest search. The neighbours continued the whole day looking for me, and
several times many of them came within a few yards of the place where I lay hid.
I then gave myself up for lost entirely, and expected every moment, when I heard
a rustling among the trees, to be found out, and punished by my master: but they
never discovered me, though they were often so near that I even heard their conjectures as they were looking about for me; and I now learned from them, that
any attempt to return home would be hopeless. Most of them supposed I had

fled towards home; but the distance was so great, and the way so intricate, that they thought I could never reach it, and that I should be lost in the woods. When I heard this I was seized with a violent panic, and abandoned myself to despair. Night too began to approach, and aggravated all my fears. I had before entertained hopes of getting home, and I had determined when it should be dark to make the attempt; but I was now convinced it was fruitless, and I began to consider that, if possibly I could escape all other animals, I could not those of the human kind; and that, not knowing the way, I must perish in the wood. Thus was I like the hunted deer:

> ——"Ev'ry leaf and ev'ry whisp'ring breath
> "Convey'd a foe, and ev'ry foe a death."[106]

I heard frequent rustlings among the leaves; and being pretty sure they were snakes I expected every instant to be stung by them. This increased my anguish, and the horror of my situation became now quite insupportable. I at length quitted the thicket, very faint and hungry, for I had not eaten or drank any thing all the day; and crept to my master's kitchen, from whence I set out at first, and which was an open shed, and laid myself down in the ashes with an anxious wish for death to relieve me from all my pains. I was scarcely awake in the morning when the old woman slave, who was the first up, came to light the fire, and saw me in the fire place. She was very much surprised to see me, and could scarcely believe her own eyes. She now promised to intercede for me, and went for her master, who soon after came, and, having slightly reprimanded me, ordered me to be taken care of, and not to be ill-treated.

Soon after this my master's only daughter, and child by his first wife, sickened and died, which affected him so much that for some time he was almost frantic, and really would have killed himself, had he not been watched and prevented. However, in a small time afterwards he recovered, and I was again sold. I was now carried to the left of the sun's rising, through many different countries, and a number of large woods. The people I was sold to used to carry me very often, when I was tired, either on their shoulders or on their backs. I saw many convenient well-built sheds along the roads, at proper distances, to accommodate the merchants and travellers, who lay in those buildings along with their wives, who often accompany them; and they always go well armed.

From the time I left my own nation I always found somebody that understood me till I came to the sea coast. The languages of different nations did not totally differ, nor were they so copious as those of the Europeans, particularly the English. They were therefore easily learned; and, while I was journeying thus through Africa, I acquired two or three different tongues. In this manner I had been travelling for a considerable time, when one evening, to my great surprise, whom should I see brought to the house where I was but my dear sister! As soon as she saw me she gave a loud shriek, and ran into my arms—I was quite overpowered: neither of us could speak; but, for a considerable time, clung to each other in mutual embraces, unable to do any thing but weep. Our meeting affected all who saw us; and indeed I must acknowledge, in honour of those sable destroyers of human rights, that I never met with any ill treatment, or saw any offered to their slaves, except tying them, when necessary, to keep them from running away. When these people knew we were brother and sister they indulged us together; and the man, to whom I supposed we belonged, lay with us, he in the middle, while she and I held one another by the hands across his breast all night; and thus for a while we forgot our misfortunes in the joy of being together; but even this small comfort was soon to have an end; for scarcely had the fatal morning appeared, when she was again torn from me for ever! I was now more miserable, if possible, than before. The small relief which her presence gave me from pain was gone, and the wretchedness of my situation was redoubled by my anxiety after her fate, and my apprehensions lest her sufferings should be greater than mine, when I could not be with her to alleviate them. Yes, thou dear partner of all my childish sports! thou sharer of my joys and sorrows! happy should I have ever esteemed myself to encounter every misery for you, and to procure your freedom by the sacrifice of my own. Though you were early forced from my arms, your image has been always rivetted in my heart, from which neither *time nor fortune* have been able to remove it; so that, while the thoughts of your sufferings have damped my prosperity, they have mingled with adversity and increased its bitterness. To that Heaven which protects the weak from the strong, I commit the care of your innocence and virtues, if they have not already received their full reward, and if your youth and delicacy have not long since fallen victims to the violence of the African trader, the pestilential stench of a Guinea ship, the seasoning in the European colonies, or the lash and lust of a brutal and unrelenting overseer.

I did not long remain after my sister. I was again sold, and carried through a number of places, till, after travelling a considerable time, I came to a town called Tinmah, in the most beautiful country I had yet seen in Africa. It was extremely rich, and there were many rivulets which flowed through it, and supplied a large pond in the centre of the town, where the people washed. Here I first saw and tasted cocoa-nuts, which I thought superior to any nuts I had ever tasted before; and the trees, which were loaded, were also interspersed amongst the houses, which had commodious shades adjoining, and were in the same manner as ours, the insides being neatly plastered and whitewashed. Here I also saw and tasted for the first time sugar-cane. Their money consisted of little white shells, the size of the finger nail. I was sold here for one hundred and seventy-two of them by a merchant who lived and brought me there. I had been about two or three days at his house, when a wealthy widow, a neighbour of his, came there one evening, and brought with her an only son, a young gentleman about my own age and size. Here they saw me; and, having taken a fancy to me, I was bought of the merchant, and went home with them. Her house and premises were situated close to one of those rivulets I have mentioned, and were the finest I ever saw in Africa: they were very extensive, and she had a number of slaves to attend her. The next day I was washed and perfumed, and when meal-time came I was led into the presence of my mistress, and ate and drank before her with her son. This filled me with astonishment; and I could scarce help expressing my surprise that the young gentleman should suffer me, who was bound, to eat with

him who was free; and not only so, but that he would not at any time either eat
or drink till I had taken first, because I was the eldest, which was agreeable to
our custom. Indeed every thing here, and all their treatment of me, made me forget that I was a slave. The language of these people resembled ours so nearly,
that we understood each other perfectly. They had also the very same customs
as we. There were likewise slaves daily to attend us, while my young master and
I with other boys sported with our darts and bows and arrows, as I had been
used to do at home. In this resemblance to my former happy state I passed about
two months; and I now began to think I was to be adopted into the family, and
was beginning to be rereconciled to my situation, and to forget by degrees my
misfortunes, when all at once the delusion vanished; for, without the least previous knowledge, one morning early, while my dear master and companion was
still asleep, I was wakened out of my reverie to fresh sorrow, and hurried away
even amongst the uncircumcised.

Thus, at the very moment I dreamed of the greatest happiness, I found myself most miserable; and it seemed as if fortune wished to give me this taste of
joy, only to render the reverse more poignant. The change I now experienced was
as painful as it was sudden and unexpected. It was a change indeed from a state
of bliss to a scene which is inexpressible by me, as it discovered to me an element
I had never before beheld, and till then had no idea of, and wherein such instances of hardship and cruelty continually occurred as I can never reflect on but
with horror.

All the nations and people I had hitherto passed through resembled our
own in their manners, customs, and language: but I came at length to a country,
the inhabitants of which differed from us in all those particulars. I was very much
struck with this difference, especially when I came among a people who did not
circumcise, and are without washing their hands. They cooked also in iron pots
and had European cutlasses and cross bows, which were unknown to us, and
fought with their fists amongst themselves. Their women were not so modest as
ours, for they ate, and drank, and slept, with their men. But, above all, I was
amazed to see no sacrifices or offerings among them. In some of those places the
people ornamented themselves with scars, and likewise filed their teeth very
sharp. They wanted sometimes to ornament me in the same manner, but I would
not suffer them; hoping that I might some time be among a people who did not
thus disfigure themselves, as I thought they did. At last I came to the banks of a
large river, which was covered with canoes, in which the people appeared to live
with their household utensils and provisions of all kinds. I was beyond measure
astonished at this, as I had never before seen any water larger than a pond or a
rivulet: and my surprise was mingled with no small fear when I was put into one
of these canoes, and we began to paddle and move along the river. We continued going on thus till night; and when we came to land, and made fires on the
banks, each family by themselves, some dragged their canoes on shore, others
stayed and cooked in theirs, and laid in them all night. Those on the land had
mats, of which they made tents, some in the shape of little houses: in these we
slept; and after the morning meal we embarked again and proceeded as before.
I was often very much astonished to see some of the women, as well as the men,

jump into the water, dive to the bottom, come up again, and swim about. Thus I continued to travel, sometimes by land, sometimes by water, through different countries and various nations, till, at the end of six or seven months after I had been kidnapped, I arrived at the sea coast. It would be tedious and uninteresting to relate all the incidents which befell me during this journey, and which I have not yet forgotten; of the various hands I passed through, and the manners and customs of all the different people among whom I lived: I shall therefore only observe, that in all the places where I was the soil was exceedingly rich; the pomkins,[107] eadas, plantains, yams, &c. &c. were in great abundance, and of incredible size. There were also vast quantities of different gums, though not used for any purpose; and every where a great deal of tobacco. The cotton even grew quite wild; and there was plenty of red-wood. I saw no mechanics[108] whatever in all the way, except such as I have mentioned. The chief employment in all these countries was agriculture, and both the males and females, as with us, were brought up to it, and trained in the arts of war.

The first object which saluted my eyes when I arrived on the coast was the sea, and a slave ship, which was then riding at anchor, and waiting for its cargo. These filled me with astonishment, which was soon converted into terror when I was carried on board. I was immediately handled and tossed up to see if I were sound by some of the crew; and I was now persuaded that I had gotten into a world of bad spirits, and that they were going to kill me. Their complexions too differing so much from ours, their long hair, and the language they spoke, (which was very different from any I had ever heard) united to confirm me in this belief. Indeed such were the horrors of my views and fears at the moment, that, if ten thousand worlds had been my own, I would have freely parted with them all to have exchanged my condition with that of the meanest slave in my own country. When I looked round the ship too and saw a large furnace or copper[109] boiling, and a multitude of black people of every description chained together, every one of their countenances expressing dejection and sorrow, I no longer doubted of my fate; and, quite overpowered with horror and anguish, I fell motionless on the deck and fainted. When I recovered a little I found some black people about me, who I believed were some of those who brought me on board, and had been receiving their pay; they talked to me in order to cheer me, but all in vain. I asked them if we were not to be eaten by those white men with horrible looks, red faces, and loose hair. They told me I was not; and one of the crew brought me a small portion of spirituous liquor in a wine glass; but, being afraid of him, I would not take it out of his hand. One of the blacks therefore took it from him and gave it to me, and I took a little down my palate, which, instead of reviving me, as they thought it would, threw me into the greatest consternation at the strange feeling it produced, having never tasted any such liquor before. Soon after this the blacks who brought me on board went off, and left me abandoned to despair. I now saw myself deprived of all chance of returning to my native country, or even the least glimpse of hope of gaining the shore, which I now considered as friendly; and I even wished for my former slavery in preference to my present situation, which was filled with horrors of every kind, still heightened by my ignorance of what I was to undergo. I was not long suffered to indulge my grief; I was soon put down under the decks, and there I received such a salutation in my nostrils as I had never experienced in my life: so that, with the loathsomeness of the stench, and crying together, I became so sick and low that I was not able to eat, nor had I the least desire to taste anything. I now wished for the last friend, death, to relieve me; but soon, to my grief, two of the white men offered me eatables; and, on my refusing to eat, one of them held me fast by the hands, and laid me across I think the windlass, and tied my feet, while the other flogged me severely. I had never experienced any thing of this kind before; and although, not being used to the water, I naturally feared that element the first time I saw it, yet nevertheless, could I have got over the nettings,[110] I would have jumped over the side, but I could not; and, besides, the crew used to watch us very closely who were not chained down to the decks, lest we should leap into the water: and I have seen some of these poor African prisoners most severely cut for attempting to do so, and hourly whipped for not eating. This indeed was often the case with myself. In a little time after, amongst the poor chained men, I found some of my own nation, which in a small degree gave ease to my mind. I inquired of these what was to be done with us; they gave me to understand we were to be carried to these white people's country to work for them. I then was a little revived, and thought, if it were no worse than working, my situation was not so desperate: but still I feared I should be put to death, the white people looked and acted, as I thought, in so savage a manner; for I had never seen among any people such instances of brutal cruelty; and this not only shewn towards us blacks, but also to some of the whites themselves. One white man in particular I saw, when we were permitted to be on deck, flogged so unmercifully with a large rope near the foremast, that he died in the consequence of it; and they tossed him over the side as they would have done a brute. This made me fear these people the more; and I expected nothing less than to be treated in the same manner. I could not help expressing my fears and apprehensions to some of my countrymen: I asked them if these people had no country, but lived in this hollow place (the ship): they told at me they did not, but came from a distant one. 'Then,' said I, 'how comes it in all our country we never heard of them?' They told me because they lived so very far off. I then asked where were their women? had they any like themselves? I was told they had: 'and why,' said I, 'do we not see them?' they answered, because they were left behind. I asked how the vessel could go? they told me they could not tell; but that there were cloths put upon the masts by the help of the ropes I saw, and then the vessel went on; and the white men had some spell or magic they put in the water when they liked in order to stop the vessel. I was exceedingly amazed at this account, and really thought they were spirits. I therefore wished much to be from amongst them, for I expected they would sacrifice me: but my wishes were vain; for we were so quartered that it was impossible for any of us to make our escape. While we stayed on the coast I was mostly on deck; and one day, to my great astonishment, I saw one of these vessels coming in with the sails up. As soon as the whites saw it, they gave a great shout, at which we were amazed; and the more so as the vessel appeared larger by approaching nearer. At last she came to an anchor in my sight, and when the anchor was let go I and my countrymen who saw it were lost in astonishment to observe the vessel stop; and were now convinced it was done by magic. Soon after this the other ship got her boats out, and they came on board of us, and the people of both ships seemed very glad to see each other. Several of the strangers also shook hands with us black people, and made motions with their hands, signifying I suppose we were to go to their country; but we did not understand them. At last, when the ship we were in had got in all her cargo, they made ready with many fearful noises, and we were all put under deck, so that we could not see how they managed the vessel. But this disappointment was the least of my sorrow. The stench of the hold while we were on the coast was so intolerably loathsome, that it was dangerous to remain there for any time, and some of us had been permitted to stay on the deck for the fresh air; but now that the whole ship's cargo were confined together, it became absolutely pestilential. The closeness of the place, and the heat of the climate, added to the number in the ship, which was so crowded that each had scarcely room to turn himself, almost suffocated us. This produced copious perspirations, so that the air soon became unfit for respiration, from a variety of loathsome smells, and brought on a sickness among the slaves, of which many died, thus falling victims to the improvident avarice, as I may call it, of their purchasers. This wretched situation was again aggravated by the galling of the chains, now become insupportable; and the filth of the necessary tubs, into which the children often fell, and were almost suffocated. The shrieks of the women, and the groans of the dying, rendered the whole a scene of horror almost inconceivable. Happily perhaps for myself I was soon reduced so low here that it was thought necessary to keep me almost always on deck; and from my extreme youth I was not put in fetters. In this situation I expected every hour to share the fate of my companions, some of whom were almost daily brought upon deck at the point of death, which I began to hope would soon put an end to my miseries. Often did I think many of the inhabitants of the deep much more happy than myself. I envied them the freedom they enjoyed, and often wished I could change my condition for theirs. Every circumstance I met with served only to render my state more painful, and heighten my apprehensions, and my opinion of the cruelty of the whites. One day they had taken a number of fishes; and when they had killed and satisfied themselves with as many as they thought fit, to our astonishment who were on the deck, rather than give any of them to us to eat as we expected, they tossed the remaining fish into the sea again, although we begged and prayed for some as well as we could, but in vain; and some of my countrymen, being pressed by hunger, took an opportunity, when they thought no one saw them, of trying to get a little privately; but they were discovered, and the attempt procured them some very severe floggings. One day, when we had a smooth sea and moderate wind, two of my wearied countrymen who were chained together (I was near them at the time), preferring death to such a life of misery, somehow made through the nettings and jumped into the sea: immediately another quite dejected fellow, who, on account of his illness, was suffered to be out of irons, also followed their example; and I believe many more would very soon have done the same if they had not been prevented by the ship's crew, who were instantly alarmed. Those of us that were the most active were in a moment put down under the deck, and there was such a noise and confusion amongst the people of the ship as I never heard before, to stop her, and get the boat out to go after the slaves. However two of the wretches were drowned, but they got the other, and afterwards flogged him unmercifully for thus attempting to prefer death to slavery. In this manner we continued to undergo more hardships than I can now relate, hardships which are inseparable from this accursed trade. Many a time we were near suffocation from the want of fresh air, which we were often without for whole days together. This, and the stench of the necessary tubs, carried off many. During our passage I first saw flying fishes, which surprised me very much: they used frequently to fly across the ship, and many of them fell on the deck. I also now first saw the use of the quadrant; I had often with astonishment seen the mariners make observations with it, and I could not think what it meant. They at last took notice of my surprise; and one of them, willing to increase it, as well as to gratify my curiosity, made me one day look through it. The clouds appeared to me to be land, which disappeared as they passed along. This heightened my wonder; and I was now more persuaded than ever that I was in another world, and that every thing about me was magic. At last we came in sight of the island of Barbadoes, at which the whites on board gave a great shout, and made many signs of joy to us. We did not know what to think of this; but as the vessel drew nearer we plainly saw the harbour, and other ships of different kinds and sizes; and we soon anchored amongst them off Bridge Town. Many merchants and planters now came on board, though it was in the evening. They put us in separate parcels, and examined us attentively. They also made us jump, and pointed to the land, signifying we were to go there. We thought by this we should be eaten by these ugly men, as they appeared to us; and, when soon after we were all put down under the deck again, there was much dread and trembling among us, and nothing but bitter cries to be heard all the night from these apprehensions, insomuch that at last the white people got some old slaves from the land to pacify us. They told us we were not to be eaten, but to work, and were soon to go on land, where we should see many of our country people. This report eased us much; and sure enough, soon after we were landed, there came to us Africans of all languages. We were conducted immediately to the merchant's yard, where we were all pent up together like so many sheep in a fold, without regard to sex or age. As every object was new to me every thing I saw filled me with surprise. What struck me first was that the houses were built with stories, and in every other respect different from those in Africa: but I was still more astonished on seeing people on horseback. I did not know what this could mean; and indeed I thought these people were full of nothing but magical arts. While I was in this astonishment one of my fellow prisoners spoke to a countryman of his about the horses, who said they were the same kind they had in their country. I understood them, though they were from a distant part of Africa, and I thought it odd I had not seen any horses there; but afterwards, when I came to converse with different Africans, I found they had many horses amongst them, and much larger than those I then saw. We were not many days in the merchant's custody before we were sold after their usual manner, which is this:—On a signal given, (as the beat of a drum) the buyers rush at once into the yard where the slaves are confined, and make choice of that parcel they like best. The noise and clamour with which this is attended, and the eagerness visible in the countenances of the buyers, serve not a little to increase the apprehensions of the terrified Africans, who may well be supposed to consider them as the ministers of that destruction to which they think themselves devoted. In this manner, without scruple, are relations and friends separated, most of them never to see each other again. I remember in the vessel in which I was brought over, in the men's apartment, there were several brothers, who, in the sale, were sold in different lots; and it was very moving on this occasion to see and hear their cries at parting. O, ye nominal Christians! might not an African ask you, learned you this from your God, who says unto you, Do unto all men as you would men should do unto you? Is it not enough that we are torn from our country and friends to toil for your luxury and lust of gain? Must every tender feeling be likewise sacrificed to your avarice? Are the dearest friends and relations, now rendered more dear by their separation from their kindred, still to be parted from each other, and thus prevented from cheering the gloom of slavery with the small comfort of being together and mingling their sufferings and sorrows? Why are parents to lose their children, brothers their sisters, or husbands their wives? Surely this is a new refinement in cruelty, which, while it has no advantage to atone for it, thus aggravates distress, and adds fresh horrors even to the wretchedness of slavery.

## CHAP. III.

*The author is carried to Virginia—His distress—Surprise at seeing a picture and a watch—Is bought by Captain Pascal, and sets out for England—His terror during the voyage—Arrives in England—His wonder at a fall of snow—Is sent to Guernsey, and in some time goes on board a ship of war with his master—Some account of the expedition against Louisbourg under the command of Admiral Boscawen, in 1758.*

I NOW totally lost the small remains of comfort I had enjoyed in conversing with my countrymen; the women too, who used to wash and take care of me, were all gone different ways, and I never saw one of them afterwards.

I stayed in this island for a few days; I believe it could not be above a fortnight; when I and some few more slaves, that were not saleable amongst the rest, from very much fretting, were shipped off in a sloop for North America. On the passage we were better treated than when we were coming from Africa, and we had plenty of rice and fat pork. We were landed up a river a good way from the sea, about Virginia county, where we saw few or none of our native Africans, and not one soul who could talk to me. I was a few weeks weeding grass, and gathering stones in a plantation; and at last all my companions were distributed different ways, and only myself was left. I was now exceedingly miserable, and thought myself worse off than any of the rest of my companions; for they could talk to each other, but I had no person to speak to that I could understand. In this state I was constantly grieving and pining, and wishing for death rather than any thing else. While I was in this plantation the gentleman, to whom I suppose the estate belonged, being unwell, I was one day sent for to his dwelling house to fan him; when I came into the room where he was I was very much affrighted at some things I saw, and the more so as I had seen a black woman slave as I came through the house, who was cooking the dinner, and the poor creature was cruelly loaded with various kinds of iron machines; she had one particularly on her head, which locked her mouth so fast that she could scarcely speak; and could not eat nor drink. I was much astonished and shocked at this contrivance, which I afterwards learned was called the iron muzzle. Soon after I had a fan put into my hand, to fan the gentleman while he slept; and so I did indeed with great fear. While he was fast asleep I indulged myself a great deal in looking about the room, which to me appeared very fine and curious. The first object that engaged my attention was a watch which hung on the chimney, and was going. I was quite surprised at the noise it made, and was afraid it would tell the gentleman any thing I might do amiss: and when I immediately after observed a picture hanging in the room, which appeared constantly to look at me, I was still more affrighted, having never seen such things as these before. At one time I thought it was something relative to magic; and not seeing it move I thought it might be some way the whites had to keep their great men when they died, and offer them libation as we used to do to our friendly spirits. In this state of anxiety I remained till my master awoke, when I was dismissed out of the room, to my no small satisfaction and relief; for I thought that these people were all made up of wonders. In this place I was called Jacob; but on board the African snow[111] I was called Michael. I had been some time in this miserable, forlorn, and much dejected state, without having any one to talk to, which made my life a burden, when the kind and unknown hand of the Creator (who in very deed leads the blind in a way they know not) now began to appear, to my comfort; for one day the captain of a merchant ship, called the Industrious Bee, came on some business to my master's house. This gentleman, whose name was Michael Henry Pascal, was a lieutenant in the royal navy, but now commanded this trading ship, which was somewhere in the confines of the county many miles off. While he was at my master's house it happened that he saw me, and liked me so well that he made a purchase of me. I think I have often heard him say he gave thirty or forty pounds sterling for me; but I do not now remember which. However, he meant me for a present to some of his friends in England: and I was sent accordingly from the house of my then master, one Mr. Campbell, to the place where the ship lay; I was conducted on horseback by an elderly black man, (a mode of travelling which appeared very odd to me). When I arrived I was carried on board a fine large ship, loaded with tobacco, &c. and just ready to sail for England. I now thought my condition much mended; I had sails to lie on, and plenty of good victuals to eat; and every body on board used me very kindly, quite contrary to what I had seen of any white people before; I therefore began to think that they were not all of the same disposition. A few days after I was on board we sailed for England. I was still at a loss to conjecture my destiny. By this time, however,

I could smatter a little imperfect English; and I wanted to know as well as I could where we were going. Some of the people of the ship used to tell me they were going to carry me back to my own country, and this made me very happy. I was quite rejoiced at the sound of going back; and thought if I should get home what wonders I should have to tell. But I was reserved for another fate, and was soon undeceived when we came within sight of the English coast. While I was on board this ship, my captain and master named me *Gustavus Vasa*.[112] I at that time began to understand him a little, and refused to be called so, and told him as well as I could that I would be called Jacob; but he said I should not, and still called me Gustavus; and when I refused to answer to my new name, which at first I did, it gained me many a cuff; so at length I submitted, and was obliged to bear the present name, by which I have been known ever since.[113] The ship had a very long passage; and on that account we had very short allowance of provisions. Towards the last we had only one pound and a half of bread per week, and about the same quantity of meat, and one quart of water a-day. We spoke with only one vessel the whole time we were at sea, and but once we caught a few fishes. In our extremities the captain and people told me in jest they would kill and eat me; but I thought them in earnest, and was depressed beyond measure, expecting every moment to be my last. While I was in this situation one evening they caught, with a good deal of trouble, a large shark, and got it on board. This gladdened my poor heart exceedingly, as I thought it would serve the people to eat instead of their eating me; but very soon, to my astonishment, they cut off a small part of the tail, and tossed the rest over the side. This renewed my consternation; and I did not know what to think of these white people, though I very much feared they would kill and eat me. There was on board the ship a young lad who had never been at sea before, about four or five years older than myself: his name was Richard Baker. He was a native of America, had received an excellent education, and was of a most amiable temper. Soon after I went on board he shewed me a great deal of partiality and attention, and in return I grew extremely fond of him. We at length became inseparable; and, for the space of two years, he was of very great use to me, and was my constant companion and instructor. Although this dear youth had many slaves of his own, yet he and I have gone through many sufferings together on shipboard; and we have many nights lain in each other's bosoms when we were in great distress. Thus such a friendship was cemented between us as we cherished till his death, which to my very great sorrow, happened in the year 1759, when he was up the Archipelago, on board his majesty's ship the Preston: an event which I have never ceased to regret, as I lost at once a kind interpreter, an agreeable companion, and a faithful friend; who, at the age of fifteen, discovered a mind superior to prejudice; and who was not ashamed to notice, to associate with, and to be the friend and instructor of one who was ignorant, a stranger, of a different complexion, and a slave! My master had lodged in his mother's house in America: he respected him very much, and made him always eat with him in the cabin. He used often to tell him jocularly that he would kill me to eat. Sometimes he would say to me—the black people were not good to eat, and would ask me if we did not eat people in my country. I said, No: then he said he would kill Dick (as he always

called him) first, and afterwards me. Though this hearing relieved my mind a little as to myself, I was alarmed for Dick and whenever he was called I used to be
very much afraid he was to be killed; and I would peep and watch to see if they
were going to kill him: nor was I free from this consternation till we made the
land. One night we lost a man overboard; and the cries and noise were so great
and confused, in stopping the ship, that I, who did not know what was the matter, began, as usual, to be very much afraid, and to think they were going to make
an offering with me, and perform some magic; which I still believed they dealt
in. As the waves were very high I thought the Ruler of the seas was angry, and I
expected to be offered up to appease him. This filled my mind with agony, and
I could not any more that night close my eyes again to rest. However, when daylight appeared I was a little eased in my mind; but still every time I was called I
used to think it was to be killed. Some time after this we saw some very large
fish, which I afterwards found were called grampusses. They looked to me extremely terrible, and made their appearance just at dusk; and were so near as to
blow the water on the ship's deck. I believed them to be the rulers of the sea; and,
as the white people did not make any offerings at any time, I thought they were
angry with them; and, at last, what confirmed my belief was, the wind just then
died away, and a calm ensued, and in consequence of it the ship stopped going.
I supposed that the fish had performed this, and I hid myself in the fore part of
the ship, through fear of being offered up to appease them, every minute peeping and quaking: but my good friend Dick came shortly towards me, and I took
an opportunity to ask him, as well as I could, what these fish were. Not being
able to talk much English, I could but just make him understand my question;
and not at all, when I asked him if any offerings were to be made to them: however, he told me these fish would swallow any body; which sufficiently alarmed
me. Here he was called away by the captain, who was leaning over the quarter-
deck railing and looking at the fish; and most of the people were busied in getting a barrel of pitch to light, for them to play with. The captain now called me
to him, having learned some of my apprehensions from Dick; and having diverted himself and others for some time with my fears, which appeared ludicrous
enough in my crying and trembling, he dismissed me. The barrel of pitch was
now lighted and put over the side into the water: by this time it was just dark,
and the fish went after it; and, to my great joy, I saw them no more.

However, all my alarms began to subside when we got sight of land; and
at last the ship arrived at Falmouth,[114] after a passage of thirteen weeks. Every
heart on board seemed gladdened on our reaching the shore, and none more than
mine. The captain immediately went on shore, and sent on board some fresh provisions, which we wanted very much: we made good use of them, and our famine
was soon turned into feasting, almost without ending. It was about the beginning of the spring 1757 when I arrived in England, and I was near twelve years
of age at that time. I was very much struck with the buildings and the pavement
of the streets in Falmouth; and, indeed, any object I saw filled me with new surprise. One morning, when I got upon deck, I saw it covered all over with the
snow that fell over-night: as I had never seen any thing of the kind before, I
thought it was salt; so I immediately ran down to the mate and desired him, as

well as I could, to come and see how somebody in the night had thrown salt all over the deck. He, knowing what it was, desired me to bring some of it down to him: accordingly I took up a handful of it, which I found very cold indeed; and when I brought it to him he desired me to taste it. I did so, and I was surprised beyond measure. I then asked him what it was; he told me it was snow: but I could not in anywise understand him. He asked me if we had no such thing in my country; and I told him, No. I then asked him the use of it, and who made it; he told me a great man in the heavens, called God: but here again I was to all intents and purposes at a loss to understand him; and the more so, when a little after I saw the air filled with it, in a heavy shower, which fell down on the same day. After this I went to church; and having never been at such a place before, I was again amazed at seeing and hearing the service. I asked all I could about it; and they gave me to understand it was worshipping God, who made us and all things. I was still at a great loss, and soon got into an endless field of inquiries, as well as I was able to speak and ask about things. However, my little friend Dick used to be my best interpreter; for I could make free with him, and he always instructed me with pleasure: and from what I could understand by him of this God, and in seeing these white people did not sell one another, as we did, I was much pleased; and in this I thought they were much happier than we Africans. I was astonished at the wisdom of the white people in all things I saw; but was amazed at their not sacrificing, or making any offerings, and eating with unwashed hands, and touching the dead. I likewise could not help remarking the particular slenderness of their women, which I did not at first like; and I thought they were not so modest and shamefaced as the African women.

I had often seen my master and Dick employed in reading; and I had a great curiosity to talk to the books, as I thought they did; and so to learn how all things had a beginning: for that purpose I have often taken up a book, and have talked to it, and then put my ears to it, when alone, in hopes it would answer me; and I have been very much concerned when I found it remained silent.

My master lodged at the house of a gentleman in Falmouth, who had a fine little daughter about six or seven years of age, and she grew prodigiously fond of me; insomuch that we used to eat together, and had servants to wait on us. I was so much caressed by this family that it often reminded me of the treatment I have received from my little noble African master. After I had been here a few days, I was sent on board of the ship; but the child cried so much after me that nothing could pacify her till I was sent for again. It is ludicrous enough, that I began to fear I should be betrothed to this young lady; and when my master asked me if I would stay there with her behind him, as he was going away with the ship, which had taken in the tobacco again, I cried immediately, and said I would not leave her. At last, by stealth, one night I was sent on board the ship again; and in a little time we sailed for Guernsey, where she was in part owned by a merchant, one Nicholas Doberry. As I was now amongst a people who had not their faces scarred, like some of the African nations where I had been, I was very glad I did not let them ornament me in that manner when I was with them. When we arrived at Guernsey, my master placed me to board and lodge with one of his mates, who had a wife and family there; and some months afterwards he went to England, and left me in care of this mate, together with my friend Dick: This mate had a little daughter, aged about five or six years, with whom I used to be much delighted. I had often observed that when her mother washed her face it looked very rosy; but when she washed mine it did not look so: I therefore tried oftentimes myself if I could not by washing make my face of the same colour as my little play-mate (Mary), but it was all in vain; and I now began to be mortified at the difference in our complexions. This woman behaved to me with great kindness and attention; and taught me every thing in the same manner as she did her own child, and indeed in every respect treated me as such. I remained here till the summer of the year 1757; when my master, being appointed first lieutenant of his majesty's ship the Roebuck, sent for Dick and me, and his old mate: on this we all left Guernsey, and set out for England in a sloop bound for London. As we were coming up towards the Nore,[115] where the Roebuck lay, a man of war's boat came alongside to press our people; on which each man ran to hide himself. I was very much frightened at this, though I did not know what it meant, or what to think or do. However I went and hid myself also under a hencoop. Immediately afterwards the press-gang came on board with their swords drawn, and searched all about, pulled the people out by force, and put them into the boat. At last I was found out also: the man that found me held me up by the heels while they all made their sport of me, I roaring and crying out all the time most lustily: but at last the mate, who was my conductor, seeing this, came to my assistance, and did all he could to pacify me; but all to very little purpose, till I had seen the boat go off. Soon afterwards we came to the Nore, where the Roebuck lay; and, to our great joy, my master came on board to us, and brought us to the ship. When I went on board this large ship, I was amazed indeed to see the quantity of men and the guns. However my surprise began to diminish as my knowledge increased; and I ceased to feel those apprehensions and alarms which had taken such strong possession of me when I first came among the Europeans, and for some time after. I began now to pass to an opposite extreme; I was so far from being afraid of any thing new which I saw, that, after I had been some time in this ship, I even began to long for a battle. My griefs too, which in young minds are not perpetual, were now wearing away; and I soon enjoyed myself pretty well, and felt tolerably easy in my present situation. There was a number of boys on board, which still made it more agreeable; for we were always together, and a great part of our time was spent in play. I remained in this ship a considerable time, during which we made several cruises, and visited a variety of places: among others we were twice in Holland, and brought over several persons of distinction from it, whose names I do not now remember. On the passage, one day, for the diversion of those gentlemen, all the boys were called on the quarter-deck and were paired proportionably, and then made to fight; after which the gentleman gave the combatants from five to nine shilling each. This was the first time I ever fought with a white boy; and I never knew what it was to have a bloody nose before. This made me fight most desperately; I suppose considerably more than an hour: and at last, both of us being weary, we were parted. I had a great deal of this kind of sport afterwards, in which the captain and the ship's company used very much to encourage me. Sometime afterwards the ship went to Leith in Scotland, and from thence to the Orkneys, where I was surprised in seeing scarcely any night: and from thence we sailed with a great fleet, full of soldiers, for England. All this time we had never come to an engagement, though we were frequently cruising off the coast of France: during which we chased many vessels, and took in all seventeen prizes. I had been learning many of the maneuvers of the ship during our cruise; and I was several times made to fire the guns. One evening, off Havre de Grace, just as it was growing dark, we were standing off shore, and met with a fine large French-built frigate. We got all things immediately ready for fighting; and I now expected I should be gratified in seeing an engagement, which I had so long wished for in vain. But the very moment the word of command was given to fire we heard those on board the other ship cry 'Haul down the jib;' and in that instant she hoisted English colours. There was instantly with us an amazing cry of—Avast! or stop firing; and I think one or two guns had been let off, but happily they did no mischief. We had hailed them several times; but they not hearing, we received no answer, which was the cause of our firing. The boat was then sent on board of her, and she proved to be the Ambuscade man of war, to my no small disappointment. We returned to Portsmouth, without having been in any action, just at the trial of Admiral Byng[116] (whom I saw several times during it)ɪ and my master having left the ship, and gone to London for promotion, Dick and I were put on board the Savage sloop of war, and we went in her to assist in bringing off the St. George man of war, that had ran ashore somewhere on the coast. After staying a few weeks on board the Savage, Dick and I were sent on shore at Deal, where we remained some short time, till my master sent for us to London, the place I had long desired exceedingly to see. We therefore both with great pleasure got into a waggon, and came to London, where we were received by a Mr. Guerin, a relation of my master. This gentleman had two sisters, very amiable ladies, who took much notice and great care of me. Though I had desired so much to see London, when I arrived in it I was unfortunately unable to gratify my curiosity; for I had at this time the chilblains to such a degree that I could not stand for several months, and I was obliged to be sent to St. George's Hospital. There I grew so ill, that the doctors wanted to cut my left leg off at different times, apprehending a mortification; but I always said I would rather die than suffer it; and happily (I thank God) I recovered without the operation. After being there several weeks, and just as I had recovered, the small-pox broke out on me, so that I was again confined; and I thought myself now particularly unfortunate. However I soon recovered again; and by this time my master having been promoted to be first lieutenant of the Preston man of war of fifty guns, then new at Deptford,[117] Dick and I were sent on board her, and soon after we went to Holland to bring over the late Duke of ———[118] to England.—While I was in this ship an incident happened, which, though trifling, I beg leave to relate, as I could not help taking particular notice of it, and considering it then as a judgment of God. One morning a young man was looking up to the fore-top, and in a wicked tone, common on shipboard, d——d his eyes about something. Just at the moment some small particles of dirt fell into his left eye, and by the

evening it was very much inflamed. The next day it grew worse; and within six
or seven days he lost it. From this ship my master was appointed a lieutenant
on board the Royal George. When he was going he wished me to stay on board
the Preston, to learn the French horn; but the ship being ordered for Turkey I
could not think of leaving my master, to whom I was very warmly attached; and
I told him if he left me behind it would break my heart. This prevailed on him
to take me with him; but he left Dick on board the Preston, whom I embraced
as parting for the last time. The Royal George was the largest ship I had ever
seen; so that when I came on board of her I was surprised at the number of people, men, women, and children, of every denomination; and the largeness of the
guns, many of them also of brass, which I had never seen before. Here were also
shops of stalls of every kind of goods, and people crying their different commodities about the ship as in a town. To me it appeared a little world, into which
I was again cast without a friend, for I had no longer my dear companion Dick.
We did not stay long here. My master was not many weeks on board before he
got an appointment to be sixth lieutenant of the Namur, which was then at Spithead,[119] sitting up[120] for Vice-admiral Boscawen, who was going with a large
fleet on an expedition against Louisburgh.[121] The crew of the Royal George
were turned over to her, and the flag of the gallant admiral was hoisted on
board, the blue[122] at the maintop-gallant mast head. There was a very great fleet
of men of war of every description assembled together for this expedition, and
I was in hopes soon to have an opportunity of being gratified with a sea-fight.
All things being now in readiness, this mighty fleet (for there was also Admiral
Cornish's fleet in company, destined for the East Indies)[123] at last weighed anchor, and sailed. The two fleets continued in company for several days, and then
parted; Admiral Cornish, in the Lenox, having first saluted our admiral in the
Namur, which he returned. We then steered for America; but, by contrary
winds, we were driven to Teneriffe, where I was struck with its noted peak. Its
prodigious height, and its form, resembling a sugar-loaf,[124] filled me with wonder. We remained in sight of this island some days, and then proceeded for
America, which we soon made, and got into a very commodious harbour called
St. George, in Halifax, where we had fish in great plenty, and all other fresh provisions. We were here joined by different men of war and transport ships with
soldiers; after which, our fleet being increased to a prodigious number of ships
of all kinds, we sailed for Cape Breton in Nova Scotia. We had the good and
gallant General Wolfe[125] on board our ship, whose affability made him highly
esteemed and beloved by all the men. He often honoured me, as well as other
boys, with marks of his notice; and saved me once a flogging for fighting with
a young gentleman. We arrived at Cape Breton in the summer of 1758: and here
the soldiers were to be landed, in order to make an attack upon Louisbourgh.
My master had some part in superintending the landing; and here I was in a
small measure gratified in seeing an encounter between our men and the enemy.
The French were posted on the shore to receive us, and disputed our landing for
a long time; but at last they were driven from their trenches, and a complete
landing was effected. Our troops pursued them as far as the town of Louisbourgh. In this action many were killed on both sides. One thing remarkable I

saw this day:—A lieutenant of the Princess Amelia, who, as well as my master, superintended the landing, was giving the word of command, and while his mouth was open a musquet ball went through it, and passed out at his check. I had that day in my hand the scalp of an indian king, who was killed in the engagement: the scalp had been taken off by an Highlander. I saw this king's ornaments too, which were very curious, and made of feathers.

Our land forces laid siege to the town of Louisbourgh, while the French men of war were blocked up in the harbour by the fleet, the batteries at the same time playing upon them from the land. This they did with such effect, that one day I saw some of the ships set on fire by the shells from the batteries, and I believe two or three of them were quite burnt. At another time, about fifty boats belonging to the English men of war, commanded by Captain George Balfour of the Ætna fire-ship, and another junior captain, Laforey, attacked and boarded the only two remaining French men of war in the harbour. They also set fire to a seventy-gun ship, but a sixty-four, called the Bienfaisant, they brought off. During my stay here I had often an opportunity of being near Captain Balfour, who was pleased to notice me, and liked me so much that he often asked my master to let him have me, but he would not part with me; and no consideration could have induced me to leave him. At last Louisbourgh was taken, and the English men of war came into the harbour before it, to my very great joy; for I had now more liberty of indulging myself, and I went often on shore. When the ships were in the harbour we had the most beautiful procession on the water I ever saw. All the admirals and captains of the men of war, full dressed, and in their barges, well ornamented with pendants, came alongside of the Namur. The vice-admiral then went on shore in his barge, followed by the other officers in order of seniority, to take possession, as I suppose, of the town and fort. Some time after this the French governor and his lady, and other persons of note, came on board our ship to dine. On this occasion our ships were dressed with colours of all kinds, from the topgallant-mast head to the deck; and this, with the firing of guns, formed a most grand and magnificent spectacle.

As soon as every thing here was settled Admiral Boscawen sailed with part of the fleet of England, leaving some ships behind with Rear-admirals Sir Charles Hardy and Durell. It was now winter; and one evening, during our passage home, about dusk, when we were in the channel, or near soundings, and were beginning to look for land, we descried seven sail of large men of war, which stood off shore. Several people on board of our ship said, as the two fleets were (in forty minutes from the first sight) within hail of each other, that they were English men of war; and some of our people even began to name some of the ships. By this time both fleets began to mingle, and our admiral ordered his flag to be hoisted. At that instant the other fleet, which were French, hoisted their ensigns, and gave us a broadside as they passed by. Nothing could create greater surprise and confusion among us than this: the wind was high, the sea rough, and we had our lower and middle deck guns housed in, so that not a single gun on board was ready to be fired at any of the French ships. However, the Royal William and the Somerset being our sternmost ships, became a little prepared, and each gave the French ships a broadside as they

passed by. I afterwards heard this was a French squadron, commanded by
Mons. Conflans; and certainly had the Frenchman known our condition, and
had a mind to fight us, they might have done us great mischief. But we were
not long before we were prepared for an engagement. Immediately many things
were tossed overboard; the ships were made ready for fighting as soon as possible; and about ten at night we had bent a new main sail, the old one being
split. Being now in readiness for fighting, we wore ship,[126] and stood after[127]
the French fleet, who were one or two ships in number more than we. However we gave them chase, and continued pursuing them all night; and at daylight we saw six of them, all large ships of the line, and an English East Indiaman,[128] a prize they had taken. We chased them all day till between three and
four o'clock in the evening, when we came up with, and passed within a musquet shot of, one seventy-four gun ship, and the Indiaman also, who now
hoisted her colours, but immediately hauled them down again. On this we
made a signal for the other ships to take possession of her; and, supposing the
man of war would likewise strike,[129] we cheered, but she did not; though if we
had fired into her, from being so near, we must have taken her. To my utter
surprise the Somerset, who was the next ship a-stern of the Namur, made way
likewise; and, thinking they were sure of this French ship, they cheered in the
same manner, but still continued to follow us. The French Commodore was
about a gun-shot ahead of all, running from us with all speed; and about four
o'clock he carried his foretopmast overboard. This caused another loud cheer
with us; and a little after the topmast came close by us; but, to our great surprise, instead of coming up with her, we found she went as fast as ever, if not
faster. The sea grew now much smoother; and the wind lulling, the seventy-
four gun ship we had passed came again by us in the very same direction, and
so near, that we heard her people talk as she went by; yet not a shot was fired
on either side; and about five or six o'clock, just as it grew dark, she joined her
commodore. We chased all night, but the next day they were out of sight, so
that we saw no more of them; and we only had the old Indiaman (called
Carnarvon I think) for our trouble. After this we stood in for the channel, and
soon made the land; and, about the close of the year 1758–9, we got safe to St.
Helen's.[130] Here the Namur ran aground; and also another large ship astern of
us; but, by starting our water,[131] and tossing many things overboard to lighten
her, we got the ships off without any damage. We stayed for a short time at
Spithead, and then went into Portsmouth harbour to refit; from whence the admiral went to London; and my master and I soon followed, with a press-gang,
as we wanted some hands to complete our complement.

---

## CHAP. IV.

*The author is baptized—Narrowly escapes drowning—Goes on an expedition to the
Mediterranean—Incidents he met with there—Is witness to an engagement between some English and French ships—A particular account of the celebrated*

*engagement between Admiral Boscawen and Mons. Le Clue, off Cape Logas,
in August 1759—Dreadful explosion of a French ship—The author sails for
England—His master appointed to the command of a fire-ship—Meets a negro
boy, from whom he experiences much benevolence—Prepares for an expedition
against Belle-Isle—A remarkable story of a disaster which befel his ship—Arrives at Belle-Isle—Operations of the landing and siege—The author's danger
and distress, with his manner of extricating himself—Surrender of Belle-Isle—
Transactions afterwards on the coast of France—Remarkable instance of kidnapping—The author returns to England—Hears a talk of peace, and expects
his freedom—His ship sails for Deptford to be paid off, and when he arrives
there he is suddenly seized by his master and carried forcibly on board a West
India ship and sold.*

IT was now between two and three years since I first came to England, a great
part of which I had spent at sea; so that I became inured to that service, and began to consider myself as happily situated; for my master treated me always extremely well; and my attachment and gratitude to him were very great. From the
various scenes I had beheld on ship-board, I soon grew a stranger to terror of
every kind, and was, in that respect at least, almost an Englishman. I have often
reflected with surprise that I never felt half the alarm at any of the numerous dangers I have been in, that I was filled with at the first sight of the Europeans, and
at every act of theirs, even the most trifling, when I first came among them, and
for some time afterwards. That fear, however, which was the effect of my ignorance, wore away as I began to know them. I could now speak English tolerably
well, and I perfectly understood everything that was said. I now not only felt myself quite easy with these new countrymen, but relished their society and manners. I no longer looked upon them as spirits, but as men superior to us; and
therefore I had the stronger desire to resemble them; to imbibe their spirit, and
imitate their manners; I therefore embraced every occasion of improvement; and
every new thing that I observed I treasured up in my memory. I had long wished
to be able to read and write; and for this purpose I took every opportunity to
gain instruction, but had made as yet very little progress. However, when I went
to London with my master, I had soon an opportunity of improving myself,
which I gladly embraced. Shortly after my arrival, he sent me to wait upon the
Miss Guerins, who had treated me with much kindness when I was there before;
and they sent me to school.

While I was attending these ladies their servants told me I could not go to
Heaven unless I was baptized. This made me very uneasy; for I had now some
faint idea of a future state: accordingly I communicated my anxiety to the eldest
Miss Guerin, with whom I was become a favourite, and pressed her to have me
baptized; when to my great joy she told me I should. She had formerly asked my
master to let me be baptized, but he had refused; however she now insisted on
it; and he being under some obligation to her brother complied with her request;
so I was baptized in St. Margaret's church, Westminster, in February 1759, by
my present name. The clergyman, at the same time, gave me a book, called a
Guide to the Indians, written by the Bishop of Sodor and Man.[132] On this

occasion Miss Guerin did me the honour to stand as godmother, and afterwards gave me a treat. I used to attend these ladies about the town, in which service I was extremely happy; as I had thus many opportunities of seeing London, which I desired of all things. I was sometimes, however, with my master at his rendezvous-house,[133] which was at the foot of Westminster-bridge. Here I used to enjoy myself in playing about the bridge stairs, and often in the watermen's wherries, with other boys. On one of these occasions there was another boy with me in a wherry, and we went out into the current of the river: while we were there two more stout boys came to us in another wherry, and abusing us for taking the boat, desired me to get into the other wherry-boat. Accordingly I went to get out of the wherry I was in; but just as I had got one of my feet into the other boat the boys shoved it off, so that I fell into the Thames; and, not being able to swim, I should unavoidably have been drowned, but for the assistance of some watermen who providentially came to my relief.

The Namur being again got ready for sea, my master, with his gang, was ordered on board; and, to my no small grief, I was obliged to leave my schoolmaster, whom I liked very much, and always attended while I stayed in London, to repair on board with my master. Nor did I leave my kind patronesses, the Miss Guerins, without uneasiness and regret. They often used to teach me to read, and took great pains to instruct me in the principles of religion and the knowledge of God. I therefore parted from those amiable ladies with reluctance; after receiving from them many friendly cautions how to conduct myself, and some valuable presents.

When I came to Spithead, I found we were destined for the Mediterranean, with the large fleet, which was now ready to put to sea. We only waited for the arrival of the admiral, who soon came on board; and about the beginning of the spring 1759, having weighed anchor, and got under way, sailed for the Mediterranean; and in eleven days, from the Land's End, we got to Gibraltar. While we were here I used to be often on shore, and got various fruits in great plenty, and very cheap.

I had frequently told several people, in my excursions on shore, the story of my being kidnapped with my sister, and of our being separated, as I have related before; and I had as often expressed my anxiety for her fate, and my sorrow at having never met her again. One day, when I was on shore, and mentioning these circumstances to some persons, one of them told me he knew where my sister was, and, if I would accompany him, he would bring me to her. Improbable as this story was I believed it immediately, and agreed to go with him, while my heart leaped for joy: and, indeed, he conducted me to a black young woman, who was so like my sister, that, at first sight, I really thought it was her: but I was quickly undeceived; and, on talking to her, I found her to be of another nation.

While we lay here the Preston came in from the Levant.[134] As soon as she arrived, my master told me I should now see my old companion, Dick, who had gone in her when she sailed for Turkey. I was much rejoiced at this news, and expected every minute to embrace him; and when the captain came on board of our ship, which he did immediately after, I ran to inquire after my friend; but, with inexpressible sorrow, I learned from the boat's crew that the dear youth was dead! and that they had brought his chest, and all his other things, to my master: these he afterwards gave to me, and I regarded them as a memorial of my friend, whom I loved, and grieved for, as a brother.

While we were at Gibraltar, I saw a soldier hanging by his heels, at one of the moles*: I thought this a strange sight, as I had seen a man hanged in London by his neck. At another time I saw the master of a frigate towed to shore on a grating, by several of the men of war's boats, and discharged the fleet, which I understood was a mark of disgrace for cowardice. On board the same ship there was also a sailor hung up at the yard-arm.

After lying at Gibraltar for some time, we sailed up the Mediterranean a considerable way above the Gulf of Lyons; where we were one night overtaken with a terrible gale of wind, much greater than any I had ever yet experienced. The sea ran so high that, though all the guns were well housed, there was a great reason to fear their getting loose, the ship rolled so much; and if they had it must have proved our destruction. After we had cruised here for a short time, we came to Barcelona, a Spanish sea-port, remarkable for its silk manufactures. Here the ships were all to be watered; and my master, who spoke different languages, and used often to interpret for the admiral, superintended the watering of ours. For that purpose he and the officers of the other ships, who were on the same service, had tents pitched in the bay; and the Spanish soldiers were stationed along the shore, I suppose to see that no depredations were committed by our men.

I used constantly to attend my master; and I was charmed with this place. All the time we stayed it was like a fair with the natives, who brought us fruits of all kinds, and sold them to us much cheaper than I got them in England. They used also to bring wine down to us in hog and sheep skins, which diverted me very much. The Spanish officers here treated our officers with great politeness and attention; and some of them, in particular, used to come often to my master's tent to visit him; where they would sometimes divert themselves by mounting me on the horses or mules, so that I could not fall, and setting them off at full gallop; my imperfect skill in horsemanship all the while affording them no small entertainment. After the ships were watered, we returned to our old station of cruizing off Toulon, for the purpose of intercepting a fleet of French men of war that lay there. One Sunday, in our cruise, we came off a place where there were two small French frigates lying in shore; and our admiral, thinking to take or destroy them, sent two ships in after them—the Culloden and the Conqueror. They soon came up to the Frenchmen; and I saw a smart fight here, both by sea and land: for the frigates were covered by batteries, and they played upon our ships most furiously, which they as furiously returned, and for a long time a constant firing was kept up on all sides at an amazing rate. At last one frigate sunk; but the people escaped, though not without much difficulty: and a little after some of the people left the other frigate also, which was a mere wreck. However,

---

*He had drowned himself in endeavouring to desert.

our ships did not venture to bring her away, they were so much annoyed from the batteries, which raked them both in going and coming: their topmasts were shot away, and they were otherwise so much shattered, that the admiral was obliged to send in many boats to tow them back to the fleet. I afterwards sailed with a man who fought in one of the French batteries during the engagement, and he told me our ships had done considerable mischief that day on shore and in the batteries.

After this we sailed for Gibraltar, and arrived there about August 1759. Here we remained with all our sails unbent, while the fleet was watering and doing other necessary things. While we were in this situation, one day the admiral, with most of the principal officers, and many people of all stations, being on shore, about seven o'clock in the evening we were alarmed by signals from the frigates stationed for that purpose; and in an instant there was a general cry that the French fleet was out, and just passing through the streights. The admiral immediately came on board with some other officers; and it is impossible to describe the noise, hurry and confusion throughout the whole fleet, in bending their sails and slipping their cables; many people and ships' boats were left on shore in the bustle. We had two captains on board of our ship who came away in the hurry and left their ships to follow. We shewed lights from the gun-whale to the main topmast-head; and all our lieutenants were employed amongst the fleet to tell the ships not to wait for their captains, but to put the sails to the yards, slip their cables and follow us; and in this constitution of making ready for fighting we set out for sea in the dark after the French fleet. Here I could have exclaimed with Ajax,

"Oh Jove! O father! if it be thy will
"That we must perish, we thy will obey,
"But let us perish by the light of day."[135]

They had got the start of us so far that we were not able to come up with them during the night; but at day-light we saw seven sail of the line of battle some miles ahead. We immediately chased them till about four o'clock in the evening, when our ships came up with them; and, though we were about fifteen large ships, our gallant admiral only fought them with his own division, which consisted of seven; so that we were just ship for ship. We passed by the whole of the enemy's fleet in order to come at their commander, Mons. La Clue,[136] who was in the Ocean, an eighty-four gun ship: as we passed they all fired on us; and at one time three of them fired together, continuing to do so for some time. Notwithstanding which our admiral would not suffer a gun to be fired at any of them, to my astonishment; but made us lie on our bellies on the deck till we came quite close to the Ocean, who was ahead of them all; when we had orders to pour the whole three tiers into her at once.

The engagement now commenced with great fury on both sides: the Ocean immediately returned our fire, and we continued engaged with each other for some time; during which I was frequently stunned with the thundering of the great guns, whose dreadful contents hurried many of my companions into awful eternity. At last the French line was entirely broken, and we obtained the victory, which was immediately proclaimed with loud huzzas and acclamations. We took three prizes, La Modeste, of sixty-four guns, and Le Temeraire and Centaur, of seventy-four guns each. The rest of the French ships took to flight with all the sail they could crowd. Our ship being very much damaged, and quite disabled from pursuing the enemy, the admiral immediately quitted her, and went in the broken and only boat we had left on board the Newark, with which, and some other ships, he went after the French. The Ocean, and another large French ship, called the Redoubtable, endeavouring to escape, ran ashore at Cape Logas, on the coast of Portugal; and the French admiral and some of the crew got ashore; but we, finding it impossible to get the ships off, set fire to them both. About midnight I saw the Ocean blow up, with a most dreadful explosion. I never beheld a more awful scene. In less than a minute the midnight for a certain space seemed turned into day by the blaze, which was attended with a noise louder and more terrible than thunder, that seemed to rend every element around us.

My station during the engagement was on the middle-deck, where I was quartered with another boy, to bring powder to the aftermost gun; and here I was a witness of the dreadful fate of many of my companions, who, in the twinkling of an eye, were dashed in pieces, and launched into eternity. Happily I escaped unhurt, though the shot and splinters flew thick about me during the whole fight. Towards the latter part of it my master was wounded, and I saw him carried down to the surgeon; but though I was much alarmed for him and wished to assist him I dared not leave my post. At this station my gun-mate (a partner in bringing powder for the same gun) and I ran a very great risk for more than half an hour of blowing up the ship. For, when we had taken the cartridges out of the boxes, the bottoms of many of them proving rotten, the powder ran all about the deck, near the match tub: we scarcely had water enough at the last to throw on it. We were also, from our employment, very much exposed to the enemy's shots; for we had to go through nearly the whole length of the ship to bring the powder. I expected therefore every minute to be my last; especially when I saw our men fall so thick about me; but, wishing to guard as much against the dangers as possible, at first I thought it would be safest not to go for the powder till the Frenchmen had fired their broadside; and then, while they were charging, I could go and come with my powder: but immediately afterwards I thought this caution was fruitless; and, cheering myself with the reflection that there was a time allotted for me to die as well as to be born, I instantly cast off all fear or thought whatever of death, and went through the whole of my duty with alacrity; pleasing myself with the hope, if I survived the battle, of relating it and the dangers I had escaped to the dear Miss Guerin, and others, when I should return to London.

Our ship suffered very much in this engagement; for, besides the number of our killed and wounded, she was almost torn to pieces, and our rigging so much shattered, that our mizen-mast and main-yard, &c. hung over the side of the ship; so that we were obliged to get many carpenters, and others from some of the ships of the fleet, to assist in setting us in some tolerable order; and, notwithstanding, it took us some time before we were completely refitted; after which we left Admiral Broderick to command, and we, with the prizes, steered for England. On the passage, and as soon as my master was something recovered of his wounds, the admiral appointed him captain of the Ætna fire-ship, on

which he and I left the Namur, and went on board of her at sea. I liked this little ship very much. I now became the captain's steward, in which situation I was
very happy: for I was extremely well treated by all on board; and I had leisure to
improve myself in reading and writing. The latter I had learned a little of before
I left the Namur, as there was a school on board. When we arrived at Spithead
the Ætna went into Portsmouth harbour to refit, which being done, we returned
to Spithead and joined a large fleet that was thought to be intended against the
Havannah; but about that time the king died:[137] whether that prevented the expedition I know not; but it caused our ship to be stationed at Cowes, in the isle
of Wight, till the beginning of the year sixty-one. Here I spent my time very pleasantly; I was much on shore all about this delightful island, and found the inhabitants very civil.

While I was here, I met with a trifling incident, which surprised me agreeably. I was one day in a field belonging to a gentleman who had a black boy about
my own size; this boy having observed me from his master's house, was transported at the sight of one of his own countrymen, and ran to meet me with the
utmost haste. I not knowing what he was about turned a little out of his way at
first, but to no purpose: he soon came close to me and caught hold of me in his
arms as if I had been his brother, though we had never seen each other before.
After we had talked together for some time he took me to his master's house,
where I was treated very kindly. This benevolent boy and I were very happy in
frequently seeing each other till about the month of March 1761, when our ship
had orders to fit out again for another expedition. When we got ready, we joined
a very large fleet at Spithead, commanded by Commodore Keppel,[138] which was
destined against Belle-Isle,[139] and with a number of transport ships with troops
on board to make a descent on the place. We sailed once more in quest of fame.
I longed to engage in new adventures and see fresh wonders.

I had a mind on which every thing uncommon made its full impression, and
every event which I considered as marvellous. Every extraordinary escape, or signal deliverance, either of myself or others, I looked upon to be effected by the interposition of Providence. We had not been above ten days at sea before an incident of this kind happened; which, whatever credit it may obtain from the
reader, made no small impression on my mind.

We had on board a gunner, whose name was John Mondle; a man of very
indifferent morals. This man's cabin was between the decks, exactly over where
I lay, abreast of the quarter-deck ladder. One night, the 20th of April, being terrified with a dream, he awoke in so great a fright that he could not rest in his
bed any longer, nor even remain in his cabin; and he went upon the deck about
four o'clock in the morning extremely agitated. He immediately told those on
the deck of the agonies of his mind, and the dream which occasioned it; in which
he said he had seen many things very awful, and had been warned by St. Peter
to repent, who told him time was short. This he said had greatly alarmed him,
and he was determined to alter his life. People generally mock the fears of others when they are themselves in safety; and some of his shipmates who heard
him only laughed at him. However, he made a vow that he never would drink
strong liquors again; and he immediately got a light, and gave away his sea-

stores of liquor. After which, his agitation still continuing, he began to read the Scriptures, hoping to find some relief; and soon afterwards he laid himself down again on his bed, and endeavoured to compose himself to sleep, but to no purpose; his mind still continuing in a state of agony. By this time it was exactly half after seven in the morning: I was then under the half-deck at the great cabin door; and all at once I heard the people in the waist cry out, most fearfully— 'The Lord have mercy upon us! We are all lost! The Lord have mercy upon us!' Mr. Mondle hearing the cries, immediately ran out of his cabin; and we were instantly struck by the Lynne, a forty-gun ship, Captain Clark, which nearly ran us down. This ship had just put about, and was by the wind, but had not got full headway, or we must all have perished; for the wind was brisk. However, before Mr. Mondle had got four steps from his cabin-door, she struck our ship with her cutwater right in the middle of his bed and cabin, and ran it up to the combings of the quarter-deck hatchway, and above three feet below water, and in a minute there was not a bit of wood to be seen where Mr. Mondle's cabin stood; and he was so near being killed that some of the splinters tore his face. As Mr. Mondle must inevitably have perished from this accident had he not been alarmed in the very extraordinary way I have related, I could not help regarding this as an awful interposition of Providence for his preservation. The two ships for some time swinged alongside of each other; for ours being a fire-ship, our grappling-irons caught the Lynne every way, and the yards and rigging went at an astonishing rate. Our ship was in such a shocking condition that we all thought she would instantly go down, and every one ran for their lives, and got as well as they could on board the Lynne; but our lieutenant being the aggressor, he never quitted the ship. However, when we found she did not sink immediately, the captain came on board again, and encouraged our people to return and try to save her. Many on this came back, but some would not venture. Some of the ships in the fleet, seeing our situation, immediately sent their boats to our assistance; but it took us the whole day to save the ship with all their help. And by using every possible means, particularly frapping her together with many hawsers, and putting a great quantity of tallow below water where she was damaged, she was kept together; but it was well we did not meet with any gales of wind, or we must have gone to pieces; for we were in such a crazy condition that we had ships to attend us till we arrived at Belle-Isle, the place of our destination; and then we had all things taken out of the ship, and she was properly repaired. This escape of Mr. Mondle, which he, as well as myself, always considered as a singular act of Providence, I believe had a great influence on his life and conduct ever afterwards.

Now that I am on this subject I beg leave to relate another instance or two which strongly raised my belief of the particular interposition of Heaven, and which might not otherwise have found a place here, from their insignificance. I belonged for a few days in the year 1758 to the Jason, of fifty-four guns, at Plymouth; and one night, when I was on board, a woman, with a child at her breast, fell from the upper-deck down into the hold, near the keel. Every one thought that the mother and child must be both dashed to pieces; but, to our great surprise, neither of them was hurt. I myself one day fell headlong from the upper-deck of the Ætna down the after-hold, when the ballast was out; and all who saw me fall cried out I was killed: but I received not the least injury. And in the same ship a man fell from the masthead on the deck without being hurt. In these, and in many more instances, I thought I could plainly trace the hand of God, without whose permission a sparrow cannot fall. I began to raise my fear from man to him alone, and to call daily on his holy name with fear and reverence: and I trust he heard my supplications, and graciously condescended to answer me according to his holy word, and to implant the seeds of piety in me, even one of the meanest of his creatures.

When we had refitted or ship, and all things were in readiness for attacking the place, the troops on board the transports were ordered to disembark; and my master, as a junior captain, had a share in the command of the landing. This was on the 8th of April. The French were drawn up on the shore, and had made every disposition to oppose the landing of our men, only a small part of them this day being able to effect it; most of them, after fighting with great bravery, were cut off; and General Crawford, with a number of others, were taken prisoners. In this day's engagement we had also our lieutenant killed.

On the 21st of April we renewed our efforts to land the men, while all the men of war were stationed along the shore to cover it, and fired at the French batteries and breastworks from early in the morning till about four o'clock in the evening, when our soldiers effected a safe landing. They immediately attacked the French; and, after a sharp encounter, forced them from the batteries. Before the enemy retreated they blew up several of them, lest they should fall into our hands. Our men now proceeded to besiege the citadel, and my master was ordered on shore to superintend the landing of all the materials necessary for carrying on the siege; in which service I mostly attended him. While I was there I went about to different parts of the island; and one day, particularly, my curiosity almost cost me my life. I wanted very much to see the mode of charging the mortars and letting off the shells, and for that purpose I went to an English battery that was but a very few yards from the walls of the citadel. There, indeed, I had an opportunity of completely gratifying myself in seeing the whole operation, and that not without running a very great risk, both from the English shells that burst while I was there, but likewise from those of the French. One of the largest of their shells bursted within nine or ten yards of me: there was a single rock close by, about the size of a butt; and I got instant shelter under it in time to avoid the fury of the shell. Where it burst the earth was torn in such a manner that two of three butts might easily have gone into the hole it made, and it threw great quantities of stones and dirt to a considerable distance. Three shot were also fired at me and another boy who was along with me, one of them in particular seemed

"Wing'd with red lightening and impetuous rage;"[140]

for with a most dreadful sound it hissed close by me, and struck a rock at a little distance, which it shattered to pieces. When I saw what perilous circumstances I was in,

I attempted to return the nearest way I could find, and thereby I got between the English and the French centinels. An English sergeant, who commanded the outposts, seeing me, and surprised how I came there, (which was by stealth along the seashore), reprimanded me very severely for it, and instantly took the centinel off his post into custody, for his negligence in suffering me to pass the lines. When I was in this situation I observed at a little distance a French horse, belonging to some islanders, which I thought I would now mount, for the greater expedition of getting off. Accordingly I took some cord which I had about me, and making a kind of bridle of it, I put it round the horse's head, and the tame beast very quietly suffered me to tie him thus and mount him. As soon as I was on the horse's back I began to kick and beat him, and try every means to make him go quick, but all to very little purpose: I could not drive him out of a slow pace. While I was creeping along, still within reach of the enemy's shot, I met with a servant well mounted on an English horse. I immediately stopped; and, crying, told him my case; and begged of him to help me, and this he effectually did; for, having a fine large whip, he began to lash my horse with it so severely, that he set off full speed with me towards the sea, while I was quite unable to hold or manage him. In this manner I went along till I came to a craggy precipice. I now could not stop my horse; and my mind was filled with apprehensions of my deplorable fate should he go down the precipice, which he appeared fully disposed to do: I therefore thought I had better throw myself off him at once, which I did immediately with a great deal of dexterity, and fortunately escaped unhurt. As soon as I found myself at liberty I made the best of my way for the ship, determined I would not be so fool-hardy again in a hurry.

We continued to besiege the citadel till June, when it surrendered. During the siege I have counted above sixty shells and carcases in the air at once. When this place was taken I went through the citadel, and in the bombproofs under it, which were cut in the solid rock; and I thought it a surprising place, both for strength and building: notwithstanding which our shots and shells had made amazing devastation, and ruinous heaps all around it.

After the taking of this island our ships, with some others commanded by Commodore Stanhope in the Swiftsure, went to Basse-road,[141] where we blocked up a French fleet. Our ships were there from June till February following; and in that time I saw a great many scenes of war, and stratagems on both sides to destroy each others fleet. Sometimes we would attack the French with some ships of the line; at other times with boats; and frequently we made prizes. Once or twice the French attacked us by throwing shells with their bomb-vessels: and one day as a French vessel was throwing shells at our ships she broke from her springs, behind the isle of I de Re: the tide being complicated, she came within a gun shot of the Nassau; but the Nassau could not bring a gun to bear upon her, and thereby the Frenchman got off. We were twice attacked by their fire-floats, which they chained together, and then let them float down with the tide; but each time we sent boats with graplings, and towed them safe out of the fleet.

We had different commanders while we were at this place, Commodores Stanhope, Dennis, Lord Howe, &c. From hence, before the Spanish war[142] began, our ship and the Wasp sloop were sent to St. Sebastian in Spain,[143] by Commodore Stanhope; and Commodore Dennis afterwards sent our ship as a cartel[144] to Bayonne in France*, after which† we went in February in 1762 to Belle-Isle, and there stayed till the summer, when we left it, and returned to Portsmouth.

After our ship was fitted out again for service, in September[145] she went to Guernsey, where I was glad to see my old hostess, who was now a widow, and my former little charming companion, her daughter. I spent some time here very happily with them, till October, when we had orders to repair to Portsmouth. We parted from each other with a great deal of affection; and I promised to return soon, and see them again, not knowing what all-powerful fate had determined for me. Our ship having arrived at Portsmouth, we went into the harbour, and remained there till the latter end of November, when we heard great talk about peace; and, to our very great joy, in the beginning of December we had orders to go up to London with our ship to be paid off. We received this news with loud huzzas, and every other demonstration of gladness; and nothing but mirth was to be seen throughout every part of the ship. I too was not without my share of the general joy on this occasion. I thought now of nothing but being freed, and working for myself, and thereby getting money to enable me to get a good education; for I always had a great desire to be able at least to read and write; and while I was on ship-board I had endeavoured to improve myself in both. While I was in the Ætna particularly, the captain's clerk taught me to write, and gave me a smattering of arithmetic as far as the rule of three.[146] There was also one Daniel Queen, about forty years of age, a man very well educated, who messed with me on board this ship, and he likewise dressed and attended the captain. Fortunately this man soon became very much attached to me, and took very great pains to instruct me in many things. He taught me to shave and dress hair a little, and also to read in the bible, explaining many passages to me, which I did not comprehend. I was wonderfully surprised to see the laws and rules of my country written almost exactly here; a circumstance which I believe tended to impress our manners and customs more deeply on my memory. I used to tell him of this resemblance; and many a time we have sat up the whole night together at this employment. In short, he was like a father to me; and some even used to call me after his name; they also styled me the black Christian. Indeed I almost loved him with the affection of a son. Many things I have denied myself that he might have them; and when I used to play at marbles or any other game, and won a few halfpence,

---

*Among others whom we brought from Bayonne, two gentleman, who had been in the West Indies, where they sold slaves; and they confessed they had made at one time a false bill of sale, and sold two Portuguese white men among a lot of slaves.

†Some people have it, that sometimes shortly before persons die their ward has been seen; that is, some spirit exactly in their likeness, though they are themselves at other places at the same time. One day while we were at Bayonne Mr. Mondle saw one of our men, as he thought, in the gun-room; and a little after, coming on the quarter-deck, he spoke of some circumstances of this man to some of the officers. They told him that the man was then out of the ship, in one of the boats with the Lieutenant; but Mr. Mondle would not believe it, and we searched the ship, when he found the man was actually out of her; and when the boat returned some time afterwards, we found the man had been drowned at the very time Mr. Mondle thought he saw him.

or got any little money, which I sometimes did, for shaving any one, I used to buy him a little sugar or tobacco, as far as my stock of money would go. He used to say, that he and I never should part; and that when our ship was paid off, as I was as free as himself or any other man on board, he would instruct me his business, by which I might gain a good livelihood. This gave me new life and spirits; and my heart burned within me, while I thought the time long till I obtained my freedom. For though my master had not promised it to me, yet, besides the assurances I had received that he had no right to detain me, he always treated me with the greatest kindness, and reposed in me an unbounded confidence; he even paid attention to my morals; and would never suffer me to deceive him, or tell lies, of which he used to tell me the consequences; and that if I did so God would not love me; so that, from all this tenderness, I had never once supposed, in all my dreams of freedom, that he would think of detaining me any longer than I wished.

In pursuance of our orders we sailed from Portsmouth for the Thames, and arrived at Deptford the 10th of December, where we cast anchor just as it was high water. The ship was up about half an hour, when my master ordered the barge to be manned; and all in an instant, without having before given me the least reason to suspect any thing of the matter, he forced me into the barge; saying, I was going to leave him, but he would take care I should not. I was so struck with the unexpectedness of this proceeding, that for some time I did not make a reply, only I made an offer to go for my books and chest of clothes, but he swore I should not move out of his sight; and if I did he would cut my throat, at the same time taking his hanger.[147] I began, however, to collect myself; and, plucking up courage, I told him I was free, and he could not by law serve me so.[148] But this only enraged him the more; and he continued to swear, and said he would soon let me know whether he would or not, and at that instant sprung himself into the barge from the ship; to the astonishment and sorrow of all on board. The tide, rather unluckily for me, had just turned downward, so that we quickly fell down the river along with it, till we came among some outward-bound West Indiamen; for he was resolved to put me on board the first vessel he could get to receive me. The boat's crew, who pulled against their will, became quite faint different times, and would have gone ashore; but he would not let them. Some of them strove then to cheer me, and told me he could not sell me, and that they would stand by me, which revived me a little; and I still entertained hopes; for as they pulled along he asked some vessels to receive me, but they could not. But, just as we had got a little below Gravesend, we came alongside of a ship which was going away the next tide for the West Indies; her name was the Charming Sally, Captain James Doran; and my master went on board and agreed with him for me; and in a little time I was sent for into the cabin. When I came there Captain Doran asked me if I knew him; I answered that I did not; 'Then,' said he 'you are now my slave.' I told him my master could not sell me to him, nor to any one else. 'Why,' said he, 'did not your master buy you?' I confessed he did. 'But I have served him,' said I, 'many years, and he has taken all my wages and prize-money, for I only got one sixpence during the war; besides this I have been baptized; and by the laws of the land no man has a right to sell me:' And I added, that I had heard a lawyer and others at different times tell my master so. They both then said that those people who told me so were not my friends; but I replied—it was very extraordinary that other people did not know the law as well as they. Upon this Captain Doran said I talked too much English; and if I did not behave myself well, and be quiet, he had a method on board to make me. I was too well convinced of his power over me to doubt what he said; and my former sufferings in the slave-ship presenting themselves to my mind, the recollection of them made me shudder. However, before I retired I told him that as I could not get any right among men here I hoped I should hereafter in Heaven; and I immediately left the cabin, filled with resentment and sorrow. The only coat I had with me my master took away with him, and said if my prize-money had been 10,000 l. he had a right to it all, and would have taken it. I had about nine guineas, which, during my long sea-faring life, I had scraped together from trifling perquisites and little ventures; and I hid it that instant, lest my master should take that from me likewise, still hoping that by some means or other I should make my escape to the shore; and indeed some of my old shipmates told me not to despair, for they could get me back again; and that, as soon as they could get their pay, they would immediately come to Portsmouth to me, where this ship was going: but, alas! all my hopes were baffled, and the hour of my deliverance was yet far off. My master, having soon concluded his bargain with the captain, came out of the cabin, and he and his people got into the boat and put off; I followed them with aching eyes as long as I could, and when they were out of sight I threw myself on the deck, while my heart was ready to burst with sorrow and anguish.

## CHAP. V

*The author's reflections on his situation—Is deceived by a promise of being delivered—His despair at sailing for the West Indies—Arrives at Montserrat, where he is sold to Mr. King—Various interesting instances of oppression, cruelty, and extortion, which the author saw practised upon the slaves in the West Indies during his captivity from the year 1763 to 1766—Address on it to the planters.*

THUS, at the moment I expected all my toils to end, was I plunged, as I supposed, in a new slavery; in comparison of which all my service hitherto had been 'perfect freedom;' and whose horrors, always present to my mind, now rushed on it with tenfold aggravation. I wept very bitterly for some time: and began to think that I must have done something to displease the Lord, that he thus punished me so severely. This filled me with painful reflections on my past conduct; I recollected that on the morning of our arrival at Deptford I had rashly sworn that as soon as we reached London I would spend the day in rambling and sport. My conscience smote me for this unguarded expression: I felt that the Lord was able to disappoint me in all things, and immediately considered my present situation as a judgment of Heaven on account of my presumption in swearing: I therefore, with contrition of heart, acknowledged my transgression to God, and poured out my soul before him with unfeigned repentance, and with earnest supplications I besought him not to abandon me in my distress, or cast me from his mercy for ever. In a little time my grief, spent with its own violence, began to subside; and after the first confusion of my thoughts was over I reflected with more calmness on my present condition: I considered that trials and disappointments are some-times for our good, and I thought God might perhaps have permitted this in or-der to teach wisdom and resignation; for he had hitherto shadowed me with the wings of his mercy, and by his invisible but powerful hand brought me the way I knew not. These reflections gave me a little comfort, and I rose at last from the deck with dejection and sorrow in my countenance, yet mixed with some faint hope that the Lord would appear for my deliverance.

Soon afterwards, as my new master was going ashore, he called me to him, and told me to behave myself well, and do the business of the ship the same as any of the rest of the boys, and that I should fare the better for it; but I made him no answer. I was then asked if I could swim, and I said, No. How-ever I was made to go under the deck, and was well watched. The next tide the ship got under way, and soon after arrived at the Mother Bank, Portsmouth; where she waited a few days for some of the West India convoy. While I was here I tried every means I could devise amongst the people of the ship to get me a boat from the shore, as there was none suffered to come alongside of the ship; and their own, whenever it was used, was hoisted in again immediately. A sailor on board took a guinea from me on pretence of getting me a boat; and promised me, time after time, that it was hourly to come off. When he had the watch upon deck I watched also; and looked long enough, but all in vain; I could never see either the boat or my guinea again. And what I thought was still the worst of all, the fellow gave information, as I afterwards found, all the while to the mates, of my intention to go off, if I could in any way do it; but, rogue like, he never told them he had got a guinea from me to procure my es-cape. However, after we had sailed, and his trick was made known to the ship's crew, I had some satisfaction in seeing him detested and despised by them all for his behaviour to me. I was still in hopes that my old shipmates would not forget their promise to come for me to Portsmouth: and, indeed, at last, but not till the day before we sailed, some of them did come there, and sent me off some oranges, and other tokens of their regard. They also sent me word they would come off to me themselves the next day or the day after; and a lady also, who lived in Gosport, wrote to me that she would come and take me out of the ship at the same time. This lady had been once very intimate with my former master: I used to sell and take care of a great deal of property for her, in dif-ferent ships; and in return she always shewed great friendship for me, and used to tell my master that she would take me away to live with her: but, unfortu-nately for me, a disagreement soon afterwards took place between them; and she was succeeded in my master's good graces by another lady, who appeared sole mistress of the Ætna, and mostly lodged on board. I was not so great a favourite with this lady as with the former; she had conceived a pique against me on some occasion when she was on board, and she did not fail to instigate my master to treat me in the manner he did*.

However, the next morning, the 30th of December, the wind being brisk and easterly, the Œolus frigate, which was to escort the convoy, made a signal for sailing. All the ships the got up their anchors; and, before any of my friends had an opportunity to come off to my relief, to my inexpressible anguish our ship had got under way. What tumultuous emotions agitated my soul when the convoy got under sail, and I a prisoner on board, now without hope! I kept my swimming eyes upon the land in a state of unutterable grief; not knowing what to do, and despairing how to help myself. While my mind was in this situation the fleet sailed on, and in one day's time I lost sight of the wished-for land. In the first expressions of my grief I reproached my fate, and wished I had never been born. I was ready to curse the tide that bore us, the gale that wafted my prison, and even the ship that conducted us; and I called on death to relieve me from the horrors I felt and dreaded, that I might be in that place

> "Where slaves are free, and men oppress no more,
> "Fool that I was, inur'd so long to pain,
> "To trust to hope, or dream of joy again.
>
> \* \* \* \* \* \* \* \* \* \* \* \*
>
> "Now dragg'd once more beyond the western main,
> "To groan beneath some dastard planter's chain;
> "Where my poor countrymen in bondage wait
> "The long enfranchisement of ling'ring fate:
> "Hard ling'ring fate! while, ere the dawn of day,
> "Rous'd by the lash they go their cheerless way;
> "And as their souls with shame and anguish burn,
> "Salute with groans unwelcome morn's return,
> "And, chiding ev'ry hour the slow-pac'd sun,
> "Pursue their toils till all his race is run.
> "No eye to mark their suff'rings with a tear;
> "No friend to comfort, and no hope to cheer:
> "Then, like the dull unpity'd brutes, repair
> "To stalls as wretched, and as coarse a fare;
> "Thank heaven one day of mis'ry was o'er,
> "Then sink to sleep, and wish to wake no more.†[149]

---

*Thus was I sacrificed to the envy and resentment of this woman for knowing that the lady whom she had succeeded in my master's good graces designed to take me into her service; which, had I once got on shore, she would not have been able to prevent. She felt her pride alarmed at the superiority of her rival in being attended by a black servant: it was not less to prevent this than to be revenged on me, that she caused the captain to treat me thus cruelly.

†"The Dying Negro," a poem originally published in 1773. Perhaps it may not be deemed impertinent here to add, that this elegant and pathetic little poem was occasioned, as appears by the advertisement prefixed to it, by the following incident. "A black, who, a few days before had ran away from his master, and got himself christened, with intent to marry a white woman his fellow-servant, being taken and sent on board a ship in the Thames, took an opportunity of shooting himself through the head."

The turbulence of my emotions however naturally gave way to calmer thoughts, and I soon perceived what fate had decreed no mortal on earth could prevent. The convoy sailed on without any accident, with a pleasant gale and smooth sea, for six weeks, till February, when one morning the Œolus ran down a brig, one of the convoy, and she instantly went down and was ingulfed in the dark recessess of the ocean. The convoy was immediately thrown into great confusion till it was day-light; and the Œolus was illumined with lights to prevent any farther mischief. On the 13th of February 1763, from the masthead, we descried our destined island Montserrat; and soon after I beheld those

"Regions of sorrow, doleful shades, where peace
"And rest can rarely dwell. Hope never comes
"That comes to all, but torture without end
"Still urges."[150]

At the sight of this land of bondage, a fresh horror ran through all my frame, and chilled me to the heart. My former slavery now rose in dreadful review to my mind, and displayed nothing but misery, stripes, and chains; and, in the first paroxysm of my grief, I called upon God's thunder, and his avenging power, to direct the stroke of death to me, rather than permit me to become a slave, and be sold from lord to lord.

In this state of my mind our ship came to an anchor, and soon after discharged her cargo. I now knew what it was to work hard; I was made to help to unload and load the ship. And, to comfort me in my distress in that time, two of the sailors robbed me of all my money, and ran away from the ship. I had been so long used to an European climate that at first I felt the scorching West India sun very painful, while the dashing surf would toss the boat and the people in it frequently above high water mark. Sometimes our limbs were broken with this, or even attended with instant death, and I was day by day mangled and torn.

About the middle of May, when the ship was got ready to sail for England, I all the time believing that Fate's blackest clouds were gathering over my head, and expecting their bursting would mix me with the dead, Captain Doran sent for me ashore one morning, and I was told by the messenger that my fate was then determined. With fluttering steps and trembling heart I came to the captain, and found with him one Mr. Robert King, a quaker, and the first merchant in the place. The captain then told me my former master had sent me there to be sold; but that he had desired him to get me the best master he could, as he told him I was a very deserving boy, which Captain Doran said he found to be true; and if he were to stay in the West Indies he would be glad to keep me himself; but he could not venture to take me to London, for he was very sure that when I came there I would leave him. I at that instant burst out a crying, and begged much of him to take me to England with him, but all to no purpose. He told me he had got me the very best master in the whole island, with whom I should be as happy as if I were in England, and for that reason he chose to let him have me, though he could sell me to his own brother-in-law for a great deal more money than what he got from this gentleman. Mr. King, my new master, then made a reply, and said the reason he had bought me was on account of my good character; and, as he had not the least doubt of my good behaviour, I should be very well off with him. He also told me he did not live in the West Indies, but at Philadelphia, where he was going soon; and, as I understood something of the rules of arithmetic, when we got there he would put me to school, and fit me for a clerk. This conversation relieved my mind a little, and I left those gentlemen considerably more at ease in myself than when I came to them; and I was very grateful to Captain Doran, and even to my old master, for the character they had given me; a character which I afterwards found of infinite service to me. I went on board again, and took leave of all my shipmates; and the next day the ship sailed. When she weighed anchor I went to the waterside and looked at her with a very wishful and aching heart, and followed her with my eyes and tears until she was totally out of sight. I was so bowed down with grief that I could not hold up my head for many months; and if my new master had not been kind to me I believe I should have died under it at last. And indeed I soon found that he fully deserved the good character which Captain Doran had given me of him; for he possessed a most amiable disposition and temper, and was very charitable and humane. If any of his slaves behaved amiss he did not beat or use them ill, but parted with them. This made them afraid of disobliging him; and as he treated his slaves better than any other man on the island, so he was better and more faithfully served by them in return. By his kind treatment I did at last endeavour to compose myself; and with fortitude, though moneyless, determined to face whatever fate had decreed for me. Mr. King soon asked me what I could do; and at the same time said he did not mean to treat me as a common slave. I told him I knew something of seamanship, and could shave and dress hair pretty well; and I could refine wines, which I had learned on shipboard, where I often done it; and that I could write, and understood arithmetic tolerably well as far as the Rule of Three. He then asked me if I knew any thing of gauging; and, on my answering that I did not, he said one of his clerks should teach me to gauge.

Mr. King dealt in all manner of merchandize, and kept from one to six clerks. He loaded many vessels in a year; particularly to Philadelphia, where he was born, and was connected with a great mercantile house in that city. He had besides many vessels and droggers,[151] of different sizes, which used to go about the island; and others to collect rum, sugar, and other goods. I understood pulling and managing those boats very well; and this hard work, which was the first that he set me to, in the sugar seasons used to be my constant employment. I have rowed the boat, and slaved at the oars, from one hour to sixteen in the twenty-four; during which I had fifteen pence sterling per day to live on, though sometimes only ten pence. However this was considerably more than was allowed to other slaves that used to work with me, and belonged to other gentlemen on the island: those poor souls had never more than nine pence per day, and seldom more than six pence, from their masters or owners, though they earned them three or four pisterines*: for it is a common practice in the West Indies for men to purchase slaves though they have not plantations themselves, in order to let them out to planters and merchants at so much a piece by the day, and they give what allowance they chuse out of this produce of their daily work to their slaves for subsistence; this allowance is often very scanty. My master often gave the owners of these slaves two and a half of these pieces per day, and found the poor fellows in victuals himself, because he thought their owners did not feed them well enough according to the work they did. The slaves used to like this very well; and, as they knew my master to be a man of feeling, they were always glad to work for him in preference to any other gentleman: some of whom, after they had been paid for these poor people's labours, would not give them their allowance out of it. Many times have I even seen these unfortunate wretches beaten for asking for their pay; and often severely flogged by their owners if they did not bring them their daily or weekly money exactly to the time; though the poor creatures were obliged to wait on the gentlemen they had worked for sometimes for more than half the day before they could get their pay; and this generally on Sundays, when they wanted the time for themselves. In particular, I knew a countryman of mine who once did not bring the weekly money directly that it was earned; and though he brought it the same day to his master, yet he was staked to the ground for this pretended negligence, and was just going to receive a hundred lashes, but for a gentlemen who begged him off fifty. This poor man was very industrious; and, by his frugality, had saved so much money by working on shipboard, that he had got a white man to buy him a boat, unknown to this master. Some time after he had this little estate the governor wanted a boat to bring his sugar from different parts of the island; and, knowing this to be a negro-man's boat, he seized upon it for himself, and would not pay the owner a farthing. The man on this went to his master, and complained to him of this act of the governor; but the only satisfaction he received was to be damned very heartily by his master, who asked him how dared any of his negroes to have a boat. If the justly-merited ruin of the governor's fortune could be any gratification to the poor man he had thus robbed, he was not without consolation. Extortion and rapine are poor providers; and some time after this the governor died in the King's Bench[152] in England, as I was told, in great poverty. The last war[153] favoured this poor negro-man, and he found some means to escape from his Christian master: he came to England; where I saw him afterwards several times. Such treatment as this often drives these miserable wretches to despair, and they run away from their masters at the hazard of their lives. Many of them, in this place, unable to get their pay when they have earned it, and fearing to be flogged, as usual, if they return home without it, run away where they can for shelter, and a reward is often offered to bring them in dead or alive. My master used sometimes, in these cases, to agree with their owners, and to settle with them himself; and thereby he saved many of them a flogging.

---

*These pisterines are of the value of a shilling.

Once, for a few days, I was let out to fit a vessel, and I had no victuals allowed me by either party; at last I told my master of this treatment, and he took me away from it. In many of the estates, on the different islands where I used to be sent for rum or sugar, they would not deliver it to me, or any other negro; he was therefore obliged to send a white man along with me to those places; and then he used to pay him from six to ten pisterines a day. From being thus employed, during the time I served Mr. King, in going about the different estates on the island, I had all the opportunity I could wish for to see the dreadful usage of the poor men; usage that reconciled me to my situation, and made me bless God for the hands into which I had fallen.

I had the good fortune to please my master in every department in which he employed me; and there was scarcely any part of his business, or household affairs, in which I was not occasionally engaged. I often supplied the place of a clerk, in receiving and delivering cargoes to the ships, in tending stores, and delivering goods: and, besides this, I used to shave and dress my master when convenient, and take care of his horse; and when it was necessary, which was very often, I worked likewise on board of different vessels of his. By these means I became very useful to my master; and saved him, as he used to acknowledge, above a hundred pounds a year. Nor did he scruple to say I was of more advantage to him than any of his clerks; though their usual wages in the West Indies are from sixty to a hundred pounds current a year.

I have sometimes heard it asserted that a negro cannot earn his master the first cost; but nothing can be further from the truth. I suppose nine tenths of the mechanics throughout the West Indies are negro slaves; and I well know the coopers among them earn two dollars a day; the carpenters the same, and oftentimes more; as also the masons, smiths, and fishermen, &c. and I have known many slaves whose masters would not take a thousand pounds current for them. But surely this assertion refutes itself; for, if it be true, why do the planters and merchants pay such a price for slaves? And, above all, why do those who make this assertion exclaim the most loudly against the abolition of the slave trade? So much are men blinded, and to such inconsistent arguments are they driven by mistaken interest! I grant, indeed, that slaves are sometimes, by half-feeding, half-clothing, over-working and stripes, reduced so low, that they are turned out as unfit for service, and left to perish in the woods, or expire on a dunghill.

My master was several times offered by different gentlemen one hundred guineas for me; but he always told them he would not sell me, to my great joy: and I used to double my diligence and care for fear of getting into the hands of those men who did not allow a valuable slave the common support of life. Many of them even used to find fault with my master for feeding his slaves so well as he did; although I often went hungry, and an Englishman might think my fare very indifferent; but he used to tell them he always would do it, because the slaves thereby looked better and did more work.

While I was thus employed by my master I was often a witness to cruelties of every kind, which were exercised on my unhappy fellow slaves. I used frequently to have different cargoes of new negroes in my care for sale; and it was almost a constant practice with our clerks, and other whites, to commit violent depredations on the chastity of the female slaves; and these I was, though with reluctance, obliged to submit to at all times, being unable to help them. When we have had some of these slaves on board my master's vessels to carry them to other islands, or to America, I have known our mates to commit these acts most shamefully, to the disgrace, not of Christians only, but of men. I have even known them gratify their brutal passion with females not ten years old; and these abominations some of them practised to such scandalous excess, that one of our captains discharged the mate and others on that account. And yet in Montserrat I have seen a negro man staked to the ground, and cut most shockingly, and then his ears cut off bit by bit, because he had been connected with a white woman who was a common prostitute: as if it were no crime in the whites to rob an innocent African girl of her virtue; but most heinous in a black man only to gratify a passion of nature, where the temptation was offered by one of a different colour, though the most abandoned woman of her species. Another negro man was half hanged, and then burnt, for attempting to poison a cruel overseer. Thus by repeated cruelties are the wretched first urged to despair, and then murdered, because they still retain so much of human nature about them as to wish to put an end to their misery, and retaliate on their tyrants! These overseers are indeed for the most part persons of the worst character of any denomination of men in the West Indies. Unfortunately, many humane gentlemen, by not residing on their estates, are obliged to leave the management of them in the hands of these human butchers, who cut and mangle the slaves in a shocking manner on the most trifling occasions, and altogether treat them in every respect like brutes. They pay no regard to the situation of pregnant women, nor the least attention to the lodging of the field negroes. Their huts, which ought to be well covered, and the place dry where they take their little repose, are often open sheds, built in damp places; so that, when the poor creatures return tired from the toils of the field, they contract many disorders, from being exposed to the damp air in this uncomfortable state, while they are heated, and their pores are open. This neglect certainly conspires with many others to cause a decrease in the births as well as in the lives of the grown negroes. I can quote many instances of gentlemen who reside on their estates in the West Indies, and then the scene is quite changed; the negroes are treated with lenity and proper care, by which their lives are prolonged, and their masters are profited. To the honour of humanity, I knew several gentlemen who managed their estates in this manner; and they found that benevolence was their true interest. And, among many I could mention in several of the islands, I knew one in Montserrat* whose slaves looked remarkably well, and never needed any fresh supplies of negroes; and there are many other estates, especially in Barbadoes, which, from such judicious treatment, need no fresh stock of negroes at any time. I have the honour of knowing a most worthy and humane gentleman, who is a native of Barbadoes, and has estates

---

*Mr. Dubury, and many others, Montserrat.

there*. This gentleman has written a treatise on the usage of his own slaves.[154] He allows them two hours for refreshment at mid-day; and many other indulgencies and comforts, particularly in their lying; and, besides this, he raises more provisions on his estate than they can destroy; so that by these attentions he saves the lives of his negroes, and keeps them healthy, and as happy as the condition of slavery can admit. I myself, as shall appear in the sequel, managed an estate, where, by those attentions, the negroes were uncommonly cheerful and healthy, and did more work by half than by the common mode of treatment they usually do. For want, therefore, of such care and attention to the poor negroes, and otherwise oppressed as they are, it is no wonder that the decrease should require 20,000 new negroes annually to fill up the vacant places of the dead.

Even in Barbadoes, notwithstanding those humane exceptions which I have mentioned, and others I am acquainted with, which justly make it quoted as a place where slaves meet with the best treatment, and need fewest recruits of any in the West Indies, yet this island requires 1000 negroes annually to keep up the original stock, which is only 80,000. So that the whole term of a negro's life may be said to be there but sixteen years!† And yet the climate here is in every respect the same as that from which they are taken, except in being more wholesome. Do the British colonies decrease in this manner? And yet what a prodigious difference is there between an English and West India climate?

While I was in Montserrat I knew a negro man, named Emanuel Sankey, who endeavoured to escape from his miserable bondage, by concealing himself on board of a London ship: but fate did not favour the poor oppressed man; for, being discovered when the vessel was under sail, he was delivered up again to his master. This *Christian master* immediately pinned the wretch down to the ground at each wrist and ancle, and then took some sticks of sealing wax, and lighted them, and dropped it all over his back. There was another master who was noted for cruelty; and I believe he had not a slave but what had been cut, and had pieces fairly taken out of the flesh: and, after they had been punished thus, he used to make them get into a long wooden box or case he had for that purpose, in which he shut them up during pleasure. It was just about the height and breadth of a man; and the poor wretches had no room, when in the case, to move.

It was very common in several of the islands, particularly in St. Kitt's, for the slaves to be branded with the initial letters of their master's name; and a load of heavy iron hooks hung about their necks. Indeed on the most trifling occasions they were loaded with chains; and often instruments of torture were added. The iron muzzle, thumb-screws, &c. are so well known, as not to need a description, and were sometimes applied for the slightest faults. I have seen a negro beaten till some of his bones were broken, for even letting a pot boil over. Is

---

*Sir Philip Gibbes, Baronet, Barbadoes.
†Benezet's "Account of Guinea," p. 16.

it surprising that usage like this should drive the poor creatures to despair, and make them seek a refuge in death from those evils which render their lives intolerable—while,

> "With shudd'ring horror pale, and eyes aghast,
> "They view their lamentable lot, and find
> "No rest!"[155]

This they frequently do. A negro-man on board a vessel of my master, while I belonged to her, having been put in irons for some trifling misdemeanor, and kept in that state for some days, being weary of life, took an opportunity of jumping overboard into the sea; however, he was picked up without being drowned. Another, whose life was also a burden to him, resolved to starve himself to death, and refused to eat any victuals; this procured him a severe flogging: and he also, on the first occasion which offered, jumped overboard at Charles Town,[156] but was saved.

Nor is there any greater regard shewn to the little property than there is to the persons and lives of the negroes. I have already related an instance or two of particular oppression out of many which I have witnessed; but the following is frequent in all the islands. The wretched field-slaves, after toiling all the day for an unfeeling owner, who gives them but little victuals, steal sometimes a few moments from rest or refreshment to gather some small portion of grass,[157] according as their time will admit. This they commonly tie up in a parcel; (either a bit, worth six pence; or half a bit's-worth) and bring it to town, or to the market, to sell. Nothing is more common than for the white people on this occasion to take the grass from them without paying for it; and not only so, but too often also, to my knowledge, our clerks, and many others, at the same time have committed acts of violence on the poor, wretched, and helpless females; whom I have seen for hours stand crying to no purpose, and get no redress or pay of any kind. Is not this one common and crying sin enough to bring down God's judgment on the islands? He tells us the oppressor and the oppressed are both in his hands; and if these are not the poor, the broken-hearted, the blind, the captive, the bruised, which our Savior speaks of, who are they? One of these depredators once, in St. Eustatia,[158] came on board of our vessel, and bought some fowls and pigs of me; and a whole day after his departure with the things he returned again and wanted his money back: I refused to give it; and, not seeing my captain on board, he began the common pranks with me; and swore he would even break open my chest and take my money. I therefore expected, as my captain was absent, that he would be as good as his word: and he was just proceeding to strike me, when fortunately a British seaman on board, whose heart had not been debauched by a West India climate, interposed and prevented him. But had the cruel man struck me I certainly should have defended myself at the hazard of my life; for what is life to a man thus oppressed? He went away, however, swearing; and threatened that whenever he caught me on shore he would shoot me, and pay for me afterwards.

The small account in which the life of a negro is held in the West Indies is so universally known, that it might seem impertinent to quote the following extract, if some people had not been hardy enough of late to assert that negroes are on the same footing in that respect as Europeans. By the 329th Act, page 125, of the Assembly of Barbadoes, it is enacted 'That if any negro, or other slave, under punishment by his master, or his order, for running away, or any other crime or misdemeanor towards his said master, unfortunately shall suffer in life or member, no person whatsoever shall be liable to a fine; but if any man shall out of *wantonness, or only of bloody-mindedness, or cruel intention, wilfully kill a negro, or other slave, of his own, he shall pay into the public treasury fifteen pounds sterling.*' And it is the same in most, if not all, of the West India islands. Is not this one of the many acts of the islands which call loudly for redress? And do not the assembly which enacted it deserve the appellation of savages and brutes rather than of Christians and men? It is an act at once unmerciful, unjust, and unwise; which for cruelty would disgrace an assembly of those who are called barbarians; and for its injustice and *insanity* would shock the morality and common sense of a Samaide[159] or a Hottentot.

Shocking as this and many more acts of the bloody West India code at first view appear, how is the iniquity of it heightened when we consider to whom it may be extended! Mr. James Tobin,[160] a zealous labourer in the vineyard of slavery, gives an account of a French planter of his acquaintance, in the island of Martinico, who shewed him many mulattoes working in the fields like beasts of burden; and he told Mr. Tobin these were all the produce of his own loins! And I myself have known similar instances. Pray, reader, are these sons and daughters of the French planter less his children by being begotten on a black woman? And what must be the virtue of those legislators, and the feelings of those fathers, who estimate the lives of their sons, however begotten, at no more than fifteen pounds; though they should be murdered, as the act says, *out of wantonness and bloody-mindedness!* But is not the slave trade entirely a war with the heart of man? And surely that which is begun by breaking down the barriers of virtue involves in its continuance destruction to every principle, and buries all sentiments in ruin!

I have often seen slaves, particularly those who were meagre, in different islands, put into scales and weighed; and then sold from three pence to six pence or nine pence a pound. My master, however, whose humanity was shocked at this mode, used to sell such by the lump. And at or after a sale it was not uncommon to see negroes taken from their wives, wives taken from their husbands, and children from their parents, and sent off to other islands, and wherever else their merciless lords chose; and probably never more during life to see each other! Oftentimes my heart has bled at these partings; when the friends of the departed have been at the water side, and, with sighs and tears, have kept their eyes fixed on the vessel till it went out of sight.

A poor Creole negro I knew well, who, after having been often thus transported from island to island, at last resided in Montserrat. This man used to tell me many melancholy tales of himself. Generally, after he had done working for his master, he used to employ his few leisure moments to go a fishing. When he had caught any fish, his master would frequently take them from him without paying him; and at other times some other white people would serve him in the same manner. One day he said to me, very movingly, 'Sometimes when a white man take away my fish I go to my maser, and he get me my right; and when my maser by strength take away my fishes, what me must do? I can't go to any body to be righted; then' said the poor man, looking up above 'I must look up to God Mighty in the top for right.' This artless tale moved me much, and I could not help feeling the just cause Moses had in redressing his brother against the Egyptian.[161] I exhorted the man to look up still to the God on the top, since there was no redress below. Though I little thought then that I myself should more than once experience such imposition, and read the same exhortation hereafter, in my own transactions in the islands; and that even this poor man and I should some time after suffer together in the same manner, as shall be related hereafter.

Nor was such usage as this confined to particular places or individuals; for, in all the different islands in which I have been (and I have visited no less than fifteen) the treatment of the slaves was nearly the same; so nearly indeed, that the history of an island, or even a plantation, with a few such exceptions as I have mentioned, might serve for a history of the whole. Such a tendency has the slave-trade to debauch men's minds, and harden them to every feeling of humanity! For I will not suppose that the dealers in slaves are born worse than other men—No; it is the fatality of this mistaken avarice, that it corrupts the milk of human kindness and turns it into gall. And, had the pursuits of those men been different, they might have been as generous, as tender-hearted and just, as they are unfeeling, rapacious and cruel. Surely this traffic cannot be good, which spreads like a pestilence, and taints what it touches! which violates that first natural right of mankind, equality and independency, and gives one man a dominion over his fellows which God could never intend! For it raises the owner to a state as far above man as it depresses the slave below it; and, with all the presumption of human pride, sets a distinction between them, immeasurable in extent, and endless in duration! Yet how mistaken is the avarice even of the planters? Are slaves more useful by being thus humbled to the condition of brutes, than they would be if suffered to enjoy the privileges of men? The freedom which diffuses health and prosperity throughout Britain answers you—No. When you make men slaves you deprive them of half their virtue, you set them in your own conduct an example of fraud, rapine, and cruelty, and compel them to live with you in a state of war; and yet you complain that they are not honest or faithful! You stupify them with stripes, and think it necessary to keep them in a state of ignorance; and yet you assert that they are incapable of learning; that their minds are such a barren soil or moor, that culture would be lost on them; and that they come from a climate, where nature, though prodigal of her bounties in a degree unknown to yourselves, has left man alone scant and unfinished, and incapable of enjoying the treasures she has poured out for him!—An assertion at once impious and absurd. Why do you use those instruments of torture? Are they fit to be applied by one rational being to another? And are ye not struck with shame and mortification, to see the partakers of your nature reduced so low? But, above all, are there no dangers attending this mode of treatment? Are you not hourly in dread of an insurrection? Now would it be surprising: for when

"————No peace is given
"To us enslav'd, but custody severe;
"And stripes and arbitrary punishment
"Inflicted—What peace can we return?
"But to our power, hostility and hate;
"Untam'd reluctance, and revenge, though slow.
"Yet ever plotting how the conqueror least
"May reap his conquest, and may least rejoice
"In doing what we most in suffering feel."[162]

But by changing your conduct, and treating your slaves as men, every cause of fear would be banished. They would be faithful, honest, intelligent and vigorous; and peace, prosperity, and happiness, would attend you.

## CHAP. VI.

*Some account of Brimstone-Hill in Montserrat—Favourable change in the author's situation—He commences merchant with three pence—His various success in dealing in the different islands, and America, and the impositions he meets with in his transactions with Europeans—A curious imposition on human nature—Danger of the surfs in the West Indies—Remarkable instance of kidnapping a free mulatto—The author is nearly murdered by Doctor Perkins in Savannah.*

In the preceding chapter I have set before the reader a few of those many instances of oppression, extortion, and cruelty, which I have been a witness to in the West Indies; but, were I to enumerate them all, the catalogue would be tedious and disgusting. The punishments of the slaves on every trifling occasion are so frequent, and so well known, together with the different instruments with which they are tortured, that it cannot any longer afford novelty to recite them; and they are too shocking to yield delight either to the writer or the reader. I shall therefore hereafter only mention such as incidentally befel myself in the course of my adventures.

In the variety of departments in which I was employed by my master, I had an opportunity of seeing many curious scenes in different islands; but, above all, I was struck with a celebrated curiosity called Brimstone-Hill, which is a high and steep mountain, some few miles from the town of Plymouth in Montserrat. I had often heard of some wonders that were to be seen on this hill, and I went once with some white and black people to visit it. When we arrived at the top, I saw under different cliffs great flakes of brimstone, occasioned by the steams of various little ponds, which were then boiling naturally in the earth. Some of these ponds were as white as milk, some quite blue, and many others of different colours. I had taken some potatoes with me, and I put them into different ponds, and in a few minutes they were well boiled. I tasted some of them, but they were very sulphurous; and the silver shoe buckles, and all the other things of that metal we had among us, were, in a little time, turned as black as lead.

Some time in the year 1763 kind Providence seemed to appear rather more favourable to me. One of my master's vessels, a Bermudas sloop, about sixty tons, was commanded by one Captain Thomas Farmer, an Englishman, a very alert and active man, who gained my master a great deal of money by his good management in carrying passengers from one island to another; but very often his sailors used to get drunk and run away from the vessel, which hindered him in his business very much. This man had taken a liking to me; and many different times begged of my master to let me go a trip with him as a sailor; but he would tell him he could not spare me, though the vessel sometimes could not go for want of hands, for sailors were generally very scarce in the island. However, at last, from necessity or force, my master was prevailed on, though very reluctantly, to let me go with this captain; but he gave great charge to him to take care that I did not run away, for if I did he would make him pay for me. This being the case, the captain had for some time a sharp eye upon me whenever the vessel anchored; and as soon as she returned I was sent for on shore again. Thus was I slaving as it were for life, sometimes at one thing, and sometimes at another; so that the captain and I were nearly the most useful men in my master's employment. I also became so useful to the captain on shipboard, that many times, when he used to ask for me to go with him, though it should be but for twenty-four hours, to some of the islands near us, my master would answer he could not spare me, at which the captain would swear, and would not go the trip; and tell my master I was better to him on board than any three white men he had; for they used to behave ill in many respects, particularly in getting drunk; and then they frequently got the boat stove, so as to hinder the vessel from coming back as soon as she might have done. This my master knew very well; and at last, by the captain's constant entreaties, after I had been several times with him, one day, to my great joy, my master told me the captain would not let him rest, and asked me whether I would go aboard as a sailor, or stay on shore and mind the stores, for he could not bear any longer to be plagued in this manner. I was very happy at this proposal, for I immediately thought I might in time stand some chance by being on board to get a little money, or possibly make my escape if I should be used ill: I also expected to get better food, and in greater abundance; for I had felt much hunger oftentimes, though my master treated his slaves, as I have observed, uncommonly well. I therefore, without hesitation, answered him, that I would go and be a sailor if he pleased. Accordingly I was ordered on board directly. Nevertheless, between the vessel and the shore, when she was in port, I had little or no rest, as my master always wished to have me along with him. Indeed he was a very pleasant gentleman, and but for my expectations on shipboard I should not have thought of leaving him. But the captain liked me also very much, and I was entirely his right-hand man. I did all I could to deserve his favour, and in return I received better treatment from him than any other I believe ever met with in the West Indies in my situation.

After I had been sailing for some time with this captain, at length I endeavoured to try my luck and commence merchant. I had but a very small capital to begin with; for one single half bit, which is equal to three pence in England, made up my whole stock. However I trusted to the Lord to be with me; and at one of our trips to St. Eustatia, a Dutch island, I bought a glass tumbler with my half bit, and when I came to Montserrat I sold it for a bit, or sixpence. Luckily we made several successive trips to St. Eustatia (which was a general mart for the West Indies, about twenty leagues from Montserrat); and in our next, finding my tumbler so profitable, with this one bit I bought two tumblers more; and when I came back I sold them for two bits, equal to a shilling sterling. When we went again I bought with these two bits four more of these glasses, which I sold for four bits on our return to Montserrat: and in our next voyage to St. Eustatia I bought two glasses with one bit, and with the other three I bought a jug of Geneva,[163] nearly about three pints in measure. When we came to Montserrat I sold the gin for eight bits, and the tumblers for two, so that my capital now amounted in all to a dollar, well husbanded and acquired in the space of a month or six weeks, when I blessed the Lord that I was so rich. As we sailed to different islands, I laid this money out in various things occasionally, and it used to turn out to very good account, especially when we went to Guadaloupe, Grenada, and the rest of the French islands. Thus was I going all about the islands upwards of four years, and ever trading as I went, during which I experienced many instances of ill usage, and have seen many injuries done to other negroes in our dealings with Europeans: and, amidst our recreations, when we have been dancing and merry-making, they, without cause, have molested and insulted us. Indeed I was more than once obliged to look up to God on high, as I had advised the poor fisherman some time before. And I had not been long trading for myself in the manner I have related above, when I experienced the like trial in company with him as follows: This man being used to the water, was upon an emergency put on board of us by his master to work as another hand, on a voyage to Santa Cruz;[164] and at our sailing he had brought his little all for a venture, which consisted of six bits' worth of limes and oranges in a bag; I had also my whole stock, which was about twelve bits' worth of the same kind of goods, separate in two bags; for we had heard these fruits sold well in that island. When we came there, in some little convenient time he and I went ashore with our fruits to sell them; but we had scarcely landed when we were met by two white men, who presently took our three bags from us. We could not at first guess what they meant to do; and for some time we thought they were jesting with us; but they too soon let us know otherwise, for they took our ventures immediately to a house hard by, and adjoining the fort, while we followed all the way begging of them to give us our fruits, but in vain. They not only refused to return them, but swore at us, and threatened if we did not immediately depart they would flog us well. We told them these three bags were all we were worth in the world, and that we brought them with us to sell when we came from Montserrat, and shewed them the vessel. But this was rather against us, as they now saw we were strangers as well as slaves. They still therefore swore, and desired us to be gone, and even took sticks to beat us; while we, seeing they meant what they said, went off in the greatest confusion and despair. Thus, in the very minute of gaining more by three times then I ever did by any venture in my life before, was I deprived of every farthing I was worth. An insupportable misfortune! but how to help ourselves we knew not. In our consternation we went to the commanding officer of the fort and told him how we had been served by some of his people; but we obtained not the least redress: he answered our complaints only by a volley of imprecations against us, and immediately took a horse-whip, in order to chastise us, so that we were obliged to turn out much faster than we came in. I now, in the agony of distress and indignation, wished that the ire of God in his forked lightning might transfix these cruel oppressors among the dead. Still however we preserved; went back again to the house, and begged and besought them again and again for our fruits, till at last some other people that were in the house asked if we would be contented if they kept one bag and gave us the other two. We, seeing no remedy whatever, consented to this; and they, observing one bag to have both kinds of fruit in it, which belonged to my companion, kept that; and the other two, which were mine, they gave us back. As soon as I got them, I ran as fast as I could, and got the first negro man I could to help me off; my companion, however, stayed a little longer to plead; he told them the bag they had was his, and likewise all that he was worth in the world; but this was of no avail, and he was obliged to return without it. The poor old man, wringing his hands, cried bitterly for his loss; and, indeed, he then did look up to God on high, which so moved me with pity for him, that I gave him nearly one third of my fruits. We then proceeded to the markets to sell them; and Providence was more favourable to us than we could have expected, for we sold our fruits uncommonly well; I got for mine about thirty-seven bits. Such a surprising reverse of fortune in so short a space of time seemed like a dream to me, and proved no small encouragement for me to trust the Lord in any situation. My captain afterwards frequently used to take my part, and get me my right, when I have been plundered or used ill by these tender Christian depredators; among whom I have shuddered to observe the unceasing blasphemous execrations which are wantonly thrown out by persons of all ages and conditions, not only without occasion, but even as if they were indulgences and pleasure.

At one of our trips to St. Kitt's I had eleven bits of my own; and my friendly captain lent me five bits more, with which I bought a Bible. I was very glad to get this book, which I scarcely could meet with any where. I think there was none sold in Montserrat; and, much to my grief, from being forced out of the Ætna in the manner I have related, my Bible, and the Guide to the Indians, the two books I loved above all others, were left behind.

While I was in this place, St. Kitt's, a very curious imposition on human nature took place:—A white man wanted to marry in the church a free black woman that had land and slaves in Montserrat: but the clergyman told him it was against the law of the place to marry a white and a black in the church. The man then asked to be married on the water, to which the parson consented, and the two lovers went in one boat, and the parson and clerk in another, and thus the ceremony was performed. After this the loving pair came on board our vessel, and my captain treated them extremely well, and brought them safe to Montserrat.

The reader cannot but judge of the irksomeness of this situation to a mind like mine, in being daily exposed to new hardships and impositions, after having seen many better days, and having been as it were in a state of freedom and

plenty; added to which, every part of the world I had hitherto been in seemed to
me a paradise in comparison of the West Indies. My mind was therefore hourly
replete with inventions and thoughts of being freed, and, if possible, by honest
and honourable means; for I always remembered the old adage; and I trust it has
ever been my ruling principle, that honesty is the best policy; and likewise that
other golden precept—to do unto all men as I would they should do unto me.
However, as I was from early years a predestinarian, I thought whatever fate had
determined must ever come to pass; and therefore, if ever it were my lot to be
freed nothing could prevent me, although I should at present see no means or
hope to obtain my freedom; on the other hand, if it were my fate not to be freed
I never should be so, and all my endeavours for that purpose would be fruitless.
In the midst of these thoughts I therefore looked up with prayers anxiously to
God for my liberty; and at the same time I used every honest means, and endeavoured all that was possible on my part to obtain it. In process of time I became master of a few pounds, and in a fair way of making more, which my
friendly captain knew very well; this occasioned him sometimes to take liberties
with me: but whenever he treated me waspishly I used plainly to tell him my
mind, and that I would die before I would be imposed on as other negroes were,
and that to me life had lost its relish when liberty was gone. This I said although
I foresaw my then well-being or future hopes of freedom (humanly speaking) depended on this man. However, as he could not bear the thoughts of my not sailing with him, he always became mild on my threats. I therefore continued with
him; and, from my great attention to his orders and his business, I gained him
credit, and through his kindness to me I at last procured my liberty. While I thus
went on, filled with the thoughts of freedom, and resisting oppression as well as
I was able, my life hung daily in suspense, particularly in the surfs I have formerly mentioned, as I could not swim. These are extremely violent throughout
the West Indies, and I was ever exposed to their howling rage and devouring fury
in all the islands. I have seen them strike and toss a boat right up an end, and
maim several on board. Once in the Grenada islands, when I and about eight
others were pulling a large boat with two puncheons of water in it, a surf struck
us, and drove the boat and all in it about half a stone's throw, among some trees,
and above the high water mark. We were obliged to get all the assistance we
could from the nearest estate to mend the boat, and launch it into the water
again. At Montserrat one night, in pressing hard to get off the shore on board,
the punt was overset with us four times; the first time I was very near being
drowned; however the jacket I had on kept me up above water a little space of
time, while I called on a man near me who was a good swimmer, and told him I
could not swim; he then made haste to me, and just as I was sinking, he caught
hold of me, and brought me to sounding, and then he went and brought the punt
also. As soon as we had turned the water out of her, lest we should be used ill
for being absent, we attempted again three times more, and as often the horrid
surfs served us as at first; but at last, the fifth time we attempted, we gained our
point, at the imminent hazard of our lives. One day also, at Old Road in
Montserrat, our captain, and three men besides myself, were going in a large canoe in quest of rum and sugar, when a single surf tossed the canoe an amazing

distance from the water, and some of us even a stone's throw from each other: most of us were very much bruised; so that I and many more often said, and really thought, that there was not such another place under the heavens as this. I longed therefore much to leave it, and daily wished to see my master's promise performed of going to Philadelphia. While we lay in this place a very cruel thing happened on board of our sloop which filled me with horror; though I found afterwards such practices were frequent. There was a very clever and decent free young mulatto-man who sailed a long time with us: he had a free woman for his wife, by whom he had a child; and she was then living on shore, and all very happy. Our captain and mate, and other people on board, and several elsewhere, even the natives of Bermudas, all knew this young man from a child that he was always free, and no one had ever claimed him as their property: however, as might too often overcomes right in these parts, it happened that a Bermudas captain, whose vessel lay there for a few days in the road, came on board of us, and seeing the mulattoman, whose name was Joseph Clipson, he told him he was not free, and that he had orders from his master to bring him to Bermudas. The poor man could not believe the captain to be in earnest; but he was very soon undeceived, his men laying violent hands on him: and although he shewed a certificate of his being born free in St. Kitt's, and most people on board knew that he served his time to boat-building, and always passed for a free man, yet he was taken forcibly out of our vessel. He then asked to be carried ashore before the secretary or magistrates, and these infernal invaders of human rights promised him he should; but, instead of that, they carried him on board of the other vessel: and the next day, without giving the poor man any hearing on shore, or suffering him even to see his wife or child, he was carried away, and probably doomed never more in this world to see them again. Nor was this the only instance of this kind of barbarity I was a witness to. I have since often seen in Jamaica and other islands free men, whom I have known in America, thus villainously trepanned and held in bondage. I have heard of two similar practices even in Philadelphia: and were it not for the benevolence of the quakers in that city many of the sable race, who now breathe the air of liberty, would, I believe, be groaning indeed under some planter's chains. These things opened my mind to a new scene of horror to which I had been before a stranger. Hitherto I had thought only slavery dreadful; but the state of a free negro appeared to me now equally so at least, and in some respects even worse, for they live in constant alarm for their liberty; and even this is but nominal, for they are universally insulted and plundered without the possibility of redress; for such is the equity of the West Indian laws, that no free negro's evidence will be admitted in their courts of justice. In this situation is it surprising that slaves, when mildly treated, should prefer even the misery of slavery to such a mockery of freedom? I was now completely disgusted with the West Indies, and thought I never should be entirely free until I had left them.

> "With thoughts like these my anxious boding mind
> "Recall'd those pleasing scenes I left behind;
> "Scenes where fair Liberty in bright array

"Makes darkness bright, and e'en illumines day;
"Where nor complexion, wealth, or station, can
"Protect the wretch who makes a slave of man."[165]

I determined to make every exertion to obtain my freedom, and to return to
Old England. For this purpose I thought a knowledge of navigation might be of
use to me; for, though I did not intend to run away unless I should be ill used, yet,
in such a case, if I understood navigation, I might attempt my escape in our sloop,
which was one of the swiftest sailing vessels in the West Indies, and I could be at
no loss for hands to join me: and if I should make this attempt, I had intended to
have gone for England; but this, as I said, was only to be in the event of my meeting with any ill usage. I therefore employed the mate of our vessel to teach me
navigation, for which I agreed to give him twenty-four dollars, and actually paid
him part of the money down; though when the captain, some time after, came to
know that the mate was to have such a sum for teaching me, he rebuked him, and
said it was a shame for him to take any money from me. However, my progress
in this useful art was much retarded by the constancy of our work. Had I wished
to run away I did not want opportunities, which frequently presented themselves;
and particularly at one time, soon after this. When we were at the island of Gaurdeloupe there was a large fleet of merchantmen bound for Old France; and, seamen then being very scarce, they gave from fifteen to twenty pounds a man for
the run. Our mate, and all the white sailors, left our vessel on this account, and
went on board of the French ships. They would have had me also to go with them,
for they regarded me; and they swore to protect me, if I would go: and, as the fleet
was to sail the next day, I really believe I could have got safe to Europe at that
time. However, as my master was kind, I would not attempt to leave him; and,
remembering the old maxim, that 'honesty is the best policy,' I suffered them to
go without me. Indeed my captain was much afraid of my leaving him and the
vessel at that time, as I had so fair an opportunity: but, I thank God, this fidelity
of mine turned out much to my advantage hereafter, when I did not in the least
think of it; and made me so much in favor with the captain, that he used now and
then to teach me some parts of navigation himself: but some of our passengers,
and others, seeing this, found much fault with him for it, saying it was a very dangerous thing to let a negro know navigation; thus I was hindered again in my pursuits. About the latter end of the year 1764 my master bought a larger sloop,
called the Providence, about seventy or eighty tons, of which my captain had the
command. I went with him into this vessel, and we took a load of new slaves for
Georgia and Charles Town. My master now left me entirely to the captain, though
he still wished for me to be with him; but I, who always much wished to lose sight
of the West Indies, was not a little rejoiced at the thoughts of seeing any other
country. Therefore, relying on the goodness of my captain, I got ready all the little venture I could; and, when the vessel was ready, we sailed, to my great joy.
When we got to our destined places, Georgia and Charles Town, I expected I
should have an opportunity of selling my little property to advantage: but here,
particularly in Charles Town, I met with buyers, white men, who imposed on me
as in other places. Notwithstanding, I was resolved to have fortitude; thinking no

lot or trial is too hard when kind Heaven is the rewarder. We soon got loaded again, and returned to Montserrat; and there, amongst the rest of the islands, I sold my goods well; and in this manner I continued trading during the year 1764; meeting with various scenes of imposition, as usual. After this, my master fitted out his vessel for Philadelphia, in the year 1765; and during the time we were loading her, and getting ready for the voyage, I worked with redoubled alacrity, from the hope of getting money enough by these voyages to buy my freedom in time, if it should please God; and also to see the town of Philadelphia, which I had heard a great deal about for some years past; besides which, I had always longed to prove my master's promise the first day I came to him. In the midst of these elevated ideas, and while I was about getting my little merchandize in readiness, one Sunday my master sent for me to his house. When I came there I found him and the captain together; and, on my going in, I was struck with astonishment at his telling me he heard that I meant to run away from him when I got to Philadelphia: 'And therefore,' said he, 'I must sell you again: you cost me a great deal of money, no less than forty pounds sterling; and it will not do to lose so much. You are a valuable fellow,' continued he; 'and I can get any day for you one hundred guineas, from many gentlemen in this island.' And then he told me of Captain Doran's brother-in-law, a severe master, who ever wanted to buy me to make me his overseer. My captain also said he could get much more than a hundred guineas for me in Carolina. This I knew to be a fact; for the gentleman that wanted to buy me came off several times on board of us, and spoke to me to live with him, and said he would use me well. When I asked what work he would put me to he said, as I was a sailor, he would make me a captain of one of his rice vessels. But I refused: and fearing, at the same time, by a sudden turn I saw in the captain's temper, he might mean to sell me, I told the gentleman I would not live with him on any condition, and that I certainly would run away with his vessel: but he said he did not fear that, as he would catch me again; and then he told me how cruelly he would serve me if I should do so. My captain, however, gave him to understand that I knew something of navigation: so he thought better of it; and, to my great joy, he went away. I now told my master I did not say I would run away in Philadelphia; neither did I mean it, as he did not use me ill, nor yet the captain: for if they did I certainly would have made some attempts before now; but as I thought that if it were God's will I ever should be freed it would be so, and, on the contrary, if it was not his will it would not happen; so I hoped, if ever I were freed, whilst I was used well, it should be by honest means; but, as I could not help myself, he must do as he pleased; I could only hope and trust to the God of Heaven; and at that instant my mind was big with inventions and full of schemes to escape. I then appealed to the captain whether he ever saw any sign of my making the least attempt to run away; and asked him if I did not always come on board according to the time for which he gave me liberty; and, more particularly, when all our men left us at Gaurdeloupe and went on board of the French fleet, and advised me to go with them, whether I might not, and that he could not have got me again. To my no small surprise, and very great joy, the captain confirmed every syllable that I had said: and even more; for he said he had tried different times to see if I would make any attempt of this kind, both at St. Eustatia and in America, and he never found that I made the smallest; but, on the contrary, I always came on board according to his orders; and he did really believe, if I ever meant to run away, that, as I could never had had a better opportunity, I would have done it the night the mate and all the people left our vessel at Gaurdeloupe. The captain then informed my master, who had been thus imposed on by our mate, though I did not know who was my enemy, the reason the mate had for imposing this lie upon him; which was, because I had acquainted the captain of the provisions the mate had given away or taken out of the vessel. This speech of the captain was like life to the dead to me, and instantly my soul glorified God; and still more so on hearing my master immediately say that I was a sensible fellow, and he never did intend to use me as a common slave; and that but for the entreaties of the captain, and his character of me, he would not have let me go from the stores about as I had done; that also, in so doing, he thought by carrying one little thing or other to different places to sell I might make money. That he also intended to encourage me in this by crediting me with half a puncheon of rum and half a hogshead of sugar at a time; so that, from being careful, I might have money enough, in some time, to purchase my freedom; and, when that was the case, I might depend upon it he would let me have it for forty pounds sterling money, which was only the same price he gave for me. This sound gladdened my poor heart beyond measure; though indeed it was no more than the very idea I had formed in my mind of my master long before, and I immediately made him this reply: 'Sir, I always had that very thought of you, indeed I had, and that made me so diligent in serving you.' He then gave me a large piece of silver coin, such as I never had seen or had before, and told me to get ready for the voyage, and he would credit me with a tierce of sugar, and another of rum; he also said that he had two amiable sisters in Philadelphia, from whom I might get some necessary things. Upon this my noble captain desired me to go aboard; and, knowing the African metal,[166] he charged me not to say any thing of this matter to any body; and he promised that the lying mate should not go with him any more. This was a change indeed; in the same hour to feel the most exquisite pain, and in the turn of a moment the fullest joy. It caused in me such sensations as I was only able to express in my looks; my heart was so overpowered with gratitude that I could have kissed both of their feet. When I left the room I immediately went, or rather flew, to the vessel, which being loaded, my master, as good as his word, trusted me with a tierce of rum, and another of sugar, when we sailed, and arrived safe at the elegant town of Philadelphia. I soon sold my goods here pretty well; and in this charming place I found everything plentiful and cheap.

While I was in this place a very extraordinary occurrence befell me. I had been told one evening of a *wise* woman, a Mrs. Davis, who revealed secrets, foretold events, &c. I put little faith in this story at first, as I could not conceive that any mortal could foresee the future disposals of Providence, nor did I believe in any other revelation than that of the Holy Scriptures; however, I was greatly astonished at seeing this woman in a dream that night, though a person I never before beheld in my life; this made such an impression on me, that I could not get the idea the next day out of my mind, and I then became as anxious to see her as I was before indifferent; accordingly in the evening, after we left off working,

I inquired where she lived, and being directed to her, to my inexpressible sur-prise, beheld the very woman in the very same dress she appeared to me to wear in the vision. She immediately told me I had dreamed of her the preceding night; related to me many things that had happened with a correctness that astonished me; and finally told me I should not be long a slave: this was the more agreeable news, as I believed it the more readily from her having so faithfully related the past incidents of my life. She said I should be twice in very great danger of my life within eighteen months, which, if I escaped, I should afterwards go on well; so, giving me her blessing, we parted. After staying here some time till our ves-sel was loaded, and I had bought in my little traffic, we sailed from this agree-able spot for Montserrat, once more to encounter the raging surfs.

We arrived safe at Montserrat, where we discharged our cargo; and soon af-ter that we took slaves on board for St. Eustatia, and from thence to Georgia. I had always exerted myself and did double work, in order to make our voyages as short as possible; and from this overworking myself while we were at Georgia I caught a fever and ague. I was very ill for eleven days and near dying; eternity was now exceedingly impressed on my mind, and I feared very much that awful event. I prayed the Lord therefore to spare me; and I made a promise in my mind to God, that I would be good if ever I should recover. At length, from having an eminent doctor to attend me, I was restored again to health; and soon after we got the ves-sel loaded, and set off for Montserrat. During the passage, as I was perfectly re-stored, and had much business of the vessel to mind, all my endeavours to keep up my integrity, and perform my promise to God, began to fail; and, in spite of all I could do, as we drew nearer and nearer to the islands, my resolutions more and more declined, as if the very air of that country or climate seemed fatal to piety. When we were safe arrived at Montserrat, and I had got ashore, I forgot my for-mer resolutions.—Alas! how prone is the heart to leave that God it wishes to love! and how strongly do the things of this world strike the senses and captivate the soul!—After our vessel was discharged, we soon got her ready, and took in, as usual, some of the poor oppressed natives of Africa, and other negroes; we then set off again for Georgia and Charlestown. We arrived at Georgia, and, having landed part of our cargo, proceeded to Charlestown with the remainder. While we were there I saw the town illuminated; the guns were fired, and bonfires and other demonstrations of joy shewn, on account of the repeal of the stamp act.[167] Here I disposed of some goods on my own account; the white men buying them with smooth promises and fair words, giving me however but very indifferent payment. There was one gentlemen particularly who bought a puncheon of rum of me, which gave me a great deal of trouble; and, although I used the interest of my friendly captain, I could not obtain any thing for it; for, being a negro man, I could not oblige him to pay me. This vexed me much, not knowing how to act; and I lost some time in seeking after this Christian; and though, when the Sabbath came (which the negroes usually make their holiday) I was much inclined to go to pub-lic worship, I was obliged to hire some black men to help to pull a boat across the water to go in quest of this gentleman. When I found him, after much entreaty, both from myself and my worthy captain, he at last paid me in dollars; some of them, however, were copper, and of consequence of no value; but he took advantage of my being a negro man, and obliged me to put up with those or none, although I objected to them. Immediately after, as I was trying to pass them in the market, amongst other white men, I was abused for offering to pass bad coin; and, though I shewed them the man I got them from, I was within one minute of being tied up and flogged without either judge or jury; however, by the help of a good pair of heels, I ran off, and so escaped the bastinadoes I should have received. I got on board as fast as I could, but still continued in fear of them until we sailed, which I thanked God we did not long after; and I have never been amongst them since.

We soon came to Georgia, where we were to complete our lading; and here worse fate than ever attended me: for one Sunday night, as I was with some negroes in their master's yard in the town of Savannah, it happened that their master, one Doctor Perkins, who was a very severe and cruel man, came in drunk; and, not liking to see any strange negroes in his yard, he and a ruffian of a white man he had in his service beset me in an instant, and both of them struck me with the first weapons they could get hold of. I cried out as long as I could for help and mercy; but, though I have a good account of myself, and he knew my captain, who lodged hard by him, it was to no purpose. They beat and mangled me in a shameful manner, leaving me near dead. I lost so much blood from the wounds I received, that I lay quite motionless, and was so benumbed that I could not feel any thing for many hours. Early in the morning they took me away to the jail. As I did not return to the ship all night, my captain, not knowing where I was, and being uneasy that I did not then make my appearance, he made inquiry after me; and, having found where I was, immediately came to me. As soon as the good man saw me so cut and mangled, he could not forbear weeping; he soon got me out of jail to his lodgings, and immediately sent for the best doctors in the place, who at first declared it as their opinion that I could not recover. My captain on this went to all the lawyers in the town for their advice, but they told him they could do nothing for me as I was a negro. He then went to Doctor Perkins, the hero who had vanquished me, and menaced him, swearing he would be revenged of him, and challenged him to fight.—But cowardice is ever the companion of cruelty—and the Doctor refused. However, by the skilfulness of one Doctor Brady of that place, I began at last to amend; but, although I was so sore and bad with the wounds I had all over me that I could not rest in any posture, yet I was in more pain on account of the captain's uneasiness about me than I otherwise should have been. The worthy man nursed and watched me all the hours of the night; and I was, through his attention and that of the doctor, able to get out of bed in about sixteen or eighteen days. All this time I was very much wanted on board, as I used frequently to go up and down the river for rafts, and other parts of our cargo, and stow them when the mate was sick or absent. In about four weeks I was able to go on duty; and in a fortnight after, having got in all our lading, our vessel set sail for Montserrat; and in less than three weeks we arrived there safe towards the end of the year. This ended my adventures in 1764; for I did not leave Montserrat again till the beginning of the following year.

## END OF THE FIRST VOLUME.

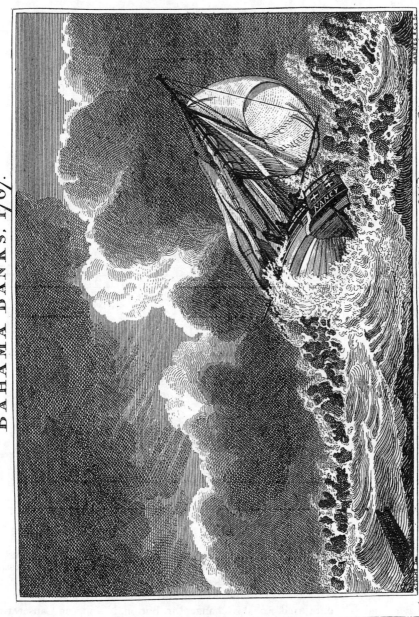

BAHAMA BANKS. 1767.

Thus God speaketh once, yea, twice, yet Man perceiveth it not. In a Dream, or a Vision of the Night, when deep sleep falleth upon Men, in slumbrings upon the Bed; Then he openeth the Ears of Men, & sealeth their instruction. Job. Ch.33.Ver.14 15.16.&29.&30.

THE

# INTERESTING NARRATIVE

OF

# THE LIFE

OF

# OLAUDAH EQUIANO,

OR

# GUSTAVUS VASSA,

THE AFRICAN.

*WRITTEN BY HIMSELF.*

VOL. II.

———

*Behold, God is my salvation; I will trust and not be afraid, for
the Lord Jehovah is my strength and my song; he also is become
my salvation.*
*And in that day shall ye say, Praise the Lord, call upon his name,
declare his doings among the people.*　　　　Isaiah xii. 2, 4.

———

## LONDON:
Printed for and sold by the AUTHOR,
No. 10, Union-Street, Middlesex Hospital.

Sold also by Mr. Johnson, St. Paul's Church-Yard; Mr. Murray, Fleet-Street; Messrs.
Robson and Clark, Bond-Street; Mr. Davis, opposite Gray's-Inn, Holborn; Messrs.
Shepperson and Reynolds, and Mr. Jackson, Oxford-Street; Mr. Lackington,
Chiswell-Street; Mr. Mathews, Strand; Mr. Murray, Prince's-Street, Soho; Mess.
Taylor and Co. South Arch, Royal Exchange; Mr. Button, Newington-Causeway;
Mr. Parsons, Paternoster-Row; and may be had of all the Booksellers in Town and
Country.

[𝔈𝔫𝔱𝔢𝔯𝔢𝔡 𝔞𝔱 𝔖𝔱𝔞𝔱𝔦𝔬𝔫𝔢𝔯'𝔰 𝔥𝔞𝔩𝔩.]

They ran the ship aground: and the fore part stuck fast, and remained unmoveable, but the hinder part was broken with the violence of the waves.

ACTS xxvii. 41.

Howbeit, we must be cast upon a certain island;
Wherefore, sirs, be of good cheer: for I believe God, that it shall be even as it was told me.

ACTS xxvii. 26, 25.

Now a thing was secretly brought to me, and mine ear received a little thereof.
In thoughts from the visions of the night, when deep sleep falleth on men.

JOB iv. 12, 13.

Lo, all these *things* worketh God oftentimes with man,
To bring back his soul from the pit, to be enlightened with the light of the living.

JOB xxxiii, 29, 30.

# CONTENTS OF VOLUME II.

### CHAP. VII.
The author's disgust at the West Indies—Forms schemes to obtain his freedom 109

### CHAP. VIII.
Three remarkable dreams—The author is shipwrecked on the Bahama-bank .. 117

### CHAP. IX
The author arrives at Martinico—Meets with new difficulties, and sails
    for England ............................................... 126

### CHAP. X.
Some account of the manner of the author's conversion to the faith of
    Jesus Christ ............................................ 136

### CHAP. XI.
Picking up eleven miserable men at sea in returning to England ........... 148

### CHAP. XII.
Different transactions of the author's life—Petition to the Queen—Conclusion 162

# THE LIFE, &c.

## CHAPTER VII.

*The author's disgust at the West Indies—Forms schemes to obtain his freedom—Ludicrous disappointment he and his Captain meet with in Georgia—At last, by several successful voyages, he acquires a sum of money sufficient to purchase it—Applies to his master, who accepts it, and grants his manumission, to his great joy—He afterwards enters as a freeman on board one of Mr. King's ships, and sails for Georgia—Impositions on free negroes as usual—His venture of turkies—Sails for Montserrat, and on his passage his friend, the Captain, falls ill and dies.*

EVERY day now brought me nearer my freedom, and I was impatient till we proceeded again to sea, that I might have an opportunity of getting a sum large enough to purchase it. I was not long ungratified; for, in the beginning of the year 1766, my master bought another sloop, named the Nancy, the largest I had ever seen. She was partly laden, and was to proceed to Philadelphia; our Captain had his choice of three, and I was well pleased he chose this, which was the largest; for, from his having a large vessel, I had more room, and could carry a larger quantity of goods with me. Accordingly, when we had delivered our old vessel, the Prudence, and completed the lading of the Nancy, having made near three hundred per cent, by four barrels of pork I brought from Charlestown, I laid in as large a cargo as I could, trusting to God's providence to prosper my undertaking. With these views I sailed for Philadelphia. On our passage, when we drew near the land, I was for the first time surprised at the sight of some whales, having never seen any such large sea monsters before; and as we sailed by the land one morning I saw a puppy whale close by the vessel; it was about the length of a wherry boat, and it followed us all the day till we got within the Capes. We arrived safe and in good time at Philadelphia, and I sold my goods there chiefly to the quakers. They always appeared to be a very honest discreet sort of people, and never attempted to impose on me; I therefore liked them, and ever after chose to deal with them in preference to any others. One Sunday morning while I was here, as I was going to church, I chanced to pass a meeting-house. The doors being open, and the house full of people, it excited my curiosity to go in. When I entered the house, to my great surprise, I saw a very tall woman standing in the midst of them, speaking in an audible voice something which I could not understand. Having never seen anything of this kind before, I stood and stared about me for some time, wondering at this odd scene. As soon as it was over I took an opportunity to make inquiry about the place and people, when I was informed they were called Quakers. I particularly asked what that woman I saw in the midst of them had said, but none of them were pleased to satisfy me; so I quitted them, and soon after, as I was returning, I came to a church crowded with people; the church-yard was full likewise, and a number of people were even mounted on ladders, looking in at the windows. I thought this a strange sight, as I had never seen churches, either in England or the West Indies, crowded in this manner before. I therefore made bold to ask some people the meaning of all this, and they told me the Rev. Mr. George Whitfield[168] was preaching. I had often heard of this gentleman, and had wished to see and hear him; but I had never before had an opportunity. I now therefore resolved to gratify myself with the sight, and I pressed in amidst the multitude. When I got into the church I saw this pious man exhorting the people with the greatest fervour and earnestness, and sweating as much as I ever did while in slavery on Montserrat beach. I was very much struck and impressed with this; I thought it strange I had never seen divines exert themselves in this manner before, and I was no longer at a loss to account for the thin congregations they preached to. When we had discharged our cargo here, and were loaded again, we left this fruitful land once more, and set sail for Montserrat. My traffic had hitherto succeeded to so well with me, that I thought, by selling my goods when we arrived at Montserrat, I should have enough to purchase my freedom. But, as soon as our vessel arrived there, my master came on board, and gave orders for us to go to St. Eustatia, and discharge our cargo there, and from thence proceed for Georgia. I was much disappointed at this; but thinking, as usual, it was of no use to encounter with the decrees of fate, I submitted without repining, and we went to St. Eustatia. After we had discharged our cargo there we took in a live cargo, as we call a cargo of slaves. Here I sold my goods tolerably well; but, not being able to lay out all my money in this small island to as much advantage as in many other places, I laid out only part, and the remainder I brought away with me neat. We sailed from hence for Georgia, and I was glad when we got there, though I had not much reason to like the place from my last adventure in Savannah; but I longed to get back to Montserrat and procure my freedom, which I expected to be able to purchase when I returned. As soon as we arrived here I waited on my careful doctor, Mr. Brady, to whom I made the most grateful acknowledgments in my power for his former kindness and attention during my illness. While we were here an odd circumstance happened to the Captain and me, which disappointed us both a good deal. A silversmith, whom we had brought to this place some voyages before, agreed with the Captain to return with us to the West Indies, and promised at the same time to give the Captain a great deal of money, having pretended to take a liking to him, and being, as we thought, very rich. But while we stayed to load our vessel this man was taken ill in a house where he worked, and in a week's time became very bad. The worse he grew the more he used to speak of giving the Captain what he had promised him, so that he expected something considerable from the death of this man, who had no wife or child, and he attended him day and night. I used also to go with the Captain, at his own desire, to attend him; especially when we saw there was no appearance of his recovery: and, in order to recompense me for my trouble, the Captain promised me ten pounds, when he should get the man's property. I thought this would be of great service to me, although I had nearly money enough to purchase my freedom, if I should get safe this voyage to Montserrat. In this expectation I laid out above eight pounds of my money for a suit of superfine clothes to dance with at my freedom, which I hoped was then at hand. We still continued to attend this man, and were with him even on the last day he lived, till very late at night, when we went on board. After we were got to bed, about one or two o'clock in the morning, the Captain was sent for, and informed the man was dead. On this he came to my bed, and, waking me, informed me of it, and desired me to get up and procure a light, and immediately go to him. I told him I was very sleepy, and wished he would take somebody else with him; or else, as the man was dead, and could want no farther attendance, to let all things remain as they were till the next morning. 'No, no,' said he, 'we will have the money to-night, I cannot wait till to-morrow; so let us go.' Accordingly I got up and struck a light, and away we both went and saw the man as dead as we could wish. The Captain said he would give him a grand burial, in gratitude for the promised treasure, and desired that all the things belonging to the deceased might be brought forth. Among others, there was a nest of trunks of which he had kept the keys whilst the man was ill, and when they were produced we opened them with no small eagerness and expectation; and as there were a great number within one another, with much impatience we took them one out of the other. At last, when we came to the smallest, and had opened it, we saw it was full of papers, which we supposed to be notes; at the sight of which our hearts leapt for joy; and that instant the Captain, clapping his hands, cried out, 'Thank God, here it is.' But when we took up the trunk, and began to examine the supposed treasure and long-looked-for bounty, (alas! alas! how uncertain and deceitful are all human affairs!) what had we found! While we thought we were embracing a substance we grasped an empty nothing. The whole amount that was in the nest of trunks was only one dollar and a half; and all that the man possessed would not pay for his coffin. Our sudden and exquisite joy was now succeeded by as sudden and exquisite pain; and my Captain and I exhibited, for some time, most ridiculous figures—pictures of chagrin and disappointment! We went away greatly mortified, and left the deceased to do as well as he could for himself, as we had taken so good care of him when alive for nothing. We set sail once more for Montserrat, and arrived there safe; but much out of humour with our friend the silversmith. When we had unladen the vessel, and I had sold my venture, finding myself master of about forty-seven pounds, I consulted my true friend, the Captain, how I should proceed in offering my master the money for my freedom. He told me to come on a certain morning, when he and my master would be at breakfast together. Accordingly, on that morning I went, and met the Captain there, as he had appointed. When I went in I made my obeisance to my master, and with my money in my hand, and many fears in my heart, I prayed him to be as good as his offer to me, when he was pleased to promise me my freedom as soon as I could purchase it. This speech seemed to confound him; he began to recoil: and my heart that instant sunk within me. 'What,' said he, 'give you your freedom? Why, where did you get the money? Have you got forty pounds sterling?' 'Yes, sir,' I answered. 'How did you get it?' replied he. I told him, very honestly. The Captain then said he knew I got the money very honestly and with much industry, and that I was particularly careful. On which my master replied, I got money much faster than he did; and said he would not have made me the promise he did if he had thought I should have got money so soon. 'Come, come,' said my worthy Captain, clapping my master on the back, 'Come, Robert, (which was his name) I think you must let him have his freedom; you have laid your money out very well; you have received good interest for it all this time, and here is now the principal at last. I know Gustavus has earned you more than an hundred a-year, and he will still save you money, as he will not leave you:—Come, Robert, take the money.' My master then said, he would not be worse than his promise; and, taking the money, told me to go to the Secretary at the Register Office, and get my manumission drawn up. These words of my master were like a voice from heaven to me: in an instant all my trepidation was turned into unutterable bliss; and I most reverently bowed myself with gratitude, unable to express my feelings, but by the overflowing of my eyes, while my true and worthy friend, the Captain, congratulated us both with a peculiar degree of heart-felt pleasure. As soon as the first transports of my joy were over, and that I had expressed my thanks to these my worthy friends in the best manner I was able, I rose with a heart full of affection and reverence, and left the room, in order to obey my master's joyful mandate of going to the Register Office. As I was leaving the house I called to mind the words of the Psalmist, in the 126th Psalm, and like him, 'I glorified God in my heart, in whom I trusted.' These words had been impressed on my mind from the very day I was forced from Deptford to the present hour, and I now saw them, as I thought, fulfilled and verified. My imagination was all rapture as I flew to the Register Office, and, in this respect, like the apostle Peter,* (whose deliverance from prison was so sudden and extraordinary, that he thought he was in a vision) I could scarcely believe I was awake. Heavens! who could do justice to my feelings at this moment! Not conquering heroes themselves, in the midst of a triumph—Not the tender mother who has just regained her long lost infant, and presses it to her heart—Not the weary hungry mariner, at the sight of the desired friendly port— Not the lover, when he once more embraces his beloved mistress, after she had been ravished from his arms!—All within my breast was tumult, wildness, and delirium! My feet scarcely touched the ground, for they were winged with joy, and, like Elijah, as he rose to Heaven, they 'were with lightning sped as I went on.' Every one I met I told of my happiness, and blazed about the virtue of my amiable master and captain.

When I got to the office and acquainted the Register with my errand he congratulated me on the occasion, and told me he would draw up my manumission for half price, which was a guinea. I thanked him for his kindness; and, having received it and paid him, I hastened to my master to get him to sign it, that I might be fully released. Accordingly he signed the manumission that day, so that,

---

*Acts, chap. xii. ver. 9.

before night, I who had been a slave in the morning, trembling at the will of another, was become my own master, and completely free. I thought this was the happiest day I had ever experienced; and my joy was still heightened by the blessings and prayers of the sable race, particularly the aged, to whom my heart had ever been attached with reverence.

---

As the form of my manumission has something peculiar in it, and expresses the absolute power and dominion one man claims over his fellow, I shall beg leave to present it before my readers at full length:

*Montserrat.*—To all men unto whom these presents shall come: I Robert King, of the parish of St. Anthony in the said island, merchant, send greeting: Know ye, that I the aforesaid Robert King, for and in consideration of the sum of seventy pounds current money of the said island, to me in hand paid, and to the intent that a negro man-slave, named Gustavus Vassa, shall and may become free, have manumitted, emancipated, enfranchised, and set free, and by these presents do manumit, emancipate, enfranchise, and set free, the aforesaid negro man-slave, named Gustavus Vassa, for ever, hereby giving, granting, and releasing unto him, the said Gustavus Vassa, all right, title, dominion, sovereignty, and property, which, as lord and master over the aforesaid Gustavus Vassa, I had, or now I have, or by any means whatsoever I may or can hereafter possibly have over him the aforesaid negro, for ever. In witness whereof I the abovesaid Robert King have unto these presents set my hand and seal, this tenth day of July, in the year of our Lord one thousand seven hundred and sixty-six.

ROBERT KING.

Signed, sealed, and delivered in the presence of Terrylegay, Montserrat.

Registered the within manumission at full length, this eleventh day of July, 1766, in liber D.

TERRYLEGAY, Register.

---

In short, the fair as well as black people immediately styled me by a new appellation, to me the most desirable in the world, which was Freeman, and at the dances I gave my Georgia superfine blue clothes made no indifferent appearance, as I thought. Some of the sable females, who formerly stood aloof, now began to relax and appear less coy; but my heart was still fixed on London, where I hoped to be ere long. So that my worthy captain and his owner, my late master, finding that the bent of my mind was towards London, said to me, 'We hope you won't leave us, but that you will still be with the vessels.' Here gratitude bowed me down; and none but the generous mind can judge of my feelings, struggling between inclination and duty. However, notwithstanding my wish to be in London, I obediently answered my benefactors that I would go in the vessel, and not leave them; and from that day I was entered on board as an able-bodied sailor, at thirty-six shillings per month, besides what perquisites I could make. My intention was to make a voyage or two, entirely to please these my honoured patrons; but I determined that the year following, if it pleased God, I would see Old England once

more, and surprise my old master, Capt. Pascal, who was hourly in my mind; for
I still loved him, notwithstanding his usage of me, and I pleased myself with thinking of what he would say when he saw what the Lord had done for me in so short
a time, instead of being, as he might perhaps suppose, under the cruel yoke of
some planter. With these kind of reveries I used often to entertain myself, and
shorten the time till my return; and now, being as in my original free African state,
I embarked on board the Nancy, after having got all things ready for our voyage.
In this state of serenity we sailed for St. Eustatia; and, having smooth seas and
calm weather, we soon arrived there: after taking our cargo on board, we proceeded to Savannah in Georgia, in August 1766. While we were there, as usual, I
used to go for the cargo up the rivers in boats; and on this business I have been
frequently beset by alligators, which were very numerous on that coast, and I have
shot many of them when they have been near getting into our boats; which we
have with great difficulty sometimes prevented, and have been very much frightened at them. I have seen a young one sold in Georgia alive for six pence. During
our stay at this place, one evening a slave belonging to Mr. Read, a merchant of
Savannah, came near our vessel, and began to use me very ill. I entreated him,
with all the patience I was master of, to desist, as I knew there was little or no law
for a free negro here; but the fellow, instead of taking my advice, persevered in
his insults, and even struck me. At this I lost all temper, and I fell on him and beat
him soundly. The next morning his master came to our vessel as we lay alongside
the wharf, and desired me to come ashore that he might have me flogged all round
the town, for beating his negro slave. I told him he had insulted me, and had given
the provocation, by first striking me. I had told my captain also the whole affair
that morning, and wished him to have gone along with me to Mr. Read, to prevent bad consequences; but he said that it did not signify, and if Mr. Read said
any thing he would make matters up, and had desired me to go to work, which I
accordingly did. The Captain being on board when Mr. Read came, he told him
I was a free man; and when Mr. Read applied to him to deliver me up, he said he
knew nothing of the matter. I was astonished and frightened at this, and thought
I had better keep where I was than go ashore and be flogged round the town, without judge or jury. I therefore refused to stir; and Mr. Read went away, swearing
he would bring all the constables in the town, for he would have me out of the
vessel. When he was gone, I thought his threat might prove too true to my sorrow; and I was confirmed in this belief, as well by the many instances I had seen
of the treatment of free negroes, as from a fact that had happened within my own
knowledge here a short time before. There was a free black man, a carpenter, that
I knew, who, for asking a gentleman that he worked for the money he had earned,
was put into gaol; and afterwards this oppressed man was sent from Georgia, with
false accusations, of an intention to set the gentleman's house on fire, and run
away with his slaves. I was therefore much embarrassed, and very apprehensive
of a flogging at least. I dreaded, of all things, the thoughts of being striped, as I
never in my life had the marks of any violence of that kind. At that instant a rage
seized my soul, and for a little I determined to resist the first man that should offer to lay violent hands on me, or basely use me without a trial; for I would sooner
die like a free man, than suffer myself to be scourged by the hands of ruffians, and

my blood drawn like a slave. The captain and others, more cautious, advised me to make haste and conceal myself; for they said Mr. Read was a very spiteful man, and he would soon come on board with constables and take me. At first I refused this counsel, being determined to stand my ground; but at length, by the prevailing entreaties of the captain and Mr. Dixon, with whom he lodged, I went to Mr. Dixon's house, which was a little out of town, at a place called Yea-ma-chra.[169] I was but just gone when Mr. Read, with the constables, came for me, and searched the vessel; but, not finding me there, he swore he would have me dead or alive. I was secreted about five days; however, the good character which my captain always gave me as well as some other gentlemen who also knew me, procured me some friends. At last some of them told my captain that he did not use me well, in suffering me thus to be imposed upon, and said they would see me redressed, and get me on board some other vessel. My captain, on this, immediately went to Mr. Read, and told him, that ever since I eloped from the vessel his work had been neglected, and he could not go on with her loading, himself and mate not being well; and, as I had managed things on board for them, my absence must retard his voyage, and consequently hurt the owner; he therefore begged of him to forgive me, as he said he never had any complaint of me before, for the many years that I had been with him. After repeated entreaties, Mr. Read said I might go to hell, and that he would not meddle with me; on which my captain came immediately to me at his lodging, and, telling me how pleasantly matters had gone on, he desired me to go on board. Some of my other friends then asked him if he had got the constable's warrant from them; the captain said, No. On this I was desired by them to stay in the house; and they said they would get me on board of some other vessel before the evening. When the captain heard this he became almost distracted. He went immediately for the warrant, and after using every exertion in his power, he at last got it from my hunters; but I had all the expenses to pay. After I had thanked all my friends for their attention, I went on board again to my work, of which I had always plenty. We were in the haste to complete our lading, and were to carry twenty head of cattle with us to the West Indies, where they are a very profitable article. In order to encourage me in working, and to make up for the time I had lost, my captain promised me the privilege of carrying two bullocks of my own with me; and this made me work with redoubled ardour. As soon as I had got the vessel loaded, in doing which I was obliged to perform the duty of the mate as well as my own work, and that the bullocks were near coming on board, I asked the captain leave to bring my two, according to his promise; but, to my great surprise, he told me there was no room for them. I then asked him to permit me to take one; but he said he could not. I was a good deal mortified at this usage, and told him I had no notion that he intended thus to impose on me; nor could I think well of any man that was so much worse than his word. On this we had some disagreement, and I gave him to understand, that I intended to leave the vessel. At this he appeared to be very much dejected; and our mate, who had been very sickly, and whose duty had long devolved upon me, advised him to persuade me to stay: in consequence of which he spoke very kindly to me, making many fair promises, telling me that, as the mate was so sickly, he could not do without me, and that, as the safety of the vessel and cargo depended greatly upon me, he therefore hoped that I would not be offended at what had passed between us, and swore he would make up all matters when we arrived in the West Indies; so I consented to slave on as before. Soon after this, as the bullocks were coming on board, one of them ran at the captain, and butted him so furiously in the breast, that he never recovered of the blow. In order to make me some amends for his treatment about the bullocks, the captain now pressed me very much to take some turkeys, and other fowls, with me, and gave me liberty to take as many as I could find room for: but I told him he knew very well I had never carried any turkeys before, as I always thought they were such tender birds that they were not fit to cross the seas. However, he continued to press me to buy them for once; and, what was very surprising to me, the more I was against it, the more he urged my taking them, insomuch that he ensured me from all losses that might happen by them, and I was prevailed on to take them; but I thought this very strange, as he had never acted so with me before. This, and not being able to dispose of my paper-money in any other way, induced me at length to take four dozen. The turkeys, however, I was so dissatisfied about that I determined to make no more voyages to this quarter, nor with this captain; and was very apprehensive that my free voyage would be the worst I had ever made. We set sail for Montserrat. The captain and mate had been both complaining of sickness when we sailed, and as we proceeded on our voyage they grew worse. This was about November, and we had not been long at sea before we began to meet with strong northerly gales and rough seas; and in about seven or eight days all the bullocks were near being drowned, and four or five of them died. Our vessel, which had not been tight at first, was much less so now; and, though we were but nine in the whole, including five sailors and myself, yet we were obliged to attend to the pumps every half or three quarters of an hour. The captain and mate came on deck as often as they were able, which was now but seldom; for they declined so fast, that they were not well enough to make observations above four or five times the whole voyage. The whole care of the vessel rested, therefore, upon me, and I was obliged to direct her by my former experience, not being able to work a traverse. The captain was now very sorry he had not taught me navigation, and protested, if ever he should get well again, he would not fail to do so; but in about seventeen days his illness increased so much, that he was obliged to keep his bed, continuing sensible, however, till the last, constantly having the owner's interest at heart; for this just and benevolent man ever appeared much concerned about the welfare of what he was intrusted with. When this dear friend found the symptoms of death approaching, he called me by my name; and, when I came to him, he asked (with almost his last breath) if he had ever done me any harm? 'God forbid I should think so,' I replied, 'I should then be the most ungrateful of wretches to the best of benefactors.' While I was thus expressing my affection and sorrow by his bedside, he expired without saying another word; and the day following we committed his body to the deep. Every man on board loved this man, and regretted his death; but I was exceedingly affected at it, and I found that I did not know, till he was gone, the strength of my regard for him. Indeed I had every reason in the world to be attached to him; for, besides, that he was in general mild, affable, generous, faithful, benevolent, and just, he was to me a friend and a father; and, had it pleased Providence that he had died but five months before, I verily believe I should not have obtained my freedom when I did; and it is not improbable that I might not have been able to get it at any rate afterwards. The captain being dead, the mate came on the deck, and made such observations as he was able, but to no purpose. In the course of a few days more, the few bullocks that remained were found dead; but the turkies I had, though on the deck, and exposed to so much wet and bad weather, did well, and I afterwards gained near three hundred per cent on the sale of them; so that in the event it proved a happy circumstance for me that I had not bought the bullocks I intended, for they must have perished with the rest; and I could not help looking on this, otherwise trifling circumstance, as a particular providence of God, and I was thankful accordingly. The care of the vessel took up all my time, and engaged my attention entirely. As we were now out of the variable winds, I thought I should not be much puzzled to hit upon the islands. I was persuaded I steered right for Antigua, which I wished to reach, as the nearest to us; and in the course of nine or ten days we made this island, to our great joy; and the next day after we came safe to Montserrat. Many were surprised when they heard of my conducting the sloop into the port, and I now obtained a new appelation, and was called Captain. This elated me not a little, and it was quite flattering to my vanity to be thus styled by as high as title as any free man in this place possessed. When the death of the captain became known, he was much regretted by all who knew him; for he was a man universally respected. At the same time the sable captain lost no fame; for the success I had met with increased the affection of my friends in no small measure.[170]

# CHAP. VIII.

*The author, to oblige Mr. King, once more embarks for Georgia in one of his vessels—A new captain is appointed—They sail, and steer a new course—Three remarkable dreams—The vessel is shipwrecked on the Bahama bank, but the crew are preserved, principally by means of the author—He sets out from the island with the captain, in a small boat, in quest of a ship—Their distress—Meet with a wrecker—Sail for Providence—Are overtaken again by a terrible storm, and are all near perishing—Arrive at New Providence—The author, after some time, sails from thence to Georgia—Meets with another storm, and is obliged to put back and refit—Arrives at Georgia—Meets new impositions—Two white men attempt to kidnap him—Officiates as a parson at a funeral ceremony—Bids adieu to Georgia, and sails for Martinico.*

As I had now, by the death of my captain, lost my great benefactor and friend, I had little inducement to remain longer in the West Indies, except my gratitude to Mr. King, which I thought I had pretty well discharged in bringing back his vessel safe, and delivering his cargo to his satisfaction. I began to think of leaving this part of the world, of which I had been long tired, and returning to England, where my heart had always been; but Mr. King still pressed me very much to stay with his vessel; and he had done so much for me that I found myself unable to refuse his requests, and consented to go another voyage to Georgia, as the mate, from his ill state of health, was quite useless in the vessel. Accordingly a new captain was appointed, whose name was William Phillips, an old acquaintance of mine; and, having refitted our vessel, and taken several slaves on board, we set sail for St. Eustatia, where we stayed but a few days; and on the 30th of January 1767 we steered for Georgia. Our new captain boasted strangely of his skill in navigating and conducting a vessel; and in consequence of this he steered a new course, several points more to the westward than we ever did before; this appeared to me very extraordinary.

On the fourth of February, which was soon after we had got into our new course, I dreamt the ship was wrecked amidst the surfs and rocks, and that I was the means of saving every one on board; and on the night following I dreamed the very same dream. These dreams however made no impression on my mind; and the next evening, it being my watch below, I was pumping the vessel a little after eight o'clock, just before I went off the deck, as is the custom; and being weary with the duty of the day, and tired at the pump, (for we made a good deal of water) I began to express my impatience, and I uttered with an oath, 'Damn the vessel's bottom out.' But my conscience instantly smote me for the expression. When I left the deck I went to bed, and had scarcely fallen asleep when I dreamed the same dream again about the ship that I had dreamt the two preceeding nights. At twelve o'clock the watch was changed; and, as I had always the charge of the captain's watch, I then went upon deck. At half after one in the morning the man at the helm saw something under the lee-beam that the sea washed against, and he immediately called to me that there was a grampus, and desired me to look at it. Accordingly I stood up and observed it for some time; but, when I saw the sea wash up against it again and again, I said it was not a fish but a rock. Being soon certain of this, I went down to the captain, and, with some confusion, told him the danger we were in, and desired him to come upon deck immediately. He said it was very well, and I went up again. As soon as I was upon deck the wind, which had been pretty high, having abated a little, the vessel began to be carried sideways towards the rock, by means of the current. Still the captain did not appear. I therefore went to him again, and told him the vessel was then near a large rock, and desired he would come up with speed. He said he would, and I returned to the deck. When I was upon the deck again I saw were were not above a pistol shot from the rock, and I heard the noise of the breakers all around us. I was exceedingly alarmed at this; and the captain having not yet come on the deck I lost all patience; and, growing quite enraged, I ran down to him again, and asked him why he did not come up, and what he could mean by all this? 'The breakers,' said I, 'are round us, and the vessel is almost on the rock.' With that he came on the deck with me, and we tried to put the vessel about, and get her out of the current, but all to no purpose, the wind being very small. We then called all hands up immediately; and after a little we got up one end of a cable, and fastened it to the anchor. By this time the surf was foaming round us, and made a dreadful noise on the breakers, and the very moment we let the anchor go the vessel struck against the rocks. One swell now succeeded another, as it were one wave calling on its fellow: the roaring of the billows increased, and, with one single heave of the swells, the sloop was pierced and transfixed among the rocks! In a moment a scene of horror presented itself to my mind, such as I never had conceived or experienced before. All my sins, stared me in the face; and especially, I thought that God had hurled his direful vengeance on my guilty head for cursing the vessel on which my life depended. My spirits at this forsook me, and I expected every moment to go the bottom: I determined if I should still be saved that I would never swear again. And in the midst of my distress, while the dreadful surfs were dashing with unremitting fury among the rocks, I remembered the Lord, though fearful that I was undeserving of forgiveness, and I thought that as he had often delivered he might yet deliver; and, calling to mind the many mercies he had shewn me in times past, they gave me some small hope that he might still help me. I then began to think how we might be saved; and I believe no mind was ever like mine so replete with inventions and confused with schemes, though how to escape death I knew not. The captain immediately ordered the hatches to be nailed down on the slaves in the hold, where there were above twenty, all of whom must unavoidably have perished if he had been obeyed. When he desired the man to nail down the hatches I thought that my sin was the cause of this, and that God would charge me with these people's blood. This thought rushed upon my mind that instant with such violence, that it quite overpowered me, and I fainted. I recovered just as the people were about to nail down the hatches; perceiving which, I desired them to stop. The captain then said it must be done: I asked him why? He said that every one would endeavour to get into the boat, which was but small, and thereby we should be drowned; for it would not have carried above ten at the most. I could no longer restrain my emotion, and I told him he deserved drowning for not knowing how to navigate the vessel; and I believe the people would have tossed him overboard if I had given them the least hint of it. However the hatches were not nailed down; and, as none of us could leave the vessel then on account of the darkness, as we knew not where to go, and were convinced besides that the boat could not survive the surfs, we all said we would remain on the dry part of the vessel, and trust to God till daylight appeared, when we should know better what to do.

I then advised to get the boat prepared against morning, and some of us began to set about it; but some abandoned all care of the ship and themselves, and fell to drinking. Our boat had a piece out of her bottom near two feet long, and we had no materials to mend her; however, necessity being the mother of invention, I took some pump leather and nailed it to the broken part, and plastered it over with tallow-grease. And, thus prepared, with the utmost anxiety of mind we watched for day-light, and thought every minute an hour till it appeared. At last it saluted our longing eyes, and kind Providence accompanied its approach with what was no small comfort to us; for the dreadful swell began to subside; and the next thing that we discovered to raise our drooping spirits, was a small key or island, about five or six miles off; but a barrier soon presented itself; for there was not water enough for our boat to go over the reefs, and this threw us again into a sad consternation; but there was no alternative, we were therefore

obliged to put but few in the boat at once; and, what is still worse, all of us were
frequently under the necessity of getting out to drag and lift it over the reefs. This
cost us much labour and fatigue; and, what was yet more distressing, we could
not avoid having our legs cut and torn very much with the rocks. There were
only four people that would work with me at the oars; and they consisted of three
black men and a Dutch creole sailor; and, though we went with the boat five
times that day, we had no others to assist us. But, had we not worked in this
manner, I really believe the people could not have been saved; for not one of the
white men did any thing to preserve their lives; and indeed they soon got so drunk
that they were not able, but lay about the deck like swine, so that we were at last
obliged to lift them into the boat and carry them on shore by force. This want of
assistance made our labour intolerably severe; insomuch, that, by putting on
shore so often that day, the skin was entirely stript off my hands.

However, we continued all day to toil and strain our exertions, till we had
brought all on board safe to the shore; so that out of thirty-two people we lost
not one. My dream now returned upon my mind with all its force; it was fulfilled
in every part; for our danger was the same I had dreamt of: and I could not help
looking on myself as the principal instrument in effecting our deliverance; for,
owing to some of our people getting drunk, the rest of us were obliged to double our exertions; and it was fortunate we did, for in a very little time longer the
patch of leather on the boat would have been worn out, and she would have been
no longer fit for service. Situated as we were, who could think that men should
be so careless of the danger they were in? for, if the wind had but raised the swell
as it was when the vessel struck, we must have bid a final farewell to all hopes
of deliverance; and though, I warned the people who were drinking and entreated them to embrace the moment of deliverance, nevertheless they persisted,
as if not possessed of the least spark of reason. I could not help thinking, that, if
any of these people had been lost, God would charge me with their lives, which,
perhaps, was one cause of my labouring so hard for their preservation, and indeed every one of them afterwards seemed so sensible of the service I had rendered them; and while we were on the key I was a kind of chieftain amongst
them. I brought some limes, oranges, and lemons ashore; and, finding it to be a
good soil where we were, I planted several of them as a token to any one that
might be cast away hereafter. This key, as we afterwards found, was one of the
Bahama islands, which consist of a cluster of large islands, with smaller ones or
keys, as they called, interspersed among them. It was about a mile in circumference, with a white sandy beach running in a regular order along it. On that part
of it where we first attempted to land there stood some very large birds, called
flamingoes: these, from the reflection of the sun, appeared to us at a little distance as large as men; and, when they walked backwards and forwards, we could
not conceive what they were: our captain swore they were cannibals. This created a great panic among us; and we held a consultation how to act. The captain
wanted to go to a key that was within sight, but a great way off; but I was against
it, as in so doing we should not be able to save all the people; 'And therefore,'
said I, 'let us go on shore here, and perhaps these cannibals may take to the water.' Accordingly we steered towards them; and when we approached them, to

our very great joy and no less wonder, they walked off one after the other very deliberately; and at last they took flight and relieved us entirely from our fears. About the key there were turtles and several sorts of fish in such abundance that we caught them without bait, which was a great relief to us after the salt provisions on board. There was also a large rock on the beach, about ten feet high, which was in the form of a punch-bowl at the top; this we could not help thinking Providence had ordained to supply us with rainwater; and it was something singular that, if we did not take the water when it rained, in some little time after it would turn as salt as sea-water.

Our first care, after refreshment, was to make ourselves tents to lodge in, which we did as well as we could with some sails we had brought from the ship. We then began to think how we might get from this place, which was quite uninhabited; and we determined to repair our boat, which was very much shattered, and to put to sea in quest of a ship or some inhabited island. It took us up however eleven days before we could get the boat ready for sea in the manner we wanted it, with a sail and other necessaries. When we had got all things prepared the captain wanted me to stay on shore while he went to sea in quest of a vessel to take all the people off the key; but this I refused; and the captain and myself, with five more, set off in the boat towards New Providence.[171] We had no more than two musket load of gun-powder with us if any thing should happen; and our stock of provisions consisted of three gallons of rum, four of water, some salt beef, some biscuit; and in this manner we proceeded to sea.

On the second day of our voyage we came to an island called Abbico, the largest of the Bahama islands. We were much in want of water; for by this time our water was expended, and we were exceedingly fatigued in pulling two days in the heat of the sun; and it being late in the evening, we hauled the boat ashore to try for water and remain during the night: when we came ashore we searched for water, but could find none. When it was dark, we made a fire around us for fear of the wild beasts, as the place was an entire thick wood, and we took it by turns to watch. In this situation we found very little rest, and waited with impatience for the morning. As soon as the light appeared we set off again with our boat, in hopes of finding assistance during the day. We were now much dejected and weakened by pulling the boat; for our sail was of no use, and we went almost famished for want of fresh water to drink. We had nothing left to eat but salt beef, and that we could not use without water. In this situation we toiled all day in sight of the island, which was very long; in the evening, seeing no relief, we made ashore again, and fastened out boat. We then went to look for fresh water, being quite faint for the want of it; and we dug and searched about for some all the remainder of the evening, but could not find one drop, so that our dejection at this period became excessive, and our terror so great, that we expected nothing but death to deliver us. We could not touch our beef, which was as salt as brine, without fresh water; and we were in the greatest terror from the apprehension of wild beasts. When unwelcome night came we acted as on the night before; and the next morning we set off again from the island in hopes of seeing some vessel. In this manner we toiled as well as we were able till four o'clock, during which we passed several keys, but could not meet with a ship; and, still famishing with thirst, went ashore on one of the those keys again in hopes of finding some water. Here we found some leaves with a few drops of water in them, which we lapped with much eagerness; we then dug in several places, but without success. As we were digging holes in search of water there came forth some very thick and black stuff; but none of us could touch it, except the poor Dutch Creole, who drank above a quart of it as eagerly as if it had been wine. We tried to catch fish, but could not; and we now began to repine our fate, and abandon ourselves to despair; when, in the midst of our murmuring, the captain all at once cried 'A sail! a sail! a sail!' This gladdening sound was like a reprieve to a convict, and we all instantly turned to look at it; but in a little time some of us began to be afraid it was not a sail. However, at a venture, we embarked and steered after it; and, in half an hour, to our unspeakable joy, we plainly saw that it was a vessel. At this our drooping spirits revived, and we made towards her with all the speed imaginable. When we came near to her, we found she was a little sloop, about the size of a Gravesend hoy,[172] and quite full of people; a circumstance which we could not make out the meaning of. Our captain, who was a Welchman, swore that they were pirates, and would kill us. I said, be that as it might, we must board her if we were to die for it; and, if they should not receive us kindly, we must oppose them as well as we could; for there was no alternative between their perishing and ours. This counsel was immediately taken; and I really believe that the captain, myself, and the Dutchman, would then have faced twenty men. We had two cutlasses and a musquet, that I brought in the boat; and, in this situation, we rowed alongside, and immediately boarded her. I believe there were about forty hands on board; but how great was our surprise, as soon as we got on board, to find that the major part of them were in the same predicament as ourselves!

They belonged to a whaling schooner that was wrecked two days before us about nine miles to the north of our vessel. When she was wrecked some of them had taken to their boats and had left some of their people and property on a key, in the same manner as we had done; and were going, like us, to New Providence in quest of a ship, when they met with this little sloop, called a wrecker; their employment in those seas being to look after wrecks. They were then going to take the remainder of the people belonging to the schooner; for which the wrecker was to have all things belonging to the vessel, and likewise their people's help to get what they could out of her, and were then to carry the crew to New Providence.

We told the people of the wrecker the condition of our vessel, and we made the same agreement with them as the schooner's people; and, on their complying, we begged of them to go to our key directly, because our people were in want of water. They agreed, therefore, to go along with us first; and in two days we arrived at the key, to the inexpressible joy of the people that we had left behind, as they had been reduced to great extremities for want of water in our absence. Luckily for us, the wrecker had now more people on board than she could carry or victual for any moderate length of time; they therefore hired the schooner's people to work on our wreck, and we left them our boat, and embarked for New Providence.

Nothing could have been more fortunate than our meeting with this wrecker, for New Providence was at such a distance that we never could have reached it in our boat. The island of Abbico was much longer than we expected; and it was not till after sailing for three or four days that we got safe to the farther end of it, towards New Providence. When we arrived there we watered, and got a good many lobsters and other shellfish; which proved a great relief to us, as our provisions and water were almost exhausted. We then proceeded on our voyage; but the day after we left the island, late in the evening, and whilst we were yet amongst the Bahama keys, we were overtaken by a violent gale of wind, so that we were obliged to cut away the mast. The vessel was very near foundering; for she parted from her anchors, and struck several times on the shoals. Here we expected every minute that she would have gone to pieces, and each moment to be our last; so much so that my old captain and sickly useless mate, and several others, fainted; and death stared us in the face on every side. All the swearers on board now began to call on the God of Heaven to assist them: and, sure enough, beyond our comprehension he did assist us, and in a miraculous manner delivered us! In the very height of our extremity the wind lulled for a few minutes; and, although the swell was high beyond expression, two men, who were expert swimmers, attempted to go to the buoy of the anchor, which we still saw on the water, at some distance, in a little punt that belonged to the wrecker, which was not large enough to carry more than two. She filled different times in their endeavours to get into her alongside of our vessel; and they saw nothing but death before them, as well as we; but they said they might as well die that way as any other. A coil of very small rope, with a little buoy, was put in along with them; and, at last, with great hazard, they got the punt clear from the vessel; and these two intrepid water heroes paddled away for life towards the buoy of the anchor. The eyes of us all were fixed on them all the time, expecting every minute to be their last: and the prayers of all those that remained in their senses were offered up to God, on their behalf, for a speedy deliverance; and for our own, which depended on them; and he heard and answered us! These two men at last reached the buoy; and, having fastened the punt to it, they tied one end of their rope to the small buoy that they had in the punt, and sent it adrift towards the vessel. We on board observing this threw out boat-hooks and leads fastened to lines, in order to catch the buoy: at last we caught it, and fastened a hawser to the end of the small rope; we then gave them a sign to pull, and they pulled the hawser to them, and fastened it to the buoy: which being done we hauled for our lives; and, through the mercy of God, we got again from the shoals into deep water, and the punt got safe to the vessel. It is impossible for any to conceive our heart-felt joy at this second deliverance from ruin, but those who have suffered the same hardships. Those whose strength and senses were gone came to themselves, and were now as elated as they were before depressed. Two days after this the wind ceased, and the water became smooth. The punt then went on shore, and we cut down some trees; and having found our mast and mended it we brought it on board, and fixed it up. As soon as we had done this we got up the anchor, and away we went once more for New Providence, which in three days more we reached safe, after having been above three weeks in a situation in which we did not expect to escape with life. The inhabitants here were very kind to us; and, when they learned our situation, shewed us a great deal of hospitality and friendship. Soon after this every one of my old fellow-sufferers that were free parted from us, and shaped their course where their inclination led them. One merchant, who had a large sloop, seeing our condition, and knowing we wanted to go to Georgia, told four of us that his vessel was going there; and, if we would work on board and load her, he would give us our passage free. As we could not get any wages whatever, and found it very hard to get off the place, we were obliged to consent to his proposal; and we went on board and helped to load the sloop, though we had only our victuals allowed us. When she was entirely loaded he told us she was going to Jamaica first, where we must go if we went in her. This, however, I refused; but my fellow-sufferers not having any money to help themselves with, necessity obliged them to accept of the offer, and to steer that course, though they did not like it.

We stayed in New Providence about seventeen or eighteen days; during which time I met with many friends, who gave me encouragement to stay there with them: but I declined it; though, had not my heart been fixed on England, I should have stayed, as I liked the place extremely, and there were some free black people here who were very happy, and we passed our time pleasantly together, with the melodious sound of the catguts,[173] under the lime and lemon trees. At length Captain Phillips hired a sloop to carry him and some of the slaves that he could not sell to Georgia; and I agreed to go with him in this vessel, meaning now to take my farewell of that place. When the vessel was ready we all embarked; and I took my leave of New Providence, not without regret. We sailed about four o'clock in the morning, with a fair wind, for Georgia; and about eleven o'clock the same morning a short and sudden gale sprung up and blew away most of our sails; and, as we were still amongst the keys, in a very few minutes it dashed the sloop against the rocks. Luckily for us the water was deep; and the sea was not so angry but that, after having for some time laboured hard, and being many in number, we were saved through God's mercy; and, by using our greatest exertions, we got the vessel off. The next day we returned to Providence, where we soon got her again refitted. Some of the people swore that we had spells set upon us by somebody in Montserrat; and others that we had witches and wizzards amongst the poor helpless slaves; and that we never should arrive safe at Georgia. But these things did not deter me; I said, 'Let us again face the winds and seas, and swear not, but trust to God, and he will deliver us.' We therefore once more set sail; and, with hard labour, in seven day's time arrived safe at Georgia.

After our arrival we went up to the town of Savannah; and the same evening I went to a friend's house to lodge, whose name was Mosa, a black man. We were very happy at meeting each other; and after supper we had a light till it was between nine and ten o'clock at night. About that time the watch or patrol came by; and, discerning a light in the house, they knocked at the door: we opened it; and they came in and sat down, and drank some punch with us: they also begged some limes of me, as they understood I had some, which I readily gave them. A little after this they told me I must go to the watch-house with them: this surprised me a good deal, after our kindness to them; and I asked them, Why so? They said that all negroes who had light in their houses after nine o'clock were to be taken into custody, and either pay some dollars or be flogged. Some of those people knew that I was a free man; but, as the man of the house was not free, and had his master to protect him, they did not take the same liberty with him they did with me. I told them I was a free man, and just arrived from Providence; that we were not making any noise, and that I was not a stranger in that place, but was very well known there; 'Besides,' said I, 'what will you do with me?'—'That you shall see,' replied they, 'but you must go to the watch-house with us.' Now whether they meant to get money from me or not I was at a loss to know; but I thought immediately of the oranges and limes at Santa Cruz: and seeing that nothing would pacify them I went with them to the watch-house, where I remained during the night. Early the next morning these imposing ruffians flogged a negro-man and woman that they had in the watch-house, and then they told me that I must be flogged too. I asked why? and if there was no law for free men? And told them if there was I would have it put in force against them. But this only exasperated them the more; and instantly they swore they would serve me as Doctor Perkins had done; and they were going to lay violent hands on me; when one of them, more humane than the rest, said that as I was a free man they could not justify stripping me by law. I then immediately sent for Doctor Brady, who was known to be an honest and worthy man; and on his coming to my assistance they let me go.

This was not the only disagreeable incident I met with while I was in this place; for, one day, while I was a little way out of the town of Savannah, I was beset by two white men, who meant to play their usual tricks with me in the way of kidnapping. As soon as these men accosted me, one of them said to the other, 'This is the very fellow we are looking for that you lost:' and the other swore immediately that I was the identical person. On this they made up to me, and were about to handle me; but I told them to be still and keep off; for I had seen those kind of tricks played upon other free blacks, and they must not think to serve me so. At this they paused a little, and one said to the other—it will not do; and the other answered that I talked too good English. I replied, I believed I did; and I had also with me a revengeful stick equal to the occasion; and my mind was likewise good. Happily however, it was not used; and, after we had talked together a little in this manner, the rogues left me. I stayed in Savannah some time, anxiously trying to get to Montserrat once more to see Mr. King, my old master, and then to take a final farewell of the American quarter of the globe. At last I met with a sloop called the Speedwell, Captain John Bunton, which belonged to Grenada, and was bound to Martinico, a French island, with a cargo of rice, and I shipped myself on board of her. Before I left Georgia a black woman, who had a child lying dead, being very tenacious of the church burial service, and not able to get any white person to perform it, applied to me for that purpose. I told her I was no parson; and besides, that the service over the dead did not affect the soul. This however did not satisfy her; she still urged me very hard: I therefore complied with her earnest entreaties, and at last consented to act the parson for the first time in my life. As she was much respected, there was a great company both of white and black people at the grave. I then accordingly assumed my new vocation, and performed the funeral ceremony to the satisfaction of all present; after which I bade adieu to Georgia, and sailed for Martinico.

## CHAP. IX.

*The author arrives at Martinico—Meets with new difficulties—Gets to Montserrat, where he takes leave of his old master, and sails for England—Meets Capt. Pascal—Learns the French horn—Hires himself with Doctor Irving, where he learns to freshen sea water—Leaves the doctor, and goes a voyage to Turkey and Portugal; and afterwards goes a voyage to Grenada, and another to Jamaica—Returns to the Doctor, and they embark together on a voyage to the North Pole, with the Hon. Capt. Phipps—Some account of that voyage, and the dangers the author was in—He returns to England.*

I THUS took a final leave of Georgia; for the treatment I had received in it disgusted me very much against the place; and when I left it and sailed for Martinico I determined never more to revisit it. My new captain conducted his vessel safer then my former one; and, after an agreeable voyage, we got safe to our intended port. While I was on this island I went about a good deal, and found it very pleasant: in particular I admired the town of St. Pierre, which is the principal one in the island, and built more like an European town than any I had seen in the West Indies. In general also, slaves were better treated, had more holidays, and looked better than those in the English islands. After we had done our business here, I wanted my discharge, which was necessary; for it was then the month of May, and I wished much to be at Montserrat to bid farewell to Mr. King, and all my other friends there, in time to sail for Old England in the July fleet. But, alas! I had put a great stumbling block in my own way, by which I was near losing my passage that season to England. I had lent my captain some money, which I now wanted to enable me to prosecute my intentions. This I told him; but when I applied for it, though I urged the necessity of my occasion, I met with so much shuffling from him, that I began at last to be afraid of losing my money, as I could not recover it by law: for I have already mentioned, that throughout the West Indies no black man's testimony is admitted, on any occasion, against any white person whatever, and therefore my own oath would have been of no use. I was obliged, therefore, to remain with him till he might be disposed to return it to me. Thus we sailed from Martinico for the Grenades.[174] I frequently pressing the captain for my money to no purpose; and, to render my condition worse, when we got there, the captain and his owners quarrelled; so that my situation became daily more irksome: for besides that we on board had little or no victuals allowed us, and I could not get my money nor wages, I could then have gotten my passage free to Montserrat had I been able to accept it. The worst of all was, that it was growing late in July, and the ships in the islands must sail by the 26th of that month. At last, however, with a great many entreaties, I got my money from the captain, and took the first vessel I could meet with for St. Eustatia. From thence I went in another to Basseterre in St. Kitts, where I arrived on the 19th of July. On the 22d, having met with a vessel bound to Montserrat, I wanted to go in her; but the captain and others would not take me on board until I should advertise myself, and give notice of my go-

ing off the island. I told him of my haste to be in Montserrat, and that the time
then would not admit of advertising, it being late in the evening, and the captain about to sail; but he insisted it was necessary, and otherwise he said he
would not take me. This reduced me to great perplexity; for if I should be compelled to submit to this degrading necessity, which every black freeman is under, of advertising himself like a slave, when he leaves an island, and which I
thought a gross imposition upon any freeman, I feared I should miss that opportunity of going to Montserrat, and then I could not get to England that year.
The vessel was just going off, and no time could be lost; I immediately therefore
set about, with a heavy heart, to try who I could get to befriend me in complying with the demands of the captain. Luckily I found, in a few minutes, some
gentlemen of Montserrat whom I knew; and having told them my situation, I
requested their friendly assistance in helping me off the island. Some of them,
on this, went with me to the captain, and satisfied him of my freedom; and, to
my very great joy, he desired me to go on board. We then set sail, and the next
day, the 23d, I arrived at the wished-for place, after an absence of six months,
in which I had more than once experienced the delivering hand of Providence,
when all human means of escaping destruction seemed hopeless. I saw my
friends with a gladness of heart which was increased by my absence and the dangers I had escaped, and I was received with great friendship by them all, but particularly by Mr. King, to whom I related the fate of his sloop, the Nancy, and
the causes of her being wrecked. I now learned with extreme sorrow, that his
house was washed away during my absence, by the bursting of a pond at the
top of a mountain that was opposite the town of Plymouth. It swept great part
of the town away, and Mr. King lost a great deal of property from the inunda-
tion, and nearly his life. When I told him I intended to go to London that season, and that I had come to visit him before my departure, the good man expressed a great deal of affection for me, and sorrow that I should leave him, and
warmly advised me to stay there; insisting, as I was much respected by all the
gentlemen in the place, that I might do very well, and in a short time have land
and slaves of my own. I thanked him for this instance of his friendship; but, as
I wished very much to be in London, I declined remaining any longer there, and
begged he would excuse me. I then requested he would be kind enough to give
me a certificate of my behavior while in his service, which he very readily complied with, and gave me the following:

*Montserrat, January 26, 1767.*
'The bearer hereof, Gustavus Vassa, was my slave for upwards of three
years, during which he has always behaved himself well, and discharged his duty
with honesty and assiduity.
                                                                'ROBERT KING.
'To all whom this may concern.'

Having obtained this, I parted from my kind master, after many sincere
professions of gratitude and regard, and prepared for my departure for London.
I immediately agreed to go with one Capt. John Hamer, for seven guineas, the

passage to London, on board a ship called the Andromache; and on the 24th and 25th I had free dances, as they are called, with some of my countrymen, previous to my setting off; after which I took leave of all my friends, and on the 26th I embarked for London, exceedingly glad to see myself once more on board of a ship; and still more so, in steering the course I had long wished for. With a light heart I bade Montserrat farewell, and never had my feet on it since; and with it I bade adieu to the sound of the cruel whip, and all other dreadful instruments of torture; adieu to the offensive sight of the violated chastity of the sable females, which has too often accosted my eyes; adieu to oppressions (although to me less severe than most of my countrymen); and adieu to the angry howling, dashing surfs. I wished for a grateful and thankful heart to praise the Lord God on high for all his mercies!

    We had a most prosperous voyage, and, at the end of seven weeks, arrived at Cherry-Garden stairs.[175] Thus were my longing eyes once more gratified with a sight of London, after having been absent from it above four years. I immediately received my wages, and I never had earned seven guineas so quick in my life before; I had thirty-seven guineas in all, when I got cleared of the ship. I now entered upon a scene, quite new to me, but full of hope. In this situation my first thoughts were to look out for some of my former friends, and amongst the first of those were the Miss Guerins. As soon, therefore, as I had regaled myself I went in quest of those kind ladies, whom I was very impatient to see; and with some difficulty and perseverence, I found them at May's-hill, Greenwich. They were most agreeably surprised to see me, and I quite overjoyed at meeting with them. I told them my history, at which they expressed great wonder, and freely acknowledged it did their cousin, Capt. Pascal, no honour. He then visited there frequently; and I met him four or five days after in Greenwich park. When he saw me he appeared a good deal surprised, and asked me how I came back? I answered, 'In a ship.' To which he replied dryly, 'I suppose you did not walk back to London on the water.' As I saw, by his manner, that he did not seem to be sorry for his behavior to me, and that I had not much reason to expect any favour from him, I told him that he had used me very ill, after I had been such a faithful servant to him for so many years; on which, without saying any more, he turned about and went away. A few days after this I met Capt. Pascal at Miss Guerin's house, and asked him for my prize-money. He said there was none due to me; for, if my prize money had been 10,000 l. he had a right to it all. I told him I was informed otherwise; on which he bade me defiance; and, in a bantering tone, desired me to commence a lawsuit against him for it: 'There are lawyers enough,' said he, 'that will take the cause in hand, and you had better try it.' I told him then that I would try it, which enraged him very much; however, out of regard to the ladies, I remained still, and never made any farther demand of my right. Sometime afterwards these friendly ladies asked me what I meant to do with myself, and how they could assist me. I thanked them, and said, if they pleased, I would be their servant; but if not, as I had thirty-seven guineas, which would support me for some time, I would be much obliged to them to recommend me to some person who would teach me a business whereby I might earn my living. They answered me very politely, that they were sorry it did not suit them to take me as their servant, and asked me what business I should like to learn? I said, hairdressing. They then promised to assist me in this; and soon after they recommended me to a gentleman whom I had known before, one Capt. O'Hara, who treated me with much kindness, and procured me a master, a hair-dresser, in Coventry-court, Haymarket, with whom he placed me. I was with this man from September till the February following. In that time we had a neighbour in the same court who taught the French horn. He used to blow it so well that I was charmed with it, and agreed with him to teach me to blow it. Accordingly he took me in hand, and began to instruct me, and I soon learned all the three parts.[176] I took great delight in blowing on this instrument, the evenings being long; and besides that I was fond of it, I did not like to be idle, and it filled up my vacant hours innocently. At this time also I agreed with the Rev. Mr. Gregory, who lived in the same court, where he kept an academy and an evening-school, to improve me in arithmetic. This he did as far as barter and alligation;[177] so that all the time I was there I was entirely employed. In February 1768 I hired myself to Dr. Charles Irving, in Pall-mall, so celebrated for his successful experiments in making sea water fresh; and here I had plenty of hair-dressing to improve my hand. This gentleman was an excellent master; he was exceedingly kind and good tempered; and allowed me in the evenings to attend my schools, which I esteemed a great blessing; therefore I thanked God and him for it, and used all my diligence to improve the opportunity. This diligence and attention recommended me to the notice and care of my three preceptors, who on their parts bestowed a great deal of pains in my instruction, and besides were all very kind to me. My wages, however, which were by two thirds less than I ever had in my life (for I had only 12 l. per annum) I soon found would not be sufficient to defray this extraordinary expense of masters, and my own necessary expenses; my old thirty-seven guineas had by this time worn all away to one. I thought it best, therefore, to try the sea again in quest of more money, as I had been bred to it, and had hitherto found the profession of it successful. I had also a very great desire to see Turkey, and I now determined to gratify it. Accordingly, in the month of May, 1768, I told the doctor my wish to go to sea again, to which he made no opposition; and we parted on friendly terms. The same day I went into the city in quest of a master. I was extremely fortunate in my inquiry, for I soon heard of a gentlemen who had a ship going to Italy and Turkey, and he wanted a man who could dress hair well. I was overjoyed at this, and went immediately on board of his ship, as I had been directed, which I found to be fitted up with great taste, and I already foreboded no small pleasure in sailing in her. Not finding the gentleman on board, I was directed to his lodgings, where I met with him the next day, and gave him a specimen of my dressing. He liked it so well that he hired me immediately, so that I was perfectly happy; for the ship, master, and voyage, and were entirely to my mind. The ship was called the Delawar, and my master's name was John Jolly, a neat smart good humoured man, just such an one as I wished to serve. We sailed from England in July following, and our voyage was extremely pleasant. We went to Villa Franca,[178] Nice, and Leghorn;[179] and in all these places

I was charmed with the richness and beauty of the countries, and struck with the elegant buildings with which they abound. We had always in them plenty of extraordinary good wines and rich fruits, which I was very fond of; and I had frequent occasions of gratifying both my taste and curiosity; for my captain always lodged on shore in those places, which afforded me opportunities to see the country around. I also learned navigation of the mate, which I was very fond of. When we left Italy we had delightful sailing among the Archipelago islands,[180] and from thence to Smyrna in Turkey. This is a very ancient city; the houses are built of stone, and most of them have graves adjoining to them; so that they sometimes present the appearance of church-yards. Provisions are very plentiful in this city, and good wine less than a penny a pint. The grapes, pomegranates, and many other fruits, were also the richest and largest I ever tasted. The natives are well looking and strong made, and treated me always with great civility. In general I believe they are fond of black people; and several of them gave me pressing invitations to stay amongst them, although they keep the franks, or Christians, separate, and do not suffer them to dwell immediately amongst them. I was astonished in not seeing women in any of their shops, and very rarely any in the streets; and whenever I did they were covered with a veil from head to foot, so that I could not see their faces, except when any of them out of curiosity uncovered them to look at me, which they sometimes did. I was surprised to see how the Greeks are, in some measure, kept under by the Turks, as the negroes are in the West Indies by the white people. The less refined Greeks, as I have already hinted, dance here in the same manner as we do in my nation. On the whole, during our stay here, which was about five months, I liked the place and the Turks extremely well. I could not help observing one very remarkable circumstance there: the tails of the sheep are flat, and so very large, that I have known the tail even of a lamb to weigh from eleven to thirteen pounds. The fat of them is very white and rich, and is excellent in puddings, for which it is much used. Our ship being at length richly loaded with silk, and other articles, we sailed for England.

In May 1769, soon after our return from Turkey, our ship made a delightful voyage to Oporto in Portugal, where we arrived at the time of the carnival. On our arrival, there were sent on board to us thirty-six articles to observe, with very heavy penalties if we should break any of them; and none of us even dared to go on board any other vessel or on shore till the Inquisition had sent on board and searched for every thing illegal, especially bibles. Such as were produced, and certain other things, were sent on shore till the ships were going away; and any person in whose custody a bible was found concealed was to be imprisoned and flogged, and sent into slavery for ten years.[181] I saw here many very magnificent sights, particularly the garden of Eden, where many of the clergy and laity went in procession in their several orders with the host, and sung Te Deum. I had a great curiosity to go into some of their churches, but could not gain admittance without using the necessary sprinkling of holy water at my entrance. From curiosity, and a wish to be holy, I therefore complied with this ceremony, but its virtues were lost on me, for I found myself nothing the better for it it. This place abounds with plenty of all kinds of provisions. The town is well built and pretty, and commands a fine prospect. Our ship having taken in a load of wine, and other commodities, we sailed for London, and arrived in July following. Our next voyage was to the Mediterranean. The ship was again got ready, and we sailed in September for Genoa. This is one of the finest cities I ever saw; some of the edifices were of beautiful marble, and made a most noble appearance; and many had very curious fountains before them. The churches were rich and magnificent, and curiously adorned both in the inside and out. But all this grandeur was in my eyes disgraced by the galley slaves, whose condition both there and in other parts of Italy is truly piteous and wretched. After we had stayed three some weeks, during which we bought many different things which we wanted, and got them very cheap, we sailed to Naples, a charming city, and remarkably clean. The bay is the most beautiful I ever saw; the moles for shiping are excellent. I thought it extraordinary to see grand operas acted here on Sunday nights, and even attended by their majesties. I too, like these great ones, went to those sights, and vainly served God in the day while I thus served mammon effectually at night. While we remained here there happened an eruption of mount Vesuvius, of which I had a perfect view. It was extremely awful; and we were so near that the ashes from it used to be thick on our deck. After we had transacted our business at Naples we sailed with a fair wind once more for Smyrna, where we arrived in December. A seraskier or officer took a liking to me here, and wanted me to stay, and offered me two wives; however I refused the temptation. The merchants here travel in caravans or large companies. I have seen many caravans from India, with some hundreds of camels, laden with different goods. The people of these caravans are quite brown. Among other articles, they brought with them a great quantity of locusts, which are a kind of pulse, sweet and pleasant to the palate, and in shape resembling French beans, but longer. Each kind of goods is sold in a street by itself, and I always found the Turks very honest in their dealings. They let no Christians into their mosques or churches, for which I was very sorry; as I was always fond of going to see the different modes of worship of the people wherever I went. The plague broke out while we were in Smyrna, and we stopped taking goods into the ship till it was over. She was then richly laden, and we sailed in about March 1770 for England. One day in our passage we met with an accident which was near burning the ship. A black cook, in melting some fat, overset the pan into the fire under the deck, which immediately began to blaze, and the flame went up very high under the foretop. With the fright the poor cook became almost white, and altogether speechless. Happily however we got the fire out without doing much mischief. After various delays in this passage, which was tedious, we arrived in Standgate creek[182] in July; and, at the latter end of the year, some new event occurred, so that my noble captain, the ship, and I all separated.

In April 1771 I shipped myself as a steward with Capt. Wm. Robertson of the ship Grenada Planter, once more to try my fortune in the West Indies; and we sailed from London for Madeira, Barbadoes, and the Grenades. When we were at this last place, having some goods to sell, I met once more with my former kind of West India customers. A white man, an islander, bought some goods of me to the amount of some pounds, and made me many fair promises as usual, but without any intention of paying me. He had likewise bought goods from some more of our people, whom he intended to serve in the same manner; but he still amused us with promises. However, when our ship was loaded, and near sailing, this honest buyer discovered no intention or sign of paying for any thing he had bought of us; but on the contrary, when I asked him for my money he threatened me and another black man he had bought goods of, so that we found we were like to get more blows than payment. On this we went to complain to one Mr. McIntosh,[183] a justice of the peace; we told his worship of the man's villainous tricks, and begged that he would be kind enough to see us redressed: but being negroes, although free, we could not get any remedy; and our ship being then just upon the point of sailing, we knew not how to help ourselves, though we thought it hard to lose our property in this manner. Luckily for us however, this man was also indebted to three white sailors, who could not get a farthing from him; they therefore readily joined us, and we all went together in search of him. When we found where he was, I took him out of a house and threatened him with vengeance; on which, finding he was likely to be handled roughly, the rogue offered each of us some small allowance, but nothing near our demands. This exasperated us much more; and some were for cutting his ears off; but he begged hard for mercy, which was at last granted him, after we had entirely stripped him. We then let him go, for which he thanked us, glad to get off so easily, and ran into the bushes, after having wished us a good voyage. We then repaired on board, and shortly after set sail for England. I cannot help remarking here a very narrow escape we had from being blown up, owing to a piece of negligence of mine. Just as our ship was under sail, I went down into the cabin to do some business, and had a lighted candle in my hand, which, in my hurry, without thinking, I held in a barrel of gunpowder. It remained in the powder until it was near catching fire, when fortunately I observed it and snatched it out in time, and providentially no harm happened; but I was so overcome with terror that I immediately fainted at this deliverance.

In twenty-eight days time we arrived in England, and I got clear of this ship. But, being still of a roving disposition, and desirous of seeing as many different parts of the world as I could, I shipped myself soon after, in the same year, as steward on board of a fine large ship, called the Jamaica, Captain David Watt; and we sailed from England in December 1771 for Nevis and Jamaica. I found Jamaica to be a very fine large island, well peopled, and the most considerable of the West India islands. There was a vast number of negroes here, whom I found as usual exceedingly imposed upon by the white people, and the slaves punished as in the other islands. There are negroes whose business it is to flog slaves, they go about to different people for employment, and the usual pay is from one to four bits. I saw many cruel punishments inflicted on the slaves in the short time I stayed here. In particular I was present when a poor fellow was tied up and kept hanging by the wrists at some distance from the ground, and then some half hundred weights were fixed to his ancles, in which posture he was flogged most unmercifully. There were also, as I heard, two different masters noted for cruelty on the island, who had staked up two negroes naked, and in two hours the vermin stung them to death. I heard a gentleman I well knew tell my captain that he passed sentence on a negro man to be burnt alive for attempting to poison an overseer. I pass over numerous other instances, in order to relieve the reader by a milder scene of roguery. Before I had been long on the island, one Mr. Smith at Port Morant bought goods of me to the amount of twenty-five pounds sterling; but when I demanded payment from him, he was going each time to beat me, and threatened that he would put me in gaol. One time he would say I was going to set his house on fire, at another he would swear I was going to run away with his slaves. I was astonished at this usage from a person who was in the situation of a gentleman, but I had no alternative; I was therefore obliged to submit. When I came to Kingston, I was surprised to to see the number of Africans who were assembled together on Sundays; particularly at a large commodious place, called Spring Path. Here each different nation of Africa meet and dance after the manner of their own country. They still retain most of their native customs: they bury their dead, and put victuals, pipes and tobacco, and other things, in the grave with the corps, in the same manner as in Africa. Our ship having got her loading we sailed for London, where we arrived in the August following. On my return to London, I waited on my old and good master, Dr. Irving, who made me an offer of his service again. Being now tired of the sea I gladly accepted it. I was very happy in living with this gentleman once more; during which time we were daily employed in reducing old Neptune's dominions by purifying the briny element and making it fresh. Thus I went on till May 1773, when I was roused by the sound of fame, to seek new adventures, and to find, towards the north pole, what our Creator never intended we should, a passage to India. An expedition was now fitting out to explore a north-east passage, conducted by the Honourable John Constantine Phipps, since Lord Mulgrave,[184] in his Majesty's sloop of war the Race Horse. My master being anxious for the reputation of this adventure, we therefore prepared every thing for our voyage, and I attended him on board the Race Horse, the 24th day of May 1773. We proceeded to Sheerness, where we were joined by his Majesty's sloop the Carcass, commanded by Captain Lutwidge. On the 4th of June we sailed towards our destined place, the pole; and on the 15th of the same month we were off Shetland. On this day I had a great and unexpected deliverance from an accident which was near blowing up the ship and destroying the crew, which made me ever after during the voyage uncommonly cautious. The ship was so filled that there was very little room on board for any one, which placed me in a very awkward situation. I had resolved to keep a journal of this singular and interesting voyage; and I had no other place for this purpose but a little cabin, or the doctor's store-room, where I slept. This little place was stuffed with all manner of combustibles, particularly with tow and aquafortis, and many other dangerous things. Unfortunately it happened in the evening as I was writing my journal, that I had occasion to take the candle out of the lanthorn, and a spark having touched a single thread of the tow, all the rest caught the flame, and immediately the whole was in a blaze. I saw nothing but present death before me, and expected to be the first to perish in the flames. In a moment the alarm was spread, and many people who were near ran to assist in putting out the fire. All this time I was in the very midst of the flames; my

shirt, and the handkerchief on my neck, were burnt, and I was almost smoth-
ered with the smoke. However, through God's mercy, as I was nearly giving up
all hopes, some people brought blankets and mattresses and threw them on the
flames, by which means in a short time the fire was put out. I was severely reprimanded and menaced by such of the officers who knew it, and strictly charged
never more to go there with a light: and, indeed, even my own fears made me
give heed to this command for a little time; but at last, not being able to write
my journal in any other part of the ship, I was tempted again to venture by
stealth with a light in the same cabin, though not without considerable fear and
dread on my mind. On the 20th of June we began to use Dr. Irving's apparatus
for making salt water fresh; I used to attend the distillery: I frequently purified
from twenty-six to forty gallons a day. The water thus distilled was perfectly
pure, well tasted, and free from salt; and was used on various occasions on
board the ship. On the 28th of June, being in lat. 78, we made Greenland, where
I was surprised to see the sun did not set. The weather now became extremely
cold; and as we sailed between north and east, which was our course, we saw
many very high and curious mountains of ice; and also a great number of very
large whales, which used to come close to our ship, and blow the water up to a
very great height in the air. One morning we had vast quantities of sea-horses[185]
about the ship, which neighed exactly like any other horses. We fired some har-
poon guns amongst them, in order to take some, but we could not get any. The
30th, the captain of a Greenland ship came on board, and told us of three ships
that were lost in the ice; however we still held on our course till July the 11th,
when we were stopt by one compact impenetrable body of ice. We ran along it
from east to west above ten degrees; and on the 27th we got as far north as 80,
37; and in 19 or 20 degrees east longitude from London. On the 29th and 30th
of July we saw one continued plain of smooth unbroken ice, bounded only by
the horizon; and we fastened to a piece of ice that was eight yards eleven inches
thick. We had generally sunshine, and constant daylight; which gave cheerfulness and novelty to the whole of this striking, grand, and uncommon scene; and,
to heighten it still more, the reflection of the sun from the ice gave the clouds a
most beautiful appearance. We killed many different animals at this time, and
among the rest nine bears. Though they had nothing in their paunches but water yet they were all very fat. We used to decoy them to the ship sometimes by
burning feathers or skins. I thought them coarse eating, but some of the ship's
company relished them very much. Some of our people once, in the boat, fired
at and wounded a sea-horse, which dived immediately; and, in a little time after, brought up with it a number of others. They all joined in an attack upon
the boat, and were with difficulty prevented from staving or oversetting her; but
a boat from the Carcass having come to assist ours, and joined it, they dispersed,
after having wrested an oar from one of the men. One of the ship's boats had
before been attacked in the same manner, but happily no harm was done.
Though we wounded several of these animals we never got but one. We remained hereabouts until the 1st of August; when the two ships got completely
fastened in the ice, occasioned by the loose ice that set in from the sea. This made
our situation very dreadful and alarming; so that on the 7th day we were in very

great apprehension of having the ships squeezed to pieces. The officers now held a council to know what was best for us to do in order to save our lives; and it was determined that we should endeavour to escape by dragging our boats along the ice towards the sea; which, however, was farther off than any of us thought. This determination filled us with extreme dejection, and confounded us with despair; for we had very little prospect of escaping with life. However, we sawed some of the ice about the ships to keep it from hurting them; and thus kept them in a kind of pond. We then began to drag the boats as well as we could towards the sea; but, after two or three days labour, we made very little progress; so that some of our hearts totally failed us, and I really began to give up myself for lost, when I saw our surrounding calamities. While we were at this hard labour I once fell into a pond we had made amongst some loose ice, and was very near being drowned; but providentially some people were near who gave me immediate assistance, and thereby I escaped drowning. Our deplorable condition, which kept up the constant apprehension of our perishing in the ice, brought me gradually to think of eternity in such a matter as I never had done before. I had the fears of death hourly upon me, and shuddered at the thoughts of meeting the grim king of terrors in the *natural* state I then was in, and was exceedingly doubtful of a happy eternity if I should die in it. I had no hopes of my life being prolonged for any time; for we saw that our existence could not be long on the ice after leaving the ships, which were now out of sight, and some miles from the boats. Our appearance now became truly lamentable; pale dejection seized every countenance; many, who had been before blasphemers, in this our distress began to call on the good God of heaven for his help; and in the time of our utter need he heard us, and against hope or human probability delivered us! It was the eleventh day of the ships being thus fastened, and the fourth of our drawing the boats in this manner, that the wind changed to the E. N. E. The weather immediately became mild, and the ice broke towards the sea, which was to the S. W. of us. Many of us on this got on board again, and with all our might we hove the ships into every open water we could find, and made all the sail on them in our power; and now, having a prospect of success, we made signals for the boats and the remainder of the people. This seemed to us like a reprieve from death; and happy was the man who could first get on board of any ship, or the first boat he could meet. We then proceeded in this manner till we got into the open water again, which we accomplished in about thirty hours, to our infinite joy and gladness of heart. As soon as we were out of danger we came to anchor and refitted; and on the 19th of August we sailed from this uninhabited extremity of the world, were the inhospitable climate affords neither food nor shelter, and not a tree or shrub of any kind grows amongst its barren rocks; but all is one desolate and expanded waste of ice, which even the constant beams of the sun for six months in the year cannot penetrate or dissolve. The sun now being on the decline the days shortened as we sailed to the southward; and, on the 28th, in latitude 73, it was dark by ten o'clock at night. September the 10th, in latitude 58–59, we met a very severe gale of wind and high seas, and shipped a great deal of water in the space of ten hours. This made us work exceedingly hard at all our pumps a whole day; and one sea, which struck the ship with more force than any thing I ever met with of the kind before, laid her under water for some time, so that we thought she would have gone down. Two boats were washed from the booms, and the long-boat from the chocks: all other moveable things on the deck were also washed away, among which were many curious things of different kinds which we had brought from Greenland; and we were obliged, in order to lighten the ship, to toss some of our guns overboard. We saw a ship, at the same time, in very great distress, and her masts were gone; but we were unable to assist her. We now lost sight of the Carcass till the 26th, when we saw land about Orfordness,[186] off which place she joined us. From thence we sailed for London, and on the 30th came up to Deptford. And thus ended our Arctic voyage, to the no small joy of all on board, after having been absent four months; in which time, at the imminent hazard of our lives, we explored nearly as far towards the Pole as 81 degrees north, and 20 degrees east longitude; being much farther, by all ac-counts, than any navigator had ever ventured before; in which we fully proved the impracticability of finding a passage that way to India.

## CHAP. X.

*The author leaves Doctor Irving and engages on board a Turkey ship—Account of a black man's being kidnapped on board and sent to the West Indies, and the author's fruitless endeavours to procure his freedom—Some account of the manner of the author's conversion to the faith of Jesus Christ.*

OUR voyage to the North Pole being ended, I returned to London with Doctor Irving, with whom I continued for sometime, during which I began seriously to reflect on the dangers I had escaped, particularly those of my last voyage, which made a lasting impression on my mind, and, by the grace of God, proved after-wards a mercy to me; it caused me to reflect deeply on my eternal state, and to seek the Lord with full purpose of heart ere it was too late. I rejoiced greatly; and heartily thanked the Lord for directing me to London, where I was determined to work out my own salvation, and in so doing procure a title to heaven, being the result of a mind blended by ignorance and sin.

In process of time I left my master, Doctor Irving, the purifier of waters, and lodged in Coventry-court, Haymarket, where I was continually oppressed and much concerned about the salvation of my soul, and was determined (in my own strength) to be a first-rate Christian. I used every means for this purpose; and, not being able to find any person amongst my acquaintance that agreed with me in point of religion, or, in scripture language, 'that would shew me any good;'[187] I was much dejected, and knew not where to seek relief; however, I first frequented the neighbouring churches, St. James's, and others, two or three times a day, for many weeks; still I came away dissatisfied; something was wanting that I could not obtain, and I really found more heartfelt relief in reading my bible at home than in attending the church; and, being resolved to be saved, I pursued other

methods still. First I went among the quakers, where the word of God was neither read or preached, so that I remained as much in the dark as ever. I then
searched into the Roman catholic principles, but was not in the least satisfied. At
length I had recourse to the Jews, which availed me nothing, for the fear of eternity daily harassed my mind, and I knew not where to seek shelter from the wrath
to come. However this was my conclusion, at all events, to read the four evan-
gelists, and whatever sect or party I found adhering thereto such I would join.
Thus I went on heavily without any guide to direct me the way that leadeth to
eternal life. I asked different people questions about the manner of going to
heaven, and was told different ways. Here I was much staggered, and could not
find any at that time more righteous than myself, or indeed so much inclined to
devotion. I thought we should not all be saved (this is agreeable to the holy scriptures), nor would all be damned. I found none among the circle of my acquaintance that kept wholly the ten commandments. So righteous was I in my own
eyes, that I was convinced I excelled many of them in that point, by keeping eight
out of ten; and finding those who in general termed themselves Christians not so
honest or so good in their morals as the Turks, I really thought the Turks were
in a safer way of salvation than my neighbours: so that between hopes and fears
I went on, and the chief comforts I enjoyed were in the musical French horn,
which I then practised, and also dressing of hair. Such was my situation some
months, experiencing the dishonesty of many people here. I determined at last to
set out for Turkey, and there to end my days. It was now early in the spring 1774.
I sought for a master, and found a captain John Hughes, commander of a ship
called Anglicania, sitting out in the river Thames, and bound to Smyrna in
Turkey. I shipped myself with him as a steward; at the same time I recommended
to him a very clever black man, John Annis, as a cook. This man was on board
the ship near two months doing his duty: he had formerly lived many years with
Mr. William Kirkpatrick, a gentleman of the island of St. Kitts, from whom he
parted by consent, though he afterwards tried many schemes to inveigle the poor
man. He had applied to many captains who traded to St. Kitts to trepan him; and
when all their attempts and schemes of kidnapping proved abortive, Mr. Kirkpatrick came to our ship at Union Stairs on Easter Monday, April the fourth, with
two wherry boats and six men, having learned that the man was on board; and
tied, and forcibly took him away from the ship, in the presence of the crew and
the chief mate, who had detained him after he had notice to come away. I believe
that this was a combined piece of business: but, at any rate, it certainly reflected
great disgrace on the mate and captain also, who, although they had desired the
oppressed man to stay on board, yet he did not in the least assist to recover him,
or pay me a farthing of his wages, which was about five pounds. I proved the only
friend he had, who attempted to regain him his liberty if possible, having known
the want of liberty myself. I sent as soon as I could to Gravesend, and got knowledge of the ship in which he was; but unluckily she had sailed the first tide after
he was put on board. My intention was then immediately to apprehend Mr. Kirkpatrick, who was about setting off for Scotland; and, having obtained a *habeas
corpus* for him, and got a tipstaff to go with me to St. Paul's church-yard, where
he lived, he, suspecting something of this kind, set a watch to look out. My being

known to them occasioned me to use the following deception: I whitened my face, that they might not know me, and this had its desired effect. He did not go out of his house that night, and next morning I contrived a well plotted stratagem notwithstanding he had a gentleman in his house to personate[188] him. My direction to the tipstaff, who got admittance into the house, was to conduct him to a judge, according to the writ. When he came there, his plea was, that he had not the body in custody, on which he was admitted to bail. I proceeded immediately to that philanthropist, Granville Sharp, Esq.[189] who received me with the utmost kindness, and gave me every instruction that was needful on the occasion. I left him in full hope that I should gain the unhappy man his liberty, with the warmest sense of gratitude towards Mr. Sharp for his kindness; but, alas! my attorney proved unfaithful; he took my money, lost me many months employ, and did not do the least good in the cause: and when the poor man arrived at St. Kitts, he was, according to custom, staked to the ground with four pins through a cord, two on his wrists, and two on his ancles, was cut and flogged most unmercifully, and afterwards loaded cruelly with irons about his neck. I had two very moving letters from him, while he was in this situation; and also was told of it by some very respectable families now in London, who saw him in St. Kitts, in the same state in which he remained till kind death released him out of the hands of his tyrants. During this disagreeable business I was under strong convictions of sin, and thought that my state was worse than any man's; my mind was unaccountably disturbed; I often wished for death, though at the same time convinced I was altogether unprepared for that awful summons. Suffering much by villains in the late cause, and being much concerned about a state of my soul, these things (but particularly the latter) brought me very low; so that I became a burden to myself, and viewed all things around me as emptiness and vanity, which could give no satisfaction to a troubled conscience. I was again determined to go to Turkey, and resolved, at that time, never more to return to England. I engaged as steward on board a Turkeyman (the Wester Hall, Capt. Linna); but was prevented by means of my late captain, Mr. Hughes, and others. All this appeared to be against me, and the only comfort I then experienced was, in reading the holy scriptures, where I saw that 'there is no new thing under the sun,' Eccles. i. 9; and what was appointed for me I must submit to. Thus I continued to travel in much heaviness, and frequently murmured against the Almighty, particularly in his providential dealings; and, awful to think! I began to blaspheme, and wished often to be any thing but a human being. In these severe conflicts the Lord answered me by awful 'visions of the night, when deep sleep falleth upon men, in slumberings upon the bed,' Job xxxiii. 15. He was pleased, in much mercy, to give me to see, and in some measure to understand, the great and awful scene of the judgment-day, that 'no unclean person, no unholy thing, can enter into the kingdom of God,' Eph. v. 5. I would then, if it had been possible, have changed my nature with the meanest worm on the earth; and was ready to say to the mountains and rocks 'fall on me,' Rev. vi. 16; but all in vain. I then requested the divine Creator that he would grant me a small space of time to repent of my follies and vile iniquities, which I felt were grievous. The Lord, in his manifold mercies, was pleased to grant my request, and being yet in a state of time, the sense of God's mercies was so great on my mind when I awoke, that my strength entirely failed me for many minutes, and I was exceedingly weak. This was the first spiritual mercy I ever was sensible of, and being on praying ground, as soon as I recovered a little strength, and got out of bed and dressed myself, I invoked Heaven from my inmost soul, and fervently begged that God would never again permit me to blaspheme his most holy name. The Lord, who is long-suffering and full of compassion to such rebels as we are, condescended to hear and answer. I felt that I was altogether unholy, and saw clearly what a bad use I had made of the faculties I was endowed with; they were given me to glorify God with; I thought, therefore, I had better want them here, and enter into life enternal, than abuse them and be cast into hell fire. I prayed to be directed, if there were any holier than those with whom I was acquainted, that the Lord would point them out to me. I appealed to the Searcher of hearts, whether I did not wish to love him more, and serve him better. Notwithstanding all this, the reader may easily discern, if he is a believer, that I was still in nature's darkness. At length I hated the house in which I lodged, because God's most holy name was blasphemed in it; then I saw the word of God versified, viz. 'Before they call, I will answer; and while they are yet speaking, I will hear.'

I had a great desire to read the bible the whole day at home; but not having a convenient place for retirement, I left the house in the day, rather than stay amongst the wicked ones; and that day as I was walking, it pleased God to direct me to a house where there was an old sea-faring man, who experienced much of the love of God shed abroad in his heart. He began to discourse with me; and, as I desired to love the Lord, his conversation rejoiced me greatly; and indeed I had never heard before the love of Christ to believers set forth in such a manner, and in so clear a point of view. Here I had more questions to put to the man than this time would permit him to answer; and in that memorable hour there came in a dissenting minister; he joined our discourse, and asked me some few questions; among others, where I heard the gospel preached. I knew not what he meant by hearing the gospel; I told him I had read the gospel: and he asked where I went to church, or whether I went at all or not. To which I replied, 'I attended St. James's, St. Martin's, and St. Ann's, Soho;'—'So,' said he, 'you are a churchman.' I answered, I was. He then invited me to a lovefeast at his chapel that evening. I accepted the offer, and thanked him; and soon after he went away, I had some further discourse with the old Christian, added to some profitable reading, which made me exceedingly happy. When I left him he reminded me of coming to the feast; I assured him I would be there. Thus we parted, and I weighed over the heavenly conversation that had passed between these two men, which cheered my then heavy and drooping spirit more than any thing I had met with for many months. However, I thought the time long in going to my supposed banquet. I also wished much for the company of these friendly men; their company pleased me much; and I thought the gentlemen very kind, in asking me, a stranger, to a feast; but how singular did it appear to me, to have it in a chapel! When the wished for hour came I went, and happily the old man was there, who kindly seated me, as he belonged to the place. I was much astonished to see the place filled with people, and no signs of eating and drinking. There were many ministers in the company. At last they began by giving out hymns, and between the singing the minister engaged in prayer; in short, I knew not what to make of this sight, having never seen any thing of the kind in my life before now. Some of the guests began to speak their experience, agreeable to what I read in the Scriptures; much was said by every speaker of the providence of God, and his unspeakable mercies, to each of them. This I knew in a great measure, and could most heartily join them. But when they spoke of a future state, they seemed to be altogether certain of their calling and election of God; and that no one could ever separate them from the love of Christ, or pluck them out of his hands. This filled me with utter consternation, intermingled with admiration. I was so amazed as not to know what to think of the company; my heart was attracted and my affections were enlarged. I wished to be as happy as them, and was per-suaded in my mind that they were different from the world 'that lieth in wicked-ness,' 1 John v. 19. Their language and singing, &c. did well harmonize; I was entirely overcome, and wished to live and die thus. Lastly, some persons in the place produced some neat baskets full of buns, which they distributed about; and each person communicated with his neighbour, and sipped water out of differ-ent mugs, which they handed about to all who were present. This kind of Chris-tian fellowship I had never seen, nor ever thought of seeing on earth; it fully re-minded me of what I had read in the holy scriptures, of the primitive Christians, who loved each other and broke bread. In partaking of it, even from house to house, this entertainment (which lasted about four hours) ended in singing and prayer. It was the first soul feast I ever was present at. This last twenty-four hours produced me things, spiritual and temporal, sleeping and waking, judgment and mercy, that I could not but admire the goodness of God, in directing the blind, blasphemous sinner in the path that he knew not of, even among the just; and instead of judgment he has shewed mercy, and will hear and answer the prayers and supplications of every returning prodigal:

> O! to grace how great a debtor
> Daily I'm constrain'd to be![190]

After this I was resolved to win Heaven if possible; and if I perished I thought it should be at the feet of Jesus, in praying to him for salvation. After having been an eye-witness to some of the happiness which attended those who feared God, I knew not how, with any propriety, to return to my lodgings, where the name of God was continually profaned, at which I felt the greatest horror. I paused in my mind for some time, not knowing what to do; whether to hire a bed elsewhere, or go home again. At last, fearing an evil report might arise, I went home, with a farewell to card-playing and vain jesting, &c. I saw that time was very short, eternity long, and very near, and I viewed those persons alone blessed who were found ready at midnight call, or when the Judge of all, both quick and dead, cometh.

The next day I took courage, and went to Holborn, to see my new and wor-thy acquaintance, the old man, Mr. C——; he, with his wife, a gracious woman, were at work at silk weaving; they seemed mutually happy, and both quite glad to see me, and I more so to see them. I sat down, and we conversed much about soul matters, &c. Their discourse was amazingly delightful, edifying, and pleasant I knew not at last how to leave this agreeable pair, till time summoned me away. As I was going they lent me a little book, entitled "The Conversion of an Indian."[191] It was in questions and answers. The poor man came over the sea to London, to inquire after the Christian's God, who, (through rich mercy) he found, and had not his journey in vain. The above book was of great use to me, and at that time was a means of strengthening my faith; however, in parting, they both invited me to call on them when I pleased. This delighted me, and I took care to make all the improvement from it I could; and so far I thanked God for such company and desires. I prayed that the many evils I felt within might be done away, and that I might be weaned from my former carnal acquaintances. This was quickly heard and answered, and I was soon connected with those whom the scripture calls the excellent of the earth. I heard the gospel preached, and the thoughts of my heart and actions were laid open by the preachers, and the way of salvation by Christ alone was evidently set forth. Thus I went on happily for near two months; and I once heard, during this period, a reverend gentlemen speak of a man who had departed this life in full assurance of his going to glory. I was much astonished at the assertion; and did very deliberately inquire how he could get at this knowledge. I was answered fully, agreeable to what I read in the oracles of truth; and was told also, that if I did not experience the new birth, and the pardon of my sins, through the blood of Christ, before I died, I could not enter the kingdom of heaven. I knew not what to think of this report, as I thought I kept eight commandments out of ten; then my worthy interpreter told me I did not do it, nor could I; and he added, that no man ever did or could keep the commandments, without offending in one point. I thought this sounded very strange, and puzzled me much for many weeks; for I thought it a hard saying. I then asked my friend, Mr. L——d, who was a clerk in a chapel, why the commandments of God were given, if we could not be saved by them? To which he replied, 'The law is a schoolmaster to bring us to Christ,' who alone could and did keep the commandments and fulfilled all their requirements for his elect people, even those to whom he had given a living faith, and the sins of those chosen vessels *were already* atoned for and forgiven them whilst living;[192] and if I did not experience the same before my exit, the Lord would say at that great day to me 'Go ye cursed,' &c. &c.[193] for God would appear faithful in his judgments to the wicked, as he would be faithful in shewing mercy to those who were ordained to it before the world was; therefore Christ Jesus seemed to be all in all to that man's soul. I was much wounded at this discourse, and brought into such a dilemma as I never expected. I asked him, if *he* was to die that moment, whether he was sure to enter the kingdom of God? and added, 'Do you *know* that your sins are forgiven you?' He answered in the affirmative. Then confusion, anger, and discontent seized me, and I staggered much at this sort of doctrine; it brought me to a stand, not knowing which to believe, whether salvation by works or by faith only in Christ. I requested him to tell me how I might know when my sins were forgiven me. He assured me he could not, and that none but God alone could do this. I told him it was very mysterious; but he said it was really matter of fact, and quoted many portions of scripture immediately to the point, to which I could make no reply. He then desired me to pray to God to shew me these things. I answered, that I prayed to God every day? He said, 'I perceive you are a churchman.' I answered I was. He then entreated me to beg of God to shew me what I was, and the true state of my soul. I thought the prayer very short and odd; so we parted for that time. I weighed all these things well over, and could not help thinking how it was possible for a man to know that his sins were forgiven him in this life. I wished that God would reveal this self same thing unto me. In a short time after this I went to Westminster chapel; the Rev. Mr. P—— preached, from Lam. iii. 39. It was a wonderful sermon; he clearly shewed that a living man had no cause to complain for the punishment of his sins; he evidently justified the Lord in all his dealings with the sons of men; he also shewed the justice of God in the eternal punishment of the wicked and impenitent. The discourse seemed to me like a two-edged sword cutting all ways; it afforded me much joy, intermingled with many fears, about my soul; and when it was ended, he gave it out that he intended, the ensuing week, to examine all those who meant to attend the Lord's table. Now I thought much of my good works, and at the same time was doubtful of my being a proper object to receive the sacrament; I was full of meditation till the day of examining. However, I went to the chapel, and, though much distressed, I addressed the reverend gentleman, thinking, if I was not right, he would endeavour to convince me of it. When I conversed with him, the first thing he asked me was, what I knew of Christ? I told him I believed in him, and had been baptized in his name. 'Then,' said he, 'when were you brought to the knowledge of God? and how were you convinced of sin?' I knew not what he meant by these questions; I told him I kept eight commandments out of ten; but that I sometimes swore on board ship, and sometimes when on shore, and broke the sabbath. He then asked me if I could read? I answered, 'Yes.'— 'Then,' said he, 'do you not read in the bible, he that offends in one point is guilty of all?' I said, 'Yes.' Then he assured me, that one sin unatoned for was as sufficient to damn a soul as one leak was to sink a ship. Here I was struck with awe; for the minister exhorted me much, and reminded me of the shortness of time, and the length of eternity, and that no unregenerate soul, or any thing unclean, could enter the kingdom of Heaven. He did not admit me as a communicant; but recommended me to read the scriptures, and hear the word preached, not to neglect fervent prayer to God, who has promised to hear the supplications of those who seek him in godly sincerity; so I took my leave of him, with many thanks, and resolved to follow his advice, so far as the Lord would condescend to enable me. During this time I was out of employ, nor was I likely to get a situation suitable for me, which obliged me to go once more to sea. I engaged as steward of a ship called the Hope, Capt. Richard Strange, bound from London to Cadiz in Spain. In a short time after I was on board I heard the name of God much blasphemed, and I feared greatly, lest I should catch the horrible infection. I thought if I sinned again, after having life and death set evidently before me, I should certainly go to hell. My mind was uncommonly chagrined, and I murmured much at God's providential dealings with me, and was discontented with the commandments, that I could not be saved by what I had done; I hated all things, and wished I had never been born; confusion seized me, and I wished to be annihilated. One day I was standing on the very edge of the stern of the ship, thinking to drown myself; but this scripture was instantly impressed on my mind—'that no murderer hath eternal life abiding in him,' 1 John iii. 15. Then I paused, and thought myself the unhappiest man living. Again I was convinced that the Lord was better to me than I deserved, and I was better off in the world than many. After this I began to fear death; I fretted, mourned, and prayed, till I became a burden to others, but more so to myself. At length I concluded to beg my bread on shore rather than go again to sea amongst a people who feared not God, and I entreated the captain three different times to discharge me; he would not, but each time gave me greater and greater encouragement to continue with him, and all on board shewed me very great civility: notwithstanding all this I was unwilling to embark again. At last some of my religious friends advised me, by saying it was my lawful calling, consequently it was my duty to obey, and that God was not confined to place, &c. &c. particularly Mr. G. S. the governor of Tothilfields Bridewell,[194] who pitied my case, and read the eleventh chapter of the Hebrews to me, with exhortations. He prayed for me, and I believed that he prevailed on my behalf, as my burden was then greatly removed, and I found a heartfelt resignation to the will of God. The good man gave me a pocket Bible and Allen's Alarm to the unconverted.[195] We parted, and the next day I went on board again. We sailed for Spain, and I found favour with the captain. It was the fourth of the month of September when we sailed from London; we had a delightful voyage to Cadiz, where we arrived the twenty-third of the same month. The place is strong, commands a fine prospect, and is very rich. The Spanish galloons frequent that port, and some arrived whilst we were there. I had many opportunities of reading the scriptures. I wrestled hard with God in fervent prayer, who had declared in his word that he would hear the groanings and deep sighs of the poor in spirit. I found this verified to my utter astonishment and comfort in the following manner:

On the morning of the 6th of October, (I pray you to attend) or all that day, I thought that I should either see or hear something supernatural. I had a secret impulse on my mind of something that was to take place, which drove me continually for that time to a throne of grace. It pleased God to enable me to wrestle with him, as Jacob did: I prayed that if sudden death were to happen, and I perished, it might be at Christ's feet.

In the evening of the same day, as I was reading and meditating on the fourth chapter of the Acts, twelfth verse,[196] under the solemn apprehensions of eternity, and reflecting on my past actions, I began to think I had lived a moral life, and that I had a proper ground to believe I had an interest in the divine favour; but still mediating on the subject, not knowing whether salvation was to be had partly for our own good deeds, or solely as the sovereign gift of God; in this deep consternation the Lord was pleased to break in upon my soul with his bright beams of heavenly light; and in an instant as it were, removing the veil, and letting light into a dark place, I saw clearly with the eye of faith the crucified Saviour bleeding on the cross on mount Calvary: the scriptures became an unsealed book, I saw myself a condemned criminal under the law, which came with its full force to my conscience, and when 'the commandment came sin revived, and I died.'[197] I saw the Lord Jesus Christ in his humiliation, loaded and bearing my reproach, sin, and shame. I then clearly perceived that by the deeds of the law no flesh living could be justified. I was then convinced that by the first Adam sin came, and by the second Adam (the Lord Jesus Christ) all that are saved must be made alive. It was given me at that time to know what it was to be born again, John iii. 5.[198] I saw the eighth chapter to the Romans, and the doctrines of God's decrees, verified agreeable to his eternal, everlasting, and unchangeable purposes. The word of God was sweet to my taste, yea sweeter than honey and the honeycomb.[199] Christ was revealed to my soul as the chiefest among ten thousand. These heavenly moments were really as life to the dead, and what John calls an earnest of the Spirit*. This was indeed unspeakable, and I firmly believe undeniable by many. Now every leading providential circumstance that happened to me, from the day I was taken from my parents to that hour, was then in my view, as if it had but just then occurred. I was sensible of the invisible hand of God, which guided and protected me when in truth I knew it not: still the Lord pursued me although I slighted and disregarded it; this mercy melted me down. When I considered my poor wretched state I wept, seeing what a great debtor I was to sovereign free grace. Now the Ethiopian was willing to be saved by Jesus Christ, the sinner's only surety, and also to rely on none other person or thing for salvation. Self was obnoxious, and good works he had none, for it is God that worketh in us both to will and to do. The amazing things of that hour can never be told—it was joy in the Holy Ghost! I felt an astonishing change; the burden of sin, the gaping jaws of hell, and the fears of death, that weighed me down before, now lost their horror; indeed I thought death would now be the best earthly friend I ever had. Such were my grief and joy as I believe are seldom experienced. I was bathed in tears, and said, What am I that God should thus look on me the vilest of sinners? I felt a deep concern for my mother and friends, which occasioned me to pray with fresh ardour; and, in the abyss of thought, I viewed the unconverted people of the world in a very awful state, being without God and without hope.

It pleased God to pour out on me the Spirit of prayer and the grace of supplication, so that in loud acclamations I was enabled to praise and glorify his most holy name. When I got out of the cabin, and told some of the people what the Lord had done for me, alas, who could understand me or believe my report!—None but to whom the arm of the Lord was revealed. I became a barbarian to them in talking of the love of Christ: his name was to me as ointment poured forth; indeed it was sweet to my soul, but to them a rock of offence. I thought my case singular, and every hour a day until I came to London, for I much longed to be with some to whom I could tell of the wonders of God's love towards me, and join in prayer to him whom my soul loved and thirsted after. I had uncommon commotions within, such as few can tell aught about. Now the bible was my only companion and comfort; I prized it much, with many thanks

---

*John xvi. 13, 14. &c.

to God that I could read it for myself, and was not left to be tossed about or led by man's devices and notions. The worth of a soul cannot be told.—May the Lord give the reader an understanding in this. Whenever I looked in the bible I saw things new, and many texts were immediately applied to me with great comfort, for I knew that to me was the word of salvation sent. Sure I was that the Spirit, which indited the word opened my heart to receive the truth of it as it is in Jesus—that the same Spirit enabled me to act faith upon the promises that were so precious to me, and enabled me to believe to the salvation of my soul. By free grace I was persuaded that I had a part in the first resurrection, and was 'enlightened with the light of the living,' Job xxxiii. 30. I wished for a man of God with whom I might converse: my soul was like the chariots of Aminidab, Canticles vi. 12. These, among others, were the precious promises that were so powerfully applied to me: 'All things whatsoever ye shall ask in prayer, believing, ye shall receive,' Mat. xxi. 22. 'Peace I leave with you, my peace I give unto you,' John xiv. 27. I saw the blessed Redeemer to be the fountain of life, and the well of salvation. I experienced him all in all; he had brought me by a way that I knew not, and he had made crooked paths straight. Then in his name I set up my Ebenezer, saying, Hitherto he hath helped me:[200] and could say to the sinners about me, Behold what a Saviour I have! Thus I was, by the teaching of that all-glorious Deity, the great One in Three, and Three in One, confirmed in the truths of the bible, those oracles of everlasting truth, on which every soul living must stand or fall eternally, agreeable to Acts iv. 12. 'Neither is there salvation in any other, for there is none other name under heaven given among men whereby we must be saved, but only Christ Jesus.' May God give the reader a right understanding in these facts! To him that believeth all things are possible, but to them that are unbelieving nothing is pure, Titus i. 15. During this period we remained at Cadiz until our ship got laden. We sailed about the fourth of November; and, having a good passage, we arrived in London the month following, to my comfort, with heartfelt gratitude to God for his rich and unspeakable mercies. On my return I had but one text which puzzled me, or that the devil endeavoured to buffet me with, viz. Rom. xi. 6.[201] and, as I had heard of the Reverend Mr. Romaine,[202] and his great knowledge in the scriptures, I wished much to hear him preach. One day I went to Blackfriars church, and, to my great satisfaction and surprise, he preached from that very text. He very clearly shewed the difference between human works and free election, which is according to God's sovereign will and pleasure. These glad tidings set me entirely at liberty, and I went out of the church rejoicing, seeing my spots were those of God's children. I went to Westminster Chapel, and saw some of my old friends, who were glad when they perceived the wonderful change that the Lord had wrought in me, particularly Mr. G—— S——, my worthy acquaintance, who was a man of a choice spirit, and had great zeal for the Lord's service. I enjoyed his correspondence till he died in the year 1784. I was again examined at that same chapel, and was received into church fellowship amongst them: I rejoiced in spirit, making melody in my heart to the God of all my mercies. Now my whole wish was to be dissolved, and to be with Christ—but, alas! I must wait mine appointed time.

## MISCELLANEOUS VERSES,

### OR

Reflections on the State of my mind during my first Convictions; of the Necessity of believing the Truth, and experiencing the inestimable Benefits of Christianity.

Well may I say my life has been
One scene of sorrow and of pain;
From early days I griefs have known,
And as I grew my griefs have grown:

Dangers were always in my path;
And fear of wrath, and sometimes, death;
While pale dejection in me reign'd
I often wept, by grief constrain'd.

When taken from my native land,
By an unjust and cruel band,
How did uncommon dread prevail!
My sighs no more I could conceal.

'To ease my mind I often strove,
'And tried my trouble to remove:
'I sung, and utter'd sighs between—
'Assay'd to stifle guilt with sin.

'But O! not all that I could do
'Would stop the current of my woe;
'Conviction still my vileness shew'd;
'How great my guilt—how lost from God!

'Prevented, that I could not die,
'Nor might to one kind refuge fly;
'An orphan state I had to mourn,—
'Forsook by all, and left forlorn.'

Those who beheld my downcast mien
Could not guess at my woes unseen:
They by appearance could not know
The troubles that I waded through.

'Lust, anger, blasphemy, and pride,
'With legions of such ills beside,
'Troubled my thoughts,' while doubts and fears
Clouded and darken'd most my years.

'Sighs now no more would be confin'd—
'They breath'd the trouble of my mind:
'I wish'd for death, but check'd the word
'And often pray'd unto the Lord.'

Unhappy, more than some on earth,
I thought the place that gave me birth—
Strange thoughts oppress'd—while I replied
"Why not in Ethiopia died?"

And why thus spared, nigh to hell?—
God only knew—I could not tell!
'A tott'ring fence, a bowing wall,'
'I thought myself ere since the fall.'

'Oft times I mused, nigh despair,
'While birds melodious fill'd the air:
'Thrice happy songsters, ever free,
'How bless'd were they compar'd to me!'

Thus all things added to my pain,
While grief compell'd me to complain;
When sable clouds began to rise
My mind grew darker than the skies.

The English nation call'd to leave,
How did my breast with sorrows heave!
I long'd for rest—cried "Help me, Lord!
"Some mitigation, Lord, afford!"

Yet on, dejected, still I went—
Heart-throbbing woes within were pent;
Nor land, nor sea, could comfort give,
Nothing my anxious mind relive.

Weary with travail, yet unknown
To all but God and self alone,
Numerous months for peace I strove,
And numerous foes I had to prove.

Inur'd to dangers, griefs, and woes,
Train'd up 'midst perils, deaths, and foes,
I said "Must it thus ever be?—
"No quiet is permitted me."

Hard hap, and more than heavy lot!
I pray'd to God "Forget me not—
"What thou ordain'st willing I'll bear;
"But O! deliver from despair!"

Strivings and wrestlings seem'd in vain;
Nothing I did could ease my pain:
Then gave I up my works and will,
Confess'd and own'd my doom was hell!

Like some poor pris'ner at the bar,
Conscious of guilt, of sin and fear,
Arraign'd, and self-condemned, I stood—
'Lost in the world, and in my blood!'

Yet here, 'midst blackest clouds confin'd,
A beam from Christ, the day-star, shin'd;
Surely, thought I, if Jesus please,
He can at once sign my release.

I, ignorant of his righteousness,
Set up my labours in its place;
'Forgot for why his blood was shed,
'And pray'd and fasted in its stead.'

He dy'd for sinners—I am one!
Might not his blood for me atone?
Tho' I am nothing else but sin,
Yet surely he can make me clean!

Thus light came in, and I believ'd;
Myself forgot, and help receiv'd!
My Saviour then I know I found,
For, eas'd from guilt, no more I groan'd.

O, happy hour, in which I ceas'd
To mourn, for then I found a rest!
My soul and Christ were now as one—
Thy light, O Jesus, in me shone!

Bless'd be they name, for now I know
I and my works can nothing do;
"The Lord alone can ransom man—
"For this the spotless Lamb was slain!"

When sacrifices, works, and pray'r,
Prov'd vain, and ineffectual were,
"Lo, then I come!" the Saviour cry'd,
And, bleeding, bow'd his head and dy'd!

He dy'd for all who ever saw
No help in them, nor by the law:—
I this have seen; and gladly own
"Salvation is by Christ alone*!"[203]

---

## CHAP. XI.

*The author embarks on board a ship bound for Cadiz—Is near being shipwrecked—
Goes to Malaga—Remarkable fine cathedral there—The author disputes with
a popish priest—Picking up eleven miserable men at sea in returning to England—Engages again with Doctor Irving to accompany him to Jamaica and the
Mosquito Shore—Meets with an Indian prince on board—The author attempts
to instruct him in the truths of the Gospel—Frustrated by the bad example of
some in the ship—They arrive on the Mosquito Shore with some slaves they
purchased at Jamaica, and begin to cultivate a plantation—Some account of
the manners and customs of the Mosquito Indians—Successful device of the*

---

*Acts iv. 12.

*author's to quell a riot among them—Curious entertainment given by them to*
*Doctor Irving and the author, who leaves the shore and goes for Jamaica—Is*
*barbarously treated by a man with whom he engaged for his passage—Escapes*
*and goes to the Mosquito admiral, who treats him kindly—He gets another ves-*
*sel and goes on board—Instances of bad treatment—Meets Doctor Irving—*
*Gets to Jamaica—Is cheated by his captain—Leaves the Doctor and goes for*
*England.*

When our ship was got ready for sea again, I was entreated by the captain to go in her once more; but, as I felt myself now as happy as I could wish to be in this life, I for some time refused; however, the advice of my friends at last prevailed; and, in full resignation to the will of God, I again embarked for Cadiz in March 1775. We had a very good passage, without any material accident, until we arrived off the Bay of Cadiz; when one Sunday, just as we were going into the harbour, the ship struck against a rock and knocked off a garboard plank, which is the next to the keel. In an instant all hands were in the greatest confusion, and began with loud cries to call on God to have mercy on them. Although I could not swim, and saw no way of escaping death, I felt no dread in my then situation, having no desire to live. I even rejoiced in spirit, thinking this death would be sudden glory. But the fulness of time was not yet come. The people near to me were much astonished in seeing me thus calm and resigned; but I told them of the peace of God, which through sovereign grace I enjoyed, and these words were that instant in my mind:

> "Christ is my pilot wise, my compass is his word;
> "My soul each storm defies, while I have such a Lord.
>    "I trust his faithfulness and power,
>    "To save me in the trying hour.
> "Though rocks and quicksands deep through all my passage lie,
> "Yet Christ shall safely keep and guide me with his eye.
>    "How can I sink with such a prop,
>    "That bears the world and all things up?"[204]

At this time there were many large Spanish flukers or passage-vessels full of people crossing the channel; who seeing our condition, a number of them came alongside of us. As many hands as could be employed began to work; some at our three pumps, and the rest unloading the ship as fast as possible. There being only a single rock called the Porpus on which we struck, we soon got off it, and providentially it was then high water, we therefore run the ship ashore at the nearest place to keep her from sinking. After many tides, with a great deal of care and industry, we got her repaired again. When we had dispatched our business at Cadiz, we went to Gibraltar, and from thence to Malaga, a very pleasant and rich city, where there is one of the finest cathedrals I had ever seen. It had been above fifty years in building, as I heard, though it was not then quite finished; great part of the inside, however, was completed and highly decorated with the richest marble columns and many superb paintings; it was lighted occasionally by an amazing number of wax tapers of different sizes, some of which were as thick as a man's thigh; these, however, were only used on some of their grand festivals.

I was very much shocked at the custom of bull-baiting, and other diversions which prevailed here on Sunday evenings, to the great scandal of Christianity and morals. I used to express my abhorrence of it to a priest whom I met with. I had frequent contests about religion with the reverend father, in which he took great pains to make a proselyte of me to his church; and I no less to convert him to mine. On these occasions I used to produce my Bible, and shew him in what points his church erred. He then said he had been in England, and that every person there read the Bible, which was very wrong; but I answered him that Christ desired us to search the Scriptures. In his zeal for my conversion, he solicited me to go to one of the universities in Spain, and declared that I should have my education free; and told me, if I got myself made a priest, I might in time become even pope; and that Pope Benedict was a black man. As I was ever desirous of learning, I paused for some time upon this temptation; and thought by being crafty I might catch some with guile; but I began to think that it would be only hypocrisy in me to embrace his offer, as I could not in conscience conform to the opinions of his church. I was therefore enabled to regard the word of God, which says, 'Come out from amongst them,' and refused Father Vincent's offer. So we parted without conviction on either side.

Having taken at this place some fine wines, fruits, and money, we proceeded to Cadiz, where we took about two tons more of money, &c. and then sailed for England in the month of June. When we were about the north latitude 42, we had contrary wind for several days, and the ship did not make in that time about six or seven miles straight course. This made the captain exceeding fretful and peevish: and I was very sorry to hear God's most holy name often blasphemed by him. One day, as he was in that impious mood, a young gentleman on board, who was a passenger, reproached him, and said he acted wrong; for we ought to be thankful to God for all things, as we were not in want of any thing on board; and though the wind was contrary for us, yet it was fair for some others, who, perhaps, stood in more need of it than we. I immediately seconded this young gentleman with some boldness, and said we had not the least cause to murmur, for that the Lord was better to us than we deserved, and that he had done all things well. I expected that the captain would be very angry with me for speaking, but he replied not a word. However, before that time on the following day, being the 21st of June, much to our great joy and astonishment, we saw the providential hand of our benign Creator, whose ways with his blind creatures are past finding out. The preceding night I dreamed that I saw a boat immediately off the starboard main shrouds; and exactly at half past one o'clock, the following day at noon, while I was below, just as we had dined in the cabin, the man at the helm cried out, A boat! which brought my dream that instant into my mind. I was the first man that jumped on the deck; and, looking from the shrouds onward, according to my dream, I descried a little boat at some distance; but, as the waves were high, it was as much as we could do sometimes to discern her; we however stopped the ship's way, and the boat, which was extremely small, came alongside with eleven miserable men, whom we took on board immediately. To all human appearance, these people must have perished in the course of one hour or less, the boat being small, it barely contained them. When we took them up they were half drowned, and had no victuals, compass, water, or any other necessary whatsoever, and had only one bit of an oar to steer with, and that right before the wind; so that they were obliged to trust entirely to the mercy of the waves. As soon as we got them all on board, they bowed themselves on their knees, and, with hands and voices lifted up to heaven, thanked God for their deliverance; and I trust that my prayers were not wanting amongst them at the same time. This mercy of the Lord quite melted me, and I recollected his words, which I saw thus verified in the 107th Psalm 'O give thanks unto the Lord, for he is good, for his mercy endureth for ever. Hungry and thirsty, their souls fainted in them. They cried unto Lord in their trouble, and he delivered them out of their distresses. And he led them forth by the right way, that they might go to a city of habitation. O that men would praise the Lord for his goodness and for his wonderful works to the children of men! For he satisfieth the longing soul, and filleth the hungry soul with goodness.

'Such as sit in darkness and in the shadow of death:

'Then they cried unto the Lord in their trouble, and he saved them out of their distress. They that go down to the sea in ships; that do business in great waters: these see the works of the Lord, and his wonders in the deep. Whoso is wise and will observe these things, even they shall understand the loving kindness of the Lord.'

The poor distressed captain said, 'that the Lord is good; for, seeing that I am not fit to die, he therefore gave me a space of time to repent.' I was very glad to hear this expression, and took an opportunity when convenient of talking to him on the providence of God. They told us they were Portuguese, and were in a brig loaded with corn, which shifted that morning at five o'clock, owing to which the vessel sunk that instant with two of the crew; and how these eleven got into the boat (which was lashed to the deck) not one of them could tell. We provided them with every necessary, and brought them all safe to London: and I hope the Lord gave them repentance unto life eternal.

I was happy once more amongst my friends and brethren, till November, when my old friend, the celebrated Doctor Irving, bought a remarkable fine sloop, about 150 tons. He had a mind for a new adventure in cultivating a plantation at Jamaica and the Musquito Shore;[205] asked me to go with him, and said that he would trust me with his estate in preference to any one. By the advice, therefore, of my friends, I accepted of the offer, knowing that the harvest was fully ripe in those parts, and hoped to be the instrument, under God, of bringing some poor sinner to my well beloved master, Jesus Christ. Before I embarked, I found with the Doctor four Musquito[206] Indians, who were chiefs in their own country, and were brought here by some English traders for some selfish ends. One of them was the Musquito king's son; a youth of about eighteen years of age; and whilst he was here he was baptized by the name of George. They were going back at the government's expense, after having been in England about twelve months, during which they learned to speak pretty good English. When I

came to talk to them about eight days before we sailed, I was very much mortified in finding that they had not frequented any churches since they were here,
to be baptized, nor was any attention paid to their morals. I was very sorry for
this mock Christianity, and had just an opportunity to take some of them once
to church before we sailed. We embarked in the month of November 1775, on
board of the sloop Morning Star, Captain David Miller, and sailed for Jamaica.
In our passage, I took all the pains that I could to instruct the Indian prince in
the doctrines of Christianity, of which he was entirely ignorant; and, to my great
joy, he was quite attentive, and received with gladness the truths that the Lord
enabled me to set forth to him. I taught him in the compass of eleven days all the
letters, and he could put even two or three of them together and spell them. I had
Fox's Martyrology[207] with cuts, and he used to be very fond of looking into it,
and would ask many questions about the papal cruelties he saw depicted there,
which I explained to him. I made such progress with this youth, especially in religion, that when I used to go to bed at different hours of the night, if he was in
his bed, he would get up on purpose to go to prayer with me, without any other
clothes than his shirt; and before he would eat any of his meals amongst the gentlemen in the cabin, he would first come to me to pray, as he called it. I was well
pleased at this, and took great delight in him, and used much supplication to God
for his conversion. I was in full hope of seeing daily every appearance of that
change which I could wish; not knowing the devices of satan, who had many of
his emissaries to sow his tares as fast as I sowed the good seed, and pull down as
fast as I built up. Thus we went on nearly four fifths of our passage, when satan
at last got the upper hand. Some of his messengers, seeing this poor heathen
much advanced in piety, began to ask him whether I had converted him to Christianity, laughed, and made their jest at him, for which I rebuked them as much
as I could; but this treatment caused the prince to halt between two opinions.
Some of the true sons of Belial, who did not believe that there was any hereafter,
told him never to fear the devil, for there was none existing; and if ever he came
to the prince, they desired he might be sent to them. Thus they teazed the poor
innocent youth, so that he would not learn his book any more! He would not
drink nor carouse with these ungodly actors, nor would he be with me, even at
prayers. This grieved me very much. I endeavoured to persuade him as well as I
could, but he would not come; and entreated him very much to tell me his reasons for acting thus. At last he asked me, 'How comes it that all the white men
on board who can read and write, and observe the sun, and know all things, yet
swear, lie, and get drunk, only excepting yourself?' I answered him, the reason
was, that they did not fear God; and that if any one of them died so they could
not go to, or be happy with God. He replied, that if these persons went to hell
he would go to hell too. I was sorry to hear this; and, as he sometimes had the
tooth-ach, and also some other persons in the ship at the same time, I asked him
if their toothach made his easy; he said, No. Then I told him if he and these people went to hell together, their pains would not make his any lighter. This answer had great weight with him: it depressed his spirits much; and he became
ever after, during the passage, fond of being alone. When we were in the latitude
of Martinico, and near making the land, one morning we had a brisk gale of

wind, and, carrying too much sail, the main-mast went over the side. Many people were then all about the deck, and the yards, masts, and rigging, came tumbling all about us, yet there was not one of us in the least hurt, although some were within a hair's breadth of being killed: and particularly, I saw two men then, by the providential hand of God, most miraculously preserved from being smashed to pieces. On the fifth of January we made Antigua and Montserrat, and ran along the rest of the islands; and on the fourteenth we arrived at Jamaica. One Sunday while we were there I took the Musquito Prince George to church, where he saw the sacrament administered. When we came out we saw all kinds of people, almost from the church door for the space of half a mile down to the waterside, buying and selling all kinds of commodities: and these acts afforded me great matter of exhortation to this youth, who was much astonished. Our vessel being ready to sail for the Musquito shore, I went with the Doctor on board a Guinea-man,[208] to purchase some slaves to carry with us, and cultivate a plantation; and I chose them all my own countrymen. On the twelfth of February we sailed from Jamaica, and on the eighteenth arrived at the Musquito shore, at a place called Dupeupy. All our Indian guests now, after I had admonished them and a few cases of liquor given them by the Doctor, took an affectionate leave of us, and went ashore, where they were met by the Musquito king, and we never saw one of them afterwards. We then sailed to the southward of the shore, to a place called Cape Gracias a Dios, where there was a large lagoon or lake, which received the emptying of two or three very fine large rivers, and abounded much in fish and land tortoise. Some of the native Indians came on board of us here; and we used them well, and told them we were come to dwell amongst them, which they seemed pleased at. So the Doctor and I, with some others, went with them ashore; and they took us to different places to view the land, in order to choose a place to make a plantation of. We fixed on a spot near a river's bank, in a rich soil; and, having got our necessaries out of the sloop, we began to clear away the woods, and plant different kinds of vegetables, which had a quick growth. While we were employed in this manner, our vessel went northward to Black River to trade. While she was there, a Spanish guarda costa met with and took her. This proved very hurtful, and a great embarrassment to us. However, we went on with the culture of the land. We used to make fires every night all around us, to keep off wild beasts, which, as soon as it was dark, set up a most hideous roaring. Our habitation being far up in the woods, we frequently saw different kinds of animals; but none of them ever hurt us, except poisonous snakes, the bite of which the Doctor used to cure by giving to the patient, as soon as possible, about half a tumbler of strong rum, with a good deal of Cayenne pepper in it. In this manner he cured two natives and one of his own slaves. The Indians were exceedingly fond of the Doctor, and they had good reason for it; for I believe they never had such an useful man amongst them. They came from all quarters to our dwelling; and some *woolwow*,[209] or flat-headed Indians, who lived fifty or sixty miles above our river, and this side of the South Sea, brought us a good deal of silver in exchange for our goods. The principal articles we could get from our neighbouring Indians, were turtle oil, and shells, little silk grass, and some provisions; but they would not work at any thing for us, except fishing; and a few times they assisted to cut some trees down, in order to build us houses; which they did exactly like the Africans, by the joint labour of men, women, and children. I do not recollect any of them to have had more than two wives. These always accompanied their husbands when they came to our dwelling; and then they generally carried whatever they brought to us, and always squatted down behind their husbands. Whenever we gave them any thing to eat, the men and their wives ate it separate. I never saw the least sign of incontinence amongst them. The women are ornamented with beads, and fond of painting themselves; the men also paint, even to excess, both their faces and shirts: their favorite colour is red. The women generally cultivate the ground, and the men are all fisherman and canoe makers. Upon the whole, I never met any nation that were so simple in their manners as these people, or had so little ornament in their houses. Neither had they, as I ever could learn, one word expressive of an oath. The worst word I ever heard amongst them when they were quarreling, was one that they had got from the English, which was, 'you rascal.' I never saw any mode of worship among them; but in this they were not worse than their European brethren or neighbours; for I am sorry to say that there was not one white person in our dwelling, nor any where else that I saw in different places I was at on the shore, that was better or more pious than those unenlightened Indians; but they either worked or slept on Sundays: and, to my sorrow, working was too much Sunday's employment with ourselves; so much so, that in some length of time we really did not know one day from another. This mode of living laid the foundation of my decamping at last. The natives are well made and warlike; and they particularly boast of having never been conquered by the Spaniards. They are great drinkers of strong liquors when they can get them. We used to distill rum from pine apples, where were very plentiful here; and then we could not get them away from our place. Yet they seemed to be singular, in point of honesty, above any other nation I was ever amongst. The country being hot, we lived under an open shed, where we had all kinds of goods, without a door or a lock to any one article; yet we slept in safety, and never lost any thing, or were disturbed. This surprised us a good deal; and the Doctor, myself, and others, used to say, if we were to lie in that manner in Europe we should have our throats cut the first night. The Indian governor goes once in a certain time all about the province or district, and has a number of men with him as attendants and assistants. He settles all the differences among the people, like the judge here, and is treated with very great respect. He took care to give us timely notice before he came to our habitation, by sending his stick as a token, for rum, sugar, and gunpowder, which we did not refuse sending; and at the same time we made the utmost preparation to receive his honour and his train. When he came with his tribe, and all our neighbouring chieftains, we expected to find him a grave reverend judge, solid and sagacious; but instead of that, before he and his gang came in sight, we heard them very clamorous; and they even had plundered some of our good neighbouring Indians, having intoxicated themselves with our liquor. When they arrived we did not know what to make of our new guests, and would gladly have dispensed with the honour of their company. However, having no alternative, we feasted them plentifully all the day till the evening; when the governor, getting quite drunk, grew very unruly, and struck one of our most friendly chiefs, who was our nearest neighbour, and also took his gold-laced hat from him. At this a great commotion taken place; and the Doctor interfered to make peace, as we could all understand one another, but to no purpose; and at last they became so outrageous that the Doctor, fearing he might get into trouble, left the house, and made the best of his way to the nearest wood, leaving me to do as well as I could among them. I was so enraged with the Governor, that I could have wished to have seen him tied fast to a tree and flogged for his behavior; but I had not people enough to cope with his party. I therefore thought of a stratagem to appease the riot. Recollecting a passage I had read in the life of Columbus, when he was amongst the Indians in Mexico or Peru,[210] where, on some occasion, he frightened them, by telling them of certain events in the heavens, I had recourse to the same expedient; and it succeeded beyond my most sanguine expectations. When I had formed my determination, I went in the midst of them; and, taking hold of the Governor, I pointed up to the heavens. I menaced him and the rest: I told them God lived there, and that he was angry with them, and they must not quarrel so; that they were all brothers, and if they did not leave off, and go away quietly, I would take the book (pointing to the Bible), read, and *tell* God to make them dead. This was something like magic. The clamour immediately ceased, and I gave them some rum and a few other things; after which they went away peaceably; and the Governor afterwards gave our neighbour, who was called Captain Plasmyah, his hat again. When the Doctor returned, he was exceedingly glad at my success in thus getting rid of our troublesome guests. The Musquito people within our vicinity, out of respect to the Doctor, myself and his people, made entertainments of the grand kind, called in their tongue *tourrie* or *dryckbot*. The English of this expression is, a feast of drinking about, of which it seems a corruption of language. The drink consisted of pine apples roasted, and casades[211] chewed or beaten in mortars; which, after lying some time, ferments, and becomes so strong as to intoxicate, when drank in any quantity. We had timely notice given to us of the entertainment. A white family, within five miles of us, told us how the drink was made, and I and two others went before the time to the village, where the mirth was appointed to be held; and there we saw the whole art of making the drink, and also the kind of animals that were to be eaten there. I cannot say the sight of either the drink or the meat were enticing to me. They had some thousands of pine apples roasting, which they squeezed, dirt and all, into a canoe they had there for the purpose. The casade drink was in beef barrels and other vessels, and looked exactly like hog-wash. Men, women, and children, were thus employed in roasting the pine apples, and squeezing them with their hands. For food they had many land torpins or tortoises, some dried turtle, and three large alligators alive, and tied fast to the trees. I asked the people what they were going to do with these alligators; and I was told they were to be eaten. I was much surprised at this, and went home, not a little disgusted at the preparations. When the day of the feast was come, we took some rum with us, and went to the appointed place, where we found a great assemblage of these people, who received us very kindly. The mirth had begun before we came; and they were dancing with music: and the musical instruments were nearly the same as those of any other sable people; but, as I thought, much less melodious than any other nation I ever knew. They had many curious gestures in dancing, and a variety of motions and postures of their bodies, which to me were in no wise attracting. The males danced by themselves, and the females also by themselves, as with us. The Doctor shewed his people the example, by immediately joining the women's party, though not by their choice. On perceiving the women disgusted, he joined the males. At night there were great illuminations, by setting fire to many pine trees, while the dryckbot went round merrily by calabashes or gourds: but the liquor might more justly be called eating than drinking. One Owden, the oldest father in the vicinity, was dressed in a strange and terrifying form. Around his body were skins adorned with different kinds of feathers, and he had on his head a very large and high head-piece, in the form of a grenadier's cap, with prickles like a porcupine; and he made a certain noise which resembled the cry of an alligator. Our people skipped amongst them out of complaisance, though some could not drink of their tourrie; but our rum met with customers enough, and was soon gone. The alligators were killed and some of them roasted. Their manner of roasting is by digging a hole in the earth, and filling it with wood, which they burn to coal, and then they lay sticks across, on which they set the meat. I had a raw piece of the alligator in my hand: it was very rich: I thought it looked like fresh salmon, and it had a most fragrant smell, but I could not eat any of it. This merry-making at last ended without the least discord in any person in the company, although it was made up of different nations and complexions. The rainy season came on here about the the latter end of May, which continued till August very heavily; so that the rivers were overflowed, and our provisions then in the ground were washed away. I thought this was in some measure a judgment upon us for working on Sundays, and it hurt my mind very much. I often wished to leave this place and sail for Europe; for our mode of procedure and living in this heathenish form was very irksome to me. The word of God saith, 'What does it avail a man if he gain the whole world, and lose his own soul?'[212] This was much and heavily impressed on my mind; and, though I did not know how to speak to the Doctor for my discharge, it was disagreeable for me to stay any longer. But about the middle of June I took courage enough to ask him for it. He was very unwilling at first to grant my request; but I gave him so many reasons for it, that at last he consented to my going, and gave me the following certificate of my behavior:

'The bearer, Gustavus Vassa, has served me several years with strict honesty, sobriety, and fidelity. I can, therefore, with justice recommend him for these qualifications; and indeed in every respect I consider him as an excellent servant. I do hereby certify that he always behaved well, and that he is perfectly trustworthy.

'CHARLES IRVING.'

*Musquito Shore, June 15, 1767.*

Though I was much attached to the doctor, I was happy when he consented. I got every thing ready for my departure, and hired some Indians, with a large canoe, to carry me off. All my poor countrymen, the slaves, when they heard of my leaving them, were very sorry, as I had always treated them with care and affection, and did every thing I could to comfort the poor creatures, and render their condition easy. Having taken leave of my old friends and companions, on the 18th of June, accompanied by the doctor, I left that spot of the world, and went southward about twenty miles along the river. There I found a sloop, the captain of which told me he was going to Jamaica. Having agreed for my passage with him and one of the owners, who was also on board, named Hughes, the doctor and I parted, not without shedding tears on both sides. The vessel then sailed along the river till night, when she stopped in a lagoon within the same river. During the night a schooner belonging to the same owners came in, and, as she was in want of hands, Hughes, the owner of the sloop, asked me to go in the schooner as a sailor, and said he would give me wages. I thanked him; but I said I wanted to go to Jamaica. He then immediately changed his tone, and swore, and abused me very much, and asked how I came to be freed. I told him, and said that I came into that vicinity with Dr. Irving, whom he had seen that day. This account was of no use; he still swore exceedingly at me, and cursed the master for a fool that sold me my freedom, and the doctor for another in letting me go from him. Then he desired me to go in the schooner, or else I should not go out of the sloop as a freeman. I said this was very hard, and begged to be put on shore again; but he swore that I should not. I said I had been twice amongst the Turks, yet had never seen any such usage with them, and much less could I have expected any thing of this kind amongst Christians. This incensed him exceedingly; and, with a volley of oaths and imprecations; he replied, 'Christians! Damn you, you are one of St. Paul's men;[213] but by G—, except you have St. Paul's or St. Peter's faith, and walk upon the water to the shore, you shall not go out of the vessel;' which I now found was going amongst the Spaniards towards Carthagena,[214] where he swore he would sell me. I simply asked him what right he had to sell me? but, without another word, he made some of his people tie ropes around each of my ancles, and also to each wrist, and another rope round my body, and hoisted me up without letting my feet touch or rest upon any thing. Thus I hung, without any crime committed, and without judge or jury; merely because I was a free man, and could not by the law get any redress from a white person in those parts of the world. I was in great pain from my situation, and cried and begged very hard for some mercy; but all in vain. My tyrant, in a great rage, brought a musquet out of the cabin, and loaded it before me and the crew, and swore that he would shoot me if I cried any more. I had now no alternative; I therefore remained silent, seeing not one white man on board who said a word on my behalf. I hung in that manner from between ten and eleven o'clock at night till about one in the morning; when, finding my cruel abuser fast asleep, I begged some of his slaves to slack the rope that was round my body, that my feet might rest on something. This they did at the risk of being cruelly used by their master, who beat some of them severely at first for not tying me when he commanded them. Whilst I remained in this condition, till between five and six o'clock next morning, I trust I prayed to God to forgive this blasphemer, who cared not what he did, but when he got up out of his sleep in the morning was the very same temper and disposition as when he left me at night. When they got up the anchor, and the vessel was getting under way, I once more cried and begged to be released; and now, being fortunately in the way of their hoisting the sails, they released me. When I was let down, I spoke to one Mr. Cox, a carpenter, whom I knew on board, on the impropriety of this conduct. He also knew the doctor, and the good opinion he ever had of me. This man then went to the captain, and told him not to carry me away in that manner; that I was the doctor's steward, who regarded me very highly, and would resent the usage when he should come to know it. On which he desired a young man to put me ashore in a small canoe I brought with me. This sound gladdened my heart, and I got hastily into the canoe and set off, whilst my tyrant was down in the cabin; but he soon spied me out, when I was not above thirty or forty years from the vessel, and running upon the deck with a loaded musket in his hand, he presented it to me, and swore heavily and dreadfully, that he would shoot me that instant, if I did not come back on board. As I knew the wretch would have done as he said, without hesitation, I put back to the vessel again; but, as the good Lord would have it, just as I was alongside he was abusing the captain for letting me go from the vessel; which the captain returned, and both of them soon got into a very great heat. The young man that was with me now got out of the canoe; the vessel was sailing on fast with a smooth sea: and I then thought it was neck or nothing, so at that instant I set off again, for my life, in the canoe, towards the shore; and fortunately the confusion was so great amongst them on board, that I got out of the reach of the musquet shot unnoticed, while the vessel sailed on with a fair wind a different way; so that they could not overtake me without tacking: but even before that could be done I should have been on shore, which I soon reached, with many thanks to God for this unexpected deliverance. I then went and told the other owner, who lived near that shore (with whom I had agreed for my passage) of the usage I had met with. He was very much astonished, and appeared very sorry for it. After treating me with kindness, he gave me some refreshment, and three heads of roasted Indian corn, for a voyage of about eighteen miles south, to look for another vessel. He then directed me to an Indian chief of a district, who was also the Musquito admiral, and had once been at our dwelling; after which I set off with the canoe across a large lagoon alone (for I could not get any one to assist me), though I was much jaded, and had pains in my bowels, by means of the rope I had hung by the night before. I was therefore at different times unable to manage the canoe, for the paddling was very laborious. However, a little before dark I got to my destined place, where some of the Indians knew me, and received me kindly. I asked for the admiral; and they conducted me to his dwelling. He was glad to see me, and refreshed me with such things as the place afforded; and I had a hammock to sleep in. They acted towards me more like Christians than those whites I was amongst the last night, though they had been baptized. I told the admiral I wanted to go to the next port to get a vessel to carry me to Jamaica; and requested him to send the canoe back which I then had, for which I was to pay him. He agreed with me, and sent five able Indians with a large canoe to carry my things to my intended place, about fifty miles; and we set off the next morning. When we got out of the lagoon and went along shore, the sea was so high that the canoe was oftentimes very near being filled with water. We were obliged to go ashore and drag across different necks of land; we were also two nights in the swamps, which swarmed with musquito flies, and they proved troublesome to us. This tiresome journey of land and water ended, however, on the third day, to my great joy; and I got on board of a sloop commanded by one Captain Jenning. She was then partly loaded, and he told me he was expecting daily to sail for Jamaica; and having agreed with me to work my passage, I went to work accordingly. I was not many days on board before we sailed; but to my sorrow and disappointment, though used to such tricks, we went to the southward along the Musquito shore, instead of steering for Jamaica. I was compelled to assist in cutting a great deal of mahogany wood on the shore as we coasted along it, and load the vessel with it, before she sailed. This fretted me much; but, as I did not know how to help myself among these deceivers, I thought patience was the only remedy I had left, and even that was forced. There was much hard work and little victuals on board, except by good luck we happened to catch turtles. On this coast there was also a particular kind of fish called manatee, which is most excellent eating, and the flesh is more like beef than fish; the scales are as large as a shilling, and the skin thicker than I ever saw that of any other fish. Within the brackish waters along shore there were likewise vast numbers of alligators, which made the fish scarce. I was on board this sloop sixteen days, during which, in our coasting, we came to another place, where there was a smaller sloop called the Indian Queen, commanded by one John Baker. He also was an Englishman, and had been a long time along the shore trading for turtle shells and silver, and had got a good quantity of each on board. He wanted some hands very much; and, understanding I was a free man, and wanted to go to Jamaica, he told me if he could get one or two, that he would sail immediately for that island: he also pretended to me some marks of attention and respect, and promised to give me forty-five shillings sterling a month if I would go with him. I thought this much better than cutting wood for nothing. I therefore told the other captain that I wanted to go to Jamaica in the other vessel; but he would not listen to me: and, seeing me resolved to go in a day or two, he got the vessel to sail, intending to carry me away against my will. This treatment mortified me extremely. I immediately, according to an agreement I had made with the captain of the Indian Queen, called for her boat, which was lying near us, and it came alongside; and, by the means of a north-pole shipmate which I met with in the sloop I was in, I got my things into the boat, and went on board of the Indian Queen, July the 10th. A few days after I was there, we got all things ready and sailed: but again, to my great mortification, this vessel still went to the south, nearly as far as Carthagena, trading along the coast, instead of going to Jamaica, as the captain had promised me: and, what was worst of all, he was a very cruel and bloody-minded man, and was a horrid blasphemer. Among others he had a white pilot, one Stoker, whom he beat often as severely as he did some negroes he had on board. One night in particular, after he had beaten this man most cruelly, he put him into the boat, and made two negroes row him to a desolate key, or small island; and he loaded two pistols, and swore bitterly that he would shoot the negroes if they brought Stoker on board again. There was not the least doubt but that he would do as he said, and the two poor fellows were obliged to obey the cruel mandate; but, when the captain was asleep, the two negroes took a blanket and carried it to the unfortunate Stoker, which I believe was the means of saving his life from the annoyance of insects. A great deal of entreaty was used with the captain the next day, before he would consent to let Stoker come on board; and when the poor man was brought on board he was very ill, from his situation during the night, and he remained so till he was drowned a little time after. As we sailed southward we came to many uninhabited islands, which were overgrown with fine large cocoa nuts. As I was very much in want of provisions, I brought a boat load of them on board, which lasted me and others for several weeks, and afforded us many a delicious repast in our scarcity. One day, before this, I could not help observing the providential hand of God, that ever supplies all our wants, though in the ways and manner we know not. I had been a whole day without food, and made signals for boats to come off, but in vain. I therefore earnestly prayed to God for relief in my need; and at the close of the evening I went off the deck. Just as I laid down I heard a noise on the deck; and, not knowing what it meant, I went directly on the deck again, when what should I see but a fine large fish about seven or eight pounds, which had jumped aboard! I took it, and admired, with thanks, the good hand of God; and, what I considered as not less extraordinary, the captain, who was very avaricious, did not attempt to take it from me, there being only him and I on board; for the rest were all gone ashore trading. Sometimes the people did not come off for some days: this used to fret the captain, and then he would vent his fury on me by beating me, or making me feel in other cruel ways. One day especially, in his wild, wicked, and mad career, after striking me several times with different things, and once across my mouth, even with a red burning stick out of the fire, he got a barrel of gunpowder on the deck, and swore that he would blow up the vessel. I was then at my wit's end, and earnestly prayed to God to direct me. The head was out of the barrel; and the captain took a lighted stick out of the fire to blow himself and me up, because there was a vessel then in sight coming in, which he supposed was a Spaniard, and he was afraid of falling into their hands. Seeing this I got an axe, unnoticed by him, and placed myself between him and the powder, having resolved in myself as soon as he attempted to put the fire in the barrel to chop him down that instant. I was more than an hour in this situation; during which he struck me often, still keeping the fire in his hand for this wicked purpose. I really should have thought myself justifiable in any other part of the world if I had killed him, and prayed to God, who gave me a mind which rested solely on himself. I prayed for resignation, that his will might be done; and the following two portions of his holy word, which occurred to my mind, buoyed up my hope, and kept me from taking the life of this wicked man. 'He hath determined the times before appointed, and set bounds to our habitations,' Acts xvii. 26. And, 'Who is there amongst you that feareth the Lord, that obeyeth the voice of his servant, that walketh in darkness and hath no light? let him trust in the name of the Lord, and stay upon his God,' Isaiah

l. 10. And thus by the grace of God I was enabled to do. I found him a present help in the time of need, and the captain's fury began to subside as the night approached: but I found,

> "That he who cannot stem his anger's tide
> "Doth a wild horse without a bridle ride."[215]

The next morning we discovered that the vessel which had caused such a fury in the captain was an English sloop. They soon came to an anchor where we were, and, to my no small surprise, I learned that Doctor Irving was on board of her on his way from the Musquito shore to Jamaica. I was for going immediately to see this old master and friend, but the captain would not suffer me to leave the vessel. I then informed the doctor, by letter, how I was treated, and begged that he would take me out of the sloop: but he informed me that it was not in his power, as he was a passenger himself; but he sent me some rum and sugar for my own use. I now learned that after I had left the estate which I managed for this gentleman on the Musquito shore, during which the slaves were well fed and comfortable, a white overseer had supplied my place: this man, through inhumanity and ill-judged avarice, beat and cut the poor slaves most unmercifully; and the consequence was, that every one got into a large Puriogua canoe, and endeavoured to escape; but not knowing where to go, or how to manage the canoe, they were all drowned; in consequence of which the doctor's plantation was left uncultivated, and he was now returning to Jamaica to purchase more slaves and stock it again. On the 14th of October the Indian Queen arrived at Kingston in Jamaica. When we were unloaded I demanded my wages, which amounted to eight pounds and five shillings sterling; but Captain Baker refused to give me one farthing, although it was the hardest-earned money I ever worked for in my life. I found out Doctor Irving upon this, and acquainted him of the captain's knavery. He did all he could to help me to get my money; and we went to every magistrate in Kingston (and there were nine), but they all refused to do any thing for me, and said my oath could not be admitted against a white man. Nor was this all; for Baker threatened that he would beat me severely if he could catch me for attempting to demand my money; and this he would have done, but that I got, by means of Dr. Irving, under the protection of Captain Douglas of the Squirrel man of war. I thought this exceedingly hard usage; though indeed I found it to be too much the practice there to pay free men for their labour in this manner. One day I went with a free negroe taylor, named Joe Diamond, to one Mr. Cochran, who was indebted to him some trifling sum; and the man, not being able to get his money, began to murmur. The other immediately took a horse-whip to pay him with it; but, by the help of a good pair of heels, the taylor got off. Such oppressions as these made me seek for a vessel to get off the island as fast as I could; and by the mercy of God I found a ship in November and bound for England, when I embarked with a convoy, after having taken a last farewell of Doctor Irving. When I left Jamaica he was employed in refining sugars; and some months after my arrival in England I learned, with much sorrow, that this my amiable friend was dead, owing to his having eaten some poisoned fish. We had many very heavy gales of wind in our passage; in the course of which no material incident occurred, except that an American privateer, falling in with the fleet, was captured and set fire to by his Majesty's ship the Squirrel. On January the seventh, 1777, we arrived at Plymouth. I was happy once more to tread upon English ground; and, after passing some little time at Plymouth and Exeter among some pious friends, whom I was happy to see, I went to London with a heart replete with thanks to God for all past mercies.

## CHAP. XII.

*Different transactions of the author's life till the present time—His application to the late Bishop of London to be appointed a missionary to Africa—Some account of his share in the conduct of the late expedition to Sierra Leona—Petition to the Queen—Conclusion.*

Such were the various scenes which I was a witness to, and the fortune I experienced until the year 1777. Since that period my life has been more uniform, and the incidents of it fewer, than in any other equal number of years preceding; I therefore hasten to the conclusion of a narrative, which I fear the reader may think already sufficiently tedious.

I had suffered so many impositions in my commercial transactions in different parts of the world, that I became heartily disgusted with the seafaring life, and I was determined not to return to it, at least for some time. I therefore once more engaged in service shortly after my return, and continued for the most part in this situation until 1784.

Soon after my arrival in London, I saw a remarkable circumstance relative to African complexion, which I thought so extraordinary, that I beg leave just to mention it: A white negro woman, that I had formerly seen in London and other parts, had married a white man, by whom she had three boys, and they were every one mulattoes, and yet they had fine light hair. In 1779 I served Governor Macnamara,[216] who had been a considerable time on the coast of Africa. In the time of my service, I used to ask frequently other servants to join me in family prayers; but this only excited their mockery. However, the Governor, understanding that I was of a religious turn, wished to know of what religion I was; I told him I was a protestant of the church of England, agreeable to the thirty-nine articles of that church, and that whomsoever I found to preach according to that doctrine, those I would hear. A few days after this, we had some more discourse on the same subject: the Governor spoke to me on it again, and said that he would, if I chose, as he thought I might be of service in converting my countrymen to the Gospel faith, get me sent out as a missionary to Africa. I at first refused going, and told him how I had been served on a like occasion by some white people the last voyage I went to Jamaica, when I attempted (if it were the will of God) to be the means of converting the Indian prince; and I said I supposed they would serve me worse than Alexander the coppersmith did St.

Paul,[217] if I should attempt to go amongst them in Africa. He told me not to fear, for he would apply to the Bishop of London to get me ordained. On these terms I consented to the Governor's proposal to go to Africa, in hope of doing good if possible amongst my countrymen; so, in order to have me sent out properly, we immediately wrote the following letters to the late Bishop of London:[218]

*To the Right Reverend Father in God,* ROBERT, *Lord Bishop of London:*

### The MEMORIAL of GUSTAVUS VASSA

SHEWETH,

THAT your memorialist is a native of Africa, and has a knowledge of the manners and customs of the inhabitants of that country.

That your memorialist has resided in different parts of Europe for twenty-two years last past, and embraced the Christian faith in the year 1759.

That your memorialist is desirious of returning to Africa as a missionary, if encouraged by your Lordship, in hopes of being able to prevail upon his countrymen to become Christians; and your memorialist is the more induced to undertake the same, from the success that has attended the like undertakings when encouraged by the Portuguese through their different settlements on the coast of Africa, and also by the Dutch: both governments encouraging the blacks, who, by their education were qualified to undertake the same, and are found more proper than European clergymen, unacquainted with the language and customs of the country.

Your memorialist's only motive for soliciting the office of a missionary is, that he may be a means, under God, of reforming his countrymen and persuading them to embrace the Christian religion. Therefore your memorialist humbly prays your Lordship's encouragement and support in the undertaking.

GUSTAVUS VASSA.

At Mr. Guthrie's, taylor, No. 17, Hedge-lane.

MY LORD,

I HAVE resided near seven years on the coast of Africa, for most part of the time as commanding officer. From the knowledge I have of the country and its inhabitants, I am inclined to think that the within plan will be attended with great success, if countenanced by your Lordship. I beg leave further to represent to your Lordship, that the like attempts, when encouraged by other governments, have met with uncommon success; and at this very time I know a very respectable character a black priest at Cape Coast Castle. I know the within named Gustavus Vassa, and believe him a moral good man.

I have the honour to be,
My Lord,
Your Lordship's
Humble and obedient servant.
MATT. MACNAMARA.

Grove, 11th March 1779.

This letter was also accompanied by the following from Doctor Wallace, who had resided in Africa for many years, and whose sentiments on the subject of an African mission were the same with Governor Macnamara's.

*March* 13, 1779

MY LORD,
I have resided near five years on Senegambia on the coast of Africa, and have had the honour of filling very considerable employments in that province. I do approve of the within plan, and think the undertaking very laudable and proper, and that it deserves your Lordship's protection and encouragement, in which case it must be attended with the intended success.

I am,
My Lord,
Your Lordship's
Humble and obedient servant,
THOMAS WALLACE.

With these letters, I waited on the Bishop by the Governor's desire, and presented them to his Lordship. He received me with much condescension and politeness; but, from some certain scruples of delicacy, declined to ordain me.

My sole motive for thus dwelling on this transaction, or inserting these papers, is the opinion which gentlemen of sense and education, who are acquainted with Africa, entertain of the probability of converting the inhabitants of it to the faith of Jesus Christ, if the attempt were countenanced by the legislature.

Shortly after this I left the Governor, and served a nobleman in the Devonshire militia, with whom I was encamped at Coxheath for some time; but the operations there were too minute and uninteresting to make a detail of.

In the year 1783 I visited eight counties in Wales, from motives of curiosity. While I was in that part of the country I was led to go down into a coal-pit in Shropshire, but my curiosity nearly cost me my life; for while I was in the pit the coals fell in, and buried one poor man, who was not far from me: upon this I got out as fast as I could, thinking the surface of the earth the safest part of it.

In the spring 1784 I thought of visiting old ocean again. In consequence of this I embarked as steward on board a fine new ship called the London, commanded by Martin Hopkins, and sailed for New-York. I admired this city very much; it is large and well-built, and abounds with provisions of all kinds. While we lay here a circumstance happened which I thought extremely singular:—One day a malefactor was to be executed on a gallows; but with a condition that if any woman, having nothing on but her shift, married the man under the gallows, his life was to be saved. This extraordinary privilege was claimed; a woman presented herself; and the marriage ceremony was performed. Our ship having got laden we returned to London in January 1785. When she was ready again for another voyage, the captain being an agreeable man, I sailed with him from hence in the spring, March 1785, for Philadelphia. On the fifth of April we took our departure from the Land's-end, with a pleasant gale; and about nine o'clock that night the moon shone bright, and the sea was smooth, while our ship was going free by the wind, at the rate of about four or five miles an hour. At this time another ship was going nearly as fast as we on the opposite point, meeting us right in the teeth, yet none on board observed either ship until we struck each other forcibly head and head, to the astonishment and consternation of both crews. She did us much damage, but I believe we did her more; for when we passed by each other, which we did very quickly, they called to us to bring to, and hoist out our boat, but we had enough to do to mind ourselves; and in about eight minutes we saw no more of her. We refitted as well as we could the next day, and proceeded on our voyage, and in May arrived at Philadelphia. I was very glad to see this favourite old town once more; and my pleasure was much increased in seeing the worthy quakers freeing and easing the burthens of many of my oppressed African brethren. It rejoiced my heart when one of these friendly people took me to see a free-school they had erected for every denomination of black people, whose minds are cultivated here and forwarded to virtue; and thus they are made useful members of the community. Does not the success of this practice say loudly to the planters in the language of scripture—"Go ye and do likewise?"[219]

In October 1785 I was accompanied by some of the Africans, and presented this address of thanks to the gentlemen called Friends or Quakers, in Gracechurch-Court Lombard-Street:

GENTLEMEN,

By reading your book, entitled a Caution to Great Britain and her Colonies, concerning the Calamitous State of the enslaved Negroes:[220] We the poor, oppressed, needy, and much-degraded negroes, desire to approach you with this address of thanks, with our inmost love and warmest acknowledgement; and with the deepest sense of your benevolence, unwearied labour, and kind interposition, towards breaking the yoke of slavery, and to administer a little comfort and ease to thousands and tens of thousands of very grievously afflicted, and too heavy burthened negroes.

Gentlemen, could you, by perseverance, at last be enabled, under God to lighten in any degree the heavy burthen of the afflicted, no doubt it would, in some measure, be the possible means, under God, of saving the souls of many of the oppressors; and, if so, sure we are that the God, whose eyes are ever upon all his creatures, and always rewards every true act of virtue, and regards the prayers of the oppressed, will give to you and yours those blessings which it is not in our power to express or conceive, but which we, as a part of those captivated, oppressed, and afflicted people, most earnestly wish and pray for.

These gentlemen received us very kindly, with a promise to exert themselves on behalf the oppressed Africans, and we parted.

While in town I chanced once to be invited to a quaker's wedding. The simple and yet expressive mode used at their solemnizations is worthy of note. The following is the true form of it:

After the company have met they have seasonable exhortations by several of the members; the bride and bridegroom stand up, and, taking each other by the hand in a solemn manner, the man audibly declares to this purpose:

"Friends, in the fear of the Lord, and in the presence of this assembly, whom I desire to be my witnesses, I take this my friend, M. N. to be my wife; promising, through divine assistance, to be unto her a loving and faithful husband till death separate us:" and the woman makes the like declaration. Then the two first sign their names to the record, and as many more witnesses as have a mind. I had the honour to subscribe mine to a register in Gracechurch-Court, Lombard-Street.[221]

We returned to London in August; and our ship not going immediately to sea, I shipped as a steward in an American ship called the Harmony, Captain John Willet, and left London in March 1786, bound to Philadelphia. Eleven days after sailing we carried our foremast away. We had a nine weeks passage, which caused our trip not to succeed well, the market for our goods proving bad; and, to make it worse, my commander began to play me the like tricks as others too often practice on free negroes in the West Indies. But I thank God I found my friends here, who in some measure prevented him. On my return to London in August I was very agreeably surprised to find that the benevolence of government had adopted the plan of some philanthropic individuals to send the Africans from hence to their native quarter; and that some vessels were then engaged to carry them to Sierra Leone; an act which redounded to the honour of all concerned in its promotion, and filled me with prayers and much rejoicing. There was then in the city a select committee of gentlemen for the black poor, to some of whom I had the honour of being known; and, as soon as they heard of my arrival they sent for me to the committee. When I came there they informed me of the intention of government; and as they seemed to think me qualified to superintend part of the undertaking, they asked me to go with the black poor to Africa. I pointed out to them many objections to my going; and particularly I expressed some difficulties on the account of the slave dealers, as I would certainly oppose their traffic in the human species by every means in my power. However, these objections were over-ruled by the gentlemen of the committee, who prevailed on me to go, and recommended me to the honourable Commissioners of his Majesty's Navy as a proper person to act as commissary for government in the intended expedition; and they accordingly appointed me in November 1786 to that office, and gave me sufficient power to act for the government in the capacity of commissary, having received my warrant and the following order.

*By the principal Officers and Commissioners of his Majesty's Navy.*

WHEREAS you were directed, by our warrant of the 4th of last month, to receive into your charge from Mr. Irving[222] the surplus provisions remaining of what was provided for the voyage, as well as the provisions for the support of the black poor, after the landing at Sierra Leone, with the cloathing, tools, and all other articles provided at government's expense; and as the provisions were laid in at the rate of two months for the voyage, and for four months after the landing, but the number embarked being so much less than was expected, whereby there may be a considerable surplus of provisions, cloathing, &c. These are, in addition to former orders, to direct and require you to appropriate or dispose of such surplus to the best advantage you can for the benefit of government, keeping and rendering to us a faithful account of what you do herein. And for your guidance in preventing any white persons going, who are not intended to have the indulgence of being carried thither, we send you herewith a list of those recommended by the Committee for the black poor as proper persons to be permitted to embark, and acquaint you that you are not to suffer any others to go who do not produce a certificate from the committee for the black poor, of their having their permission for it. For which this shall be your warrant. Dated at the Navy Office, January 16, 1787.

J. HINSLOW,<br>GEO. MARSH,<br>W. PALMER.

To Mr. Gustavus Vassa, Commissary of
   Provisions and Stores for the Black Poor
   going to Sierra Leone.

I proceeded immediately to the execution of my duty on board the vessels destined for the voyage, where I continued till the March following.

During my continuance in the employment of government, I was struck with the flagrant abuses committed by the agent, and endeavoured to remedy them, but without effect. One instance, among many which I could produce, may serve as a specimen. Government had ordered to be provided all necessaries (slops, as they are called, included) for 750 persons; however, not being able to muster more than 426, I was ordered to send the superfluous slops, &c. to the king's stores at Portsmouth; but, when I demanded them for that purpose from the agent, it appeared they had never been bought, though paid for by government. But that was not all, government were not the only objects of peculation; these poor people suffered infinitely more; their accommodations were most wretched; many of them wanted beds, and many more cloathing and other necessaries. For the truth of this, and much more, I do not seek credit from my own assertion. I appeal to the testimony of Capt. Thompson, of the Nautilus, who convoyed us, to whom I applied in February 1787 for a remedy, when I had remonstrated to the agent in vain, and even brought him to be a witness of the injustice and oppression I complained of. I appeal also to a letter written by these wretched people, so early as the beginning of the preceding January, and published in the Morning Herald of the 4th of that month, signed by twenty of their chiefs.

I could not silently suffer government to be thus cheated, and my countrymen plundered and oppressed, and even left destitute of the necessaries for almost their existence. I therefore informed the Commissioners of the Navy of the agent's proceeding; but my dismission was soon after procured, by means of a gentleman in the city, whom the agent, conscious of his peculation, had deceived by letter, and whom, moreover, empowered the same agent to receive on board, at the government expense, a number of persons as passengers, contrary to the orders I received. By this I suffered a considerable loss in my property: however, the commissioners were satisfied with my conduct, and wrote to Capt. Thompson, expressing their approbation of it.

Thus provided, they proceeded on their voyage; and at last, worn out by treatment, perhaps not the most mild, and wasted by sickness, brought on by want of medicine, cloaths, bedding, &c. they reached Sierra Leone just at the commencement of the rains. At that season of the year it is impossible to cultivate the lands; their provisions therefore were exhausted before they could derive any benefit from agriculture; and it is not surprising that many, especially the lascars, whose constitutions were very tender, and who had been cooped up in ships from October to June, and accommodated in the manner I have mentioned, should be so wasted by their confinement as not long to survive it.

Thus ended my part of the long-talked-of expedition to Sierra Leone; an expedition which, however unfortunate in the event, was humane and politic in its design, nor was its failure owing to government: every thing was done on their part; but there was evidently sufficient mismanagement attending the conduct and execution of it to defeat its success.

I should not have been so ample in my account of this transaction, had not the share I bore in it been made the subject of partial animadversion, and even my dismission from my employment thought worthy of being made by some a matter of public triumph*.[223] The motives which might influence any person to descend to a petty contest with an obscure African, and to seek gratification by his depression, perhaps it is not proper here to inquire into or relate, even if its detection were necessary to my vindication; but I thank Heaven it is not. I wish to stand by my own integrity, and not to shelter myself under the impropriety of another; and I trust the behaviour of the Commissioners of the Navy to me entitle me to make this assertion; for after I had been dismissed, March 24, I drew up a memorial thus:

To the Right Honourable the Lords Commissioners of his Majesty's Treasury:

The Memorial and Petition of GUSTAVUS VASSA a black Man, late Commissary to the black Poor going to AFRICA.

HUMBLY SHEWETH,
        THAT your Lordships' memorialist was, by the Honourable the Commissioners of his Majesty's navy, on the 4th of December last, appointed to the above employment by warrant from that board;

That he accordingly proceeded to the execution of his duty on board of the Vernon, being one of the ships appointed to proceed to Africa with the above poor;

That your memorialist, to his great grief and astonishment, received a letter of dismission from the Honourable Commissioners of the Navy, by your Lordships' orders;

That, conscious of having acted with the most perfect fidelity and the greatest assiduity in discharging the trust reposed in him, he is altogether at a loss to conceive the reasons of your Lordships' having altered the favourable opinion you were pleased to conceive him, sensible that your Lordships would not proceed to

*See the Public Advertiser, July 14, 1787.

so severe a measure without some apparent good cause; he therefore has every reason to believe that his conduct has been grossly misrepresented to your Lordships; and he is the more confirmed in his opinion, because, by opposing measures of others concerned in the same expedition, which tended to defeat your Lordships' humane intentions, and to put the government to a very considerable additional expense, he created a number of enemies, whose misrepresentations, he has too much reason to believe, laid the foundation of his dismission. Unsupported by friends, and unaided by the advantages of a liberal education, he can only hope for redress from the justice of his cause, in addition to the mortification of having been removed from his employment, and the advantage which he reasonably might have expected to have derived therefrom. He has had the misfortune to have sunk a considerable part of his little property in fitting himself out, and in other expenses arising out of his situation, an account of which he here annexes. Your memorialist will not trouble your Lordships with a vindication of any part of his conduct, because he knows not of what crimes he is accused; he, however, earnestly entreats that you will be pleased to direct an inquiry into his behavior during the time he acted in the public service; and, if it be found that this dismission arose from false representations, he is confident that in your Lordships' justice he shall find redress.

Your petitioner therefore humbly prays that your Lordships will take his case into consideration, and that you will be pleased to order payment of the above referred-to account, amounting to 32 l. 4 s. and also the wages intended, which is most humbly submitted.

*London, May* 12, 1787.

The above petition was delivered into the hands of their Lordships, who were kind enough, in the space of some few months afterwards, without hearing, to order me 50 l. sterling—that is, 18 l. wages for the time (upwards of four months) I acted a faithful part in their service. Certainly the sum is more than a free negro would have had in the western colonies!!!

March the 21st, 1788, I had the honour of presenting the Queen[224] with a petition of behalf of my African brethren, which was received most graciously by her Majesty*;

*To the* QUEEN's *most Excellent Majesty.*

MADAM,

YOUR Majesty's well known benevolence and humanity emboldens me to approach your royal presence, trusting that the obscurity of my situation will not prevent your Majesty from attending to the sufferings for which I plead.

Yet I do not solicit your royal pity for my own distress; my sufferings, although numerous, are in a measure forgotten. I supplicate your Majesty's compassion for millions of my African countrymen, who groan under the lash of tyranny in the West Indies.

---

*At the request of some of my most particular friends, I take the liberty of inserting it here.

The oppression and cruelty exercised to the unhappy negroes there, have at length reached the British legislature, and they are now deliberating on its redress; even several persons of property in slaves in the West Indies, have petitioned parliament against its continuance, sensible that it is as impolitic as it is unjust—and what is inhuman must ever be unwise.

Your Majesty's reign has been hitherto distinguished by private acts of benevolence and bounty; surely the more extended the misery is, the greater claim it has to your Majesty's compassion, and the greater must be your Majesty's pleasure in administering to its relief.

I presume, therefore, gracious Queen, to implore your interposition with your royal consort, in favour of the wretched Africans; that, by your Majesty's benevolent influence, a period may now be put to their misery; and that they may be raised from the condition of brutes, to which they are at present degraded, to the rights and situation of freemen, and admitted to partake of the blessings of your Majesty's happy government; so shall your Majesty enjoy the heart-felt pleasure of procuring happiness to millions, and be rewarded in the grateful prayers of themselves, and of their posterity.

And may the all-bountiful Creator shower on your Majesty, and the Royal Family, every blessing that this world can afford, and every fulness of joy which divine revelation has promised us in the next.

I am your Majesty's most dutiful and devoted servant to command,

GUSTAVUS VASSA,

The Oppressed Ethiopean.

No. 53, Baldwin's Gardens.

The negro consolidated act, made by the assembly of Jamaica last year,[225] and the new act of amendment now in agitation there, contain a proof of the existence of those charges that have been made against the planters relative to the treatment of their slaves.

I hope to have the satisfaction of seeing the renovation of liberty and justice resting on the British government, to vindicate the honour of our common nature. These are concerns which do not perhaps belong to any particular office: but, to speak more seriously to every man of sentiment, actions like these are the just and sure foundation of future fame; a reversion, though remote, is coveted by some noble minds as a substantial good. It is upon these grounds that I hope and expect the attention of gentlemen in power. These are designs consonant to the elevation of their rank, and the dignity of their stations: they are ends suitable to the nature of a free and generous government; and, connected with views of empire and dominion, suited to the benevolence and solid merit of the legislature. It is a pursuit of substantial greatness.—May the time come—at least the speculation to me is pleasing—when the sable people shall gratefully commemorate the auspicious æra of extensive freedom. Then shall those persons*[226] particularly be named with

---

*Grenville Sharp, Esq; the Reverend Thomas Clarkson; the Reverend James Ramsay; our approved friends, men of virtue, are an honour to their country, ornamental to human nature, happy in themselves, and benefactors to mankind!

praise and honour, who generously proposed and stood forth in the cause of humanity, liberty, and good policy; and brought to the ear of the legislature designs worthy of royal patronage and adoption. May Heaven make the British senators the dispersers of light, liberty, and science, to the uttermost parts of the earth: then will be glory to God on the highest, on earth peace, and good-will to men:—Glory, honour, peace, &c. to every soul of man that worketh good, to the Britons first, (because to them the Gospel is preached) and also to the nations. 'Those that honour their Maker have mercy on the poor.'[227] 'It is righteousness exalteth a nation; but sin is a reproach to any people; destruction shall be to the workers of iniquity, and the wicked shall fall by their own wickedness.'[228] May the blessings of the Lord be upon the heads of all those who commiserated the cases of the oppressed negroes, and the fear of God prolong their days; and may their expectations be filled with gladness! 'The liberal devise liberal things, and by liberal things shall stand,' Isaiah xxxii. 8. They can say with pious Job, 'Did not I weep for him that was in trouble? was not my soul grieved for the poor?' Job xxx. 25.

As the inhuman traffic of slavery is to be taken into the consideration of the British legislature, I doubt not, if a system of commerce was established in Africa, the demand for manufactures would most rapidly augment, as the native inhabitants will insensibly adopt the British fashions, manners, customs, &c. In proportion to the civilization, so will be the consumption of British manufactures.

The wear and tear of a continent, nearly twice as large as Europe, and rich in vegetable and mineral productions, is much easier conceived than calculated.

A case in point.—It cost the Aborigines of Britain little or nothing in clothing, &c. The difference between their forefathers and the present generation, in point of consumption, is literally infinite. The supposition is most obvious. It will be equally immense in Africa—The same cause, viz. civilization, will ever have the same effect.

It is trading upon safe grounds. A commercial intercourse with Africa opens an inexhaustible source of wealth to the manufacturing interests of Great Britain, and to all which the slave trade is an objection.

If I am not misinformed, the manufacturing interest is equal, if not superior, to the landed interest, as to the value, for reasons which will soon appear. The abolition of slavery, so diabolical, will give a most rapid extension of manufactures, which is totally and diametrically opposite to what some interested people assert.

The manufacturers of this country must and will, in the nature and reason of things, have a full and constant employ by supplying the African markets.

Population, the bowels and surface of Africa, abound in valuable and useful returns; the hidden treasures of centuries will be brought to light and into circulation. Industry, enterprize, and mining, will have their full scope, proportionably as they civilize. In a word, it lays open an endless field of commerce to the British manufactures and merchant adventurer. The manufacturing interest and the general interests are synonymous. The abolition of slavery would be in reality an universal good.

Tortures, murder, and every other imaginable barbarity and iniquity, are

practised upon the poor slaves with impunity. I hope the slave trade will be abolished. I pray it may be an event at hand. The great body of manufacturers, uniting in the cause, will considerably facilitate and expedite it; and, as I have already
stated, it is most substantially their interest and advantage, and as such the nation's at large, (except those persons concerned in the manufacturing neck-yokes,
collars, chains, hand-cuffs, leg-bolts, drags,[229] thumbscrews, iron muzzles, and
coffins; cats,[230] scourges, and other instruments of torture used in the slave trade).
In a short time one sentiment alone will prevail, from motives of interest as well
as justice and humanity. Europe contains one hundred and twenty millions of inhabitants. Query—How many millions doth Africa contain? Supposing the
Africans, collectively and individually, to expend 5 l. a head in raiment and furniture yearly when civilized, &c. an immensity beyond the reach of imagination!

I this I conceive to be a theory founded upon facts, and therefore an infallible one. If the blacks were permitted to remain in their own country, they would
double themselves every fifteen years. In proportion of such increase will be the
demand for manufactures. Cotton and indigo grow spontaneously in most parts
of the Africa; a consideration this of no small consequence to the manufacturing
towns of Great Britain. It opens a most immense, glorious, and happy prospect—
the clothing, &c. of a continent ten thousand miles in circumference, and immensely rich in production of every denomination in return for manufactures.

I have only therefore to request the reader's indulgence and conclude. I am
far from the vanity of thinking there is any merit in this narrative: I hope censure
will be suspended, when it is considered that it was written by one who was as
unwilling as unable to adorn the plainness of truth by the colouring of imagination. My life and fortune have been extremely chequered, and my adventures various. Even those I have related are considerably abridged. If any incident in this
little work should appear uninteresting and trifling to most readers, I can only
say, as my excuse for mentioning it, that almost every event of my life made an
impression on my mind and influenced my conduct. I early accustomed myself
to look for the hand of God in the minutest occurrence, and to learn from it a
lesson of morality and religion; and in this light every circumstance I have related
was to me of importance. After all, what makes any event important, unless by
its observation we become better and wiser, and learn 'to do justly, to love mercy,
and to walk humbly before God?'[231] To those who are possessed of this spirit,
there is scarcely any book or incident so trifling that does not afford some profit,
while to others the experience of ages seems of no use; and even to pour out to
them the treasures of wisdom is throwing the jewels of instruction away.


THE END.



1. Gates, *Classic Slave Narratives,* xiv.
2. Andrews, *Free Story,* 56.

3. Loggins, *Negro Author,* 46.

4. Carretta, *Interesting Narrative,* xxv. (I am greatly indebted to this source for a good number of the annotations below, particularly the attributions of the poetic citations.)

5. Carretta, *Interesting Narrative,* xiii–xiv.

6. Ibid., xxv–xxvii.

7. Potkay and Burr, *Black Atlantic Writers,* 162–164; Edwards, *Olaudah Equiano,* I:vii–x; Carretta, *Interesting Narrative,* xxix, 345.

8. Costanzo, *Surprizing Narrative,* 50, 125–126.

9. Andrews, *Free Story,* 60.

10. Gates, *Classic Slave Narratives,* xiv.

11. Carretta, *Interesting Narrative,* 345.

12. Edwards, *Olaudah Equiano,* I:lxxi–lxxii.

13. Edwards, "West African Writers," 187–188.

14. The Lords Spiritual refers to the bishops who are peers of the realm; the Lords Temporal to the lay peers. Together they constitute the House of Lords.

15. These were people who had promised in advance to buy the book upon its publication. Annotated below are the most prominent of those subscribers whose identification is relatively certain.

16. George, Prince of Wales (later King George IV; 1762–1830) was a whig partisan and an extravagant drunkard and gambler who squandered fortunes and went deeply into debt. He became regent in 1788, when his father, George III, went mad; upon the King's recovery the following year, the two were almost entirely estranged.

17. Frederick Augustus, Duke of York (1763–1827) was the second son of King George III. He was popular not only with his father and older brother, but with the British people. He spent most of his life in the military, and served for eleven years as commander-in-chief of the British army.

18. James Adair (?–1798) was recorder of London and king's serjeant-at-law.

19. William Aldridge (1737–97) was a nonconformist minister who was for many years in Countess Huntingdon's service.

20. John Almon (1737–1805) was a journalist, bookseller, editor, and political writer best known for his close friendship with the agitator, journalist, and mayor of London, John Wilkes.

21. Samuel Atkins (?–1808) was a marine painter of some note.

22. Thomas Atwood (?–1793) was chief judge of the island of Dominica and afterward of the Bahamas; he was the author of *Observations on the True Method of Treatment and Usage of the Negro Slaves in the British West India Islands* (1790).

23. Francis Russell, Duke of Bedford (1765–1802) was a whig peer and friend of the Prince of Wales.

24. John Warren (1730–1800) was nominated Bishop of St. David's in 1779 and elected Bishop of Bangor in 1783, a post he held until his death. He was highly respected for his business acumen and integrity.

25. Matthew Baillie (1761–1823) was at the time physician to St. George's Hospital in London and became in 1789 a fellow of the College of Physicians. In 1795 he would publish the first English-language morbid anatomy, and would make many important medical discoveries.

26. Probably Joanna Baillie (1762–1851), who would soon become an important dramatist and poet.

27. Thomas Bellamy (1745–1800) was a writer of miscellaneous pieces and editor of two short-lived magazines.

28. Bart. is an abbreviation for *baronet.*

29. Sir William Schaw, Baron Cathcart (1755–1843) commanded the British legion during the siege of Charleston in 1780; at the time of the book's publication, he was a Scottish M.P.

30. Henry Seymour Conway (1721–95) was secretary of state, leader of the House of Commons, and field-marshal. A close friend of Horace Walpole, he was an immensely well-liked man, esteemed for his integrity, looks, and graciousness. He was one of the most influential British speakers on behalf of American independence and was instrumental in having it granted.

31. Thomas Clarkson (1760–1846) was perhaps the most effective antislavery agitator of his day. He distributed tracts and tirelessly investigated the facts of the slave trade; by 1789 he had published three antislavery works.

32. Richard Cosway (1740–1821) painted miniature portraits of London high society and was principal painter to the Prince of Wales.

33. Ottobah Cugoano (c. 1757–?) was an African ex-slave who worked for some time as a servant of Richard Cosway, and wrote *Thoughts and Sentiments on the Evil and Wicked Traffic of the Slavery and Commerce of the Human Species* (1787). Potkay and Burr, *Black Atlantic Writers*, 126–127.

34. William Legge, Earl of Dartmouth (1731–1801) was lord privy seal from 1775 to 1782. A pious man, he was intimate with both George III and Countess Huntingdon; owing to his Methodism, he was known as "The Psalm-Singer." Dartmouth College in New Hampshire was named in his honor.

35. Charles Edward de Coetlogon (c. 1746–1820) was a popular Calvinist preacher, writer, and editor of *The Theological Miscellany*.

36. Charles Dilly (1739–1807) was an important publisher, bookseller, and host to the London literati.

37. Sir Gilbert Elliott (1751–1814) was a lawyer and whig M.P. He later governed first Corsica, then India.

38. John Eyre (1754–1803) was a minister under the Countess of Huntingdon's patronage, and founded and edited the *Evangelical Magazine*.

39. John Fell (1735–97) was a minister, classical tutor, and author of a number of essays and lectures.

40. Richard Grosvenor, Earl of Grosvenor (1731–1802) was mayor of Chester, grand cupbearer at the coronation of George III, and the greatest racehorse breeder of his day.

41. Probably Daniel Gardner (c. 1750–1805), a fashionable portrait painter.

42. James Hope (1741–1816) was one of the largest landowners in Scotland.

43. Selina Hastings, Countess of Huntingdon (1707–91), was one of the most important Methodist leaders of her day. She was close to John and Charles Wesley and George Whitefield, the founders of Methodism, and when they split took the part of Whitefield. The patron and protector of dozens of prominent clergymen, she was largely responsible for introducing Methodism to the upper classes. In addition, she was the patron of many black writers, including James Albert Ukawsaw Gronniosaw, Phillis Wheatley, John Marrant, and Equiano.

44. Sir Richard Hill (1732–1808) was a champion of Calvinist Methodism, a member of parliament, and a polemical writer.

45. Rowland Hill (1744–1833) was a controversial and popular preacher.

46. William Hodges (1744–97) was a painter of exotic landscapes.

47. Probably John Jackson (?–1792), an actor and dramatist whose most famous roles included that of Oroonoko, the slave.

48. Probably Edward King (c. 1735–1807), who wrote widely and eccentrically on political, religious, and archeological subjects.

49. Andrew Kippis (1725–95) was the nonconformist pastor of a church in Westminster for forty-three years. He was largely responsible for the second edition of the *Biographia Brittanica,* of which the first five volumes, covering *A–Fastolf,* appeared in 1778 through 1793. He also wrote several other biographies.

50. Probably John Knight (1748–1831), an admiral who fought in the American Revolution and, in 1780–82, the West Indies.

51. Beilby Porteus (1731–1808) was in turn chaplain to King George III, bishop of Chester, and bishop of London. He was deeply interested in the welfare of slaves, and helped form the Society for the Conversion and Religious Instruction of the Negroes in the West Indies.

52. James Lackington (1746–1815) was a major London bookseller who sold about one hundred thousand volumes a year.

53. Bennett Langton (1737–1801) was a close friend of Samuel Johnson.

54. Charles Lloyd (1748–1828) was a Quaker philanthropist who helped pioneer the movement to emancipate West Indian slaves.

55. George Spencer, Duke of Marlborough (1739–1817) was appointed lord chamberlain in 1762, was lord privy seal from 1763 to 1765, and was later high steward of Oxford and Woodstock.

56. George Brudenell, Duke of Montagu (1712–90) was the governor of the young Prince of Wales and Duke of York, governor of Windsor Castle, a privy councillor, lord-lieutenant of Huntingdon, and president of both the London Hospital and the Society of Arts.

57. Constantine John Phipps, Baron Mulgrave (1744–92) served in the navy in the West Indies during the Seven Years' War, was elected to the House of Commons, and attempted— with Equiano on board—to find a northern passage to India via the North Pole in 1773. He published *A Voyage towards the North Pole* in 1774; it served as a valuable resource for Equiano in the writing of his autobiography (see Chapter IX).

58. Probably Thomas Mitchell (?–1790), a marine painter, shipwright, and surveyor.

59. Probably Elizabeth Montagu (1720–1800), a wealthy writer who played the supreme hostess for London's intellectual society: her guests included Horace Walpole, Samuel Johnson, Edmund Burke, David Garrick, Joshua Reynolds, Samuel Richardson, William Cowper, and King George III.

60. Hannah More (1745–1833) wrote poems, plays, and philosophical and religious essays. While in her early years she had been intimate with Samuel Johnson, David Garrick, and Elizabeth Montagu, by the 1780s she had become more involved with religious society; she was close to William Wilberforce, who was beginning to protest the slave trade. Her 1788 poem "Slavery" was one of many well-received and popular polemical writings.

61. Thomas Morris (c. 1750–1800) was a landscape engraver.

62. Maurice Morgann (1726–1802) was an intellectual figure who wrote pamphlets on many of the important issues of the day, including *Remarks on the Slave Trade*. He is best remembered for his 1777 *Essay on the Dramatic Character of Sir John Falstaff*.

63. Hugh Percy, Duke of Northumberland (1742–1817) fought in the Seven Years' War and the American Revolution, in which he became a general. He was a friend of the Prince of Wales.

64. George Pitt, Baron Rivers (c. 1722–1803) served in the House of Commons for over thirty years, and, after being created Baron Rivers, in the House of Lords another twenty-five. He was a great favorite of Lady Montagu.

65. James Ramsay (1733–89) was a pastor in the West Indies, where he began a scheme for the religious instruction of the slaves; opposition from slaveowners forced him to return to England. The 1784 publication of his first abolitionist tract, *An Essay on the Treatment and Conversion of African Slaves in the British Sugar Colonies,* was a signal event that helped to augment antislavery forces in England; he subsequently wrote several other works on the subject.

66. George Rose (1744–1818) fought in the West Indies during the Seven Years' War, and was later secretary to the treasury and a member of parliament. He was an intimate friend of the Duke of Northumberland and William Pitt.

67. Samuel Harsley, Bishop of St. David's (1733–1806), was an important intellectual and religious figure; his accomplishments included an edition of the works of Sir Isaac Newton, an influential antirevolutionary sermon, and a 1774 letter to Commodore Phipps entitled "Remarks on the Observations Made in the Late Voyage towards the North Pole."

68. Charles Stanhope, Earl Stanhope (1753–1816) was an M.P. in the House of Commons from 1780 until his accession to the peerage in 1786. An opponent of the slave trade and a close friend of William Pitt, he became infamous for his support of the American and, later, the French revolutions. He was also an important scientist and inventor.

69. Ignatius Sancho (1729–80) was a personal servant to the Duke of Montagu, and a black writer whose *Letters* were published posthumously in 1782 to considerable popularity.

70. Thomas Seddon (1753–96) was a curate and political writer.

71. Probably William Seward (1747–99), who wrote, among other things, Samuel Johnson's epitaph and five volumes of anecdotes. He was popular in intellectual society.

72. Thomas Scott (1747–1821), a priest, wrote a remarkable spiritual autobiography entitled *The Force of Truth* (1779), as well as an important commentary on the Bible.

73. Granville Sharp (1735–1813) was a pioneer in antislavery activism, and was primarily

responsible for the 1772 decision by which the British courts declared "that as soon as a slave sets his foot upon English territory, he becomes free." He supported the Americans during the revolution, argued against the impressment of seamen, published a score of antislavery tracts, and originated the idea of establishing a colony of free blacks in Sierra Leone.

74. Sir William Sidney Smith (1764–1840) fought in the American Revolution and, in 1782, in the West Indies. Much later he became a hero of the Napoleonic wars.

75. John Graves Simcoe (1752–1806) fought in the American Revolution; he later became the first governor of Upper Canada.

76. George Smith (?–1784) managed a jail called Tothill-Fields; he was praised by prison reformers for his exertions to civilize the prisoners. Carretta, *Interesting Narrative,* 289.

77. Probably William Smith (1756–1835), a member of the House of Commons and an opponent of the slave trade.

78. Richard Southgate (1729–95) was curate of St.-Giles-in-the-Fields in London from 1765 to 1795.

79. Henry Thornton (1760–1815) was a vocal opponent of the slave trade in the House of Commons, took a leading part in the foundation of the colony at Sierra Leone, and was founder and chairman of the Sierra Leone Company. He was renowned for his integrity, generosity, and calm.

80. Christian Ignatius Latrobe (1758–1836) was secretary to the Society for the Furtherance of the Gospel, and a composer of religious and secular music.

81. Sir John Vaughan (c. 1748–1795) was a lieutenant-colonel in the West Indies during the Seven Years' War and distinguished himself at the capture of Martinique. He fought in the American Revolution, and was commander-in-chief of the Leeward Islands for several years.

82. Richard Hurd, Bishop of Worcester (1720–1808), wrote numerous works, most significantly a series of *Moral and Political Dialogues,* and *Letters on Chivalry and Romance.* He was appointed Bishop of Lichfield and Coventry in 1774, preceptor to the Prince of Wales and the Duke of York in 1776, and Bishop of Worcester in 1781.

83. William Windham (1750–1810) started, with Equiano, on Commodore Phipps's voyage to the North Pole in 1773, but was compelled by seasickness to land in Norway. A close friend of Samuel Johnson and Edmund Burke, he was rich, eloquent, and a brilliant social success. He opposed the American war, and was elected to parliament in 1784; he much later became secretary at war.

84. Josiah Wedgwood (1730–95) was an innovator who is considered the father of modern pottery. Both his useful and ornamental ware was popular throughout Europe.

85. John Wesley (1703–91) was the founder and leader of Methodism. His commitment to missionary work gained him worldwide fame; his practical and religious writings fill thirty-two volumes. He was the first high-ranking religious leader to oppose slavery, and he read Equiano's narrative with evident delight.

86. Probably Joseph Wright (1734–97), a painter of portraits, sentimental and mythical scenes, and landscapes.

87. The equator.

88. Ethiopia.

89. These last three sentences, like other portions of this chapter, are more or less lifted from Anthony Benezet (1713–84), *Some Historical Account of Guinea, its Situation, Produce, and the General Disposition of its Inhabitants* (1788). Costanzo, *Surprizing Narrative,* 55.

90. Ibo.

91. Paul Edwards, relying on the assistance of Chinua Achebe, convincingly argues that Equiano was born east of the modern Nigerian city of Onitsha. See Edwards, *Olaudah Equiano,* I:v, xviii–xxv. According to Nigerian scholar Catherine Obianuju Acholonu, his birthplace is the village of Isseke, in Igboland, in the modern Anambra State, Nigeria (Potkay and Burr, *Black Atlantic Writers,* 159). However, Acholonu's scholarship has been questioned.

92. Equiano's footnote refers to the work cited in note 89 above.

93. A kind of xylophone.

94. An African edible tuberous plant. Edwards, *Olaudah Equiano,* I:lxxiii; Carretta, *Interesting Narrative,* 242.

95. Subsequent editions read, "by pouring out a small portion of the drink, and tossing a small quantity of the food . . ."

96. Ensnare.

97. Equiano's footnote refers to Benezet's *A Short Account of that Part of Africa, Inhabited by the Negroes* (1762).

98. According to Acholonu, his real name was Adipuoerie Olaude Ekwealuo. Potkay and Burr, *Black Atlantic Writers,* 159.

99. Equiano's footnote refers to John Matthews, *A Voyage to the River Sierra-Leone, on the Coast of Africa* (1788).

100. John Gill (1697–1771), *An Exposition of the Old Testament, in Which are Recorded the Original of Mankind, of the Several Nations of the World, and of the Jewish Nation in Particular* (1788).

101. John Clarke (1682–1757) translated *The Truth of the Christian Religion* by Hugo Grotius (1583–1645).

102. Arthur Bedford (1668–1745), *The Scripture Chronology Demonstrated by Astronomical Calculations, and Also by the Year of Jubilee, and the Sabbatical Year among the Jews; or, An Account of Time from the Creation of the World to the Destruction of Jerusalem; as it May be Proved from the Writings of the Old and New Testament* (1730).

103. Thomas Clarkson (1760–1846), *An Essay on the Slavery and Commerce of the Human Species, Particularly the African* (1786). Clarkson was on Equiano's subscription list, above.

104. John Mitchel wrote a paper called "Causes of the Different Colours of Persons in Different Climates," which was published in *Philosophical Transactions.* Carretta, *Interesting Narrative,* 246–247.

105. See *Isaiah* 55:8.

106. Adapted from Sir John Denham (1615–69), *Cooper's Hill* (1642).

107. Pumpkins.

108. People employed in manual occupations.

109. A large cooking pot.

110. These were placed along the sides of slave ships to prevent slaves from jumping overboard. Carretta, *Interesting Narrative,* 250.

111. Small sailing vessel, often employed as a warship.

112. Gustavus Vasa was King Gustavus I of Sweden (1496–1560), who led an uprising against the tyrannical Danish king, Christian II, and went on to found the modern Swedish state.

113. The only time Equiano ever used the name Olaudah Equiano in his public life subsequent to this was on the title page of his narrative; in all his other writings he called himself Gustavus Vassa. Carretta, *Interesting Narrative,* 252.

114. A port town in Cornwall, about forty-five miles from Plymouth.

115. An anchorage in the Thames estuary.

116. John Byng (1704–57) tried unsuccessfully to defend Minorca from the French in 1755; after the defeat of his fleet he was court-martialled and sentenced to death. His 1757 execution was widely denounced as "a judicial murder."

117. The site of London's royal dockyard.

118. Identified in later editions as the Duke of Cumberland, William Augustus (1721–65), who had just resigned from the army after a humiliating defeat. Carretta, *Interesting Narrative,* 258.

119. The east part of the English Channel, between Hampshire and the Isle of Wight.

120. Waiting.

121. Edward Boscawen (1711–61) defeated the French off Cape Finisterre in 1747, captured two French ships off Newfoundland in 1755, and in 1758 captured Louisbourg, a fort on Cape Breton Island off the coast of Nova Scotia, which guarded the mouth of the St. Lawrence River.

122. The square flag of the Blue Squadron, one of the three divisions of the English fleet.

123. Sir Samuel Cornish (?–1770) was sent to the East Indies in February 1759 to reinforce Vice Admiral Pocock. Later, in 1762, he captured the Philippines from Spain.

124. A conical pile of refined sugar.

125. James Wolfe (1727–59) was largely responsible for the 1758 capture of Louisbourg; he later commanded the British Army at the 1759 capture of Quebec.

126. Changed course.

127. Gave chase to.

128. A ship belonging to the British East India Company.

129. Lower their colors to signal surrender.

130. A town on the east coast of the Isle of Wight.

131. Pumping water out of the ship.

132. Thomas Wilson, Bishop of Sodor and Man (1663–1755), *An Essay towards an Instruction for the Indians; Explaining the Most Essential Doctrines of Christianity* (1740).

133. Base of operations.

134. The eastern part of the Mediterranean.

135. Adapted from Alexander Pope's translation of Homer's *Iliad*.

136. Jean-François de Bertet, Marquis de la Clue (c. 1703–59), was an eminent French admiral.

137. King George II died on October 25, 1760.

138. George Keppel, Earl of Albemarle (1724–72), commanded ten thousand troops in Admiral Pocock's fleet.

139. An island off the coast of Brittany.

140. John Milton (1608–74), *Paradise Lost*.

141. The Basque Road, an anchorage between the Ile de Ré and the Ile d'Orleans, both in the Bay of Biscay in western France.

142. Britain declared war on Spain, France's ally in the Seven Years' War, on January 4, 1762.

143. In northern Spain, on the Bay of Biscay.

144. A ship whose purpose is the exchange of prisoners or the carrying of proposals between enemy forces.

145. Also in September, Equiano was promoted from the status of a servant to that of able-bodied seaman, thus complicating his relationship with his master. Carretta, *Interesting Narrative*, 267.

146. A method of finding a fourth number given three numbers, of which the first is in the same proportion to the second as the third is to the fourth.

147. A small sword used by seamen.

148. Although it was popularly believed that a baptized slave was by law freed upon landing on English soil, Equiano was mistaken; only after 1772 was this the case.

149. By Thomas Day (1748–89) and John Bicknell.

150. Adapted from Milton, *Paradise Lost*.

151. West Indian coasting vessels.

152. A jail for debtors and criminals.

153. The American Revolution.

154. Philip Gibbes (1731–1815), *Instructions for the Treatment of Negroes* (1786).

155. Adapted from Milton, *Paradise Lost*.

156. Charleston, South Carolina.

157. Probably asparagus ("sparrow-grass").

158. An island of the Dutch West Indies.

159. Samoyed.

160. Author of *Cursory Remarks upon the Reverend Mr. Ramsay's Essay on the Treatment and Conversion of African Slaves in the Sugar Colonies* (1785), a proslavery tract. Edwards, *Olaudah Equiano*, I:lxxvii.

161. Moses slew an Egyptian who had been smiting a fellow Hebrew. See *Exodus* 2:11–12.

162. Adapted from Milton, *Paradise Lost*.

163. A spirit distilled from grain and flavored with juniper berries. The word *gin* is derived from *geneva*.

164. Saint Croix, now part of the U.S. Virgin Islands.

165. These verses may well have been written by Equiano himself.

166. Corrected in later editions to *mettle*.

167. The Stamp Act (1765) taxed all commercial and legal papers, newspapers, pamphlets, cards, almanacs, and dice. American colonists refused to pay the tax and rioted against the Act, which was repealed in 1766. (This conflicts with other dates given in this chapter.)

168. George Whitefield (1714–70) was an evangelist and the leader of the Calvinistic Methodist Church. An extraordinarily popular preacher, he gave open-air sermons throughout England and the American colonies, was an influential figure in the Great Awakening, and kept a house in Savannah, where he had established a home for orphans. Whitefield broke with John and Charles Wesley in 1741, which resulted in the establishment of two branches of Methodism. Although he welcomed blacks into Methodism, in 1747 he bought a plantation and slaves in South Carolina, and defended slavery on biblical grounds.

169. An Indian name for Savannah. Potkay and Burr, *Black Atlantic Writers*, 264.

170. In later editions Equiano adds, "and I was offered, by a gentleman of the place, the command of his sloop to go amongst the islands, but I refused."

171. An island of the Bahamas.

172. A small ship built in Gravesend, a British shipbuilding city.

173. Fiddles.

174. The Grenadines.

175. A landing place on the south bank of the Thames.

176. The French horn has three distinct ranges; to master all three is quite difficult.

177. *Barter* is the computation of the quantity or value of one commodity to be exchanged for a known quantity and value of another; *alligation* is the method of solving questions concerning the mixing of articles of different qualities or values.

178. A town in northern Spain, near Tudela.

179. Livorno, Italy.

180. The islands of the Aegean Sea.

181. Roman Catholics at this time held that the Bible should be transmitted to laypeople only through the mediation of the Church; hence the importation of Bibles, especially Protestant ones, was illegal.

182. Stangate Stairs is a landing bank on the south side of the Thames in London.

183. McIntosh was also on Equiano's subscription list, above.

184. See note 57 above.

185. Walrus.

186. A promontory on the North Sea, in Suffolk.

187. See *Psalms* 4:6.

188. Impersonate.

189. See note 73 above.

190. Robert Robinson (1735–90), "Come Thou Fount of Every Blessing" (a Methodist hymn).

191. Lawrence Harlow, *The Conversion of an Indian, in a Letter to a Friend* (1774).

192. See *Romans* 8:1–3.

193. See *Matthew* 25:41.

194. See note 76 above.

195. Joseph Alleine (1634–68), *An Allarme to Unconverted Sinners* (1673).

196. "Neither is there salvation in any other: for there is none other name under heaven given among men, whereby we must be saved."

197. *Romans* 7:9.

198. "Jesus answered, 'Verily, verily, I say unto thee, Except a man be born of water and of the Spirit, he cannot enter into the kingdom of God.'"

199. *Psalms* 19:9–10.

200. When the Israelites defeated the Philistines near Mizpah, the prophet Samuel set up a stone there, and called it Eben-ezer, saying, "Hitherto hath the Lord helped us." See *I Samuel* 7:12.

201. "And if by grace, then is it no more of works: otherwise grace is no more grace. But if it be of works, then is it no more grace, otherwise work is no more work."

202. William Romaine (1714–95) was a follower of George Whitefield and the ablest exponent of Calvinist Methodist doctrine. He was persecuted for his popular preaching, and was one of Lady Huntingdon's chaplains. From 1766 on, he preached at Blackfriars, St. Anne's.

203. Of course, the author of these verses is Equiano himself.

204. From a Methodist hymn.

205. A vast, undeveloped stretch of the Caribbean coast stretching from 11° to 16° N (currently shared by Honduras and Nicaragua).

206. Miskito.

207. John Fox (1517–87), *The Acts and Monuments of the Church, or Book of Martyrs.*

208. A slave ship.

209. Ulua.

210. Actually in Jamaica. Equiano corrected this in the ninth edition. Carretta, *Interesting Narrative,* 293.

211. Cassava.

212. *Matthew* 16:26.

213. Possibly refers to the con artists found around St. Paul's Cathedral in London. Carretta, *Interesting Narrative,* 294; Edwards, *Olaudah Equiano,* I:lxxx.

214. In present-day Colombia.

215. Adapted from Colley Cibber (1671–1757), *Love's Last Shift.*

216. Matthias Macnamara had been governor of Senegambia from 1775 to 1778. Carretta, *Interesting Narrative,* 295.

217. See *Timothy* 4:14.

218. Robert Lowth (1710–1787) was Bishop of London from 1777 until his death.

219. *Luke* 10:37.

220. Written by Anthony Benezet (1766).

221. In the second, third, and fourth editions, Equiano adds, "—My hand is ever free—if any female Debonair wished to obtain it, this mode I recommend." Carretta, *Interesting Narrative,* 297.

222. Joseph Irwin, the agent conductor of the resettlement project.

223. Equiano's footnote refers to a letter he wrote vindicating his conduct.

224. Queen Charlotte (1744–1818), Royal Consort of King George III.

225. The 1788 Consolidated Slave Act of Jamaica penalized some of the brutalities of slaveowners, and established humane guidelines for the slaves' treatment. Edwards, *Olaudah Equiano,* I:lxxxi.

226. Regarding Equiano's footnote, see notes 73, 31, and 65 above.

227. *Proverbs* 14:31.

228. *Proverbs* 14:34, 10:29, 11:5.

229. Hooks.

230. Cat-o'-nine-tails.

231. *Micah* 6:8.

WILLIAM GRIMES

WILLIAM GRIMES (1784–?) wrote and published the first book-length American fugitive slave narrative; at the time it was the longest autobiography written by an African American.[1] Written without the aid of abolitionists— seemingly even without exposure to their ideas—it surpasses in complexity all later narratives. Here the common trajectory of the slave narrative is notably absent, for though the writer passes from slavery to freedom, he does not heroically triumph over adversity. Instead, like the large majority of his enslaved brethren, he succumbs to it. Unredeemed, he becomes fearful, angry, bitter, disconsolate.

Grimes underwent an extraordinary range of experiences. He suffered under ten different owners, was haunted by ghosts and ridden by a witch, went on a hunger strike and beat his overseer, tried to break his own leg and bit off the nose of a fellow slave, and was accused of thievery, pimping, and rape. Furthermore, his life as a free man was as cruel as his life as a slave. As if this weren't complicated enough, in his narrative Grimes refuses to resolve the contradictions between his religious faith and his willingness to sin, between his desire for freedom and his disparagement of its advantages over slavery, and between his identification as a black ex-slave and as an indigent, three-quarters-white man.

William Andrews claims that the narrative's complexity is mostly psychological, but its contradictions may equally be due to the author's uncertainty about how he would be perceived by his readers. For example, Grimes claims near the close of his narrative that he does not know his true age, while he earlier gives his birthdate as 1784. It seems that here Grimes, anxious to excuse the faults of his narrative, desired to adopt the modest persona of the ignorant and unlettered slave. Some of his other contradictory statements may be equally disingenuous. After all, Grimes could clearly be crafty when he chose.

At any rate, the narrative offers no clear answers to questions about the nature of slavery, race, class, or faith—which again sets it apart from many subsequent narratives. But although at times it verges on incoherence, its unforgettable conclusion comprises perhaps the most profound and poetic comment on slavery in the United States to be found in any narrative—even inviting a reading of the narrative as a kind of reverse U.S. constitution. As Andrews puts it, "The *Life* has stood as a loaded gun, a 'death weapon,' as Roger Rosenblatt has termed modern black autobiography, as much a threat to the literary system of autobiography as to the social system of slavery."[2]

In 1855, at the age of seventy-one, Grimes published a second edition of his narrative, to which he added a "Conclusion" describing his last thirty years. He had eighteen children, the last at the age of sixty-three; after that his wife, Clarissa Caesar, left him in order to travel to California to look for gold. Grimes himself moved from town to town in Connecticut before settling in New Haven, spent some time in jail for assaulting a butcher who had insulted him, continued his work as a barber, and then became a broker instead, selling lottery tickets. He was, in the end, "a fixed institution" of New Haven, as a newspaper put it— or, in his own words, "one who has often been called one of the most remarkable personages of modern times."[3]

# LIFE

OF

# WILLIAM GRIMES,

THE

## RUNAWAY SLAVE.

*WRITTEN BY HIMSELF.*

NEW-YORK:

1825.

DISTRICT OF CONNECTICUT, ss.

BE IT REMEMBERED, That on the twenty-eighth day of January, in the forty-ninth year of the Independence of the United States of America, WILLIAM GRIMES of the said District, hath deposited in this Office the title of a Book, the right whereof he claims as Author, in the words following, to wit:

*"The Life of William Grimes, the Runaway Slave. Written by Himself"*

In conformity to the Act of the Congress of the United States, entitled, "An Act for the encouragement of learning, by securing the copies of Maps, Charts, and Books, to the Authors and Proprietors of such copies, during the times therein mentioned."

CHARLES A. INGERSOLL,
*Clerk of the District of Connecticut.*

A true copy of Record, examined and sealed by me.

CHARLES A. INGERSOLL,
*Clerk of the District of Connecticut.*

# TO THE PUBLIC.

---

THOSE who are acquainted with the subscriber, he presumes will readily purchase his history. Those who are not, but wish to know who Grimes is, and what is his history, he would inform them, generally, that he is now living in Litchfield, Connecticut, that he is about 40 years of age, that he is married to a black woman and passes for a negro, though three parts white; that he was born in a place in Virginia, has lived in several different States, and been owned by ten different masters; that about ten years since, he ran away, and came to Connecticut, where, after six years, he was recognized by some of his former master's friends, taken up, and compelled to purchase his freedom with the sacrifice of all he had earned. That his history is an account of his fortune, or rather of his suffering, in all these various situations, in which he has seen, heard, and felt, not a little.

To those who still think the Book promises no entertainment, he begs leave to suggest another motive why they should purchase it. To him who has feeling, the condition of a slave, under any possible circumstances, is painful and unfortunate, and will excite the sympathy of all who have any. Such was my condition for more than thirty years, and in circumstances not only painful, but often intolerable. But after having tasted the sweets of liberty, (embittered, indeed, with constant apprehension,) and after having, by eight years labor and exertion, accumulated about a thousand dollars, then to be stripped of all these hard earnings and turned pennyless upon the world with a family, and to purchase freedom, this gives me a claim upon charity, which, I presume, few possess, and I think, none will deny. Let any one suppose himself a husband and father, possessed of a house, home, and livelihood: a stranger enters that house; before his children, and in fair day light, puts the chain on his leg, where it remains till the last cent of his property buys from avarice and cruelty, the remnant of a life, whose best years had been spent in misery! Let any one imagine this, and think what I have felt.

WILLIAM GRIMES.

*Litchfield, October 1, 1824.*

# LIFE OF WILLIAM GRIMES.

———

I WAS born in the year 1784, in J——, County of King George, Virginia; in a land boasting its freedom, and under a government whose motto is Liberty and Equality. I was yet born a slave. My father, ———, was one of the most wealthy planters in Virginia. He had four sons; two by his wife, one, myself, by a slave of Doct. Steward, and another by his own servant maid. In all the Slave States, the children follow the condition of their mother; so that, although in fact, the son of ———, I was in law, a bastard and slave, and owned by Doct. Steward. My father was a wild sort of man, and very much feared by all his neighbors. I recollect he shot a man by the name of Billy Hough, through the arm, who came to my master's and staid. He was, however, finally taken up and committed to Fredericksburg jail, for shooting Mr. Gallava, a gentleman of that country. He refused however to be taken, until a military force was called out. Then he gave up, went to jail, was tried and acquitted, on the ground of insanity. Doct. Steward's house was about a mile from my father's, where I went frequently, to carry newspapers, &c. He always used to laugh and talk with me, and send me to the kitchen to get something to eat. I also at those times, saw and played with his other children. My brother, the mulatto, was sent to school, and I believe had his freedom when he grew up. My father, I have no doubt, would have bought and freed me, if I had not been sold and taken off while he was in jail. I supposed my father would have been hung; and whether wealth and powerful friends procured his escape, I know not. It is, however, a sufficient commentary upon that event, and upon my fortune, that I then thought and now speak on the subject with indifference. He died at his own house, in J——, about the year 1804. That he suffered his blood to run in the veins of a slave, is the only reflection I would cast upon his memory, which is just none at all, in the slave States. He was a very brave man, I reckon; and when it was attempted to take him, armed his slaves, and would never have been taken alive, if some of his friends had not persuaded him to yield quietly. Mr. Gallava was passing my father's when my father met him, and asked him to stop; he said, no, he could not. My father then drew his pistol, and shot him dead. Mr. Gallava's servant came directly to Doct. Steward's and gave the alarm. My father inherited the house and plantation where he lived, from his father, who was a man of considerable notoriety, and I believe, both respected and beloved. His character I cannot give. His name however, has been embalmed by the muses, and lives in song; he being the very person on whom that famous song called "Old Grimes," was written. The lines are as follows.

TUNE.—"John Gilpin was a citizen."

Old Grimes is dead.—That good old man
    We never shall see more;
He us'd to wear a long black coat,
    All button'd down before.

His heart was open as the day;
    His feelings all were true;
His hair was some inclin'd to gray—
    He wore it in a queue.

Whene'er was heard the voice of pain
    His breast with pity burn'd—
The large, round head, upon his cane
    From ivory was turn'd.

Thus, ever prompt at pity's call,
    He knew no base design—
His eyes were dark, and rather small;
    His nose was aquiline.

He liv'd at peace with all mankind,
    In friendship he was true;
His coat had pocket-holes behind—
    His pantaloons were blue.

Unharm'd—the sin which earth pollutes,
    He pass'd securely o'er:
And never wore a pair of boots,
    For thirty years, or more.

But poor *old Grimes* is now at rest,
    Nor fears misfortune's frown;
He had a double-breasted vest—
    The stripes ran up and down.

He modest merit sought to find,
    And pay it its desert:
He had no malice in his mind—
    No ruffles on his shirt.

His neighbors he did not abuse,
    Was sociable and gay;
He wore large buckles in his shoes,
    And chang'd them every day.

His knowledge hid from public gaze,
    He did not bring in view—
Nor make a noise town-meeting days,
    As many people do.

His worldly goods he never threw
    In trust to fortune's chances;
But liv'd (as all his brothers do)
    In easy circumstances.

Thus, undisturb'd by anxious care,
  His peaceful moments ran;
And ev'ry body said he was
  A fine old gentleman.

Good people all, give cheerful thought
  To Grimes's memory:
As doth his cousin ESEK SHORT,
  Who made this poetry.

Such, according to Esek Short, was the character of my grandfather; and if it is impartially given, I think the family has degenerated. One would think, though, Mr. Short admired old Grimes's virtues, more than he lamented his death.

Doct. Steward kept me until I was ten years old. I used to ride behind his carriage, to open gates, and hold his horse. He was very fond of me, and always treated me kindly. This made my old mistress, his wife, hate me; and when she caught me in the house, she would beat me until I could hardly stand. Young as I was then, I can yet remember her cruelty with emotions of indignation that almost drive me to curses. She is dead, thank God, and if I ever meet her again, I hope I shall know her.

When I was ten years of age, Col. William Thornton came down from the mountains, in Culpepper County, to buy negroes, and he came to my master's house, who was his brother-in-law, and seeing me, thought me a smart boy. He asked my master what he would take for me; he replied, he thought I was worth £60. Col. Thornton immediately offered £65, and the bargain was made. The next morning I started with him for Culpepper. It grieved me to see my mother's tears at our separation. I was a heart-broken child, although too young to realize the afflictions of a tender mother, who was also a slave, the hopes of freedom for her already lost; but I was compelled to go and leave her. After two days travel on horseback, we arrived at my new master's plantation, which was called Montpelier. After residing there a few weeks, my mistress, finding me an honest servant boy, I was then intrusted with all the keys, which made some of the other servants jealous, who had, when in the situation which I held, pilfered from the stores entrusted to their care, for the purpose of giving to their acquaintances and relations; one in particular, my mistress's head servant and seamstress, who had as many children as my mistress, and who were then working on the plantation. They fared much harder there than they would in my situation. She tried every art she could invent to set my master and mistress against me. As I had to make the coffee every morning in the nursery, where this servant, whose name was Patty, sat sewing, she would, when I was out, often take medicine from the cupboard, and put it in the coffee; and her object in doing this, was to compel me to go on the plantation, and have one of her children in my place. But as I was a poor friendless boy, without any connexions or inducement to that, if I had been disposed, my mistress was determined to keep me in my present situation. But the favorable opinion my mistress had of my integrity, (which was correct) has cost me many a severe flagellation, in the manner which I will now relate. I had always made the coffee to the satisfaction of my mistress, until one morning, my young master, George Thornton, after taking two or three sips at it, observed, this coffee has a particular taste; and Doct. Hawes, whom I shall hereafter mention, being then at the table, observed the same, adding that it tasted as if some medicine had been put in it. Upon this remark of the Doctor, my mistress rose up from the table and went to the cupboard, where the medicine was kept; and after examining, said, "here is where he has just taken it from, this morning." My master then rose up in anger and took me behind the ice-house, and whipped me severely, in the following manner: First, he caused me to be what they call horsed up, by being raised upon the shoulders of another slave, and the slave to confine my hands around his breast; in this situation they gave me about forty or fifty lashes; they whipped me until I hardly had any feeling in me. The crime was sufficiently deserving the punishment, but for a young boy, who had tried and exerted himself to the utmost, to give good satisfaction to his master, mistress, and all the family, never intending to injure any other servant, but rather participate in their wrongs, and render assistance if it could lawfully be done; and all for the malicious temper and disposition of this same Patty, it was too much for me to bear. It indeed sometimes happened, that every morning I was taken and whipped severely, for this very act of that malicious (I must call her brute,) when I was entirely innocent. There without friends, torn from the arms of my mother, who has since died in slavery, not being allowed to see me, her only son, during her illness: (I knew of course she would suffer for what she wanted while confined and unable to help herself, and no one willing to help her that could be allowed to see her,) this, together with my suffering, is sufficient to convince my readers, that any boy of my age would endeavor to find, and also improve an opportunity to clear themselves from the house of bondage.

Doct. Hawes, aforementioned, was present at the time I was whipped on account of the coffee, and advised my master not to whip me any more, as he said he thought I could not bear it much longer. He was my master's son in-law, and a member of Congress, and married my master's eldest daughter. He did not whip me any more at that time, after the advice of the Doctor. Oftentimes, my mistress would have me make the coffee in the dining room, before her. At such times, Patty had no opportunity for putting in the drugs, and the coffee was then good. I was satisfied in my own mind, that (as she was the overseer of the house, and her husband of the plantation, there being about ten or fifteen servants about the house, and no one of them allowed to interfere with this business in which I was employed) that it must be through her machinations which she employed to injure me, and get me severely flogged. One time they had what they call a spell, on the plantation, at which all the servants were compelled to turn out, and assist in hoeing corn. I then requested my master to let me go and assist them. He finally consented, and I went. After working there two days, they requested me to come back in the house again, but I refused; and in order that I should be punished for refusing to return, my master and mistress consented to my staying, thinking that my labour and fare would be so much harder that I would willingly return; but the fear of making the coffee, and of the whipping I should receive, induced me still to refuse to return; although at the same time I longed to return, on account of my food, (as did the children of Israel to the flesh pots of Egypt.) Patty and her husband were then better satisfied, for they had me just where they wanted me; that is, out of the house into the field, where I suffered every thing but death itself. When I was in waiting at the house, Maj. Jones, brother-in-law to my master, saw me waiting about the house, and thinking me a smart active boy to wait about the house, asked my master if he would sell me. He refused, saying he wanted me to wait on his son, William Thornton, jr. who was study-ing with lawyer Thompson, near Culpepper Court House, as soon as he should go into business for himself. So I was not sold this time.

I remained on the plantation about two years, under a black overseer, by the name of Voluntine, who punished me repeatedly, to make me perform more labour than the rest of the boys. My master then procured another overseer, a white man, by the name of Coleman Thead; he treated us somewhat better than old Voluntine, but he was very severe, flogged me severely several times, for al-most nothing. The overseers have an unlimited control over the slaves on the plantation, and exercise their authority in the most tyranical manner. I was one day at work on the plantation, with nothing on but my shirt, when the overseer (Thead) came to me, threatening to whip me, and caught hold of me for that pur-pose. I clinched him and told him that if he struck me, I would inform my mas-ter about his riding a favorite horse without my masters consent; that my mas-ter had already enquired of me why the horse grew so poor, but I would not then tell him; the fear of detection induced him to let me go, telling me to be a good boy, and he would not flog me. I worked under this overseer about nine months, when he left us and went to Georgia. I then worked under old Voluntine again for about six months, when my master engaged a new overseer by the name of *Burrows:* he was more severe than either of the former. After working with him some time, he set us to making fence, and would compel us to *run* with the rails on our backs, whipping us all the time most unmercifully. This hard treatment continuing for some time I at length resolved to run away. I accordingly repaired to the cabin of a slave called *Planter George,* and informed him that I intended to run away the next morning. I asked him for an old jacket and some meal, both of which he promised to give me. I then baked what meal I had, for my supper, and went to sleep. Old George immediately repaired to the house of the overseer and informed him of my intention to run away in the morning. The overseer came directly to the cabin and sent in George to question me, while he should listen without. George asked me if I intended to run away, provided he would give me the jacket and some meal; being partly asleep I answered that I did not know. He repeated the question several times and still received the same answer. The overseer then hallowed out, hey, you son of a bitch, you are going to run away are you, I'll give it to you: bring him out here. So they brought me out and horsed me upon the back of Planter George, and whipped me until I could hardly stand, and then told me if I did not run away, he would whip me three times a day, and make me carry three rails to one, all day.

In this manner do the overseers impose on their Planters, and compel their slaves to run away, by cruel treatment. The next morning came, and I knew not what to do. If I went to the field, I was sure to be whipped, and to run away I

did not like to. However, like most, I presume, in my situation, I chose the latter alternative, so away I ran for the mountain. I passed close by the field where
my young master, Philip Thornton was shooting. His gun burst, and blew off
part of his thumb. I crept along under the fence, and got to the mountains, where
I staid until night: then I began to be hungry, and thought I would go to some of
the neighbors to get something to eat. I went to Mr. Pallam's, and asked for some
tobacco seed for my master, for an excuse, and stayed there all night. I got some
corn bread for my supper, and picked up a little about the kitchen for the next
day. The next morning I went to the mountain, and staid till night again, when
I went down to Mr. Pallam's to get something to eat, pretending that I had come
on an errand from my master. Mr. Pallam immediately seized me, and called to
Daniel to bring the hame strings.[4] He had been down to my master's that day,
and they told him I had gone off, and if I came there again, to take me, which he
did, and would have carried me home that night, but his wife persuaded him to
wait till morning. I was then put under the care of old Daniel. Mr. Pallam told
me if I run away from him he would catch me with his dogs, for they would track
me any where. Daniel took me to his hovel, and for greater security took away
my shoes. I lay peaceable till near morning, when the fear of my master came
over me again, and I wished to get away. I begged old Daniel to let me go out,
under pretence of necessity, but he refused. He finally gave me one of his shoes,
and I went to the door to look out. It was just the dawn of day. I had been waiting the cock crowing all night, and it was now time to go if I went at all. The
ground was covered with a light snow. I gave a jump, and Daniel after me, but
my step was as light as the snow flake, and the last glimpse I had of Daniel
showed him prostrate over a log. I escaped to a corn field in sight of my master's
house, and secreted myself in an old log which I had picked out before. While in
the log I fell asleep, and dreamed they had caught and was tying me to be
whipped; and such was my agony, that I awoke, from a dream, indeed, but to
reality not less painful. I stayed in that place about three days, when I became so
pinched with hunger, that I thought I might as well be whipped to death as to
starve; so I concluded to give myself up, if I could get to my master before the
overseer should get me. In that I succeeded. They gave me something to eat, and
Doct. Hawes, my master's son-in-law, who was at the house, advised them not
to whip me. My master asked me what made me go off: I told him the cruelty of
the overseer. He then told the overseer not to whip me again without his knowledge. I was so hungry that they were afraid to give me as much as I wanted, lest
I should kill myself. Not long after, however, the overseer came into the field
where we were at work, and after trying to find some fault, whipped us all round.
This was the first time he had done it since my master told him not; but I dare
not tell my master, for if I did, the overseer would whip me for that. If it were
not for our hopes, our hearts would break; we poor slaves always cherish hopes
of better times. We are human beings, sensible of injuries, and capable of gratitude towards our masters. This overseer whipped me a great many times before
I escaped from his hands. Shortly after this I recollect my master came home late
at night, and getting off his horse, got entangled, and would have fallen if I had
not been near, and caught him; and being a very large man, the fall might have

injured him very much, nay, killed him. Afterwards, when he was angry with me, I could sometimes appease him somewhat, by hinting this to him. There is a holyday which our master gave us, called Easter Sunday, or Monday. On one of those days I asked my young master, Stuart Thornton, to let me go and see Miss Jourdine, a mulatto girl who was brought up with me and sold by Doct. Steward, to Mr. Glassel. It was eight years before that. When I saw her last, she was then a beautiful girl. I cannot describe the emotions of pleasure with which her presence filled my bosom, nor forget the hour when fate parted us forever. I presume the heart, and the feelings of an illiterate peasant, or an ignorant slave, are as susceptible and as ardent as those of men more enlightened, at least when warmed and excited by the influence of female attractions. The last look of a woman whom you know loves you, which is given through tears and with a consciousness that you are leaving her forever, troubles my heart beyond any thing I have since experienced. My young master did not like me to go, but I did. On the way my bosom burned and my heart almost leaped from me, as I thought on this girl. I felt as though I could, unarmed, have flogged half a dozen lions, if they had crossed my path. I did not find her at Mr. Glassel's, she having been sold to Mr. Jourdine, who had bought her and kept her for his wife; but I did not return without seeing her. One of the Miss Glassel's sent a book to my young mistress, to whom I presented it on my return. She asked me where I had been; I told her I had been to see Miss Jourdine. And because I called the girl Miss instead of Betty, my young mistress was extremely angry with me, and said she would have me whipped in the morning. In the morning, Burrows, the overseer came after me to Aaron's cabin, where I stayed. As I came towards the house, my master came out. The little rascal, says he, had the impertinence to call that wench Miss Jourdine, to his mistress; take him and give it to him. So they took me, and tied me on a bench, and as soon as they began to whip, I would slip out from the rope, until my master told the overseer to horse me upon another's back, and after he had whipped me a while, to stop and let me rest; for he said he wanted to whip me about a month. They began to whip again in a few minutes, though not so hard, and kept it up three or four hours; I begging all the while to be forgiven, and promising to offend no more. I was so weak after this, I could hardly stand, but they would not have got me to whip if it had not snowed, and prevented me from running away to the mountain. My master gave me many very severe floggings; but I had rather be whipped by him than the overseer, and especially, the black overseers. Oh, how much have I suffered from these black drivers!

Sometime during this year, my master's son, George, wanted me to wait on him. He came to the field where I was at work, to see me. I had been fighting with Moses, and had cut off my hair as close as possible, for the purpose of having the advantage. Seeing this, he refused to take me, I looked so bad. So I was obliged to remain in the field and live on my peck of meal a week. Colonel Thornton was a severe master, and he made his slaves work harder than any one about there, and kept them poorer. Sometimes we had a little meat, or fish, but not often any thing more than our peck of meal. We used to steal meat whenever we could get a chance; and such was my craving for it, that if the punishment had been death, I could not have resisted the temptation. How much I suffered, I will not pretend to say; but I recollect one Saturday I had been to work hard all day: in the evening, I found, back of the garden, some hog's entrails which had been thrown out a few days before. I was so hungry for meat, that I took these guts, washed them, and put them into a skillet and boiled them. I then wet some corn meal in cold water, put it in the ashes, and made a fire over it. After it had baked, I mixed it with the guts and eat it; but before morning, I was so much swollen that I like to have died. When any of the hogs died, we always eat them. But we did not wait for pigs and geese to die of old age, when we could get a chance to steal them. Steal? Yes, steal them. Why, I have been so hungry for meat that I could have eat my mother.

One instance of cruelty from my mistress I can never forget. It was my turn to beat homony that night. So I began at dark and beat most all night. Having been at work hard all day, before morning I was so hungry that I took and fanned the chaff and husks from the corn I was beating, wet it up with water, and baked it, and this without one grain of salt or fat. I had worked as hard as I could, and beat the homony as I thought sufficiently. About an hour before day, I lay down and went to sleep. In the morning, my mistress sent to the overseer to give me a severe whipping for she said the homony was not beat quite enough, though very good. Notwithstanding, I had worked all night as hard as I could spring, I was taken and flogged. (Homony is a kind of food used at breakfast and dinner. It is made of corn pounded till the skin is all off, then boiled, mashed and fried.) It seems as though I should not forget this flogging when I die: it grieved my soul beyond the power of time to cure. I should not have been alive now if I had remained a slave, for I would have resisted with my life, when I became older, treatment, which I have witnessed towards others, from the overseers, and such as I should probably have met with, nay, such as I have received when a boy from overseers.

While I was with Col. Wm. Thornton, a great many of his slaves were taken sick and died. Doct. Hawes, married one of Col. Thornton's daughters, Fanny Thornton. My master gave him a tract of land in Culpepper, on which he built himself a house, about a mile from my master's, and came up there to live, from Caroline, Spotsylvania county. We always supposed that some of his slaves poisoned my Master's; and I heard one of the servants say, that he saw an old woman of Doct. Hawes', put something like red earth into the bread. Several of the servants in the spinning room died, and after that there was a groaning heard in that room; and I have myself heard the spirits groan in that room. If ever there was a room haunted it was that. I will believe it as long as I have my breath to draw. I slept in the passage, close by the door of my master and mistress. Sometimes when I was as wide awake as I am now, the spirits would unlock the doors, and come upstairs, and trample on me, press me to the floor, and squeeze me almost to death: I should have screamed, but the fear of my master, who would not believe, but would have whipped me, prevented.

There was, not long after this, a great hurricane and earthquake; and I saw the sky part, and it looked as red as crimson. The earth shook, and every thing that was on it; and I heard them talk of many thousands who were drowned.[5]

There was, I recollect, at my master's, two gentlemen from Connecticut,

Parson Beebe, and Doct. Goodsell.—They staid there some time, and it was supposed Doctor Goodsell was courting my young mistress. One of my young masters came on to court with them. I heard them talk about New-Haven, but I little thought I should ever see it.

While I was at work under Burrows, the overseer, my master's son, George, returned from Philadelphia, where he had been studying physic. He went to Northumberland county to practice, and took me from the plantation to wait on him.

In going to Northumberland, we passed through Leedstown, where I saw my mother and brothers. It was, I suppose, ten years since I had seen my mother. She was living with her old mistress, Doct. Steward's former wife, but now married to George Fitchue, Doct. Steward being dead. There is nothing in slavery, perhaps, more painful, than the unavoidable separation of parents and children. It is not uncommon to hear mothers say, that they have half a dozen children, but the Lord only knows where they are. Oh! my poor mother! but she is gone, and I presume her skin is now as white as that of her mistress.

Master George hired a house in Northumberland, and I took care of the house when he was gone. I always had been praying to God, ever since I knew what God was; and I thought, like Peter, I had faith. One day when I was alone in the house, I shut all the doors in the house, and went up into the third story to pray; and just as I entered the room, I saw, to my astonishment, a number of skeletons hanging up about it. It was a terrible sight to me, and I was so frightened that I could not stop. The holes in the skull, where the eyes are, seemed to look right at me. I turned round as slowly and softly as possible, without taking my eyes from them until I shut the door. I have often thought it strange, that a skeleton or a corpse should terrify us, though they might shock our feelings. But my poor heart never walloped so before; and I had never thought that our garret was a sepulchre.

My master sent me to Fredericksburg, to get another doctor to come and help him cut off a woman's thigh. I had helped him once, but I almost fainted. When I had got in town and done my errand, I put out my horse at the tavern, and went into the kitchen, where, who should I find but my old master's cook, Philip. He told me that my brother Benjamin was in town. I went to see him, and told him who I was. He gave me seventy-five cents.—With this I went and bought some cake and rum, and drank, not thinking, until I got drunk and fell down in the street. Some of my friends took me up, and carried me in, and I slept till most night, when I started for home, and rode with all haste, lest my master should flog me for staying. I pretended to him that I rode slow. However, as I did not let him see the horse he never found out my scrape, and it is well he did not, for if he had, I might not have been here to record it. He was cross to me and I feared him like death. I reccollect once his whipping me, after our return from Northumberland, so severely on the naked back, that I carry the stripes to this day, and all because his mother told him that I had been telling his younger brother something that was done when he lived at Northumberland. He gave me once a tumbler of spirits, and made me drink it, which almost killed me. This he did to conceal from my knowledge, a scrape which he was going to have, as I supposed. If the cook had not blown tobacco smoke through me, I believe I should have been a corpse before morning.

After staying at Northumberland six or eight months, master George left there, and I went back to his father's plantation. I went sorrowing too. Master George was going to Philadelphia again, so there was no other place for me but his father's plantation, where I must work all day, and some times most all night, with my peck of meal a week, and the hell-hound Burrows, to flog me, for he gloried in doing it. One instance in which my master disappointed his savage heart, I remember. He told Burrows to take me down to the stable, tie my legs, put a rail between them, then stretch me up and whip me. While going down to the stable, which was about thirty or forty rods distant, I thought if the order was put in execution, I could not endure it, but must die in the operation. My master and Burrows went forward, and I followed behind. I looked up to heaven, and prayed fervently to God to hear my prayer, and grant me relief in this hour of adversity; expecting every moment to be whipped until I could not stand: and *blessed be God* that he turned their hearts before they arrived at the place of destination; for on arriving there I was acquitted. God delivered me from the power of the adversary. Blessed be his name, he heard my prayer in the hour of adversity, and delivered me from the enemy. I will here inform my readers, that in the time of going down to the stable, I did not make a feeble attempt to induce my master not to flog me; but put my trust, and offered my prayers to my heavenly father, who heard and answered them.

On my arriving at the stable, I was surprised to hear my master express himself in terms that I could not reasonably from former treatment expect. He said to me, "go, behave yourself well and you shall not be whipped." In the mean time, Burrows, the overseer, who had stood by wanting and waiting for the privilege of whipping me, stood in suspence and astonishment, at the lenity of my master in not having me flogged after he, Burrows, had every thing prepared for the purpose; such as a bundle of hickories, ropes to bind me, and a good stout hand to lay it on; ah! and a good resolution.

At one time my master having caused an oven to be built in the yard, for the purpose of baking bread for the negroes, I went there and finding it not quite dry, made impressions with my fingers, such as letters &c. on it, while the mortar was green on the outside. Gabriel, one of the servants, a son of old Volentine, was ordered to strip my shirt up and whip me; (the word severely, has been so many times used it needs no repetition) my master stood by to see the thing well executed: and as he thought he did not be severe enough, he ordered me to strip him and perform the same ceremony, which I did. He then ordered Gabriel to try to whip me harder than he did before. Then Gabriel knew what the old man meant, *to wit,* to whip me as severe as lay in his power, which he affected on the second trial, exerting all his strength and agility to the utmost to make me suffer, only to please his master. This being so often the case, the negro drivers and indeed the slaves, show much less humanity in punishment, than the masters themselves.

Again, while living with my present, or old master, Col. William Thornton, I had the care of some cows, two of which had calves; and I tried to invent some method to get some milk from these cows, to eat with my corn bread; but dared not let any person know that I did it, fearing that if I did I should receive a severe whipping. But a stratagem occurred to me. We had gourds growing on the side of the fence. I had often used and seen used, the shell of the gourd for a ladle, or scoup dish, and I took a gourd that was green, and excoriated a part, took out the seeds, &c., and without any further cleansing, I filled it with milk from the cow, and then hid it in the chaff pen.—I then went home and baked some bread, and got another gourd and carried there the milk. Being in an open place and it requiring straining, I had nothing at all to strain it through; but being under necessity, I took a part of my shirt tail, which being made of coarse tow cloth, and not having been washed for five or six weeks, I being a poor motherless boy, and no one to wash it but myself, and I all the time kept busy in the field, under the overseer, my shirt was what would be generally termed, full of lice at the time; but as I had no other cloth for straining, I made use of that. But when I went to get the milk, the gourd being green, the milk had contracted a bitterness of which no one can judge, unless they have had a trial. I was however driven to the necessity of eating it, or eating my bread dry. I was quite fearful of being taken by old James, a black servant, who was very much respected by my master and mistress, although very deceitful, but escaped his vigilance. He died before I began to wait on any of my young master's; and peace be to his soul.

Master George returned from Philadelphia in about a year. He courted his cousin, who lived about six miles from his father's, and married her. His father gave him a plantation a mile from his own, where I was now placed. My master lived at my wife's father's, intending to move in the spring; this being the fall season. The name of his overseer was Bennet. This Bennet, and his mother, had lived on land rented to them by my former master, Colonel Thornton. They were then very poor, and secretly bot' things from the negroes, which they had stolen from my master. This Bennett, having now become overseer, was severe. My master had a servant by his wife's estate called James. I saw Bennet strip off James' shirt, and whip his naked back part as if he had been cutting down a tree. I thought what was to be my fate.

One day I was sick and did not go to ploughing. Bennet came after me, and told me he would whip me if I did not. I took up a stick, and told him if he put his hand upon me I would strike him: and marched towards him as bold as a lion. But he knew that I had lived so poor that I had not much strength; and seeing that he did not fear but was in a great rage, I took to my heels. But he caught me, and dragged me up to the negro houses, and called two of them to come and assist him. While they were tying me, I made one pitch at Bennet with my head. I missed him, but he hit me with a club, and knocked me speechless. The blood ran from my mouth and nose very fast. I was then so weak that I could hardly stand; so I gave up, and told the overseer to whip me as much as he pleased, but if he did not whip me to death he should drink sorrow for it. When I was tied, James brought the sticks, I spoke out brave, and said to the overseer, why don't you get some better ones; whip me till your soul is satisfied, but I'll remember every stick. He began to whip, and I counted out loud every stroke. After he had struck me eleven times, he said, if you will say that you are drunk, and hold your peace, I will stop. I said, you might as well whip me to death; for if you don't master will, when he hears of this. But he promised me that if I would hold my tongue, and say nothing about this, he would see that I should not be whipped. He knew that it was for his interest to keep me from exposing their buying things which they knew the slaves had stolen. My master however, heard something about this scrape, and was going to whip me, but Mr. Bennet interfered, and told him that I was drunk, as I said, and that he had whipped me enough.

I ought perhaps, to blame slavery more than my master's. The disposition to tyrannize over those under us, is universal; and there is no one who will not occasionally do it. I had too much sense and feeling to be a slave: too much of the blood of my father, whose spirit feared nothing. I was therefore perhaps, difficult to *govern in the way in which it was attempted.* I was at this time the property of George Thornton, to whom I was given by his father—Doct. P. T. an older brother, at this time came up from his father's plantation to buy me, which he did.

I was then in the ice house, he called me up, and the moment I saw him my heart leaped for joy. He asked me if I was willing to go and wait on him, as it would be much easier for me than it would to work on the plantation? I answered, yes sir, if you please. He then said he had bought me, and was going to Port Royal, to practice physic, and wanted me to go with him on another horse, carry his portmanteau and wait on him. He then sent me to the tailors to get some clothes, and fitted me out very handsomely. We travelled on to Port Royal, where he went into practice. I had two horses to take care of. After remaining there a couple of months, he formed an acquaintance with a young lady, who he afterwards married. After he had been married one month and four days, his wife died. Soon after that we returned to his father's plantation in Montpelier. After remaining there a few days we went on to Frederickstown in Maryland, where we staid a short time, and returned again to his father's. After a short stay there, we went to Monticello, and resided at the house of Thomas Jefferson, formerly President of the United States, for a few weeks. While we were there he met with his brother-in-law from Port Royal, and we returned to that place, when he stayed long enough to settle up his business, and then went to Richmond, Virginia, to practice physic, where he had a very good run of business. After some time, having an opportunity to earn something, I had laid up a few dollars, and being very fond of having my fortune told, being anxious to know whether I should be a free man or not, I went to an old woman who told fortunes in order to have her tell mine, a number of times. She told me that I should be sold to a gentleman, and be taken to the south. I asked her what kind of a man he was: she told me his head was white, which I afterwards found to be true, for he used powder. What she told me proved to be true: she told me he was a crabbed sort of a man and that I should be severely dealt with. She said to me, don't you go, your master will not compel you to go, but you will finally consent to it, and will go. I told her I would not go. She again told me that I would. I have since thought it strange how this old creature could tell me exactly as it was; but it was so. The man who bought me was at this time in New-York, some hundreds of miles off. Some months after this, one morning as I was busily engaged about the yard, cleaning my masters boots, and doing other work as usual, a gentleman came into the yard at the bell tavern where my master boarded, and enquired of one of the servants for Doct. Thornton. He told him he did not know where he was, but pointing to me said, there is his servant sir. He then said to me, are you his servant boy? I answered him that I was. He then told me to go up and tell my master (who was then in bed) that he wanted to see him. I went and told my master there was a gentleman below who wished to see him. He told me to invite him up into his room. I did so and showed him the way up, where I left them together. A short time after this he came down and asked me if I should be willing to go to Savannah with him, provided he should buy me. I told him I did not know where it was. He then told me to go up and see my master. I did so, and he asked me if I wanted to go with that gentleman. I told him I was very well contented to live with him. (He had always treated me perfectly well, we never had any difficulty) I found that this gentleman had enquired on the road for a good servant, and being informed that my master had one that he would sell, he came to buy me. My master told me that this gentleman was rich and would be likely to give me my time after a few years, but I did not agree to go still. The gentleman again returned from the eagle tavern to our boarding house, the bell tavern. He then slipped two dollars into my hand and said here boy take this and say you will go; and after a great deal of coaxing and flattering, I finally consented to go, for which I have many a time and often heartily repented. He then went to my master and I followed him. He told him that I had consented to go. My master said he would not force me to go, but if I was willing he would consent to it. Mr. A——, (for that was my new masters name, who was a Jew) then paid him five hundred dollars. Doct. Thornton, then ordered his horse up: he would not stay to see me start, but bade me good bye, and rode off with tears in his eyes. I then started with my new master for Savannah, with a carriage and four horses: we travelled about twelve miles the first day. I was dissatisfied with him before I had got two miles. We travelled the next day twenty five miles, as far as Petersburgh. I was so much dissatisfied with him, that I offered a black man at that place, two silver dollars to take an axe and break my leg, in order that I could not go on to Savannah; but he refused, saying he could tell me a better way. I asked him how? He said runaway. I told him I would not run away unless I was sure of gaining my freedom by doing it. We then travelled on the next day about thirty miles, and put up for the night. I then attempted to break my leg myself. Accordingly I took up an axe, and laying my leg on a log, I struck at it several times with an axe endeavouring to break it, at the same time I put up my fervent prayers to God to be my guide, saying, "if it be thy will that I break my leg in order that I may not go on to Georgia, grant that my blows may take effect; but thy will not mine be done." Finding I could not hit my leg after a number of fruitless attempts, I was convinced by my feelings then, that God had not left me in my sixth trouble, and would be with me in the seventh. Accordingly I tried no more to destroy myself. I then prayed to God, that if it was his will that I should go, that I might willingly. My old master and mistress to Virginia, had often threatend to sell me to the negro buyer from Georgia, for any trifling offence, and in order to make me dislike to go there, they would tell me I should have to eat cotton seed, and make indigo, and not have corn bread to eat as I did in Virginia. The next day we went as far as Columbia, in South Carolina. This was Saturday evening.

I was quite fatigued, and after taking care of the horses, I laid myself down in the stable to rest. I soon fell asleep, and slept for an hour or two. My master missing me, and thinking I had run away, made a thorough search for me, but could not find me until I awoke and went into the house. He was very angry with me: he cursed me and asked me where I had been. I told him I had been asleep in the stable. He told me I lied, and that I had attempted to make my escape; threatening to whip me. I told him I had not attempted any thing of the kind; but he would not believe me. Here again I was in great trouble. I went to bed and slept as well as I could, which was but little. The next day we again pursued our journey, and nothing of any consequence, different from what had before taken place, until we arrived at Savannah, which was in about six weeks. As we entered the city, we were about to pass a man who had a gun on his shoulder, loaded with shot. It accidentally went off, the contents within a very few inches of me. Here again, I escaped a wound, if not death. After residing in Savannah for a few months, and perceiving that he grew more severe and inhuman with me every day, I began to despair of ever living with him in peace. I however found some friends in Savannah, after a short time, and they advised me (after being made acquainted with the manner in which I was used) to get away from him as soon as possible. He would never allow me to leave the yard, unless it was for the purpose of taking out his horses to exercise them. At such times, I would often go to the fortune-teller, and by paying her twenty-five cents, she would tell me what she said my fortune would be. She told me I should eventually get away, but that it would be attended with a great deal of trouble; and truly, I experienced a vast deal of trouble before I could get away.

I will state to my readers some facts relative to the treatment I received from him, and others, during the time I lived there. He had an old black female slave whom he called Frankee. I always believed her to be a witch: circumstances to prove this, I shall hereafter state. He also had at one time, a number of carpenters at work in his yard. One of them, a man about my size, and resembling me very much in his dress, being dressed in a blue round-about jacket. He came into the yard to his work one morning, with an umbrella in his hand. This old woman saw him come in, and thinking it was me, or pretending so to do, was the cause of my receiving a severe whipping, in the following manner. My master having mislaid his umbrella, had been looking for it for some time, and on enquiring of her about it, she told him that she saw me come into the yard with it in my hand. I was then in the yard; he called to me, and said, where have you been sir? I replied, only to work about the yard sir. He then asked me where I was all night with his umbrella. I told him I had not been out of the yard, nor had I seen his umbrella. He said I was a liar, and that I had taken his umbrella away, and was seen to return with it in my hand this morning when coming into the yard. I told him it was not so, and that I knew nothing about it. He immediately fell foul of me with a large stick, and beat me most unmercifully, until I really thought he would kill me. I begged of him to desist, as I was perfectly innocent. He not believing me, still continued to beat me, until his strength was entirely exhausted.

Some time after this, my mistress found his umbrella where she had placed it herself, having removed it from the place where he had left it, and gave it to him, saying, you have beat him for nothing, he was innocent of it. I was afterwards informed by another servant, of the circumstance. I then went to my master, and told him that he had beaten me most unmercifully, for a crime I was not guilty of, all through the insinuation of that old woman. He replied, "no, by Gad, I never hit you a blow amiss; if you did not deserve it now, you did some other time." I told him she must have been drunk or she would not have told him such a story. He said that could not be, as she never was allowed to have any liquor by her. I told him to look in her chest, and convince himself. He then enquired of her if she had any rum. She said, no sir, I have not a drop. I then told him that if he would look in her chest, he would find it. He accordingly went, and found it. He then said to her, hey, you old bitch I have caught you in a lie. On this same account she appeared to be determined to kill me, by some means or other. I slept in the same room with her under the kitchen. My blankets were on the floor. She had a straw bed on a bed-stead about four paces from mine. My master slept directly over my head. I have heretofore stated that I was convinced that this creature was a witch, and would turn herself into almost any different shape she chose. I have at different times of the night felt a singular sensation, such as people generally call the night-mare: I would feel her coming towards me, and endeavouring to make a noise, which I could quite plainly at first; but the nearer she approached me the more faintly I would cry out. I called to her, aunt Frankee, aunt Frankee, as plain as I could, until she got upon me and began to exercise her enchantments on me. I was then entirely speechless; making a noise like one apparently choking, or strangling. My master had often heard me make this noise in the night, and had called to me, to know what was the matter; but as long as she remained there I could not answer. She would then leave me and go to her own bed. After my master had called to her a number of times, Frankee, Frankee, when she got to her own bed, she would answer, sair. What ails Theo? (a name I went by there, cutting short the name Theodore) She answered, hag ride him sair. He then called to me, telling me to go and sleep with her. I could then, after she had left me, speak myself, and also have use of my limbs. I got up and went to her bed, and tried to get under her coverlid; but could not find her. I found her bed clothes wet. I kept feeling for her, but could not find her. Her bed was tumbled from head to foot. I was then convinced she was a witch, and that she rode me. I then lay across the corner of her bed without any covering, because I thought she would not dare to ride me on her own bed, although she was a witch. I have often, at the time she started from her own bed, in some shape or other, felt a shock, and the nigher she advanced towards me, the more severe the shock would be. The next morning my master asked me what was the matter of me last night. I told him that some old witch rode me, and that old witch, is no other than old Frankee. He cursed me and called me a damned fool, and told me that if he heard any more of it, he would whip me. I then knew he did not believe in witch-craft. He said, why don't she ride me? I will give her a dollar. Ride me you old hag, and I will give you a dollar. I told him she would not dare to ride him.

One morning after he had given me such a severe pounding concerning the umbrella, and I was determined not to stay with him long, but to get away from him as soon as possible; he ordered me to fetch up my horse and saddle him, and put the other horse to the chaise, in order to go out to Bonaventure. I did so, and whilst I was gone I tried to invent some project, to make him believe me unwell. The next morning I pretended to be sick. He asked me what the matter was with me. I told him I had a pain in my side. He then said to Miss A——, go and weigh out a pound of salts for him. She did so. He then came to me with the salts in a cup, and said, do you see this sir? Do you see this? By Gad, you shall take every bit of this. He then mixed up a slight dose and gave it to me, which I took. He then sent for a doctor, who came and felt my pulse, and then said it would be well enough to put a blister plaister on my side. He accordingly went home, spread a very large plaister, and sent it over, which my master caused to be put on my side, which drew a large blister there. All this I bore without being sick, or unwell in the least. There was a man who had been to him repeatedly, to see if he would sell me. He always refused, saying no, I did not buy him to sell, and I will be damned if I do sell him, I bought him for my own use. I saw that he knew I was determined to get a new master, and he was the more determined to keep me. At length I refused to eat any thing at all. He would often ask me why I would not eat. I answered him that I could not, I was very weak and unwell. Still he invented every method he could, to induce me to eat, often setting victuals by my bed side &c. At length, one day he wanted me to go and fetch a load of wood: he said, come, make haste and get your dinner ready, I want you to be a clever fellow, and eat your dinner, then to take the horse and cart, and go out and fetch in a load of wood. The dinner was soon ready: he cut off some meat and other victuals, and gave me before he eat himself, saying, here now take this, be a clever fellow; eat it, and go and fetch a load of wood. I told him I did not want it. He says take it sir, and eat it. I replied, I thank you sir, I don't want it. Got tam your soul; you don't want it ha, you Got tam son of a bitch, you don't want it do you? He then took up a chair and came towards me, threatning to kill me. His wife being afraid he would, called to him in order to prevent him; saying, do not kill him, do not strike him with that chair. He set it down and called to Frankee, fetch me a rope God dam you, fetch me a rope. I will bind him fast, send him to jail, and let him have Moses law. (which is thirty-nine lashes on the naked back)[6] She fetched the rope, and he bound me, and was on the point of having me taken to jail; when I dreading the whipping I knew I should be obliged to take if I went there, finally consented to eat my victuals, and behave myself well. I then eat the victuals, which relished exceedingly well. Then I went to the woods, and fetched home a load of wood. After that I again refused to eat any thing at all, but pretended to be sick all the time. I also told Frankee, to tell my master, that I was subject to such turns every spring, and I should not live through this. She told him, which frightened him very much, thinking he should lose me. (which would grieve him as much as it would to lose a fine horse of the same value.) He then again tried to make me eat by the same means, often leaving victuals by my bed side at night, or order Frankee to do it. He would then enquire of her if I had eaten any thing yet. She replied, no, sir, I have not seen him eat anything since last Friday noon. I had his horse to water every day; and as I went out of, or across the yard, where I knew he would see me, I would pretend to be so weak that I could scarcely go. I would stagger along, to make him think that I should fall every moment. He one time called his wife to the window, saying, Missess, Missess, by Gad come here, do you see him? He is almost gone, by Gad I shall lose him; see how he staggers. By Gad he has not eat a mouthfull now for these three weeks. I must lose him by Gad; do you see that? I would however have it understood, that during all this time, I did not go without victuals. I sometimes could steal a little provision, and after driving my master to his plantation, I could sometimes run into the potatoe house, where I could find a few of them, which I ate raw. At other times I could find a bone, not quite stripped clean, which together with what I stole, made me a comfortable subsistance; or as much so, as the slaves generally receive. I was determined not to eat any thing in his sight, or to his knowledge, in order to make him think he must either sell me or lose me. One morning he sent me to eat my breakfast, I told him I did not want any. He said, go along and get your breakfast. I went, and returned. When I came back, he asked me if I had eaten my breakfast. I told him, no, sir, I thank you, I did not wish for any. You did not, did you? Gad dam you, you are sick, are you? You may die and be damned, by Gad: you may die and be damned: your coffin shall not cost me a quarter of a dollar, by Gad: you shall be buried on your face, by Gad: you may die and be damned.

Which of us is most likely to receive that part of this blessing which is to take effect in the next life, I will not say. However being determined to change my situation if possible, I went to one Major Lewis, a free black man, and very cunning. I gave him money, to go to my master, and run me down, and endeavour to convince him that I was really sick, and should never be good for any thing. In a few days from this, my master came down in the kitchen and says, boy get up, there boy, (holding it out in his hand,) there is the very money I gave for you: I have got my money again, and you may go and be damned; and don't you never step into my house again; if you do I will split your dam brains out. I then went to my new master's, Mr. Oliver Sturges, who came from Fairfield, Connecticut. He bought me to drive his carriage. A new coachman's dress, which he gave me, would have felt much better, if it had not been for the large blister, that had been drawn upon my side. However, I rode down by my old master's, and cracked my whip with as much pride, spirit and activity, as one of Uncle Sam's Mail carriers, who drives four horses, on a general post road, drunk or sober. My old master happening to see me pass in this manner, was very much chagrined, to think he had sold me under the impression that I was just ready to die. He called his wife to the window, and complained to her, that she had urged him to sell me, and swore, and cursed outrageously. I was now under my sixth master, Mr. Sturges, who bought me from the Jew. Mr. Sturges, was a very kind master, but exceedingly severe when angry. He had a new negro, by the name of Cato, with whom I got a fighting, and bit off his nose, just as my master was going to sell him, which injured the sale of Cato, very much. For this I had to beg very hard to escape being whipped. I went to the fortune tellers, who told me that my master said, that if he should take me on with him to New-York, I should be free: so I knew that I should not go with him. I had always been in the habit of praying, ever since I knew what it meant; and whenever I went to church, to drive the carriage, I used to stand upon the steps, and listen to the preaching. About this time, I began to realize that I was a sinner, and that hell would be my portion if I should die in my present situation: and afterwards while I was living with Doct. Collock, and under the advice of the Rev. Mr. Collock, whose voice and preaching, harrowed up my soul with awful apprehensions, I sought and obtained the hope of salvation. Blessed be God, I know the path to heaven. I have had sweet communion with the Lord; but alas! I have erred, and gone astray from holiness.

My conscience used sometimes to upbraid me with having done wrong, after I had run away from my master and arrived in Connecticut; and while I was living in Southington, Conn. (where I spent some time, as will afterwards be told) I went up on a high mountain, and prayed to the Lord, to teach me my duty, that I might know whether or not I ought to go back to my master. Before I came down I felt satisfied, and it did seem to me that the Lord heard my prayers, when I was a poor wretched slave, and delivered me out of the land of Egypt, and out of the house of bondage; and that it was his hand, and not my own artfulness and cunning, which had enabled me to escape: therefore if we trust in God, we need have no fear of the greatest trials; and though my heart has been pierced with sufferings keen as death, and drank from the cup of slavery, the bitterest dregs ever mingled in it; yet under the consolations of religion, my fortitude never left me.

As Mr. Sturges was intending to remove to New-York, he sold out all his property, and every thing he could wish to part with. He talked very strong of taking me on with him to New-York, but after consideration altered his mind, and hired me out to a Mr. Wolhopter, a printer in Savannah. I lived with Mr. Wolhopter all that summer, and drove his horses and carriages all about there, and out to White Bluff, where he had hired a seat for the summer, supposing it to be a healthy situation, which indeed it was; but we were tormented with moschetos and such other insects as infest that country (called by different names) to a great degree, so that we could hardly sleep nights. We were alternately at this place and at Savannah for the space of four or five months. At the expiration of that time, Mr. Wolhopter removed back to Savannah, with his family, and I accompanied them. I will here mention that during the time I resided at White Bluff, at the request of Mr. Wolhopter, I often went a fishing, and the rays of the sun beating down more severe there, than where I had formerly lived, it created an ague and fever, which reduced me so low that even my attending physician, Doct. Collock (who attended me strictly for about four months) dispaired of my life, and often since that time being borne down under the afflictions that a slave often experiences, and indeed too often, I have wished his predictions had proved true. But after Doct. Collock perceived I was convalescent, and gaining my health and strength rapidly, he enquired of me, that provided he should buy me, if I would be contented to live with him, drive his horses and carriage, occasionally wait in the house and at the table, and do such other business as is necessarily required in a family.

With but few remarks I endeavour to give my readers but a faint representation of the hard treatment, ill usage and horrid abuse the poor slave experiences while groaning under the yoke of bondage; that yoke which is not easy, nor the burden light; but being placed in that situation, to repine is useless, we must submit to our fate and bear up as well as we can under the cruel treatment of our despotic tyrant. After Doct. Collock made this proposition to me, I replied that I had been sold from my parents in Virginia, and felt anxious to see them again once more, but if he would buy me, I would serve him faithfully and freely for the term of five years, provided that at the expiration of that time he would grant me my freedom, to be specified in writing, to which he consented and promised to have it done and give me the writing to keep, but he never fulfilled his promise. He however wrote to Mr. Sturges, in New-York, and told me that he had received a letter from him, in which he consented I should go and live with him, and directed me to leave Mr. Wolhopter's house, and come to his place of residence, which I accordingly did being then very low in health, not having recovered from the ague and fever, but after living with him for some time I recovered my health so far as to be able to perform my duty. When I first went there, on account of my being unwell, my mistress did not like to have me sleep in the house, and so gave me a room up over the carriage house to sleep in. In this room there was a bed-stead, or bunk made of boards. I understood by some of the servants that a man lately died there in a fit. In the course of the day I laid myself down on the bed-stead with a blanket, to rest, not being able to be about, as a very little exercise overcame me. After lying there about an hour, I was looking very steady up towards the roof of the building, when to my great horror and surprise I could plainly perceive a large bright sparkling pair of eyes intently fixed on me, staring me full in the face. It instantly occurred to me that the bed-stead I was then lying on, belonged to the man who had died there, and that I (not having any liberty to use it) was doing wrong and that this was a token for me to leave it. I accordingly took my blanket, spread it on the floor and lay on that. Presently after, the cook *Jane* came up to fetch me something to eat, she enquired of me why I left the bed-stead and lay on the floor. I replied to her that I was afraid I had done wrong in lying on it as long as I already had done, for I had received no liberty from any person so to do, and I was convinced in my own mind that the bed-stead placed there, belonged to the man who had died there, and that I thought I had seen a token for me to leave it, which I accordingly had done. I then told her the circumstances of the eyes and of my conjectures at the time, that I had no business there. She replied to me, sleep on it if you please, you are perfectly welcome to the use of it. My mistress now knowing any thing of what had happened, sent me word that I might have a lamp there to keep burning through the night. She then was very kind to me and used me well; but I could not endure the thoughts of sleeping there, and as soon as bedtime came, I took my blanket and went in the house and slept in the parlour with the two boys who were then waiting in the house, named Sandy and Cyrus. (commonly called Cy) This being all unknown to my mistress at that time, but she afterwards consented to have me sleep in the house, which I did during the time I lived there. My readers, or many of them who are not credulous, will very likely be apt to disbelieve the assertion already made, but I can assure them that the whole is true. Where is the person who would be made easily to believe a story of this kind, unless he positively did know it to be a fact, and the circumstances can be attested to even now. Although they did not see what I did, they were some of them acquainted with the circumstances. This cook, who brought me my victuals, told me the place was said to be haunted. She had her information from the other servants who also told me the same, also that strange noises were heard, which had been heard by other persons who were sick and put up there by my master's orders to be taken care of; many of them had been removed on the same account, as they told that they were positive of hearing strange noises, and also seeing frightful sights. These stories combined with what I myself saw, warranted me in my opinion to make this assertion. I think the house without any doubt is what people in general would call haunted. My readers may put their own constructions and draw inferences, I can barely state that I tell the truth.

This circumstance happened in the winter. The next summer, my master, Doct. Collock, ordered me to get the horses and carriage ready, to take all the family off to Darien; which I accordingly did. They went from thence to Cumberland Island, and I returned to Savannah with the horses and carriage, alone. My master gave me a piece of bacon, or shoulder, smoked, which I suppose would weigh about six or eight pounds, which was the whole he left me, to last all summer. He also left a tierce[7] of rice, to be divided amongst us, about the house, in all, eight or ten of us. After the rice was gone, we were allowed to each of us, eight quarts of Indian corn per week; this was all we had to subsist upon during his absence, which was about six or seven months. I also had a great deal to do about the house, and out on the plantation I had as much mowing as I could attend to. At another time, when I was at work out in the country, at my master's country seat, I had slipped the head stalls or bridles over the horses heads in order to let them eat while they were harnessed to a waggon, as I had been using them to draw hay. I left them to eat while I went to eat my dinner. In the mean time, two or three small negro children got into the waggon and frightened the horses, so that they ran round the house in the yard, a number of times; and in so doing, they dragged the waggon over, or so nigh a young tree which my master set great store by, that it was torn up or broken down. When my master returned from Cumberland Island, he enquired of the driver, (old Ben) what had become of the tree. Old Ben replied, the torm broke him down, massa; and my master knew no more afterwards about it. The waggon that was also badly broken, we mended up as well as we could among ourselves: the harness, which being considerably injured, I carried to Mr. Kitchen, who being used to make and repair harnesses for my master, fixed it so that he (my master) never found that it had been broken or injured—all of this passed unnoticed by my master.

At the time Doct. Collock left Savannah, he left in his office an old man called Doct. Sherman, to take charge of his office, and attend on such persons as should request his attendance, when he was gone. There were also, at the same time, two young gentlemen in the office, studying with my master; one of them named James M'Call, and the other, a young man, I think they called Mr. Ginneylack. He at different times had insulted these young gentlemen to such a degree, that they left the office. A short time after this, he found a large paper, containing a number of images drawn out with a pencil; one, representing himself, and others, representing ducks, with their bills open, apparently in the attitude of squalling. On the paper was written something like this; "how do you do, my good old friend? how do you do? how are your sore legs? We know that ducks quack, and Sherman is a quack, &c." It was supposed that he was a quack in the greatest degree. Doct. Collock was considered one of the best physicians in Savannah; but as he was obliged to go to Cumberland Island, and could get no other person of any repute to remain in his office and take charge of his business, readily, and this old man (or Doctor) being an indigent person, he out of charity, let him remain in his office until his return, and transact such business in his line as the people should see fit to set him about. The old man, not knowing to whom to ascribe the (what he termed libel,) vented his malice on me, by asserting that I was the author of it, of which I was perfectly innocent: but he made my master believe it. He wrote to him while he was at Cumberland Island, and persuaded him that I was actually the author. At the time my master wished to return to Savannah, he wrote to his brother-in-law, Edward Campbell, Esq. attorney at law, requesting him to come with me, with the carriage and horses to Darien, in order to take him and his family home. We accordingly went on one day, met them there, and returned the next. After our return, my master took me into his office, and enquired of me about these images. I told him I knew nothing about it. He was very inquisitive about it, but I still told him I knew nothing about it; but as Sherman made him believe that I had done all this mischief, of course my mistress also believed it, and after that I could never please them, let me try my best endeavours, they still appeared to be dissatisfied.

I was one evening, ordered to take my mistress and her sisters to Mr. Andrews'. I accordingly harnessed the horses, put them to the carriage, and drove (with the ladies) to the house where I was directed. They went in the house and stayed, I do not know how long. I stayed with the horses and carriage at the door, in order to take care of them. I waited for them until I fell asleep and was dreaming. When they came out of the house, they awoke me by their talking and laughing at the door. I did not know where I was, where I had been, nor where I was a going. I knew no more where I was than if I had been blind-folded. But I was afraid to let them know that I had been asleep, so I drove on directly towards the market, looking on the right hand and on the left, to see if I could recognize some house that I had before been acquainted with; but finding none I drove on. I had passed a number of turns which would have taken us directly home. My mistress observing this, enquired of me why I did not take that route home, but I made her no reply, then turned towards the bay thinking I was driving towards the commons. I then saw Mrs. Telfure's house, and then I knew where I was. I then drove down to Judge Jones's, and left her sisters there, and continued on home with my mistress to broad street. I do not think that my mistress, or either of the ladies ever suspected the reason why I took such a round-about road to get home; but it was owing entirely to my falling asleep in the carriage while waiting at the door, and on awaking, not knowing where I was.

At another time I was severely attacked with a tooth-ache. My master drew one of my teeth which fractured my jaw and made it ache worse. He had often given me a great many bottles to clean and scour, and at this time gave me a great number. I went down under the bluff to get some sand for the purpose of cleaning them. While I was there I kept drinking spirits, (in order to ease my jaw where the tooth was drawn) till I got completely intoxicated, and did not return until nearly evening. *I was then a praying soul.* As I was returning back to my master's house, I called in at the Rev. Henry Collock's study, or office. He seeing my condition, or the condition I then was in, immediately offered to attend prayers with me, which he did; we prayed there nearly half an hour. I went into his office with tears rolling down my bosom, and the floor of his office will be a witness to my tears until the day of judgement. After our prayers were ended I came out, and the next time I saw him, was within the walls of a cold prison: he came to the diamond hole, and spoke to me, and asked me how I did, (I was at the time lying down on my blanket on the floor.) I answered him, I had a very bad jaw-ache. I then asked him to give me a book containing the Psalms of David, such an one as I was then reading. The next day he sent me a Bible. I however, at the time I left this Parson Collock at his office, went directly home to my master, who was his cousin. One was a worldly man, the other was a christian. Immediately after I went into the yard, my master had information of it, and took me in his office; he asked me where I had been? I told him I had been after gravel to clean his bottles, and on account of the pain in my jaw, I had drank spirits until I was so much intoxicated that I dare not come back until then. He then after having a long conversation with me, ordered me to go up stairs and lie down. I did so, but after I had lain there a few minutes he came up, took me by the collar and ordered me to go into a room where he wanted to lock me up. At this time I suspected his intention of wishing to lock me up, in order that as soon as night came, he could send me to jail. I then pretended to be much more intoxicated than I really was, in hopes by that means to induce him to let me remain where I then was until morning; but he would not, and after a severe struggle he affected the purpose he intended, and I was locked up in a room in the third story, or in the garret. After sitting some time, I began to consider my situation. I observed a bed-stead with a cord in it, which I concluded best for me to take out and let myself down from the window, and clear myself for the woods; but upon examination, I found the window so high from the ground, (after I had taken the cord from the bed-stead) that I feared to attempt the leap; I threw back the cord with despair, and then determined to force the door; it was in me a desperate undertaking, but I finally effected it. After coming down the stairs as still and sly as possible, that creature, Jane the cook, perceived me and gave the alarm. Immediately the cry of stop thief! stop thief! re-echoed from every quarter. I run and they pursued, caught me, and brought me back. I was then bound and pinioned, my hands were closely tied behind, and I was conducted in this manner (in a more shameful manner than one half the prisoners, malefactors, or high way robbers, after having the sentence of death pronounced upon them, are taken to the place of execution) to jail. There I staid eight long weeks, and what do you think my diet was during that time? Why I will tell you my reader, our allowance was to each person one quart of corn, ground and the husks fanned out of it, and then boiled, which we sometimes are allowed salt for, and at other times we are not. Oftentimes we were obliged to eat it without even salt or any other seasoning. As for meat we are entirely a stranger to it, we know nothing about it, as an allowance either from our masters or the jailor. Our jailor having considerable to be done in and about the house, and knowing me to be expert in what he wanted to have done, released me from solitary confinement, and let me work for him about the prison at his own discretion; but one day Doct. Collock saw me out of jail on my ordinary business while he was passing by, and came in and told Capt. M'Call, the jailor, that I would run away if he gave me such liberties. Mr. Griffin, then clerk of the jail, came and called to me and said, Grimes, your master says you will run away, and that you must be shut up again, for he does not like to see you out here. I was then conducted back to the cell again, where I remained until he again returned to Savannah; then I was restored as it were to liberty again, that is, to do what was necessary in and about the house; but I being a barber fared rather better than the other prisoners.

I will state that I have seen women brought there and tied hand and foot, and their clothes turned up and tied there, up to their shoulders, leaving their body perfectly naked, then whipped with a keen raw-hide (or cow-skin sometimes called) until the blood run down to their heels. I was then in expectation that my turn would be next, every moment looking for it. While I was in confinement, I myself, as well as the other prisoners, were used to the sound of Oh pray! Oh pray! which came from those poor slaves, then in preparation for being whipped, or experiencing then at the same time, the smart of the lash which was so often used without mercy. As large, stout and athletic a negro as I was ever acquainted with, was selected for the purpose of whipping those who were doomed to receive the lash. He himself being there confined for some crime he had committed. In a case of whipping, he was compelled to put it on as severely as lay in his power, or take a severe flogging himself. One man who was confined in the same room with me, by the name of Reuben, belonging to John Bolton, (one of the richest men in Savannah.) This poor man's back was cut up with the lash, until I could compare it to nothing but a field lately ploughed. He was whipped three times in one week, forty stripes, save one, and well put on by this strong athletic fellow. You may well think this poor negro's back was well lacerated, ah, indeed, not only well lacerated, but brutally and inhumanly bruised.

I at this time was in such dread of the whipping post, where I daily saw so many human beings sacrificed to the lash of the tyrant, that it struck me with horror. I prayed constantly to my God (who had relieved me before in the hour of danger,) to protect and defend me in this adversity, being now in a prison, from whence I knew no means of escape. And early one morning, while pondering on the miseries I was compelled to endure, I thought, and indeed, I was convinced, that I heard a voice from heaven, saying, Be of good cheer; and other words, which I do not conceive necessary to mention in this history. At the same time I heard this, I had a glimpse of something, most glorious to behold. I immediately felt a comfort in my soul, which cheered me up, and made me feel joyful. I was then convinced that my prayers had ascended to the high throne of

Grace, for which I returned my most fervent thanks to the Almighty Ruler of the universe.

After remaining some time in jail, Doct. Collock came and took me out, and said his reason for keeping me there so long, was, that he had expected a ship from New-Orleans, and intended to send me there to work on the sugar plantation; but as the ship did not arrive, and he having considerable mowing to do on his plantation, he would take me out and set me at work to do his mowing, the other slaves not understanding it. So, after remaining in my solitary cell for eight long weeks, I was then permitted to breathe the fresh air again, and put to my task in the meadows, where I continued during that season, cutting and curing his grass. The winter following, I was employed in clearing and grubbing new ground. The next summer I was kept on the plantation as usual, under the negro driver. When the season came for cutting oats, I was one day sent to mow them. I mowed one forenoon, and having a severe boil under each arm, I did not feel able, nor indeed was I able to rake them up. I went to the room where I slept, it being out from Savannah about two or three miles, in a large house where the driver and his family slept. I there laid down to rest myself. After about half an hour, the old negro driver came to me, and asked me why I did not rake up my oats, or those I had cut. I replied, that I had a large boil under each arm, and was unable to do it. He swore I should do it, and went for a stick to beat me, in order to compel me to do it. I heard him coming back, and when he burst open the door, I let him have it in old Virginia stile, (which generally consists in gouging, biting and butting.) I drove my head against him, (hardly knowing what I was about, being so much terrified,) until he could scarcely stand or go. I then compelled him to give up the stick to me, which I kept in my hand, walking to and fro, while he, as soon as he recovered from the bruising I had given him, called aloud to the other slaves to come to his assistance. They immediately gathered together, to the number of about twenty. He ordered them to seize me, and was in hopes they would: but one of the stoutest of them, on whom he placed the greatest reliance, came up to me to inquire what was the matter, and why I had treated the driver so. I asked how I had treated him. He replied, how did you. I then seized him by the shoulders, and said to him, I will show you. So I served him in the same way I had the driver, and almost as severe. The other negroes seeing me use this stout fellow so harshly, were afraid to touch me. I kept walking with the stick I had taken from my enemy, to and fro as before. They did not attempt after that to touch me. The driver then called to one of the slaves, to get a horse, and go to town, to give my master information; saying, Robert, Robert, gitta up a horse, and go uppa town, tella massa Pero a whippa me. But they not attempting to meddle with me any more, I went myself to town, to see my master first. I arrived there after Robert had been there a short time. I went into my master's office and told him the whole affair. He enquired of me very particularly concerning it. I convinced him of my innocence, and he sent me back to the plantation again, to work as before. During the conversation I had with my master, he asked me how I dare strike the driver. I replied, that I must defend myself. He said to me, would you dare to strike me if I was out there? Do you not know that your arm would be cut off if you did? I answered, yes, sir, I know my arm would be cut off if I should attempt to strike you; but, sir, if you had been there you would not have used me in the way the driver did: he is an iggorant old African, or Guinea negro, and has not judgment sufficient to superintend any one in my present situation. I then showed him my biles. He was satisfied I was not able to rake the oats, but said, when I leave my driver there, I put him in my shoes: go back to the plantation, I shall be there soon myself. I told him I had no friend, except it was himself, and if he did not whip me when he came to the plantation, I should be convinced he was my friend; and furthermore I was convinced that not one negro on the plantation was friendly to me. He knew me to be a stranger, and a man of good sense. After this conversation, I went back to the plantation, and staid there until he came. When he arrived there, he called the old driver, and talked to him very severely, saying, you should have examined into his situation before you undertook to whip him; you would then have been satisfied he was not able to work. He said not three words to me in anger. I continued to work on the plantation until towards winter, when I was again sent to the woods, and employed in cutting and splitting rails. I should have mentioned, that while workings on the plantation the summer past, I undertook to raise for myself a small crop of rice, of perhaps twenty rods of ground. It being the first I had ever undertook to raise, it cost me considerable trouble. All that I knew about it, was what little information I could get from seeing the negroes raise here and there a small piece for themselves; and I was obliged to do it in the same way; that is, to take an opportunity occasionally, when not being observed by the driver, to slip in and do a little at it. After it was in a situation to cut, I reaped it and carried it to town, where I sold it for $1 25 per hundred, amounting in the whole, to about five or six dollars. I kept this money, that in case of emergency, I could occasionally purchase a small piece of meat, or other necessary articles, for my subsistence. I sometimes went to town in order to procure something to eat with our common allowance, (a peck of corn per week) and have often carried on my head a bundle of wood, perhaps three miles, weighing more than one hundred pounds, which I would sell for twelve cents, in order to get a supply of necessary food. I would then, it being late in the evening, go to my master's house unknown to him, and lodge there. It has frequently been the case, that I have been so much fatigued with my day's work, and then carrying my bundle of wood that distance, that I have overslept myself, or slept longer than I intended. In that case, I have been obliged to get out at the window, or in some other way avoid my master, who used to visit his plantation early each morning, so that I could get there first. I would then, after running three miles, start the negroes out to work, telling them my master was coming. They would all go out at once, and by the time he arrived, be steadily engaged at their work. Thus I gained for my master a great many hours work in the course of the season, which he knew nothing about, and all for the purpose of clearing myself from blame, and perhaps a severe flogging.

By this manner, I was enabled to acquire a very comfortable subsistence through the winter, or during the time I lived with Doct. Collock. He sold me some time in the winter. To do the Doctor justice, I must say that he was the best and most humane man I ever lived with, or worked under. Some time previous to my master's selling me, I had heard that A. S. Bullock, Esq. agent for the navy, (who had engaged a carriage and pair of horses, coming on from New-York, which he expected very soon,) wanted to buy a servant, to drive and take care of them. I went to see him, and enquired whether he would buy me. He replied, yes, if your master will sell you. I then went to my master, and told him Mr. Bullock wished to buy me, provided he would sell me. He then said to me, where did you see Mr. Bullock? have you been there to try to induce him to buy you? I replied, no, sir, he saw me in the street and enquired of me whether my master wished to sell me. I told him you did. He then said go and tell your master I will buy you if he will sell you, he then asked me what price my master would require for me, I told him $500, was the price for which I was last sold, he replied I will give that sum for you if Doct. Collock will accept of it. He added, tell your master if he wants to sell you, that I wish him to come and see me. My master replied, if Mr. Bullock wants to see me, let him come here, I shall not go to see him. I then went and told Mr. Bullock the answer my master gave me; he asked me if my master would give me a recommend. I answered him that he said he would give me none. He then observed to me, I perceive your master does not want to sell you. He then called his little son to him (aged about twelve years) and gave him between five and six hundred dollars, telling him to go to Doct. Collock, give him the money, and tell him that if he was willing to sell Grimes, to take that and send back as much change as he pleased. He took $500, and sent back the remainder. I was now sold to Mr. Bullock, where I stayed without returning to see my old master. I felt very uneasy whilst the boy was gone, fearing my master would not sell me, as I was satisfied his intention was not to sell me in Savannah, but to send me off to New-Orleans, or some other place at a distance, being as I was convinced in my own mind, so much prejudiced against me by that old quack, (so called) *Sherman,* that he was determined if he sold me at all, that it should not be in Savannah. It is generally known that when a man sells a servant, he intends by that means to punish him, and endeavors to sell him where he shall never see him again. For this same reason I was afraid Doct. Collock, would not sell me, my mistress also being opposed to my being sold in Savannah. I shall here mention a very narrow escape I had while I lived with Doct. Collock. As I was occasionally tending his horses and driving them, I was exposed very often to be hurt by them, to be killed, bit, thrown off them, &c. He had one very ill-natured cross horse, no one could approach him or pass behind him with any safety. I was one day compelled to go in great haste in the reach of him. As I got almost past him, he threw both his feet against me with such violence that my breath was entirely beat out of my body, and I was completely stunned; he sent me at a distance where I lay completely senseless for some time; I merely escaped with my life. After some time I got up, went and informed my master and mistress of the circumstance, when the necessary remedy was administered, and I finally recovered. This I mention, merely to inform my readers of the dangers and narrow escapes I have experienced during my slavery.

This same parson Collock, whom I have heretofore mentioned, was a very fine, candid and humane man; he was beloved by every one who was acquainted with him; a friend to the poor slave, as well as the richest planter, or gentleman, he was in a habit of holding meetings in the evening, as often as two or three times each week, which I always attended to strictly, and very often it was as late as 10 o'clock, or later, before I reached my master's house. He had a number of times on finding me not at home in the evening, enquired of the other servants where I was, and being generally by them told that they did not know unless I was at meeting; he one evening after my return, appeared to be very angry with me, and asked me where I had been so late for a number of evenings. I replied, I have been to meeting sir. He then said by what means do you escape the vigilance of the guard? (or what they term in the northern states *Watch*.) I replied, the guard do not meddle with me in returning from meeting. He then said, why do they not? they ought to. I said nothing to this, but I knew very well what he wished, that was, he would be very well pleased to have the guard take me up, and take me to gaol, in order to punish me for attending meeting; but the guard never attempted to meddle with me, they always took me to be a *white man*. I have frequently walked the streets of Savannah in an evening, and being pretty well dressed, (generally having on a good decent suit of clothes,) and having a light complexion, (being at least three parts white,) on meeting the guard I would walk as bold as I knew how, and as much like a gentleman; they would always give me the wall.[8] One time in particular, while walking home late in the evening, I saw two or three of them together, I was afraid, but summoned all my resolution, and marched directly on towards them, not turning to the right hand nor to the left, until I came up to them. They at first did not notice me being engaged in conversation. I continued on, head up, walked past them and happened to brush one of them a little in passing, they immediately turned off the walk; one of them spoke and said we ask your pardon sir. At another time I deceived them in the following manner. One evening a coloured man from Richmond, Virginia, called on me while sitting in the kitchen and told me he had lately been waiting on my old master, Doct. Philip Thornton of Richmond, and had taken him from there to his father's country-seat, at Montpelier in Culpepper county, in a carriage with four horses, but was at present waiting on a gentleman from Richmond, then in town, who lodged at Col. Shelman's tavern, some distance from my master's. He told me his name was William Patterson, he was a free man, and was hired by people occasionally to drive their horses. He had heard of me while at Doct. Thornton's, and by enquiring of Major Lewis, a black man, who was a great groom in Savannah, he found where I lived. He stayed with me, taking something to drink, and smoked a segar (my master knowing nothing of it,) until about eleven o'clock, when he wanted to return to his lodgings. I told him the guard were all out at their posts, and it would be dangerous for him to attempt it alone; but if he would consent to walk behind me in the capacity of a servant, (to all appearances) I would accompany him home, and I had no doubt but I could deceive the watch as I had done before. He readily consented to this, and I put on my best suit, took a rattan in my hand, he walked behind me and continued on until we reached the tavern, where we found about fifteen or twenty of the guard seated on the steps of the door; he trembled, but I walked directly on, when they rose up to make room for me to enter and him to follow, I opened the door and went in, he closed it. After he had followed me as a servant through the streets, and made the watch believe it, when we were alone by our selves, he flourished his hands and snapped his fingers a great number of times, saying, well done, well done for you; I will tell this when I get home to Virginia, I should not dared to have undertaken so desperate a thing.

During the time I lived with A. S. Bullock, Esq. the navy agent, at first, he treated me very well. After living with him about a fortnight, the horses and carriage he had expected arrived. The horses were very low in flesh. I took them into my care, attended to them strictly, and they soon began to thrive: in about three or four weeks they were in good order. By this time, my master knew, or at least thought, I understood the business of taking care of horses, and was very well pleased with my performance, as I kept the carriage, horses and harness very clean and nice. During the winter and summer after, I used to drive the horses and carriage, carrying some part or the whole of his family out for a ride every evening, about five o'clock. The distance was generally from three to five miles. The winter following, I was employed generally as during the one past. The next spring he sold his horses and carriage to Doct. Jones, who was an enemy to me, and exerted all the arts he could invent, to influence my master against me; but all availed nothing, my master being well pleased with me, and I with him, he could not effect this purpose. At this time, my mistress, her sister, Mrs. Hunter, with her daughter, Miss Catherine, and a brother of my mistress, Mr. Glen, took passage in a packet, with a great number besides, for New-York. My master concluded to go by land, and to buy a light carriage, with a pair of horses; one Mr. Lyon to join with him, and for me to go and drive the horses. After having every thing almost completed for the journey, they altered their minds, and concluded to take passage in the stage. If I had gone on with Mr. Bullock to the northward, I should have returned, had it been for no other purpose than to make out my enemies to be liars, who had instilled into my master a belief that if he took me with him, I should never return, but run away and leave him. I was then left, by my master's order, to work out, and pay him three dollars per week, and find myself. I then went to work for Mr. Irving, on board the Epervier, who was manager on board. He gave me one dollar for each day I worked there. The Epervier was a vessel taken from the British in the last war. I saw seven truck loads of gold and silver, in boxes, taken from her and carried to the bank in Savannah. I worked for Mr. Irving about a month, he paid me off, and I worked about town for a few days after. I then went out on a plantation, and worked for a Mr. Housten. He also gave a dollar a day. I worked for him about a week at mowing. After that, I came back, and went to work on board the James Monroe, a national vessel, for Capt. Skinner, of New-London, Con. He gave me seventy-five cents a day. I acted as cook and steward on board of her. After this I went to work about town, and Mr. Burrows, a brother-in-law of my master, hired me to drive his horses and carriage. He gave me twenty dollars a month. I carried him and his family to Augusta. I resided with him all that summer, and drove his horses and carriage from there, up to the same hills, back and forth, each day, when the weather was good, for about five or six months, which was as long as my master would spare me. Mr. Stephen Bullock, a relative to my master, (as he was left superintendent of his affairs during the time he was absent,) wrote to Mr. Burrows that he must send me home. Accordingly I went back to Savannah on horseback. A few weeks after my return, my master and family arrived from New-York, with a carriage and four elegant horses. I now had six horses to take care of, and the carriage to keep clean and in order. I took such good care of the horses, and kept the carriage so nice, that Mr. Bullock was well pleased with me. After I had got the four new horses in good order, and fat, he sold one pair of them, which relieved me from some trouble and labor. We have never had any disagreement, yet he had been on to the northward, and but just returned. Some time after this, my master bottled up a few dozen of wine, counted them, and delivered them into my care for keeping. At this time he had a number of workmen, joiners and carpenters, at work about the house. When I took the wine into my care, I took it out of the cellar, and as I was gone after a basket, one of the workmen took a bottle and secreted it. My object in going after a basket was to carry it up into the garret, and this man passing that way, took that opportunity to steal a bottle of it, perhaps not considering at the same time that I was responsible for it, and should be liable to receive a severe punishment if the bottles were not all found: but he did not even return the bottle, after drinking the contents. After I carried them up stairs, my master went and counted them, and finding one missing, called to me to know where it was. I told him I had set them all out of the cellar, and then went for a basket to carry them up; and I had carried the whole that I found up garret. He said there was one missing, and ordered me to fetch it immediately. I told him I thought I had carried up the whole of them. We then went together, and counted them a number of times, but found one missing. He was very angry with me. I asserted my innocence repeatedly, but all to no purpose. I could not make him believe me not guilty. I was suspicious that some one of the mechanics had taken it. I went to them and enquired about it. One of them acknowledged to me that he had taken it, and was willing to pay my master for it. I then immediately went and informed my master, but he would not believe me. I returned to the man who took it, and requested him to go with me to my master, in order to convince him of my innocence. He consented, and we went together. He made a statement to him of the whole affair, and also told him he was willing to pay him to his full satisfaction. But whether my master had an idea that there was a connivance between us to clear myself, or what his motive was I cannot tell, but he did not appear to be any more satisfied than before; still telling me I took it. It grieved me very much to be blamed, when I was innocent. I knew I had been faithful to him; perfectly so. At this time I was quite serious, and used constantly to pray to my God. I would not lie, nor steal. My master knew nothing of that, I kept it a profound secret from him. When I considered his accusing me of stealing when I was so innocent and had endeavored to make him satisfied by every means in my power, that I was so, but he still persisted in disbelieving me, I then said to myself, if this thing is done in a green tree, what must be done in a dry. I forgave my master in my own heart for all this, and prayed to God to forgive him and turn his heart. I was dissatisfied to think that my master had so bad an opinion of me at the time I was so honest; and tried by best endeavors to please him.

I then wanted some person to buy me, and let me work until I had paid $800. I accordingly applied to a man, who promised me he would try to buy me. I must here state the circumstance that prevented him from doing so. Sometime previous to this, I had told the other servants that something would happen to me, that my master would be very angry with me for something, he would beat me unmercifully and send me to prison. They were very much surprised to hear me talk in this manner as they well knew that we were on very good terms at that time. So after this happened concerning the wine, I having a number of articles in and about the yard, such as boxes, clothes, trunks &c. and as I have before mentioned, being determined to get some person to buy me, I used occasionally to carry some of them off and hide them in the woods, well knowing that if my master should sell me, he would never allow me to enter his yard again, and the things being my own, would be of service to me in another place, should I be so fortunate as to have a new master. After obtaining the promise of this man to buy me, he being unwilling to speak to him on the subject, fearing my master might think he was endeavouring to entice me away, he told me to ask my master if he *wanted* to sell me. I shall not mention the name of this man, for as it so happened he did not buy me, it might make some difficulty. Ever since the circumstance of the wine, my master not appearing to be satisfied with me about it, had treated me very severely. I determined one day when my master was in the parlour, to ask him the question. So I went into the kitchen which was in the lower room where the other servants were, (having been myself in the stable attending to the horses,) and told them that what I had prophesied would soon take place, saying, my hour is come, I am now going up to see my master, and he will beat me and put me in prison. They then enquired of me what was the matter. I answered them that I was going to ask my master a question, for which I shall receive this. They endeavored to persuade me not to go, saying, you will only bring trouble on yourself by going. But being determined on doing it, I went, not heeding what they said, begging of me not to go. I went up, he was walking backwards and forwards (with his hands thrust in his pockets) across the room, waiting for his dinner. I stood for a few moments behind a chair, with my hand on the back of it, fearing to speak, at length he stepped up towards me, saying, well what's wanting Grimes? I being so fearful to irritate him, dared not to speak immediately. He repeated, well Grimes what's wanting. I then with a great deal of diffidence (after many fruitless attempts to speak) said, master are you willing to sell me? It was exactly as I had anticipated, he flew in a violent passion, caught hold of a chair and came toward me in the attitude of attempting to strike me, he made one or two passes at me with it, dropping it seized me by the collar, and beat me with his fist most unmercifully; at the same time exclaiming, sell you? yes, you damned son of a bitch. God dam you, I'll sell you; I'll sell you by God; who wants to buy you; God dam you, who wants to buy you? I made no reply, but cleared myself from him and his house as soon as possible for the stable; while going towards the stable, not dareing to turn my head, and expecting him every moment at my heels, I pretended to stop to pick up something, at the same time casting my eyes behind me, I saw him coming very rapidly towards me. I had hoped as his dinner was nigh ready, he would not undertake to come after me until after dinner, and had determined on quitting him immediately, thinking it best to go then, as I was convinced he would when he next saw me finish what he had began, that is a severe beating; but seeing him so near, and pretending not to have seen him, I went into the stable, took my fork, and went to work stirring up the straw, not noticing him at all, or at least not letting him know that I did. He came into the stable and seized me by the collar with his left hand, while with his right fist clenched, he beat me with that in my breast and face, until all in a gore of blood. I dared not say a word, but pretended to be very much hurt; he all the time exclaiming who wants to buy you? God dam you, I say who wants to buy you? you rascal. He then dragged me to the platform under the Piazza, continuing all the time to beat me in the same manner, but calling frequently to Jack to bring a rope and bind me. He said, bring me a rope Jack, bring a rope God dam you, and bind this rascal. Jack went for a rope, but not being able to find one as soon as he wanted, my master was quite enraged at him, and fell to beating him severely. After some time Jack found a rope and fetched it to my master, but he was so much enraged at me, that he kept beating him, saying, tie him you rascal, tie him sir. All that poor Jack could do was to smart under his chastisement, and keep saying, yes sir, yes sir, I will. I was then placed in such a situation that my arms were pinioned, and my hands tied behind. He then sent Jack for a constable, saying, go you rascal and find a constable, have this damn'd rascal taken to gaol. Jack went but soon came back, saying, I could not find master Noble. He then told him to go and get any constable he could find. He soon came with another; my master told this constable to take me to jail, and give me a flogging and lock me up. This man seeing my situation, my face all blood, my hands bound behind me, and I standing there trembling with the bruises I had received, together with the fear of another more barbarous flogging, appeared to take pity on me. He whispered to my master and said, I think by his looks you have given him a severe whipping, I would put him in jail without any more chastisement. My master replied, by God I have not hurt him, all I have done was with my knuckles. I had repeatedly told my master before, that my hands were so closely bound the blood was almost ready to start through my fingers, he replied, I don't care if it should. He then directed the constable (as he had persuaded him not to flog me any more) to take me to jail. We started and got as far as the gate, when he called him back, saying, let Jack wash the blood off his face, it has not been washed for six months, people will think I have been murdering. He then told Jack to go and get my hat and put on me, and also my coat and spread over my shoulders, which he did. I then went with the constable to jail and was locked in. I knew my master's disposition so well, that I was convinced he did not wish to have me imprisoned, but only for me to make an acknowledgment and ask his pardon, for merely my asking him the question I did. I had before anticipated this, for I knew he could not do without me, all he wanted of me, to set me at liberty, was for me to ask his pardon, and promise never to ask him to sell me again. Had he (at the time the constable advised him not to have me whipped again) persisted in having his orders executed, which I knew to be Moses' law, (that is) 40 stripes save one, which I must receive before I entered the jail, I should have begged his pardon, and made most any acknowledgement he should require, knowing my constitution could not bear it. But I pretended to be ignorant of the whole and acted stupid, and dull, not regarding what I knew to be his wish; and when I heard him order the constable to commit me without whipping, my heart leapt for joy, for I knew what I had to endure before I should be sold. After lying in jail some time, I sent word to this same man who had promised to buy me, to come and buy me out of jail; but he refused, thinking my master would conjecture he had enticed me to leave him; notwithstanding I had assured him that my master wished to sell me. After that I was compelled to lie there in my solitary cell for the space of three weeks, before any person appeared to buy me. The room in which I was placed, was so foul and full of vermin, it was almost insupportable. The lice were so thick and large, that I was obliged to spread a blanket (which I had procured myself) on the floor, and as they crawled up on it, take a junk or porter bottle which I found in the jail, and rolled it over the blanket repeatedly, and in the same way that I have seen people grind or power mustard seed on a board. I could always hear the death of some announced by their cracking. This I had to observe daily, and indeed often two or three and perhaps more times each day. Besides all this, I had often to take off my shirt, pick them out of my collar, pile them up as fast as I could, and take the bottle to crush them. My readers will here understand, that this room had constantly previous to my imprisonment therein, been occupied as a prison for negroes. They no more than myself having a privilege of a change of linnen, or water wherewith to cleanse it. Any person would naturally suppose the place to be (vulgarly speaking,) filled with lice; and it was when I went there, as nigh filled as any building I ever entered. I will here mention that a few days previous to the time that I told the servants something would take place between my master and myself dissatisfactory to us both, that for some trivial fault, which I cannot now recollect, he came to the stable, took the reins of the harness, bound my hands and led me along the stables (the doors being open,) backwards and forwards for some time, threatning to whip me. The windows in the house being open, my mistress saw him. She then went to the back door and called Ben (a servant) from the kitchen. He came to her. She immediately seized him by his ear and shaking him severely, pointing at the same time to me, (having a fair view and grinning horridly a ghastly smile,) said, you see there! you see there! Do you see how your master does with Grimes? he will do so with you too. She then called Jack, a poor honest Guinea negro, and a faithful servant, to her and used him in the same way, saying, if you do not behave yourself well you shall be served in the same manner. They replied, yes mistress, I will, I will. It was a practice of my master to have a soup almost every day. My master Stephen, usually went to market each day to procure meat for dinner for the family, and always purchased a shin of beef. Jack accompanied him with the market basket to fetch home what he bought. The richest part of the soup was consumed by the family, and the remainder consisting of the lean meat and the shin and course pieces remaining on the bones, were then left for us in the kitchen. Gulla Jack, who was a servant about the house, to scour, &c, the same that fetched the meat home, after noticing this for a number of months began to be dissatisfied with it. One day in particular we were standing together under the platform back of the house, my master being in the necessary but a few yards from us, heard his conversation, which amounted to nearly what I now am about to state. Jack said to me, (not knowing our master was so near) by God I don't want to stay here for my master to licka me, an licka me, and all he give me a sin of beef, he eata all de meat an den he licka me wid de bone, be God me do not lika stay here to be usa so: using such kind of broken language as he had often before used to me, when I would laugh and join with him merely for sport and to hear him talk; at this time I joined with him and laughed heartily. After this I went to the stable to work, and Jack went to his work. My master went into the house and went up stairs, when he told my mistress what he had heard. Whilst he was telling her, one of the servant girls happened to over hear him. She came directly and informed Jack and myself of it, saying our master was quite angry with us for it. We were both very much frightened at this information, and knew not what to do. I had cleaned his shoes for him and sent them up by the girl; he sent them back again, saying they were not half cleaned. I did it again and made them very nice and sent them up again. He sent them back a second time with orders for me to fetch them up myself. I was now more afraid than before, but I took them up to him in the parlour: when I went in he was very angry, he snatched up the poker and thrust it hastily into the fire with the greatest fury, ex-claiming, what, you are above cleaning my shoes are you? by God you are above cleaning my shoes; you can carry on with Jack about a shin of beef, but you are above cleaning my shoes. I replied that I did not mean any harm by that, but only laughed to hear him use his broken language. He then said Jack was not to blame, but it was me altogether, for I knew better, but he was a poor ignorant Guinea negro, and therefore not so much to blame.

My master would always when the weather was bad, order me to drive the horse and chaise to his office and carry him home to dinner, precisely at two o'clock. One time I being detained rather longer than usual, did not arrive there until after the clock had struck; I met him about fifty yards from his office on his way home; I drove up to him in order to have him get in, but he took no notice of me at all, and continued on towards home; I drove a little forwards and turned about, overtook him and asked him if he would ride; he looked at me very sternly and replied, no, I'll walk as I began it. I then drove home and told Ben about it. He said to me, ah! you look out for that. I might mention a great many similar circumstances, but it would be too tedious a task, and I will leave it here.

After I had got through with all my troubles with Mr. Bullock, a Mr. White came and bought me out of jail for five hundred dollars. He came to the jail and spoke to me, saying he would buy me if I would consent to drive his horses. I told him I would. I was accordingly let out of jail soon after, and went to his house. I found him to be a cross crabbed man. I did not stay with him long. I lived with him perhaps two or three months, when a certain Mr. Welman came to my master's and bought me. This was the eighth time that I had been sold for five hundred dollars each time. My master did not buy me for his present use. He hired me out to Mr. Oliver Sturges, the man who had once owned me before. I worked for Mr. Sturges about four or five months. He had a man from New-York, who he hired for thirty dollars per month. He wanting to go home, Mr.

Sturges offered Mr. Welman the same wages for me. Whilst I was there I drove his horses, took care of his carriage, and occasionally attended the people in the house.

I have experienced the sufferings of a slave in the Southern States. I have travelled from Frederickstown in Maryland, to Darien in Georgia, and from there to Savannah, from whence I made my escape in the following manner. While I belonged to Mr. Welman, he went with his family to Bermuda, and left me to work for what I could get by my paying him three dollars per week. During this time, the Brig Casket from Boston arrived. I went with a number more to assist in loading her. I soon got acquainted with some of these Yankee sailors, and they appeared to be quite pleased with me. Her cargo chiefly consisted of cotton in bales. After filling her hold, they were obliged to lash a great number of bales on deck. The sailors growing more and more attached to me, they proposed to me to leave in the centre of the cotton bales on deck, a hole or place sufficiently large for me to stow away in, with my necessary provisions. Whether they then had any idea of my coming away with them or not I cannot tell, but this I can say safely, a place was left, and I occupied it during the passage, and by that means made my escape. The evening before the Brig was to sail, I went with a coloured man (a sailor on board) up into town and procured some bread, water, dried beef, and such other necessaries that I should naturally want. It was late in the evening and he being a Yankee sailor, I directed him to walk behind me in the capacity of a servant. (as they would consider me his master, the watch or guard being all on their posts,) He did so, and we procured every thing necessary for me, took them on board and I stowed them away in the hole left for me, where I myself went and remained until we arrived at the quarantine ground New-York. I will here mention that during my passage I lay concealed as much as possible; some evenings I would crawl out and go and lie down with the sailors on deck, the night being dark, the captain would not distinguish me from the hands, having a number on board of different complexions. He or some one would often in the night when there was something to be done, come on deck and call, forward, there, boys. Aye, aye sir, was the reply; then they would immediately be at their posts, I remaining on the floor not perceived by him. We cast off from the wharf at Savannah Saturday night, and remained in the Savannah river until Monday morning; we then crossed the bar near the light-house. After we had got into the ocean the sailors gave three cheers, and gave me to understand that I was clear; we were out of sight of land they said. Nothing more of any consequence occurred until we arrived at the quarantine ground New-York. I remained concealed from the Captain, Mate, and Steward, until after we arrived. One morning after I had left my place of concealment and was in the forecastle of the vessel, intending to change my clothes, as I was putting on a clean shirt, the mate came down; (the captain and passengers having gone before to New-York,) he perceived me with my shirt half on, (being so frightened that I stood motionless,) said, why Grimes, how came you here? I could make him no answer. He then called some of the crew and enquired of them how I came there. They replied, poor fellow he stole aboard. He then enquired if the steward knew that I was aboard. I told him that he did not. He replied know well that you do not let him know it. He then enquired if the captain knew it. I answered him, no sir. He then said to me, let no one know any thing of it, I wish that I myself knew nothing of it; here boys put him over the bows and set him ashore on Staten Island. Upon that, one of the sailors took me ashore in the boat. On landing, he found another sailor with whom he was acquainted, and told him my circumstances, requesting him to assist me in getting to New-York. He promised him that he would. After staying on the Island a few hours, this man told me to follow him down to the river where the packet boat lay, as she would sail soon. There being some of the crew on board the Casket sick, it was necessary that all who passed from the Island, having been on board of her, and all other persons who went from the Island to New-York, should be examined by a Doctor, stationed there for that purpose. This was what I most feared. This man had once spoken to the Doctor, and his name entered on his book; the Doctor stood on the wharf to receive the names of all those who passed into the packet, and none to pass without giving their names, the same to be recorded in his book which he held in his hand. As we approached the wharf, I felt as if my heart was in my mouth, or in other words very much afraid that I should be compelled to give my name, together with an account from where I came, and where I was going, and in what manner I came there. To all this I should not dare to answer, (fearing in one case to implicate the master of the vessel in which I came, who was perfectly innocent; and in the second, of being taken and again returned to my master, there to remain in slavery during the rest of my life.) but I followed him down to the packet boat. I perceived the Doctor had his head turned a little to the left, looking at something in that direction. He perceived the sailor who was my conductor, and recognized him as one he had examined; but not noticing me, I slipped aboard without being interrogated at all. I was in the greatest fear of being detected, so much so that I almost fainted; but when I heard the word given to push off, I rejoiced heartily. I then told the sailor who had been my friend, that I was convinced I should meet with some person on my landing whom I had formerly known. He replied, never mind that, take hold of my chest and come along with me. I did so, and soon after we arrived at the lodgings of this sailor who proved to be my friend. (Which I made my place of abode for the present) In the course of the afternoon I saw a coloured girl near the house in the street, I enquired of her if she would walk with me a little ways, in order to see the town, and that I could again find my lodgings. I being a stranger there was afraid of being lost.

We walked about the city some time; at length, as we were walking up Broadway, who should I see but Mr. Oliver Sturges, of Fairfield, who once had been my master in Savannah. To my great astonishment, he came up to me, and said, why, Theodore, how came you here? I lied to him, and told him I had been there about two weeks; being so frightened, I knew not what to say, never intending to tell a lie, wilfully or maliciously. He asked me how all things were going on at his yard in Savannah. I answered, all well, I just came from there, sir. After a few moments conversation, he passed on one way, and I went on towards my lodgings, where I rested that night. The next morning, after purchasing a loaf of bread, and a small piece of meat, I started on foot for New-Haven. I could often get an opportunity to ride; sometimes behind the stage, at others, I could sometimes persuade a teamster to take me on for a short distance. In this manner, I arrived at New-Haven. After I arrived there, and even before, every carriage or person I saw coming behind me, I fancied were in pursuit of me. Lying still on board the vessel so long, made it fatiguing for me to walk far at a time without stopping to rest: my situation there being quite confined, and no opportunity for exercise. I often was obliged to go off the road and lie down for some time; and whenever I saw any person coming on, that I suspected, I took that opportunity for a resting spell, and went out of sight until they passed by. Finding my money growing short, I found that I must live prudent. I met a couple of boys on the road who had some apples. I bought them, which together with what little provision I took with me, was all I had to subsist on until I arrived at New-Haven, which was three days. I lodged the two nights I was on the road at private houses. When I arrived at New-Haven, I found that all the money I had left amounted to no more than seventy-five cents. That night I lodged at a boarding house, kept by a certain Mrs. W. who took me to be a white man; and although I have lived in New-Haven since that time a number of years, she never knew to this day, but what it was a white man that lodged there that night. The next morning I went to work for Abel Lanson, who kept a livery stable. He set me at work in a ledge of rocks, getting out stone for building. This I found to be the hardest work I had ever done, and began to repent that I had ever come away from Savannah, to this hard cold country. After I had worked at this for about three months, I got employment in taking care of a sick person, who called his name Carr, who had been a servant to Judge Clay, of Kentucky; he was then driving for Lanson. I took care of him, and took his place as driver for some time. One day, as I was assisting Isaac (a son of Lanson) to harness a horse, to my great astonishment and surprise, master Stephen Bullock, whom I have heretofore mentioned, as the relation to, and superintendent of my master's office in Savannah, came up to me and said, Why, John, it is as hot here as in Savannah. (I will here mention, that as it may appear strange for me to have so many names, to those who are not acquainted with the circumstance, that it is a practice among the slave holders, whenever one buys a slave of another, if the name does not suit him, or if he has one of the same name already, he gives him what name he pleases. I for these reasons, have had three different names.) I was so much surprised to see Mr. Bullock, that I could scarce give him an answer. He spoke to me several times. I was so much afraid and astonished, that I could give him no answer. I was afraid he would ask me how I came in New-Haven. Who can express my feelings at first seeing him. I behaved so bashful and afraid to speak, that after saying a few words, he walked down Church street, and I saw no more of him. After he had gone, Isaac said to me, why, he appears to know you. I replied, yes, it is no wonder that he knows me. I then went and informed my friends that I had seen my young master, and I did not think it prudent for me to stay in New-Haven long. Accordingly I left town, and went on to a place called Southington, a few miles back in the country, where I went to work on a farm. Here an accident befel me, which I will mention. I one day went to assist Capt. Potter to pick up apples, and having on a red flannel shirt, the cattle were afraid of it as I was attempting to take them from the cart. Having stepped between them, in order to let the tongue of the cart down, which was filled with apples, they started and ran down a hill as fast as they possibly could. I held on to the tongue of the cart as long as I had strength enough. They were constantly kicking me in the face. I durst not attempt to quit my hold, fearing I should be crushed to pieces by the loaded cart; but not being able to hold on any longer, after they had run down the hill, and through a pair of bars, I fell, and the cart passed over me and crushed my ancle severely. The neighbors gathered round me, expecting every moment to see me breathe my last. They took me up and carried me to a house, sent for a doctor, and he came. I being so much bruised and kicked, the blood was streaming from me in many places. The Doctor soon stopped it, and bound up my ancle. I recovered slowly, and was obliged to crawl on my hands and knees a great while, and supported myself on what little money I had acquired, until I procured a pair of crutches. I then used to go around amongst the neighbors in Southington, husking corn, and doing such kind of work as I could do in my situation. I found it much harder at this time to be a free man, than I had to be a slave; but finally got to be able to earn fifty cents per day. After I had so far recovered as to be able to walk, or rather limp without crutches, I returned to New-Haven. After staying there a short time, I was taken sick, and continued unable to work for a week or two. I put up with Abel Lanson, and assisted him in digging a well. I then worked about the Colleges, cutting wood, at which I earned about one dollar a day, of which I was very saving, until I had collected about twenty dollars. I then left New-Haven, and started for Providence, where I spent the chief part of my money. I then went into partnership with a man by the name of Boham, and kept a barbers shop. After a few months, we dissolved partnership. I then went on to Newport, and after waiting some time for a passage to New-Bedford, at length found a packet bound for that port; but the wind blowing very hard, I did not think it safe to go on board, so I put my trunk on board, and went on myself on foot, it being thirty miles, and arrived there before the packet. I had not money sufficient to pay for my board one week. Wishing to get a place to work as soon as I could, and hearing that Mr. John Howland wanted a servant, I applied to him for employ; we soon struck a bargain at the rate of nine dollars a month: this was in June. In the fall after, I kept shop for myself some part of the time; the rest part I worked for Mr. Howland, until it began to grow cold. I also kept a few groceries. The colored people being often in there evenings, had finally become so much habituated to take their own heads in rioting and carousing, (which I endeavored to suppress in vain,) that Mr. Hazzet, my landlord, asked me a number of times, if I had not better give up the shop. To which I replied, yes sir, I will very gladly, for I see the colored people have imposed upon me. I being a stranger, and the only barber in the place, except white people, they would often come in with their families and dance evenings, until late; and being noisy and riotous, I would endeavor to stop them, but to no purpose; they still persisted in it, until I was obliged to give up my shop.

There was a women who lived in the room below me: she kept house there, and was not pleased with the noise, saying she would not have it there. I suppose she complained to my landlord, and for that reason I was obliged to give up my shop. After one quarter, I did it, and paid him up my rent. After I had left the shop about two months, this woman was heard to cry murder in the night. The neighbors immediately assembled, when two sailors were seen to escape out of her window, go down on to the wharf, and go on board a vessel. The morning following the authority made enquiry about it. On questioning her, she said that two persons came into her room and offered her violence, she resisted as long as her strength held out, and after they had accomplished their design, they then abused and whipped her until she made the outcry. They then enquired of her if she knew who it was. She replied, no. They then enquired, do you suspect any one. She said, no. On enquiring again if she had any reason to mistrust any one, on any account. She replied, I know of no one who owes me grudge except William Grimes: Whilst he lived in this house, over my room, he used to have a great deal of noise there, which disturbed me; I said considerable about it, which was the means of his quitting his shop. He then threatened to be revenged for it. I can think of no other person. I was then taken before a Justice, Esq. Williams, to answer to this charge. I proved by Mr. John Howland, Jr. to whom I had hired out for the winter, for seven dollars a month, that I was in his house all that night. He knew me to go to bed, and as a light snow was then falling, he said it was impossible for me to go out of the house without his knowledge. After three days time I was discharged, they not being able to prove any thing against me. Before I left the room, I was again arrested and taken to this woman's room, where they questioned her very close. They asked her if she could or would swear to the voice of the person or persons that had been seen to come out of her window. She replied, no, I cannot. They then asked her if she was willing to swear that she was afraid of her life. She answered yes. I was again taken back to the court for another trial; I was well convinced that the woman knew it was not me, and also knew who it was. If it had been me, she would have said so at once. Esq. Williams, asked me if I would have a lawyer. I not knowing what to answer, never having been brought up in a court before, answered, yes, sir, I will have you for my lawyer. He replied, I am bound to do you all the good I can; I must do justice. You had better get some other attorney; but there being no one handy, they (my opponents) said, as you have no attorney, we will have none. Esq. Williams then said to me, you must be recognized together with some other person in the sum of $300, for your appearance at Taunton court, in about three months. I not being acquainted with any person to whom I wished to apply, and having no money, I therefore went to gaol, where I stayed until the court set. When the trial came on, two witnesses were brought forward, who testified that they heard me say I would injure the woman. The Judge enquired of them, was that all you heard? is that all you know? They answered, yes. He then acquitted me, cautioning me to behave myself well. I then went directly to Providence, where I remained a few days, then continued on to Norwich, where I went to work for a few weeks, for Mr. Christopher Starr. From thence I went on to New-London, where I purchased a set of barbers tools. Having been informed previous to this that a barber might do well at Stonington point, after crossing the river I pursued my journey, it being through woods. I had not gone more than one or two miles before I saw four or five men, who made directly towards me.

I was very much frightened when I saw them, but could not tell why. I was much more so, when they came up to me and said where are you going, boy? I answered them to Stonington point. Where did you come from? I came from New-London. What have you got there in your bundle? I have got nothing but some barber's tools. You are a barber then are you? Yes, I was told that Stonington point was a good place for a barber, and I purchased a set of tools in New-London, with the intention of going there to establish a shop. They then replied, there has lately been a store broken open, and we are now in pursuit of the rogues; we have orders to search every person we meet with; we are therefore under the necessity of searching you. I replied, you may search me gentlemen if you please. They then proceeded to search my bundle, and finding nothing there more than I had told them, let me go on; but advised me not to go there: that the people were not civil, but would raise the devil with any person, who should undertake to establish a barber's shop there. They advised me to return back to Mr. Starr's; and after considerable conversation I resolved to return; which I did, and worked on Mr. Starr's farm about two weeks longer. I then went to New-London, and took the steam-boat for New-Haven, where I arrived sometime in May. I then went to work about the Colleges, as I had formerly done; also, shaving, cutting hair, &c. such as waiting on the scholars in their rooms, and all other kinds of work that I could do when not employed at this. I worked about the Colleges about six or eight months. I had then accumulated about fifty dollars, and hearing that there was no barber in Litchfield, (a very pleasant town, about 36 miles back in the country, where the celebrated Law school, under the direction of Tapping Reeve Esq. was kept,) and as there were between twenty and thirty law students, I thought it a good place for me. I accordingly went and established myself as a barber. I very soon had a great deal of custom, amounting to fifty or sixty dollars per month. After I had resided there about a year with about as good success, I undertook to keep one or two horses and gigs to let. For sometime I made money very fast; that at length trading horses a number of times, the horse rookies would cheat me, and to get restitution I was compelled to sue them. I would sometimes win the case; but the lawyers would alone reap the benefit of it. At other times I lost my case, fiddle and all; besides paying my Attorney.

Let it not be imagined that the poor and friendless are entirely free from oppression where slavery does not exist: this would be fully illustrated if I should give all the particulars of my life, since I have been in Connecticut. This I may do in a future Edition, and when I feel less delicacy about mentioning names.

While at Litchfield, I sold a waggon to a neighbor and took his note, which I was compelled to sue. My debtor lived in a house with another man, whom I had made my enemy, by dunning him in the street for cutting his hair. They out of revenge went to a Grand-Juror, and made complaint against me for keeping a bad girl at my house. I always kept a girl, as we took in washing, and this girl who had been living with an inhabitant there, my wife hired about ten days before. The trial was before Squire M. who got another Esq. to set with him, and a great court it was too. They asked me if I had a lawyer. I said I would plead my own case, as I was sure they had nothing against me. I however told one of

Judge G's. son's, that he might answer for me if he was a mind to. There were a great many of the inhabitants summoned to testify, and all of them testified in my favour, except *two*. The jail keeper who lived second door from me, said he knew, nor heard nothing against me; and he was no friend of mine. Trowbridge, and Hungerford, said they had heard thus and so: but were not questioned where they got their information. If I had plead my own case, I could have done better than any lawyer or rather student. M. Smith, managed the case against me. Esq. one of the court as before mentioned, by invitation in giving his opinion, made a long speech against me; or rather, he said there was proof enough that such report was enough to convict me; he said more than the lawyer against me. I had got most of my business by activity, from his servant, who before I went to Litchfield, was the principle waiter &c. for the students. I thought this trial showed his master, and some others thought as much of this as of the crime of which I was accused; particularly as it was one at which they were not likely to feel much indignation in their hearts. The girl was of a bad character; but I did not know it. She was white. I sent her away as soon as I heard any thing against her. I asked my lawyer why he did not question the witness against me, where they heard reports; and he said there was nothing proved against me. The court, he said, did as they was a mind to. I being a negro, I suppose they thought no one would ever notice it. I had money, and if I had not, the town *would* have to pay the cost. I say before my God, that I was convicted of keeping a bad house, when I had only kept this girl in my house ten days, and knew nothing but that she was virtuous.

I was warned out of town shortly after I went to Litchfield by one of the select-men, and through the influence of this servant before mentioned, or his friends. But I went to Esq. B. who told them to let me stay, and I heard no more about it. After I was put under bonds, I was obliged to give a mortgage of my house; and this same trial was five hundred dollars damage to me: it injured my character of course, and those who suppose I have no feelings are mistaken.

A few days after my trial, I went down to cut the Governor's hair, and he said to me, Grimes, I am sorry that you got in such a scrape.[9] I supposed his since secretary would persuade him that I was guilty. I only said I was not guilty; and I do wish that the Governor only did know the truth about it. I after this met Esq. B. in the street, and he said William, they did not do you justice at the *trial*. I talked with him, and he told me when the county court set, he would get the bonds taken off if the states attorney did not object; but the attorney did object at the instigation of ———.

This servant had been tried for the same offence which I had, and was convicted; but found friends. I presume if I had been actually guilty, I should have met with different treatment.

It has been my fortune most always to be suspected by the good, and to be cheated and abused by the vicious. An instance of rascability I will now mention, which took place at Litchfield: one J. swapped horses with me, and by fraud, induced me to give twenty dollars to boot. The horse I swapped cost me five. I sold the horse I had of him for fifteen dollars. I sued him though, and recovered, I believe thirty dollars. I bought a mare of one P. and paid him good money. Afterwards he came to me with a counterfeit bill, and said I paid it to him. I knew I

did not, for it was torn and ragged. He threatened me and I took it, being ignorant of the law. But I understand the law now, pretty well, at least that part which
consists in paying *fees*. My case with the horse jockey cost me a great deal of
money. It was curious to hear his witnesses testify: some who knew nothing
about the horse or the bargain, swore, just as if they were reciting their cate-
chism. God help them! One of my children was sick, and I sold a buffaloe skin
to the physician while he was visiting the child, for which he was to give me six
dollars. Before I left Litchfield, I could not get him to make out his bill: but after
I went to New-Haven, this doctor sent his bill down there for collection. I
thought I had paid enough and refused paying any more than the six dollars, unless he swore to his account. This he did, but what was strange, he went up into
Tolland County, about forty miles off to do it. I was in as good credit as any man
in Litchfield and as good a paymaster. Quackery and extortion generally go together.

I used to carry to the student's rooms, their meals when they wanted. One
of them from Charleston, a graduate of Yale College, sent for his dinner one day.
I carried a variety of dishes, a very large dinner, and a plenty of wine and brandy.
He had several gentlemen in the room with him that day, and they did all set
down at the table, and they would have me to set down to the table too. One of
them would say, Mr. Grimes, a glass of wine with you, sir; and the next gentleman would say the same, and so they kept on, until I had got two glasses to their
one all around the table. I began to feel myself on a footing with them, and made
as free with them as they did with me, and drank to them, and they would set
me to making speeches. They not only drank with me themselves, until they got
me as drunk as a fool, but they called in Peter Hamden, who was going along,
and made him drink a glass of brandy and water with me. At last I took the floor,
and lay there speechless some hours. I had two or three apprentice boys; towards
night, they came after me and led me home. I never was so drunk in my life before. I looked so like death, my wife was shocked at the sight of me.

Harry, the servant whom I have mentioned before, as my great rival and enemy, I knew kept a lewd house. His protector had been so active in the prosecution against me, that I thought I would retaliate a little. I went to a grand juror
therefore and made a complaint against Harry. The grand juror did not understand
managing the case at all, as he was just appointed. The trial was before Esq. B. Mr.
Beers managed the case for Harry, and got him clear; the witnesses being all
Harry's friends. And when a lawyer makes a justice, the justice sometimes is very
apt to remember his creator. Harry then turned round and sued me for damages
in getting him complained of. He employed two lawyers, Mr. Sanford and Mr.
Beers, and I employed two. Before I made complaint against Harry, I was riding
in the stage with a man to New-Haven, who told me all about Harry's house. I
now went to New-Haven, and took this man's deposition before Esq. Dennison.
At the trial, which made some noise in Litchfield, we called on Harry's lawyers to
give bonds, which they did, and at it they went until dinner, when the court adjourned. Only one of Harry's lawyers returned after dinner, and all he did was to
pay the cost and be off. So I came off triumphant. At one time, while I was living
in New-Haven, I applied to the jail keeper in Litchfield, to borrow two hundred

dollars. He said if I would buy his horse and cutter, he would let me have fifty dollars cash, and I must give my note for two hundred dollars, with a mortgage on my place, for security. I did so. The horse and cutter I suppose was worth seventy-five dollars. But while my ignorance thus exposed me to imposition, it was perhaps the only way in which I could learn wisdom: indeed, those to whom I have done kindness, have often proved ungrateful. One Barnes I recollect was confined in Litchfield jail for the fine and cost which had been imposed for a fighting scrape. He told me if I would pay it, which was twelve dollars, he would let me have his cow to get my pay. I paid it, gave him some change after I had taken him out, and shaved him, so that he might go home and see his wife. But I found the cow was not his. His brother is a cabinet maker, and rich, but would not help him I believe. I got into a quarrel with a student. He struck me in a passion, and I sued. He gave me twenty dollars, and I settled it; and having about this time an opportunity to let my place, I did so. The rent was seventy dollars a year. My object was to go to New-Haven, which I now did. I hired a place of Esq. Dagget in New-Haven, close by the Colleges, and gave him one hundred dollars rent. I kept a victualing shop, and waited on the students. I kept money to let, and soon got into full business. I bought furniture too of the students; in this my business interfered with Mr. E. my next neighbor, which brought upon me his displeasure. In fact I had such a run of custom, that all the shop keepers, that is of these huckster shops about college, and who get their living out of the students fell upon me, to injure me in every possible manner: they had more sense than I had, about keeping in with the Faculty, and others about there, but I can swear they were not more honest in my opinion. They took pains to prejudice the college steward against me. When I wanted wood, I used to get some student who owed me, to sign a bill and then got the wood delivered at my house; the wood is furnished by college to the students. This was the only way in which I could get my pay often. I had got a load at my house, which had been delivered in this manner. The cartman had thrown it part off, when the steward came up and ordered him to carry it back. I ordered him to unload. He began to put the wood back, when I seized him and stopped it. The steward says you rascal, this is my wood, and are you not going to give up. I said I am not, it is in my possession. He took back however, what was not thrown off. But I went immediately up to the stewards office and demanded it again, and told him I would sue him if he did not restore it; and he gave it up. I told him that it was all I could get from the student. The steward knew if I sued him it would make a great noise and laugh about town, and he knew (being a lawyer,) that I could recover. Being in opposition to all these fellows who get their living about College, they all hated me, and would go to the Tutors and throw out insinuations against me, would tell the students if they had me in their rooms they would be suspected. But notwithstanding their efforts, I did a mighty good business.

As I have spoken of a wife, it may seem strange that I have not related the tale of love which must have preceded matrimony. It would be indelicate to relate many things, necessary to a full understanding of a courtship, from beginning to end. One might tell how he got acquainted; whether he was welcomed or repulsed at first. Praise his wife's beauty, or commend her temper, before the die is cast. Somehow I did not like, did not know how to tell it. I got married.

Though before I went to Litchfield to live, and shortly after I returned to New-Haven, from Taunton, as is mentioned before, I used to hear students say something about taking Yankee girls for wives, and I thought I would look round and see if I could not find one. I had a great many clothes from the students, and I could rig myself up mighty well. And I have always seen that the girls seemed to like those best who dressed the finest. Yet I do reckon, the generality of girls are sluttish, though my wife is not. When a servant, and since too, I have seen so much behind the curtain, that I don't want telling. I recollect one student telling a story of this sort, when I was in the room. An acquaintance of his had been courting a lady some time, and, I forget how it was exactly, but after he married her, come to see her in the morning, with all the curls, ribbons, combs, caps, ear rings, wreaths, &c. &c. stripped off, he did not know her. While I was looking round, I found a plain looking girl in New-Haven, and I found she was the very one providence had provided for me; though her beauty, before it faded, and her figure before it was spoiled, as it always must be soon, were such as a fine Virginian like me, might be proud to embrace. I paid my attention to her. I loved her into an engagement. After a while I got one of the students to write a publishment, and sent it to the Rev. Mr. M.; he did not read it the next sabbath, as is customary, and I went to see him. He said he would read it next Sunday, though he thought it was a hoax. So next Sunday he made proclamation. I was then married in the Episcopal manner. I reckon my wife did belong, originally, at Middlebury, twenty miles from New-Haven. I had at that time, become much alarmed about being taken up and carried back to my master, which was one reason why I left New-Haven for Litchfield. My wife's mother came down to see her, and she went home with her, and came down in a waggon after me, and as I was walking in the street that evening she came, I thought I heard the constable after me, and Mr. Sturges, who formerly owned me. I heard them say, the constable and another, that fellow ran away from Savannah. I was so frightened, my strength left me. But I began to run. I stopped at Lanson's, and left word for my wife, and then went on as swift as a deer, over the fences. I never thought where I was going. I travelled until two or three o'clock. Oh, how the sweat did run off me! I crept into a barn and slept; and the next day I arrived at Middlebury. Here I went to work among the farmers, until I left for Litchfield, as aforementioned, and commenced my barber's shop and waiting. I suppose I staid at Litchfield four years, until when I rented my house, and came to New-Haven, as above stated.

While living in New-Haven, one C. a student, gave me a room in the house where he roomed, and I waited on him. He sent me to the College Hall after his breakfast. Mr. Kennedy, one of the Cooks, ordered me out, and we had a considerable scrumage in the Hall, but I got the breakfast. I told Corbett, and he advised me to sue him. I went to lawyer Thomas, and got a writ drawn, and had it served that day. Mr. Kennedy got Mr. Twining for his attorney: indeed, I think he had two lawyers. I lost my case. They had president Dwight's deposition, who stated that he put these men in the hall to do for him as they would in their own houses. Therefore, Kennedy had according to law, a right to put me out. I was at this time a stranger in New-Haven, but I knew a great many of the students, and they were very good to me. They paid the cost of this case, or gave me clothes and money, so that I made money, if any thing, by the suit.

My acquaintance among the black people were friendly to me in New-Haven, and it is no more than just that I should preserve the name of one of them, who is now dead, from oblivion, particularly as he was a runaway slave, like myself, and very distinguished in his profession. As soon as I came from New-Bedford to New-Haven, I went up to College to see Barber Thompson, and to see how he came on; and I found him very sick. He was very glad to see me, and gave the shop into my possession, to keep for him. Barber Thompson, for that was the name he went by in New-Haven, was a slave to Mr. Benly, of Port Royal, Va. He came on to the north with a gentleman, to wait on him, and ran away during the last war. He was honest and clever, was called the greatest barber in America, kept shop by the College, and was often called to officiate at parties and weddings, being the politest servant in town. He died last winter, and I had him buried in my burying ground. That poverty which often leaves my wife and children without a supper, may well excuse me for leaving his grave nameless. A stone I intended to erect, with this epitaph.

> Here lies Old Thompson! and now he is dead,
> I think some one should tell his story;
> For while men's faces must be shaved,
> His name should live in glory.

But I have not for the reason above, put up a stone.

The enmity of some of my rivals in business, led them to make representations about town against my character, and one of them had some authority in town affairs. My conduct was good, and the strict laws of Connecticut could find nothing to punish; but the select-men have power to warn any man out of town who had not gained a settlement, which is a difficult thing for a poor man. This was the only course my enemies could take with me. There was certainly no danger of my coming upon the town, which is all the object of the law to prevent. It is very mean and cruel, to drive a man out of town because he is suspected of some crime, or breach of law. If he is guilty, punish him, but not set him adrift on suspicion, or from mere tyranny, because his poverty exposes him to it. If I was a pimp why not punish me for it, not warn a man out of town, because his enemies accuse him of crime. Such was the fact though. They then brought a suit for the penalty, one dollar and sixty-seven cents a week. The suit was before a justice in Woodbridge. I saw him in town and told him I wished to have the case adjourned to New-Haven. They got judgment against me, as I did not appear. I was then in this predicament, liable to be whipped at the post, if I did not pay the fine or depart, in ten days. I think I should not have left, but paid my dollar and sixty-seven cents a week and staid, if I had not at this time become alarmed about being taken up by my old master in Savannah. I was often recognized by students, and others from the south; and my master knew where I was. I thought if I went back in the country, if I was taken up I should have more chance to buy myself free; I therefore returned to Litchfield.

After I retuned to Litchfield, Mr. Thompson came on as I had anticipated, with power from my master, to free me or take me back. He said he would put me in irons and send me down to New-York, and then on to Savannah, if I did not buy myself. I instantly offered to give up my house and land, all I had. The house was under a mortgage to Dr. Cottin. A Mr. Burrows, from the south had before this, seen me in New-Haven, and said my master would send on for me. I got a gentleman in Litchfield to write to my master, to know what he would do, and he wrote back he would take five hundred dollars for me, tho' I was worth eight. Mr. Thompson had now come on, with discretionary power. My house would sell for only $425, under the incumbrance. Mr. T. wished me to give my note for fifty dollars, in addition. I went to the Governor, and told him the whole story: and the governor said, not so, Grimes; you must have what you get hereafter, for yourself. The governor did pity my case, and was willing to assist me, for such is his feeling to the poor.

To be put in irons and dragged back to a state of slavery, and either leave my wife and children in the street, or take them into servitude, was a situation, in which my soul now shudders at the thought of having been placed. It would have exhibited an awful spectacle of the conduct and inconsistency of men, to have done it; yet I was undoubtedly the lawful property of my master according to the laws of the country, and though many would justify him, perhaps aid in taking me back, yet if there is any man in God's whole creation, who will say with respect to himself, (only bring the case home) that there are any possible circumstances in which it is just that he should be at the capricious disposal of a fellow being, if he will say, that nature within him, that feeling, that reason tells him so, or can convince him so, that man lies! The soul of man cannot be made to feel it, to think it, to own it, or believe it. I may give my life for the good or the safety of others. But no law, no consequences, not the lives of millions, can authorize them to take my life or liberty from me, while innocent of any crime.

I have to thank my master, however, that he took what I had, and freed me. I gave a deed of my house to a gentleman in Litchfield. He paid the money for it to Mr. T., who then gave me my free papers. Oh! how my heart did rejoice, and thank God! From what anxiety, what pain and heart ache did it relieve me. For even though I might have fared better the rest of life under my master, yet the thought of being snatched up and taken back, was awful. Accustomed as I had been to freedom for years, the miseries of slavery which I had felt, and knew, and tasted, were presented to my mind in no faint image. To say that a man is better off in one situation than another, if in the one he is better clothed and better fed, and has less care than in the other, is false. It is true if you regard him as a brute, as destitute of the feelings of human nature. But I will not speak on the subject more. Those slaves who have kind masters, are perhaps as happy as the generality of mankind. They are not aware that their condition can be better, and I don't know as it can: indeed it cannot by their own exertions. I would advise no slave to leave his master. If he runs away, he is most sure to be taken. If he is not, he will ever be in the apprehension of it. And I do think there is no inducement for a slave to leave his master, and be set free in the northern states. I have had to work hard; I have been often cheated, insulted, abused, and injured; yet a black man, if he will be industrious and honest, he can get along here as well as any one who is poor, and in a situation to be imposed on. I have been very unfortunate in life in this respect. Notwithstanding all my struggles and sufferings, and injuries, I have been an honest man. There is no one who can come forward and say he knows any thing against Grimes. This I know, that I have been punished for being suspected of things, of which, some of those who were loudest against me, were actually guilty. The practice of warning poor people out of town is very cruel. It may be necessary that towns should have that power, otherwise some might be overrun with paupers. But it is mighty apt to be abused. A poor man just gets a going in business, and is then warned to depart. Perhaps he has a family, and don't know where to go, or what to do. I am a poor man, and ignorant. But I am a man of sense. I have seen them contributing at church for the heathen, to build churches, and send out preachers to them, yet there was no place where I could get a seat in the church. I knew in New-Haven, Indians and negroes, come from a great many thousand miles, sent to be educated, while there were people I knew in the town, cold and hungry, and ignorant. They have kind of societies to make clothes, for those, who they say, go naked in their own countries. The ladies sometimes do this at one end of a town, while their father's who may happen to be selectmen, may be warning a poor man and his family, out at the other end, for fear they may have to be buried at the state expense. It sounds rather strange upon a man's ear, who feels that he is friendless and abused in society, to hear so many speeches about charity; for I was always inclined to be observing.

I have forebore to mention names in my history where it might give the least pain, in this I have made it less interesting and injured myself.

I may sometimes be a little mistaken, as I have to write from memory, and there is a great deal I have omitted from want of recollection at the time of writing. I cannot speak as I feel on some subjects. If those who read my history, think I have not led a life of trial, I have failed to give a correct representation. I think I must be Forty years of age but don't know; I could not tell my wife my age. I have learned to read and write pretty well; if I had opportunity I could learn very fast. My wife has a tolerable good education, which has been a help to me.

I hope some will buy my books from charity, but I am no beggar. I am now entirely destitute of property; where and how I shall live I don't know; where and how I shall die I don't know, but I hope I may be prepared. If it were not for the stripes on my back which were made while I was a slave, I would in my will, leave my skin a legacy to the government, desiring that it might be taken off and made into parchment, and then bind the constitution of glorious happy *and free* America. Let the skin of an American slave, bind the charter of American Liberty.

WILLIAM GRIMES.

1. Solomon Bayley, also a fugitive slave, had the first edition of his narrative published in 1820, but this tract was by no means "book-length," as it numbered only eight pages. The first edition of Grimes's narrative, on the other hand, was sixty-eight pages long. The autobiographies of Olaudah Equiano and John Jea are longer than Grimes's, but neither of these writers can properly be considered African American.

2. Andrews, *Free Story*, 81. I am indebted to Andrews's book, 77–81, for some of the insights in this and the previous paragraphs, as well as to Nichols, "Case of William Grimes."

3. Grimes, *Life*, 2d ed., 121–128.

4. Traces attaching a draft horse's collar to a cart or plough.

5. There is no record of a hurricane, cyclone, or earthquake in Virginia during this period in which "many thousands" drowned. Grimes may have heard exaggerated reports about the storm he saw.

6. See *Deuteronomy* 25:2–3.

7. A cask larger than a barrel and smaller than a hogshead.

8. They would allow him the privilege of walking next to the wall as the safer and cleaner side of the pavement or sidewalk.

9. Oliver Wolcott II (1760–1833) was governor of Connecticut from 1817 to 1827.

# NAT TURNER

NAT TURNER (1800–31) led the deadliest slave revolt in U.S. history. In the predawn hours of August 22, 1831, this slave of the cotton and tobacco fields of southeastern Virginia, whose father had long since run away to freedom, gathered together a small band of followers who esteemed him as a prophet. Over the next forty hours, armed with axes, they killed between fifty-seven and sixty-five white men, women, and children (although Turner himself killed only one person, a white woman).[1]

As the revolt was quashed, thousands of troops converged on Southampton County. We will never know exactly how many slaves died during the fighting and in subsequent reprisals, but some scholars estimate as many as two hundred, or about three times the number that actually participated. A cavalry company from Murfreesboro, North Carolina, slaughtered forty blacks in two days, placing fifteen of their severed heads on poles as a public warning. In a three-week period, nearly fifty slaves and free blacks were tried for participation in the rebellion; thirty of them were sentenced to death, although only nineteen were actually hanged.

Turner himself, however, escaped and remained hidden for close to six weeks. On the day after his capture, Monday, October 31, he was questioned by two court justices, with several other witnesses present. Only sketchy accounts of this interrogation survive, but it is evident that much of what he told them he repeated or elaborated on in the interviews that resulted in the *Confessions*. However, three elements of his initial confession did not reappear there. He claimed that God had given him power over the weather and seasons, that "by the efficacy of prayer" he could cause thunderstorms or droughts, that he could heal the sick. Regarding the revolt, he stated that if he could do it all over again, "he must necessarily act in the same way." And most importantly, he explained that "indiscriminate massacre was not their intention after they obtained foothold, and was resorted to in the first instance to strike terror and alarm. Women and children would afterwards have been spared, and men too who ceased to resist."[2]

Probably one of the men present at the questioning was an attorney named Thomas Ruffin Gray. He was born, like Turner, in 1800; in December 1830 he had become an attorney. But his last few months had been disastrous: his wife had died, leaving him an infant daughter; many of his friends, neighbors, and acquaintances were killed in the revolt; and while he was acting as a public defender for four slaves during the subsequent trials, his father died, disinheriting him. Over the space of the last two years his property had dwindled from twenty-one slaves and eight hundred acres to one slave and three hundred acres (and would dwindle still further—to one horse, no slaves, and no land—by 1832).[3] From these facts alone, it would be reasonable to infer that Gray was a some-

what desperate man, and that the prospect of publishing the confessions of so famous a criminal would be too financially appealing to pass up.

It appears that for the following three days, November 1 through 3, Gray
interviewed Turner extensively, with the explicit understanding that the result
would be published as Turner's confessions. Clearly, Turner was willing to talk.
As Stephen Oates conjectures, "Though Nat never said so, this would be his last
opportunity to strike back at the slave world he hated, to flay it with verbal bril-
liance and religious prophecy (was not exhortation his forte?). Indeed, a published confession would ensure Nat a kind of immortality; it would recount his
extraordinary life in his own words and on his own terms."[4]

The end result was *The Confessions of Nat Turner,* which Peter Wood has
justly called "one of the most extraordinary firsthand texts in American history."[5] It is a unique document, since it was produced by a collaboration between
a slave who held whites in contempt and a slave owner who had little if any respect for blacks. Nat Turner compared himself to Christ; Thomas Gray regarded
Turner as a kind of devil. For Turner, his confession, like his life, would be a revelation of Holy Scripture; for Gray, it would simply confirm that Turner was a
deluded maniac. The *Confessions* presents two texts, Turner's and Gray's, working against each other, yet inseparable.[6]

The part that is most clearly Turner's is the apocalyptic rhetoric, which in
this context was nothing short of revolutionary. As the narrative of Charles Ball
put it only five years later, "The idea of a revolution in the conditions of the
whites and the blacks, is the corner-stone of the religion of the latter." For
Turner, religion and revolution went hand in hand—it was no coincidence that
the revolt was originally slated for Independence Day.

It is striking, then, that the published *Confessions* barely mentions freedom. Could Turner have failed to state to Gray his final objective? Or did Gray
distort Turner's words in order to give the impression that Turner was a fiendish
madman? Although Gray was intimately familiar with every detail of the revolt,
he fails to mention two vitally important facts. First, Turner was married, with
two children, and he deliberately spared from bloodshed the family of his wife's
owner. Second, the massacre was only the first step in a much bigger plan. These
omissions make it easier for Gray to paint Turner as a lone fanatic rather than a
family man and revolutionary thinker, and in doing so to implicitly justify rather
than condemn the institution of slavery.

The omissions go hand in hand with other self-serving distortions. The ex-
cerpt from the trial that appears at the end of the *Confessions* bears little resemblance to the trial transcript. The confession that was read at the trial appears to
be the one taken by the justices on October 31, not the one given to Gray; Turner
probably did not state that he had "made a full confession to Mr. Gray"; and
the justice's final speech in the *Confessions* was clearly embellished, if not wholly
fabricated, by Gray.[7]

In addition, Gray attributes to Turner certain words that Turner was unlikely to have uttered. He has Turner say, "a circumstance occurred which . . .
laid the ground work of that enthusiasm, which has terminated so fatally to
many, both white and black, and for which I am about to atone at the gallows."

Yet it is clear from the rest of the *Confessions,* from accounts of the interview with the justices, and from Turner's plea of not guilty at his trial, that he felt no remorse for the killings; and he hardly would have belittled his religious convictions as an "enthusiasm." Turner's account of the killings is replete with phrases that were most likely inserted by Gray: "but it was only to sleep the sleep of death"; "Vain hope!"; "to an untimely grave"; "[I] viewed the mangled bodies as they lay, in silent satisfaction"; "to arrest the progress of these barbarous villains"; "we found no more victims to gratify our thirst for blood."[8]

Yet one can also infer that the majority of Turner's confession remains intact, for its details are very close to those of the justices' interrogation. In addition, Gray does not censor or simplify Nat's accounts of his own intelligence, his black rage, his complex and audacious interpretation of Scripture, or his faithfulness to it.[9] According to Eric Sundquist, this interpretation "makes Christ a typological prefiguring of [Turner], the slave rebel. . . . In Turner's prophecy slavery is the Antichrist, Revelation is equivalent to revolution, and he is the Redeemer whose acts of chastening, completed by martyrdom, will inaugurate the holy utopia. . . . In the moment of the eclipse, Turner became the black Christ of the South."[10] Gray allows Turner to present this prophecy without denying the scriptural basis for Turner's significance in this world. Instead, as William Andrews notes, "The lawyer simply tries to counter Turner's view of himself as Savior with an opposing estimate of him as Satanically inspired. This in itself constitutes a rhetorical victory for Turner."[11]

But this victory was posthumous. At his trial on November 5, the judge pronounced Turner guilty as charged and asked if he had anything to say before sentencing. "Nothing but what I've said before," he replied. He went to his execution six days later bravely and with his head up. According to interviews conducted in 1900 by William Sidney Drewry, "Nat Turner's body was delivered to the doctors, who skinned it and made grease of the flesh. His skeleton was for many years in the possession of Dr. Massenberg, but has since been misplaced. . . . Mr. R. S. Barham's father owned a money purse made of his hide."[12] As Kenneth Greenberg comments, "Apparently unaware of the bizarre mixture of horror and irony in their actions, Southampton whites consumed the body and the blood of the black rebel who likened himself to Christ."[13]

"It would be difficult to exaggerate the psychic toll which the Turner massacre exacted from the southern mind," write Seymour Gross and Eileen Bender. "As is evidenced in the ritualistic desecration of Turner's body, the event had cut through to the lower layers of the psyche where the nightmares are transacted."[14] In addition to barbarous reprisals and paralyzing fear, this was evident in new Virginia laws prohibiting blacks, both slave and free, from preaching or conducting religious meetings and from learning to read or write. And throughout the South abolitionist literature was seized and burned. In the North, on the other hand, Turner's revolt helped catalyze three decades of increased abolitionist agitation.

Incendiary as it was, *The Confessions of Nat Turner* found singular success in both North and South. Gray had produced it extraordinarily quickly, copyrighting it on November 10 and publishing it less than two weeks later.

Thomas Wentworth Higginson, writing in 1861, estimated that fifty thousand copies had been sold, although he later revised that estimate to forty thousand. It was reprinted in Virginia in 1832, and went through at least five editions in the nineteenth century.

Although the legend of Nat Turner has been supplemented by a great deal of myth-making, the *Confessions* has been the basis for almost all that has been written about him and his revolt. Harriet Beecher Stowe was one writer who was fascinated by Turner, and based her 1856 novel *Dred* on the *Confessions,* which she appended to it. More recently, William Styron entitled his controversial 1967 novel *The Confessions of Nat Turner,* as if he were attempting to supplant the original. And Stephen B. Oates's highly acclaimed 1975 biography, *The Fires of Jubilee,* also owes its primary debt to the *Confessions.* As Sundquist eloquently notes, "in the enigmatic Scripture he left in the wake of his uprising, Turner continued his confession in a dimension certain to outlast the historical moment of his death."[15]

# THE
# CONFESSIONS
OF
# NAT TURNER,

THE LEADER OF THE LATE

INSURRECTION IN SOUTHAMPTON, VA.

As fully and voluntarily made to

## THOMAS R. GRAY,

In the prison where he was confined, and acknowledged by
him to be such when read before the Court of Southampton; with the certificate, under seal of
the Court convened at Jerusalem,[16]
Nov. 5, 1831, for his trial.

ALSO, AN AUTHENTIC

ACCOUNT OF THE WHOLE INSURRECTION,

WITH LISTS OF THE WHITES WHO WERE MURDERED,

AND OF THE NEGROES BROUGHT BEFORE THE COURT OF
SOUTHAMPTON, AND THERE SENTENCED, &c.

———

Baltimore:
PUBLISHED BY THOMAS R. GRAY.
Lucas & Deaver, print.
1831.

DISTRICT OF COLUMBIA, TO WIT:

*Be it remembered,* That on this tenth day of November, Anno Domini, eighteen hundred and thirty-one, Thomas R. Gray of the said District, deposited in this office the title of a book, which is in the words as following:

"The Confessions of Nat Turner, the leader of the late insurrection in Southampton, Virginia, as fully and voluntarily made to Thomas R. Gray, in the prison where he was confined, and acknowledged by him to be such when read before the Court of Southampton; with the certificate, under seal, of the Court convened at Jerusalem, November 5, 1831, for his trial. Also, an authentic account of the whole insurrection, with lists of the whites who were murdered, and of the negroes brought before the Court of Southampton, and there sentenced, &c. the right whereof he claims as proprietor, in conformity with an Act of Congress, entitled "An act to amend the several acts respecting Copy Rights."

EDMUND J. LEE, Clerk of the District.

(Seal.)

In testimony that the above is a true copy, from the record of the District Court for the District of Columbia, I, Edmund J. Lee, the Clerk thereof, have hereunto set my hand and affixed the seal of my office, this 10th day of November, 1831.

EDMUND J. LEE, C. D. C.

# TO THE PUBLIC

THE late insurrection in Southampton has greatly excited the public mind, and led to a thousand idle, exaggerated and mischievous reports. It is the first instance in our history of an open rebellion of the slaves, and attended with such atrocious circumstances of cruelty and destruction, as could not fail to leave a deep impression, not only upon the minds of the community where this fearful tragedy was wrought, but throughout every portion of our country, in which this population is to be found. Public curiosity has been on the stretch to understand the origin and progress of this dreadful conspiracy, and the motives which influences its diabolical actors. The insurgent slaves had all been destroyed, or apprehended, tried and executed, (with the exception of the leader,) without revealing any thing at all satisfactory, as to the motives which governed them, or the means by which they expected to accomplish their object. Every thing connected with this sad affair was wrapt in mystery, until Nat Turner, the leader of this ferocious band, whose name has resounded throughout our widely extended empire, was captured. This "great Bandit" was taken by a single individual, in a cave near the residence of his late owner, on Sunday, the thirtieth of October, without attempting to make the slightest resistance, and on the following day safely lodged in the jail of the County. His captor was Benjamin Phipps, armed with a shot gun well charged. Nat's only weapon was a small light sword which he immediately surrendered, and begged that his life might be spared. Since his confinement, by permission of the jailor, I have had ready access to him, and finding that he was willing to make a full and free confession of the origin, progress and consummation of the insurrectory movements of the slaves of which he was the contriver and head; I determined for the gratification of public curiosity to commit his statements to writing, and publish them, with little or no variation, from his own words. That this is a faithful record of his confessions, the annexed certificate of the County Court of Southampton, will attest. They certainly bear one stamp of truth and sincerity. He makes no attempt (as all the other insurgents who were examined did,) to exculpate himself, but frankly acknowledges his full participation in all the guilt of the transaction. He was not only the contriver of the conspiracy, but gave the first blow towards its execution.

It will thus appear, that whilst every thing upon the surface of society wore a calm and peaceful aspect; whilst not one note of preparation was heard to warn the devoted inhabitants of woe and death, a gloomy fanatic was revolving in the recesses of his own dark, bewildered, and overwrought mind, schemes of indiscriminate massacre to the whites. Schemes too fearfully executed as far as his fiendish band proceeded in their desolating march. No cry for mercy penetrated their flinty bosoms. No acts of remembered kindness made the least impression upon these remorseless murderers. Men, women and children, from hoary age to helpless infancy were involved in the same cruel fate. Never did a band of savages do their work of death more unsparingly. Apprehension for their own personal safety seems to have been the only principle of restraint in the whole course of their bloody proceedings. And it is not the

least remarkable feature in this horrid transaction, that a band actuated by such hell-
ish purposes, should have resisted so feebly, when met by the whites in arms. Desperation alone, one would think, might have led to greater efforts. More than twenty
of them attacked Dr. Blunt's house on Tuesday morning, a little before day-break, defended by two men and three boys. They fled precipitately at the first fire; and their
future plans of mischief, were entirely disconcerted and broken up. Escaping thence,
each individual sought his own safety either in concealment, or by returning home,
with the hope that his participation might escape detection, and all were shot down
in the course of a few days, or captured and brought to trial and punishment. Nat has
survived all his followers, and the gallows will speedily close his career. His own account of the conspiracy is submitted to the public, without comment. It reads an awful, and it is hoped, a useful lesson, as to the operations of a mind like his, endeavoring to grapple with things beyond its reach. How it first became bewildered and
confounded, and finally corrupted and led to the conception and perpetration of the
most atrocious and heart-rending deeds. It is calculated also to demonstrate the policy of our laws in restraint of this class of our population, and to induce all those entrusted with their execution, as well as our citizens generally, to see that they are
strictly and rigidly enforced. Each particular community should look to its own safety,
whilst the general guardians of the laws, keep a watchful eye over all. If Nat's statements can be relied on, the insurrection in this county was entirely local, and his designs confided but to a few, and these in his immediate vicinity. It was not instigated
by motives of revenge or sudden anger, but the results of long deliberation, and a settled purpose of mind. The offspring of gloomy fanaticism, acting upon materials but
too well prepared for such impressions. It will be long remembered in the annals of
our country, and many a mother as she presses her infant darling to her bosom, will
shudder at the recollection of Nat Turner, and his band of ferocious miscreants.

Believing the following narrative, by removing doubts and conjectures from the
public mind which otherwise must have remained, would give general satisfaction, it
is respectfully submitted to the public by their ob't serv't,

T. R. GRAY.

*Jerusalem, Southampton, Va. Nov. 5, 1831.*

We the undersigned, members of the Court convened at Jerusalem, on Saturday, the 5th day of Nov. 1831, for the trial of Nat, *alias* Nat Turner, a negro slave,
late the property of Putnam Moore, deceased, do hereby certify, that the confessions
of Nat, to Thomas R. Gray, was read to him in our presence, and that Nat acknowledged the same to be full, free, and voluntary; and that furthermore, when
called upon by the presiding Magistrate of the Court, to state if he had any thing to
say, why sentence of death should not be passed upon him, replied he had nothing
further than he had communicated to Mr. Gray. Given under our hands and seals at
Jerusalem, this 5th day of November, 1831.

|  |  |
|---|---|
| JEREMIAH COBB, | [*Seal.*] |
| THOMAS PRETLOW, | [*Seal.*] |
| JAMES W. PARKER, | [*Seal.*] |
| CARR BOWERS, | [*Seal.*] |
| SAMUEL B. HINES, | [*Seal.*] |
| ORRIS A. BROWNE, | [*Seal.*] |

*State of Virginia, Southampton County, to wit:*

    I, James Rochelle, Clerk of the County Court of Southampton in the State of Virginia, do hereby certify, that Jeremiah Cobb, Thomas Pretlow, James W. Parker, Carr Bowers, Samuel B. Hines, and Orris A. Browne, esqr's are acting Justices of the Peace, in and for the County aforesaid, and were members of the Court which convened at Jerusalem, on Saturday the 5th day of November, 1831, for the trial of Nat *alias* Nat Turner, a negro slave, late the property of Putnam Moore, deceased, who was tried and convicted, as an insurgent in the late insurrection in the county of Southampton aforesaid, and that full faith and credit are due, and ought to be given to their acts as Justices of the peace aforesaid.

    In testimony whereof, I have hereunto set my hand and caused the seal of the Court [Seal.] aforesaid, to be affixed this 5th day of November, 1831.

JAMES ROCHELLE, C. S. C. C.

―――――――――

# CONFESSION

———————

Agreeable to his own appointment, on the evening he was committed to prison, with permission of the jailer, I visited NAT on Tuesday the 1st November, when, without being questioned at all, he commenced his narrative in the following words:—

SIR,—You have asked me to give a history of the motives which induced me to undertake the late insurrection, as you call it—To do so I must go back to the days of my infancy, and even before I was born. I was thirty-one years of age the 2d of October last, and born the property of Benj. Turner, of this county. In my childhood a circumstance occurred which made an indelible impression on my mind, and laid the ground work of that enthusiasm, which has terminated so fatally to many, both white and black, and for which I am about to atone at the gallows. It is here necessary to relate this circumstance—trifling as it may seem, it was the commencement of that belief which has grown with time, and even now, sir, in this dungeon, helpless and forsaken as I am, I cannot divest myself of. Being at play with other children, when three or four years old, I was telling them something, which my mother overhearing, said it had happened before I was born—I stuck to my story, however, and related somethings which went, in her opinion, to confirm it—others being called on were greatly astonished, knowing that these things had happened, and caused them to say in my hearing, I surely would be a prophet, as the Lord had shewn me things that had happened before my birth. And my father and mother strengthened me in this my first impression, saying in my presence, I was intended for some great purpose, which they had always thought from certain marks on my head and breast—[a parcel of excrescences which I believe are not at all uncommon, particularly among negroes, as I have seen several with the same. In this case he has either cut them off or they have nearly disappeared]—My grandmother, who was very religious, and to whom I was much attached—my master, who belonged to the church, and other religious persons who visited the house, and whom I often saw at prayers, noticing the singularity of my manners, I suppose, and my uncommon intelligence for a child, remarked I had too much sense to be raised, and if I was, I would never be of any service to any one as a slave—To a mind like mine, restless, inquisitive and observant of every thing that was passing, it is easy to suppose that religion was the subject to which it would be directed, and although this subject principally occupied my thoughts—there was nothing that I saw or heard of to which my attention was not directed—The manner in which I learned to read and write, not only had great influence on my own mind, as I acquired it with the most perfect ease, so much so, that I have no recollection whatever of learning the alphabet—but to the astonishment of the family, one day, when a book was shewn me to keep me from crying, I began spelling the names of different objects—this was a source of wonder to all in the neighborhood, particularly the blacks—and this learning was constantly improved at all opportunities—when I got large enough to go to work, while employed, I was reflecting on many things that would present themselves to my imagination, and whenever an opportunity occurred of looking at a book, when the school children were getting their lessons, I would find many things that the fertility of my own imagination had depicted to me before; all my time, not devoted to my master's service, was spent either in prayer, or in making experiments in casting different things in moulds made of earth, in attempting to make paper, gunpowder, and many other experiments, that although I could not perfect, yet convinced me of its practicability if I had the means.* I was not addicted to stealing in my youth, nor have ever been—Yet such was the confidence of the negroes in the neighborhood, even at this early period of my life, in my superior judgment, that they would often carry me with them when they were going on any roguery, to plan for them. Growing up among them, with this confidence in my superior judgment, and when this, in their opinions, was perfected by Divine inspiration, from the circumstances already alluded to in my infancy, and which belief was ever afterwards zealously inculcated by the austerity of my life and manners, which became the subject of remark by white and black.—Having soon discovered to be great, I must appear so, and therefore studiously avoided mixing in society, and wrapped myself in mystery, devoting my time to fasting and prayer—By this time, having arrived to man's estate, and hearing the scriptures commented on at meetings, I was struck with that particular passage which says: "Seek ye the kingdom of Heaven and all things shall be added unto you."[17] I reflected much on this passage, and prayed daily for light on this subject—As I was praying one day at my plough, the spirit spoke to me, saying "Seek ye the kingdom of Heaven and all things shall be added unto you." *Question*—what do you mean by the Spirit. *Ans.* The Spirit that spoke to the prophets in former days—and I was greatly astonished, and for two years prayed continually, whenever my duty would permit—and then again I had the same revelation, which fully confirmed me in the impression that I was ordained for some great purpose in the hands of the Almighty. Several years rolled round, in which many events occurred to strengthen me in this my belief. At this time I reverted in my mind to the remarks made of me in my childhood, and the things that had been shewn me—and as it had been said of me in my childhood by those by whom I had been taught to pray, both white and black, and in whom I had the greatest confidence, that I had too much sense to be raised, and if I was, I would never be of any use to any one as a slave. Now finding I had arrived to man's estate, and was a slave, and these revelations being made known to me, I began to direct my attention to this great object, to fulfil the purpose for which, by this time, I felt assured I was intended. Knowing the influence I had obtained

---

*When questioned as to the manner of manufacturing those different articles, he was found well informed on the subject.

over the minds of my fellow servants, (not by the means of conjuring and such like tricks—for to them I always spoke of such things with contempt) but by the communion of the Spirit whose revelations I often communicated to them, and they believed and said my wisdom came from God. I now began to prepare them for my purpose, by telling them something was about to happen that would terminate in fulfilling the great promise that had been made to me—About this time I was placed under an overseer, from whom I ran away—and after remaining in the woods thirty days, I returned, to the astonishment of the negroes on the plantation, who thought I had made my escape to some other part of the country, as my father had done before. But the reason of my return was, that the Spirit appeared to me and said I had my wishes directed to the things of this world, and not to the kingdom of Heaven, and that I should return to the service of my earthly master—"For he who knoweth his Master's will, and doeth it not, shall be beaten with many stripes, and thus have I chastened you."[18] And the negroes found fault, and murmured against me, saying that if they had my sense they would not serve any master in the world. And about this time I had a vision— and I saw white spirits and black spirits engaged in battle, and the sun was darkened—the thunder rolled in the Heavens, and blood flowed in streams—and I heard a voice saying, "Such is your luck, such you are called to see, and let it come rough or smooth, you must surely bare it." I now withdrew myself as much as my situation would permit, from the intercourse of my fellow servants, for the avowed purpose of serving the Spirit more fully—and it appeared to me, and reminded me of the things it had already shown me, and that it would then reveal to me the knowledge of the elements, the revolution of the planets, the operation of tides, and changes of the seasons. After this revelation in the year 1825, and the knowledge of the elements being made known to me, I sought more than ever to obtain true holiness before the great day of judgment should appear, and then I began to receive the true knowledge of faith. And from the first steps of righteousness until the last, was I made perfect; and the Holy Ghost was with me, and said, "Behold me as I stand in the Heavens"—and I looked and saw the forms of men in different attitudes—and there were lights in the sky to which the children of darkness gave other names than what they really were—for they were the lights of the Saviour's hands, stretched forth from east to west, even as they were extended on the cross on Calvary for the redemption of sinners. And I wondered greatly at these miracles, and prayed to be informed of a certainty of the meaning thereof—and shortly afterwards, while laboring in the field, I discovered drops of blood on the corn as though it were dew from heaven—and I communicated it to many, both white and black, in the neighborhood—and I then found on the leaves in the woods hieroglyphic characters, and numbers, with the forms of men in different attitudes, portrayed in blood, and representing the figures I had seen before in the heavens. And now the Holy Ghost had revealed itself to me, and made plain the miracles it had shown me—For as the blood of Christ had been shed on this earth, and had ascended to heaven for the salvation of sinners, and was now returning to earth again in the form of dew—and as the leaves on the trees bore the impression of the figures I had seen in the heavens, it was plain to me that the Saviour was about to lay down the yoke he had borne for the sins of men, and the great day of judgment was at hand. About this time I told these things to a white man, (Etheldred T. Brantley) on whom it had a wonderful effect—and he ceased from his wickedness, and was attacked immediately with a cutaneous eruption, and blood ozed from the pores of his skin, and after praying and fasting nine days, he was healed, and the Spirit appeared to me again, and said, as the Saviour had been baptised so should we be also—and when the white people would not let us be baptised by the church, we went down into the water together, in the sight of many who reviled us, and were baptised by the Spirit—After this I rejoiced greatly, and gave thanks to God. And on the 12th of May, 1828, I heard a loud noise in the heavens, and the Spirit instantly appeared to me and said the Serpent was loosened, and Christ had laid down the yoke he had borne for the sins of men, and that I should take it on and fight against the Serpent, for the time was fast approaching when the first should be last and the last should be first.[19] *Ques.* Do you not find yourself mistaken now? *Ans.* Was not Christ crucified. And by signs in the heavens that it would make known to me when I should commence the great work—and until the first sign appeared, I should conceal it from the knowledge of men—And on the appearance of the sign, (the eclipse of the sun last February) I should arise and prepare myself, and slay my enemies with their own weapons. And immediately on the sign appearing in the heavens, the seal was removed from my lips, and I communicated the great work laid out for me to do, to four in whom I had the greatest confidence. (Henry, Hark, Nelson, and Sam)—It was intended by us to have begun the work of death on the 4th July last—Many were the plans formed and rejected by us, and it affected my mind to such a degree, that I fell sick, and the time passed without our coming to any determination how to commence—Still forming new schemes and rejecting them, when the sign appeared again, which determined me not to wait longer.

Since the commencement of 1830, I had been living with Mr. Joseph Travis, who was to me a kind master, and placed the greatest confidence in me; in fact, I had no cause to complain of his treatment to me. On Saturday evening, the 20th of August, it was agreed between Henry, Hark and myself, to prepare a dinner the next day for the men we expected, and then to concert a plan, as we had not yet determined on any. Hark, on the following morning, brought a pig, and Henry brandy, and being joined by Sam, Nelson, Will and Jack, they prepared in the woods a dinner, where, about three o'clock, I joined them.

*Q.* Why were you so backward in joining them.

*A.* The same reason that had caused me not to mix with them for years before.

I saluted them on coming up, and asked Will how came he there, he answered, his life was worth no more than others, and his liberty as dear to him. I asked him if he thought to obtain it? He said he would, or loose his life. This was enough to put him in full confidence. Jack, I knew, was only a tool in the hands of Hark, it was quickly agreed we should commence at home (Mr. J. Travis') on that night, and until we had armed and equipped ourselves, and gathered sufficient force, neither age nor sex was to be spared, (which was invariably adhered to.) We remained at the feast, until about two hours in the night, when we went to the house and found Austin; they all went to the cider press and drank, except myself. On returning to the house, Hark went to the door with an axe, for the purpose of breaking it open, as we knew we were strong enough to murder the family, if they were awaked by the noise; but reflecting that it might create an alarm in the neighborhood, we determined to enter the house secretly, and murder them whilst sleeping. Hark got a ladder and set it against the chimney, on which I ascended, and hoisting a window, entered and came down stairs, unbarred the door, and removed the guns from their places. It was then observed that I must spill the first blood. On which, armed with a hatchet, and accompanied by Will, I entered my master's chamber, it being dark, I could not give a death blow, the hatchet glanced from his head, he sprang from the bed and called his wife, it was his last word, Will laid him dead, with a blow of his axe, and Mrs. Travis shared the same fate, as she lay in bed. The murder of this family, five in number, was the work of a moment, not one of them awoke; there was a little infant sleeping in a cradle, that was forgotten, until we had left the house and gone some distance, when Henry and Will returned and killed it; we got here, four guns that would shoot, and several old muskets, with a pound or two of powder. We remained some time at the barn, where we paraded; I formed them in a line as soldiers, and after carrying them through all the manoevres I was master of, marched them off to Mr. Salathul Francis', about six hundred yards distant. Sam and Will went to the door and knocked. Mr. Francis asked who was there, Sam replied it was him, and he had a letter for him, on which he got up and came to the door; they immediately seized him, and dragging him out a little from the door, he was dispatched by repeated blows on the head; there was no other white person in the family. We started from there for Mrs. Reese's, maintaining the most perfect silence on our march, where finding the door unlocked, we entered, and murdured Mrs. Reese in her bed, while sleeping; her son awoke, but it was only to sleep the sleep of death, he had only time to say who is that, and he was no more. From Mrs. Reese's we went to Mrs. Turner's, a mile distant, which we reached about sunrise, on Monday morning. Henry, Austin, and Sam, went to the still, where, finding Mr. Peebles, Austin shot him, and the rest of us went to the house; as we approached, the family discovered us, and shut the door. Vain hope! Will, with one stroke of his axe, opened it, and we entered and found Mrs. Turner and Mrs. Newsome in the middle of a room, almost frightened to death. Will immediately killed Mrs. Turner, with one blow of his axe. I took Mrs. Newsome by the hand, and with the sword I had when I was apprehended, I struck her several blows over the head, but not being able to kill her, as the sword was dull. Will turning around and discovering it, despatched her also. A general destruction of property and search for money and ammunition, always succeeded the murders. By this time my company amounted to fifteen, and nine men mounted, who started for Mrs. Whitehead's, (the other six were to go through a by way to Mr. Bryant's, and rejoin us at Mrs. Whitehead's,) as we approached the house we discovered Mr. Richard Whitehead standing in the cotton patch, near the lane fence; we called him over into the lane, and Will, the executioner, was near at hand, with his fatal axe, to send him to an untimely grave. As we pushed on to the house, I discovered some one run round the garden, and thinking it was some of the white family, I pursued them, but finding it was a servant girl belonging to the house, I returned to commence the work of death, but they whom I left, had not been idle; all the family were already murdered, but Mrs. Whitehead and her daughter Margaret. As I came round to the door I saw Will pulling Mrs. Whitehead out of the house, and at the step he nearly severed her head from her body, with his broad axe. Miss Margaret, when I discovered her, had concealed herself in the corner, formed by the projection of the cellar cap from the house; on my approach she fled, but was soon overtaken, and after repeated blows with a sword, I killed her by a blow on the head, with a fence rail. By this time, the six who had gone by Mr. Bryant's, rejoined us, and informed me they had done the work of death assigned them. We again divided, part going to Mr. Richard Porter's, and from thence to Nathaniel Francis', the others to Mr. Howell Harris', and Mr. T. Doyles. On my reaching Mr. Porter's, he had escaped with his family. I understood there, that the alarm had already spread, and I immediately returned to bring up those sent to Mr. Doyles, and Mr. Howell Harris'; the party I left going on to Mr. Francis', having told them I would join them in that neighborhood. I met these sent to Mr. Doyles' and Mr. Harris' returning, having met Mr. Doyle on the road and killed him; and learning from some who joined them, that Mr. Harris was from home, I immediately pursued the course taken by the party gone on before; but knowing they would complete the work of death and pillage, at Mr. Francis' before I could get there, I went to Mr. Peter Edwards', expecting to find them there, but they had been here also. I then went to Mr. John T. Barrow's, they had been here and murdered him. I pursued on their track to Capt. Newit Harris', where I found the greater part mounted, and ready to start; the men now amounting to about forty, shouted and hurraed as I rode up, some were in the yard, loading their guns, others drinking. They said Captain Harris and his family had escaped, the property in the house they destroyed, robbing him of money and other valuables. I ordered them to mount and march instantly, this was about nine or ten o'clock, Monday morning. I proceeded to Mr. Levi Waller's, two or three miles distant. I took my station in the rear, and as it 'twas my object to carry terror and devastation wherever we went, I placed fifteen or twenty of the best armed and most to be relied on, in front, who generally approached the house as fast as their horses could run; this was for two purposes, to prevent their escape and strike terror to the inhabitants—on this account I never got to the houses, after leaving Mrs. Whitehead's, until the murders were committed, except in one case. I sometimes got in sight in time to see the work of death completed, viewed the mangled bodies as they lay, in silent satisfaction, and immediately started in quest of other victims—Having murdered Mrs. Waller and ten children, we started for Mr. William Williams'—having killed him and two little boys that were there; while engaged in this, Mrs. Williams fled and got some distance from the house, but she was pursued, overtaken, and compelled to get up behind one of the company, who brought her back, and after showing her the mangled body of her lifeless husband, she was told to get down and lay by his side, where she was shot dead. I then started for Mr. Jacob Williams, where the family were murdered—Here we found a young man named Drury, who had come on business with Mr. Williams—he was pursued, overtaken and shot. Mrs. Vaughan was the

next place we visited—and after murdering the family here, I determined on starting for Jerusalem—Our number amounted now to fifty or sixty, all mounted and
armed with guns, axes, swords and clubs—On reaching Mr. James W. Parkers'
gate, immediately on the road leading to Jerusalem, and about three miles distant,
it was proposed to me to call there, but I objected, as I knew he was gone to Jerusalem, and my object was to reach there as soon as possible; but some of the men
having relations at Mr. Parker's it was agreed that they might call and get his people. I remained at the gate on the road, with seven or eight; the others going across
the field to the house, about half a mile off. After waiting some time for them, I
became impatient, and started to the house for them, and on our return we were
met by a party of white men, who had pursued our blood-stained track, and who
had fired on those at the gate, and dispersed them, which I new nothing of, not
having been at that time rejoined by any of them—Immediately on discovering
the whites, I ordered my men to halt and form, as they appeared to be alarmed—
The white men, eighteen in number, approached us in about one hundred yards,
when one of them fired, (this was against the positive orders of Captain Alexander P. Peete, who commanded, and who had directed the men to reserve their fire
until within thirty paces). And I discovered about half of them retreating, I then
ordered my men to fire and rush on them; the few remaining stood their ground
until we approached within fifty yards, when they fired and retreated. We pursued and overtook some of them who we thought we left dead; (they were not
killed) after pursuing them about two hundred yards, and rising a little hill, I discovered they were met by another party, and had haulted, and were re-loading
their guns, (this was a small party from Jerusalem who knew the negroes were in
the field, and had just tied their horses to await their return to the road, knowing
that Mr. Parker and family were in Jerusalem, but knew nothing of the party that
had gone in with Captain Peete; on hearing the firing they immediately rushed to
the spot and arrived just in time to arrest the progress of these barbarous villians,
and save the lives of their friends and fellow citizens.) Thinking that those who
retreated first, and the party who fired on us at fifty or sixty yards distant, had all
only fallen back to meet others with amunition. As I saw them re-loading their
guns, and more coming up than I saw at first, and several of my bravest men being wounded, the others became panick struck and squandered over the field; the
white men pursued and fired on us several times. Hark had his horse shot under
him, and I caught another for him as it was running by me; five or six of my men
were wounded, but none left on the field; finding myself defeated here I instantly
determined to go through a private way, and cross the Nottoway river at the Cypress Bridge, three miles below Jerusalem, and attack that place in the rear, as I
expected they would look for me on the other road, and I had a great desire to
get there to procure arms and amunition. After going a short distance in this private way, accompanied by about twenty men, I overtook two or three who told
me the others were dispersed in every direction. After trying in vain to collect a
sufficient force to proceed to Jerusalem, I determined to return, as I was sure they
would make back to their old neighborhood, where they would rejoin me, make
new recruits, and come down again. On my way back, I called at Mrs. Thomas's,
Mrs. Spencer's, and several other places, the white families having fled, we found

no more victims to gratify our thirst for blood, we stopped at Majr. Ridley's quarter for the night, and being joined by four of his men, with the recruits made since my defeat, we mustered now about forty strong. After placing out sentinels, I laid down to sleep, but was quickly roused by a great racket; starting up, I found some mounted, and others in great confusion; one of the sentinels having given the alarm that we were about to be attacked, I ordered some to ride round and reconnoitre, and on their return the others being more alarmed, not knowing who they were, fled in different ways, so that I was reduced to about twenty again; with this I determined to attempt to recruit, and proceed on to rally in the neighborhood, I had left. Dr. Blunt's was the nearest house, which we reached just before day; on riding up the yard, Hark fired a gun. We expected Dr. Blunt and his family were at Maj. Ridley's, as I knew there was a company of men there; the gun was fired to ascertain if any of the family were at home; we were immediately fired upon and retreated, leaving several of my men. I do not know what became of them, as I never saw them afterwards. Pursuing our course back and coming in sight of Captain Harris', where we had been the day before, we discovered a party of white men at the house, on which all deserted me but two, (Jacob and Nat,) we concealed ourselves in the woods until near night, when I sent them in search of Henry, Sam, Nelson, and Hark, and directed them to rally all they could, at the place we had had our dinner the Sunday before, where they would find me, and I accordingly returned there as soon as it was dark and remained until Wednesday evening, when discovering white men riding around the place as though they were looking for some one, and none of my men joining me, I concluded Jacob and Nat had been taken, and compelled to betray me. On this I gave up all hope for the present; and on Thursday night after having supplied myself with provisions from Mr. Travis's, I scratched a hole under a pile of fence rails in a field, where I concealed myself for six weeks, never leaving my hiding place but for a few minutes in the dead of night to get water which was very near; thinking by this time I could venture out, I began to go about in the night and eaves drop the houses in the neighborhood; pursuing this course for about a fortnight and gathering little or no intelligence, afraid of speaking to any human being, and returning every morning to my cave before the dawn of day. I know not how long I might have led this life, if accident had not betrayed me, a dog in the neighborhood passing by my hiding place one night while I was out, was attracted by some meat I had in my cave, and crawled in and stole it, and was coming out just as I returned. A few nights after, two negroes having started to go hunting with the same dog, and passed that way, the dog came again to the place, and having just gone out to walk about, discovered me and barked, on which thinking myself discovered, I spoke to them to beg concealment. On making myself known they fled from me. Knowing then they would betray me, I immediately left my hiding place, and was pursued almost incessantly until I was taken a fortnight afterwards by Mr. Benjamin Phipps, in a little hole I had dug out with my sword, for the purpose of concealment, under the top of a fallen tree. On Mr. Phipps' discovering the place of my concealment, he cocked his gun and aimed at me. I requested him not to shoot and I would give up, upon which he demanded my sword. I delivered it to him, and he brought me to prison. During the time I was pursued, I had many hair breadth escapes, which your time will not permit you to relate. I am here loaded with chains, and willing to suffer the fate that awaits me.

I here proceeded to make some inquiries of him, after assuring him of the certain death that awaited him, and that concealment would only bring destruction on the innocent as well as guilty, of his own color, if he knew of any extensive or concerted plan. His answer was, I do not. When I questioned him as to the insurrection in North Carolina happening about the same time, he denied any knowledge of it; and when I looked him in the face as though I would search his inmost thoughts, he replied, "I see sir, you doubt my word; but can you not think the same ideas, and strange appearances about this time in the heaven's might prompt others, as well as myself, to this undertaking." I now had much conversation with and asked him many questions, having forborne to do so previously, except in the cases noted in parenthesis; but during his statement, I had, unnoticed by him, taken notes as to some particular circumstances, and having the advantage of his statement before me in writing, on the evening of the third day that I had been with him, I began a cross examination, and found his statement corroborated by every circumstance coming within my own knowledge or the confessions of others whom had been either killed or executed, and whom he had not seen nor had any knowledge since 22d of August last, he expressed himself fully satisfied as to the impracticability of his attempt. It has been said he was ignorant and cowardly, and that his object was to murder and rob for the purpose of obtaining money to make his escape. It is notorious, that he was never known to have a dollar in his life; to swear an oath, or drink a drop of spirits. As to his ignorance, he certainly never had the advantages of education, but he can read and write, (it was taught him by his parents,) and for natural intelligence and quickness of apprehension, is surpassed by few men I have ever seen. As to his being a coward, his reason as given for not resisting Mr. Phipps, shews the decision of his character. When he saw Mr. Phipps present his gun, he said he knew it was impossible for him to escape as the woods were full of men; he therefore thought it was better to surrender, and trust to fortune for his escape. He is a complete fanatic, or plays his part most admirably. On other subjects he possesses an uncommon share of intelligence, with a mind capable of attaining any thing; but warped and perverted by the influence of early impressions. He is below the ordinary stature, though strong and active, having the true negro face, every feature of which is strongly marked. I shall not attempt to describe the effect of his narrative, as told and commented on by himself, in the condemned hole of the prison. The calm, deliberate composure with which he spoke of his late deeds and intentions, the expression of his fiend-like face when excited by enthusiasm, still bearing the stains of the blood of helpless innocence about him; clothed with rags and covered with chains; yet daring to raise his manacled hands to heaven, with a spirit soaring above the attributes of man; I looked on him and my blood curdled in my veins.

I will not shock the feelings of humanity, nor wound afresh the bosoms of the disconsolate sufferers in this unparalleled and inhuman massacre, by detailing the deeds of their fiend-like barbarity. There were two or three who were in the power of these wretches, had they known it, and who escaped in the most providential manner. There were two whom they thought they left dead on the field at Mr. Parker's, but who were only stunned by the blows of their guns, as they did not take time to re-load when they charged on them. The escape of a little girl who went to school at Mr. Waller's, and where the children were collecting for that purpose, excited general sympathy. As their teacher had not arrived, they were at play in the yard, and seeing the negroes approach, she ran up on a dirt chimney, (such as are common to log houses,) and remained there unnoticed during the massacre of the eleven that were killed at this place. She remained on her hiding place till just before the arrival of a party, who were in pursuit of the murderers, when she came down and fled to a swamp, where, a mere child as she was, with the horrors of the late scene before her, she lay concealed until the next day, when seeing a party go up to the house, she came up, and on being asked how she escaped, replied with the utmost simplicity, "The Lord helped her." She was taken up behind a gentleman of the party, and returned to the arms of her weeping mother. Miss Whitehead concealed herself between the bed and the mat that supported it, while they murdered her sister in the same room, without discovering her. She was afterwards carried off, and concealed for protection by a slave of the family, who gave evidence against several of them on their trial. Mrs. Nathaniel Francis, while concealed in a closet heard their blows, and the shrieks of the victims of these ruthless savages; they then entered the closet where she was concealed, and went out without discovering her. While in this hiding place, she heard two of her women in a quarrel about the division of her clothes. Mr. John T. Baron, discovering them approaching his house, told his wife to make her escape, and scorning to fly, fell fighting on his own threshold. After firing his rifle, he discharged his gun at them, and then broke it over the villain who first approached him, but he was overpowered, and slain. His bravery, however, saved from the hands of these monsters, his lovely and amiable wife, who will long lament a husband so deserving of her love. As directed by him, she attempted to escape through the garden, when she was caught and held by one of her servant girls, but another coming to her rescue, she fled to the woods, and concealed herself. Few indeed, were those who escaped their work of death. But fortunate for society, the hand of retributive justice has overtaken them; and not one that was known to be concerned has escaped.

*The Commonwealth,*
        vs.
    *Nat Turner.*            Charged with making insurrection, and plotting to take away the lives of divers free white persons, &c. on the 22d of August, 1831.

The court composed of ———, having met for the trial of Nat Turner, the prisoner was brought in and arraigned, and upon his arraignment pleaded *Not guilty;* saying to his counsel, that he did not feel so.

On the part of the Commonwealth, Levi Waller was introduced, who being sworn, deposed as follows: *(agreeably to Nat's own Confession.)* Col. Trezvant* was then introduced, who being sworn, narrated Nat's Confession to him, as follows: *(his Confession as given to Mr. Gray.)* The prisoner introduced no evidence, and the case was submitted without argument to the court, who having found him guilty, Jeremiah Cobb, Esq. Chairman, pronounced the sentence of the court, in the following words: "Nat Turner! Stand up. Have you any thing to say why sentence of death should not be pronounced against you?

*Ans.* I have not. I have made a full confession to Mr. Gray, and I have nothing more to say.

Attend then to the sentence of the Court. You have been arraigned and tried before this court, and convicted of one of the highest crimes in our criminal code. You have been convicted of plotting in cold blood, the indiscriminate destruction of men, of helpless women, and of infant children. The evidence before us leaves not a shadow of doubt, but that your hands were often imbrued in the blood of the innocent; and your own confession tells us that they were stained with the blood of a master; in your own language, "too indulgent." Could I stop here, your crime would be sufficiently aggravated. But the original contriver of a plan, deep and deadly, one that never can be effected, you managed so far to put it into execution, as to deprive us of many of our most valuable citizens; and this was done when they were asleep, and defenceless; under circumstances shocking to humanity. And while upon this part of the subject, I cannot but call your attention to the poor misguided wretches who have gone before you. They are not few in number—they were your bosom associates; and the blood of all cries aloud, and calls upon you, as the author of their misfortune. Yes! You forced them unprepared, from Time to Eternity. Borne down by this load of guilt, your only justification is, that you were led away by fanaticism. If this be true, from my soul I pity you; and while you have my sympathies, I am, nevertheless called upon to pass the sentence of the court. The time between this and your execution, will necessarily be very short; and your only hope must be in another world. The judgment of the court is, that you be taken hence to the jail from whence you came, thence to the place of execution, and on Friday next, between the hours of 10 A. M. and 2 P. M. be hung by the neck until you are dead! dead! dead and may the Lord have mercy upon your soul.

---

*The committing Magistrate.

## A LIST OF PERSONS MURDERED IN THE INSURRECTION, ON THE 21ST AND 22D OF AUGUST, 1831.

Joseph Travers and wife and three children, Mrs. Elizabeth Turner, Hartwell Prebles, Sarah Newsome, Mrs. P. Reese and son William, Trajan Doyle, Henry Bryant and wife and child, and wife's mother, Mrs. Catharine Whitehead, son Richard and four daughters and grand-child, Salathiel Francis, Nathaniel Francis' overseer and two children, John T. Barrow, George Vaughan, Mrs. Levi Waller and ten children, William Williams, wife and two boys, Mrs. Caswell Worrell and child, Mrs. Rebecca Vaughan, Ann Eliza Vaughan, and son Arthur, Mrs. John K. Williams and child, Mrs. Jacob Williams and three children, and Edwin Drury—amounting to fifty-five.

## A LIST OF NEGROES BROUGHT BEFORE THE COURT OF SOUTHAMPTON, WITH THEIR OWNERS' NAMES, AND SENTENCE.

| | | |
|---|---|---|
| Daniel, | Richard Porter, | Convicted. |
| Moses, | J. T. Barrow, | Do.[20] |
| Tom, | Caty Whitehead, | Discharged. |
| Jack and Andrew, | Caty Whitehead, | Con. and transported. |
| Jacob, | Geo. H. Charlton, | Disch'd without trial. |
| Isaac, | Ditto, | Convi. and transported. |
| Jack, | Everett Bryant, | Discharged. |
| Nathan, | Benj. Blunt's estate, | Convicted. |
| Nathan, Tom, and Davy, (boys,) | Nathaniel Francis, | Convicted and transported. |
| Davy | Elizabeth Turner, | Convicted. |
| Curtis, | Thomas Ridley, | Do. |
| Stephen, | Do. | Do. |
| Hardy and Isham, | Benjamin Edwards, | Convicted and transp'd. |
| Sam, | Nathaniel Francis, | Convicted. |
| Hark, | Joseph Travis' estate. | Do. |
| Moses, (a boy,) | Do. | Do. and transported |
| Davy, | Levi Waller, | Convicted. |
| Nelson, | Jacob Williams, | Do. |
| Nat, | Edm'd Turner's estate, | Do. |
| Jack, | Wm. Reese's estate, | Do. |
| Dred | Nathaniel Francis, | Do. |
| Arnold, Artist, (free,) | | Discharged. |
| Sam, | J. W. Parker, | Acquitted. |
| Ferry and Archer, | J. W. Parker, | Disch'd without trial. |
| Jim, | William Vaughan, | Acquitted. |
| Bob, | Temperance Parker, | Do. |
| Davy, | Joseph Parker, | |
| Daniel, | Solomon D. Parker, | Disch'd without trial. |
| Thomas Haithcock, (free,) | | Sent on for further trial. |
| Joe, | John C. Turner, | Convicted. |
| Lucy, | John T. Barrow, | Do. |
| Matt, | Thomas Ridley, | Acquitted. |
| Jim, | Richard Porter, | Do. |

| | | |
|---|---|---|
| Exum Artes, (free,) | .......................... | Sent on for further trial. |
| Joe, | .................. Richard P. Briggs, | Disch'd without trial. |
| Bury Newsome, (free,) | ..................... | Sent on for further trial. |
| Stephen, | ............. James Bell, | Acquitted. |
| Jim and Isaac, | ......... Samuel Champion, | Convicted and trans'd. |
| Proston, | ............ Hannah Williamson, | Acquitted. |
| Frank, | ............... Solomon D. Parker, | Convi'd and transp'd. |
| Jack and Shadrach, | ...... Nathaniel Simmons, | Acquitted. |
| Nelson, | .............. Benj. Blunt's estate, | Do. |
| Sam, | ................. Peter Edwards, | Convicted. |
| Archer, | .............. Arthur G. Reese, | Acquitted. |
| Isham Turner, (free,) | ...................... | Sent on for further trial. |
| Nat Turner, | ........... Putnam Moore, dec'd,.. | Convicted. |

1. The historical information throughout this introduction to Turner's *Confessions* was gleaned from a variety of sources, including Aptheker, "Turner, Nat"; Fabricant, "Thomas R. Gray"; Greenberg, *Confessions of Nat Turner*; Oates, *Fires of Jubilee*; Sundquist, *To Wake the Nations*; Tragle, *Southampton Slave Revolt*; and Wood, "Nat Turner's Rebellion."

2. Oates, *Fires of Jubilee*, 118–119; Tragle, *Southampton Slave Revolt*, 134–135, 137–138.

3. Parramore, *Southampton County*, 105–107, as cited in Fabricant, "Thomas R. Gray," 340; Greenberg, *Confessions of Nat Turner*, 8; and Sundquist, *To Wake the Nations*, 38.

4. Oates, *Fires of Jubilee*, 121.

5. Wood, "Nat Turner's Rebellion," 1970.

6. See Andrews, *Free Story*, 72–77.

7. Fabricant, "Thomas R. Gray," 343–354.

8. Gross and Bender, "History," 497; Oates, *Fires of Jubilee*, 123.

9. Andrews, *Free Story*, 72; Oates, *Fires of Jubilee*, 123.

10. Sundquist, *To Wake the Nations*, 79–81.

11. Andrews, *Free Story*, 76.

12. Drewry, *Southampton Insurrection*, 102, as cited in Greenberg, *Confessions of Nat Turner*, 19–20.

13. Ibid., 20.

14. Gross and Bender, "History," 491.

15. Sundquist, *To Wake the Nations*, 83.

16. Southampton County is located just over the border from Murfreesboro, North Carolina. Jerusalem was the county seat, with a population of 175 at the time.

17. See *Luke* 12:31.

18. See *Luke* 12:47.

19. See *Matthew* 19:30, 20:16, *Mark* 10:31, and *Luke* 13:30.

20. Ditto.

CHARLES BALL

CHARLES BALL (c. 1781–?) was the pseudonym of an anonymous slave who collaborated with Isaac Fisher, a prominent attorney of Lewistown, Pennsylvania, to produce the longest and most detailed slave narrative of the antebellum period.[1] No other source more fully describes plantation life from the slave's point of view; indeed, the book rivals Frederick Law Olmsted's *A Journey in the Seaboard Slave States* as one of the best antebellum portraits of the region. Ball possessed a prodigious memory and seems to have recalled almost every meal he ate and every plant or animal he came into contact with. This profusion of detail rarely bogs down his narrative, however, which reads less like an exposition of its title, *Slavery in the United States,* than an exceptionally well written adventure novel. It includes alligators, snakes, a panther, and, through the eyes of a fellow slave, an African lion; no less than four hair-raising escapes and as many kidnapping attempts; military action in the War of 1812; and an unusual and chilling tale—remarkable for its evenhanded sobriety—of black-on-white crime and its consequences. A surprising twist at the end casts a shadow on all that has come before.

The book has had a long and complex history. In 1835, prepublication advertisements boasted that the book would expose "the actual condition of the slaves, moral as well as physical, mental as well as corporeal, with greater certainty, and with more accuracy of detail than could be obtained by many years of travel"; and continued, "To those who take delight in lonely and desperate undertakings, pursued with patient and unflinching courage, we recommend the flight and journey from Georgia to Maryland, which exhibits the curious spectacle of a man wandering six months in the United States without speaking to a human creature."[2] The narrative was eagerly anticipated, and, when published in 1836, it met with immediate success; in large part it set the mold for subsequent slave narratives.

Its popularity notwithstanding, the narrative's veracity was challenged. Even favorable reviewers could not help but notice the lack of documentary evidence. The *Quarterly Anti-Slavery Magazine* wrote:

> Whether the narrative, . . . is real or fictitious, we think its reader will not retain, through many pages, a doubt of the perfect accuracy of its picture of slavery. . . . We are led to this remark, not because we feel ourselves at liberty to doubt the genuineness and reality of the whole, but because the book itself does not answer a number of preliminary questions which the public will not fail to ask. . . .
>
> It is due to the writer to say, and perhaps a higher compliment could not be paid him, that he has accomplished his very important and difficult object, in a manner that would have done credit to the author of Robinson Crusoe. He has traced his hero through all the vicissitudes of slavery, with a minuteness of detail that is truly astonishing, while at the same time the interest of his narrative is ever fresh and grow-

ing. The book is not merely readable. It has charm and potency about it. It is one of those books which always draws the reader on by the irresistible magnetism of the next paragraph to the unwelcome appearance of "The end." . . .

Believing, as we have privately good reason to do, that this book contains, in the language of a faithful interpreter, a true narrative which has fallen from the lips of a veritable fugitive, we have only to regret that there is not an appendix of some sort, containing some documentary evidence to that effect.[3]

A few months after the book's publication, another narrative entitled *The Slave; or, Memoirs of Archy Moore* was published anonymously in Boston, purporting to be the autobiography of a Virginia slave. When it became known that the latter was a novel written by the abolitionist Richard Hildreth, Southern sympathizers lumped both books together and condemned them as fiction.[4]

This did not prevent the publication of further editions of Ball's narrative, totaling at least nine in the United States, two in England, and one in Germany. The 1837 (second U.S.) edition included a testimonial signed by two of Lewistown's most prominent citizens, certifying that they "know the black man whose narrative is given in this book, and have heard him relate the principal matters contained in the book concerning himself, long before the book was published"; but its introduction also included this disclaimer: "How far this personal narrative is true is a question which each reader must, of course, decide for himself."[5] The 1858 edition was, in the words of John Herbert Nelson, "condensed slightly, bound in a fiery red cover, with great wavering gilt letters staring out at the reader, and handed out to an eager public under the astonishing [and completely inaccurate] title, *Fifty Years in Chains*";[6] and Marion Starling wrote in 1946, "more copies are to be found of [the 1859 edition of *Fifty Years in Chains*] than are to be found of any other edition of this slave narrative, or any other slave narrative, in the libraries throughout this country."[7] In sum, Charles Ball's narrative probably rivaled in popularity those of Olaudah Equiano, Nat Turner, Frederick Douglass, Josiah Henson, and Solomon Northup.

But the accuracy of Ball's narrative continued to be questioned. One of the most zealous attempts to discredit it was published in the *Southern Quarterly Review* in January 1853. Vernon Loggins, in his 1931 *The Negro Author,* wrote "the book has a notorious reputation as a work of deception." In 1977 John W. Blassingame refuted the 1853 article at length, and, in doing so, substantiated many details of the narrative. But as recently as 1989 Blyden Jackson, in *A History of Afro-American Literature,* repeated Loggins's unsubstantiated claim that Charles Ball and Archy Moore were equally fictitious, ignoring Blassingame's research.[8]

The presentation of Ball's story by his amanuensis certainly hasn't helped its acceptance by historians and literary scholars. Fisher's preface makes explicit the practices of most of the amanuenses of slave narrators: he admits to omitting or suppressing Ball's opinions and sentiments and to excluding his "bitterness of heart." The publisher's introduction to the 1837 edition goes further:

Mr. Fisher, (the author) intimates in his preface, what is, indeed, sufficiently obvious from the felicity of his style, that the *language* of the book is not that of the unlettered slave, whose adventures he records. A similar intimation might with equal propriety have been given, in reference to the various profound and interesting reflections interspersed throughout the work. The author states, in a private communication, that many of the anecdotes in the book illustrative of Southern society, were not obtained from Ball, but from other and creditable sources; he avers, however, that all the facts which relate personally to the fugitive, were received from his own lips.[9]

Clearly, Fisher transformed Ball's personal narrative into a wide-ranging exposition of the conditions of the slave, and in the process all but erased Ball's own voice. However, almost all slave narratives, whether self-penned or dictated, deemphasized the psychology of the narrator in the interest of providing a quasi-documentary account. And the hero of Ball's narrative, while perhaps lacking the psychological depth of William Grimes, Douglass, or Harriet Jacobs, nonetheless emerges as an unforgettable figure in his own right.

# SLAVERY

## IN THE

# UNITED STATES:

## A NARRATIVE

### OF

## THE LIFE AND ADVENTURES OF

# CHARLES BALL,

## *A BLACK MAN,*

Who lived forty years in Maryland, South Carolina and Georgia, as a
Slave, under various masters, and was one year in the Navy,
with Commodore Barney, during the late war. Containing
an account of the manners and usages of the Planters
and Slaveholders of the South, a description of the
condition and treatment of the Slaves, with
observations upon the state of morals
amongst the cotton planters, and the
perils and sufferings of a fugitive
slave, who twice escaped
from the cotton country.

LEWISTOWN, PA.
PRINTED AND PUBLISHED BY JOHN W. SHUGERT.
1836.

# PREFACE.

---

IN the following pages, the reader will find embodied the principal incidents that have occurred in the life of a slave, in the United States of America. The narrative is taken from the mouth of the adventurer himself; and if the copy does not retain the identical words of the original, the sense and import, at least, are faithfully preserved.

Many of his opinions have been cautiously omitted, or carefully suppressed, as being of no value to the reader; and his sentiments upon the subject of slavery, have not been embodied in this work. The design of the writer, who is no more than the recorder of the facts detailed to him by another, has been to render the narrative as simple, and the style of the story as plain, as the laws of the language would permit. To introduce the reader, as it were, to a view of the cotton fields, and exhibit, not to his imagination, but to his very eyes, the mode of life to which the slaves on the southern plantations must conform, has been the primary object of the compiler.

The book has been written without fear or prejudice, and no opinions have been consulted in its composition. The sole view of the writer has been to make the citizens of the United States acquainted with each other, and to give a faithful portrait of the manners, usages, and customs of the southern people, so far as those manners, usages, and customs have fallen under the observations of a common negro slave, endued by nature with a tolerable portion of intellectual capacity. The more reliance is to be placed upon his relations of those things that he saw in the southern country, when it is recollected that he had been born and brought up in a part of the state of Maryland, in which, of all others, the spirit of the "old aristocracy," as it has not unaptly been called, retained much of its pristine vigour in his youth; and where he had an early opportunity of seeing many of the most respectable, best educated, and most highly enlightened families of both Maryland and Virginia, a constant succession of kind offices, friendly visits, and family alliances, having at that day united the most distinguished inhabitants of the two sides of the Potomac, in the social relations of one people.

It might naturally be expected, that a man who had passed through so many scenes of adversity, and had suffered so many wrongs at the hands of his fellow-man, would feel much of the bitterness of heart that is engendered by a remembrance of unatoned injuries; but every sentiment of this kind has been carefully excluded from the following pages, in which the reader will find nothing but an unadorned detail of acts, and the impressions those acts produced on the mind of him upon whom they operated.

# NARRATIVE.[10]

## CHAPTER I.

THE system of slavery, as practised in the United States, has been, and is now, but little understood by the people who live north of the Potomac and the Ohio; for, although individual cases of extreme cruelty and oppression occasionally occur in Maryland, yet the general treatment of the black people, is far more lenient and mild in that state, than it is farther south. This, I presume, is mainly to be attributed to the vicinity of the free state of Pennsylvania; but, in no small degree, to the influence of the population of the cities of Baltimore and Washington, over the families of the planters of the surrounding counties. For experience has taught me, that both masters and mistresses, who, if not observed by strangers, would treat their slaves with the utmost rigour, are so far operated upon, by a sense of shame or pride, as to provide them tolerably with both food and clothing, when they know their conduct is subject to the observation of persons, whose good opinion they wish to preserve. A large number of the most respectable and wealthy people in both Washington and Baltimore, being altogether opposed to the practice of slavery, hold a constant control over the actions of their friends, the farmers, and thus prevent much misery; but in the south, the case is widely different. There, every man, and every woman too, except prevented by poverty, is a slave-holder; and the entire white population is leagued together by a common bond of the most sordid interest, in the torture and oppression of the poor descendants of Africa. If the negro is wronged, there is no one to whom he can complain—if suffering for want of the coarsest food, he dare not steal—if flogged till the flesh falls from his bones, he must not murmur—and if compelled to perform his daily toil in an iron collar, no expression of resentment must escape his lips.

People of the northern states, who make excursions to the south, visit the principal cities and towns, travel the most frequented highways, or even sojourn for a time at the residences of the large planters, and partake of their hospitality and amusements, know nothing of the condition of the southern slaves. To acquire this knowledge, the traveller must take up his abode for a season, in the lodge of the overseer, pass a summer in the remote cotton fields, or spend a year within view of the rice swamps. By attending for one month, the court which the overseer of a large estate holds every evening in the cotton-gin yard, and witnessing the execution of his decrees, a Turk or a Russian would find the tribunals of his country far outdone.

It seems to be a law of nature, that slavery is equally destructive to the master and the slave; for, whilst it stupifies the latter with fear, and reduces him below the condition of man, it brutalizes the former, by the practice of continual tyranny; and makes him the prey of all the vices which render human nature loathsome.

In the following simple narrative of an unlearned man, I have endeavoured, faithfully and truly, to present to the reader, some of the most material accidents which occurred to myself, in a period of thirty years of slavery in the free Republic of the United States; as well as many circumstances, which I observed in the condition and conduct of other persons during that period.

It has been supposed, by many, that the state of the southern slaves is constantly becoming better; and that the treatment which they receive at the hands of their masters, is progressively milder and more humane; but the contrary of all this is unquestionably the truth; for, under the bad culture which is practised in the south, the land is constantly becoming poorer, and the means of getting food, more and more difficult. So long as the land is new and rich, and produces corn and sweet potatoes abundantly, the black people seldom suffer greatly for food; but, when the ground is all cleared, and planted in rice or cotton, corn and potatoes become scarce; *and when corn has to be bought on a cotton plantation, the people must expect to make acquaintance with hunger.*

My grandfather was brought from Africa, and sold as a slave in Calvert county, in Maryland,[11] about the year 1730. I never understood the name of the ship in which he was imported, nor the name of the planter who bought him on his arrival, but at the time I knew him, he was a slave in a family called Mauel, who resided near Leonardtown. My father was a slave in a family named Hantz, living near the same place. My mother was the slave of a tobacco planter, an old man, who died, according to the best of my recollection, when I was about four years old, leaving his property in such a situation that it became necessary, as I suppose, to sell a part of it to pay his debts. Soon after his death, several of his slaves, and with others myself, were sold at public vendue. My mother had several children, my brothers and sisters, and we were all sold on the same day to different purchasers. Our new master took us away, and I never saw my mother, nor any of my brothers and sisters afterwards. This was, I presume, about the year 1785. I learned subsequently, from my father, that my mother was sold to a Georgia trader, who soon after that carried her away from Maryland. Her other children were sold to slave-dealers from Carolina, and were also taken away, so that I was left alone in Calvert county, with my father, whose owner lived only a few miles from my new master's residence. At the time I was sold I was quite naked, having never had any clothes in my life; but my new master had brought with him a child's frock or wrapper, belonging to one of his own children; and after he had purchased me, he dressed me in this garment, took me before him on his horse, and started home; but my poor mother, when she saw me leaving her for the last time, ran after me, took me down from the horse, clasped me in her arms, and wept loudly and bitterly over me. My master seemed to pity her, and endeavoured to soothe her distress by telling her that he would be a good master to me, and that I should not want any thing. She then, still holding me in her arms, walked along the road beside the horse as he moved slowly, and earnestly and imploringly besought my master to buy her and the rest of her children, and not permit them to be carried away by the negro buyers; but whilst thus entreating him to save her and her family, the slave-driver, who had first bought her, came running in pursuit of her with a raw hide in his hand. When he overtook us he told her he was her master now, and ordered her to give that little negro to its owner, and come back with him.

My mother then turned to him and cried, "Oh, master, do not take me from my child!" Without making any reply, he gave her two or three heavy blows on the shoulders with his raw hide, snatched me from her arms, handed me to my master, and seizing her by one arm, dragged her back towards the place of sale. My master then quickened the pace of his horse; and as we advanced, the cries of my poor parent became more and more indistinct—at length they died away in the distance, and I never again heard the voice of my poor mother. Young as I was, the horrors of that day sank deeply into my heart, and even at this time, though half a century has elapsed, the terrors of the scene return with painful vividness upon my memory. Frightened at the sight of the cruelties inflicted upon my poor mother, I forgot my own sorrows at parting from her and clung to my new master, as an angel and a saviour, when compared with the hardened fiend into whose power she had fallen. She had been a kind and good mother to me; had warmed me in her bosom in the cold nights of winter; and had often divided the scanty pittance of food allowed her by her mistress, between my brothers, and sisters, and me, and gone supperless to bed herself. Whatever victuals she could obtain beyond the coarse food, salt fish, and corn-bread, allowed to slaves on the Patuxent and Potomac rivers, she carefully distributed among her children, and treated us with all the tenderness which her own miserable condition would permit. I have no doubt that she was chained and driven to Carolina, and toiled out the residue of a forlorn and famished existence in the rice swamps, or indigo fields of the south.

My father never recovered from the effects of the shock, which this sudden and overwhelming ruin of his family gave him. He had formerly been of a gay social temper, and when he came to see us on a Saturday night, he always brought us some little present, such as the means of a poor slave would allow— apples, melons, sweet potatoes, or, if he could procure nothing else, a little parched corn, which tasted better in our cabin, because he had brought it.

He spent the greater part of the time, which his master permitted him to pass with us, in relating such stories as he had learned from his companions, or in singing the rude songs common amongst the slaves of Maryland and Virginia. After this time I never heard him laugh heartily, or sing a song. He became gloomy and morose in his temper, to all but me; and spent nearly all his leisure time with my grandfather, who claimed kindred with some royal family in Africa, and had been a great warrior in his native country. The master of my father was a hard penurious man, and so exceedingly avaricious, that he scarcely allowed himself the common conveniences of life. A stranger to sensibility, he was incapable of tracing the change in the temper and deportment of my father, to its true cause; but attributed it to a sullen discontent with his condition as a slave, and a desire to abandon his service, and seek his liberty by escaping to some of the free states. To prevent the perpetration of this suspected crime of *running away from slavery,* the old man resolved to sell my father to a southern slave-dealer, and accordingly applied to one of those men, who was at that time in Calvert, to become the purchaser. The price was agreed on, but, as my father was a very strong, active, and resolute man, it was deemed unsafe for the Georgian to attempt to seize him, even with the aid of others, in the day-time, when he was at work, as it was known he carried upon his person a large knife. It was therefore determined to secure him by stratagem, and for this purpose, a farmer in the neighbourhood, who was made privy to the plan, alleged that he had lost a pig, which must have been stolen by some one, and that he suspected my father to be the thief. A constable was employed to arrest him, but as he was afraid to undertake the business alone, he called on his way, at the house of the master of my grandfather, to procure assistance from the overseer of the plantation. When he arrived at the house, the overseer was at the barn, and thither he repaired to make his application. At the end of the barn was the coach-house, and as the day was cool, to avoid the wind which was high, the two walked to the side of the coach-house to talk over the matter, and settle their plan of operations. It so happened, that my grandfather, whose business it was to keep the coach in good condition, was at work at this time, rubbing the plated handles of the doors, and brightening the other metallic parts of the vehicle. Hearing the voice of the overseer without, he suspended his work, and listening attentively, became a party to their councils. They agreed that they would delay the execution of their project until the next day, as it was then late. They supposed they would have no difficulty in apprehending their intended victim, as, knowing himself innocent of the theft, he would readily consent to go with the constable to a justice of the peace, to have the charge examined. That night, however, about midnight, my grandfather silently repaired to the cabin of my father, a distance of about three miles, aroused him from his sleep, made him acquainted with the extent of his danger, gave him a bottle of cider and a small bag of parched corn, and then praying to the God of his native country to protect his son, enjoined him to fly from the destruction which awaited him. In the morning, the Georgian could not find his newly purchased slave, who was never seen or heard of in Maryland from that day. He probably had prudence enough to conceal himself in the day, and travel only at night; by this means making his way slowly up the country, between the Patapsco and Patuxent, until he was able to strike across to the north, and reach Pennsylvania.

After the flight of my father, my grandfather was the only person left in Maryland, with whom I could claim kindred. He was at that time an old man, as he himself said, nearly eighty years of age, and he manifested towards me all the fondness which a person so far advanced in life could be expected to feel for a child. As he was too feeble to perform much hard labour, his master did not require him either to live or to work with the common field hands, who were employed the greater part of the year in cultivating tobacco, and preparing it for market, that being the staple crop of all the lower part of the western shore of Maryland at that time. Indeed, old Ben, as my grandfather was called, had always expressed great contempt for his fellow slaves, they being, as he said, a mean and vulgar race, quite beneath his rank, and the dignity of his former station. He had, during all the time that I knew him, a small cabin of his own, with about half an acre of ground attached to it, which he cultivated on his own account, and from which he drew a large portion of his subsistence. He entertained strange and peculiar notions of religion, and prayed every night, though he said he ought to pray oftener; but that his God would excuse him for the non-performance of this duty in consideration of his being a slave, and compelled to devote his whole time to the service of his master. He never went to church or meeting, and held, that the religion of this country was altogether false, and indeed, no religion at all; being the mere invention of priests and crafty men, who hoped thereby to profit through the ignorance and credulity of the multitude. In support of this opinion, he maintained that there could only be one true standard of faith, which was the case in his country, where all the people worshipped together in the same assembly, and believed in the same doctrines which had been of old time delivered by the true God to a holy man, who was taken up into heaven for that purpose, and after he had received the divine communication, had returned to earth, and spent a hundred years in preaching and imparting the truth which had been revealed to him, to mankind. This inspired man resided in some country, at a great distance from that of my grandfather, but had come there, across a part of the sea, in company with an angel; and instructed the people in the mysteries of the true faith, which had ever since been preserved in its utmost purity, by the descendants of those who received it, through a period of more than ten thousand years. My grandfather said, that the tenets of this religion were so plain and self-evident, that any one could understand them, without any other instruction, than the reading of a small book, a copy of which was kept in every family, and which contained all the rules both of faith and practice, necessary for any one to know or exercise. No one was permitted to expound or explain this book, as it was known to be the oracle of the true God, and it was held impious for any person to give a construction to his words, different from that which was so palpably and manifestly expressed on the face of the book.

This book was likewise written in such plain and intelligible language, that only one meaning could possibly be given to any one part of it; and was withal so compendious and brief, that people could, with very little labour, commit the whole of its precepts to memory. The priests had, at several times, attempted to publish commentaries and glossaries upon this book; but as often as this had been attempted, the perpetrators had been tried, found guilty of conspiring to corrupt the public morals, and then banished from the country. People who were disposed to worship publicly, convened together in summer, under the boughs of a large tree, and the eldest person present read the inspired book from beginning to end, which could be done in two hours, at most. Sometimes a priest was employed to read the book, but he was never, by any means, allowed to add any observations of his own, as it would have been considered absurd as well as very wicked, for a mere man to attempt to add to, alter, amend, or in any manner give a colouring to the revealed word of God. In winter, when it rained constantly, the worshippers met under the roof of a house covered with the leaves of a certain tree, which grew in great abundance on the margins of all the streams.

The law imposed no penalties on those who did not profess to believe the contents of the sacred book; but those who did not live according to its rules were deemed bad subjects, and were compelled to become soldiers, as being fit only for a life of bloodshed and cruelty.

The book inculcated no particular form of belief, and left men free to profess what faith they pleased; but its principles of morality were extremely rigid
and uncompromising. Love of country, charity, and social affection, were the
chief points of duty enjoined by it. Lying and drunkenness were strictly prohibited, and those guilty of these vices were severely punished. Cruelty was placed
in the same rank of crimes; but the mode of punishment was left entirely to the
civil law-giver. The book required neither fastings, penances, nor pilgrimages;
but tenderness to wives and children, was one of its most positive injunctions.

## CHAPTER II.

THE name of the man who purchased me at the vendue, and became my master, was John Cox; but he was generally called Jack Cox. He was a man of kindly
feelings towards his family, and treated his slaves, of whom he had several besides me, with humanity. He permitted my grandfather to visit me as often as he
pleased, and allowed him sometimes to carry me to his own cabin, which stood
in a lonely place, at the head of a deep hollow, almost surrounded by a thicket
of cedar trees, which had grown up in a worn out and abandoned tobacco field.
My master gave me better clothes than the little slaves of my age generally received in Calvert, and often told me that he intended to make me his waiter, and
that if I behaved well I should become his overseer in time. These stations of
waiter and overseer appeared to me to be the highest points of honour and greatness in the whole world, and had not circumstances frustrated my master's plans,
as well as my own views, I should probably have been living at this time in a
cabin on the corner of some tobacco plantation.

Fortune had decreed otherwise. When I was about twelve years old, my
master, Jack Cox, died of a disease which had long confined him to the house. I
was sorry for the death of my master, who had always been kind to me; and I
soon discovered that I had good cause to regret his departure from this world.
He had several children at the time of his death, who were all young; the oldest
being about my own age. The father of my late master, who was still living, became administrator of his estate, and took possession of his property, and
amongst the rest, of myself. This old gentleman treated me with the greatest
severity, and compelled me to work very hard on his plantation for several years,
until I suppose I must have been near or quite twenty years of age. As I was always very obedient, and ready to execute all his orders, I did not receive much
whipping, but suffered greatly for want of sufficient and proper food. My master allowed his slaves a peck of corn, each, per week, throughout the year; and
this we had to grind into meal in a hand mill for ourselves. We had a tolerable
supply of meat for a short time, about the month of December, when he killed
his hogs. After that season we had meat once a week, unless bacon became
scarce, which very often happened, in which case we had no meat at all. However, as we fortunately lived near both the Patuxent river and the Chesapeake
Bay, we had abundance of fish in the spring, and as long as the fishing season

continued. After that period, each slave received, in addition to his allowance of corn, one salt herring every day.

My master gave me one pair of shoes, one pair of stockings, one hat, one jacket of coarse cloth, two coarse shirts, and two pair of trousers yearly. He allowed me no other clothes. In the winter time I often suffered very much from the cold; as I had to drive the team of oxen which hauled the tobacco to market, and frequently did not get home until late at night, the distance being considerable, and my cattle travelling very slow.

One Saturday evening, when I came home from the corn field, my master told me that he had hired me out for a year at the city of Washington, and that I would have to live at the navy-yard.

On the new-year's-day following, which happened about two weeks afterwards, my master set forward for Washington, on horseback, and ordered me to accompany him on foot. It was night when we arrived at the navy-yard, and every thing appeared very strange to me.

I was told by a gentleman who had epaulets on his shoulders, that I must go on board a large ship, which lay in the river. He at the same time told a boy to show me the way. This ship proved to be the Congress frigate, and I was told that I had been brought there to cook for the people belonging to her. In the course of a few days the duties of my station became quite familiar to me; and in the enjoyment of a profusion of excellent provisions, I felt very happy. I strove by all means to please the officers and gentlemen who came on board, and in this I soon found my account. One gave me a half-worn coat, another an old shirt, and a third, a cast off waistcoat and pantaloons. Some presented me with small sums of money, and in this way I soon found myself well clothed, and with more than a dollar in my pocket. My duties, though constant, were not burthensome, and I was permitted to spend Sunday afternoon in my own way. I generally went up into the city to see the new and splendid buildings; often walked as far as Georgetown, and made many new acquaintances amongst the slaves, and frequently saw large numbers of people of my colour chained together in long trains, and driven off towards the south. At that time the Slave-trade was not regarded with so much indignation and disgust, as it is now. It was a rare thing to hear of a person of colour running away, and escaping altogether from his master: my father being the only one within my knowledge, who had, before this time, obtained his liberty in this manner, in Calvert county; and, as before stated, I never heard what became of him after his flight.

I remained on board the Congress, and about the navy-yard, two years, and was quite satisfied with my lot, until about three months before the expiration of this period, when it so happened that a schooner, loaded with iron and other materials for the use of the yard, arrived from Philadelphia. She came and lay close by the Congress, to discharge her cargo, and amongst her crew I observed a black man, with whom, in the course of a day or two, I became acquainted. He told me he was free, and lived in Philadelphia, where he kept a house of entertainment for sailors, which he said was attended to in his absence by his wife.

His description of Philadelphia, and of the liberty enjoyed there by the black people, so charmed my imagination that I determined to devise some plan of escaping from the Congress, and making my way to the north. I communicated my designs to my new friend, who promised to give me his aid. We agreed that the night before the schooner should sail, I was to be concealed in the hold, amongst a parcel of loose tobacco, which he said the captain had undertaken to carry to Philadelphia. The sailing of the schooner was delayed longer than we expected; and, finally, her captain purchased a cargo of flour in Georgetown, and sailed for the West Indies. Whilst I was anxiously awaiting some other opportunity of making my way to Philadelphia, (the idea of crossing the country to the western part of Pennsylvania never entered my mind,) new-year's-day came, and with it came my old master from Calvert, accompanied by a gentleman named Gibson, to whom he said he had sold me, and to whom he delivered me over in the navy-yard. We all three set out that same evening for Calvert, and reached the residence of my new master the next day. Here I was informed that I had become the subject of a law-suit. My new master claimed me under his purchase from old Mr. Cox; and another gentleman of the neighbourhood, named Levin Ballard, had bought me of the children of my former master, Jack Cox. This suit continued in the courts of Calvert county more than two years; but was finally decided in favour of him who had bought me of the children.

I went home with my master, Mr. Gibson, who was a farmer, and with whom I lived three years. Soon after I came to live with Mr. Gibson, I married a girl of colour named Judah, the slave of a gentleman by the name of Symmes, who resided in the same neighborhood. I was at the house of Mr. Symmes every week; and became as well acquainted with him and his family, as I was with my master.

Mr. Symmes also married a wife about the time I did. The lady whom he married lived near Philadelphia, and when she first came to Maryland, she refused to be served by a black chambermaid, but employed a white girl, the daughter of a poor man, who lived near. The lady was reported to be very wealthy, and brought a large trunk full of plate, and other valuable articles. This trunk was so heavy that I could scarcely carry it, and it impressed my mind with the idea of great riches in the owner, at that time. After some time Mrs. Symmes dismissed her white chambermaid, and placed my wife in that situation, which I regarded as a fortunate circumstance, as it insured her good food, and at least one good suit of clothes.

The Symmes' family was one of the most ancient in Maryland, and had been a long time resident in Calvert county. The grounds had been laid out, and all the improvements projected about the family abode, in a style of much magnificence, according to the custom of the old aristocracy of Maryland and Virginia.

Appendant to the domicile, and at no great distance from the house, was a family vault, built of brick, in which reposed the occupants of the estate, who had lived there for many previous generations. This vault had not been opened or entered for fifteen years previous to the time of which I speak; but it so happened, that at this period, a young man, a distant relation of the family, died, having requested on his death-bed, that he might be buried in this family resting place. When I came on Saturday evening to see my wife and child, Mr. Symmes desired me, as I was older than any of his black men, to take an iron pick and go and open the vault, which I accordingly did, by cutting away the mortar, and removing a few bricks from one side of the building; but I could not remove more than three or four bricks before I was obliged, by the horrid effluvia which issued at the aperture, to retire. It was the most deadly and sickening scent that I have ever smelled, and I could not return to complete the work until after the sun had risen the next day, when I pulled down so much of one of the side walls, as to permit persons to walk in upright. I then went in alone, and examined this house of the dead, and surely no picture could more strongly and vividly depict the emptiness of all earthly vanity, and the nothingness of human pride. Dispersed over the floor lay the fragments of more than twenty human skeletons, each in the place where it had been deposited by the idle tenderness of surviving friends. In some cases nothing remained but the hair and the larger bones, whilst in several the form of the coffin was yet visible, with all the bones resting in their proper places. One coffin, the sides of which were yet standing, the lid only having decayed and partly fallen in, so as to disclose the contents of this narrow cell, presented a peculiarly moving spectacle. Upon the centre of the lid was a large silver plate, and the head and foot were adorned with silver stars. The nails which had united the parts of the coffin had also silver heads. Within lay the skeletons of a mother and her infant child, in slumbers only to be broken by the peal of the last trumpet. The bones of the infant lay upon the breast of the mother, where the hands of affection had shrouded them. The ribs of the parent had fallen down, and rested on the back bone. Many gold rings were about the bones of the fingers. Brilliant ear-rings lay beneath where the ears had been; and a glittering gold chain encircled the ghastly and haggard vertebrae of a once beautiful neck. The shroud and flesh had disappeared, but the hair of the mother appeared strong and fresh. Even the silken locks of the infant were still preserved. Behold the end of youth and beauty, and of all that is lovely in life! The coffin was so much decayed that it could not be removed. A thick and dismal vapour hung embodied from the roof and walls of this charnal house, in appearance somewhat like a mass of dark cobwebs; but which was impalpable to the touch, and when stirred by the hand vanished away. On the second day we deposited with his kindred, the corpse of the young man, and at night I again carefully closed up the breach which I had made in the walls of this dwelling-place of the dead.

## CHAPTER III.

SOME short time after my wife became chambermaid to her mistress, it was my misfortune to change masters once more. Levin Ballard, who, as before stated, had purchased me of the children of my former master, Jack Cox, was successful in his law suit with Mr. Gibson, the object of which was to determine the right of property in me; and one day, whilst I was at work in the corn-field, Mr. Ballard came and told me I was his property; asking me at the same time if I was willing to go with him. I told him I was not willing to go; but that if I belonged to him I knew I must. We then went to the house, and Mr. Gibson not being at home, Mrs. Gibson told me I must go with Mr. Ballard.

I accordingly went with him, determining to serve him obediently and faithfully. I remained in his service almost three years, and as he lived near the residence of my wife's master, my former mode of life was not materially changed, by this change of home.

Mrs. Symmes spent much of her time in exchanging visits with the families of the other large planters, both in Calvert, and the neighbouring counties; and through my wife, I became acquainted with the private family history of many of the principal persons in Maryland.

There was a great proprietor, who resided in another county, who owned several hundred slaves; and who permitted them to beg of travellers on the highway. This same gentleman had several daughters, and according to the custom of the time, kept what they called open house: that is, his house was free to all persons of genteel appearance, who chose to visit it. The young ladies were supposed to be the greatest fortunes in the country, were reputed beautiful, and consequently were greatly admired.

Two gentlemen, who were lovers of these girls, desirous of amusing their mistresses, invited a young man, whose standing in society they supposed to be beneath theirs, to go with them to the manor, as it was called. When there, they endeavoured to make him an object of ridicule, in presence of the ladies; but he so well acquitted himself, and manifested such superior wit and talents, that one of the young ladies fell in love with him, and soon after, wrote him a letter, which led to their marriage. His two pretended friends were never afterwards countenanced by the family, as gentlemen of honour; but the fortunate husband avenged himself of his heartless companions, by inviting them to his wedding, and exposing them to the observation of the vast assemblage of fashionable people, who always attended a marriage, in the family of a great planter.

The two gentlemen, who had been thus made to fall into the pit that they had dug for another, were so much chagrined at the issue of the adventure, that one, soon left Maryland; and the other became a common drunkard, and died a few years afterwards.

My change of masters, realised all the evil apprehensions which I had entertained. I found Mr. Ballard sullen and crabbed in his temper, and always prone to find fault with my conduct—no matter how hard I had laboured, or how careful I was to fulfil all his orders, and obey his most unreasonable commands. Yet, it so happened, that he never beat me, for which, I was altogether indebted to the good character, for industry, sobriety, and humility, which I had established in the neighbourhood. I think he was ashamed to abuse me, lest he should suffer in the good opinion of the public; for he often fell into the most violent fits of anger against me, and overwhelmed me with coarse and abusive language. He did not give me clothes enough to keep me warm in winter, and compelled me to work in the woods, when there was deep snow on the ground, by which I suffered very much. I had determined at last to speak to him to sell me to some person in the neighbourhood, so that I might still be near my wife and children—but a different fate awaited me.

My master kept a store at a small village on the bank of the Patuxent river, called B——, although he resided at some distance on a farm. One morning he rose early, and ordered me to take a yoke of oxen and go to the village, to bring home a cart which was there, saying he would follow me. He arrived at the village soon after I did, and took his breakfast with his store-keeper. He then told me to come into the house and get my breakfast. Whilst I was eating in the kitchen, I observed him talking earnestly, but lowly, to a stranger near the kitchen door. I soon after went out, and hitched my oxen to the cart, and was about to drive off, when several men came round about me, and amongst them the stranger whom I had seen speaking with my master. This man came up to me, and, seizing me by the collar, shook me violently, saying I was his property, and must go with him to Georgia. At the sound of these words, the thoughts of my wife and children rushed across my mind, and my heart died away within me. I saw and knew that my case was hopeless, and that resistance was vain, as there were near twenty persons present, all of whom were ready to assist the man by whom I was kidnapped. I felt incapable of weeping or speaking, and in my despair I laughed loudly. My purchaser ordered me to cross my hands behind, which were quickly bound with a strong cord; and he then told me that we must set out that very day for the south. I asked if I could not be allowed to go to see my wife and children, or if this could not be permitted, if they might not have leave to come to see me; but was told that I would be able to get another wife in Georgia.

My new master, whose name I did not hear, took me that same day across the Patuxent, where I joined fifty-one other slaves, whom he had bought in Maryland. Thirty-two of these were men, and nineteen were women. The women were merely tied together with a rope, about the size of a bed cord,[12] which was tied like a halter round the neck of each; but the men, of whom I was the stoutest and strongest, were very differently caparisoned. A strong iron collar was closely fitted by means of a padlock round each of our necks. A chain of iron, about a hundred feet in length, was passed through the hasp of each padlock, except at the two ends, where the hasps of the padlocks passed through a link of the chain. In addition to this, we were handcuffed in pairs, with iron staples and bolts, with a short chain, about a foot long, uniting the handcuffs and their wearers in pairs. In this manner we were chained alternately by the right and left hand; and the poor man, to whom I was thus ironed, wept like an infant when the blacksmith, with his heavy hammer, fastened the ends of the bolts that kept the staples from slipping from our arms. For my own part, I felt indifferent to my fate. It appeared to me that the worst had come, that could come, and that no change of fortune could harm me.

After we were all chained and handcuffed together, we sat down upon the ground; and here reflecting upon the sad reverse of fortune that had so suddenly overtaken me, and the dreadful suffering which awaited me, I became weary of life, and bitterly execrated the day I was born. It seemed that I was destined by fate to drink the cup of sorrow to the very dregs, and that I should find no respite from misery but in the grave. I longed to die, and escape from the hands of my tormentors; but even the wretched privilege of destroying myself was denied me; for I could not shake off my chains, nor move a yard without the consent of my master. Reflecting in silence upon my forlorn condition, I at length concluded that as things could not become worse—and as the life of man is but a continued round of changes, they must, of necessity, take a turn in my favour at some future day. I found relief in this vague and indefinite hope, and when we received orders to go on board the scow, which was to transport us over the Patuxent, I marched down to the water with a firmness of purpose of which I did not believe myself capable, a few minutes before.

We were soon on the south side of the river, and taking up our line of march, we travelled about five miles that evening, and stopped for the night at one of those miserable public houses, so frequent in the lower parts of Maryland and Virginia, called "*ordinaries.*"

Our master ordered a pot of mush to be made for our supper; after despatching which, we all lay down on the naked floor to sleep in our handcuffs and chains. The women, my fellow-slaves, lay on one side of the room; and the men who were chained with me, occupied the other. I slept but little this night, which I passed in thinking of my wife and little children, whom I could not hope ever to see again. I also thought of my grandfather, and of the long nights I had passed with him, listening to his narratives of the scenes through which he had passed in Africa. I at length fell asleep, but was distressed by painful dreams. My wife and children appeared to be weeping and lamenting my calamity; and beseeching and imploring my master on their knees, not to carry me away from them. My little boy came and begged me not to go and leave him, and endeavoured, as I thought, with his little hands to break the fetters that bound me. I awoke in agony and cursed my existence. I could not pray, for the measure of my woes seemed to be full, and I felt as if there was no mercy in heaven, nor compassion on earth, for a man who was born a slave. Day at length came, and with the dawn, we resumed our journey towards the Potomac. As we passed along the road, I saw the slaves at work in the corn and tobacco-fields. I knew they toiled hard and lacked food; but they were not, like me, dragged in chains from their wives, children, and friends. Compared with me, they were the happiest of mortals. I almost envied them their blessed lot.

Before night we crossed the Potomac, at Hoe's Ferry, and bade farewell to Maryland. At night we stopped at the house of a poor gentleman, at least he appeared to wish my master to consider him a gentleman; and he had no difficulty in establishing his claim to poverty. He lived at the side of the road, in a framed house, which had never been plastered within—the weather-boards being the only wall. He had about fifty acres of land enclosed by a fence, the remains of a farm which had once covered two or three hundred acres; but the cedar bushes had encroached upon all sides, until the cultivation had been confined to its present limits. The land was the very picture of sterility, and there was neither barn nor stable on the place. The owner was ragged, and his wife and children were in a similar plight. It was with difficulty that we obtained a bushel of corn, which our master ordered us to parch at a fire made in the yard, and to eat for our supper. Even this miserable family possessed two slaves, half-starved, half-naked wretches, whose appearance bespoke them familiar with hunger, and victims of the lash; but yet there was one pang which they had not known,—they had not been chained and driven from their parents, or children, into hopeless exile.

We left this place early in the morning, and directed our course toward the south-west; our master riding beside us, and hastening our march, sometimes by words of encouragement, and sometimes by threats of punishment. The women took their place in the rear of our line. We halted about nine o'clock for breakfast, and received as much cornbread as we could eat, together with a plate of broiled herrings, and about three pounds of pork amongst us. Before we left this place, I was removed from near the middle of the chain, and placed at the front end of it; so that I now became the leader of the file, and held this post of honour until our irons were taken from us, near the town of Columbia in South Carolina. We continued our route this day along the high road between the Potomac and Rappahannock: and I several times saw each of those rivers before night. Our master gave us no dinner to day, but we halted a short time before sundown, and got as much corn mush, and sour milk, as we could eat for supper. It was now the beginning of the month of May, and the weather, in the fine climate of Virginia, was very mild and pleasant; so that our master was not obliged to provide us with fire at night.

From this time, to the end of our journey southward, we all slept, promiscuously, men and women, on the floors of such houses as we chanced to stop at. We had no clothes except those we wore, and a few blankets; the larger portion of our gang being in rags at the time we crossed the Potomac. Two of the women were pregnant; the one far advanced—and she already complained of inability to keep pace with our march; but her complaints were disregarded. We crossed the Rappahannock at Port Royal, and afterwards passed through the village of Bowling Green; a place with which I became better acquainted in after times; but which now presented the quiet so common to all the small towns in Virginia, and indeed in all the southern states. Time did not reconcile me to my chains, but it made me familiar with them; and in a few days the horrible sensations attendant upon my cruel separation from my wife and children, in some measure subsided; and I began to reflect upon my present hopeless and desperate situation, with some degree of calmness; hoping that I might be able to devise some means of escaping from the hands of my new master, who seemed to place particular value on me, as I could perceive from his conversation with such persons as we happened to meet at our resting places. I heard him tell a tavern-keeper where we halted, that if he had me in Georgia, he could get five hundred dollars for me; but he had bought me for his brother, and he believed he would not sell me; but in this he afterwards changed his opinion. I examined every part of our long chain, to see if there might not be some place in it at which it could be severed; but found it so completely secured, that with any means in my power, its separation was impossible. From this time I endeavoured to beguile my sorrows, by examining the state of the country through which we were travelling, and observing the condition of my fellow-slaves, on the plantations along the high-road upon which we sojourned.

We all had as much corn bread as we could eat. This was procured by our owner at the small dram shops, or *ordinaries,* at which we usually tarried all night. In addition to this, we generally received a salt herring, though not *every* day. On Sunday, our master bought as much bacon, as, when divided amongst us, gave about a quarter of a pound to each person in our gang.

In Calvert county, where I was born, the practice amongst slave-holders, was to allow each slave one peck of corn weekly, which was measured out every Monday morning; at the same time each one receiving seven salt herrings. This formed the week's provision, and the master who did not give it, was called a *hard master,* whilst those who allowed their people any thing more, were deemed kind and indulgent. It often happened, that the stock of salt herrings laid up by a master in the spring, was not sufficient to enable him to continue this rate of distribution through the year; and when the fish failed nothing more than the corn was dealt out. On the other hand, some planters, who had large stocks of cattle, and many cows, kept the sour milk, after all the cream had been skimmed from it, and made a daily distribution of this amongst the working slaves. Some who had large apple orchards, gave their slaves a pint of cider each per day, through the autumn. It sometimes happened, too, in the lower counties of Maryland, that there was an allowance of pork, made to the slaves one day in each week; though on some estates this did not take place more than once in a month. This allowance of meat was disposed of in such a manner as to permit each slave to get a slice; very often amounting to half a pound. The slaves were also permitted to work for themselves at night, and on Sunday. If they chose to fish, they had the privilege of selling whatever they caught. Some expert fishermen caught and sold as many fish and oysters, as enabled them to buy coffee, sugar, and other luxuries for their wives, besides keeping themselves and their families in Sunday clothes; for, the masters in Maryland only allowed the men one wool hat, one pair of shoes, two shirts, two pair of trousers—one pair of tow cloth, and one of woollen—and one woollen jacket in the year. The women were furnished in proportion. All other clothes they had to provide for themselves. Children not able to work in the field, were not provided with clothes at all, by their masters. It is, however, honourable to the Maryland slave-holders, that they never permit women to go naked in the fields, or about the house; and if the men are industrious and *employ themselves well on Sundays and holydays,* they can always keep themselves in comfortable clothes.

In Virginia, it appeared to me that the slaves were more rigorously treated than they were in my native place. It is easy to tell a man of colour who is poorly fed, from one who is well supplied with food, by his personal appearance. A half-starved negro is a miserable looking creature. His skin becomes dry, and appears to be sprinkled over with whitish husks, or scales; the glossiness of his face vanishes, his hair loses its colour, becomes dry, and when stricken with a rod, the dust flies from it. These signs of bad treatment I perceived to be very common in Virginia; many young girls who would have been beautiful, if they had been allowed enough to eat, had lost all their prettiness through mere starvation; their fine glossy hair had become of a reddish colour, and stood out round their heads like long brown wool.

## CHAPTER IV.

OUR master at first expressed a determination to pass through the city of Richmond; but for some reason, which he did not make known to us, he changed his mind, and drove us up the country, crossing the Matepony, North Anna and South Anna rivers. For several days we traversed a region, which had been deserted by the occupants—being no longer worth culture—and immense thickets of young red cedars, now occupied the fields, in diging of which, thousands of wretched slaves had worn out their lives in the service of merciless masters.

In some places these cedar thickets, as they are called, continued for three or four miles together, without a house to enliven the scene, and with scarcely an original forest tree to give variety to the landscape. One day, in the midst of a wilderness of cedars, we came in view of a stately and venerable looking brick edifice, which, on nearer inspection, I discovered to be a church. On approaching it, our driver ordered us to halt, and dismounting from his horse, tied him to a young cedar tree, and sat himself down upon a flat tomb-stone, near the west end of the church, ordering us, at the same time, to sit down among the grass and rest ourselves. The grave yard in which we were now encamped, occupied about two acres of ground, which was surrounded by a square brick wall, much dilapidated, and in many places broken down nearly to the ground. The gates were decayed and gone, but the gate-ways were yet distinct. The whole enclosure was thickly strewed with graves, many of which were surmounted by beautiful marble slabs; others were designated by plain head and foot stones; whilst far the larger number only betrayed the resting places of their sleeping tenants, by the simple mounds of clay, which still maintained their elevation above the level of the surrounding earth. From the appearance of this burial place, I suppose no one had been interred there for thirty years. Several hollies, planted by the hands of friendship, grew amongst the hillocks, and numerous flowering shrubs and bushes, now in bloom, gave fragrance to the air of the place. The cedars which covered the surrounding plain, with a forest impervious to the eye, had respected this lonely dwelling of the dead, and not one was to be seen within the walls.

Though it was now the meridian of day in spring, the stillness of midnight pervaded the environs of this deserted and forsaken temple; the pulpit, pews, and gallery of which were still standing, as I could perceive through the broken door-way; and maintained a freshness and newness of appearance, little according with the time-worn aspect of the exterior scenery.

It was manifest that this earthly dwelling of the Most High, now so desolate and ruinous, was once the resort of a congregation of people, gay, fashionable, and proud; who had disappeared from the land, leaving only this fallen edifice, and these grassy tombs, as the mementos of their existence. They had passed away, even as did the wandering red men, who roamed through the lofty oak forests which once shaded the ground where we now lay. As I sat musing upon the desolation that surrounded me, my mind turned to the cause which had converted a former rich and populous country, into the solitude of a deserted wilderness.

The ground over which we had travelled, since we crossed the Potomac, had generally been a strong reddish clay, with an admixture of sand, and was of the same quality with the soil of the counties of Chester, Montgomery, and Bucks, in Pennsylvania. It had originally been highly fertile and productive, and had it been properly treated, would doubtlessly have continued to yield abundant and prolific crops; but the gentlemen who became the early proprietors of this fine region, supplied themselves with slaves from Africa, cleared large plantations of many thousands of acres—cultivated tobacco—and became suddenly wealthy; built spacious houses and numerous churches, such as this; but, regardless of their true interest, they valued their lands less than their slaves, exhausted the kindly soil by unremitting crops of tobacco, declined in their circumstances, and finally grew poor, upon the very fields that had formerly made their possessors rich; abandoned one portion after another, as not worth planting any longer, and, pinched by necessity, at last sold their slaves to Georgian planters, to procure a subsistence; and when all was gone, took refuge in the wilds of Kentucky, again to act the same melancholy drama, leaving their native land to desolation and poverty. The churches then followed the fate of their builders. The revolutionary war deprived the parsons of their legal support, and they fled from the altar which no longer maintained them. Virginia has become poor by the folly and wickedness of slavery, and dearly has she paid for the anguish and sufferings she has inflicted upon our injured, degraded, and fallen race.

After remaining about two hours in this place, we again resumed our march; and wretched as I was, I felt relieved when we departed from this abode of the spirit of ruin.

We continued our course up the country westward, for two or three days, moving at a slow pace, and at length turning south, crossed James river, at a place about thirty miles above Richmond, as I understood at the time. We continued our journey from day to day, in a course and by roads which appeared to me to bear generally about south-west, for more than four weeks, in which time we entered South Carolina, and in this state, near Camden, I first saw a field of cotton in bloom.

I had endeavoured through the whole journey, from the time we crossed the Rappahannock river, to make such observations upon the country, the roads we travelled, and the towns we passed through, as would enable me at some future period, to find my way back to Maryland. I was particularly careful to note the names of the towns and villages through which we passed, and to fix on my memory, not only the names of all the rivers, but also the position and bearing of the ferries over those streams.

After leaving James river, I assumed an air of cheerfulness and even gaiety—I often told stories to my master of the manners and customs of the Maryland planters, and asked him if the same usages prevailed in Georgia, whither we were destined. By repeatedly naming the rivers that we came to, and in the order which we had reached them, I was able at my arrival in Georgia, to repeat the name of every considerable stream from the Potomac to the Savannah, and to tell at what ferries we had crossed them. I afterwards found this knowledge of great service to me; indeed, without it I should never have been able to extricate myself from slavery.

After leaving James river, our road led us southwest, through that region of country, which, in Virginia and the Carolinas, they call the upper country. It lies between the head of the tides, in the great rivers, and the lower ranges of the Alleghany Mountains. I had, at that time, never seen a country cultivated by the labour of freemen, and consequently, was not able to institute any comparison between the southern plantations and the farms in Pennsylvania, the fields of which are ploughed and reaped by the hands of their owners; but my recollection of the general aspect of upper Virginia and Carolina is still vivid. When contrasted with the exhausted and depopulated portion of Virginia, lying below the head of the tide, much of which I had seen, the lands traversed by us in the month of May and early part of June, were indeed fertile and beautiful; but when compared with what the same plantations would have been, in the hands of such farmers as I have seen in Pennsylvania, divided into farms of the proper size, the cause of the general poverty and weakness of the slave-holding slates is at once seen. The plantations are large in the south, often including a thousand acres or more; the population is consequently thin, as only one white family, beside the overseer, ever resides on one plantation.

As I advanced southward, even in Virginia, I perceived that the state of cultivation became progressively worse. Here, as in Maryland, the practice of the best farmers who cultivate grain, of planting the land every alternate year in corn, and sowing it in wheat or rye in the autumn of the same year in which the corn is planted, and whilst the corn is yet standing in the field, so as to get a crop from the same ground every year, without allowing it time to rest or recover, exhausts the finest soil in a few years, and in one or two generations reduces the proprietors to poverty. Some, who are supposed to be very superior farmers, only plant the land in corn once in three years; sowing it in wheat or rye as in the former case; however, without any covering of clover or other grass to protect it from the rays of the sun. The culture of tobacco prevails over a large portion of Virginia, especially south of James river, to the exclusion of almost every other crop, except corn. This destructive crop ruins the best land in a short time; and in all the lower parts of Maryland and Virginia the traveller will see large old family mansions, of weather-beaten and neglected appearance, standing in the middle of vast fields of many hundred acres, the fences of which have rotted away, and have been replaced by a wattled work in place of a fence, composed of short cedar stakes driven into the ground, about two feet apart, and standing about three feet above the earth, the intervals being filled up by branches cut from the cedar trees, and worked into the stakes horizontally, after the manner of splits in a basket.

Many of these fields have been abandoned altogether, and are overgrown by cedars, which spring up in infinite numbers almost as soon as a field ceases to be ploughed, and furnish materials for fencing such parts of the ancient plantation as are still kept enclosed. In many places the enclosed fields are only partially cultivated, all the hills and poorest parts being given up to the cedars and chinquopin bushes. These estates, the seats of families that were once powerful,

wealthy, and proud, are universally destitute of the appearance of a barn, such
as is known among the farmers of Pennsylvania. The out houses, stables, gardens, and offices, have fallen to decay, and the dwelling-house is occupied by the
descendants of those who erected it, still pertinaciously adhering to the halls of
their ancestry, with a half dozen or ten slaves, the remains of the two or three
hundred who toiled upon these grounds in former days. The residue of the stock
has been distributed in marriage portions to the daughters of the family gone to
a distance—have been removed to the west by emigrating sons, or have been sold
to the southern traders, from time to time, to procure money to support the dignity of the house, as the land grew poorer, and the tobacco crop shorter, from
year to year.

In Maryland and Virginia, although the slaves are treated with so much
    Industry, enterprise, and ambition, have fled from these abodes, and sought
refuge from sterility and barrenness in the vales of Kentucky, or the plains of Alabama; whilst the present occupants, vain of their ancestral monuments, and
proud of an obscure name, contend with all the ills that poverty brings upon
fallen greatness, and pass their lives in a contest between mimic state and actual
penury—too ignorant of agriculture to know how to restore fertility to a once
prolific and still substantial soil, and too spiritless to sell their effects and search
a new home under other skies. The sedge grass every where takes possession of
the worn out fields, until it is supplanted by the chinquopin and the cedar. This
grass grows in thick set bunches or stools, and no land is too poor for it. It rises
to the height of two or three feet, and grows, in many places, in great profusion—
is utterly worthless, either for hay or pasturage, but affords shelter to numerous
rabbits, and countless flocks of partridges, and, at a short distance, has a beautiful appearance, as its elastic blue tops wave in the breeze.

    In Maryland and Virginia, although the slaves are treated with so much
rigour, and oftentimes with so much cruelty, I have seen instances of the greatest tenderness of feeling on the part of their owners. I myself had three masters
in Maryland, and I cannot say now, even after having resided so many years in
a state where slavery is not tolerated, that either of them (except the last, who
sold me to the Georgians, and was an unfeeling man,) used me worse than they
had a moral right to do, regarding me merely as an article of property, and not
entitled to any rights as a man, political or civil. My mistresses, in Maryland,
were all good women; and the mistress of my wife, in whose kitchen I spent my
Sundays and many of my nights, for several years, was a lady of most benevolent and kindly feelings. She was a true friend to me, and I shall always venerate
her memory.

    It is now my opinion, after all I have seen, that there are no better-hearted
women in the world, than the ladies of the ancient families, as they are called, in
old Virginia, or the country below the mountains, and the same observations will
apply to the ladies of Maryland. The stock of slaves has belonged to the family
for several generations, and there is a kind of family pride, in being the proprietors of so many human beings, which, in many instances, borders on affection
for people of colour.

    If the proprietors of the soil in Maryland and Virginia, were skilful culti-
vators—had their lands in good condition—and kept no more slaves on each es-

tate than would be sufficient to work the soil in a proper manner, and keep up the repairs of the place—the condition of the coloured people would not be, by any means, a comparatively unhappy one. I am convinced, that in nine cases in ten, the hardships and sufferings of the coloured population of lower Virginia, is attributable to the poverty and distress of its owners. In many instances, an estate scarcely yields enough to feed and clothe the slaves in a comfortable manner, without allowing any thing for the support of the master and family; but it is obvious, that the family must first be supported, and the slaves must be content with the surplus—and this, on a poor, old, worn out tobacco plantation, is often very small, and wholly inadequate to the comfortable sustenance of the hands, as they are called. There, in many places, nothing is allowed to the poor negro, but his peck of corn per week, without the sauce of a salt herring, or even a little salt itself.

Wretched as may be the state of the negroes, in the quarter, that of the master and his wife and daughters, is, in many instances, not much more enviable in the old apartments of the *great house*. The sons and daughters of the family are gentlemen and ladies by birthright—and were the former to be seen at the plough, or the latter at the churn, or the wash tub, the honour of the family would be stained, and the dignity of the house degraded. People must and will be employed about something, and if they cannot be usefully occupied, they will most surely engage in some pursuit wholly unprofitable. So it happens in Virginia—the young men spend their time in riding about the country, whilst they ought to be ploughing or harrowing in the cornfield; and the young women are engaged in reading silly books, or visiting their neighbours' houses, instead of attending to the dairy, or manufacturing cloth for themselves and their brothers. During all this, the father is too often defending himself against attorneys, or making such terms as he can with the sheriff, for debts, in which he has been involved by the vicious idleness of his children, and his own want of virtue and courage, to break through the evil tyranny of old customs, and compel his offspring to learn, in early life, to procure their subsistence by honest and honourable industry. In this state of things there is not enough for all. Pride forbids the sale of the slaves, as long as it is possible to avoid it, and their meagre allowance of corn is stinted rather than it shall be said, the master was obliged to sell them. Somebody must suffer, and "self-preservation is the first law of nature," says the proverb—hunger must invade either the great house or the quarter, and it is but reasonable to suppose, that so unwelcome an intruder would be expelled, to the last moment, from the former. In this conflict of pride and folly, against industry and wisdom, the slave-holders have been unhappily engaged for more than fifty years.

They are attempting to perform impossibilities—to draw the means of supporting a life of idleness, luxury, and splendour, from a once generous, but long since worn out and exhausted soil—a soil, which, carefully used, would at this day have richly repaid the toils of the husbandman, by a noble abundance of all the comforts of life; but which, tortured into barrenness by the double curse of slavery and tobacco, stands—and until its proprietors are regenerated, and learn the difference between a land of slaves and a nation of freemen—must continue to stand, *a monument of the poverty and punishment which Providence has de-creed as the reward of idleness and tyranny.* The general features of slavery are the same everywhere; but the utmost rigour of the system is only to be met with on the cotton plantations of Carolina and Georgia, or in the rice fields which skirt the deep swamps and morasses of the southern rivers. In the tobacco fields of Maryland and Virginia, great cruelties are practised—not so frequently by the owners, as by the overseers of the slaves; but yet, the tasks are not so excessive as in the cotton region, nor is the press of labour so incessant throughout the year. It is true, that from the period when the tobacco plants are set in the field, there is no resting time until it is housed; but it is planted out about the first of May, and must be cut and taken out of the field before the frost comes. After it is hung and dried, the labour of stripping and preparing it for the hogshead in leaf, or of manufacturing it into twist, is comparatively a work of leisure and ease. Besides, on almost every plantation the hands are able to complete the work of preparing the tobacco by January, and sometimes earlier; so that the winter months form some sort of respite from the toils of the year. The people are obliged, it is true, to occupy themselves in cutting wood for the house, making rails and repairing fences, and in clearing new land, to raise the tobacco plants for the next year; but as there is usually time enough, and to spare, for the com-pletion of all this work, before the season arrives for setting the plants in the field, the men are seldom flogged much, unless they are very lazy or negligent, and the women are allowed to remain in the house, in very cold, snowy, or rainy weather. I who am intimately acquainted with the slavery, both of Maryland and Virginia, and know that there is no material difference between the two, aver, that a de-scription of one is a description of both; and that the coloured people here have many advantages over those of the cotton region. There are seldom more than one hundred, of all ages and conditions, kept on one tobacco plantation; though there are sometimes many more; but this is not frequent; whilst on the cotton es-tates, I have seen four or five hundred, working together in the same vast field. In Maryland, the owners of the estates, generally, reside at home throughout the year; and the mistress of the mansion is seldom absent more than a few weeks in the winter, when she visits Baltimore or Washington,—the same is the case in Virginia. Her constant residence on the estate makes her acquainted, personally, with all the slaves, and she frequently interests herself in their welfare, often in-terceding with the master, her husband, to prevent the overseer from beating them unmercifully.

The young ladies of the family also, if there be any, after they have left school, are generally at home until they are married. Each of them universally claims a young black girl as her own, and takes her under her protection. This enables the girl to extend the protection and friendship of her *young mistress* to her father, mother, brothers and sisters. The sons of the family likewise have their favourites among the black boys, and have many disputes with the *overseer* if he abuses them. All these advantages accrue to the black people, from the circum-stance of the master and his family living at home. In Maryland I never knew a mistress, or a young mistress, who would not listen to the complaints of the slaves. It is true, we were always obliged to approach the door of the mansion, in the most humble and supplicating manner, with our hats in our hands, and the most subdued and beseeching language in our mouths—but, in return, we generally received words of kindness, and very often a redress of our grievances; though I have known very great ladies, who would never grant any request from the *plantation hands,* but always referred them and their petitions to their master, under a pretence that they could not meddle with things that did not belong to the house. The mistresses of the great families, generally gave mild language to the slaves; though they sometimes sent for the overseer and had them severely flogged; but I have never heard any mistress, in either Maryland or Virginia, indulge in the low, vulgar and profane vituperations, of which I was myself the object in Georgia, for several years, whenever I came into the presence of my mistress. Flogging—though often severe and excruciating in Maryland, is not practised with the order, regularity, and system, to which it is reduced in the south. On the Potomac, if a slave gives offence, he is generally chastised on the spot, in the field where he is at work, as the overseer always carries a whip—sometimes a twisted cow-hide, sometimes a kind of horsewhip, and very often a simple hickory switch or gad,[13] cut in the adjoining woods. For stealing meat, or other provisions, or for any of the *higher* offences, the slaves are stripped, tied up by the hands—sometimes by the thumbs—and whipped at the quarter—but, many times, on a large tobacco plantation, there is not more than one of these regular whippings in a week—though on others, where the master happens to be a bad man, or a drunkard, the back of the unhappy Maryland slave, is seamed with scars from his neck to his hips.

It was my fortune, whilst I was a slave in Maryland, always to have comparatively mild masters; and as I uniformly endeavoured to do whatever was held to be the duty of a good slave, according to the customs of the country, I was never tied up to be flogged there, and never received a blow from my master, after I was fifteen years old. I was never under the control of an overseer in Maryland; or, it is very likely that I should not have been able to give this account of myself.

It is the custom of all the tobacco planters, in Maryland and Virginia, to plant a certain portion of their land in corn every year; so much as they suppose will be sufficient to produce bread, as they term it, for the negroes. By bread, is understood, a peck of corn per week, for each of their slaves.

After my return from the navy-yard, at Washington, I was generally employed in the culture of tobacco; but my attention was necessarily divided between the tobacco and the corn. The corn crop is, however, only a matter of secondary consideration, as no grain, of any kind, is grown for sale, by the planters; and if they raised as much, in my time, as supplied the wants of the *people,* and the horses of the stable, it was considered good farming. The sale of the tobacco was regarded as the only means of obtaining money, or any commodity which did not grow on the plantation.

It is unfortunate for the slaves, that in a tobacco or cotton growing country, no attention whatever is paid to the rearing of sheep—consequently, there is no wool to make winter clothes for the *people,* and oftentimes they suffer, excessively, from the cold; whereas, if their masters kept a good flock of sheep to

supply them with wool, they could easily spin and weave in their cabins, a sufficiency of cloth to clothe them comfortably.

As many persons may be unacquainted with the process of cultivating tobacco, a short account of the growth of this plant, may not be uninteresting. The
operation is to be commenced in the month of February, by clearing a piece of
new land, and burning the timber cut from it, on the ground, so as to form a coat
of ashes over the whole space, if possible. This ground is then to be dug up with
a hoe, and the sticks and roots are to be carefully removed from it. In this bed,
the tobacco seeds are sown about the beginning of March, not in hills, or in rows,
but by broad cast, as in sowing turnips. The seeds do not spring soon, but generally the young plant appears early in April. If the weather, at the time the tobacco comes up, as it is called, is yet frosty, a covering of pine tops, or red cedar
branches, is thickly spread over the whole patch, which consists of from one to
four or five acres, according to the dimensions of the plantation to be provided
with plants. As soon as the weather becomes fine, and the young tobacco begins
to grow, the covering of the branches is removed, and the bed is exposed to the
rays of the sun. From this time, the patch must be carefully attended, and kept
clear of all grass and weeds. In the months of March and April the *people* are
busily employed in ploughing the fields in which the tobacco is to be planted in
May. Immediately after the corn is planted, every one, man, woman, and child,
able to work with a hoe, or carry a tobacco plant, is engaged in working up the
whole plantation, already ploughed a second time, into hills about four feet
apart, laid out in regular rows across the field, by the course of the furrows. These
hills are formed into squares or diamonds, at equal distances, both ways, and
into these are transplanted the tobacco plants from the beds in which the seeds
were sown. This transplantation must be done when the earth is wet with rain,
and it is best to do it, if possible, just before, or at the time the rain falls, as cabbages are transplanted in a kitchen garden; but as the planting a field of one or
two hundred acres, with tobacco, is not the work of an hour, as soon as it is
deemed certain that there will be a sufficient fall of rain, to answer the purpose
of planting out tobacco, all hands are called to the tobacco field, and no matter
how fast it may rain, or how violent the storm may be, the removal of the plants
from the bed, and fixing them in the hills where they are to grow in the field, goes
on, until the crop is planted out, or the rain ceases, and the sun begins to shine.
Nothing but the darkness of night, and the short respite, required by the scanty
meal of the slaves, produces any cessation in the labour of tobacco planting, until the work is done, or the rain ceases, and the clouds disappear. Some plants die
under the operation of removal, and their places are to be supplied from those
left in the bed, at the fall of the next rain.

Sometimes the tobacco worm appears amongst the plants, before their removal from the bed, and from the moment this loathsome reptile is seen, the
plants are to be carefully examined every day, for the purpose of destroying any
worms that may be found. It is, however, not until the plants have been set in
the field, and have begun to grow and flourish, that the worms come forth in
their full strength. If unmolested, they would totally destroy the largest field of
tobacco in the months of June and July. At this season of the year, every slave

that is able to kill a tobacco worm, is kept in the field, from morning until night. Those who are able to work with hoes, are engaged in weeding the tobacco, and at the same time destroying all the worms they find. The children do nothing but search for, and destroy the worms. All this labour and vigilance, however, would not suffice to keep the worms under, were it not for the aid of turkeys and ducks. On some large estates, they raise from one to two hundred turkeys, and as many ducks—not for the purpose of sale; but for the destruction of tobacco worms. The ducks, live in the tobacco field, day and night, except when they go to water; and as they are great gormandizers, they take from the plants and destroy an infinite number of worms. They are fond of them as an article of food, and require no watching to keep them in their place; but it is otherwise with the turkeys. These require very peculiar treatment. They must be kept all night in a large coop spacious enough to contain the whole flock, with poles for them to roost on. As soon as it is light in the morning, the coop is opened, the flock turned out, and driven to the tobacco field.

Two hundred turkeys should be followed by four or five active lads, or young men, to keep them together, and at their duty. One turkey will destroy as many worms, as five men could do in the same period of time; but it seems that tobacco worms are not the natural food of turkeys; and they are prone to break out of the field, and escape to the woods or pastures in search of grasshoppers, which they greatly prefer to tobacco worms, for breakfast. However, if kept amongst the tobacco, they commit terrible ravages amongst the worms, and will eat until they are filled up to the throat. When they cease eating worms, they are to be driven back to the coop, and shut up, where they must have plenty of water, and a peck of corn to a hundred turkeys. If they get no corn, and are forced to live on tobacco worms only, they droop, become sickly, and would doubtlessly die. In the evening, they are again driven to the field, and treated again in the same manner as in the morning.

The tobacco worm, is of a bright green colour, with a series of rings or circles round its body. I have seen them as large as a man's longest finger. I was never able to discover in what manner they originate. They certainly do not change into a butterfly as some other worms do; and I could never perceive that they deposite eggs anywhere. I am of opinion that there is something in the very nature of the tobacco plant, which produces these nauseous reptiles, for they are too large, when at full growth, to be ranked with insects.[14]

In the month of August, the tobacco crop is laid by, as it is termed; which means that they cease working in the fields, for the purpose of destroying the weeds and grass; the plants having now become so large, as not to be injured by the under vegetation. Still, however, the worms continue their ravages, and it is necessary to employ all hands in destroying them. In this month, also, the tobacco is to be topped, if it has not been done before. When the plants have reached the height of two or three feet, according to the goodness of the soil, and the vigour of the growth, the top is to be cut off, to prevent it from going to seed. This topping, causes all the powers of the plant, which would be exhausted in the formation of flowers and seeds, to expand in leaves fit for use. After the tobacco is fully grown, which in some plants happens early in August, it is to be carefully watched, to see when it is ripe, or fit for cutting. The state of the plant is known by its colour, and by certain pale spots which appear on the leaves. It does not all arrive at maturity at the same time; and although some plants ripen early in August, others are not ripe before the middle of September. When the plants are cut down, they are laid on the ground for a short time, then taken up, and the stalks split open to facilitate the drying of the leaves. In this condition it is removed to the drying house, and there hung up under sheds, until it is fully dry. From thence it is removed into the tobacco house, and laid up in bulk, ready for stripping and manufacturing.

---

## CHAPTER V.

IT is time to resume the narrative of my journey southward. At the period of which I now write, tobacco was universally cultivated in those parts of Virginia through which I travelled; and that, with the corn crops, constituted nearly the whole objects of agricultural labour.

The quantity of wheat and rye, which I saw on my journey, was very small. A little oats was growing on the estates of some gentlemen, who were fond of breeding fine horses. I did not perceive any material difference in the condition of the country, as I passed south, until after crossing the Roanoke river. Near this stream we passed a very large estate, on which, there appeared to me, to be nearly a thousand acres of tobacco growing. Our master was informed, by a gentleman whom we met here, that this property belonged to Mr. Randolph,[15] a member of Congress, and one of the largest planters in Virginia. The land appeared to me not to be any better than the tobacco lands in Maryland, though a little more sandy. The mansion house was low, and of ordinary appearance. The fields were badly fenced, and the whole place was in poor condition. We passed close by a gang of near a hundred hands—men and women, at work with hoes, in a tobacco field. I had not, in all Virginia, seen any slaves more destitute of clothes. Many of the men, and some of the young women, were without shirts; and several young lads had only a few rags about their loins. Their skins looked dry and husky, which proved that they were not well fed. They were followed by an overseer who carried in his hand a kind of whip which I had never before seen; though I afterward became familiar with this terrible weapon. South of the Roanoke, the land became more sandy, and pine timber generally prevailed—in many places, to the exclusion of all other trees. In North Carolina, the same course of culture is pursued, as that which I have noted in Virginia; and the same disastrous consequences result from it; though, as the country has not been settled so long as the northern part of Virginia and Maryland, so great a portion of the land has not been worn out and abandoned in the former, as in the latter. Here, also, the red cedar is seldom seen; as the pitch-pine takes possession of all waste and deserted fields. In this state the houses are not so well built as they are further north; there are fewer carriages, and the number of good horses, judging from those I saw on the road, must be much less. The inhabitants of the country are plainer in their dress, and they have fewer people of fashion, than are to be met in Virginia. The plantations here were not so large as those I saw on the north of the Roanoke; but larger tracts of country are covered with wood, than any I had heretofore seen. The condition of the slaves is not worse here, than it is in Virginia; nor is there any wheat in Carolina, worth speaking of.

As we approached the Yadkin river, the tobacco disappeared from the fields, and the cotton plant took its place, as an article of general culture. We passed the Yadkin by a ferry, on Sunday morning; and on the Wednesday following, in the evening, our master told us we were in the state of South Carolina. We staid this night in a small town called Lancaster; and I shall never forget the sensations which I experienced this evening, on finding myself in chains, in the state of South Carolina. From my earliest recollections, the name of South Carolina had been little less terrible to me than that of the bottomless pit. In Maryland, it had always been the practice of masters and mistresses, who wished to terrify their slaves, to threaten to sell them to South Carolina; where, it was represented, that their condition would be a hundred fold worse than it was in Maryland. I had regarded such a sale of myself, as the greatest of evils that could befall me, and had striven to demean myself in such manner, to my owners, as to preclude them from all excuse for transporting me to so horrid a place. At length I found myself, without having committed any crime, or even the slightest transgression, in the place and condition, of which I had, through life, entertained the greatest dread. I slept but little this night, and for the first time felt weary of life. It appeared to me that the cup of my misery was full—that there was no hope of release from my present chains, unless it might be to exchange them for the long lash of the overseers of the cotton plantations; in each of whose hands I observed such a whip as I saw in possession of Mr. Randolph's slave driver in Virginia. I seriously meditated on self-destruction, and had I been at liberty to get a rope, I believe I should have hanged myself at Lancaster. It appeared to me that such an act, done by a man in my situation, could not be a violation of the precepts of religion, nor of the laws of God.

I had now no hope of ever again seeing my wife and children, or of revisiting the scenes of my youth. I apprehended that I should, if I lived, suffer the most excruciating pangs that extreme and long continued hunger could inflict; for I had often heard, that in South Carolina, the slaves were compelled in times of scarcity, to live on cotton seeds.

From the dreadful apprehensions of future evil, which harrassed and harrowed my mind that night, I do not marvel, that the slaves who are driven to the south often destroy themselves. Self-destruction is much more frequent among the slaves in the cotton region than is generally supposed. When a negro kills himself, the master is unwilling to let it be known, lest the deed should be attributed to his own cruelty. A certain degree of disgrace falls upon the master whose slave has committed suicide—and the same man, who would stand by, and see his overseer give his slave a hundred lashes, with the long whip, on his bare back, without manifesting the least pity for the sufferings of the poor tortured wretch, will express very profound regret if the same slave terminates his own life, to avoid a repetition of the horrid flogging. Suicide amongst the slaves is regarded as a matter of dangerous example, and one which it is the business and the interest of all proprietors to discountenance and prevent. All the arguments which can be devised against it are used to deter the negroes from the perpetration of it; and such as take this dreadful means of freeing themselves from their miseries, are always branded in reputation after death, as the worst of criminals; and their bodies are not allowed the small portion of Christian rites which are awarded to the corpses of other slaves.

Surely if any thing can justify a man in taking his life into his own hands, and terminating his existence, no one can attach blame to the slaves on many of the cotton plantations of the south, when they cut short their breath, and the agonies of the present being, by a single stroke. What is life worth, amidst hunger, nakedness and excessive toil, under the continually uplifted lash?

It was long after midnight before I fell asleep; but the most pleasant dreams succeeded to these sorrowful forebodings. I thought I had, by some means, escaped from my master, and through infinite and unparalleled dangers and sufferings, had made my way back to Maryland; and was again in the cabin of my wife, with two of my little children on my lap; whilst their mother was busy in preparing for me a supper of fried fish, such as she often dressed, when I was at home, and had taken to her the fish I had caught in the Patuxent river. Every object was so vividly impressed upon my imagination in this dream, that when I awoke, a firm conviction settled upon my mind, that by some means, at present incomprehensible to me, I should yet again embrace my wife, and caress my children in their humble dwelling. Early in the morning, our master called us up; and distributed to each of the party, a cake made of corn meal, and a small piece of bacon. On our journey, we had only eaten twice a day, and had not received breakfast until about nine o'clock; but he said this morning meal was given to welcome us to South Carolina. He then addressed us all, and told us we might now give up all hope of ever returning to the places of our nativity; as it would be impossible for us to pass through the states of North Carolina and Virginia, without being taken up and sent back. He further advised us to make ourselves contented, as he would take us to Georgia, a far better country than any we had seen; and where we would be able to live in the greatest abundance. About sunrise we took up our march on the road to Columbia, as we were told. Hitherto our master had not offered to sell any of us, and had even refused to stop to talk to any one on the subject of our sale, although he had several times been addressed on this point, before we reached Lancaster; but soon after we departed from this village, we were overtaken on the road by a man on horseback, who accosted our driver by asking him if his *niggers* were for sale. The latter replied, that he believed he would not sell any yet, as he was on his way to Georgia, and cotton being now much in demand, he expected to obtain high prices for us from persons who were going to settle in the new purchase. He, however, contrary to his custom, ordered us to stop, and told the stranger he might look at us, and that he would find us as fine a lot of hands, as were ever imported into the country—that we were all prime property, and he had no doubt would command his own prices in Georgia.

The stranger, who was a thin, weather-beaten, sun-burned figure, then said, he wanted a couple of breeding-wenches, and would give as much for them as they would bring in Georgia—that he had lately heard from Augusta, and that *niggers* were not higher there than in Columbia, and, as he had been in Columbia the week before, he knew what *niggers* were worth. He then walked along our line, as we stood chained together, and looked at the whole of us—then turning to the women, asked the prices of the two pregnant ones. Our master replied, that these were two of the best breeding-wenches in all Maryland—that one was twenty-two, and the other only nineteen—that the first was already the mother of seven children, and the other of four—that he had himself seen the children at the time he bought their mothers—and that such wenches would be cheap at a thousand dollars each; but as they were not able to keep up with the gang, he would take twelve hundred dollars for the two. The purchaser said this was too much, but that he would give nine hundred dollars for the pair. This price was promptly refused; but our master, after some consideration, said he was willing to sell a bargain in these wenches, and would take eleven hundred dollars for them, which was objected to on the other side; and many faults and failings were pointed out in the merchandise. After much bargaining, and many gross jests on the part of the stranger, he offered a thousand dollars for the two; and said he would give no more. He then mounted his horse, and moved off; but after he had gone about one hundred yards, he was called back; and our master said, if he would go with him to the next blacksmith's shop on the road to Columbia, and pay for taking the irons off the rest of us, he might have the two women.

This proposal was agreed to, and as it was now about nine o'clock, we were ordered to hasten on to the next house, where, we were told, we must stop for breakfast. At this place we were informed that it was ten miles to the next smith's shop, and our new acquaintance was obliged by the terms of his contract, to accompany us thither. We received, for breakfast, about a pint of boiled rice to each person, and after this was despatched, we again took to the road, eager to reach the blacksmith's shop, at which we expected to be relieved of the iron rings and chains, which had so long galled and worried us. About two o'clock, we arrived at the longed-for residence of the smith; but, on inquiry, our master was informed that he was not at home, and would not return before evening. Here a controversy arose, whether we should all remain here until the smith returned, or the stranger should go on with us to the next smithery, which was said to be only five miles distant. This was a point not easily settled, between two such spirits as our master and the stranger; both of whom had been overseers in their time, and both of whom had risen to the rank of proprietors of slaves.

The matter had already produced angry words, and much vaunting on the part of the stranger;—"that a freeman of South Carolina was not to be imposed upon; that by the constitution of the state, his rights were sacred, and he was not to be deprived of his liberty, at the arbitrary will of a man just from amongst the Yankees, and who had brought with him to the south, as many Yankee tricks as he had *niggers,* and he believed many more." He then swore, that "all the *niggers* in the drove were Yankee *niggers.*"

"When I *overseed* for Colonel Polk," said he, "on his rice plantation, he had two Yankee *niggers* that he brought from Maryland, and they were running away every day. I gave them a hundred lashes more than a dozen times; but they never quit running away, till I chained them together, with iron collars round their necks, and chained them to spades, and made them do nothing but dig ditches to drain the rice swamps. They could not run away then, unless they went together, and carried their chains and spades with them. I kept them in this way two years, and better *niggers* I never had. One of them died one night, and the other was never good for any thing after he lost his mate. He never ran away afterwards, but he died too, after a while." He then addressed himself to the two women, whose master he had become, and told them that if ever they ran away, he would treat them in the same way. Wretched as I was myself, my heart bled for these poor creatures, who had fallen into the hands of a tiger in human form. The dispute between the two masters was still raging, when, unexpectedly, the blacksmith rode up to his house, on a thin, bony-looking horse, and, dismounting, asked his wife what these gentlemen were making such a *frolick* about. I did not hear her answer, but both the disputants turned and addressed themselves to the smith—the one to know what price he would demand, to take the irons off all these *niggers,* and the other to know how long it would take him to perform the work. It is here proper for me to observe, that there are many phrases of language in common use in Carolina and Georgia, which are applied in a way that would not be understood by persons from one of the northern states. For instance, when several persons are quarrelling, brawling, making a great noise, or even fighting, they say, "*the gentlemen are frolicking!*" I heard many other terms equally strange, whilst I resided in the southern country, amongst such white people as I became acquainted with; though my acquaintance was confined, in a great measure, to overseers, and such people as did not associate with the rich planters and great families.

The smith at length agreed to take the irons from the whole of us for two dollars and fifty cents, and immediately set about it, with the air of indifference that he would have manifested in tearing a pair of old shoes from the hoofs of a wagon-horse. It was four weeks and five days, from the time my irons had been riveted upon me, until they were removed, and great as had been my sufferings whilst chained to my fellow-slaves, I cannot say that I felt any pleasure in being released from my long confinement; for I knew that my liberation was only preparatory to my final, and, as I feared, perpetual subjugation to the power of some such monster, as the one then before me, who was preparing to drive away the two unfortunate women whom he had purchased, and whose life's-blood he had acquired the power of shedding at pleasure, for the sum of a thousand dollars. After we were released from our chains, our master sold the whole lot of irons, which we had borne, from Maryland, to the blacksmith, for seven dollars.

The smith then procured a bottle of rum, and treated his two new acquaintances to a part of its contents—wishing them both good luck with their *niggers.* After these civilities were over, the two women were ordered to follow their new master, who shaped his course across the country, by a road leading westward. At parting from us, they both wept aloud, and wrung their hands in despair. We all went to them, and bade them a last farewell. Their road led into a wood, which they soon entered, and I never saw them, nor heard of them again.

These women had both been driven from Calvert county, as well as myself, and the fate of the younger of the two, was peculiarly severe.

She had been brought up as the waiting-maid of a young lady, the daughter of a gentleman, whose wife and family often visited the mistress of my own wife. I had frequently seen this woman when she was a young girl, in attendance upon her young mistress, and riding in the same carriage with her. The father of the young lady died, and soon after, she married a gentleman who resided a few miles off. The husband received a considerable fortune with his bride, and amongst other things, her waiting-maid, who was reputed a great beauty among people of colour. He had been addicted to the fashionable sports of the country, before marriage, such as horse-racing, fox-hunting, &c. and I had heard the black people say he drank too freely; but it was supposed that he would correct all these irregularities after marriage, more especially as his wife was a great belle, and withal very handsome. The reverse, however, turned out to be the fact. Instead of growing better, he became worse; and in the course of a few years, was known all over the country, as a drunkard and a gambler. His wife, it was said, died of grief, and soon after her death, his effects were seized by his creditors, and sold by the sheriff. The former waiting-maid, now the mother of several children, was purchased by our present master, for three hundred dollars, at the sheriff's sale, and this poor wretch, whose employment in early life had been to take care of her young mistress, and attend her in her chamber, and at her toilet, after being torn from her husband and her children, had now gone to toil out a horrible existence beneath the scorching sun of a South Carolina cotton field, under the dominion of a master, as void of the manners of a gentleman, as he was of the language of humanity.

It was now late in the afternoon; but, as we had made little progress to-day, and were now divested of the burden of our chains, as well as freed from the two women, who had hitherto much retarded our march, our master ordered us to hasten on our way, as we had ten miles to go that evening. I had been so long oppressed by the weight of my chains, and the iron collar about my neck, that for some time after I commenced walking at my natural liberty, I felt a kind of giddiness, or lightness of the head. Most of my companions complained of the same sensation, and we did not recover our proper feelings, until after we had slept one night. It was after dark when we arrived at our lodging-place, which proved to be the house of a small cotton-planter, who, it appeared, kept a sort of a house of entertainment for travellers, contrary to what I afterwards discovered to be the usual custom of cotton-planters. This man and my master had known each other before, and seemed to be well acquainted. He was the first person that we had met since leaving Maryland, who was known to my master, and as they kept up a very free conversation, through the course of the evening, and the house in which they were, was only separated from the kitchen, in which we were lodged, by a space of a few feet, I had an opportunity of hearing much that was highly interesting to me. The landlord, after supper, came with our master to look at us, and to see us receive our allowance of boiled rice from the hands of a couple of black women, who had prepared it in a large iron kettle. Whilst viewing us, the former asked the latter, what he intended to do with his drove;

but no reply was made to this inquiry—and as our master had, through our whole journey, maintained a studied silence on this subject, I felt a great curiosity to know what disposition he intended to make of the whole gang, and of myself in particular. On their return to the house, I advanced to a small window in the kitchen, which brought me within a few yards of the place where they sat, and from which I was able to hear all they said, although they spoke in a low tone of voice. I here learned, that so many of us as could be sold for a good price, were to be disposed of in Columbia, on our arrival at that place, and that the residue would be driven to Augusta and sold there.

The landlord assured my master that at this time slaves were much in demand, both in Columbia and Augusta; that purchasers were numerous and prices good; and that the best plan of effecting good sales would be to put up each *nigger,* separately, at auction, after giving a few days' notice, by an advertisement, in the neighbouring country. Cotton, he said, had not been higher for many years, and as a great many persons, especially young men, were moving off to the new purchase in Georgia, prime hands were in high demand, for the purpose of clearing the land in the new country—that the boys and girls, under twenty, would bring almost any price at present, in Columbia, for the purpose of picking the growing crop of cotton, which promised to be very heavy; and as most persons had planted more than their hands would be able to pick, young *niggers,* who would soon learn to pick cotton, were prime articles in the market. As to those more advanced in life, he seemed to think the prospect of selling them at an unusual price, not so good, as they could not so readily become expert cotton-pickers—he said further, that from some cause, which he could not comprehend, the price of rice had not been so good this year as usual; and that he had found it cheaper to purchase rice to feed his own *niggers* than to provide them with corn, which had to be brought from the upper country. He therefore, advised my master, not to drive us towards the rice plantation of the low country. My master said he would follow his advice, at least so far as to sell a portion of us in Carolina, but seemed to be of opinion that his prime hands would bring him more money in Georgia, and named me, in particular, as one who would be worth, at least, a thousand dollars, to a man who was about making a settlement, and clearing a plantation in the new purchase. I therefore concluded, that in the course of events, I was likely to become the property of a Georgian, which turned out in the end, to be the case, though not so soon as I at this time apprehended. I slept but little this night, feeling a restlessness when no longer in chains; and pondering over the future lot of my life, which appeared fraught only with evil and misfortune. Day at length dawned, and with its first light we were ordered to betake ourselves to the road, which, we were told, would lead us to Columbia, the place of intended sale of some, if not all of us. For several days past, I had observed that in the country through which we travelled, little attention was paid to the cultivation of any thing but cotton. Now this plant was almost the sole possessor of the fields. It covered the plantations adjacent to the road, as far as I could see, both before and behind me, and looked not unlike buckwheat before it blossoms. I saw some small fields of corn, and lots of sweet potatoes, amongst which the young vines of the water-melon were frequently visible. The improvements on the plantations were not good. There were no barns, but only stables and sheds, to put the cotton under, as it was brought from the field. Hay seemed to be unknown in the country, for I saw neither hay-stacks nor meadows; and the few fields that were lying fallow, had but small numbers of cattle in them, and these were thin and meagre. We had met with no flocks of sheep of late, and the hogs that we saw on the road-side, were in bad condition. The horses and mules that I saw at work in the cotton-fields, were poor and badly harnessed, and the half-naked condition of the negroes, who drove them, or followed with the hoe, together with their wan complexions, proved to me that they had too much work, or not enough food. We passed a cotton-gin this morning, the first that I ever saw; but they were not at work with it. We also met a party of ladies and gentlemen on a journey of pleasure, riding in two very handsome carriages, drawn by sleek and spirited horses, very different in appearance from the moving skeletons that I had noticed drawing the ploughs in the fields. The black drivers of the coaches were neatly clad in gay-coloured clothes, and contrasted well with their half-naked brethren, a gang of whom were hoeing cotton by the road-side, near them, attended by an overseer in a white linen shirt and pantaloons, with one of the long negro whips in his hand.

I observed that these poor people did not raise their heads, to look either at the fine coaches and horses then passing, or at us; but kept their faces steadily bent towards the cotton-plants, from among which they were removing the weeds. I almost shuddered at the sight, knowing, that I myself was doomed to a state of servitude, equally cruel and debasing, unless, by some unforeseen occurrence, I might fall into the hands of a master of less inhumanity of temper than the one who had possession of the miserable creatures before me.

---

## CHAPTER VI.

IT was manifest, that I was now in a country, where the life of a black man was no more regarded than that of an ox, except as far as the man was worth the more money in the market. On all the plantations that we passed, there was a want of live stock of every description, except slaves, and they were deplorably abundant.

The fields were destitute of every thing that deserved the name of grass, and not a spear of clover was anywhere visible. The few cattle that existed, were browsing on the boughs of the trees, in the woods. Every thing betrayed a scarcity of the means of supplying the slaves, who cultivated the vast cotton-fields, with a sufficiency of food. We travelled this day more than thirty miles, and crossed the Catawba river in the afternoon, on the bottoms of which I saw, for the first time, fields of rice, growing in swamps, covered with water. Causeways were raised through the low-lands in which the rice grew, and on these, the road was formed on which we travelled. These rice-fields, or rather swamps, had, in my eyes, a beautiful appearance. The rice was nearly two feet in height above the water, and of a vivid green colour, covering a large space, of at least a hundred acres. Had it not been for the water, which appeared stagnant and sickly, and swarmed with frogs and thousands of snakes, it would have been as fine a sight as one need wish to look upon. After leaving the low grounds along the river, we again entered plantations of cotton, which lined the roads on both sides, relieved, here and there, by corn-fields, and potato-patches. We stopped for the night at a small tavern, and our master said we were within a day's journey of Columbia.

We here, again, received boiled rice for supper, without salt, or any kind of seasoning; a pint was allotted to each person, which we greedily devoured, having had no dinner to-day, save an allowance of corn-cakes, with the fat of about five pounds of bacon, extracted by frying, in which we dipped our bread. I slept soundly after this day's march, the fatigues of the body having, for once, overcome the agitations of the mind. The next day, which was, if my recollection is accurate, the ninth of June, was the last of our journey before our company separated; and we were on the road before the stars had disappeared from the sky. Our breakfast, this morning, consisted of bacon soup, a dish composed of corn meal, boiled in water, with a small piece of bacon to give the soup a taste of meat. For dinner we had boiled Indian peas, with a small allowance of bacon. This was the first time that we had received two rations of meat in the same day, on the whole journey, and some of our party were much surprised at the kindness of our master; but I had no doubt that his object was to make us look fat and hearty, to enable him to obtain better prices for us at Columbia.

At supper this night, we had corn mush, in large wooden trays, with melted lard to dip the mush in before eating it. We might have reached Columbia this day if we had continued our march, but we stopped, at least an hour before sunset, about three miles from town, at the house of a man who supported the double character of planter, and keeper of a house of entertainment; for I learned from his slaves that their master considered it disreputable to be called a tavern-keeper, and would not put up a sign, although he received pay of such persons as lodged with him. His house was a frame building, weather-boarded with pine boards, but had no plastering within. The furniture corresponded with the house which contained it, and was both scanty and mean, consisting of pine tables and wooden chairs, with bottoms made of corn husks. The house was only one story high, and all the rooms, six or seven in number, parlour, bed-rooms, and kitchen, were on the first floor. As the weather was warm and the windows open, I had an opportunity of looking into the sleeping rooms of the family, as I walked round the house, which I was permitted freely to do. The beds and their furniture answered well to the chairs and tables; yet in the large front room I observed on an old fashioned sideboard, a great quantity of glass ware, of various descriptions, with two or three dozen silver spoons, a silver tea urn, and several knives and forks with silver handles. In the corner of this room stood a bed with gaudy red curtains, with figures of lions, elephants, naked negroes, and other representations of African scenery.

The master of the house was not at home when we arrived, but came in from the field shortly afterwards. He met my master with the cordiality of an old friend, though he had never seen him before, said he was happy to see him at his house, and that the greatest pleasure he enjoyed was derived from the entertainment of such gentlemen as thought proper to visit his house; that he was always glad to see strangers, and more especially gentlemen who were adding so much to the wealth and population of Carolina, as those merchants who imported servants from the north. He then observed that he had never seen a finer lot of property pass his house than we were, and that any gentleman who brought such a stock of hands into the country was a public benefactor, and entitled to the respect and gratitude of every friend of the south. He assured my master that he was happy to see him at his house, and that if he thought proper to remain a few days with him, it would be his chief business to introduce him to the gentlemen of the neighbourhood, who would all be glad to become acquainted with a merchant of his respectability. In the state of Maryland, my master had been called a *negro buyer, or Georgia trader,* sometimes a *negro driver;* but here, I found that he was elevated to the rank of merchant, and a merchant of the first order too; for it was very clear that in the opinion of the landlord, no branch of trade was more honourable than the traffic in us poor slaves. Our master observed that he had a mind to remain here a short time, and try what kind of market Columbia would present, for the sale of his lot of servants; and that he would make this house his home, until he had ascertained what could be done in town, and what demand there was in the neighbourhood for servants. We were not called *slaves* by these men, who talked of selling us, and of the price we would bring, with as little compunction of conscience as they would have talked of the sale of so many mules.

It is the custom throughout all the slave-holding states, amongst people of fashion, never to speak of their negroes as slaves, but always as servants; but I had never before met with the keeper of a public house, in the country, who had arrived at this degree of refinement. I had been accustomed to hear this order of men, and indeed the greater number of white people, speak of the people of colour as *niggers*. We remained at this place more than two weeks; I presume because my master found it cheaper to keep us here than in town, or perhaps, because he supposed we might recover from the hardships of our journey more speedily in the country.

As it was here that my real acquaintance with South Carolina commenced, I have noted, with more particularity the incidents that occurred, than I otherwise should have done. This family was composed of the husband, wife, three daughters, all young women, and two sons, one of whom appeared to be about twenty, and the other, perhaps seventeen years old. They had nine slaves in all, one very old man, quite crooked with years and labour—two men of middle age—one lad, perhaps sixteen—one woman, with three children, the oldest about seven,—and a young girl of twelve or fourteen. The farm, or plantation, they lived on, contained about one hundred and fifty acres of cleared land, sandy, and the greater part of it poor, as was proved by the stinted growth of the cotton.

At the time of our arrival at this house, I saw no persons about it, except the four ladies—the mother and her three daughters—the husband being in the field, as noticed above. According to the orders of my master, I had taken the saddle from his horse and put him in a stable; and it was not until after the first salutations of the new landlord to my master were over, that he seemed to think of asking him whether he had come on foot, on horse-back, or in a coach. He at length, however, turned suddenly and asked him, with an air of surprise, where he had left his horses and carriage. My master said he had no carriage, that he travelled on horseback, and that his horse was in the stable. The landlord then apologized for the trouble he must have had, in having his horse put away himself; and said that at this season of the year, the planters were so hurried by their crops, and found so much difficulty in keeping down the grass, that they were generally obliged to keep all their servants in the field; that for his part, he had been compelled to put his coachman, and even the waiting-maids of his daughters into the cotton fields, and that at this time, his family were without servants, a circumstance that had never happened before! "For my part," said he, "I have always prided myself on bringing up my family well, and can say, that although I do not live in so fine a house as some of the other planters of Carolina, yet my children are as great ladies and gentlemen as any in the state. Not one of them has ever had to do a day's work yet, and as long as I live, never shall. I sent two of my daughters to Charleston last summer, and they were there three months; and I intend to send the youngest there this summer. They have all learned to dance here in Columbia, where I sent them two quarters to a Frenchman, and he made me pay pretty well for it. They went to the same dancing school with the daughters of Wade Hampton and Colonel Fitzhugh.[16] I am determined that they shall never marry any but gentlemen of the first character, and I know they will always follow my advice in matters of this kind. They are prudent and sensible girls, and are not going to do as Major Pollack's daughter did this spring, who ran away with a Georgia cracker who brought a drove of cattle for sale from the Indian country, and who had not a *nigger* in the world. He staid with me sometime, and wished to have something to say to my second daughter, but the thing would not do."

Here he stopped short in his narrative, and seeming to muse a moment, said to his guest, "I presume, as you travel alone, you have no family." "No," replied my master, "I am a single man." "I thought so by your appearance," said the loquacious landlord, "and I shall be glad to introduce you to my family this evening. My sons are two as fine fellows as there are in all Carolina. My oldest boy is lieutenant in the militia, and in the same company that marched with Gen. Marion[17] in the war. He was on the point of fighting a duel last winter, with young M'Corkle in Columbia; but the matter was settled between them. You will see him this evening, when he returns from the coit-party.[18] A coit-party of young bucks meets once every week about two miles from this, and as I wish my sons to keep the best company, they both attend it. There is to be a cock-fight there this afternoon, and my youngest son, Edmund, has the finest cock in this country. He is of the true game blood,—the real Dominica game breed; and I sent to Charleston for his gaffs. There is a bet of ten dollars a side between my son's cock, and one belonging to young Blainey, the son of Major Blainey. Young Blainey is a hot-headed young blood, and has been concerned in three duels, though I believe he never fought but one; but I know Edmund will not take a word from him, and it will be well if he and his cock do not both get well licked."

Here the conversation was arrested by the sound of horses' feet on the road, and in the next instant, two young men rode up at a gallop, mounted on lean looking horses; one of the riders carrying a pole on his shoulder, with a game cock in a net bag, tied to one end of it. On perceiving them the landlord exclaimed with an oath, "There's two lads of spirit! stranger,—and if you will allow me the liberty of asking you your name, I will introduce you to them." At the suggestion of his name, my master seemed to hesitate a little, but after a moment's pause, said, "They call me M'Giffin, sir." "My name is Hulig, sir," replied the landlord, "and I am very happy to be acquainted with you, Mr. M'Giffin," at the same time shaking him by the hand, and introducing his two sons, who were by this time at the door.

This was the first time I had ever heard the name of my master, although I had been with him five weeks. I had never seen him before the day on which he seized and bound me in Maryland, and as he took me away immediately, I did not hear his name at the time. The people who assisted to fetter me, either from accident or design, omitted to name him, and after we commenced our journey, he had maintained so much distant reserve and austerity of manner towards us all, that no one ventured to ask him his name. We had called him nothing but "master," and the various persons at whose houses we had stopped on our way, knew as little of his name as we did. We had frequently been asked the name of our master, and perhaps had not always obtained credence, when we said we did not know it.

Throughout the whole journey, until after we were released from our irons, he had forbidden us to converse together beyond a few words in relation to our temporary condition and wants; and as he was with us all day, and never slept out of hearing of us at night, he rigidly enforced his edict of silence. I presume that the reason of this prohibition of all conversation, was to prevent us from devising plans of escape; but he had imposed as rigid a silence on himself as was enforced upon us; and after having passed from Maryland to South Carolina, in his company, I knew no more of my master, than, that he knew how to keep his secrets, guard his slaves, and make a close bargain. I had never heard him speak of his home or family; and therefore had concluded that he was an unmarried man, and an adventurer, who felt no more attachment for one place than another, and whose residence was not very well settled; but, from the large sums of money which he must have been able to command and carry with him to the north, to enable him to purchase so large a number of slaves, I had no doubt that he was a man of consequence and consideration in the place from whence he came.

In Maryland, I had always observed that men, who were the owners of large stocks of negroes, were not averse to having publicity given to their names; and that the possession of this species of property even there, gave its owner more vanity and egotism, than fell to the lot of the holders of any other kind of estate; and in truth, my subsequent experience proved, that without the possession of slaves, no man could ever arrive at, or hope to rise to any honourable station in society;—yet, my master seemed to take no pride in having at his disposal the lives of so many human beings. He never spoke to us in words of either pity or hatred; and never spoke of us, except to order us to be fed or watered, as he would have directed the same offices to be performed for so many horses, or to inquire where the best prices could be obtained for us. He regarded us only as objects of traffic and the materials of his commerce; and although he had lived several years in Carolina and Georgia, and had there exercised the profession of an overseer, he regarded the southern planters as no less the subjects of trade and speculation, than the slaves he sold to them; as will appear in the sequel. It was to this man that the landlord introduced his two sons, and upon whom he was endeavouring to impose a belief, that he was the head of a family which took rank with those of the first planters of the district. The ladies of the household, though I had seen them in the kitchen when I walked round the house, had not yet presented themselves to my master, nor indeed were they in a condition to be seen anywhere but in the apartment they occupied at the time. The young gentlemen gave a very gasconading account of the coit-party and cock-fight, from which they had just returned, and according to their version of the affair, it might have been an assemblage of at least half the military officers of the state; for all the persons of whom they spoke, were captains, majors, and colonels. The eldest said, he had won two bowls of punch at coits; and the youngest, whose cock had been victor in the battle, on which ten dollars were staked, vaunted much of the qualities of his bird; and supported his veracity by numerous oaths, and reiterated appeals to his brother for the truth of his assertions. Both these young men were so much intoxicated, that they with difficulty maintained an erect posture in walking.

By this time the sun was going down, and I observed two female slaves, a woman and girl, approaching the house on the side of the kitchen from the cotton field. They were coming home to prepare supper for the family; the ladies whom I had seen in the kitchen not having been there for the purpose of performing the duties appropriate to that station, but having sought it as a place of refuge from the sight of my master, who had approached the front of their dwelling silently, and so suddenly as not to permit them to gain the foot of the stairway in the large front room, without being seen by him, to whose view they by no means wished to expose themselves, before they had visited their toilets. About dark the supper was ready in the large room, and, as it had two fronts, one of which looked into the yard where my companions and I had been permitted to seat ourselves, and had an opportunity of seeing, by the light of the candle, all that was done within, and of hearing all that was said. The ladies, four in number, had entered the room before the gentlemen; and when the latter came in my master was introduced, by the landlord to his wife and daughters, by the name and title of *Colonel M'Giffin,* which, at that time, impressed me with a belief that he was really an officer, and that he had disclosed this circumstance without out my knowledge; but I afterwards perceived that in the south it is deemed respectful to address a stranger by the title of Colonel, or Major, or General, if his appearance will warrant the association of so high a rank with his name. My master had declared his intention of becoming the inmate of this family for some time, and no pains seemed to be spared on their part to impress upon his mind the high opinion that they entertained of the dignity of the owner of fifty slaves; the possession of so large a number of human creatures being, in Carolina, a certificate of character, which entitles its bearer to enter whatever society he may choose to select, without any thing more being known of his birth, his life, or reputation. The man who owns fifty servants must needs be a gentleman amongst the higher ranks, and the owner of half a hundred *niggers* is a sort of nobleman amongst the low, the ignorant, and the vulgar. The mother and three daughters, whose appearance, when I saw them in the kitchen, would have warranted the conclusion that they had just risen from bed, without having time to adjust their dress, were now gaily, if not neatly attired; and the two female slaves, who had come from the field at sundown to cook the supper, now waited at the table. The landlord talked much of his crops, his plantation and slaves, and of the distinguished families who exchanged visits with his own; but my master took very little part in the conversation of the evening, and appeared disposed to maintain the air of mystery which had hitherto invested his character.

After it was quite dark, the slaves came in from the cotton-field, and taking little notice of us, went into the kitchen, and each taking thence a pint of corn, proceeded to a little mill, which was nailed to a post in the yard, and there commenced the operation of grinding meal for their suppers, which were afterwards to be prepared by baking the meal into cakes at the fire. The woman who was the mother of the three small children, was permitted to grind her allowance of corn first, and after her came the old man, and the others in succession. After the corn was converted into meal, each one kneaded it up with cold water into a thick dough, and raking away the ashes from a small space on the kitchen hearth, placed the dough, rolled up in green leaves, in the hollow, and covering it with hot embers, left it to be baked into bread, which was done in about half an hour. These loaves constituted the only supper of the slaves belonging to this family; for I observed that the two women who had waited at the table, after the supper of the white people was disposed of, also came with their corn to the mill on the post, and ground their allowance like the others. They had not been permitted to taste even the fragments of the meal that they had cooked for their masters and mistresses. It was eleven o'clock before these people had finished their supper of cakes, and several of them, especially the younger of the two lads, were so overpowered with toil and sleep, that they had to be roused from their slumbers when their cakes were done, to devour them.

We had for our supper to-night, a pint of boiled rice to each person, and a small quantity of stale and very rancid butter, from the bottom of an old keg, or firkin, which contained about two pounds, the remnant of that which once filled it. We boiled the rice ourselves, in a large iron kettle; and, as our master now informed us that we were to remain here some time, many of us determined to avail ourselves of this season of respite from our toils, to wash our clothes, and free our persons from the vermin which had appeared amongst our party several weeks before, and now begun to be extremely tormenting. As we were not allowed any soap, we were obliged to resort to the use of a very fine and unctuous kind of clay, resembling fullers' earth, but of a yellow colour, which was found on the margin of a small swamp near the house. This was the first time that I had ever heard of clay being used for the purpose of washing clothes; but I often availed myself of this resource afterwards, whilst I was a slave in the south. We wet our clothes, then rubbed this clay all over the garments, and by scouring it out in warm water with our hands, the cloth, whether of woollen, cotton, or linen texture, was left entirely clean. We subjected our persons to the same process, and in this way freed our camp from the host of enemies that had been generated in the course of our journey.

This washing consumed the whole of the first day of our residence on the plantation of Mr. Hulig. We all lay the first night in a shed, or summer kitchen, standing behind the house, and a few yards from it, a place in which the slaves of the plantation washed their clothes, and passed their Sundays in warm weather, when they did not work; but as this place was quite too small to accommodate our party, or indeed to contain us, without crowding us together in such a manner as to endanger our health, we were removed, the morning after our arrival, to an old decayed frame building, about one hundred yards from the house, which had been erected, as I learned, for a cotton-gin, but into which its possessor, for want of means I presume, had never introduced the machinery of the gin. This building was near forty feet square; was without any other floor than the earth, and had neither doors nor windows, to close the openings which had been left for the admission of those who entered it. We were told that in this place the cotton of the plantation was deposited in the picking season, as it was brought from the field, until it could be removed to a neighbouring plantation, where there was a gin to divest it of its seeds.

Here we took our temporary abode—men and women promiscuously. Our provisions, whilst we remained here, were regularly distributed to us; and the daily allowance to each person, consisted of a pint of corn, a pint of rice, and about three or four pounds of butter, such as we had received on the night of our arrival, divided amongst us, in small pieces from the point of a table knife. The rice we boiled in the iron kettle,—we ground our corn at the little mill on the post in the kitchen, and converted the meal into bread, in the manner we had been accustomed to at home—sometimes on the hearth, and sometimes before the fire, on a hoe. The butter was given us as an extraordinary ration, to strengthen and recruit us after our long march, and give us a healthy and expert appearance at the time of our future sale.

We had no beds of any kind to sleep on, but each one was provided with a blanket, which had been the companion of our travels. We were left entirely at liberty to go out or in when we pleased, and no watch was kept over us either by night or day.

Our master had removed us so far from our native country, that he supposed it impossible for any of us ever to escape from him, and surmount all the obstacles that lay between us and our former homes. He went away immediately after we were established in our new lodgings, and remained absent until the second evening about sundown, when he returned, came into our shed, sat down on a block of wood in the midst of us, and asked if any one had been sick; if we had got our clothes clean; and if we had been supplied with an allowance of rice, corn, and butter. After satisfying himself upon these points, he told us that we were now at liberty to run away if we chose to do so; but if we made the attempt we should most certainly be re-taken, and subjected to the most terrible punishment. "I never flog," said he, "my practice is to *cat-haul;* and if you run away, and I catch you again—as I surely shall do—and give you one cat-hauling, you will never run away again, nor attempt it." I did not then understand the import of cat-hauling, but in after times, became well acquainted with its signification.

We remained in this place nearly two weeks, during which time our allowance of food was not varied, and was regularly given to us. We were not required to do any work; and I had liberty and leisure to walk about the plantation, and make such observations as I could upon the new state of things around me. Gentlemen and ladies came every day to look at us, with a view of becoming our purchasers; and we were examined with minute care as to our ages, former occupations, and capacity of performing labour. Our persons were inspected, and more especially the hands were scrutinized, to see if all the fingers were perfect, and capable of the quick motions necessary in picking cotton. Our master only visited us once a day, and sometimes he remained absent two days; so that he seldom met any of those who came to see us; but, whenever it so happened that he did meet them, he laid aside his silence and became very talkative, and even animated in his conversation, extolling our good qualities, and averring that he had purchased some of us of one colonel, and others of another general in Virginia; that he could by no means have procured us, had it not been that, in some instances, our masters had ruined themselves, and were obliged to sell us to save their families from ruin; and in others, that our owners were dead, their estates deeply in debt, and we had been sold at public sale; by which means he had become possessed of us. He said our habits were unexceptionable, our characters good, and that there was not one amongst us all who had ever been known to run away, or steal any thing from our former masters. I observed that running away, and stealing from his master, were regarded as the highest crimes of which a slave could be guilty; but I heard no questions asked concerning our propensity to steal from other people besides our masters, and I afterwards learned, that this was not always regarded as a very high crime by the owner of a slave, provided he would perpetrate the theft so adroitly as not to be detected in it.

We were severally asked by our visiters, if we would be willing to live with them, if they would purchase us, to which we generally replied in the affirmative; but our owner declined all the offers that were made for us, upon the ground that we were too poor—looked too bad to be sold at present—and that in our condition he could not expect to get a fair value for us.

One evening, when our master was with us, a thin, sallow-looking man rode up to the house, and alighting from his horse, came to us, and told him that he had come to buy a boy; that he wished to get a good field hand, and would pay a good price for him. I never saw a human countenance that expressed more of the evil passions of the heart than did that of this man, and his conversation corresponded with his physiognomy. Every sentence of his language was accompanied with an oath of the most vulgar profanity, and his eyes appeared to me to be the index of a soul as cruel as his visage was disgusting and repulsive.

After looking at us for some time, this wretch singled *me* out as the object of his choice, and coming up to me, asked me how I would like him for a master.

In my heart I detested him; but a slave is often afraid to speak the truth, and divulge all he feels; so with myself in this instance, as it was doubtful whether I
might not fall into his hands, and be subject to the violence of his temper, I told
him that if he was a good master, as every gentleman ought to be, I should be
willing to live with him. He appeared satisfied with my answer, and turning to
my master, said he would give a high price for me. "I can," said he, "by going
to Charleston, buy as many Guinea negroes as I please for two hundred dollars
each, but as I like this fellow, I will give you four hundred for him." This offer
struck terror into my very heart, for I knew it was as much as was generally given
for the best and ablest slaves, and I expected that it would immediately be accepted as my price, and that I should be at once consigned to the hands of this
man, of whom I had formed so abhorrent an opinion. To my surprise and satisfaction, however, my master made no reply to the proposition; but stood for a
moment, with one hand raised to his face and his fore-finger on his nose, and
then turning suddenly to me said, "Charles, go into the house; I shall not sell you
to-day." It was my business to obey the order of departure, and as I went beyond
the sound of their voices, I could not understand the purport of the conversation
which followed between these two traffickers in human blood; but after a par-
ley of about a quarter of an hour, the hated stranger started abruptly away, and
going to the road, mounted his horse, and rode off at a gallop, banishing himself and my fears together.

I did not see my master again this evening, and when I came out of our bar-
racks in the morning, although it was scarcely daylight, I saw him standing near
one corner of the building, with his head inclined towards the wall, evidently listening to catch any sounds within. He ordered me to go and feed his horse, and
have him saddled for him by sunrise. About an hour afterwards he came to the
stable in his riding dress; and told me that he should remove us all to Columbia
in a few days. He then rode away, and did not return until the third day afterwards.

---

## CHAPTER VII.

It was now about the middle of June, the weather excessively warm, and from
eleven o'clock, A. M. until late in the afternoon, the sand about our residence
was so hot, that we could not stand on it with our bare feet in one posture, more
than one or two minutes. The whole country, so far as I could see, appeared to
be a dead plain, without the least variety of either hill or dale. The pine was so
far the predominating timber of the forest, that at a little distance the entire
woods appeared to be composed of this tree.

I had become weary of being confined to the immediate vicinity of our lodgings, and determined to venture out into the fields of the plantation, and see the
manner of cultivating cotton. Accordingly, after I had made my morning meal
upon corn cakes, I sallied out in the direction which I had seen the slaves of the
plantation take at the time they left the house at daylight, and following a path

through a small field of corn, which was so tall as to prevent me from seeing beyond it, I soon arrived at the field in which the people were at work with hoes amongst the cotton, which was about two feet and a half high, and had formed such long branches, that they could no longer plough in it without breaking it. Expecting to pass the remainder of my life in this kind of labour, I felt anxious to know the evils, if any, attending it, and more especially the manner in which the slaves were treated on the cotton estates.

The people now before me, were all diligently and laboriously weeding and hilling the cotton with hoes, and when I approached them, they scarcely took time to speak to me, but continued their labour as if I had not been present. As there did not appear to be any overseer with them, I thought I would go amongst them, and enter into conversation with them; but upon addressing myself to one of the men, and telling him, if it was not disagreeable to him, I should be glad to become acquainted with him, he said he should be glad to be acquainted with me, but master Tom did not allow him to talk much to people when he was at work. I asked him where his master Tom was; but before he had time to reply, some one called—"Mind your work there, you rascals." Looking in the direction of the sound, I saw master Tom, sitting under the shade of a sassafras tree, at the distance of about a hundred yards from us. Deeming it unsafe to continue in the field without the permission of its lord, I approached the sassafras tree, with my hat in my hand, and in a very humble manner, asked leave to help the people work awhile, as I was tired of staying about the house and doing nothing. He said he did not care; I might go and work with them awhile, but I must take care not to talk too much, and keep his hands from their work.

Now, having authority on my side, I returned, and taking a hoe from the hands of a small girl, told her to pull up weeds, and I would take her row for her. When we arrived at the end of the rows which we were then hilling, master Tom, who still held his post under the sassafras tree, called his people to come to breakfast. Although I had already broken my fast, I went with the rest for the purpose of seeing what their breakfast was composed of. At the tree I saw a keg which contained about five gallons, with water in it; and a gourd lying by it; near this was a basket made of splits, large enough to hold more than a peck. It contained the breakfast of the people, covered by some green leaves of the magnolia, or great bay tree of the south. When the leaves were removed, I found that the supply of provisions consisted of one cake of corn meal, weighing about half a pound, for each person. This bread had no sort of seasoning, not even salt, and constituted the only breakfast of these poor people, who had been toiling from early dawn until about eight o'clock. There was no cake for me, and master Tom did not say any thing to me on the state of my stomach; but the young girl, whose hoe I had taken in the field, offered me a part of her cake, which I refused. After the breakfast was despatched, we again returned to our work; but the master ordered the girl, whose hoe I had, to go and get another hoe which lay at some distance in the field, and take her row again. I continued in the field until dinner, which took place about one o'clock, and was the same, in all respects, as the breakfast had been.

Master Tom was the younger of the two brothers who returned from the cock-fight on the evening of our arrival at this place,—he left the field about ten o'clock, and was succeeded by his elder brother, as overseer for the remainder of the day. After this change of superintendents, my companions became more loquacious, and in the course of an hour or two, I had become familiar with the condition of my fellow-labourers who told me that the elder of their young masters was much less tyrannical than his younger brother; and that whilst the former remained in the field they would be at liberty to talk as much as they pleased, provided they did not neglect their work. One of the men who appeared to be about forty years of age, and who was the foreman of the field, told me that he had been born in South Carolina, and had always lived there, though he had only belonged to his present master about ten years. I asked him if his master allowed him no meat, nor any kind of provisions except bread; to which he replied that they never had any meat except at Christmas, when each hand on the place received about three pounds of pork; that from September, when the sweet potatoes were at the maturity of their growth, they had an allowance of potatoes as long as the crop held out, which was generally until about March; but that for the rest of the year, they had nothing but a peck of corn a week, with such weeds and other vegetables as they could gather from the fields for greens—that their master did not allow them any salt, and that the only means they had of procuring this luxury, was, by working on Sundays for the neigbouring planters, who paid them in money at the rate of fifty cents per day, with which they purchased salt and some other articles of convenience.

This man told me that his master furnished him with two shirts of tow linen, and two pair of trousers, one of woollen and the other of linen cloth, one woollen jacket, and one blanket every year. That he received the woollen clothes at Christmas, and the linen at Easter; and all the other clothes, if he had any, he was obliged to provide for himself by working on Sunday. He said, that for several years past, he had not been able to provide any clothes for himself; as he had a wife with several small children, on an adjoining plantation, whose master gave only one suit of clothes in the year to the mother, and none of any kind to the children, which had compelled him to lay out all his savings in providing clothes for his family, and such little necessaries as were called for by his wife, from time to time. He had not had a shoe on his foot for several years, but in winter made a kind of moccasin for himself of the bark of a tree, which he said was abundant in the swamps, and could be so manufactured as to make good ropes, and tolerable moccasins, sufficient at least, to defend the feet from the frost though not to keep them dry.

The old man whom I have alluded to before, was in the field with the others, though he was not able to keep up his row. He had no clothes on him except the remains of an old shirt, which hung in tatters from his neck and arms; the two young girls had nothing on them but petticoats, made of coarse tow cloth, and the woman who was the mother of the children, wore the remains of a tow linen shift, the front part of which was entirely gone; but a piece of old cotton bagging tied round her loins, served the purposes of an apron. The younger of the two boys was entirely naked.

The man who was foreman of the field, was a person of good sense for the condition of life in which fortune had placed him, and spoke to me freely of his hard lot. I observed that under his shirt, which was very ragged, he wore a piece of fine linen cloth, apparently part of an old shirt, wrapped closely round his back, and confined in front by strings, tied down his breast. I asked him why he wore that piece of gentleman's linen under his shirt, and shall give his reply in his own words as well as I can recollect them, at a distance of near thirty years.

"I have always been a hard working man, and have suffered a great deal from hunger in my time. It is not possible for a man to work hard every day for several months, and get nothing but a peck of corn a week to eat, and not feel hungry. When a man is hungry, you know, (if you have ever been hungry,) he must eat whatever he can get. I have not tasted meat since last Christmas, and we have had to work uncommonly hard this summer. Master has a flock of sheep, that run in the woods, and they come every night to sleep in the lane near the house. Two weeks ago last Saturday, when we quit work at night, I was very hungry, and as we went to the house we passed along the lane where the sheep lay. There were nearly fifty of them, and some were very fat. The temptation was more than I could bear. I caught one of them, cut its head off with the hoe that I carried on my shoulder, and threw it under the fence. About midnight, when all was still about the house, I went out with a knife, took the sheep into the woods, and dressed it by the light of the moon. The carcass I took home, and after cutting it up, placed it in the great kettle over a good fire, intending to boil it and divide it, when cooked, between my fellow-slaves (whom I knew to be as hungry as I was) and myself. Unfortunately for me, master Tom, who had been out amongst his friends that day, had not returned at bed-time; and about one o'clock in the morning, at the time when I had a blazing fire under the kettle, I heard the sound of the feet of a horse coming along the lane. The kitchen walls were open so that the light of my fire could not be concealed, and in a moment I heard the horse blowing at the front of the house. Conscious of my danger, I stripped my shirt from my back, and pushed it into the boiling kettle, so as wholly to conceal the flesh of the sheep. I had scarcely completed this act of precaution, when master Tom burst into the kitchen, and with a terrible oath, asked me what I was doing so late at night, with a great fire in the kitchen. I replied, 'I am going to wash my shirt, master, and am boiling it to get it clean.' 'Washing your shirt at this time of night!' said he, 'I will let you know that you are not to sit up all night and be lazy and good for nothing all day. There shall be no boiling of shirts here on Sunday morning,' and thrusting his cane into the kettle, he raised my shirt out and threw it on the kitchen floor.

"He did not at first observe the mutton, which rose to the surface of the water as soon as the shirt was removed; but, after giving the shirt a kick towards the door, he again turned his face to the fire, and seeing a leg standing several inches out of the pot, he demanded of me what I had in there and where I had got this meat? Finding that I was detected, and that the whole matter must be discovered, I said,—'Master, I am hungry, and am cooking my supper.' 'What is it you have in here?' 'A sheep,' said I, and as the words were uttered, he knocked me down with his cane, and after beating me severely, ordered me to cross my hands until he bound me fast with a rope that hung in the kitchen, and answered the double purpose of a clothes' line, and a cord to tie us with when we were to be whipped. He put out the fire under the kettle, drew me into the yard, tied me fast to the mill-post, and leaving me there for the night, went and called one of the negro boys to put his horse in the stable, and went to his bed. The cord was bound so tightly round my wrists, that before morning, the blood had burst out under my finger nails; but I suppose my master slept soundly for all that, I was afraid to call any one to come and release me from my torment, lest a still more terrible punishment might overtake me.

"I was permitted to remain in this situation until long after sunrise the next morning, which being Sunday, was quiet and still; my fellow-slaves being permitted to take their rest after the severe toil of the past week, and my old master and two young ones having no occasion to rise to call the hands to the field, did not think of interrupting their morning slumbers, to release me from my painful confinement. However, when the sun was risen about an hour, I heard the noise of persons moving in the great house, and soon after, a loud and boisterous conversation, which I well knew portended no good to me. At length they all three came into the yard where I lay, lashed to the post, and approaching me, my old master asked me if I had any accomplices in stealing the sheep. I told them none—that it was entirely my own act—and that none of my fellow-slaves had any hand in it. This was the truth; but if any of my companions had been concerned with me, I should not have betrayed them; for such an act of treachery could not have alleviated the dreadful punishment which I knew awaited me, and would only have involved them in the same misery.

"They called me a thief, loaded me with oaths and imprecations, and each one proposed the punishment which he deemed the most appropriate to the enormity of the crime that I had committed. Master Tom was of opinion, that I should be lashed to the post at the foot of which I lay, and that each of my fellow-slaves should be compelled to give me a dozen lashes in turn, with a roasted and greased hickory *gad,* until I had received, in the whole, two hundred and fifty lashes on my bare back, and that he would stand by, with the whip in his hand, and *compel* them not to spare me; but after a short debate this was given up, as it would probably render me unable to work in the field again for several weeks. My master Ned was in favour of giving me a dozen lashes every morning for a month, with the whip; but my old master said, this would be attended with too much trouble, and besides, it would keep me from my work, at least half an hour every morning, and proposed, in his turn, that I should not be whipped at all, but that the carcass of the sheep should be taken from the kettle in its half-boiled condition, and hung up in the kitchen loft without salt; and that I should be compelled to subsist on this putrid mutton without any other food, until it should be consumed. This suggestion met the approbation of my young masters, and would have been adopted, had not mistress at this moment come into the yard, and hearing the intended punishment, loudly objected to it, because the mutton would, in a day or two, create such an offensive stench, that she and my young mistresses would not be able to remain in the house. My mistress swore dreadfully, and cursed me for an ungrateful sheep thief, who, after all her kindness in giving me soup and warm bread when I was sick last winter, was always stealing every thing I could get hold of. She then said to my master, that such villany ought not to be passed over in a slight manner, and that as crimes, such as this, concerned the whole country, my punishment ought to be public for the purpose of example; and advised him to have me whipped that same afternoon, at five o'clock; first giving notice to the planters of the neighbourhood to come and see the spectacle, and to bring with them their slaves, that they might be witnesses to the consequences of stealing sheep.

"They then returned to the house to breakfast; but as the pain in my hands and arms produced by the ligatures of the cord with which I was bound, was greater than I could bear, I now felt exceedingly sick, and lost all knowledge of my situation. They told me I fainted; and when I recovered my faculties I found myself lying in the shade of the house, with my hands free, and all the white persons in my master's family, standing around me. As soon as I was able to stand, the rope was tied round my neck, and the other end again fastened to the mill post. My mistress said I had only pretended to faint; and master Tom said, I would have something worth fainting for before night. He was faithful to his promise; but, for the present, I was suffered to sit on the grass in the shade of the house.

"As soon as breakfast was over, my two young masters had their horses saddled, and set out to give notice to their friends of what had happened, and to invite them to come and see me punished for the crime I had committed. My mistress gave me no breakfast, and when I begged one of the black boys whom I saw looking at me through the pales, to bring me some water in a gourd to drink, she ordered him to bring it from a puddle in the lane. My mistress has always been very cruel to all her black people.

"I remained in this situation until about eleven o'clock, when one of my young mistresses came to me and gave me a piece of jonny-cake about the size of my hand, perhaps larger than my hand, telling me at the same time, that my fellow-slaves had been permitted to re-boil the mutton that I had left in the kettle, and make their breakfast of it, but that her mother would not allow her to give me any part of it. It was well for them that I had parboiled it with my shirt, and so defiled it, that it was unfit for the table of my master, otherwise, no portion of it would have fallen to the black people—as it was, they had as much meat as they could consume in two days, for which I had to suffer.

"About twelve o'clock, one of my young masters returned, and soon afterwards the other came home. I heard them tell my old master that they had been round to give notice of my offence to the neighbouring planters, and that several of them would attend to see me flogged and would bring with them some of their slaves, who might be able to report to their companions what had been done to me for stealing.

"It was late in the afternoon before any of the gentlemen came; but, before five o'clock, there were more than twenty white people, and at least fifty black ones present, the latter of whom had been compelled, by their masters, to come and see me punished. Amongst others, an overseer from a neighbouring estate attended, and to him was awarded the office of executioner. I was stripped of my shirt, and the waist-band of my trousers was drawn closely round me, below my hips, so as to expose the whole of my back, in its entire length.

"It seems that it had been determined to beat me with thongs of raw cow-hide, for the overseer had two of these in his hands, each about four feet long; but one of the gentlemen present said this might bruise my back so badly, that I could not work for some time; perhaps not for a week or two; and as I could not be spared from the field without great disadvantage to my master's crop, he suggested a different plan, by which, in his opinion, the greatest degree of pain could be inflicted on me, with the least danger of rendering me unable to work. As he was a large planter, and had more than fifty slaves, all were disposed to be guided by his counsels, and my master said he would submit the matter entirely to him as a man of judgment and experience in such cases. He then desired my master to have a dozen pods of red pepper boiled in half a gallon of water, and desired the overseer to lay aside his thongs of raw hide, and put a new cracker of silk, to the lash of his negro whip. Whilst these preparations were being made, each of my thumbs was lashed closely to the end of a stick about three feet long, and a chair being placed beside the mill post, I was compelled to raise my hands and place the stick, to which my thumbs were bound, over the top of the post, which is about eighteen inches square; the chair was then taken from under me, and I was left hanging by the thumbs, with my face towards the post, and my feet about a foot from the ground. My two great toes were then tied together, and drawn down the post as far as my joints could be stretched; the cord was passed round the post two or three times and securely fastened. In this posture I had no power of motion, except in my neck, and could only move that at the expense of beating my face against the side of the post.

"The pepper tea was now brought, and poured into a basin to cool, and the overseer was desired to give me a dozen lashes just above the waist-band; and not to cover a space of more than four inches on my back, from the waist-band upwards. He obeyed the injunction faithfully, but slowly, and each crack of the whip was followed by a sensation as painful as if a red hot iron had been drawn across my back. When the twelve strokes had been given, the operation was suspended, and a black man, one of the slaves present, was compelled to wash the gashes in my skin, with the scalding pepper tea, which was yet so hot that he could not hold his hand in it. This doubly-burning liquid was thrown into my raw and bleeding wounds, and produced a tormenting smart, beyond the description of language. After a delay of ten minutes, by the watch, I received another dozen lashes, on the part of my back which was immediately above the bleeding and burning gashes of the former whipping; and again the biting, stinging, pepper tea was applied to my lacerated and trembling muscles. This operation was continued at regular intervals, until I had received ninety-six lashes, and my back was cut and scalded from end to end. Every stroke of the whip had drawn blood; many of the gashes were three inches long; my back burned as if it had been covered by a coat of hot embers, mixed with living coals; and I felt my flesh quiver like that of animals that have been slaughtered by the butcher and are flayed whilst yet half alive. My face was bruised, and my nose bled profusely, for in the madness of my agony, I had not been able to refrain from beating my head violently against the post.

"Vainly did I beg and implore for mercy. I was kept bound to the post with my whole weight hanging upon my thumbs, an hour and a half, but it appeared to me that I had entered upon eternity, and that my sufferings would never end. At length, however, my feet were unbound, and afterwards my hands; but when released from the cords, I was so far exhausted as not to be able to stand, and my thumbs were stiff and motionless. I was carried into the kitchen, and laid on a blanket, where my mistress came to see me; and after looking at my lacerated back, and telling me that my wounds were only skin deep, said I had come off well, after what I had done, and that I ought to be thankful that it was not worse with me. She then bade me not to groan so loud, nor make so much noise, and left me to myself. I lay in this condition until it was quite dark, by which time the burning of my back had much abated, and was succeeded by an aching soreness, which rendered me unable to turn over, or bend my spine in the slightest manner. My mistress again visited me, and brought with her about half a pound of fat bacon, which she made one of the black women roast before the fire on a fork, until the oil ran freely from it, and then rub it warm over my back. This was repeated until I was greased from the neck to the hips, effectually. An old blanket was then thrown over me, and I was left to pass the night alone. Such was the terror stricken into my fellow-slaves, by the example made of me, that, although they loved and pitied me, not one of them dared to approach me during this night.

"My strength was gone, and I at length fell asleep, from which I did not awake until the horn was blown the next morning, to call the people to the corn crib, to receive their weekly allowance of a peck of corn. I did not rise, nor attempt to join the other people, and shortly afterwards my master entered the kitchen, and in a soft and gentle tone of voice, asked me if I was dead. I answered him that I was not dead, and making some effort, found I was able to get upon my feet. My master had become frightened when he missed me at the corn crib, and being suddenly seized with an apprehension that I was dead, his heart had become softened, not with compassion for my sufferings, but with the fear of losing his best field hand; but when he saw me stand before him erect, and upright, the recollection of the lost sheep revived in his mind, and with it, all his feelings of revenge against the author of its death.

" 'So you are not dead yet, you thieving rascal,' said he; and cursing me with many bitter oaths, ordered me to go along to the crib and get my corn, and go to work with the rest of the hands. I was forced to obey, and taking my basket of corn from the door of the crib, placed it in the kitchen loft, and went to the field with the other people.

"Weak and exhausted as I was, I was compelled to do the work of an able hand, but was not permitted to taste the mutton, which was all given to the others, who were carefully guarded whilst they were eating, lest they should give me some of it."

This man's back was not yet well. Many of the gashes made by the lash were yet sore, and those that were healed had left long white stripes across his body. He had no notion of leaving the service of his tyrannical master, and his spirit was so broken and subdued, that he was ready to suffer and to bear all his hardships; not, indeed, without complaining, but without attempting to resist his oppressors, or to escape from their power. I saw him often whilst I remained at this place, and ventured to tell him once that if I had a master who would abuse me as his had abused him, I would run away. "Where could I run, or in what place could I conceal myself?" said he. "I have known many slaves who ran away, but they were always caught, and treated worse afterwards than they had been before. I have heard that there is a place called Philadelphia, where the black people are all free, but I do not know which way it lies, nor what road I should take to go there; and if I knew the way, how could I hope to get there? would not the patrol be sure to catch me?"

I pitied this unfortunate creature, and was at the same time fearful, that, in a short time, I should be equally the object of pity myself. How well my fears were justified the sequel of my narrative will show.

---

## CHAPTER VIII.

WE had been stationed in the old cotton-gin house, about twenty days, had recovered from the fatigues of our journey, and were greatly improved in our strength and appearance, when our master returned one evening, after an absence of two days, and told us that we must go to Columbia the next day; and must, for this purpose, have our breakfast ready by sunrise. On the following morning he called us at daylight, and we made all despatch in preparing our morning repast, the last that we were to take in our present residence.

As our equipments consisted of the few clothes we had on our persons, and a solitary blanket to each individual, our baggage was easily adjusted, and we were on the road before the sun was up half an hour; and in less than an hour we were in Columbia, drawn up in a long line in the street opposite the courthouse.

The town, which was small and mean looking, was full of people, and I believe that more than a thousand gentlemen came to look at us within the course of this day. We were kept in the street about an hour, and were then taken into the jail-yard and permitted to sit down; but were not shut up in the jail. The court was sitting in Columbia at this time, and either this circumstance, or the intelligence of our arrival in the country, or both, had drawn together a very great crowd of people.

We were supplied with victuals by the jailer, and had a small allowance of salt pork for dinner. We slept in the jail at night, and as none of us had been sold on the day of our arrival in Columbia, and we had not heard any of the persons who came to look at us make proposals to our master for our purchase, I supposed it might be his intention to drive us still farther south before he offered us for sale; but I discovered my error on the second day, which was Tuesday. This day the crowd in town was much greater than it had been on Monday; and, about ten o'clock, our master came into the yard, in company with the jailer, and after looking at us some time, the latter addressed us in a short speech, which continued perhaps five minutes. In this harangue he told us we had come to live in the finest country in the world; that South Carolina was the richest and best part of the United States; and that he was going to sell us to gentlemen who would make us all very happy, and would require us to do no hard work; but only raise cotton and pick it. He then ordered a handsome young lad, about eighteen years of age, to follow him into the street, where we observed a great concourse of persons collected. Here the jailer made another harangue to the multitude, in which he assured them that he was just about to sell the most valuable lot of slaves that had ever been offered in Columbia. That we were all young, in excellent health, of good habits, having been all purchased in Virginia, from the estates of tobacco planters; and that there was not one in the whole lot who had lost the use of a single finger, or was blind of an eye.

He then cried the poor lad for sale, and the first bid he received was two hundred dollars. Others quickly succeeded, and the boy, who was a remarkably handsome youth, was striken off in a few minutes to a young man who appeared not much older than himself, at three hundred and fifty dollars. The purchaser paid down his price to our master on a table in the jail, and the lad, after bidding us farewell, followed his new master with tears running down his cheeks.

He next sold a young girl, about fifteen or sixteen years old, for two hundred and fifty dollars, to a lady who attended the sales in her carriage, and made her bids out of the window. In this manner the sales were continued for about two hours and a half, when they were adjourned until three o'clock. In the afternoon they were again resumed, and kept open until about five o'clock, when they were closed for the day. As my companions were sold, they were taken from amongst us, and we saw them no more.

The next morning, before day, I was awakened from my sleep by the sound of several heavy fires of cannon which were discharged, as it seemed to me, within a few yards of the place where I lay. These were succeeded by fifes and drums, and all the noise with which I had formerly heard the fourth of July ushered in, at the navy-yard in Washington.

Since I had left Maryland I had carefully kept the reckoning of the days of the week; but had not been careful to note the dates of the month; yet as soon as daylight appeared, and the door of our apartment was opened, I inquired and learned, that this was, as I had supposed it to be, the day of universal rejoicing.

I understood that the court did not sit this day, but a great crowd of people gathered, and remained around the jail, all the morning; many of whom were intoxicated, and sang and shouted in honour of free government, and the rights of man. About eleven o'clock, a long table was spread under a row of trees which grew in the street, not far from the jail, and which appeared to me, to be of the kind called in Pennsylvania, the pride of China.[19] At this table, several hundred persons sat down to dinner, soon after noon; and continued to eat, and drink, and sing songs in honour of liberty, for more than two hours. At the end of the dinner, a gentleman rose and stood upon his chair, near one end of the table, and begged the company to hear him for a few minutes. He informed them that he was a candidate for some office—but what office it was I do not recollect—and said, that as it was an acknowledged principle of our free government, that all

men were born free and equal, he presumed it would not be deemed an act of ar-
rogance in him, to call upon them for their votes, at the coming election.

This first speaker was succeeded by another, who addressed his audience
in nearly the same language; and after he had concluded, the company broke up.
I heard a black man that belonged to the jailer, or, who was at least in his service, say that there had been a great meeting that morning in the court house, at
which several gentlemen had made speeches.

When I lived at the navy-yard, the officers sometimes permitted me to go
up town with them, on the fourth of July, and listen to the fine speeches that were
made there, on such occasions.

About five o'clock, the jailer came and stood at the front door of the jail,
and proclaimed, in a very loud voice, that a sale of most valuable slaves would
immediately take place; that he had sold many fine hands yesterday, but they
were only the refuse and most worthless part of the whole lot;—that those who
wished to get great bargains and prime property, had better attend now; as it
was certain that such negroes had never been offered for sale in Columbia
before.

In a few minutes the whole assembly, that had composed the dinner party,
and hundreds of others, were convened around the jail door, and the jailer again
proceeded with his auction. Several of the stoutest men, and handsomest women
in the whole company, had been reserved for this day; and I perceived that the
very best of us, were kept back for the last. We went off at rather better prices
than had been obtained on the former day; and I perceived much eagerness
amongst the bidders, many of whom were not sober. Within less than three
hours, only three of us remained in the jail; and we were ordered to come and
stand at the door, in front of the crier who made a most extravagant eulogium
upon our good qualities, and capacity to perform labour. He said, "These three
fellows are as strong as horses, and as patient as mules; one of them can do as
much work as two common men, and they are perfectly honest. Mr. M'Giffin
says, he was assured by their former masters, that they were never known to
steal, or run away. They must bring good prices gentlemen, or they will not be
sold. Their master is determined, that if they do not bring six hundred dollars,
he will not sell them, but will take them to Georgia next summer, and sell them
to some of the new settlers. These boys can do any thing. This one," referring to
me, "can cut five cords of wood in a day, and put it up. He is a rough carpenter,
and a first rate field hand." "This one," laying his hand on the shoulder of one
of my companions, "is a blacksmith; and can lay a ploughshare; put new steel
upon an axe; or mend a broken chain." The other, he recommended as a good
shoemaker; and well acquainted with the process of tanning leather.

We were all nearly of the same age; and very stout, healthy, robust young
men, in full possession of our corporal powers; and if we had been shut up in a
room, with ten of the strongest of those who had assembled to purchase us, and
our liberty had depended on tying them fast to each other, I have no doubt that
we should have been free, if ropes had been provided for us.

After a few minutes of hesitancy amongst the purchasers, and a closer examination of our persons than had been made in the jail-yard, an elderly gentle-

man said he would take the carpenter; and the blacksmith, and shoemaker, were immediately taken by others, at the required price.

It was now sundown. The heat of the day had been very oppressive, and I was glad to be released from the confined air of the jail; and the hot atmosphere, in which so many hundreds were breathing. My new master asked me my name, and ordered me to follow him.

We proceeded to a tavern, where a great number of persons were assembled, at a short distance from the jail. My master entered the house, and joined in the conversation of the party, in which the utmost hilarity prevailed. They were drinking toasts in honour of liberty and independence, over glasses of toddy; a liquor composed of a mixture of rum, water, sugar, and nutmeg.

It was ten o'clock at night before my master and his companions had finished their toasts and toddy; and all this time, I had been standing before the door, or sitting on a log of wood, that lay in front of the house. At one time, I took a seat on a bench, at the side of the house; but was soon driven from this position by a gentleman, in military clothes, with a large gilt epaulet on each shoulder, and a profusion of glittering buttons on his coat; who passing near me in the dark, and happening to cast his eye on me, demanded of me, in an imperious tone, how I dared to sit on that seat. I told him I was a stranger, and did not know that it was wrong to sit there. He then ordered me with an oath, to begone from there; and said, if he caught me on that bench again, he would cut my head off. "Did you not see white people sit upon that bench, you saucy rascal?" said he. I assured him I had not seen any white gentleman sit on the bench, as it was near night when I came to the house; that I had not intended to be saucy, or misbehave myself; and that I hoped he would not be angry with me, as my master had left me at the door, and had not told me where I was to sit.

I remained on the log until the termination of the festival, in honour of liberty and equality; when my master came to the door, and observed in my hearing, to some of his friends, that they had celebrated the day in a handsome manner.

No person, except the military gentleman, had spoken to me, since I came to the house, in the evening with my master, who seemed to have forgotten me; for he remained at the door, warmly engaged in conversation, on various political subjects, a full hour after he rose from the toast party. At length, however, I heard him say—"I bought a negro this evening,—I wonder where he is." Rising immediately from the log on which I had been so long seated, I presented myself before him, and said, "Here, master." He then ordered me to go to the kitchen of the inn, and go to sleep; but said nothing to me about supper. I retired to the kitchen, where I found a large number of servants, who belonged to the house; and amongst them two young girls, who had been purchased by a gentleman, who lived near Augusta; and who, they told me, intended to set out for his plantation the next morning, and take them with him.

These girls had been sold out of our company on the first day; and had been living in the tavern kitchen since that time. They appeared quite contented, and evinced no repugnance to setting out the next morning for their master's plantation. They were of that order of people who never look beyond the present day;

and so long as they had plenty of victuals, in this kitchen, they did not trouble themselves with reflections upon the cotton field.

One of the servants gave me some cold meat, and a piece of wheaten bread; which was the first I had tasted since I left Maryland, and indeed, it was the last that I tasted, until I reached Maryland again.

I here met with a man, who was born and brought up in the Northern Neck of Virginia, on the banks of the Potomac, and within a few miles of my native place. We soon formed an acquaintance; and sat up nearly all night. He was the chief hostler in the stable of this tavern; and told me, that he had often thought of attempting to escape, and return to Virginia. He said he had little doubt of being able to reach the Potomac; but having no knowledge of the country, beyond that river, he was afraid that he should not be able to make his way to Philadelphia; which he regarded as the only place in which he could be safe, from the pursuit of his master. I was myself then young, and my knowledge of the country, north of Baltimore, was very vague and undefined. I, however, told him, that I had heard, that if a black man could reach any part of Pennsylvania, he would be beyond the reach of his pursuers. He said he could not justly complain of want of food; but the services required of him were so unreasonable, and the punishment frequently inflicted upon him, so severe, that he was determined to set out for the north, as soon as the corn was so far ripe, as to be fit to be roasted. He felt confident, that by lying in the woods, and unfrequented places all day, and travelling only by night, he could escape the vigilance of all pursuit; and gain the Northern Neck, before the corn would be gathered from the fields. He had no fear of wanting food, as he could live well on roasting ears, as long as the corn was in the milk; and afterwards, on parched corn, as long the grain remained in the field. I advised him, as well as I could, as to the best means of reaching the state of Pennsylvania; but was not able to give him any very definite instructions.

This man possessed a very sound understanding; and having been five years in Carolina, was well acquainted with the country. He gave me such an account of the sufferings of the slaves, on the cotton and indigo plantations—of whom I now regarded myself as one—that I was unable to sleep any this night. From the resolute manner in which he spoke of his intended elopement, and the regularity with which he had connected the various combinations of the enterprise, I have no doubt that he undertook that which he intended to perform. Whether he was successful or not, in the enterprise, I cannot say; as I never saw him, nor heard of him, after the next morning.

This man certainly communicated to me the outlines of the plan, which I afterwards put in execution; and by which I gained my liberty, at the expense of sufferings, which none can appreciate, except those who have borne all that the stoutest human constitution can bear, of cold and hunger, toil and pain. The conversation of this slave, aroused in my breast so many recollections of the past, and fears of the future, that I did not lie down; but sat on an old chair until daylight.

From the people of the kitchen I again received some cold victuals for my breakfast, but I did not see my master until about nine o'clock; the toddy of the last evening, causing him to sleep late this morning. At length, a female slave gave me notice that my master wished to see me in the dining room, whither I repaired, without a moment's delay. When I entered the room, he was sitting near the window, smoking a pipe, with a very long handle—I believe more than two feet in length.

He asked no questions, but addressing me by the title of "boy," ordered me to go with the hostler of the inn, and get his horse and chaise ready. As soon as this order could be executed, I informed him that his chaise was at the door, and we immediately commenced our journey to the plantation of my master, which, he told me, lay at the distance of twenty miles from Columbia. He said I must keep up with him; and, as he drove at the rate of five or six miles an hour, I was obliged to run, nearly half the time; but I was then young, and could easily travel fifty or sixty miles in a day. It was with great anxiety that I looked for the place, which was in future to be my home; but this did not prevent me from making such observations upon the state of the country through which we travelled, as the rapidity of our march permitted.

This whole region had originally been one vast wilderness of pine forest, except the low grounds and river bottoms, here called swamps; in which all the varieties of trees, shrubs, vines, and plants, peculiar to such places, in southern latitudes, vegetated in unrestrained luxuriance. Nor is pine the only timber that grows on the uplands, in this part of Carolina; although it is the predominant tree, and in some places, prevails to the exclusion of every other—oak, hickory, sassafras, and many others are found.

Here, also, I first observed groves of the most beautiful of all the trees of the wood—the great Southern Magnolia, or Green Bay. No adequate conception can be formed of the appearance, or the fragrance, of this most magnificent tree, by any one who has not seen it, or scented the air when tainted by the perfume of its flowers. It rises in a right line to the height of seventy or eighty feet; the stem is of a delicate taper form, and casts off numerous branches, in nearly right angles with itself; the extremities of which, decline gently towards the ground, and become shorter and shorter in the ascent, until at the apex of the tree, they are scarcely a foot in length; whilst below they are many times found twenty feet long. The immense cones formed by these trees are as perfect as those diminutive forms which nature exhibits in the bur of the pine tree. The leaf of the magnolia is smooth, of an oblong taper form, about six inches in length, and half as broad. Its colour is the deepest and purest green. The foliage of the Bay tree is as impervious as a brick wall to the rays of the sun, and its refreshing coolness, in the heat of a summer day, affords one of the greatest luxuries of a cotton plantation. It blooms in May, and bears great numbers of broad, expanded white flowers, the odour of which is exceedingly grateful, and so abundant, that I have no doubt, that a grove of these trees, in full bloom, may be smelled at a distance of fifteen or twenty miles. I have heard it asserted in the south, that their scent has been perceived by persons fifty or sixty miles from them.

This tree is one of nature's most splendid, and in the climate where she has placed it, one of her most agreeable productions. It is peculiar to the southern temperate latitudes, and cannot bear the rigours of a northern winter; though I have heard that groves of the Bay are found on Fishing Creek, in Western

Virginia, not far from Wheeling, and near the Ohio river. Could this tree be nat-
uralized in Pennsylvania, it would form an ornament to her towns, cities, and
country seats, at once the most tasteful and the most delicious. A forest of these
trees, in the month of May, resembles a wood, enveloped in an untimely fall of
snow at midsummer, glowing in the rays of a morning sun.

We passed this day through cotton fields and pine woods, alternately; but
the scene was sometimes enlivened by the appearance of lots of corn, and sweet
potatoes, which, I observed, were generally planted near the houses. I afterwards
learned that this custom of planting the corn and potatoes near the house of the
planter, is general over all Carolina. The object is, to prevent the slaves from
stealing; and thus procuring more food, than, by the laws of the plantation, they
are entitled to.

In passing through a lane, I this day saw a field, which appeared to me to
contain about fifty acres, in which people were at work with hoes, amongst a
sort of plants that I had never seen before. I asked my master what this was,
and he told me it was indigo. I shall have occasion to say more of this plant
hereafter.

We at length arrived at the residence of my master, who descended from
his chaise, and leaving me in charge of the horse at the gate, proceeded to the
house, across a long court yard. In a few minutes two young ladies, and a young
gentleman, came out of the house, and walked to the gate, near which I was with
the horse. One of the ladies said, they had come to look at me, and see what kind
of a boy her pa had brought home with him. The other one said I was a very
smart looking boy; and this compliment flattered me greatly; they being the first
kind words that had been addressed to me since I left Maryland. The young gentleman asked me if I could run fast, and if I had ever picked cotton. His manner
did not impress me so much in his favour, as the address of his sister had done
for her. These three young persons were the son and daughters of my master. After looking at me a short time, my young master, (for so I must now call him,)
ordered me to take the harness from the horse, give him water at a well which
was near, and come into the kitchen, where some boiled rice was given me for
my dinner.

I was not required to go to work this first day of my abode in my new residence; but after I had eaten my rice, my young master told me I might rest myself or walk out and see the plantation, but that I must be ready to go with the
overseer the next morning.

---

## CHAPTER IX.

By the laws of the United States I am still a slave; and though I am now growing old, I might even yet be deemed of sufficient value to be worth pursuing as
far as my present residence, if those to whom the law gives the right of dominion over my person and life, knew where to find me. For these reasons I have
been advised, by those whom I believe to be my friends, not to disclose the true

names of any of those families in which I was a slave, in Carolina or Georgia, lest this narrative should meet their eyes, and in some way lead them to a discovery of my retreat.

I was now the slave of one of the most wealthy planters in Carolina, who planted cotton, rice, indigo, corn, and potatoes; and was the master of two hundred and sixty slaves.[20]

The description of one great cotton plantation will give a correct idea of all others; and I shall here present an outline of that of my master.

He lived about two miles from Caugaree river; which bordered his estate on one side, and in the swamps of which were his rice fields. The country hereabout is very flat; the banks of the river are low; and in wet seasons large tracts of country are flooded by the superabundant water of the river. There are no springs; and the only means of procuring water, on the plantations, is from wells, which must be sunk in general about twenty feet deep, before a constant supply of water can be obtained. My master had two of these wells on his plantation; one at the mansion house, and one at the quarter.

My master's house was of brick, (brick houses are by no means common amongst the planters, whose residences are generally built of frame work, weather boarded with pine boards, and covered with shingles of the white cedar or juniper cypress,) and contained two large parlours, and a spacious hall or entry on the ground door. The main building was two stories high; and attached to this was a smaller building, one story and a half high, with a large room, where the family generally took breakfast; with a kitchen at the farther extremity from the main building.

There was a spacious garden behind the house, containing, I believe, about five acres, well cultivated, and handsomely laid out. In this garden grew a great variety of vegetables; some of which I have never seen in the market of Philadelphia. It contained a profusion of flowers, three different shrubberies, a vast number of ornamental and small fruit trees, and several small hot houses, with glass roofs. There was a head gardener, who did nothing but attend to this garden through the year; and during the summer he generally had two men and two boys to assist him. In the months of April and May this garden was one of the sweetest and most pleasant places that I ever was in. At one end of the main building was a small house, called the library, in which my master kept his books and papers, and where he spent much of his time.

At some distance from the mansion was a pigeon house, and near the kitchen was a large wooden building, called the kitchen quarter, in which the house servants slept; and where they generally took their meals. Here, also, the washing of the family was done; and all the rough or unpleasant work of the kitchen department,—such as cleaning and salting fish, putting up pork, &c. was assigned to this place.

There was no barn on this plantation, according to the acceptation of the word *barn* in Pennsylvania; but there was a wooden building, about forty feet long, called the coach-house; in one end of which the family carriage, and the chaise in which my master rode, were kept. Under the same roof was a stable, sufficiently capacious to contain ten or twelve horses. In one end of the building the corn intended for the horses was kept; and the whole of the loft, or upper story, was occupied by the fodder, or blades and tops of the corn.

About a quarter of a mile from the dwelling-house were the huts or cabins of the plantation slaves, or field hands, standing in rows, much like the Indian villages which I have seen in the country of the Cherokees. These cabins were thirty-eight in number, generally about fifteen or sixteen feet square, built of hewn logs, covered with shingles, and provided with floors of pine boards. These houses were all dry and comfortable, and were provided with chimnies, so that the people when in them, were well sheltered from the inclemencies of the weather. In this practice of keeping their slaves well sheltered at night, the south-ern planters are pretty uniform; for they know that upon this circumstance, more than any other in that climate, depends the health of the slave, and consequently his value.

In these thirty-eight cabins were lodged two hundred and fifty people of all ages, sexes, and sizes. Ten or twelve were generally employed in the garden, and about the house.

At a distance of about one hundred yards from the lines of cabins stood the house of the overseer; a small two-story log building, with a yard and garden at-tached to it of proportionate dimensions. This small house was the abode of a despot, more absolute, and more cruel than were any of those we read of in the Bible, who so grievously oppressed the children of Israel. In one corner of the overseer's garden stood the corn crib, also a log building, in which was stored up the corn, constituting the yearly provisions of the coloured people. In another corner of the same garden was a large vault, covered with sods, very like some ice-houses that I have seen. This was the potato-house, and in it were deposited the sweet potatoes, also intended to supply the people.

At a short distance beyond the garden of the overseer stood a large build-ing, constituting the principal feature in the landscape of every great cotton plan-tation. This was the house containing the cotton-gin, and the sheds to contain the cotton, when brought from the field in the seed; and also the bales, after be-ing pressed and prepared for market.

As I shall be obliged to make frequent references to the cotton-gin, it may perhaps be well to describe it. Formerly there was no way of separating the cot-ton from the seed, but by pulling it off with the fingers—a very tedious and trou-blesome process—but a person from the north, by the name of Whitney,[21] at length discovered the gin, which is a very simple though very powerful machine. It is composed of a wooden cylinder, about six or eight feet in length, surrounded at very short intervals, with small circular saws, in such a manner that as the cylinder is turned rapidly round, by a leather strap on the end, similar to a turner's lathe, the teeth of the saws, in turning over, continually cut downwards in front of the cylinder, which is placed close to a long hopper, extending the whole length of the cylinder, and so close to it that the seeds of the cotton can-not pass between them. This cylinder revolves, with almost inconceivable rapid-ity, and great caution is necessary in working with the gin, not to touch the saws. One end of the cylinder and hopper being slightly elevated, the seeds as they are stripped of the wool, are gradually but certainly moved toward the lower end, where they drop down into a heap, after being as perfectly divested of the cotton as they could be by the most careful picking with the fingers.

The rapid evolutions of the cylinder are procured by the aid of cogs and wheels, similar to those used in small grist mills.

It is necessary to be very careful in working about a cotton-gin; more especially in removing the seeds from before the saws; for if they do but touch the hand the injury is very great. I knew a black man who had all the sinews of the inner part of his right hand torn out—some of them measuring more than a foot in length—and the flesh of his palm cut into tatters, by carelessly putting his hand too near the saws, when they were in motion, for the idle purpose of feeling the strength of the current of air created by the motions of the cylinder. A good gin will clean several thousand pounds of cotton, in the seed, in a day. To work the gin two horses are necessary; though one is often compelled to perform the labour.

There was no smoke-house, nor any other place, for curing or preserving meat, attached to the quarter; and whilst I was on this plantation no pork was ever salted for the use of the slaves.

After remaining in the kitchen some time, I went into the garden, and remained with the gardener, assisting him to work until after sundown; when my old master came to the gate, and called one of the garden boys to him. The boy soon returned, and told me I must go with him to the quarter, as his master had told him to take me to the overseer. When we arrived at the overseer's house he had not yet returned from the field; but in a few minutes we saw him coming at some distance through a cotton field, followed by a great number of black people. As he approached us, the boy that was with me handed him a small piece of paper, which he carried in his hand, and without saying a word, ran back toward the house, leaving me to become acquainted with the overseer in the best way I could. But I found this to be no difficult task; for he had no sooner glanced his eye over the piece of paper, than, turning to me, he asked me my name; and calling to a middle-aged man who was passing us at some distance, told him he must take me to live with him, and that my supper should be sent to me from his own house.

I followed my new friend to his cabin, which I found to be the habitation of himself, his wife, and five children. The only furniture in this cabin, consisted of a few blocks of wood for seats; a short bench, made of a pine board, which served as a table; and a small bed in one corner composed of a mat, made of common rushes, spread upon some corn husks, pulled and split into fine pieces, and kept together by a narrow slip of wood, confined to the floor by wooden pins. There was a common iron pot, standing beside the chimney; and several wooden spoons and dishes hung against the wall. Several blankets also hung against the wall upon wooden pins. An old box, made of pine boards, without either lock or hinges, occupied one corner.

At the time I entered this humble abode the mistress was not at home. She had not yet returned from the field; having been sent, as the husband informed me, with some other people late in the evening, to do some work in a field about two miles distant. I found a child, about a year old, lying on the mat-bed, and a little girl about four years old sitting beside it.

These children were entirely naked, and when we came to the door, the elder rose from its place and ran to its father, and clasping him round one of his knees, said, "Now we shall get good supper." The father laid his hand upon the head of his naked child, and stood silently looking in its face—which was turned upwards toward his own for a moment—and then turning to me, said, "Did you leave any children at home?" The scene before me—the question propounded—and the manner of this poor man and his child, caused my heart to swell until my breast seemed too small to contain it. My soul fled back upon the wings of fancy to my wife's lowly dwelling in Maryland; where I had been so often met on a Saturday evening, when I paid them my weekly visit, by my own little ones, who clung to my knees for protection and support, even as the poor little wretch now before me, seized upon the weary limb of its hapless and destitute father, hoping that, naked as he was, (for he too was naked, save only the tattered remains of a pair of old trousers,) he would bring with his return at evening its customary scanty supper. I was unable to reply; but stood motionless, leaning against the walls of the cabin. My children seemed to flit by the door in the dusky twilight; and the twittering of a swallow, which that moment fluttered over my head, sounded in my ear as the infantile tittering of my own little boy; but on a moment's reflection I knew that we were separated without the hope of ever again meeting; that they no more heard the welcome tread of my feet, and could never again receive the little gifts with which, poor as I was, I was accustomed to present them. I was far from the place of my nativity, in a land of strangers, with no one to care for me beyond the care that a master bestows upon his ox; with all my future life, one long, waste, barren desert, of cheerless, hopeless, lifeless slavery; to be varied only by the pangs of hunger and the stings of the lash.

My revery was at length broken by the appearance of the mother of the family, with her three eldest children. The mother wore an old ragged shift; but the children, the eldest of whom appeared to be about twelve, and the youngest six years old, were quite naked. When she came in, the husband told her that the overseer had sent me to live with them; and she and her oldest child, who was a boy, immediately set about preparing their supper, by boiling some of the leaves of the weed called lamb's-quarter, in the pot. This, together with some cakes of cold corn bread, formed their supper. My supper was brought to me from the house of the overseer by a small girl, his daughter. It was about half a pound of bread, cut from a loaf made of corn meal. My companions gave me a part of their boiled greens, and we all sat down together to my first meal in my new habitation.

I had no other bed than the blanket which I had brought with me from Maryland; and I went to sleep in the loft of the cabin which was assigned to me as my sleeping room; and in which I continued to lodge as long as I remained on this plantation.

The next morning I was waked, at the break of day, by the sound of a horn, which was blown very loudly. Perceiving that it was growing light, I came down, and went out immediately in front of the house of the overseer, who was standing near his own gate, blowing the horn. In a few minutes the whole of the working people, from all the cabins were assembled; and as it was now light enough for me distinctly to see such objects as were about me, I at once perceived the nature of the servitude to which I was, in future, to be subject.

As I have before stated, there were altogether on this plantation, two hundred and sixty slaves; but the number was seldom stationary for a single week. Births were numerous and frequent, and deaths were not uncommon. When I joined them I believe we counted in all two hundred and sixty-three; but of these only one hundred and seventy went to the field to work. The others were children, too small to be of any service as labourers; old and blind persons, or incurably diseased. Ten or twelve were kept about the mansion-house and garden, chosen from the most handsome and sprightly of the gang.

I think about one hundred and sixty-eight assembled this morning, at the sound of the horn—two or three being sick, sent word to the overseer that they could not come.

The overseer wrote something on a piece of paper, and gave it to his little son. This I was told was a note to be sent to our master, to inform him that some of the hands were sick—it not being any part of the duty of the overseer to attend to a sick negro.

The overseer then led off to the field, with his horn in one hand and his whip in the other; we following—men, women, and children, promiscuously—and a wretched looking troop we were. There was not an entire garment amongst us.

More than half of the gang were entirely naked. Several young girls, who had arrived at puberty, wearing only the livery with which nature had ornamented them, and a great number of lads, of an equal or superior age, appeared in the same costume. There was neither bonnet, cap, nor head dress of any kind amongst us, except the old straw hat that I wore; and which my wife had made for me in Maryland. This I soon laid aside to avoid the appearance of singularity; and, as owing to the severe treatment I had endured whilst travelling in chains, and being compelled to sleep on the naked floor, without undressing myself, my clothes were quite worn out, I did not make a much better figure than my companions; though still I preserved the semblance of clothing so far, that it could be seen that my shirt and trousers had once been distinct and separate garments. Not one of the others had on even the remains of two pieces of apparel. Some of the men had old shirts, and some ragged trousers, but no one wore both. Amongst the women, several wore petticoats, and many had shifts. Not one of the whole number wore both of these vestments.

We walked nearly a mile through one vast cotton field, before we arrived at the place of our intended day's labour. At last the overseer stopped at the side of the field, and calling to several of the men by name, ordered them to call their companies and turn into their rows. The work we had to do today was to hoe and weed cotton, for the last time; and the men whose names had been called, and who were, I believe, eleven in number, were designated as captains, each of whom had under his command a certain number of the other hands. The captain was the foreman of his company, and those under his command had to keep up with him. Each of the men and women had to take one row; and two, and in some cases where they were very small, three of the children had one. The first captain, whose name was Simon, took the first row,—and the other captains were compelled to keep up with him. By this means the overseer had nothing to do but to keep Simon hard at work, and he was certain that all the others must work equally hard.

Simon was a stout, strong man, apparently about thirty-five years of age; and for some reason unknown to me, I was ordered to take the row next to his. The overseer with his whip in his hand walked about the field after us, to see that our work was well done. As we worked with hoes, I had no difficulty in learning how the work was to be performed.

The fields of cotton at this season of the year are very beautiful. The plants, amongst which we worked this day, were about three feet high, and in full bloom, with branches so numerous that they nearly covered the whole ground— leaving scarcely space enough between them to permit us to move about, and work with our hoes.

About seven o'clock in the morning the overseer sounded his horn; and we all repaired to the shade of some perscimmon trees, which grew in a corner of the field, to get our breakfast. I here saw a cart drawn by a yoke of oxen, driven by an old black man, nearly blind. The cart contained three barrels, filled with water, and several large baskets' full of corn bread, that had been baked in the ashes. The water was for us to drink, and the bread was our breakfast. The little son of the overseer was also in the cart, and had brought with him the breakfast of his father, in a small wooden bucket.

The overseer had bread, butter, cold ham, and coffee for his breakfast. Ours was composed of a corn cake, weighing about three quarters of a pound, to each person, with as much water as was desired. I at first supposed that this bread was dealt out to the people as their allowance; but on further inquiry I found this not to be the case. Simon, by whose side I was now at work, and who seemed much pleased with my agility and diligence in my duty, told me that here, as well as every where in this country, each person received a peck of corn at the crib door, every Sunday evening, and that in ordinary times, every one had to grind this corn and bake it, for him or herself, making such use of it as the owner thought proper; but that for some time past, the overseer, for the purpose of saving the time which had been lost in baking the bread, had made it the duty of an old woman, who was not capable of doing much work in the field, to stay at the quarter, and bake the bread of the whole gang. When baked, it was brought to the field in a cart, as I saw, and dealt out in loaves.

They still had to grind their own corn, after night; and as there were only three hand-mills on the plantation, he said they experienced much difficulty in converting their corn into meal. We worked in this field all day; and at the end of every hour, or hour and a quarter, we had permission to go to the cart, which was moved about the field, so as to be near us, and get water.

Our dinner was the same, in all respects, as our breakfast, except that, in addition to the bread, we had a little salt, and a radish for each person. We were not allowed to rest at either breakfast or dinner, longer than while we were eating; and we worked in the evening as long as we could distinguish the weeds from the cotton plants.

Simon informed me, that formerly, when they baked their own bread, they had left their work soon after sundown, to go home and bake for the next day, but the overseer had adopted the new policy for the purpose of keeping them at work until dark.

When we could no longer see to work, the horn was again sounded, and we returned home. I had now lived through one of the days—a succession of which make up the life of a slave—on a cotton plantation.

As we went out in the morning, I observed several women, who carried their young children in their arms to the field. These mothers laid their children at the side of the fence, or under the shade of the cotton plants, whilst they were at work; and when the rest of us went to get water, they would go to give suck to their children, requesting some one to bring them water in gourds, which they were careful to carry to the field with them. One young woman did not, like the others, leave her child at the end of the row, but had contrived a sort of rude knapsack, made of a piece of coarse linen cloth, in which she fastened her child, which was very young, upon her back; and in this way carried it all day, and performed her task at the hoe with the other people.

I pitied this woman; and as we were going home at night, I came near her, and spoke to her. Perceiving as soon as she spoke that she had not been brought up amongst the slaves of this plantation—for her language was different from theirs—I asked her why she did not do as the other women did, and leave her child at the end of the row in the shade. "Indeed," said she, "I cannot leave my child in the weeds amongst the snakes. What would be my feelings if I should leave it there, and a scorpion were to bite it? Besides, my child cries so piteously, when I leave it alone in the field, that I cannot bear to hear it. Poor thing, I wish we were both in the grave, where all sorrow is forgotten."

I asked this woman, who did not appear to be more than twenty years old, how long she had been here, and where she came from. "I have been here," said she, "almost two years, and came from the Eastern Shore. I once lived as well as any lady in Maryland. I was born a slave, in the family of a gentleman whose name was Le Compt. My master was a man of property; lived on his estate, and entertained much company. My mistress, who was very kind to me, made me her nurse, when I was about ten years old, and put me to live with her own children. I grew up amongst her daughters; not as their equal and companion, but as a favoured and indulged servant. I was always well dressed, and received a portion of all the delicacies of their table. I wanted nothing, and had not the trouble of providing even for myself. I believe there was not a happier being in the world than I was. At present none can be more wretched.

"When I was yet a child, my master had given me to his oldest daughter, who was about one year older than I was. To her, I had always looked as my future mistress; and expected that whenever she became a wife, I should follow her person, and cease to be a member of the family of her father. When I was almost seventeen, my young mistress married a gentleman of the Eastern Shore of Virginia, who had been addressing her, more than a year.

"Soon after the wedding was over, my new master removed his wife to his own residence; and took me and a black boy of my own age, that the lady's father had given her, with him. He had caused it to be reported in Maryland, that he was very wealthy; and was the owner of a plantation, with a large stock of slaves and other property. It was supposed at the time of the marriage, that my young mistress was making a very good match, and all her friends were pleased with it. When her lover came to visit her, he always rode in a handsome gig, accompanied by a black man on horseback, as his servant. This man told us in the kitchen, that his master was one of the most fashionable men in Virginia; was a man of large fortune, and that all the young ladies in the county he lived in, had their eyes upon him. These stories I repeated carefully to my young mistress; and added every persuasion that I could think of, to induce her to accept her lover, as her husband. My feelings had become deeply interested in the issue of this matter; for whilst the master was striving to win the heart of my young mistress, the servant had already conquered mine.

"It was more than a hundred miles from the residence of my old master, to that of my young one; and when we arrived at the latter place my mistress and I soon found, that we had been equally credulous, and were equally deceived. We were taken to an old dilapidated mansion, which was quite in keeping with every thing on the estate to which it was attached. The house was almost without furniture; and there were no servants in it, except myself and my companion. The black man who had so effectually practiced upon me, belonged to one of my new master's companions,—and had a wife and three children in the neighborhood.

"My mistress, soon discovered that her husband's companions were gamblers and horse racers; who frequently convened at her house, to concert or mature some scheme; the object of which was to cheat some one.

"My old master was a member of the church, and was very scrupulous in the observance of his moral duties. His precepts had been deeply implanted in the mind of my young mistress; and the society of these sportsmen, (as the friends of my young master denominated themselves,) became so revolting to her feelings, that after she had been married nearly a year, and had exhausted all her patience, and all her fortitude, in endeavouring to reclaim her husband from the vile associations and pursuits, by which his time and his affections were engaged, she determined at last to return to her father, for a time, and to take me with her, for the purpose of ascertaining whether this would not bring him to reflect upon the wrong he had done her, as well as himself.

"She communicated to me her designs, and we were waiting for an opportunity of carrying them into effect, when one evening, near sundown, my master came to me in the kitchen; and told me he wished me to go to the house of a gentleman who lived about a mile distant, and deliver a letter for him; without letting my mistress know any thing of the matter, I immediately set out, expecting to return in half an hour. As I left the house I saw my mistress in the garden; and I never saw her again.

"Between the house of my master, and that to which he had sent me, was a grove of young pine trees, that had grown up in a field, that had formerly been cultivated; but which had been neglected, on account of its poverty, for many years. Through this thicket, the path which I had to travel led; and when near the middle of the wood, I saw a white man step into the path, only a few yards before me, with a rope in his hand. Sometime before this, my mistress had told me, that she wished to get me back to her father's house in Maryland, because she was afraid that my master would sell me to the negro buyers; and the moment I saw the man with the rope, in my path, the words of my mistress were recollected.

"I screamed, and turned to fly towards home; but at the first step was met by the coloured man, who had attended my master, as his servant, when he visited Maryland, at the time he was courting my mistress—and who had made so deep an impression on my heart. This was the first time I had seen him, since I came to live in Virginia; and base as I knew he must be, from his former conduct to me, yet at sight of him, my former affection for a moment revived, and I rushed into his arms which were extended towards me, hoping that he would save me from the danger I so much dreaded from behind. He saw that I was frightened, and had fled to him for protection, and only said, 'Come with me.' I followed him, more by instinct than by reason, and holding to his arm, ran as fast as I could—knew not whither. I did not observe whether we were on the path or not. I do not know how far we had run, when he stopped, and said—'We must remain here for some time.'

"In a few minutes the white man whom I had seen in the path, came up with us, and seizing me by the hands, he and my pretended protector bound them together, at my back, and to suppress my cries, tied a large handkerchief round my head, and over my mouth. It was now becoming dark, and they hurried out of the wood, and across the fields, to a small creek, the water of which fell into the Chesapeake Bay. Here was a boat; and another white man in it. They forced me on board; and the white men taking the oars whilst the black managed the rudder, we were quickly out in the bay, and in less than an hour, I was on board a small schooner, lying at anchor; where I found eleven others, who like myself, had been dragged from their homes and their friends, to be sold to the southern traders.

"I have no doubt, that my master had sold me without the knowledge of my mistress; and that he endeavoured to persuade her, that I had run away: perhaps he was successful in this endeavour.

"I heard no more of my mistress, for whom I was very sorry, for I knew she would be greatly distressed at losing me.

"The vessel remained at anchor where we found her that night, and the next day until evening, when she made sail, and beat up the bay all night against a head wind. When she approached the western shore, she hoisted a red handkerchief at her mast head, and a boat came off from the land, large enough to carry us all, and we were removed to a house on the bank of York river, where I found about thirty men and women, all imprisoned in the cellar of a small tavern. The men were in irons, but the women were not bound with any thing. The cords and handkerchief had been taken from me, whilst on board the vessel. We remained at York river more than a week; and whilst there, twenty-five or thirty persons were brought in, and shut up with us.

"When we commenced our journey for the south, we were about sixty in number. The men were chained together, but the women were all left quite at liberty. At the end of three weeks, we reached Savannah river, opposite the town of Augusta, where we were sold out by our owner. Our present master was there, and purchased me and another woman who has been at work in the field to-day.

"Soon after I was brought home, the overseer compelled me to be married to a man I did not like. He is a native of Africa, and still retains the manner and religion of his country. He has not been with us to day, as he is sick, and under the care of the doctor. I must hasten home to get my supper, and go to rest; and glad I should be, if I were never to rise again.

"I have several times been whipped unmercifully, because I was not strong enough to do as much work with the hoe, as the other women, who have lived all their lives on this plantation, and have been accustomed from their infancy to work in the field.

"For a long time after I was brought here, I thought it would be impossible for me to live, on the coarse and scanty food, with which we are supplied. When I contrast my former happiness with my present misery, I pray for death to deliver me from my sufferings."

I was deeply affected by the narrative of this woman, and as we had loitered on our way, it was already dark, whilst we were at some distance from the quarter; but the sound of the overseer's horn, here interrupted our conversation—at hearing which, she exclaimed, "We are too late, let us run, or we shall be whipped;" and setting off as fast as she could carry her child, she left me alone. A moment's reflection, however, convinced me that I too had better quicken my pace—I quickly passed the woman, encumbered with her infant, and arrived in the crowd of the people, some time, perhaps a minute, before her.

---

## CHAPTER X.

At the time I joined the company, the overseer was calling over the names of the whole, from a little book; and the first name that I heard was that of my companion whom I had just left, which was Lydia—called by him Lyd. As she did not answer, I said, "Master, Lydia, the woman that carries the baby on her back, will be here in a minute—I left her just behind." The overseer took no notice of what I said, but went on with his roll-call.

As the people answered to their names, they passed off to the cabins, except three—two women and a man; who, when their names were called, were ordered to go into the yard, in front of the overseer's house. My name was the last on the list; and when it was called I was ordered into the yard with the three others. Just as we had entered, Lydia came up out of breath, with the child in her arms; and following us into the yard, dropped on her knees before the overseer, and begged him to forgive her. "Where have you been?" said he. Poor Lydia now burst into tears, and said, "I only stopped to talk awhile to this man," pointing to me; "but, indeed, master overseer, I will never do so again." "Lie down," was his reply. Lydia immediately fell prostrate upon the ground; and in this position he compelled her to remove her old tow linen shift, the only garment she wore, so as to expose her hips, when he gave her ten lashes, with his long whip, every touch of which brought blood, and a shriek from the sufferer. He then ordered her to go and get her supper, with an injunction never to stay behind again. The other three culprits were then put upon their trial.

The first was a middle aged woman, who had, as her overseer said, left several hills of cotton in the course of the day, without cleaning and hilling them in a proper manner. She received twelve lashes. The other two were charged in general terms, with having been lazy, and of having neglected their work that day. Each of these received twelve lashes.

These people all received punishment in the same manner that it had been inflicted upon Lydia, and when they were all gone, the overseer turned to me and said—"Boy, you are a stranger here yet, but I called you in, to let you see how things are done here, and to give you a little advice. When I get a new negro under my command, I never whip at first; I always give him a few days to learn his duty, unless he is an outrageous villain, in which case I anoint him a little at the beginning. I call over the names of all the hands twice every week, on Wednesday and Saturday evenings, and settle with them according to their general conduct, for the last three days. I call the names of my captains every morning, and it is their business to see that they have all their hands in their proper places. You ought not to have staid behind to-night with Lyd; but as this is your first offence, I shall overlook it, and you may go and get your supper." I made a low bow, and thanked master overseer for his kindness to me, and left him. This night for supper, we had corn bread and cucumbers; but we had neither salt, vinegar, nor pepper, with the cucumbers.

I had never before seen people flogged in the way our overseer flogged his people. This plan of making the person who is to be whipped, lie down upon the ground, was new to me, though it is much practiced in the south; and I have since seen men and women too, cut nearly in pieces by this mode of punishment. It has one advantage over tying people up by the hands, as it prevents all accidents from sprains in the thumbs or wrists. I have known people to hurt their joints very much, by struggling when tied up by the thumbs, or wrists, to undergo a severe whipping. The method of ground whipping, as it is called, is, in my opinion, very indecent, as it compels females to expose themselves in a very shameful manner.

The whip used by the overseers on the cotton plantations, is different from all other whips, that I have ever seen. The staff is about twenty or twenty-two inches in length, with a large and heavy head, which is often loaded with a quarter or half a pound of lead, wrapped in cat-gut, and securely fastened on, so that nothing but the greatest violence can separate it from the staff. The lash is ten feet long, made of small strips of buckskin, tanned so as to be dry and hard, and plaited carefully and closely together, of the thickness, in the largest part, of a man's little finger, but quite small at each extremity. At the farthest end of this thong is attached a cracker,[22] nine inches in length, made of strong sewing silk, twisted and knotted, until it feels as firm as the hardest twine.

This whip, in an unpractised hand, is a very awkward and inefficient weapon; but the best qualification of the overseer of a cotton plantation is the ability of using this whip with adroitness; and when wielded by an experienced arm, it is one of the keenest instruments of torture ever invented by the ingenuity of man. The cat-o'-nine tails, used in the British military service, is but a clumsy instrument beside this whip; which has superseded the cow-hide, the hickory, and every other species of lash, on the cotton plantations. The cow-hide and hickory, bruise and mangle the flesh of the sufferer; but this whip cuts, when expertly applied, almost as keen as a knife, and never bruises the flesh, nor injures the bones.

It was now Saturday night, and I wished very much for Sunday morning to come that I might see the manner of spending the Sabbath, on a great cotton plantation. I expected, that as these people had been compelled to work so hard, and fare so poorly all the week, they would be inclined to repose themselves on Sunday; and that the morning of this day would be passed in quietness, if not in sleep, by the inhabitants of our quarter. No horn was blown by the overseer, to awaken us this morning, and I slept, in my little loft, until it was quite day; but when I came down, I found our small community a scene of universal bustle and agitation.

Here it is necessary to make my readers acquainted with the rules of polity, which governed us on Sunday, (for I now speak of myself, as one of the slaves on this plantation,) and with the causes which gave rise to these rules.

All over the south, the slaves are discouraged, as much as possible, and by all possible means, from going to any place of religious worship on Sunday. This is to prevent them from associating together, from different estates, and distant parts of the country; and plotting conspiracies and insurrections. On some estates, the overseers are required to prohibit the people from going to meeting off the plantation, at any time, under the severest penalties. White preachers cannot come upon the plantations, to preach to the people, without first obtaining permission of the master, and afterwards procuring the sanction of the overseer. No slave dare leave the plantation to which he belongs, a single mile, without a written pass from the overseer, or master; but by exposing himself to the danger of being taken up and flogged. Any white man who meets a slave off the plantation without a pass, has a right to take him up, and flog him at his discretion. All these causes combined, operate powerfully to keep the slave at home. But, in addition to these principles of restraint, it is a rule on every plantation, that no overseer ever departs from, to flog every slave, male or female, that leaves the estate for a single hour, by night or by day—Sunday not excepted—without a written pass.

The overseer who should permit the people under his charge to go about the neighbourhood without a pass, would soon lose his character, and no one would employ him; nor would his reputation less certainly suffer in the estimation of the planters, were he to fall into the practice of granting passes, except on the most urgent occasions; and for purposes generally to be specified in the pass.

A cotton planter has no more idea of permitting his slaves to go at will, about the neighbourhood on Sunday, than a farmer in Pennsylvania has of letting his horses out of his field on that day. Nor would the neighbours be less inclined to complain of the annoyance, in the former, than in the latter case.

There has always been a strong repugnance, amongst the planters, against their slaves becoming members of any religious society, Not, as I believe, because they are so maliciously disposed towards their people as to wish to deprive them of the comforts of religion—provided the principles of religion did not militate against the principles of slavery—but they fear that the slaves, by attending meetings, and listening to the preachers, may imbibe with the morality they teach, the notions of equality and liberty, contained in the gospel. This, I have no doubt, is the ground of all the dissatisfaction, that the planters express, with the itinerant preachers, who have from time to time, sought opportunities of instructing the slaves in their religious duties.

The cotton planters have always, since I knew any thing of them, been most careful to prevent the slaves from learning to read; and such is the gross ignorance that prevails, that many of them could not name the four cardinal points.

At the time I first went to Carolina, there were a great many African slaves in the country, and they continued to come in for several years afterwards. I became intimately acquainted with some of these men. Many of them believed there were several gods; some of whom were good, and others evil, and they prayed as much to the latter as to the former. I knew several who must have been, from what I have since learned, Mohamedans; though at that time, I had never heard of the religion of Mohamed.

There was one man on this plantation, who prayed five times every day, always turning his face to the east, when in the performance of his devotion.

There is, in general, very little sense of religious obligation, or duty, amongst the slaves on the cotton plantations; and Christianity cannot be, with propriety, called the religion of these people. They are universally subject to the grossest and most abject superstition; and uniformly believe in witchcraft, conjuration, and the agency of evil spirits in the affairs of human life. Far the greater part of them are either natives of Africa, or the descendants of those who have always, from generation to generation, lived in the south, since their ancestors were landed on this continent; and their superstition, for it does not deserve the name of religion, is no better, nor is it less ferocious, than that which oppresses the inhabitants of the wildest regions of Negro-land.

They have not the slightest religious regard for the Sabbath-day, and their masters make no efforts to impress them with the least respect for this sacred institution. My first Sunday on this plantation was but a prelude to all that followed; and I shall here give an account of it.

At the time I rose this morning, it wanted only about fifteen or twenty minutes of sunrise; and a large number of the men, as well as some of the women, had already quitted the quarter, and gone about the business of the day. That is, they had gone to work for wages for themselves—in this manner: our overseer had, about two miles off, a field of near twenty acres, planted in cotton, on his own account. He was the owner of this land; but as he had no slaves, he was obliged to hire people to work it for him, or let it lie waste. He had procured this field to be cleared, as I was told, partly by letting white men make tar and turpentine from the pine wood which grew on it; and partly by hiring slaves to work upon it on Sunday. About twenty of our people went to work for him to-day, for which he gave them fifty cents each. Several of the others, perhaps forty in all, went out through the neighbourhood, to work for other planters.

On every plantation, with which I ever had any acquaintance, the people are allowed to make patches, as they are called—that is, gardens, in some remote and unprofitable part of the estate, generally in the woods, in which they plant corn, potatoes, pumpkins, melons, &c. for themselves.

These patches they must cultivate on Sunday, or let them go uncultivated. I think, that on this estate, there were about thirty of these patches, cleared in the woods, and fenced—some with rails, and others with brush—the property of the various families.

The vegetables that grew in these patches, were always consumed in the families of the owners; and the money that was earned by hiring out, was spent in various ways; sometimes for clothes, sometimes for better food than was allowed by the overseer, and sometimes for rum; but those who drank rum, had to do it by stealth.

By the time the sun was up an hour, this morning, our quarter was nearly as quiet and clear of inhabitants, as it had been at the same period on the previous day.

As I had nothing to do for myself, I went with Lydia, whose husband was still sick, to help her to work in her patch, which was about a mile and a half from our dwelling. We took with us some bread, and a large bucket of water; and worked all day. She had onions, cabbages, cucumbers, melons, and many other things in her garden.

In the evening, as we returned home, we were joined by the man who prayed five times a day; and at the going down of the sun, he stopped and prayed aloud in our hearing, in a language I did not understand.

This man told me, he formerly lived on the confines of a country, which had no trees, nor grass upon it; and that in some places, no water was to be found for several days' journey. That this barren country was, nevertheless, inhabited by a race of men, who had many camels and goats, and some horses. They had no settled place of residence; but removed from one part of the country to another, in quest of places where green herbage was to be found—their chief food being the milk of their camels, and goats; but that they also ate the flesh of these animals, sometimes. The hair of these people, was not short and woolly, like that of the negroes; nor were they of a shining black. They were continually at war with some of the neighbouring people, and very often with his own countrymen. He was himself once taken prisoner by them, when a lad, in a great battle fought between them and his own people, in which his party were defeated. The victors kept him in their possession, more than two years, compelling him to attend to their camels and goats.

Whilst he was with these people, they travelled a great way towards the rising sun; and came to a river, running through a country inhabited by yellow people, where the land was very rich, and produced great quantities of rice, such as grows here—and many other kinds of grain.

The people who had taken him prisoner, professed the same religion that he did; and it was forbidden by its precepts, for one man to sell another into slavery, who held the same faith with himself; otherwise he should have been sold to these yellow people. In the river of this country he saw alligators, in great abundance, like those that he had seen in Carolina; and the musquitos were, in some places, so numerous, that it was difficult to breathe without inhaling them.

"When we turned the camels out to graze, we used to tie their fore-feet together, with a rope made of the hair of this animal, spun upon small sticks, and twisted into a rope. Sometimes they broke these ropes, and slipped their feet out of its coils; and it was then very difficult to retake them. They would sometimes strike off at a trot, across the open country, and we would be obliged to mount of her camels, and follow them for a day or two, before we could retake them. I had been with these people so long, and being of the same religion with themselves, had become so familiar with their customs and manner of life, that they seemed almost to regard me as one of their own nation; and frequently sent me alone, in pursuit of the stray camels, giving me instructions how to direct my course, so as to rejoin them; for they never waited for me, to return to them, at the place where I left them, if the beasts had consumed the bushes, and green herbage, growing there, before I came back.

"When I had been a captive with them fully two years, we came one evening, and encamped at a little well, the mouth of which was about a yard over; and the water in which was very sweet and good.

"This well, seemed to have been scooped out of the hard and flinty sand, with men's hands, and was scarcely more than four feet deep; though it contained an abundant supply of water. We encamped by this fountain all night; and I remembered that we had been at the same place, soon after I was made a prisoner; and that when we had formerly come to it, we travelled with our backs to the mid-day sun. There was no herbage hereabout, except a few stunted and thorny bushes; and in wandering abroad in quest of something to eat, one of the best and fleetest camels, entangled the rope which bound his fore-feet, amongst these bushes, and broke it. I found part of the rope fast to a bush in the morning; but the camel was at a great distance from us, towards the setting sun.

"The chief of our party ordered me to mount another camel, and go with a long rope, in pursuit of the stray; and told me that they should travel towards the south, that day, and encamp at a place where there was much grass. I went in pursuit of the lost camel; but when I came near him, he took off at a great trot over the country,—and I pursued him until noon, without being able to overtake him, or even to change the line of his march. His course was towards the southwest; and when I found it impossible to overtake him, as his speed was superior to that of the beast I rode, I resolved to strive to accomplish that, by stratagem, which force could not effect. I knew the beasts were both hungry; and that having received as much water as they could drink, the night before, they would devour with the utmost avidity, the first green herbage that they might meet with.

"I slackened the speed of my camel, and followed at a leisure gait, after the one I pursued, suffering him to leave me behind him at a considerable distance. He still, however, kept on in the same direction, and with nearly the same speed, with which he had advanced all the morning; so that it became necessary for me to quicken my pace, to prevent him from passing out of my sight, and escaping from me altogether.

"About five o'clock in the afternoon, I came in sight of trees, the tops of which were only visible across the open plain. The camel I rode was now as desirous to advance rapidly, as his leader had been throughout the day. I was carried forward as quickly as the swiftest horse could trot; and awhile before sundown, I approached a small grove of tall straight trees, which are greatly valued in Africa, and which bear large quantities of nuts, of a very good quality. Under and about these trees, was a small tract of ground, covered with long green grass; and here my stray camel stopped.

"I have no doubt that he had scented the odour of this grass, soon after I first gave chase to him in the morning; though the distance at which he was from it, was so great, that the best horse could not have travelled it in one day. When I came up to the trees, I dismounted from the camel I rode, and tying its feet together with a short rope, preserved my long one, for the purpose of taking the runaway. I gathered as many nuts as I could eat, and after satisfying my hunger, lay down to sleep.

"This was the first time that I had ever attempted to pass a night alone, in this open country; and after I had made my bed in the grass, I became fearful that some wild beast might fall in with me before morning, as I had often heard lions, and other creatures of prey, breaking the stillness of night, in those desolate regions, by their yells and roaring. I therefore ascended a tree, and placed myself amongst some spreading limbs, in such a position as to be in no danger of falling, even if I should be overtaken by deep.

"The moon was now full; and in that country where there are no clouds, and where there is seldom any dew, objects can be distinguished at the distance of several miles over the plains, by moonlight. When I had been in the tree about an hour, I heard at a great distance, a loud sullen noise, between a growl and a roar, which I knew to proceed from a lion; for I was well acquainted with the habits and noise of this animal; having frequently assisted in hunting him, in my own country.

"I was greatly terrified by this circumstance; not for my own safety, for I knew that no beast of prey could reach me in the tree, but I feared that my camels might be devoured, and I be left to perish in the desert.

"My fears were in part, well founded; for keeping my eye steadily directed towards the point from which the sound had proceeded, it was not long before I saw some object, moving over the naked plain.

"The runaway camel now joined his tethered companion, and both quitting the herbage, came and stood at the root of the tree, upon the branches of which I was. I still kept my eye steadily fixed upon the moving body which was evidently advancing nearer to me over the plain. I had no longer any doubt that it was coming to the grove of trees, which were only twelve or fifteen in number; and so bare of branches that I could distinctly see in every direction around me.

"In a few minutes, the animal approached me. It was a monstrous lion, of the black maned species. It was now within one hundred paces of me, and the poor camels raised their heads, as high as they could, towards me, and crouched close to the trunk of the tree, apparently so stupified by fear, as to be incapable of attempting to fly. The lion approached with a kind of circular motion; and at length dropping on his belly, glided along the ground, until within about ten yards of the tree, when uttering a terrific roar, which shook the stillness of the night for many a league around, he sprang upon and seized the unbound camel by the neck.

"Finding that I afforded no protection, the animal, after striving in vain to shake off his assailant, rushed out upon the open plain, carrying on his back the lion, which I could perceive, had already fastened upon the throat of his victim, which did not go more than a stone's cast from the trees, before he fell, and after a short struggle, ceased to move his limbs. The lion held the poor beast by the throat for some time after he was dead, and until, I suppose, the blood had ceased to flow from his veins—then, quitting the neck, he turned to the side of the slain, and tearing a hole into the cavity of the body, extracted the intestines, and devoured the liver and heart, before he began to gorge himself with the flesh.

"The moon was now high in the heavens, and shone with such exceeding brilliancy, that I could see distinctly for many miles round me. In that country, the smooth and glittering surface of the hard and baked sandy plains, reflects the light of the moon, as strongly as a sheet of snow in winter does in this; and the atmosphere being free from all humidity, is so clear and transparent, that I could perceive the quivering motion of the camel's lips, in his last agony, as well as the tongue of the lion, when he licked the blood from his paws.

"As soon as my fright had a little subsided, I looked for my surviving camel which, to my terror, I could not see, either at the foot of the tree on which I was, and where I had last seen it, or anywhere in the grove.

"I now concluded, that in the alarm caused by the lion, and the destruction of his companion, my surviving beast had broken the cord which bound its feet, and had taken to flight, leaving me alone, and without any means of escaping from the desert; for I had no hope of being able to reach, on foot, either the people with whom I had so long lived, or the inhabitants of the woody countries, lying far to the south of me. No condition can be more miserable than that to which I was now reduced.

"My late masters were distant from me, at least one day's journey, on a swift camel; and were removing farther from me every day, as fast as their beasts could carry them; and I had no knowledge of the various watering places, and spots of herbage, which lie scattered over the wide expanse of those unfrequented regions, in the midst of which I then was. I had not seen any water at this place, since I came to it; and had not the poor consolation of knowing, that I could remain here, and live on the fruit of the trees, until some chance should bring hither some of the wandering tribes, that roam over those solitudes.

"After a lapse of two or three hours, not being able to discover my living camel anywhere, although the moon had now passed her meridian, and shone with a splendour which enabled me to distinguish small pebbles at some distance, I gave him up for lost, and again turned my attention to the lion, which still continued at intervals, to utter deep and sullen growls over his prey. I expected, that at the approach of day, the lion would leave the dead carcass, and retire to his lair in some distant place; and I determined to await the period of his departure, to descend the tree, and search for water amongst the grass, which rose in some places to the height of my shoulders.

"I slept none this night,—but from my couch in the boughs, watched the motions of the lion, which, after swallowing at least one third of the camel, stretched himself at full length on his belly, about twenty paces from it, and laying his head between his fore-feet, prepared to guard his spoil against all the intruders of the night. In this position he remained, until the sun was up in the morning, and began to dart his rays across the naked and parched plain, upon which he lay—when rising and stretching himself, he walked slowly towards the grove—passed under me—went to the other side of the trees and entered some very tall herbage, where I heard him lap water. I now knew that I was in no danger of dying from thirst, provided I could escape wild beasts, on my way to and from the fountain.

"The trees afforded me both food and shelter; but I quickly found myself deprived of tasting water, at the present—for the lion, after slaking his thirst, returned by the same way that he had gone to the water, and coming to the tree in the boughs of which I lay, rubbed himself against its trunk, raising his tail, and exposing his sides alternately to the friction of the rough bark. After continuing this exercise for some time, he rested his weight on his hind-feet, licked his breast, fore-legs and paws, and then lying down on his side in the shade, appeared to fall into a deep sleep. Great as my anxiety was to leave my present lodgings, I dared not attempt to pass the sentinel that kept guard at the root of the tree, even though he slept on his post; for whenever I made the least rustling in the branches, I perceived that he moved his ears, and opened his eyes, but closed the latter again, when the noise ceased.

"The lion lay all day under the tree, only removing so as to place himself in the shade in the afternoon; but soon after the sun descended below the horizon, in the evening, he aroused himself, and resting upon his hind-feet, as he had done in the morning, uttered a roar that shook all the leaves about my head, and caused a tremulous motion in the branches upon which I rested. This horrid noise, together with the sight of the great beast that uttered it, so agitated my whole frame, that I was near leaping from my seat, and falling to the ground. I was so overcome with fear, that all prudence and self-possession forsook me; and I uttered a loud shout, as if in defiance of the monster below me.

"The moment the lion heard my voice, he raised his head, looked directly at me, with his fiery eyes and crouched down in the attitude of springing; but perceiving me to be quite out of the reach of his longest leap, he walked slowly off, and lay down about half way between me and the dead camel, with his head towards my tree. I had no doubt that his object was to watch me, until my descent from the tree, that he might make his supper of me this night, as he had of my camel, the night before.

"I had now been without water two days—my thirst was tormenting, and I had no prospect before me but of remaining in this tree, until driven to delirium for water, I should voluntarily descend, and deliver myself into the jaws of my enemy.

"The moon did not rise this night until long after the disappearance of daylight; but in the country where I then was, the stars shed such abundant light, that objects of magnitude can be seen at a great distance by their rays, without the aid of the moon. The lion moved frequently from place to place, but I could perceive that his attention was still fixed upon me: at last, however, he started away across the plain, and went farther and farther from me, until at length I lost sight of him in the distance; and all remained as quiet and noiseless, in the immense expanse around me, as the land of the dead.

"I now thought of descending, to go in quest of water; but whilst I deliberated upon this subject the moon rose, and cast her broad and glorious light upon these wide fields of desolation. As I could now see every thing, I resolved to descend; but before doing this, thought it prudent to cast a look about me, to see if there might not be some other beast of prey near. This thought saved my life; for on turning my eyes in a direction quite different from that in which the lion had departed, I saw him returning, within two or three stone's cast, creeping along the ground. I watched him, and he came and placed himself between me and the water.

"All was again silent; and I remained in the tree, burning with thirst, until the moon was elevated high in the heavens, when the silence was interrupted by the roaring of a lion, at a great distance, which was again repeated after a short interval. At the end of half an hour I again heard the same lion, apparently not far off. Casting my eye in the direction of the sound, I saw the beast advancing rapidly, as I thought towards me, and began to apprehend that a whole den of lions were lying in wait for me.

"The stranger soon undeceived me, for he was coming to partake of the dead camel, whose flesh or blood he had doubtlessly smelled, though it was not putrid, for, in this dry atmosphere, flesh is preserved a long time free from taint, and is sometimes dried in the sun, in a state of perfect soundness. I knew the nature of the lion too well, to suppose that the stranger was going to get his supper free of cost; and before he had reached the carcass, my jailer quitted his post, and set off to defend his acquisition of the last night.

"The new comer arrived first, and fell upon the dead camel, with the fury of a hungry lion—as he was; but he had scarcely swallowed a second morsel when the rightful owner, uttering a roar yet more dreadful than any that had preceded it, leaped upon the intruder, and brought him to the ground. For a moment I heard nothing but the gnashing of teeth, the clashing of talons, and the sounds caused by the laceration of the flesh and hides of the combatants; but anon, they rolled along the ground, and filled the whole canopy of heaven with their yells of rage—then the roaring would cease, and only the rending of the flesh of these lords of the waste could be heard—then the roaring would again burst forth, with renewed energy.

"This battle lasted more than an hour; but at length both appearing to be exhausted, they lay for some minutes on their sides, each with the other wrapped in his fierce embrace. In the end, I perceived that one of them rose and walked away, leaving the other upon the ground. The victor, which I could perceive was the stranger, for his mane was not black, returned to the remnant of the camel, and lay down panting beside it. After he had taken time to breathe, he recommenced his attack, and consumed far the larger part of the carcass. Having eaten to fulness, he took up the bones and remaining flesh of the camel, and set out across the desert,—I followed him with my eye for more than an hour.

"Parched as my throat was, but still afraid to descend from my place of safety, I remained on the tree until the light of the next morning, when I examined carefully around, to see that there was no beast of prey lurking about the place, where I knew the water to be. Perceiving no danger, I descended before the sun was up, and going to the water, knelt down, and drank as long and as much as I thought I could with safety.

"I then proceeded to make a more minute examination of this place, and saw numerous tracks of wild goats, and of other animals, that had come here, as well to drink as to eat the grass. I also saw the tracks of lions, and other beasts of prey, which satisfied me that these had come to lie in wait for other animals coming to drink: it also convinced me that it was not safe for me to remain in this grove alone; but I knew of no means by which I could escape from it.

"It now occurred to my mind that if my living camel had not escaped from me, I might have made my way to my own country, for on my camel I had two leather bottles, which I had neglected to fill with water, the morning I left the company of my former masters. By replenishing these from the fountain, giving my camel as much as he could drink, and filling two small sacks attached to my saddle, with the nuts from these trees, I should have been equipped for a journey of ten days, within which period, I had no doubt, I should have been able to reach my own people; but my camel was gone, and these reflections served only to aggravate the bitterness of my anguish.

"I walked out upon the desert, and prayed to be delivered from the perils that environed me. At the distance of two or three miles from me, I now observed a small sand hill, rising to the height of eight or ten feet; easily perceived when looking along the level surface of the ground, but which had escaped my observation from my elevated post in the tree. Such sand hills are often found in those deserts, and sometimes contain the bones of men and animals that have been buried in them.

"In my situation, I could not remain idle; and urged forward by restlessness, bordering on despair, I resolved to go to the little hill before me, without having any definite object in view. I soon approached the hill, and having reached its foot, walked along its base for some distance. I then turned to go back to the trees; but after advancing a few steps, was seized with a sudden impulse, which urged me to go to the top of the sand hill. I again turned and walked slowly to the summit, beyond which I saw only the same dreary expanse that I was so well used to look upon. Advancing along the top of this sand hill, which had been blown up by the wind in a long narrow ridge, I saw a recess or hollow place, on the side opposite to that by which I had ascended it; and on coming to this spot, beheld my camel crouched down close to the ground, with his neck extended at full length. My joy was unbounded—I leaped with delight, and was wild for some minutes, with a delirium of gladness.

"My camel had fled from the grove, at the time his companion was killed by the lion, and reaching this place, had here taken refuge, and had not moved since. I hastened to loose his feet from the cords with which I had bound them; mounted upon his back, and was quickly at the watering place. I filled my two water skins with water, and gathering as many nuts as my sacks would contain, caused my camel to take a full draught, and fill his stomach with grass, and then directed my course to the south, with a quick pace.

"It was now noon when I left this watering place; and I travelled hard all that day and the succeeding night, until the moon rose. I then alighted, and causing my camel to lie down, crept close to his side, and betook myself to sleep. I rested well this night, and recommencing my journey at the dawn of day, I pursued my route, without any thing worthy of relating happening to me until the eighth day, when I discovered trees, and all the appearance of a woody country, before me.

"Soon after entering the forest, I came to a small stream of water. Descending this stream a few miles, I found some people, who were cutting grass for the purpose of making mats to sleep on. These people spoke my own language, and told me that one of them had been in my native village lately. They took me and my camel to their village, and treated me very kindly; promising me that after I had recovered from my fatigue, they would go with me to my friends.

"My protectors were at war with a nation whose religion was different from ours; and about a month after I came to the village we were alarmed one morning, just at break of day, by the horrible uproar caused by mingled shouts of men, and blows given with heavy sticks upon large wooden drums. The village was surrounded by enemies, who attacked us with clubs, long wooden spears, and bows and arrows. After fighting for more than an hour, those who were not fortunate enough to run away, were made prisoners. It was not the object of our enemies to kill; they wished to take us alive, and sell us as slaves. I was knocked down by a heavy blow of a club, and when I recovered from the stupor that followed, I found myself tied fast with the long rope that I had brought from the desert, and in which I had formerly led the camels of my masters.

"We were immediately led away from this village, through the forest, and were compelled to travel all day, as fast as we could walk. We had nothing to eat on this journey, but a small quantity of grain, taken with ourselves. This grain we were compelled to carry on our backs, and roast by the fires which we kindled at nights, to frighten away the wild beasts. We travelled three weeks in the woods,—sometimes without any path at all; and arrived one day at a large river, with a rapid current. Here we were forced to help our conquerors, to roll a great number of dead trees into the water, from a vast pile that had been thrown together by high floods.

"These trees being dry and light, floated high out of the water; and when several of them were fastened together, with the tough branches of young trees, formed a raft, upon which we all placed ourselves, and descended the river for three days, when we came in sight of what appeared to me the most wonderful object in the world; this was a large ship, at anchor, in the river. When our raft came near the ship, the white people—for such they were on board—assisted to take us on deck, and the logs were suffered to float down the river.

"I had never seen white people before; and they appeared to me the ugliest creatures in the world. The persons who brought us down the river received payment for us of the people in the ship, in various articles, of which I remember that a keg of liquor, and some yards of blue and red cotton cloth, were the principal. At the time we came into this ship, she was full of black people, who were all confined in a dark and low place, in irons. The women were in irons as well as the men.

"About twenty persons were seized in our village, at the time I was; and amongst these were three children, so young that they were not able to walk, or to eat any hard substance. The mothers of these children had brought them all the way with them; and had them in their arms when we were taken on board this ship.

"When they put us in irons, to be sent to our place of confinement in the ship, the men who fastened the irons on these mothers, took the children out of their hands, and threw them over the side of the ship, into the water. When this was done, two of the women leaped overboard after the children—the third was already confined by a chain to another woman, and could not get into the water, but in struggling to disengage herself she broke her arm, and died a few days after, of a fever. One of the two women who were in the river, was carried down by the weight of her irons, before she could be rescued; but the other was taken up by some men in a boat, and brought on board. This woman threw herself overboard one night, when we were at sea.

"The weather was very hot, whilst we lay in the river, and many of us died every day; but the number brought on board greatly exceeded those who died, and at the end of two weeks the place in which we were confined was so full that no one could lie down; and we were obliged to sit all the time, for the room was not high enough for us to stand. When our prison would hold no more, the ship sailed down the river, and on the night of the second day after she sailed, I heard the roaring of the ocean, as it dashed against her sides.

"After we had been at sea some days, the irons were removed from the women, and they were permitted to go upon deck; but whenever the wind blew high, they were driven down amongst us.

"We had nothing to eat but yams, which were thrown amongst us at random—and of these we had scarcely enough to support life. More than one-third of us died on the passage; and when we arrived at Charleston, I was not able to stand. It was more than a week after I left the ship, before I could straighten my limbs. I was bought by a trader, with several others; brought up the country, and sold to our present master: I have been here five years."

---

## CHAPTER XI.

It was dusky twilight when this narrative was ended, and we hastened home to the quarter. When we arrived, the overseer had not yet come. He had been at his cotton field, with the people he had hired in the morning to work for him; but he soon made his appearance, and going into his house, came out with a small bag of money, and paid each one the price he had a right to receive. In this transaction the overseer acted with entire fairness to the people who worked for him; and with the exception of the moral turpitude of violating the Sabbath, in this shameful manner, the business was conducted with propriety.

I must here observe, that when the slaves go out to work for wages on Sunday, their employers never flog them; and so far as I know never give them abusive language. I have often hired myself to work on Sunday, and have been employed in this way by more than twenty different persons, not one of whom ever insulted or maltreated me in any way. They seldom took the trouble of coming to look at me until towards evening, and sometimes not then. I worked faithfully, because I knew that if I did not, I could not expect payment; and those who hired me, knew that if I did not work well, they need not employ me.

The practice of working on Sunday, is so universal amongst the slaves on the cotton plantations, that the immorality of the matter is never spoken of.

We retired to rest this evening at the usual hour; and no one could have known, by either our appearance or our manners, that this was Sunday evening. There were no clean clothes amongst us; for few of our people were acquainted with the luxury of a suit of clean vestments, and those who could afford a clean garment, reserved it for Monday morning. Sunday is the customary wash-day on cotton plantations.

It is here proper to observe, that it is usual, on the cotton estates, to deal out the weekly allowance of corn to the slaves, on Sunday evening; but our overseer, at this period, had changed this business from Sunday to Monday morning, for the reason, I believe, that he wished to keep the hired people at work, in his own cotton field, until night. He, however, soon afterwards resumed the practice of distributing the allowance on Sunday evening, and continued it as long as I remained on the estate. The business was conducted in the same manner, when performed on Sunday, as when attended to on Monday, only the time was changed.

On Monday morning I heard the sound of the horn, at the usual hour, and repairing to the front of the overseer's house, found that he had already gone to the corn crib, for the purpose of distributing corn amongst the people, for the bread of the week; or rather, for the week's subsistence; for this corn was all the provision that our master, or his overseer, usually made for us;—I say usually, for whatever was given to us beyond the corn, which we received on Sunday evening, was considered in the light of a bounty bestowed upon us, over and beyond what we were entitled to, or had a right to expect to receive.

When I arrived at the crib, the door was unlocked and open, and the distribution had already commenced. Each person was entitled to half a bushel of ears of corn, which was measured out by several of the men who were in the crib. Every child above six months old drew this weekly allowance of corn; and in this way, women who had several small children, had more corn than they could consume, and sometimes bartered small quantities with the other people, for such things as they needed, and were not able to procure.

The people received their corn in baskets, old bags, or any thing with which they could most conveniently provide themselves. I had not been able, since I came here, to procure a basket, or any thing else to put my corn in, and desired the man with whom I lived to take my portion in his basket, with that of his family. This he readily agreed to do, and as soon as we had received our share we left the crib.

The overseer attended in person to the measuring of this corn; and it is only justice to him to say, that he was careful to see that justice was done us. The men who measured the corn always heaped the measure as long as an ear would lie on; and he never restrained their generosity to their fellow-slaves.

In addition to this allowance of corn, we received a weekly allowance of salt, amounting, in general, to about half a gill to each person; but this article was not furnished regularly, and sometimes we received none for two or three weeks.

The reader must not suppose, that, on this plantation we had nothing to eat beyond the corn and salt. This was far from the case. I have already described the gardens, or patches, cultivated by the people, and the practice which they universally followed of working on Sunday, for wages. In addition to all these, an industrious, managing slave would contrive to gather up a great deal to eat.

I have before observed, that the planters are careful of the health of their slaves, and in pursuance of this rule, they seldom expose them to rainy weather, especially in the sickly seasons of the year, if it can be avoided.

In the spring and early parts of the summer, the rains are frequently so violent, and the ground becomes so wet, that it is injurious to the cotton to work it, at least whilst it rains. In the course of the year there are many of these rainy days, in which the people cannot go to work with safety; and it often happens that there is nothing for them to do in the house. At such time they make baskets, brooms, horse collars, and other things, which they are able to sell amongst the planters.

The baskets are made of wooden splits, and the brooms of young white oak or hickory trees. The mats are sometimes made of splits, but more frequently of flags as they are called—a kind of tall rush, which grows in swampy ground. The horse or mule collars are made of husks of corn, though sometimes of rushes, but the latter are not very durable.

The money procured by these, and various other means, which I shall explain hereafter, is laid out by the slaves in purchasing such little articles of necessity or luxury, as it enables them to procure. A part is disbursed in payment for sugar, molasses, and sometimes a few pounds of coffee, for the use of the family; another part is laid out for clothes for winter; and no inconsiderable portion of his pittance is squandered away by the misguided slave for tobacco, and an occasional bottle of rum. Tobacco is deemed so indispensable to comfort, nay to existence, that hunger and nakedness are patiently endured, to enable the slave to indulge in this highest of enjoyments.

There being few towns in the cotton country, the shops, or stores, are frequently kept at some cross road, or other public place, in or adjacent to a rich district of plantations. To these shops the slaves resort, sometimes with, and at other times without, the consent of the overseer, for the purpose of laying out the little money they get. Notwithstanding all the vigilance that is exercised by the planters, the slaves, who are no less vigilant than their masters, often leave the plantation after the overseer has retired to his bed, and go to the store.

The store-keepers are always ready to accommodate the slaves, who are frequently better customers than many white people; because the former always pay cash, whilst the latter almost always require credit. In dealing with the slave, the shop-keeper knows he can demand whatever price he pleases for his goods, without danger of being charged with extortion; and he is ready to rise at any time of the night to oblige friends, who are of so much value to him.

It is held highly disgraceful, on the part of store-keepers, to deal with the slaves for any thing but money, or the coarse fabrics that it is known are the usual products of the ingenuity and industry of the negroes; but, notwithstanding this, a considerable traffic is carried on between the shop-keepers and slaves, in which the latter make their payments by barter. The utmost caution and severity of masters and overseers, are sometimes insufficient to repress the cunning contrivances of the slaves.

After we had received our corn, we deposited it in our several houses, and immediately followed the overseer to the same cotton field, in which we had been at work on Saturday. Our breakfast this morning was bread, to which was added a large basket of apples, from the orchard of our master. These apples served us for a relish with our bread, both for breakfast and dinner, and when I returned to the quarter in the evening, Dinah (the name of the woman who was at the head of our family) produced at supper, a black jug, containing molasses, and gave me some of the molasses for my supper.

I felt grateful to Dinah for this act of kindness, as I well knew that her children regarded molasses as the greatest of human luxuries, and that she was depriving them of their highest enjoyment to afford me the means of making a gourd full of molasses and water. I therefore proposed to her and her husband, whose name was Nero, that whilst I should remain a member of the family, I would contribute as much towards its support as Nero himself; or, at least, that I would bring all my earnings into the family stock, provided I might be treated as one of its members, and be allowed a portion of the proceeds of their patch or garden. This offer was very readily accepted, and from this time we constituted one community, as long as I remained among the field hands on this plantation. After supper was over, we had to grind our corn; but as we had to wait for our turn at the mill, we did not get through this indispensable operation before one o'clock in the morning. We did not sit up all night to wait for our turn at the mill, but as our several turns were assigned us by lot, the person who had the first turn, when done with the mill, gave notice to the one entitled to the second, and so on. By this means nobody lost more than half an hour's sleep, and in the morning every one's grinding was done.

We worked very hard this week. We were now laying by the cotton, as it is termed; that is, we were giving the last weeding and hilling to the crop, of which there was, on this plantation, about five hundred acres, which looked well, and promised to yield a fine picking.

In addition to the cotton, there was on this plantation, one hundred acres of corn, about ten acres of indigo, ten or twelve acres in sweet potatoes, and a rice swamp of about fifty acres. The potatoes and indigo had been laid by, (that is, the season of working in them was past,) before I came upon the estate; and we were driven hard by the overseer to get done with the cotton, to be ready to give the corn another harrowing, and hoeing, before the season should be too far advanced. Most of the corn in this part of the country, was already laid by, but the crop here had been planted late, and yet required to be worked.

We were supplied with an abundance of bread, for a peck of corn is as much as a man can consume in a week, if he has other vegetables with it; but we were obliged to provide ourselves with the other articles, necessary for our subsistence. Nero had corn in his patch, which was now hard enough to be fit for boiling, and my friend Lydia had beans in her garden. We exchanged corn for beans, and had a good supply of both; but these delicacies we were obliged to reserve for supper. We took our breakfast in the field, from the cart, which seldom afforded us any thing better than bread, and some raw vegetables from the garden. Nothing of moment occurred amongst us, in this first week of my residence here. On Wednesday evening, called settlement-night, two men and a woman were whipped; but circumstances of this kind were so common, that I shall, in future, not mention them, unless something extraordinary attended them.

I could make wooden bowls and ladles, and went to work with a man who was clearing some new land about two miles off—on the second Sunday of my sojourn here, and applied the money I earned in purchasing the tools necessary to enable me to carry on my trade. I occupied all my leisure hours, for several months after this, in making wooden trays, and such other wooden vessels as were most in demand. These I traded off, in part, to a store-keeper, who lived about five miles from the plantation; and for some of my work I obtained money. Before Christmas, I had sold more than thirty dollars worth of my manufactures; but the merchant with whom I traded, charged such high prices for his goods, that I was poorly compensated for my Sunday toils, and nightly labours; nevertheless, by these means, I was able to keep our family supplied with molasses, and some other luxuries, and at the approach of winter, I purchased three coarse blankets, to which Nero added as many, and we had all these made up into blanket-coats for Dinah, ourselves, and the children.

About ten days after my arrival, we had a great feast at the quarter. One night, after we had returned from the field, the overseer sent for me by his little son, and when I came to his house, he asked me if I understood the trade of a butcher—I told him I was not a butcher by trade, but that I had often assisted my master and others, to kill hogs and cattle, and that I could dress a hog, or a bullock, as well as most people. He then told me he was going to have a beef killed in the morning at the great house, and I must do it—that he would not spare any of the hands to go with me, but he would get one of the house-boys to help me.

When the morning came, I went, according to orders, to butcher the beef, which I expected to find in some enclosure on the plantation; but the overseer told me I must take a boy named Toney, from the house, whose business it was to take care of the cattle, and go to the woods and look for the beef. Toney and I set out sometime before sunrise, and went to a cow-pen, about a mile from the house, where he said he had seen the young cattle only a day or two before. At this cow-pen, we saw several cows waiting to be milked, I suppose, for their calves were in an adjoining field, and separated from them only by a fence. Toney then said, we should have to go to the long savanna, where the dry cattle generally ranged, and thither we set off. This long savanna lay at the distance of three miles from the cow-pen, and when we reached it, I found it to be literally what it was called, a long savanna. It was a piece of low, swampy ground, several miles in extent, with an open space in the interior part of it, about a mile long, and perhaps a quarter of a mile in width. It was manifest that this open space was covered with water through the greater part of the year, which prevented the growth of timber in this place; though at the time it was dry, except a pond near one end, which covered, perhaps, an acre of ground. In this natural meadow, every kind of wild grass, common to such places in the southern country, abounded.

Here I first saw the scrub and saw grasses—the first of which is so hard and rough, that it is gathered to scrub coarse wooden furniture, or even pewter; and the last is provided with edges, somewhat like saw teeth, so hard and sharp that it would soon tear the skin off the legs of any one who should venture to walk through it with bare limbs.

As we entered this savanna, we were enveloped in clouds of musquitos, and swarms of galinippers,[23] that threatened to devour us. As we advanced through the grass, they rose up until the air was thick, and actually darkened with them. They rushed upon us with the fury of yellow-jackets, whose hive has been broken in upon, and covered every part of our persons. The clothes I had on, which were nothing but a shirt and trousers of tow linen, afforded no protection, even against the musquitos, which were much larger than those found along the Chesapeake Bay; and nothing short of a covering of leather could have defended me against the galinippers.

I was pierced by a thousand stings at a time, and verily believe I could not have lived beyond a few hours in this place. Toney ran into the pond, and rolled himself in the water to get rid of his persecutors; but he had not been long there before he came running out, as fast as he had gone in, hallooing and clamouring in a manner wholly unintelligible to me. He was terribly frightened; but I could not imagine what could be the cause of his alarm, until he reached the shore, when he turned round with his face to the water, and called out—"the biggest alligator in the whole world—did not you see him?" I told him I had not seen any thing but himself in the water; but he insisted that he had been chased in the pond by an alligator, which had followed him until he was close to the shore. We waited a few minutes for the alligator to rise to the surface, but were soon compelled by the musquitos, to quit this place.

Toney said, we need not look for the cattle here; no cattle could live amongst these musquitos, and I thought he was right in his judgment. We then proceeded into the woods and thickets, and after wandering about for an hour or more, we found the cattle, and after much difficulty, succeeded in driving a part of them back to the cow-pen, and enclosing them in it. I here selected the one that appeared to me to be the fattest, and securing it with ropes, we drove the animal to the place of slaughter.

This beef was intended as a feast for the slaves, at the laying by of the corn and cotton; and when I had it hung up, and had taken the hide off, my young master, whom I had seen on the day of my arrival, came out to me, and ordered me to cut off the head, neck, legs, end tail, and lay them, together with the empty stomach and the harslet,[24] in a basket. This basket was sent home, to the kitchen of the great house, by a woman and a boy, who attended for that purpose. I think there was at least one hundred and twenty or thirty pounds of this offal. The residue of the carcass I cut into four quarters, and we carried it to the cellar of the great house. Here one of the hind quarters was salted in a tub, for the use of the family, and the other was sent, as a present, to a planter, who lived about four miles distant. The two fore-quarters were cut into very small pieces, and salted by themselves. These, I was told, would be cooked for our dinner on the next day, (Sunday,) when there was to be a general rejoicing amongst all the slaves of the plantation.

After the beef was salted down, I received some bread and milk for my breakfast, and went to join the hands in the corn field, where they were now harrowing and hoeing the crop for the last time. The overseer had promised us that we should have holiday, after the completion of this work, and by great exertion, we finished it about five o'clock in the afternoon.

On our return to the quarter, the overseer, at roll-call—which he performed this day before night—told us that every family must send a bowl to the great house, to get our dinners of meat. This intelligence diffused as much joy amongst us, as if each one had drawn a prize in a lottery. At the assurance of a meat dinner, the old people smiled and showed their teeth, and returned thanks to master overseer; but many of the younger ones shouted, clapped their hands, leaped, and ran about with delight.

Each family, or mess, now sent its deputy, with a large wooden bowl in his hand, to receive the dinner at the great kitchen. I went on the part of our family, and found that the meat dinner of this day, was made up of the basket of tripe, and other offal, that I had prepared in the morning. The whole had been boiled in four great iron kettles, until the flesh had disappeared from the bones, which were broken in small pieces—a flitch of bacon, some green corn, squashes, tomatos, and onions, had been added, together with other condiments, and the whole converted into about a hundred gallons of soup, of which I received in my bowl, for the use of our family, more than two gallons. We had plenty of bread, and a supply of black-eyed peas, gathered from our garden, some of which Dinah had boiled in our kettle, whilst I was gone for the soup, of which there was as much as we could consume, and I believe that every one in the quarter had enough.

I doubt if there was in the world a happier assemblage than ours, on this Saturday evening. We had finished one of the grand divisions of the labours of a cotton plantation, and were supplied with a dinner, which to the most of my fellow-slaves, appeared to be a great luxury, and most liberal donation on the part of our master, whom they regarded with sentiments of gratitude, for this manifestation of his bounty.

In addition to present gratification, they looked forward to the enjoyments of the next day, when they were to spend a whole Sunday in rest and banqueting; for it was known that the two fore-quarters of the bullock, were to be dressed for Sunday's dinner; and I had told them that each of these quarters weighed at least one hundred pounds.

Our quarter knew but little quiet this night; singing—playing on the banjoe, and dancing, occupied nearly the whole community, until the break of day. Those who were too old to take any part in our active pleasures, beat time with their hands, or recited stories of former times. Most of these stories referred to affairs that had been transacted in Africa, and were sufficiently fraught with demons, miracles, and murders, to fix the attention of many hearers.

To add to our happiness, the early peaches were now ripe, and the overseer permitted us to send, on Sunday morning, to the orchard, and gather at least ten bushels of very fine fruit.

In South Carolina they have very good summer apples, but they fall from the trees, and rot immediately after they are ripe; indeed, very often they speckrot on the trees, before they become ripe. This "speck-rot," as it is termed, appears to be a kind of epidemic disease amongst apples; for in some seasons whole orchards are subject to it, and the fruit is totally worthless, whilst in other years, the fruit in the same orchard continues sound and good, until it is ripe. The climate of Carolina is, however, not favourable to the apple, and this fruit of so much value in the north, is in the cotton region, only of a few weeks continuance—winter apples being unknown. Every climate is congenial to the growth of some kind of fruit tree; and in Carolina and Georgia, the peach arrives at its utmost perfection: the fig also ripens well, and is a delicious fruit.

None of our people went out to work for wages, to-day. Some few, devoted a part of the morning to such work as they deemed necessary, in or about their patches, and some went to the woods, or the swamps, to collect sticks for brooms, and splits, or to gather flags for mats; but far the greater number remained at the quarter, occupied in some small work, or quietly awaiting the hour of dinner, which we had been informed, by one of the house-servants, would be at one o'clock. Every family made ready some preparation of vegetables, from their own garden, to enlarge the quantity, if not to heighten the flavour of the dinner of this day.

One o'clock at length arrived, but not before it had been long desired; and we proceeded with our bowls a second time, to the great kitchen. I acted, as I had done yesterday, the part of commissary for our family; but when we were already at the place where we were to receive our soup and meat, into our bowls, (for it was understood that we were, with the soup, to have an allowance of both beef and bacon, to-day,) we were told that puddings had been boiled for us, and that we must bring dishes to receive them in. This occasioned some delay, until we obtained vessels from the quarter. In addition to at least two gallons of soup, about a pound of beef, and a small piece of bacon, I obtained nearly two pounds of pudding, made of corn meal, mixed with lard, and boiled in large bags. This pudding, with the molasses that we had at home, formed a very palatable second course, to our bread, soup, and vegetables.

On Sunday afternoon, we had a meeting, at which many of our party attended. A man named Jacob, who had come from Virginia, sang and prayed; but a great many of the people went out about the plantation, in search of fruits; for there were many peach and some fig trees, standing along the fences, on various parts of the estate. With us, this was a day of uninterrupted happiness.

A man cannot well be miserable, when he sees every one about him immersed in pleasure; and though our fare of to-day, was not of a quality to yield me much gratification, yet such was the impulse given to my feelings, by the universal hilarity and contentment, which prevailed amongst my fellows, that I forgot for the time, all the subjects of grief that were stored in my memory, all the acts of wrong that had been perpetrated against me, and entered with the most sincere and earnest sentiments, in the participation of the felicity of our community.

## CHAPTER XII.

AT the time of which I now speak, the rice was ripe, and ready to be gathered. On Monday morning, after our feast, the overseer took the whole of us to the rice field, to enter upon the harvest of this crop. The field lay in a piece of low ground, near the river, and in such a position that it could be flooded by the water of the stream, in wet seasons. The rice is planted in drills, or rows, and grows more like oats than any of the other grain, known in the north.

The water is sometimes let in to the rice fields, and drawn off again, several times, according to the state of the weather. Watering and weeding the rice is considered one of the most unhealthy occupations on a southern plantation, as the people are obliged to live for several weeks in the mud and water, subject to all the unwholesome vapours that arise from stagnant pools, under the rays of a summer sun, as well as the chilly autumnal dews of night. At the time we came to cut this rice, the field was quite dry; and after we had reaped and bound it, we hauled it upon wagons, to a piece of hard ground, where we made a threshing floor, and threshed it. In some places, they tread out the rice, with mules or horses, as they tread wheat in Maryland; but this renders the grain dusty, and is injurious to its sale.

After getting in the rice, we were occupied for some time in clearing and ditching swampy land, preparatory to a more extended culture of rice, the next year; and about the first of August, twenty or thirty of the people, principally women and children, were employed for two weeks in making cider, of apples which grew in an orchard of nearly two hundred trees, that stood on a part of the estate. After the cider was made, a barrel of it was one day brought to the field, and distributed amongst us; but this gratuity was not repeated. The cider that was made by the people, was converted into brandy, at a still in the corner of the orchard.

I often obtained cider to drink, at the still, which was sheltered from the weather by a shed, of boards and slabs. We were not permitted to go into the orchard at pleasure; but as long as the apples continued, we were allowed the privilege of sending five or six persons every evening, for the purpose of bringing apples to the quarter, for our common use; and by taking large baskets, and filling them well, we generally contrived to get as many as we could consume.

When the peaches ripened, they were guarded with more rigour—peach brandy being an article which is nowhere more highly prized than in South Carolina. There were on the plantation, more than a thousand peach trees, growing on poor sandy fields which were no longer worth the expense of cultivation. The best peaches grow upon the poorest sandhills.

We were allowed to take three bushels of peaches every day, for the use of the quarter; but we could, and did eat, at least three times that quantity, for we stole at night that which was not given us by day. I confess, that I took part in these thefts, and I do not feel that I committed any wrong, against either God or man, by my participation in the common danger that we ran, for we well knew the consequences that would have followed detection.

After the feast at laying by the corn and cotton, we had no meat for several weeks; and it is my opinion that our master lost money, by the economy he practised at this season of the year.

In the month of August, we had to save the fodder. This fodder-saving is the most toilsome, and next to working in the rice swamps, the most unhealthy job, that has to be performed on a cotton plantation, in the whole year. The manner of doing it is to cut the tops from the corn, as is done in Pennsylvania; but in addition to this, the blades below the ear, are always pulled off by the hand. Great pains is taken with these corn-blades. They constitute the chosen food of race, and all other horses, that are intended to be kept with extraordinary care, and in superior condition. For the purpose of procuring the best blades, they are frequently stripped from the stock, sometimes before the corn is ripe enough in the ear, to permit the top of the stalk to be cut off, without prejudice to the grain. After the blades are stripped from the stem, they are stuck between the hills of corn until they are cured, ready for the stack. They are then cut, and bound in sheaves, with small bands of the blades themselves. This binding, and the subsequent hauling from the field, must be done either early in the morning, before the dew is dried up, or in the night, whilst the dew is falling.

This work exposes the people who do it, to the fogs and damps of the climate, at the most unhealthy season of the year. Agues, fevers, and all the diseases which follow in their train, have their dates at the time of fodder-saving. It is the only work, appertaining to a cotton estate, which must of necessity be done in the night, or in the fogs of the morning; and the people at this season of the year, and whilst engaged in this very fatiguing work, would certainly be better able to go through with it, if they were regularly supplied, with proper portions of sound and wholesome salted provisions.

If every master would, through the months of August and September, supply his people with only a quarter of a pound of good bacon flitch to each person, daily, I have no doubt but that he would save money by it; to say nothing of the great comfort it would yield to the slaves, at this period, when the human frame is so subject to debility and feebleness.

Early in August, disease made its appearance amongst us. Several were attacked by the ague, with its accompanying fever; but in South Carolina, the "ague," as it is called, is scarcely regarded as a disease, and if a slave has no ailment that is deemed more dangerous, he is never withdrawn from the roll of the field hands. I have seen many of our poor people compelled to pick cotton, when their frames were shaken so violently, by the ague, that they were unable to get hold of the cotton in the burs, without difficulty. In this, masters commit a great error. Many fine slaves are lost, by this disease, which superinduces the dropsy, and sometimes the consumption, which could have been prevented by arresting the ague at its onset. When any of our people were taken so ill that they were not able to go to the field, they were removed to the great house, and placed in the "sick room," as it was termed. This sick room was a large, airy apartment, in the second story of a building which stood in the garden.

The lower part of this building was divided into two apartments, in one of which was kept the milk, butter, and other things connected with the dairy. In the other, the salt provisions of the family, including fish, bacon, and other articles, were secured. This apartment also constituted the smoke house; but as the ceiling was lathed, and plastered with a thick coat of lime and sand, no smoke could penetrate the "sick room," which was at all seasons of the year, a very comfortable place to sleep in.

Though I was never sick myself, whilst on this plantation, I was several times in this "sick room," and always observed, when there, that the sick slaves were well attended to. There was a hanging partition, which could be let down at pleasure, and which was let down when it was necessary, to divide the rooms into two apartments, which always happened when there were several slaves of different sexes, sick at the same time.

The beds, upon which the sick lay, were of straw, but clean and wholesome, and the patients when once in this room, were provided with every thing necessary for persons in their situation. A physician attended them daily, and proper food, and even wines, were not wanting.

The contrast between the cotton and rice fields, and this little hospital, was very great; and it appeared to me at the time, that if a part of the tenderness and benevolence, displayed here, had been bestowed upon the people whilst in good health, very many of the inmates of this infirmary, would never have been here.

I have often seen the same misapplication of the principles of philanthropy in Pennsylvania,—the subjects only being varied, from slaves to horses. The finest, and most valuable horses, are often overworked, or driven beyond their capacity of endurance, (it cannot be said that horses are not generally well fed in Pennsylvania,) without mercy or consideration, on the part of their owners; or more frequently of unfeeling hirelings, who have no interest in the life of the poor animal; and when his constitution is broken, and his health gone, great care and even expense, are bestowed upon him, for the purpose of restoring him to his former strength; the one half of which care or expense, would have preserved him in beauty and vigour, had they been bestowed upon him before he had suffered the irreparable injuries, attendant upon his cruel treatment.

In Pennsylvania, the horse is regarded, and justly regarded, only on account of the labour he is able to perform. Being the subject of property, his owner considers, not how he shall add most to the comforts and enjoyments of his horse, but by what means he shall be able to procure the greatest amount of labour from him, with the least expense to himself. In devising the means of saving expense, the life of the horse, and the surest and cheapest method of its preservation, are taken into consideration.

Precisely in this way, do the cotton planters reason and act, in relation to their slaves. Regarding the negroes merely as objects of property, like prudent calculators, they study how to render this property of the greatest value, and to obtain the greatest yearly income, from the capital invested in the slaves, and the lands they cultivate.

Experience has proved to me, that a man who eats no animal food, may yet be healthy, and able to perform the work usually done on a cotton plantation. Corn bread, sweet potatoes, some garden vegetables, with a little molasses and salt, assisted by the other accidental supplies that a thrifty slave is able to procure, on a plantation, are capable of sustaining life and health; and a slave who lives on such food, and never tastes flesh, stands at least an equal chance, for long life, with his master or mistress, "who are clad in purple and fine linen, and fare sumptuously every day." More people are killed by eating and drinking too much, than die of the effects of starvation, in the south; but the diseases of the white man, do not diminish the sufferings of the black one. A man who lives upon vegetable diet, may be healthy, and active; but I know he is not so strong and vigorous, as if he enjoyed a portion of animal food.

The labour usually performed by slaves, on a cotton plantation, does not require great bodily strength, but rather superior agility, and wakefulness. The hoes in use, are not heavy, and the art of picking cotton depends not upon superior strength, but upon the power of giving quick and accelerated motion to the fingers, arms, and legs. The fences have to be made, and repaired, and ditches dug—wood must also be cut, for many purposes, and all these operations call for strength; but they consume only a very small portion of the whole year,— more than three fourths of which is spent in the cotton, corn, rice, and indigo fields, where the strength of a boy, or a woman is sufficient to perform any kind of labour, necessary in the culture of the plants; but men are able to do more, even of this work, than either boys or women.

We scarcely had time to complete the securing of the fodder, and working up the apples, and peaches, when the cotton was ready for picking. This business of picking cotton, constitutes about half the labour of the year, on a large plantation. In Carolina, it is generally commenced about the first of September; though in some years, much cotton is picked in August. The manner of doing the work is this. The cotton being planted in hills, in straight rows, from four to five feet apart, each hand or picker, provided with a bag, made of cotton bagging, holding a bushel or more, hung round the neck, with cords, proceeds from one side of the field to the other, between two of these rows, picking all the cotton from the open burs, on the right and left, as he goes. It is the business of the picker to take all the cotton, from each of the rows, as far as the lines of the rows or hills. In this way he picks half the cotton from each of the rows, and the pickers who come on his right and left, take the remainder from the opposite sides of the rows.

The cotton is gathered into the bag, and when it becomes burdensome by its weight, it is deposited in some convenient place, until night, when it is taken home, either in a large bag or basket, and weighed under the inspection of the overseer. A day's work is not estimated by the number of hills, or rows, that are picked in the day, but by the number of pounds of cotton in the seed, that the picker brings into the cotton house, at night.

In a good field of cotton, fully ripe, a day's work is sixty pounds; but where the cotton is of inferior quality, or the burs are not in full blow, fifty pounds is the day's work; and where the cotton is poor, or in bad order, forty, or even thirty pounds, is as much as one hand can get in a day.

The picking of cotton, continues from August until December, or January; and in some fields, they pick from the old plants, until they are ploughed up in February or March, to make room for the planting of the seeds of another crop.

On all estates, the standard of a day's work is fixed by the overseer, according to the quality of the cotton; and if a hand gathers more than this standard, he is paid for it; but if, on the other hand, when his or her cotton is weighed at the cotton-house, in the evening, it is found that the standard quantity has not been picked, the delinquent picker is sure to receive a whipping.

On some estates, settlements are made every evening; and the whipping follows immediately; on others, the whipping does not occur until the next morning, whilst on a few plantations, the accounts are closed twice, or three times a week.

I have stated heretofore, that our overseer whipped twice a week, for the purpose of saving time; but if this method saved time to the overseer and the hands, it also saved the latter of a great many hard stripes; for very often, when one of us had displeased the overseer, he would tell us that on Wednesday or Saturday night, as the case might be, we should be remembered; yet the matter was either forgotten, or the passion of the overseer subdued, before the time of retribution arrived, and the delinquent escaped altogether from the punishment, which would certainly have fallen upon him, if it had been the custom of the overseer to chastise for every offence, at the moment, or even on the day, of its perpetration. A short day's work was always punished.

The cotton does not all ripen at the same time, on the same plant, which is picked and repicked, from six to ten times. The burs ripen, and burst open on the lower branches of the plant, whilst those at the top are yet in flower; or perhaps only in leaf or bud. The plant grows on, taller and larger, until it is arrested by the frost, or cool weather in autumn, continually throwing out new branches, new stems, new blossoms, and new burs, ceasing only with the first frost, at which time there are always some green burs, at the top of the plant, that never arrive at maturity. This state of things is, however, often prevented by topping the plant, in August or September, which prevents it from throwing out new branches, and blossoms, and forwards the growth and ripening of those already formed.

The first picking, takes the cotton from the burs of the lowest branches; the second from those a little higher, and so on, until those of the latest growth, at the top of the plant, are reached.

When the season has been bad, or from any other cause, the crop is light, the picking is sometimes complete, and the field clear of the cotton, before the first of January; but when the crop is heavy, or the people have been sickly in the fall, the picking is frequently protracted until February, or even the first of March. The winter does not injure the cotton, standing in the field, though the wind blows some of it out of the expanded burs, which is thus scattered over the field and lost.

An acre of prime land, will yield two thousand pounds of cotton in the seed. I have heard of three thousand pounds having been picked from an acre, but have not seen it. Four pounds of cotton in the seed, yields one pound when cleaned, and prepared for market.

It is estimated by the planters, or rather by the overseers, that a good hand can cultivate and pick five acres of cotton, and raise as much corn as will make his bread, and feed a mule or a horse. I know this to be a very hard task for a single hand, if the land is good, and the crops at all luxuriant. One man may, with great diligence, and continued good health, be able to get through with the cotton, and two or three, or even five acres of corn, up to the time when the cotton is ready to be picked; but from this period, he will find the labour more than he can perform, if the cotton is to be picked clean from the plants. Five acres of good cotton will yield ten thousand pounds of rough, or seed cotton. If he can pick sixty pounds a day, and works twenty-five days in a month, the picking of ten thousand pounds will occupy him more than six months.

From my own observations, on the plantations of South Carolina and Georgia, I am of opinion, that the planters in those states, do not get more than six or seven thousand pounds of cotton in the seed, for each hand employed; and I presume, that fifteen hundred pounds of clean cotton, is a full average of the product of the labour of each hand.

I now entered upon a new scene of life. My true value had not yet been ascertained by my present owner; and whether I was to hold the rank of a first, or second rate hand, could only be determined by an experience of my ability to pick cotton; nor was this important trait in my character, to be fully understood by a trial of one, or only a few days. It requires some time to enable a stranger, or new hand, to acquire the sleight of picking cotton.

I had ascertained, that at the hoe, the spade, the axe, the sickle, or the flail, I was a full match for the best hands on the plantation; but soon discovered, when we came to the picking of cotton, that I was not equal to a boy of twelve or fifteen years of age. I worked hard the first day, and made every effort to sustain the character that I had acquired, amongst my companions, but when evening came, and our cotton was weighed, I had only thirty-eight pounds, and was vexed to see that two young men, about my own age, had, one fifty-eight, and the other fifty-nine pounds. This was our first day's work; and the overseer had not yet settled the amount of a day's picking. It was necessary for him to ascertain, by the experience of a few days, how much the best hands could pick in a day, before he established the standard of the season. I hung down my head, and felt very much ashamed of myself, when I found that my cotton was so far behind that of many, even of the women, who had heretofore regarded me as the strongest and most powerful man of the whole gang.

I had exerted myself to-day, to the utmost of my power; and as the picking of cotton seemed to be so very simple a business, I felt apprehensive that I should never be able to improve myself, so far as to become even a second rate hand. In this posture of affairs, I looked forward to something still more painful than the loss of character which I must sustain, both with my fellows and my master; for I knew that the lash of the overseer would soon become familiar with my back, if I did not perform as much work as any of the other young men.

I expected indeed, that it would go hard with me even now, and stood by with feelings of despondence and terror, whilst the other people were getting their cotton weighed. When it was all weighed, the overseer came to me where I stood, and told me to show him my hands. When I had done this, and he had looked at them, he observed—"You have a pair of good hands—you will make a good picker." This faint praise of the overseer revived my spirits greatly, and I went home with a lighter heart than I had expected to possess, before the termination of cotton-picking.

When I came to get my cotton weighed, on the evening of the second day, I was rejoiced to find that I had forty-six pounds, although I had not worked harder than I did the first day. On the third evening I had fifty-two pounds; and before the end of the week, there were only three hands in the field—two men and a young woman—who could pick more cotton in a day, than I could.

On the Monday morning of the second week when we went to the field, the overseer told us, that he fixed the day's work at fifty pounds; and that all those who picked more than that, would be paid a cent a pound, for the over-plus. Twenty-five pounds was assigned as the daily task of the old people, as well as a number of boys and girls, whilst some of the women, who had children, were required to pick forty pounds, and several children had ten pounds each as their task.

Picking of cotton may almost be reckoned among the arts. A man who has arrived at the age of twenty-five, before he sees a cotton field, will never, in the language of the overseer, become a *crack picker*.

By great industry and vigilance, I was able, at the end of a month, to return every evening a few pounds over the daily rate, for which I received my pay; but the business of picking cotton was an irksome, and fatiguing labour to me, and one to which I could never become thoroughly reconciled; for the reason, I believe, that in every other kind of work in which I was engaged in the south, I was able to acquire the character of a first rate hand; whilst in picking cotton, I was hardly regarded as a *prime hand*.

---

## CHAPTER XIII.

IN a community of near three hundred persons, governed by laws as severe and unbending as those which regulated our actions, it is not to be expected that universal content can prevail, or that crimes will not be imagined, and even sometimes perpetrated. Ignorant men estimate those things which fortune has placed beyond their reach, not by their real value, but by the strength of their own desires and passions. Objects in themselves indifferent, which they are forbidden to touch, or even approach, excite in the minds of the unreflecting, ungovernable impulses. The slave, who is taught from infancy, to regard his condition as unchangeable, and his fate as fixed, by the laws of nature, fancies that he sees his master in possession of that happiness which he knows has been denied to himself. The lower men are sunk in the scale of civilization, the more violent become their animal passions. The native Africans are revengeful, and unforgiving in their tempers, easily provoked, and cruel in their designs. They generally place little, or even no value, upon the fine houses, and superb furniture of their masters; and discover no beauty in the fair complexions, and delicate forms of their mistresses. They feel indignant at the servitude that is imposed upon them, and only want power to inflict the most cruel retribution upon their oppressors; but they desire only the means of subsistence, and temporary gratification in this country, during their abode here.

They are universally of opinion, and this opinion is founded in their religion, that after death they shall return to their own country, and rejoin their former companions and friends, in some happy region, in which they will be provided with plenty of food, and beautiful women, from the lovely daughters of their own native land.

The case is different with the American negro, who knows nothing of Africa, her religion, or customs, and who has borrowed all his ideas of present and future happiness, from the opinions and intercourse of white people, and of Christians. He is, perhaps, not so impatient of slavery, and excessive labour, as the native of Congo; but his mind is bent upon other pursuits, and his discontent works out for itself other schemes, than those which agitate the brain of the imported negro. His heart pants for no heaven beyond the waves of the ocean; and he dreams of no delights in the arms of sable beauties, in groves of immortality, on the banks of the Niger, or the Gambia; nor does he often solace himself with the reflection, that the day will arrive when all men will receive the awards of immutable justice, and live together in eternal bliss, without any other distinctions than those of superior virtue, and exalted mercy. Circumstances oppose great obstacles in the way of these opinions.

The slaves who are natives of the country, (I now speak of the mass of those on the cotton plantations, as I knew them,) like all other people, who suffer wrong in this world, are exceedingly prone to console themselves with the delights of a future state, when the evil that has been endured in this life, will not only be abolished, and all injuries be compensated by proper rewards, bestowed upon the sufferers, but, as they have learned that wickedness is to be punished, as well as goodness compensated, they do not stop at the point of their own enjoyments and pleasures, but believe that those who have tormented them here, will most surely be tormented in their turn hereafter. The gross and carnal minds of these slaves, are not capable of arriving at the sublime doctrines taught by the white preachers; in which they are encouraged to look forward to the day when all distinctions of colour, and of condition, will be abolished, and they shall sit down in the same paradise, with their masters, mistresses, and even with the overseer. They are ready enough to receive the faith, which conducts them to heaven, and eternal rest, on account of their present sufferings; but they by no means so willingly admit the master and mistress to an equal participation in their enjoyments—this would only be partial justice, and half way retribution. According to their notions, the master and mistress are to be, in future, the companions of wicked slaves, whilst an agreeable recreation of the celestial inhabitants of the negro's heaven, will be a return to the overseer of the countless lashes that he has lent out so liberally here.

It is impossible to reconcile the mind of the native slave to the idea of living in a state of perfect equality, and boundless affection, with the white people. Heaven will be no heaven to him, if he is not to be avenged of his enemies. I know from experience, that these are the fundamental rules of his religious creed; because I learned them in the religious meetings of the slaves themselves. A favourite and kind master or mistress, may now and then be admitted into heaven, but this rather as a matter of favour, to the intercession of some slave, than as matter of strict justice to the whites, who will, by no means, be of an equal rank with those who shall be raised from the depths of misery, in this world.

The idea of a revolution in the conditions of the whites and the blacks, is the corner-stone of the religion of the latter; and indeed, it seems to me, at least, to be quite natural, if not in strict accordance with the precepts of the Bible; for in that book, I find it every where laid down, that those who have possessed an inordinate portion of the good things of this world, and have lived in ease and luxury, at the expense of their fellow men will surely have to render an account of their stewardship, and be punished, for having withheld from others the participation of those blessings, which they themselves enjoyed.

There is no subject which presents to the mind of the male slave a greater contrast between his own condition and that of his master, than the relative station and appearance of his wife and his mistress. The one, poorly clad, poorly fed, and exposed to all the hardships of the cotton field; the other dressed in clothes of gay and various colours, ornamented with jewelry, and carefully protected from the rays of the sun, and the blasts of the wind.

As I have before observed, the Africans have feelings peculiar to themselves; but with an American slave, the possession of the spacious house, splendid furniture, and fine horses of his master, are but the secondary objects of his desires. To fill the measure of his happiness, and crown his highest ambition, his young and beautiful mistress must adorn his triumph, and enliven his hopes.

I have been drawn into the above reflections, by the recollection of an event of a most melancholy character, which took place when I had been on this plantation about three months. Amongst the house-servants of my master, was a young man, named Hardy, of a dark yellow complexion—a quadroon, or mulatto—one fourth of whose blood was transmitted from white parentage.

Hardy was employed in various kinds of work about the house, and was frequently sent of errands; sometimes on horseback. I had become acquainted with the boy, who had often come to see me at the quarter, and had sometimes staid all night with me, and often told me of the ladies and gentlemen, who visited at the great house.

Amongst others, he frequently spoke of a young lady, who resided six or seven miles from the plantation, and often came to visit the daughters of the family, in company with her brother, a lad about twelve or fourteen years of age. He described the great beauty of this girl, whose mother was a widow, living on a small estate of her own. This lady did not keep a carriage; but her son and daughter, when they went abroad, travelled on horseback.

One Sunday, these two young people came to visit at the house of my master, and remained until after tea in the evening. As I did not go out to work that day, I went over to the great house, and from the house to a place in the woods, about a mile distant, where I had set snares for rabbits. This place was near the road, and I saw the young lady and her brother, on their way home. It was after sundown, when they passed me; but, as the evening was clear and pleasant, I supposed they would get home soon after dark, and that no accident would befall them.

No more was thought of the matter this evening, and I heard nothing further of the young people, until the next day, about noon, when a black boy came into the field, where we were picking cotton, and went to the overseer with a piece of paper. In a short time the overseer called me to come with him; and, leaving the field with the hands under the orders of Simon, the first captain, we proceeded to the great house.

As soon as we arrived at the mansion, my master, who had not spoken to me since the day we came from Columbia, appeared at the front door, and ordered me to come in and follow him. He led me through a part of the house, and passed into the back yard, where I saw the young gentleman, his son, another gentleman, whom I did not know, the family doctor, and the overseer, all standing together, and in earnest conversation. At my appearance, the overseer opened a cellar door, and ordered me to go in. I had no suspicion of evil, and obeyed the order immediately: as, indeed, I must have obeyed it, whatever might have been my suspicions.

The overseer, and the gentlemen, all followed; and as soon as the cellar door was closed after us, by some one whom I could not see, I was ordered to pull off my clothes, and lie down on my back. I was then bound by the hands and feet, with strong cords, and extended at full length between two of the beams that supported the timbers of the building.

The stranger, who, I now observed, was much agitated, spoke to the doctor, who then opened a small case of surgeons' instruments, which he took from his pocket, and told me he was going to skin me, for what I had done last night; "But," said the doctor, "before you are skinned, you had better confess your crime." "What crime, master, shall I confess? I have committed no crime—what has been done, that you are going to murder me?" was my reply. My master then asked me, why I had followed the young lady and her brother, who went from the house the evening before, and murdered her? Astonished and terrified at the charge of being a murderer, I knew not what to say; and only continued the protestations of my innocence, and my entreaties not to be put to death. My young master was greatly enraged against me, and loaded me with maledictions, and imprecations; and his father appeared to be as well satisfied as he was, of my guilt, but was more calm, and less vociferous in his language.

The doctor, during this time, was assorting his instruments, and looking at me—then stooping down, and feeling my pulse, he said, it would not do to skin a man so full of blood as I was. I should bleed so much that he could not see to do his work; and he should probably cut some large vein, or artery, by which I should bleed to death in a few minutes: it was necessary to bleed me in the arms, for some time, so as to reduce the quantity of blood that was in me, before taking my skin off. He then bound a string round my right arm, and opened a vein near the middle of the arm, from which the blood ran in a large and smooth stream. I already began to feel faint, with the loss of blood, when the cellar door was thrown open, and several persons came down, with two lighted candles.

I looked at these people attentively, as they came near, and stood around me, and expressed their satisfaction at the just and dreadful punishment that I was about to undergo. Their faces were all new, and unknown to me, except that of a lad, whom I recognized as the same, who had ridden by me, the preceding evening, in company with his sister.

My old master spoke to this boy, by name, and told him to come and see the murderer of his sister receive his due. The boy was a pretty youth, and wore his hair long, on the top of his head, in the fashion of that day. As he came round near my head, the light of a candle, which the doctor held in his hand, shone full in my face, and seeing that the eyes of the boy met mine, I determined to make one more effort to save my life, and said to him, in as calm a tone as I could, "Young master, did I murder young mistress, your sister?" The youth immediately looked at my master, and said, "This is not the man,—this man has short wool, and he had long wool, like your Hardy."

My life was saved. I was snatched from the most horrible of tortures; and from a slow and painful death. I was unbound, the bleeding of my arm stopped, and I was suffered to put on my clothes, and go up into the back yard of the house, where I was required to tell what I knew of the young lady and her brother, on the previous day. I stated that I had seen them in the court yard of the house, at the time I was in the kitchen; that I had then gone to the woods, to set my snares, and had seen them pass along the road, near me, and that this was all the knowledge I had of them. The boy was then required to examine me particularly, and ascertain whether I was, or was not, the man who had murdered his sister. He said, he had not seen me at the place, where I stated I was, and that he was confident I was not the person who had attacked him and his sister. That my hair, or wool, as he called it, was short; but that of the man who committed the crime was long, like Hardy's, and that he was about the size of Hardy—not so large as I was, but black like me, and not yellow like Hardy. Some one now asked where Hardy was, and he was called for, but could not be found in the kitchen. Persons were sent to the quarter, and other places, in quest of him, but returned without him. Hardy was nowhere to be found. Whilst this inquiry, or rather search, was going on,—perceiving that my old master had ceased to look upon me as a murderer, I asked him to please to tell me what had happened, that had been so near proving fatal to me.

I was now informed, that the young lady who had left the house on the previous evening, in company with her brother, had been assailed on the road, about four miles off, by a black man, who had sprung from a thicket, and snatched her from her horse, as she was riding at a short distance behind her brother. That the assassin, as soon as she was on the ground, struck her horse a blow with a long stick, which, together with the fright caused by the screams of its rider, when torn from it, had caused it to fly off at full speed; and the horse of the brother also taking fright, followed in pursuit, notwithstanding all the exertions of the lad to stop it. All the account the brother could give of the matter was, that as his horse ran with him, he saw the negro drag his sister into the woods, and heard her screams for a short time. He was not able to stop his horse, until he reached home, when he gave information to his mother, and her family. That people had been scouring the woods all night, and all the morning, without being able to find the young lady.

When intelligence of this horrid crime was brought to the house of my master, Hardy was the first to receive it; he having gone to take the horse of the person,—a young gentleman of the neighbourhood,—who bore it, and who immediately returned to join his friends, in their search for the dead body.

As soon as the messenger was gone, Hardy had come to my master, and told him, that if he would prevent me from murdering him, he would disclose the perpetrator of the crime. He was then ordered to communicate all he knew, on the subject; and declared, that, having gone into the woods the day before, to hunt squirrels, he staid until it was late, and on his return home, hearing the shrieks of a woman, he had proceeded cautiously to the place; but before he could arrive at the spot, the cries had ceased; nevertheless, he had found me, after some search, with the body of the young lady, whom I had just killed, and that I was about to kill him too, with a hickory club, but he had saved his life by promising that he would never betray me. He was glad to leave me; and what I had done with the body, he did not know.

Hardy was known in the neighbourhood, and his character had been good. I was a stranger, and on inquiry, the black people in the kitchen supported Hardy, by saying, that I had been seen going to the woods, before night, by the way of the road, which the deceased had travelled. These circumstances were deemed conclusive against me by my master; and as the offence, of which I was believed to be guilty, was the highest that can be committed by a slave, according to the opinion of owners, it was determined to punish me in a way unknown to the law, and to inflict tortures upon me which the law would not tolerate. I was now released, and though very weak from the effects of bleeding, I was yet able to return to my own lodgings.

I had no doubt, that Hardy was the perpetrator of the crime, for which I was so near losing my life; and now recollected, that when I was at the kitchen of the great house, on Sunday, he had disappeared, a short time before sundown, as I had looked for him when I was going to set my snares, but could not find him. I went back to the house, and communicated this fact to my master.

By this time, nearly twenty white men had collected about the dwelling, with the intention of going to search for the body of the lost lady; but it was now resolved to make the look-out double, and to give it the twofold character of a pursuit of the living, as well as a seeking for the dead.

I now returned to my lodgings, in the quarter, and soon fell into a profound sleep, from which I did not awake until long after night, when all was quiet, and the stillness of undisturbed tranquility prevailed over our little community. I felt restless, and sunk into a labyrinth of painful reflections, upon the horrid and perilous condition, from which I had this day escaped, as it seemed, merely by chance; and as I slept until all sensations of drowsiness had left me, I rose from my bed, and walked out by the light of the moon, which was now shining. After being in the open air some time, I thought of the snares that I had set on Sunday evening, and determined to go, and see if they had taken any game. I sometimes caught oppossums in my snares; and as these animals were very fat, at this season of the year, I felt a hope that I might be fortunate enough to get one tonight. I had been at my snares, and had returned, as far as the road, near where I had seen the young lady and her brother, on horseback, on Sunday evening, and had seated myself under the boughs of a holly bush, that grew there. It so happened, that the place where I sat, was in the shade of the bush, within a few feet of the road, but screened from it by some small boughs. In this position, which I had taken by accident, I could see a great distance along the road, towards the end of my master's lane. Though covered as I was, by the shade, and enveloped in boughs, it was difficult for a person in the road to see me.

The occurrence that had befallen me, in the course of the previous day, had rendered me nervous, and easily susceptible of all the emotions of fear. I had not been long in this place, when I thought I heard sounds, as of a person walking on the ground at a quick pace; and looking along the road, towards the lane, I saw the form of some one, passing through a space in the road, where the beams of the moon, piercing between two trees, reached the ground. When the moving body passed into the shade, I could not see it; but in a short time, it came so near, that I could distinctly see that it was a man, approaching me by the road. When he came opposite me, and the moon shone full in his face, I knew him to be a young mulatto, named David, the coachman of a widow lady, who resided somewhere near Charleston; but who had been at the house of my master, for two or three weeks, as a visiter, with her two daughters.

This man passed on at a quick step, without observing me; and the suspicion instantly riveted itself in my mind, that he was the murderer, for whose crime I had already suffered so much, and that he was now on his way to the place where he had left the body, for the purpose of removing, or burying it in the earth. I was confident, that no honest purpose could bring him to this place, at this time of night, alone. I was about two miles from home, and an equal distance from the spot, where the girl had been seized.

Of her subsequent murder, no one entertained a doubt; for it was not to be expected, that the fellow who had been guilty of one great crime, would flinch from the commission of another, of equal magnitude, and suffer his victim to exist, as a witness to identify his person.

I felt animated, by a spirit of revenge, against the wretch, whoever he might be, who had brought me so near to torture and death; and feeble and weak as I was, resolved to pursue the foot-steps of this coachman, at a wary and cautious distance, and ascertain, if possible, the object of his visit to these woods, at this time of night.

I waited until he had passed me, more than a hundred yards; and until I could barely discover his form, in the faint light of the deep shade of the trees, when stealing quietly into the road, I followed, with the caution of a spy, traversing the camp of an enemy. We were now in a dark pine forest, and on both sides of us, were tracts of low swampy ground, covered with thickets so dense, as to be difficult of penetration, even by a person on foot. The road led along a neck of elevated, and dry ground, that divided these swamps for more than a mile, when they terminated, and were succeeded by ground that produced scarcely any other timber, than a scrubby kind of oak, called black jack. It was amongst these black jacks, about half a mile beyond the swamps, that the lady had been carried off. I had often been here, for the purpose of snaring, and trapping, the small game of these woods, and was well acquainted with the topography of this forest, for some distance, on both sides of the road.

It was necessary for me to use the utmost caution, in the enterprise I was now engaged in. The road we were now travelling, was in no place very broad, and at some points, barely wide enough to permit a carriage to pass between the trees, that lined its sides. In some places, it was so dark that I could not see the man, whose steps I followed: but was obliged to depend on the sound, produced by the tread of his feet, upon the ground. I deemed it necessary to keep as close as possible, to the object of my pursuit, lest he should suddenly turn into the swamp, on one side or the other of the road, and elude my vigilance; for I had no doubt that he would quit the road, somewhere. As we approached the termination of the low grounds, my anxiety became intense, lest he should escape me; and at one time, I could not have been more than one hundred feet behind him; but he continued his course, until he reached the oak woods, and came to a place where an old cart-road led off to the left, along the side of the Dark Swamp, as it was termed in the neighbourhood.

This road, the mulatto took, without turning to look behind him. Here my difficulties, and perils increased, for I now felt myself in danger, as I had no longer any doubt, that I was on the trail of the murderer, and that, if discovered by him, my life would be the price of my curiosity. I was too weak to be able to struggle with him, for a minute; though if the blood which I had lost, through his wickedness, could have been restored to my veins, I could have seized him by the neck, and strangled him.

The road I now had to travel, was so little frequented, that bushes of the ground oak, and bilberry, stood thick, in almost every part of it. Many of these bushes were full of dry leaves, which had been touched by the frost, but had not yet fallen. It was easy for me to follow him, for I pursued by the noise he made, amongst these bushes; but it was not so easy for me to avoid, on my part, the making of a rustling, and agitation of the bushes, which might expose me to detection. I was now obliged to depend wholly on my ears, to guide my pursuit, my eyes being occupied in watching my own way, to enable me to avoid every object, the touching of which was likely to produce sound.

I followed this road more than a mile, led by the cracking of the sticks, or the shaking of the leaves. At length, I heard a loud, shrill whistle, and then a total silence succeeded. I now stood still, and in a few seconds, heard a noise in the swamp like the drumming of a pheasant. Soon afterwards, I heard the breaking of sticks, and the sounds caused by the bending of branches of trees. In a little time, I was satisfied, that something having life was moving in the swamp, and coming towards the place where the mulatto stood.

This was at the end of the cart-road, and opposite some large pine trees, which grew in the swamp, at the distance of two or three hundred yards from its margin. The noise in the swamp, still approached us; and at length a person came out of the thicket, and stood for a minute, or more, with the mulatto whom I had followed; and then they both entered the swamp, and took the course of the pine trees, as I could easily distinguish by my ears.

When they were gone, I advanced to the end of the road, and sat down upon a log, to listen to their progress, through the swamp. At length, it seemed that they had stopped, for I no longer heard any thing of them. Anxious, however, to ascertain more of this mysterious business, I remained in silence on the log, determined to stay there until day, if I could not sooner learn something to satisfy me, why these men had gone into the swamp. All uncertainty upon this subject was, however, quickly removed from my mind; for within less than ten minutes, after I had ceased to hear them moving in the thicket, I was shocked by the faint, but shrill wailings of a female voice, accompanied with exclamations, and supplications, in a tone so feeble, that I could only distinguish a few solitary words.

My mind comprehended the whole ground of this matter, at a glance. The lady supposed to have been murdered, on Sunday evening, was still living; and concealed by the two fiends who had passed out of my sight, but a few minutes before. The one I knew, for I had examined his features, within a few feet of me, in the full light of the moon; and, that the other was Hardy, I was as perfectly convinced, as if I had seen him also.

I now rose to return home; the cries of the female in the swamp, still continuing; but growing weaker, and dying away, as I receded from the place where I had sat.

I was now in possession of the clearest evidence, of the guilt of the two murderers; but I was afraid to communicate my knowledge to my master, lest he should suspect me of being an accomplice in this crime; and, if the lady could not be recovered alive, I had no doubt, that Hardy and his companion, were sufficiently depraved, to charge me as a participator with themselves, to be avenged upon me. I was confident that the mulatto, David, would return to the house before day, and be found in his bed in the morning; which he could easily do, for he slept in a part of the stable loft; under pretence of being near the horses of his mistress.

I thought it possible, that Hardy might also return home, that night, and endeavour to account for his absence from home on Monday afternoon, by some ingenious lie; in the invention of which I knew him to be very expert. In this case, I saw that I should have to run the risk, of being overpowered by the number of my false accusers; and, as I stood alone, they might yet be able to sacrifice my life, and escape the punishment due to their crimes. After much consideration, I came to the resolution at returning, as quick as possible, to the quarter—calling up the overseer—and acquainting him with all that I had seen, heard, and done, in the course of this night.

As I did not know what time of night it was, when I left my bed, I was apprehensive that day might break before I could so far mature my plans, as to have persons to way-lay, and arrest the mulatto, on his return home; but when I roused the overseer, he told me it was only one o'clock, and seemed but little inclined to credit my story; but, after talking to me several minutes, he told me he now, more than ever, suspected me to be the murderer; but he would go with me, and see if I had told the truth. When we arrived at the great house, some members of the family had not yet gone to bed, having been kept up by the arrival of several gentlemen, who had been searching the woods all day for the lost lady, and who had come here to seek lodgings, when it was near midnight. My master was in bed, but was called up and listened attentively to my story—at the close of which, he shook his head, and said with an oath, "You ——, I believe you to be the murderer; but we will go and see if all you say is a lie; if it is, the torments of —— will be pleasure to what awaits you. You have escaped once, but you will not get off a second time." I now found that somebody must die; and if the guilty could not be found, the innocent would have to atone for them. The manner in which my master had delivered his words, assured me, that the life of somebody must be taken.

This new danger aroused my energies,—and I told them I was ready to go, and take the consequences. Accordingly, the overseer, my young master, and three other gentlemen, immediately set out with me. It was agreed that we should all travel on foot; the overseer and I going a few paces in advance of the others. We proceeded silently, but rapidly, on our way; and as we passed it, I shewed them the place where I sat under the holly bush, when the mulatto passed me. We neither saw nor heard any person on the road, and reached the log at the end of the cart-road, where I sat, when I heard the cries in the swamp. All was now quiet, and our party lay down in the bushes, on each side of a large gum tree; at the root of which the two murderers stood, when they talked together, before they entered the thicket. We had not been here more than an hour, when I heard, as I lay with my head near the ground, a noise in the swamp, which I believed could only be made by those whom we sought.

I, however, said nothing, and the gentlemen did not hear it. It was caused, as I afterwards ascertained, by dragging the fallen branch of a tree, along the ground, for the purpose of lighting the fire.

The night was very clear and serene—its silence only being broken at intervals, by the loud hooting of the great long-eared owls, which are numerous in these swamps. I felt oppressed by the cold, and was glad to hear the crowing of a cock, at a great distance, announcing the approach of day. This was followed, after a short interval, by the cracking of sticks, and by other tokens, which I knew could proceed only from the motions of living bodies. I now whispered to the overseer, who lay near me, that it would soon appear whether I had spoken the truth or not.

All were now satisfied that people were coming out of the swamp, for we heard them speak to each other. I desired the overseer to advise the other gentlemen to let the culprits come out of the swamp, and gain the high ground, before we attempted to seize them; but this counsel was, unfortunately, not taken; and when they came near to the gum-tree, and it could be clearly seen that there were two men, and no more, one of the gentlemen called out to them to stop, or they were dead. Instead, however, of stopping, they both sprang forward, and took to flight. They did not turn into the swamp, for the gentleman who ordered them to stop, was in their rear—they having already passed him. At the moment they had started to run, each of the gentlemen fired two pistols at them. The pistols made the forest ring, on all sides; and I supposed it was impossible for either of the fugitives to escape from so many balls. This was, however, not the case; for only one of them was injured. The mulatto, David, had one arm and one leg broken, and fell about ten yards from us; but Hardy escaped, and when the smoke cleared away, he was nowhere to be seen. On being interrogated, David acknowledged that the lady was in the swamp, on a small island, and was yet alive—that he and Hardy had gone from the house on Sunday, for the purpose of waylaying and carrying her off; and intended to kill her little brother—this part of the duty being assigned to him, whilst Hardy was to drag the sister from her horse. As they were both mulattos, they blacked their faces with charcoal, taken from a pine stump, partially burned. The boy was riding before his sister, and when Hardy seized her and dragged her from her horse, she screamed and frightened both the horses, which took off at full speed, by which means the boy escaped. Finding that the boy was out of his reach, David remained in the bushes, until Hardy brought the sister to him. They immediately tied a handkerchief round her face, so as to cover her mouth and stifle her shrieks; and taking her in their arms, carried her back toward my master's house, for some distance, through the woods, until they came to the cart-road leading along the swamp. They then followed this road as far as it led, and, turning into the swamp, took their victim to a place they had prepared for her the Sunday before, on a small knoll in the swamp, where the ground was dry.

Her hands were closely confined, and she was tied by the feet to a tree. He said he had stolen some bread, and taken it to her this night; but when they unbound her mouth to permit her to eat, she only wept and made a noise, begging them to release her, until they were obliged again to bandage her mouth.

It was now determined by the gentlemen, that as the lady was still alive, we ought not to lose a moment in endeavouring to rescue her from her dreadful situation. I pointed out the large pine trees, in the direction of which I heard the cries of the young lady, and near which I believed she was—undertaking, at the same time, to act as pilot, in penetrating the thicket. Three of the gentlemen and myself, accordingly set out, leaving the other two with the wounded mulatto, with directions to inform us when we deviated from a right line to the pine trees. This they were able to do by attending to the noise we made, with nearly as much accuracy as if they had seen us.

The atmosphere had now become a little cloudy, and the morning was very dark, even in the oak woods; but when we had entered the thickets of the swamp, all objects became utterly invisible; and the obscurity was as total as if our eyes had been closed. Our companions on the dry ground, lost sight of the pine trees, and could not give us any directions in our journey. We became entangled in briers, and vines, and mats of bushes, from which the greatest exertions were necessary to disengage ourselves.

It was so dark, that we could not see the fallen trees; and, missing these, fell into quagmires, and sloughs of mud and water, into which we sunk up to the arm-pits, and from which we were able to extricate ourselves, only by seizing upon the hanging branches of the surrounding trees. After struggling in this half-drowned condition, for at least a quarter of an hour, we reached a small dry spot, where the gentlemen again held a council, as to ulterior measures. They called to those left on the shore, to know if we were proceeding toward the pine trees; but received for answer that the pines were invisible, and they knew not whether we were right or wrong. In this state of uncertainty, it was thought most prudent to wait the coming of day, in our present resting place.

The air was frosty, and in our wet clothes, loaded as we were with mud, it may be imagined that our feelings were not pleasant; and when the day broke, it brought us but little relief, for we found, as soon as it was light enough to enable us to see around, that we were on one of those insulated dry spots, called "*tussocks*," by the people of the south. These *tussocks* are formed by clusters of small trees, which, taking root in the mud, are, in process of time, surrounded by long grass, which, entwining its roots with those of the trees, overspread and cover the surface of the muddy foundation, by which the superstructure is supported. These *tussocks* are often several yards in diameter. That upon which we now were, stood in the midst of a great miry pool, into which we were again obliged to launch ourselves, and struggle onward for a distance of ten yards, before we reached the line of some fallen and decaying trees.

It was now broad daylight, and we saw the pine trees, at the distance of about a hundred yards from us; but even with the assistance of the light, we had great difficulty in reaching them,—to do which, we were compelled to travel at least a quarter of a mile by the angles and curves of the fallen timber, upon which alone we could walk; this part of the swamp being a vast half-fluid bog.

It was sunrise when we reached the pines, which we found standing upon a small islet of firm ground, containing, as well as I could judge, about half an acre, covered with a heavy growth of white maples, swamp oaks, a few large pines, and a vast mat of swamp laurel, called in the south *ivy*. I had no doubt, that the object of our search was somewhere on this little island; but small as it was, it was no trifling affair to give every part of it a minute examination, for the stems and branches of the ivy were so minutely interwoven with each other, and spread along the ground in so many curves and crossings, that it was impossible to proceed a single rod, without lying down and creeping along the earth.

The gentlemen agreed, that if any one discovered the young lady, he should immediately call to the others; and we all entered the thicket. I, however, turned along the edge of the island, with the intention of making its circuit, for the purpose of tracing, if possible, the footsteps of those who had passed between it and the main shore. I made my way more than half round the island, without much difficulty, and without discovering any signs of persons having been here before me; but in crossing the trunk of a large tree which had fallen, and the top of which extended far into the ivy, I perceived some stains of mud, on the bark of the log. Looking into the swamp, I saw that the root of this tree was connected with other fallen timber, extending beyond the reach of my vision which was obstructed by the bramble of the swamp, and the numerous ever-greens, growing here. I now advanced along the trunk of the tree, until I reached its topmost branches, and here discovered evident signs of a small trail, leading into the thicket of ivy. Creeping along, and following this trail, by the small bearberry bushes that had been trampled down, and had not again risen to an erect position, I was led almost across the island, and found that the small bushes were discomposed, quite up to the edge of a vast heap of the branches of ever-green trees, produced by the falling of several large juniper cypress trees, which grew in the swamp in a cluster, and, having been blown down, had fallen with their tops athwart each other, and upon the almost impervious mat of ivies, with which the surface of the island was coated over.

I stood and looked at this mass of entangled green brush, but could not perceive the slightest marks of any entrance into its labyrinths; nor did it seem possible for any creature, larger than a squirrel, to penetrate it. It now for the first time struck me as a great oversight in the gentlemen, that they had not compelled the mulatto, David, to describe the place where they had concealed the lady; and, as the forest was so dense, that no communication could be had with the shore, either by words or signs, we could not now procure any information on this subject. I therefore called to the gentlemen, who were on the island with me, and desired them to come to me without delay.

Small as this island was, it was after the lapse of many minutes, that the overseer, and the other gentlemen, arrived where I stood; and when they came, they would have been the subjects of mirthful emotions, had not the tragic circumstances, in which I was placed, banished from my heart, every feeling but that of the most profound melancholy.

When the gentlemen had assembled, I informed them of signs of footsteps, that I had traced from the other side of the island; and told them, that I believed the young lady lay somewhere under the heap of brushwood, before us. This opinion obtained but little credit, because there was no opening in the brush, by which any one could enter it; but on going a few paces round the heap, I perceived a small, snaggy pole, resting on the brush, and nearly concealed by it, with the lower end stuck in the ground. The branches had been cut from this pole, at the distance of three or four inches from the main stem, which made it a tolerable substitute for a ladder. I immediately ascended the pole, which led me to the top of the pile; and here I discovered an opening in the brush, between the forked top of one of the cypress trees, through which a man might easily pass. Applying my head to this aperture, I distinctly heard a quick, and laborious breathing, like that of a person in extreme illness; and again called the gentlemen to follow me.

When they came up the ladder, the breathing was audible to all; and one of the gentlemen, whom I now perceived to be the stranger, who was with us in my master's cellar, when I was bled, slid down into the dark and narrow passage, without uttering a word. I confess, that some feelings of trepidation passed through my nerves, when I stood alone; but now that a leader had preceded me, I followed, and glided through the smooth and elastic cypress tops, to the bottom of this vast labyrinth of green boughs.

When I reached the ground, I found myself in contact with the gentleman, who was in advance of me, and near one end of a large concave, oblong, open space, formed by the branches of the trees, having been supported and kept above the ground, partly by a cluster of very large and strong ivies, that grew here, and partly by a young gum tree, which had been bent into the form of an arch, by the falling timber.

Though we could not see into this leafy cavern from above, yet when we had been in it, a few moments, we had light enough to see the objects around us, with tolerable clearness; but that which surprised us both greatly, was, that the place was totally silent, and we could not perceive the appearance of any living thing, except ourselves.

After we had been here some minutes, our vision became still more distinct; and I saw, at the other end of the open space, ashes of wood, and some extinguished brands, but there was no smoke. Going to these ashes, and stirring them with a stick, I found coals of fire carefully covered over, in a hole six or eight inches deep.

When he saw the fire, the gentleman spoke to me, and expressed his astonishment, that we heard the breathing no longer; but he had scarcely uttered these words, when a faint groan, as of a woman in great pain, was heard to issue, apparently from the ground; but a motion of branches on our right, assured me that the sufferer was concealed there. The gentleman sprung to the spot, pushed aside the pendant boughs, stooped low beneath the bent ivies, and came out, bearing in his hands, a delicate female figure. As he turned round, and exposed her half-closed eye and white forehead, to the light, he exclaimed, "Eternal God, Maria, is it you?" He then pressed her to his bosom, and sunk upon the ground, still holding her closely in his embrace.

The lady lay motionless in his arms, and I thought she was dead. Her hair hung matted and dishevelled from her head; a handkerchief, once white, but now soiled with dust, and stained with blood, was bound firmly round her head, covering her mouth and chin, and was fastened at the back of the neck, by a double knot, and secured by a ligature of cypress bark.

I knew not whom most to pity,—the lady, who now lay insensible, in the arms that still clasped her tenderly; or the unhappy gentleman, who having cut the cords from her limbs, and the handkerchief from her face, now sat, and silently gazed upon her death-like countenance. He uttered not a sigh, and moved not a joint; but his breast heaved with agony; the sinews, and muscles of his neck rose and fell, like those of a man in convulsions; all the lineaments of his face were, alternately, contracted and expanded, as if his last moments were at hand; whilst great drops of sweat rolled down his forehead, as though he struggled against an enemy, whose strength was more than human.

Oppressed by the sight of so much wretchedness, I turned from its contemplation; and called aloud to the gentlemen without, (who had all this time been waiting to hear from us,) to come up the ladder, to the top of the pile of boughs. The overseer was quickly at the top of the opening, by which I had descended; and I now informed him that we had found the lady. He ordered me to hand her up—and I desired the gentleman, who was with me, to permit me to do so; but this he refused—and mounting the boughs of the fallen trees, and supporting himself by the strong branches of the ivies, he quickly reached the place, where the overseer stood.

He even here refused to part from his charge, but bore her down the ladder alone. He was, however, obliged to accept aid, in conveying her through the swamp, to the place where we had left the two gentlemen, with the wounded mulatto, whose sufferings, demon as he was, were sufficient to move the hardest heart. His right arm, and left leg were broken; and he had lost much blood, before we returned from the island; and as he could not walk, it was necessary to carry him home. We had not brought any horses; and until the lady was recovered, no one seemed to think any more about the mulatto, after he was shot down.

It was proposed to send for a horse, to take David home; but it was finally agreed, that we should leave him in the woods, where he was, until a man could be sent for him, with a cart. At the time we left him, his groans and lamentations seemed to excite no sympathy, in the breast of any. More cruel sufferings yet awaited him.

The lady was carried home, in the arms of the gentlemen; and she did not speak, until after she was bathed, and put to bed in my master's house, as I afterwards heard. I know she did not speak on the way. She died on the fourth day after her rescue; and before her death, related the circumstances of her misfortune, as I was told by a coloured woman, who attended her in her illness, in the following manner:

As she was riding in the dusk of the evening, at a rapid trot, a few yards behind her brother, a black man sprang from behind a tree standing close by the side of the road; seized her by her riding dress, and dragged her to the ground, but failed to catch the bridle of the horse, which sprang off at full speed. Another negro immediately came to the aid of the first, and said, "I could not catch him— we must make haste." They carried her as fast as they could go, to the place where we found her; when they bound her hands, feet, and mouth, and left her until the next night; and had left her the second morning, only a few minutes, when she heard the report of guns. Soon after this, by great efforts, she extricated one of her feet from the bark, with which she was bound; but finding herself too weak to stand, she crawled, as far as she could, under the boughs of the trees, hoping that when her assassins returned again, they would not be able to find her; and that she might there die alone.

Exhausted by the efforts she had made, to remove herself, she fell into the stupor of sleep, from which she was aroused by the noise we made, when we descended into the cavern. She then, supposing us to be her destroyers returned again, lay still, and breathed as softly as possible, to prevent us from hearing her; but when she heard the voice of the gentleman who was with me, the tones of which were familiar to her, she groaned, and moved her feet, to let us know where she was. This exertion, and the idea of her horrid condition, overcame the strength of her nerves; and when her deliverer raised her from the ground, she had swooned, and was unconscious of all things.

We had no sooner arrived at the house, than inquiry was made for Hardy; but it was ascertained in the kitchen, that he had not been seen, since the previous evening, at night fall, when he had left the kitchen for the purpose of going to sleep at the stable, with David, as he had told one of the black women; and preparation was immediately made, to go in pursuit of him.

For this purpose all the gentlemen present equipped themselves with pistols, fowling pieces, and horns—such as are used by fox hunters. Messengers were despatched round the country, to give notice to all the planters, within the distance of many miles, of the crime that had been committed, and of the escape of one of its perpetrators, with a request to them to come without delay, and join in the pursuit, intended to be given. Those who had dogs, trained to chase thieves, were desired to bring them; and a gentleman who lived twelve miles off, and who owned a blood hound, was sent for, and requested to come with his dog, in all haste.

In consequence, I suppose, of the information I had given, I was permitted to be present at these deliberations; and though my advice was not asked, I was often interrogated, concerning my knowledge of the affair. Some proposed to go at once, with dogs and horses, into the woods, and traverse the swamp and thickets, for the purpose of rousing Hardy from the place of concealment, he might have chosen; but the opinion of the overseer prevailed, who thought, that from the intimate knowledge possessed by him, of all the swamps and coverts in the neighbourhood, there would be little hope of discovering him in this manner. The overseer advised them, to wait the coming of the gentleman with his blood hound, before they entered the woods; for the reason, that if the blood hound could be made to take the trail, he would certainly find his game, before he quit it, if not thrown off the scent by the men, horses, and dogs crossing his course; but if the blood hound could not take the scent, they might then adopt the proposed plan of pursuit, with as much success as at present. This counsel being adopted, the horses were ordered into the stable; and the gentlemen entered the house to take their breakfast, and wait the arrival of the blood hound.

Nothing was said of the mulatto, David, who seemed to be forgotten—not a word being spoken by any one of bringing him from the woods. I knew that he was suffering the most agonizing pains, and great as were his crimes, his groans and cries of anguish still seemed to echo in my ears; but I was afraid to make any application in his behalf, lest, even yet, I might be suspected of some participation in his offences; for I knew that the most horrid punishments were often inflicted upon slaves, merely on suspicion.

As the morning advanced, the number of men and horses in front of my master's mansion increased; and before ten o'clock, I think there were, at least, fifty of each—the horses standing hitched and the men conversing in groups without, or assembled together within the house.

At length the owner of the blood hound came, bringing with him his dog, in a chaise, drawn by one horse. The harness was removed from the horse, its place supplied by a saddle and bridle, and the whole party set off for the woods. As they rode away, my master, who was one of the company, told me to follow them; but we had proceeded only a little distance, when the gentlemen stopped, and my master after speaking with the owner of the dog, told the overseer to go back to the house, and get some piece of the clothes of Hardy, that had been worn by him lately. The overseer returned, and we all proceeded forward to the place where David lay.

We found him where we had left him, greatly weakened by the loss of blood, and complaining that the cold air caused his wounds to smart intolerably. When I came near him, he looked at me and told me I had betrayed him. None of the gentlemen seemed at all moved by his sufferings, and when any of them spoke to him, it was with derision, and every epithet of scorn and contumely. As it was apparent that he could not escape, no one proposed to remove him to a place of greater safety; but several of the horsemen, as they passed, lashed him with the thongs of their whips; but I do not believe he felt these blows—the pain he endured from his wounds being so great, as to drown the sensation of such minor afflictions.

The day had already become warm, although the night had been cold; the sun shone with great clearness, and many carrion crows, attracted by the scent of blood, were perched upon the trees near where we now were.

When the overseer came up with us, he brought an old blanket, in which Hardy had slept for some time, and handed it to the owner of the dog; who, having first caused the hound to smell of the blanket, untied the cord in which he had been led, and turned him into the woods. The dog went from us fifty or sixty yards, in a right line, then made a circle around us, again commenced his circular movement, and pursued it nearly half round. Then he dropped his nose to the ground, snuffed the tainted surface, and moved off through the woods, slowly, almost touching the earth with his nose. The owner of the dog, and twelve or fifteen others followed him, whilst the residue of the party dispersed themselves along the edge of the swamp; and the overseer ordered me to stay, and watch the horses of those who dismounted, going himself on foot in the pursuit.

When the gentlemen were all gone out of sight, I went to David, who lay all this time within my view, for the purpose of asking him if I could render him any assistance. He begged me to bring him some water, as he was dying of thirst, no less than with the pain of his wounds. One of the horsemen had left a large tin horn, hanging on his saddle; this I took, and stopping the small end closely with leaves, filled it with water from the swamp, and gave it to the wounded man, who drank it, and then turning his head towards me, said—"Hardy and I had laid a plan to have this thing brought upon you, and to have you hung for it— but you have escaped." He then asked me if they intended to leave him to die in the woods, or to take him home and hang him. I told him I had heard them talk of taking him home in a cart, but what was to be done with him I did not know. I felt a horror of the crimes committed by this man; was pained by the sight of his sufferings, and being unable to relieve the one, or to forgive the other, went to a place where I could neither see nor hear him, and sat down to await the return of those who had gone in pursuit of Hardy.

In the circumstances which surrounded me, it cannot be supposed that my feelings were pleasant, or that time moved very fleetly; but painful as my situation was, I was obliged to bear it for many hours. From the time the gentlemen left me, I neither saw nor heard them, until late in the afternoon, when five or six of them returned, having lost their companions in the woods.

Toward sundown, I heard a great noise of horns blown, and of men shouting at a distance in the forest; and soon after, my master, the owner of the blood hound, and many others returned, bringing with them, Hardy, whom the hound had followed ten or twelve miles, through the swamps and thickets; had at last caught him, and would soon have killed him, had he not been compelled to relinquish his prey. When the party had all returned, a kind of court was held in the woods, where we then were, for the purpose of determining what punishment should be indicted upon Hardy and David. All agreed at once, that an example of the most terrific character ought to be made of such atrocious villains, and that it would defeat the ends of justice to deliver these fellows up to the civil authority, to be hanged like common murderers. The next measure was, to settle upon the kind of punishment to be inflicted upon them, and the manner of executing the sentence.

Hardy was, all this time, sitting on the ground, covered with blood, and yet bleeding profusely, in hearing of his inexorable judges. The dog had mangled both his arms, and hands, in a shocking manner; torn a large piece of flesh entirely away from one side of his breast, and sunk his fangs deep in the side of his neck. No other human creature that I have ever seen, presented a more deplorable spectacle of mingled crime and cruelty.

It was now growing late, and the fate of these miserable men was to be decided before the company separated to go to their several homes. One proposed to burn them, another to flay them alive, and a third to starve them to death, and many other modes of slowly and tormentingly extinguishing life, were named; but that which was finally adopted, was, of all others, the most horrible. The wretches were unanimously sentenced to be stripped naked, and bound down securely upon their backs, on the naked earth, in sight of each other; to have their mouths closely covered with bandages, to prevent them from making a noise to frighten away the birds, and in this manner to be left, to be devoured alive by the carrion crows and buzzards, which swarm in every part of South Carolina.

The sentence was instantly carried into effect, so far as its execution depended on us. Hardy, and his companion, were divested of their clothes, stretched upon their backs on the ground; their mouths bandaged with handkerchiefs—their limbs extended—and these, together with their necks, being crossed by numerous poles, were kept close to the earth by forked sticks driven into the ground, so as to prevent the possibility of moving any part of their persons; and in this manner these wicked men were left to be torn in pieces, by birds of prey. The buzzards, and carrion crows, always attack dead bodies by pulling out and consuming the eyes first. They then tear open the bowels, and feed upon the intestines.

We returned to my master's plantation, and I did not see this place again until the next Sunday, when several of my fellow-slaves went with me to see the remains of the dead, but we found only their bones. Great flocks of buzzards, and carrion crows, were assembled in the trees, giving a dismal aspect to the woods; and I hastened to abandon a place, fraught with so many afflicting recollections.

The lady, who had been the innocent sacrifice of the brutality of the men, whose bones I had seen bleaching in the sun, had died on Saturday evening, and her corpse was buried on Monday, in a grave-yard on my master's plantation. I have never seen a large cotton plantation, in Carolina, without its burying ground. This burying ground is not only the place of sepulture of the family, who are the proprietors of the estate, but also of many other persons, who have lived in the neighbourhood. Half an acre, or an acre of ground, is appropriated as a grave-yard, on one side of which the proprietors of the estate, from age to age, are buried; whilst the other parts of the ground are open to strangers, poor people of their vicinity, and, in general, to all who choose to inter their dead within its boundaries. This custom prevails as far north as Maryland; and it seems to me to be much more consonant to the feelings of solitude and tender recollections, which we always associate with the memory of departed friends, than the practice of promiscuous interment in a church-yard, where all idea of seclusion is banished, by the last home of the dead being thrown open to the rude intrusions of strangers; where the sanctity of the sepulchre is treated as a common, and where the grave itself is, in a few years, torn up, or covered over, to form a temporary resting place for some new tenant.

The family of the deceased lady, though not very wealthy, was amongst the most ancient and respectable in this part of the country; and, on Sunday, whilst the dead body lay in my master's house, there was a continual influx and efflux of visiters, in carriages, on horse-back, and on foot. The house was open to all who chose to come; and the best wines, cakes, sweet-meats and fruits, were handed about to the company, by the servants; though I observed that none remained for dinner, except the relations of the deceased, those of my master's family, and the young gentleman who was with me on the island. The visiters remained but a short time when they came, and were nearly all in mourning. This was the first time that I had seen a large number of the fashionable people of Carolina assembled together, and their appearance impressed me with an opinion favourable to their character. I had never seen an equal number of people anywhere, whose deportment was more orderly and decorous, nor whose feelings seemed to be more in accordance with the solemnity of the event, which had brought them together.

I had been ordered by the overseer, to remain at the great house until the afternoon, for the purpose, as I afterwards learned, of being seen by those who came to see the corpse; and many of the ladies and gentlemen inquired for me, and when I was pointed out to them, commended my conduct and fidelity, in discovering the authors of the murder—condoled with me for having suffered innocently, and several gave me money. One old lady, who came in a pretty carriage, drawn by two black horses, gave me a dollar.

On Monday, the funeral took place, and several hundred persons followed the corpse to the grave, over which a minister delivered a short sermon. The young gentleman who was with me when we found the deceased on the island, walked with her mother to the grave-yard, and the little brother followed, with a younger sister.

After the interment, wines and refreshments were handed round to the whole assembly, and, at least a hundred persons remained for dinner, with my master's family. At four o'clock in the afternoon, the carriages and horses were ordered to the door of the court-yard of the house, and the company retired. At sundown, the plantation was as quiet as if its peace had never been disturbed.

---

# CHAPTER XIV.

I HAVE before observed, that the negroes of the cotton plantations are exceedingly superstitious; and they are indeed, prone, beyond all other people that I have ever known, to believe in ghosts, and the existence of an infinite number of supernatural agents. No story of a miraculous character, can be too absurd to obtain credit with them; and a narrative is not the less eagerly listened to, nor the more cautiously received, because it is impossible in its circumstances. Within a few weeks after the deaths of the two malefactors, to whose horrible crimes were awarded equally horrible punishments, the forest that had been the scene of these bloody deeds, was reported, and believed to be visited at night by beings of unearthly make, whose groans, and death-struggles, were heard in the darkest recesses of the woods, amidst the flapping of the wings of vultures, the fluttering of carrion crows, and the dismal croaking of ravens. In the midst of this nocturnal din, the noise caused by the tearing of the flesh from the bones, was heard, and the panting breath of the agonized sufferer, quivering under the beaks of his tormentors, as they consumed his vitals, floated audibly upon the evening breeze.

The murdered lady was also seen walking by moonlight, near the spot where she had been dragged from her horse, wrapped in a blood-stained mantle; overhung with gory and dishevelled locks.

The little island in the swamp, was said to present spectacles too horrible for human eyes to look upon, and sounds were heard to issue from it, which no human ear could bear. Terrific and ghastly fires were seen to burst up, at midnight, amongst the ever-greens that clad this lonely spot, emitting scents too suffocating and sickly to be endured; whilst demoniac yells, shouts of despair and groans of agony, mingled their echos in the solitude of the woods.

Whilst I remained in this neighbourhood, no coloured person ever travelled this road, alone, after night-fall; and many white men would have ridden ten miles round the country, to avoid the passage of the ridge road, after dark. Generations must pass away, before the tradition of this place will be forgotten; and many a year will open and close, before the last face will be pale, or the last heart beat, as the twilight traveller, skirts the borders of the Murderers' Swamp.

We had allowances of meat distributed to all the people twice this fall— once when we had finished the saving of the fodder, and again soon after the murder of the young lady. The first time we had beef, such as I had driven from the woods when I went to the alligator pond; but now we had two hogs given to us, which weighed, one a hundred and thirty, and the other a hundred and fifty-six pounds. This was very good pork, and I received a pound and a quarter as my share of it. This was the first pork that I had tasted in Carolina, and it afforded a real feast. We had, in our family, full seven pounds of good fat meat; and as we now had plenty of sweet potatoes, both in our gardens and in our weekly allowance, we had on the Sunday following the funeral, as good a dinner of stewed pork and potatoes, as could have been found in all Carolina. We did not eat all our meat on Sunday, but kept part of it until Tuesday, when we warmed it in a pot, with an addition of parsley and other herbs, and had another very comfortable meal.

I had, by this time, become in some measure, acquainted with the country, and began to lay and execute plans to procure supplies of such things as were not allowed me by my master. I understood various methods of entrapping rackoons, and other wild animals that abounded in the large swamps of this country; and besides the skins, which were worth something for their furs, I generally procured as many rackoons, opossums, and rabbits, as afforded us two or three meals in a week. The woman with whom I lived, understood the way of dressing an opossum, and I was careful to provide one for our Sunday dinner every week, so long as these animals continued fat and in good condition.

All the people on the plantation did not live as well as our family did, for many of the men did not understand trapping game, and others were too indolent to go far enough from home to find good places for setting their traps. My principal trapping ground was three miles from home, and I went three times a week, always after night, to bring home my game, and keep my traps in good order. Many of the families in the quarter caught no game, and had no meat, except that which we received from the overseer, which averaged about six or seven meals in the year.

Lydia, the woman whom I have mentioned heretofore, was one of the women whose husbands procured little or nothing for the sustenance of their families, and I often gave her a quarter of a rackoon or a small opossum, for which she appeared very thankful. Her health was not good—she had a bad cough, and often told me, she was feverish and restless at night. It appeared clear to me that this woman's constitution was broken by hardships, and sufferings, and that she could not live long in her present mode of existence. Her husband, a native of a country far in the interior of Africa, said he had been a priest in his own nation, and had never been taught to do any kind of labour, being supported by the contributions of the public; and he now maintained, as far as he could, the same kind of lazy dignity, that he had enjoyed at home. He was compelled by the overseer to work, with the other hands, in the field, but as soon as he had come into his cabin, he took his seat, and refused to give his wife the least assistance in doing any thing. She was consequently obliged to do the little work that it was necessary to perform in the cabin; and also to bear all the labour of weeding and cultivating the family patch or garden. The husband was a morose, sullen man, and said, he formerly had ten wives in his own country, who all had to work for, and wait upon him; and he thought himself badly off here, in having but one woman to do any thing for him. This man was very irritable, and often beat and otherwise maltreated his wife, on the slightest provocation, and the overseer refused to protect her, on the ground, that he never interfered in the family quarrels of the black people. I pitied this woman greatly, but as it was not in my power to remove her from the presence and authority of her husband, I thought it prudent not to say nor do any thing to provoke him further against her. As the winter approached, and the autumnal rains set in, she was frequently exposed in the field, and was wet for several hours together: this, joined to the want of warm and comfortable woollen clothes, caused her to contract colds, and hoarseness, which increased the severity of her cough. A few days before Christmas, her child died, after an illness of only three days. I assisted her and her husband to inter the infant—which was a little boy—and its father buried with it, a small bow and several arrows; a little bag of parched meal; a miniature canoe, about a foot long, and a little paddle, (with which he said it would cross the ocean to his own country) a small stick, with an iron nail, sharpened, and fastened into one end of it; and a piece of white muslin, with several curious and strange figures painted on it in blue and red, by which, he said, his relations and countrymen would know the infant to be his son, and would receive it accordingly, on its arrival amongst them.

Cruel as this man was to his wife, I could not but respect the sentiments which inspired his affection for his child; though it was the affection of a barbarian. He cut a lock of hair from his head, threw it upon the dead infant, and closed the grave with his own hands. He then told us the God of his country was looking at him, and was pleased with what he had done. Thus ended the funeral service.

As we returned home, Lydia told me she was rejoiced that her child was dead, and out of a world in which slavery and wretchedness must have been its only portion. I am now, said she, ready to follow my child, and the sooner I go, the better for me. She went with us to the field until the month of January, when, as we were returning from our work, one stormy and wet evening, she told me she should never pick any more cotton—that her strength was gone, and she could work no more. When we assembled, at the blowing of the horn, on the following morning, Lydia did not appear. The overseer, who had always appeared to dislike this woman, when he missed her, swore very angrily, and said he supposed she was pretending to be sick, but if she was, he would soon cure her. He then stepped into his house and took some copperas from a little bag, and mixed it with water. I followed him to Lydia's cabin, where he compelled her to drink this solution of copperas. It caused her to vomit violently, and made her exceedingly sick. I think to this day, that this act of the overseer, was the most inhuman of all those that I have seen perpetrated upon defenceless slaves.

Lydia was removed that same day to the sick room, in a state of extreme debility and exhaustion. When she left this room again she was a corpse. Her disease was a consumption of the lungs, which terminated her life early in March. I assisted in carrying her to the grave, which I closed upon her, and covered with green turf. She sleeps by the side of her infant, in a corner of the negro grave-yard, of this plantation. Death was to her a welcome messenger, who came to remove her from toil that she could not support, and from misery that she could not sustain.

Her life had been a morning of pleasure, but a day of bitterness, upon which no sunlight had fallen. Had she known no other mode of existence than that which she saw on this plantation, her lot would have been happiness itself, in comparison with her actual destiny. Trained up as she had been in Maryland, no greater cruelty could have been devised by the malice of her most cunning enemy, than to transfer her from the service, and almost companionship, of an indulgent and affectionate mistress, to the condition in which I saw her, and knew her, in the cotton fields of South Carolina.

In Maryland, it is a custom as widely extended as the state itself, I believe, to give the slaves a week of holidays, at Christmas; and the master, who should attempt to violate this usage, would become an object of derision amongst his neighbours. But I learned, long before Christmas, that the force of custom was not so binding here, as it is farther north. In Maryland, Christmas comes at a season of leisure, when the work of the farm, or the tobacco plantation, is generally closed for the year; and, if a good supply of firewood has been provided, there seems to be but little for the people to do, and a week lost to the master, is a matter of little moment, at a period when the days are short and cold; but in the cotton country, the case is very different.

Christmas comes in the very midst of cotton picking. The richest and best part of the crop has been secured before this period, it is true; but large quantities of cotton still remain in the field, and every pound that can be saved from the winds, or the plough of the next spring, is a gain of its value, to the owner of the estate.

For these reasons, which are very powerful on the side of the master, there is but little Christmas on a large cotton plantation. In lieu of the week of holiday, which formerly prevailed even in Carolina, before cotton was cultivated as a crop, the master now gives the people a dinner of meat, on Christmas-day, and distributes amongst them their annual allowance of winter clothes, on estates where such an allowance is made; and where it is not, some small gratuity supplies its place.

There are cotton planters who give no clothes to their slaves, but expect them to supply themselves with apparel, out of the proceeds of their Sunday labour and nightly earnings. Clothes of a certain quality were given to the people of the estate on which I lived, at the time of which I now speak; but they were not at all sufficient to keep us warm and comfortable in the winter; and the residue, we had to procure for ourselves. In Georgia, I lived three years with one master, and the best master, too, that I ever had in the south, who never gave me any clothes during that period, except an old great coat, and a pair of boots.—I shall have occasion to speak of him hereafter.

As Christmas of the year 1805, approached, we were all big with hope of obtaining three or four days, at least, if not a week of holiday; but when the day at length arrived, we were sorely disappointed, for on Christmas eve, when we had come from the field, with our cotton, the overseer fell into a furious passion, and swore at us all for our laziness, and many other bad qualities. He then told us that he had intended to give us three days, if we had worked well, but that we had been so idle, and had left so much cotton yet to be picked in the field, that he found it impossible to give us more than one day; but that he would go to the house, and endeavour to procure a meat dinner for us, and a dram in the morning. Accordingly, on the next morning, we received a dram of peach brandy, for each person; and two hogs, weighing together more than three hundred, were slaughtered and divided amongst us.

I went to the field and picked cotton all day, for which I was paid by the overseer, and at night I had a good dinner of stewed pork and sweet potatoes.— Such were the beginning and end of my first Christmas, on a cotton plantation. We went to work as usual the next morning, and continued our labour through the week, as if Christmas had been stricken from the calender. I had already saved and laid by a little more than ten dollars in money, but part of it had been given to me at the funeral. I was now much in want of clothes, none having been given me since I came here. I had, at the commencement of the cold weather, cut up my old blanket, and, with the aid of Lydia, who was a very good seamstress, converted it into a pair of trousers, and a long roundabout jacket; but this deprived me of my bed, which was imperfectly supplied by mats, which I made of rushes. The mats were very comfortable things to lie upon, but they were by no means equal to blankets for covering.

A report had been current amongst us, for some time, that there would be a distribution of clothes, to the people, at new-year's-day; but how much, or what kind of clothes we were to get, no one pretended to know, except that we were to get shoes, in conformity to a long-established rule of this plantation. From Christmas to new-year, appeared a long week to me, and I have no doubt that it appeared yet longer to some of my fellow-slaves, most of whom were entirely barefoot. I had made mockasins for myself, of the skins of squirrels, that I had caught in my traps, and by this means protected my feet from the frost, which was sometimes very heavy and sharp, in the morning.

On the first day of January, when we met at the blowing of the morning horn, the overseer told us, we must all proceed to the great house, where we were to receive our winter clothes; and surely, no order was ever more willingly obeyed. When we arrived at the house, our master was up, and we were all called into the great court yard in front of the dwelling. The overseer now told us, that shoes would be given to all those who were able to go to the field, to pick cotton. This deprived of shoes, the children, and several old persons, whose eyesight was not sufficiently clear, to enable them to pick cotton. A new blanket was then given to every one above seven years of age—children under seven, received no blanket, being left to be provided for by their parents. Children of this age, and under, go entirely naked, in the day-time, and sleep with their mothers at night, or are wrapped up together, in such bedding as the mother may possess. Children under seven years of age are of little use in picking cotton, and it is not supposed that their labour can repay the expense of clothing them in a manner to fit them to go to the field—they are, therefore, suffered to remain in the house or quarter, without clothes, from October to April. In summer they do not require clothes, and can perform such work as they are able to do, as well without garments as with them.

At the time we received our shoes, and blankets, there was not a good shirt in our quarter—but all the men, and women, had provided themselves with some sort of woollen clothes, out of their own savings. Woollen stuff, for a petticoat and short-gown, had also been given, before Christmas, to each of the women who were mothers of small children, or in such a condition as to render it certain, that they must, in a short time, become so. Many of the women could pick as much cotton as a man; and any good hand could earn sixty cents, by picking cotton on Sunday—the overseer paying us punctually for all the cotton we brought in, on Sunday evening. Besides this, a good hand could always, in a fine day, pick more cotton than was required to be brought home, as a day's work. I could not pick as much in a day, as some of the others, by four or five pounds; but I could generally carry home as much beyond the day's work, or task, as it is called, as entitled me to receive from five to ten cents every evening, from the overseer. This money was punctually paid to me every Saturday night; and in some weeks I cleared, in this way, as high as fifty cents, over and above what I earned on Sunday. One of the men cleared to himself, including his Sunday work, two dollars a week, for several weeks; and his savings, on this entire crop of cotton, were thirty-one dollars—but he was a first-rate cotton picker, and worked late and early. One of the women cleared twenty-six dollars to herself, in the same way. We were expected to clothe ourselves with these, and our other extra earnings; but some of the people performed no more work, through the week, than their regular task, and would not work constantly on Sunday. Such were not able to provide themselves with good clothes; and many of them suffered greatly from the cold, in the course of the winter. When the weather was mild and pleasant, some of the children, who were not required to go to the field, to do a day's work, would go out, in the warmest part of the day, and pick a few pounds of cotton, for which their parents received pay, and were obliged, in return, to find the children in bedding for the winter.

A man can plant and cultivate more cotton plants, than he is afterwards able to pick the wool from, if the season is good, and no disaster befalls the crop. Here every effort is made, from the commencement of the picking season until its close, to procure as much work as possible from the hands; and, spite of all that can be done, much cotton is lost—the people not being able to pick it all from the stalks, before the field is ploughed up to prepare the ground for the reception of the seeds of a new crop. In such cases, every pound that the hands can be induced to pick, beyond their daily task, is a clear gain to the master; and slaves often leave the fields of their masters, where the cotton is nearly all gathered, and the picking is poor, to go to the field of some neighbouring planter, where the cotton is more abundant, to work on Sunday. It is a matter of indifference to the slave, whether his master gets his cotton all picked or not; his object is to get employment in a field where he can make the best wages. In such cases, the masters often direct the overseers to offer their own slaves one half as much as the cotton is worth, for each pound they will pick on Sunday—and this, for the purpose of preventing them from going to some other field, to work on that day.

The usual price only, is paid for extra cotton, picked on working days; for after a hand has picked his task, he would not have time to go anywhere else to work; nor indeed, would he be permitted to leave his plantation. The slave is a kind of freeman on Sunday all over the southern country; and it is in truth, by the exercise of his liberty on this day, that he is enabled to provide himself and his family, with many of the necessaries of life that his master refuses to supply him with.

It is altogether impossible, to make a person residing in any of the middle or northern states of the Union, and who has never been in the south, thoroughly acquainted with all the minute particulars of the life of a slave on a cotton plantation; or to give him an idea of the system of parsimonious economy, that the slave is obliged to exercise and maintain in his little household. Poor as the slave is, and dependent at all times upon the arbitrary will of his master, or yet more fickle caprice of the overseer, his children look up to him in his little cabin, as their protector and supporter. There is always in every cabin, except in times of scarcity, after there has been a failure of the corn crop, a sufficient supply of either corn bread or sweet potatoes; and either of these, is sufficient to give health and vigour to children, who are not required to do any work; but a person who is grown up, and is obliged to labour hard, finds either bread or potatoes, or even both together, quite inadequate to sustain the body in the full and powerful tone of muscular action, that more generous food would bestow. A mother will imagine the painful feelings experienced by a parent, in the cabin of a slave, when a small portion of animal food is procured, dressed and made ready for the table. The father and mother know, that it is not only food, but medicine to them, and their appetites keenly court the precious morsel; whilst the children, whose senses are all acute, seem to be indued with taste and smell in a tenfold degree, and manifest a ravenous craving for fresh meat, which it is painful to witness, without being able to gratify it.

During the whole of this fall and winter, we usually had something to roast, at least twice a week, in our cabin. These roasts were rackoons, opossums, and other game—the proceeds of my trapping. All the time the meat was hanging at the fire, as well as while it was on the table, our house was surrounded by the children of our fellow-slaves; some begging for a piece, and all expressing, by their eager countenances, the keen desire they felt to partake with us of our dainties. It was idle to think of sharing with them, the contents of our board; for they were often thirty or forty in number; and the largest rackoon would scarcely have made a mouthful for each of them. There was one little boy, four years old, a very fine little fellow, to whom I had become warmly attached; and who used to share with me in all the good things I possessed. He was of the same age with my own little son, whom I had left in Maryland; and there was nothing that I possessed in the world, that I would not have divided with him, even to my last crust.

It may well be supposed, that in our society, although we were all slaves, and all nominally in a condition of the most perfect equality, yet there was in fact a very great difference in the manner of living, in the several families. Indeed, I doubt, if there is as great a diversity in the modes of life, in the several families of any white village in New-York, or Pennsylvania, containing a population of three hundred persons, as there was in the several households of our quarter. This may be illustrated by the following circumstance: Before I came to reside in the family with whom I lived at this time, they seldom tasted animal food, or even fish, except on meat-days, as they were called; that is, when meat was given to the people by the overseer, under the orders of our master. The head of the family was a very quiet, worthy man; but slothful and inactive in his habits. When he had come from the field at night, he seldom thought of leaving the cabin again before morning. He would, and did, make baskets and mats, and earned some money by these means; he also did his regular day's work on Sunday; but all his acquirements were not sufficient to enable him to provide any kind of meat for his family. All that his wife and children could do, was to provide him with work at his baskets and mats; and they lived even then better than some of their neighbours. After I came among them and had acquired some knowledge of the surrounding country, I made as many baskets and mats as he did; and took time to go twice a week to look at all my traps.

As the winter passed away and spring approached, the proceeds of my hunting began to diminish. The game became scarce, and both rackoons and opossums grew poor and worthless. It was necessary for me to discover some new mode of improving the allowance allotted to me by the overseer. I had all my life been accustomed to fishing, in Maryland, and I now resolved to resort to the water for a living; the land having failed to furnish me a comfortable subsistence. With these views, I set out one Sunday morning, early in February, and went to the river at a distance of three miles from home. From the appearance of the stream, I felt confident that it must contain many fish; and I went immediately to work to make a weir. With the help of an axe that I had with me, I had finished, before night, the frame work of a weir of pine sticks, lashed together with white oak splits. I had no canoe, but made a raft of dry logs, upon which I went to a suitable place in the river, and set my weir. I afterwards made a small net of twine, that I bought at the store; and on next Thursday night I took as many fish from my weir as filled a half bushel measure. This was a real treasure—it was the most fortunate circumstance that had happened with me since I came to the country.

I was enabled to show my generosity; but, like all mankind, even in my liberality, I kept myself in mind. I gave a large fish to the overseer, and took three more to the great house. These were the first fresh fish that had been in the family this season; and I was much praised by my master and young mistresses, for my skill and success in fishing; but this was all the advantage I received from this effort to court the favour of the great:—I did not even get a dram. The part I had performed in the detection of the murderers of the young lady was forgotten; or, at least, not mentioned now. I went away from the house, not only disappointed, but chagrined, and thought with myself, that if my master and young mistresses had nothing but words to give me for my fish, we should not carry on a very large traffic.

On next Sunday morning, a black boy came from the house, and told me that our master wished to see me. This summons was not to be disobeyed. When I returned to the mansion, I went round to the kitchen, and sent word by one of the house-slaves, that I had come. The servant returned and told me, that I was to stay in the kitchen and get my breakfast; and after that, to come into the house. A very good breakfast was sent to me from my master's table, after the family had finished their morning meal; and when I had done with my repast, I went into the parlour. I was received with great affability by my master, who told me he had sent for me to know if I had been accustomed to fish in the place I had come from. I informed him, that I had been employed at a fishery on the Patuxent, every spring, for several years; and that I thought I understood fishing with a seine, as well as most people. He then asked me, if I could knit a seine; to which I replied in the affirmative. After some other questions, he told me, that as the picking of cotton was nearly over for this season, and the fields must soon be ploughed up for a new crop, he had a thought of having a seine made; and of placing me at the head of a fishing party, for the purpose of trying to take a supply of fish for his hands. No communication could have been more unexpected than this was, and it was almost as pleasing to me as it was unexpected by me. I now began to hope that there would be some respite from the labours of the cotton field, and that I should not be doomed to drag out a dull and monotonous existence, within the confines of the enclosures of the plantation.

In Maryland, the fishing season was always one of hard labour, it is true; but also a time of joy and hilarity. We then had, throughout the time of fishing, plenty of bread, and, at least, bacon enough to fry our fish with. We had also a daily allowance of whiskey, or brandy, and we always considered ourselves fortunate when we left the farm to go to the fishery.

A few days after this, I was again sent for by my master, who told me, that he had bought twine and ropes for a seine; and that I must set to work and knit it as quickly as possible; that as he did not wish the twine to be taken to the quarter, I must remain with the servants in the kitchen, and live with them whilst employed in constructing the seine. I was assisted in making the seine by a black boy, whom I had taught to work with me; and by the end of two weeks we had finished our job.

While at work on this seine, I lived rather better than I had formerly done, when residing at the quarter. We received amongst us—twelve in number, including the people who worked in the garden—the refuse of our master's table. In this way we procured a little cold meat every day; and when there were many strangers visiting the family, we sometimes procured considerable quantities of cold and broken meats.

My new employment afforded me a better opportunity, than I had hitherto possessed, of making correct observations upon the domestic economy of my master's household, and of learning the habits and modes of life of the persons who composed it. On a great cotton plantation, such as this of my master's, the field hands, who live in the quarter, are removed so far from the domestic circle of their master's family, by their servile condition and the nature of their employment, that they know but little more of the transactions within the walls of the great house, than if they lived ten miles off. Many a slave has been born, lived to old age, and died on a plantation, without ever having been within the walls of his master's domicil.

My master was a widower; and his house was in charge of his sister, a maiden lady, apparently of fifty-five or sixty. He had six children, three sons and three daughters, and all unmarried; but only one of the sons was at home, at the time I came upon the estate; the other two were in some of the northern cities: the one studying medicine, and the other at college. At the time of knitting the twine, these young gentlemen had returned, on a visit, to their relations, and all the brothers and sisters were now on the place. The young ladies were all grown up; and marriageable; their father was known to be a man of great wealth; and the girls were reputed very pretty in Carolina; one of them, the second of the three, was esteemed a great beauty.

The reader might deem my young mistress' pretty face and graceful person, altogether impertinent to the narrative of my own life; but they had a most material influence upon my fortunes, and changed the whole tenor of my existence. Had she been less beautiful, or of a temper less romantic and adventurous, I should still have been a slave in South Carolina, if yet alive, and the world would have been saved the labour of perusing these pages.

Any one at all acquainted with southern manners, will at once see that my master's house possessed attractions which would not fail to draw within it numerous visiters; and that the head of such a family as dwelt under its roof was not likely to be without friends.

I had not been at work upon the seine a week before I discovered, by listening to the conversation of my master, and the other members of the family, that they prided themselves not a little, upon the antiquity of their house, and the long practice of a generous hospitality to strangers, and to all respectable people, who chose to visit their homestead. All circumstances seemed to conspire to render this house one of the chief seats of the fashion, the beauty, the wit, and the gallantry of South Carolina. Scarcely an evening came but it brought a carriage, and ladies and gentlemen, and their servants; and every day brought dashing young planters, mounted on horseback, to dine with the family; but Sunday was the day of the week on which the house received the greatest accession of company. My master and family were members of the Episcopal Church, and attended service every Sunday, when the weather was fine, at a church eight miles distant. Each of my young masters and mistresses had a saddlehorse, and in pleasant weather, they frequently all went to church on horseback, leaving my old master and mistress to occupy the family carriage alone. I have seen fifteen or twenty young people come to my master's for dinner, on Sunday from church; and very often the parson, a young man of handsome appearance, was amongst them. I had observed these things long before, but now I had come to live at the house, and became more familiar with them. Three Sundays intervened while I was at work upon the seine, and on each of these Sundays more than twenty persons, besides the family, dined at my master's. During these three weeks, my young masters were absent far the greater part of the time; but I observed that they generally came home on Sunday for dinner. My young mistresses were not from home much, and I believe they never left the plantation unless either their father or some one of their brothers was with them. Dinner parties were frequent in my master's house; and on these occasions of festivity, a black man, who belonged to a neighbouring estate, and who played the violin, was sent for. I observed that whenever this man was sent for, he came, and sometimes even came before night, which appeared a little singular to me, as I knew the difficulty that coloured people had to encounter in leaving the estate to which they were attached. I felt curious to ascertain how it happened, that Peter (that was the name of the fiddler,) enjoyed such privileges and contrived to become acquainted with him, when he came to get his supper in the kitchen. He informed me that his master was always ready to let him go to a ball; and would permit him to leave the cotton field at any time for that purpose, and even lend him a horse to ride. I afterwards learned from this man, that his master compelled him to give him half the money that he received as gratuities from the gentlemen for whom he played at the dinner parties; but as his master had enjoined him, under pain of being whipped, not to divulge this circumstance, I never betrayed the poor fellow's confidence. Peter's master was a planter, who owned thirty slaves, and his children (several of whom were young ladies and gentlemen) moved in highly respectable circles of society; but I believe my master's family did not treat them as quite their equals; not so much on account of their inferiority in point of wealth, as because they were new in the country, having only been settled here but a few years, and the master of Peter having, when a young man, acted as overseer on a rice plantation near Charleston.

## CHAPTER XV.

I HAVE, though always in a very humble station in life, travelled more, and seen more of the people in the United States, than some who occupy elevated ranks, and claim for themselves a knowledge of the world far greater than I pretend to possess; but a man's knowledge is to be valued, not by that which he has imagined, but by that which experience has taught him; and in estimating his ability to give information to others, we are to judge him, not by what he says he would wish men and the world to be, but by what he has seen, and by the just inferences he draws from those actions, that he has witnessed in the various conditions of human society, that have passed in review before him. In this book I do not pretend to discuss systems, or advance theories. I am content to give facts as I saw them.

In the northern and middle states, so far as I have known them, very little respect is paid to family pretensions; and this disregard of ancestry seems to me to be the necessary offspring of the condition of things. In the states of New-York and Pennsylvania, there are so many ways by which men may and do arrive at distinction, and so many, and such various means of acquiring wealth, that all claim of superiority on account of the possession of any particular kind of property, is prohibited by public opinion. A great landholder is counterbalanced by a great manufacturer, and perhaps surpassed by a great merchant, whilst a successful and skilful mechanic is the rival of all these. Family distinction can obtain no place amongst these men. In the plantation states, the case is widely different. There, lands and slaves constitute the only property of the country that is worthy of being taken into an estimate of public wealth. Cattle and horses, hogs, sheep and mules exist, but in numbers so few, and of qualities so inferior, that the portion of them, possessed by any individual planter, would compose an aggregate value of sufficient magnitude only to raise him barely beyond the lines that divide poverty from mediocrity of condition.

The mechanic is a sort of journeyman to the planters, and works about the country as he may chance to find a job, in building a house, erecting a cotton-gin, or constructing a horse-mill, if he is a carpenter or mill-wright; if he is a tai-lor, he seeks employment from house to house, never remaining longer in one place than to allow himself time to do the work of the family. The mechanic holds a kind of half-way rank between the gentleman and the slave. He is not, and never can be, a gentleman, for the reason that he does, and must do his own work. Hence mechanics and artizans of every description avoid the southern country; or, if found there, they are only sojourners. The country they are in is not their home: they are there from necessity, or with a hope of acquiring money to establish themselves in business, in places where their occupations are held more in honour. Manufacturers are not in existence in the cotton country, there-fore no comparison can be instituted between them and the planters.

I believe, from what I saw, that all the commerce of the cotton country is in the hands of strangers, and that a large portion of these strangers are foreign-ers. The planters deal with them from necessity, as they must have such things as they need, and must obtain them somewhere, and from somebody. The store-keeper lives as well, dresses as well, and often lives in as good a house as the planter—perhaps in one that is better than that of the planter; but his wealth is not so material, his means of subsistence do not strike the eye so powerfully as a hundred field hands, and three hundred acres of cotton. The country has no hold on him, and he has no hold on the country. His habits of life are not simi-lar to those of his neighbours—he is not "one of us."

All the families who visited at my master's were those of planters; and the families of the cotton planters have nothing to do but visit, or read, hunt, or fish, or run into some vicious amusements, or sit down and do nothing. Every kind of labour is as strictly prohibited to the sons and daughters of the planters, by universal custom, as if a law of the land made it punishable by fine and impris-onment, and gave one-half of the fine to a common informer. The only line that divides the gentleman from the simple man, is that the latter works for his liv-ing, whilst the former has slaves to work for him. No man who works with his hands, can or will be received into the highest orders of society, on a footing of equality, nor can he hope to see his family treated better than himself. This un-happy fiat of public opinion has done infinite mischief in the south.

Men of fortune will not work, nor permit their sons to work in the field, because this exemption from labour is their badge of gentility, and the circum-stance that distinguishes them from the less favoured members of the commu-nity. As the wealthy, the great, and the fashionable, are never seen at labour and as it is known that they hold it to be beneath the rank of a gentleman to work in the field, those who are more sparingly endowed with the advantages of fortune, imbibe an opinion that it is disgraceful to plough, or to dig, and that it is necessary to lead a life of idleness, to maintain their *caste* in society.

No man works in South Carolina, except under the impulse of necessity. In this state of things, many men of limited fortunes rear up families of children without education, and without the means of supporting an expensive style of living. The sons, when grown up, of necessity, commingle with the other young people of the country, and bring with them into the affairs of the world, nothing upon which they can pride themselves, except that they are white men, and are not obliged to work for a living.

This false pride has infected the whole mass of the white population; and the young man, whose father has half a dozen children, and an equal number of slaves, looks with affected disdain upon the son of his father's neighbour, who owns no slaves, because the son of the non-slaveholder must work for his bread, whilst the son of the master of half a dozen negroes, contrives to support himself in a sort of lazy poverty, only one remove from actual penury.

Every man who is able to procure a subsistence, without labour, regards himself a gentleman, from this circumstance alone, if he has nothing else to sustain his pretensions. These poor gentlemen, are the worst members of society, and the least productive of benefit, either to themselves or their country. They are prone to horse-racing, cock-fighting, gambling, and all sorts of vices common to the country. Having no livelihood, and being engaged in no pursuit, they hope to distinguish themselves by running to excess in what they call fashionable amusements, or sporting exercises. These people are universally detested by the slaves, and are indeed far more tyrannical than the great slave-holders themselves, or any other portion of the white population, the overseers excepted.

A man who is master of only four or five slaves, is generally the most ready of all to apprehend a black man, whom he may happen to catch straying from his plantation; and generally whips him the most unmercifully for this offence. The law gives him the same authority to arrest the person of a slave, seen travelling without his pass, that it vests in the owner of five hundred negroes; and the experience of all ages, that petty tyrants are the most oppressive, seems fully verified in the cotton country.

A person who has not been in the slave-holding states, can never fully understand the bonds that hold society together there, or appreciate the rules which prescribe the boundaries of the pretensions of the several orders of men who compose the body politic of those communities; and after all that I have written, and all that I shall write, in this book, the reader who has never resided south of the Potomac, will never be able to perceive things precisely as they present themselves to my vision, or to comprehend the spirit that prevails in a country, where the population is divided into three separate classes. Those will fall into great error, who shall imagine that in Carolina and Georgia there are but two orders of men; and that the artificial distinctions of society have only classified the people into white and black, freemen and slaves. It is true, that the distinctions of colour are the most obvious, and present themselves more readily than any others to the inspection of a stranger; but he who will take time to examine into the fundamental organization of society, in the cotton planting region, will easily discover that there is a third order of men located there, little known to the world, but who, nevertheless, hold a separate station, occupying a place of their own, and who do not come into direct contrast with either the master or the slave.

The white man, who has no property, no possession, and no education, is, in Carolina, in a condition no better than that to which the slave has been reduced; except only that he is master of his own person, and of his own time, and may, if he chooses, emigrate and transfer himself to a country where he can better his circumstances, whilst the slave is bound, by invisible chains, to the plantation on which his master may think proper to place him.

In my opinion, there is no order of men in any part of the United States, with which I have any acquaintance, who are in a more debased and humiliated state of moral servitude, than are those white people who inhabit that part of the southern country, where the landed property is all, or nearly all, held by the great planters. Many of these white people live in wretched cabins, not half so good as the houses which judicious planters provide for their slaves. Some of these cabins of the white men are made of mere sticks, or small poles notched, or rather thatched together, and filled in with mud, mixed with the leaves, or *shats,* as they are termed, of the pine tree. Some fix their residence far in the pine forest, and gain a scanty subsistence by notching the trees and gathering the turpentine; others are seated upon some poor, and worthless point of land, near the margin of a river, or creek, and draw a precarious livelihood from the water, and the badly cultivated garden that surrounds, or adjoins the dwelling.

These people do not occupy the place held in the north by the respectable and useful class of day labourers, who constitute so considerable a portion of the numerical population of the country.

In the south, these white cottagers are never employed to work on the plantations for wages. Two things forbid this. The white man, however poor and necessitous he may be, is too proud to go to work in the same field with the negro slaves by his side; and the owner of the slaves is not willing to permit white men, of the lowest order, to come amongst them, lest the morals of the negroes should be corrupted, and illicit traffic should be carried on, to the detriment of the master.

The slaves generally believe, that however miserable they may be, in their servile station, it is nevertheless preferable to the degraded existence of these poor white people. This sentiment is cherished by the slaves, and encouraged by their masters, who fancy that they subserve their own interests in promoting an opinion amongst the negroes, that they are better off in the world than are many white persons, who are free, and have to submit to the burthen of taking care of, and providing for themselves.

I never could learn nor understand how, or by what means, these poor cottagers came to be settled in Carolina. They are a separate and distinct race of men from the planters, and appear to have nothing in common with them. If it were possible for any people to occupy a grade in human society below that of the slaves, on the cotton plantations, certainly the station would be filled by these white families, who cannot be said to possess any thing in the shape of property. The contempt in which they are held, and the contumely with which they are treated, by the great planters, to be comprehended, must be seen.

These observations are applicable in their fullest extent, only to the lower parts of Georgia and Carolina, and to country places. In the upper country, where slaves are not so numerous, and where less of cotton and more of grain is cultivated, there is not so great a difference between the white man, who holds slaves and a plantation, and another white man who has neither slaves nor plantation. In the towns, also, more especially in Charleston and Savannah, where the number of white men who have no slaves is very great, they are able, from their very numbers, to constitute a moral force sufficiently powerful to give them some degree of weight in the community.

I shall now return to my narrative. Early in March, or perhaps on one of the last days of February, my seine being now completed, my master told me I must take with me three other black men, and go to the river to clear out a fishery. This task of clearing out a fishery, was a very disagreeable job; for it was nothing less than dragging out of the river, all the old trees and brush that had sunk to the bottom, within the limits of our intended fishing ground. My master's eldest son had been down the river, and had purchased two boats, to be used at the fishery; but when I saw them I declared them to be totally unfit for the purpose. They were old batteaux,[25] and so leaky, that they would not have supported the weight of a wet seine, and the men necessary to lay it out. I advised the building of two good canoes, from some of the large yellow pines, in the woods. My advice was accepted, and together with five other hands, I went to work at the canoes, which we completed in less than a week.

So far things went pretty well, and I flattered myself that I should become the head man at this new fishery, and have the command of the other hands. I also expected that I should be able to gain some advantage to myself, by disposing of a part of the small fish that might be taken at the fishery. I reckoned without my host.

My master had only purchased this place a short time before he bought me. Before that time he did not own any place on the river, fit for the establishment of a fishery. His lands adjoined the river for more than a mile in extent, along its margin; but an impassable morass separated the channel of the river, from the firm ground, all along his lines. He had cleared the highest parts of this morass, or swamp, and had here made his rice fields; but he was as entirely cut off from the river, as if an ocean had separated it from him.

On the day that we launched the canoes into the river, and while we were engaged in removing some snags, and old trees that had stuck in the mud, near the shore, an ill-looking stranger came to us, and told us that our master had sent him to take charge of the fishery, and superintend all the work that was to be done at it. This man, by his contract with my master, was to receive a part of all the fish caught, in lieu of wages; and was invested with the same authority over us that was exercised by the overseer in the cotton field.

I soon found that I had cause to regret my removal from the plantation. It was found quite impossible to remove the old logs, and other rubbish from the bottom of the river, without going into the water, and wrenching them from their places with long hand-spikes. In performing this work we were obliged to wade up to our shoulders, and often to dip our very heads under water, in raising the sunken timber. However, within less than a week, we had cleared the ground, and now began to haul our seine. At first, we caught nothing but common river fish; but after two or three days, we began to take shad. Of the common fish, such as pike, perch, suckers, and others, we had the liberty of keeping as many as we could eat; but the misfortune was, that we had no pork, or fat of any kind, to fry them with; and for several days we contented ourselves with broiling them on the coals, and eating them with our corn bread, and sweet potatoes. We could have lived well, if we had been permitted to broil the shad on the coals, and eat them; for a fat shad will dress itself in being broiled, and is very good, without any oily substance added to it.

All the shad that we caught, were carefully taken away by a black man, who came three times every day to the fishery, with a cart.

The master of the fishery had a family that lived several miles up the river. In the summer time, he fished with hooks, and small nets, when not engaged in running turpentine, in the pine woods. In the winter he went back into the pine forest, and made tar of the dead pine trees; but returned to the river at the opening of the spring, to take advantage of the shad fishery. He was supposed to be one of the most skilful fishermen on the Congaree river, and my master employed him to superintend his new fishery, under an expectation, I presume, that as he was to get a tenth part of all the fish that might be caught, he would make the most of his situation. My master had not calculated with accuracy the force of habit, nor the difficulty which men experience, in conducting very simple affairs, of which they have no practical knowledge.

The fish-master did very well for the interest of his employer, for a few days; compelling us to work, in hauling the seine, night and day, and scarcely permitting us to take rest enough to obtain necessary sleep. We were compelled to work full sixteen hours every day, including Sunday; for in the fishing season, no respect is paid to Sunday by fishermen, anywhere. We had our usual quantity of bread and potatoes, with plenty of common fish; but no shad came to our lot; nor had we any thing to fry our fish with. A broiled fresh-water fish is not very good, at best, without salt or oil; and after we had eaten them every day, for a week, we cared very little for them.

By this time, our fish-master began to relax in his discipline; not that he became more kind to us, or required us to do less work; but to compel us to work all night, it was necessary for him to sit up all night and watch us. This was a degree of toil and privation to which he could not long submit; and one evening soon after dark, he called me to him and told me, that he intended to make me overseer of the fishery that night; and he had no doubt, I would keep the hands at work, and attend to the business as well without him as with him. He then went into his cabin, and went to bed; whilst I went and laid out the seine, and made a very good haul. We took more than two hundred shad at this draught; and followed up our work with great industry all night, only taking time to eat our accustomed meal at midnight.

Every fisherman knows that the night is the best time for taking shad; and the little rest that had been allowed us, since we began to fish, had always been from eight o'clock in the morning, until four in the afternoon; unless within that period there was an appearance of a school of fish in the river; when we had to rise, and lay out the seine, no matter at what hour of the day. The fish-master had been very severe with the hands, since he came amongst us; and had made very free use of a long hickory gad that he sometimes carried about with him; though at times he would relax his austerity, and talk quite familiarly with us: especially with me, whom he perceived to have some knowledge of the business in which we were engaged. The truth was, that this man knew nothing of fishing with a seine, and I had been obliged from the beginning to direct the operations of laying out and drawing in the seine; though the master was always very loud and boisterous in giving his commands, and directing us in what part of the river we should let down the seine.

Having never been accustomed to regular work, or to the pursuit of any constant course of personal application, the master was incapable of long continued exertion; and I feel certain, that he could not have been prevailed upon to labour twelve hours each day, for a year, if in return he had been certain of receiving ten thousand dollars. Notwithstanding this, he was capable of rousing himself, and of undergoing any degree of fatigue or privation, for a short time; even for a few days. He had not been trained to habits of industry, and could not bear the restraints of uniform labour.

We worked hard all night, the first night of my superintendence, and when the sun rose the next morning, the master had not risen from his bed. As it was now the usual time of dividing the fish, I called to him to come and see this business fairly done; but as he did not come down immediately to the landing, I proceeded to make the division myself, in as equitable a manner as I could: giving, however, a full share of large fish to the master. When he came down to us, and overlooked both the piles of fish—his own and that of my master—he was so well satisfied with what I had done, that he said, if he had known that I would do so well for him, he would not have risen. I was glad to hear this, as it led me to hope, that I should be able to induce him to stay in his cabin during the greater part of the time; to do which, I was well assured, he felt disposed.

When the night came, the master again told me he should go to bed, not being well; and desired me to do as I had done the night before. This night we cooked as many shad as we could all eat; but were careful to carry, far out into the river, the scales and entrails of the stolen fish. In the morning I made a division of the fish before I called the master, and then went and asked him to come and see what I had done. He was again well pleased, and now proposed to us all, that if we would not let the affair be known to our master, he would leave us to manage the fishery at night according to our discretion. To this proposal we all readily agreed, and I received authority to keep the other hands at work, until the master would go and get his breakfast. I had now accomplished the object that I had held very near my heart, ever since we began to fish at this place.

From this time, to the end of the fishing season, we all lived well, and did not perform more work than we were able to bear. I was in no fear of being punished by the fish-master; for he was now at least as much in my power, as I was in his; for if my master had known the agreement, that he had made with us, for the purpose of enabling himself to sleep all night in his cabin, he would have been deprived of his situation, and all the profits of his share of the fishery.

There never can be any affinity of feeling between master and slave, except in some few isolated cases, where the master has treated his slave in such a manner, as to have excited in him strong feelings of gratitude; or where the slave entertains apprehensions, that by the death of his master, or by being separated from him in any other way, he may fall under the power of a more tyrannical ruler, or may in some shape be worsted by the change. I was never acquainted with a slave who believed, that he violated any rule of morality by appropriating to himself any thing that belonged to his master, if it was necessary to his comfort. The master might call it theft, and brand it with the name of crime; but the slave reasoned differently, when he took a portion of his master's goods, to satisfy his hunger, keep himself warm, or to gratify his passion for luxurious enjoyment.

The slave sees his master residing in a spacious mansion, riding in a fine carriage, and dressed in costly clothes, and attributes the possession of all these enjoyments to his own labour; whilst he who is the cause of so much gratification and pleasure to another, is himself deprived of even the necessary accommodations of human life. Ignorant men do not and cannot reason logically; and in tracing things from cause to effect, the slave attributes all that he sees in possession of his master, to his own toil, without taking the trouble to examine, how far the skill, judgment, and economy of his master may have contributed to the accumulation of the wealth by which his residence is surrounded. There is, in fact, a mutual dependence between the master and his slave. The former could not acquire any thing without the labour of the latter, and the latter would always remain in poverty, without the judgment of the former in directing labour to a definite and profitable result.

After I had obtained the virtual command of the fishery, I was careful to awaken the master every morning at sunrise, that he might be present when the division of the fish was made; and when the morning cart arrived, that the carter might not report to my master, that the fish-master was in bed. I had now become interested in preserving the good opinion of my master in favour of his agent.

Since my arrival in Carolina I had never enjoyed a full meal of bacon; and now determined, if possible, to procure such a supply of that luxury, as would enable me and all my fellow-slaves at the fishery to regale ourselves at pleasure. At this season of the year, boats frequently passed up the river, laden with merchandise and goods of various kinds, amongst which were generally large quantities of salt, intended for curing fish, and for other purposes on the plantations. These boats also carried bacon and salted pork up the river, for sale; but as they never moved at night, confining their navigation to day-light, and as none of them had hitherto stopped near our landing, we had not met with an opportunity of entering into a traffic with any of the boat masters. We were not always to be so unfortunate. One evening, in the second week of the fishing season, a large keel-boat was seen working up the river about sundown; and shortly after, came to for the night, on the opposite side of the river, directly against our landing. We had at the fishery a small canoe called a punt, about twelve feet long; and when we went to lay out the seine, for the first haul after night, I attached the punt to the side of the canoe, and when we had finished letting down the seine, I left the other hands to work it toward the shore, and ran over in the punt to the keel-boat. Upon inquiring of the captain if he had any bacon that he would exchange for shad, he said, he had a little; but, as the risk he would run in dealing with a slave was great, I must expect to pay him more than the usual price. He at length proposed to give me a hundred pounds of bacon for three hundred shad. This was at least twice as much as the bacon was worth; but we did not bargain as men generally do, where half of the bargain is on each side; for here the captain of the keel-boat settled the terms for both parties. However, he ran the hazard of being prosecuted for dealing with slaves, which is a very high offence in Carolina; and I was selling that which, in point of law, did not belong to me; but to which, nevertheless, I felt in my conscience that I had a better right than any other person. In support of the right, which I felt to be on my side in this case, came a keen appetite for the bacon, which settled the controversy, upon the question of the morality of this traffic, in my favour. It so happened, that we made a good haul with our seine this evening, and at the time I returned to the landing, the men were all on shore, engaged in drawing in the seine. As soon as we had taken out the fish, we placed three hundred of them in one of our canoes, and pushed over to the keel-boat, where the fish were counted out, and the bacon was received into our craft with all possible despatch. One part of this small trade exhibited a trait of human character which I think worthy of being noticed. The captain of the boat was a middle-aged, thin, sallow man, with long bushy hair; and he looked like one who valued the opinions of men but little. I expected that he would not be scrupulous in giving me my full hundred pounds of bacon; but in this I was mistaken; for he weighed the flitches with great exactness, in a pair of large steelyards, and gave me good weight. When the business was ended, and the bacon in my canoe, he told me, he hoped I was satisfied with him; and assured me, that I should find the bacon excellent. When I was about pushing from the boat, he told me in a low voice, though there was no one who could hear us, except his own people—that he should be down the river again in about two weeks, when he should be very glad to buy any produce that I had for sale; adding, "I will give you half as much for cotton as it is worth in Charleston, and pay you either in money or groceries, as you may choose. Take care, and do not betray yourself, and I shall be honest with you."

I was so much rejoiced, at being in possession of a hundred pounds of good flitch bacon, that I had no room in either my head or my heart, for the consideration of this man's notions of honesty, at the present time; but paddled with all strength for our landing, where we took the bacon from the canoe, stowed it away in an old salt barrel, and safely deposited it in a hole, dug for the purpose in the floor of my cabin.

About this time, our allowance of sweet potatoes was withheld from us altogether, in consequence of the high price paid for this article by the captains of the keel-boats; for the purpose, as I heard, of sending them to New-York and Philadelphia. Ever since Christmas, we had been permitted to draw, on each

Sunday evening, either a peck of corn, as usual, or half a peck of corn, and half a bushel of sweet potatoes, at our discretion. The half a peck of corn, and the half a bushel of potatoes was worth much more than a peck of corn; but potatoes were so abundant this year, that they were of little value, and the saving of corn was an object worth attending to by a large planter. The boatmen now offered half a dollar a bushel for potatoes, and we were again restricted to our corn ration.

Notwithstanding the privation of our potatoes, we at the fishery lived sumptuously; although our master certainly believed, that our fare consisted of corn bread and river fish, cooked without lard or butter. It was necessary to be exceedingly cautious in the use of our bacon; and to prevent the suspicions of the master and others, who frequented our landing, I enjoined our people never to fry any of the meat, but to boil it all. No one can smell boiled bacon far; but fried flitch can be smelled a mile by a good nose.

We had two meals every night, one of bacon and the other of fried shad; which nearly deprived us of all appetite for the breakfasts and dinners that we prepared in the daytime; consisting of cold corn bread without salt, and broiled fresh water fish, without any sort of seasoning. We spent more than two weeks in this happy mode of life, unmolested by our master, his son, or the master of the fishery; except when the latter complained, rather than threatened us, because we sometimes suffered our seine to float too far down the river, and get entangled amongst some roots and brush that lay on the bottom, immediately below our fishing ground. We now expected, every evening, to see the return of the boatman who had sold us the bacon; and the man who was with me in the canoe, at the time we received it, had not forgotten the invitation of the captain to trade with him in cotton on his return. My fellow-slave was a native of Virginia, as he told me and had been sold and brought to Carolina about ten years before this time. He was a good natured, kind hearted man, and did many acts of benevolence to me, such as one slave is able to perform for another, and I felt a real affection for him; but he had adopted the too common rule of moral action, that there is no harm in a slave robbing his master.

The reader may suppose, from my account of the bacon, that I, too, had adopted this rule as a part of my creed; but I solemnly declare, that this was not the case, and that I never deprived any one of all the masters that I have served, of any thing against his consent, unless it was some kind of food; and that of all I ever took, I am confident, I have given away more than the half to my fellow-slaves, whom I knew to be equally needy with myself.

The man who had been with me at the keel-boat told me one day, that he had laid a plan by which we could get thirty or forty dollars, if I would join him in the execution of his project. Thirty or forty dollars was a large sum of money to me. I had never possessed so much money at one time in my life; and I told him that I was willing to do any thing by which we could obtain such a treasure. He then told me, that he knew where the mule and cart that were used by the man who carried away our fish, were kept at night; and that he intended to set out, on the first dark night, and go to the plantation—harness the mule to the cart—go to the cotton-gin house—put two bags of cotton into the cart—bring them to a thicket of small pines that grew on the river bank, a short distance below the fishery, and leave them there until the keel-boat should return. All that he desired of me was, to make some excuse for his absence, to the other hands; and assist him to get his cotton into the canoe, at the coming of the boat.

I disliked the whole scheme, both on account of its iniquity, and of the danger which attended it; but my companion was not to be discouraged by all the arguments which I could use against it, and said, if I would not participate in it, he was determined to undertake it alone: provided I would not inform against him. To this I said nothing; but he had so often heard me express my detestation of one slave betraying another, that I presume he felt easy on that score. The next night but one after this conversation, was very dark; and when we went to lay out the seine after night, Nero was missing. The other people inquired of me, if I knew where he was, and when I replied in the negative, little more was said on the subject; it being common for the slaves to absent themselves from their habitations at night, and if the matter is not discovered by the overseer or master, nothing is ever said of it by the slaves. The other people supposed that, in this instance, Nero had gone to see a woman whom he lived with as his wife, on a plantation a few miles down the river; and were willing to work a little harder to permit him to enjoy the pleasure of seeing his family. He returned before day, and said he had been to see his wife, which satisfied the curiosity of our companions. The very next evening after Nero's absence, the keel-boat descended the river, came down on our side, hailed us at the fishery, and, drawing in to the shore below our landing, made her ropes fast among the young pines of which I have spoken above. After we made our first haul, I missed Nero; but he returned to us before we had laid out the seine, and told us that he had been in the woods to collect some *light-wood*—dry, resinous pine,—which he brought on his shoulder. When the morning came, the keel-boat was gone, and every thing wore the ordinary aspect about our fishery; but when the man came with the mule and the cart, to take away the fish, he told us that there was great trouble on the plantation. The overseer had discovered, that some one had stolen two bags of cotton the last night, and all the hands were undergoing an examination on the subject. The slaves on the plantation, one and all, denied having any knowledge of the matter, and, as there was no evidence against any one, the overseer threatened, at the time he left the quarter, to whip every hand on the estate, for the purpose of making them discover who the thief was.

The slaves on the plantation differed in opinion as to the perpetrator of this theft; but the greater number concurred in charging it upon a free negro man, named Ishmael, who lived in a place called the White Oak Woods, and followed making ploughs and harrow frames. He also made handles for hoes, and the frame work of cart bodies.

This man was generally reputed a thief for a great distance round the country, and the black people charged him with stealing the cotton on no other evidence than his general bad character. The overseer, on the other hand, expressed his opinion without hesitation; which was, that the cotton had been stolen by some of the people of the plantation, and sold to a poor white man, who resided at the distance of three miles back in the pine woods, and was believed to have dealt with slaves, as a receiver of their stolen goods, for many years.

This white man was one of the class of poor cottagers to whom I have heretofore referred, in this narrative. The house, or cabin, in which he resided, was built of small poles of the yellow pine, with the bark remaining on them; the roof was of clap-boards of pine, and the chimney was made of sticks and mud, raised to the height of eight or ten feet. The appearance of the man and his wife was such as one might expect to find in such a dwelling. The lowest poverty had, through life, been the companion of these poor people, of which their clayey complexions, haggard figures, and tattered garments, gave the strongest proof. It appeared to me, that the state of destitution in which these people lived, afforded very convincing evidence that they were not in possession of the proceeds of the stolen goods of any person. I had often been at the cabin of this man, in my trapping expeditions, the previous autumn and winter; and I believe the overseer regarded the circumstance, that black people often called at his house, as conclusive evidence that he held criminal intercourse with them. However this might be, the overseer determined to search the premises of this harmless forester, whom he resolved, beforehand, to treat as a guilty man.

It being known that I was well acquainted with the woods, in the neighbourhood of the cabin, I was sent for, to leave the fishery, and come to assist in making search for the lost bags of cotton—perhaps it was also believed, that I was in the secrets of the suspected house. It was not thought prudent to trust any of the hands on the plantation in making the intended search, as they were considered the principal thieves; whilst we, of the fishery, against whom no suspicion had arisen, were required to give our assistance, in ferreting out the perpetrators of an offence of the highest grade that can be committed by a slave, on a cotton estate.

Before leaving the fishery, I advised the master to be very careful not to let the overseer, or my master know, that he had left us to manage the fishery at night, by ourselves; since, as a theft had been committed, it might possibly be charged upon him, if it were known that he had allowed us so much liberty. I said this to put the master on his guard against surprise; and to prevent him from saying any thing that might turn the attention of the overseer to the hands at the fishery; for I knew that if punishment were to fall amongst us, it would be quite as likely to reach the innocent as the guilty—besides, though I was innocent of the bags of cotton, I was guilty of the bacon, and, however I might make distinctions between the moral turpitude of the two cases, I knew that if discovered, they would both be treated alike.

When I arrived at the quarter, whither I repaired, in obedience to the orders I received, I found the overseer with my master's eldest son, and a young white man, who had been employed to repair the cotton-gin, waiting for me. I observed when I came near the overseer, that he looked at me very attentively, and afterwards called my young master aside, and spoke to him in a tone of voice too low to be heard by me. The white gentlemen then mounted their horses, and set off by the road for the cabin of the white man. I had orders to take a short route, through the woods and across a swamp, by which I could reach the cabin as soon as the overseer.

The attentive examination that the overseer had given me, caused me to feel uneasy, although I could not divine the cause of his scrutiny, nor of the subject of the short conversation between him and my young master. By travelling at a rapid pace, I arrived at the cabin of the suspected man before the gentlemen, but thought it prudent not to approach it before they came up, lest it might be imagined that I had gone in to give information to the occupants of the danger that threatened them.

Here I had a hard struggle with my conscience, which seemed to say to me, that I ought at once to disclose all I knew concerning the lost bags of cotton, for the purpose of saving these poor people from the terror that they must necessarily feel at the sight of those who were coming to accuse them of a great crime, perhaps from the afflictions and sufferings attendant upon a prosecution in a court of justice. These reflections were cut short by the arrival of the party of gentlemen, who passed me where I sat, at the side of the path, with no other notice than a simple command of the overseer to come on. I followed them into the cabin, where we found the man and his wife, with two little children, eating roasted potatoes.

The overseer saluted this family by telling them that we had come to search the house for stolen cotton. That it was well known that he had long been dealing with negroes, and they were now determined to bring him to punishment. I was then ordered to tear up the floor of the cabin, whilst the overseer mounted into the loft. I found nothing under the floor, and the overseer had no better success above. The wife was then advised to confess where her husband had concealed the cotton, to save herself from being brought in as a party to the affair; but this poor woman protested with tears that they were totally ignorant of the whole matter. Whilst the wife was interrogated, the father stood without his own door, trembling with fear, but, as I could perceive, indignant with rage.

The overseer, who was fluent in the use of profane language, exerted the highest degree of his vulgar eloquence upon these harmless people, whose only crime was their poverty, and whose weakness alone had invited the ruthless aggression of their powerful and rich neighbours.

Finding nothing in the house, the gentlemen set out to scour the woods around the cabin, and commanded me to take the lead in tracing out tree tops and thickets, where it was most likely that the stolen cotton might be found. Our search was in vain, as I knew it would be beforehand; but when weary of ranging in the woods, the gentlemen again returned to the cabin, which we now found without inhabitants. The alarm caused by our visit, and the manner in which the gentlemen had treated this lonely family, had caused them to abandon their dwelling, and seek safety in flight. The door of the house was closed and fastened with a string to a nail in the post of the door. After calling several times for the fugitives, and receiving no answer, the door was kicked open by my young master; the few articles of miserable furniture that the cabin contained, including a bed, made of flags, were thrown into a heap in the corner, and fire was set to the dwelling by the overseer.

We remained until the flames had reached the roof of the cabin, when the gentlemen mounted their horses and set off for home, ordering me to return by the way that I had come. When we again reached the house of my master, several gentlemen of the neighbourhood had assembled, drawn together by common interest that is felt amongst the planters to punish theft, and particularly a theft of cotton in the bag. My young master related to his neighbours, with great apparent satisfaction, the exploits of the morning; said he had routed one receiver of stolen goods out of the country, and that all others of his character ought to be dealt with in the same manner. In this opinion all the gentlemen present concurred, and after much conversation on the subject, it was agreed to call a general meeting for the purpose of devising the best, surest, and most peaceful method of removing from the country the many white men who, residing in the district without property, or without interest in preserving the morals of the slaves, were believed to carry on an unlawful and criminal traffic with the negroes, to the great injury of the planters in general, and of the masters of the slaves who dealt with the offenders in particular.

I was present at this preliminary consultation, which took place at my master's cotton-gin, whither the gentlemen had repaired for the purpose of looking at the place where the cotton had been removed. So many cases of this forbidden traffic between the slaves and these "white negro dealers," as they were termed, were here related by the different gentlemen, and so many white men were referred to by name as being concerned in this criminal business, that I began to suppose the losses of the planters in this way must be immense. This conference continued until I had totally forgotten the scrutinizing look that I had received from our overseer at the time I came up from the fishery in the morning; but the period had now come when I again was to be reminded of this circumstance, for on a sudden the overseer called me to come forward and let the gentlemen see me. I again felt a sort of vague and undefinable apprehension that no good was to grow out of this examination of my person, but a command of our overseer was not to be disobeyed. After looking at my face, with a kind of leer or side glance, one of the gentlemen, who was an entire stranger to me, and whom I had never before seen, said, "Boy, you appear to live well; how much meat does your master allow you in a week?" I was almost totally confounded at the name of meat, and felt the blood rush to my heart, but nevertheless forced a sort of smile upon my face, and replied, "My master has been very kind to all his people of late, but has not allowed us any meat for some weeks. We have plenty of good bread, and abundance of river fish, which, together with the heads and roes of the shad that we have salted at the landing, makes a very excellent living for us; though if master would please to give us a little meat now and then, we should be very thankful for it."

This speech, which contained all the eloquence I was master of at the time, seemed to produce some effect in my favour, for the gentleman said nothing in reply, until the overseer, rising from a board on which he had been sitting, came close up to me and said, "Charles, you need not tell lies about it; you have been eating meat, I know you have, no negro could look as fat, and sleek, and black, and greasy, as you, if he had nothing to eat but corn bread and river chubs. You do not look at all as you did before you went to the fishery; and all the hands on the plantation have had as many chubs and other river fish as they could eat, as well as you, and yet they are as poor as snakes in comparison with you. Come, tell us the truth, let us know where you get the meat that you have been eating, and you shall not be whipped." I begged the overseer and the other gentlemen not to ridicule or make sport of me, because I was a poor slave, and was obliged to live on bread and fresh water fish; and concluded this second harangue by expressing my thankfulness to God Almighty, for giving me such good health and strength as to enable me to do my work, and look so well as I did upon such poor fare; adding, that if I only had as much bacon as I could eat, they would soon see a man of a different appearance from that which I now exhibited. "None of your palaver," rejoined the overseer—"Why, I smell the meat in you this moment. Do I not see the grease as it runs out of your face?" I was by this time in a profuse sweat, caused by the anxiety of my feelings, and simply said, "Master sees me sweat, I suppose."

All the gentlemen present then declared, with one accord, that I must have been living on meat for a long time, as no negro, who had no meat to eat, could look as I did; and one of the company advised the overseer to whip me, and compel me to confess the truth. I have no doubt but this advice would have been practically followed, had it not been for a happy, though dangerous suggestion of my own mind, at this moment. It was no other than a proposal on my part, that I should be taken to the landing, and if all the people there did not look as well, and as much like meat-eaters as I did, then I would agree to be whipped in any way the gentlemen should deem expedient. This offer on my part was instantly accepted by the gentlemen, and it was agreed amongst them that they would all go to the landing with the overseer, partly for the purpose of seeing me condemned by the judgment to which I had voluntarily chosen to submit myself, and partly for the purpose of seeing my master's new fishery.

We were quickly at the landing, though four miles distant; and I now felt confident that I should escape the dangers that beset me, provided the master of the fishery did not betray his own negligence, and lead himself, as well as us, into new troubles.

Though on foot, I was at the landing as soon as the gentlemen, and was first to announce to the master the feats we had performed in the course of the day, adding, with great emphasis, and even confidence in my manner, "You know, master fish-master, whether we have had any meat to eat here or not. If we had meat here, would not you see it? You have been up with us every night, and know that we have not been allowed to take even shad, let alone having meat to eat." The fish-master supported me in all I said; declared we had been good boys—had worked night and day, of his certain knowledge, as he had been with us all night and every night since we began to fish. That he had not allowed us to eat any thing but fresh water fish, and the heads and roes of the shad that were salted at the landing. As to meat, he said he was willing to be qualified on a cart load of testaments that there had not been a pound at the landing since the commencement of the season, except that which he had in his own cabin. I had now acquired confidence, and desired the gentlemen to look at Nero and the other hands, all of whom had as much the appearance of bacon eaters as myself. This was the truth, especially with regard to one of the men, who was much fatter than I was.

The gentlemen now began to doubt the evidence of their own senses, which they had held infallible heretofore. I showed the fine fish that we had to eat; cat, perch, mullets, and especially two large pikes, that had been caught to-day, and assured them that upon such fare as this men must needs get fat. I now perceived that victory was with me for once. All the gentlemen faltered, hesitated, and began to talk of other affairs, except the overseer, who still ran about the landing, swearing and scratching his head, and saying it was strange that we were so fat, whilst the hands on the plantation were as lean as sand-hill cranes. He was obliged to give the affair over. He was no longer supported by my young master and his companions, all of whom congratulated themselves upon a discovery so useful and valuable to the planting interest; and all determined to provide, as soon as possible, a proper supply of fresh river-fish for their hands.

The two bales of cotton were never once named, and, I suppose, were not thought of by the gentlemen, when at the landing; and this was well for Nero; for such was the consternation and terror into which he was thrown, by the presence of the gentlemen, and their inquiries concerning our eating of meat, that the sweat rolled off him like rain from the plant *never-wet;*[26] his countenance was wild and haggard, and his knees shook like the wooden spring of a wheat-fan. I believe, that if they had charged him at once with stealing the cotton, he would have confessed the deed.

---

## CHAPTER XVI.

AFTER this, the fishing season passed off without any thing having happened, worthy of being noticed here. When we left the fishery, and returned to the plantation, which was after the middle of April, the corn and cotton had all been planted, and the latter had been replanted. I was set to plough, with two mules for my team; and having never been accustomed to ploughing with these animals, I had much trouble with them at first. My master owned more than forty mules, and at this season of the year, they were all at work in the cotton field, used instead of horses for drawing ploughs. Some of the largest were hitched single to a plough; but the smallest were coupled together.

On the whole, the fishery had been a losing affair with me; for although I had lived better at the landing, than I usually did at the plantation, yet I had been compelled to work all the time, by night and by day, including Sunday, for my master; by which I had lost all that I could have earned for my own benefit, had I been on the plantation. I had now become so well acquainted with the rules of the plantation, and the customs of the country where I lived, that I experienced less distress than I did at my first coming to the south.

We now received a shad every Sunday evening with our peck of corn. The fish were those that I had caught in the spring; and were tolerably preserved. In addition to all this, each one of the hands now received a pint of vinegar, every week. This vinegar was a great comfort to me. As the weather became hot, I gathered lettuce, and other salads, from my garden in the woods; which, with the vinegar and bread, furnished me many a cheerful meal. The vinegar had been furnished to us by our master, more out of regard to our health, than to our comfort; but it greatly promoted both.

The affairs of the plantation now went on quietly, until after the cotton had been ploughed, and hoed the first time, after replanting. The working of the cotton crop is not disagreeable labour—no more so than the culture of corn—but we were called upon to perform a kind of labour, than which none can be more toilsome to the body, or dangerous to the health.

I have elsewhere informed the reader, that my master was a cultivator of rice, as well as of cotton. Whilst I was at the fishery in the spring, thirty acres of swamp land had been cleared off, ploughed, and planted in rice. The water had now been turned off the plants, and the field was to be ploughed and hoed. When we were taken to the rice field, the weather was very hot, and the ground was yet muddy and wet. The ploughs were to be dragged through the wet soil, and the young rice had to be cleaned of weeds, by the hand, and hilled up with the hoe.

It is the common opinion, that no stranger can work a week in a rice swamp, at this season of the year, without becoming sick; and all the new hands, three in number, besides myself, were taken ill within the first five days, after we had entered this field. The other three were removed to the sick room; but I did not go there, choosing rather to remain at the quarter, where I was my own master, except that the doctor, who called to see me, took a large quantity of blood from my arm, and compelled me to take a dose of some sort of medicine that made me very sick, and caused me to vomit violently. This happened on the second day of my illness, and from this time I recovered slowly, but was not able to go to the field again for more than a week. Here it is but justice to my master to say, that during all the time of my illness, some one came from the great house, every day, to inquire after me, and to offer me some kind of light and cool refreshment. I might have gone to the sick room at any time, if I had chosen to do so.

An opinion generally prevails, amongst the people of both colours, that the drug *copperas* is very poisonous—and perhaps it may be so, if taken in large quantities—but the circumstance, that it is used in medicine, seems to forbid the notion of its poisonous qualities. I believe copperas was mingled with the potion the doctor gave to me. Some overseers keep copperas by them, as a medicine, to be administered to the hands whenever they become sick; but this I take to be a bad practice; for although, in some cases, this drug may be very efficacious, it certainly should be administered by a more skilful hand than that of an overseer. It, however, has the effect of deterring the people from complaining of illness, until they are no longer able to work; for it is the most nauseous and sickening medicine that was ever taken into the stomach. Ignorant, or malicious overseers may, and often do, misapply it; as was the case with our overseer, when he compelled poor Lydia to take a draught of its solution. After the restoration of my health, I resumed my accustomed labour in the field, and continued it without intermission, until I left this plantation.

We had, this year, as a part of our crop, ten acres of indigo. This plant is worked nearly after the manner of rice, except, that it is planted on high and dry ground, whilst the rice is always cultivated in low swamps, where the ground may be inundated with water; but notwithstanding its location on dry ground, the culture of indigo is not less unpleasant than that of rice. When the rice is ripe, and ready for the sickle, it is no longer disagreeable; but when the indigo is ripe and ready to cut, the troubles attendant upon it have only commenced.

The indigo plant bears more resemblance to the weed called wild indigo, which is common in the woods of Pennsylvania, than to any other herb with which I am acquainted.

The root of the indigo plant is long and slender, and emits a scent somewhat like that of parsley. From the root issues a single stem, straight, hard, and slender, covered with a bark, a little cracked on its surface, of a gray colour towards the bottom, green in the middle, reddish at the extremity, and without the appearance of pith in the inside. The leaves ranged in pairs around the stalk, are of an oval form,—smooth, soft to the touch, furrowed above, and of a deep green on the under side. The upper parts of the plant are loaded with small flowers, destitute of smell. Each flower changes into a pod, enclosing seed.

This plant thrives best in a rich, moist soil. The seeds are black, very small, and sowed in straight drills. This crop requires very careful culture, and must be kept free from every kind of weeds and grass. It ripens within less than three months from the time it is sown. When it begins to flower, the top is cut off, and, as new flowers appear, the plant is again pruned, until the end of the season.

Indigo impoverishes land more rapidly than almost any other crop, and the plant must be gathered in with great caution, for fear of shaking off the valuable farina that lies in the leaves. When gathered, it is thrown into the steeping vat— a large tub filled with water—here it undergoes a fermentation, which, in twenty-four hours, at farthest, is completed. A cock is then turned to let the water run into the second tub, called the mortar, or pounding tub: the steeping vat is then cleaned out, that fresh plants may be thrown in; and thus the work is continued, without interruption. The water in the pounding tub is stirred with wooden buckets, with holes in their bottoms, for several days; and, after the sediment contained in the water, has settled to the bottom of the tub, the water is let off, and the sediment, which is the indigo of commerce, is gathered into bags, and hung up to drain. It is afterwards pressed, and laid away to dry in cakes, and then packed in chests for market.

Washing at the tubs is exceedingly unpleasant, both on account of the filth and the stench, arising from the decomposition of the plants.

In the early part of June, our shad, that each one had been used to receive, was withheld from us, and we no longer received any thing but the peck of corn, and pint of vinegar. This circumstance, in a community less severely disciplined than ours, might have procured murmurs; but to us it was only announced by the fact of the fish not being distributed to us on Sunday evening.

This was considered a fortunate season by our people. There had been no exemplary punishment inflicted amongst us, for several months; we had escaped entirely upon the occasion of the stolen bags of cotton, though nothing less was to have been looked for, on that occurrence, than a general whipping of the whole gang.

There was more or less of whipping amongst us, every week; frequently, one was flogged every evening, over and above the punishments that followed on each settlement day; but these chastisements, which seldom exceeded ten or twenty lashes, were of little import. I was careful, for my own part, to conform to all the regulations of the plantation.

When I no longer received my fish from the overseer, I found it necessary again to resort to my own expedients, for the purpose of procuring something in the shape of animal food, to add to my bread and greens.

I had, by this time, become well acquainted with the woods and swamps, for several miles round our plantation; and this being the season when the turtles came upon the land, to deposite their eggs, I availed myself of it, and going out one Sunday morning, caught, in the course of the day, by travelling cautiously around the edges of the swamps, ten snapping turtles, four of which were very large. As I caught these creatures, I tied each one with hickory bark, and hung it up to the bough of a tree, so that I could come and carry it home at my leisure.

I afterwards carried my turtles home, and put them into a hole that I dug in the ground, four or five feet deep, and secured the sides by driving small pieces of split timber into the ground, quite round the circumference of the hole, the upper ends of the timber standing out above the ground. Into this hole I poured water at pleasure, and kept my turtles until I needed them.

On the next Sunday, I again went to the swamps to search for turtles; but as the period of laying their eggs had nearly passed, I had poor success to day, only taking two turtles of the species called skill-pots—a kind of large terrapin, with a speckled back and red belly.

This day, when I was three or four miles from home, in a very solitary part of the swamps, I heard the sound of bells, similar to those which wagoners place on the shoulders of their horses. At first, the noise of bells of this kind, in a place where they were so unexpected, alarmed me, as I could not imagine who or what it was that was causing these bells to ring. I was standing near a pond of water, and listening attentively; I thought the bells were moving in the woods, and coming toward me. I therefore crouched down upon the ground, under cover of a cluster of small bushes that were near me, and lay, not free from disquietude, to await the near approach of these mysterious bells.

Sometimes they were quite silent for a minute or more at a time, and then again would jingle quick, but not loud. They were evidently approaching me; and at length I heard footsteps distinctly in the leaves, which lay dry upon the ground. A feeling of horror seized me at this moment, for I now recollected that I was on the verge of the swamp, near which the vultures and carrion crows had mangled the living bodies of the two murderers; and my terror was not abated, when, a moment after, I saw come from behind a large tree, the form of a brawny, famished-looking black man, entirely naked, with his hair matted and shaggy, his eyes wild and rolling, and bearing over his head something in the form of an arch, elevated three feet above his hair, beneath the top of which were suspended the bells, three in number, whose sound had first attracted my attention. Upon a closer examination of this frightful figure, I perceived that it wore a collar of iron about its neck, with a large padlock pendent from behind, and carried in its hand a long staff, with an iron spear in one end. The staff, like every thing else belonging to this strange spectre, was black. It slowly approached within ten paces of me, and stood still.

The sun was now down, and the early twilight produced by the gloom of the heavy forest, in the midst of which I was, added approaching darkness to heighten my dismay. My heart was in my mouth; all the hairs of my head started from their sockets; I seemed to be rising from my hiding place into the open air, in spite of myself, and I gasped for breath.

The black apparition moved past me, went to the water and kneeled down. The forest re-echoed with the sound of the bells, and their dreadful peals filled the deepest recesses of the swamps, as their bearer, drank the water of the pond, in which I thought I heard his irons hiss, when they came in contact with it. I felt confident that I was now in the immediate presence of an inhabitant of a nether and fiery world, who had been permitted to escape, for a time, from the place of his torment, and come to revisit the scenes of his former crimes. I now gave myself up for lost, without other aid than my own, and began to pray aloud to heaven to protect me. At the sound of my voice, the supposed evil one appeared to be scarcely less alarmed than I was. He sprang to his feet, and, at a single bound, rushed mid-deep into the water, then turning, he besought me in a suppliant and piteous tone of voice, to have mercy upon him, and not carry him back to his master.

The suddenness with which we pass from the extreme of one passion, to the utmost bounds of another, is inconceivable, and must be assigned to the catalogue of unknown causes and effects, unless we suppose the human frame to be an involuntary machine, operated upon by surrounding objects which give it different and contrary impulses, as a ball is driven to and fro by the batons of boys, when they play in troops upon a common. I had no sooner heard a human voice than all my fears fled, as a spark that ascends from a heap of burning charcoal, and vanishes to nothing.

I at once perceived, that the object that had well nigh deprived me of my reason, so far from having either the will or the power to injure me, was only a poor destitute African negro, still more wretched and helpless than myself.

Rising from the bushes, I now advanced to the water side, and desired him to come out without fear, and to be assured that if I could render him any assistance, I would do it most cheerfully. As to carrying him back to his master, I was more ready to ask help to deliver me from my own, than to give aid to any one in forcing him back to his.

We now went to a place in the forest, where the ground was, for some distance, clear of trees, and where the light of the sun was yet so strong, that every object could be seen. My new friend now desired me to look at his back, which was seamed and ridged with scars of the whip, and the hickory, from the pole of his neck to the lower extremity of the spine. The natural colour of the skin had disappeared, and was succeeded by a streaked and speckled appearance of dusky white and pale flesh colour, scarcely any of the original black remaining. The skin of this man's back had been again and again cut away by the thong, and renewed by the hand of nature, until it was grown fast to the flesh, and felt hard and turbid.

He told me his name was Paul; that he was a native of Congo, in Africa, and had been a slave five years; that he had left an aged mother, a widow, at home, as also a wife and four children; that it had been his misfortune to fall into the hands of a master, who was frequently drunk, and whose temper was so savage, that his chief delight appeared to consist in whipping and torturing his slaves, of whom he owned near twenty; but through some unaccountable caprice, he had contracted a particular dislike against Paul, whose life he now declared to me, was insupportable. He had then been wandering in the woods, more than three weeks, with no other subsistence than the land tortoises, frogs, and other reptiles that he had taken in the woods, and along the shores of the ponds, with the aid of his spear. He had not been able to take any of the turtles in the laying season, because the noise of his bells frightened them, and they always escaped to the water before he could catch them. He had found many eggs, which he had eaten raw, having no fire, nor any means of making fire, to cook his food. He had been afraid to travel much in the middle of the day, lest the sound of his bells should be heard by some one, who would make his master acquainted with the place of his concealment. The only periods when he ventured to go in search of food, were early in the morning, before people could have time to leave their homes and reach the swamp; or late in the evening, after those who were in pursuit of him had gone to their dwellings for the night.

This man spoke our language imperfectly, but possessed a sound and vigorous understanding; and reasoned with me upon the propriety of destroying a life which was doomed to continual distress. He informed me that he had first run away from his master more than two years ago, after being whipped, with long hickory switches, until he fainted. That he concealed himself in a swamp, at that time, ten or fifteen miles from this place, for more than six months, but was finally betrayed by a woman whom he sometimes visited; that when taken, he was again whipped until he was not able to stand, and had a heavy block of wood chained to one foot, which he was obliged to drag after him at his daily labour, for more than three months, when he found an old file, with which he cut the irons from his ancle, and again escaped to the woods, but was retaken within little more than a week after his flight, by two men who were looking for their cattle, and came upon him in the woods where he was asleep.

On being returned to his master, he was again whipped; and then the iron collar that he now wore, with the iron rod, extending from one shoulder over his head to the other, with the bells fastened at the top of the arch, were put upon him. Of these irons he could not divest himself, and wore them constantly from that time to the present.

I had no instruments with me, to enable me to release Paul from his manacles, and all I could do for him was to desire him to go with me to the place where I had left my terrapins, which I gave to him, together with all the eggs that I had found to-day. I also caused him to lie down, and having furnished myself with a flint-stone, (many of which lay in the sand near the edge of the pond) and a handful of dry moss, I succeeded in striking fire from the iron collar, and made a fire of sticks, upon which he could roast the terrapins and the eggs. It was now quite dark, and I was full two miles from my road, with no path to guide me towards home, but the small traces made in the woods by the cattle.

I advised Paul to bear his misfortunes as well as he could, until the next Sunday, when I would return and bring with me a file, and other things necessary to the removal of his fetters.

I now set out alone, to make my way home, not without some little feeling of trepidation, as I passed along in the dark shade of the pine trees, and thought of the terrific deeds that had been done in these woods.

This was the period of the full moon, which now rose, and cast her brilliant rays through the tops of the trees that overhung my way, and enveloped my path in a gloom more cheerless than the obscurity of total darkness. The path I travelled led by sinuosities around the margin of the swamp, and finally ended at the extremity of the cart-road terminating at the spot where David and Hardy had been given alive for food to vultures; and over this ground I was now obliged to pass, unless I chose to turn far to the left, through the pathless forest, and make my way to the high road near the spot where the lady had been torn from her horse. I hated the idea of acknowledging to my own heart, that I was a coward, and dared not look upon the bones of a murderer at midnight; and there was little less of awe attached to the notion of visiting the ground where the ghost of the murdered woman was reported to wander in the moonbeams, than in visiting the scene where diabolical crimes had been visited by fiend-like punishment.

My opinion is, that there is no one who is not at times subject to a sensation approaching fear, when placed in situations similar to that in which I found myself this night. I did not believe that those who had passed the dark line, which separates the living from the dead, could again return to the earth, either for good or for evil; but that solemn foreboding of the heart which directs the minds of all men to a contemplation of the just judgment, which a superior, and unknown power, holds in reservation for the deeds of this life, filled my soul with a dread conception of the unutterable woes which a righteous and unerring tribunal must award to the blood-stained spirits of the two men whose lives had been closed in such unspeakable torment by the side of the path I was now treading.

The moon had risen high above the trees, and shone with a clear and cloudless light; the whole firmament of heaven was radiant with the lustre of a mild and balmy summer evening. Save only the droppings of the early dew from the lofty branches of the trees into the water, which lay in shallow pools on my right, and the light trampling of my own footsteps; the stillness of night pervaded the lonely wastes around me. But there is a deep melancholy in the sound of the heavy drop as it meets the bosom of the wave in a dense forest at night, that revives in the memory the recollection of the days of other years, and fills the heart with sadness.

I was now approaching the unhallowed ground where lay the remains of the remorseless and guilty dead, who had gone to their final account, reeking in their sins, unatoned, unblest, and unwept. Already I saw the bones, whitened by the rain, and bleached in the sun, lying scattered and dispersed, a leg here and an arm there, whilst a scull with the under jaw in its place, retaining all its teeth, grinned a ghastly laugh, with its front full in the beams of the moon, which, falling into the vacant sockets of the eye-balls, reflected a pale shadow from these deserted caverns, and played in twinkling lustre upon the bald, and skinless forehead.

In a moment, the night-breeze agitated the leaves of the wood and moaned in dreary sighs through the lofty pine tops; the gale shook the forest in the depth of its solitudes: a cloud swept across the moon, and her light disappeared; a flock of carrion crows disturbed in their roosts, flapped their wings and fluttered over my head; and a wolf, who had been gnawing the dry bones, greeted the darkness with a long and dismal howl.

I felt the blood chill in my veins, and all my joints shuddered, as if I had been smitten by electricity. At least a minute elapsed before I recovered the power of self-government. I hastened to fly from a place devoted to crime, where an evil genius presided in darkness over a fell assembly of howling wolves, and blood-snuffing vultures.

When I arrived at the quarter, all was quiet. The inhabitants of this mock-village were wrapped in forgetfulness; and I stole silently into my little loft, and joined my neighbours in their repose. Experience had made me so well acquainted with the dangers that beset the life of a slave, that I determined, as a matter of prudence, to say nothing to any one, of the adventures of this Sunday; but went to work on Monday morning, at the summons of the overseer's horn, as if nothing unusual had occurred. In the course of the week, I often thought of the forlorn and desponding African, who had so terrified me in the woods, and who seemed so grateful for the succour I gave him. I felt anxious to become better acquainted with this man, who possessed knowledge superior to the common race of slaves, and manifested a moral courage in the conversation that I had with him, worthy of a better fate than that to which fortune had consigned him. On the following Sunday, having provided myself with a large file, which I procured from the blacksmith's shop, belonging to the plantation, I again repaired to the place, at the side of the swamp, where I had first seen the figure of this ill-fated man. I expected that he would be in waiting for me at the appointed place, as I had promised him that I would certainly come again, at this time; but on arriving at the spot where I had left him, I saw no sign of any person. The remains of the fire that I had kindled were here, and it seemed that the fire had been kept up for several days, by the quantity of ashes that lay in a heap, surrounded by numerous small brands. The impressions of human feet, were thickly disposed around this decayed fire: and the bones of the terrapins that I had given to Paul, as well as the skeletons of many frogs, were scattered upon the ground; but there was nothing that showed that any one had visited this spot, since the fall of the last rain, which I now recollected had taken place on the previous Thursday. From this circumstance I concluded, that Paul had relieved himself of his irons, and gone to seek concealment in some other place; or that his master had discovered his retreat, and carried him back to the plantation.

Whilst standing at the ashes I heard the croaking of ravens at some distance in the woods, and immediately afterwards a turkey-buzzard passed over me pursued by an eagle, coming from the quarter in which I had just heard the ravens. I knew that the eagle never pursued the buzzard for the purpose of preying upon him, but only to compel him to disgorge himself of his own prey for the benefit of the king of birds. I therefore concluded that there was some dead animal in my neighbourhood that had called all these ravenous fowls together. It might be that Paul had killed a cow by knocking her down with a pine knot, and that he had removed his residence to this slaughtered animal. Curiosity was aroused in me, and I proceeded to examine the woods.

I had not advanced more than two hundred yards when I felt oppressed by a most sickening stench, and saw the trees swarming with birds of prey, buzzards perched upon their branches, ravens sailing amongst their boughs, and clouds of carrion crows flitting about, and poising themselves in the air in a stationary position, after the manner of that most nauseous of all birds, when it perceives, or thinks it perceives, some object of prey. Proceeding onward, I came in view of a large sassafras tree, around the top of which was congregated a cloud of crows, some on the boughs and others on the wing, whilst numerous buzzards were sailing low and nearly skimming the ground. This sassafras tree had many low horizontal branches, attached to one of which I now saw the cause of so vast an assembly of the obscene fowls of the air. The lifeless and putrid body of the unhappy Paul hung suspended by a cord made of twisted hickory bark, passed in the form of a halter round the neck, and firmly bound to a limb of the tree.

It was manifest that he had climbed the tree, fastened the cord to the branch, and then sprung off. The smell that assailed my nostrils was too overwhelming to permit me to remain long in view of the dead body, which was much mangled and torn, though its identity was beyond question, for the iron collar, and the bells with the arch that bore them, were still in their place. The bells had preserved the corpse from being devoured; for whilst I looked at it I observed a crow descend upon it, and make a stroke at the face with its beak, but the motion that this gave to the bells caused them to rattle, and the bird took to flight.

Seeing that I could no longer render assistance to Paul, who was now beyond the reach of his master's tyranny, as well as of my pity, I returned without delay to my master's house, and going into the kitchen, related to the household servants that I had found a black man hung in the woods with bells upon him. This intelligence was soon communicated to my master, who sent for me to come into the house to relate the circumstance to him. I was careful not to tell that I had seen Paul before his death; and when I had finished my narrative, my master observed to a gentleman who was with him, that this was a heavy loss to the owner, and told me to go.

The body of Paul was never taken down, but remained hanging where I had seen it until the flesh fell from the bones, or was torn off by the birds. I saw the bones hanging in the sassafras tree more than two months afterwards, and the last time that I was ever in these swamps.

---

## CHAPTER XVII.

AN affair was now in progress, which, though the persons who were actors in it were far removed from me, had in its effects a great influence upon the fortunes of my life. I have informed the reader that my master had three daughters, and that the second of the sisters was deemed a great beauty. The eldest of the three was married about the time of which I now write, to a planter of great wealth, who resided near Columbia; but the second had formed an attachment to a young gentleman whom she had frequently seen at the church attended by my master's family. As this young man, either from want of wealth, or proper persons to introduce him, had never been at my master's house, my young mistress had no opportunity of communicating to him the sentiments she entertained towards him, without violating the rules of modesty in which she had been educated. Before she would attempt any thing which might be deemed a violation of the decorum of her sex, she determined to take a new method of obtaining a husband. She communicated to her father, my master, a knowledge of the whole affair, with a desire that he would invite the gentleman of her choice to his house. This the father resolutely opposed, upon the ground that the young man upon whom his daughter had fixed her heart was without property, and consequently destitute of the means of supporting his daughter in a style suitable to the rank she occupied in society. A woman in love is not easily foiled in her purposes; my young mistress, by continual entreaties, so far prevailed over the affections, or more probably the fears of her father, that he introduced the young man to his family, and about two months afterwards my young mistress was a bride; but it had been agreed amongst all the parties, as I understood, before the marriage, that as the son-in-law had no land or slaves of his own, he should remove with his wife to a large tract of land that my master owned in the new purchase in the state of Georgia.

In the mouth of September, 1806, my master came to the quarter one evening, at the time of our return from the field, in company with his son-in-law, and informed me that he had given me, with a number of others of his slaves, to his daughter; and that I, with eight other men and two or three women, must set out on the next Sunday with my new master, for his estate in Georgia, whither we were to go, to clear land, build houses, and make other improvements, necessary for the reception of the newly-married lady, in the following spring.

I was much pleased with the appearance and manners of my new master; who was a young man apparently about twenty-seven or eight years old, and of good figure. We were to take with us, in our expedition to Georgia, a wagon, to be drawn by six mules, and I was appointed to drive the team. Before we set off my young mistress came in person to the quarter, and told us that all those who were going to the new settlement must come to the house, where she furnished each of us with two full suits of clothes, one of coarse woollen, and the other of hempen cloth. She also gave a hat to each of us, and two pairs of shoes, with a trifle in money, and enjoined us to be good boys and girls, and get things ready for her, and that when she should come to live with us we should not be forgotten. The conduct of this young lady was so different from that which I had been accustomed to witness since I came to Carolina, that I considered myself highly fortunate in becoming her slave, and now congratulated myself with the idea that I should, in future, have a mistress who would treat me kindly, and if I behaved well, would not permit me to want.

At the time appointed we set out for Georgia, with all the tools and implements necessary to the prosecution of a new settlement. My young master accompanied us, and travelled slowly for several days to enable me to keep up with him. We continued our march in this order until we reached the Savannah river at the town of Augusta, where my master told me that he was so well satisfied with my conduct, that he intended to leave me with the team to bring on the goods and the women and children; but that he would take the men and push on, as fast as possible, to the new settlement, and go to work until the time of my arrival. He gave me directions to follow on and inquire for Morgan county Court House, and said that he would have a person ready there on my arrival to guide me to him and the people with him. He then gave me twenty dollars to buy food for the mules and provisions for myself and those with me, and left me on the high road master of myself and the team. I was resolved that this striking proof of confidence on the part of my master should not be a subject of regret to him, and pursued my route with the greatest diligence, taking care to lay out as little money as possible for such things as I had to buy. On the sixth day, in the morning, I arrived at our new settlement in the middle of a heavy forest of such timber as is common to that country, with three dollars and twenty-five cents in my pocket, part of the money given to me at Augusta. This I offered to return, but my master refused to take it, and told me to keep it for my good conduct. I now felt assured that all my troubles in this world were ended, and that, in future, I might look forward to a life of happiness and ease; for I did not consider labour any hardship, if I was well provided with good food and clothes, and my other wants properly regarded.

My master, and the people who were with him, had, before our arrival with the wagon, put up the logs of two cabins, and were engaged, when we came, in covering one of them with clapboards. In the course of the next day we completed both these cabins, with puncheon floors and small glass windows, the sash and glass for which I had brought in the wagon. We put up two other cabins, and a stable for the mules, and then began to clear land. After a few days, my master told me he meant to go down into the settlements to buy provisions for the winter, and that he should leave me to oversee the hands, and carry on the work in his absence. He accordingly left us, taking with him the wagon and two boys, one to drive the team, and another to drive cattle and hogs, which he intended to buy and drive to our settlement. I now felt myself almost proprietor of our new establishment, and believe the men left under my charge did not consider me a very lenient overseer. I in truth compelled them to work very hard, as I did myself. At the end of a week my master returned with a heavy load of meal and bacon, with salt and other things that we needed, and the day following a white man drove to our station several cows, and more than twenty hogs, the greater part of which were breeders. At this season of the year neither the hogs nor the cattle required any feeding at our hands. The woods were full of nuts, and the grass was abundant; but we gave salt to our stock, and kept the hogs in a pen, two or three days, to accustom them to the place.

We now lived very differently from what we did on my old master's plantation. We had as much bacon every day as we could eat; which, together with bread and sweet potatoes, which we had at will, constituted our fare. My master remained with us more than two months; within which time we had cleared forty acres of ground, ready for the plough; but, a few days before Christmas, an event took place, which, in its consequences, destroyed all my prospects of happiness, and totally changed the future path of my life. A messenger one day came to our settlement, with a letter, which had been forwarded in this manner, by the postmaster at the Court House, where the post-office was kept. This letter contained intelligence of the sudden death of my old master; and that difficulties had arisen in the family which required the immediate attention of my young one. The letter was written by my mistress. My master, forthwith, took an account of the stock of provisions, and other things that he had on hand, and putting the whole under my charge, gave me directions to attend to the work, and set off on horseback that evening; promising to return within one month at furthest. We never saw him again, and heard nothing of him until late in the month of January, 1807, when the eldest son of my late master came to our settlement, in company with a strange gentleman. The son of my late master informed me, to my surprise and sorrow, that my young master, who had brought us to Georgia, was dead; and that he, and the gentleman with him, were administrators of the deceased, and had come to Georgia for the purpose of letting out on lease, for the period of seven years, our place, with all the people on it, including me.

To me, the most distressing part of this news, was the death of my young master; and I was still more sorry when I learned, that he had been killed in a duel. My young mistress, whose beauty had drawn around her numerous suiters, many of whom were men of base minds and cowardly hearts, had chosen her husband, in the manner I have related; and his former rivals, after his return from Georgia, confederated together, for the dastardly purpose of revenging themselves, of both husband and wife, by the murder of the former.

In all parts of the cotton country, there are numerous taverns, which answer the double purpose of drinking and gambling houses. These places are kept by men who are willing to abandon all pretensions to the character and standing of gentlemen, for the hope of sordid gain; and are frequented by all classes of planters; though it is not to be understood, that all the planters resort to these houses. There are men of high and honourable virtue amongst the planters, who equally detest the mean cupidity of the men who keep these houses, and the silly wickedness of those who support them. Billiards is the game regarded as the most polite, amongst men of education and fashion; but cards, dice, and every kind of game, whether of skill or of hazard, are openly played in these sinks of iniquity. So far as my knowledge extends, there is not a single district of ten miles square, in all the cotton region, without at least one of these vile ordinaries, as they are frequently and justly termed. The keeping of these houses is a means of subsistence resorted to by men of desperate reputation, or reckless character; and they invite, as guests, all the profligate, the drunken, the idle, and the unwary of the surrounding country. In a community, where the white man never works, except at the expense of forfeiting all claim to the rank of a gentleman, and where it is beneath the dignity of a man, to oversee the labour of his own plantation, the number of those who frequent these gaming houses, may be imagined.

My young master, fortunately for his own honour, was of those who kept aloof from the precincts of the tavern, unless compelled by necessary business to go there; but the band of conspirators, who had resolved on his destruction, invited him through one of their number, who pretended to wish to treat with him concerning his property, to meet them at an ordinary, one evening. Here a quarrel was sought with him, and he was challenged to fight with pistols, over the table around which they sat.

My master, who, it appears, was unable to bear the reproach of cowardice, even amongst fools, agreed to fight; and as he had no pistols with him, was presented with a pair belonging to one of the gang; and accepted their owner, as his friend, or second in the business. The result was as might have been expected. My master was killed, at the first fire, by a ball which passed through his breast, whilst his antagonist escaped unharmed.

A servant was immediately despatched, with a letter to my mistress, informing her of the death of her husband. She was awakened in the night, to read the letter, the bearer having informed her maid that it was necessary for her to see it immediately. The shock drove her into a feverish delirium, from which she never recovered. At periods, her reason resumed its dominion; but in the summer following, she became a mother, and died in child-bed, of puerperal fever. I obtained this account from the mouth of a black man, who was the travelling servant of the eldest son of my old master, and who was with his master at the time he came to visit the tenant, to whom he let his sister's estate in Georgia, in the year 1807.

The estate to which I was now attached, was advertised to be rented for the term of seven years, with all the stock of mules, cattle, and so forth, upon it— together with seventeen slaves, six of whom were too young to be able to work at present. The price asked, was one thousand dollars for the first year, and two thousand dollars for each of the six succeeding years; the tenant to be bound to clear thirty acres of land annually.

Before the day on which the estate was to be let, by the terms of the advertisement, a man came up from the neighbourhood of Savannah, and agreed to take the new plantation, on the terms asked. He was immediately put into possession of the premises, and from this moment, I became his slave for the term of seven years.

Fortune had now thrown me into the power of a new master, of whom, when I considered the part of the country from whence he came, which had always been represented to me, as distinguished for the cruelty with which slaves were treated in it, I had no reason to expect much that was good. I had indeed, from the moment I saw this new master, and had learned the place of his former residence, made up my mind to prepare myself for a harsh servitude; but as we are often disappointed for the worse, so it sometimes happens, that we are deceived for the better. This man was by no means so bad as I was prepared to find him; and yet, I experienced all the evils in his service, that I had ever apprehended: but I could never find in my heart, to entertain a revengeful feeling towards him, for he was as much a slave as I was; and I believe of the two, the greater sufferer. Perhaps the evils he endured himself, made him more compassionate of the sorrows of others; but notwithstanding the injustice that was done me while with him, I could never look upon him as a bad man.

At the time he took possession of the estate, he was alone, and did not let us know that he had a wife, until after he had been with us, at least two weeks. One day, however, he called us together, and told us that he was going down the country, to bring up his family—that he wished us to go on with the work on the place in the manner he pointed out; and telling the rest of the hands that they must obey my orders, he left us. He was gone full two weeks; and when he returned, I had all the cleared land planted in cotton, corn, and sweet potatoes, and had progressed with the business of the plantation so much to his satisfaction, that he gave me a dollar, with which I bought a pair of new trousers—my old ones having been worn out in clearing the new land, and burning logs.

My master's family, a wife and one child, came with him; and my new mistress soon caused me to regret the death of my former young master, for other reasons, than those of affection and esteem.

This woman (though she was my mistress, I cannot call her lady) was the daughter of a very wealthy planter, who resided near Milledgeville, and had several children, besides my mistress. My master was a native of North Carolina—had removed to Georgia several years before this—had acquired some property, and was married to my mistress more than two years, when I became his slave, for a term of years as I have stated. I saw many families, and was acquainted with the moral character of many ladies, while I lived in the south; but I must, in justice to the country, say, that my new mistress was the worst woman I ever saw amongst the southern people. Her temper was as bad as that of a speckled viper; and her language, when she was enraged, was a mere vocabulary of profanity and virulence.

My master and mistress brought with them when they came, twelve slaves, great and small, seven of whom were able to do field work. We now had on our new place, a very respectable force; and my master was a man, who understood the means of procuring a good day's work from his hands, as well as any of his neighbours. He was also a man who, when left to pursue his own inclinations, was kind and humane in his temper, and conduct towards his people; and if he had possessed courage enough, to whip his wife two or three times, as he sometimes whipped his slaves, and to compel her to observe a rule of conduct befitting her sex, I should have had a tolerable time of my servitude with him; and should, in all probability, have been a slave in Georgia until this day. Before my mistress came, we had meat in abundance; for my master had left his keys with me, and I dealt out the provisions to the people.

Lest my master should complain of me at his return, or suspect that I had not been faithful to my trust, I had only allowed ourselves (for I fared in common with the others) one meal of meat in each day. We had several cows, that supplied us with milk, and a barrel of molasses was amongst the stores of provisions. We had mush, sweet potatoes, milk, molasses, and sometimes butter for breakfast and supper, and meat for dinner. Had we been permitted to enjoy this fine fare, after the arrival of our mistress, and had she been a woman of kindly disposition, and lady-like manners, I should have considered myself well off in the world; for I was now living in as good a country as I ever saw; and I much doubt if there is a better one anywhere.

Our mistress gave us a specimen of her character, on the first morning after her arrival amongst us, by beating severely, with a raw cow-hide, the black girl who nursed the infant, because the child cried, and could not be kept silent. I perceived by this, that my mistress possessed no control over her passions; and that, when enraged, she would find some victim to pour her fury upon, without regard to justice or mercy.

When we were called to dinner to-day, we had no meat, and a very short supply of bread; our meal being composed of badly cooked sweet potatoes, some bread, and a very small quantity of sour milk. From this time our allowance of meat was withdrawn from us altogether, and we had to live upon our bread, potatoes, and the little milk that our mistress permitted us to have. The most vexatious part of the new discipline, was the distinction that was made between us, who were on the plantation before our mistress came to it, and the slaves that she brought with her. To these latter, she gave the best part of the sour milk, all the buttermilk, and I believe, frequently rations of meat.

We were not on our part (I mean us of the old stock) wholly without meat, for our master sometimes gave us a whole flitch of bacon at once; this he had stolen from his own smoke-house—I say stolen, because he took it without the knowledge of my mistress, and always charged us in the most solemn manner not to let her know that we had received it. She was as negligent of the duties of a good housewife, as she was arrogant in assuming the control of things not within the sphere of her domestic duties, and never missed the bacon that our master gave to us, because she had not taken the trouble of examining the state of the meat-house. Obtaining all the meat we ate by stealth, through our master, our supplies were not regular, coming once or twice a-week, according to circumstances. However, as I was satisfied of the good intentions of my master towards me, I felt interested in his welfare, and in a short time became warmly attached to him. He fared but little better at the hands of my mistress than I did, except that as he ate at the same table with her, he always had enough of comfortable food; but in the matter of ill language, I believe my master and I might safely have put our goods together as a joint stock in trade, without either the one or the other being greatly the loser. I had secured the good opinion of my master, and it was perceivable by any one that he had more confidence in me than in any of his other slaves, and often treated me as the foreman of his people.

This aroused the indignation of my mistress, who, with all her ill qualities, retained a sort of selfish esteem for the slaves who had come with her from her father's estate. She seldom saw me without giving me her customary salutation of profanity; and she exceeded all other persons that I have ever known in the quickness and sarcasm of the jibes and jeers with which she seasoned her oaths. To form any fair conception of her volubility and scurrilous wit, it was necessary to hear her, more especially on Sunday morning or a rainy day, when the people were all loitering about the kitchens, which stood close round her dwelling. She treated my master with no more ceremony than she did me. Misery loves company, it is said, and I verily believe that my master and I felt a mutual attachment on account of our mutual sufferings.

## CHAPTER XVIII.

THE country I now lived in was new, and abounded with every sort of game common to a new settlement. Wages were high, and I could sometimes earn a dollar and a half a day by doing job work on Sunday. The price of a day's work here was a dollar. My master paid me regularly and fairly for all the work I did for him on Sunday, and I never went anywhere else to procure work. All his other hands were treated in the same way. He also gave me an old gun that had seen much hard service, for the stock was quite shattered to pieces, and the lock would not strike fire. I took my gun to a blacksmith in the neighbourhood, and he repaired the lock, so that my musket was as sure fire as any piece need be. I found upon trial, that though the stock and lock had been worn out, the barrel was none the worse for the service it had undergone.

I now, for the first time in my life, became a hunter, in the proper sense of the word; and generally managed my affairs in such a way as to get the half of Saturday to myself. This I did by prevailing on my master to set my task for the week on Monday morning.

Saturday was appropriated to hunting, if I was not obliged to work all day, and I soon became pretty expert in the use of my gun. I made salt licks in the woods, to which the deer came, at night, and I shot them from a seat of clapboards that was placed on the branches of a tree. Rackoons abounded here, and were of a large size, and fat at all seasons. In the month of April I saw the ground thickly strewed with nuts, the growth of the last year. I now began to live well, notwithstanding the persecution that my mistress still directed against me, and to feel myself, in some measure, an independent man.

Serpents of various kinds swarmed in this country. I have killed more than twenty rattle-snakes in a day, and copper-heads were innumerable; but the snake that I most dreaded was the moccason, which is quite as venomous as the copperhead or rattle-snake, and much more active and malicious. Vipers and other poisonous reptiles were innumerable; and in the swamps was a monstrous serpent, though of rare occurrence, which was really dangerous on account of its prodigious size. This snake is of a blown colour, with ashy white spots distributed over its body. It lives by catching rabbits and squirrels, rackoons and other animals. I have no doubt that some of this species would attack and swallow children several years old. I once shot one of these snakes that was more than eight feet long, and as thick as the leg of an ordinary man. When coiled up it appeared as large as a small calf lying in its resting place. Panthers, wolves, and other beasts of prey, were common in the woods.

I had always observed that snakes congregate, either in large groups or in pairs; and that if one snake is killed, another is soon after seen near the same place. I one day killed an enormous rattle-snake in the cotton field near my master's house. This snake was full six feet in length, of a corresponding thickness, and had fangs an inch and three-quarters in length. When dead, I skinned it, and stretched the skin on a board. A few days after, having occasion to cross a fence near where I had killed the large snake, and jumping from the top of the fence

upon the ground, without looking down, I alighted close beside another rattle-
snake, quite as large as the one I had killed. This one was lying at full length, and
I was surprised that it did not attempt to bite me, nor even to throw itself into
coil. It only sounded its rattles, making a noise sufficiently loud to be heard a
hundred yards. I killed this snake also, and seeing it appear to be full of something that it had eaten, I ripped it open with my knife, and found the whole cavity of its body stuffed full of corn meal that it had eaten in the house where my
master kept his stores, to which it had found access through some aperture in the
logs of the house. The snake was so full of meal that it could not coil itself, and
thus saved my life, for the bite of such a snake as this was, is almost certain death.
I knew a white man, some time afterwards, who was bitten by one of these large
rattle-snakes in the hand, as he was trying to punch it to death with a stick in a
hollow stump, and he died before he could be taken to his own house, which was
little more than a mile from the place where he was bitten.

A neighbour of my master was one day hunting deer in the woods with
hounds; and hearing one of his hounds cry out as if hurt by something, the gentleman proceeded to the spot, and found his dog lying in the agonies of death,
and a great rattlesnake near him. On examining the dog it was found that the
snake had struck him with its fangs in the side, and cut a deep gash in the skin.
The dog being heated with running, death ensued almost instantly.

I had a dog of my own which I had brought with me from Carolina, and
which was an excellent hunting dog. He would tree rackoons and bears, and
chase deer, and was so faithful, that I thought he would lose his life, if necessary,
in my defence; but dogs, like men, have a certain limit, beyond which their friendship will not carry them, at least it was so with my dog.

Being in the woods one Sunday, at a place called the goose-pond, a shallow pool of water to which wild geese resorted, my dog came out of the cane to
me, with his bristles raised, and showing by his conduct that he had seen something in the canes of which he was afraid. I had gone to the pond that day for
the purpose of cutting and putting into the water some sticks of a tree that grows
in that part of Georgia, of which very good ropes can be made. The timber is cut
and thrown into the water until the bark becomes soft and loose, and it is then
peeled off, beaten, and split to pieces; and of this bark ropes can be made nearly
equal to hempen ropes. I got a good deal of money by making ropes of this bark
and selling them. At the time I speak of, I had my axe with me, but was without
my gun. I endeavoured in vain to induce my dog to enter into the cane-brake,
and started on my way home, my dog keeping a little in advance of me, and frequently looking back. I had not proceeded far before the cause of my dog's alarm
became manifest. Looking behind me, I saw a huge panther creeping along the
path after me, in the manner that a cat creeps when stealing upon her prey. I felt
myself in danger, and again endeavoured to urge my dog to attack the panther,
but I could not prevail on him to place himself between me and the wild beast. I
stood still for some time, and the panther lay down on the ground, still, however, looking attentively at me. When I again moved forward, the panther moved
after me; and when I stopped and turned round, it stopped also. In this way I
proceeded, alternately advancing and halting, with the panther sometimes within

twenty steps of me, until I came in view of my master's clearing, when the panther turned off into the woods, and I saw it no more. I do not know whether this panther was in pursuit of me or my dog; but whether of the one or the other, it showed but little fear of both of us; and I believe that, if alone, it would not have hesitated to attack either of us. As soon as the panther disappeared I went home and told my master of my adventure. He sent immediately to the house of a gentleman who lived two miles distant, who came, and brought his dogs with him. These dogs, when joined to my master's made five in number. I went to the woods, and showed the place where the panther had left me, and the dogs immediately scented the trail. It was then late in the evening, and the chase was continued until near day-break the next morning, when the panther was forced to take a tree ten miles from my master's house. It was shot by my master with his rifle, and after it was dead, we measured it, from the end of the nose to the tip of the tail, and found the whole length to be eleven feet and ten inches.

In the fall of this year I went with my master to the Indian country, to purchase and bring to the settlement cattle and Indian horses. We travelled a hundred miles from the residence of my master, nearly west, before we came to any Indian village.

The country where the Indians lived was similar in soil and productions to that in which my master had settled; and I saw several fields of corn amongst the Indians of excellent quality, and well enclosed with substantial fences. I also saw amongst these people several log-houses, with square hewn logs. Some cotton was growing in small patches in the fields, but this plant was not extensively cultivated. Large herds of cattle were ranging in the woods, and cost their owners nothing for their keeping, except a small quantity of salt. These cattle were of the Spanish breed, generally speckled, but often of a dun or mouse colour, and sometimes of a leaden gray. They universally had long horns, and dark muzzles, and stood high on their legs, with elevated and bold fronts. When ranging in droves in the woods, they were the finest cattle in appearance that I ever saw. They make excellent working oxen, but their quarters are not so heavy and fleshy as those of the English cattle. The cows do not give large quantities of milk.

The Indian horses run at large in the woods like the cattle, and receive no feed from their owners, unless on some very extraordinary occasion. They are small, but very handsome little horses. I do not know that I ever saw one of these horses more than fourteen hands high; but they are very strong and active, and when brought upon the plantation, and broken to work, they are hardy and docile, and keep fat on very little food. The prevailing colour of these horses is black; but many of them are beautiful grays, with flowing manes and tails, and, of their size, are fine horses.

My master bought fifty horses, and more than a hundred of the cattle; and hired seven Indians, to help us to drive them into the settlement. We had only a path to travel in—no road having been opened to the Indian country, of width sufficient for wagons to pass upon it; and I was often surprised at the agility of the Indians, in riding the unbroken horses along this path, and through the cane-brakes, which lined it on either side, in pursuit of the cattle, when any of them attempted to leave the drove. With the horses we had but little trouble, after we had them once started on the path; but the cattle were much inclined to separate and wander in the woods, for several days after we set out from the Nation,— but the greatest trouble was experienced at the time we halted in the evening, for the night. Some of the cattle, and many of the horses, would wander off from the fire, to a great distance in the woods, if not prevented; and might attempt to return to the Indian country. To obviate this, as soon as the fire was kindled, and the Indians had taken their supper, they would take off into the woods in all directions, and, stationing themselves at the distance of about half a quarter of a mile from the fire, would set up such a horrible yelling and whooping, that the whole forest appeared to be full of demons, come to devour us and our drove too. This noise never failed to cause both horse and cattle to keep within the circle formed by the Indians; and I believe we did not lose a single beast on the whole journey.

My master kept many of the cattle, and several of the horses, which he used on the plantation, instead of mules. The residue he sold among the planters, and I believe the expedition yielded him a handsome profit in the end; it also afforded me an opportunity of seeing the Cherokee Indians in their own country, and of contrasting the immense difference that exists between man in a state of civilization and industry, and man in a state of barbarism and indolence.

Ever since I had been in the southern country, vast numbers of African negroes had been yearly imported; but this year the business ceased altogether, and I did not see any African who was landed in the United States after this date.[27]

I shall here submit to the reader, the results of the observations I have made on the regulations of southern society. It is my opinion, that the white people in general, are not nearly so well informed in the southern states, as they are in those lying farther north. The cause of this may not be obvious to strangers; but to a man who has resided amongst the cotton plantations, it is quite plain.

There is a great scarcity of schools, throughout all the cotton country, that I have seen; because the white population is so thinly scattered over the country, and the families live so far apart, that it is not easy to get a sufficient number of children together to constitute a school. The young men of the country, who have received educations proper to qualify them for the profession of teachers, are too proud to submit to this kind of occupation; and strangers, who come from the north, will not engage in a service that is held in contempt, unless they can procure large salaries from individuals, or get a great number of pupils to attend their instructions, whose united contributions may amount, in the aggregate, to a large sum.

Great numbers of the young men of fortune are sent abroad to be educated: but thousands of the sons of land and slave-holders receive very little education, and pass their lives in ignorant idleness. The poor white children are not educated at all. It is my opinion, that the women are not better educated than the men.

A few of the great families live in a style of luxury and magnificence on their estates, that people in the north are not accustomed to witness; but this splendour is made up of crowds of slaves, employed as household servants, and a gaudy show of silver plate, rather than in good houses, or convenient furniture. Good beef and good mutton, such as are seen in Philadelphia and New-York, are not known on the cotton plantations. Good butter is also a rarity; and, in the summer time, sweet flour, or sweet wheaten bread, is scarcely to be looked for. The flour is imported from the north, or west; and in the hot, damp climate of the southern summer, it cannot be kept from souring, more than four or five weeks.

The temper of my mistress grew worse daily—if that could grow worse, which was already as bad as it could be—and her enmity against me increased, the more she observed that my master confided in me. To enhance my misfortunes, the health of my master began, about this time, visibly to decline, and towards the latter end of the autumn of this year, he one day told me, that he believed he should not live long, as he already felt the symptoms of approaching decay and death.

This was a source of much anxiety and trouble to me; for I clearly foresaw, that if ever I fell under the unbridled dominion of my mistress, I should regret the worst period of my servitude in South Carolina. I was much afraid, as the winter came on, that my master might grow worse, and pass to the grave in the spring, for his disease was a consumption of the lungs; and it is well known, that the spring of the year, which brings joy, gladness, and vitality, to all creation, animate and inanimate, except the victim of consumption, is often the season that consigns him to the grave.

## CHAPTER XIX.

WE passed this winter in clearing land, after we had secured the crops of cotton and corn, and nothing happened on our plantation, to disturb the usual monotony of the life of a slave, except, that in the month of January, my master informed me, that he intended to go to Savannah for the purpose of purchasing groceries, and such other supplies as might be required on the plantation, in the following season; and that he intended to take down a load of cotton with our wagon and team; and that I must prepare to be the driver. This intelligence was not disagreeable to me, as the trip to Savannah would, in the first place, release me for a short time, from the tyranny of my mistress; and, in the second, would give me an opportunity of seeing a great deal of strange country. I derived a third advantage, in after times, from this journey; but which did not enter into my estimate of this affair, at that time.

My master had not yet erected a cotton-gin on his place—the land not being his own—and we hauled our cotton, in the seed, nearly three miles to be ginned, for which we had to give one-fourth to the owner of the gin.

When the time of my departure came, I loaded my wagon with ten bales of cotton, and set out with the same team of six mules that I had driven from South Carolina. Nothing of moment happened to me until the evening of the fourth day, when we were one hundred miles from home. My master stopped to-night (for he travelled with me on his horse) at the house of an old friend of his; and I heard my master, in conversation with this gentleman, (for such he certainly was) give me a very good character, and tell him, that I was the most faithful and trusty negro that he had ever owned. He also said that if he lived to see the expiration of the seven years for which he had leased me, he intended to buy me. He said much more of me; and I thought I heard him tell his friend something about my mistress, but this was spoken in a low tone of voice, and I could not distinctly understand it. When I was going away in the morning with my team, this gentleman came out to the wagon, and ordered one of his own slaves to help me to put the harness on my mules. At parting, he told me to stop at his house on my return, and stay all night; and said, I should always be welcome to the use of his kitchen, if it should ever be my lot to travel that way again.

I mention these trifles to show, that if there are hard and cruel masters in the south, there are also others of a contrary character. The slave-holders are neither more nor less than men, some of whom are good, and very many are bad. My master and this gentleman, were certainly of the number of the good; but the contrast between them and some others that I have seen, was, unhappily for many of the slaves, very great. I shall, hereafter, refer to this gentleman, at whose house I now was; and shall never name him without honour, nor think of him without gratitude.

As I travelled through the country with my team, my chief employment, beyond my duty of a teamster, was to observe the condition of the slaves on the various plantations by which we passed on our journey, and to compare things in Georgia, as I now saw them, with similar things in Carolina, as I had heretofore seen them.

There is as much sameness amongst the various cotton plantations, in Georgia, as there is amongst the various farms in New-York, or New-Jersey. He who has seen one cotton field, has seen all other cotton fields, bating the difference that naturally results from good and bad soils, or good and bad culture; but the contrast that prevails in the treatment of the slaves, on different plantations, is very remarkable. We travelled a road that was not well provided with public houses, and we frequently stopped for the night at the private dwellings of the planters; and I observed that my master was received as a visiter, and treated as a friend in the family, whilst I was always left at the road with my wagon, my master supplying me with money to buy food for myself and my mules.

It was my practice, when we remained all night at these gentlemen's houses, to go to the kitchen in the evening, after I had fed my mules and eaten my supper, and pass some time in conversation with the black people I might chance to find there. One evening, we halted before sundown, and I unhitched my mules at the road, about two hundred yards from the house of a planter, to which my master went to claim hospitality for himself.

After I had disposed of my team for the night, and taken my supper, I went as usual to see the people of colour in the kitchen, belonging to this plantation. The sun had just set when I reached the kitchen, and soon afterwards, a black boy came in and told the woman who was the only person in the kitchen when I came to it, that she must go down to the overseer's house. She immediately started, in obedience to this order, and not choosing to remain alone in a strange house, I concluded to follow the woman, and see the other people of this estate.

When we reached the house of the overseer, the coloured people were coming in from the field, and with them came the overseer, and another man, better dressed than overseers usually are.

I stood at some distance from these gentlemen, not thinking it prudent to be too forward amongst strangers. The black people were all called together, and the overseer told them, that some one of them had stolen a fat hog from the pen, carried it to the woods, and there killed and dressed it; that he had that day found the place where the hog had been slaughtered, and that if they did not confess, and tell who the perpetrators of this theft were, they would all be whipped in the severest manner. To this threat, no other reply was made than a universal assertion of the innocence of the accused. They were all then ordered to lie down upon the ground, and expose their backs, to which the overseer applied the thong of his long whip, by turns, until he was weary. It was fortunate for these people, that they were more than twenty in number, which prevented the overseer from inflicting many lashes on any one of them.

When the whole number had received, each in turn, a share of the lash, the overseer returned to the man, to whom he had first applied the whip, and told him he was certain that he knew who stole the hog; and that if he did not tell who the thief was, he would whip him all night. He then again applied the whip to the back of this man, until the blood flowed copiously; but the sufferer hid his face in his hands, and said not a word. The other gentleman then asked the overseer, if he was confident this man had stolen the pig; and, receiving an affirmative answer, he said he would make the fellow confess the truth, if he would follow his directions. He then asked the overseer if he had ever tried cat-hauling, upon an obstinate negro; and was told that this punishment had been heard of, but never practised on this plantation.

A boy was then ordered to get up, run to the house, and bring a cat, which was soon produced. The cat, which was a large gray tom-cat, was then taken by the well-dressed gentleman, and placed upon the bare back of the prostrate black man, near the shoulder, and forcibly dragged by the tail down the back, and along the bare thighs of the sufferer. The cat sunk his nails into the flesh, and tore off pieces of the skin with his teeth. The man roared with the pain of this punishment, and would have rolled along the ground, had he not been held in his place by the force of four other slaves, each one of whom confined a hand or a foot. As soon as the cat was drawn from him, the man said he would tell who stole the hog, and confessed that he and several others, three of whom were then holding him, had stolen the hog—killed, dressed, and eaten it. In return for this confession, the overseer said he should have another touch of the cat, which was again drawn along his back, not as before, from the head downwards, but from below the hips to the head. The man was then permitted to rise, and each of those who had been named by him as a participator in stealing the hog, was compelled to lie down, and have the cat twice drawn along his back; first downwards, and then upwards. After the termination of this punishment, each of the sufferers was washed with salt water, by a black woman, and they were then all dismissed. This was the most excruciating punishment that I ever saw inflicted on black people, and, in my opinion, it is very dangerous; for the claws of the cat are poisonous, and wounds made by them are very subject to inflammation.

During all this time, I had remained at the distance of fifty yards from the place of punishment, fearing either to advance or retreat, lest I too, might excite the indignation of these sanguinary judges. After the business was over, and my feelings became a little more composed, I thought the voice of the gentleman, in good clothes, was familiar to me; but I could not recollect who he was, nor where I had heard his voice, until the gentlemen at length left this place, and went towards the great house, and as they passed me, I recognized in the companion of the overseer, my old master, the negro trader, who had bought me in Maryland, and brought me to Carolina.

I afterwards learned from my master, that this man had formerly been engaged in the African slave-trade, which he had given up some years before, for the safer and less arduous business of buying negroes in the north, and bringing them to the south, as articles of merchandise, in which he had acquired a very respectable fortune—had lately married in a wealthy family, in this part of the country, and was a great planter.

Two days after this, we reached Savannah, where my master sold his cotton, and purchased a wagon load of sugar, molasses, coffee, shoes, dry goods, and such articles as we stood in need of at home; and on the next day after I entered the city, I again left it, and directed my course up the country. In Savannah I saw many black men, who were slaves, and who yet acted as freemen so far, that they went out to work, where and with whom they pleased, received their own wages, and provided their own subsistence; but were obliged to pay a certain sum at the end of each week to their masters. One of these men told me, that he paid six dollars on every Saturday evening, to his master; and yet he was comfortably dressed, and appeared to live well. Savannah was a very busy place, and I saw vast quantities of cotton, piled up on the wharves; but the appearance of the town itself, was not much in favour of the people who lived in it.

On my way home I travelled for several days, by a road different from that which we had pursued in coming down; and at the distance of fifty or sixty miles from Savannah, I passed by the largest plantation that I had ever seen. I think I saw at least a thousand acres of cotton in one field, which was all as level as a bowling-green. There were, as I was told, three hundred and fifty hands at work in this field, picking the last of the cotton from the burs; and these were the most miserable looking slaves that I had seen in all my travels.

It was now the depth of winter, and although the weather was not cold, yet it was the winter of this climate; and a man who lives on the Savannah river a few years, will find himself almost as much oppressed with cold, in winter there, as he would be in the same season of the year, on the banks of the Potomac, if he had always resided there.

These people were, as far as I could see, totally without shoes; and there was no such garment as a hat of any kind amongst them. Each person had a coarse blanket, which had holes cut for the arms to pass through, and, the top was drawn up round the neck, so as to form a sort of loose frock, tied before with strings. The arms, when the people were at work, were naked, and some of them had very little clothing of any kind, besides this blanket frock. The appearance of these people, afforded the most conclusive evidence that they were not eaters of pork; and that lent lasted with them throughout the year.

I again staid all night, as I went home, with the gentleman whom I have before noticed, as the friend of my master, who had left me soon after we quitted Savannah, and I saw him no more, until I reached home.

Soon after my return from Savannah, an affair of a very melancholy character took place in the neighbourhood of my master's plantation. About two miles from our residence, lived a gentleman who was a bachelor, and who had for his housekeeper a mulatto woman. The master was a young man, not more than twenty-five years old, and the housekeeper must have been at least forty. She had children grown up, one of whom had been sold by her master, the father of the bachelor, since I lived here, and carried away to the west. This woman had acquired a most unaccountable influence over her young master, who lived with her as his wife, and gave her the entire command of his house, and of every thing about it. Before he came to live where he now did, and whilst he still resided with his father, to whom the woman then belonged, the old gentleman perceiving the attachment of his son to this female, had sold her to a trader, who was on his way to the Mississippi river, in the absence of the young man; but when the latter returned home, and learned what had been done, he immediately set off in pursuit of the purchaser, overtook him somewhere in the Indian territory, and bought the woman of him, at an advanced price. He then brought her back, and put her, as his housekeeper, on the place where he now lived; left his father, and came to reside in person with the woman.

On a plantation adjoining that of the gentleman bachelor, lived a planter, who owned a young mulatto man, named Frank, not more than twenty-four or five years old, a very smart, as well as handsome fellow. Frank had become as much enamoured of this woman, who was old enough to have been his mother, as her master, the bachelor was; and she returned Frank's attachment, to the prejudice of her owner. Frank was in the practice of visiting his mistress at night, a circumstance of which her master was suspicious; and he forbade Frank from coming to the house. This only heightened the flame that was burning in the bosoms of the lovers; and they resolved, after many and long deliberations, to destroy the master. She projected the plot, and furnished the means for the murder, by taking her master's gun from the place where he usually kept it, and giving it to Frank, who came to the house in the evening, when the gentleman was taking his supper alone.

Lucy always waited upon her master at his meals, and knowing his usual place of sitting, had made a hole between two of the logs of the house, towards which, she knew his back would be at supper. At a given signal, Frank came quietly up to the house, levelled the gun through the hole prepared for him, and discharged a load of buck-shot between the shoulders of the unsuspecting master, who sprang from his seat and fell dead beside the table. This murder was not known in the neighbourhood until the next morning, when the woman herself went to a house on an adjoining plantation, and told it.

The murdered gentleman had several other slaves, none of whom were at home at the time of his death, except one man; and he was so terrified that he was afraid to run and alarm the neighbourhood. I knew this man well, and believe he was afraid of the woman and her accomplice. I never had any doubt of his innocence, though he suffered a punishment, upon no other evidence than mere suspicion, far more terrible than any ordinary form of death.

As soon as the murder was known to the neighbouring gentlemen, they hastened to visit the dead body, and were no less expeditious in instituting inquiries after those who had done the bloody deed. My master was amongst the first who arrived at the house of the deceased; and in a short time, half the slaves of the neighbouring plantations were arrested, and brought to the late dwelling of the dead man. For my own part, from the moment I heard of the murder, I had no doubt of its author.

Silence is a great virtue when it is dangerous to speak; and I had long since determined never to advance opinions, uncalled for, in controversies between the white people and the slaves. Many witnesses were examined by a justice of the peace, before the coroner arrived, but after the coming of the latter, a jury was called; and more than half a day was spent in asking questions of various black people, without the disclosure of any circumstance, which tended to fix the guilt of the murder upon any one. My master, who was present all this time, at last desired them to examine me, if it was thought that my testimony could be of any service in the matter, as he wished me to go home to attend to my work. I was sworn on the testament to tell the whole truth; and stated at the commencement of my testimony, that I believed Frank and Lucy to be the murderers, and proceeded to assign the reasons upon which my opinion was founded. Frank had not been present at this examination, and Lucy who had been sworn, had said she knew nothing of the matter; that at the time her master was shot, she had gone into the kitchen for some milk for his supper, and that on hearing the gun, she had come into the room, at the moment he fell to the floor and expired; but when she opened the door and looked out, she could neither hear nor see any one.

When Frank was brought in and made to touch the dead body, which he was compelled to do, because some said that if he was the murderer, the corpse would bleed at his touch, he trembled so much, that I thought he would fall; but no blood issued from the wound of the dead man. This compulsory touching of the dead had, however, in this instance, a much more powerful effect, in the conviction of the criminal, than the flowing of any quantity of blood could have had; for as soon as Frank had withdrawn his hand from the touch of the dead, the coroner asked him, in a peremptory tone, as if conscious of the fact, why he had done this. Frank was so confounded with fear, and overwhelmed by this interrogatory, that he lost all self-possession, and cried out in a voice of despair, that Lucy had made him do it.

Lucy, who had left the room when Frank was brought in, was now recalled, and confronted with her partner in guilt; but nothing could wring a word of confession from her. She persisted, that if Frank had murdered her master, he had done it of his own accord, and without her knowledge or advice. Some one now, for the first time, thought of making search for the gun of the dead man, which was not found in the place where he usually had kept it. Frank said he had committed the crime with this gun, which had been placed in his hands by Lucy. Frank, Lucy, and Billy, a black man, against whom there was no evidence, nor cause of suspicion, except that he was in the kitchen at the time of the murder, were committed to prison in a new log-house on an adjoining plantation, closely confined in irons, and kept there a little more than two weeks,when they were all tried before some gentlemen of the neighbourhood, who held a court for that purpose. Lucy and Frank were condemned to be hung; but Billy was found not guilty; although he was not released, but kept in confinement until the execution of his companions, which took place ten days after the trial.

On the morning of the execution, my master told me, and all the rest of the people, that we must go to the *hanging,* as it was termed by him as well as others. The place of punishment was only two miles from my master's residence, and I was there in time to get a good stand, near the gallows' tree, by which I was enabled to see all the proceedings connected with this solemn affair. It was estimated by my master, that there were at least fifteen thousand people present at this scene, more than half of whom were blacks; all the masters, for a great distance round the country, having permitted, or compelled, their people to come to this *hanging* .

Billy was brought to the gallows with Lucy and Frank, but was permitted to walk beside the cart in which they rode. Under the gallows, after the rope was around her neck, Lucy confessed that the murder had been designed by her, in the first place, and that Frank had only perpetrated it at her instance. She said she had at first intended to apply to Billy to assist her in the undertaking, but had afterwards communicated her designs to Frank, who offered to shoot her master, if she would supply him with a gun, and let no other person be in the secret.

A long sermon was preached by a white man under the gallows, which was only the limb of a tree, and afterwards an exhortation was delivered by a black man. The two convicts were hung together, and after they were quite dead, a consultation was held among the gentlemen as to the future disposition of Billy, who, having been in the house when his master was murdered, and not having given immediate information of the fact, was held to be guilty of concealing the death, and was accordingly sentenced to receive five hundred lashes. I was in the branches of a tree close by the place where the court was held, and distinctly heard its proceedings and judgment. Some went to the woods to cut hickories, whilst others stripped Billy and tied him to a tree. More than twenty long switches, some of them six or seven feet in length, had been procured, and two men applied the rods at the same time, one standing on each side of the culprit, one of them using his left hand.

I had often seen black men whipped, and had always, when the lash was applied with great severity, heard the sufferer cry out and beg for mercy; but in this case, the pain inflicted by the double blows of the hickory was so intense, that Billy never uttered so much as a groan; and I do not believe he breathed for the space of two minutes after he received the first strokes. He shrank his body close to the trunk of the tree, around which his arms and legs were lashed, drew his shoulders up to his head like a dying man, and trembled, or rather shivered, in all his members. The blood flowed from the commencement, and in a few minutes lay in small puddles at the root of the tree. I saw flakes of flesh as long as my finger fall out of the gashes in his back; and I believe he was insensible during all the time that he was receiving the last two hundred lashes. When the whole five hundred lashes had been counted by the person appointed to perform this duty, the half dead body was unbound and laid in the shade of the tree upon which I sat. The gentlemen who had done the whipping, eight or ten in number, being joined by their friends, then came under the tree and drank punch until their dinner was made ready, under a booth of green boughs at a short distance.

After dinner, Billy, who had been groaning on the ground where he was laid, was taken up, placed in the cart in which Lucy and Frank had been brought to the gallows, and conveyed to the dwelling of his late master, where he was confined to the house and his bed more than three months, and was never worth much afterwards while I remained in Georgia.

Lucy and Frank, after they had been half an hour upon the gallows, were cut down, and suffered to drop into a deep hole that had been dug under them whilst they were suspended. As they fell, so the earth was thrown upon them, and the grave closed over them for ever.

They were hung on Thursday, and the vast assemblage of people that had convened to witness their death did not leave the place altogether until the next Monday morning. Wagons, carts, and carriages had been brought upon the ground; booths and tents erected for the convenience and accommodation of the multitude; and the terrible spectacles that I have just described were succeeded by music, dancing, trading in horses, gambling, drinking, fighting, and every other species of amusement and excess to which the southern people are addicted.

I had to work in the day-time, but went every night to witness this funereal carnival, the numbers that joined in which appeared to increase, rather than diminish, during the Friday and Saturday that followed the execution. It was not until Sunday afternoon that the crowd began sensibly to diminish; and on Monday morning, after breakfast time, the last wagons left the ground, now trampled into dust as dry and as light as ashes, and the grave of the murderers was left to the solitude of the woods.

Certainly those who were hanged well deserved their punishment; but it was a very arbitrary exercise of power to whip a man until he was insensible, because he did not prevent a murder which was committed without his knowledge; and I could not understand the right of punishing him, because he was so weak or timorous as to refrain from the disclosure of the crime the moment it came to his knowledge.

It is necessary for the southern people to be vigilant in guarding the moral condition of their slaves, and even to punish the intention to commit crimes, when that intention can be clearly proved; for such is the natural relation of master and slave, in by far the greater number of cases, that no cordiality of feeling can ever exist between them; and the sentiments that bind together the different members of society in a state of freedom and social equality, being absent, the master must resort to principles of physical restraint, and rules of mental coercion, unknown in another and a different condition of the social compact.

It is a mistake to suppose that the southern planters could ever retain their property, or live amongst their slaves, if those slaves were not kept in terror of the punishment that would follow acts of violence and disorder. There is no difference between the feelings of the different races of men, so far as their personal rights are concerned. The black man is as anxious to possess and to enjoy liberty as the white one would be, were he deprived of this inestimable blessing. It is not for me to say that the one is as well qualified for the enjoyment of liberty as the other. Low ignorance, moral degradation of character, and mental depravity, are inseparable companions; and in the breast of an ignorant man, the passions of envy and revenge hold unbridled dominion.

It was in the month of April that I witnessed the painful spectacle of two fellow-creatures being launched into the abyss of eternity, and a third, being tortured beyond the sufferings of mere death, not for his crimes, but as a terror to others; and this, not to deter others from the commission of crimes, but to stimulate them to a more active and devoted performance of their duties to their owners. My spirits had not recovered from the depression produced by that scene, in which my feelings had been awakened in the cause of others, when I was called to a nearer and more immediate apprehension of sufferings, which, I now too clearly saw, were in preparation for myself.

My master's health became worse continually, and I expected he would not survive this summer. In this, however, I was disappointed; but he was so ill that he was seldom able to come to the field, and paid but little attention to his plantation, or the culture of his crops. He left the care of the cotton field to me after the month of June, and was not again out on the plantation before the following October; when he one day came out on a little Indian pony that he had used as his hackney, before he was so far reduced as to decline the practice of riding. I suffered very much this summer for want of good and substantial provisions, my master being no longer able to supply me, with his usual liberality, from his own meat house. I was obliged to lay out nearly all my other earnings, in the course of the summer, for bacon, to enable me to bear the hardship and toil to which I was exposed. My master often sent for me to come to the house, and talked to me in a very kind manner; and I believe that no hired overseer could have carried on the business more industriously than I did, until the crop was secured the next winter.

Soon after my master was in the field, in October, he sent for me to come to him one day, and gave me, on parting, a pretty good great coat of strong drab cloth, almost new, which he said would be of service to me in the coming winter. He also gave me at the same time a pair of boots which he had worn half out, but the legs of which were quite good. This great coat and these boots were afterwards of great service to me.

As the winter came on my master grew worse, and though he still continued to walk about the house in good weather, it was manifest that he was approaching the close of his earthly existence. I worked very hard this winter. The crop of cotton was heavy, and we did not get it all out of the field until some time after Christmas, which compelled me to work hard myself, and cause my fellow-slaves to work hard too, in clearing the land that my master was bound to clear every year on this place. He desired me to get as much of the land cleared in time for cotton as I could, and to plant the rest with corn when cleared off.

As I was now entrusted with the entire superintendence of the plantation by my master, who never left his house, it became necessary for me to assume the authority of an overseer of my fellow-slaves, and I not unfrequently found it proper to punish them with stripes to compel them to perform their work. At first I felt much repugnance against the use of the hickory, the only instrument with which I punished offenders, but the longer I was accustomed to this practice, the more familiar and less offensive it became to me; and I believe that a few years of perseverance and experience would have made me as inveterate a negro-driver as any in Georgia, though I feel conscious that I never should have become so hardened as to strip a person for the purpose of whipping, nor should I ever have consented to compel people to work without a sufficiency of good food, if I had it in my power to supply them with enough of this first of comforts.

In the month of February, my master became so weak, and his cough was so distressing, that he took to his bed, from which he never again departed, save only once, before the time when he was removed to be wrapped in his winding-sheet. In the month of March, two of the brothers of my mistress came to see her, and remained with her until after the death of my master.

When they had been with their sister about three weeks, they came to the kitchen one day when I had come in for my dinner, and told me that they were going to whip me. I asked them what they were going to whip me for? to which they replied, that they thought a good whipping would be good for me, and that at any rate, I must prepare to take it. My mistress now joined us, and after swearing at me in the most furious manner, for a space of several minutes, and bestowing upon me a multitude of the coarsest epithets, told me that she had long owed me a whipping, and that I should now get it.

She then ordered me to take off my shirt, (the only garment I had on, except a pair of old tow linen trowsers,) and the two brothers backed the command of their sister, the one by presenting a pistol at my breast, and the other by drawing a large club over his head in the attitude of striking me. Resistance was vain, and I was forced to yield. My shirt being off, I was tied by the hands with a stout bed-cord, and being led to a tree, called the Pride of China, that grew in the yard, my hands were drawn by the rope, being passed over a limb, until my feet no longer touched the ground. Being thus suspended in the air by the rope, and my whole weight hanging on my wrists, I was unable to move any part of my person, except my feet and legs. I had never been whipped since I was a boy, and felt the injustice of the present proceeding with the utmost keenness; but neither justice nor my feelings had any influence upon the hearts of my mistress and her brothers, two men as cruel in temper and as savage in manners as herself.

The first strokes of the hickory produced a sensation that I can only liken to streams of scalding water, running along my back; but after a hundred, or hundred and fifty lashes had been showered upon me, the pain became less acute and piercing, but was succeeded by a dead and painful aching, which seemed to extend to my very backbone.

As I hung by the rope, the moving of my legs sometimes caused me to turn round, and soon after they began to beat me I saw the pale and deathlike figure of my master standing at the door, when my face was turned toward the house, and heard him, in a faint voice, scarcely louder than a strong breathing, commanding his brothers-in-law to let me go. These commands were disregarded, until I had received full three hundred lashes; and doubtlessly more would have been inflicted upon me, had not my master, with an effort beyond his strength, by the aid of a stick on which he supported himself, made his way to me, and placing his skeleton form beside me as I hung, told his brothers-in-law that if they struck another stroke, he would send for a lawyer and have them both prosecuted at law. This interposition stopped the progress of my punishment, and after cutting me down, they carried my master again into the house. I was yet able to walk, and went into the kitchen, whither my mistress followed, and compelled me to submit to be washed in brine by a black woman, who acted as her cook. I was then permitted to put my shirt on, and to go to my bed.

This was Saturday, and on the next day, when I awoke late in the morning, I found myself unable to turn over or to rise. I felt too indignant at the barbarity with which I had been treated to call for help from any one, and lay in my bed made of corn husks until after twelve o'clock, when my mistress came to me and asked me how I was. A slave must not manifest feelings of resentment, and I answered with humility, that I was very sore and unable to get up. She then called a man and a woman, who came and raised me up; but I now found that my shirt was as fast to my back as if it had grown there. The blood and bruised flesh having become incorporated with the substance of the linen, it formed only the outer coat of the great scab that covered my back.

After I was down stairs, my mistress had me washed in warm water, and warm grease was rubbed over my back and sides, until the shirt was saturated with oil, and becoming soft, was at length separated from my back. My mistress then had my back washed and greased, and put upon me one of my master's old linen shirts. She had become alarmed, and was fearful either that I should die, or would not be able to work again for a long time. As it was, she lost a month of my labour at this time, and in the end, she lost myself, in consequence of this whipping.

As soon as I was able to walk, my master sent for me to come to his bedside, and told me that he was very sorrow for what had happened; that it was not his fault, and that if he had been well I should never have been touched. Tears came in his eyes as he talked to me, and said that as he could not live long, he hoped I would continue faithful to him whilst he did live. This I promised to do, for I really loved my master; but I had already determined, that as soon as he was in his grave, I would attempt to escape from Georgia and the cotton country, if my life should be the forfeiture of the attempt.

As soon as I had recovered of my wounds, I again went to work, not in my former situation of superintendent of my master's plantation, for this place was now occupied by one of the brothers of my mistress, but in the woods, where my mistress had determined to clear a new field. After this time, I did nothing but grub and clear land, while I remained in Georgia, but I was always making preparations for my departure from that country.

My master was an officer of militia, and had a sword which he wore on parade days, and at other times he hung it up in the room where he slept. I conceived an idea that this sword would be of service to me in the long journey that I intended to undertake. One evening, when I had gone in to see my master, and had remained standing at his bed-side some time, he closed his eyes as if going to sleep, and it being twilight, I slipped the sword from the place where it hung, and dropped it out of the window. I knew my master could never need this weapon again, but yet I felt some compunction of conscience at the thought of robbing so good a man. When I left the room, I took up the sword, and afterwards secreted it in a hollow tree in the woods, near the place at which I worked daily.

## CHAPTER XX.

MY master died in the month of May, and I followed him to his grave with a heavy heart, for I felt that I had lost the only friend I had in the world, who possessed at once the power and the inclination to protect me against the tyranny and oppression to which slaves on a cotton plantation are subject.

Had he lived, I should have remained with him, and never have left him, for he had promised to purchase the residue of my time of my owners in Carolina; but when he was gone, I felt the parting of the last tie that bound me to the place where I then was, and my heart yearned for my wife and children, from whom I had now been separated more than four years.

I held my life in small estimation, if it was to be worn out under the dominion of my mistress and her brothers, though since the death of my master she had greatly meliorated my condition by giving me frequent allowances of meat and other necessaries. I believe she entertained some vague apprehensions that I might run away, and betake myself to the woods for a living, perhaps go to the Indians; but I do not think she ever suspected that I would hazard the untried undertaking of attempting to make my way back to Maryland. My purpose was fixed, and now nothing could shake it. I only waited for a proper season of the year to commence my toilsome and dangerous journey. As I must of necessity procure my own subsistence on my march, it behoved me to pay regard to the time at which I took it up.

I furnished myself with a fire-box, as it is called, that is, a tin case containing flints, steel, and tinder, this I considered indispensable. I took the great coat that my master had given me, and with a coarse needle and thread quilted a scabbard of old cloth in one side of it, in which I could put my sword and carry it with safety. I also procured a small bag of linen that held more than a peck. This bag I filled with the meal of parched corn, grinding the corn after it was parched in the woods where I worked at the mill at night. These operations, except the grinding of the corn, I carried on in a small conical cabin that I had built in the woods. The boots that my master gave me, I had repaired by a Spaniard who lived in the neighbourhood, and followed the business of a cobbler.

Before the first of August I had all my preparations completed, and had matured them with so much secrecy, that no one in the country, white or black, suspected me of entertaining any extraordinary design. I only waited for the corn to be ripe, and fit to be roasted, which time I had fixed as the period of my departure. I watched the progress of the corn daily, and on the eighth of August I perceived, on examining my mistress' field, that nearly half of the ears were so far grown, that by roasting them, a man could easily subsist himself; and as I knew that this corn had been planted later than the most of the corn in the country, I resolved to take leave of the plantation and its tenants, for ever, on the next day.

I had a faithful dog, called Trueman, and this poor animal had been my constant companion for more than four years, without ever showing cowardice or infidelity, but once, and that was when the panther followed us from the woods. I was accordingly anxious to bring my dog with me; but as I knew the success of my undertaking depended on secrecy and silence, I thought it safest to abandon my last friend, and engage in my perilous enterprise alone. On the morning of the ninth, I went to work as usual, carrying my dinner with me, and worked diligently at grubbing until about one o'clock in the day. I now sat down and took my last dinner as the slave of my mistress, dividing the contents of my basket with my dog. After I had finished, I tied my dog with a rope to a small tree; I set my gun against it, for I thought I should be better without the gun than with it; tied my knapsack with my bag of meal on my shoulders, and then turned to take a last farewell of my poor dog, that stood by the tree to which he was bound, looking wistfully at me. When I approached him, he licked my hands, and then rising on his hind feet, and placing his fore paws on my breast, he uttered a long howl, which thrilled through my heart, as if he had said, "My master, do not leave me behind you." All the affection that the poor animal had testified for me in the course of his life, now rose fresh in my memory. I recollected that he had always been ready to lay down his life for me; that when I was tied and bound to the tree to be whipped, they were forced to compel me to order my dog to be quiet, to prevent him from attacking my executioner in my defence; and even when he fled from the panther, he had not left me, only advancing a few feet before me, and beckoning me to fly from an enemy whose strength was too great for us to contend against with hope of success; and I now felt assured, that had the panther attacked me, my dog would have conquered at my side, or have died in defending me. This was the first time that I had ever tied him. I had often left him for a whole day to guard my coat, my basket, or my gun, which he never deserted; and he now seemed to feel that I charged him with ingratitude and infidelity, when I bound him to a charge which I had never known him to forsake.

As I was now leaving my dog for ever, I talked to him as to a creature that understood language, and was sensible of the dangers I was going to meet.

"Poor Trueman, faithful Trueman, fare thee well. Thou hast been an honest dog, and sure friend to thy master in all his shades of fortune. When my basket was well filled, how cheerfully we have partaken together of its contents. I did not then upbraid thee, that thou atest in idleness the proceeds of my labour, for I knew that thy heart was devoted to thy protector. In the day of my adversity, when all the world had forsaken me, when my master was dead, and I had no friend to protect me, still, poor Trueman, thou wert the same. Thou laidest thyself down at my feet when the world had united to oppress me. How often, when I was sick, and the fever raged in my veins, didst thou come at the going down of the sun, and lick my feet in token of thy faith; and how patiently didst thou watch with thy poor master through the long and lonely night.

"When I had no crumbs in my basket to give thee, nor crust in my pocket to divide with thee, thy faithful heart failed not; and a glance from the eye of thy hungry master filled thee with gratitude and joy. Poor dog, I must bid thee farewell. To-morrow they will come and release thee. Perhaps they will hate thee for my sake, and persecute thee as they have persecuted me; but I leave thee my gun to secure thee protection at the hands of those who will be the arbiters of thy fate when I am gone. It is all the legacy I can give thee; and surely they will not kill so good a dog when they see him possessed of so true a gun. Man is selfish and heartless—the richest of them all are as wretched slaves as I am, and are only minions of fear and avarice. Could pride and ambition witness thy fidelity and gratitude to thy forsaken master, and learn humility from thy example, how many tears would be wiped from the eyes of sorrow. Follow the new master who shall possess my gun, and may he be as kind to thee as thou hast been faithful to me."

I now took to the forest, keeping, as nearly as I could, a north course all the afternoon. Night overtook me, before I reached any watercourse, or any other object worthy of being noticed; and I lay down and slept soundly, without kindling a fire, or eating any thing. I was awake before day, and as soon as there was light enough to enable me to see my way, I resumed my journey and walked on, until about eight o'clock, when I came to a river, which I knew must be the Appalachie. I sat down on the bank of the river, opened my bag of meal, and made my breakfast of a part of its contents. I used my meal very sparingly, it being the most valuable treasure that I now possessed; though I had in my pocket three Spanish dollars; but in my situation, this money could not avail me any thing, as I was resolved not to show myself to any person, either white or black. After taking my breakfast, I prepared to cross the river, which was here about a hundred yards wide, with a sluggish and deep current. The morning was sultry, and the thickets along the margin of the river teemed with insects and reptiles. By sounding the river with a pole, I found the stream too deep to be waded, and I therefore prepared to swim it. For this purpose, I stripped myself, and bound my clothes on the top of my knapsack, and my bag of meal on the top of my clothes; then drawing my knapsack close up to my head, I threw myself into the river. In my youth I had learned to swim in the Patuxent, and have seldom met with any person who was more at ease in deep water than myself. I kept a straight line from the place of my entrance into the Appalachie, to the opposite side, and when I had reached it, stepped on the margin of the land, and turned round to view the place from which I had set out on my aquatic passage; but my eye was arrested by an object nearer to me than the opposite shore. Within twenty feet of me, in the very line that I had pursued in crossing the river, a large alligator was moving in full pursuit of me, with his nose just above the surface, in the position that creature takes when he gives chase to his intended prey in the water.

The alligator can swim more than twice as fast as a man, for he can overtake young ducks on the water; and had I been ten seconds longer in the river, I should have been dragged to the bottom, and never again been heard of.

Seeing that I had gained the shore, my pursuer turned, made two or three circles in the water close by me, and then disappeared.

I received this admonition as a warning of the dangers that I must encounter in my journey to the north. After adjusting my clothes, I again took to the woods, and bore a little to the east of north; it now being my determination to turn down the country, so as to gain the line of the roads by which I had come to the south. I travelled all day in the woods; but a short time before sundown, came within view of an opening in the forest, which I took to be cleared fields, but upon a closer examination, finding no fences or other enclosures around it, I advanced into it and found it to be an open savannah, with a small stream of water creeping slowly through it. At the lower side of the open space, were the remains of an old beaver dam, the central part of which had been broken away by the current of the stream at the time of some flood. Around the margin of this former pond, I observed several decayed beaver lodges, and numerous stumps of small trees, that had been cut down for the food or fortifications of this industrious little nation, which had fled at the approach of the white man, and all its people were now, like me, seeking refuge in the deepest solitudes of the forest, from the glance of every human eye. As it was growing late, and I believed I must now be near the settlements, I determined to encamp for the night, beside this old beaver dam. I again took my supper from my bag of meal, and made my bed for the night, amongst the canes that grew in the place. This night I slept but little: for it seemed as if all the owls in the country had assembled in my neighbourhood to perform a grand musical concert. Their hooting and chattering commenced soon after dark, and continued until the dawn of day. In all parts of the southern country, the owls are very numerous, especially along the margins of streams, and in the low grounds, with which the waters are universally bordered; but since I had been in the country, although I had passed many nights in the woods, at all seasons of the year, I had never before heard so clamorous and deafening a chorus of nocturnal music. With the coming of the morning, I arose from my couch, and proceeded warily along the woods, keeping a continual lookout for plantations, and listening attentively to every noise that I heard in the trees, or amongst the canebrakes. When the sun had been up two or three hours, I saw an appearance of blue sky at a distance, through the trees, which proved that the forest had been removed from a spot somewhere before me, and at no great distance from me; and, as I cautiously advanced, I heard the voices of people in loud conversation. Sitting down amongst the palmetto plants, that grew around me in great numbers, I soon perceived that the people whose conversation I heard, were coming nearer to me. I now heard the sound of horses' feet, and immediately afterwards, saw two men on horseback, with rifles on their shoulders, riding through the woods, and moving on a line that led them past me, at a distance of about fifty or sixty yards. Perceiving that these men were equipped as hunters, I remained almost breathless, for the purpose of hearing their conversation. When they came so near that I could distinguish their words, they were talking of the best place to take a stand, for the purpose of seeing the deer; from which I inferred, that they had sent men to some other point, for the purpose of rousing the deer with dogs. After they had passed that point of their way that was nearest to me, and were beginning to recede from me, one of them asked the other, if he had heard that a negro had run away the day before yesterday, in Morgan county; to which his companion answered in the negative. The first then said, he had seen an advertisement at the store, which offered a hundred dollars reward for the runaway, whose name was Charles.

The conversation of these horsemen was now interrupted by the cry of hounds, at a distance in the woods, and heightening the speed of their horses, they were soon out of my sight and hearing.

Information of the state of the country through which I was travelling, was of the highest value to me; and nothing could more nearly interest me than a knowledge of the fact, that my flight was known to the white people, who resided round about, and before me. It was now necessary for me to become doubly vigilant, and to concert with myself measures of the highest moment.

The first resolution that I took was, that I would travel no more in the daytime. This was the season of hunting deer, and knowing that the hunters were under the necessity of being as silent as possible in the woods, I saw at a glance that they would be at least as likely to discover me in the forest, before I could see them, as I should be to see them, before I myself could be seen.

I was now very hungry, but exceedingly loath to make any further breaches on my bag of meal, except in extreme necessity. Feeling confident that there was a plantation within a few rods of me, I was anxious to have a view of it, in hope that I might find a corn-field upon it, from which I could obtain a supply of roasting ears. Fearful to stand upright, I crept along through the low ground, where I then was, at times raising myself to my knees, for the purpose of obtaining a better view of things about me. In this way I advanced until I came in view of a high fence, and beyond this saw cotton, tall and flourishing, but no sign of corn. I crept up close to the fence, where I found the trunk of a large tree, that had been felled in clearing the field. Standing upon this, and looking over the plantation, I saw the tassels of corn, at the distance of half a mile, growing in a field which was bordered on one side by the wood, in which I stood.

It was now nine or ten o'clock in the morning, and as I had slept but little the night before, I crept into the bushes, great numbers of which grew in and about the top of the fallen tree, and, hungry as I was, fell asleep. When I awoke, it appeared to me from the position of the sun, which I had carefully noted, before I lay down, to be about one or two o'clock. As this was the time of the day, when the heat is most oppressive, and when every one was most likely to be absent from the forest, I again moved, and taking a circuitous route at some distance from the fields, reached the fence opposite the corn-field, without having met with any thing to alarm me. Having cautiously examined every thing around me, as well by the eye as by the ear, and finding all quiet, I ventured to cross the fence and pluck from the standing stalks, about a dozen good ears of corn, with which I stole back to the thicket in safety. This corn was of no use to me without fire to roast it; and it was equally dangerous to kindle fire by night, as by day, the light at one time, and the smoke at another, might betray me to those who I knew were ever ready to pursue and arrest me. "Hunger eats through stone walls," says the proverb; and an empty stomach is a petitioner, whose solicitations cannot be refused, if there is any thing to satisfy them with.

Having regained the woods in safety, I ventured to go as far as the side of a swamp, which I knew to be at the distance of two or three hundred yards, by the appearance of the timber. When in the swamp, I felt pretty secure, but determined that I would never again attempt to travel in the neighbourhood of a plantation in the daytime.

When in the swamp a quarter of a mile, I collected some dry wood, and lighted it with the aid of my tinder-box, flint, and steel. This was the first fire that I kindled on my journey, and I was careful to burn none but dry wood, to prevent the formation of smoke. Here I roasted my corn, and ate as much of it as I could. After my dinner, I lay down and slept for three or four hours. When I awoke, the sun was scarcely visible through the tree tops. It was evening, and prudence required me to leave the swamp before dark, lest I should not be able to find my way out.

Approaching the edge of the swamp, I watched the going down of the sun, and noted the stars as they appeared in the heavens. I had long since learned to distinguish the north-star, from all the other small luminaries of the night; and the seven pointers[28] were familiar to me. These heavenly bodies were all the guides I had to direct me on my way, and as soon as the night had set in, I commenced my march through the woods, bearing as nearly due east as I could.

I took this course for the purpose of getting down the country, as far as the road leading from Augusta to Morgan County, with the intention of pursuing the route by which I had come out from South Carolina; deeming it more safe to travel the high road by night, than to attempt to make my way at random over the country, guided only by the stars. I travelled all night, keeping the north-star on my left hand as nearly as I could, and passing many plantations, taking care to keep at a great distance from the houses. I think I travelled at least twenty-five miles to-night, without passing any road that appeared so wide, or so much beaten, as that which I had travelled when I came from South Carolina. This night I passed through a peach orchard, laden with fine ripe fruit, with which I filled my pockets and hat; and before day, in crossing a corn-field, I pulled a supply of roasting-ears, with which and my peaches, I retired at break of day to a large wood, into which I travelled more than a mile before I halted. Here, in the midst of a thicket of high whortleberry bushes, I encamped for the day. I made my breakfast upon roasted corn and peaches, and then lay down and slept, unmolested, until after twelve o'clock, when I awoke and rose up for the purpose of taking a better view of my quarters; but I was scarcely on my feet, when I was attacked by a swarm of hornets, that issued from a large nest that hung on the limb of a tree, within twenty or thirty feet of me.

I knew that the best means of making peace with my hostile neighbours, was to lie down with my face to the ground; and this attitude I quickly took, not however before I had been stung by several of my assailants, which kept humming through the air about me for a long time, and prevented me from leaving this spot until after sundown, and after they had retired to rest for the night. I now commenced the attack on my part, and taking a handful of dry leaves, approached the nest, which was full as large as a half bushel, and thrusting the leaves into the hole at the bottom of the nest, through which its tenants passed in and out, secured the whole garrison prisoners in their own citadel. I now cut off the branch upon which the nest hung, and threw it, with its contents, into my evening fire, over which I roasted a supply of corn, for my night's journey.

Commencing my march this evening, soon after nightfall, I travelled until about one o'clock in the morning, as nearly as I could estimate the time, by the appearance of the stars, when I came upon a road, which from its width, and beaten appearance, I took to be the road leading to Augusta, and determined to pursue it.

I travelled on this road until I saw the appearance of daylight, when I turned into the woods, and went full a mile before I ventured to stop for the day. I concealed myself to-day in a thicket of young pine trees, that had sprung up round about an old pen of logs, which had formerly been used, either as a wolf or turkey trap. In this retreat nothing disturbed me this day, and at dark I again returned to the road, which I travelled in silence, treading as lightly as possible with my feet, and listening most attentively to every sound that I heard. After being on the road more than an hour, I heard the sound of the feet of horses, and immediately stepped aside, and took my place behind the trunk of a large tree. Within a minute or two, several horses with men on them, passed me. The men were talking to each other, and one of them asked another, in my hearing, if it was not about five miles to the Oconee. The reply was too low to be understood by me; but I was now satisfied that I was on the high road, leading down the country, on the Savannah side of Oconee.

Waiting until these horsemen were out of hearing, I followed them at a brisk walk, and within less than an hour, came to the side of a river, the width of which I could not ascertain, by reason of the darkness of the night, some fog having risen from the water.

I had no doubt that this stream was the Oconee; and as I had heretofore forded that river with a wagon and team, I procured a long stick from the shore, and entered the river with all my clothes on me, except my great coat and pantaloons, which I carried on my back. The river proved shallow, not being more than four feet deep in the deepest part; and I had proceeded in safety beyond the middle of the stream, when I heard the noise produced by horses' feet in front of me, and within two or three minutes several horsemen rode into the river directly before me, and advanced towards me. I now stooped down into the water, so as to leave nothing but my head, and the upper part of my pack above its surface, and waited the passage of the strangers, who, after riding into the river until the water washed the bellies of their horses, stopped to permit the animals to drink; two of them being, at this time, not more than ten yards from me. Here they entered into conversation with each other, and one said, it was his opinion that "that fellow had not come this way at all." The other then asked what his name was, and the first replied that he was called Charles, in the advertisements, but that he would no doubt call himself by some other name; as runaway negroes always took some false name, and assumed a false character. I now knew that I was within a few feet of a party, who were patrolling the country in search of me, and that nothing could save me from falling into their hands, but the obscurity produced by the fog.

There were no clouds, and if the fog had not been in the air, they must have perceived my head, on the smooth surface of the water, and have known that it was no stump or log of wood. After a few minutes of pause, these gentlemen all rode on to the side of the river from which I had come, and in a short time were out of hearing.

Notwithstanding they were gone, I remained in the water full a quarter of an hour, until I was certain that no other persons were moving along the road near me. These were the same gentlemen who had passed me, early in the night, and from whom I learned the distance to the river. From these people I had gained intelligence, which I considered of much value to me. It was now certain, that the whole country had been advised of my flight; but it was equally certain that no one had any knowledge of the course I had taken, nor of the point I was endeavouring to reach. To prevent any one from acquiring a knowledge of my route, was a primary object with me; and I determined from this moment, so to regulate my movements, as to wrap my very existence, in a veil of impenetrable secrecy. After leaving the river one or two miles, I turned aside from the road, and wrung the water from my clothes, which were all wet. This occupied some time, and after being again equipped for my journey, I made all haste to gain as much distance this night, as possible. The fog extended only a few miles from the river, and from the top of an eminence which I gained, an hour after wringing my clothes, the stars were distinctly visible. Here I discovered that the road I was travelling bore nearly east, and was not likely to take me to the Savannah river, for a long time. Nevertheless, I travelled hard until daylight appeared before me, which was my signal for turning into the woods, and seeking a place of safety for the day.

The country in which I now was, appeared high and dry, without any swamps or low grounds, in which an asylum might be found; I therefore determined to go to the top of a hill, that extended on my right for some distance either way. The summit of this ridge was gained before there was enough of daylight to enable me to see objects clearly; but, as soon as a view of the place could be had, I discovered, that it was a thicket of pine trees; and that the road which I had left, led through a plantation that lay within sight: the house and other buildings on which, appeared to be such as I had before seen; but I could not at once recollect where, or at what time I had seen them.

Going to an open space in the thicket, from which I could scan the plantation at leisure, I became satisfied, after the sun had risen, and thrown his light upon the earth, that this was no other than the residence of the gentleman, who had so kindly entertained my master and me, as we went to, and returned from, Savannah with the wagon. I now remembered, that this gentleman was the friend of my late master, and that he had told me, to come and see him if ever I passed this way again; but I knew that he was a slave-holder and a planter; and that when he gave me liberty to visit his plantation, he expected that my visits would always be the visits of a slave, and not the clandestine calls of a runaway negro.

It seemed to me, that this gentleman was too benevolent a man, to arrest and send me back to my cruel mistress; and yet, how could I expect, or even hope, that a cotton planter would see a runaway slave on his premises, and not cause him to be taken up and sent home? Failing to seize a runaway slave, when he has him in his power, is held to be one of the most dishonourable acts, to which a southern planter can subject himself. Nor should the people of the north be surprised at this. Slaves are regarded, in the south, as the most precious of all earthly possessions; and at the same time, as a precarious and hazardous kind of property, in the enjoyment of which the master is not safe. The planters may well be compared to the inhabitants of a national frontier, which is exposed to the inroads of hostile invading tribes. Where all are in like danger; and subject to like fears, it is expected that all will be governed by like sentiments, and act upon like principles.

I stood and looked at the house of this good planter, for more than an hour after the sun had risen, and saw all the movements which usually take place on a cotton plantation in the morning. Long before the sun was up, the overseer had proceeded to the field, at the head of the hands; the black women who attended to the cattle, and milked the cows, had gone to the cow-pen with their pails; and the smoke ascended from the chimney of the kitchen, before the doors of the great house were opened, or any of the members of the family were seen abroad. At length, two young ladies opened the door, and stood in the freshness of the morning air. These were soon joined by a brother; and at last, I saw the gentleman himself leave the house, and walk towards the stables, that stood at some distance from the house, on my left. I think even now, that it was a foolish resolution that emboldened me to show myself to this gentleman. It was like throwing one's self in the way of a lion who is known sometimes to spare those whom he might destroy; but I resolved to go and meet this planter at his stables, and tell him my whole story. Issuing from the woods, I crossed the fields unperceived by the people at the house, and going directly to the stables, presented myself to their proprietor, as he stood looking at a fine horse, in one of the yards. At first, he did not know me, and asked me whose man I was. I then asked him if he did not remember me; and named the time when I had been at his house. I then told at once, that I was a runaway: that my master was dead, and my mistress so cruel, that I could not live with her: not omitting to show the scars on my back, and to give a full account of the manner in which they had been made. The gentleman stood and looked at me more than a minute, without uttering a word, and then said, "Charles, I will not betray you, but you must not stay here. It must not be known that you were on this plantation, and that I saw and conversed with you. However, as I suppose you are hungry, you may go to the kitchen and get your breakfast with my house servants."

He then set off for the house, and I followed, but turning into the kitchen, as he ordered me, I was soon supplied with a good breakfast of cold meat, warm bread, and as much new butter-milk as I chose to drink. Before I sat down to breakfast, the lady of the house came into the kitchen, with her two daughters, and gave me a dram of peach brandy. I drank this brandy, and was very thankful for it; but I am fully convinced now that it did me much more harm than good;

and that this part of the kindness of this most excellent family, was altogether misplaced.

Whilst I was taking my breakfast, a black man came into the kitchen, and gave me a dollar that he said his master had sent me, at the same time laying on the table before me a package of bread and meat, weighing at least ten pounds, wrapped up in a cloth. On delivering these things, the black man told me that his master desired me to quit his premises as soon as I had finished my breakfast.

This injunction I obeyed; and within less than an hour after I entered this truly hospitable house, I quitted it forever, but not without leaving behind me my holiest blessings upon the heads of its inhabitants. It was yet early in the morning when I regained the woods on the opposite side of the plantation, from that by which I had entered it.

## CHAPTER XXI.

I COULD not believe it possible that the white people whom I had just left, would give information of the route I had taken; but as it was possible that all who dwelt on this plantation might not be so pure of heart as were they who possessed it, I thought it prudent to travel some distance in the woods, before I stopped for the day, notwithstanding the risk of moving about in the open light. For the purpose of precluding the possibility of being betrayed, I now determined to quit this road, and travel altogether in the woods, or through open fields, for two or three nights, guiding my march by the stars. In pursuance of this resolution, I bore away to the left of the high road, and travelled five or six miles before I stopped, going round all the fields that I saw in my way, and keeping them at a good distance from me.

In the afternoon of this day, it rained, and I had no other shelter than the boughs and leaves of a large magnolia tree; but this kept me tolerably dry, and as it cleared away in the evening, I was able to continue my journey by starlight. I have no definite idea of the distance that I travelled in the course of this and the two succeeding nights, as I had no road to guide me, and was much perplexed by the plantations and houses, the latter of which I most carefully eschewed; but on the third night after this, I encountered a danger, which was very nearly fatal to me.

At the time of which I now speak, the moon having changed lately, shone until about eleven o'clock. I had been on my way two or three hours this evening, and all the world seemed to be quiet, when I entered a plantation that lay quite across my way. In passing through these fields, I at last saw the houses, and other improvements, and about a hundred yards from the house, a peach orchard, which I could distinguish by the faint light of the moon. This orchard was but little out of my way, and a quarter of a mile, as nearly as I could judge, from the woods. I resolved to examine these peach trees, and see what fruit was on them. Coming amongst them, I found the fruit of the kind called Indian peaches, in Georgia.

These Indian peaches are much the largest and finest peaches that I have ever seen, one of them oftentimes being as large as a common quince. I had filled all my pockets, and was filling my handkerchief with this delicious fruit, which is of deep red, when I heard the loud growl of a dog toward the house, the roof of which I could see. I stood as still as a stone, but yet the dog growled on, and at length barked out. I presume he smelled me, for he could not hear me. In a short time I found that the dog was coming towards me, and I then started and ran as fast as I could for the woods. He now barked louder, and was followed by another dog, both making a terrible noise. I was then pretty light of foot, and was already close by the woods when the first dog overtook me. I carried a good stick in my hand, and with this I kept the dogs at bay, until I gained the fence, and escaped into the woods; but now I heard the shouts of men encouraging the dogs, both of which were now up with me, and the men were coming as fast as they could. The dogs would not permit me to run, and unless I could make free use of my heels, it was clear that I must be taken in a few minutes. I now thought of my master's sword, which I had not removed from its quilted scabbard, in my great coat, since I commenced my journey. I snatched it from its sheath, and, at a single cut, laid open the head of the largest and fiercest of the dogs, from his neck to his nose. He gave a loud yell and fell dead on the ground. The other dog, seeing the fate of his companion, leaped the fence, and escaped into the field, where he stopped, and like a cowardly cur, set up a clamorous barking at the enemy he was afraid to look in the face. I thought this no time to wait to ascertain what the men would say, when they came to their dead dog, but made the best of my way through the woods and did not stop to look behind me, for more than an hour. In my battle with the dogs, I lost all my peaches, except a few that remained in my pockets; and in running through the woods I tore my clothes very badly, a disaster not easily repaired in my situation; but I had proved the solidity of my own judgment in putting up my sword as a part of my travelling equipage.

I now considered it necessary to travel as fast as possible, and get as far as I could before day, from the late battle-ground, and certainly I lost no time; but from the occurrences of the next day, I am of opinion, that I had not continued in a straight line all night, but that I must have travelled in a circular or zigzag route. When a man is greatly alarmed, and in a strange country, he is not able to note courses, or calculate distances, very accurately.

Daylight made its appearance, when I was moving to the south, for the daybreak was on my left hand; but I immediately stopped, went into a thicket of low white oak bushes, and lay down to rest myself for I was very weary, and soon fell asleep, and did not awake until it was ten or eleven o'clock. Before I fell asleep, I noted the course of the rising sun, from the place where I lay, in pursuance of a rule that I had established; for by this means I could tell the time of day at any hour, within a short period of time, by taking the bearing of the sun in the heavens, from where I lay, and then comparing it with the place of his rising.

When I awoke to-day, I felt hungry, and after eating my breakfast, again lay down, but felt an unusual sense of disquietude and alarm. It seemed to me that this was not a safe place to lie in, although it looked as well as any other spot, that I could see. I rose and looked for a more secure retreat, but not seeing any, lay down again—still I was uneasy, and could not lie still. Finally I determined to get up, and remove to the side of a large and long black log, that lay at the distance of seventy or eighty yards from me. I went to the log and lay down by it, placing my bundle under my head, with the intention of going to sleep again, if I could; but I had not been here more than fifteen or twenty minutes, when I heard the noise of men's voices, and soon after the tramping of horses on the ground. I lay with my back to the log in such a position, that I could see the place where I had been in the bushes. I saw two dogs go into this little thicket, and three horsemen rode over the very spot where I had lain when asleep in the morning, and immediately horses and voices were at my back, around me, and over me. Two horses jumped over the log by the side of which I lay, one about ten feet from my feet, and the other within two yards from my head. The horses both saw me, took fright, and started to run; but fortunately their riders, who were probably looking for me in the tops of the trees, or expecting to see me start before them in the woods, and run for my life, did not see me, and attributed the alarm of their horses to the black appearance of the log, for I heard one of them say—"Our horses are afraid of black logs—I wonder how they would stand the sight of the negro, if we should meet him."

There must have been in the troop, at least twenty horsemen; and the number of dogs was greater than I could count, as they ran in the woods. I knew, that all these men and dogs were in search of me, and that if they could find me, I should be hunted down like a wild beast. The dogs that had gone into the thicket where I had been, fortunately for me, had not been trained to hunt negroes in the woods, and were probably brought out for the purpose of being trained. Doubtless, if some of the kept dogs, as they are called, of which there were certainly several in this large pack, had happened to go into that thicket, instead of those that did go there, my race would soon have been run.

I lay still by the side of the log for a long time after the horses, dogs, and men, had ceased to trouble the woods with their noise; if it can be said that a man lies still, who is trembling in every joint, nerve, and muscle, like a dog lying upon a cake of ice; and when I arose and turned round, I found myself so completely bereft of understanding, that I could not tell south from north, nor east from west. I could not even distinguish the thicket of bushes, from which I had removed to come to this place, from the other bushes of the woods. I remained here all day, and at night it appeared to me, that the sun set in the south-east. After sundown, the moon appeared to my distempered judgment, to stand due north from me; and all the stars were out of their places. Fortunately I had sense enough remaining to know, that it would not be safe for me to attempt to travel, until my brain had been restored to its ordinary stability; which did not take place until the third morning after my fright. The three days that I passed in this place, I reckon the most unhappy of my life; for surely it is the height of human misery, to be oppressed with alienation of mind, and to be conscious of the affliction.

Distracted as I was, I had determined never to quit this wood, and voluntarily return to slavery; and the joy I felt on the third morning, when I saw the sun rise in his proper place in the heavens; the black log, the thicket of bushes, and all other things resume the positions in which I found them, may be imagined by those who have been saved from apparently hopeless shipwreck on a barren rock, in the midst of the ocean; but cannot be described by any but a poetic pen.

I spent this day in making short excursions through the woods, for the purpose of ascertaining whether any road was near to me or not; and in the afternoon I came to one, about a mile from my camp, which was broad, and had the appearance of being much travelled. It appeared to me to lead to the north.

Awhile before sundown, I brought my bundle to this road, and lay down quietly to await the approach of night. When it was quite dark, except the light of the moon, which was now brilliant, I took to this road, and travelled all night, without hearing or seeing any person, and on the succeeding night, about two o'clock in the morning, I came to the margin of a river, so wide that I could not see across it; but the fog was so dense at this time, that I could not have seen across a river of very moderate width. I procured a long pole, and sounded the depth of the water, which I found not very deep; but as I could not see the opposite shore, was afraid to attempt to ford the stream.

In this dilemma, I turned back from the river, and went more than a mile to gain the cover of a small wood, where I might pass the day in safety, and wait a favourable moment for obtaining a view of the river, preparatory to crossing it. I lay all day in full view of the high road, and saw, at least, a hundred people pass; from which I inferred, that the country was populous about me. In the evening, as soon as it was dark, I left my retreat, and returned to the river side. The atmosphere was now clear, and the river seemed to be at least a quarter of a mile in width; and whilst I was divesting myself of my clothes, preparatory to entering the water, happening to look down the shore, I saw a canoe, with its head drawn high on the beach. On reaching the canoe, I found that it was secured to the trunk of a tree by a lock and chain; but after many efforts, I broke the lock and launched the canoe into the river. The paddles had been removed, but with the aid of my sounding-pole, I managed to conduct the canoe across the water.

I was now once more in South Carolina, where I knew it was necessary for me to be even more watchful than I had been in Georgia. I do not know where I crossed the Savannah river, but I think it must have been only a few miles above the town of Augusta.

After gaining the Carolina shore, I took an observation of the rising moon and of such stars as I was acquainted with, and hastened to get away from the river, from which I knew that heavy fogs rose every night, at this season of the year, obscuring the heavens for many miles on either side. I travelled this night at least twenty miles, and provided myself with a supply of corn, which was now hard, from a field at the side of the road. At daybreak I turned into the woods, and went to the top of a hill on my left, where the ground was overgrown by the species of pine-tree called spruce in the south. I here kindled a fire, and parched corn for my breakfast.

In the afternoon of this day the weather became cloudy, and before dark the rain fell copiously, and continued through the night, with the wind high. I took shelter under a large stooping tree that was decayed and hollow on the lower side, and kept me dry until the morning. When daylight appeared, I could see that the country around me was well inhabited, and that the forest in which I lay was surrounded by plantations, at the distance of one or two miles from me. I did not consider this a safe position, and waited anxiously for night, to enable me to change my quarters. The weather was foul throughout the day; and when night returned, it was so dark that I could not see a large tree three feet before me. Waiting until the moon rose, I made my way back to the road, but had not proceeded more than two or three miles on my way, when I came to a place where the road forked, and the two roads led away almost at right angles from each other. It was so cloudy that I could not see the place of the moon in the heavens, and I knew not which of these roads to take. To go wrong was worse than to stand still, and I therefore determined to look out for some spot in which I could hide myself, and remain in this neighbourhood until the clearing up of the weather. Taking the right hand road, I followed its course until I saw at the distance, as I computed it in the night, of two miles from me a large forest which covered elevated ground. I gained it by the shortest route across some cotton fields. Going several hundred yards into this wood, I attempted to kindle a fire, in which I failed, every combustible substance being wet. This compelled me to pass the night as well as I could amongst the damp bushes and trees that overhung me. When day came, I went farther into the woods, and on the top of the highest ground that I could see, established my camp, by cutting bushes with my knife, and erecting a sort of rude booth.

It was now, by my computation, about the twenty-fifth of August, and I remained here eleven days without seeing one clear night; and in all this time the sun never shone for half a day at once. I procured my subsistence while here from a field of corn which I discovered at the distance of a mile and a half from my camp. This was the first time that I was weather-bound, and my patience had been worn out and renewed repeatedly before the return of the clear weather; but one afternoon I perceived the trees to be much agitated by the wind, the clouds appeared high, and were driven with velocity over my head. I saw the clear sky appear in all its beauty, in the northwest.

Before sundown the wind was high, the sun shone in full splendour, and a few fleecy clouds, careering high in the upper vault of heaven, gave assurance that the rains were over and gone.

At nightfall I returned to the forks of the road, and after much observation, finally concluded to follow the right hand road, in which I am satisfied that I committed a great error. Nothing worthy of notice occurred for several days after this. As I was now in a thickly-peopled country, I never moved until long after night, and was cautious never to permit daylight to find me on the road; but I observed that the north-star was always on my left hand. My object was to reach the neighbourhood of Columbia, and get upon the road which I had travelled and seen years before in coming to the south; but the road I was now on must have been the great Charleston road, leading down the country, and not across the courses of the rivers. So many people travelled this road, as well by night as by day, that my progress was very slow; and in some of the nights I did not travel more than eight miles. At the end of a week, after leaving the forks, I found myself in a flat, sandy, poor country; and as I had not met with any river on this road, I now concluded that I was on the way to the sea-board instead of Columbia. In my perplexity, I resolved to try to get information concerning the country I was in, by placing myself in some obscure place in the side of the road, and listening to the conversation of travellers as they passed me. For this purpose I chose the corner of a cotton field, around which the road turned, and led along the fence for some distance. Passing the day in the woods among the pine-trees I came to this corner in the evening, and lying down within the field, waited patiently the coming of travellers, that I might hear their conversation, and endeavour to learn from that which they said, the name at least of some place in this neighbourhood. On the first and second evenings that I lay here, I gleaned nothing from the passengers that I thought could be of service to me; but on the third night, about ten o'clock, several wagons drawn by mules passed me, and I heard one of the drivers call to another and tell him that it was sixty miles to Charleston; and that they should be able to reach the river to-morrow. I could not at first imagine what river this could be; but another of the wagoners enquired how far it was to the Edisto, to which it was replied by some one, that it was near thirty miles. I now perceived that I had mistaken my course; and was as completely lost as a wild goose in cloudy weather.

Not knowing what to do, I retraced the road that had led me to this place for several nights, hoping that something would happen from which I might learn the route to Columbia; but I gained no information that could avail me anything. At length I determined to quit this road altogether, travel by the north-star for two or three weeks, and after that to trust to Providence to guide me to some road that might lead me back to Maryland. Having turned my face due north, I made my way pretty well for the first night; but on the second, the fog was so dense that no stars could be seen. This compelled me to remain in my camp, which I had pitched in a swamp. In this place I remained more than a week, waiting for clear nights; but now the equinoctial storm came on, and raged with a fury which I had never before witnessed in this annual gale; at least it had never before appeared so violent to me, because, perhaps, I had never been exposed to its blasts, without the shelter of a house of some kind. This storm continued four days; and no wolf ever lay closer in his lair, or moved out with more stealthy caution than I did during this time. My subsistence was drawn from a small corn-field at the edge of the swamp in which I lay.

After the storm was over, the weather became calm and clear, and I fell into a road which appeared to run nearly north-west. Following the course of this road by short marches, because I was obliged to start late at night and stop before day, I came on the first day, or rather night, of October, by my calender, to a broad and well-frequented road that crossed mine at nearly right angles. These roads crossed in the middle of a plantation, and I took to the right hand along this great road, and pursued it in the same cautious and slow manner that I had travelled for the last month.

When the day came I took refuge in the woods as usual, choosing the highest piece of ground that I could find in the neighbourhood. No part of this country was very high, but I thought people who visited these woods, would be less inclined to walk to the tops of the hills, than to keep their course along the low grounds.

I had lately crossed many small streams; but on the second night of my journey on this road, came to a narrow but deep river, and after the most careful search, no boat or craft of any kind could be found on my side. A large flat, with two or three canoes, lay on the opposite side, but they were as much out of my reach as if they had never been made. There was no alternative but swimming this stream, and I made the transit in less than three minutes, carrying my packages on my back.

I had as yet fallen in with no considerable towns, and whenever I had seen a house near the road, or one of the small hamlets of the south in my way, I had gone round by the woods or fields, so as to avoid the inhabitants; but on the fourth night after swimming the small river, I came in sight of a considerable village, with lights burning and shining through many of the windows. I knew the danger of passing a town, on account of the patrols with which all southern towns are provided, and making a long circuit to the right, so as totally to avoid this village, I came to the banks of a broad river, which, upon further examination, I found flowing past the village, and near its border. This compelled me to go back, and attempt to turn the village on the left, which was performed by wandering a long time in swamps and pine woods.

It was break of day when I regained the road beyond the village, and returning to the swamps from which I had first issued, I passed the day under their cover. On the following night, after regaining the road, I soon found myself in a country almost entirely clear of timber, and abounding in fields of cotton and corn.

The houses were numerous, and the barking of dogs was incessant. I felt that I was in the midst of dangers, and that I was entering a region very different from those tracts of country through which I had lately passed, where the gloom of the wilderness was only broken by solitary plantations or lonely huts. I had no doubt that I was in the neighbourhood of some town, but of its name, and the part of the country in which it was located, I was ignorant. I at length found that I was receding from the woods altogether, and entering a champaign country, in the midst of which I now perceived a town of considerable magnitude, the inhabitants of which were entirely silent, and the town itself presented the appearance of total solitude. The country around was so open, that I despaired of turning so large a place as this was, and again finding the road I travelled, I therefore determined to risk all consequences, and attempt to pass this town under cover of darkness.

Keeping straight forward, I came unexpectedly to a broad river, which I now saw running between me and the town. I took it for granted that there must be a ferry at this place, and on examining the shore, found several small boats fastened only with ropes to a large scow. One of these boats I seized, and was quickly on the opposite shore of the river. I entered the village and proceeded to its centre, without seeing so much as a rat in motion. Finding myself in an open space I stopped to examine the streets, and upon looking at the houses around me, I at once recognized the jail of Columbia, and the tavern in which I had lodged on the night after I was sold.

This discovery made me feel almost at home, with my wife and children. I remembered the streets by which I had come from the country to the jail, and was quickly at the extremity of the town, marching towards the residence of the paltry planter, at whose house I had lodged on my way south. It was late at night, when I left Columbia, and it was necessary for me to make all speed, and get as far as possible from that place before day. I ran rather than walked, until the appearance of dawn, when I left the road and took shelter in the pine woods, with which this part of the country abounds.

I had now been travelling almost two months, and was still so near the place from which I first departed, that I could easily have walked to it in a week, by daylight; but I hoped, that as I was now on a road with which I was acquainted, and in a country through which I had travelled before, that my future progress would be more rapid, and that I should be able to surmount, without difficulty, many of the obstacles that had hitherto embarrassed me so greatly.

It was now in my power to avail myself of the knowledge I had formerly acquired, of the customs of South Carolina. The patrol are very rigid in the execution of the authority, with which they are invested; but I never had much difficulty with these officers, anywhere. From dark until ten or eleven o'clock at night, the patrol are watchful, and always traversing the country in quest of negroes, but towards midnight these gentlemen grow cold, or sleepy, or weary, and generally betake themselves to some house, where they can procure a comfortable fire.

I now established, as a rule of my future conduct, to remain in my hiding place until after ten o'clock, according to my computation of time; and this night I did not come to the road, until I supposed it to be within an hour of midnight, and it was well for me that I practised so much caution, for when within two or three hundred yards of the road, I heard people conversing. After standing some minutes in the woods, and listening to the voices at the road, the people separated, and a party took each end of the road, and galloped away upon their horses. These people were certainly a band of patrollers, who were watching this road, and had just separated to return home for the night. After the horsemen were quite out of hearing, I came to the road, and walked as fast as I could for hours, and again came into the lane leading to the house, where I had first remained a few days, in Carolina. Turning away from the road I passed through this plantation, near the old cotton-gin house, in which I had formerly lodged, and perceived that every thing on this plantation was nearly as it was when I left it. Two or three miles from this place I again left the road, and sought a place of concealment, and from this time until I reached Maryland, I never remained in the road until daylight but once, and I paid dearly then for my temerity.

I was now in an open, thickly-peopled country, in comparison with many other tracts through which I had passed; and this circumstance compelled me to observe the greater caution. As nearly as possible, I confined my travelling within the hours of midnight and three o'clock in the morning. Parties of patrollers were heard by me almost every morning, before day. These people sometimes moved directly along the roads, but more frequently lay in wait near the side of the road, ready to pounce upon any runaway slave that might chance to pass; but I knew

by former experience that they never lay out all night, except in times of apprehended danger; and the country appearing at this time to be quiet, I felt but little apprehension of falling in with these policemen, within my travelling hours.

There was now plenty of corn in the fields, and sweet potatoes had not yet
been dug. There was no scarcity of provisions with me, and my health was good,
and my strength unimpaired. For more than two weeks, I pursued the road that
had led me from Columbia, believing I was on my way to Camden. Many small
streams crossed my way, but none of them were large enough to oblige me to
swim in crossing them.

## CHAPTER XXII.

ON the twenty-fourth of October, according to my computation, in a dark
night, I came to a river, which appeared to be both broad and deep. Sounding its
depth with a pole, I found it too deep to be forded, and after the most careful
search along the shore, no boat could be discovered. This place appeared altogether strange to me, and I began to fear that I was again lost. Confident that I
had never before been where I now found myself, and ignorant of the other side
of the stream, I thought it best not to attempt to cross this water until I was better informed of the country through which it flowed. A thick wood bordered the
road on my left, and gave me shelter until daylight. Ascending a tree at sunrise,
that overlooked the stream, which appeared to be more than a mile in width, I
perceived on the opposite shore a house, and one large, and several small boats
in the river. I remained in this tree the greater part of the day, and saw several
persons cross the river, some of whom had horses; but in the evening the boats
were all taken back to the place at which I had seen them in the morning. The
river was so broad, that I felt some fear of failing in the attempt to swim it; but
seeing no prospect of procuring a boat to transport me, I resolved to attempt the
navigation as soon as it was dark. About nine o'clock at night, having equipped
myself in the best manner I was able, I undertook this hazardous navigation, and
succeeded in gaining the farther shore of the river, in about an hour, with all my
things in safety. On the previous day I had noted the bearing of the road, as it
led from the river, and in the middle of the night I again resumed my journey, in
a state of perplexity bordering upon desperation; for it was now evident that this
was not the road by which we had travelled when we came to the southern country, and on which hand to turn to reach the right way, I knew not.

After travelling five or six miles on this road, and having the north-star in
view all the time, I became satisfied that my course lay northwest, and that I was
consequently going out of my way; and to heighten my anxiety, I had not tasted
any animal food since I crossed the Savannah river—a sensation of hunger harrassed me constantly; but fortune, which had been so long adverse to me, and
had led me so often astray, had now a little favour in store for me. The leaves
were already fallen from some of the more tender trees, and near the road I this
night perceived a persimmon tree, well laden with fruit, and whilst gathering the

fallen persimmons under the tree, a noise over head arrested my attention. This noise was caused by a large opossum, which was on the tree gathering fruit like myself. With a long stick the animal was brought to the ground, and it proved to be very fat, weighing at least ten pounds. With such a luxury as this in my possession, I could not think of travelling far without tasting it, and accordingly halted about a mile from the persimmon tree, on a rising ground in a thick wood, where I killed my opossum, and took off its skin, a circumstance that I much regretted, for with the skin I took at least a pound of fine fat. Had I possessed the means of scalding my game, and dressing it like a pig, it would have afforded me provision for a week; but as it was, I made a large fire and roasted my prize before it, losing all the oil that ran out in the operation, for want of a dripping-pan to catch it. It was daylight when my meat was ready for the table, and a very sumptuous breakfast it yielded me.

Since leaving Columbia, I had followed as nearly as the course of the roads permitted, the index of the north-star; which, I supposed, would lead me on the most direct route to Maryland; but I now became convinced, that this star was leading me away from the line by which I had approached the cotton country.

I slept none this day, but passed the whole time, from breakfast until night, in considering the means of regaining my lost way. From the aspect of the country I arrived at the conclusion, that I was not near the sea-coast; for there were no swamps in all this region; the land lay rather high and rolling, and oak timber abounded.

At the return of night, I resumed my journey earlier than usual: paying no regard to the roads, but keeping the north-star on my left hand, as nearly as I could. This night I killed a rabbit, which had leaped from the bushes before me, by throwing my walking stick at it. It was roasted at my stopping place in the morning, and was very good.

I pursued the same course, keeping the north-star on my left hand for three nights; intending to get as far east as the road leading from Columbia to Richmond, in Virginia; but as my line of march lay almost continually in the woods, I made but little progress; and on the third day, the weather became cloudy, so that I could not see the stars. This again compelled me to lie by, until the return of fair weather.

On the second day, after I had stopped this time, the sun shone out bright in the morning, and continued to shed a glorious light during the day; but in the evening, the heavens became overcast with clouds; and the night that followed was so dark, that I did not attempt to travel. This state of the weather continued more than a week: obliging me to remain stationary all this time. These cloudy nights were succeeded by a brisk wind from the north-west, accompanied by fine clear nights, in which I made the best of my way towards the north-east, pursuing my course across the country without regard to roads, forests, or streams of water: crossing many of the latter, none of which were deep, but some of them were extremely muddy. One night I became entangled in a thick and deep swamp; the trees that grew in which, were so tall, and stood so close together, that the interlocking of their boughs, and the deep foliage in which they were clad, prevented me from seeing the stars. Wandering there for several hours, most of the time with mud and water over my knees, and frequently wading in stagnant pools, with deep slimy bottoms, I became totally lost, and was incapable of seeing the least appearance of fast land. At length, giving up all hope of extricating myself from this abyss of mud, water, brambles, and fallen timber, I scrambled on a large tussock, and sat down to await the coming of day, with the intention of going to the nearest high land, as soon as the sun should be up. The nights were now becoming cool, and though I did not see any frost in the swamp where I was in the morning, I have no doubt, that hoar frost was seen in the dry and open country. After daylight I found myself as much perplexed as I was at midnight. No shore was to be seen; and in every direction there was the same deep, dreary, black solitude. To add to my misfortune, the morning proved cloudy, and when the sun was up, I could not tell the east from the west. After waiting several hours for a sight of the sun, and failing to obtain it, I set out in search of a running stream of water, intending to strike off at right angles, with the course of the current, and endeavour to reach the dry ground by this means: but after wandering about, through tangled bushes, briars, and vines, clambering over fallen tree-tops, and wading through fens overgrown with saw grass, for two or three hours, I sat down in despair of finding any guide to conduct me from this detestable place.

My bag of meal that I took with me at the commencement of my journey, was long since gone; and the only provisions that I now possessed, were a few grains of parched corn, and near a pint of chestnuts that I had picked up under a tree the day before I entered the swamp. The chestnut-tree was full of nuts, but I was afraid to throw sticks or to shake the tree, lest hunters or other persons hearing the noise, might be drawn to the place.

About ten o'clock I sat down under a large cypress tree, upon a decaying log of the same timber, to make my breakfast on a few grains of parched corn. Near me was an open space without trees, but filled with water that seemed to be deep, for no grass grew in it, except a small quantity near the shore. The water was on my left hand, and as I sat cracking my corn, my attention was attracted by the playful gambols of two squirrels that were running and chasing each other on the boughs of some trees near me. Half pleased with the joyous movements of the little animals, and half covetous of their carcasses, to roast and devour them, I paid no attention to a succession of sounds on my left, which I thought proceeded from the movement of frogs at the edge of the water, until the breaking of a stick near me caused me to turn my head, when I discovered that I had other neighbours than spring-frogs.

A monstrous alligator had left the water, and was crawling over the mud, with his eyes fixed upon me. He was now within fifteen feet of me, and in a moment more, if he had not broken the stick with his weight, I should have become his prey. He could easily have knocked me down with a blow of his tail; and if his jaws had once been closed on a leg or an arm, he would have dragged me into the water, spite of any resistance that I could have made.

At the sight of him, I sprang to my feet, and running to the other end of the fallen free on which I sat, and being there out of danger, had an opportunity of viewing the motions of the alligator at leisure. Finding me out of his reach, he raised his trunk from the ground, elevated his snout, and gave a wistful look, the import of which I well understood; then turning slowly round, he retreated to the water, and sank from my vision.

I was much alarmed by this adventure with the alligator, for had I fallen in with this huge reptile in the night-time, I should have had no chance of escape from his tusks.

The whole day was spent in the swamp, not in travelling from place to place, but in waiting for the sun to shine, to enable me to obtain a knowledge of the various points of the heavens. The day was succeeded by a night of unbroken darkness; and it was late in the evening of the second day before I saw the sun. It being then too late to attempt to extricate myself from the swamp for that day, I was obliged to pass another night in the lodge that I had formed for myself in the thick boughs of a fallen cypress tree, which elevated me several feet from the ground, where I believed the alligator could not reach me, if he should come in pursuit of me.

On the morning of the third day, the sun rose beautifully clear, and at sight of him I set off for the east. It must have been five miles from the place where I lay to the dry land on the east of the swamp; for with all the exertion that fear and hunger compelled me to make, it was two or three o'clock in the afternoon when I reached the shore, after swimming in several places, and suffering the loss of a very valuable part of my clothes, which were torn off by the briars and snags. On coming to high ground I found myself in the woods, and hungry as I was, lay down to await the coming of night, lest some one should see me moving through the forest in daylight.

When night came on, I resumed my journey by the stars, which were visible, and marched several miles before coming to a plantation. The first that I came to was a cotton field; and after much search, I found no corn nor grain of any kind on this place, and was compelled to continue on my way.

Two or three miles further on, I was more fortunate, and found a field of corn which had been gathered from the stalks and thrown in heaps along the ground. Filling my little bag, which I still kept, with this corn, I retreated a mile or two in the woods, and striking fire, encamped for the purpose of parching and eating it. After despatching my meal, I lay down beside the fire and fell into a sound sleep, from which I did not awake until long after sunrise; but on rising and looking around me, I found that my lodge was within less than a hundred yards of a new house that people were building in the woods, and upon which men were now at work. Dropping instantly to the ground, I crawled away through the woods, until being out of sight of the house, I ventured to rise and escape on my feet. After I lay down in the night, my fire had died away, and emitted no smoke; this circumstance saved me. This affair made me more cautious as to my future conduct.

Hiding in the woods until night again came on, I continued my course eastward, and some time after midnight came upon a wide, well beaten road, one end of which led, at this place, a little to the left of the north-star, which I could plainly see. Here I deliberated a long time, whether to take this road, or continue my course across the country by the stars; but at last resolved to follow the road, more from a desire to get out of the woods, than from a conviction that it would lead me in the right way. In the course of this night I saw but few plantations, but was so fortunate as to see a ground hog crossing the road before me. This animal I killed with my stick, and carried it until morning.

At the approach of daylight, turning away to the right, I gained the top of an eminence, from which I could see through the woods for some distance around me. Here I kindled a fire and roasted my ground-hog, which afforded me a most grateful repast, after my late fasting and severe toils. According to custom, my meal being over, I betook myself to sleep, and did not awake until the afternoon; when descending a few rods down the hill, and standing still to take a survey of the woods around me, I saw, at the distance of half a mile from me, a man moving slowly about in the forest, and apparently watching, like myself, to see if any one was in view. Looking at this man attentively, I saw that he was a black, and that he did not move more than a few rods from the same spot where I first saw him. Curiosity impelled me to know more of the condition of my neighbour; and descending quite to the foot of the hill, I perceived that he had a covert of boughs of trees, under which I saw him pass, and after some time return again from his retreat. Examining the appearance of things carefully, I became satisfied that the stranger was, like myself, a negro slave, and I determined, without more ceremony, to go and speak to him, for I felt no fear of being betrayed by one as badly off in the world as myself.

When this man first saw me, at the distance of a hundred yards from him, he manifested great agitation, and at once seemed disposed to run from me; but when I called to him, and told him not to be afraid, he became more assured, and waited for me to come close to him. I found him to be a dark mulatto, small and slender in person, and lame in one leg. He had been well bred, and possessed good manners and fine address. I told him I was travelling, and presumed this was not his dwelling-place. Upon which he informed me that he was a native of Kent county, in the state of Delaware, and had been brought up as a house-servant by his master, who, on his death-bed, had made his will, and directed him to be set free by his executors, at the age of twenty-five, and that in the meantime he would be hired out as a servant to some person who should treat him well. Soon after the death of his master, the executors hired him to a man in Wilmington, who employed him as a waiter in his house for three or four months, and then took him to a small town called Newport, and sold him to a man who took him immediately to Baltimore, where he was again sold or transferred to another man, who brought him to South Carolina, and sold him to a cotton planter, with whom he had lived more than two years, and had run away three weeks before the time I saw him, with the intention of returning to Delaware.

That being lame, and becoming fatigued by travelling, he had stopped here and made this shelter of boughs and bark of trees, under which he had remained more than a week before I met him. He invited me to go into his camp, as he termed it, where he had an old skillet, more than a bushel of potatoes, and several fowls, all of which he said he had purloined from the plantations in the neighbourhood.

This encampment was in a level open wood, and it appeared surprising to me that its occupant had not been discovered and conveyed back to his master before this time. I told him that I thought he ran great risk of being taken up by remaining here, and advised him to break up his lodge immediately, and pursue his journey, travelling only in the night time. He then proposed to join me, and travel in company with me; but this I declined, because of his lameness and great want of discretion, though I did not assign these reasons to him.

I remained with this man two or three hours, and ate dinner of fowls dressed after his rude fashion. Before leaving him, I pressed upon him the necessity of immediately quitting the position he then occupied; but he said he intended to remain there a few days longer, unless I would take him with me.

On quitting my new acquaintance, I thought it prudent to change my place of abode for the residue of this day, and removed along the top of the hill that I occupied at least two miles, and concealed myself in a thicket until night, when returning to the road I had left in the morning, and travelling hard all night, I came to a large stream of water just at the break of day. As it was too late to pass the river with safety this morning, at this ford, I went half a mile higher, and swam across the stream in open daylight, at a place where both sides of the water were skirted with woods. I had several large potatoes that had been given to me by the man at his camp in the woods, and these constituted my rations for this day.

At the rising and setting of the sun, I took the bearing of the road by the course of the stream that I had crossed, and found that I was travelling to the northwest, instead of the north or northeast, to one of which latter points I wished to direct my march.

Having perceived the country in which I now was to be thickly peopled, I remained in my resting place until late at night, when returning to the road, and crossing it, I took once more to the woods, with the stars for my guides, and steered for the northeast.

This was a fortunate night for me in all respects. The atmosphere was clear, the ground was high, dry, and free from thickets. In the course of the night I passed several corn fields, with the corn still remaining in them, and passed a potato lot, in which large quantities of fine potatoes were dug out of the ground, and lay in heaps covered with vines; but my most signal good luck occurred just before day, when passing under a dog-wood tree, and hearing a noise in the branches above me, I looked up and saw a large opossum amongst the berries that hung upon the boughs. The game was quickly shaken down, and turned out as fat as a well-fed pig, and as heavy as a full-grown rackoon. My attention was now turned to searching for a place in which I could secrete myself for the day, and dress my provisions in quietness.

This day was clear and beautiful until the afternoon, when the air became damp, and the heavens were overhung with clouds. The night that followed was dark as pitch, compelling me to remain in my camp all night. The next day brought with it a terrible storm of rain and wind, that continued with but little intermission, more than twenty-four hours, and the sun was not again visible until the third day; nor was there a clear night for more than a week. During all this time I lay in my camp, and subsisted upon the provisions that I had brought with me to this place. The corn and potatoes looked so tempting, when I saw them in the fields, that I had taken more than I should have consumed, had not the bad weather compelled me to remain at this spot; but it was well for me, for this time, that I had taken more than I could eat in one or two days.

At the end of the cloudy weather, I felt much refreshed and strengthened, and resumed my journey in high spirits, although I now began to feel the want of shoes—those which I wore when I left my mistress having long since been worn out, and my boots were now beginning to fail so much, that I was obliged to wrap straps of hickory bark about my feet, to keep the leather from separating, and falling to pieces.

It was now, by my computation, the month of November, and I was yet in the state of South Carolina. I began to consider with myself, whether I had gained or lost, by attempting to travel on the roads; and, after revolving in my mind all the disasters that had befallen me, determined to abandon the roads altogether, for two reasons:—the first of which was, that on the highways, I was constantly liable to meet persons, or to be overtaken by them; and a second, no less powerful, was, that as I did not know what roads to pursue, I was oftener travelling on the wrong route than on the right one.

Setting my face once more for the north-star, I advanced with a steady, though slow pace, for four or five nights, when I was again delayed by dark weather, and forced to remain in idleness nearly two weeks; and when the weather again became clear, I was arrested, on the second night, by a broad and rapid river, that appeared so formidable, that I did not dare to attempt its passage, until after examining it in daylight. On the succeeding night, however, I crossed it by swimming—resting at some large rocks near the middle. After gaining the north side of this river, which I believed to be the Catawba, I considered myself in North Carolina, and again steered towards the north.

## CHAPTER XXIII.

THE month of November is, in all years, a season of clouds and vapours; but at the time of which I write, the good weather vanished early in the month, and all the clouds of the universe seemed to have collected in North Carolina. From the second night after crossing the Catawba, I did not see the north-star for the space of three weeks; and during all this time, no progress was made in my journey; although I seldom remained two days in the same place, but moved from one position to another, for the purpose of eluding the observation of the people of the country, whose attention might have been attracted by the continual appearance of the smoke of my fires in one place.

There had, as yet, been no hard frost, and the leaves were still on the oak trees, at the close of this cloudy weather; but the northwest wind which dispelled the mist, also brought down nearly all the leaves of the forest, except those of the evergreen trees; and the nights now became clear, and the air keen with frost.

Hitherto the oak woods had afforded me the safest shelter, but now I was obliged to seek for groves of young pines to retire to at dawn. Heretofore I had found a plentiful subsistence in every corn-field and potato-lot, that fell in my way: but now began to find some of the fields in which corn had grown, destitute of the corn, and containing nothing but the stalks. The potatoes had all been taken out of the lots where they grew, except in some few instances where they had been buried in the field; and the means of subsistence became every day more difficult to be obtained; but as I had fine weather, I made the best use of those hours in which I dared to travel, and was constantly moving from a short time after dark until daylight. The toil that I underwent for the first half of the month of December was excessive, and my sufferings for want of food were great. I was obliged to carry with me a stock of corn, sufficient to supply me for two or three days; for it frequently happened that I met with none in the fields for a long time. In the course of this period, I crossed innumerable streams, the greater portion of which were of small size, but some were of considerable magnitude; and in all of them the water had become almost as cold as ice. Sometimes I was fortunate enough to find boats or canoes tied at the side of the streams, and when this happened, I always made free use of that which no one else was using at the time; but this did not occur often, and I believe that in these two weeks I swam over nine rivers, or streams, so deep, that I could not ford them. The number of creeks and rivulets through which I waded, was far greater; but I cannot now fix the number.

In one of these fine nights, passing near the house of a planter, I saw several dry hides hanging on poles, under a shed. One of these hides I appropriated to myself, for the purpose of converting it into moccasins, to supply the place of my boots, which were totally worthless. By beating the dry hide with a stick it was made sufficiently pliable to bear making it into moccasins; of which I made for myself three pair, wearing one, and carrying the others on my back.

One day as I lay in a pine thicket, several pigs, which appeared to be wild, having no marks on their ears, came near me, and one of them approached so close without seeing me, that I knocked it down with a stone, and succeeded in killing it. This pig was very fat, and would have weighed thirty if not forty pounds. Feeling now greatly exhausted with the fatigues that I had lately undergone, and being in a very great forest, far removed from white inhabitants, I resolved to remain a few days in this place, to regale myself with the flesh of the pig, which I preserved by hanging it up in the shade, after cutting it into pieces. Fortune, so adverse to me heretofore, seemed to have been more kind to me at this time, for the very night succeeding the day on which I killed the pig, a storm of hail, snow, and sleet, came on, and continued fifteen or sixteen hours. The snow lay on the ground four inches in depth, and the whole country was covered with a crust almost hard enough to bear a man. In this state of the weather I could not travel, and my stock of pork was invaluable to me. The pork was frozen where it hung on the branches of the trees, and was as well preserved as if it had been buried in snow; but on the fourth day after the snow fell, the atmosphere underwent a great change. The wind blew from the south, the snow melted away, the air became warm, and the sun shone with the brightness, and almost with the warmth of spring. It was manifest that my pork, which was now soft and oily, would not long be in a sound state. If I remained here, my provisions would become putrid on my hands in a short time, and compel me to quit my residence to avoid the atmosphere of the place.

I resolved to pursue my journey, and prepared myself by roasting before the fire, all my pork that was left, wrapping it up carefully in green pine leaves, and enveloping the whole in a sort of close basket, that I made of small boughs of trees. Equipping myself for my journey with my meat in my knapsack, I again took to the woods, with the stars for my guide, keeping the north-star over my left eye.

The weather had now become exceedingly variable, and I was seldom able to travel more than half of the night. The fields were muddy, the low grounds in the woods were wet, and often covered with water, through which I was obliged to wade—the air was damp and cold by day, the nights were frosty, very often covering the water with ice an inch in thickness. From the great degree of cold that prevailed, I inferred, either that I was pretty far north, or that I had advanced too much to the left, and was approaching the mountain country.

To satisfy myself as far as possible of my situation, one fair day, when the sky was very clear, I climbed to the top of a pine-tree that stood on the summit of a hill, and took a wide survey of the region around me. Eastward, I saw nothing but a vast continuation of plantations, intervened by forests; on the south, the faint beams of a winter sun shed a soft lustre over the woods, which were dotted at remote distances, with the habitations of men, and the openings that they had made in the green champaign of the endless pine-groves, that nature had planted in the direction of the midday sun. On the north, at a great distance, I saw a tract of low and flat country, which, in my opinion, was the vale of some great river, and beyond this, at the farthest stretch of vision, the eye was lost in the blue transparent vault, where the extremity of the arch of the world touches the abode of perpetual winter. Turning westward, the view passed beyond the region of pine-trees, which was followed afar off by naked and leafless oaks, hickories, and walnuts; and still beyond these rose high in air, elevated tracts of country, clad in the white livery of snow, and bearing the impress of mid-winter.

It was now apparent that I had borne too far westward, and was within a few days travel of the mountains. Descending from my observations, I determined, on the return of night, to shape my course, for the future, nearly due east, until I should at least be out of the mountains.

According to my calendar, it was the day before Christmas that I ascended the pine-tree; and I believe I was at that time in the north-western part of North Carolina, not far from the banks of the Yadkin river. On the following night I travelled from dark until, as I supposed, about three or four o'clock in the morning, when I came to a road which led, as I thought, in an easterly direction. This road I travelled until daylight, and encamped near it in an old field, overgrown with young pines, and holly-trees.

This was Christmas-day, and I celebrated it by breakfasting on fat pork, without salt, and substituted parched corn for bread. In the evening, the weather became cloudy and cold, and when night came, it was so dark, that I found difficulty in keeping in the road, at some points where it made short angles. Before midnight it began to snow, and at break of day the snow lay more than a foot deep. This compelled me to seek winter quarters; and fortunately, at about half a mile from the road, I found, on the side of a steep hill, a shelving rock that formed a dry covert, with a southern prospect.

Under this rock I took refuge, and kindling a fire of dry sticks, considered myself happy to possess a few pounds of my roasted pork, and more than half a gallon of corn that I carried in my pockets. The snow continued falling, until it was full two feet deep around me, and the danger of exposing myself to discovery by my tracks in the snow, compelled me to keep close to my hiding place until the third day, when I ventured to go back to the road, which I found broken by the passage of numerous wagons, sleds, and horses, and so much beaten that I could travel it with ease at night, the snow affording good light.

Accordingly at night I again advanced on my way, which indeed I was obliged to do, for my corn was quite gone, and not more than a pound of my pork remained to me. I travelled hard through the night, and after the morning star rose, came to a river, which I think must have been the Yadkin. It appeared to be about two hundred yards wide, and the water ran with great rapidity in it.

Waiting until the eastern horizon was tinged with the first rays of the morning light, I entered the river at the ford, and waded until the water was nearly three feet deep, when it felt as if it was cutting the flesh from the bones of my limbs, and a large cake of ice floating downward, forced me off my balance, and I was near falling. My courage failed me, and I returned to the shore; but found the pain that already tormented me, greatly increased, when I was out of the water, and exposed to the action of the open air. Returning to the river, I plunged into the current to relieve me from the pinching frost, that gnawed every part of my skin that had become wet; and rushing forward as fast as the weight of the water, that pressed me downward, would permit, was soon up to my chin in melted ice, when rising to the surface, I exerted my utmost strength and skill to gain the opposite shore by swimming in the shortest space of time. At every stroke of my arms and legs, they were cut and bruised by cakes of solid ice, or weighed down by floating masses of congealed snow.

It is impossible for human life to be long sustained in such an element as that which encompassed me; and I had not been afloat five minutes before I felt chilled in all my members, and in less than the double of that time, my limbs felt numbed, and my hands became stiff, and almost powerless.

When at the distance of thirty feet from the shore, my body was struck by a violent current, produced by a projecting rock above me, and driven with resistless violence down the stream. Wholly unable to contend with the fury of the waves, and penetrated by the coldness of death, in my inmost vitals, I gave myself up for lost, and was commending my soul to God, whom I expected to be my immediate judge, when I perceived the long hanging branch of a large tree, sweeping to and fro, and undulating backward and forward, as its extremities were washed by the surging current of the river, just below me. In a moment I was in contact with the tree, and making the effort of despair, seized one of its limbs. Bowed down by the weight of my body, the branch yielded to the power of the water, which rushing against my person, swept me round like the quadrant of a circle, and dashed me against the shore, where clinging to some roots that grew near the bank, the limb of the tree left me, and springing with elastic force to its former position, again dipped its slender branches in the mad stream.

Crawling out of the water, and being once more on dry land, I found my circumstances little less desperate, than when I was struggling with the floating ice. The morning was frosty, and icicles hung in long pendant groups from the trees along the shore of the river, and the hoar frost glistened in sparkling radiance, upon the polished surface of the smooth snow, as it whitened all the plain before me, and spread its chill but beautiful covering through the woods.

There were three alternatives before me, one of which I knew must quickly be adopted. The one was to obtain a fire, by which I could dry and warm my stiffened limbs; the second was to die, without the fire; the third, to go to the first house, if I could reach one, and surrender myself as a runaway slave.

Staggering, rather than walking forward, until I gained the cover of a wood, at a short distance from the river, I turned into it, and found that a field bordered the wood within less than twenty rods of the road. Within a few yards of this fence I stopped, and taking out my fire apparatus, to my unspeakable joy, found them dry and in perfect safety. With the aid of my spunk, and some dry moss gathered from the fence, a small flame was obtained, to which dry leaves being added from the boughs of a white oak tree, that had fallen before the frost of the last autumn had commenced, I soon had fire of sufficient intensity, to consume dry wood, with which I supplied it, partly from the fence, and partly from the branches of the fallen tree. Having raked away the snow from about the fire, by the time the sun was up, my frozen clothes were smoking before the coals—warming first one side and then the other—I felt the glow of returning life, once more invigorating my blood, and giving animation to my frozen limbs.

The public road was near me on one hand, and an enclosed field was before me on the other, but in my present condition, it was impossible for me to leave this place to-day, without danger of perishing in the woods, or of being arrested on the road.

As evening came on, the air became much colder than it was in the forenoon, and after night the wind rose high, and blew from the northwest, with intense keenness. My limbs were yet stiff from the effects of my morning adventure, and to complete my distress, I was totally without provisions, having left a few ears of corn, that I had in my pocket, on the other side of the river.

Leaving my fire in the night, and advancing into the field near me, I discovered a house at some distance, and as there was no light, or sign of fire about it, I determined to reconnoitre the premises, which turned out to be a small barn, standing alone, with no other inhabitants about it than a few cattle and a flock of sheep. After much trouble, I succeeded in entering the barn by starting the nails that confined one of the boards at the corner. Entering the house I found it nearly filled with corn, in the husks, and some from which the husks had been removed, was lying in a heap in one corner.

Into these husks I crawled, and covering myself deeply under them, soon became warm, and fell into a profound sleep, from which I was awakened by the noise of people walking about in the barn, and talking of the cattle and sheep, which it appeared they had come to feed, for they soon commenced working in the corn husks, with which I was covered, and throwing them out to the cattle. I expected at every moment that they would uncover me; but fortunately before they saw me, they ceased their operations, and went to work, some husking corn, and throwing the husks on the pile over me, while others were employed in loading the husked corn into carts, as I learned by their conversation, and hauling it away to the house. The people continued working in the barn all day, and in the evening gave more husks to the cattle and went home.

Waiting two or three hours after my visiters were gone, I rose from the pile of husks, and filling my pockets with ears of corn, issued from the barn, at the same place by which I had entered it, and returned to the woods, where I kindled a fire in a pine thicket, and parched more than half a gallon of corn. Before day I returned to the barn, and again secreted myself in the corn husks. In the morning the people again returned to their work, and husked corn until the evening. At night I again repaired to the woods, and parched more corn. In this manner I passed more than a month, lying in the barn all day, and going to the woods at night; but at length the corn was all husked, and I watched daily the progress that was made in feeding the cattle with the husks, knowing that I must quit my winter retreat, before the husks were exhausted. Before the husked corn was removed from the barn, I had conveyed several bushels of the ears into the husks, near my bed, and concealed them for my winter's stock.

Whilst I lay in this barn, there were frequent and great changes of weather. The snow that covered the earth to the depth of two feet, when I came here, did not remain more than ten days, and was succeeded by more than a week of warm rainy weather, which was in turn succeeded by several days of dry weather, with cold high winds from the north. The month of February was cloudy and damp, with several squalls of snow and frequent rains. About the first of March, the atmosphere became clear and dry, and the winds boisterous from the west.

On the third of this month, having filled my little bag and all my pockets with parched corn, I quitted my winter quarters about ten o'clock at night, and again proceeded on my way to the north, leaving a large heap of corn husks still lying in the corner of the barn.

On leaving this place, I again pursued the road that had led me to it, for several nights; crossing many small streams in my way, all of which I was able to pass without swimming, though several of them were so deep, that they wet me as high as my arm-pits. This road led nearly northeast, and was the only road that I had fallen in with, since I left Georgia, that had maintained that direction for so great a distance. Nothing extraordinary befell me until the twelfth of March, when venturing to turn out earlier than usual in the evening, and proceeding along the road, I found that my way led me down a hill, along the side of which the road had been cut into the earth ten or twelve feet in depth, having steep banks on each side, which were now so damp and slippery, that it was impossible for a man to ascend either the one or the other.

Whilst in this narrow place, I heard the sound of horses proceeding up the hill to meet me. Stopping to listen, in a moment almost two horsemen were close before me, trotting up the road. To escape on either hand was impossible, and to retreat backwards would have exposed me to certain destruction. Only one means of salvation was left, and I embraced it. Near the place where I stood, was a deep gully cut in one side of the road, by the water which had run down here in time of rains. Into this gully I threw myself, and lying down close to the ground, the horsemen rode almost over me, and passed on. When they were gone I arose, and descending the hill, found a river before me.

In crossing this stream, I was compelled to swim at least two hundred yards; and found the cold so oppressive, after coming out of the water, that I was forced to stop at the first thick woods that I could find and make a fire to dry myself. I did not move again until the next night; and on the fourth night after this, came to a great river, which I suppose was the Roanoke. I was obliged to swim this stream, and was carried a great way down by the rapidity of the current. It must have been more than an hour from the time that I entered the water, until I reached the opposite shore, and as the rivers were yet very cold, I suffered greatly at this place.

Judging by the aspect of the country, I believed myself to be at this time in Virginia; and was now reduced to the utmost extremity, for want of provisions. The corn that I had parched at the barn, and brought with me, was nearly exhausted, and no more was to be obtained in the fields, at this season of the year. For three or four days I allowed myself only my two hands full of parched corn per day; and after this I travelled three days without tasting food of any kind; but being nearly exhausted with hunger, I one night entered an old stack-yard,[29] hoping that I might fall in with pigs, or poultry of some kind. I found, instead of these, a stack of oats, which had not been threshed. From this stack I took as much oats in the sheaf, as I could carry, and going on a few miles, stopped in a pine forest, made a large fire, and parched at least half a gallon of oats, after rubbing the grain from the straw. After the grain was parched, I again rubbed it in my hands, to separate it from the husks, and spent the night in feasting on parched oats.

The weather was now becoming quite warm, though the water was cold in the rivers; and I perceived the farmers had everywhere ploughed their fields, preparatory to planting corn. Every night I saw people burning brush in the new grounds that they were clearing of the wood and brush; and when the day came, in the morning after I obtained the oats, I perceived people planting corn in a field about half a mile from my fire. According to my computation of time, it was on the night of the last day of March that I obtained the oats; and the appearance of the country satisfied me, that I had not lost many days in my reckoning.

I lay in this pine-wood two days, for the purpose of recruiting my strength, after my long fast; and when I again resumed my journey, determined to seek some large road leading towards the north, and follow it in future; the one that I had been pursuing of late, not appearing to be a principal high-way of the country. For this purpose, striking off across the fields, in an easterly direction, I travelled a few hours, and was fortunate enough to come to a great road, which was manifestly much travelled, leading towards the northeast.

My bag was now replenished with more than a gallon of parched oats, and

I had yet one pair of moccasins made of raw hide; but my shirt was totally gone, and my last pair of trousers was now in actual service. A tolerable waistcoat still remained to me, and my great coat, though full of honourable scars, was yet capable of much service.

Having resolved to pursue the road I was now in, it was necessary again to resort to the utmost degree of caution, to prevent surprise. Travelling only after it was dark, and taking care to stop before the appearance of day, my progress was not rapid, but my safety was preserved.

The acquisition of food had now become difficult, and when my oats began to fail, I resorted to the dangerous expedient of attacking the corn-crib of a planter that was near the road. The house was built of round logs, and was covered with boards. One of these boards I succeeded in removing, on the side of the crib opposite from the dwelling, and by thrusting my arm downwards, was able to reach the corn—of which I took as much as filled my bag, the pockets of my great coat, and a large handkerchief, that I had preserved through all the vicissitudes of my journey. This opportune supply of corn furnished me with food more than a week, and before it was consumed, I reached the Appomattox river, which I crossed in a canoe, that I found tied at the shore, a few miles above the town of Petersburg. Having approached Petersburg in the night, I was afraid to attempt to pass through it, lest the patrol should fall in with me; and turning to the left through the country, reached the river, and crossed in safety.

The great road leading to Richmond is so distinguishingly marked above the other ways in this part of Virginia, that there was no difficulty in following it, and on the third night after passing Petersburg, I obtained a sight of the capitol of Virginia. It was only a little after midnight, when the city presented itself to my sight; but here, as well as at Petersburg, I was afraid to attempt to go through the town, under cover of the darkness, because of the patrol. Turning, therefore, back into a forest, about two miles from the small town on the south-side of the river, I lay there until after twelve o'clock in the day, when loosening the package from my back, and taking it in my hand in the form of a bundle, I advanced into the village, as if I had only come from some plantation in the neighbourhood.

This was on Sunday, I believe, though according to my computation, it was Monday; but it must have been Sunday, for the village was quiet, and in passing it, I only saw two or three persons, whom I passed as if I had not seen them. No one spoke to me, and I gained the bridge in safety, and crossed it without attracting the least attention.

Entering the city of Richmond, I kept along the principal street, walking at a slow pace, and turning my head from side to side, as if much attracted by the objects around me. Few persons were in the street, and I was careful to appear more attentive to the houses than to the people. At the upper end of the city I saw a great crowd of ladies and gentlemen, who were, I believe, returning from church. Whilst these people were passing me, I stood in the street, on the outside of the foot pavement, with my face turned to the opposite side of the street. They all went by without taking any notice of me; and when they were gone, I again resumed my leisure walk along the pavement, and reached the utmost limit of the town without being accosted by any one. As soon as I was clear of the city I quickened my pace, assumed the air of a man in great haste, sometimes actually ran, and in less than an hour was safely lodged in the thickest part of the woods that lay on the north of Richmond, and full four miles from the river. This was the boldest exploit that I had performed since leaving my mistress, except the visit I paid to the gentleman in Georgia.

My corn was now failing, but as I had once entered a crib secretly, I felt but little apprehension on account of future supplies. After this time I never wanted corn, and did not again suffer by hunger, until I reached the place of my nativity.

After leaving Richmond, I again kept along the great road by which I had travelled on my way south, taking great care not to expose my person unnecessarily. For several nights I saw no white people on the way, but was often met by black ones, whom I avoided by turning out of the road; but one moonlight night, five or six days after I left Richmond, a man stepped out of the woods almost at my side, and accosting me in a familiar manner, asked me which way I was travelling, how long I had been on the road, and made many inquiries concerning the course of my late journey. This man was a mulatto, and carried a heavy cane, or rather club, in his hand. I did not like his appearance, and the idea of a familiar conversation with any one seemed to terrify me. I determined to watch my companion closely, and he appeared equally intent on observing me; but at the same time that he talked with me, he was constantly drawing closer to, and following behind me. This conduct increased my suspicion, and I began to wish to get rid of him, but could not at the moment imagine how I should effect my purpose. To avoid him, I crossed the road several times; but still he followed me closely. The moon, which shone brightly upon our backs, cast his shadow far before me, and enabled me to perceive his motions with the utmost accuracy, without turning my head towards him. He carried his club under his left arm, and at length raised his right hand gently, took the stick by the end, and drawing it slowly over his head, was in the very act of striking a blow at me, when, springing backward, and raising my own staff at the same moment, I brought him to the ground by a stroke on his forehead; and when I had him down, beat him over the back and sides with my weapon, until he roared for mercy, and begged me not to kill him. I left him in no condition to pursue me, and hastened on my way, resolved to get as far from him before day as my legs would carry me.

This man was undoubtedly one of those wretches who are employed by white men to kidnap and betray such unfortunate people of colour as may chance to fall into their hands; but for once the deceiver was deceived, and he who intended to make prey of me, had well nigh fallen a sacrifice himself.

The same night I crossed the Pammunky river, near the village of Hanover by swimming, and secreted myself before day in a dense cedar thicket. The next night, after I had travelled several miles, in ascending a hill, I saw the head of a man rise on the opposite side, without having heard any noise. I instantly ran into the woods, and concealed myself behind a large tree. The traveller was on horseback, and the road being sandy, and his horse moving only at a walk, I had

not heard his approach until I saw him. He also saw me; for when he came opposite the place where I stood, he stopped his horse in the road, and desired me
to tell him how far it was to some place, the name of which I have forgotten. As
I made no answer, he again repeated the inquiry; and then said, I need not be
afraid to speak, as he did not wish to hurt me; but no answer being given him,
he at last said I might as well speak, and rode on.

Before day I reached the Matapony river, and crossed it by wading; but
knowing that I was not far from Maryland, I fell into a great indiscretion, and
forgot the wariness and caution that had enabled me to overcome obstacles apparently insurmountable. Anxious to get forward, I neglected to conceal myself
before day; but travelled until daybreak before I sought a place of concealment,
and unfortunately, when I looked for a hiding place, none was at hand. This
compelled me to keep on the road, until gray twilight, for the purpose of reaching a wood that was in view before me; but to gain this wood I was obliged to
pass a house, that stood at the road side, and when only about fifty yards beyond
the house, a white man opened the door, and seeing me in the road, called to me
to stop. As this order was not obeyed, he set his dog upon me. The dog was
quickly vanquished by my stick, and setting off to run at full speed, I at the same
moment heard the report of a gun, and received its contents in my legs, chiefly
about, and in my hams. I fell on the road, and was soon surrounded by several
persons, who it appeared were a party of patrollers, who had gathered together
in this house. They ordered me to cross my hands, which order not being immediately obeyed, they beat me with sticks and stones until I was almost senseless,
and entirely unable to make resistance. They then bound me with cords, and
dragged me by the feet back to the house, and threw me into the kitchen, like a
dead dog. One of my eyes was almost beaten out, and the blood was running
from my mouth, nose and ears; but in this condition they refused to wash the
blood from my face, or even to give me a drink of water.

In a short time, a justice of the peace arrived, and when he looked at me,
ordered me to be unbound, and to have water to wash myself, and also some
bread to eat. This man's heart appeared not to be altogether void of sensibility,
for he reprimanded, in harsh terms, those who had beaten me; told them that
their conduct was brutal, and that it would have been more humane to kill me
outright, than to bruise and mangle me in the manner they had done.

He then interrogated me as to my name, place of abode, and place of destination, and afterwards demanded the name of my master. To all these inquiries
I made no reply, except that I was going to Maryland, where I lived. The justice
told me it was his duty under the law, to send me to jail; and I was immediately
put into a cart, and carried to a small village called Bowling Green, which I
reached before ten o'clock.

There I was locked up in the jail, and a doctor came to examine my legs,
and extract the shot from my wounds. In the course of the operation he took out
thirty-four duck shot, and after dressing my legs left me to my own reflections.
No fever followed in the train of my disasters, which I attributed to the reduced
state of my blood, by long fasting, and the fatigues I had undergone.

In the afternoon the jailer came to see me, and brought my daily allowance of provisions, and a jug of water. The provisions consisted of more than a pound of corn-bread, and some boiled bacon. As my appetite was good, I immediately devoured more than two-thirds of this food, but reserved the rest for supper.

For several days I was not able to stand, and in this period found great difficulty in performing the ordinary offices of life for myself, no one coming to give me any aid; but I did not suffer for want of food, the daily allowance of the jailer being quite sufficient to appease the cravings of hunger. After I grew better, and was able to walk in the jail, the jailer frequently called to see me, and endeavoured to prevail on me to tell where I had come from; but in this undertaking, he was no more successful than the justice had been in the same business.

I remained in the jail more than a month, and in this time became quite fat and strong, but saw no way by which I could escape. The jail was of brick, the floors were of solid oak boards, and the door, of the same material, was secured by iron bolts, let into its posts, and connected together by a strong band of iron, reaching from the one to the other.

Every thing appeared sound and strong, and to add to my security, my feet were chained together, from the time my wounds were healed. This chain I acquired the knowledge of removing from my feet, by working out of its socket a small iron pin that secured the bolt that held the chain round one of my legs.

The jailer came to see me with great regularity, every morning and evening, but remained only a few minutes, when he came, leaving me entirely alone at all other times.

---

# CHAPTER XXIV.

WHEN I had been in prison thirty-nine days, and had quite recovered from the wounds that I had received, the jailer was late in coming to me with my breakfast, and going to the door I began to beat against it with my fist, for the purpose of making a noise. After beating some time against the door I happened, by mere accident, to strike my fist against one of the posts, which, to my surprise, I discovered by its sound, to be a mere hollow shell, encrusted with a thin coat of sound timber, and as I struck it, the rotten wood crumbled to pieces within. On a more careful examination of this post, I became satisfied that I could easily split it to pieces, by the aid of the iron bolt that confined my feet. The jailer came with my breakfast, and reprimanded me for making a noise. This day appeared as long to me, as a week had done heretofore; but night came at length, and as soon as the room in which I was confined, had become quite dark, I disentangled myself from the irons with which I was bound, and with the aid of the long bolt, easily wrenched from its place, the large staple that held one end of the bar, that lay across the door. The hasps that held the lock in its place, were drawn away almost without force, and the door swung open of its own weight.

I now walked out into the jail-yard, and found that all was quiet, and that only a few lights were burning in the village windows. At first I walked slowly along the road, but soon quickened my pace, and ran along the high-way, until

I was more than a mile from the jail, then taking to the woods, I travelled all night, in a northern direction. At the approach of day I concealed myself in a cedar thicket, where I lay until the next evening, without any thing to eat.

On the second night after my escape, I crossed the Potomac, at Hoe's ferry, in a small boat that I found tied at the side of the ferry flat; and on the night following crossed the Patuxent, in a canoe, which I found chained at the shore.

About one o'clock in the morning, I came to the door of my wife's cabin, and stood there, I believe, more than five minutes, before I could summon sufficient fortitude to knock. I at length rapped lightly on the door, and was immediately asked, in the well-known voice of my wife, "Who is there?"—I replied "Charles." She then came to the door, and opening it slowly, said, "Who is this that speaks so much like my husband?" I then rushed into the cabin and made myself known to her, but it was some time before I could convince her, that I was really her husband, returned from Georgia. The children were then called up, but they had forgotten me.

When I attempted to take them in my arms, they fled from me, and took refuge under the bed of their mother. My eldest boy, who was four years old when I was carried away, still retained some recollections of once having had a father, but could not believe that I was that father. My wife, who at first was overcome by astonishment at seeing me again in her cabin, and was incapable of giving credit to the fidelity of her own vision, after I had been in the house a few minutes, seemed to awake from a dream; and gathering all three of her children in her arms, thrust them into my lap, as I sat in the corner, clapped her hands, laughed, and cried by turns; and in her ecstasy forgot to give me any supper, until I at length told her that I was hungry. Before I entered the house I felt as if I could eat any thing in the shape of food; but now that I attempted to eat, my appetite had fled, and I sat up all night with my wife and children.

When on my journey I thought of nothing but getting home, and never reflected, that when at home, I might still be in danger; but now that my toils were ended, I began to consider with myself how I could appear in safety in Calvert county, where everybody must know that I was a runaway slave. With my heart thrilling with joy, when I looked upon my wife and children, who had not hoped ever to behold me again; yet fearful of the coming of daylight, which must expose me to be arrested as a fugitive slave, I passed the night between the happiness of the present and the dread of the future. In all the toils, dangers, and sufferings of my long journey, my courage had never forsaken me. The hope of again seeing my wife and little ones, had borne me triumphantly through perils, that even now I reflect upon as upon some extravagant dream; but when I found myself at rest under the roof of my wife, the object of my labours attained, and no motive to arouse my energies, or give them the least impulse, that firmness of resolution which had so long sustained me, suddenly vanished from my bosom; and I passed the night, with my children around me, oppressed by a melancholy foreboding of my future destiny. The idea that I was utterly unable to afford protection and safeguard to my own family, and was myself even more helpless than they, tormented my bosom with alternate throbs of affection and fear, until the dawn broke in the east, and summoned me to decide upon my future conduct.

When morning came, I went to the great house, and showed myself to my wife's master and mistress who treated me with great kindness, and gave me a good breakfast. Mr. Symmes at first advised me to conceal myself, but soon afterwards told me to go to work in the neigbourhood for wages. I continued to hire myself about among the farmers, until after the war broke out; and until Commodore Barney came into the Patuxent with his flotilla, when I enlisted on board one of his barges, and was employed sometimes in the capacity of a seaman, and sometimes as cook of the barge.[30]

I had been on board, only a few days, when the British fleet entered the Patuxent, and forced our flotilla high up the river. I was present when the flotilla was blown up, and assisted in the performance of that operation upon the barge that I was in. The guns and the principal part of the armament of the flotilla, were sunk in the river and lost.

I marched with the troops of Barney, from Benedict to Bladensburg, and travelled nearly the whole of the distance, through heavy forests of timber, or numerous and dense cedar thickets. It is my opinion, that if General Winder had marched the half of the troops that he had at Bladensburg, down to the lower part of Prince George county, and attacked the British in these woods and cedar thickets, not a man of them would ever have reached Bladensburg.[31]

I feel confident that in the country through which I marched, one hundred Americans would have destroyed a thousand of the enemy, by felling trees across the road, and attacking them in ambush.

When we reached Bladensburg, and the flotilla men were drawn up in line, to work at their cannon, armed with their cutlasses, I volunteered to assist in working the cannon, that occupied the first place, on the left of the Commodore. We had a full and perfect view of the British army, as it advanced along the road, leading to the bridge over the East Branch; and I could not but admire the handsome manner in which the British officers led on their fatigued and worn-out soldiers. I thought then, and think yet, that General Ross was one of the finest looking men that I ever saw on horseback.

I stood at my gun, until the Commodore was shot down, when he ordered us to retreat, as I was told by the officer who commanded our gun. If the militia regiments, that lay upon our right and left, could have been brought to charge the British, in close fight, as they crossed the bridge, we should have killed or taken the whole of them in a short time; but the militia ran like sheep chased by dogs.

My readers will not, perhaps, condemn me if I here make a short digression from my main narrative, to give some account of the part that I took in the war, on the shores of the Chesapeake, and the Patuxent. I did not enlist with Commodore Barney until the month of December, 1813; but as I resided in Calvert county, in the summer of 1813, I had an opportunity of witnessing many of the evils that followed in the train of war, before I assumed the profession of arms myself.

In the spring of the year 1813, the British fleet came into the bay, and from this time, the origin of the troubles and distresses of the people of the Western Shore, may be dated. I had been employed at a fishery, near the mouth of the

Patuxent, from early in March, until the latter part of May, when a British vessel of war came off the mouth of the river, and sent her boats up to drive us away from our fishing gound. There was but little property at the fishery that could be destroyed; but the enemy cut the seines to pieces, and burned the sheds belonging to the place. They then marched up two miles into the country, burned the house of a planter, and brought away with them several cattle, that were found in his fields. They also carried off more than twenty slaves, which were never again restored to their owner; although, on the following day, he went on board the ship, with a flag of truce, and offered a large ransom for these slaves.

These were the first black people whom I had known to desert to the British, although the practice was afterwards so common. In the course of this summer, and the summer of 1814, several thousand black people deserted from their masters and mistresses, and escaped to the British fleet. None of these people were ever regained by their owners, as the British naval officers treated them as free people, and placed them on the footing of military deserters.

In the fall of this year, a lady by the name of Wilson, who owned more than a hundred slaves, lost them all in one night, except one man, who had a wife and several children on an adjoining estate, and as he could not take his family with him, on account of the rigid guard that was kept over them, he refused to go himself.

The slaves of Mrs. Wilson effected their escape in the following manner. Two or three of the men having agreed amongst themselves, that they would run away and go to the fleet, they stole a canoe one night, and went off to the ship, that lay nearest the shore. When on board, they informed the officer of the ship that their mistress owned more than a hundred other slaves, whom they had left behind them. They were then advised to return home, and remain there until the next night, and then bring with them to the beach, all the slaves on the plantation—the officer promising that he would send a detachment of boats to the shore, to bring them off. This advice was followed, and the fugitives returned before day, to their cabins, on the plantation of their mistress.

On the next night, having communicated their plans to some of their fellow-slaves, they rose about midnight, and partly by persuasion, partly by compulsion, carried off all the slaves on the plantation, with the exception of the man already named.

When they reached the beach, they kindled a fire, as had been concerted with the British officers, and the boats of the fleet came off, and removed this whole party on board. In the morning, when the overseer of Mrs. Wilson arose, and went to call his hands to the field, he found only empty cabins in the quarter, with a single man remaining, to tell what had become of his fellows.

This was the greatest disaster that had befallen any individual in our neighbourhood, in the course of the war; and as the sufferer was a lady, much sympathy was excited in her favour. A large number of gentlemen met together, for the purpose of endeavouring to devise some means of recovering the fugitive slaves. Their consultations ended in sending a deputation of gentlemen, on board the fleet, with a flag of truce, to solicit the restoration of the deserters, either as a matter of favour, or for such ransom, as might be agreed upon. Strong hopes were entertained, that the runaways might be induced voluntarily to return to the service of their mistress, as she had never treated them with great severity.

To accomplish, if possible, this latter end, I was spoken to, to go along with the flag of truce, in the assumed character of the servant of one of the gentlemen who bore it; but in the real character of the advocate of the mistress, for the purpose of inducing her slaves to return to her service.

We went on board the ship in the afternoon, and I observed, that the gentlemen who went with me, were received by the British officers with very little ceremony. The captain did not show himself on deck, nor were the gentlemen invited into his cabin. They were shown into a large square room under the first deck of the ship, which was a 74,[32] and here a great number of officers came to talk to them, and ask them questions concerning the war, and the state of the country.

The whole of the runaways were on board this ship, lounging about on the main deck, or leaning against the sides of the ship's bulwarks. I went amongst them, and talked to them a long time, on the subject of returning home; but found that their heads were full of notions of liberty and happiness in some of the West India islands.

In the afternoon, all the gentlemen, except one, returned home in the boat that they had come off in. The gentleman, who remained on board, was a young man of pleasing manners and lively conversation, who appeared, even before the other gentlemen who had come with the flag had left the ship, to have become quite a favourite with the younger British officers. Permission was obtained of the British captain, for this young gentleman to remain on board a few days, for the purpose, as he alleged, of seeing the curiosities of the ship. He had permission to retain me with him as his servant; and I was instructed to exert myself to the utmost, to prevail on the runaway slaves to return to their mistress. The ship lay at anchor off the shore of Calvert county, until the second night after I came on board, when, from some cause which I was not able to understand, this ship and all the rest of the fleet, got under weigh, and stood down the Bay to the neighbourhood of Tangier Islands; where she again cast anchor, soon after sunrise the next morning, in ten fathoms water. I was now at least seventy or eighty miles from home, in a ship of the public enemies of the country, and liable to be carried off to sea, and to be conveyed to the most distant part of the world. To increase my alarm, about noon of this day, a sloop of war cast anchor under the stern of our ship; and all the black people that were with us, were immediately removed on board the sloop. I was invited, and even urged to go with the others, who, I was told, were bound to the island of Trinidad, in the West Indies, where they would have lands given to them, and where they were to be free. I returned many thanks for their kind offers; but respectfully declined them; telling those who made them, that I was already a freeman, and though I owned no land myself, yet I could have plenty of land of other people to cultivate.

In the evening, the sloop weighed anchor, and stood down the Bay, with more than two hundred and fifty black people on board. I watched her as she sailed away from us, until the darkness of the night shut her out from my sight. In the morning she was not to be seen. What became of the miserable mass of black fugitives, that this vessel took to sea, I never learned.[33]

My mission was now at an end, and I spoke this day to the young gentleman, under whose care I was, to endeavour to procure some means of conveying both him and me back again to Calvert. My protector seemed no less embarrassed than I was, and informed me, that the officers of the ship said they would not land us on the Western Shore, within less than two weeks. I was obliged to content myself in the best way I could, in my confinement on shipboard; and I amused myself by talking to the sailors, and giving them an account of the way in which I had passed my life on the tobacco and cotton plantations; in return for which, the seamen gave many long stories of their adventures at sea, and of the battles they had been engaged in.

I lived well whilst on board this ship, as they allowed me to share in a mess. In compensation for their civility, I gave them many useful instructions in the art of taking fish in the Bay.

This great ship lay at anchor like a vast castle, moored by the cable; but there were many small vessels, used as tenders to the fleet, that were continually sailing up and down the Bay, by night, as well as by day, in pursuit of any thing that they might fall in with, that they could take from the Americans. Whilst I was on board, I saw more than thirty vessels, chiefly Bay craft, brought to our anchorage, and there burned, after being stripped of every thing valuable that could be taken from them. The people who manned and navigated these vessels, were made prisoners, and dispersed amongst the several ships of the fleet, until they could be removed to Halifax, or the West Indies. One day a small schooner was seen standing out of the mouth of Nanticoke river, and beating up the Bay. Chase was immediately given by several of the light vessels belonging to the fleet, and continued until nightfall, when I could no longer see the sails; but the next day, the British vessels returned, bringing in their company the little schooner, which was manned by her owner, who acted as captain, and two boys. On board the schooner, besides her crew, were several passengers, seven in number, I believe. The people were taken out of this little vessel, which was laden with Indian corn, and after her cargo had been removed, she was burned in view of her owner, who seemed much affected at the sight, and said that it was all the property he owned in the world, and that his wife and children were now beggars. The passengers and crew of this little vessel, were all retained as prisoners of war, on board the 74, in which I was; and were shut up every night in a room on the lower gun-deck. In this room there were several port-holes, which were suffered to remain open for the benefit of the air.

After these people had been on board three or four days, a boat's crew, that had been out somewhere in the evening, when they returned to the ship, tied the boat with a long rope to one of the halyards of the ship, and left the boat floating near the ship's bows. Some time after night the tide turned, moved the boat along the side of the ship, and floated it directly under the port-holes of the prisoners' room. The night was dark and warm, and I had taken a station on the upper deck, and was leaning over the bulwarks, when my attention was drawn towards the water, by hearing something drop into the boat that lay along side. Dark as it was, I could see the forms of men passing out of the port-holes into the boat. In less than two minutes, nine persons had entered the boat; and I then heard a low whisper, which I could not understand; but immediately afterwards, saw the boat drifting with the tide; which convinced me that she was loose, and that the prisoners were in her. I said nothing, and in a short time the boat was out of sight. She had, however, not been long gone, when the watch on deck passed near me and looking over the side of the ship, called to the officer on deck, that the yawl was gone. The officer on deck instantly called to some one below to examine the room of the prisoners; and received for answer, that the prisoners had fled. A gun was immediately fired under me, on one of the lower decks; the ship's bells were tolled; numerous blue lights were made ready, and cast high into the air, which performing a curve in the atmosphere, illuminated the face of the water all the way from the ship to the place where they fell. The other ships in the fleet all answered by firing guns, casting out lights, and ringing their large bells. Three boats put off from our ship, in search of the fugitives, with as little delay as possible; and, after being absent more than an hour, returned without finding those who had escaped.

This affair presented one of the finest night scenes that can well be imagined. The deep thunder of the heavy artillery, as it broke upon the stillness of the night, and re-echoed from the distant shores; the solemn and mournful tones of the numerous bells, as they answered each other from ship to ship, as the sounds rose in the air, and died away in the distance, on the wide expanse of waters; with the shouts of the seamen, and the pale and ghastly appearance of the blue lights, as they rose into the atmosphere, and then descended and died away in the water—all combined together, to affect both the eye and the ear, in a manner the most impressive.

One of the prisoners remained in the ship; not having courage to undertake, with his companions, the daring and dangerous exploit of escaping from the ship in her own boat. When the morning came, this man explained, to the officers of the ship, the whole plan that had been devised, and pursued by his companions. When they found that the boat had floated under the port-holes of their room, some one of the number proposed to the rest, to attempt to escape, as the oars of the boat had been left in her; but a difficulty suggested itself, at the outset, which was this: the oars could not be worked on the boat without making a great noise, sufficient to alarm the watch on deck. To avoid this, one of the prisoners said he would undertake to pull off his coat, and muffle one of the oars with it, and scull the boat until they should be clear of the fleet; when they could lay both oars on the boat, and row to shore. We lay much nearer to the Western Shore, than we were to the Eastern but this man said, the design of the prisoners was to pull to the Eastern Shore. All the boats that went from our ship pulled for the Western Shore, and by this means the prisoners escaped, without being seen.

The captain of the ship was much enraged at the escape of these prisoners, and swore he would be avenged of the Yankees in a short time. In this he was as good as his word; for the very next day he fitted out an expedition, consisting of eleven long boats, and more than two hundred men, who landed on the Western Shore, and burned three houses, with all their furniture, and killed a great number of cattle.

The officer who headed this expedition, brought back with him a large silk handkerchief full of silver spoons, and other articles of silver plate. I saw him exhibit these trophies of his valour amongst his brother officers, on the deck of the ship.

After I had been on board nearly a week, a furious northeast storm came on and blew for three days, accompanied with frequent gusts of rain. In the evening of the second day, we saw two schooners standing down the bay, and sailing close on the wind, so as to pass between the fleet and the Eastern Shore. As it was dangerous for large ships to approach much nearer the Eastern Shore than where we lay, several of the tenders of the fleet, amounting in all to more than a dozen, were ordered, by signal, to intercept the strange sails, and bring them to the fleet.

The tenders got under weigh and stood before the wind, for the purpose of encountering the schooners, as they came down the Bay. These schooners proved to be two heavy armed American privateers, and when the tenders approached them a furious battle commenced, with cannon, which lasted more than an hour, and until the privateers had passed quite below the anchorage of the fleet.

Several of the tenders were much damaged in their hulls and rigging; and it was said that they lost more than twenty men. I could not perceive that the privateers sustained the least injury, as they never shortened sail, nor altered their course, until they had passed to the windward of all the ships of the fleet, when they changed their bearing, and stood for the Capes of Virginia. There were nearly forty vessels in the fleet, great and small; and yet these two privateers braved the whole of them in open daylight, and went to sea in spite of them.

On the ninth day after we came on board, the fleet again moved up the Bay, and when we were off the mouth of the Potomac, the captain sent the young gentleman, in whose service I was, together with myself, on shore in his own gig.

The lieutenant who had command of the gig, after he set us on shore, went up to the house of a farmer, whose estate lay open to the Bay, and after pilfering the premises of every thing that he could carry away, set fire to the house, and returned to his boat. In the course of the summer and fall of the year 1813, I witnessed many other atrocities, of equal enormity.

I continued with the army after the sack of Washington, and assisted in the defence of Baltimore; but in the fall of 1814, I procured my discharge from the army, and went to work in Baltimore, as a free black man. From this time, until the year 1820, I worked in various places in Maryland, as a free man; sometimes in Baltimore, sometimes in Annapolis, and frequently in Washington. My wife died in the year 1816, and from that time I was not often in Calvert county. I was fortunate in the enjoyment of good health; and by constant economy I found myself in possession, in the year 1820, of three hundred and fifty dollars in money, the proceeds of my labour.

I now removed to the neighbourhood of Baltimore, and purchased a lot of twelve acres of ground, upon which I erected a small house, and became a farmer on my own account, and upon my own property. I purchased a yoke of oxen and two cows, and became a regular attendant of the Baltimore market, where I sold the products of my own farm and dairy. In the course of two or three years, I had brought my little farm into very good culture, and had increased my stock of cattle to four cows and several younger animals. I now lived very happily, and had an abundance of all the necessaries of life around me. I had married a second wife, who bore me four children, and I now looked forward to an old age of comfort, if not of ease; but I was soon to be awakened from this dream.

## CHAPTER XXV.

IN the month of June, 1830, as I was ploughing in my lot, three gentlemen rode up to my fence, and alighting from their horses, all came over the fence and approached me, when one of them told me he was the sheriff, and had a writ in his pocket, which commanded him to take me to Baltimore. I was not conscious of having done any thing injurious to any one; but yet felt a distrust of these men, who were all strangers to me. I told them I would go with them, if they would permit me to turn my oxen loose from the plough; but it was my intention to seek an opportunity of escaping to the house of a gentleman, who lived about a mile from me. This purpose I was not able to effect, for whilst I was taking the yoke from the oxen, one of the gentlemen came behind me, and knocked me down, with a heavy whip, that he carried in his hand.

When I recovered from the stunning effects of this blow, I found myself bound with my hands behind me, and strong cords closely wrapped about my arms. In this condition I was forced to set out immediately, for Balitmore, without speaking to my wife, or even entering my door. I expected that, on arriving at Baltimore, I should be taken before a judge for the purpose of being tried, but in this I was deceived. They led me to the city jail, and there shut me up, with several other black people, both men and women, who told me that they had lately been purchased by a trader from Georgia.

I now saw the extent of my misfortune, but could not learn who the persons were, who had seized me. In the evening however, one of the gentlemen, who had brought me from home, came into the jail with the jailer, and asked me if I knew him. On being answered in the negative, he told me that he knew me very well; and asked me if I did not recollect the time when he and his brother had whipped me, before my master's door, in Georgia.

I now recognised the features of the younger of the two brothers of my mistress; but this man was so changed in his appearance, from the time when I had last seen him, that if he had not declared himself, I should never have known him. When I left Georgia, he was not more than twenty-one or two years of age, and had black, bushy hair. His hair was now thin and gray, and all his features were changed.

After lying in jail a little more than two weeks, strongly ironed, my fellow prisoners and I were one day chained together, handcuffed in pairs, and in this way driven about ten miles out of Baltimore, where we remained all night.

On the evening of the second day, we halted at Bladensburg, and were shut up in a small house, within full view of the very ground, where sixteen years before I had fought in the ranks of the army of the United States, in defence of the liberty and independence of that which I then regarded as my country. It seemed as if it had been but yesterday that I had seen the British columns, advancing across the bridge now before me, directing their fire against me, and my companions in arms.

The thought now struck me, that if I had deserted that day, and gone over to the enemies of the United States, how different would my situation at this moment have been. And this, thought I, is the reward of the part I bore in the dangers and fatigues of that disastrous battle.

On the next morning, we marched through Washington, and as we passed in front of the President's house, I saw an old gentleman walking in the grounds, near the gate. This man I was told was the President of the United States.[34]

Within four weeks after we left Washington, I was in Milledgeville in Georgia, near which the man who had kidnapped me, resided. He took me home with him, and set me to work on his plantation; but I had now enjoyed liberty too long to submit quietly to the endurance of slavery. I had no sooner come here, than I began to devise ways of escaping again from the hands of my tyrants, and of making my way to the northern states.

The month of August was now approaching, which is a favourable season of the year to travel, on account of the abundance of food that is to be found in the corn fields and orchards; but I remembered the dreadful sufferings that I had endured in my former journey from the south, and determined, if possible, to devise some scheme of getting away, that would not subject me to such hardships.

After several weeks of consideration, I resolved to run away, go to some of the seaports, and endeavour to get a passage on board a vessel, bound to a northern city. With this view, I assumed the appearance of resignation and composure, under the new aspect of my fortune; and even went so far as to tell my new master that I lived more comfortably with him, in his cotton fields, than I had formerly done, on my own small farm in Maryland; though I believe my master did me the justice to give no credit to my assertions, on this subject.

From the moment I discovered in Maryland, that I had fallen into the hands of the brother of my former mistress, I gave up all hope of contesting his right to arrest me, with success, at law, as I supposed he had come with authority to reclaim me as the property of his sister; but after I had returned to Georgia, and had been at work some weeks on the plantation of my new master, I learned that he now claimed me as his own slave, and that he had reported he had purchased me in Baltimore. It was now clear to me that this man, having by some means learned the place of my residence, in Maryland, had kidnapped and now held me as his slave, without the colour of legal right; but complaint on my part was useless, and resistance vain.

I was again reduced to the condition of a common field slave, on a cotton plantation in Georgia, and compelled to subsist on the very scanty and coarse food, allowed to the southern slaves. I had been absent from Georgia, almost twenty years, and in that period, great changes had doubtlessly taken place in the face of the country, as well as in the condition of human society.

I had never been in Milledgeville, until I was brought there by the man who had kidnapped me in Maryland; and I was now a slave among entire strangers, and had no friend to give me the consolation of kind words, such as I had formerly received from my master in Morgan county. The plantation on which I was now a slave, had formerly belonged to the father of my mistress; and some of my fellow-slaves had been well acquainted with her, in her youth. From these people I learned, that after the death of my master, and my flight from Georgia, my mistress had become the wife of a second husband, who had removed with her to the state of Louisiana, more than fifteen years ago.

After ascertaining these facts, which proved beyond all doubt that my present master had no right whatsoever to me, in either law or justice, I determined, that before encountering the dangers and sufferings, that must necessarily attend my second flight from Georgia, I would attempt to claim the protection of the laws of the country, and try to get myself discharged from the unjust slavery in which I was now held. For this purpose, I went to Milledgeville, one Sunday, and inquired for a lawyer, of a black man whom I met in the street. This person told me that his master was a lawyer, and went with me to his house.

The lawyer, after talking to me some time, told me that my master was his client, and that he therefore could not undertake my cause; but referred me to a young gentleman, who he said would do my business for me. Accordingly to this young man I went, and after relating my whole story to him, he told me that he believed he could not do any thing for me, as I had no witnesses to prove my freedom.

I rejoined, that it seemed hard that I must be compelled to prove myself a freeman: and that it would appear more consonant to reason, that my master should prove me to be a slave. He, however, assured me that this was not the law of Georgia, where every man of colour was presumed to be a slave, until he could prove that he was free. He then told me that if I expected him to talk to me, I must give him a fee; whereupon I gave him all the money I had been able to procure, since my arrival in the country, which was two dollars and seventy-five cents.

When I offered him this money, the lawyer tossed his head, and said such a trifle was not worth accepting; but nevertheless he took it, and then asked me if I could get some more money before the next Sunday. That if I could get another dollar, he would issue a writ and have me brought before the court; but if he succeeded in getting me set free, I must engage to serve him a year. To these conditions I agreed, and signed a paper which the lawyer wrote, and which was signed by two persons as witnesses.

The brother of my pretended master, was yet living in this neighbourhood, and the lawyer advised me to have him brought forward, as a witness, to prove that I was not the slave of my present pretended owner.

On the Wednesday following my visit to Milledgeville, the sheriff came to my master's plantation, and took me from the field to the house, telling me as I walked beside him, that he had a writ which commanded him to take me to Milledgeville. Instead, however, of obeying the command of his writ, when we arrived at the house, he took a bond of my master that he would produce me at the court-house on the next day, Friday, and then rode away, leaving me at the mercy of my kidnapper.

Since I had been on this plantation, I had never been whipped, although all the other slaves, of whom there were more than fifty, were frequently flogged without any apparent cause. I had all along attributed my exemption from the lash to the fears of my master. He knew I had formerly run away from his sister, on account of her cruelty, and his own savage conduct to me; and I believed that he was still apprehensive that a repetition of his former barbarity might produce the same effect that it had done twenty years before.

His evil passions were like fire covered with ashes, concealed, not extinguished. He now found that I was determined to try to regain my liberty at all events, and the sheriff was no sooner gone, than the overseer was sent for, to come from the field, and I was tied up and whipped, with the long lashed negro whip, until I fainted, and was carried in a state of insensibility, to my lodgings in the quarter. It was night when I recovered my understanding, sufficiently to be aware of my true situation. I now found that my wounds had been oiled, and that I was wrapped in a piece of clean linen cloth; but for several days I was unable to leave my bed. When Friday came, I was not taken to Milledgeville, and afterwards learned that my master reported to the court, that I had been taken ill, and was not able to leave the house. The judge asked no questions as to the cause of my illness.

At the end of two weeks, I was taken to Milledgeville, and carried before a judge, who first asked a few questions of my master, as to the length of time that he had owned me, and the place where he had purchased me. He stated in my presence that he had purchased me, with several others, at public auction, in the city of Baltimore, and had paid five hundred and ten dollars for me. I was not permitted to speak to the court, much less to contradict this falsehood in the manner it deserved.

The brother of my master was then called as a witness, by my lawyer; but the witness refused to be sworn or examined, on account of his interest in me, as his slave. In support of his refusal, he produced a bill of sale from my master to himself, for an equal, undivided half part of the slave Charles. This bill of sale was dated several weeks previous to the time of trial, and gave rise to an argument between the opposing lawyers, that continued until the court adjourned in the evening.

On the next morning I was again brought into court, and the judge now delivered his opinion, which was that the witness could not be compelled to give evidence in a cause to which he was really, though not nominally, a party.

The court then proceeded to give judgment in the cause now before it, and declared that the law was well settled in Georgia, that every negro was presumed to be a slave, until he proved his freedom by the clearest evidence. That where a negro was found in the custody or keeping of a white man, the law declared that white man to be his master, without any evidence on the subject. But the case before the court, was exceedingly plain and free from all doubt or difficulty. Here the master has brought this slave into the state of Georgia, as his property, has held him as a slave ever since, and still holds him as a slave. The title of the master in this case, is the best title that a man can have to any property, and the order of the court is that the slave Charles be returned to the custody of his master.

I was immediately ordered to return home, and from this time until I left the plantation, my life was a continual torment to me. The overseer often came up to me in the field, and gave me several lashes with his long whip, over my naked back, through mere wantonness; and I was often compelled, after I had done my day's work in the field, to cut wood, or perform some other labour at the house, until long after dark. My sufferings were too great to be borne long by any human creature; and to a man who had once tasted the sweets of liberty, they were doubly tormenting.

There was nothing in the form of danger that could intimidate me, if the road on which I had to encounter it, led me to freedom. That season of the year, most favourable to my escape from bondage, had at length arrived. The corn in the fields was so far grown, as to be fit for roasting; the peaches were beginning to ripen, and the sweet potatoes were large enough to be eaten; but notwithstanding all this, the difficulties that surrounded me were greater than can easily be imagined by any one who has never been a slave in the lower country of Georgia.

In the first place I was almost naked, having no other clothes than a ragged shirt of tow cloth, and a pair of old trousers of the same material, with an old woollen jacket that I had brought with me from home. In addition to this, I was closely watched every evening, until I had finished the labour assigned me, and then I was locked up in a small cabin by myself for the night.

This cabin was really a prison, and had been built for the purpose of confining such of the slaves of this estate, as were tried in the evening, and sentenced to be whipped in the morning. It was built of strong oak logs, hewn square, and dovetailed together at the corners. It had no window in it; but as the logs did not fit very close together, there was never any want of air in this jail, in which I had been locked up every night since my trial before the court.

On Sundays I was permitted to go to work in the fields, with the other people who worked on that day, if I chose so to do; but at this time I was put under the charge of an old African negro, who was instructed to give immediate information, if I attempted to leave the field. To escape on Sunday was impossible, and there seemed to be no hope of getting out of my sleeping room, the door of which was made of strong pine plank.

Fortune at length did for me that which I had not been able to accomplish, by the greatest efforts, for myself. The lock that was on the door of my nightly prison, was a large stock lock, and had been clumsily fitted on the door, so that the end of the lock pressed against the door-case, and made it difficult to shut the door even in dry weather. When the weather was damp, and the wood was swollen with moisture, it was not easy to close the door at all.

Late in the month of September, the weather became cloudy, and much rain fell. The clouds continued to obscure the heavens for four or five days. One evening, when I was ordered to my house, as it was called, the overseer followed me without a light, although it was very dark. When I was in the house, he pushed the door after me, with all his strength. The violence of the effort caused the door to pass within the case at the top, for one or two feet, and this held it so fast that he could not again pull it open.

Supposing in the extreme darkness, that the door was shut, he turned the

key; and the bolt of the lock passing on the outside of the staple intended to receive it, completely deceived him. He then withdrew the key, and went away.
Soon after he was gone, I went to the door, and feeling with my hands, ascertained that it was not shut. An opportunity now presented itself for me to escape
from my prison-house, with a prospect of being able to be so far from my master's residence before morning, that none could soon overtake me, even should
the course of my flight be ascertained. Waiting quietly, until every one about the
quarter had ceased to be heard, I applied one of my feet to the door, and giving
it a strong push, forced it open.

The world was now all before me, but the darkness was so profound, as to
obscure from my vision the largest objects, even a house, at the distance of a few
yards. But dark as it was, necessity compelled me to leave the plantation without delay, and knowing only the great road that led to Milledgeville, amongst
the various roads of this country, I set off at a brisk walk on this public highway,
assured that no one could apprehend me in so dark a night.

It was only about seven miles to Milledgeville, and when I reached that
town several lights were burning in the windows of the houses; but keeping on
directly through the village, I neither saw nor heard any person in it, and after
gaining the open country, my first care was to find some secure place where shelter could be found for the next day; but no appearance of thick woods was to be
seen for several miles, and two or three hours must have elapsed before a forest
of sufficient magnitude was found to answer my purposes.

It was perhaps three o'clock in the morning, when I took refuge in a thick
and dismal swamp that lay on the right hand of the road, intending to remain
here until daylight, and then look out for a secret place to conceal myself in, during the day. Hitherto, although the night was so extremely dark, it had not rained
any, but soon after my halt in the swamp, the rain began to fall in floods, rather
than in showers, which made me as wet as if I had swum a river.

Daylight at length appeared, but brought with it very little mitigation of
my sufferings; for the swamp, in which my hiding-place was, lay in the midst of
a well-peopled country, and was surrounded, on all sides, by cotton and corn
fields, so close to me, that the open spaces of the cleared land could be seen from
my position. It was dangerous to move, lest some one should see me; and painful
to remain without food, when hunger was consuming me.

My resting place, in the swamp, was within view of the road; and, soon after sunrise, although it continued to rain fast, numerous horsemen were seen
passing along the road by the way that had led me to the swamp. There was little doubt on my mind, that these people were in search of me, and the sequel
proved that my surmises were well founded. It rained throughout this day, and
the fear of being apprehended by those who came in pursuit of me, confined me
to the swamp, until after dark the following evening, when I ventured to leave
the thicket, and return to the high road, the bearing of which it was impossible
for me to ascertain, on account of the dense clouds that obscured the heavens.
All that could be done in my situation, was to take care not to follow that end
of the road which had led me to the swamp. Turning my back once more upon
Milledgeville, and walking at a quick pace, every effort was made to remove my-

self, as far as possible this night, from the scene of suffering, for which that swamp will be always memorable in my mind.

The rain had ceased to fall at the going down of the sun; and the darkness of this second night, was not so great as that of the first had been. This circumstance was regarded by me, as a happy presage of the final success that awaited my undertaking. Events proved that I was no prophet; for the dim light of this night, was the cause of the dreadful misfortune that awaited me.

In a former part of this volume, the reader is made acquainted with the deep interest that is taken by all the planters, far and wide, around the plantation from which a slave has escaped, by running away. Twenty years had wrought no change in favour of the fugitive; nor had the feuds and dissensions, that agitate and distract the communities of white men, produced any relaxation in the friendship that they profess to feel, and really do feel, for each other, on a question of so much importance to them all.

More than twenty miles of road had been left behind me this night; and it must have been two or three o'clock in the morning, when, as I was passing a part of the road that led through a dense pine grove, where the trees on either side grew close to the wheel tracks, five or six men suddenly rushed upon me, from both sides of the road, and with loud cries of "Kill him! kill him!" accompanied with oaths and opprobrious language, seized me, dragged me to the ground, and bound me fast with a long cord, which was wrapped round my arms and body, so as to confine my hands below my hips.

In this condition, I was driven, or rather dragged, about two miles to a kind of tavern or public house, that stood by the side of the road; where my captors were joined, soon after daylight, by at least twenty of their companions, who had been out all night waiting and watching for me, on the other roads of this part of the country. Those who had taken me were loudly applauded by their fellows; and the whole party passed the morning in drinking, singing songs, and playing cards, at this house. At breakfast time, they gave me a large cake of corn bread, and some sour milk, for breakfast.

About ten o'clock in the morning, my master arrived at the tavern, in company with two or three other gentlemen, all strangers to me. My master, when he came into my presence, looked at me, and said, "Well, Charles, you had bad luck in running away this time;" and immediately asked aloud, what any person would give for me. One man, who was slightly intoxicated, said he would give four hundred dollars for me. Other bids followed, until my price was soon up to five hundred and eighty dollars, for which I was stricken off, by my master himself, to a gentleman, who immediately gave his note for me, and took charge of me as his property.

---

## CHAPTER XXVI.

THE name of my new master was Jones, a planter, who was only a visiter in this part of the country; his residence being about fifty miles down the country. The next day, my new master set off with me to the place of his residence; permitting me to walk behind him, as he rode on horseback, and leaving me entirely unshackled. I was resolved, that as my owner treated me with so much liberality, the trust he reposed in me should not be broken until after we had reached his home; though the determination of again running away, and attempting to escape from Georgia, never abandoned me for a moment.

The country through which we passed, on our journey, was not rich. The soil was sandy, light, and, in many places, much exhausted by excessive tillage. The timber, in the woods where the ground was high, was almost exclusively pine; but many swamps, and extensive tracts of low ground intervened, in which maple, gum, and all the other trees common to such land in the south, abounded.

No improvement in the condition of the slaves on the plantations, was here perceptible; but it appeared to me, that there was now even a greater want of good clothes, amongst the slaves on the various plantations that we passed, than had existed twenty years before. Everywhere, the overseers still kept up the same custom of walking in the fields with the long whip, that has been elsewhere described; and everywhere, the slaves proved, by the husky appearance of their skins, and the dry, sunburnt aspect of their hair, that they were strangers to animal food.

On the second day of our journey, in the evening, we arrived at the residence of my master; about eighty miles from Savannah. The plantation, which had now become the place of my residence, was not large: containing only about three hundred acres of cleared land, and having on it, about thirty working slaves of all classes.

It was now the very midst of the season of picking cotton, and, at the end of twenty years from the time of my first flight, I again had a daily task assigned me, with the promise of half a cent a pound, for all the cotton I should pick, beyond my day's work. Picking cotton, like every other occupation requiring active manipulation, depends more upon sleight, than strength; and I was not now able to pick so much in a day, as I was once able to do.

My master seemed to be a man ardently bent on the acquisition of wealth, and came into the field, where we were at work, almost every day; frequently remonstrating, in strong language, with the overseer, because he did not get more work done.

Our rations, on this place, were a half peck of corn per week; in addition to which, we had rather more than a peck of sweet potatoes allowed to each person.

Our provisions were distributed to us on every Sunday morning by the overseer; but my master was generally present, either to see that justice was done to us, or that injustice was not done to himself.

When I had been here about a week, my master came into the field one day, and, in passing near me, stopped and told me, that I had now fallen into good hands, as it was his practice not to whip his people much. That he, in truth, never whipped them, nor suffered his overseer to whip them, except in flagrant cases. That he had discovered a mode of punishment much more mild, and, at the same time, much more effectual, than flogging; and that he governed his negroes exclusively under this mode of discipline. He then told me, that when I came home in the evening, I must come to the house; and that he would then make me acquainted with the principles upon which he chastised his slaves.

Going to the house in the evening, according to orders, my master showed me a pump, set in a well in which the water rose within ten feet of the surface of the ground. The spout of this pump, was elevated at least thirteen feet above the earth, and when the water was to be drawn from it, the person who worked the handle ascended by a ladder to the proper station. The water in this well, although so near the surface, was very cold; and the pump discharged it in a large stream. One of the women employed in the house, had committed some offence for which she was to be punished; and the opportunity was embraced of exhibiting to me, the effect of this novel mode of torture upon the human frame. The woman was stripped quite naked, and tied to a post that stood just under the stream of water, as it fell from the spout of the pump. A lad was then ordered to ascend the ladder, and pump water upon the head and shoulders of the victim; who had not been under the waterfall more than a minute, before she began to cry and scream in a most lamentable manner. In a short time, she exerted her strength, in the most convulsive throes, in trying to escape from the post; but as the cords were strong, this was impossible. After another minute or a little more, her cries became weaker, and soon afterwards her head fell forward upon her breast; and then the boy was ordered to cease pumping the water. The woman was removed in a state of insensibility; but recovered her faculties in about an hour. The next morning she complained of lightness of head; but was able to go to work.

This punishment of the pump, as it is called, was never inflicted on me; and I am only able to describe it, as it has been described to me, by those who have endured it.

When the water first strikes the head and arms, it is not at all painful; but in a very short time, it produces the sensation that is felt when heavy blows are inflicted with large rods, of the size of a man's finger. This perception becomes more and more painful, until the skull bone and shoulder blades appear to be broken in pieces. Finally, all the faculties become oppressed; breathing becomes more and more difficult; until the eye-sight becomes dim, and animation ceases. This punishment is in fact a temporary murder; as all the pains are endured, that can be felt by a person who is deprived of life by being beaten with bludgeons;— but after the punishment of the pump, the sufferer is restored to existence by being laid in a bed, and covered with warm clothes. A giddiness of the head, and oppression of the breast, follows this operation, for a day or two, and sometimes longer. The object of calling me to be a witness of this new mode of torture, doubtlessly, was to intimidate me from running away; but like medicines administered by empirics, the spectacle had precisely the opposite effect, from that which it was expected to produce.

After my arrival on this estate, my intention had been to defer my elopement until the next year, before I had seen the torture inflicted on this unfortunate woman; but from that moment my resolution was unalterably fixed, to escape as quickly as possible. Such was my desperation of feeling, at this time, that I deliberated seriously upon the project of endeavouring to make my way southward, for the purpose of joining the Indians in Florida. Fortune reserved a more agreeable fate for me.

On the Saturday night after the woman was punished at the pump, I stole a yard of cotton bagging from the cotton-gin house, and converted it into a bag, by means of a coarse needle and thread that I borrowed of one of the black women. On the next morning, when our weekly rations were distributed to us, my portion was carefully placed in my bag, under pretence of fears that it would be stolen from me, if it was left open in the loft of the kitchen that I lodged in.

This day being Sunday, I did not go to the field to work as usual, on that day, but under pretence of being unwell, remained in the kitchen all day, to be the better prepared for the toils of the following night. After daylight had totally disappeared, taking my bag under my arm, under pretence of going to the mill to grind my corn, I stole softly across the cotton fields to the nearest woods, and taking an observation of the stars, directed my course to the eastward, resolved that in no event should any thing induce me to travel a single yard, on the high road, until at least one hundred miles from this plantation.

Keeping on steadily through the whole of this night, and meeting with no swamps, or briery thickets in my way, I have no doubt that before daylight, the plantation was more than thirty miles behind me.

Twenty years before this, I had been in Savannah, and noted at that time that great numbers of ships were in that port, taking in loading of cotton. My plan now was to reach Savannah, in the best way I could, by some means to be devised after my arrival in the city, to procure a passage to some of the northern cities.

When day appeared before me, I was in a large cotton field, and before the woods could be reached, it was gray dawn; but the forest bordering on the field was large and afforded me good shelter through the day, under the cover of a large thicket of swamp laurel, that lay at the distance of a quarter of a mile from the field. It now became necessary to kindle a fire, for all my stock of provisions, consisting of corn and potatoes, was raw and undressed. Less fortunate now than in my former flight, no fire apparatus was in my possession, and driven at last to the extremity, I determined to endeavour to produce fire by rubbing two sticks together, and spent at least two hours of incessant toil, in this vain operation, without the least prospect of success. Abandoning this project at length, I turned my thoughts to searching for a stone of some kind, with which to endeavour to extract fire from an old jack knife, that had been my companion in Maryland for more than three years. My labours were fruitless. No stone could be found in this swamp; and the day was passed in anxiety and hunger, a few raw potatoes being my only food.

Night at length came, and with it a renewal of my travelling labours. Avoiding with the utmost care, every appearance of a road, and pursuing my way until daylight, I must have travelled at least thirty miles this night. Awhile before day, in crossing a field, I fortunately came upon a bed of large pebbles, on the side of a hill. Several of these were deposited in my bag, which enabled me when day arrived to procure fire, with which I parched corn and roasted potatoes sufficient to subsist me for two or three days. On the fourth night of my journey, fortune directed me to a broad, open highway, that appeared to be much travelled.

Near the side of this road, I established my quarters for the day in a thick pine wood, for the purpose of making observations upon the people who travelled it, and of judging thence of the part of the country to which it led.

Soon after daylight, a wagon passed along, drawn by oxen, and loaded with bales of cotton; then followed some white men on horseback, and soon after sunrise, a whole train of wagons and carts, all loaded with bales of cotton, passed by, following the wagon first seen by me. In the course of the day, at least one hundred wagons and carts passed along this road, towards the south-east, all laden with cotton bales; and at least an equal number came towards the west, either laden with casks of various dimensions, or entirely empty. Numerous horsemen, many carriages, and great numbers of persons on foot, also passed to and fro on this road, in the course of the day.

All these indications satisfied me, that I must be near some large town, the seat of an extensive cotton market. The next consideration with me was to know how far it was to this town, for which purpose I determined to travel on the road, the succeeding night.

Lying in the woods, until about eleven o'clock, I rose, came to the road, and travelled it until within an hour of daylight, at which time the country around me appeared almost wholly clear of timber; and houses became much more numerous than they had been in the former part of my journey.

Things continued to wear this aspect until daylight, when I stopped, and sat down by the side of a high fence that stood beside the road. After remaining here a short time, a wagon laden with cotton, passed along, drawn by oxen, whose driver, a black man, asked me if I was going towards town. Being answered in the affirmative, he then asked me if I did not wish to ride in his wagon. I told him I had been out of town all night, and should be very thankful to him for a ride; at the same time ascending his wagon and placing myself in a secure and easy position, on the bags of cotton.

In this manner we travelled on for about two hours, when we entered the town of Savannah. In my situation there was no danger of any one suspecting me to be a runaway slave; for no runaway had ever been known to flee from the country, and seek refuge in Savannah.

The man who drove the wagon, passed through several of the principal streets of the city, and stopped his team before a large warehouse, standing on a wharf, looking into the river. Here I assisted my new friend to unload his cotton and when we were done, he invited me to share his breakfast with him, consisting of corn bread, roasted potatoes, and some cold boiled rice.

Whilst we were at our breakfast, a black man came along the street, and asked us if we knew where he could hire a hand, to help him to work a day or two. I at once replied that my master had sent me to town, to hire myself out for a few weeks, and that I was ready to go with him immediately. The joy I felt at finding employment, so overcame me, that all thought of my wages was forgotten. Bidding farewell to the man who had given me my breakfast, and thanking him in my heart for his kindness, I followed my new employer, who informed me that he had engaged to remove a thousand bales of cotton from a large warehouse, to the end of a wharf at which a ship lay, that was taking in the cotton as a load.

This man was a slave, but hired his time of his master at two hundred and fifty dollars a year, which he said he paid in monthly instalments. He did what he called job work, which consisted of undertaking jobs, and hiring men to work under him, if the job was too great to be performed by himself. In the present instance he had seven or eight black men, beside me, all hired to help him to remove the cotton in wheel-barrows, and lay it near the end of the wharf, when it was taken up by sailors and carried on board the ship, that was receiving it.

We continued working hard all day; and amongst the crew of the ship was a black man, with whom I resolved to become acquainted by some means. Accordingly at night, after we had quit our work, I went to the end of the wharf against which the ship lay moored, and stood there a long time, waiting for the black sailor to make his appearance on deck. At length my desires were gratified. He came upon the deck, and sat down near the main-mast, with a pipe in his mouth, which he was smoking with great apparent pleasure. After a few minutes, I spoke to him, for he had not yet seen me, as it appeared, and when he heard my voice, he rose up and came to the side of the ship near where I stood. We entered into conversation together, in the course of which he informed me that his home was in New-York; that he had a wife and several children there, but that he followed the sea for a livelihood, and knew no other mode of life. He also asked me where my master lived, and if Georgia had always been the place of my residence.

I deemed this a favourable opportunity of effecting the object I had in view, in seeking the acquaintance of this man, and told him at once that by law and justice I was a free man, but had been kidnapped near Baltimore, forcibly brought to Georgia, and sold there as a slave. That I was now a fugitive from my master, and in search of some means of getting back to my wife and children.

The man seemed moved by the account of my sufferings, and at the close of my narrative, told me he could not receive me on board the ship, as the captain had given positive orders to him, not to let any of the negroes of Savannah come on board, lest they should steal something belonging to the ship. He further told me that he was on watch, and should continue on deck two hours. That he was forced to take a turn of watching the ship every night, for two hours; but that his turn would not come the next night until after midnight.

I now begged him to enable me to secrete myself on board the ship, previous to the time of her sailing, so that I might be conveyed to Philadelphia, whither the ship was bound with her load of cotton. He at first received my application with great coldness, and said he would not do any thing contrary to the orders of the captain; but before we parted, he said he should be glad to assist me if he could, but that the execution of the plan proposed by me, would be attended with great dangers, if not ruin.

In my situation there was nothing too hazardous for me to undertake, and I informed him that if he would let me hide myself in the hold of the ship, amongst the bags of cotton, no one should ever know that he had any knowledge of the fact; and that all the danger, and all the disasters that might attend the affair, should fall exclusively on me. He finally told me to go away, and that he would think of the matter until the next day.

It was obvious that his heart was softened in my favour; that his feelings of compassion almost impelled him to do an act in my behalf, that was forbidden by his judgment, and his sense of duty to his employers. As the houses of the city were now closed, and I was a stranger in the place, I went to a wagon that stood in front of the warehouse, and had been unladen of the cotton that kind been brought in it, and creeping into it, made my bed with the driver, who permitted me to share his lodgings amongst some corn tops, that he had brought to feed his oxen.

When the morning came, I went again to the ship, and when the people came on deck, asked them for the captain, whom I should not have known by his dress, which was very nearly similar to that of the sailors. On being asked if he did not wish to hire a hand, to help to load his ship, he told me I might go to work amongst the men, if I chose, and he would pay me what I was worth.

My object was to procure employment on board the ship, and not to get wages; and in the course of this day I found means to enter the hold of the ship several times, and examine it minutely. The black sailor promised that he would not betray me, and that if I could find the means of escaping on board the ship he would not disclose it.

At the end of three days, the ship had taken in her loading, and the captain said in my presence, that he intended to sail the day after. No time was now to be lost, and asking the captain what he thought I had earned, he gave me three dollars, which was certainly very liberal pay, considering that during the whole time that I had worked for him, my fare had been the same as that of the sailors, who had as much as they could consume, of excellent food.

The sailors were now busy in trimming the ship, and making ready for sea, and observing, that this work required them to spend much time in the hold of the ship, I went to the captain and told him, that as he had paid me good wages, and treated me well, I would work with his people, the residue of this day, for my victuals and half a gallon of molasses; which he said he would give me. My first object now, was to get into the hold of the ship with those who were adjusting the cargo. The first time the men below called for aid, I went to them, and being there, took care to remain with them. Being placed at one side of the hold, for the purpose of packing the bags close to the ship's timbers, I so managed, as to leave a space between two of the bags, large enough for a man to creep in, and conceal himself. This cavity was near the opening in the centre of the hold, that was left to let men get down, to stow away the last of the bags that were put in. In this small hollow retreat amongst the bags of cotton, I determined to take my passage to Philadelphia, if by any means I could succeed in stealing on board the ship at night.

When the evening came, I went to a store near the wharf, and bought two jugs, one that held half a gallon, and the other, a large stone jug, holding more than three gallons. When it was dark, I filled my large jug with water; purchased twenty pounds of pilot bread[35] at a bakery, which I tied in a large handkerchief;

and taking my jugs in my hand, went on board the ship to receive my molasses of the captain, for the labour of the day. The captain was not on board, and a boy gave me the molasses; but, under pretence of waiting to see the captain, I sat down between two rows of cotton bales, that were stowed on deck. The night was very dark, and, watching a favourable opportunity, when the man on deck had gone forward, I succeeded in placing both my jugs upon the bags of cotton that rose in the hold, almost to the deck. In another moment, I glided down amongst the cargo; and lost no time in placing my jugs in the place provided for them, amongst the bales of cotton, beside the lair provided for myself.

Soon after I had taken my station for the voyage, the captain came on board, and the boy reported to him, that he had paid me off, and dismissed me. In a short time, all was quiet on board the ship, except the occasional tread of the man on watch. I slept none at all this night; the anxiety that oppressed me, preventing me from taking any repose.

Before day the captain was on deck, and gave orders to the seamen, to clear the ship for sailing, and to be ready to descend the river with the ebb tide, which was expected to flow at sunrise. I felt the motion of the ship when she got under weigh, and thought the time long before I heard the breakers of the ocean surging against her sides.

In the place where I lay, when the hatches were closed, total darkness prevailed; and I had no idea of the lapse of time, or of the progress we made, until, having at one period crept out into the open space, between the rows of cotton bags, which I have before described, I heard a man, who appeared from the sound of his voice to be standing on the hatch, call out and say, "That is Cape Hatteras." I had already come out of my covert, several times, into the open space; but the hatches were closed so tightly, as to exclude all light. It appeared to me that we had already been at sea a long time; but as darkness was unbroken with me, I could not make any computation of periods.

Soon after this, the hatch was opened, and the light was let into the hold. A man descended for the purpose of examining the state of the cargo; who returned in a short time. The hatch was again closed; and nothing of moment occurred from this time, until I heard and felt the ship strike against some solid body. In a short time I heard much noise, and a multitude of sounds of various kinds. All this satisfied me, that the ship was in some port; for I no longer heard the sound of the waves, nor perceived the least motion in the ship.

At length the hatch was again opened, and the light was let in upon me. My anxiety now was, to escape from the ship, without being discovered by any one; to accomplish which I determined to issue from the hold as soon as night came on, if possible. Waiting until sometime after daylight had disappeared, I ventured to creep to the hatchway, and raise my head above deck. Seeing no one on board, I crawled out of the hold, and stepped on board a ship that lay alongside of that in which I had come a passenger. Here a man seized me, and called me a thief, saying I had come to rob his ship; and it was with much difficulty that I prevailed upon him to let me go. He at length permitted me to go on the wharf; and I once more felt myself a freeman.

I did not know what city I was in; but as the sailors had all told me, at Savannah, that their ship was bound to Philadelphia, I had no doubt of being in that city. In going along the street, a black man met me, and I asked him if I was in Philadelphia. This question caused the stranger to laugh loudly: and he passed on without giving me any answer. Soon afterwards I met an old gentleman, with drab clothes on, as I could see by the light of the lamps. To him I propounded the same question, that had been addressed a few moments before to the black man. This time, however, I received a civil answer: being told that I was in Philadelphia.

This gentleman seemed concerned for me, either because of my wretched and ragged appearance, or because I was a stranger, and did not know where I was. Whether for the one cause or the other, I know not; but he told me to follow him, and led me to the house of a black man, not far off, whom he directed to take care of me until the morning. In this house I was kindly entertained all night, and when the morning came, the old gentleman in drab clothes returned, and brought with him an entire suit of clothes, not more than half worn, of which he made me a present, and gave me money to buy a hat and some muslin for a couple of shirts. He then turned to go away, and said, "I perceive that thee is a slave, and has run away from thy master. Thee can now go to work for thy living; but take care that they do not catch thee again." I then told him, that I had been a slave, and had twice run away and escaped from the state of Georgia. The gentleman seemed a little incredulous of that which I told him; but when I explained to him the cause of the condition in which he found me, he seemed to become more than ever interested in my fate. This gentleman, whose name I shall not publish, has always been a kind friend to me.

After remaining in Philadelphia a few weeks, I resolved to return to my little farm in Maryland, for the purpose of selling my property for as much as it would produce, and of bringing my wife and children to Pennsylvania.

On arriving in Baltimore, I went to a tavern keeper, whom I had formerly supplied with vegetables from my garden. This man appeared greatly surprised to see me; and asked me how I had managed to escape from my master in Georgia. I told him, that the man who had taken me to Georgia was not my master; but had kidnapped me, and carried me away by violence. The tavern keeper then told me, that I had better leave Baltimore as soon as possible, and showed me a hand-bill that was stuck up against the wall of his bar-room, in which a hundred and fifty dollars reward was offered for my apprehension. I immediately left this house, and fled from Baltimore that very night.

When I reached my former residence, I found a white man living in it, whom I did not know. This man, on being questioned by me, as to the time he had owned this place, and the manner in which he had obtained possession, informed me, that a black man had formerly lived here; but he was a runaway slave, and his master had come, the summer before, and carried him off. That the wife of the former owner of the house, was also a slave; and that her master had come about six weeks before the present time, and taken her and her children, and sold them in Baltimore to a slave-dealer from the south.

This man also informed me, that he was not in this neighbourhood at the time the woman and her children were carried away; but that he had received his information from a black woman, who lived half a mile off.

This black woman I was well acquainted with; she had been my neighbour, and I knew her to be my friend. She had been set free, some years before by a gentleman of this neighbourbood, and resided under his protection, on a part of his land. I immediately went to the house of this woman, who could scarcely believe the evidence of her own eyes, when she saw me enter her door. The first words she spoke to me were, "Lucy and her children have all been stolen away." At my request, she gave me the following account of the manner in which my wife and children, all of whom had been free from their birth, were seized and driven into southern slavery.

"A few weeks," said she, "after they took you away, and before Lucy had so far recovered from the terror produced by that event, as to remain in her house all night with her children, without some other company, I went one evening to stay all night with her; a kindness that I always rendered her, if no other person came to remain with her.

"It was late when we went to bed, perhaps eleven o'clock; and after we had been asleep some time, we were awakened by a loud rap at the door. At first we said nothing; but upon the rap being several times repeated, Lucy asked who was there. She was then told, in a voice that seemed by its sound to be that of a woman, to get up and open the door; adding, that the person without had something to tell her that she wished to hear. Lucy, supposing the voice to be that of a black woman, the slave of a lady living near, rose and opened the door; but, to our astonishment, instead of a woman coming in, four or five men rushed into the house, and immediately closed the door; at which one of the men stood, with his back against it, until the others made a light in the fire place, and proceeded deliberately to tie Lucy with a rope. Search was then made in the bed for the children; and I was found, and dragged out. This seemed to produce some consternation amongst the captors, whose faces were all black, but whose hair and visages were those of white men. A consultation was held amongst them, the object of which was to determine whether I should also be taken along with Lucy and the children, or be left behind, on account of the interest which my master was supposed to feel for me.

"It was finally agreed, that as it would be very dangerous to carry me off, lest my old master should cause pursuit to be made after them, they would leave me behind, and take only Lucy and the children. One of the number then said it would not do to leave me behind, and at liberty, as I would immediately go and give intelligence of what I had seen, and if the affair should be discovered by the members of the abolition society, before they had time to get out of Maryland, they would certainly be detected and punished for the crimes they were committing.

"It was finally resolved to tie me with cords, to one of the logs of the house, gag me by tying a rope in my mouth, and confining it closely at the back of my neck. They immediately confined me, and then took the children from the bed. The oldest boy they tied to his mother, and compelled them to go out of the house together. The three youngest children were then taken out of bed, and carried off in the hands of the men who had tied me to the log. I never saw nor heard any more of Lucy or her children.

"For myself, I remained in the house, the door of which was carefully closed, and fastened after it was shut, until the second night after my confinement, without any thing to eat or drink. On the second night some unknown persons came and cut the cords that bound me, when I returned to my own cabin."

This intelligence almost deprived me of life; it was the most dreadful of all the misfortunes that I had ever suffered. It was now clear that some slave-dealer had come in my absence, and seized my wife and children as slaves, and sold them to such men as I had served in the south. They had now passed into hopeless bondage, and were gone forever beyond my reach. I myself was advertised as a fugitive slave, and was liable to be arrested at each moment, and dragged back to Georgia. I rushed out of my own house in despair and returned to Pennsylvania with a broken heart.

For the last few years, I have resided about fifty miles from Philadelphia, where I expect to pass the evening of my life, in working hard for my subsistence, without the least hope of ever again seeing my wife and children:—fearful, at this day, to let my place of residence be known, lest even yet it may be supposed, that as an article of property, I am of sufficient value to be worth pursuing in my old age.

## THE END.

1. Although the page count of the first edition of Ball's narrative (four hundred) is lower than that of certain other narratives (Olaudah Equiano's, Frederick Douglass's *My Bondage and My Freedom,* and Samuel Ringgold Ward's), if one considers the number of words per page, Ball's turns out the longest.

2. Starling, *Slave Narrative,* 226; Foster, *Witnessing Slavery,* 143.

3. "Life and Adventures," 6–8.

4. Starling, *Slave Narrative,* 227.

5. Fisher, *Slavery* [2d ed.], i–ii.

6. Nelson, *Negro Character,* 61.

7. Starling, *Slave Narrative,* 232.

8. Loggins, *Negro Author,* 99; Blassingame, *Slave Testimony,* xxiii–xxvi; Jackson, *History,* 132.

9. Fisher, *Slavery* [2d ed.], i–ii.

10. The version of Ball's narrative republished herein reflects the text of the 1836 edition, but the orthography and punctuation of the 1837 edition.

11. On the west side of Chesapeake Bay, about twenty miles southeast of Washington, D.C.

12. A cord interwoven in a bedstead, supporting the bed or mattress.

13. A stiff whip or switch.

14. Tobacco worms are caterpillars, larvae of hawkmoths.

15. John Randolph (1773–1833). His estate, "Roanoke," included more than 8,000 acres of land and nearly 400 slaves.

16. Wade Hampton (c. 1752–1835) was the wealthiest planter of his day, a Revolutionary War hero, and a U.S. congressman. Colonel William Fitzhugh (1741–1809) was a planter and Virginia delegate to the Continental Congress.

17. Francis Marion (1732–95), also known as "the Swamp Fox," commanded a regiment of South Carolina militia.

18. Coits is a game in which the players throw a heavy, flattish ring of iron at a pin stuck in the ground.

19. Chinaberry tree (*Melia azedarach*).

20. Blassingame (*Slave Testimony*, xxv) claims, "In all probability, Ball's South Carolina owner was General Wade Hampton. The description of Hampton by his contemporaries closely parallels that of Ball. . . . Hampton's account books and travelers' descriptions of his estate verify many details of Ball's account of the plantation regimen." However, Ball's account of the significant events in his master's life does not at all agree with the details of Hampton's; e.g., his death date.

21. Eli Whitney (1765–1825) invented the cotton gin in 1793.

22. An attachment to the end of a whip that produces a cracking sound.

23. Large mosquitoes or other biting insects.

24. The heart, liver, and other edible innards.

25. Small, flat-bottomed boats.

26. Golden club, a perennial herb (*Orontium aquaticum*).

27. The importation of slaves from Africa to the United States was halted in 1808.

28. The Big Dipper.

29. A farmyard containing stacks of corn, hay, etc.

30. A congressional act of March 3, 1813, authorized the enlistment of free blacks in the U.S. Navy.

31. Commodore Joshua Barney (1759–1818) commanded a flotilla in Chesapeake Bay from August 1813 to August 1814. The flotilla, however, got bottled up in the Patuxent River while being pursued by the British, and Barney was forced to destroy his boats on August 22, 1814. At the disastrous battle of Bladensburg two days later, Barney directed the fire of a battery of five guns, and his troops—unlike the majority of American soldiers, led by Maryland Governor Levin Winder (1757–1819)—courageously tried to prevent the British, under General Robert Ross (1766–1814), from advancing on Washington, D.C., that night. Needless to say, they failed, and Ross sacked and burned the capitol.

32. A ship carrying seventy-four guns.

33. Many were enlisted by the British as Colonial Marines and garrisoned on Tangier Island, near the eastern shore of Chesapeake Bay. After the war, they were resettled in Trinidad. Weiss, *Trinidad,* 8–19.

34. Andrew Jackson.

35. Hardtack, a saltless, hard bread.

MOSES ROPER

MOSES ROPER (1816–?) was the first fugitive slave to widely publicize his experiences to British audiences. His horrifyingly vivid and popular narrative was probably written with some assistance from the Reverend Thomas Price (1802–68), the editor of the short-lived British journal *Slavery in America* (1836–37) and author of *The History of Protestant Nonconformity in England*. *A Narrative of the Adventures and Escape of Moses Roper* was first published in London in 1837 and Philadelphia in 1838. Over the next twenty years it went through ten editions, many of them substantially expanded, and was even translated into Welsh;[1] an 1844 edition announced it was the twenty-eighth thousand copy printed. The narrative is notable for Roper's explicit concern with questions of truth-telling, and for the nightmarish and ingenious tortures practiced upon him by his master Mr. Gooch, whose name soon became a popular symbol for the worst kind of slaveholder.[2]

Roper had been giving speeches on his slave experiences since his arrival in England in 1835. In 1844 he wrote to the Committee of the British and Foreign Anti-Slavery Society:

> I have been in England now rather more than eight years, and have employed myself during that period partly in pursuing my studies and partly lecturing through the country, & by the sale of my book (the only remuneration I received for my lectures), have paid for my education and supported myself. I have addressed meetings in upwards of two thousand towns and villages as I often lectured twice in one day. . . . Thousand[s] I have addressed in *remote places,* did not know there was such a curse as Slavery in America.[3]

In 1839, Roper had married a white woman from Bristol, and in this letter he begged the Committee for assistance in moving his wife, child, and himself to the Cape of Good Hope in Africa, where he hoped to purchase a farm with the proceeds from his *Narrative*. He moved instead to West Canada that year. He returned to England at least twice thereafter, in 1846 and 1854.[4]

# A NARRATIVE

## OF THE

# ADVENTURES AND ESCAPE

## OF

# MOSES ROPER,

### FROM

# AMERICAN SLAVERY;

### WITH A PREFACE

## BY THE REV. T. PRICE, D.D.

---

"Slaves cannot breathe in England; if their lungs
Receive our air, that moment they are free:
They touch our country, and their shackles fall.
That's noble! and bespeaks a nation proud
And jealous of the blessing. Spread it then,
And let it circulate through every vein."[5]

---

## PHILADELPHIA:

## MERRIHEW & GUNN, PRINTERS.

1838.

# PREFACE.

THE following narrative was to have appeared under the auspices of the Rev. Dr. Morison,[6] of Chelsea, whose generous exertions on behalf of Moses Roper have entitled him to the admiration and gratitude of every philanthropist. But the illness of the doctor having prevented him from reading the manuscript, I have been requested to supply his lack of service. To this request I assent reluctantly, as the narrative would have derived a fuller sanction and wider currency, had circumstances permitted the original purpose to be carried out. Moses Roper was introduced to Dr. Morison by an eminent American abolitionist, in a letter, dated November 9th, 1835, in which honourable testimony is borne to his general character, and the soundness of his religious profession. "He has spent about ten days in my house," says Dr. Morison's correspondent; "I have watched him attentively, and have no doubt that he is an excellent young man, that he possesses uncommon intelligence, sincere piety, and a strong desire to preach the gospel. He can tell you his own story better than any one else; and I believe that if he should receive an education, he would be able to counteract the false and wicked misrepresentations of American slavery, which are made in your country by our Priests and Levites who visit you."

Dr. Morison, as might have been anticipated from his well-known character, heartily responded to the appeal of his American correspondent. He sent his letter to the Patriot newspaper, remarking in his own communication to the editor, "I have seen Moses Roper, the fugitive slave. He comes to this country, as you will perceive, well authenticated as to character and religious standing; and my anxiety is, that the means may forthwith be supplied by some of your generous readers, for placing him in some appropriate seminary, for the improvement of his mind, that he may be trained for future usefulness in the church. His thirst for knowledge is great; and he may yet become a most important agent in liberating his country from the curse of slavery."

Moses Roper brought with him to this country several other testimonies, from persons residing in different parts of the States; but it is unnecessary to extend this preface by quoting them. They all speak the same language, and bear unequivocal witness to his sobriety, intelligence, and honesty.

He is now in the land of freedom, and is earnestly desirous of availing himself of the advantages of his position. His great ambition is to be qualified for usefulness amongst his own people; and the progress he has already made justifies the belief that if the means of education can be secured for a short time longer, he will be eminently qualified to instruct the children of Africa in the truths of the gospel of Christ. He has drawn up the following narrative, partly with the hope of being assisted in this legitimate object, and partly to engage the sympathies of our countrymen on behalf of his oppressed brethren. I trust that he will not be disappointed in either of these expectations, but that all the friends of humanity and religion among us will cheerfully render him their aid, by promoting the circulation of his volume. Should this be done to the extent that is quite possible, the difficulties now lying in his way will be removed.

Of the narrative itself, it is not necessary that I should say much. It is his own production, and carries with it internal evidence of truth. Some of its statements will probably startle those readers who are unacquainted with the details of the slave system; but no such feeling will be produced in any who are conversant with the practice of slavery, whether in America or our own colonies. There is no vice too loathsome—no passion too cruel or remorseless, to be engendered by this horrid system. It brutalizes all who administer it; and seeks to efface the likeness of God, stamped on the brow of its victims. It makes the former class demons, and reduces the latter to the level of brutes.

I could easily adduce from the records of our own slave system, as well as from those of America, several instances of equal atrocity to any which Moses Roper has recorded. But this is unnecessary; and I shall therefore merely add the unqualified expression of my own confidence in the truth of his narrative, and my strong recommendation of it to the patronage of the British public.

THOMAS PRICE.

HACKNEY, July 22d.

# INTRODUCTION.

THE determination of laying this little narrative before the public did not arise from any desire to make myself conspicuous, but with the view of exposing the cruel system of slavery, as will here be laid before my readers; from the urgent calls of nearly all the friends to whom I had related any part of the story, and also from the recommendation of anti-slavery meetings, which I have attended, through the suggestion of many warm friends of the cause of the oppressed.

The general narrative, I am aware, may seem to many of my readers, and especially to those who have not been before put in possession of the actual features of this accursed system, somewhat at variance with the dictates of humanity. But the facts related here do not come before the reader unsubstantiated by collateral evidence, nor highly colored to the disadvantage of cruel taskmasters.

My readers may be put in possession of facts respecting this system which equal in cruelty my own narrative, on an authority which may be investigated with the greatest satisfaction. Besides which, this little book will not be confined to a small circle of my own friends in London, or even in England. The slave-holder, the colonizationist, and even Mr. Gooch himself, will be able to obtain this document, and be at liberty to draw from it whatever they are honestly able, in order to set me down as the tool of a party. Yea, even friend Breckenridge, a gentleman known at Glasgow, will be able to possess this, and to draw from it all the forcible arguments on his own side, which in his wisdom, honesty, and candor he may be able to adduce.[7]

The earnest wish to lay this narrative before my friends as an impartial statement of facts, has led me to develope some part of my conduct which I now deeply deplore. The ignorance in which the poor slaves are kept by their masters, precludes almost the possibility of their being alive to any moral duties.

With these remarks, I leave the statement before the public. May this little volume be the instrument of opening the eyes of the ignorant to this system; of convincing the wicked, cruel, and hardened slave-holder; and of befriending generally the cause of oppressed humanity.

MOSES ROPER.

LONDON, June 28, 1837.

# ESCAPE, &c.

I WAS born in North Carolina, in Caswell county,[8] I am not able to tell in what year or month. What I shall now relate is, what was told me by my mother and grandmother. A few months before I was born, my father married my mother's young mistress. As soon as my father's wife heard of my birth, she sent one of my mother's sisters to see whether I was white or black, and when my aunt had seen me, she returned back as soon as she could, and told her mistress that I was white, and resembled Mr. Roper very much. Mr. R.'s wife being not pleased with this report, she got a large club stick and knife, and hastened to the place in which my mother was confined. She went into my mother's room with full intention to murder me with her knife and club, but as she was going to stick the knife into me, my grandmother happening to come in, caught the knife and saved my life. But as well as I can recollect from what my mother told me, my father sold her and myself soon after her confinement. I cannot recollect any thing that is worth notice till I was six or seven years old. My mother being half white, and my father a white man, I was at that time very white. Soon after I was six or seven years of age, my mother's old master died, that is, my father's wife's father. All his slaves had to be divided among the children.* I have mentioned before of my father disposing of me; I am not sure whether he exchanged me and my mother for another slave or not, but think it very likely he did exchange me with one of his wife's brothers or sisters, because I remember when my mother's old master died, I was living with my father's wife's brother-in-law, whose name was Mr. Durham. My mother was drawn with the other slaves.

The way they divide their slaves is this: they write the names of different slaves on a small piece of paper, and put it into a box, and let them all draw. I think that Mr. Durham drew my mother, and Mr. Fowler drew me, so we were separated a considerable distance, I cannot say how far. My resembling my father so very much, and being whiter than the other slaves, caused me to be soon sold to what they call a negro trader, who took me to the southern states of America, several hundred miles from my mother. As well as I can recollect, I was then about six years old. The trader, Mr. Michael, after travelling several hundred miles and selling a good many of his slaves, found he could not sell me very well, (as I was so much whiter than the other slaves were,) for he had been trying several months—left me with a Mr. Sneed, who kept a large boarding-house, who took me to wait at table, and sell me if he could. I think I stayed with Mr.

---

*Slaves are usually a part of the marriage portion, but lent rather than given, to be returned to the estate at the decease of the father, in order that they may be divided equally among his children.

Sneed about a year, but he could not sell me. When Mr. Michael had sold his slaves, he went to the north and bought up another drove, and returned to the south with them, and sent his son-in-law into Washington, in Georgia, after me; so he came and took me from Mr. Sneed, and met his father-in-law with me, in a town called Lancaster,⁹ with his drove of slaves. We stayed in Lancaster a week, because it was court week, and there were a great many people there, and it was a good opportunity for selling the slaves, and there he was enabled to sell me to a gentleman, Dr. Jones, who was both a doctor and a cotton planter. He took me into his shop to beat up and to mix medicines, which was not a very hard employment, but I did not keep it long, as the doctor soon sent me to his cotton plantation, that I might be burnt darker by the sun. He sent for me to be with a tailor to learn the trade, but all the journeymen being white men, Mr. Bryant, the tailor, did not let me work in the shop; I cannot say whether it was the prejudice of his journeymen in not wanting me to sit in the shop with them, or whether Mr. Bryant wanted to keep me about the house to do the domestic work instead of teaching me the trade. After several months my master came to know how I got on with the trade; I am not able to tell Mr. Bryant's answer, but it was either that I could not learn, or that his journeymen were not willing that I should sit in the shop with them. I was only once in the shop all the time I was there, and then only for an hour or two, before his wife called me out to do some other work. So my master took me home, and as he was going to send a load of cotton to Camden,¹⁰ about forty miles distance, he sent me with the bales of cotton to be sold with it, where I was soon sold to a gentleman named Allen, but Mr. Allen soon exchanged me for a female slave to please his wife. The traders who bought me were named Cooper and Linsey, who took me for sale, but could not sell me, people objecting to my being rather white. They then took me to the city of Fayetteville, North Carolina, where he swopt me for a boy that was blacker than me, to Mr. Smith, who lived several miles off.

I was with Mr. Smith nearly a year. I arrived at the first knowledge of my age when I lived with him. I was then between twelve and thirteen years old; it was when President Jackson was elected the first time, and he has been president eight years, so I must be nearly twenty-one years of age. At this time I was quite a small boy, and was sold to Mr. Hodge, a negro trader. Here I began to enter into hardships. After travelling several hundred miles, Mr. Hodge sold me to Mr. Gooch, the cotton planter, Cashaw county,¹¹ South Carolina; he purchased me at a town called Liberty Hill, about three miles from his home. As soon as he got home, he immediately put me on his cotton plantation to work, and put me under overseers, gave me allowance of meat and bread with the other slaves, which was not half enough for me to live upon, and very laborious work. Here my heart was almost broke with grief at leaving my fellow slaves. Mr. Gooch did not mind my grief, for he flogged me nearly every day, and very severely. Mr. Gooch bought me for his son-in-law, Mr. Hammans, about five miles from his residence. This man had but two slaves besides myself; he treated me very kindly for a week or two, but in summer, when cotton was ready to hoe, he gave me task work connected with this department, which I could not get done, not having worked on cotton farms before. When I failed in my task, he commenced flogging me, and set me to work without any shirt in the cotton field, in a very hot sun, in the month of July. In August, Mr. Condell, his overseer, gave me a task at pulling fodder. Having finished my task before night, I left the field; the rain came on, which soaked the fodder. On discovering this, he threatened to flog me for not getting in the fodder before the rain came. This was the first time I attempted to run away, knowing that I should get a flogging. I was then between thirteen and fourteen years of age. I ran away to the woods half naked; I was caught by a slave-holder, who put me in Lancaster jail. When they put slaves in jail, they advertise for their masters to own them; but if the master does not claim his slave in six months from the time of imprisonment, the slave is sold for jail fees. When the slave runs away, the master always adopts a more rigorous system of flogging; this was the case in the present instance. After this, having determined from my youth to gain my freedom, I made several attempts, was caught and got a severe flogging of one hundred lashes each time. Mr. Hammans was a very severe and cruel master, and his wife still worse; she used to tie me up and flog me while naked.

After Mr. Hammans saw that I was determined to die in the woods, and not live with him, he tried to obtain a piece of land from his father-in-law, Mr. Gooch; not having the means of purchasing it, he exchanged me for the land.

As soon as Mr. Gooch had possession of me again, knowing that I was averse to going back to him, he chained me by the neck to his chaise. In this manner he took me to his home at MacDaniel's Ferry, in the county of Chester, a distance of fifteen miles. After which, he put me into a swamp, to cut trees, the heaviest work which men of twenty-five or thirty years of age have to do, I being but sixteen. Here I was on very short allowance of food, and having heavy work, was too weak to fulfil my tasks. For this I got many severe floggings; and after I had got my irons off, I made another attempt at running away. He took my irons off in the full anticipation that I could never get across the Catauba River, even when at liberty. On this I procured a small Indian canoe, which was tied to a tree, and ultimately got across the river in it. I then wandered through the wilderness for several days without any food, and but a drop of water to allay my thirst, till I became so starved, that I was obliged to go to a house to beg for something to eat, when I was captured, and again imprisoned.

Mr. Gooch, having heard of me through an advertisement, sent his son after me; he tied me up, and took me back to his father. Mr. Gooch then obtained the assistance of another slave-holder, and tied me up in his blacksmith's shop, and gave me fifty lashes with a cow-hide. He then put a long chain, weighing twenty-five pounds, round my neck, and sent me into a field, into which he followed me with the cow-hide, intending to set his slaves to flog me again. Knowing this, and dreading to suffer again in this way, I gave him the slip, and got out of his sight, he having stopped to speak with the other slave-holder.

I got to a canal on the Catauba River, on the banks of which, and near to a lock, I procured a stone and a piece of iron, with which I forced the ring off my chain, and got it off, and then crossed the river, and walked about twenty miles, when I fell in with a slave-holder named Ballad, who had married the sister of Mr. Hammans. I knew that he was not so cruel as Mr. Gooch, and, therefore, begged of him to buy me. Mr. Ballad, who was one of the best planters in the neighbourhood, said, that he was not able to buy me, and stated, that he was obliged to take me back to my master, on account of the heavy fine attaching to a man harbouring a slave. Mr. Ballad proceeded to take me back. As we came in sight of Mr. Gooch's, all the treatment that I had met with there came forcibly upon my mind, the powerful influence of which is beyond description. On my knees, with tears in my eyes, with terror in my countenance, and fervency in all my features, I implored Mr. Ballad to buy me, but he again refused, and I was taken back to my dreaded and cruel master. Having reached Mr. Gooch's, he proceeded to punish me. This he did by first tying my wrists together, and placing them over the knees; he then put a stick through, under my knees and over my arms, and having thus secured my arms, he proceeded to flog me, and gave me five hundred lashes on my bare back. This may appear incredible, but the marks which they left at present remain on my body, a standing testimony to the truth of this statement of his severity. He then chained me down in a log-pen with a 40 lb. chain, and made me lie on the damp earth all night. In the morning after his breakfast he came to me, and without giving me any breakfast, tied me to a large heavy barrow, which is usually drawn by a horse, and made me drag it to the cotton field for the horse to use in the field. Thus, the reader will see, that it was of no possible use to my master to make me drag it to the field, and not through it; his cruelty went so far as actually to make me the slave of his horse, and thus to degrade me. He then flogged me again, and set me to work in the corn field the whole of that day, and at night chained me down in the log-pen as before. The next morning he took me to the cotton field, and gave me a third flogging, and set me to hoe cotton. At this time I was dreadfully sore and weak with the repeated floggings and harsh treatment I had endured. He put me under a black man with orders, that if I did not keep my row up in hoeing with this man, he was to flog me. The reader must recollect here, that not being used to this kind of work, having been a domestic slave, it was quite impossible for me to keep up with him, and, therefore, I was repeatedly flogged during the day.

Mr. Gooch had a female slave about eighteen years old, who also had been a domestic slave, and through not being able to fulfil her task, had run away; which slave he was at this time punishing for that offence. On the third day, he chained me to this female slave, with a large chain of 40 lbs. weight round the neck. It was most harrowing to my feelings thus to be chained to a young female slave, for whom I would rather have suffered a hundred lashes than she should have been thus treated. He kept me chained to her during the week, and repeatedly flogged us both while thus chained together, and forced us to keep up with the other slaves, although retarded by the heavy weight of the log-chain.

Here again words are insufficient to describe the misery which possessed both body and mind whilst under this treatment, and which was most dreadfully increased by the sympathy which I felt for my poor degraded fellow sufferer. On the Friday morning, I entreated my master to set me free from my chains, and promised him to do the task which was given me, and more if possible, if he would desist from flogging me. This he refused to do until Saturday night, when he did set me free. This must rather be ascribed to his own interest in preserving me from death, as it was very evident I could no longer have survived under such treatment.

After this, though still determined in my own mind to escape, I stayed with him several months, during which he frequently flogged me, but not so severely as before related. During this time I had opportunity for recovering my health, and using means to heal my wounds. My master's cruelty was not confined to me, it was his general conduct to all his slaves. I might relate many instances to substantiate this, but will confine myself to one or two. Mr. Gooch, it is proper to observe, was a member of a Baptist church, called Black Jack Meeting-House, in Cashaw county, which church I attended for several years, but was never inside. This is accounted for by the fact, that the coloured population are not permitted to mix with the white population. Mr. Gooch had a slave named Phil,* who was a member of a Methodist church. This man was between seventy and eighty years of age; he was so feeble that he could not accomplish his tasks, for which his master used to chain him round the neck, and run him down a steep hill; this treatment he never relinquished to the time of his death. Another case was that of a slave named Peter, who, for not doing his task, he flogged nearly to death, and afterwards pulled out his pistol to shoot him, but his (Mr. Gooch's) daughter snatched the pistol from his hand. Another mode of punishment which this man adopted was, that of using iron horns, with bells, attached to the back of the slave's neck.

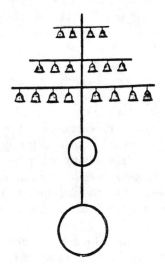

This instrument he used to prevent the negroes running away, being a very ponderous machine, seven feet in height, and the cross pieces being two feet four, and six feet in length. This custom is generally adopted among the slave-holders in South Carolina, and some other slave states. One morning, about an hour before daybreak, I was going on an errand for my master. Having proceeded about a quarter of a mile, I came up to a man named King, (Mr. Sumlin's overseer,) who had caught a young girl that had run away with the above-described

*This is an abbreviation of Philip.

machine on her. She had proceeded four miles from her station, with the intention of getting into the hands of a more humane master. She came up with this overseer nearly dead, and could get no farther. He immediately secured her, and took her back to her master, a Mr. Johnston.

Having been in the habit of going over many slave states with my master, I had good opportunities of witnessing the harsh treatment which was adopted by masters towards their slaves. As I have never read or heard of any thing connected with slavery so cruel as what I have myself witnessed, it will be well to mention a case or two.

A large farmer, Colonel M'Quiller, in Cashaw county, South Carolina, was in the habit of driving nails into a hogshead so as to leave the point of the nail just protruding in the inside of the cask. Into this he used to put his slaves for punishment, and roll them down a very long and steep hill. I have heard from several slaves, (though I had no means of ascertaining the truth of the statement,) that in this way he killed six or seven of his slaves. This plan was first adopted by a Mr. Perry, who lived on the Catauba River, and has since been adopted by several planters. Another was that of a young lad, who had been hired by Mr. Bell, a member of a Methodist church, to hoe three quarters of an acre of cotton per day. Having been brought up as a domestic slave, he was not able to accomplish the task assigned to him. On the Saturday night, he left three or four rows to do on the Sunday; on the same night it rained very hard, by which the master could tell that he had done some of the rows on Sunday. On Monday his master took and tied him up to a tree in the field, and kept him there the whole of that day, and flogged him at intervals. At night, when he was taken down, he was so weak that he could not get home, having a mile to go. Two white men, who were employed by Mr. Bell, put him on a horse, took him home, and threw him down on the kitchen floor, while they proceeded to their supper. In a little time they heard some deep groans proceeding from the kitchen; they went to see him die; he had groaned his last. Thus, Mr. Bell flogged this poor boy even to death; for what? for breaking the Sabbath, when he (his master) had set him a task on Saturday which it was not possible for him to do, and which, if he did not do, no mercy would be extended towards him. So much for the regard of this Methodist for the observance of the Sabbath. The general custom in this respect is, that if a man kills his own slave, no notice is taken of it by the civil functionaries; but if a man kills a slave belonging to another master, he is compelled to pay the worth of the slave. In this case, a jury met, returned a verdict of "Wilful murder" against this man, and ordered him to pay the value. Mr. Bell was unable to do this, but a Mr. Cunningham paid the debt, and took this Mr. Bell, with this recommendation for cruelty, to be his overseer.

It will be observed, that most of the cases here cited are those in respect to males. Many instances, however, in respect to females might be mentioned, but are too disgusting to appear in this narrative. The cases here brought forward are not rare, but the continued feature of slavery. But I must now follow up the narrative as regards myself in particular. I stayed with this master for several months, during which time we went on very well in general. In August, 1831, (this was my first acquaintance with any date,) I happened to hear a man men-

tion this date, and, as it excited my curiosity, I asked what it meant; they told me
it was the number of the year from the birth of Christ. On this date, August,
1831, some cows broke into a crib where the corn is kept, and ate a great deal.
For this his slaves were tied up and received several floggings; but myself and another man, hearing the groans of those who were being flogged, stayed back in
the field, and would not come up. Upon this I thought to escape punishment. On
the Monday morning, however, I heard my master flogging the other man who
was in the field. He could not see me, it being a field of Indian corn, which grows
to a great height. Being afraid that he would catch me, and dreading a flogging
more than many others, I determined to run for it, and after travelling forty miles
I arrived at the estate of Mr. Crawford, in North Carolina, Mecklinburgh
county. Having formerly heard people talk about the free states, I determined
upon going thither, and if possible, in my way, to find out my poor mother, who
was in slavery several hundred miles from Chester; but the hope of doing the latter was very faint, and, even if I did, it was not likely that she would know me,
having been separated from her when between five and six years old.

The first night I slept in a barn upon Mr. Crawford's estate, and, having
overslept myself, was awoke by Mr. Crawford's overseer, upon which I was
dreadfully frightened. He asked me what I was doing there? I made no reply to
him then, and he making sure that he had secured a runaway slave, did not press
me for an answer. On my way to his house, however, I made up the following
story, which I told him in the presence of his wife:—I said, that I had been bound
to a very cruel master when I was a little boy, and that having been treated very
badly, I wanted to get home to see my mother. This statement may appear to some
to be a direct lie, but as I understood the word *bound*, I considered it to apply to
my case, having been sold to him, and thereby bound to serve him; though still, I
rather hope that he would understand it, that I was bound, when a boy, till
twenty-one years of age. Though I was white at the time, he would not believe my
story, on account of my hair being curly and woolly, which led him to conclude
I was possessed of enslaved blood. The overseer's wife, however, who seemed
much interested in me, said she did not think I was of African origin, and that she
had seen white men still darker than me. Her persuasion prevailed; and, after the
overseer had given me as much buttermilk as I could drink, and something to eat,
which was very acceptable, having had nothing for two days, I set off for Charlotte in North Carolina, the largest town in the county. I went on very quickly the
whole of that day, fearful of being pursued. The trees were very thick on each side
of the road, and only a few houses at the distance of two or three miles apart. As
I proceeded, I turned round in all directions to see if I was pursued, and if I caught
a glimpse of any one coming along the road, I immediately rushed into the thickest part of the wood, to elude the grasp of what I was afraid might be my master.
I went on in this way the whole day; at night I came up with two wagons: they
had been to market. The regular road wagons do not generally put up at inns, but
encamp in the roads and fields. When I came to them, I told them the same story
I had told Mr. Crawford's overseer, with the assurance that the statement would
meet the same success. After they had heard me, they gave me something to eat,
and also a lodging in the camp with them.

I then went on with them about five miles, and they agreed to take me with them as far as they went, if I would assist them. This I promised to do. In the morning, however, I was much frightened by one of the men putting several questions to me; we were then about three miles from Charlotte. When within a mile of that town, we stopped at a brook to water the horses. While stopping here, I saw the men whispering, and fancying I overheard them say they would put me in Charlotte jail when they got there, I made my escape into the woods, pretending to be looking after something till I got out of their sight. I then ran on as fast as I could, but did not go through the town of Charlotte, as had been my intention; being a large town, I was fearful it might prove fatal to my escape. Here I was at a loss how to get on, as houses were not very distant from each other for nearly two hundred miles.

While thinking what I should do, I observed some wagons before me, which I determined to keep behind, and never go nearer to them than a quarter of a mile; in this way I travelled till I got to Salisbury. If I happened to meet any person on the road, I was afraid they would take me up; I asked them how far the wagons had got on before me, to make them suppose I belonged to the wagons. At night I slept on the ground in the woods, some little distance from the wagons, but not near enough to be seen by the men belonging to them. All this time I had but little food, principally fruit, which I found on the road. On Thursday night, I got into Salisbury, having left Chester on the Monday morning preceding. After this, being afraid my master was in pursuit of me, I left the usual line of road, and took another direction, through Huntsville and Salem, principally through fields and woods. On my way to Caswell Court-house, a distance of nearly two hundred miles from Salisbury,[12] I was stopped by a white man, to whom I told my old story, and again succeeded in my escape. I also came up with a small cart, driven by a poor man who had been moving into some of the western territories, and was going back to Virginia to move some more of his luggage. On this, I told him I was going the same way to Hilton, thirteen miles from Caswell Court-house. He took me up in his cart, and we went to the Red House, two miles from Hilton, the place where Mr. Mitchell took me from when six years old, to go to the southern states. This was a very providential circumstance, for it happened that at the time I had to pass through Caswell Court-house, a fair or election was going on, which caused the place to be much crowded with people, and rendered it more dangerous for me to pass through.

At the Red House I left the cart and wandered about a long time, not knowing which way to go to find my mother. After some time, I took the road leading over to Ikeo Creek. I shortly came up with a little girl about six years old, and asked her where she was going; she said to her mother's, pointing to a house on a hill about half a mile off. She had been to the overseer's house, and was returning to her mother. I then felt some emotions arising in my breast which I cannot describe, but will be fully explained in the sequel. I told her that I was very thirsty, and would go with her to get something to drink. On our way, I asked her several questions, such as her name, that of her mother: she said hers was Maria, and her mother's Nancy. I inquired if her mother had any more children? She said five besides herself, and that they had been told that one had been sold when a little boy. I then asked the name of this child? She said, it was Moses. These answers, as we approached the house, led me nearer and nearer to the finding out the object of my pursuit, and of recognising in the little girl the person of my own sister.[13] At last I got to my mother's house! My mother was at home; I asked her if she knew me? She said, No. Her master was having a house built just by, and the men were digging a well; she supposed that I was one of the diggers. I told her I knew her very well, and thought that if she looked at me a little she would know me; but this had no effect. I then asked her if she had any sons? She said, Yes; but none so large as me. I then waited a few minutes, and narrated some circumstances to her attending my being sold into slavery, and how she grieved at my loss. Here the mother's feelings on that dire occasion, and which a mother only can know, rushed to her mind; she saw her own son before her, for whom she had so often wept; and in an instant we were clasped in each other's arms, amidst the ardent interchange of caresses and tears of joy. Ten years had elapsed since I had seen my dear mother. My own feelings, and the circumstances attending my coming home, have often brought to mind since, on a perusal of the 42d, 43d, 44th, and 45th chapters of Genesis. What could picture my feelings so well, as I once more beheld the mother who had brought me into the world and had nourished me, not with the anticipation of my being torn from her maternal care when only six years old, to become the prey of a mercenary and blood-stained slave-holder,—I say, what picture so vivid in description of this part of my tale, as the 7th and 8th verses of the 42d chapter of Genesis, "And Joseph saw his brethren and he knew them, but made himself strange unto them. And Joseph knew his brethren, but they knew not him." After the first emotion of the mother on recognising her first-born had somewhat subsided, could the reader not fancy the little one, my sister, as she told her simple tale of meeting with me to her mother, how she would say, while the parent listened with intense interest, "The man asked me straitly of our state and of our kindred, saying, Is your father yet alive, and have ye another brother?" Or, when at last, I could no longer refrain from making myself known, I say I was ready to burst into a frenzy of joy. How applicable the 1st, 2d, and 3d verses of the 45th chapter, "Then Joseph could not refrain himself before all them that stood by him; and he wept aloud, and said unto his brethren, I am Joseph; doth my father still live?" Then when the mother knew her son, when the brothers and sisters owned their brother; "He kissed all his brethren and wept over them, and after that his brethren talked with him," 15th verse. At night, my mother's husband, a blacksmith, belonging to Mr. Jefferson, at the Red House, came home. He was suprised to see me with the family, not knowing who I was. He had been married to my mother when I was a babe, and had always been very fond of me. After the same tale had been told him, and the same emotions filled his soul, he again kissed the object of his early affection. The next morning I wanted to go on my journey, in order to make sure of my escape to the free states. But, as might be expected, my mother, father, brothers, and sisters, could ill part with their long lost one, and persuaded me to go into the woods in the daytime, and at night come home and sleep there. This I did for about a week. On the next Sunday night, I laid me down to sleep between my two brothers, on a pallet which my mother had prepared for me. About twelve o'clock I was suddenly awoke, and found my bed surrounded by twelve slave-holders with pistols in hand, who took me away (not allowing me to bid farewell to those I loved so dearly) to the Red House, where they confined me in a room the rest of the night, and in the morning lodged me in the jail of Caswell Courthouse.

What was the scene at home, what sorrow possessed their hearts, I am unable to describe, as I never after saw any of them more. I heard, however, that my mother, who was in the family-way when I went home, was soon after confined, and was very long before she recovered the effects of this disaster. I was told afterwards that some of those men who took me were professing Christians, but to me they did not seem to live up to what they professed. They did not seem, by their practices, at least, to recognise that God as their God, who hath said, "Thou shalt not deliver unto his master, the servant which is escaped from his master unto thee; he shall dwell with thee, even among you, in that place which he shall choose, in one of thy gates, where it liketh him best; thou shalt not oppress him." Deut. xxiii. 15, 16.

I was confined here in a dungeon under ground, the grating of which looked to the door of the jailer's house. His wife had a great antipathy to me. She was Mr. Roper's wife's cousin. My grandmother used to come to me nearly every day, and bring me something to eat, besides the regular jail allowance, by which my sufferings were somewhat decreased. Whenever the jailer went out, which he often did, his wife used to come to my dungeon and shut the wooden door over the grating, by which I was nearly suffocated, the place being very damp and noisome. My master did not hear of my being in jail for thirty-one days after I had been placed there. He immediately sent his son and son-in-law, Mr. Anderson, after me. They came in a horse and chaise, took me from the jail to a blacksmith's shop, and got an iron collar fitted round my neck, with a heavy chain attached, then tied up my hands, and fastened the other end of the chain on another horse, and put me on its back. Just before we started, my grandmother came to bid me farewell; I gave her my hand as well as I could, and she having given me two or three presents, we parted. I had felt enough, far too much, for the weak state I was in; but how shall I describe my feelings upon parting with the *last* relative that I *ever saw*? The reader must judge by what would be his own feelings under similar circumstances. We then went on for fifty miles; I was very weak, and could hardly sit on the horse. Having been in prison so long, I had lost the southern tan; and, as the people could not see my hair, having my hat on, they thought I was a white man, a criminal, and asked what crime I had committed. We arrived late at night at the house of Mr. Britton. I shall never forget the journey that night. The thunder was one continued roar, and the lightning blazing all around. I expected every minute that my iron collar would attract it, and I should be knocked off the horse and dragged along the ground. This gentleman, a year or two before, had liberated his slaves, and sent them into Ohio, having joined the society of Friends, which society does not allow the holding of slaves. I was, therefore, treated very well there, and they gave me a hearty supper, which did me much good in my weak state.

They secured me in the night by locking me to the post of the bed on which they slept. The next morning we went on to Salisbury. At that place we stopped to water the horses; they chained me to a tree in the yard, by the side of their chaise. On my horse they had put the saddle bags which contained the provisions. As I was in the yard, a black man came and asked me what I had been doing; I told him I had run away from my master; after which he told me several tales about the slaves, and among them, he mentioned the case of a Quaker, who was then in prison, waiting to be hung, for giving a free pass to a slave. I had been considering all the way how I could escape from my horse, and once had an idea of cutting his head off, but thought it too cruel, and at last thought of trying to get a rasp and cut the chain by which I was fastened to the horse. As they often let me get on nearly a quarter of a mile before them, I thought I should have a good opportunity of doing this without being seen. The black man procured me a rasp, and I put it into the saddle-bags which contained the provisions. We then went on our journey, and one of the sons asked me if I wanted any thing to eat; I answered, No, though very hungry at the time, as I was afraid of their going to the bags and discovering the rasp. However, they had not had their own meal at the inn, as I supposed, and went to the bags to supply themselves, where they discovered the rasp. Upon this, they fastened my horse beside the horse in their chaise, and kept a stricter watch over me. Nothing remarkable occurred, till we got within eight miles of Mr. Gooch's, where we stopped a short time; and, taking advantage of their absence, I broke a switch from some boughs above my head, lashed my horse, and set off at full speed. I had got about a quarter of a mile before they could get their horse loose from the chaise; one then rode the horse, and the other ran as fast as he could after me. When I caught sight of them, I turned off the main road into the woods, hoping to escape their sight; their horse, however, being much swifter than mine, they soon got within a short distance of me. I then came to a rail fence, which I found it very difficult to get over, but breaking several rails away, I effected my object. They then called upon me to stop, more than three times, and I not doing so, they fired after me, but the pistol only snapped. This is according to law; after three calls they may shoot a runaway slave. Soon after the one on the horse came up with me, and catching hold of the bridle of my horse, pushed the pistol to my side; the other soon came up, and breaking off several stout branches from the trees, they gave me about a hundred blows. They did this very near to a planter's house; the gentleman was not at home, but his wife came out, and begged them not to *kill* me *so near the house;* they took no notice of this, but kept on beating me. They then fastened me to the axle-tree of their chaise, one of them got into the chaise, the other took my horse, and they run me all the eight miles as fast as they could, the one on my horse going behind to guard me. In this way we came to my old master, Mr. Gooch. The first person I saw was himself; he unchained me from the chaise, and at first seemed to treat me very gently, asking me where I had been, &c. The first thing the sons did, was to show the rasp which I had got to cut my chain. My master gave me a hearty dinner, the best he ever did give me, but it was to keep me from dying before he had given me all the flogging he intended. After dinner he took me to a log-house, stripped me quite naked, fastened a rail up very high, tied my hands to the rail, fastened my feet together, put a rail between my feet, and stood on one end of it to hold it down; the two sons then gave me fifty lashes each, the eldest another fifty, and Mr. Gooch himself fifty more. While doing this, his wife came out and begged him not to kill me, the first act of sympathy I ever noticed in her. When I called for water, they brought a pail-full and threw it over my back, ploughed up by the lashes. After this, they took me to the blacksmith's shop, got two large bars of iron, which they bent round my feet, each bar weighing twenty pounds, and put a heavy log-chain on my neck. This was on Saturday. On the Monday, he chained me to the same female slave as before. As he had to go out that day, he did not give me the punishment which he intended to give me every day, but at night when he came home, he made us walk round his estate, and by all the houses of the slaves, for them to taunt us. When we came home, he told us we must be up very early in the morning, and go to the fields before the other slaves. We were up at daybreak, but we could not get on fast, on account of the heavy irons on my feet. We walked about a mile in two hours, but knowing the punishment he was going to inflict on us, we made up our minds to escape into the woods, and secrete ourselves. This we did, and he not being able to find us, sent all his slaves, about forty, and his sons, to find us, which they could not do; and about twelve o'clock, when we thought they would give up looking for us at that time, we went on, and came to the banks of the Catauba. Here I got a stone, and prized the ring of the chain on her neck, and got it off; and as the chain round my neck was only passed through a ring, as soon as I had got hers off, I slipped the chain through my ring and got it off my own neck. We then went on by the banks of the river for some distance, and found a little canoe about two feet wide. I managed to get in, although the irons on my feet made it very dangerous, for if I had upset the canoe I could not swim. The female got in after me, and gave me the paddles, by which we got some distance down the river. The current being very strong, it drove us against a small island; we paddled round the island to the other side, and then made towards the opposite bank. Here again we were stopped by the current, and made up to a large rock in the river, between the island and the opposite shore. As the weather was very rough, we landed on the rock and secured the canoe, as it was not possible to get back to the island. It was a very dark night and rained tremendously, and as the water was rising rapidly towards the top of the rock, we gave all up for lost, and sometimes hoped, and sometimes feared to hope, that we should never see the morning. But Providence was moving in our favour; the rain ceased, the water reached the edge of the rock, then receded, and we were out of danger from this cause. We remained all night upon the rock, and in the morning reached the opposite shore, and then made our way through the woods, till we came to a field of Indian corn, where we plucked some of the green ears and eat them, having had nothing for two days and nights. We came to the estate of ———, where we met with a colored man who knew me, and having run away himself from a bad master, he gave us some food, and told us we might sleep in the barn that night. Being very fatigued, we overslept ourselves; the proprietor came to the barn, but as I was in one corner under some Indian corn tops, and she in another, he did not perceive us, and we did not leave the barn before night, (Wednesday). We then went out, got something to eat, and stayed about the estate till Sunday. On that day, I met with some men, one of whom had had irons on his feet the same as me; he told me, that his master was going out to see his friends, and that he would try and get my feet loose. For this purpose I parted with this female, fearing, that if she were caught with me, she would be forced to tell who took my irons off. The man tried some time without effect; he then gave me a file and I tried myself, but was disappointed, on account of their thickness.

On the Monday, I went on towards Lancaster, and got within three miles of it that night, and went towards the plantation of Mr. Crockett, as I knew some of his slaves, and hoped to get some food given me. When I got there, however, the dogs smelt me out and barked; upon which Mr. Crockett came out, followed me with his rifle, and came up with me. He put me on a horse's back, which put me to extreme pain, from the great weight hanging from my feet. We reached Lancaster jail that night, and he lodged me there. I was placed in the next dungeon to a man who was going to be hung. I shall never forget his cries and groans, as he prayed all night for the mercy of God. Mr. Gooch did not hear of me for several weeks; when he did, he sent his son-in-law, Mr. Anderson, after me. Mr. Gooch himself came within a mile of Lancaster, and waited until Mr. Anderson brought me. At this time I had but one of the irons on my feet, having got so thin round my ankles that I had slipped one off while in jail. His son-in-law tied my hands, and made me walk along till we came to Mr. Gooch. As soon as we arrived at M'Daniel's Ford, two miles above the ferry, on the Catauba River, they made me wade across, themselves going on horseback. The water was very deep, and having irons on one foot and round my neck, I could not keep a footing. They dragged me along by my chain, floating on the top of the water. It was as much as they could do to hold me by the chain, the current being very strong. They then took me home, flogged me, put extra irons on my neck and feet, and put me under the driver, with more work than ever I had before. He did not flog me so severely as before, but continued it every day. Among the instruments of torture employed, I here describe one:

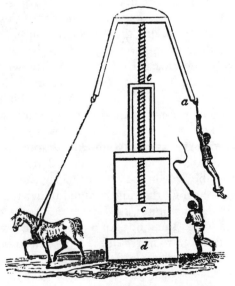

A COTTON SCREW.

This is a machine used for packing and pressing cotton. By it he hung me up by the hands at letter *a,* a horse moving round the screw *e,* and carrying it up and down, and pressing the block *c* into the box *d,* into which the cotton is put. At this time he hung me up for a quarter of an hour. I was carried up ten feet from the ground, when Mr. Gooch asked me if I was tired. He then let me rest for five minutes, then carried me round again, after which he let me down and put me into the box *d,* and shut me down in it for about ten minutes. After this torture, I stayed with him several months, and did my work very well. It was about the beginning of 1832 when he took off my irons, and being in dread of him, he having threatened me with more punishment, I attempted again to escape from him. At this time I got into North Carolina; but a reward having been offered for me, a Mr. Robinson caught me, and chained me to a chair, upon which he sat up with me all night, and next day proceeded home with me. This was Saturday, Mr. Gooch had gone to church, several miles from his house. When he came back, the first thing he did was to pour some tar on my head, then rubbed it all over my face, took a torch, with pitch on, and set it on fire. He put it out before it did me very great injury, but the pain which I endured was most excruciating, nearly all my hair having been burnt off. On Monday he put irons on me again, weighing nearly fifty pounds. He threatened me again on the Sunday with another flogging; and on the Monday morning, before day-break, I got away again, with my irons on, and was about three hours going a distance of two miles. I had gone a good distance, when I met with a colored man, who got some wedges and took my irons off. However, I was caught again, and put into prison in Charlotte, where Mr. Gooch came, and took me back to Chester. He asked me how I got my irons off? They having been got off by a slave, I would not answer his question, for fear of getting the man punished. Upon this, he put the fingers of my left hand into a vice, and squeezed all my nails off. He then had my feet put on an anvil, and ordered a man to beat my toes, till he smashed some of my nails off. The marks of this treatment still remain upon me, my nails never having grown perfect since. He inflicted this punishment, in order to get out of me how I got my irons off, but never succeeded. After this he hardly knew what to do with me, the whole stock of his cruelties seemed to be exhausted. He chained me down in the log-house. Soon after this, he sent a female slave to see if I was safe. Mr. Gooch had not secured me as he thought, but had only run my chain through the ring, without locking it. This I observed; and while the slave was coming, I was employed in loosening the chain with the hand that was not wounded. As soon as I observed her coming, I drew the chain up tight, and she observing that I seemed fast, went away and told her master who was in the field ordering the slaves. When she was gone, I drew the chain through the ring, escaped under the flooring of the log-house, and went on under his house, till I came out at the other side, and ran on; but being sore and weak, I had not got a mile before I was caught, and again carried back. He tied me up to a tree in the woods at night and made his slaves flog me. I cannot say how many lashes I received, but it was the worst flogging I ever had, and the last which Mr. Gooch ever gave me.

There are several circumstances which occurred on this estate while I was there, relative to other slaves, which it may be interesting to mention. Hardly a day ever passed without some one being flogged. To one of his female slaves he had given a dose of castor oil and salts together, as much as she could take; he then got a box, about six feet by two and a half, and one and a half feet deep; he put this slave under the box, and made the men fetch as many stones as they could get, and put them on the top of it; under this she was made to stay all night. I believe, that if he had given this slave one, he had given her three thousand lashes. Mr. Gooch was a member of a Baptist church. His slaves, thinking him a very bad sample of what a professing Christian ought to be, would not join the connexion he belonged to, thinking they must be a very bad set of people; there were many of them members of the Methodist church. On Sunday, the slaves can only go to church at the will of their master, when he gives them a pass for the time they are to be out. If they are found by the patrole after the time to which their pass extends, they are severely flogged.

On Sunday nights, a slave, named Allen, used to come to Mr. Gooch's estate for the purpose of exhorting and praying with his brother slaves, by whose instrumentality many of them had been converted. One evening Mr. Gooch caught them all in a room, turned Allen out, and threatened his slaves with a hundred lashes each, if they ever brought him there again. At one time Mr. Gooch was ill and confined to his room; if any of the slaves had done any thing which he thought deserving a flogging, he would have them brought into his bed-room and flogged before his eyes.

With respect to food, he used to allow us one peck of Indian meal each, per week, which, after being sifted and the bran taken from it, would not be much more than half a peck. Meat we did not get for sometimes several weeks together; however, he was proverbial for giving his slaves more food than any other slave-holder. I stayed with Mr. Gooch a year and a half. During that time the scenes of cruelty I witnessed and experienced, are not at all fitted for these pages. There is much to excite disgust in what has been narrated, but hundreds of other cases might be mentioned. After this, Mr. Gooch, seeing that I was determined to get away from him, chained me, and sent me with another female slave, whom he had treated very cruelly, to Mr. Britton, son of the before-mentioned, a slave-dealer. We were to have gone to Georgia to be sold, but a bargain was struck before we arrived there. Mr. Britton had put chains on me to please Mr. Gooch; but having gone some little distance, we came up with a white man, who begged Mr. Britton to unchain me; he then took off my hand-cuffs. We then went on to Union Court-house, where we met a drove of slaves; the driver came to me, and ultimately bought me, and sent me to his drove; the girl was sold to a planter in the neighbourhood, as bad as Mr. Gooch. In court week, the negro traders and slaves encamp a little way out of the town. The traders here will often sleep with the best-looking female slaves among them, and they will often have many children in the year, which are said to be slave-holder's children, by which means, through his villany, he will make an immense profit of this intercourse, by selling the babe with its mother. They often keep an immense stock of slaves on hand. Many of them will be with the trader a year or more before they are sold. Mr. Marcus Rowland, the drover who bought me, then returned with his slaves to his brother's house, (Mr. John Rowland,) where he kept his drove, on his way to Virginia. He kept me as a kind of servant. I had to grease the faces of the blacks every morning with sweet oil, to make them shine before they are put up to sell. After he had been round several weeks and sold many slaves, he left me and some more at his brother's house, while he went on to Washington, about six hundred miles, to buy some more slaves, the drove having got very small. We were treated very well while there, having plenty to eat, and little work to do, in order to make us fat. I was brought up more as a domestic slave, as they generally prefer slaves of my colour for that purpose. When Mr. Rowland came back, having been absent about five months, he found all the slaves well, except one female, who had been grieving very much at being parted from her parents, and at last died of grief. He dressed us very nicely, and went on again. I travelled with him for a year, and had to look over the slaves, and see that they were dressed well, had plenty of food, and to oil their faces. During this time, we stopped once at White House Church, a Baptist association; a protracted camp meeting was holding there, on the plan of the revival meetings in this country. We got there at the time of the meeting, and sold two female slaves on the Sunday morning, at the time the meeting broke up, to a gentleman who had been attending the meeting the whole of the week. While I was with Mr. Rowland we were at many such meetings, and the members of the churches are by this means so well influenced towards their fellow creatures, at these meetings for the worship of God, that it becomes a fruitful season for the drover, who carries on immense traffic with the attendants at these places. This is common to Baptists and Methodists. At the end of the year he exchanged me to a farmer, Mr. David Goodley, for a female slave, in Greenville, about fourteen miles from Greenville Court-house. The gentleman was going to Missouri to settle, and on his way had to pass through Ohio, a free state. But having learnt, after he bought me, that I had before tried to get away to the free states, he was afraid to take me with him, and I was again exchanged to a Mr. Marvel Louis. He was in the habit of travelling a great deal, and took me as a domestic slave to wait on him. Mr. Louis boarded at the house of Mr. Clevelin, a very rich planter at Greenville, South Carolina. Mr. L. was paying his addresses to the daughter of this gentleman, but was surprised and routed in his approaches, by a Colonel Dorkin, of Union Court-house, who ultimately carried her off in triumph. After this Mr. Louis took to drinking, to drown his recollection of disappointed love. One day he went to Pendleton races, and I waited on the road for him; returning intoxicated, he was thrown from his horse into a brook, and was picked up by a gentleman and taken to an inn, and I went there to take care of him. Next day he went on to Punkintown with Mr. Warren R. Davis, a member of Congress; I went with him. This was at the time of the agitation of the Union and Nullifying party, which was expected to end in a general war.[14] The Nullifying party had a grand dinner on the occasion, after which they gave their slaves all the refuse, for the purpose of bribing them to fight on the side of their party. The scene on this occasion was most humorous, all the slaves scrambling after bare bones and crumbs, as if they had had nothing for months. When Mr. Louis had got over this fit of drunkenness, we returned to Greenville, where I had little to do, except in the warehouse. There was preaching in the Court-house on the Sunday, but scarcely had the sweet savour of the worship of God passed away, when, on Monday, a public auction was held for the sale of slaves, cattle, sugar, iron, &c., by Z. Davis, the high constable, and others.

On these days, I was generally very busy in handing out the different articles for inspection, and was employed in this way for several months. After which, Mr. Louis left this place for Pendleton;[15] but his health getting worse, and fast approaching consumption, he determined to travel. I went with him over Georgia to the Indian springs, and from there to Columbus; here he left me with Lawyer Kemp, a member of the State Assembly, to take care of his horses and carriage till he came back from Cuba, where he went for the benefit of his health. I travelled round with Mr. Kemp, waiting until my master came back. I soon after heard that Mr. Louis had died at Appalachicola, and had been buried at Tennessee Bluff. I was very much attached to the neighbourhood of Pendleton and Greenville, and feared, from Mr. Louis's death, I should not get back there.

As soon as this information arrived, Mr. Kemp put me, the carriage and horses, a gold watch, and cigars, up to auction, on which I was much frightened, knowing there would be some very cruel masters at the sale, and fearing I should again be disappointed in my attempt to escape from bondage. Mr. Beveridge, a Scotchman, from Appalachicola, bought me, the horses, and cigars. He was not a cruel master; he had been in America eighteen years, and, I believe, I was the first slave he ever bought. Mr. Kemp had no right to sell me, which he did, before he had written to Mr. Louis's brother.

Shortly after this, Mr. Kemp, having some altercation with General Woodfork, it ended in a duel, in which Mr. W. was killed. A few weeks after, as Mr. Kemp was passing down a street, he was suddenly shot dead by Mr. Milton, a rival lawyer. When I heard this, I considered it a visitation of God on Mr. Kemp for having sold me unjustly, as I did not belong to him. This was soon discovered by me, Mr. Louis's brother having called at Mackintosh Hotel, Columbus, to claim me, but which he could not effect. After this, I travelled with Mr. Beveridge, through Georgia to the warm springs, and then came back to Columbus, going on to Marianna, his summer house, in Florida.

Here I met with better treatment than I had ever experienced before; we travelled on the whole summer; at the fall, Mr. Beveridge went to Appalachicola on business. Mr. Beveridge was contractor for the mail from Columbus to Appalachicola, and owner of three steamboats, the Versailles, Andrew Jackson, and Van Buren. He made me steward on board the Versailles, the whole winter. The river then got so low that the boats could not run. At this time Mr. Beveridge went to Mount Vernon. On our way we had to pass through the Indian nation. We arrived at Columbus, where I was taken dangerously ill of a fever. After I got well, Mr. Beveridge returned to Marianna, through the Indian nation. Having gone about twelve miles, he was taken very ill. I took him out of the carriage to a brook, and washed his hands and feet until he got better, when I got him into the carriage again, and drove off till we came to General Irving's, where he stopped several days on account of his health. While there, I observed on the floor of the kitchen several children, one about three months old, without anybody to take care of her; I asked where her mother was, and was told that Mrs. Irving had given her a very hard task to do at washing in a brook about a quarter of a mile distant. We heard after, that not being able to get it done, she had got some cords, tied them round her neck, climbed up a tree, swung off, and hung herself. Being missed, persons were sent after her, who observed several buzzards flying about a particular spot, to which they directed their steps, and found the poor woman nearly eaten up.

After this, we travelled several months without any thing remarkable taking place.

In the year 1834, Mr. Beveridge, who was now residing in Appalachicola, a town in West Florida, became a bankrupt, when all his property was sold, and I fell into the hands of a very cruel master, Mr. Register, a planter in the same state, of whom, knowing his savage character, I always had a dread. Previously to his purchasing me, he had frequently taunted me, by saying, "You have been a gentleman long enough, and, whatever may be the consequences, I intend to buy you." To which I remarked, that I would on no account live with him if I could help it. Nevertheless, intent upon his purpose, in the month of July, 1834, he bought me, after which, I was so exasperated that I cared not whether I lived or died; in fact, whilst I was on my passage from Appalachicola, I procured a quart bottle of whiskey, for the purpose of so intoxicating myself, that I might be able, either to plunge myself into the river, or so to enrage my master, that he should despatch me forthwith. I was, however, by a kind Providence, prevented from committing this horrid deed by an old slave on board, who, knowing my intention, secretly took the bottle from me; after which my hands were tied, and I was led into the town of Ochesa, to a warehouse, where my master was asked, by the proprietor of the place, the reason for his confining my hands; in answer to which, Mr. Register said, that he had purchased me. The proprietor, however, persuaded him to untie me; after which my master being excessively drunk, asked for a cow-hide, intending to flog me, from which the proprietor dissuaded him, saying, that he had known me for some time, and he was sure that I did not require to be flogged. From this place, we proceeded about mid-day on our way, he placing me on the bare back of a half starved old horse, which he had purchased, and upon which sharp *surface* he kindly intended I should ride about eighty miles, the distance we were then from his home. In this unpleasant situation, I could not help reflecting upon the prospects before me, not forgetting that I had heard that my new master had been in the habit of stealing cattle and other property, and among other things, a slave woman, and that I had said, as it afterwards turned out, in the hearing of some one who communicated the saying to my master, that I had been accustomed to live with a gentleman, and not with a rogue; and, finding that he had been informed of this, I had the additional dread of a few hundred lashes for it, on my arrival at my destination.

About two hours after we started, it began to rain very heavily, and continued to do so until we arrived at Marianna, about twelve at night, where we were to rest till morning. My master here questioned me, as to whether I intended to run away or not; and I not then knowing the sin of lying, at once told him that I would not. He then gave me his clothes to dry; I took them to the kitchen for that purpose, and he retired to bed, taking a bag of clothes belonging to me with him, as a kind of security, I presume, for my safety. In an hour or two afterwards I took his clothes to him dried, and found him fast asleep. I placed them by his side, and said, that I would then take my own to dry too, taking care to speak loud enough to ascertain whether he was asleep or not, knowing that he had a dirk and a pistol by his side, which he would not have hesitated using against me, if I had attempted secretly to have procured them. I was glad to find, that the effects of his drinking the day before had caused his sleeping very soundly, and I immediately resolved on making my escape; and without loss of time, started with my few clothes into the woods, which were in the immediate neighbourhood; and, after running many miles, I came to the river Chapoli, which is very deep, and so beset with alligators, that I dared not attempt to swim across. I paced up and down this river, with the hope of finding a conveyance across, for a whole day, the succeeding night, and till noon the following day, which was Saturday. About twelve o'clock on that day I discovered an Indian canoe, which had not, from all appearance, been used for some time; this, of course, I used to convey myself across, and after being obliged to go a little way down the river, by means of a piece of wood I providentially found in the boat, I landed on the opposite side. Here I found myself surrounded by planters looking for me, in consequence of which I hid myself in the bushes until night, when I again travelled several miles, to the farm of a Mr. Robinson, a large sugar-planter, where I rested till morning in a field. Afterwards I set out, working my way through the woods about twenty miles towards the east; this I knew by my knowledge of the position of the sun at its rising. Having reached the Chattahoochee River, which divides Florida from Georgia, I was again puzzled to know how to cross. It was three o'clock in the day, when a number of persons were fishing; having walked for some hours along the banks, I at last, after dark, procured a ferry-boat, which not being able, from the swiftness of the river, to steer direct across, I was carried many miles down the river, landing on the Georgian side, from whence I proceeded on through the woods two or three miles, and came to a little farm-house about twelve at night; at a short distance from the house, I found an old slave hut, into which I went, and informed the old man, who appeared seventy or eighty years old, that I had had a very bad master, from whom I had run away; and asked him, if he could give me something to eat, having had no suitable food for three or four days; he told me, he had nothing but a piece of dry Indian bread, which he cheerfully gave me; having eaten it, I went on a short distance from the hut, and laid down in

the wood to rest for an hour or two. All the following day, (Monday,) I continued travelling through the woods, was greatly distressed for want of water
to quench my thirst, it being a very dry country, till I came to Spring Creek,
which is a wide, deep stream, and with some of which I gladly quenched my
thirst. I then proceeded to cross the same by a bridge close by, and continued
my way till dusk. I came to a gentleman's house in the woods, where I inquired
how far it was to the next house, taking care to watch an opportunity to ask
some individual whom I could master, and get away from, if any interruption
to my progress was attempted. I went on for some time, it being a very fine
moonlight night, and was presently alarmed by the howling of a wolf very near
me, which I concluded was calling other wolves to join him in attacking me,
having understood that they always assemble in numbers for such a purpose.
The howling increased, and I was still pursued, and the numbers were evidently
increasing fast; but I was happily rescued from my dreadful fright, by coming
to some cattle, which attracted the wolves, and saved my life; for I could not get
up the trees for safety, they being very tall pines, the lowest branches of which
were at least forty or fifty feet from the ground, and the trunks very large and
smooth.

About two o'clock I came to the house of a Mr. Cherry, on the borders of
the Flint River; I went up to the house, and called them up to beg something to
eat; but having nothing cooked, they kindly allowed me to lie down in the porch,
where they made me a bed. In conversation with this Mr. Cherry, I discovered
that I had known him before, having been in a steamboat, the Versailles, some
months previous, which sunk very near his house, but which I did not at first discern to be the same. I then thought that it would not be prudent for me to stop
there, and therefore told them I was in a hurry to get on, and must start very
early again, he having no idea who I was; and I gave his son six cents to take me
across the river, which he did when the sun was about half an hour high, and unfortunately landed me where there was a man building a boat, who knew me very
well, and my former master too; he calling me by name, asked me where I was
going.

I was very much frightened at being discovered, but summoned up courage,
and said, that my master had gone on to Tallyhassa by the coach, and that there
was not room for me, and I had to walk round to meet him. I then asked the man
to put me into the best road to get there, which, however, I knew as well as he
did, having travelled there before; he directed me the best way, but I of course
took the contrary direction, wanting to get on to Savannah. By this hasty and
wicked deception I saved myself from going to Bainbridge prison, which was
close by, and to which I should surely have been taken had it been known that I
was making my escape.

Leaving Bainbridge, I proceeded about forty miles, travelling all day under
a scorching sun through the woods, in which I saw many deer and serpents, until I reached Thomas Town in the evening. I there inquired the way to Augusta
of a man whom I met, and also asked where I could obtain lodgings, and was
told that there was a poor minister about a mile from the place who would give
me lodgings. I accordingly went and found them in a little log-house, where, hav-

ing awakened the family, I found them all lying on the bare boards, where I joined them for the remainder of the night.

In the morning the old gentleman prayed for me that I might be preserved on my journey; he had previously asked me where I was going, and I knowing, that if I told him the right place, any that inquired of him for me would be able to find me, asked the way to Augusta instead of Savannah, my real destination. I also told him that I was partly Indian and partly white, but I am also partly African; but this I omitted to tell him, knowing if I did I should be apprehended. After I had left this hut, I again inquired for Augusta, for the purpose of mis-leading my pursuers, but I afterwards took my course through the woods, and came into a road, called the Coffee road, which General Jackson cut down for his troops, at the time of the war between the Americans and Spaniards, in Florida; in which road there are but few houses, and which I preferred for the purpose of avoiding detection.

After several days I left this road, and took a more direct way to Savannah, where I had to wade through two rivers before I came to the Alatamah, which I crossed in a ferry-boat, about a mile below the place where the rivers Oconee and Ocmulgee run together into one river, called the Alatamah. I here met with some cattle drovers, who were collecting cattle to drive to Savannah. On walk-ing on before them, I began to consider in what way I could obtain a passport for Savannah, and determined on the following plan:—

I called at a cottage, and after I had talked some time with the wife, who began to feel greatly for me, in consequence of my telling her a little of my his-tory, (her husband being out hunting,) I pretended to show her my passport, feel-ing for it everywhere about my coat and hat, and not finding it, I went back a lit-tle way pretending to look for it, but came back saying I was very sorry, but I did not know where it was. At last the man came home, carrying a deer upon his shoulders, which he brought into the yard and began to dress it. The wife then went out to tell him my situation, and after long persuasion he said he could not write, but that if I could tell his son what was in my passport he should write me one; and knowing that I should not be able to pass Savannah without one, and having heard several free colored men read theirs, I thought I could tell the lad what to write. The lad sat down and wrote what I told him, nearly filling a large sheet of paper for the passport, and another sheet with recommendations. These being completed, I was invited to partake of some of the fresh venison, which the woman of the house had prepared for dinner, and having done so, and feeling grateful for their kindness, I proceeded on my way. Going along I took my pa-pers out of my pocket, and looking at them, although I could not read a word, I perceived that the boy's writing was very unlike other writing that I had seen, and was greatly blotted besides; consequently I was afraid that these documents would not answer my purpose, and began to consider what other plan I could pursue to obtain another pass.

I had now to wade through another river to which I came, and which I had great difficulty in crossing in consequence of the water overflowing the banks of several rivers to the extent of upwards of twenty miles. In the midst of the water I passed one night upon a small island, and the next day I went through the remainder of the water. On many occasions I was obliged to walk upon my toes, and consequently found the advantage of being six feet two inches high, and at other times was obliged to swim. In the middle of this extremity I felt it would be imprudent for me to return; for if my master was in pursuit of me, my safest place from him was in the water, if I could keep my head above the surface. I was, however, dreadfully frightened, and most earnestly prayed that I might be kept from a watery grave, and resolved that if again I landed, I would spend my life in the service of God.

Having through mercy again started on my journey, I met with the drovers, and having, whilst in the water, taken the pass out of my hat, and so dipped it in the water as to spoil it, I showed it to the men, and asked them where I could get another. They told me, that in the neighbourhood there lived a rich cotton merchant, who would write me one. They took me to him, and gave their word, that they saw the passport before it was wet, (for I had previously showed it to them,) upon which the cotton planter wrote a free pass and a recommendation, to which the cow-drovers affixed their marks.

The recommendation was as follows:

"John Roper, a very interesting young lad, whom I have seen and travelled with for eighty or ninety miles on his road from Florida, is a free man, descended from Indian and white. I trust, he will be allowed to pass on without interruption, being convinced from what I have seen that he is free, and though dark, is not an African. I had seen his papers before they were wetted."

These cow-drovers, who procured me the passport and recommendation from the cotton planter, could not read; and they were intoxicated when they went with me to him. I am part African, as well as Indian and white, my father being a white man, Henry Roper, Esq., Caswell county, North Carolina, U. S., a very wealthy slave-holder, who sold me when quite a child, for the strong resemblance I bore to him. My mother is part Indian, part African; but I dared not disclose that, or I should have been taken up. I then had eleven miles to go to Savannah, one of the greatest slave-holding cities in America, and where they are always looking out for runaway slaves. When at this city, I had travelled about five hundred miles.* It required great courage to pass through this place. I went through the main street with apparent confidence, though much alarmed; did not stop at any house in the city, but went down immediately to the dock, and inquired for a berth, as a steward to a vessel to New York. I had been in this capacity before on the Appalachicola River. The person whom I asked to procure me a berth was steward of one of the New York packets; he knew Captain Deckay, of the schooner Fox, and got me a situation on board that vessel, in five minutes after I had been at the docks. The schooner Fox was a very old vessel, twenty-seven years old, laden with lumber and cattle for New York; she was rotten and could not be insured. The sailors were afraid of her; but I ventured on board, and five minutes after we dropped from the docks into the river. My spirits then began to revive, and I thought I should get to

---

*The distance between these two places is much less than five hundred miles; but I was obliged to travel round about, in order to avoid being caught.

a free country directly. We cast anchor in the stream, to keep the sailors on, as they were so dissatisfied with the vessel, and lay there four days; during which time I had to go into the city several times, which exposed me to great danger, as my master was after me, and I dreaded meeting with him in the city.

Fearing the Fox would not sail before I should be seized, I deserted her, and went on board a brig sailing to Providence, that was towed out by a steamboat, and got thirty miles from Savannah. During this time I endeavoured to persuade the steward to take me as an assistant, and hoped to have accomplished my purpose; but the captain had observed me attentively, and thought I was a slave; he therefore ordered me, when the steamboat was sent back, to go on board her to Savannah, as the fine for taking a slave from that city to any of the free states is five hundred dollars. I reluctantly went back to Savannah, among slave-holders and slaves. My mind was in a sad state, and I was under strong temptation to throw myself into the river. I had deserted the schooner Fox, and knew that the captain might put me into prison till the vessel was ready to sail; if this had happened, and my master had come to the jail in search of me, I must have gone back to slavery. But when I reached the docks at Savannah, the first person I met was the captain of the Fox, looking for another steward in my place. He was a very kind man, belonging to the free states, and inquired if I would go back to his vessel. This usage was very different to what I expected, and I gladly accepted his offer. This captain did not know that I was a slave. In about two days we sailed from Savannah for New York.

I am (August, 1834) unable to express the joy I now felt. I never was at sea before, and, after I had been out about an hour, was taken with sea-sickness, which continued five days. I was scarcely able to stand up, and one of the sailors was obliged to take my place. The captain was very kind to me all this time; but even after I recovered, I was not sufficiently well to do my duty properly, and could not give satisfaction to the sailors, who swore at me, and asked me why I shipped, as I was not used to the sea. We had a very quick passage, and in six days after leaving Savannah, we were in the harbour at Staten Island, where the vessel was quarantined for two days, six miles from New York. The captain went to the city, but left me aboard with the sailors, who had most of them been brought up in the slave-holding states, and were very cruel men. One of the sailors was particularly angry with me because he had to perform the duties of my place; and while the captain was in the city, the sailors called me to the fore-hatch, where they said they would treat me. I went, and while I was talking, they threw a rope round my neck and nearly choked me. The blood streamed from my nose profusely. They also took up ropes with large knots, and knocked me over the head. They said I was a negro; they despised me; and I expected they would have thrown me into the water. When we arrived at the city, these men, who had so ill-treated me, ran away, that they might escape the punishment which would otherwise have been inflicted on them. When I arrived in the city of New York, I thought I was free; but learned I was not, and could be taken there. I went out into the country several miles, and tried to get employment, but failed, as I had no recommendation. I then returned to New York, but finding the same difficulty there to get work as in the country, I went back to the vessel, which was to sail eighty miles up the Hudson River, to Poughkeepsie. When I arrived, I obtained employment at an inn, and after I had been there about two days, was seized with the cholera, which was at that place. The complaint was, without doubt, brought on by my having subsisted on fruit only for several days, while I was in the slave states. The landlord of the inn came to me when I was in bed, suffering violently from cholera, and told me he knew I had that complaint, and as it had never been in his house, I could not stop there any longer. No one would enter my room, except a young lady, who appeared very pious and amiable, and had visited persons with the cholera. She immediately procured me some medicine at her own expense, and administered it herself; and whilst I was groaning with agony, the landlord came up and ordered me out of the house directly. Most of the persons in Poughkeepsie had retired for the night, and I lay under a shed on some cotton bales. The medicine relieved me, having been given so promptly, and next morning I went from the shed, and laid on the banks of the river below the city. Towards evening I felt much better, and went on in a steamboat to the city of Albany, about eighty miles. When I reached there, I went into the country, and tried for three or four days to procure employment, but failed.

At that time I had scarcely any money, and lived upon fruit; so I returned to Albany, where I could get no work, as I could not show the recommendations I possessed, which were only from slave states, and I did not wish any one to know I came from them. After a time, I went up the western canal[16] as steward in one of the boats. When I had gone about 350 miles up the canal, I found I was going too much towards the slave states, in consequence of which I returned to Albany, and went up the northern canal into one of the New England states, Vermont. The distance I had travelled, including the 350 miles I had to return from the west, and the 100 to Vermont, was 2300 miles. When I reached Vermont, I found the people very hospitable and kind; they seemed opposed to slavery, so I told them I was a runaway slave. I hired myself to a firm in Sudbury.* After I had been in Sudbury some time, the neighboring farmers told me that I had hired myself for much less money than I ought. I mentioned it to my employers, who were very angry about it; I was advised to leave by some of the people round, who thought the gentlemen I was with would write to my former master, informing him where I was, and obtain the reward fixed upon me. Fearing I should be taken, I immediately left and went into the town of Ludlow, where I met with a kind friend Mr. ———,† who sent me to school for several weeks. At this time I was advertised in the papers, and was obliged to leave; I went a little way out of Ludlow to a retired place, and lived

---

*During my stay in this town, I thought of the vow I made in the water, (Page 72 [page 514 in this edition],) and I became more thoughtful about the salvation of my soul. I attended the Methodist chapel, where a Mr. Benton preached, and there I began to feel that I was a great sinner. During the latter part of my stay here, I became more anxious about salvation, and I entertained the absurd notion that religion would come to me in some extraordinary way. With this impression, I used to go into the woods two hours before daylight to pray, and expected something would take place, and I should become religious.

†It would not be proper to mention any names, as a person in any of the states of America found harboring a slave, would have to pay a heavy fine.

two weeks with a Mr. ———, deacon of a church at Ludlow; at this place I could have obtained education, had it been safe to have remained.* From there I went to New Hampshire, where I was not safe, so went to Boston, Massachusetts, with the hope of returning to Ludlow, to which place I was much attached. At Boston I met with a friend, who kept a shop, and took me to assist him for several weeks. Here I did not consider myself safe, as persons from all parts of the country were continually coming to the shop, and I feared some might come who knew me. I now had my head shaved and bought a wig, and engaged myself to a Mr. Perkins of Brookline, three miles from Boston, where I remained about a month. Some of the family discovered that I wore a wig, and said that I was a runaway slave, but the neighbors all round thought I was a white, to prove which, I have a document in my possession to call me to military duty. The law is, that no slave or colored person performs this, but every other person in America of the age of twenty-one is called upon to perform military duty, once or twice in the year, or pay a fine.

### COPY OF THE DOCUMENT

"Mr. Moses Roper,
"You being duly enrolled as a soldier in the company, under the command of Captain Benjamin Bradley, are hereby notified and ordered to appear at the Town House in Brookline, on Friday 28th instant, at 3 o'clock, P. M., for the purpose of filling the vacancy in said company occasioned by the promotion of Lieut. Nathaniel M. Weeks, and of filling any other vacancy which may then and there occur in said company, and there wait further orders.

"By order of the captain,
"F. P. WENTWORTH, clerk.

"*Brookline, August 14th, 1835.*"†

I then returned to the city of Boston, to the shop where I was before.‡ Several weeks after I had returned to my situation two colored men informed me that

---

*While in this neighborhood, I attended the Baptist meeting, and trust the preaching of the gospel was much blessed to my soul. As this was the first time I was ever favored with any education, I was very intent upon learning to read the Bible, and in a few weeks I was able, from my own reading, to repeat by heart the whole of the last chapter of Matthew. I also attended the prayer and inquiry meetings, where the attendants used to relate their experience, and I was requested to do the same. I found these meetings a great blessing, and they were the means, under God, of communicating to my mind a more clear and distinct knowledge of the way of salvation by Jesus Christ.
†Being very tall, I was taken to be twenty-one, but my correct age, as far as I can tell, is stated in page 13 [page 494 in this edition].
‡During the first part of my abode in this city, I attended at the colored church in Bellnap street; and I hope I found both profit and pleasure in attending the means of divine grace. I now saw the wicked part I had taken in using so much deception in making my escape. After a time, I found slave-owners were in the habit of going to this colored chapel to look for runaway slaves. I became alarmed and afterwards attended the preaching of the Rev. Dr. Sharp. I waited upon the doctor to request he would baptize me, and admit me a member of his church; and after hearing my experience, he wished me to call again. This I did, but he was gone into the county, and I saw him no more.

a gentleman had been inquiring for a person whom, from the description, I knew to be myself, and offered them a considerable sum if they would disclose my place of abode; but they being much opposed to slavery, came and told me, upon which information I secreted myself till I could get off. I went into the Green Mountains for several weeks, from thence to the city of New York, and remained in secret several days, till I heard of a ship, the Napoleon, sailing to England, and on the 11th of November, 1835, I sailed, taking with me letters of recommendation to the Rev. Drs. Morison and Raffles, and the Rev. Alex. Fletcher. The time I first started from slavery was in July, 1834, so that I was nearly sixteen months in making my escape.

On the 29th of November, 1835, I reached Liverpool, and my feelings when I first touched the shores of Britain were indescribable, and can only be properly understood by those who have escaped from the cruel bondage of slavery.

> " 'Tis liberty alone that gives the flower of fleeting life its lustre and perfume;
> And we are weeds without it."

> "Slaves cannot breathe in England;
> If their lungs receive our air, that moment they are free;
> They touch our country and their shackles fall." — *Cowper*.[17]

When I reached Liverpool, I proceeded to Dr. Raffles, and handed my letters of recommendation to him. He received me very kindly, and introduced me to a member of his church, with whom I stayed the night. Here I met with the greatest attention and kindness. The next day, I went on to Manchester, where I met with many kind friends, among others Mr. Adshead, a hosier of that town, to whom I desire through this medium, to return my most sincere thanks for the many great services which he rendered me, adding both to my spiritual and temporal comfort. I would not, however, forget to remember here, Mr. Leese, Mr. Childs, Mr. Crewdson, and Mr. Clare, the latter of whom gave me a letter to Mr. Scoble, the secretary of the Anti-slavery Society. I remained here several days, and then proceeded to London, December 12th, 1835, and immediately called on Mr. Scoble, to whom I delivered my letter; this gentleman procured me a lodging. I then lost no time in delivering my letters to Dr. Morison and the Rev. Alexander Fletcher, who received me with the greatest kindness, and shortly after this Dr. Morison sent my letter from New York, with another from himself, to the *Patriot* newspaper, in which he kindly implored the sympathy of the public in my behalf. The appeal was read by Mr. Christopherson, a member of Dr. Morison's church, of which gentleman I express but little of my feelings and gratitude, when I say, that throughout he has been towards me a parent, and for whose tenderness and sympathy, I desire ever to feel that attachment which I do not know how to express.

I stayed at his house several weeks, being treated as one of the family. The appeal in the *Patriot,* referred to getting a suitable academy for me, which the Rev. Dr. Cox recommended at Hackney, where I remained half a year, going through the rudiments of an English education. At this time I attended the min-

istry of Dr. Cox, which I enjoyed very much, and to which I ascribe the attainment of clearer views of divine grace than I had before. I had attended here several months, when I expressed my wish to Dr. Cox to become a member of his
church; I was proposed, and after stating my experience was admitted, March
31st, 1836. Here I feel it a duty to present my tribute of thankfulness, however
feebly expressed, to the affectionate and devoted attention of the Rev. Doctor,
from whom, under God, I received very much indeed of spiritual advice and
consolation, as well as a plentiful administration to my temporal necessities. I
would not forget also to mention the kindness of his church generally, by whom
I was received with Christian love and charity. Never, I trust, will be effaced
from my memory, the parental care of the Rev. Dr. Morison, from whom I can
strictly say, I received the greatest kindness I ever met with, and to whom, as
long as God gives me lips to utter, or mind to reflect, I desire to attribute the
comfort which I have experienced since I set my foot upon the happy shores of
England.

Here it is necessary that I should draw this narrative to a close, not that my
materials are exhausted, but that I am unwilling to extend it to a size which might
preclude many well-wishers from the possession of it.

But I must remark, that my feelings of happiness at having escaped from
cruel bondage, are not unmixed with sorrow of a very touching kind. "*The
land of the Free*" still contains the mother, the brothers, and the sisters of
Moses Roper, not enjoying liberty, not the possessors of like feelings with me,
not having even a distant glimpse of advancing towards freedom, but still
slaves! This is a weight which hangs heavy on me. As circumstances at present
stand, there is not much prospect of ever again seeing those dear ones—that
dear mother, from whom, on the Sunday night, I was torn away by armed
slave-holders, and carried into cruel bondage.* And, nothing would contribute
so much to my entire happiness, if the kindness of a gracious Providence
should ever place me in such favorable circumstances as to be able to purchase
the freedom of so beloved a parent. But I desire to express my entire resignation to the will of God. Should that Divine Being who made of one flesh all the
kindreds of the earth, see fit that I should again clasp them to my breast, and
see in them the reality of free men and free women, how shall I, a poor mortal, be enabled to sing a strain of praise sufficiently appropriate to such a boon
from heaven?

But if the all-wise Disposer of all things should see fit to keep them still in
suffering and bondage, it is a mercy to know that he orders all things well, that
he is still the Judge of all the earth, and that under such dispensations of his
Providence, he is working out that which shall be most for the advantage of his
creatures.

Whatever I may have experienced in America, at the hands of cruel taskmasters, yet I am unwilling to speak in any but respectful terms of the land of
my birth. It is far from my wish to attempt to degrade America in the eyes of
Britons. I love her institutions in the free states, her zeal for Christ; I bear no en-

---

*See page 36 [page 502 in this edition].

mity even to the slave-holders, but regret their delusions; many I am aware are deeply sensible of the fault, but some I regret to say are not, and I could wish to open their eyes to their sin; may the period come when God shall wipe off this deep stain from her constitution, and may America soon be indeed the land of the free.

In conclusion, I thank my dear friends in England for their affectionate attentions, and may God help me to show by my future walk in life, that I am not wanting in my acknowledgments of their kindness. But above all, to the God of all grace, I desire here before his people, to acknowledge that all the way in which he has led me, has been the right way; and as in his mercy and wisdom, he has led me to this country, where I am allowed to go free, may all my actions tend to lead me on, through the mercy of God in Christ, in the right way, to a city of habitation.

THE END.

1. Starling, *Slave Narrative*, 108; Roper, "Anti-Slavery Society," 136.
2. Starling, *Slave Narrative*, 110.
3. Roper, "Anti-Slavery Society," 134–136.
4. Ripley, *Black Abolitionist Papers*, I:62.
5. William Cowper, *The Task*. See note 17 below.
6. John Morison, D.D. (1791–1859) was an eminent British congregational minister and, for thirty years, editor of the *Evangelical Magazine*.
7. The Reverend R. J. Breckenridge, according to a letter Roper wrote to Thomas Price in 1836, "question[ed] the accuracy of a statement made by me in reference to the burning alive of a slave in the United States." Roper, "To Thomas Price," 23–24.
8. On the Virginia border, not far from Greensboro.
9. South Carolina.
10. South Carolina.
11. Kershaw County; not far from Columbia.
12. Actually closer to one hundred miles.
13. In the second British edition (1848), Roper adds the following footnote here: "Providence has been profuse in its blessings on me. When I wrote the foregoing statement, about my meeting with my sister Maria, and when I met with some who regarded this fact as bordering on the 'marvellous,' I little thought of such a proof of the truth of it, as I have now the pleasure of recording:—A gentleman of great respectability, at Manchester, having read the account in the first edition, has sent to America to purchase the freedom of Maria, and I know not, but she may be at this moment free, and is likely to be in this country in a short time." Roper, *Narrative*, 2d British ed., 32.
14. After Congress enacted the 1832 tariff act, proclaiming protection tariffs a permanent policy, the South Carolina nullifying party won control of the state legislature and called a state convention for November 19, 1832. The convention adopted an Ordinance of Nullification declaring the tariff acts of 1828 and 1832 oppressive, unconstitutional, null and void, and not binding on the people of South Carolina. In response to the state's enforcement of the Ordinance, President Jackson denounced nullification as treason and asked Congress to pass a "Force Bill" to enable him to use the army and navy to enforce the law. The crisis was averted when Congress passed a Compromise Tariff in February 1833.

15. South Carolina.

16. The Erie Canal.

17. William Cowper, *The Task*. Cowper (1731–1800) was a forerunner of the British romantic poets, and wrote a number of antislavery verses. *The Task* (1785) was probably his most famous poem.

FREDERICK DOUGLASS

FREDERICK DOUGLASS (1818–95), a slave, orator, autobiographer, editor, activist, and statesman, was the most famous African American of the nineteenth century. His 1845 *Narrative of the Life of Frederick Douglass, an American Slave* has taken its place on the short shelf of canonical American books, and is currently the most widely studied slave narrative. It owes its enduring popularity to its superb craftsmanship, to its reputation as the most representative or exemplary slave narrative, and to its expression of the American ideals of freedom, self-determination, self-education, and political activism. As David Blight writes, "In American letters, we have no better illustration of liberation through the power of language than Douglass's *Narrative*."[1]

On May 23, 1845, *The Liberator,* the preeminent abolitionist newspaper, published the following advertisement:

> Narrative of the Life of Frederick Douglass. This long-desired Narrative is now presented to the public, in a neat volume occupying 125 pages. It was written entirely by Mr. Douglass, and reveals all the facts in regard to his birthplace—the names of his mother, master, overseer, etc., etc. It cannot fail to produce a great sensation wherever it may happen to circulate, especially in the slaveocracy. The edition is going off rapidly . . . It is for sale at 25 Cornhill. Price 50 cents. Accompanying it is a finely executed and admirable likeness of the author.[2]

Douglass had escaped from slavery in 1838 and had given his first public speech in 1841. But by 1844 many skeptics were beginning to openly doubt that he had ever been a slave. He spoke too well; his English was too pure; his appearance was too elegant and self-confident; he refused to make known his slave name or verifiable slave experiences for fear of kidnapping.[3] As one letter-writer put it,

> Many persons in the audience seemed unable to credit the statements which he gave of himself, and could not believe that he was actually a slave. How a man, only six years out of bondage, and who had never gone to school a day in his life, could speak with such eloquence—with such precision of language and power of thought—they were utterly at a loss to devise.[4]

By this time, Douglass had no doubt read a number of slave narratives and was well aware of their appeal and persuasiveness.[5] So he took up his pen and composed a slave narrative that would simultaneously confound his skeptics and increase his popularity as an orator.

The book was enormously popular. Its first printing of five thousand copies sold out in four months. Within a year, four additional reprintings of two thousand copies each were exhausted. By 1850 approximately thirty thousand copies had been sold in the United States and Great Britain, including a sale of six and a half thousand copies in Belfast in a space of three months, and the *Narrative* had been translated into Dutch and French.[6]

The book was no less well received by reviewers than by the public. The Lynn, Massachusetts, *Pioneer* wrote:

> It is the most thrilling work which the American press ever issued—and the most important. If it does not open the eyes of this people, they must be petrified into eternal sleep. . . . There are passages in it which would brighten the reputation of any living author,—while the book, as a whole, judged as a mere work of art, would widen the fame of Bunyan and DeFoe.[7]

And Margaret Fuller, in a front-page review in the New York *Tribune,* wrote:

> He has had the courage to name the persons, times and places, thus exposing himself to obvious danger, and setting the seal on his deep convictions as to the religious need of speaking the whole truth. Considered merely as a narrative, we have never read one more simple, true, coherent, and warm with genuine feeling. It is an excellent piece of writing, and on that score to be prized as a specimen of the powers of the Black Race, which Prejudice persists in disputing.[8]

On first reading, Douglass's *Narrative* appears to be a remarkably integrated, linear work that presents himself and his stories simply and straightforwardly. His allegiance to himself he declares as absolute: "I prefer to be true to myself, even at the hazard of incurring the ridicule of others, rather than to be false, and incur my own abhorrence." His self-knowledge is at first incomplete, and is only realized when he learns to read. As James Olney points out, "Literacy, identity, and a sense of freedom are all acquired simultaneously and without the first, according to Douglass, the latter two would never have been."[9] His self-mastery is thus dependent on his mastery of the word. While the incidents he relates are fairly standard for the slave narrative genre, his unparalleled rhetorical skill, as evidenced by his use of a wide variety of sophisticated rhetorical devices, draws attention not so much to the incidents themselves, but to their significance for himself and his cause. Thus, as William Andrews comments, Douglass "repossesses autobiography as a self-expressive, not simply a fact-assertive, act."[10] In writing about the events of his life as a slave he becomes their master.

Almost as if he were proving his literary mastery, Douglass audaciously refuses to divulge any of the details of his escape from slavery. As Lucinda Mac-Kethan writes, "This might have been disastrous, like leaving the filling out of a pie, since the escape portion of the slave narrative would have been eagerly awaited as the most suspenseful and thrilling segment."[11] This unusual omission makes it difficult to portray Douglass's *Narrative* as exemplary of the genre. For rather than the attainment of liberty, its climax is Douglass's assumption of a new identity, his affirmation of his mastery over his name, his freedom, and his selfhood. As Olney states, "In that lettered utterance [of his name] is assertion of identity and in identity is freedom—freedom from slavery, freedom from ignorance, freedom from non-being, freedom even from time."[12]

But Douglass's new identity was indissolubly bound to the abolitionist cause. His allegiance to it is evident not only in his choice of Garrison and Wendell Phillips, the two most prominent white abolitionists of the day, to contribute to his narrative; he also closes his narrative with an antislavery meeting at which

Garrison was present, and calls the latter's doctrines as put forth in the *Liberator* "my meat and my drink." The tenets of abolitionism are everywhere apparent in the *Narrative*. As Blyden Jackson notes,

> It dichotomizes the people it portrays, and most of the action it presents, quite symmetrically according to a formula which surrounds with a bright and presumably celestial light all that is antislavery, including the slaves, and shrouds within a Stygian gloom the exact opposite of a heavenly radiance everything and anything of supposed aid to slavery.[13]

Although Douglass takes great care to stick to the facts, in interpreting those facts he reinvents his history and himself along abolitionist lines. As a slave, Douglass presents himself as "a heroic loner whose relationship to his environment was largely adversarial," as Andrews points out. "Slavery was 'hell,' a state of deprivation epitomized by the absence of mother, father, family, and, except during a short interlude at Mr. Freeland's, community with others."[14] The degree to which he exaggerates his isolation in the *Narrative* becomes clear from the fuller, more nuanced description of his family and the slave community in his subsequent autobiography, *My Bondage and My Freedom* (1855), written eight years after his split with Garrison.

In his speeches and other writings of the 1840s and 1850s, Douglass subjects the United States and its institutions to withering scorn, denouncing institutionalized racism and the Constitution's protection of slaveholders. But the *Narrative* presents itself as an American story of "An American Slave," never hinting—as Douglass would write in a letter to Garrison only seven months after its publication, and would repeat in *My Bondage and My Freedom*— that "in thinking of America, . . . I am filled with unutterable loathing, and led to reproach myself that any thing could fall from my lips in praise of such a land."[15]

The result of Douglass's abstraction of his experiences and his fidelity to his brand of abolitionism is that, as Henry Louis Gates, Jr. makes clear, "Douglass's rhetorical power convinces us that he is 'the' black slave, that he embodies the structures of thoughts and feelings of all black slaves, that he is the resplendent, articulate part that stands for the whole, for the collective black slave community."[16] Although this may belie Douglass's insistence on being true to himself, it reinforces his rhetorical power over his audience. And, after all, that rhetorical power—precisely because it was so persuasive—was likely Douglass's main concern when composing his narrative. As Eric Sundquist remarks, "The *Narrative* is, in fact, something of a memorized lecture performance transferred to paper."[17]

The book would in turn establish on firm ground Douglass's subsequent career as an orator and statesman. Now that he had identified himself as a fugitive slave, it was no longer safe for him to remain in the United States, so he reluctantly departed for a lecture tour of the British Isles, where his reputation had preceded him. As Peter Ripley notes, "The *Narrative* blended with the tour, one contributing to the success of the other. By providing advance publicity, the book helped launch Douglass's tour of the British Isles, and its sales sustained him while there."[18]

Like other slave narratives, Douglass's then fell out of print for over one hundred years, and was not reprinted until 1960. Its subsequent recuperation and canonization, however, was rapid. As Blight puts it, "During the 1970s and 1980s, . . . analysis of the text became a kind of rite of passage in the burgeoning field of black literary criticism."[19] The amount of writing devoted to Douglass's *Narrative* now exceeds that of all other slave narratives, and over a dozen editions are currently available.

As for Douglass, friends purchased his freedom from Hugh Auld in December 1846,[20] and the following April he returned to the United States. From 1847 to 1863 he edited his own publication, at first called the *North Star,* then *Frederick Douglass' Paper,* and finally *Douglass' Monthly.* In 1855 he published *My Bondage and My Freedom,* a less heroic, equally militant, and far longer, more sophisticated, playful, detached, nuanced, and inclusive autobiography. In the meantime he was involved in the national Negro convention movement, various black conferences, and the women's suffrage movement. During the Civil War Douglass was on close terms with President Lincoln, and urged him to enlist black troops in the Union army. While he had long been the preeminent spokesman for his race, after the war he was even more widely known and respected. In the 1870s and 1880s he held various governmental offices, continued his career as an orator and activist, and published a third autobiography, the *Life and Times of Frederick Douglass* (1881). Throughout his life he tried to transcend issues of race, claiming ultimate allegiance to the human race. Yet he nonetheless personified—and will continue to personify—his people's struggle from slavery to freedom.

*Frederick Douglass*

# NARRATIVE

OF THE

# LIFE

OF

# FREDERICK DOUGLASS,

AN

# AMERICAN SLAVE.

———

## WRITTEN BY HIMSELF.

———

BOSTON

PUBLISHED AT THE ANTI-SLAVERY OFFICE,

No. 25 CORNHILL

1845

# PREFACE.

In the month of August, 1841, I attended an anti-slavery convention in Nantucket, at which it was my happiness to become acquainted with FREDERICK DOUGLASS, the writer of the following Narrative. He was a stranger to nearly every member of that body; but, having recently made his escape from the southern prison-house of bondage, and feeling his curiosity excited to ascertain the principles and measures of the abolitionists,—of whom he had heard a somewhat vague description while he was a slave,—he was induced to give his attendance, on the occasion alluded to, though at that time a resident in New Bedford.

Fortunate, most fortunate occurrence!—fortunate for the millions of his manacled brethren, yet panting for deliverance from their awful thraldom!—fortunate for the cause of negro emancipation, and of universal liberty!—fortunate for the land of his birth, which he has already done so much to save and bless!—fortunate for a large circle of friends and acquaintances, whose sympathy and affection he has strongly secured by the many sufferings he has endured, by his virtuous traits of character, by his ever-abiding remembrance of those who are in bonds, as being bound with them!—fortunate for the multitudes, in various parts of our republic, whose minds he has enlightened on the subject of slavery, and who have been melted to tears by his pathos, or roused to virtuous indignation by his stirring eloquence against the enslavers of men!—fortunate for himself, as it at once brought him into the field of public usefulness, "gave the world assurance of a MAN,"[21] quickened the slumbering energies of his soul, and consecrated him to the great work of breaking the rod of the oppressor, and letting the oppressed go free!

I shall never forget his first speech at the convention—the extraordinary emotion it excited in my own mind—the powerful impression it created upon a crowded auditory, completely taken by surprise—the applause which followed from the beginning to the end of his felicitous remarks. I think I never hated slavery so intensely as at that moment; certainly, my perception of the enormous outrage which is inflicted by it, on the godlike nature of its victims, was rendered far more clear than ever. There stood one, in physical proportion and stature commanding and exact—in intellect richly endowed—in natural eloquence a prodigy—in soul manifestly "created but a little lower than the angels"[22]—yet a slave, ay, a fugitive slave,—trembling for his safety, hardly daring to believe that on the American soil, a single white person could be found who would befriend him at all hazards, for the love of God and humanity! Capable of high attainments as an intellectual and moral being—needing nothing but a comparatively small amount of cultivation to make him an ornament to society and a blessing to his race—by the law of the land, by the voice of the people, by the terms of the slave code, he was only a piece of property, a beast of burden, a chattel personal, nevertheless!

A beloved friend from New Bedford prevailed on Mr. DOUGLASS to address the convention: He came forward to the platform with a hesitancy and embarrassment, necessarily the attendants of a sensitive mind in such a novel position. After apologizing for his ignorance, and reminding the audience that slavery was a poor school for the human intellect and heart, he proceeded to narrate some of the facts in his own history as a slave, and in the course of his speech gave utterance to many noble thoughts and thrilling reflections. As soon as he had taken his seat, filled with hope and admiration, I rose, and declared that PATRICK HENRY, of revolutionary fame, never made a speech more eloquent in the cause of liberty, than the one we had just listened to from the lips of that hunted fugitive. So I believed at that time—such is my belief now. I reminded the audience of the peril which surrounded this self-emancipated young man at the North,—even in Massachusetts, on the soil of the Pilgrim Fathers, among the descendants of revolutionary sires; and I appealed to them, whether they would ever allow him to be carried back into slavery,—law or no law, constitution or no constitution. The response was unanimous and in thunder-tones—"NO!" "Will you succor and protect him as a brother-man—a resident of the old Bay State?" "YES!" shouted the whole mass, with an energy so startling, that the ruthless tyrants south of Mason and Dixon's line might almost have heard the mighty burst of feeling, and recognized it as the pledge of an invincible determination, on the part of those who gave it, never to betray him that wanders, but to hide the outcast, and firmly to abide the consequences.

It was at once deeply impressed upon my mind, that, if Mr. DOUGLASS could be persuaded to consecrate his time and talents to the promotion of the anti-slavery enterprise, a powerful impetus would be given to it, and a stunning blow at the same time inflicted on northern prejudice against a colored complexion. I therefore endeavored to instil hope and courage into his mind, in order that he might dare to engage in a vocation so anomalous and responsible for a person in his situation; and I was seconded in this effort by warm-hearted friends, especially by the late General Agent of the Massachusetts Anti-Slavery Society, Mr. JOHN A. COLLINS, whose judgment in this instance entirely coincided with my own. At first, he could give no encouragement; with unfeigned diffidence, he expressed his conviction that he was not adequate to the performance of so great a task; the path marked out was wholly an untrodden one; he was sincerely apprehensive that he should do more harm than good. After much deliberation, however, he consented to make a trial; and ever since that period, he has acted as a lecturing agent, under the auspices either of the American or the Massachusetts Anti-Slavery Society. In labors he has been most abundant; and his success in combating prejudice, in gaining proselytes, in agitating the public mind, has far surpassed the most sanguine expectations that were raised at the commencement of his brilliant career. He has borne himself with gentleness and meekness, yet with true manliness of character. As a public speaker, he excels in pathos, wit, comparison, imitation, strength of reasoning, and fluency of language. There is in him that union of head and heart, which is indispensable to an enlightenment of the heads and a winning of the hearts of others. May his strength continue to be equal to his day! May he continue to "grow in grace, and in the knowledge of God,"[23] that he may be increasingly serviceable in the cause of bleeding humanity, whether at home or abroad!

It is certainly a very remarkable fact, that one of the most efficient advocates of the slave population, now before the public, is a fugitive slave, in the person of FREDERICK DOUGLASS; and that the free colored population of the United States are as ably represented by one of their own number, in the person of CHARLES LENOX

REMOND,[24] whose eloquent appeals have extorted the highest applause of multitudes on both sides of the Atlantic. Let the calumniators of the colored race despise themselves for their baseness and illiberality of spirit, and henceforth cease to talk of the natural inferiority of those who require nothing but time and opportunity to attain to the highest point of human excellence.

It may, perhaps, be fairly questioned, whether any other portion of the population of the earth could have endured the privations, sufferings and horrors of slavery, without having become more degraded in the scale of humanity than the slaves of African descent. Nothing has been left undone to cripple their intellects, darken their minds, debase their moral nature, obliterate all traces of their relationship to mankind; and yet how wonderfully they have sustained the mighty load of a most frightful bondage, under which they have been groaning for centuries! To illustrate the effect of slavery on the white man,—to show that he has no powers of endurance, in such a condition, superior to those of his black brother,—DANIEL O'CONNELL, the distinguished advocate of universal emancipation, and the mightiest champion of prostrate but not conquered Ireland,[25] relates the following anecdote in a speech delivered by him in the Conciliation Hall, Dublin, before the Loyal National Repeal Association, March 31, 1845. "No matter," said Mr. O'CONNELL, "under what specious term it may disguise itself, slavery is still hideous. *It has a natural, an inevitable tendency to brutalize every noble faculty of man.* An American sailor, who was cast away on the shore of Africa, where he was kept in slavery for three years, was, at the expiration of that period, found to be imbruted and stultified—he had lost all reasoning power; and having forgotten his native language, could only utter some savage gibberish between Arabic and English, which nobody could understand, and which even he himself found difficulty in pronouncing. So much for the humanizing influence of THE DOMESTIC INSTITUTION!" Admitting this to have been an extraordinary case of mental deterioration, it proves at least that the white slave can sink as low in the scale of humanity as the black one.

Mr. DOUGLASS has very properly chosen to write his own Narrative, in his own style, and according to the best of his ability, rather than to employ some one else. It is, therefore, entirely his own production; and, considering how long and dark was the career he had to run as a slave,—how few have been his opportunities to improve his mind since he broke his iron fetters,—it is, in my judgment, highly creditable to his head and heart. He who can peruse it without a tearful eye, a heaving breast, an afflicted spirit,—without being filled with an unutterable abhorrence of slavery and all its abettors, and animated with a determination to seek the immediate overthrow of that execrable system,—without trembling for the fate of this country in the hands of a righteous God, who is ever on the side of the oppressed, and whose arm is not shortened that it cannot save,—must have a flinty heart, and be qualified to act the part of a trafficker "in slaves and the souls of men."[26] I am confident that it is essentially true in all its statements; that nothing has been set down in malice, nothing exaggerated, nothing drawn from the imagination; that it comes short of the reality, rather than overstates a single fact in regard to SLAVERY AS IT IS.[27] The experience of FREDERICK DOUGLASS, as a slave, was not a peculiar one; his lot was not especially a hard one; his case may be regarded as a very fair specimen of the treatment of slaves in Maryland, in which State it is conceded that they are better fed and less cruelly treated than in Georgia, Alabama, or Louisiana. Many have suffered incomparably more, while very few on the plantations have suffered less, than himself. Yet how deplorable was his situation! what terrible chastisements were inflicted upon his person! what still more shocking outrages were perpetrated upon his mind! with all his noble powers and sublime aspirations, how like a brute was he treated, even by those professing to have the same mind in them that was in Christ Jesus! to what dreadful liabilities was he continually subjected! how destitute of friendly counsel and aid, even in his greatest extremities! how heavy was the midnight of woe which shrouded in blackness the last ray of hope, and filled the future with terror and gloom! what longings after freedom took possession of his breast, and how his misery augmented, in proportion as he grew reflective and intelligent,—thus demonstrating that a happy slave is an extinct man! how he thought, reasoned, felt, under the lash of the driver, with the chains upon his limbs! what perils he encountered in his endeavors to escape from his horrible doom! and how signal have been his deliverance and preservation in the midst of a nation of pitiless enemies!

This Narrative contains many affecting incidents, many passages of great eloquence and power; but I think the most thrilling one of them all is the description DOUGLASS gives of his feelings, as he stood soliloquizing respecting his fate, and the chances of his one day being a freeman, on the banks of the Chesapeake Bay—viewing the receding vessels as they flew with their white wings before the breeze, and apostrophizing them as animated by the living spirit of freedom. Who can read that passage, and be insensible to its pathos and sublimity? Compressed into it is a whole Alexandrian library[28] of thought, feeling, and sentiment—all that can, all that need be urged, in the form of expostulation, entreaty, rebuke, against that crime of crimes,—making man the property of his fellow-man! O, how accursed is that system, which entombs the godlike mind of man, defaces the divine image, reduces those who by creation were crowned with glory and honor to a level with four-footed beasts, and exalts the dealer in human flesh above all that is called God! Why should its existence be prolonged one hour? Is it not evil, only evil, and that continually? What does its presence imply but the absence of all fear of God, all regard for man, on the part of the people of the United States? Heaven speed its eternal overthrow!

So profoundly ignorant of the nature of slavery are many persons, that they are stubbornly incredulous whenever they read or listen to any recital of the cruelties which are daily inflicted on its victims. They do not deny that the slaves are held as property; but that terrible fact seems to convey to their minds no idea of injustice, exposure to outrage, or savage barbarity. Tell them of cruel scourgings, of mutilations and brandings, of scenes of pollution and blood, of the banishment of all light and knowledge, and they affect to be greatly indignant at such enormous exaggerations, such wholesale misstatements, such abominable libels on the character of the southern planters! As if all these direful outrages were not the natural results of slavery! As if it were less cruel to reduce a human being to the condition of a thing, than to give him a severe flagellation, or to deprive him of necessary food and clothing! As if whips, chains, thumb-screws, paddles, bloodhounds, overseers, drivers, patrols, were not all indispensable to keep the slaves down, and to give protection to their ruthless oppressors! As if, when the marriage institution is abolished, concubinage, adultery, and incest, must not necessarily abound; when all the rights of humanity are annihilated, any barrier remains to protect the victim from the fury of the spoiler; when absolute power is assumed over life and liberty, it will not be wielded with destructive sway! Skeptics of this character abound in society. In some few instances, their incredulity arises from a want of reflection; but, generally, it indicates a hatred of the light, a desire to shield slavery from the assaults of its foes, a contempt of the colored race, whether bond or free. Such will try to discredit the shocking tales of slaveholding cruelty which are recorded in this truthful Narrative; but they will labor in vain. Mr. DOUGLASS has frankly disclosed the place of his birth, the names of those who claimed ownership in his body and soul, and the names also of those who committed the crimes which he has alleged against them. His statements, therefore, may easily be disproved, if they are untrue.

In the course of his Narrative, he relates two instances of murderous cruelty,— in one of which a planter deliberately shot a slave belonging to a neighboring plantation, who had unintentionally gotten within his lordly domain in quest of fish; and in the other, an overseer blew out the brains of a slave who had fled to a stream of water to escape a bloody scourging. Mr. DOUGLASS states that in neither of these instances was any thing done by way of legal arrest or judicial investigation. The Baltimore American, of March 17, 1845, relates a similar case of atrocity, perpetrated with similar impunity—as follows:—"*Shooting a slave.*—We learn, upon the authority of a letter from Charles county, Maryland, received by a gentleman of this city, that a young man, named Matthews, a nephew of General Matthews, and whose father, it is believed, holds an office at Washington, killed one of the slaves upon his father's farm by shooting him. The letter states that young Matthews had been left in charge of the farm; that he gave an order to the servant, which was disobeyed, when he proceeded to the house, *obtained a gun, and, returning, shot the servant.* He immediately, the letter continues, fled to his father's residence, where he still remains unmolested."—Let it never be forgotten, that no slaveholder or overseer can be convicted of any outrage perpetrated on the person of a slave, however diabolical it may be, on the testimony of colored witnesses, whether bond or free. By the slave code, they are adjudged to be as incompetent to testify against a white man, as though they were indeed a part of the brute creation. Hence, there is no legal protection in fact, whatever there may be in form, for the slave population; and any amount of cruelty may be inflicted on them with impunity. Is it possible for the human mind to conceive of a more horrible state of society?

The effect of a religious profession on the conduct of southern masters is vividly described in the following Narrative, and shown to be any thing but salutary. In the nature of the case, it must be in the highest degree pernicious. The testimony of Mr. DOUGLASS, on this point, is sustained by a cloud of witnesses, whose veracity is unimpeachable. "A slaveholder's profession of Christianity is a palpable imposture. He is a felon of the highest grade. He is a man-stealer. It is of no importance what you put in the other scale."

Reader! are you with the man-stealers in sympathy and purpose, or on the side of their down-trodden victims? If with the former, then are you the foe of God and man. If with the latter, what are you prepared to do and dare in their behalf? Be faithful, be vigilant, be untiring in your efforts to break every yoke, and let the oppressed go free. Come what may—cost what it may—inscribe on the banner which you unfurl to the breeze, as your religious and political motto—"NO COMPROMISE WITH SLAVERY! NO UNION WITH SLAVEHOLDERS!"

WM. LLOYD GARRISON.[29]

BOSTON, *May* 1, 1845.

# LETTER
## FROM WENDELL PHILLIPS, ESQ.[30]

BOSTON, *April 22,* 1845.

My Dear Friend:

YOU remember the old fable of "The Man and the Lion," where the lion complained that he should not be so misrepresented "when the lions wrote history."[31]

I am glad the time has come when the "lions write history." We have been left long enough to gather the character of slavery from the involuntary evidence of the masters. One might, indeed, rest sufficiently satisfied with what, it is evident, must be, in general, the results of such a relation, without seeking farther to find whether they have followed in every instance. Indeed, those who stare at the half-peck of corn a week, and love to count the lashes on the slave's back, are seldom the "stuff" out of which reformers and abolitionists are to be made. I remember that, in 1838, many were waiting for the results of the West India experiment,[32] before they could come into our ranks. Those "results" have come long ago; but, alas! few of that number have come with them, as converts. A man must be disposed to judge of emancipation by other tests than whether it has increased the produce of sugar,—and to hate slavery for other reasons than because it starves men and whips women,—before he is ready to lay the first stone of his anti-slavery life.

I was glad to learn, in your story, how early the most neglected of God's children waken to a sense of their rights, and of the injustice done them. Experience is a keen teacher; and long before you had mastered your A B C, or knew where the "white sails" of the Chesapeake were bound, you began, I see, to gauge the wretchedness of the slave, not by his hunger and want, not by his lashes and toil, but by the cruel and blighting death which gathers over his soul.

In connection with this, there is one circumstance which makes your recollections peculiarly valuable, and renders your early insight the more remarkable. You come from that part of the country where we are told slavery appears with its fairest features. Let us hear, then, what it is at its best estate—gaze on its bright side, if it has one; and then imagination may task her powers to add dark lines to the picture, as she travels southward to that (for the colored man) Valley of the Shadow of Death, where the Mississippi sweeps along.

Again, we have known you long, and can put the most entire confidence in your truth, candor, and sincerity. Every one who has heard you speak has felt, and, I am confident, every one who reads your book will feel, persuaded that you give them a fair specimen of the whole truth. No one-sided portrait,—no wholesale complaints,—but strict justice done, whenever individual kindliness has neutralized, for a moment, the deadly system with which it was strangely allied. You have been with us, too, some years, and can fairly compare the twilight of rights, which your race enjoy at the North, with that "noon of night"[33] under which they labor south of Mason and Dixon's line. Tell us whether, after all, the half-free colored man of Massachusetts is worse off than the pampered slave of the rice swamps!

In reading your life, no one can say that we have unfairly picked out some rare specimens of cruelty. We know that the bitter drops, which even you have drained from the cup, are no incidental aggravations, no individual ills, but such as must mingle always and necessarily in the lot of every slave. They are the essential ingredients, not the occasional results, of the system.

After all, I shall read your book with trembling for you. Some years ago, when you were beginning to tell me your real name and birthplace, you may remember I stopped you, and preferred to remain ignorant of all. With the exception of a vague description, so I continued, till the other day, when you read me your memoirs. I hardly knew, at the time, whether to thank you or not for the sight of them, when I reflected that it was still dangerous, in Massachusetts, for honest men to tell their names! They say the fathers, in 1776, signed the Declaration of Independence with the halter about their necks. You, too, publish your declaration of freedom with danger compassing you around. In all the broad lands which the Constitution of the United States overshadows, there is no single spot,—however narrow or desolate,—where a fugitive slave can plant himself and say, "I am safe." The whole armory of Northern Law has no shield for you. I am free to say that, in your place, I should throw the MS. into the fire.

You, perhaps, may tell your story in safety, endeared as you are to so many warm hearts by rare gifts, and a still rarer devotion of them to the service of others. But it will be owing only to your labors, and the fearless efforts of those who, trampling the laws and Constitution of the country under their feet, are determined that they will "hide the outcast," and that their hearths shall be, spite of the law, an asylum for the oppressed, if, some time or other, the humblest may stand in our streets, and bear witness in safety against the cruelties of which he has been the victim.

Yet it is sad to think, that these very throbbing hearts which welcome your story, and form your best safeguard in telling it, are all beating contrary to the "statute in such case made and provided."[34] Go on, my dear friend, till you, and those who, like you, have been saved, so as by fire, from the dark prison-house, shall stereotype these free, illegal pulses into statutes; and New England, cutting loose from a blood-stained Union, shall glory in being the house of refuge for the oppressed;—till we no longer merely "*hide* the outcast," or make a merit of standing idly by while he is hunted in our midst; but, consecrating anew the soil of the Pilgrims as an asylum for the oppressed, proclaim our *welcome* to the slave so loudly, that the tones shall reach every hut in the Carolinas, and make the broken-hearted bondman leap up at the thought of old Massachusetts.

God speed the day!
Till then, and ever,
Yours truly,
WENDELL PHILLIPS.

Frederick Douglass.

# NARRATIVE

## OF THE

# LIFE OF FREDERICK DOUGLASS.

---

### CHAPTER I.

I WAS born in Tuckahoe, near Hillsborough, and about twelve miles from Easton, in Talbot county, Maryland. I have no accurate knowledge of my age, never having seen any authentic record containing it. By far the larger part of the slaves know as little of their ages as horses know of theirs, and it is the wish of most masters within my knowledge to keep their slaves thus ignorant. I do not remember to have ever met a slave who could tell of his birthday. They seldom come nearer to it than planting-time, harvest-time, cherry-time, spring-time, or fall-time. A want of information concerning my own was a source of unhappiness to me even during childhood. The white children could tell their ages. I could not tell why I ought to be deprived of the same privilege. I was not allowed to make any inquiries of my master concerning it. He deemed all such inquiries on the part of a slave improper and impertinent, and evidence of a restless spirit. The nearest estimate I can give makes me now between twenty-seven and twenty-eight years of age. I come to this, from hearing my master say, some time during 1835, I was about seventeen years old.

My mother was named Harriet Bailey. She was the daughter of Isaac and Betsey Bailey, both colored, and quite dark. My mother was of a darker complexion than either my grandmother or grandfather.

My father was a white man. He was admitted to be such by all I ever heard speak of my parentage. The opinion was also whispered that my master was my father; but of the correctness of this opinion, I know nothing; the means of knowing was withheld from me. My mother and I were separated when I was but an infant—before I knew her as my mother. It is a common custom, in the part of Maryland from which I ran away, to part children from their mothers at a very early age. Frequently, before the child has reached its twelfth month, its mother is taken from it, and hired out on some farm a considerable distance off, and the child is placed under the care of an old woman, too old for field labor. For what this separation is done, I do not know, unless it be to hinder the development of the child's affection toward its mother, and to blunt and destroy the natural affection of the mother for the child. This is the inevitable result.

I never saw my mother, to know her as such, more than four or five times in my life; and each of these times was very short in duration, and at night. She was hired by a Mr. Stewart, who lived about twelve miles from my home. She made her journeys to see me in the night, travelling the whole distance on foot, after the performance of her day's work. She was a field hand, and a whipping is the penalty of not being in the field at sunrise, unless a slave has special permission from his or her master to the contrary—a permission which they seldom get, and one that gives to him that gives it the proud name of being a kind master. I do not recollect of ever seeing my mother by the light of day. She was with me in the night. She would lie down with me, and get me to sleep, but long before I waked she was gone. Very little communication ever took place between us. Death soon ended what little we could have while she lived, and with it her hardships and suffering. She died when I was about seven years old, on one of my master's farms, near Lee's Mill. I was not allowed to be present during her illness, at her death, or burial. She was gone long before I knew any thing about it. Never having enjoyed, to any considerable extent, her soothing presence, her tender and watchful care, I received the tidings of her death with much the same emotions I should have probably felt at the death of a stranger.

Called thus suddenly away, she left me without the slightest intimation of who my father was. The whisper that my master was my father, may or may not be true; and, true or false, it is of but little consequence to my purpose whilst the fact remains, in all its glaring odiousness, that slaveholders have ordained, and by law established, that the children of slave women shall in all cases follow the condition of their mothers; and this is done too obviously to administer to their own lusts, and make a gratification of their wicked desires profitable as well as pleasurable; for by this cunning arrangement, the slaveholder, in cases not a few, sustains to his slaves the double relation of master and father.

I know of such cases; and it is worthy of remark that such slaves invariably suffer greater hardships, and have more to contend with, than others. They are, in the first place, a constant offence to their mistress. She is ever disposed to find fault with them; they can seldom do any thing to please her; she is never better pleased than when she sees them under the lash, especially when she suspects her husband of showing to his mulatto children favors which he withholds from his black slaves. The master is frequently compelled to sell this class of his slaves, out of deference to the feelings of his white wife; and, cruel as the deed may strike any one to be, for a man to sell his own children to human flesh-mongers, it is often the dictate of humanity for him to do so; for, unless he does this, he must not only whip them himself, but must stand by and see one white son tie up his brother, of but few shades darker complexion than himself, and ply the gory lash to his naked back; and if he lisp one word of disapproval, it is set down to his parental partiality, and only makes a bad matter worse, both for himself and the slave whom he would protect and defend.

Every year brings with it multitudes of this class of slaves. It was doubtless in consequence of a knowledge of this fact, that one great statesman of the south predicted the downfall of slavery by the inevitable laws of population.[35] Whether this prophecy is ever fulfilled or not, it is nevertheless plain that a very different-looking class of people are springing up at the south, and are now held in slavery, from those originally brought to this country from Africa; and if their increase do no other good, it will do away the force of the argument, that God cursed Ham, and therefore American slavery is right. If the lineal descendants of Ham are alone to be scripturally enslaved, it is certain that slavery at the south must soon become unscriptural; for thousands are ushered into the world, annually, who, like myself, owe their existence to white fathers, and those fathers most frequently their own masters.

I have had two masters. My first master's name was Anthony. I do not remember his first name.[36] He was generally called Captain Anthony—a title which, I presume, he acquired by sailing a craft on the Chesapeake Bay. He was not considered a rich slaveholder. He owned two or three farms, and about thirty slaves. His farms and slaves were under the care of an overseer. The overseer's name was Plummer. Mr. Plummer was a miserable drunkard, a profane swearer, and a savage monster. He always went armed with a cowskin and a heavy cudgel. I have known him to cut and slash the women's heads so horribly, that even master would be enraged at his cruelty, and would threaten to whip him if he did not mind himself. Master, however, was not a humane slaveholder. It required extraordinary barbarity on the part of an overseer to affect him. He was a cruel man, hardened by a long life of slaveholding. He would at times seem to take great pleasure in whipping a slave. I have often been awakened at the dawn of day by the most heart-rending shrieks of an own aunt of mine, whom he used to tie up to a joist, and whip upon her naked back till she was literally covered with blood. No words, no tears, no prayers, from his gory victim, seemed to move his iron heart from its bloody purpose. The louder she screamed, the harder he whipped; and where the blood ran fastest, there he whipped longest. He would whip her to make her scream, and whip her to make her hush; and not until overcome by fatigue, would he cease to swing the blood-clotted cowskin. I remember the first time I ever witnessed this horrible exhibition. I was quite a child, but I well remember it. I never shall forget it whilst I remember any thing. It was the first of a long series of such outrages, of which I was doomed to be a witness and a participant. It struck me with awful force. It was the blood-stained gate, the entrance to the hell of slavery, through which I was about to pass. It was a most terrible spectacle. I wish I could commit to paper the feelings with which I beheld it.

This occurrence took place very soon after I went to live with my old master, and under the following circumstances. Aunt Hester went out one night,—where or for what I do not know,—and happened to be absent when my master desired her presence. He had ordered her not to go out evenings, and warned her that she must never let him catch her in company with a young man, who was paying attention to her belonging to Colonel Lloyd.[37] The young man's name was Ned Roberts, generally called Lloyd's Ned. Why master was so careful of her, may be safely left to conjecture. She was a woman of noble form, and of graceful proportions, having very few equals, and fewer superiors, in personal appearance, among the colored or white women of our neighborhood.

Aunt Hester had not only disobeyed his orders in going out, but had been found in company with Lloyd's Ned; which circumstance, I found, from what he said while whipping her, was the chief offence. Had he been a man of pure morals himself, he might have been thought interested in protecting the innocence of my aunt; but those who knew him will not suspect him of any such virtue. Before he commenced whipping Aunt Hester, he took her into the kitchen, and stripped her from neck to waist, leaving her neck, shoulders, and back, entirely naked. He then told her to cross her hands, calling her at the same time a d——d b——h. After crossing her hands, he tied them with a strong rope, and led her to a stool under a large hook in the joist, put in for the purpose. He made her get upon the stool, and tied her hands to the hook. She now stood fair for his infernal purpose. Her arms were stretched up at their full length, so that she stood upon the ends of her toes. He then said to her, "Now, you d——d b——h, I'll learn you how to disobey my orders!" and after rolling up his sleeves, he commenced to lay on the heavy cowskin, and soon the warm, red blood (amid heart-rending shrieks from her, and horrid oaths from him) came dripping to the floor. I was so terrified and horror-stricken at the sight, that I hid myself in a closet, and dared not venture out till long after the bloody transaction was over. I expected it would be my turn next. It was all new to me. I had never seen any thing like it before. I had always lived with my grandmother on the outskirts of the plantation, where she was put to raise the children of the younger women. I had therefore been, until now, out of the way of the bloody scenes that often occurred on the plantation.

## CHAPTER II.

MY master's family consisted of two sons, Andrew and Richard; one daughter, Lucretia, and her husband, Captain Thomas Auld. They lived in one house, upon the home plantation of Colonel Edward Lloyd. My master was Colonel Lloyd's clerk and superintendent. He was what might be called the overseer of the overseers. I spent two years of childhood on this plantation in my old master's family. It was here that I witnessed the bloody transaction recorded in the first chapter; and as I received my first impressions of slavery on this plantation, I will give some description of it, and of slavery as it there existed. The plantation is about twelve miles north of Easton, in Talbot county, and is situated on the border of Miles River. The principal products raised upon it were tobacco, corn, and wheat. These were raised in great abundance; so that, with the products of this and the other farms belonging to him, he was able to keep in almost constant employment a large sloop, in carrying them to market at Baltimore. This sloop was named Sally Lloyd, in honor of one of the colonel's daughters. My master's son-in-law, Captain Auld, was master of the vessel; she was otherwise manned by the colonel's own slaves. Their names were Peter, Isaac, Rich, and Jake. These were esteemed very highly by the other slaves, and looked upon as the privileged ones of the plantation; for it was no small affair, in the eyes of the slaves, to be allowed to see Baltimore.

Colonel Lloyd kept from three to four hundred slaves on his home plantation, and owned a large number more on the neighboring farms belonging to him. The names of the farms nearest to the home plantation were Wye Town and New Design. "Wye Town" was under the overseership of a man named Noah Willis. New Design was under the overseership of a Mr. Townsend. The overseers of these, and all the rest of the farms, numbering over twenty, received advice and direction from the managers of the home plantation. This was the great business place. It was the seat of government for the whole twenty farms. All disputes among the overseers were settled here. If a slave was convicted of any high misdemeanor, became unmanageable, or evinced a determination to run away, he was brought immediately here, severely whipped, put on board the sloop, carried to Baltimore, and sold to Austin Woolfolk,[38] or some other slave-trader, as a warning to the slaves remaining.

Here, too, the slaves of all the other farms received their monthly allowance of food, and their yearly clothing. The men and women slaves received, as their monthly allowance of food, eight pounds of pork, or its equivalent in fish, and one bushel of corn meal. Their yearly clothing consisted of two coarse linen shirts, one pair of linen trousers, like the shirts, one jacket, one pair of trousers for winter, made of coarse negro cloth, one pair of stockings, and one pair of shoes; the whole of which could not have cost more than seven dollars. The allowance of the slave children was given to their mothers, or the old women having the care of them. The children unable to work in the field had neither shoes, stockings, jackets, nor trousers, given to them; their clothing consisted of two coarse linen shirts per year. When these failed them, they went naked until the next allowance-day. Children from seven to ten years old, of both sexes, almost naked, might be seen at all seasons of the year.

There were no beds given the slaves, unless one coarse blanket be considered such, and none but the men and women had these. This, however, is not considered a very great privation. They find less difficulty from the want of beds, than from the want of time to sleep; for when their day's work in the field is done, the most of them having their washing, mending, and cooking to do, and having few or none of the ordinary facilities for doing either of these, very many of their sleeping hours are consumed in preparing for the field the coming day; and when this is done, old and young, male and female, married and single, drop down side by side, on one common bed,—the cold, damp floor,—each covering himself or herself with their miserable blankets; and here they sleep till they are summoned to the field by the driver's horn. At the sound of this, all must rise, and be off to the field. There must be no halting; every one must be at his or her post; and woe betides them who hear not this morning summons to the field; for if they are not awakened by the sense of hearing, they are by the sense of feeling: no age nor sex finds any favor. Mr. Severe,[39] the overseer, used to stand by the door of the quarter, armed with a large hickory stick and heavy cowskin, ready to whip any one who was so unfortunate as not to hear, or, from any other cause, was prevented from being ready to start for the field at the sound of the horn.

Mr. Severe was rightly named: he was a cruel man. I have seen him whip a woman, causing the blood to run half an hour at the time; and this, too, in the midst of her crying children, pleading for their mother's release. He seemed to take pleasure in manifesting his fiendish barbarity. Added to his cruelty, he was a profane swearer. It was enough to chill the blood and stiffen the hair of an ordinary man to hear him talk. Scarce a sentence escaped him but that was commenced or concluded by some horrid oath. The field was the place to witness his cruelty and profanity. His presence made it both the field of blood and of blasphemy. From the rising till the going down of the sun, he was cursing, raving, cutting, and slashing among the slaves of the field, in the most frightful manner. His career was short. He died very soon after I went to Colonel Lloyd's; and he died as he lived, uttering, with his dying groans, bitter curses and horrid oaths. His death was regarded by the slaves as the result of a merciful providence.

Mr. Severe's place was filled by a Mr. Hopkins. He was a very different man. He was less cruel, less profane, and made less noise, than Mr. Severe. His course was characterized by no extraordinary demonstrations of cruelty. He whipped, but seemed to take no pleasure in it. He was called by the slaves a good overseer.

The home plantation of Colonel Lloyd wore the appearance of a country village. All the mechanical operations for all the farms were performed here. The shoemaking and mending, the blacksmithing, cartwrighting, coopering, weaving, and grain-grinding, were all performed by the slaves on the home plantation. The whole place wore a business-like aspect very unlike the neighboring farms. The number of houses, too, conspired to give it advantage over the neighboring farms. It was called by the slaves the *Great House Farm*. Few privileges were esteemed higher, by the slaves of the out-farms, than that of being selected to do errands at the Great House Farm. It was associated in their minds with greatness. A representative could not be prouder of his election to a seat in the American Congress, than a slave on one of the out-farms would be of his election to do errands at the Great House Farm. They regarded it as evidence of great confidence reposed in them by their overseers; and it was on this account, as well as a constant desire to be out of the field from under the driver's lash, that they esteemed it a high privilege, one worth careful living for. He was called the smartest and most trusty fellow, who had this honor conferred upon him the most frequently. The competitors for this office sought as diligently to please their overseers, as the office-seekers in the political parties seek to please and deceive the people. The same traits of character might be seen in Colonel Lloyd's slaves, as are seen in the slaves of the political parties.

The slaves selected to go to the Great House Farm, for the monthly allowance for themselves and their fellow-slaves, were peculiarly enthusiastic. While on their way, they would make the dense old woods, for miles around, reverberate with their wild songs, revealing at once the highest joy and the deepest sadness. They would compose and sing as they went along, consulting neither time nor tune. The thought that came up, came out—if not in the word, in the sound;—and as frequently in the one as in the other. They would sometimes sing the most pathetic sentiment in the most rapturous tone, and the most rapturous sentiment in the most pathetic tone. Into all of their songs they would manage to weave something of the Great House Farm. Especially would they do this, when leaving home. They would then sing most exultingly the following words:—

> "I am going away to the Great House Farm!
> O, yea! O, yea! O!"

This they would sing, as a chorus, to words which to many would seem unmeaning jargon, but which, nevertheless, were full of meaning to themselves. I have sometimes thought that the mere hearing of those songs would do more to impress some minds with the horrible character of slavery, than the reading of whole volumes of philosophy on the subject could do.

I did not, when a slave, understand the deep meaning of those rude and apparently incoherent songs. I was myself within the circle; so that I neither saw nor heard as those without might see and hear. They told a tale of woe which was then altogether beyond my feeble comprehension; they were tones loud, long, and deep; they breathed the prayer and complaint of souls boiling over with the bitterest anguish. Every tone was a testimony against slavery, and a prayer to God for deliverance from chains. The hearing of those wild notes always depressed my spirit, and filled me with ineffable sadness. I have frequently found myself in tears while hearing them. The mere recurrence to those songs, even now, afflicts me; and while I am writing these lines, an expression of feeling has already found its way down my cheek. To those songs I trace my first glimmering conception of the dehumanizing character of slavery. I can never get rid of that conception. Those songs still follow me, to deepen my hatred of slavery, and quicken my sympathies for my brethren in bonds. If any one wishes to be impressed with the soul-killing effects of slavery, let him go to Colonel Lloyd's plantation, and, on allowance-day, place himself in the deep pine woods, and there let him, in silence, analyze the sounds that shall pass through the chambers of his soul,—and if he is not thus impressed, it will only be because "there is no flesh in his obdurate heart."[40]

I have often been utterly astonished, since I came to the north, to find persons who could speak of the singing, among slaves, as evidence of their contentment and happiness. It is impossible to conceive of a greater mistake. Slaves sing most when they are most unhappy. The songs of the slave represent the sorrows of his heart; and he is relieved by them, only as an aching heart is relieved by its tears. At least, such is my experience. I have often sung to drown my sorrow, but seldom to express my happiness. Crying for joy, and singing for joy, were alike uncommon to me while in the jaws of slavery. The singing of a man cast away upon a desolate island might be as appropriately considered as evidence of contentment and happiness, as the singing of a slave; the songs of the one and of the other are prompted by the same emotion.

---

## CHAPTER III.

COLONEL LLOYD kept a large and finely cultivated garden, which afforded almost constant employment for four men, besides the chief gardener, (Mr. M'Durmond.) This garden was probably the greatest attraction of the place. During the summer months, people came from far and near—from Baltimore, Easton, and Annapolis—to see it. It abounded in fruits of almost every description, from the hardy apple of the north to the delicate orange of the south. This garden was not the least source of trouble on the plantation. Its excellent fruit was quite a temptation to the hungry swarms of boys, as well as the older slaves, belonging to the colonel, few of whom had the virtue or the vice to resist it.

Scarcely a day passed, during the summer, but that some slave had to take the lash for stealing fruit. The colonel had to resort to all kinds of stratagems to keep his slaves out of the garden. The last and most successful one was that of tarring his fence all around; after which, if a slave was caught with any tar upon his person, it was deemed sufficient proof that he had either been into the garden, or had tried to get in. In either case, he was severely whipped by the chief gardener. This plan worked well; the slaves became as fearful of tar as of the lash. They seemed to realize the impossibility of touching *tar* without being defiled.

The colonel also kept a splendid riding equipage. His stable and carriage-house presented the appearance of some of our large city livery establishments. His horses were of the finest form and noblest blood. His carriage-house contained three splendid coaches, three or four gigs, besides dearborns[41] and barouches of the most fashionable style.

This establishment was under the care of two slaves—old Barney and young Barney—father and son. To attend to this establishment was their sole work. But it was by no means an easy employment; for in nothing was Colonel Lloyd more particular than in the management of his horses. The slightest inattention to these was unpardonable, and was visited upon those, under whose care they were placed, with the severest punishment; no excuse could shield them, if the colonel only suspected any want of attention to his horses—a supposition which he frequently indulged, and one which, of course, made the office of old and young Barney a very trying one. They never knew when they were safe from punishment. They were frequently whipped when least deserving, and escaped whipping when most deserving it. Every thing depended upon the looks of the horses, and the state of Colonel Lloyd's own mind when his horses were brought to him for use. If a horse did not move fast enough, or hold his head high enough, it was owing to some fault of his keepers. It was painful to stand near the stable-door, and hear the various complaints against the keepers when a horse was taken out for use. "This horse has not had proper attention. He has not been sufficiently rubbed and curried, or he has not been properly fed; his food was too wet or too dry; he got it too soon or too late; he was too hot or too cold; he had too much hay, and not enough of grain; or he had too much grain, and not enough of hay; instead of old Barney's attending to the horse, he had very improperly left it to his son." To all these complaints, no matter how unjust, the slave must answer never a word. Colonel Lloyd could not brook any contradiction from a slave. When he spoke, a slave must stand, listen, and tremble; and such was literally the case. I have seen Colonel Lloyd make old Barney, a man between fifty and sixty years of age, uncover his bald head, kneel down upon the cold, damp ground, and receive upon his naked and toil-worn shoulders more than thirty lashes at the time. Colonel Lloyd had three sons—Edward, Murray, and Daniel,—and three sons-in-law, Mr. Winder, Mr. Nicholson, and Mr. Lowndes. All of these lived at the Great House Farm, and enjoyed the luxury of whipping the servants when they pleased, from old Barney down to William Wilkes, the coach-driver. I have seen Winder make one of the house-servants stand off from him a suitable distance to be touched with the end of his whip, and at every stroke raise great ridges upon his back.

To describe the wealth of Colonel Lloyd would be almost equal to describing the riches of Job. He kept from ten to fifteen house-servants. He was said to own a thousand slaves, and I think this estimate quite within the truth. Colonel Lloyd owned so many that he did not know them when he saw them; nor did all the slaves of the out-farms know him. It is reported of him, that, while riding along the road one day, he met a colored man, and addressed him in the usual manner of speaking to colored people on the public highways of the south: "Well, boy, whom do you belong to?" "To Colonel Lloyd," replied the slave. "Well, does the colonel treat you well?" "No, sir," was the ready reply. "What, does he work you too hard?" "Yes, sir." "Well, don't he give you enough to eat?" "Yes, sir, he gives me enough, such as it is."

The colonel, after ascertaining where the slave belonged, rode on; the man also went on about his business, not dreaming that he had been conversing with his master. He thought, said, and heard nothing more of the matter, until two or three weeks afterwards. The poor man was then informed by his overseer that, for having found fault with his master, he was now to be sold to a Georgia trader. He was immediately chained and handcuffed; and thus, without a moment's warning, he was snatched away, and forever sundered, from his family and friends, by a hand more unrelenting than death. This is the penalty of telling the truth, of telling the simple truth, in answer to a series of plain questions.

It is partly in consequence of such facts, that slaves, when inquired of as to their condition and the character of their masters, almost universally say they are contented, and that their masters are kind. The slaveholders have been known to send in spies among their slaves, to ascertain their views and feelings in regard to their condition. The frequency of this has had the effect to establish among the slaves the maxim, that a still tongue makes a wise head. They suppress the truth rather than take the consequences of telling it, and in so doing prove themselves a part of the human family. If they have any thing to say of their masters, it is generally in their masters' favor, especially when speaking to an untried man. I have been frequently asked, when a slave, if I had a kind master, and do not remember ever to have given a negative answer; nor did I, in pursuing this course, consider myself as uttering what was absolutely false; for I always measured the kindness of my master by the standard of kindness set up among slaveholders around us. Moreover, slaves are like other people, and imbibe prejudices quite common to others. They think their own better than that of others. Many, under the influence of this prejudice, think their own masters are better than the masters of other slaves; and this, too, in some cases, when the very reverse is true. Indeed, it is not uncommon for slaves even to fall out and quarrel among themselves about the relative goodness of their masters, each contending for the superior goodness of his own over that of the others. At the very same time, they mutually execrate their masters when viewed separately. It was so on our plantation. When Colonel Lloyd's slaves met the slaves of Jacob Jepson,[42] they seldom parted without a quarrel about their masters; Colonel Lloyd's slaves contending that he was the richest, and Mr. Jepson's slaves that he was the smartest, and most of a man. Colonel Lloyd's slaves would boast his ability to buy and sell Jacob Jepson. Mr. Jepson's slaves would boast his ability to whip Colonel Lloyd.

These quarrels would almost always end in a fight between the parties, and those that whipped were supposed to have gained the point at issue. They seemed to think that the greatness of their masters was transferable to themselves. It was considered as being bad enough to be a slave; but to be a poor man's slave was deemed a disgrace indeed!

---

## CHAPTER IV.

MR. HOPKINS remained but a short time in the office of overseer. Why his career was so short, I do not know, but suppose he lacked the necessary severity to suit Colonel Lloyd. Mr. Hopkins was succeeded by Mr. Austin Gore,[43] a man possessing, in an eminent degree, all those traits of character indispensable to what is called a first-rate overseer. Mr. Gore had served Colonel Lloyd, in the capacity of overseer, upon one of the out-farms, and had shown himself worthy of the high station of overseer upon the home or Great House Farm.

Mr. Gore was proud, ambitious, and persevering. He was artful, cruel, and obdurate. He was just the man for such a place, and it was just the place for such a man. It afforded scope for the full exercise of all his powers, and he seemed to be perfectly at home in it. He was one of those who could torture the slightest look, word, or gesture, on the part of the slave, into impudence, and would treat it accordingly. There must be no answering back to him; no explanation was allowed a slave, showing himself to have been wrongfully accused. Mr. Gore acted fully up to the maxim laid down by slaveholders,—"It is better that a dozen slaves suffer under the lash, than that the overseer should be convicted, in the presence of the slaves, of having been at fault." No matter how innocent a slave might be—it availed him nothing, when accused by Mr. Gore of any misdemeanor. To be accused was to be convicted, and to be convicted was to be punished; the one always following the other with immutable certainty. To escape punishment was to escape accusation; and few slaves had the fortune to do either, under the overseership of Mr. Gore. He was just proud enough to demand the most debasing homage of the slave, and quite servile enough to crouch, himself, at the feet of the master. He was ambitious enough to be contented with nothing short of the highest rank of overseers, and persevering enough to reach the height of his ambition. He was cruel enough to inflict the severest punishment, artful enough to descend to the lowest trickery, and obdurate enough to be insensible to the voice of a reproving conscience. He was, of all the overseers, the most dreaded by the slaves. His presence was painful; his eye flashed confusion; and seldom was his sharp, shrill voice heard, without producing horror and trembling in their ranks.

Mr. Gore was a grave man, and, though a young man, he indulged in no jokes, said no funny words, seldom smiled. His words were in perfect keeping with his looks, and his looks were in perfect keeping with his words. Overseers will sometimes indulge in a witty word, even with the slaves; not so with Mr. Gore. He spoke but to command, and commanded but to be obeyed; he dealt sparingly with his words, and bountifully with his whip, never using the former where the latter would answer as well. When he whipped, he seemed to do so from a sense of duty, and feared no consequences. He did nothing reluctantly, no matter how disagreeable; always at his post, never inconsistent. He never promised but to fulfil. He was, in a word, a man of the most inflexible firmness and stone-like coolness.

His savage barbarity was equalled only by the consummate coolness with which he committed the grossest and most savage deeds upon the slaves under his charge. Mr. Gore once undertook to whip one of Colonel Lloyd's slaves, by the name of Demby. He had given Demby but few stripes, when, to get rid of the scourging, he ran and plunged himself into a creek, and stood there at the depth of his shoulders, refusing to come out. Mr. Gore told him that he would give him three calls, and that, if he did not come out at the third call, he would shoot him. The first call was given. Demby made no response, but stood his ground. The second and third calls were given with the same result. Mr. Gore then, without consultation or deliberation with any one, not even giving Demby an additional call, raised his musket to his face, taking deadly aim at his standing victim, and in an instant poor Demby was no more. His mangled body sank out of sight, and blood and brains marked the water where he had stood.

A thrill of horror flashed through every soul upon the plantation, excepting Mr. Gore. He alone seemed cool and collected. He was asked by Colonel Lloyd and my old master, why he resorted to this extraordinary expedient. His reply was, (as well as I can remember,) that Demby had become unmanageable. He was setting a dangerous example to the other slaves,—one which, if suffered to pass without some such demonstration on his part, would finally lead to the total subversion of all rule and order upon the plantation. He argued that if one slave refused to be corrected, and escaped with his life, the other slaves would soon copy the example; the result of which would be, the freedom of the slaves, and the enslavement of the whites. Mr. Gore's defence was satisfactory. He was continued in his station as overseer upon the home plantation. His fame as an overseer went abroad. His horrid crime was not even submitted to judicial investigation. It was committed in the presence of slaves, and they of course could neither institute a suit, nor testify against him; and thus the guilty perpetrator of one of the bloodiest and most foul murders goes unwhipped of justice, and uncensured by the community in which he lives. Mr. Gore lived in St. Michael's, Talbot county, Maryland, when I left there; and if he is still alive, he very probably lives there now; and if so, he is now, as he was then, as highly esteemed and as much respected as though his guilty soul had not been stained with his brother's blood.

I speak advisedly when I say this,—that killing a slave, or any colored person, in Talbot county, Maryland, is not treated as a crime, either by the courts or the community. Mr. Thomas Lanman,[44] of St. Michael's, killed two slaves, one of whom he killed with a hatchet, by knocking his brains out. He used to boast of the commission of the awful and bloody deed. I have heard him do so laughingly, saying, among other things, that he was the only benefactor of his country in the company, and that when others would do as much as he had done, we should be relieved of "the d——d niggers."

The wife of Mr. Giles Hick, living but a short distance from where I used to live, murdered my wife's cousin, a young girl between fifteen and sixteen years of age, mangling her person in the most horrible manner, breaking her nose and breastbone with a stick, so that the poor girl expired in a few hours afterward. She was immediately buried, but had not been in her untimely grave but a few hours before she was taken up and examined by the coroner, who decided that she had come to her death by severe beating. The offence for which this girl was thus murdered was this:—She had been set that night to mind Mrs. Hick's baby, and during the night she fell asleep, and the baby cried. She, having lost her rest for several nights previous, did not hear the crying. They were both in the room with Mrs. Hicks. Mrs. Hicks, finding the girl slow to move, jumped from her bed, seized an oak stick of wood by the fireplace, and with it broke the girl's nose and breastbone, and thus ended her life. I will not say that this most horrid murder produced no sensation in the community. It did produce sensation, but not enough to bring the murderess to punishment. There was a warrant issued for her arrest, but it was never served. Thus she escaped not only punishment, but even the pain of being arraigned before a court for her horrid crime.

Whilst I am detailing bloody deeds which took place during my stay on Colonel Lloyd's plantation, I will briefly narrate another, which occurred about the same time as the murder of Demby by Mr. Gore.

Colonel Lloyd's slaves were in the habit of spending a part of their nights and Sundays in fishing for oysters, and in this way made up the deficiency of their scanty allowance. An old man belonging to Colonel Lloyd, while thus engaged, happened to get beyond the limits of Colonel Lloyd's, and on the premises of Mr. Beal Bondly.[45] At this trespass, Mr. Bondly took offence, and with his musket came down to the shore, and blew its deadly contents into the poor old man.

Mr. Bondly came over to see Colonel Lloyd the next day, whether to pay him for his property, or to justify himself in what he had done, I know not. At any rate, this whole fiendish transaction was soon hushed up. There was very little said about it at all, and nothing done. It was a common saying, even among little white boys, that it was worth a half-cent to kill a "nigger," and a half-cent to bury one.

---

# CHAPTER V.

As to my own treatment while I lived on Colonel Lloyd's plantation, it was very similar to that of the other slave children. I was not old enough to work in the field, and there being little else than field work to do, I had a great deal of leisure time. The most I had to do was to drive up the cows at evening, keep the fowls out of the garden, keep the front yard clean, and run of errands for my old master's daughter, Mrs. Lucretia Auld. The most of my leisure time I spent in helping Master Daniel Lloyd in finding his birds, after he had shot them. My connection with Master Daniel was of some advantage to me. He became quite attached to me, and was a sort of protector of me. He would not allow the older boys to impose upon me, and would divide his cakes with me.

I was seldom whipped by my old master, and suffered little from any thing else than hunger and cold. I suffered much from hunger, but much more from cold. In hottest summer and coldest winter, I was kept almost naked—no shoes, no stockings, no jacket, no trousers, nothing on but a coarse tow linen shirt, reaching only to my knees. I had no bed. I must have perished with cold, but that, the coldest nights, I used to steal a bag which was used for carrying corn to the mill. I would crawl into this bag, and there sleep on the cold, damp, clay floor, with my head in and feet out. My feet have been so cracked with the frost, that the pen with which I am writing might be laid in the gashes.

We were not regularly allowanced. Our food was coarse corn meal boiled. This was called *mush*. It was put into a large wooden tray or trough, and set down upon the ground. The children were then called, like so many pigs, and like so many pigs they would come and devour the mush; some with oyster-shells, others with pieces of shingle, some with naked hands, and none with spoons. He that ate fastest got most; he that was strongest secured the best place; and few left the trough satisfied.

I was probably between seven and eight years old when I left Colonel Lloyd's plantation. I left it with joy. I shall never forget the ecstasy with which I received the intelligence that my old master (Anthony) had determined to let me go to Baltimore, to live with Mr. Hugh Auld, brother to my old master's son-in-law, Captain Thomas Auld. I received this information about three days before my departure. They were three of the happiest days I ever enjoyed. I spent the most part of all these three days in the creek, washing off the plantation scurf, and preparing myself for my departure.

The pride of appearance which this would indicate was not my own. I spent the time in washing, not so much because I wished to, but because Mrs. Lucre-tia had told me I must get all the dead skin off my feet and knees before I could go to Baltimore; for the people in Baltimore were very cleanly, and would laugh at me if I looked dirty. Besides, she was going to give me a pair of trousers, which I should not put on unless I got all the dirt off me. The thought of owning a pair of trousers was great indeed! It was almost a sufficient motive, not only to make me take off what would be called by pig-drovers the mange, but the skin itself. I went at it in good earnest, working for the first time with the hope of reward.

The ties that ordinarily bind children to their homes were all suspended in my case. I found no severe trial in my departure. My home was charmless; it was not home to me; on parting from it, I could not feel that I was leaving any thing which I could have enjoyed by staying. My mother was dead, my grandmother lived far off, so that I seldom saw her. I had two sisters and one brother, that lived in the same house with me; but the early separation of us from our mother had well nigh blotted the fact of our relationship from our memories. I looked for home elsewhere, and was confident of finding none which I should relish less than the one which I was leaving. If, however, I found in my new home hardship, hunger, whipping, and nakedness, I had the consolation that I should not have es-caped any one of them by staying. Having already had more than a taste of them in the house of my old master, and having endured them there, I very naturally inferred my ability to endure them elsewhere, and especially at Baltimore; for I had something of the feeling about Baltimore that is expressed in the proverb, that "being hanged in England is preferable to dying a natural death in Ireland." I had the strongest desire to see Baltimore. Cousin Tom, though not fluent in speech, had inspired me with that desire by his eloquent description of the place. I could never point out any thing at the Great House, no matter how beautiful or powerful, but that he had seen something at Baltimore far exceeding, both in beauty and strength, the object which I pointed out to him. Even the Great House itself, with all its pictures, was far inferior to many buildings in Baltimore. So strong was my desire, that I thought a gratification of it would fully compensate for whatever loss of comforts I should sustain by the exchange. I left without a regret, and with the highest hopes of future happiness.

We sailed out of Miles River for Baltimore on a Saturday morning. I remember only the day of the week, for at that time I had no knowledge of the days of the month, nor the months of the year. On setting sail, I walked aft, and gave to Colonel Lloyd's plantation what I hoped would be the last look. I then placed myself in the bows of the sloop, and there spent the remainder of the day in looking ahead, interesting myself in what was in the distance rather than in things near by or behind.

In the afternoon of that day, we reached Annapolis, the capital of the State. We stopped but a few moments, so that I had no time to go on shore. It was the first large town that I had ever seen, and though it would look small compared with some of our New England factory villages, I thought it a wonderful place for its size—more imposing even than the Great House Farm!

We arrived at Baltimore early on Sunday morning, landing at Smith's Wharf, not far from Bowley's Wharf. We had on board the sloop a large flock of sheep; and after aiding in driving them to the slaughterhouse of Mr. Curtis on Louden Slater's Hill, I was conducted by Rich, one of the hands belonging on board of the sloop, to my new home in Alliciana Street, near Mr. Gardner's shipyard, on Fells Point.

Mr. and Mrs. Auld were both at home, and met me at the door with their little son Thomas, to take care of whom I had been given. And here I saw what I had never seen before; it was a white face beaming with the most kindly emotions; it was the face of my new mistress, Sophia Auld. I wish I could describe the rapture that flashed through my soul as I beheld it. It was a new and strange sight to me, brightening up my pathway with the light of happiness. Little Thomas was told, there was his Freddy,—and I was told to take care of little Thomas; and thus I entered upon the duties of my new home with the most cheering prospect ahead.

I look upon my departure from Colonel Lloyd's plantation as one of the most interesting events of my life. It is possible, and even quite probable, that but for the mere circumstance of being removed from that plantation to Baltimore, I should have to-day, instead of being here seated by my own table, in the enjoyment of freedom and the happiness of home, writing this Narrative, been confined in the galling chains of slavery. Going to live at Baltimore laid the foundation, and opened the gateway, to all my subsequent prosperity. I have ever regarded it as the first plain manifestation of that kind providence which has ever since attended me, and marked my life with so many favors. I regarded the selection of myself as being somewhat remarkable. There were a number of slave children that might have been sent from the plantation to Baltimore. There were those younger, those older, and those of the same age. I was chosen from among them all, and was the first, last, and only choice.

I may be deemed superstitious, and even egotistical, in regarding this event as a special interposition of divine Providence in my favor. But I should be false to the earliest sentiments of my soul, if I suppressed the opinion. I prefer to be true to myself, even at the hazard of incurring the ridicule of others, rather than to be false, and incur my own abhorrence. From my earliest recollection, I date the entertainment of a deep conviction that slavery would not always be able to hold me within its foul embrace; and in the darkest hours of my career in slavery, this living word of faith and spirit of hope departed not from me, but remained like ministering angels to cheer me through the gloom. This good spirit was from God, and to him I offer thanksgiving and praise.

## CHAPTER VI.

MY new mistress proved to be all she appeared when I first met her at the door,—a woman of the kindest heart and finest feelings. She had never had a slave under her control previously to myself, and prior to her marriage she had been dependent upon her own industry for a living. She was by trade a weaver; and by constant application to her business, she had been in a good degree preserved from the blighting and dehumanizing effects of slavery. I was utterly astonished at her goodness. I scarcely knew how to behave towards her. She was entirely unlike any other white woman I had ever seen. I could not approach her as I was accustomed to approach other white ladies. My early instruction was all out of place. The crouching servility, usually so acceptable a quality in a slave, did not answer when manifested toward her. Her favor was not gained by it; she seemed to be disturbed by it. She did not deem it impudent or unmannerly for a slave to look her in the face. The meanest slave was put fully at ease in her presence, and none left without feeling better for having seen her. Her face was made of heavenly smiles, and her voice of tranquil music.

But, alas! this kind heart had but a short time to remain such. The fatal poison of irresponsible power was already in her hands, and soon commenced its infernal work. That cheerful eye, under the influence of slavery, soon became red with rage; that voice, made all of sweet accord, changed to one of harsh and horrid discord; and that angelic face gave place to that of a demon.

Very soon after I went to live with Mr. and Mrs. Auld, she very kindly commenced to teach me the A, B, C. After I had learned this, she assisted me in learning to spell words of three or four letters. Just at this point of my progress, Mr. Auld found out what was going on, and at once forbade Mrs. Auld to instruct me further, telling her, among other things, that it was unlawful, as well as unsafe, to teach a slave to read. To use his own words, further, he said, "If you give a nigger an inch, he will take an ell. A nigger should know nothing but to obey his master—to do as he is told to do. Learning would *spoil* the best nigger in the world. Now," said he, "if you teach that nigger (speaking of myself) how to read, there would be no keeping him. It would forever unfit him to be a slave. He would at once become unmanageable, and of no value to his master. As to himself, it could do him no good, but a great deal of harm. It would make him discontented and unhappy." These words sank deep into my heart, stirred up sentiments within that lay slumbering, and called into existence an entirely new train of thought. It was a new and special revelation, explaining dark and mysterious things, with which my youthful understanding had struggled, but struggled in vain. I now understood what had been to me a most perplexing difficulty—to wit, the white man's power to enslave the black man. It was a grand achievement, and I prized it highly. From that moment, I understood the pathway from slavery to freedom. It was just what I wanted, and I got it at a time when I the least expected it. Whilst I was saddened by the thought of losing the aid of my kind mistress, I was gladdened by the invaluable instruction which, by the merest accident, I had gained from my master. Though conscious of the difficulty of learning without a teacher, I set out with high hope, and a fixed purpose, at whatever cost of trouble, to learn how to read. The very decided manner with which he spoke, and strove to impress his wife with the evil consequences of giving me instruction, served to convince me that he was deeply sensible of the truths he was uttering. It gave me the best assurance that I might rely with the utmost confidence on the results which, he said, would flow from teaching me to read. What he most dreaded, that I most desired. What he most loved, that I most hated. That which to him was a great evil, to be carefully shunned, was to me a great good, to be diligently sought; and the argument which he so warmly urged, against my learning to read, only served to inspire me with a desire and determination to learn. In learning to read, I owe almost as much to the bitter opposition of my master, as to the kindly aid of my mistress. I acknowledge the benefit of both.

     I had resided but a short time in Baltimore before I observed a marked difference, in the treatment of slaves, from that which I had witnessed in the country. A city slave is almost a freeman, compared with a slave on the plantation. He is much better fed and clothed, and enjoys privileges altogether unknown to the slave on the plantation. There is a vestige of decency, a sense of shame, that does much to curb and check those outbreaks of atrocious cruelty so commonly enacted upon the plantation. He is a desperate slaveholder, who will shock the humanity of his nonslaveholding neighbors with the cries of his lacerated slave. Few are willing to incur the odium attaching to the reputation of being a cruel master; and above all things, they would not be known as not giving a slave enough to eat. Every city slaveholder is anxious to have it known of him, that he feeds his slaves well; and it is due to them to say, that most of them do give their slaves enough to eat. There are, however, some painful exceptions to this rule. Directly opposite to us, on Philpot Street, lived Mr. Thomas Hamilton. He owned two slaves. Their names were Henrietta and Mary. Henrietta was about twenty-two years of age, Mary was about fourteen; and of all the mangled and emaciated creatures I ever looked upon, these two were the most so. His heart must be harder than stone, that could look upon these unmoved. The head, neck, and shoulders of Mary were literally cut to pieces. I have frequently felt her head, and found it nearly covered with festering sores, caused by the lash of her cruel mistress. I do not know that her master ever whipped her, but I have been an eye-witness to the cruelty of Mrs. Hamilton. I used to be in Mr. Hamilton's house nearly every day. Mrs. Hamilton used to sit in a large chair in the middle of the room, with a heavy cowskin always by her side, and scarce an hour passed during the day but was marked by the blood of one of these slaves. The girls seldom passed her without her saying, "Move faster, you *black gip!*" at the same time giving them a blow with the cowskin over the head or shoulders, often drawing the blood. She would then say, "Take that, you *black gip!*"—continuing, "If you don't move faster, I'll move you!" Added to the cruel lashings to which these slaves were subjected, they were kept nearly half-starved. They seldom knew what it was to eat a full meal. I have seen Mary contending with the pigs for the offal thrown into the street. So much was Mary kicked and cut to pieces, that she was oftener called "*pecked*" than by her name.

## CHAPTER VII.

I LIVED in Master Hugh's family about seven years. During this time, I succeeded in learning to read and write. In accomplishing this, I was compelled to resort to various stratagems. I had no regular teacher. My mistress, who had kindly commenced to instruct me, had, in compliance with the advice and direction of her husband, not only ceased to instruct, but had set her face against my being instructed by any one else. It is due, however, to my mistress to say of her, that she did not adopt this course of treatment immediately. She at first lacked the depravity indispensable to shutting me up in mental darkness. It was at least necessary for her to have some training in the exercise of irresponsible power, to make her equal to the task of treating me as though I were a brute.

My mistress was, as I have said, a kind and tender-hearted woman; and in the simplicity of her soul she commenced, when I first went to live with her, to treat me as she supposed one human being ought to treat another. In entering upon the duties of a slaveholder, she did not seem to perceive that I sustained to her the relation of a mere chattel, and that for her to treat me as a human being was not only wrong, but dangerously so. Slavery proved as injurious to her as it did to me. When I went there, she was a pious, warm, and tender-hearted woman. There was no sorrow or suffering for which she had not a tear. She had bread for the hungry, clothes for the naked, and comfort for every mourner that came within her reach. Slavery soon proved its ability to divest her of these heavenly qualities. Under its influence, the tender heart became stone, and the lamb-like disposition gave way to one of tiger-like fierceness. The first step in her downward course was in her ceasing to instruct me. She now commenced to practise her husband's precepts. She finally became even more violent in her opposition than her husband himself. She was not satisfied with simply doing as well as he had commanded; she seemed anxious to do better. Nothing seemed to make her more angry than to see me with a newspaper. She seemed to think that here lay the danger. I have had her rush at me with a face made all up of fury, and snatch from me a newspaper, in a manner that fully revealed her apprehension. She was an apt woman; and a little experience soon demonstrated, to her satisfaction, that education and slavery were incompatible with each other.

From this time I was most narrowly watched. If I was in a separate room any considerable length of time, I was sure to be suspected of having a book, and was at once called to give an account of myself. All this, however, was too late. The first step had been taken. Mistress, in teaching me the alphabet, had given me the *inch,* and no precaution could prevent me from taking the *ell.*

The plan which I adopted, and the one by which I was most successful, was that of making friends of all the little white boys whom I met in the street. As many of these as I could, I converted into teachers. With their kindly aid, obtained at different times and in different places, I finally succeeded in learning to read. When I was sent of errands, I always took my book with me, and by going one part of my errand quickly, I found time to get a lesson before my return. I used also to carry bread with me, enough of which was always in the house, and to which I was always welcome; for I was much better off in this regard than many of the poor white children in our neighborhood. This bread I used to bestow upon the hungry little urchins, who, in return, would give me that more valuable bread of knowledge. I am strongly tempted to give the names of two or three of those little boys, as a testimonial of the gratitude and affection I bear them; but prudence forbids;—not that it would injure me, but it might embarrass them; for it is almost an unpardonable offence to teach slaves to read in this Christian country. It is enough to say of the dear little fellows, that they lived on Philpot Street, very near Durgin and Bailey's ship-yard. I used to talk this matter of slavery over with them. I would sometimes say to them, I wished I could be as free as they would be when they got to be men. "You will be free as soon as you are twenty-one, *but I am a slave for life!* Have not I as good a right to be free as you have?" These words used to trouble them; they would express for me the liveliest sympathy, and console me with the hope that something would occur by which I might be free.

I was now about twelve years old, and the thought of being *a slave for life* began to bear heavily upon my heart. Just about this time, I got hold of a book entitled "The Columbian Orator."[46] Every opportunity I got, I used to read this book. Among much of other interesting matter, I found in it a dialogue between a master and his slave.[47] The slave was represented as having run away from his master three times. The dialogue represented the conversation which took place between them, when the slave was retaken the third time. In this dialogue, the whole argument in behalf of slavery was brought forward by the master, all of which was disposed of by the slave. The slave was made to say some very smart as well as impressive things in reply to his master—things which had the desired though unexpected effect; for the conversation resulted in the voluntary emancipation of the slave on the part of the master.

In the same book, I met with one of Sheridan's mighty speeches on and in behalf of Catholic emancipation.[48] These were choice documents to me. I read them over and over again with unabated interest. They gave tongue to interesting thoughts of my own soul, which had frequently flashed through my mind, and died away for want of utterance. The moral which I gained from the dialogue was the power of truth over the conscience of even a slaveholder. What I got from Sheridan was a bold denunciation of slavery, and a powerful vindication of human rights. The reading of these documents enabled me to utter my thoughts, and to meet the arguments brought forward to sustain slavery; but while they relieved me of one difficulty, they brought on another even more painful than the one of which I was relieved. The more I read, the more I was led to abhor and detest my enslavers. I could regard them in no other light than a band of successful robbers, who had left their homes, and gone to Africa, and stolen us from our homes, and in a strange land reduced us to slavery. I loathed them as being the meanest as well as the most wicked of men. As I read and contemplated the subject, behold! that very discontentment which Master Hugh had predicted would follow my learning to read had already come, to torment and sting my soul to unutterable anguish. As I writhed under it, I would at times feel that learning to read had been a curse rather than a blessing. It had given me a view of my wretched condition, without the remedy. It opened my eyes to the horrible pit, but to no ladder upon which to get out. In moments of agony, I envied my fellow-slaves for their stupidity. I have often wished myself a beast. I preferred the condition of the meanest reptile to my own. Any thing, no matter what, to get rid of thinking! It was this everlasting thinking of my condition that tormented me. There was no getting rid of it. It was pressed upon me by every object within sight or hearing, animate or inanimate. The silver trump of freedom had roused my soul to eternal wakefulness. Freedom now appeared, to disappear no more forever. It was heard in every sound, and seen in every thing. It was ever present to torment me with a sense of my wretched condition. I saw nothing without seeing it, I heard nothing without hearing it, and felt nothing without feeling it. It looked from every star, it smiled in every calm, breathed in every wind, and moved in every storm.

I often found myself regretting my own existence, and wishing myself dead; and but for the hope of being free, I have no doubt but that I should have killed myself, or done something for which I should have been killed. While in this state of mind, I was eager to hear any one speak of slavery. I was a ready listener. Every little while, I could hear something about the abolitionists. It was some time before I found what the word meant. It was always used in such connections as to make it an interesting word to me. If a slave ran away and succeeded in getting clear, or if a slave killed his master, set fire to a barn, or did any thing very wrong in the mind of a slaveholder, it was spoken of as the fruit of *abolition*. Hearing the word in this connection very often, I set about learning what it meant. The dictionary afforded me little or no help. I found it was "the act of abolishing;" but then I did not know what was to be abolished. Here I was perplexed. I did not dare to ask any one about its meaning, for I was satisfied that it was something they wanted me to know very little about. After a patient

waiting, I got one of our city papers, containing an account of the number of petitions from the north, praying for the abolition of slavery in the District of Columbia, and of the slave trade between the States. From this time I understood
the words *abolition* and *abolitionist,* and always drew near when that word was
spoken, expecting to hear something of importance to myself and fellow-slaves.
The light broke in upon me by degrees. I went one day down on the wharf of
Mr. Waters; and seeing two Irishmen unloading a scow of stone, I went, unasked,
and helped them. When we had finished, one of them came to me and asked me
if I were a slave. I told him I was. He asked, "Are ye a slave for life?" I told him
that I was. The good Irishman seemed to be deeply affected by the statement. He
said to the other that it was a pity so fine a little fellow as myself should be a
slave for life. He said it was a shame to hold me. They both advised me to run
away to the north; that I should find friends there, and that I should be free. I
pretended not to be interested in what they said, and treated them as if I did not
understand them; for I feared they might be treacherous. White men have been
known to encourage slaves to escape, and then, to get the reward, catch them
and return them to their masters. I was afraid that these seemingly good men
might use me so; but I nevertheless remembered their advice, and from that time
I resolved to run away. I looked forward to a time at which it would be safe for
me to escape. I was too young to think of doing so immediately; besides, I wished
to learn how to write, as I might have occasion to write my own pass. I consoled
myself with the hope that I should one day find a good chance. Meanwhile, I
would learn to write.

The idea as to how I might learn to write was suggested to me by being in
Durgin and Bailey's ship-yard, and frequently seeing the ship carpenters, after
hewing, and getting a piece of timber ready for use, write on the timber the name
of that part of the ship for which it was intended. When a piece of timber was
intended for the larboard side, it would be marked thus—"L." When a piece was
for the starboard side, it would be marked thus—"S." A piece for the larboard
side forward, would be marked thus—"L.F." When a piece was for starboard
side forward, it would be marked thus—"S.F." For larboard aft, it would be
marked thus—"L.A." For starboard aft, it would be marked thus—"S.A." I soon
learned the names of these letters, and for what they were intended when placed
upon a piece of timber in the ship-yard. I immediately commenced copying them,
and in a short time was able to make the four letters named. After that, when I
met with any boy who I knew could write, I would tell him I could write as well
as he. The next word would be, "I don't believe you. Let me see you try it." I
would then make the letters which I had been so fortunate as to learn, and ask
him to beat that. In this way I got a good many lessons in writing, which it is
quite possible I should never have gotten in any other way. During this time, my
copy-book was the board fence, brick wall, and pavement; my pen and ink was
a lump of chalk. With these, I learned mainly how to write. I then commenced
and continued copying the Italics in Webster's Spelling Book,[49] until I could
make them all without looking on the book. By this time, my little Master
Thomas had gone to school, and learned how to write, and had written over a
number of copy-books. These had been brought home, and shown to some of

our near neighbors, and then laid aside. My mistress used to go to class meeting at the Wilk Street meetinghouse every Monday afternoon, and leave me to take care of the house. When left thus, I used to spend the time in writing in the spaces left in Master Thomas's copy-book, copying what he had written. I continued to do this until I could write a hand very similar to that of Master Thomas. Thus, after a long, tedious effort for years, I finally succeeded in learning how to write.

## CHAPTER VIII.

IN a very short time after I went to live at Baltimore, my old master's youngest son Richard died; and in about three years and six months after his death, my old master, Captain Anthony, died, leaving only his son, Andrew, and daughter, Lucretia, to share his estate. He died while on a visit to see his daughter at Hillsborough. Cut off thus unexpectedly, he left no will as to the disposal of his property. It was therefore necessary to have a valuation of the property, that it might be equally divided between Mrs. Lucretia and Master Andrew. I was immediately sent for, to be valued with the other property. Here again my feelings rose up in detestation of slavery. I had now a new conception of my degraded condition. Prior to this, I had become, if not insensible to my lot, at least partly so. I left Baltimore with a young heart overborne with sadness, and a soul full of apprehension. I took passage with Captain Rowe, in the schooner Wild Cat, and, after a sail of about twenty-four hours, I found myself near the place of my birth. I had now been absent from it almost, if not quite, five years. I, however, remembered the place very well. I was only about five years old when I left it, to go and live with my old master on Colonel Lloyd's plantation; so that I was now between ten and eleven years old.

We were all ranked together at the valuation. Men and women, old and young, married and single, were ranked with horses, sheep, and swine. There were horses and men, cattle and women, pigs and children, all holding the same rank in the scale of being, and were all subjected to the same narrow examination. Silvery-headed age and sprightly youth, maids and matrons, had to undergo the same indelicate inspection. At this moment, I saw more clearly than ever the brutalizing effects of slavery upon both slave and slaveholder.

After the valuation, then came the division. I have no language to express the high excitement and deep anxiety which were felt among us poor slaves during this time. Our fate for life was now to be decided. We had no more voice in that decision than the brutes among whom we were ranked. A single word from the white men was enough—against all our wishes, prayers, and entreaties—to sunder forever the dearest friends, dearest kindred, and strongest ties known to human beings. In addition to the pain of separation, there was the horrid dread of falling into the hands of Master Andrew. He was known to us all as being a most cruel wretch,—a common drunkard, who had, by his reckless mismanagement and profligate dissipation, already wasted a large portion of his father's property. We all felt that we might as well be sold at once to the Georgia traders,

as to pass into his hands; for we knew that that would be our inevitable condition,—a condition held by us all in the utmost horror and dread.

I suffered more anxiety than most of my fellow-slaves. I had known what
it was to be kindly treated; they had known nothing of the kind. They had seen
little or nothing of the world. They were in very deed men and women of sorrow, and acquainted with grief. Their backs had been made familiar with the
bloody lash, so that they had become callous; mine was yet tender; for while at
Baltimore I got few whippings, and few slaves could boast of a kinder master and
mistress than myself; and the thought of passing out of their hands into those of
Master Andrew—a man who, but a few days before, to give me a sample of his
bloody disposition, took my little brother by the throat, threw him on the
ground, and with the heel of his boot stamped upon his head till the blood gushed
from his nose and ears—was well calculated to make me anxious as to my fate.
After he had committed this savage outrage upon my brother, he turned to me,
and said that was the way he meant to serve me one of these days,—meaning, I
suppose, when I came into his possession.

Thanks to a kind Providence, I fell to the portion of Mrs. Lucretia, and was
sent immediately back to Baltimore, to live again in the family of Master Hugh.
Their joy at my return equalled their sorrow at my departure. It was a glad day
to me. I had escaped a worse than lion's jaws. I was absent from Baltimore, for
the purpose of valuation and division, just about one month, and it seemed to
have been six.

Very soon after my return to Baltimore, my mistress, Lucretia, died, leaving her husband and one child, Amanda; and in a very short time after her death,
Master Andrew died. Now all the property of my old master, slaves included,
was in the hands of strangers,—strangers who had had nothing to do with accumulating it. Not a slave was left free. All remained slaves, from the youngest
to the oldest. If any one thing in my experience, more than another, served to
deepen my conviction of the infernal character of slavery, and to fill me with unutterable loathing of slaveholders, it was their base ingratitude to my poor old
grandmother. She had served my old master faithfully from youth to old age. She
had been the source of all his wealth; she had peopled his plantation with slaves;
she had become a great grandmother in his service. She had rocked him in infancy, attended him in childhood, served him through life, and at his death wiped
from his icy brow the cold death-sweat, and closed his eyes forever. She was nevertheless left a slave—a slave for life—a slave in the hands of strangers; and in
their hands she saw her children, her grandchildren, and her great-grandchildren,
divided, like so many sheep, without being gratified with the small privilege of a
single word, as to their or her own destiny. And, to cap the climax of their base
ingratitude and fiendish barbarity, my grandmother, who was now very old, having outlived my old master and all his children, having seen the beginning and
end of all of them, and her present owners finding she was of but little value, her
frame already racked with the pains of old age, and complete helplessness fast
stealing over her once active limbs, they took her to the woods, built her a little
hut, put up a little mud-chimney, and then made her welcome to the privilege of
supporting herself there in perfect loneliness; thus virtually turning her out to die!

If my poor old grandmother now lives, she lives to suffer in utter loneliness; she lives to remember and mourn over the loss of children, the loss of grandchildren, and the loss of great-grandchildren.[50] They are, in the language of the slave's poet, Whittier,[51]—

> "Gone, gone, sold and gone
> To the rice swamp dank and lone,
> Where the slave-whip ceaseless swings,
> Where the noisome insect stings,
> Where the fever-demon strews
> Poison with the falling dews,
> Where the sickly sunbeams glare
> Through the hot and misty air:—
>   Gone, gone, sold and gone
>   To the rice swamp dank and lone,
>   From Virginia hills and waters—
>   Woe is me, my stolen daughters!"

The hearth is desolate. The children, the unconscious children, who once sang and danced in her presence, are gone. She gropes her way, in the darkness of age, for a drink of water. Instead of the voices of her children, she hears by day the moans of the dove, and by night the screams of the hideous owl. All is gloom. The grave is at the door. And now, when weighed down by the pains and aches of old age, when the head inclines to the feet, when the beginning and ending of human existence meet, and helpless infancy and painful old age combine together—at this time, this most needful time, the time for the exercise of that tenderness and affection which children only can exercise towards a declining parent—my poor old grandmother, the devoted mother of twelve children, is left all alone, in yonder little hut, before a few dim embers. She stands—she sits— she staggers—she falls—she groans—she dies—and there are none of her children or grandchildren present, to wipe from her wrinkled brow the cold sweat of death, or to place beneath the sod her fallen remains. Will not a righteous God visit for these things?

In about two years after the death of Mrs. Lucretia, Master Thomas married his second wife. Her name was Rowena Hamilton. She was the eldest daughter of Mr. William Hamilton.[52] Master now lived in St. Michael's.[53] Not long after his marriage, a misunderstanding took place between himself and Master Hugh; and as a means of punishing his brother, he took me from him to live with himself at St. Michael's. Here I underwent another most painful separation. It, however, was not so severe as the one I dreaded at the division of property; for, during this interval, a great change had taken place in Master Hugh and his once kind and affectionate wife. The influence of brandy upon him, and of slavery upon her, had effected a disastrous change in the characters of both; so that, as far as they were concerned, I thought I had little to lose by the change. But it was not to them that I was attached. It was to those little Baltimore boys that I felt the strongest attachment. I had received many good lessons from them, and was still receiving them, and the thought of leaving them was painful indeed. I was leaving, too, without the hope of ever being allowed to return. Master Thomas had said he would never let me return again. The barrier betwixt himself and brother he considered impassable.

I then had to regret that I did not at least make the attempt to carry out my resolution to run away; for the chances of success are tenfold greater from the city than from the country.

I sailed from Baltimore for St. Michael's in the sloop Amanda, Captain Edward Dodson. On my passage, I paid particular attention to the direction which the steamboats took to go to Philadelphia. I found, instead of going down, on reaching North Point they went up the bay, in a north-easterly direction. I deemed this knowledge of the utmost importance. My determination to run away was again revived. I resolved to wait only so long as the offering of a favorable opportunity. When that came, I was determined to be off.

## CHAPTER IX.

I HAVE now reached a period of my life when I can give dates. I left Baltimore, and went to live with Master Thomas Auld, at St. Michael's, in March, 1832. It was now more than seven years since I lived with him in the family of my old master, on Colonel Lloyd's plantation. We of course were now almost entire strangers to each other. He was to me a new master, and I to him a new slave. I was ignorant of his temper and disposition; he was equally so of mine. A very short time, however, brought us into full acquaintance with each other. I was made acquainted with his wife not less than with himself. They were well matched, being equally mean and cruel. I was now, for the first time during a space of more than seven years, made to feel the painful gnawings of hunger—a something which I had not experienced before since I left Colonel Lloyd's plantation. It went hard enough with me then, when I could look back to no period at which I had enjoyed a sufficiency. It was tenfold harder after living in Master Hugh's family, where I had always had enough to eat, and of that which was good. I have said Master Thomas was a mean man. He was so. Not to give a slave enough to eat, is regarded as the most aggravated development of meanness even among slaveholders. The rule is, no matter how coarse the food, only let there be enough of it. This is the theory; and in the part of Maryland from which I came, it is the general practice,—though there are many exceptions. Master Thomas gave us enough of neither coarse nor fine food. There were four slaves of us in the kitchen—my sister Eliza, my aunt Priscilla, Henny, and myself; and we were allowed less than a half of a bushel of corn-meal per week, and very little else, either in the shape of meat or vegetables. It was not enough for us to subsist upon. We were therefore reduced to the wretched necessity of living at the expense of our neighbors. This we did by begging and stealing, whichever came handy in the time of need, the one being considered as legitimate as the other. A great many times have we poor creatures been nearly perishing with hunger, when food in abundance lay mouldering in the safe and smoke-house, and our pious mistress was aware of the fact;

and yet that mistress and her husband would kneel every morning, and pray that God would bless them in basket and store!

Bad as all slaveholders are, we seldom meet one destitute of every element of character commanding respect. My master was one of this rare sort. I do not know of one single noble act ever performed by him. The leading trait in his character was meanness; and if there were any other element in his nature, it was made subject to this. He was mean; and, like most other mean men, he lacked the ability to conceal his meanness. Captain Auld was not born a slaveholder. He had been a poor man, master only of a Bay craft. He came into possession of all his slaves by marriage; and of all men, adopted slaveholders are the worst. He was cruel, but cowardly. He commanded without firmness. In the enforcement of his rules, he was at times rigid, and at times lax. At times, he spoke to his slaves with the firmness of Napoleon and the fury of a demon; at other times, he might well be mistaken for an inquirer who had lost his way. He did nothing of himself. He might have passed for a lion, but for his ears. In all things noble which he attempted, his own meanness shone most conspicuous. His airs, words, and actions, were the airs, words, and actions of born slaveholders, and, being assumed, were awkward enough. He was not even a good imitator. He possessed all the disposition to deceive, but wanted the power. Having no resources within himself, he was compelled to be the copyist of many, and being such, he was forever the victim of inconsistency; and of consequence he was an object of contempt, and was held as such even by his slaves. The luxury of having slaves of his own to wait upon him was something new and unprepared for. He was a slaveholder without the ability to hold slaves. He found himself incapable of managing his slaves either by force, fear, or fraud. We seldom called him "master;" we generally called him "Captain Auld," and were hardly disposed to title him at all. I doubt not that our conduct had much to do with making him appear awkward, and of consequence fretful. Our want of reverence for him must have perplexed him greatly. He wished to have us call him master, but lacked the firmness necessary to command us to do so. His wife used to insist upon our calling him so, but to no purpose. In August, 1832, my master attended a Methodist camp-meeting held in the Bay-side, Talbot county, and there experienced religion. I indulged a faint hope that his conversion would lead him to emancipate his slaves, and that, if he did not do this, it would, at any rate, make him more kind and humane. I was disappointed in both these respects. It neither made him to be humane to his slaves, nor to emancipate them. If it had any effect on his character, it made him more cruel and hateful in all his ways; for I believe him to have been a much worse man after his conversion than before. Prior to his conversion, he relied upon his own depravity to shield and sustain him in his savage barbarity; but after his conversion, he found religious sanction and support for his slaveholding cruelty. He made the greatest pretensions to piety. His house was the house of prayer. He prayed morning, noon, and night. He very soon distinguished himself among his brethren, and was soon made a class-leader and exhorter. His activity in revivals was great, and he proved himself an instrument in the hands of the church in converting many souls. His house was the preachers' home. They used to take great pleasure in coming there to put up; for while he starved us, he stuffed them. We have had three or four preachers there at a time. The names of those who used to come most frequently while I lived there, were Mr. Storks, Mr. Ewery, Mr. Humphry, and Mr. Hickey. I have also seen Mr. George Cookman[54] at our house. We slaves loved Mr. Cookman. We believed him to be a good man. We thought him instrumental in getting Mr. Samuel Harrison, a very rich slaveholder, to emancipate his slaves; and by some means got the impression that he was laboring to effect the emancipation of all the slaves. When he was at our house, we were sure to be called in to prayers. When the others were there, we were sometimes called in and sometimes not. Mr. Cookman took more notice of us than either of the other ministers. He could not come among us without betraying his sympathy for us, and, stupid as we were, we had the sagacity to see it.

While I lived with my master in St. Michael's, there was a white young man, a Mr. Wilson, who proposed to keep a Sabbath school for the instruction of such slaves as might be disposed to learn to read the New Testament. We met but three times, when Mr. West and Mr. Fairbanks, both class-leaders, with many others, came upon us with sticks and other missiles, drove us off, and forbade us to meet again. Thus ended our little Sabbath school in the pious town of St. Michael's.

I have said my master found religious sanction for his cruelty. As an example, I will state one of many facts going to prove the charge. I have seen him tie up a lame young woman, and whip her with a heavy cowskin upon her naked shoulders, causing the warm red blood to drip; and, in justification of the bloody deed, he would quote this passage of Scripture—"He that knoweth his master's will, and doeth it not, shall be beaten with many stripes."[55]

Master would keep this lacerated young woman tied up in this horrid situation four or five hours at a time. I have known him to tie her up early in the morning, and whip her before breakfast; leave her, go to his store, return at dinner, and whip her again, cutting her in the places already made raw with his cruel lash. The secret of master's cruelty toward "Henny" is found in the fact of her being almost helpless. When quite a child, she fell into the fire, and burned herself horribly. Her hands were so burnt that she never got the use of them. She could do very little but bear heavy burdens. She was to master a bill of expense; and as he was a mean man, she was a constant offence to him. He seemed desirous of getting the poor girl out of existence. He gave her away once to his sister; but, being a poor gift, she was not disposed to keep her. Finally, my benevolent master, to use his own words, "set her adrift to take care of herself." Here was a recently-converted man, holding on upon the mother, and at the same time turning out her helpless child, to starve and die! Master Thomas was one of the many pious slaveholders who hold slaves for the very charitable purpose of taking care of them.

My master and myself had quite a number of differences. He found me unsuitable to his purpose. My city life, he said, had had a very pernicious effect upon me. It had almost ruined me for every good purpose, and fitted me for every thing which was bad. One of my greatest faults was that of letting his horse run away, and go down to his father-in-law's farm, which was about five miles from St. Michael's. I would then have to go after it. My reason for this kind of carelessness, or carefulness, was, that I could always get something to eat when I went there. Master William Hamilton, my master's father-in-law, always gave his slaves enough to eat. I never left there hungry, no matter how great the need of my speedy return. Master Thomas at length said he would stand it no longer. I had lived with him nine months, during which time he had given me a number of severe whippings, all to no good purpose. He resolved to put me out, as he said, to be broken; and, for this purpose, he let me for one year to a man named Edward Covey. Mr. Covey was a poor man, a farm-renter. He rented the place upon which he lived, as also the hands with which he tilled it. Mr. Covey had acquired a very high reputation for breaking young slaves, and this reputation was of immense value to him. It enabled him to get his farm tilled with much less expense to himself than he could have had it done without such a reputation. Some slaveholders thought it not much loss to allow Mr. Covey to have their slaves one year, for the sake of the training to which they were subjected, without any other compensation. He could hire young help with great ease, in consequence of this reputation. Added to the natural good qualities of Mr. Covey, he was a professor of religion—a pious soul—a member and a class-leader in the Methodist church. All of this added weight to his reputation as a "nigger-breaker." I was aware of all the facts, having been made acquainted with them by a young man who had lived there. I nevertheless made the change gladly; for I was sure of getting enough to eat, which is not the smallest consideration to a hungry man.

## CHAPTER X.

I LEFT Master Thomas's house, and went to live with Mr. Covey, on the 1st of January, 1833.[56] I was now, for the first time in my life, a field hand. In my new employment, I found myself even more awkward than a country boy appeared to be in a large city. I had been at my new home but one week before Mr. Covey gave me a very severe whipping, cutting my back, causing the blood to run, and raising ridges on my flesh as large as my little finger. The details of this affair are as follows: Mr. Covey sent me, very early in the morning of one of our coldest days in the month of January, to the woods, to get a load of wood. He gave me a team of unbroken oxen. He told me which was the in-hand ox, and which the off-hand one.[57] He then tied the end of a large rope around the horns of the in-hand ox, and gave me the other end of it, and told me, if the oxen started to run, that I must hold on upon the rope. I had never driven oxen before, and of course I was very awkward. I, however, succeeded in getting to the edge of the woods with little difficulty; but I had got a very few rods into the woods, when the oxen took fright, and started full tilt, carrying the cart against trees, and over stumps, in the most frightful manner. I expected every moment that my brains would be dashed out against the trees. After running thus for a considerable distance, they finally upset the cart, dashing it with great force against a tree, and threw themselves into a dense thicket. How I escaped death, I do not know. There I was, entirely alone, in a thick wood, in a place new to me. My cart was upset and shattered, my oxen were entangled among the young trees, and there was none to help me. After a long spell of effort, I succeeded in getting my cart righted, my oxen disentangled, and again yoked to the cart. I now proceeded with my team to the place where I had, the day before, been chopping wood, and loaded my cart pretty heavily, thinking in this way to tame my oxen. I then proceeded on my way home. I had now consumed one half of the day. I got out of the woods safely, and now felt out of danger. I stopped my oxen to open the woods gate; and just as I did so, before I could get hold of my ox-rope, the oxen again started, rushed through the gate, catching it between the wheel and the body of the cart, tearing it to pieces, and coming within a few inches of crushing me against the gate-post. Thus twice, in one short day, I escaped death by the merest chance. On my return, I told Mr. Covey what had happened, and how it happened. He ordered me to return to the woods again immediately. I did so, and he followed on after me. Just as I got into the woods, he came up and told me to stop my cart, and that he would teach me how to trifle away my time, and break gates. He then went to a large gum-tree, and with his axe cut three large switches, and, after trimming them up neatly with his pocket-knife, he ordered me to take off my clothes. I made him no answer, but stood with my clothes on. He repeated his order. I still made him no answer, nor did I move to strip myself. Upon this he rushed at me with the fierceness of a tiger, tore off my clothes, and lashed me till he had worn out his switches, cutting me so savagely as to leave the marks visible for a long time after. This whipping was the first of a number just like it, and for similar offences.

I lived with Mr. Covey one year. During the first six months, of that year, scarce a week passed without his whipping me. I was seldom free from a sore back. My awkwardness was almost always his excuse for whipping me. We were worked fully up to the point of endurance. Long before day we were up, our horses fed, and by the first approach of day we were off to the field with our hoes and ploughing teams. Mr. Covey gave us enough to eat, but scarce time to eat it. We were often less than five minutes taking our meals. We were often in the field from the first approach of day till its last lingering ray had left us; and at saving-fodder time, midnight often caught us in the field binding blades.

Covey would be out with us. The way he used to stand it, was this. He would spend the most of his afternoons in bed. He would then come out fresh in the evening, ready to urge us on with his words, example, and frequently with the whip. Mr. Covey was one of the few slaveholders who could and did work with his hands. He was a hard-working man. He knew by himself just what a man or a boy could do. There was no deceiving him. His work went on in his absence almost as well as in his presence; and he had the faculty of making us feel that he was ever present with us. This he did by surprising us. He seldom approached the spot where we were at work openly, if he could do it secretly. He always aimed at taking us by surprise. Such was his cunning, that we used to call him, among ourselves, "the snake." When we were at work in the cornfield, he would sometimes crawl on his hands and knees to avoid detection, and all at once he would rise nearly in our midst, and scream out, "Ha, ha! Come, come! Dash on, dash on!" This being his mode of attack, it was never safe to stop a single minute. His comings were like a thief in the night. He appeared to us as being ever at hand. He was under every tree, behind every stump, in every bush, and at every window, on the plantation. He would sometimes mount his horse, as if bound to St. Michael's, a distance of seven miles, and in half an hour afterwards you would see him coiled up in the corner of the wood-fence, watching every motion of the slaves. He would, for this purpose, leave his horse tied up in the woods. Again, he would sometimes walk up to us, and give us orders as though he was upon the point of starting on a long journey, turn his back upon us, and make as though he was going to the house to get ready; and, before he would get half way thither, he would turn short and crawl into a fence-corner, or behind some tree, and there watch us till the going down of the sun.

Mr. Covey's *forte* consisted in his power to deceive. His life was devoted to planning and perpetrating the grossest deceptions. Every thing he possessed in the shape of learning or religion, he made conform to his disposition to deceive. He seemed to think himself equal to deceiving the Almighty. He would make a short prayer in the morning, and a long prayer at night; and, strange as it may seem, few men would at times appear more devotional than he. The exercises of his family devotions were always commenced with singing; and, as he was a very poor singer himself, the duty of raising the hymn generally came upon me. He would read his hymn, and nod at me to commence. I would at times do so; at others, I would not. My non-compliance would almost always produce much confusion. To show himself independent of me, he would start and stagger through with his hymn in the most discordant manner. In this state of mind, he prayed with more than ordinary spirit. Poor man! such was his disposition, and success at deceiving, I do verily believe that he sometimes deceived himself into the solemn belief, that he was a sincere worshipper of the most high God; and this, too, at a time when he may be said to have been guilty of compelling his woman slave to commit the sin of adultery. The facts in the case are these: Mr. Covey was a poor man; he was just commencing in life; he was only able to buy one slave; and, shocking as is the fact, he bought her, as he said, for *a breeder*. This woman was named Caroline. Mr. Covey bought her from Mr. Thomas Lowe, about six miles from St. Michael's. She was a large, able-bodied woman, about twenty years old. She had already given birth to one child, which proved her to be just what he wanted. After buying her, he hired a married man of Mr. Samuel Harrison, to live with him one year; and him he used to fasten up with her every night! The result was, that, at the end of the year, the miserable woman gave birth to twins. At this result Mr. Covey seemed to be highly pleased, both with the man and the wretched woman. Such was his joy, and that of his wife, that nothing they could do for Caroline during her confinement was too good, or too hard, to be done. The children were regarded as being quite an addition to his wealth.

If at any one time of my life more than another, I was made to drink the bitterest dregs of slavery, that time was during the first six months of my stay with Mr. Covey. We were worked in all weathers. It was never too hot or too cold; it could never rain, blow, hail, or snow, too hard for us to work in the field. Work, work, work, was scarcely more the order of the day than of the night. The longest days were too short for him, and the shortest nights too long for him. I was somewhat unmanageable when I first went there, but a few months of this discipline tamed me. Mr. Covey succeeded in breaking me. I was broken in body, soul, and spirit. My natural elasticity was crushed, my intellect languished, the disposition to read departed, the cheerful spark that lingered about my eye died; the dark night of slavery closed in upon me; and behold a man transformed into a brute!

Sunday was my only leisure time. I spent this in a sort of beast-like stupor, between sleep and wake, under some large tree. At times I would rise up, a flash of energetic freedom would dart through my soul, accompanied with a faint beam of hope, that flickered for a moment, and then vanished. I sank down again, mourning over my wretched condition. I was sometimes prompted to take my life, and that of Covey, but was prevented by a combination of hope and fear. My sufferings on this plantation seem now like a dream rather than a stern reality.

Our house stood within a few rods of the Chesapeake Bay, whose broad bosom was ever white with sails from every quarter of the habitable globe. Those beautiful vessels, robed in purest white, so delightful to the eye of freemen, were to me so many shrouded ghosts, to terrify and torment me with thoughts of my wretched condition. I have often, in the deep stillness of a summer's Sabbath, stood all alone upon the lofty banks of that noble bay, and traced, with saddened heart and tearful eye, the countless number of sails moving off to the mighty ocean. The sight of these always affected me powerfully. My thoughts would compel utterance; and there, with no audience but the Almighty, I would pour out my soul's complaint, in my rude way, with an apostrophe to the moving multitude of ships:—

"You are loosed from your moorings, and are free; I am fast in my chains, and am a slave! You move merrily before the gentle gale, and I sadly before the bloody whip! You are freedom's swift-winged angels, that fly round the world; I am confined in bands of iron! O that I were free! O, that I were on one of your gallant decks, and under your protecting wing! Alas! betwixt me and you, the turbid waters roll. Go on, go on. O that I could also go! Could I but swim! If I could fly! O, why was I born a man, of whom to make a brute! The glad ship is gone; she hides in the dim distance. I am left in the hottest hell of unending slavery. O God, save me! God, deliver me! Let me be free! Is there any God? Why am I a slave? I will run away. I will not stand it. Get caught, or get clear, I'll try it. I had as well die with ague as the fever. I have only one life to lose. I had as well be killed running as die standing. Only think of it; one hundred miles straight north, and I am free! Try it? Yes! God helping me, I will. It cannot be that I shall live and die a slave. I will take to the water. This very bay shall yet bear me into freedom. The steamboats steered in a north-east course from North Point. I will do the same; and when I get to the head of the bay, I will turn my canoe adrift, and walk straight through Delaware into Pennsylvania. When I get there, I shall not be required to have a pass; I can travel without being disturbed. Let but the first opportunity offer, and, come what will, I am off. Meanwhile, I will try to bear up under the yoke. I am not the only slave in the world. Why should I fret? I can bear as much as any of them. Besides, I am but a boy, and all boys are bound to some one. It may be that my misery in slavery will only increase my happiness when I get free. There is a better day coming."

Thus I used to think, and thus I used to speak to myself; goaded almost to madness at one moment, and at the next reconciling myself to my wretched lot.

I have already intimated that my condition was much worse, during the first six months of my stay at Mr. Covey's, than in the last six. The circumstances leading to the change in Mr. Covey's course toward me form an epoch in my humble history. You have seen how a man was made a slave; you shall see how a slave was made a man. On one of the hottest days of the month of August, 1833, Bill Smith, William Hughes, a slave named Eli, and myself, were engaged in fanning wheat. Hughes was clearing the fanned wheat from before the fan, Eli was turning, Smith was feeding, and I was carrying wheat to the fan. The work was simple, requiring strength rather than intellect; yet, to one entirely unused to such work, it came very hard. About three o'clock of that day, I broke down; my strength failed me; I was seized with a violent aching of the head, attended with extreme dizziness; I trembled in every limb. Finding what was coming, I nerved myself up, feeling it would never do to stop work. I stood as long as I could stagger to the hopper with grain. When I could stand no longer, I fell, and felt as if held down by an immense weight. The fan of course stopped; every one had his own work to do; and no one could do the work of the other, and have his own go on at the same time.

Mr. Covey was at the house, about one hundred yards from the treading-yard where we were fanning. On hearing the fan stop, he left immediately, and came to the spot where we were. He hastily inquired what the matter was. Bill answered that I was sick, and there was no one to bring wheat to the fan. I had by this time crawled away under the side of the post and rail-fence by which the yard was enclosed, hoping to find relief by getting out of the sun. He then asked where I was. He was told by one of the hands. He came to the spot, and, after looking at me awhile, asked me what was the matter. I told him as well as I could, for I scarce had strength to speak. He then gave me a savage kick in the side, and told me to get up. I tried to do so, but fell back in the attempt. He gave me another kick, and again told me to rise. I again tried, and succeeded in gaining my feet; but, stooping to get the tub with which I was feeding the fan, I again staggered and fell. While down in this situation, Mr. Covey took up the hickory slat with which Hughes had been striking off the half-bushel measure, and with it gave me a heavy blow upon the head, making a large wound, and the blood ran freely; and with this again told me to get up. I made no effort to comply, having now made up my mind to let him do his worst. In a short time after receiving this blow, my head grew better. Mr. Covey had now left me to my fate. At this moment I resolved, for the first time, to go to my master, enter a complaint, and ask his protection. In order to this, I must that afternoon walk seven miles; and this, under the circumstances, was truly a severe undertaking. I was exceedingly feeble; made so as much by the kicks and blows which I received, as by the severe fit of sickness to which I had been subjected. I, however, watched my chance, while Covey was looking in an opposite direction, and started for St. Michael's. I succeeded in getting a considerable distance on my way to the woods, when Covey discovered me, and called after me to come back, threatening what he would do if I did not come. I disregarded both his calls and his threats, and made my way to the woods as fast as my feeble state would allow; and thinking I might be overhauled by him if I kept the road, I walked through the woods, keeping far enough from the road to avoid detection, and near enough to prevent losing my way. I had not gone far before my little strength again failed me. I could go no farther. I fell down, and lay for a considerable time. The blood was yet oozing from the wound on my head. For a time I thought I should bleed to death; and think now that I should have done so, but that the blood so matted my hair as to stop the wound. After lying there about three quarters of an hour, I nerved myself up again, and started on my way, through bogs and briers, barefooted and bareheaded, tearing my feet sometimes at nearly every step; and after a journey of about seven miles, occupying some five hours to perform it, I arrived at master's store. I then presented an appearance enough to affect any but a heart of iron. From the crown of my head to my feet, I was covered with blood. My hair was all clotted with dust and blood; my shirt was stiff with blood. My legs and feet were torn in sundry places with briers and thorns, and were also covered with blood. I suppose I looked like a man who had escaped a den of wild beasts, and barely escaped them. In this state I appeared before my master, humbly entreating him to interpose his authority for my protection. I told him all the circumstances as well as I could, and it seemed, as I spoke, at times to affect him. He would then walk the floor, and seek to justify Covey by saying he expected I deserved it. He asked me what I wanted. I told him, to let me get a new home; that as sure as I lived with Mr. Covey again, I should live with but to die with him; that Covey would surely kill me; he was in a fair way for it. Master Thomas ridiculed the idea that there was any danger of Mr. Covey's killing me, and said that he knew Mr. Covey; that he was a good man, and that he could not think of taking me from him; that, should he do so, he would lose the whole year's wages; that I belonged to Mr. Covey for one year, and that I must go back to him, come what might; and that I must not trouble him with any more stories, or that he would himself *get hold of me.* After threatening me thus, he gave me a very large dose of salts, telling me that I might remain in St. Michael's that night, (it being quite late,) but that I must be off back to Mr. Covey's early in the morning; and that if I did not, he would *get hold of me,* which meant that he would whip me. I remained all night, and, according to his orders, I started off to Covey's in the morning, (Saturday morning,) wearied in body and broken in spirit. I got no supper that night, or breakfast that morning. I reached Covey's about nine o'clock; and just as I was getting over the fence that divided Mrs. Kemp's fields from ours, out ran Covey with his cowskin, to give me another whipping. Before he could reach me, I succeeded in getting to the cornfield; and as the corn was very high, it afforded me the means of hiding. He seemed very angry, and searched for me a long time. My behavior was altogether unaccountable. He finally gave up the chase, thinking, I suppose, that I must come home for something to eat; he would give himself no further trouble in looking for me. I spent that day mostly in the woods, having the alternative before me,—to go home and be whipped to death, or stay in the woods and be starved to death. That night, I fell in with Sandy Jenkins, a slave with whom I was somewhat acquainted. Sandy had a free wife who lived about four miles from

Mr. Covey's; and it being Saturday, he was on his way to see her. I told him my circumstances, and he very kindly invited me to go home with him. I went home with him, and talked this whole matter over, and got his advice as to what course it was best for me to pursue. I found Sandy an old adviser. He told me, with great solemnity, I must go back to Covey; but that before I went, I must go with him into another part of the woods, where there was a certain *root,* which, if I would take some of it with me, carrying it *always on my right side,* would render it impossible for Mr. Covey, or any other white man, to whip me. He said he had carried it for years; and since he had done so, he had never received a blow, and never expected to while he carried it. I at first rejected the idea, that the simple carrying of a root in my pocket would have any such effect as he had said, and was not disposed to take it; but Sandy impressed the necessity with much earnestness, telling me it could do no harm, if it did no good. To please him, I at length took the root, and, according to his direction, carried it upon my right side. This was Sunday morning. I immediately started for home; and upon entering the yard gate, out came Mr. Covey on his way to meeting. He spoke to me very kindly, bade me drive the pigs from a lot near by, and passed on towards the church. Now, this singular conduct of Mr. Covey really made me begin to think that there was something in the *root* which Sandy had given me; and had it been on any other day than Sunday, I could have attributed the conduct to no other cause than the influence of that root; and as it was, I was half inclined to think the *root* to be something more than I at first had taken it to be. All went well till Monday morning. On this morning, the virtue of the *root* was fully tested. Long before daylight, I was called to go and rub, curry, and feed, the horses. I obeyed, and was glad to obey. But whilst thus engaged, whilst in the act of throwing down some blades from the loft, Mr. Covey entered the stable with a long rope; and just as I was half out of the loft, he caught hold of my legs, and was about tying me. As soon as I found what he was up to, I gave a sudden spring, and as I did so, he holding to my legs, I was brought sprawling on the stable floor. Mr. Covey seemed now to think he had me, and could do what he pleased; but at this moment—from whence came the spirit I don't know—I resolved to fight; and, suiting my action to the resolution, I seized Covey hard by the throat; and as I did so, I rose. He held on to me, and I to him. My resistance was so entirely unexpected, that Covey seemed taken all aback. He trembled like a leaf. This gave me assurance, and I held him uneasy, causing the blood to run where I touched him with the ends of my fingers. Mr. Covey soon called out to Hughes for help. Hughes came, and, while Covey held me, attempted to tie my right hand. While he was in the act of doing so, I watched my chance, and gave him a heavy kick close under the ribs. This kick fairly sickened Hughes, so that he left me in the hands of Mr. Covey. This kick had the effect of not only weakening Hughes, but Covey also. When he saw Hughes bending over with pain, his courage quailed. He asked me if I meant to persist in my resistance. I told him I did, come what might; that he had used me like a brute for six months, and that I was determined to be used so no longer. With that, he strove to drag me to a stick that was lying just out of the stable door. He meant to knock me down. But just as he was leaning over to get the stick, I seized him with both hands by his collar, and brought him by a sudden snatch to the ground. By this time, Bill came. Covey called upon him for assistance. Bill wanted to know what he could do. Covey said, "Take hold of him, take hold of him!" Bill said his master hired him out to work, and not to help to whip me; so he left Covey and myself to fight our own battle out. We were at it for nearly two hours. Covey at length let me go, puffing and blowing at a great rate, saying that if I had not resisted, he would not have whipped me half so much. The truth was, that he had not whipped me at all. I considered him as getting entirely the worst end of the bargain; for he had drawn no blood from me, but I had from him. The whole six months afterwards, that I spend with Mr. Covey, he never laid the weight of his finger upon me in anger. He would occasionally say, he didn't want to get hold of me again. "No," thought I, "you need not; for you will come off worse than you did before."

This battle with Mr. Covey was the turning-point in my career as a slave. It rekindled the few expiring embers of freedom, and revived within me a sense of my own manhood. It recalled the departed self-confidence, and inspired me again with a determination to be free. The gratification afforded by the triumph was a full compensation for whatever else might follow, even death itself. He only can understand the deep satisfaction which I experienced, who has himself repelled by force the bloody arm of slavery. I felt as I never felt before. It was a glorious resurrection, from the tomb of slavery, to the heaven of freedom. My long-crushed spirit rose, cowardice departed, bold defiance took its place; and I now resolved that, however long I might remain a slave in form, the day had passed forever when I could be a slave in fact. I did not hesitate to let it be known of me, that the white man who expected to succeed in whipping, must also succeed in killing me.

From this time I was never again what might be called fairly whipped, though I remained a slave four years afterwards. I had several fights, but was never whipped.

It was for a long time a matter of surprise to me why Mr. Covey did not immediately have me taken by the constable to the whipping-post, and there regularly whipped for the crime of raising my hand against a white man in defence of myself. And the only explanation I can now think of does not entirely satisfy me; but such as it is, I will give it. Mr. Covey enjoyed the most unbounded reputation for being a first-rate overseer and negro-breaker. It was of considerable importance to him. That reputation was at stake; and had he sent me—a boy about sixteen years old—to the public whipping-post, his reputation would have been lost; so, to save his reputation, he suffered me to go unpunished.

My term of actual service to Mr. Edward Covey ended on Christmas day, 1833. The days between Christmas and New Year's day are allowed as holidays; and, accordingly, we were not required to perform any labor, more than to feed and take care of the stock. This time we regarded as our own, by the grace of our masters; and we therefore used or abused it nearly as we pleased. Those of us who had families at a distance, were generally allowed to spend the whole six days in their society. This time, however, was spent in various ways. The staid, sober, thinking and industrious ones of our number would employ themselves in making corn-brooms, mats, horse-collars, and baskets; and another class of us would spend the time in hunting opossums, hares, and coons. But by far the larger part engaged in such sports and merriments as playing ball, wrestling, running foot-races, fiddling, dancing, and drinking whisky; and this latter mode of spending the time was by far the most agreeable to the feelings of our masters. A slave who would work during the holidays was considered by our masters as scarcely deserving them. He was regarded as one who rejected the favor of his master. It was deemed a disgrace not to get drunk at Christmas; and he was regarded as lazy indeed, who had not provided himself with the necessary means, during the year, to get whisky enough to last him through Christmas.

From what I know of the effect of these holidays upon the slave, I believe them to be among the most effective means in the hands of the slaveholder in keeping down the spirit of insurrection. Were the slaveholders at once to abandon this practice, I have not the slightest doubt it would lead to an immediate insurrection among the slaves. These holidays serve as conductors, or safety-valves, to carry off the rebellious spirit of enslaved humanity. But for these, the slave would be forced up to the wildest desperation; and woe betide the slaveholder, the day he ventures to remove or hinder the operation of those conductors! I warn him that, in such an event, a spirit will go forth in their midst, more to be dreaded than the most appalling earthquake.

The holidays are part and parcel of the gross fraud, wrong, and inhumanity of slavery. They are professedly a custom established by the benevolence of the slaveholders; but I undertake to say, it is the result of selfishness, and one of the grossest frauds committed upon the down-trodden slave. They do not give the slaves this time because they would not like to have their work during its continuance, but because they know it would be unsafe to deprive them of it. This will be seen by the fact, that the slaveholders like to have their slaves spend those days just in such a manner as to make them as glad of their ending as of their beginning. Their object seems to be, to disgust their slaves with freedom, by plunging them into the lowest depths of dissipation. For instance, the slaveholders not only like to see the slave drink of his own accord, but will adopt various plans to make him drunk. One plan is, to make bets on their slaves, as to who can drink the most whisky without getting drunk; and in this way they succeed in getting whole multitudes to drink to excess. Thus, when the slave asks for virtuous freedom, the cunning slaveholder, knowing his ignorance, cheats him with a dose of vicious dissipation, artfully labelled with the name of liberty. The most of us used to drink it down, and the result was just what might be supposed: many of us were led to think that there was little to choose between liberty and slavery. We felt, and very properly too, that we had almost as well be slaves to man as to rum. So, when the holidays ended, we staggered up from the filth of our wallowing, took a long breath, and marched to the field,—feeling, upon the whole, rather glad to go, from what our master had deceived us into a belief was freedom, back to the arms of slavery.

I have said that this mode of treatment is a part of the whole system of fraud and inhumanity of slavery. It is so. The mode here adopted to disgust the slave with freedom, by allowing him to see only the abuse of it, is carried out in other things. For instance, a slave loves molasses; he steals some. His master, in many cases, goes off to town, and buys a large quantity; he returns, takes his whip, and commands the slave to eat the molasses, until the poor fellow is made sick at the very mention of it. The same mode is sometimes adopted to make the slaves refrain from asking for more food than their regular allowance. A slave runs through his allowance, and applies for more. His master is enraged at him; but, not willing to send him off without food, gives him more than is necessary, and compels him to eat it within a given time. Then, if he complains that he cannot eat it, he is said to be satisfied neither full nor fasting, and is whipped for being hard to please! I have an abundance of such illustrations of the same principle, drawn from my own observation, but think the cases I have cited sufficient. The practice is a very common one.

On the first of January, 1834, I left Mr. Covey, and went to live with Mr. William Freeland, who lived about three miles from St. Michael's. I soon found Mr. Freeland a very different man from Mr. Covey. Though not rich, he was what would be called an educated southern gentleman. Mr. Covey, as I have shown, was a well-trained negro-breaker and slave-driver. The former (slaveholder though he was) seemed to possess some regard for honor, some reverence for justice, and some respect for humanity. The latter seemed totally insensible to all such sentiments. Mr. Freeland had many of the faults peculiar to slaveholders, such as being very passionate and fretful; but I must do him the justice to say, that he was exceedingly free from those degrading vices to which Mr. Covey was constantly addicted. The one was open and frank, and we always knew where to find him. The other was a most artful deceiver, and could be understood only by such as were skilful enough to detect his cunningly-devised frauds. Another advantage I gained in my new master was, he made no pretensions to, or profession of, religion; and this, in my opinion, was truly a great advantage. I assert most unhesitatingly, that the religion of the south is a mere covering for the most horrid crimes,—a justifier of the most appalling barbarity,—a sanctifier of the most hateful frauds,—and a dark shelter under, which the darkest, foulest, grossest, and most infernal deeds of slaveholders find the strongest protection. Were I to be again reduced to the chains of slavery, next to that enslavement, I should regard being the slave of a religious master the greatest calamity that could befall me. For of all slaveholders with whom I have ever met, religious slaveholders are the worst. I have ever found them the meanest and basest, the most cruel and cowardly, of all others. It was my unhappy lot not only to belong to a religious slaveholder, but to live in a community of such religionists. Very near Mr. Freeland lived the Rev. Daniel Weeden, and in the same neighborhood lived the Rev. Rigby Hopkins. These were members and ministers in the Reformed Methodist Church. Mr. Weeden owned, among others, a woman slave, whose name I have forgotten. This woman's back, for weeks, was kept literally raw, made so by the lash of this merciless, *religious* wretch. He used to hire hands. His maxim was, Behave well or behave ill, it is the duty of a master occasionally to whip a slave, to remind him of his master's authority. Such was his theory, and such his practice.

Mr. Hopkins was even worse than Mr. Weeden. His chief boast was his ability to manage slaves. The peculiar feature of his government was that of whipping slaves in advance of deserving it. He always managed to have one or more of his slaves to whip every Monday morning. He did this to alarm their fears, and strike terror into those who escaped. His plan was to whip for the smallest offences, to prevent the commission of large ones. Mr. Hopkins could always find some excuse for whipping a slave. It would astonish one, unaccustomed to a slaveholding life, to see with what wonderful ease a slaveholder can find things, of which to make occasion to whip a slave. A mere look, word, or motion,—a mistake, accident, or want of power,—are all matters for which a slave may be whipped at any time. Does a slave look dissatisfied? It is said, he has the devil in him, and it must be whipped out. Does he speak loudly when spoken to by his master? Then he is getting high-minded, and should be taken down a button-hole lower. Does he forget to pull off his hat at the approach of a white person? Then he is wanting in reverence, and should be whipped for it. Does he ever venture to vindicate his conduct, when censured for it? Then he is guilty of impudence,—one of the greatest crimes of which a slave can be guilty. Does he ever venture to suggest a different mode of doing things from that pointed out by his master? He is indeed presumptuous, and getting above himself; and nothing less than a flogging will do for him. Does he, while ploughing, break a plough,—or, while hoeing, break a hoe? It is owing to his carelessness, and for it a slave must always be whipped. Mr. Hopkins could always find something of this sort to justify the use of the lash, and he seldom failed to embrace such opportunities. There was not a man in the whole county, with whom the slaves who had the getting their own home, would not prefer to live, rather than with this Rev. Mr. Hopkins. And yet there was not a man any where round, who made higher professions of religion, or was more active in revivals,—more attentive to the class, love-feast, prayer and preaching meetings, or more devotional in his family,—that prayed earlier, later, louder, and longer,—than this same reverend slave-driver, Rigby Hopkins.

But to return to Mr. Freeland, and to my experience while in his employment. He, like Mr. Covey, gave us enough to eat; but, unlike Mr. Covey, he also gave us sufficient time to take our meals. He worked us hard, but always between sunrise and sunset. He required a good deal of work to be done, but gave us good tools with which to work. His farm was large, but he employed hands enough to work it, and with ease, compared with many of his neighbors. My treatment, while in his employment, was heavenly, compared with what I experienced at the hands of Mr. Edward Covey.

Mr. Freeland was himself the owner of but two slaves. Their names were Henry Harris and John Harris. The rest of his hands he hired. These consisted of myself, Sandy Jenkins,* and Handy Caldwell. Henry and John were quite intelligent, and in a very little while after I went there, I succeeded in creating in them a strong desire to learn how to read. This desire soon sprang up in the

---

* This is the same man who gave me the roots to prevent my being whipped by Mr. Covey. He was "a clever soul." We used frequently to talk about the fight with Covey, and as often as we did so, he would claim my success as the result of the roots which he gave me. This superstition is very common among the more ignorant slaves. A slave seldom dies but that his death is attributed to trickery.

others also. They very soon mustered up some old spelling-books, and nothing would do but that I must keep a Sabbath school. I agreed to do so, and accordingly devoted my Sundays to teaching these my loved fellow-slaves how to read. Neither of them knew his letters when I went there. Some of the slaves of the neighboring farms found what was going on, and also availed themselves of this little opportunity to learn to read. It was understood, among all who came, that there must be as little display about it as possible. It was necessary to keep our religious masters at St. Michael's unacquainted with the fact, that, instead of spending the Sabbath in wrestling, boxing, and drinking whisky, we were trying to learn how to read the will of God; for they had much rather see us engaged in those degrading sports, than to see us behaving like intellectual, moral, and accountable beings. My blood boils as I think of the bloody manner in which Messrs. Wright Fairbanks and Garrison West,[58] both class-leaders, in connection with many others, rushed in upon us with sticks and stones, and broke up our virtuous little Sabbath school, at St. Michael's—all calling themselves Christians! humble followers of the Lord Jesus Christ! But I am again digressing.

I held my Sabbath school at the house of a free colored man, whose name I deem it imprudent to mention; for should it be known, it might embarrass him greatly, though the crime of holding the school was committed ten years ago. I had at one time over forty scholars, and those of the right sort, ardently desiring to learn. They were of all ages, though mostly men and women. I look back to those Sundays with an amount of pleasure not to be expressed. They were great days to my soul. The work of instructing my dear fellow-slaves was the sweetest engagement with which I was ever blessed. We loved each other, and to leave them at the close of the Sabbath was a severe cross indeed. When I think that these precious souls are to-day shut up in the prison-house of slavery, my feelings overcome me, and I am almost ready to ask, "Does a righteous God govern the universe? and for what does he hold the thunders in his right hand, if not to smite the oppressor, and deliver the spoiled out of the hand of the spoiler?" These dear souls came not to Sabbath school because it was popular to do so, nor did I teach them because it was reputable to be thus engaged. Every moment they spent in that school, they were liable to be taken up, and given thirty-nine lashes. They came because they wished to learn. Their minds had been starved by their cruel masters. They had been shut up in mental darkness. I taught them, because it was the delight of my soul to be doing something that looked like bettering the condition of my race. I kept up my school nearly the whole year I lived with Mr. Freeland; and, beside my Sabbath school, I devoted three evenings in the week, during the winter, to teaching the slaves at home. And I have the happiness to know, that several of those who came to Sabbath school learned how to read; and that one, at least, is now free through my agency.

The year passed off smoothly. It seemed only about half as long as the year which preceded it. I went through it without receiving a single blow. I will give Mr. Freeland the credit of being the best master I ever had, *till I became my own master.* For the ease with which I passed the year, I was, however, somewhat indebted to the society of my fellow-slaves. They were noble souls; they not only possessed loving hearts, but brave ones. We were linked and interlinked with each other. I loved them with a love stronger than any thing I have experienced since. It is sometimes said that we slaves do not love and confide in each other. In answer to this assertion, I can say, I never loved any or confided in any people more than my fellow-slaves, and especially those with whom I lived at Mr. Freeland's. I believe we would have died for each other. We never undertook to do any thing, of any importance, without a mutual consultation. We never moved separately. We were one; and as much so by our tempers and dispositions, as by the mutual hardships to which we were necessarily subjected by our condition as slaves.

At the close of the year 1834, Mr. Freeland again hired me of my master, for the year 1835. But, by this time, I began to want to live *upon free land* as well as *with Freeland;* and I was no longer content, therefore, to live with him or any other slaveholder. I began, with the commencement of the year, to prepare myself for a final struggle, which should decide my fate one way or the other. My tendency was upward. I was fast approaching manhood, and year after year had passed, and I was still a slave. These thoughts roused me—I must do something. I therefore resolved that 1835 should not pass without witnessing an attempt, on my part, to secure my liberty. But I was not willing to cherish this determination alone. My fellow-slaves were dear to me. I was anxious to have them participate with me in this, my life-giving determination. I therefore, though with great prudence, commenced early to ascertain their views and feelings in regard to their condition, and to imbue their minds with thoughts of freedom. I bent myself to devising ways and means for our escape, and meanwhile strove, on all fitting occasions, to impress them with the gross fraud and inhumanity of slavery. I went first to Henry, next to John, then to the others. I found, in them all, warm hearts and noble spirits. They were ready to hear, and ready to act when a feasible plan should be proposed. This was what I wanted. I talked to them of our want of manhood, if we submitted to our enslavement without at least one noble effort to be free. We met often, and consulted frequently, and told our hopes and fears, recounted the difficulties, real and imagined, which we should be called on to meet. At times we were almost disposed to give up, and try to content ourselves with our wretched lot; at others, we were firm and unbending in our determination to go. Whenever we suggested any plan, there was shrinking—the odds were fearful. Our path was beset with the greatest obstacles; and if we succeeded in gaining the end of it, our right to be free was yet questionable—we were yet liable to be returned to bondage. We could see no spot, this side of the ocean, where we could be free. We knew nothing about Canada. Our knowledge of the north did not extend farther than New York; and to go there, and be forever harassed with the frightful liability of being returned to slavery—with the certainty of being treated tenfold worse than before—the thought was truly a horrible one, and one which it was not easy to overcome. The case sometimes stood thus: At every gate through which we were to pass, we saw a watchman—at every ferry a guard—on every bridge a sentinel—and in every wood a patrol. We were hemmed in upon every side. Here were the difficulties, real or imagined—the good to be sought, and the evil to be shunned. On the one hand, there stood slavery, a stern reality, glaring frightfully upon us,—its robes already crimsoned with the blood of millions, and even now feasting itself greedily upon our own flesh. On the other hand, away back in the dim distance, under the flickering light of the north star, behind some craggy hill or snow-covered mountain, stood a doubtful freedom—half frozen—beckoning us to come and share its hospitality. This in itself was sometimes enough to stagger us; but when we permitted ourselves to survey the road, we were frequently appalled. Upon either side we saw grim death, assuming the most horrid shapes. Now it was starvation, causing us to eat our own flesh;—now we were contending with the waves, and were drowned;—now we were overtaken, and torn to pieces by the fangs of the terrible bloodhound. We were stung by scorpions, chased by wild beasts, bitten by snakes, and finally, after having nearly reached the desired spot,—after swimming rivers, encountering wild beasts, sleeping in the woods, suffering hunger and nakedness,—we were overtaken by our pursuers, and, in our resistance, we were shot dead upon the spot! I say, this picture sometimes appalled us, and made us

> "rather bear those ills we had,
> Than fly to others, that we knew not of."[59]

In coming to a fixed determination to run away, we did more than Patrick Henry, when he resolved upon liberty or death. With us it was a doubtful liberty at most, and almost certain death if we failed. For my part, I should prefer death to hopeless bondage.

Sandy, one of our number, gave up the notion, but still encouraged us. Our company then consisted of Henry Harris, John Harris, Henry Bailey, Charles Roberts, and myself. Henry Bailey was my uncle, and belonged to my master. Charles married my aunt: he belonged to my master's father-in-law, Mr. William Hamilton.

The plan we finally concluded upon was, to get a large canoe belonging to Mr. Hamilton, and upon the Saturday night previous to Easter holidays, paddle directly up the Chesapeake Bay. On our arrival at the head of the bay, a distance of seventy or eighty miles from where we lived, it was our purpose to turn our canoe adrift, and follow the guidance of the north star till we got beyond the limits of Maryland. Our reason for taking the water route was, that we were less liable to be suspected as runaways; we hoped to be regarded as fishermen; whereas, if we should take the land route, we should be subjected to interruptions of almost every kind. Any one having a white face, and being so disposed, could stop us, and subject us to examination.

The week before our intended start, I wrote several protections, one for each of us. As well as I can remember, they were in the following words, to wit:—

"This is to certify that I, the undersigned, have given the bearer, my servant, full liberty to go to Baltimore, and spend the Easter holidays. Written with mine own hand, &c., 1835.

"WILLIAM HAMILTON,
"Near St. Michael's, in Talbot county, Maryland."

We were not going to Baltimore; but, in going up the bay, we went toward Baltimore, and these protections were only intended to protect us while on the bay.

As the time drew near for our departure, our anxiety became more and more intense. It was truly a matter of life and death with us. The strength of our determination was about to be fully tested. At this time, I was very active in explaining every difficulty, removing every doubt, dispelling every fear, and inspiring all with the firmness indispensable to success in our undertaking; assuring them that half was gained the instant we made the move; we had talked long enough; we were now ready to move; if not now, we never should be; and if we did not intend to move now, we had as well fold our arms, sit down, and acknowledge ourselves fit only to be slaves. This, none of us were prepared to acknowledge. Every man stood firm; and at our last meeting, we pledged ourselves afresh, in the most solemn manner, that, at the time appointed, we would certainly start in pursuit of freedom. This was in the middle of the week, at the end of which we were to be off. We went, as usual, to our several fields of labor, but with bosoms highly agitated with thoughts of our truly hazardous undertaking. We tried to conceal our feelings as much as possible; and I think we succeeded very well.

After a painful waiting, the Saturday morning, whose night was to witness our departure, came. I hailed it with joy, bring what of sadness it might. Friday night was a sleepless one for me. I probably felt more anxious than the rest, because I was, by common consent, at the head of the whole affair. The responsibility of success or failure lay heavily upon me. The glory of the one, and the confusion of the other, were alike mine. The first two hours of that morning were such as I never experienced before, and hope never to again. Early in the morning, we went, as usual, to the field. We were spreading manure; and all at once, while thus engaged, I was overwhelmed with an indescribable feeling, in the fulness of which I turned to Sandy, who was near by, and said, "We are betrayed!" "Well," said he, "that thought has this moment struck me." We said no more. I was never more certain of any thing.

The horn was blown as usual, and we went up from the field to the house for breakfast. I went for the form, more than for want of any thing to eat that morning. Just as I got to the house, in looking out at the lane gate, I saw four white men, with two colored men. The white men were on horseback, and the colored ones were walking behind, as if tied. I watched them a few moments till they got up to our lane gate. Here they halted, and tied the colored men to the gate-post. I was not yet certain as to what the matter was. In a few moments, in rode Mr. Hamilton, with a speed betokening great excitement. He came to the door, and inquired if Master William was in. He was told he was at the barn. Mr. Hamilton, without dismounting, rode up to the barn with extraordinary speed. In a few moments, he and Mr. Freeland returned to the house. By this time, the three constables rode up, and in great haste dismounted, tied their horses, and met Master William and Mr. Hamilton returning from the barn; and after talking awhile, they all walked up to the kitchen door. There was no one in the kitchen but myself and John. Henry and Sandy were up at the barn. Mr. Freeland put his head in at the door, and called me by name, saying, there were some gentlemen at the door who wished to see me. I stepped to the door, and inquired what they wanted. They at once seized me, and, without giving me any satisfaction, tied me—lashing my hands closely together. I insisted upon know-ing what the matter was. They at length said, that they had learned I had been in a "scrape," and that I was to be examined before my master; and if their in-formation proved false, I should not be hurt.

In a few moments, they succeeded in tying John. They then turned to Henry, who had by this time returned, and commanded him to cross his hands. "I won't!" said Henry, in a firm tone, indicating his readiness to meet the con-sequences of his refusal. "Won't you?" said Tom Graham, the constable. "No, I won't!" said Henry, in a still stronger tone. With this, two of the constables pulled out their shining pistols, and swore, by their Creator, that they would make him cross his hands or kill him. Each cocked his pistol, and, with fingers on the trigger, walked up to Henry, saying, at the same time, if he did not cross his hands, they would blow his damned heart out. "Shoot me, shoot me!" said Henry; "you can't kill me but once. Shoot, shoot,—and be damned! *I won't be tied!*" This he said in a tone of loud defiance; and at the same time, with a mo-tion as quick as lightning, he with one single stroke dashed the pistols from the hand of each constable. As he did this, all hands fell upon him, and, after beat-ing him some time, they finally overpowered him, and got him tied.

During the scuffle, I managed, I know not how, to get my pass out, and, without being discovered, put it into the fire. We were all now tied; and just as we were to leave for Easton jail, Betsy Freeland, mother of William Freeland, came to the door with her hands full of biscuits, and divided them between Henry and John. She then delivered herself of a speech, to the following effect:—ad-dressing herself to me, she said, "*You devil! You yellow devil!* it was you that put it into the heads of Henry and John to run away. But for you, you long-legged mulatto devil! Henry nor John would never have thought of such a thing." I made no reply, and was immediately hurried off towards St. Michael's. Just a moment previous to the scuffle with Henry, Mr. Hamilton suggested the propri-ety of making a search for the protections which he had understood Frederick had written for himself and the rest. But, just at the moment he was about car-rying his proposal into effect, his aid was needed in helping to tie Henry; and the excitement attending the scuffle caused them either to forget, or to deem it un-safe, under the circumstances, to search. So we were not yet convicted of the in-tention to run away.

When we got about half way to St. Michael's, while the constables having us in charge were looking ahead, Henry inquired of me what he should do with his pass. I told him to eat it with his biscuit, and own nothing; and we passed the word around, "*Own nothing;*" and "*Own nothing!*" said we all. Our confidence in each other was unshaken. We were resolved to succeed or fail together, after the calamity had befallen us as much as before. We were now prepared for any thing. We were to be dragged that morning fifteen miles behind horses, and then to be placed in the Easton jail. When we reached St. Michael's, we underwent a sort of examination. We all denied that we ever intended to run away. We did this more to bring out the evidence against us, than from any hope of getting clear of being sold; for, as I have said, we were ready for that. The fact was, we cared but little where we went, so we went together. Our greatest concern was about separation.

We dreaded that more than any thing this side of death. We found the evidence against us to be the testimony of one person; our master would not tell who it was; but we came to a unanimous decision among ourselves as to who their informant was. We were sent off to the jail at Easton. When we got there, we were delivered up to the sheriff, Mr. Joseph Graham, and by him placed in jail. Henry, John, and myself, were placed in one room together—Charles, and Henry Bailey, in another. Their object in separating us was to hinder concert.

We had been in jail scarcely twenty minutes, when a swarm of slave traders, and agents for slave traders, flocked into jail to look at us, and to ascertain if we were for sale. Such a set of beings I never saw before! I felt myself surrounded by so many fiends from perdition. A band of pirates never looked more like their father, the devil. They laughed and grinned over us, saying, "Ah, my boys! we have got you, haven't we?" And after taunting us in various ways, they one by one went into an examination of us, with intent to ascertain our value. They would impudently ask us if we would not like to have them for our masters. We would make them no answer, and leave them to find out as best they could. Then they would curse and swear at us, telling us that they could take the devil out of us in a very little while, if we were only in their hands.

While in jail, we found ourselves in much more comfortable quarters than we expected when we went there. We did not get much to eat, nor that which was very good; but we had a good clean room, from the windows of which we could see what was going on in the street, which was very much better than though we had been placed in one of the dark, damp cells. Upon the whole, we got along very well, so far as the jail and its keeper were concerned. Immediately after the holidays were over, contrary to all our expectations, Mr. Hamilton and Mr. Freeland came up to Easton, and took Charles, the two Henrys, and John, out of jail, and carried them home, leaving me alone. I regarded this separation as a final one. It caused me more pain than any thing else in the whole transaction. I was ready for any thing rather than separation. I supposed that they had consulted together, and had decided that, as I was the whole cause of the intention of the others to run away, it was hard to make the innocent suffer with the guilty; and that they had, therefore, concluded to take the others home, and sell me, as a warning to the others that remained. It is due to the noble Henry to say, he seemed almost as reluctant at leaving the prison as at leaving home to come to the prison. But we knew we should, in all probability, be separated, if we were sold; and since he was in their hands, he concluded to go peaceably home.

I was now left to my fate. I was all alone, and within the walls of a stone prison. But a few days before, and I was full of hope. I expected to have been safe in a land of freedom; but now I was covered with gloom, sunk down to the utmost despair. I thought the possibility of freedom was gone. I was kept in this way about one week, at the end of which, Captain Auld, my master, to my surprise and utter astonishment, came up, and took me out, with the intention of sending me, with a gentleman of his acquaintance, into Alabama. But, from some cause or other, he did not send me to Alabama, but concluded to send me back to Baltimore, to live again with his brother Hugh, and to learn a trade.

Thus, after an absence of three years and one month, I was once more permitted to return to my old home at Baltimore. My master sent me away, because there existed against me a very great prejudice in the community, and he feared I might be killed.

In a few weeks after I went to Baltimore, Master Hugh hired me to Mr. William Gardner, an extensive ship-builder, on Fell's Point. I was put there to learn how to calk. It, however, proved a very unfavorable place for the accomplishment of this object. Mr. Gardner was engaged that spring in building two large man-of-war brigs, professedly for the Mexican government. The vessels were to be launched in the July of that year, and in failure thereof, Mr. Gardner was to lose a considerable sum; so that when I entered, all was hurry. There was no time to learn any thing. Every man had to do that which he knew how to do. In entering the shipyard, my orders from Mr. Gardner were, to do whatever the carpenters commanded me to do. This was placing me at the beck and call of about seventy-five men. I was to regard all these as masters. Their word was to be my law. My situation was a most trying one. At times I needed a dozen pair of hands. I was called a dozen ways in the space of a single minute. Three or four voices would strike my ear at the same moment. It was—"Fred., come help me to cant this timber here."—"Fred., come carry this timber yonder."—"Fred., bring that roller here."—"Fred., go get a fresh can of water."—"Fred., come help saw off the end of this timber."—"Fred., go quick, and get the crowbar."—"Fred., hold on the end of this fall."[60]—"Fred., go to the blacksmith's shop, and get a new punch."—"Hurra, Fred.! run and bring me a cold chisel."—"I say, Fred., bear a hand, and get up a fire as quick as lightning under that steambox."—"Halloo, nigger! come, turn this grindstone."—"Come, come! move, move! and *bowse* this timber forward."—"I say, darky, blast your eyes, why don't you heat up some pitch?"—"Halloo! halloo! halloo!" (Three voices at the same time.) "Come here!—Go there!—Hold on where you are! Damn you, if you move, I'll knock your brains out!"

This was my school for eight months; and I might have remained there longer, but for a most horrid fight I had with four of the white apprentices, in which my left eye was nearly knocked out, and I was horribly mangled in other respects. The facts in the case were these: Until a very little while after I went there, white and black ship-carpenters worked side by side, and no one seemed to see any impropriety in it. All hands seemed to be very well satisfied. Many of the black carpenters were freemen. Things seemed to be going on very well. All at once, the white carpenters knocked off, and said they would not work with free colored workmen. Their reason for this, as alleged, was, that if free colored carpenters were encouraged, they would soon take the trade into their own hands, and poor white men would be thrown out of employment. They therefore felt called upon at once to put a stop to it. And, taking advantage of Mr. Gardner's necessities, they broke off, swearing they would work no longer, unless he would discharge his black carpenters. Now, though this did not extend to me in form, it did reach me in fact. My fellow-apprentices very soon began to feel it degrading to them to work with me. They began to put on airs, and talk about the "niggers" taking the country, saying we all ought to be killed; and, being encouraged by the journeymen, they commenced making my condition as hard as they could, by hectoring me around, and sometimes striking me. I, of course, kept the vow I made after the fight with Mr. Covey, and struck back again, regardless of consequences; and while I kept them from combining, I succeeded very well; for I could whip the whole of them, taking them separately. They, however, at length combined, and came upon me, armed with sticks, stones, and heavy handspikes. One came in front with a half brick. There was one at each side of me, and one behind me. While I was attending to those in front, and on either side, the one behind ran up with the handspike, and struck me a heavy blow upon the head. It stunned me. I fell, and with this they all ran upon me, and fell to beating me with their fists. I let them lay on for a while, gathering strength. In an instant, I gave a sudden surge, and rose to my hands and knees. Just as I did that, one of their number gave me, with his heavy boot, a powerful kick in the left eye. My eyeball seemed to have burst. When they saw my eye closed, and badly swollen, they left me. With this I seized the handspike, and for a time pursued them. But here the carpenters interfered, and I thought I might as well give it up. It was impossible to stand my hand against so many. All this took place in sight of not less than fifty white ship-carpenters, and not one interposed a friendly word; but some cried, "Kill the damned nigger! Kill him! kill him! He struck a white person." I found my only chance for life was in flight. I succeeded in getting away without an additional blow, and barely so; for to strike a white man is death by Lynch law,—and that was the law in Mr. Gardner's ship-yard; nor is there much of any other out of Mr. Gardner's ship-yard.

I went directly home, and told the story of my wrongs to Master Hugh; and I am happy to say of him, irreligious as he was, his conduct was heavenly, compared with that of his brother Thomas under similar circumstances. He listened attentively to my narration of the circumstances leading to the savage outrage, and gave many proofs of his strong indignation at it. The heart of my once overkind mistress was again melted into pity. My puffed-out eye and blood-covered face moved her to tears. She took a chair by me, washed the blood from my face, and, with a mother's tenderness, bound up my head, covering the wounded eye with a lean piece of fresh beef. It was almost compensation for my suffering to witness, once more, a manifestation of kindness from this, my once affectionate old mistress. Master Hugh was very much enraged. He gave expression to his feelings by pouring out curses upon the heads of those who did the deed. As soon as I got a little the better of my bruises, he took me with him to Esquire Watson's, on Bond Street, to see what could be done about the matter. Mr. Watson inquired who saw the assault committed. Master Hugh told him it was done in Mr. Gardner's ship-yard, at midday, where there were a large company of men at work. "As to that," he said, "the deed was done, and there was no question as to who did it." His answer was, he could do nothing in the case, unless some white man would come forward and testify. He could issue no warrant on my word. If I had been killed in the presence of a thousand colored people, their testimony combined would have been insufficient to have arrested one of the murderers. Master Hugh, for once, was compelled to say this state of things was too bad. Of course, it was impossible to get any white man to volunteer his testimony in my behalf, and against the white young men. Even those who may have sympathized with me were not prepared to do this. It required a degree of courage unknown to them to do so; for just at that time, the slightest manifestation of humanity toward a colored person was denounced as abolitionism, and that name subjected its bearer to frightful liabilities. The watchwords of the bloody-minded in that region, and in those days, were, "Damn the abolitionists!" and "Damn the niggers!" There was nothing done, and probably nothing would have been done if I had been killed. Such was, and such remains, the state of things in the Christian city of Baltimore.

Master Hugh, finding he could get no redress, refused to let me go back again to Mr. Gardner. He kept me himself, and his wife dressed my wound till I was again restored to health. He then took me into the ship-yard of which he was foreman, in the employment of Mr. Walter Price. There I was immediately set to calking, and very soon learned the art of using my mallet and irons. In the course of one year from the time I left Mr. Gardner's, I was able to command the highest wages given to the most experienced calkers. I was now of some importance to my master. I was bringing him from six to seven dollars per week. I sometimes brought him nine dollars per week: my wages were a dollar and a half a day. After learning how to calk, I sought my own employment, made my own contracts, and collected the money which I earned. My pathway became much more smooth than before; my condition was now much more comfortable. When I could get no calking to do, I did nothing. During these leisure times, those old notions about freedom would steal over me again. When in Mr. Gardner's employment, I was kept in such a perpetual whirl of excitement, I could think of nothing, scarcely, but my life; and in thinking of my life, I almost forgot my liberty. I have observed this in my experience of slavery,—that whenever my condition was improved, instead of its increasing my contentment, it only increased my desire to be free, and set me to thinking of plans to gain my freedom. I have found that, to make a contented slave, it is necessary to make a thoughtless one. It is necessary to darken his moral and mental vision, and, as far as possible, to annihilate the power of reason. He must be able to detect no inconsistencies in slavery; he must be made to feel that slavery is right; and he can be brought to that only when he ceases to be a man.

I was now getting, as I have said, one dollar and fifty cents per day. I contracted for it; I earned it; it was paid to me; it was rightfully my own; yet, upon each returning Saturday night, I was compelled to deliver every cent of that money to Master Hugh. And why? Not because he earned it,—not because he had any hand in earning it,—not because I owed it to him,—nor because he possessed the slightest shadow of a right to it; but solely because he had the power to compel me to give it up. The right of the grim-visaged pirate upon the high seas is exactly the same.

## CHAPTER XI.

I NOW come to that part of my life during which I planned, and finally succeeded in making, my escape from slavery. But before narrating any of the peculiar circumstances, I deem it proper to make known my intention not to state all the facts connected with the transaction. My reasons for pursuing this course may be understood from the following: First, were I to give a minute statement of all the facts, it is not only possible, but quite probable, that others would thereby be involved in the most embarrassing difficulties. Secondly, such a statement would most undoubtedly induce greater vigilance on the part of slaveholders than has existed heretofore among them; which would, of course, be the means of guarding a door whereby some dear brother bondman might escape his galling chains. I deeply regret the necessity that impels me to suppress any thing of importance connected with my experience in slavery. It would afford me great pleasure indeed, as well as materially add to the interest of my narrative, were I at liberty to gratify a curiosity, which I know exists in the minds of many, by an accurate statement of all the facts pertaining to my most fortunate escape. But I must deprive myself of this pleasure, and the curious of the gratification which such a statement would afford. I would allow myself to suffer under the greatest imputations which evil-minded men might suggest, rather than exculpate myself, and thereby run the hazard of closing the slightest avenue by which a brother slave might clear himself of the chains and fetters of slavery.

I have never approved of the very public manner in which some of our western friends have conducted what they call the *underground railroad*, but which, I think, by their open declarations, has been made most emphatically the *upperground railroad*. I honor those good men and women for their noble daring, and applaud them for willingly subjecting themselves to bloody persecution, by openly avowing their participation in the escape of slaves. I, however, can see very little good resulting from such a course, either to themselves or the slaves escaping; while, upon the other hand, I see and feel assured that those open declarations are a positive evil to the slaves remaining, who are seeking to escape. They do nothing towards enlightening the slave, whilst they do much towards enlightening the master. They stimulate him to greater watchfulness, and enhance his power to capture his slave. We owe something to the slaves south of the line as well as to those north of it; and in aiding the latter on their way to freedom, we should be careful to do nothing which would be likely to hinder the former from escaping from slavery. I would keep the merciless slaveholder profoundly ignorant of the means of flight adopted by the slave. I would leave him to imagine himself surrounded by myriads of invisible tormentors, ever ready to snatch from his infernal grasp his trembling prey. Let him be left to feel his way in the dark; let darkness commensurate with his crime hover over him; and let him feel that at every step he takes, in pursuit of the flying bondman, he is running the frightful risk of having his hot brains dashed out by an invisible agency. Let us render the tyrant no aid; let us not hold the light by which he can trace the footprints of our flying brother. But enough of this. I will now proceed to the statement of those facts, connected with my escape, for which I am alone responsible, and for which no one can be made to suffer but myself.

In the early part of the year 1838, I became quite restless. I could see no reason why I should, at the end of each week, pour the reward of my toil into the purse of my master. When I carried to him my weekly wages, he would, after counting the money, look me in the face with a robber-like fierceness, and ask, "Is this all?" He was satisfied with nothing less than the last cent. He would, however, when I made him six dollars, sometimes give me six cents, to encourage me. It had the opposite effect. I regarded it as a sort of admission of my right to the whole. The fact that he gave me any part of my wages was proof, to my mind, that he believed me entitled to the whole of them. I always felt worse for having received any thing; for I feared that the giving me a few cents would ease his conscience, and make him feel himself to be a pretty honorable sort of robber. My discontent grew upon me. I was ever on the look-out for means of escape; and, finding no direct means, I determined to try to hire my time, with a view of getting money with which to make my escape. In the spring of 1838, when Master Thomas came to Baltimore to purchase his spring goods, I got an opportunity, and applied to him to allow me to hire my time. He unhesitatingly refused my request, and told me this was another stratagem by which to escape. He told me I could go nowhere but that he could get me; and that, in the event of my running away, he should spare no pains in his efforts to catch me. He exhorted me to content myself, and be obedient. He told me, if I would be happy, I must lay out no plans for the future. He said, if I behaved myself properly, he would take care of me. Indeed, he advised me to complete thoughtlessness of the future, and taught me to depend solely upon him for happiness. He seemed to see fully the pressing necessity of setting aside my intellectual nature, in order to contentment in slavery. But in spite of him, and even in spite of myself, I continued to think, and to think about the injustice of my enslavement, and the means of escape.

About two months after this, I applied to Master Hugh for the privilege of hiring my time. He was not acquainted with the fact that I had applied to Master Thomas, and had been refused. He too, at first, seemed disposed to refuse; but, after some reflection, he granted me the privilege, and proposed the following terms: I was to be allowed all my time, make all contracts with those for whom I worked, and find my own employment; and, in return for this liberty, I was to pay him three dollars at the end of each week; find myself in calking tools, and in board and clothing. My board was two dollars and a half per week. This, with the wear and tear of clothing and calking tools, made my regular expenses about six dollars per week. This amount I was compelled to make up, or relinquish the privilege of hiring my time. Rain or shine, work or no work, at the end of each week the money must be forthcoming, or I must give up my privilege. This arrangement, it will be perceived, was decidedly in my master's favor. It relieved him of all need of looking after me. His money was sure. He received all the benefits of slaveholding without its evils; while I endured all the evils of a slave, and suffered all the care and anxiety of a freeman. I found it a hard bargain. But, hard as it was, I thought it better than the old mode of getting along. It was a step towards freedom to be allowed to bear the responsibilities of a freeman, and I was determined to hold on upon it. I bent myself to the work of making money. I was ready to work at night as well as day, and by the most untiring perseverance and industry, I made enough to meet my expenses, and lay up a little money every week. I went on thus from May till August. Master Hugh then refused to allow me to hire my time longer. The ground for his refusal was a failure on my part, one Saturday night, to pay him for my week's time. This failure was occasioned by my attending a camp meeting about ten miles from Baltimore. During the week, I had entered into an engagement with a number of young friends to start from Baltimore to the camp ground early Saturday evening; and being detained by my employer, I was unable to get down to Master Hugh's without disappointing the company. I knew that Master Hugh was in no special need of the money that night. I therefore decided to go to camp meeting, and upon my return pay him the three dollars. I staid at the camp meeting one day longer than I intended when I left. But as soon as I returned, I called upon him to pay him what he considered his due. I found him very angry; he could scarce restrain his wrath. He said he had a great mind to give me a severe whipping. He wished to know how I dared go out of the city without asking his permission. I told him I hired my time, and while I paid him the price which he asked for it, I did not know that I was bound to ask him when and where I should go. This reply troubled him; and, after reflecting a few moments, he turned to me, and said I should hire my time no longer; that the next thing he should know of, I would be running away. Upon the same plea, he told me to bring my tools and clothing home forthwith. I did so; but instead of seeking work, as I had been accustomed to do previously to hiring my time, I spent the whole week without the performance of a single stroke of work. I did this in retaliation. Saturday night, he called upon me as usual for my week's wages. I told him I had no wages; I had done no work that week. Here we were upon the point of coming to blows. He raved, and swore his determination to get hold of me. I did not allow myself a single word; but was resolved, if he laid the weight of his hand upon me, it should be blow for blow. He did not strike me, but told me that he would find me in constant employment in future. I thought the matter over during the next day, Sunday, and finally resolved upon the third day of September, as the day upon which I would make a second attempt to secure my freedom. I now had three weeks during which to prepare for my journey. Early on Monday morning, before Master Hugh had time to make any engagement for me, I went out and got employment of Mr. Butler, at his ship-yard near the drawbridge, upon what is called the City Block, thus making it unnecessary for him to seek employment for me. At the end of the week, I brought him between eight and nine dollars. He seemed very well pleased, and asked me why I did not do the same the week before. He little knew what my plans were. My object in working steadily was to remove any suspicion he might entertain of my intent to run away; and in this I succeeded admirably. I suppose he thought I was never better satisfied with my condition than at the very time during which I was planning my escape. The second week passed, and again I carried him my full wages; and so well pleased was he, that he gave me twenty-five cents, (quite a large sum for a slaveholder to give a slave,) and bade me to make a good use of it. I told him I would.

Things went on without very smoothly indeed, but within there was trouble. It is impossible for me to describe my feelings as the time of my contemplated start drew near. I had a number of warm-hearted friends in Baltimore,—friends that I loved almost as I did my life,—and the thought of being separated from them forever was painful beyond expression. It is my opinion that thousands would escape from slavery, who now remain, but for the strong cords of affection that bind them to their friends. The thought of leaving my friends was decidedly the most painful thought with which I had to contend. The love of them was my tender point, and shook my decision more than all things else. Besides the pain of separation, the dread and apprehension of a failure exceeded what I had experienced at my first attempt. The appalling defeat I then sustained returned to torment me. I felt assured that, if I failed in this attempt, my case would be a hopeless one—it would seal my fate as a slave forever. I could not hope to get off with any thing less than the severest punishment, and being placed beyond the means of escape. It required no very vivid imagination to depict the most frightful scenes through which I should have to pass, in case I failed. The wretchedness of slavery, and the blessedness of freedom, were perpetually before me. It was life and death with me. But I remained firm, and, according to my resolution, on the third day of September, 1838, I left my chains, and succeeded in reaching New York without the slightest interruption of any kind. How I did so,—what means I adopted,—what direction I travelled, and by what mode of conveyance,—I must leave unexplained, for the reasons before mentioned.[61]

I have been frequently asked how I felt when I found myself in a free State. I have never been able to answer the question with any satisfaction to myself. It was a moment of the highest excitement I ever experienced. I suppose I felt as one may imagine the unarmed mariner to feel when he is rescued by a friendly man-of-war from the pursuit of a pirate. In writing to a dear friend, immediately after my arrival at New York, I said I felt like one who had escaped a den of hungry lions. This state of mind, however, very soon subsided; and I was again seized with a feeling of great insecurity and loneliness. I was yet liable to be taken back, and subjected to all the tortures of slavery. This in itself was enough to damp the ardor of my enthusiasm. But the loneliness overcame me. There I was in the midst of thousands, and yet a perfect stranger; without home and without friends, in the midst of thousands of my own brethren—children of a common Father, and yet I dared not to unfold to any one of them my sad condition. I was afraid to speak to any one for fear of speaking to the wrong one, and thereby falling into the hands of money-loving kidnappers, whose business it was to lie in wait for the panting fugitive, as the ferocious beasts of the forest lie in wait for their prey. The motto which I adopted when I started from slavery was this—"Trust no man!" I saw in every white man an enemy, and in almost every colored man cause for distrust. It was a most painful situation; and, to understand it, one must needs experience it, or imagine himself in similar circumstances. Let him be a fugitive slave in a strange land—a land given up to be the hunting-ground for slaveholders—whose inhabitants are legalized kidnappers—where he is every moment subjected to the terrible liability of being seized upon by his fellow-men, as the hideous crocodile seizes upon his prey!—I say, let him place himself in my situation—without home or friends—without money or credit—wanting shelter, and no one to give it—wanting bread, and no money to buy it,—and at the same time let him feel that he is pursued by merciless men-hunters, and in total darkness as to what to do, where to go, or where to stay,—perfectly helpless both as to the means of defence and means of escape,—in the midst of plenty, yet suffering the terrible gnawings of hunger,—in the midst of houses, yet having no home,—among fellow-men, yet feeling as if in the midst of wild beasts, whose greediness to swallow up the trembling and half-famished fugitive is only equalled by that with which the monsters of the deep swallow up the helpless fish upon which they subsist,—I say, let him be placed in this most trying situation,—the situation in which I was placed,—then, and not till then, will he fully appreciate the hardships of, and know how to sympathize with, the toil-worn and whip-scarred fugitive slave.

Thank Heaven, I remained but a short time in this distressed situation. I was relieved from it by the humane hand of Mr. DAVID RUGGLES,[62] whose vigilance, kindness, and perseverance, I shall never forget. I am glad of an opportunity to express, as far as words can, the love and gratitude I bear him. Mr. Ruggles is now afflicted with blindness, and is himself in need of the same kind offices which he was once so forward in the performance of toward others. I had been in New York but a few days, when Mr. Ruggles sought me out, and very kindly took me to his boarding-house at the corner of Church and Lespenard Streets. Mr. Ruggles was then very deeply engaged in the memorable *Darg* case,[63] as well as attending to a number of other fugitive slaves, devising ways and means for their successful escape; and, though watched and hemmed in on almost every side, he seemed to be more than a match for his enemies.

Very soon after I went to Mr. Ruggles, he wished to know of me where I wanted to go; as he deemed it unsafe for me to remain in New York. I told him I was a calker, and should like to go where I could get work. I thought of going to Canada; but he decided against it, and in favor of my going to New Bedford, thinking I should be able to get work there at my trade. At this time, Anna,* my intended wife, came on; for I wrote to her immediately after my arrival at New York, (notwithstanding my homeless, houseless, and helpless condition,) informing her of my successful flight, and wishing her to come on forthwith. In a few days after her arrival, Mr. Ruggles called in the Rev. J. W. C. Pennington,[64] who, in the presence of Mr. Ruggles, Mrs. Michaels, and two or three others, performed the marriage ceremony, and gave us a certificate, of which the following is an exact copy:—

"THIS may certify, that I joined together in holy matrimony Frederick Johnson† and Anna Murray, as man and wife, in the presence of Mr. David Ruggles and Mrs. Michaels.

"JAMES W. C. PENNINGTON.

"*New York, Sept. 15, 1838.*"

Upon receiving this certificate, and a five-dollar bill from Mr. Ruggles, I shouldered one part of our baggage, and Anna took up the other, and we set out forthwith to take passage on board of the steamboat John W. Richmond for Newport, on our way to New Bedford. Mr. Ruggles gave me a letter to a Mr. Shaw in Newport, and told me, in case my money did not serve me to New

---

* She was free.
† I had changed my name from Frederick *Bailey* to that of *Johnson*.

Bedford, to stop in Newport and obtain further assistance; but upon our arrival at Newport, we were so anxious to get to a place of safety, that, notwithstanding we lacked the necessary money to pay our fare, we decided to take seats in the stage, and promise to pay when we got to New Bedford. We were encouraged to do this by two excellent gentlemen, residents of New Bedford, whose names I afterward ascertained to be Joseph Ricketson and William C. Taber. They seemed at once to understand our circumstances, and gave us such assurance of their friendliness as put us fully at ease in their presence. It was good indeed to meet with such friends, at such a time. Upon reaching New Bedford, we were directed to the house of Mr. Nathan Johnson, by whom we were kindly received, and hospitably provided for. Both Mr. and Mrs. Johnson took a deep and lively interest in our welfare. They proved themselves quite worthy of the name of abolitionists. When the stage-driver found us unable to pay our fare, he held on upon our baggage as security for the debt. I had but to mention the fact to Mr. Johnson, and he forthwith advanced the money.

We now began to feel a degree of safety, and to prepare ourselves for the duties and responsibilities of a life of freedom. On the morning after our arrival at New Bedford, while at the breakfast-table, the question arose as to what name I should be called by. The name given me by my mother was, "Frederick Augustus Washington Bailey." I, however, had dispensed with the two middle names long before I left Maryland so that I was generally known by the name of "Frederick Bailey." I started from Baltimore bearing the name of "Stanley." When I got to New York, I again changed my name to "Frederick Johnson," and thought that would be the last change. But when I got to New Bedford, I found it necessary again to change my name. The reason of this necessity was, that there were so many Johnsons in New Bedford, it was already quite difficult to distinguish between them. I gave Mr. Johnson the privilege of choosing me a name, but told him he must not take from me the name of "Frederick." I must hold on to that, to preserve a sense of my identity. Mr. Johnson had just been reading the "Lady of the Lake," and at once suggested that my name be "Douglass."[65] From that time until now I have been called "Frederick Douglass;" and as I am more widely known by that name than by either of the others, I shall continue to use it as my own.

I was quite disappointed at the general appearance of things in New Bedford. The impression which I had received respecting the character and condition of the people of the north, I found to be singularly erroneous. I had very strangely supposed, while in slavery, that few of the comforts, and scarcely any of the luxuries, of life were enjoyed at the north, compared with what were enjoyed by the slaveholders of the south. I probably came to this conclusion from the fact that northern people owned no slaves. I supposed that they were about upon a level with the non-slaveholding population of the south. I knew *they* were exceedingly poor, and I had been accustomed to regard their poverty as the necessary consequence of their being non-slaveholders. I had somehow imbibed the opinion that, in the absence of slaves, there could be no wealth, and very little refinement. And upon coming to the north, I expected to meet with a rough, hard-handed, and uncultivated population, living in the most Spartan-like simplicity, knowing nothing of the ease, luxury, pomp, and grandeur of southern slaveholders. Such being my conjectures, any one acquainted with the appearance of New Bedford may very readily infer how palpably I must have seen my mistake.

In the afternoon of the day when I reached New Bedford, I visited the wharves, to take a view of the shipping. Here I found myself surrounded with the strongest proofs of wealth. Lying at the wharves, and riding in the stream, I saw many ships of the finest model, in the best order, and of the largest size. Upon the right and left, I was walled in by granite warehouses of the widest dimensions, stowed to their utmost capacity with the necessaries and comforts of life. Added to this, almost every body seemed to be at work, but noiselessly so, compared with what I had been accustomed to in Baltimore. There were no loud songs heard from those engaged in loading and unloading ships. I heard no deep oaths or horrid curses on the laborer. I saw no whipping of men; but all seemed to go smoothly on. Every man appeared to understand his work, and went at it with a sober, yet cheerful earnestness, which betokened the deep interest which he felt in what he was doing, as well as a sense of his own dignity as a man. To me this looked exceedingly strange. From the wharves I strolled around and over the town, gazing with wonder and admiration at the splendid churches, beautiful dwellings, and finely-cultivated gardens; evincing an amount of wealth, comfort, taste, and refinement, such as I had never seen in any part of slaveholding Maryland.

Every thing looked clean, new, and beautiful. I saw few or no dilapidated houses, with poverty-stricken inmates; no half-naked children and barefooted women, such as I had been accustomed to see in Hillsborough, Easton, St. Michael's, and Baltimore. The people looked more able, stronger, healthier, and happier, than those of Maryland. I was for once made glad by a view of extreme wealth, without being saddened by seeing extreme poverty. But the most astonishing as well as the most interesting thing to me was the condition of the colored people, a great many of whom, like myself, had escaped thither as a refuge from the hunters of men. I found many, who had not been seven years out of their chains, living in finer houses, and evidently enjoying more of the comforts of life, than the average of slaveholders in Maryland. I will venture to assert that my friend Mr. Nathan Johnson (of whom I can say with a grateful heart, "I was hungry, and he gave me meat; I was thirsty, and he gave me drink; I was a stranger, and he took me in") lived in a neater house; dined at a better table; took, paid for, and read, more newspapers; better understood the moral, religious, and political character of the nation,—than nine tenths of the slaveholders in Talbot county Maryland. Yet Mr. Johnson was a working man. His hands were hardened by toil, and not his alone, but those also of Mrs. Johnson. I found the colored people much more spirited than I had supposed they would be. I found among them a determination to protect each other from the blood-thirsty kidnapper, at all hazards. Soon after my arrival, I was told of a circumstance which illustrated their spirit. A colored man and a fugitive slave were on unfriendly terms. The former was heard to threaten the latter with informing his master of his whereabouts. Straightway a meeting was called among the colored people, under the stereotyped notice, "Business of importance!" The betrayer was invited to attend. The people came at the appointed hour, and organized the meeting by appointing a very religious old gentleman as president, who, I believe, made a prayer, after which he addressed the meeting as follows: *"Friends, we have got him here, and I would recommend that you young men just take him outside the door, and kill him!"* With this, a number of them bolted at him; but they were intercepted by some more timid than themselves, and the betrayer escaped their vengeance, and has not been seen in New Bedford since. I believe there have been no more such threats, and should there be hereafter, I doubt not that death would be the consequence.

I found employment, the third day after my arrival, in stowing a sloop with a load of oil. It was new, dirty, and hard work for me; but I went at it with a glad heart and a willing hand. I was now my own master. It was a happy moment, the rapture of which can be understood only by those who have been slaves. It was the first work, the reward of which was to be entirely my own. There was no Master Hugh standing ready, the moment I earned the money, to rob me of it. I worked that day with a pleasure I had never before experienced. I was at work for myself and newly-married wife. It was to me the starting-point of a new existence. When I got through with that job, I went in pursuit of a job of calking; but such was the strength of prejudice against color, among the white calkers, that they refused to work with me, and of course I could get no employment.* Finding my trade of no immediate benefit, I threw off my calking habiliments, and prepared myself to do any kind of work I could get to do. Mr. Johnson kindly let me have his wood-horse and saw, and I very soon found myself a plenty of work. There was no work too hard—none too dirty. I was ready to saw wood, shovel coal, carry the hod, sweep the chimney, or roll oil casks,— all of which I did for nearly three years in New Bedford, before I became known to the anti-slavery world.

In about four months after I went to New Bedford, there came a young man to me, and inquired if I did not wish to take the "Liberator."[66] I told him I did; but, just having made my escape from slavery, I remarked that I was unable to pay for it then. I, however, finally became a subscriber to it. The paper came, and I read it from week to week with such feelings as it would be quite idle for me to attempt to describe. The paper became my meat and my drink. My soul was set all on fire. Its sympathy for my brethren in bonds—its scathing denunciations of slaveholders—its faithful exposures of slavery—and its powerful attacks upon the upholders of the institution—sent a thrill of joy through my soul, such as I had never felt before!

I had not long been a reader of the "Liberator," before I got a pretty correct idea of the principles, measures and spirit of the anti-slavery reform. I took right hold of the cause. I could do but little; but what I could, I did with a joyful heart, and never felt happier than when in an anti-slavery meeting. I seldom had

---

* I am told that colored persons can now get employment at calking in New Bedford—a result of anti-slavery effort.

much to say at the meetings, because what I wanted to say was said so much better by others. But, while attending an anti-slavery convention at Nantucket, on the 11th of August, 1841, I felt strongly moved to speak, and was at the same time much urged to do so by Mr. William C. Coffin, a gentleman who had heard me speak in the colored people's meeting at New Bedford. It was a severe cross, and I took it up reluctantly. The truth was, I felt myself a slave, and the idea of speaking to white people weighed me down. I spoke but a few moments, when I felt a degree of freedom, and said what I desired with considerable ease. From that time until now, I have been engaged in pleading the cause of my brethren—with what success, and with what devotion, I leave those acquainted with my labors to decide.

# APPENDIX.

I FIND, since reading over the foregoing Narrative, that I have, in several instances, spoken in such a tone and manner, respecting religion, as may possibly lead those unacquainted with my religious views to suppose me an opponent of all religion. To remove the liability of such misapprehension, I deem it proper to append the following brief explanation. What I have said respecting and against religion, I mean strictly to apply to the *slaveholding religion* of this land, and with no possible reference to Christianity proper; for, between the Christianity of this land, and the Christianity of Christ, I recognize the widest possible difference—so wide, that to receive the one as good, pure, and holy, is of necessity to reject the other as bad, corrupt, and wicked. To be the friend of the one, is of necessity to be the enemy of the other. I love the pure, peaceable, and impartial Christianity of Christ: I therefore hate the corrupt, slaveholding, women-whipping, cradle-plundering, partial and hypocritical Christianity of this land. Indeed, I can see no reason, but the most deceitful one, for calling the religion of this land Christianity. I look upon it as the climax of all misnomers, the boldest of all frauds, and the grossest of all libels. Never was there a clearer case of "stealing the livery of the court of heaven to serve the devil in."[67] I am filled with unutterable loathing when I contemplate the religious pomp and show, together with the horrible inconsistencies, which every where surround me. We have men-stealers for ministers, women-whippers for missionaries, and cradle-plunderers for church members. The man who wields the blood-clotted cowskin during the week fills the pulpit on Sunday, and claims to be a minister of the meek and lowly Jesus. The man who robs me of my earnings at the end of each week meets me as a class-leader on Sunday morning, to show me the way of life, and the path of salvation. He who sells my sister, for purposes of prostitution, stands forth as the pious advocate of purity. He who proclaims it a religious duty to read the Bible denies me the right of learning to read the name of the God who made me. He who is the religious advocate of marriage robs whole millions of its sacred influence, and leaves them to the ravages of wholesale pollution. The warm defender of the sacredness of the family relation is the same that scatters whole families,—sundering husbands and wives, parents and children, sisters and brothers,—leaving the hut vacant, and the hearth desolate. We see the thief preaching against theft, and the adulterer against adultery. We have men sold to build churches, women sold to support the gospel, and babes sold to purchase Bibles for the *poor heathen! all for the glory of God and the good of souls!* The slave auctioneer's bell and the church-going bell chime in with each other, and the bitter cries of the heart-broken slave are drowned in the religious shouts of his pious master. Revivals of religion and revivals in the slave-trade go hand in hand together. The slave prison and the church stand near each other. The clanking of fetters and the rattling of chains in the prison, and the pious psalm and solemn prayer in the church, may be heard at the same time. The dealers in the bodies and souls of men erect their stand in the presence of the pulpit, and they mutually help each other. The dealer gives his blood-stained gold to support the pulpit, and the pulpit, in return, covers his infernal business with the garb of Christianity. Here we have religion and robbery the allies of each other—devils dressed in angels' robes, and hell presenting the semblance of paradise.

"Just God! and these are they,
  Who minister at thine altar, God of right!
Men who their hands, with prayer and blessing, lay
  On Israel's ark of light.

"What! preach, and kidnap men?
  Give thanks, and rob thy own afflicted poor?
Talk of thy glorious liberty, and then
  Bolt hard the captive's door?

"What! servants of thy own
  Merciful Son, who came to seek and save
The homeless and the outcast, fettering down
  The tasked and plundered slave!

"Pilate and Herod friends!
  Chief priests and rulers, as of old, combine!
Just God and holy! is that church which lends
  Strength to the spoiler thine?"[68]

The Christianity of America is a Christianity, of whose votaries it may be as truly said, as it was of the ancient scribes and Pharisees, "They bind heavy burdens, and grievous to be borne, and lay them on men's shoulders, but they themselves will not move them with one of their fingers. All their works they do for to be seen of men.—They love the uppermost rooms at feasts, and the chief seats in the synagogues, . . . . . . and to be called of men, Rabbi, Rabbi.—But woe unto you, scribes and Pharisees, hypocrites! for ye shut up the kingdom of heaven against men; for ye neither go in yourselves, neither suffer ye them that are entering to go in. Ye devour widows' houses, and for a pretence make long prayers; therefore ye shall receive the greater damnation. Ye compass sea and land to make one proselyte, and when he is made, ye make him twofold more the child of hell than yourselves.—Woe unto you, scribes and Pharisees, hypocrites! for ye pay tithe of mint, and anise, and cumin, and have omitted the weightier matters of the law, judgment, mercy, and faith; these ought ye to have done, and not to leave the other undone. Ye blind guides! which strain at a gnat, and swallow a camel. Woe unto you, scribes and Pharisees, hypocrites! for ye make clean the outside of the cup and of the platter; but within, they are full of extortion and excess.—Woe unto you, scribes and Pharisees, hypocrites! for ye are like unto whited sepulchres, which indeed appear beautiful outward, but are within full of dead men's bones, and of all uncleanness. Even so ye also outwardly appear righteous unto men, but within ye are full of hypocrisy and iniquity."[69]

Dark and terrible as is this picture, I hold it to be strictly true of the overwhelming mass of professed Christians in America. They strain at a gnat, and swallow a camel. Could any thing be more true of our churches? They would be shocked at the proposition of fellowshipping a *sheep*-stealer; and at the same time they hug to their communion a *man*-stealer, and brand me with being an infidel, if I find fault with them for it. They attend with Pharisaical strictness to the outward forms of religion, and at the same time neglect the weightier matters of the law, judgment, mercy, and faith. They are always ready to sacrifice, but seldom to show mercy. They are they who are represented as professing to love God whom they have not seen, whilst they hate their brother whom they have seen. They love the heathen on the other side of the globe. They can pray for him, pay money to have the Bible put into his hand, and missionaries to instruct him; while they despise and totally neglect the heathen at their own doors.

Such is, very briefly, my view of the religion of this land; and to avoid any misunderstanding, growing out of the use of general terms, I mean, by the religion of this land, that which is revealed in the words, deeds, and actions, of those bodies, north and south, calling themselves Christian churches, and yet in union with slaveholders. It is against religion, as presented by these bodies, that I have felt it my duty to testify.

I conclude these remarks by copying the following portrait of the religion of the south, (which is, by communion and fellowship, the religion of the north,) which I soberly affirm is "true to the life," and without caricature or the slightest exaggeration. It is said to have been drawn, several years before the present anti-slavery agitation began, by a northern Methodist preacher, who, while residing at the south, had an opportunity to see slaveholding morals, manners, and piety, with his own eyes. "Shall I not visit for these things? saith the Lord. Shall not my soul be avenged on such a nation as this?"[70]

## "A PARODY.

"Come, saints and sinners, hear me tell
How pious priests whip Jack and Nell,
And women buy and children sell,
And preach all sinners down to hell,
    And sing of heavenly union.

"They'll bleat and baa, dona like goats,
Gorge down black sheep, and strain at motes,
Array their backs in fine black coats,
Then seize their negroes by their throats,
    And choke, for heavenly union.

"They'll church you if you sip a dram,
And damn you if you steal a lamb;
Yet rob old Tony, Doll, and Sam,
Of human rights, and bread and ham;
    Kidnapper's heavenly union.

"They'll loudly talk of Christ's reward,
And bind his image with a cord,
And scold, and swing the lash abhorred,
And sell their brother in the Lord
    To handcuffed heavenly union.

"They'll read and sing a sacred song,
And make a prayer both loud and long,
And teach the right and do the wrong,
Hailing the brother, sister throng,
    With words of heavenly union.

"We wonder how such saints can sing,
Or praise the Lord upon the wing,
Who roar, and scold, and whip, and sting,
And to their slaves and mammon cling,
    In guilty conscience union.

"They'll raise tobacco, corn, and rye,
And drive, and thieve, and cheat, and lie,
And lay up treasures in the sky,
By making switch and cowskin fly,
   In hope of heavenly union.

"They'll crack old Tony on the skull,
And preach and roar like Bashan bull,[71]
Or braying ass, of mischief full,
Then seize old Jacob by the wool,
   And pull for heavenly union.

"A roaring, ranting, sleek man-thief,
Who lived on mutton, veal, and beef,
Yet never would afford relief
To needy, sable sons of grief,
   Was big with heavenly union.

"'Love not the world,' the preacher said,
And winked his eye, and shook his head;
He seized on Tom, and Dick, and Ned,
Cut short their meat, and clothes, and bread,
   Yet still loved heavenly union.

"Another preacher whining spoke
Of One whose heart for sinners broke:
He tied old Nanny to an oak,
And drew the blood at every stroke,
   And prayed for heavenly union.

"Two others oped their iron jaws,
And waved their children-stealing paws;
There sat their children in gewgaws;
By stinting negroes' backs and maws,
   They kept up heavenly union.

"All good from Jack another takes,
And entertains their flirts and rakes,
Who dress as sleek as glossy snakes,
And cram their mouths with sweetened cakes;
   And this goes down for union."[72]

    Sincerely and earnestly hoping that this little book may do something toward throwing light on the American slave system, and hastening the glad day of deliverance to the millions of my brethren in bonds—faithfully relying upon the power of truth, love, and justice, for success in my humble efforts—and solemnly pledging my self anew to the sacred cause,—I subscribe myself,

FREDERICK DOUGLASS.

LYNN, *Mass., April 28,* 1845.


# THE END.

1. Blight, *Narrative,* 4.

2. Douglass, *Autobiographies,* 1078–1079.

3. John W. Blassingame, as cited in Gates, "From Wheatley to Douglass," 60–61; Jackson, *History,* 107.

4. Foner, *Life and Writings,* I:59.

5. Foster, *Witnessing Slavery,* 56.

6. Andrews, "Narrative," 526; Starling, *Slave Narrative,* 40.

7. Starling, *Slave Narrative,* 251–252.

8. Fuller's review is reprinted in Blight, *Narrative,* 122–123, and Andrews and McFeely, *Narrative,* 83–84.

9. Olney, "'I Was Born,'" 156.

10. Andrews, *Free Story,* 134.

11. MacKethan, "Metaphors of Mastery," 59.

12. Olney, "'I Was Born,'" 157.

13. Jackson, *History,* 111.

14. Andrews, *Free Story,* 218.

15. Foner, *Life and Writings,* I:126; Douglass, *My Bondage,* 369.

16. Gates, *Classic Slave Narratives,* xiii.

17. Sundquist, *To Wake the Nations,* 89.

18. Ripley, "Autobiographical Writings," 140.

19. Blight, *Narrative,* 18.

20. Foner, *Life and Writings,* I:432.

21. William Shakespeare (1564–1616), *Hamlet.*

22. See *Psalms* 8:5, *Hebrews* 2:7, 9.

23. *2 Peter* 3:18.

24. Charles Lenox Remond (1810–73) was a renowned black abolitionist speaker.

25. Daniel O'Connell (1755–1847) was an Irish political leader known as the Liberator. He was largely responsible for Catholic Emancipation (the removal of oppressive restrictions on Catholics) in the British Isles in 1829.

26. *Revelations* 18:13.

27. A reference to Theodore Dwight Weld (1803–95), *American Slavery As It Is: Testimony of a Thousand Witnesses* (1839), the most influential abolitionist book of its time.

28. The greatest library of the ancient world was in Alexandria, Egypt.

29. William Lloyd Garrison (1805–79) published *The Liberator,* the most popular abolitionist newspaper, from 1831 to 1865. He helped organize the American Anti-Slavery Society, of which he was president from 1843 to 1865. He advocated Northern secession, publicly burned the Constitution, and was widely regarded as the foremost leader of the antislavery movement.

30. Wendell Phillips (1811–84) was a prominent abolitionist orator and writer, perhaps at this time second only to Garrison in fame.

31. This ancient fable appears in the collections of Aesop, Avianus, La Fontaine, and others. In it, the man shows the lion an image of a man triumphant over a lion as proof of man's superiority. The lion replies that if lions could make such images, the man would be shown prostrate under the lion's paw.

32. The British abolished slavery throughout their territories, including the West Indies, in 1833. The transition, however, was gradual, and white planters suffered major losses. Andrews and McFeely, *Narrative,* 10.

33. A poetic phrase for midnight, which clearly carries a double meaning here.

34. A phrase common in legal documents. Indictments often include it as follows: "contrary to the form of the Statute in such case made and provided and against the peace and dignity of the State" (or "of the United States").

35. It is unclear to whom Douglass is referring. While a number of Southerners considered slavery a temporary state that would pass away on its own, few if any attributed this gradual change to "the laws of population" in the sense that Douglass uses the phrase.

36. Aaron Anthony (1767–1826), an overseer on the Lloyd plantation. Blight, *Narrative,* 110.

37. Colonel Edward Lloyd (1779–1834) was governor of Maryland, a U.S. senator, and owner of over five hundred slaves. Ibid.

38. An infamous Baltimore slave trader. Ibid., 111.

39. William Sevier oversaw about 165 slaves. Ibid.

40. William Cowper (1731–1800), *The Task* (1785).

41. Light, four-wheeled wagons.

42. Actually Jacob Gibson. Blight, *Narrative,* 111.

43. Actually Orson Gore. Ibid.

44. Actually Thomas Lambdin. Ibid.

45. Actually John Beale Bordley, Jr. Ibid.

46. Caleb Bingham (1757–1817), *The Columbian Orator: Containing a Variety of Original and Selected Pieces Together with Rules Calculated to Improve Youth and Others in the Ornamental and Useful Art of Eloquence* (1797).

47. "Dialogue between a Master and a Slave," attributed in at least one edition of *The Columbian Orator* to "AIKEN."

48. Actually a speech by Arthur O'Connor (1763–1852), entitled in the *Orator* "Part of Mr. O'Connor's Speech in the Irish House of Commons, in Favour of the Bill for Emancipating the Roman Catholics, 1795."

49. Noah Webster (1758–1843), *The American Spelling Book* (1783).

50. In his *Life and Times,* Douglass wrote:

> I told [Captain Thomas Auld] that I had made a mistake in my narrative, a copy of which I had sent him, in attributing to him ungrateful and cruel treatment of my grandmother; that I had done so on the supposition that in the division of the property of my old master, Mr. Aaron Anthony, my grandmother had fallen to him, and that he had left her in her old age, when she could no longer be of service to him, to pick up her living in solitude with none to help her, or, in other words, had turned her out to die like an old horse. "Ah!" he said, "that was a mistake, I never owned your grandmother; she in the division of the slaves was awarded to my brother-in-law, Andrew Anthony; but," he added quickly, "I brought her down here and took care of her as long as she lived." The fact is, that, after writing my narrative describing the condition of my grandmother, Capt. Auld's attention being thus called to it, he rescued her from her destitution.

Douglass, *Autobiographies,* 877.

51. John Greenleaf Whittier (1807–92) was a Quaker poet, pioneer regionalist, close friend of Garrison, ardent abolitionist, one of the founders of the Republican Party, and the amanuensis for the 1838 *Narrative of James Williams, an American Slave.* The lines Douglass quotes are from "The Farewell of a Virginia Slave Mother to her Daughters, Sold into Southern Bondage" (1838).

52. Actually William Hambleton. Quarles, *Narrative,* xxii.

53. On the eastern shore of Maryland.

54. George Grimston Cookman (1800–41) was a prominent Methodist minister who was twice chaplain of the House of Representatives. Douglass, *Autobiographies,* 1084–1085.

55. *Luke* 12:47.

56. Actually 1834. Blight, *Narrative,* 113.

57. *In-hand* meant the one to be hitched to the left; *off-hand* to the right.

58. Actually Garretson West. Quarles, *Narrative,* xxii.

59. Shakespeare, *Hamlet.*

60. The loose end of the tackle—holding it is necessary for hoisting materials.

61. It was not until 1881, in his *Life and Times,* that Douglass revealed the manner of his escape, as follows:

> I had one friend—a sailor—who owned a sailor's protection, which answered somewhat the purpose of free papers—describing his person and certifying to the fact that he was a free American sailor. The instrument had at its head the American eagle, which at once gave it the appearance of an authorized document. This protection did not,

when in my hands, describe its bearer very accurately. Indeed, it called for a man much darker than myself, and close examination of it would have caused my arrest at the start. In order to avoid this fatal scrutiny on the part of the railroad official, I had arranged with Isaac Rolls, a hackman, to bring my baggage to the train just on the moment of starting, and jumped upon the car myself when the train was already in motion. Had I gone into the station and offered to purchase a ticket, I should have been instantly and carefully examined, and undoubtedly arrested. In choosing this plan upon which to act, I considered the jostle of the train, and the natural haste of the conductor in a train crowded with passengers, and relied upon my skill and address in playing the sailor as described in my protection, to do the rest. One element in my favor was the kind feeling which prevailed in Baltimore and other seaports at the time, towards "those who go down to the sea in ships." "Free trade and sailors' rights" expressed the sentiment of the country just then. In my clothing I was rigged out in sailor style. I had on a red shirt and tarpaulin hat and black cravat, tied in sailor fashion, carelessly and loosely about my neck. My knowledge of ships and sailor's talk came much to my assistance, for I knew a ship from stem to stern, and from keelson to cross-trees, and could talk sailor like an "old salt." On sped the train, and I was well on the way to Havre de Grace before the conductor came into the negro car to collect tickets and examine the papers of his black passengers. This was a critical moment in the drama. My whole future depended upon the decision of this conductor. Agitated I was while this ceremony was proceeding, but still, externally at least, I was apparently calm and self-possessed. He went on with his duty—examining several colored passengers before reaching me. He was somewhat harsh in tone and peremptory in manner until he reached me, when, strangely enough, and to my surprise and relief, his whole manner changed. Seeing that I did not readily produce my free papers, as the other colored persons in the car had done, he said to me in a friendly contrast with that observed towards the others: "I suppose you have your free papers?" To which I answered: "No, sir; I never carry my free papers to sea with me." "But you have something to show that you are a freeman, have you not?" "Yes, sir," I answered; "I have a paper with the American eagle on it, that will carry me around the world." With this I drew from my deep sailor's pocket my seaman's protection, as before described. The merest glance at the paper satisfied him, and he took my fare and went on about his business. This moment of time was one of the most anxious I ever experienced. Had the conductor looked closely at the paper, he could not have failed to discover that it called for a very different looking person from myself, and in that case it would have been his duty to arrest me on the instant and send me back to Baltimore from the first station. When he left me with the assurance that I was all right, though much relieved, I realized that I was still in great danger: I was still in Maryland, and subject to arrest at any moment. I saw on the train several persons who would have known me in any other clothes, and I feared they might recognize me, even in my sailor "rig," and report me to the conductor, who would then subject me to a closer examination, which I knew well would be fatal to me.

Though I was not a murderer fleeing from justice, I felt, perhaps, quite as miserable as such a criminal. The train was moving at a very high rate of speed for that time of railroad travel, but to my anxious mind, it was moving far too slowly. Minutes were hours, and hours were days during this part of my flight. After Maryland I was to pass through Delaware—another slave State, where slave-catchers generally awaited their prey, for it was not in the interior of the State, but on its borders, that these human hounds were most vigilant and active. The border lines between slavery and freedom were the dangerous ones, for the fugitives. The heart of no fox or deer, with hungry hounds on his trail, in full chase, could have beaten more anxiously or noisily than did mine from the time I left Baltimore till I reached Philadelphia. The passage of the Susquehanna river at Havre de Grace was at that time made by ferry-boat, on board of which I met a young colored man by the name of Nichols, who came very near betraying me. He was a "hand" on the boat, but instead of minding his business, he insisted upon knowing me, and asking me dangerous questions as to where I was going, and when I was coming back, etc. I got away from my old and inconvenient acquaintance as soon as I could decently do so, and went to another part of the boat. Once across the river I encountered a new danger. Only a few days before I had been at work on a revenue cutter, in Mr. Price's ship-yard, under the care of Captain McGowan. On the meeting at this point of the two trains, the one going south stopped on the track just opposite to the one going north, and it so happened that this Captain McGowan sat at a window where he could see me very distinctly, and would certainly have recognized me had he looked at me but for a second. Fortunately, in the hurry of the moment, he did not see me, and the trains soon passed each other on their respective ways. But this was not the only hair-breadth escape. A German blacksmith, whom I knew well, was on the train with me, and looked at me very intensely, as if he thought he had seen me somewhere before in his travels. I really believe he knew me, but had no heart to betray me. At any rate he saw me escaping and held his peace.

The last point of imminent danger, and the one I dreaded most, was Wilmington. Here we left the train and took the steamboat for Philadelphia. In making the change I again apprehended arrest, but no one disturbed me, and I was soon on the broad and beautiful Delaware, speeding away to the Quaker City. On reaching Philadelphia in the afternoon I inquired of a colored man how I could get on to New York? He directed me to the Willow street depot, and thither I went, taking the train that night. I reached New York Tuesday morning, having completed the journey in less than twenty-four hours. Such is briefly the manner of my escape from slavery—and the end of my experience as a slave.

Douglass, *Autobiographies*, 643–646.

62. David Ruggles (1810–49) was a freeborn black abolitionist who opened the first known black bookstore in New York City, published several pamphlets, founded the New York Vigilance Committee to protect free blacks from kidnapping, and published the first African American magazine, the *Mirror of Liberty*.

63. Ruggles was arrested in September 1839 for harboring a fugitive slave alleged to have stolen money from his owner John P. Darg. The case was eventually dropped. Douglass, *Autobiographies*, 1085.

64. James William Charles Pennington (1807–70) was a fugitive slave, minister, abolitionist, schoolteacher, writer, and historian. See his narrative on pp. II:103–158.

65. See Sir Walter Scott (1771–1832), *The Lady of the Lake* (1810). This tremendously popular long historical poem is set in sixteenth-century Scotland and retells a legend concerning the Douglas clan, recounting their banishment, exile, and eventual restoration. The name *Douglas* would have resonated with readers of the time, suggesting chivalry, bravery, honesty, and autonomy—all qualities of its romantic hero, James of Douglas.

66. See note 29 above.

67. Robert Pollok (1798–1827), *The Course of Time* (1827).

68. Whittier, *Clerical Oppressors* (1836).

69. See *Matthew* 23:4–28.

70. *Jeremiah* 5:9.

71. Bashan "was called the land of the giants." *Deuteronomy* 3:13.

72. Most scholars attribute this parody of the popular hymn "Heavenly Union" to Douglass himself.

LEWIS AND MILTON CLARKE

LEWIS AND MILTON CLARKE (1815–97; c. 1817–?) were two of the most engaging slave storytellers. Their vivid narratives display a unique blend of biting sarcasm, vituperation, self-deprecation, informality, and comedy.

Lewis Clarke's narrative was first published in 1845, simultaneously with Frederick Douglass's. They have much the same flavor, the same combination of outrage and wit. In fact, they probably knew each other: they had both been lecturing for the American Anti-Slavery Society for years. Lewis's brother Milton was also a popular antislavery lecturer; when their narratives were published together in 1846, the book's success increased their popularity on the lecture circuit.[1]

In 1842, three years prior to dictating his narrative, Lewis Clarke gave a series of speeches in Brooklyn, which the abolitionist Lydia Marie Child attended. She commented:

> I have seldom been more entertained by any speaker. His obvious want of education was one guaranty of the truth of his story; and the uncouth awkwardness of his language had a sort of charm, like the circuitous expression, and stammering utterance, of a foreign tongue, striving to speak our most familiar phrases. His mind was evidently full of ideas, which he was eager to express; but the medium was wanting. "I've got it in *here*," said he, laying his hand on his heart; "but I don't know how to get it out." However, in his imperfect way, I believed he conveyed much information to many minds; and that few who heard him went away without being impressed by the conviction that he was sincerely truthful, and testified of things which he did know. . . . What he *might* have been, with common advantages for education, is shown by his shrewd conclusions, and large ideas which his soul struggled so hard to utter in imperfect language.

Child inscribed from memory a large portion of what Clarke said. A brief sample will impart the flavor of his speech:

> Preacher Raymond didn't used to flog his slaves; he used to duck 'em. He had a little slave girl, about eight years old, that he used to duck very often. One day, the family went to meeting, and left her to take care of a young child. The child fretted, and she thought she would serve it as master served her; so she ducked it, and it slipped out of her hands, and got drowned. They put her in prison, and sentenced her to be hung; but she, poor child, didn't know nothing at all what it meant.—When they took her to the gallows, she was guarded all round by men; but she was so innocent, she didn't know what they was going to do with her. She stooped to pick up a pin, and stuck it in her frock, as she went.—The poor young thing was so glad to get out of prison, that she was as merry as if she was going to her mother's house.[2]

Lewis and Milton Clarke's narratives were taken down from their dictation by the abolitionist Joseph C. Lovejoy, who also probably provided the appendices, poems, and letters, which are similar to those included in his other books.[3] From Child's testimony, however, it is clear that he was not solely responsible for the homespun flavor and colloquial rhetoric that made their narratives so successful.

Subsequent to the narratives' publication, Lewis Clarke continued to be active in abolitionist causes, helping other runaway slaves and lecturing widely. He was interviewed repeatedly by Harriet Beecher Stowe in her own home; she based the character of George Harris in *Uncle Tom's Cabin* on his personality. By 1861, Lewis Clarke had married and made his home near Windsor, Ontario; after his wife's death in 1875, he returned to Oberlin, Ohio, with his children. Upon his death in Lexington, Kentucky, his body lay in state in the City Auditorium by order of the governor—making him the first black man in the state to be honored thus. He is buried in Oberlin.[4]

Engraved at 148 State St.

*Lewis Clarke*

# NARRATIVES

OF THE SUFFERINGS OF

# LEWIS AND MILTON CLARKE,

SONS OF A SOLDIER OF THE REVOLUTION,

DURING A

CAPTIVITY OF MORE THAN TWENTY YEARS

AMONG THE

# SLAVEHOLDERS OF KENTUCKY,

ONE OF THE

SO CALLED CHRISTIAN STATES OF NORTH AMERICA.

DICTATED BY THEMSELVES.

BOSTON:
PUBLISHED BY BELA MARSH,
NO. 25 CORNHILL.
1846.

All Orders to be sent to the Publisher.

# PREFACE

I FIRST became acquainted with LEWIS CLARKE in December, 1842. I well remember the deep impression made upon my mind on hearing his Narrative from his own lips. It gave a new and more vivid impression of the wrongs of Slavery than I had ever before felt. Evidently a person of good native talents and of deep sensibilities, such a mind had been under the dark cloud of slavery for more than twenty-five years. Letters, reading, all the modes of thought awakened by them, had been utterly hid from his eyes; and yet his mind had evidently been active, and trains of thought were flowing through it which he was utterly unable to express. I well remember, too, the wave on wave of deep feeling excited in an audience of more than a thousand persons, at Hallowell, Me., as they listened to his story, and looked upon his energetic and manly countenance, and wondered if the dark cloud of slavery could cover up—hide from the world, and degrade to the condition of brutes—*such* immortal minds. His story, there and wherever since told, has aroused the most utter abhorrence of the Slave System.

For the last two years, I have had the most ample opportunity of becoming acquainted with Mr. Clarke. He has made this place his home, when not engaged in giving to public audiences the story of his sufferings and the sufferings of his fellow-slaves. Soon after he came to Ohio, by the faithful instruction of pious friends, he was led, as he believes, to see himself a sinner before God, and to seek pardon and forgiveness through the precious blood of the Lamb. He has ever manifested an ardent thirst for religious, as well as for other kinds of knowledge. In the opinion of all those best acquainted with him, he has maintained the character of a sincere Christian. That he is what he professes to be,—a slave escaped from the grasp of avarice and power,—there is not the least shadow of doubt. His Narrative bears the most conclusive internal evidence of its truth. Persons of discriminating minds have heard it repeatedly, under a great variety of circumstances, and the story, in all substantial respects, has been always the same. He has been repeatedly recognized in the Free States, by persons who knew him in Kentucky, when a slave. During the summer of 1844, Cassius M. Clay[5] visited Boston, and, on seeing Milton Clarke, recognized him as one of the Clarke family, well known to him in Kentucky. Indeed, nothing can be more surely established than the fact that Lewis and Milton Clarke are no impostors. For three years they have been engaged in telling their story in seven or eight different states, and no one has appeared to make an attempt to contradict them. The capture of Milton in Ohio, by the kidnappers, as a *slave,* makes assurance doubly strong. Wherever they have told their story, large audiences have collected, and every where they have been listened to with great interest and satisfaction.

Cyrus is fully equal to either of the brothers in sprightliness of mind—is withal a great wit, and would make an admirable lecturer, but for an unfortunate impediment in his speech. They all feel deeply the wrongs they have suffered, and are by no means forgetful of their brethren in *bonds.* When Lewis first came to this place, he was frequently noticed in silent and deep meditation. On being asked what he was thinking of, he would reply, "O, of the poor slaves! Here I am free, and they suffering *so much*." Bitter tears are often seen coursing down his manly cheeks, as he recurs to the scenes of his early suffering. Many persons, who have heard him lecture, have expressed a strong desire that his story might be recorded in a connected form. He has, therefore, concluded to have it printed. He was anxious to spread the story of his sufferings as extensively as possible before the community, that he might awaken more hearts to feel for his down-trodden brethren. Nothing seems to grieve him to the heart, like finding a minister of the gospel, or a professed Christian, indifferent to the condition of the slave. As to doing much for the instruction of the minds of the slaves, or for the salvation of their souls, till they are EMANCIPATED, *restored* to the rights of men, in his opinion it is utterly impossible.

When the master, or his representative, the man who justifies slaveholding, comes with the whip in one hand and the Bible in the other, the slave says, at least in his heart, Lay down *one* or the *other*. Either make the tree good and the fruit good, or else both corrupt together. Slaves do not believe that THE RELIGION which is from God, bears *whips and chains*. They ask, emphatically, concerning their FATHER in heaven,

> "Has HE bid you buy and sell us;
> Speaking from his throne, the sky?"[6]

For the facts contained in the following Narrative, Mr. Clarke is of course alone responsible. Yet, having had the most ample opportunities for testing his accuracy, I do not hesitate to say, that I have not a shadow of doubt but in all material points every word is true. Much of it is in his own language, and all of it according to his own dictation.

J. C. LOVEJOY.[7]

CAMBRIDGEPORT, APRIL, 1845.

# NARRATIVE OF LEWIS CLARKE.

I WAS born in March, as near as I can ascertain, in the year 1815, in Madison county, Kentucky, about seven miles from Richmond, upon the plantation of my grandfather, Samuel Campbell. He was considered a very respectable man, among his fellow-robbers, the slaveholders. It did not render him less honorable in their eyes, that he took to his bed Mary, his slave, perhaps half white, by whom he had one daughter, LETITIA CAMPBELL. This was before his marriage.

My father was from "beyond the flood"—from Scotland, and by trade a weaver. He had been married in his own country, and lost his wife, who left to him, as I have been told, two sons. He came to this country in time to be in the earliest scenes of the American revolution. He was at the battle of Bunker Hill, and continued in the army to the close of the war. About the year 1800, or before, he came to Kentucky, and married Miss Letitia Campbell, then held as a slave by her *dear* and *affectionate* father. My father died, as near as I can recollect, when I was about ten or twelve years of age. He had received a wound in the war, which made him lame as long as he lived. I have often heard him tell of Scotland, sing the merry songs of his native land, and long to see its hills once more.

Mr. Campbell promised my father that his daughter Letitia should be made free in his will. It was with this promise that he married her. And I have no doubt that Mr. Campbell was as good as his word, and that, by his *will,* my mother and her nine children were made free. But ten persons in one family, each worth three hundred dollars, are not easily set free among those accustomed to live by continued robbery. We did not, therefore, by an instrument from the hand of the dead, escape the avaricious grab of the slaveholder. It is the common belief that the will was destroyed by the heirs of Mr. Campbell.

The night in which I was born, I have been told, was dark and terrible—black as the night for which Job prayed, when he besought the clouds to pitch their tent round about the place of his birth;[8] and my life of slavery was but too exactly prefigured by the stormy elements that hovered over the first hour of my being. It was with great difficulty that any one could be urged out for a necessary attendant for my mother. At length, one of the sons of Mr. Campbell, William, by the promise from his mother of the child that should be born, was induced to make an effort to obtain the necessary assistance. By going five or six miles, he obtained a female professor of the couch.

William Campbell, by virtue of this title, always claimed me as his property. And well would it have been for me if this claim had been regarded. At the age of six or seven years, I fell into the hands of his sister, Mrs. Betsey Banton, whose character will be best known when I have told the horrid wrongs which she heaped upon me for ten years. If there are any *she* spirits that come up from hell, and take possession of one part of mankind, I am sure she is one of that sort. I was consigned to her under the following circumstances: When she was married, there was given her, as part of her dower, as is common among the Algerines of Kentucky, a *girl,* by the name of Ruth, about fourteen or fifteen years old. In a short time, Ruth was dejected and injured, by beating and abuse of different kinds, so that she was sold, for a half-fool, to the more tender mercies of the sugar-planter in Louisiana. The amiable Mrs. Betsey obtained then, on loan from her parents, another slave, named Phillis. In six months she had suffered so severely, under the hand of this monster-woman, that she made an attempt to kill herself, and was taken home by the parents of Mrs. Banton. This produced a regular slaveholding family brawl; a regular war, of *four* years, between the *mild* and peaceable Mrs. B. and her own parents. These wars are very common among the Algerines in Kentucky; indeed, slaveholders have not arrived at that degree of civilization that enables them to live in tolerable peace, though united by the nearest family ties. In them is fulfilled what I have heard read in the Bible—"The father is against the son, and the daughter-in-law against the mother-in-law, and their *foes* are of their own household." Some of the slaveholders may have a *wide* house; but one of the *cat-handed,* snake-eyed, brawling women, which slavery produces, can fill it from cellar to garret. I have heard every place I could get into any way ring with their screech-owl voices. Of all the animals on the face of this earth, I am most afraid of a real mad, passionate, raving, slaveholding woman. Somebody told me, once, that Edmund Burke declared that the natives of India fled to the jungles, among tigers and lions, to escape the more barbarous cruelty of Warren Hastings.[9] I am sure I would sooner lie down to sleep by the side of tigers than near a raging-mad slave woman. But I must go back to *sweet* Mrs. Banton. I have been describing her in the *abstract.* I will give a full-grown portrait of her right away. For four years after the trouble about Phillis she never came near her father's house. At the end of this period, another of the amiable sisters was to be married, and sister Betsey could not repress the tide of curiosity urging her to be present at the nuptial ceremonies. Beside, she had another motive. Either shrewdly suspecting that she might deserve less than any member of the family, or that some ungrounded partiality would be manifested toward her sister, she determined, at all hazards, to be present, and see that the scales which weighed out the children of the plantation should be held with even hand. The wedding-day was appointed; the sons and daughters of this joyful occasion were gathered together, and then came also the fair-faced, but black-hearted, Mrs. B. Satan, among the sons of God, was never less welcome than this fury among her kindred. They all knew what she came for,—to make mischief, if possible. "Well, now, if there aint Bets!" exclaimed the old lady. The father was moody and silent, knowing that she inherited largely of the disposition of her mother; but he had experienced too many of her retorts of courtesy to say as much, for dear experience had taught him the discretion of silence. The brothers smiled at the prospect of fun and frolic; the sisters trembled for fear, and word flew round among the slaves, "The old she-bear has come home! look out! look out!"

The wedding went forward. Polly, a very good sort of a girl to be raised in that region, was married, and received, as the first instalment of her dower, a *girl* and a *boy*. Now was the time for Mrs. Banton, sweet, good Mrs. Banton. "Poll has a girl and a *boy*, and I only had that fool of a girl. I reckon, if I go home without a boy too, this house wont be left standing."

This was said, too, while the sugar of the wedding-cake was yet melting upon her tongue. How the bitter words would flow when the guests had retired, all began to imagine. To arrest this whirlwind of rising passion, her mother promised any boy upon the plantation, to be taken home on her return. Now, my evil star was right in the top of the sky. Every boy was ordered in, to pass before this female sorceress, that she might select a victim for her unprovoked malice, and on whom to pour the vials of her wrath for years. I was that unlucky fellow. Mr. Campbell, my grandfather, objected, because it would divide a family, and offered her Moses, whose father and mother had been sold south. Mrs. Campbell put in for William's claim, dated *ante natum*—before I was born; but objections and claims of every kind were swept away by the wild passion and shrill-toned voice of Mrs. B. Me she would have, and none else. Mr. Campbell went out to hunt, and drive away bad thoughts; the old lady became quiet, for she was sure none of her blood run in my veins, and, if there was any of her husband's there, it was no fault of hers. Slave women are always revengeful toward the children of slaves that have any of the blood of their husbands in them. I was too young, only seven years of age, to understand what was going on. But my poor and affectionate mother understood and appreciated it all. When she left the kitchen of the mansion-house, where she was employed as cook, and came home to her own little cottage, the tear of anguish was in her eye, and the image of sorrow upon every feature of her face. She knew the female Nero, whose rod was now to be over me. That night sleep departed from her eyes. With the youngest child clasped firmly to her bosom, she spent the night in walking the floor, coming ever and anon to lift up the clothes and look at me and my poor brother, who lay sleeping together. *Sleeping,* I said. Brother slept, but not I. I saw my mother when she first came to me, and I could not sleep. The vision of that night—its deep, ineffaceable impression—is now before my mind with all the distinctness of yesterday. In the morning, I was put into the carriage with Mrs. B. and her children, and my weary pilgrimage of suffering was fairly begun. It was her business on the road, for about twenty-five or thirty miles, to initiate her children into the art of tormenting their new victim. I was seated upon the bottom of the carriage, and these little imps were employed in pinching me, pulling my ears and hair; and they were stirred up by their mother, like a litter of young wolves, to torment me in every way possible. In the mean time, I was compelled by the old she-wolf to call them "Master," "Mistress," and bow to them, and obey them at the first call.

During that day, I had, indeed, no very agreeable foreboding of the torments to come; but, sad as were my anticipations, the reality was infinitely beyond them. Infinitely more bitter than death were the cruelties I experienced at the hand of this merciless woman. Save from one or two slaves on the plantation, during my ten years of captivity here, I scarcely heard a kind word, or saw a smile toward me from any living being. And now that I am where people look kind, and act kindly toward me, it seems like a dream. I hardly seem to be in the same world that I was then. When I first got into the free states, and saw every body look like they loved one another, sure enough, I thought, this must be the "*Heaven*" of LOVE I had heard something about. But I must go back to what I suffered from that wicked woman. It is hard work to keep the mind upon it; I hate to think it over—but I must tell it—the world must know what is done in Kentucky. I cannot, however, tell all the ways by which she tormented me. I can only give a few instances of my suffering, as specimens of the whole. A book of a thousand pages would not be large enough to tell of all the tears I shed, and the sufferings endured, in THAT TEN YEARS OF PURGATORY.

A very trivial offence was sufficient to call forth a great burst of indignation from this woman of ungoverned passions. In my simplicity, I put my lips to the same vessel, and drank out of it, from which her children were accustomed to drink. She expressed her utter abhorrence of such an act, by throwing my head violently back, and dashing into my face two dippers of water. The shower of water was followed by a heavier shower of *kicks;* yes, delicate reader, this *lady* did not hesitate to *kick,* as well as cuff in a very plentiful manner; but the words, bitter and cutting, that followed, were like a storm of hail upon my young heart. "She would teach me better manners than that; she would let me know I was to be brought up to her hand; she would have *one* slave that knew his place; if I wanted water, go to the spring, and not drink there in the house." This was new times for me; for some days I was completely benumbed with my sorrow. I could neither eat nor sleep. If there is any human being on earth, who has been so blessed as never to have *tasted* the cup of sorrow, and therefore is unable to conceive of *suffering;* if there be one so lost to all feeling as even to say, that the slaves do not suffer when *families* are separated, let such a one go to the ragged quilt which was my couch and pillow, and stand there night after night, for long, weary hours, and see the bitter tears streaming down the face of that more than orphan boy, while, with half-suppressed sighs and sobs, he calls again and again upon his absent mother.

> "Say, mother, wast thou conscious of the tears I shed?
> Hovered thy spirit o'er thy sorrowing son?
> Wretch even *then!* life's journey just begun."[10]

Let him stand by that couch of bitter sorrow through the terribly lonely night, and then wring out the wet end of those rags, and see how many tears yet remain, after the burning temples had absorbed all they could. He will not doubt, he cannot doubt, but the slave has feeling. But I find myself running away again from Mrs. Banton—and I don't much wonder neither.

There were several children in the family, and my first main business was to wait upon them. Another young slave and myself have often been compelled to sit up by turns all night, to rock the cradle of a little, peevish scion of slavery. If the cradle was stopped, the moment they awoke a dolorous cry was sent forth to mother or father, that Lewis had gone to sleep. The reply to this call would be a direction from the mother for these petty tyrants to get up and take the whip, and give the good-for-nothing scoundrel a smart whipping. This was the midnight pastime of a child ten or twelve years old. What might you expect of the future man?

There were four house-slaves in this family, including myself; and though we had not, in all respects, so hard work as the field hands, yet in many things our condition was much worse. We were constantly exposed to the whims and passions of every member of the family; from the least to the greatest their anger was wreaked upon us. Nor was our life an easy one, in the hours of our toil or in the amount of labor performed. We were always required to sit up until all the family had retired; then we must be up at early dawn in summer, and before day in winter. If we failed, through weariness or for any other reason, to appear at the first morning summons, we were sure to have our hearing quickened by a severe chastisement. Such horror has seized me, lest I might not hear the first shrill call, that I have often in dreams fancied I heard that unwelcome voice, and have leaped from my couch, and walked through the house and out of it before I awoke. I have gone and called the other slaves, in my sleep, and asked them if they did not hear master call. Never, while I live, will the remembrance of those long, bitter nights of fear pass from my mind.

But I want to give you a few specimens of the abuse which I received. During the ten years that I lived with Mrs. Banton, I do not think there were as many days, when she was at home, that I, or some other slave, did not receive some kind of beating or abuse at her hands. It seemed as though she could not live nor sleep unless some poor back was smarting, some head beating with pain, or some eye filled with tears, around her. Her tender mercies were indeed cruel. She brought up her children to imitate her example. Two of them manifested some dislike to the cruelties taught them by their mother, but they never stood high in favor with her; indeed, any thing like humanity or kindness to a slave, was looked upon by her as a great offence.

Her instruments of torture were ordinarily the raw hide, or a bunch of hickory-sprouts seasoned in the fire and tied together. But if these were not at hand, nothing came amiss. She could relish a beating with a chair, the broom, tongs, shovel, shears, knife-handle, the heavy heel of her slipper, or a bunch of keys; her zeal was so active in these barbarous inflictions, that her invention was wonderfully quick, and some way of inflicting the requisite torture was soon found out.

One instrument of torture is worthy of particular description. *This was an oak club, a foot and a half in length and an inch and a half square.* With this delicate weapon she would beat us upon the hands and upon the feet until they were blistered. This instrument was carefully preserved for a period of four years. Every day, for that time, I was compelled to see that hated tool of cruelty lying in the chair by my side. The least degree of delinquency either in not doing all the appointed work, or in look or behavior, was visited with a beating from this oak club. That club will always be a prominent object in the picture of horrors of my life of more than twenty years of bitter bondage.

When about nine years old, I was sent in the evening to catch and kill a turkey. They were securely sleeping in a tree—their accustomed resting-place for the night. I approached as cautiously as possible, and selected the victim I was directed to catch; but, just as I grasped him in my hand, my foot slipped, and he made his escape from the tree, and fled beyond my reach. I returned with a heavy heart to my mistress with the story of my misfortune. She was enraged beyond measure. She determined, at once, that I should have a whipping of the worst kind, and she was bent upon adding all the aggravations possible. Master had gone to bed drunk, and was now as fast asleep as drunkards ever are. At any rate, he was filling the house with the noise of his snoring and with the perfume of his breath. I was ordered to go and call him—wake him up—and ask him to be *kind* enough to give me fifty good smart lashes. To be *whipped* is bad enough—to *ask* for it is worse—to ask a drunken man to whip you is too bad. I would sooner have gone to a nest of rattlesnakes, than to the bed of this drunkard. But go I must. Softly I crept along, and gently shaking his arm, said, with a trembling voice, "Master, master, mistress wants you to wake up." This did not go to the extent of her command, and in a great fury she called out, "What, you wont ask him to whip you, will you?" I then added, "Mistress wants you to give me fifty lashes." A bear at the smell of a lamb was never roused quicker. "Yes, yes, that I will; I'll give you such a whipping as you will never want again." And, sure enough, so he did. He sprang from the bed, seized me by the hair, lashed me with a handful of switches, threw me my whole length upon the floor; beat, kicked, and cuffed me worse than he would a dog, and then threw me, with all his strength, out of the door, more dead than alive. There I lay for a long time, scarcely able and not daring to move, till I could hear no sound of the furies within, and then crept to my couch, longing for death to put an end to my misery. I had no friend in the world to whom I could utter one word of complaint, or to whom I could look for protection.

Mr. Banton owned a blacksmith's shop, in which he spent some of his time, though he was not a very efficient hand at the forge. One day, mistress told me to go over to the shop and let master give me a flogging. I knew the mode of punishing there too well. I would rather die than go. The poor fellow who worked in the shop, a very skilful workman, one day came to the determination that he would work no more, unless he could be paid for his labor. The enraged master put a handful of nail-rods into the fire, and when they were *red-hot,* took them out, and *cooled* one after another of them in the blood and flesh of the poor slave's back. I knew this was the shop mode of punishment. I would not go; and Mr. Banton came home, and his amiable lady told him the story of my refusal. He broke forth in a great rage, and gave me a most unmerciful beating; adding that, if I had come, he would have burned the hot nail-rods into my back.

Mrs. Banton, as is common among slaveholding women, seemed to hate and abuse me all the more, because I had some of the blood of her father in my veins. There are no slaves that are so badly abused, as those that are related to some of the women, or the children of their own husband; it seems as though they never could hate these quite bad enough. My sisters were as white and good-looking as any of the young ladies in Kentucky. It happened once of a time, that a young man called at the house of Mr. Campbell, to see a sister of Mrs. Banton. Seeing one of my sisters in the house, and pretty well dressed, with a strong family look, he thought it was Miss Campbell; and, with that supposition, addressed some conversation to her which he had intended for the private ear of Miss C. The mistake was noised abroad, and occasioned some amusement to young people. Mrs. Banton heard of it, and it made her caldron of wrath sizzling hot; every thing that diverted and amused other people seemed to enrage her. There are hot-springs in Kentucky; she was just like one of them, only brimful of boiling poison.

She must wreak her vengeance, for this innocent mistake of the young man, upon me. "She would fix me, so that nobody should ever think I was white." Accordingly, in a burning hot day, she *made me take off every rag of clothes, go out into the garden,* and pick herbs for hours, in order to *burn* me black. When I went out, she threw cold water on me, so that the sun might take effect upon me; when I came in, she gave me a severe beating on my blistered back.

After I had lived with Mrs. B. three or four years, I was put to spinning hemp, flax, and tow, on an old-fashioned foot-wheel. There were four or five slaves at this business, a good part of the time. We were kept at our work from daylight to dark in summer, from long before day to nine or ten o'clock in the evening in winter. Mrs. Banton, for the most part, was near, or kept continually passing in and out, to see that each of us performed as much work as she thought we ought to do. Being young, and sick at heart all the time, it was very hard work to go through the day and evening and not suffer exceedingly for want of more sleep. Very often, too, I was compelled to work beyond the ordinary hour, to finish the appointed task of the day. Sometimes I found it impossible not to drop asleep at the wheel.

On these occasions, Mrs. B. had her peculiar contrivances for keeping us awake. She would sometimes sit, by the hour, with a dipper of vinegar and salt, and throw it in my eyes to keep them open. My hair was pulled till there was no longer any pain from that source. *And I can now suffer myself to be lifted by the hair of the head, without experiencing the least pain.*

She very often kept me from getting water to satisfy my thirst, and in one instance kept me for two entire days without a particle of food. This she did, in order that I might make up for lost time. But, of course, I lost rather than gained upon my task. Every meal taken from me made me less able to work. It finally ended in a terrible beating.

But all my severe labor, and bitter and cruel punishments, for these ten years of captivity with this worse than Arab family, all these were as nothing to the sufferings I experienced by being separated from my mother, brothers, and sisters; the same things, with them near to sympathize with me, to hear my story of sorrow, would have been comparatively tolerable.

They were distant only about thirty miles; and yet, in ten long, lonely years of childhood, I was only permitted to see them three times.

My mother occasionally found an opportunity to send me some token of remembrance and affection, a sugar-plum or an apple; but I scarcely ever ate them; they were laid up, and handled and wept over till they wasted away in my hand.

My thoughts continually by day, and my dreams by night, were of mother and home; and the horror experienced in the morning, when I awoke and behold it was a dream, is beyond the power of language to describe.

But I am about to leave this den of robbers, where I had been so long imprisoned. I cannot, however, call the reader from his new and pleasant acquaintance with this amiable pair, without giving a few more incidents of their history. When this is done, and I have taken great pains, as I shall do, to put a copy of this portrait in the hands of this Mrs. B., I shall bid her farewell. If she sees something awfully hideous in her picture, as here presented, she will be constrained to acknowledge it is true to nature. I have given it from no malice, no feeling of resentment towards her, but that the world may know what is done by *slavery,* and that slaveholders may know that their crimes will come to light. I hope and pray that Mrs. B. will repent of her many and aggravated sins before it is too late.

The scenes between her and her husband, while I was with them, strongly illustrate the remark of Jefferson, that slavery fosters the worst passions of the master. Scarcely a day passed, in which bitter words were not bandied from one to the other. I have seen Mrs. B., with a large knife drawn in her right hand, the other upon the collar of her husband, swearing and threatening to cut him *square in two.* They both drank freely, and swore like highwaymen. He was a gambler and a counterfeiter. I have seen and handled his moulds and his false coin. They finally quarrelled openly, and separated; and the last I knew of them, he was living a sort of poor vagabond life in his native state, and she was engaged in a protracted lawsuit with some of her former friends, about her father's property.

Of course, such habits did not produce great thrift in their worldly condition, and myself and other slaves were mortgaged, from time to time, to make up the deficiency between their income and expenses. I was transferred, at the age of sixteen or seventeen, to a Mr. K., whose name I forbear to mention, lest, if he or any other man should ever claim *property* where they never had any, this, my own testimony, might be brought in to aid their wicked purposes.

In the exchange of masters, my condition was, in many respects, greatly improved. I was free, at any rate, from that kind of suffering experienced at the hand of Mrs. B., as though she delighted in cruelty for its own sake. My situation, however, with Mr. K. was far from enviable. Taken from the work in and around the house, and put at once, at that early age, to the constant work of a full-grown man, I found it not an easy task always to escape the lash of the overseer. In the four or five years that I was with this man, the overseers were often changed. Sometimes we had a man that seemed to have some consideration, some mercy; but generally their eye seemed to be fixed upon one object, and that was, to get the greatest possible amount of work out of every slave upon the plantation. When stooping to clear the tobacco-plants from the worms which infest them,—a work which draws most cruelly upon the back,—some of these men would not allow us a moment to rest at the end of the row; but, at the crack of the whip, we were compelled to jump to our places, from row to row, for hours, while the poor back was crying out with torture. Any complaint or remonstrance under such circumstances is sure to be answered in no other way than by the lash. As a sheep before her shearers is dumb, so a slave is not permitted to open his mouth.

There were about one hundred and fifteen slaves upon this plantation. Generally, we had enough, in quantity, of food. We had, however, but two meals a day, of corn-meal bread and soup, or meat of the poorest kind. Very often, so little care had been taken to cure and preserve the bacon, that, when it came to us, though it had been fairly killed once, it was more alive than dead. Occasionally, we had some refreshment over and above the two meals, but this was extra, beyond the rules of the plantation. And, to balance this gratuity, we were also frequently deprived of our food, as a punishment. We suffered greatly, too, for want of water. The slave-drivers have the notion that slaves are more healthy, if allowed to drink but little, than they are if freely allowed nature's beverage. The slaves quite as confidently cherish the opinion that, if the master would drink less peach brandy and whisky, and give the slave more water, it would be better all round. As it is, the more the master and overseer drink, the less they seem to think the slave needs.

In the winter, we took our meals before day in the morning, and after work at night; in the summer, at about nine o'clock in the morning, and at two in the afternoon. When we were cheated out of our two meals a day, either by the cruelty or caprice of the overseer, we always felt it a kind of special duty and privilege to make up, in some way, the deficiency. To accomplish this, we had many devices; and we sometimes resorted to our peculiar methods, when incited only by a desire to taste greater variety than our ordinary bill of fare afforded.

This sometimes led to very disastrous results. The poor slave who was caught with a chicken or a pig, killed from the plantation, had his back scored most unmercifully. Nevertheless, the pigs would die without being sick or squealing once; and the hens, chickens, and turkeys sometimes disappeared, and never stuck up a feather to tell where they were buried. The old goose would sometimes exchange her whole nest of eggs for round pebbles; and, patient as that animal is, this quality was exhausted, and she was obliged to leave her nest with no train of offspring behind her.

One old slave woman upon this plantation was altogether too keen and shrewd for the best of them. She would go out to the corn-crib with her basket, watch her opportunity, with one effective blow pop over a little pig, slip him into her basket, and put the cobs on top, trudge off to her cabin, and look just as innocent as though she had a right to eat of the work of her own hands. It was a kind of first principle, too, in her code of morals, that they that *worked* had a right to eat. The moral of all questions in relation to taking food was easily settled by aunt Peggy. The only question with her was, *how* and *when* to do it.

It could not be done openly, that was plain. It must be done secretly; if not in the daytime, by all means in the night. With a dead pig in the cabin, and the water all hot for scalding, she was at one time warned by her son that the Philistines were upon her. Her resources were fully equal to the sudden emergency. Quick as thought, the pig was thrown into the boiling kettle, a door was put over it, her daughter seated upon it, and, with a good, thick quilt around her, the overseer found little Clara taking a steam-bath for a terrible cold. The daughter, acting well her part, groaned sadly; the mother was very busy in tucking in the quilt, and the overseer was blinded, and went away without seeing a bristle of the pig.

Aunt P. cooked for herself, for another slave named George, and for me. George was very successful in bringing home his share of the plunder. He could capture a pig or a turkey without exciting the least suspicion. The old lady often rallied me for want of courage for such enterprises. At length, I summoned resolution, one rainy night, and determined there should be one from the herd of swine brought home by my hands. I went to the crib of corn, got my ear to shell, and my cart-stake to despatch a little roaster. I raised my arm to strike, summoned courage again and again, but to no purpose. The scattered kernels were all picked up, and no blow struck. Again I visited the crib, selected my victim, and *struck!* The blow glanced upon the side of the head, and, instead of falling, he ran off, squealing louder than ever I heard a pig squeal before. I ran as fast, in an opposite direction, made a large circuit, and reached the cabin, emptied the hot water, and made for my couch as soon as possible. I escaped detection, and only suffered from the ridicule of old Peggy and young George.

Poor Jess, upon the same plantation, did not so easily escape. More successful in his effort, he killed his pig; but he was found out. He was hung up by the hands, with a rail between his feet, and full three hundred lashes scored in upon his naked back. For a long time his life hung in doubt; and his poor wife, for becoming a partaker after the fact, was most severely beaten.

Another slave, employed as a driver upon the plantation, was compelled to whip his own wife, for a similar offence, so severely that she never recovered from the cruelty. She was literally *whipped to death by her own husband.*

A slave, called Hall, the hostler on the plantation, made a successful sally, one night, upon the animals forbidden to the Jews. The next day, he went into the barn-loft, and fell asleep. While sleeping over his abundant supper, and dreaming, perhaps, of his feast, he heard the shrill voice of his master, crying out, "The hogs are at the horse-trough; where is Hall?" The "hogs" and "Hall," coupled together, were enough for the poor fellow. He sprung from the hay, and made the best of his way off the plantation. He was gone six months; and, at the end of this period, he procured the intercession of the son-in-law of his master, and returned, escaping the ordinary punishment. But the transgression was laid up. Slaveholders seldom *forgive;* they only *postpone* the time of revenge. When about to be severely flogged, for some pretended offence, he took two of his grandsons, and escaped as far towards Canada as Indiana. He was followed, captured, brought back, and whipped most horribly. All the old score had been treasured up against him, and his poor back atoned for the whole at once.

On this plantation was a slave, named Sam, whose wife lived a few miles distant; and Sam was very seldom permitted to go and see his family. He worked in the blacksmith's shop. For a small offence, he was hung up by the hands, a rail between his feet, and whipped in turn by the master, overseer, and one of the waiters, till his back was torn all to pieces; and, in less than two months, Sam was in his grave. His last words were, "Mother, tell master he has killed me at last, for nothing; but tell him if God will forgive him I will."

A very poor white woman lived within about a mile of the plantation house. A female slave, named Flora, knowing she was in a very suffering condition, shelled out a peck of corn, and carried it to her in the night. Next day, the old man found it out, and this deed of charity was atoned for by one hundred and fifty lashes upon the bare back of poor Flora.

The master with whom I now lived was a very passionate man. At one time he thought the work on the plantation did not go on as it ought. One morning, when he and the overseer waked up from a drunken frolic, they swore the hands should not eat a morsel of any thing, till a field of wheat of some sixty acres was all cradled. There were from thirty to forty hands to do the work. We were driven on to the extent of our strength, and, although a brook ran through the field, not one of us was permitted to stop and taste a drop of water. Some of the men were so exhausted that they reeled for very weakness; two of the women fainted, and one of them was severely whipped, to revive her. They were at last carried helpless from the field and thrown down under the shade of a tree. At about five o'clock in the afternoon the wheat was all cut, and we were permitted to eat. Our suffering for want of water was excruciating. I trembled all over from the inward gnawing of hunger and from burning thirst.

In view of the sufferings of this day, we felt fully justified in making a foraging expedition upon the milk-room that night. And when master, and overseer, and all hands were locked up in sleep, ten or twelve of us went down to the spring house; a house built over a spring, to keep the milk and other things cool. We pressed altogether against the door, and open it came. We found half of a good baked pig, plenty of cream, milk, and other delicacies; and, as we felt in some measure delegated to represent all that had been cheated of their meals the day before, we ate plentifully. But after a successful plundering expedition within the gates of the enemy's camp, it is not easy always to cover the retreat. We had a *reserve* in the pasture for this purpose. We went up to the herd of swine, and, with a milk-pail in hand, it was easy to persuade them there was more where that came from, and the whole tribe followed readily into the spring house, and we left them there to wash the dishes and wipe up the floor, while we retired to rest. This was not malice in us; we did not love the waste which the hogs made; but we must have something to eat, to pay for the cruel and reluctant fast; and when we had obtained this, we must of course cover up our track. They watch us narrowly; and to take an egg, a pound of meat, or any thing else, however hungry we may be, is considered a great crime; we are compelled, therefore, to waste a good deal sometimes, to get a little.

I lived with this Mr. K. about four or five years; I then fell into the hands of his son. He was a drinking, ignorant man, but not so cruel as his father. Of him I hired my time at $12 a month; boarded and clothed myself. To meet my payments, I split rails, burned coal, peddled grass seed, and took hold of whatever I could find to do. This last master, or owner, as he would call himself, died about one year before I left Kentucky. By the administrators I was hired out for a time, and at last put up upon the auction block, for sale. No *bid* could be obtained for me. There were two reasons in the way. One was, there were two or three old mortgages which were not settled, and the second reason given by the bidders was, I had had too many privileges; had been permitted to trade for myself and go over the state; in short, to use their phrase, I was a "spoilt nigger." And sure enough I was, for all their purposes. I had long thought and dreamed of LIBERTY; I was now determined to make an effort, to gain it. No tongue can tell the doubt, the perplexities, the anxiety which a slave feels, when making up his mind upon this subject. If he makes an effort, and is not successful, he must be laughed at by his fellows; he will be beaten unmercifully by the master, and then watched and used the harder for it all his life.

And then, if he gets away, *who, what* will he find? He is ignorant of the world. All the white part of mankind, that he has ever seen, are enemies to him and all his kindred. How can he venture where none but white faces shall greet him? The master tells him, that abolitionists *decoy* slaves off into the free states, to catch them and sell them to Louisiana or Mississippi; and if he goes to Canada, the British will put him in a *mine under ground, with both eyes put out, for life.* How does he know what, or whom, to believe? A horror of great darkness comes upon him, as he thinks over what may befall him. Long, very long time did I think of escaping before I made the effort.

At length, the report was started that I was to be sold for Louisiana. Then I thought it was time to act. My mind was made up. This was about two weeks before I started. The first plan was formed between a slave named Isaac and my-self. Isaac proposed to take one of the horses of his mistress, and I was to take my pony, and we were to ride off together; I as master, and he as slave. We started together, and went on five miles. My want of confidence in the plan in-duced me to turn back. Poor Isaac plead like a good fellow to go forward. I am satisfied from experience and observation that both of us must have been cap-tured and carried back. I did not know enough at that time to travel and man-age a waiter. Every thing would have been done in such an awkward manner that a keen eye would have seen through our plot at once. I did not know the roads, and could not have read the guide-boards; and ignorant as many people are in Kentucky, they would have thought it strange to see a man with a waiter, who could not read a guide-board. I was sorry to leave Isaac, but I am satisfied I could have done him no good in the way proposed.

After this failure, I staid about two weeks; and after having arranged every thing to the best of my knowledge, I saddled my pony, went into the cellar where I kept my grass-seed apparatus, put my clothes into a pair of saddle-bags, and them into my seed-bag, and, thus equipped, set sail for the north star. O what a day was that to me! This was on Saturday, in August, 1841. I wore my common clothes, and was very careful to avoid special suspicion, as I already imagined the administrator was very watchful of me. The place from which I started was about fifty miles from Lexington. The reason why I do not give the *name* of the place, and a more accurate location, must be obvious to any one who remem-bers that, in the eye of the law, I am yet accounted a slave, and no spot in the United States affords an asylum for the wanderer. True, I feel protected in the hearts of the many warm friends of the slave by whom I am surrounded; but this protection does not come from the LAWS of any one of the United States.

But to return. After riding about fifteen miles, a Baptist minister overtook me on the road, saying, "How do you do, boy? are you free? I always thought you were free, till I saw them try to sell you the other day." I then wished him a thousand miles off, preaching, if he would, to the whole plantation, "Servants, obey your masters;" but I wanted neither sermons, questions, nor advice from him. At length I mustered resolution to make some kind of a reply. "What made you think I was free?" He replied, that he had noticed I had great privileges, that I did much as I liked, and that I was almost white. "O yes," I said, "but there are a great many slaves as white as I am." "Yes," he said, and then went on to name several; among others, one who had lately, as he said, run away. This was touching altogether too near upon what I was thinking of. Now, said I, he must know, or at least reckons, what I am at—*running away.*

However, I blushed as little as possible, and made strange of the fellow who had lately run away, as though I knew nothing of it. The old fellow looked at me, as it seemed to me, as though he would read my thoughts. I wondered what in the world *slaves could* run away for, especially if they had such a chance as I had had for the last few years. He said, "I suppose you would not run away on any account, you are so well treated." "O," said I, "I do very well, very well, sir. If you should ever hear that I had run away, be certain it must be because there is some great change in my treatment."

He then began to talk with me about the seed in my *bag,* and said that he should want to buy some. Then, I thought, he means to get at the truth by looking in my *seed bag,* where, sure enough, he would not find *grass* seed, but the seeds of Liberty. However, he dodged off soon, and left me alone. And although I have heard say, poor company is better than none, I felt much better without him than with him.

When I had gone on about twenty-five miles, I went down into a deep valley by the side of the road, and changed my clothes. I reached Lexington about seven o'clock that evening, and put up with brother Cyrus. As I had often been to Lexington before, and stopped with him, it excited no attention from the slaveholding gentry. Moreover, I had a pass from the administrator, of whom I had hired my time. I remained over the Sabbath with Cyrus, and we talked over a great many plans for future operations, if my efforts to escape should be successful. Indeed, we talked over all sorts of ways for me to proceed. But both of us were very ignorant of the roads, and of the best way to escape suspicion. And I sometimes wonder that a slave, so ignorant, so timid, as he is, *ever* makes the attempt to get his freedom. "*Without* are *foes, within* are *fears.*"[11]

Monday morning, bright and early, I set my face in good earnest toward the Ohio River, determined to see and tread the north bank of it, or *die* in the attempt. I said to myself, One of two things,—FREEDOM or DEATH! The first night I reached Mayslick, fifty odd miles from Lexington. Just before reaching this village, I stopped to think over my situation, and determine how I would pass that night. On that night hung all my hopes. I was within twenty miles of Ohio. My horse was unable to reach the river that night. And besides, to travel and attempt to cross the river in the night, would excite suspicion. I must spend the night *there.* But *how?* At one time, I thought, I will take my pony out into the field and give him some corn, and sleep myself on the grass. But then the *dogs* will be out in the evening, and, if caught under such circumstances, they will take me for a *thief* if not for a runaway. That will not do. So, after weighing the matter all over, I made a plunge right into the heart of the village, and put up at the tavern.

After seeing my pony disposed of, I looked into the bar-room, and saw some persons that I thought were from my part of the country, and would know me. I shrunk back with horror. What to do I did not know. I looked across the street, and saw the shop of a silversmith. A thought of a pair of spectacles, to hide my face, struck me. I went across the way, and began to barter for a pair of double-eyed green spectacles. When I got them on, they blind-folded *me*, if they did not others. Every thing seemed right up in my eyes. Some people buy spectacles to see out of; I bought mine to keep from being seen. I hobbled back to the tavern, and called for supper. This I did to avoid notice, for I felt like any thing but eating. At tea, I had not learned to measure distances with my new eyes, and the first pass I made with my knife and fork at my plate went right into my lap. This confused me still more, and, after drinking one cup of tea, I left the table, and got off to bed as soon as possible. But not a wink of sleep that night. All was confusion, dreams, anxiety, and trembling.

As soon as day dawned, I called for my horse, paid my reckoning, and was on my way, rejoicing that *that* night was gone, any how. I made all diligence on my way, and was across the Ohio, and in Aberdeen by noon, that day!

What my feelings were, when I reached the free shore, can be better imagined than described. I trembled all over with deep emotion, and I could feel my hair rise up on my head. I was on what was called a *free* soil, among a people who had no slaves. I saw white men at work, and no slave smarting beneath the lash. Every thing was indeed *new* and wonderful. Not knowing where to find a friend, and being ignorant of the country—unwilling to inquire, lest I should betray my ignorance, it was a whole week before I reached Cincinnati. At one place, where I put up, I had a great many more questions put to me than I wished to answer. At another place, I was very much annoyed by the officiousness of the landlord, who made it a point to supply every guest with newspapers. I took the copy handed me, and turned it over, in a somewhat awkward manner, I suppose. He came to me to point out a veto, or some other very important news. I thought it best to decline his assistance, and gave up the paper, saying my eyes were not in a fit condition to read much.

At another place, the neighbors, on learning that a Kentuckian was at the tavern, came, in great earnestness, to find out what my business was. Kentuckians sometimes came there to kidnap their citizens. They were in the habit of watching them close. I at length satisfied them, by assuring them that I was not, nor my father before me, any slaveholder at all; but, lest their suspicions should be excited in another direction, I added, my grandfather was a slaveholder.

At Cincinnati, I found some old acquaintances, and spent several days. In passing through some of the streets, I several times saw a great slave-dealer from Kentucky, who knew me, and, when I approached him, I was very careful to give him a wide berth. The only advice that I here received was from a man who had once been a slave. He urged me to sell my pony, go up the river, to Portsmouth, then take the canal for Cleveland, and cross over to Canada. I acted upon this suggestion, sold my horse for a small sum, as he was pretty well used up, took passage for Portsmouth, and soon found myself on the canal-boat, headed for Cleveland. On the boat, I became acquainted with a Mr. Conoly, from New

York. He was very sick with fever and ague, and, as he was a stranger, and alone, I took the best possible care of him, for a time. One day, in conversation with him, he spoke of the slaves, in the most harsh and bitter language, and was especially severe on those who *attempted to run away*. Thinks I, you are not the man for me to have much to do with. I found the *spirit* of slaveholding was not all south of the Ohio River.

No sooner had I reached Cleveland, than a trouble came upon me from a very unexpected quarter. A rough, swearing, reckless creature, in the shape of a man, came up to me, and declared I had passed a bad five dollar bill upon his wife, in the boat, and he demanded the silver for it. I had never seen him, nor his wife, before. He pursued me into the tavern, swearing and threatening all the way. The travellers, that had just arrived at the tavern, were asked to give their names to the clerk, that he might enter them upon the book. He called on me for my name, just as this ruffian was in the midst of his assault upon me. On leaving Kentucky, I thought it best, for my own security, to take a new name, and I had been entered on the boat as Archibald Campbell. I knew, with such a charge as this man was making against me, it would not do to change my name from the boat to the hotel. At the moment, I could not recollect what I had called myself, and, for a few minutes, I was in a complete puzzle. The clerk kept calling, and I made believe deaf, till, at length, the name popped back again, and I was duly enrolled a guest at the tavern, in Cleveland. I had heard, before, of persons being frightened out of their *Christian* names, but I was fairly scared out of both mine for a while. The landlord soon protected me from the violence of the bad-meaning man, and drove him away from the house.

I was detained at Cleveland several days, not knowing how to get across the lake, into Canada. I went out to the shore of the lake again and again, to try and see the other side, but I could see no hill, mountain, nor city of the asylum I sought. I was afraid to inquire *where* it was, lest it would betray such a degree of ignorance as to excite suspicion at once. One day, I heard a man ask another, employed on board a vessel, "and where does this vessel trade?" Well, I thought, if that is a proper question for you, it is for me. So I passed along, and asked of every vessel, "Where does this vessel trade?" At last, the answer came, "over here in Kettle Creek, near Port Stanley." And where is that? said I. "O, right over here, in *Canada*." That was the sound for me; "over here in Canada." The captain asked me if I wanted a passage to Canada. I thought it would not do to be too earnest about it, lest it would betray me. I told him I some thought of going, if I could get a passage cheap. We soon came to terms on this point, and that evening we set sail. After proceeding only nine miles, the wind changed, and the captain returned to port again. This, I thought, was a very bad omen. However, I stuck by, and the next evening, at nine o'clock, we set sail once more, and at daylight we were in Canada.

When I stepped ashore here, I said sure enough, I AM FREE. Good heaven! what a sensation, when it first visits the bosom of a full-grown man; one *born* to bondage—one who had been taught, from early infancy, that this was his inevitable lot for life. Not till *then* did I dare to cherish, for a moment, the feeling that *one* of the limbs of my body was my own. The slaves often say, when cut in the hand or foot, "Plague on the old foot" or "the old hand; it is master's—let him take care of it. Nigger don't care, if he never get well." My hands, my feet, were now my own. But what to do with them, was the next question. A strange sky was over me, a new earth under me, strange voices all around; even the animals were such as I had never seen. A flock of prairie-hens and some black geese were altogether new to me. I was entirely alone; no human being, that I had ever seen before, where I could speak to him or he to me.

And could I make that country ever seem like *home?* Some people are very much afraid all the slaves will run up north, if they are ever free. But I can assure them that they will run *back* again, if they do. If I could have been assured of my freedom in Kentucky, then, I would have given any thing in the world for the prospect of spending my life among my old acquaintances, where I first saw the sky, and the sun rise and go down. It was a long time before I could make the sun work right at all. It would rise in the wrong place, and go down wrong; and, finally, it behaved so bad, I thought it could not be the same sun.

There was a little something added to this feeling of strangeness. I could not forget all the horrid stories slaveholders tell about Canada. They assure the slave that, when they get hold of slaves in Canada, they make various uses of them. Sometimes they *skin* the *head,* and wear the wool on their coat collars— put them into the lead-mines, with both eyes out—the young slaves they eat; and as for the red coats, they are sure death to the slave. However ridiculous to a well-informed person such stories may appear, they work powerfully upon the excited imagination of an ignorant slave. With these stories all fresh in mind, when I arrived at St. Thomas,[12] I kept a bright look-out for the red coats. As I was turning the corner of one of the streets, sure enough, there stood before me a *red coat,* in full uniform, with his tall bear-skin cap, a foot and a half high, his gun shouldered, and he standing as erect as a guide-post. Sure enough, that is the fellow that they tell about catching the slave. I turned on my heel, and sought another street. On turning another corner, the *same* soldier, as I thought, faced me, with his black cap and stern look. Sure enough, my time has come now. I was as near scared to death, then, as a man can be and breathe. I could not have felt any worse if he had shot me right through the heart. I made off again, as soon as I dared to move. I inquired for a tavern. When I came up to it, there was a great brazen lion sleeping over the door, and, although I knew it was not alive, I had been so well frightened that I was almost afraid to go in. Hunger drove me to it at last, and I asked for something to eat.

On my way to St. Thomas I was also badly frightened. A man asked me who I was. I was afraid to tell him a runaway slave, lest he should have me to the mines. I was afraid to say, "I am an American," lest he should shoot me, for I knew there had been trouble between the British and Americans. I inquired, at length, for the place where the greatest number of colored soldiers were. I was told there were a great many at New London; so for New London I started. I got a ride, with some country people, to the latter place. They asked me who I was, and I told them from Kentucky; and they, in a familiar way, called me "Old Kentuck." I saw some soldiers, on the way, and asked the men what they had soldiers for. They said they were kept "to get *drunk* and be *whipped;*" that was the chief use they made of them. At last, I reached New London, and here I found soldiers in great numbers. I attended at their parade, and saw the guard driving the people back; but it required no guard to keep me off. I thought, "If you will let me alone, I will not trouble you." I was as much afraid of a red coat as I would have been of a bear. Here I asked again for the colored soldiers. The answer was, "Out at Chatham, about seventy miles distant." I started for Chatham. The first night, I stopped at a place called the Indian Settlement. The door was barred, at the house where I was, which I did not like so well, as I was yet somewhat afraid of their Canadian tricks. Just before I got to Chatham, I met two colored soldiers, with a white man, bound, and driving him along before them. This was something quite new. I thought, then, sure enough, this is the land for me. I had seen a great many colored people bound, and in the hands of the whites, but this was changing things right about. This removed all my suspicions, and, ever after, I felt quite easy in Canada. I made diligent inquiry for several slaves, that I had known in Kentucky, and at length found one, named Henry. He told me of several others, with whom I had been acquainted, and from him, also, I received the first correct information about brother Milton. I knew that he had left Kentucky about a year before I did, and I supposed, until now, that he was in Canada. Henry told me he was at Oberlin, Ohio.

At Chatham, I hired myself for a while, to recruit my purse a little, as it had become pretty well drained by this time. I had only about sixty-four dollars, when I left Kentucky, and I had been living upon it now for about six weeks. Mr. Everett, with whom I worked, treated me kindly, and urged me to stay in Canada, offering me business on his farm. He declared "there was no 'free state' in America; all were *slave* states, bound to slavery, and the slave could have no asylum in any of them." There is certainly a great deal of truth in this remark. I have *felt*, wherever I may be in the United States, the kidnappers may be upon me at any moment. If I should creep up to the top of the monument on Bunker's Hill, beneath which my father fought, I should not be safe, even there. The slave-mongers have a right, by the laws of the United States, to seek me, even upon the top of the monument, whose base rests upon the bones of those who fought for freedom.

I soon after made my way to Sandwich, and crossed over to Detroit, on my way to Ohio, to see Milton. While in Canada, I swapped away my pistol, as I thought I should not need it, for an old watch. When I arrived at Detroit, I found my watch was gone. I put my baggage, with nearly every cent of money I had, on board the boat for Cleveland, and went back to Sandwich to search for the old watch. The ferry here was about three-fourths of a mile, and, in my zeal for the old watch, I wandered so far that I did not get back in season for the boat, and had the satisfaction of hearing her *last* bell just as I was about to leave the Canada shore. When I got back to Detroit I was in a fine fix; my money and my clothes gone, and I left to wander about in the streets of Detroit. A man may be a man for all clothes or money, but he don't feel quite so well, any how. What to do now I could hardly tell. It was about the first of November. I wandered about and picked up something very cheap for supper, and paid ninepence for lodging. All the next day no boat for Cleveland. Long days and nights to me. At length another boat was up for Cleveland. I went to the Captain, to tell him my story; he was very cross and savage; said a man had no business from home without money; that so many told stories about losing money that he did not know what to believe. He finally asked me how much money I had. I told him sixty-two and a half cents. Well, he said, give me that, and pay the balance when you get there. I gave him every cent I had. We were a day and a night on the passage, and I had nothing to eat except some cold potatoes, which I picked from a barrel of fragments, and cold victuals. I went to the steward, or cook, and asked for something to eat, but he told me his orders were strict to give away nothing, and, if he should do it, he would lose his place at once.

When the boat came to Cleveland it was in the night, and I thought I would spend the balance of the night in the boat. The steward soon came along, and asked if I did not know that the boat had landed, and the passengers had gone ashore. I told him I knew it, but I had paid the captain all the money I had, and could get no shelter for the night unless I remained in the boat. He was very harsh and unfeeling, and drove me ashore, although it was very cold, and snow on the ground. I walked around a while, till I saw a light in a small house of entertainment. I called for lodging. In the morning, the Frenchman, who kept it, wanted to know if I would have breakfast. I told him, no. He said then I might pay for my lodging. I told him I would do so before I left, and that my outside coat might hang there till I paid him.

I was obliged at once to start on an expedition for raising *some cash*. My resources were not very numerous. I took a *hair* brush, that I had paid three York shillings for a short time before, and sallied out to make a sale. But the wants of every person I met seemed to be in the same direction with my own; they wanted *money* more than hair brushes. At last, I found a customer who paid me ninepence *cash*, and a small balance in the shape of something to eat for breakfast. I was started square for that day, and delivered out of my present distress. But hunger will return, and all the quicker when a man don't know how to satisfy it when it does come. I went to a plain boarding-house, and told the man just my situation; that I was waiting for the boat to return from Buffalo, hoping to get my baggage and money. He said he would board me two or three days and risk it. I tried to get work, but no one seemed inclined to employ me. At last, I gave up in despair, about my luggage, and concluded to start as soon as possible for Oberlin. I sold my great-coat for two dollars, paid one for my board, and with the other I was going to pay my fare to Oberlin. That night, after I had made all my arrangements to leave in the morning, the boat came. On hearing the bell of a steam-boat, in the night, I jumped up and went to the wharf, and found my baggage; paid a quarter of a dollar for the long journey it had been carried, and glad enough to get it again at that.

The next morning, I took the stage for Oberlin; found several abolitionists from that place in the coach. They mentioned a slave named Milton Clarke, who was living there, that he had a brother in Canada, and that he expected him there soon. They spoke in a very friendly manner of Milton, and of the slaves; so, after we had had a long conversation, and I perceived they were all friendly, I made myself known to them. To be thus surrounded at once with friends, in a land of strangers, was something quite new to me. The impression made by the kindness of these strangers upon my heart, will never be effaced. I thought, there must be some new principle at work here, such as I had not seen much of in Kentucky. That evening I arrived at Oberlin, and found Milton boarding at a Mrs. Cole's. Finding here so many friends, my first impression was that all the abolitionists in the country must live right there together. When Milton spoke of going to Massachusetts, "No," said I, "we better stay here where the *abolitionists* live." And when they assured me that the friends of the slave were more numerous in Massachusetts than in Ohio, I was greatly surprised.

Milton and I had not seen each other for a year; during that time we had passed through the greatest change in outward condition, that can befall a man in this world. How glad we were to greet each other in what we then *thought* a *free* State may be easily imagined. We little dreamed of the dangers sleeping around us. Brother Milton had not encountered so much danger in getting away as I had. But his time for suffering was soon to come. For several years before his escape, Milton had hired his time of his master, and had been employed as a steward in different steamboats upon the river. He had paid as high as two hundred dollars a year for his time. From his master he had a written pass, permitting him to go up and down the Mississippi and Ohio rivers when he pleased. He found it easy, therefore, to land on the north side of the Ohio river, and concluded to take his own time for returning. He had caused a letter to be written to Mr. L., his pretended owner, telling him to give himself no anxiety on his account; that he had found by experience he had wit enough to take care of himself, and he thought the care of his master was not worth the two hundred dollars a year which he had been paying for it, for four years; that, on the whole, if his master would be quiet and contented, he thought he should do very well. This letter, the escape of two persons belonging to the same family, and from the same region, in one year, waked up the fears and the *spite* of the slaveholders. However, they let us have a little respite, and, through the following winter and spring, we were employed in various kinds of work at Oberlin and in the neighborhood.

All this time I was deliberating upon a plan by which to go down and rescue Cyrus, our youngest brother, from bondage. In July, 1842, I gathered what little money I had saved, which was not a large sum, and started for Kentucky again. As near as I remember, I had about twenty dollars. I did not tell my plan to but one or two at Oberlin, because there were many slaves there, and I did not know but that it might get to Kentucky in some way through them sooner than I should. On my way down through Ohio, I advised with several well known friends of the slave. Most of them pointed out the dangers I should encounter, and urged me not to go. One young man told me to go, and the God of heaven would prosper me. I knew it was dangerous, but I did not then dream of all that I must suffer in body and mind before I was through with it. It is not a very comfortable feeling, to be creeping round day and night, for nearly two weeks together, in a den of lions, where, if one of them happens to put his paw on you, it is certain death, or something much worse.

At Ripley, I met a man who had lived in Kentucky; he encouraged me to go forward, and directed me about the roads. He told me to keep on a back route not much travelled, and I should not be likely to be molested. I crossed the river at Ripley, and when I reached the other side, and was again upon the soil on which I had suffered so much, I *trembled, shuddered,* at the thoughts of what might happen to me. My fears, my feelings, overcame for the moment all my resolution, and I was for a time completely overcome with emotion. Tears flowed like a brook of water. I had just left kind friends; I was now where every man I met would be my enemy. It was a long time before I could summon courage sufficient to proceed. I had with me a rude map, made by the Kentuckian whom I saw at Ripley. After examining this as well as I could, I proceeded. In the afternoon of the first day, as I was sitting in a stream to bathe and cool my feet, a man rode up on horseback, and entered into a long conversation with me. He asked me some questions about my travelling, but none but what I could easily answer. He pointed out to me a house where a white woman lived, who, he said, had recently suffered terribly from a fright. Eight slaves, that were running away, called for something to eat, and the poor woman was sorely scared by them. For his part, the man said, he hoped they never would find the slaves again. Slavery was the curse of Kentucky. He had been brought up to work, and he liked to work, but slavery made it disgraceful for any white man to work. From this conversation I was almost a good mind to trust this man, and tell him my story; but, on second thought, I concluded it might be just as *safe* not to do it. A hundred or two dollars for returning a slave, for a poor man, is a heavy temptation. At night, I stopped at the house of a widow woman, not a tavern, exactly; but they often entertained people there. The next day, when I got as far as Cynthiana, within about twenty miles of Lexington, I was sore all over, and lame, from having walked so far. I tried to hire a horse and carriage, to help me a few miles. At last, I agreed with a man to send me forward to a certain place, which he said was twelve miles, and for which I paid him, in advance, three dollars. It proved to be only seven miles. This was now Sabbath day, as I had selected that as the most suitable day for making my entrance into Lexington. There is much more passing in and out on that day, and I thought I should be much less observed than on any other day.

When I approached the city, and met troops of idlers, on foot and on horseback, sauntering out of the city, I was very careful to keep my umbrella before my face, as people passed, and kept my eyes right before me. There were many persons in the place who had known me, and I did not care to be recognized by any of them. Just before entering the city, I turned off to the field, and lay down under a tree and waited for night. When its curtains were fairly over me, I started up, took two pocket handkerchiefs, tied one over my forehead, the other under my chin, and marched forward for the city. It was not then so dark as I wished it was. I met a young slave, driving cows. He was quite disposed to condole with me, and said, in a very sympathetic manner, "Massa sick?" "Yes, boy," I said, "Massa sick; drive along your cows." The next colored man I met, I knew him in a moment, but he did not recognize me. I made for the wash-house of the man with whom Cyrus lived. I reached it without attracting any notice, and found there an old slave, as true as steel. I inquired for Cyrus; he said he was at home.

He very soon recollected me; and, while the boy was gone to call Cyrus, he uttered a great many exclamations of wonder, to think I should return.

"Good Heaven, boy! what you back here for? What on arth you here for, my son? O, I scared for you! They kill you, just as sure as I alive, if they catch you! Why, in the name of liberty, didn't you stay away, when you gone so slick? Sartin, I never did 'spect to see you again!" I said, "Don't be scared." But he kept repeating, "I scared for you! I scared for you!" When I told him my errand, his wonder was somewhat abated; but still his exclamations were repeated all the evening, "What brought you back here?" In a few minutes, Cyrus made his appearance, filled with little less of wonder than the old man had manifested. I had intended, when I left him, about a year before, that I would return for him, if I was successful in my effort for freedom. He was very glad to see me, and entered, with great animation, upon the plan for his own escape. He had a wife, who was a free woman, and consequently he had a home. He soon went out, and left me in the wash-room with the old man. He went home to apprize his wife, and to prepare a room for my concealment. His wife is a very active, industrious woman, and they were enabled to rent a very comfortable house, and, at this time, had a spare room in the attic, where I could be thoroughly concealed.

He soon returned, and said every thing was ready. I went home with him, and, before ten o'clock at night, I was stowed away in a little room, that was to be my prison-house for about a week. It was a comfortable room; still the confinement was close, and I was unable to take exercise, lest the people in the other part of the house should hear. I got out, and walked around a little, in the evening, but suffered a good deal, for want of more room to live and move in. During the day, Cyrus was busy making arrangements for his departure. He had several little sums of money, in the hands of the foreman of the tan-yard, and in other hands. Now, it would not do to go right boldly up and demand his pay of every one that owed him; this would lead to suspicion at once. So he contrived various ways to get in his little debts. He had seen the foreman, one day, counting out some singular coin of some foreign nation. He pretended to take a great liking to that foreign money, and told the man, if he would pay him what was due him in *that* money, he would give him two or three dollars. From another person he took an order on a store; and so, in various ways, he got in his little debts as well as he could. At night, we contrived to plan the ways and means of escaping. Cyrus had never been much accustomed to walking, and he dreaded, very much, to undertake such a journey. He proposed to take a couple of horses, as he thought he had richly earned them, over and above all he had received. I objected to this, because, if we were caught, either in Kentucky or out of it, they would bring against us the charge of stealing, and this would be far worse than the charge of running away.

I firmly insisted, therefore, that we must go on foot. In the course of a week, Cyrus had gathered something like twenty dollars, and we were ready for our journey. A family lived in the same house with Cyrus, in a room below. How to get out, in the early part of the evening, and not be discovered, was not an easy question. Finally, we agreed that Cyrus should go down and get into conversation with them, while I slipped out with his bundle of clothes, and repaired to a certain street, where he was to meet me.

As I passed silently out at the door, Cyrus was cracking his best jokes, and raising a general laugh, which completely covered my retreat. Cyrus soon took quiet and unexpected leave of his friends in that family, and leave, also, of his wife above, for a short time only. At a little past eight of the clock we were beyond the bounds of the city. His wife did all she could to assist him in his effort to gain his inalienable rights. She did not dare, however, to let the slaveholders know that she knew any thing of his attempt to run away. He had told the slaves that he was going to see his sister, about twelve miles off. It was Saturday night, when we left Lexington. On entering the town, when I went in, I was so intent upon covering up my face, that I took but little notice of the roads. We were very soon exceedingly perplexed to know what road to take. The moon favored us, for it was a clear, beautiful night. On we came, but, at the cross of the roads, what to do we did not know. At length, I climbed one of the guide-posts, and *spelled* out the names as well as I could. We were on the road to freedom's boundary, and, with a strong step, we measured off the path: but again the cross roads perplexed us. This time, we took hold of the sign-post and lifted it out of the ground, and turned it upon one of its horns, and spelled out the way again. As we started from this goal, I told Cyrus we had not put up the sign-post. He pulled forward, and said he guessed we would do that when we came back. Whether the sign-board is up or down, we have never been there to see.

Soon after leaving the city, we met a great many of the patrols; but they did not arrest us, and we had no disposition to trouble them.

While we were pressing on, by moonlight, and sometimes in great doubt about the road, Cyrus was a good deal discouraged. He thought, if we got upon the wrong road, it would be almost certain death for us, or something worse. In the morning, we found that, on account of our embarrassment in regard to the roads, we had only made a progress of some twenty or twenty-five miles. But we were greatly cheered to find they were so many miles in the right direction. Then we put the best foot forward, and urged our way as fast as possible. In the afternoon it rained very hard; the roads were muddy and slippery. We had slept none the night before, and had been, of course, very much excited. In this state of mind and of body, just before dark, we stopped in a little patch of bushes, to discuss the expediency of going to a house, which we saw at a distance, to spend the night.

As we sat there, Cyrus became very much excited, and, pointing across the road, exclaimed, "Don't you see that animal there?" I looked, but saw nothing; still he affirmed that he saw a dreadful ugly animal looking at us, and ready to make a spring. He began to feel for his pistols, but I told him not to fire there; but he persisted in pointing to the animal, although I am persuaded he saw nothing, only by the force of his imagination. I had some doubts about telling this story, lest people would not believe me; but a friend has suggested to me that such things are not uncommon, when the imagination is strongly excited.

In travelling through the rain and mud, this afternoon, we suffered beyond all power of description. Sometimes we found ourselves just ready to stand, fast asleep, in the middle of the road. Our feet were blistered all over. When Cyrus would get almost discouraged, I urged him on, saying we were walking for *freedom now.* "Yes," he would say, "freedom is good, Lewis, but this is a *hard, h-a-r-d* way to get it." This he would say, half asleep. We were so weak, before night, that we several times fell upon our knees in the road. We had crackers with us, but we had no appetite to eat. *Fears* were behind us; *hope* before; and we were driven and drawn as hard as ever men were. Our limbs and joints were so stiff that, if we took a step to the right hand or left, it seemed as though it would shake us to pieces. It was a dark, weary day to us both.

At length, I succeeded in getting the consent of Cyrus to go to a house for the night. We found a plain farmer's family. The good man was all taken up in talking about the camp-meeting held that day, about three miles from his house. He only asked us where we were from, and we told him our home was in Ohio. He said the young men had behaved unaccountably bad at the camp-meeting, and they had but little comfort of it. They mocked the preachers, and disturbed the meeting badly.

We escaped suspicion more readily, as I have no doubt, from the supposition, on the part of many, that we were going to the camp-meeting. Next morning, we called at the meeting, as it was on our way, bought up a little extra gingerbread against the time of need, and marched forward for the Ohio. When any one inquired why we left the meeting so soon, we had an answer ready: "The young men behave so bad, we can get no good of the meeting."

By this time we limped badly, and we were sore all over. A young lady whom we met, noticing that we walked lame, cried out, mocking us, "O my feet, my feet, how sore!" At about eleven o'clock, we reached the river, two miles below Ripley. The boatman was on the other side. We called for him. He asked us a few questions. This was a last point with us. We tried our best to appear unconcerned. I asked questions about the boats, as though I had been there before; went to Cyrus, and said, "Sir, I have no change; will you lend me enough to pay my toll? I will pay you before we part." When we were fairly landed upon the northern bank, and had gone a few steps, Cyrus stopped suddenly, on seeing the water gush out at the side of the hill. Said he, "Lewis, give me that tin cup." "What in the world do you want of a tin cup now? We have not time to stop." The cup he would have. Then he went up to the spring, dipped and drank, and dipped and drank; then he would look round, and drink again. "What in the world," said I, "are you fooling there for?" "O," said he, "this is the first time I ever had a chance to drink water that ran out of the *free* dirt." Then we went a little further, and he sat down on a log. I urged him forward. "O," said he, "I must sit on this free timber a little while."

A short distance further on, we saw a man, who seemed to watch us very closely. I asked him which was the best way to go, *over* the hill before us, or *around* it. I did this, to appear to know something about the location. He went off, without offering any obstacles to our journey. In going up the hill, Cyrus would stop, and lay down and roll over. "What in the world are you about, Cyrus? Don't you see Kentucky is over there?" He still continued to roll and kiss the ground; said it was a game horse that could roll clear over. Then he would put face to the ground, and roll over and over. "First time," he said, "he ever rolled on *free* grass."

After he had recovered a little from his sportive mood, we went up to the house of a good friend of the slave at Ripley. We were weary and worn enough; though ever since we left the river, it seemed as though Cyrus was young and spry as a colt; but when we got where we could *rest,* we found ourselves *tired.* The good lady showed us into a good bedroom. Cyrus was skittish. He would not go in and lie down. "I am afraid," said he, "of old mistress. She is too good—too good—can't be so—they want to catch us both." So, to pacify him, I had to go out into the orchard and rest there. When the young men came home, he soon got acquainted, and felt sure they were his friends. From this place we were sent on by the friends, from place to place, till we reached Oberlin, Ohio, in about five weeks after I left there to go for Cyrus. I had encountered a good deal of peril; had suffered much from anxiety of feeling; but felt richly repaid in seeing another brother free.

We stopped at Oberlin a few days, and then Cyrus started for Canada. He did not feel exactly safe. When he reached the lake, he met a man from Lexington who knew him perfectly; indeed, the very man of whom his wife hired her house. This man asked him if he was free. He told him yes, he was free, and he was hunting for brother Milton, to get him to go back and settle with the old man for his freedom. Putnam told him that was all right. He asked Cyrus if he should still want that house his wife lived in. "O, yes," said Cyrus, "we will notify you when we don't want it any more. You tell them, I shall be down there in a few days. I have heard of Milton, and expect to have him soon to carry back with me." Putnam went home, and, when he found what a fool Cyrus had made of him, he was vexed enough. "A rascal," he said, "I could have caught him as well as not."

Cyrus hastened over to Canada. He did not like that country so well as the states, and in a few weeks returned. He had already sent a letter to his wife, giving her an account of his successful escape, and urging her to join him as soon as possible. He had the pleasure of meeting his wife, and her three children by a former husband, and they have found a quiet resting-place, where, if the rumor of oppression reaches them, they do not feel its scourge, nor its chains. And there is no doubt entertained by any of his friends but he can take care of himself.

He begins already to appreciate his rights, and to maintain them as a freeman. The following paragraph concerning him was published in the Liberty Press about one year since:—

## "PROGRESS OF FREEDOM

### "*Scene at Hamilton Village, N.Y.*

"Mr. Cyrus Clarke, a brother of the well-known Milton and Lewis Clarke, (all of whom, till within a short time since, for some twenty-five years, were slaves in Kentucky,) mildly, but firmly, presented his ballot at the town meeting board. Be it known that said Cyrus, as well as his brothers, are *white,* with only a sprinkling of the African; just enough to make them bright, quick, and intelligent, and scarcely observable in the color except by the keen and scenting slaveholder. Mr. Clarke had all the necessary qualifications of white men to vote.

"*Slave*. Gentlemen, here is my ballot; I wish to vote. (Board and by-standers well knowing him, all were aghast—the waters were troubled—the slave legions were 'up in their might.')

"*Judge E.* You can't vote! Are you not, and have you not been a slave?

"*Slave*. I shall not *lie* to vote. I am and have been a slave, so called; but I wish to vote, and I believe it my right and duty.

"*Judge E.* Slaves can't vote.

"*Slave*. Will you just show me in your books, constitution, or whatever you call them, where it says a slave can't vote?

"*Judge E.* (Pretending to look over the law, &c., well knowing he was 'used up.') Well, well, you are a colored man, and can't vote without you are worth $250.

"*Slave*. I am as white as *you;* and don't *you vote?*

"(Mr. E. is well known to be very dark; indeed, as dark or darker than Clarke. The current began to set against Mr. E. by murmurs, sneers, laughs, and many other demonstrations of dislike.)

"*Judge E.* Are you not a *colored man?* and is not your hair curly?

"*Slave*. We are both colored men; and all we differ is, that you have not the handsome wavy curl; you raise *Goat's wool,* and I come, as you see, a little nearer *Saxony.*

"At this time the fire and fun was at its height, and was fast consuming the judge with public opprobrium.

"*Judge E.* I challenge this man's vote, he being a colored man, and not worth $250.

"Friends and foes warmly contested what constituted a colored man by the New York statute. The board finally came to the honorable conclusion that, to be a *colored* man, he must be at least one half blood African. Mr. Clarke, the SLAVE, then voted, he being nearly full white. I have the history of this transaction from Mr. Clarke, in person. In substance it is as told me, but varying more or less from his language used.

J. THOMPSON.

"PARIS, *March,* 12, 1844."

Martha, the wife of Cyrus, had a long story of the wrath of the slaveholders, because he ran away. Monday morning she went down, in great distress, to the overseer to inquire for her husband. She, of course, was in great anxiety about him. Mr. Logan threatened her severely, but she, having a little mixture of the Indian, Saxon, and African blood, was quite too keen for them. She succeeded in so far lulling their suspicions as to make her escape, and was very fortunate in her journey to her husband.

We remained but a short time after this in Ohio. I spent a few days in New York; found there a great many warm friends; and, in the autumn of 1843, I came to old Massachusetts. Since that time, I have been engaged a large part of the time in telling the story of what I have felt and seen of slavery.

I have generally found large audiences, and a great desire to hear about slavery. I have been in all the New England States except Connecticut; have held, I suppose, more than five hundred meetings in different places, sometimes two or three in a place. These meetings have been kindly noticed by many of the papers, of all parties and sects. Others have been very bitter and unjust in their remarks, and tried to throw every possible obstacle in my way. A large majority of ministers have been willing to give notice of my meetings, and many of them have attended them. I find that most ministers say they are abolitionists, but truth compels me to add, that, in talking with them, I find many are more zealous to apologize for the slave-holders, than they are to take any active measures to do away slavery.

Since coming to the free states, I have been struck with great surprise at the quiet and peaceable manner in which families live. I had no conception that *women* could live without quarrelling, till I came into the free states.

After I had been in Ohio a short time, and had not seen nor heard any scolding or quarrelling in the families where I was, I did not know how to account for it. I told Milton, one day, "What a faculty these women have of keeping all their bad feelings to themselves! I have not seen them quarrel with their husbands, nor with the girls, or children, since I have been here." "O," said Milton, "these women are not like our women in Kentucky; they don't fight at all." I told him I doubted that; "I guess they do it somewhere; in the kitchen, or down cellar. It can't be," said I, "that a woman can live, and not scold or quarrel." Milton laughed, and told me to watch them, and see if I could catch them at it. I have kept my eyes and ears open from that day to this, and I have not found the place where the women get mad and rave like they do in Kentucky yet. If they do it here, they are uncommon sly; but I have about concluded that they are altogether different here from what they are in the slave states. I reckon slavery must work upon their minds and dispositions, and make them ugly.

It has been a matter of great wonder to me, also, to see all the children, rich and poor, going to school. Every few miles I see a school-house, here; I did not know what it meant when I saw these houses, when I first came to Ohio. In Kentucky, if you should feed your horse only when you come to a schoolhouse, he would starve to death.

I never had heard a church bell only at Lexington, in my life. When I saw steeples and meeting-houses so thick, it seemed like I had got into another world. Nothing seems more wonderful to me now, than the different way they keep the Sabbath there, and here. In the country, in summer, there the people gather in groups around the meeting-house, *built of logs,* or around in the groves where they often meet; one company, and perhaps the minister with them, are talking about the price of niggers, pork, and corn; another group are playing cards; others are swapping horses, or horse-racing; all in sight of the meeting-house or place of worship. After a while the minister tells them it is time to begin. They stop playing and talking for a while. If they call him right smart, they hear him out; if he is "no account," they turn to their cards and horses, and finish their devotion in this manner.

The slaveholders are continually telling how poor the white people are in the free states, and how much they suffer from poverty; no masters to look out for them. When, therefore, I came into Ohio, and found nearly every family living in more real comfort than almost any slaveholder, you may easily see I did not know what to make of it. I see how it is now; every man in the free states *works;* and as they work for themselves, they do twice as much as they would do for another.

In fact, my wonder at the contrast between the slave and the free states has not ceased yet. The more I see here, the more I *know* slavery curses the master as well as the slave. It curses the soil, the houses, the churches, the schools, the burying-grounds, the flocks, and the herds; it curses man and beast, male and female, old and young. It curses the child in the cradle, and heaps curses upon the old man as he lies in his grave. Let all the people, then, of the civilized world get up upon Mount Ebal,[13] and curse it with a long and bitter curse, and with a loud voice, till it withers and dies; till the year of jubilee dawns upon the south, till the sun of a FREE DAY sends a beam of light and joy into every cabin.

I wish here sincerely to recognize the hand of a kind Providence in leading me from that terrible house of bondage, for raising me up friends in a land of strangers, and for leading me, as I hope, to a saving knowledge of the truth as it is in Christ. A slave cannot be sure that he will always enjoy his religion in peace. Some of them are beaten for acts of devotion. I can never express to God all the gratitude which I owe him for the many favors I now enjoy. I try to live in love with all men. Nothing would delight me more than to take the worst slaveholder by the hand, even Mrs. Banton, and freely forgive her, if I thought she had repented of her sins. While she, or any other man or woman, is trampling down the image of God, and *abusing* the life out of the poor slave, I cannot believe they are Christians, or that they ought to be allowed the Christian name for one moment. I testify against them now, as having none of the spirit of Christ. There will be a cloud of swift witnesses against them at the day of judgment. The testimony of the slave will be heard then. He has no voice at the tribunals of earthly justice, but he will one day be heard; and then such revelations will be made, as will fully justify the opinion which I have been compelled to form of slaveholders. They are a SEED of *evil-doers—corrupt* are they—they have done abominable works.

J. Milton Clarke

# NARRATIVE

OF

# MILTON CLARKE.

# PREFACE.

---

THE Narrative of LEWIS CLARKE was published a year since; and a large edition—three thousand copies—was exhausted in less than a year. There is a call for more; and MILTON CLARKE has concluded to add a few of the incidents of his life, and a more particular account of the attempt to kidnap him in Ohio. I have no doubt, that, with the slight mistakes in regard to circumstances incident to things so long kept only in memory, the following Narrative, as well as that which precedes, may be relied on as true. It is not among the least interesting of the marks of progress in the cause of Freedom, that now, from Ohio, the assistant kidnappers of Jerry Phinney[14] are calling loudly upon their principals in Kentucky to help them out of prison, where they suffer justly. This shows that neither Ohio, nor any other free state, can much longer be made the hunting-ground of the slaveholders.

J. C. L.

MAY, 1846.

# NARRATIVE OF MILTON CLARKE.

WHEN I was about six years of age, the estate of Samuel Campbell, my grand-father, was sold at auction. His sons and daughters were all present at the sale, except Mrs. Banton. Among the articles and animals put upon the catalogue, and placed in the hands of the auctioneer, were a large number of slaves. When every thing else had been disposed of, the question arose among the heirs, "What shall be done with Letty (my mother) and her children?" John and William Campbell came to mother, and told her they would divide her family among the heirs, but none of them should go out of the family. One of the daughters—to her ever-lasting honor be it spoken—remonstrated against any such proceeding. Judith, the wife of Joseph Logan, told her brothers and sisters, "Letty is our own half sister, and you know it; father never intended they should be sold." Her protest was disregarded, and the auctioneer was ordered to proceed. My mother, and her infant son Cyrus, about one year old, were put up together and sold for $500!! Sisters and brothers selling their own sister and her children!! My vener-able old father, who was now in extreme old age, and debilitated from the *wounds* received in the war of the Revolution, was, nevertheless, roused by this outrage upon his rights and upon those of his children.

"He had never expected," he said, "when fighting for the liberties of this country, to see his own wife and children sold in it to the highest bidder." But what were the entreaties of a quivering old man, in the sight of eight or ten hun-gry heirs? The bidding went on; and the whole family, consisting of mother and eight children, were sold at prices varying from $300 to $800. Lewis, the reader will recollect, had been previously given to that paragon of excellence, Mrs. Ban-ton. It was my fortune, with my mother, brother Cyrus, and sister Delia, to fall into the hands of aunt Judith; and had she lived many years, or had her husband shared with her the virtues of humanity, I should probably have had far less to complain of, for myself and some of the family. She was the only one of all the family that I was ever willing to own, or call my aunt.

The third day after the sale, father, mother, Delia, Cyrus, and myself, started for our home at Lexington, with Mr. Joseph Logan, a tanner. He was a tall, lank, gray-eyed, hard-hearted, cruel wretch; coarse, vulgar, debauched, cor-rupt and corrupting; but in good and regular standing in the Episcopalian church. We were always protected, however, from any very great hardships dur-ing the life of his first wife.

At her death, which happened in about two years, we were sincere mourn-ers; although her husband was probably indulging far other emotions than those of sorrow. He had already entered, to a considerable extent, into arrangements for marrying a younger sister of his wife, Miss Minerva Campbell. She was a half fool, besides being underwitted. If any body falls into such hands, they will know what Solomon meant, when he said, "Let a bear robbed of her whelps meet a man, rather than a *fool* in his folly."[15] There are a great many bears in Kentucky, but none of them quite equal to a slaveholding woman.

I had a regular battle with this young mistress, when I was about eleven years old. She had lived in the family while her sister was alive, and from the clemency of Judith, in protecting the slaves, the authority of Miss Minerva was in a very doubtful state when she came to be installed mistress of the house. Of course, every occasion was sought to show her authority. She attempted to give me a regular breaking-in, at the age above stated. I used the weapons of defence "God and nature gave me;" I bit and scratched, and well nigh won the battle; but she sent for Logan, whose shadow was more than six feet, and I had to join the *non-resistance* society right off. It was all day with me then. He dashed me down upon my head, took the raw hide and ploughed up my young back, and that grinning fool, his wife, was looking on; this was a great aggravation of the flogging, that she should see it and rejoice over it.

When I was about twelve years old, I was put to grinding bark in the tannery. Not understanding the business, I did not make such progress as Logan thought I ought to make. Many a severe beating was the consequence. At one time, the shoulder of the horse was very sore, and Logan complained that I did not take good care of him. I tried to defend myself as well as I could, but his final argument was thumping my head against the post. Kings have their *last* argument, and so have slaveholders. I took the old horse into the stable, and, as I had no one else to talk with, I held quite a dialogue with old Dobbin. Unluckily for me, Logan was hid in another stall, to hear his servant curse him. I told the horse, "Master complains that I don't grind bark enough; complains that I work you too hard; don't feed you enough; now, you old rascal, you know it is a lie, the whole of it; I have given you fifteen ears of corn three times a day, and that is enough for any horse; Caesar says that is enough, and Moses says that is enough; now eat your corn, and grow fat." At the end of this apostrophe, I gave the old horse three good cuts on the face, and told him to walk up and eat the corn. I then stepped out into the floor and threw in fifteen ears more, and said, "See if the old man will think that is enough."

Scarcely had the words passed my lips, when I heard a rustling in the next stall, and Joe Logan was before me, taller than ever I saw him before, and savage as a cannibal. I made for the door, but he shut it upon me, and caught me by one leg. He began kicking and cuffing, till, in my despair, I seized him, like a young bear, by the leg, with my teeth, and, with all his tearing and wrenching, he could not get me off. He called one of the white hands from the tanyard, and just as he came in, Logan had his knife out, and was about to cut my throat. The man spoke, and told him not to do that. They tied me and gave me *three hundred lashes;* my back was peeled from my shoulders to my heels.

Mother was in the house, and heard my screams, but did not dare to come near me. Logan left me weltering in my blood; mother then came and took me up, and carried me into her own room. About 8 o'clock that evening, Logan came out and asked mother if I was alive or dead. She told him I was alive. I laid there four weeks, before I went out of the door. Let fathers and mothers think what it would be to see a child whipped to the very gate of death, and not be permitted to say a word in their behalf. Words can never tell what I suffered, nor what mother suffered. I shuddered at the countenance of Joseph Logan for many months after. The recollection now makes me shudder, as I go back to that bitter day.

Such a cruel wretch could not, of course, manage with much discretion a silly, but high-tempered wife. Their social intercourse was like the meeting of the sirocco and the earthquake. She would scorch terribly with her provoking tongue; he would *shake* her terribly in his anger. Finally, he held her out at arms length and gave her the horsewhip to the tune of about thirty stripes. She hopped and danced at this, to the infinite amusement of the slaves when we were alone; of course, in their presence we were very serious. We had good reason for rejoicing in this flogging, for she was never known to prescribe raw hide for a slave after that. She soon, however, left her husband and went to live with Mrs. Anderson, where, by her cruelty, she showed her reform was only temporary.

Then began that series of bitter cruelties by which Logan attempted to subdue sister Delia to his diabolical wishes. She was, at this time, some sixteen or eighteen years of age. At first, persuasion was employed. This was soon exchanged for stripes.

One morning, I was a witness of the torture which he inflicted. Sister asked me to speak to mother; I ran and called her; she hesitated a good deal, but the shrieks of her child at length overcame every fear, and she rushed into the presence of, and began to remonstrate with, this brute. He was only the more enraged. He turned around with all the vengeance of a fury, and knocked poor mother down, and injured her severely; when I saw the blood streaming from the shoulders of my sister, and my mother knocked down, I became completely frantic, and ran and caught an axe, and intended to cut him down at a blow. My mother had recovered her feet just in time to meet me at the door. She persuaded me not to go into the spinning-room, where this whipping took place. Sister soon came out, covered with blood. Mother washed her wounds as well as she could. In six days after this, sister was chained to a gang of a hundred and sixty slaves, and sent down to New Orleans. Mother begged for her daughter; said she would get some one to buy her; a gentleman offered to do this, after she was sold to the slave-driver; but the inhuman monster was inexorable; this was the punishment threatened, if he was refused the sacrifice of her innocence.

Sister was therefore carried down the river to New Orleans, kept three or four weeks, and then put up for sale. The day before the sale, she was taken to the barber's, her hair dressed, and she was furnished with a new silk gown, and gold watch, and every thing done to set off her personal attractions, previous to the time of the bidding. The first bid was $500; then $800. The auctioneer began to extol her virtues. Then $1000 was bid. The auctioneer says, "If you only knew the *reason* why she is sold, you would give any sum for her. She is a *pious*, good girl, member of the Baptist church, *warranted* to be a virtuous girl." The bidding grew brisk. "*Twelve!*" "thirteen," "fourteen," "fifteen," "sixteen hundred," was at length bid, and she was knocked off to a Frenchman, named Coval. He wanted her to live with him as his housekeeper and mistress. This she utterly refused, unless she were emancipated and made his wife. In about one month, he took her to Mexico, emancipated, and married her. She visited France with her husband, spent a year or more there and in the West Indies. In four or five years after her marriage, her husband died, leaving her a fortune of twenty or thirty thousand dollars. A more just and remarkable reward of sterling virtue in an unprotected girl, cannot be found in all the books of romance.

But I must return to my own story. Soon after the sale of my sister, the father of Joseph Logan, Deacon Archibald Logan, purchased his estate in Lexington, and all his slaves; mother, Cyrus, and myself, among the number. I was then valued at one thousand dollars. Mother, I should rather say, was given away in her old age to old Mrs. Logan, the wife of the deacon. In three or four years after this, Joseph Logan came to the house of his father, sick with the consumption, and died. He professed to be penitent upon his death-bed, and asked forgiveness of mother and myself for all the wrong done to our family.

I was then taken by the deacon for his body servant; travelled with him, and was often supposed to be his son.

I have little complaint to make of the old man, except that he kept me a *slave.* Cyrus was put into the tanyard, and fared very differently. For some reason, the old deacon treated him with great cruelty.

In 1833, my poor mother ended her sorrows, cut off very suddenly by the cholera. Our condition was then desolate indeed. Father had died several years before. The prospect before us was interminable, lonely bondage. The thought of it sometimes drove us almost to despair. I soon began to hire my time, by the day, or week, as I could make a bargain. I was a very good bass drummer, and had learned to play on the bugle. The deacon would hire me out to play for volunteers, that were then and soon after *training* for a campaign in Texas. He received three dollars for half a day for my services. When I found this out, I sold my bugle and drum. He was very sorry I had sold them; would have bought them himself, if he had known I wanted to sell. I told him, I was tired of playing. We soon compromised the matter, however; I bought my instruments, and was to have half I earned with them. I then began to lay up money, and had a shrewd notion that I could take care of myself. I frequently heard the Declaration of Independence read; and listened with great wonder to the Texas orators, as they talked about liberty. I thought it might be as good for me as for others. I could never reason myself into the belief, that the old deacon had any right to the annual rent which I paid for my own body. I then was paying to this old miser two hundred dollars a year for my time, boarding and clothing myself. I joined a company of musicians, and we made money fast and easy by attending balls and parties.

But before leaving the deacon, I wish to give a few recollections of his family matters, to illustrate the workings of good society among slaveholders. The deacon lost his wife about the time of the death of my mother. He was an elder of the Presbyterian church, and afterwards became a deacon of a Congregational church; and there was a widow named Robb, of the same communion; a good name for the whole clan of slaveholding tyrants, male and female; they are all *robbers* of the worst kind. The good women of the deacon's acquaintance visited him, and pitied his lonely condition, and hinted, that Mrs. Robb would be a great comfort to him in his affliction.

The negotiation was commenced, and soon terminated, to the *present* satisfaction of both parties. But two old people, with habits firmly fixed, do not often, like kindred drops, mingle into one. Each one wanted to keep their household fixings for their own children.

She was younger than the deacon, more artful, and could easily outwit him. The daughters of Mr. Logan had come to the house, before the marriage, and carefully marked the bedding. The deacon gave me the keys of his rooms, and attempted to limit the freedom of his new spouse in the house of which she was installed mistress. This produced confusion and abundance of sparring. She treated *her* slaves better than she did *his,* and this set all the old servants against her. She got to the old man's closet, drank his wine, and then charged it to the slaves. We were not long in pointing out to the deacon the true channel in which his wine flowed. Her servants were frequently despatched, with buckets of sugar and coffee, to the daughters of Mrs. Logan. It was nuts[16] for us to find this out and tell the deacon. Here was new fuel for the fires of dispute that crackled every day in this habitation of the *Patriarchs.* They quarrelled openly; it was a public scandal; till, one day, his old withered hand seized the horsewhip and crowned their bliss with a dozen or two good smart lashes. The flame was all abroad, then. Many waters could not quench the *fires* of this loving pair. She left him, and her son-in-law threatened the old man's back with the cowskin.

The church interposed and called him to account. He owned up, as to the whipping; but justified, under the plea, that he afflicted the *body* for the good of the *soul.* It would not do. He bought off from his wife,[17] and she left him. The church excommunicated the deacon. He made application, very soon, for admission to a Congregational church. They would not receive him, till he made some sort of a confession. He acknowledged the fact, but plead a good motive—the benefit of her soul. He was at length received, and presently began to garner the sanctuary of oppression—a southern church. The house was soon carpeted; the pulpit was renovated, dressed in velvet; a new bell hung, and new life infused into the waning church, which had just received such an ornament to its virtues and holiness. The unlucky minister had a little bit of decency, if not of conscience left. He had opposed the whole proceeding. Educated at the north, he one day dropped some word of condemnation of the sin of oppression. This was too much for the deacon. The minister was forthwith dismissed, and a more supple tool employed. The old man could hardly be trained to the exemplary habits becoming an office-bearer of the standards of Zion. Frequent attempts were made to discipline him; but the deacon, with his great wealth, had such ascendency over the minds of his brethren, that a vote of censure or suspension could never be obtained. He lived and died in "good and regular standing," so far as came to my knowledge or belief.

The only beating that I had, after I came into the hands of Deacon Logan, was at the instigation of his son Joseph. Only about thirty lashes were put on by the public whipper, in the watch-house. I was tied, hands and feet, and whipped by the servile wretch, who does this business at a dollar a head for men—the *same* for women.

I did not witness as many scenes of cruelty among the slaves as many have; I was usually employed about the house, and was not in a situation to see what others have. One or two instances I can mention of what I personally knew of the cruelty of slaveholders. Joseph Logan had a slave, named Priscilla. She did the work in the kitchen. One morning, the biscuit came upon the table badly scorched. Mistress Minerva threw them in her face, struck her with the shovel, then heated the tongs, and took her by the nose. She raised her hand, to resist this act of wanton cruelty. Logan was called for, came out, and knocked her down with a large club; called in his men, and had her tied and beaten most unmercifully. He then put a log chain on her, and compelled her to drag it for days. She never recovered; her mind was destroyed, and she was soon after sold, for little or nothing, as an idiot.

Joseph Logan had another slave, named Peter. The wife of Peter was the slave of Thomas Kennedy, who lived forty-five miles from Lexington. Kennedy consented to sell Milly only on condition that, if she was ever resold, he should have the refusal of her. She lived with her husband till she had two children, and then her mistress, Minerva, resolved she should be sold. The tears and entreaties of her husband, the despair upon the countenance of the victim herself, were all in vain. She, with her two children, was sold to Warren Orford, one of the *soul* drivers, for twelve or thirteen hundred dollars. The husband became melancholy, sank down under his burden, turned to the intoxicating cup, and became a drunkard.

In the year 1838, I hired my time of Deacon Logan, for the purpose of going in a steamboat up and down the Ohio and Mississippi Rivers. I was at New Orleans three or four times, before I could find any thing of sister Delia. At last, through the assistance of an old acquaintance, I found where she lived. I went to the house, but I was so changed, by the growth of seven or eight years, that she did not know me. When I told her who I was, she was very incredulous; and, to test my identity, brought forward a small article of clothing, and asked me if ever I had seen it. I told her it once belonged to mother. "Ah! then," she said, "you must be my brother." She was very glad to see me, and hear from her brothers and sisters.

The next summer, she visited Kentucky with me, and spent two or three months. Deacon Logan treated her with great politeness; said his son did very wrong to sell her as he did; that, if he had then owned the family, it should not have been done. While in Kentucky, she advanced the money, in part, to pay for the freedom of Dennis, and, as soon as she returned to New Orleans, she sent up the balance.

She also made arrangements with Deacon Logan, to purchase brother Cyrus and myself for sixteen hundred dollars.

In the autumn of 1840, I started to go to New Orleans, to get the money to pay for Cyrus and myself. When I arrived at Louisville, I met the sorrowful tidings that sister was dead! This was a sudden, withering blast of all my well-founded hopes of deliverance from slavery. The same letter that brought the tidings of her death also informed me that she had left her property, by will, to me, for the purpose of buying myself, and all the family, from bondage. I was now told that, if I went down and took the property, my master could claim and take the whole of it. I went directly back to Lexington, and asked Mr. Logan to make me free, and I would pay him a thousand dollars, the first money that I received from the estate of my sister. This he said he would not do; but he gave me a free paper, to pass up and down the river as I pleased, and to transact any business as though I was free. With this paper, I started for New Orleans, but could get no more than sixty dollars and a suit of clothes. The person with whom it was left, said it was in real estate, and he had no authority to sell it. I then began to think that the day of my freedom was a great way off. I concluded, with a great many other persons in desperate circumstances, to go to Texas. I took boat for Galveston. Here it looked worse than slavery, if any thing can be worse. I soon returned, and came up to Louisville. Here I met three slaves of Doctor Graham, of Harrodsburg, Kentucky. Their names were Henry, Reuben, and George; all smart, fine fellows, good musicians, and yielding the doctor a handsome income. In the same company were three others, all of the same craft.

"Now," said I, "boys, is the time to strike for liberty. I go for Ohio tomorrow. What say you?" They pondered the question, and we all determined to start, as a company of musicians, to attend a great *ball* in Cincinnati—and, sure enough, it was the grandest ball we ever played for. We came to Cincinnati, and the friends there advised us to go farther north. Doctor Graham's boys struck for Canada, while I stopped at Oberlin, Ohio. It was well they did, for the doctor was close upon them, offering a large reward. He reached Detroit within a few hours after they had crossed the ice to Malden. He attempted to hire some one to go over, and capture them; no one would attempt this. He hired a man, at last, to go over and hire them to get on a boat, and go to Toledo, to play for a ball. Doctor Graham was to be in the boat, when it touched at Malden. For some reason, the boys were quite cautious, and very reluctant to go. When the wolf in sheep's clothing offered them five hundred dollars to go and play for one ball, they were more suspicious than ever. When the boat touched at the wharf, the boys were on the wharf, playing a gypsy waltz, a great favorite of Doctor Graham's. When the doctor found his plan did not work, sure enough, he came out to hear his favorite singers. He landed, and spent several days in fruitless endeavors to persuade them to return to Kentucky. They still persist in preferring a monarchy to the *patriarchal* form of government.

While at Oberlin, there was an attempt to capture a Mr. Johnson and his wife, residents in that place. They had once, to be sure, had a more southern home; but they believed the world was free for them to choose a home in, as well as for others. Johnson worked in a blacksmith's shop, with another man. To this individual he confided the name and place of the robber who had claimed him in Ohio. This wretch went to another, blacker-hearted one, named *Benedict,* of Illyria. Let no mother ever use that name again for her new-born son. It was disgraced enough by Benedict Arnold—it should, with him, be covered in oblivion. But this lawyer, Benedict of Illyria, has made the infamy around that name thicker and blacker than it was before. He wrote to the pretended owner of Johnson where he could be found. In hot haste he came; but, thanks to an honest justice, his evidence was not sufficient. He returned for better testimony; as he came back, he was suddenly grasped by the hand of death, and died within ten miles of Oberlin, with an oath upon his lips. Johnson and his wife broke jail, and were carried forward to Canada. There were a great many forwarding houses in Ohio at that time; they have greatly increased since, and nearly all of them are doing a first-rate business.

During the summer of 1841, the emigration to Canada, through Oberlin, was very large. I had the pleasure of giving the "right hand of fellowship" to a goodly number of my former acquaintances and fellow-sufferers. The masters accused me of *stealing* several of them. This is a great lie. I never stole one in my life. I have assisted several to get into possession of the true owner, but I never assisted any man to steal another away from himself. God has given every man the true title-deed to himself, written upon his face. It cannot be blotted entirely out. The slaveholders try hard to do it, but it can yet be read; all other titles are shams and forgeries. Among others, I assisted a Mrs. Swift, and her two children, to get over to Canada, where they can read titles more clearly than they do in some of the states. This was brought up as a heavy charge against me by Mr. Postlewaite, the illustrious catchpole of the slaveholders.

In the autumn of this year, I was delighted to meet brother Lewis at Oberlin. The happiness which we both experienced at meeting each other, as we supposed, securely free, in a free state, may be well imagined.

In 1842, there were nine slaves reached Oberlin by one arrival, all from one plantation. A Mr. Benningale, of Kentucky, was close upon them, impiously claiming that he had property in these images of God; ay, that they were *property*, and entirely his, to all intents and purposes. This is not the doctrine taught by a great many good men in Ohio. These men came to Oberlin. The next day, Benningale arrived. He lined the lake with watchmen. Benedict (do, printers, put that name in *black* type, if you can) of Illyria was on the alert; thirty pieces of silver were always the full price of innocent blood with him. Benningale, finding they were hid in the village, threatened to burn the town. The colored people were on guard all night. They met two persons, whom they suspected as spies of the kidnappers. They told them, if they caught them out again, they should be hung right up, as spies against liberty. The fugitives were at length put into a wagon, carried to the lake, and shipped for Canada. The pursuers offered a thousand dollars for their arrest. No one was found sufficiently enterprising to claim the reward. They landed safe upon the other side. Soon after this, there were seven more slaves arrived at Oberlin. The miserable Benedict, assisted by the Chapmans, set their traps around the village. Seven hundred dollars reward was offered for their arrest. Power of attorney had been sent on to the traitor Benedict. The slaves were kept concealed, till, as in the case of Moses, it was no longer safe for them. There were six men and one woman in the company. A plan was contrived to put the kidnappers upon a false scent. Six colored men were selected to personate the men, and I was dressed in female attire, to be passed off for the woman. A telltale was informed that the slaves would start for the lake at such a time, and go in a certain direction. He was solemnly enjoined not to tell a word of it. Those who knew him understood what he would do. The secret was too precious for him to keep. He ran right to Benedict with it. We left Oberlin in one direction, and the real objects of pursuit started, soon after, upon another road. The *ruse* took; Benedict and Company were in full pursuit, with sheriff, writ, and all the implements of kidnapping. We selected one of our number, George Perry, to act as spokesman for the gang. Just as we arrived at the village of Illyria, eight miles from Oberlin, Benedict and Company surrounded our carriage, and ordered the driver to stop. Platt, the driver, challenged his authority. Benedict pulled out his advertisement, six men and one woman, with the description of their persons. Platt told him he thought they were not the persons he was after. The traitor affirmed he knew they were. The driver turned to his passengers, and said he could do no more for them. George then began to play his part: "Well, 'den, 'dis nigger must get out." We accordingly left the carriage, and were conducted into the tavern. In the tavern were two travellers, who were very inquisitive. "Where are you from?" George answered, "Don't care where I from." Benedict, when he began to suspect that all was not exactly right, came up to me for a more minute examination of my person. I had kept my head and face under my hood and cloak. He ordered me to hold up my head. George says, "Let 'dat gal alone, Mr. white man; de nigger gal plague enough in slave state—you just let her alone, here, if you please." One of the travellers called for cider; George stepped up and drank it for him. The table was furnished for some of the guests, and George, without any ceremony, declared "'Dis nigger hungry," and swept the table for himself and comrades. The landlord threatened to flog him. The colored men all spoke up together, "You strike 'dat nigger if you dare." At last, they got a justice of the peace; but he had been let into the whole secret. Benedict began his plea; produced his evidence; said that ungrateful girl (pointing to me) had left a kind mistress, right in the midst of a large ironing!!! The justice finally said, he did not see but he must give us up to Mr. Benedict as slaves, fugitives from service. Our friends then gave the signal, and I threw off my bonnet and cloak, and stood up a man. Such a shout as the spectators raised would do the heart of freedom good. "Why, your woman has turned into a man, Mr. Benedict." "It may be these others, that appear to be men, are all women." Benedict saw through the plot, and took his saddle without any rejoinder to his plea. The tavern-keeper ordered us out of the house, and we took carriage for Oberlin. Meanwhile the real objects of pursuit were sailing on the waters of the blue lake.

Benedict was terribly angry at me. He swore he would have me captured. He wrote immediately to Deacon Logan, that no slaves could be captured there while Milton Clarke was at large.

The slaveholders of Lexington had a meeting, and determined to send a Mr. Postlewaite, a crack slavebreaker, and a Mr. M'Gowan, after me. They came and lingered about Oberlin, watching their opportunity. They engaged two wretches named Chapman, of Illyria, to assist in the capture. Brother Lewis and I went up to Madison, Lake county, to spend a few days. We had a meeting on Sabbath evening, at which we addressed the people. There was a traitor there named Warner, from Lexington, who told Postlewaite where we were. Monday morning, my brother and myself rode up to Dr. Merriam's, accompanied by two or three of Mr. Winchester's family, with whom we had spent the Sabbath. I sat a few minutes in the carriage; and a little girl out of health, the niece of Dr. Merriam, and his own daughter, came out and wanted to ride. I took them in, and had not driven a mile when a close carriage overtook and passed me, wheeled right across the road, and four men leaped out of it and seized my horse. I had no conjecture who they were. I asked them what they wanted—"if money, I have only fifty cents in the world; you are welcome to that." "We want not *money,* but *you!*" The truth then flashed upon my mind in a moment—"They are kidnappers."

I jumped from the carriage for the purpose of running for life. My foot slipped, and I fell. In a moment, four men were upon me. They thrust my head down upon the ground, bound me hand and foot, put me into the carriage, and started for Judge Page's; a judge prepared beforehand for their purposes. Soon after we started, we met a man in the road. I spoke to him, and asked him to take care of the girls in the buggy, and to tell Lewis the kidnappers from Kentucky had got me. Postlewaite and M'Gowan took off my hat, and gave me a beating upon the head. One of the Chapmans spoke and said, "Now we have got you, my good fellow; you are the chap that has enticed away so many slaves; we will take care of you; we will have Lewis soon." They then took me to Mr. Judge Page. The sheriff of the county was there. He asked me what I had done, that they had tied me up so close. "Have you murdered any body?" I said, "No." "Have you been stealing?" "No, sir." "What have you done?" "Nothing, sir." "What have they tied you for, then?" Postlewaite told him it was none of his business. The sheriff said it was his business, and, "if he has committed no crime, you must untie him." He then came up to take off the cords from me. Postlewaite drew his pistols, and threatened to shoot him. Judge Page told the sheriff he had better not touch the gentleman's *property*. The sheriff said he would see whose property he was. By this time the alarm was spread, and a large company had gathered around the tavern. The sheriff told the people to see that that man was not removed till he came back. He went out, and summoned the posse of farmers in every direction. They left their ploughs, and jumped upon their horses, with the collars yet on their necks, and rode with all speed for the scene of action. "The kidnappers had got the white nigger," was the watchword.

Postlewaite began to be alarmed. He asked Mr. Page which was the best way for him to go. Could he go safely to the lake, and take a steamboat for Cleveland? "Why, no, the abolitionists watch all the landing-places." Could he go to Painesville? "Why, no, General Paine,[18] a red-hot abolitionist, is there." Postlewaite asked for a place to take me, where I should be secure. They carried me to the counting room of the judge. They then began to coax. The judge said, "You better go back, Clarke, willingly; it will be better for you, when you get there." "Did not your master treat you well?" asked the very gracious Mr. Postlewaite. "Yes," I said, "he treated me well; no fault to find with him on that score." "What did you run away for, then?" "I came, sir, to get my freedom. I offered him eight hundred dollars for my liberty, and he would not take it. I had paid him about that much for my time, and I thought I might as well have what I earned, as to pay it to him." "Well, sir, if you had come off alone, the deacon would not have cared so much about it; but you led others off; and now we are going to carry you back, and whip you, on the public square in Lexington."

The judge had appointed three o'clock in the afternoon for my trial, as my friends said they wished to procure evidence that I came away with the consent of Deacon Logan. In the mean time, Postlewaite & Co. were full of joy at their success, and despatched a letter to Lexington, announcing the capture of Milton Clarke, and assuring their friends there, that they should have Lewis before sundown. "We shall be in Lexington with them about Thursday or Friday." This was great news to the deacon and his friends; but, alas for them, the result was not exactly to answer to the expectation. They assembled in great numbers on both days, as I have been told, and watched, with eager interest, the arrival of the stage; but no Clarke, and no Postlewaite, were in it. Many a triumph has been enjoyed only in anticipation.

Dinner came on, at length, and I was moved back into the tavern. Postlewaite had a rope around me, which he kept in his hand all the time. They called for dinner for six—the driver and myself among the number. When they sat down, I was placed at a short distance from the table. The landlady asked if I was not to sit down. Postlewaite said, no nigger should sit at table with him. She belabored him in good womanly style; told him he was a thief, and a scoundrel, and that, if she was a *man,* he should never carry me away. The people were gathered, all this time, around the windows, and in the road, discussing the matter, and getting up the steam, to meet the Kentucky bowie knives and pistols. Postlewaite sent out, and got a man to come in and watch me, while he eat his dinner. The people at the windows were preparing to take me out. He watched the movement, and had me brought up nearer to the table.

At three o'clock, my trial came on. My friends claimed, that I should have a trial as a *white* man. Robert Harper plead for the oppressors, assisted by another, whose name is unknown to me. For me, lawyer Chase,[19] and another, appeared. To these gentlemen, and all others, who were friendly to me on this occasion, I feel an obligation which I can never express. It was to me, indeed, a dark hour, and they were friends in time of need. General Paine arrived about the commencement of the trial, and presented a firm front to the tyrants. My lawyer asked by what law they claimed me. They said, under the black law of Ohio. The reply was, that I was not a black man. Postlewaite said he arrested me, as the property of Archibald Logan, under the article of the constitution, that persons *"owing service,"* and fleeing from one state to another, shall be given up to the person to whom such service is due. He then read the power of attorney, from Deacon Logan to him, authorizing him to seize one Milton Clarke—describing me as a person five feet two and a half inches tall, probably trying to pass myself off as white. "His hair is straight, but curls a little at the lower end." After reading this, he read his other papers, showing that I was the slave of Logan. He produced a bill of sale, from Joseph to Deacon Logan. He then asked me if I had not lived, for several years, with Deacon Logan. General Paine said, if I spoke at all, I might tell the whole story—that I had a free pass to go where I chose, (and this was the fact.) The suggestion of General Paine frightened Postlewaite; he told me to shut up my jaws, or he would smash my face in for me. The people cried out, "Touch him if you dare; we will string you up, short metre." He then said to me, "D—n you; we will pay you for all this, when we get home." The anxiety on my part, by this time, was beyond any thing I ever felt in my life. I sometimes hoped the people would rescue me, and then feared they would not. Many of them showed sympathy in their countenances, and I could see that the savageism of Postlewaite greatly increased it. My lawyer then asked, for what I *owed* service to Deacon Logan; told Harper & Co., if Mr. Clarke owed the deacon, present his bill, and, if it is a reasonable one, his friends will pay it. He then asked me if I owed Deacon Logan, of Kentucky. I told him no—the deacon owed me about eight hundred dollars; I owed him nothing. Postlewaite said, then, he arrested me as the *goods* and *chattels* of Logan. Mr. Chase said, "Mr. Clarke had permission to come into the free states." "Yes," said Postlewaite, "but not to *stay* so long." Finally, Mr. Chase asked, "Where did Joseph Logan get *his* right to Clarke?" On this point, he had no specific evidence. He then resorted to the general testimony of several letters, which he took from his pocket. One was from General Coombs, another from McCauly, one from John Crittenden, one from Morehead, Governor Lecher, John Speed Smith, and, last of all, from HENRY CLAY.[20] These gentlemen all represented Mr. Postlewaite as a most *pious* and excellent man, whose word was to be taken in every thing; stating, also, that they knew Milton Clarke, and that he was the property of Deacon A. Logan. This array of names closed the testimony. Bob Harper then made his infamous plea; said, finally, the judge could possibly do no otherwise than give me up, on the testimony of so many great names. Judge Page had received his fee, as I verily believe, before he gave judgment; and he very soon came to the conclusion, that Deacon Logan had proved his claim. I was delivered over to the tender mercies of Postlewaite & Co. Just as we were going out at the door, the sheriff met us, and arrested Postlewaite, McGowan, and the Chapmans, for assault and battery on the person of Milton Clarke. They were told, their trial would come on the next day, at ten o'clock, before Justice Cunningham. Postlewaite swore terribly at this; said it was an abolition concern. Some one asked the sheriff what should be done with me. He said he did not want me—it was the others that he had arrested. I was then tied to Postlewaite. Some one said, "Cut him loose." Postlewaite replied, "The first that attempts to touch him, I will blow him through." I asked the people if I should be carried back, as I had committed no crime. They said, "No, no; never." General Paine said he would call out the militia, before I should be carried back.

Postlewaite ordered out his carriage, to accompany the sheriff. He drove me into it, came in with his partners, McGowan and the Chapmans, and Judge Page. We then started for Unionville, distant about two miles from Centreville. A very great crowd followed us, on every side. My friends had not been idle; they had been over to Jeffersonville, in Ashtabula county, and obtained a writ of Habeas Corpus for me. Unionville was upon the border of *two* counties. The road through it divided them. The people had fixed their carriages so that ours must pass upon the Ashtabula side. Soon as the wheels passed the border of this county, the carriage was stopped, and the sheriff of Ashtabula demanded the body of Milton Clarke. The people shouted, came up and unhitched the horses, and turned them face to the carriage. Postlewaite cried out, "Drive on." Driver replied, "The horses are faced about." P. began to be very angry. The people asked the driver what he was there for, assisting in such business as this. The poor fellow begged they would not harm his horses; he did not know what they wanted him for, or he never would have come. He begged for his horses, and himself. Postlewaite said, if they meddled with the horses, he would shoot a hundred of them. The people told him, if he put his head out of that carriage, he would never shoot again. At this stage of the business, Robert Harper, Esq., came up, to read the riot act. The people were acting under a charter broader and older than any statutes passed on earth. Harper was glad to escape himself, or justice would have speedily been meted out to him. The friends came up to the carriage, and told me not to be alarmed; they would have me, at any rate. Among others in the crowd, was a huge Buckeye blacksmith, six feet tall. At first, he took sides with the thieves; said he wanted no niggers there. My friends told him to come up to the carriage, and pick out the nigger, if there was any there. He came, and looked into the carriage some time, and at last, pointing to Postlewaite, said, "That is the nigger." The chivalric Mr. P. told him no man called him nigger with impunity. The Buckeye insisted upon it he was the nigger. P. told him he lied, three times. The northern lion was waked up, and he slapped the armed knight in the face. Postlewaite drew his bowie knife, and threatened to cut him. The Ohioan asked him what it was. He said, a bowie knife. "What are you going to do with it?" "Put it into you, if you put your head in here again." "Ay, ay, you are going to booy me, are you? Then I'll booy you." He ran to the fence, and seized a sharp rail, and said he was going to booy, too. The sheriff, that had the writ to take me, let down the steps; and the people called out, "Let us kill them." The man armed with the rail, began to beat the door, and told them to let me out. General Paine spoke, and urged the multitude not to proceed to violence. Judge Page began to feel quite uneasy, in his new position. He exhorted me to keep still, or they would kill us all. The sheriff then gave Postlewaite and Company five minutes' time to release me, or take the consequences; said the carriage would be demolished in two minutes, when he spoke the word to the people. The pistols and bowie knives were quietly put away, and the tone of the stationary passengers, inside the carriage, very suddenly changed. Judge Page said, "Better let Clarke get out; they will kill us, if you don't." The cowardly Chapmans began to plead for mercy: "You can't say that we touched you, Clarke." "Yes you did," I told them; "you all jumped on me at once." The people became more and more clamorous outside the carriage—those inside more and more uneasy. They at length were more eager to get rid of me than they ever had been to catch me. "Get out; get out, Clarke," rung round on every side of me.

Soon as my feet touched the ground, the rope was cut, and once more I felt free. I was hurried into a wagon, and, under the care of the sheriff, driven off toward Austinburg, while the other sheriff took the kidnappers in another direction into Lake county. They soon stopped to give me something to eat; but I had no appetite for food, either then or for a week afterwards.

Postlewaite hired a man to follow and watch me. But my friends soon contrived to put him on a false scent. It was now dark, and I exchanged seats with a Mr. Winchester, and the watch-dog soon found he was on the wrong trail. The sheriff that had me in keeping was not very careful of his charge, and he soon lost all knowledge of my whereabouts. I was concealed for two or three days at Austinburg, as lonely as mortal man could well be. One night I went out and slept upon the haystack in the field, fearing they might search the house. The man who owned it came next day to Mr. Austin's, where I stopped, to know if it was so; said, if he had known that a nigger slept there, he would have burned the hay and him all up together. "Let him go back, where he belongs."

He then turned to me, and asked me if I had seen that nigger. I told him I had; I knew him very well. Mr. Austin asked him what he would say, if they should come and attempt to take me into slavery; why, said he, "I would shoot them." His philanthropy was graduated, like many others, upon nothing more substantial than color.

In a few days I had the pleasure to learn that Postlewaite and Company, after a trial before Mr. Cunningham, had returned to Kentucky. I have since been told they crept into the city of Lexington as silently as possible; that they left the stage before it entered the city, and went in under the shade of night. When they were visible, the inquiries were thick and fast, "Where are the Clarkes? What have you done with the Clarkes?"

Both the little girls in the carriage when I left it were thrown out, and one so injured that she never recovered. She died in a few days.

The citizens called a meeting at Austinburg, and Lewis and I began to lecture on the subject of slavery. From that time to the present, we have had more calls for meetings than we could attend. We have been in eight different states, and hundreds of thousands have listened with interest to the story of our wrongs, and the wrongs of our countrymen in bonds. If God spares our lives, we hope to see the day when the trump of jubilee shall sound, and liberty shall be proclaimed throughout the land to all the inhabitants thereof.

# APPENDIX.

## A SKETCH OF THE CLARKE FAMILY.

### BY LEWIS CLARKE.

MY mother was called a very handsome woman. She was very much esteemed by all who knew her; the slaves looked up to her for advice. She died, much lamented, of the cholera, in the year 1833. I was not at home, and had not even the melancholy pleasure of following her to her grave.

1. The name of the oldest member of the family was Archy. He never enjoyed very good health, but was a man of great ingenuity, and very much beloved by all his associates, colored and white. Through his own exertions, and the kindness of C. M. Clay, and one or two other friends, he procured his freedom. He lived to repay Mr. Clay and others the money advanced for him, but not long enough to enjoy for many years the freedom for which he had struggled so hard. He paid six hundred dollars for himself. He died about seven years since, leaving a wife and four or five children in bondage; the inheritance of the widow and poor orphans is, LABOR WITHOUT WAGES; WRONGS WITH NO REDRESS; SEPARATION FROM EACH OTHER FOR LIFE, and no being to hear their complaint, but that God who is the *widow's God and Judge*. "Shall I not be avenged on such a nation as this?"[21]

2. Sister Christiana was next to Archy in age. She was first married to a free colored man. By him she had several children. Her master did not like this connection, and her husband was driven away, and told never to be seen there again. The name of her master is Oliver Anderson; he is a leading man in the Presbyterian church, and is considered one of the best among slaveholders. Mr. Anderson married Polly Campbell, at the time I was given to Mrs. Betsey Banton. I believe she and Mrs. Banton have not spoken together since they divided the slaves at the death of their father. They are the only two sisters now living of the Campbell family.

3. Dennis is the third member of our family. He is a free man in Kentucky, and is doing a very good business there. He was assisted by a Mr. William L. Stevenson, and also by his sister, in getting his freedom. He never had any knowledge of our intention of running away, nor did he assist us in any manner whatever.

4. Alexander is the fourth child of my mother. He is the slave of a Dr. Richardson; has with him a very easy time; lives as well as a man can and be a slave; has no intention of running away. He lives very much like a second-hand gentleman, and I do not know as he would leave Kentucky on any condition.

5. My mother lost her fifth child soon after it was born.

6. Delia came next. Hers was a most bitter and tragical history. She was so unfortunate as to be uncommonly handsome, and, when arrived at woman's estate, was considered a great prize for the guilty passions of the slaveholders.

7. To No. 7 I, Lewis Clarke, respond, and of me you have heard enough already.

8. Milton comes next, and he is speaking for himself. He is almost constantly engaged in giving lectures upon the subject of slavery; has more calls usually than he can attend to.

9. Manda, the ninth child, died when she was about fifteen or sixteen years of age. She suffered a good deal from Joseph Logan's second wife.

10. Cyrus is the youngest of the family, and lives at Hamilton, New York.

---

## QUESTIONS AND ANSWERS.

### BY LEWIS CLARKE.

THE following questions are often asked me, when I meet the people in public, and I have thought it would be well to put down the answers here.

*How many holidays in a year do the slaves in Kentucky have?*—They usually have six days at Christmas, and two or three others in the course of the year. Public opinion generally seems to require this much of slaveholders; a few give more, some less; some *none*, not a day nor an hour.

*How do slaves spend the Sabbath?*—Every way the master pleases. There are certain kinds of work which are respectable for Sabbath day. Slaves are often sent out to salt the cattle, collect and count the pigs and sheep, mend fences, drive the stock from one pasture to another. Breaking young horses and mules, to send them to market, yoking young oxen, and training them, is proper Sabbath work; piling and burning brush, on the back part of the lot, grubbing brier patches that are out of the way, and where they will not be seen. Sometimes corn must be shelled in the corn-crib; hemp is baled in the hemp-house. The still-house must be attended on the Sabbath. In these, and various other such like employments, the more avaricious slave-holders keep their slaves busy a good part of every Sabbath. It is a great day for visiting and eating, and the house servants often have more to do on that than on any other day.

*What if strangers come along, and see you at work?*—We must quit shelling corn, and go to play with the cobs; or else we must be clearing land, on our own account. We must cover up master's sins as much as possible, and take it all to ourselves. It is hardly fair; for he ought rather to account for our sins, than we for his.

*Why did you not learn to read?*—I did not *dare* to learn. I attempted to spell some words when a child. One of the children of Mrs. Banton went in, and told her that she heard Lewis spelling. Mrs. B. jumped up as though she had been shot. "Let me ever know you to spell another word, I'll take your *heart* right out of you." I had a strong desire to learn. But it would not do to have slaves learn to read and write. They could read the guide-boards. They could write passes for each other. They cannot leave the plantation on the Sabbath without a written pass.

*What proportion of slaves attend church on the Sabbath?*—In the country, not *more* than *one in ten on an average*.

*How many slaves have you ever known that could read?*—I never saw more than three or four that could properly read at all. I never saw but one that could write.

*What do slaves know about the Bible?*—They generally believe there is somewhere a real Bible, that came from God; but they frequently say the Bible now used is master's Bible; most that they hear from it being, "Servants, obey your masters."

*Are families often separated? How many such cases have you personally known?*—*I never knew a whole family to live together till all were grown up, in my life.* There is almost always, in every family, some one or more keen and bright, or else sullen and stubborn slave, whose influence they are afraid of on the rest of the family, and such a one must take a walking ticket to the south.

There are other causes of separation. The death of a large owner is the occasion usually of many families being broken up. Bankruptcy is another cause of separation, and the hard-heartedness of a majority of slaveholders another and a more fruitful cause than either or all the rest. *Generally* there is but little more scruple about separating families than there is with a man who keeps sheep in selling off the lambs in the fall. On one plantation where I lived, there was an old slave named Paris. He was from fifty to sixty years old, and a very honest and apparently pious slave. A slave-trader came along one day, gathering hands for the south. The old master ordered the waiter or coachman to take Paris into the back room, *pluck out all his gray hairs*, rub his face with a greasy towel, and then had him brought forward and sold for a *young* man. His wife consented to go with him, upon a promise from the trader that they should be sold together, with their youngest child, which she carried in her arms. They left two behind them, who were only from four to six or eight years of age. The speculator collected his drove, started for the market, and, before he left the state, he *sold that infant child* to pay one of his tavern bills, and took the balance in cash. This was the news which came back to us, and was never disputed.

I saw one slave mother, named Lucy, with seven children, put up by an administrator for sale. At first the mother and three small children were put up together. The purchasers objected: one says, "I want the woman and the babe, but not the other children;" another says, "I want that little girl;" and another, "I want the boy." "Well," says the administrator, "I must let you have them to the best advantage." So the children were taken away; the mother and infant were first sold, then child after child—the mother looking on in perfect agony; and as one child after another came down from the auction block, they would run and cling, weeping, to her clothes. The poor mother stood, till nature gave way; she fainted and fell, with her child in her arms. The only sympathy she received from most of the hard-hearted monsters, who had riven her heart-strings asunder, was, "She is a d—d deceitful bitch; I wish she was mine; I would teach her better than to cut up such shines as that here." When she came to, she moaned wofully, and prayed that she might die, to be relieved from her sufferings.

I knew another slave, named Nathan, who had a slave woman for a wife. She was killed by hard usage. Nathan then declared he would never have another slave wife. He selected a free woman for a companion. His master opposed it violently. But Nathan persevered in his choice, and in consequence was sold to go down south. He returned once to see his wife, and she soon after died of grief and disappointment. On his return south, he leaped from the boat, and attempted to swim ashore; his master, on board the boat, took a gun and deliberately shot him, and he drifted down the current of the river.

On this subject of separation of families, I must plant one more rose in the garland that I have already tied upon the brow of the sweet Mrs. Banton. The reader cannot have forgotten her; and in the delectable business of tearing families asunder, she, of course, would have a hand. A slave by the name of Susan was taken by Mrs. Banton on mortgage. She had been well treated where she was brought up, had a husband, and they were very happy together. Susan mourned in bitterness over her separation, and pined away under the cruel hand of Mrs. Banton. At length she ran away, and hid herself in the neighborhood of her husband. When this came to the knowledge of Mrs. B., she charged her husband to go for "Suke," and never let her see his face unless she was with him. "No," said she, "if you are offered a double price, don't you take it. I want my satisfaction out of her, and then you may sell her as soon as you please." Susan was brought back in fetters, and Mr. and Mrs. B. both took their *satisfaction;* they beat and tortured poor Susan till her premature offspring perished, and she almost sank beneath their merciless hands, and then they sold her to be carried a hundred miles farther away from her husband. Ah! slavery is like running the dissecting knife around the heart, among all the tender fibres of our being.

A man by the name of Bill Myers, in Kentucky, went to a large number of auctions, and purchased women about forty years old, with their youngest children in their arms. As they are about to cease bearing at that age, they are sold cheap. The children he took and shut up in a log pen, and set some old worn-out slave women to make broth and feed them. The mothers he gathered in a large drove, and carried them south and sold them. He was detained there for months longer than he expected; and, winter coming on, and no proper provision having been made for the children, many of them perished with cold and hunger, some were frostbitten, and all were emaciated to skeletons. This was the only attempt that I ever knew for gathering young children together, like a litter of pigs, to be raised for the market. The success was not such as to warrant a repetition on the part of Myers.

Jockey Billy Barnett had a slave-prison, where he gathered his droves of husbands, fathers, and wives, separated from their friends: and he tried to keep up their spirits by employing one or two fiddlers to play for them, while they danced over and upon the torn-off fibres of their hearts. Several women were known to have died in that worse than Calcutta Black Hole of grief. They mourned for their children, and would not be comforted, because they were not.

*How are the slave cabins usually built?*—They are made of small logs, about from ten to twenty feet square. The roof is covered with splits, and *dirt* is thrown in to raise the bottom, and then it is beat down hard for a floor. The chimneys are made of cut sticks and clay. In the corners, or at the sides, there are pens made, filled with straw, for sleeping. Very commonly, two or three families are huddled together in one cabin, and in cold weather they sleep together promiscuously, old and young. Some few families are indulged in the privilege of having a few hens or ducks around them; but this is not very common.

*What amount of food do slaves have in Kentucky?*—They are not put on allowance; they generally have enough of corn bread; and meat and soup are dealt to them occasionally.

*What is the clothing of a slave for a year?*—For summer, he has usually a pair of tow and linen pants, and two shirts of the same material. He has a pair of shoes, a pair of woolsey pants, and a round jacket for winter.

The account current of a slave with his master stands about thus:—

ICHABOD LIVE-WITHOUT-WORK, *in account with*
JOHN WORK-WITHOUT-PAY.
Dr.[22]

To one man's work, one year, ............................. $100 00

*Contra,* Cr.[23]

By 13 bushels of corn meal, at 10 cents, .................. $1 30
"100 lbs. mean bacon and pork, at 1½ cents, .............. 1 50
"Chickens, pigs, &c., taken without leave, say, ............ 1 50
"9 yds. of tow and linen, for shirts and pants, at 12½ cents, ... 1 12½
"1 pair of shoes, ..................................... 1 50
"Cloth for jacket and winter pants, 5½ yds., at 2 shillings, .... 1 84
"Making clothes, ..................................... 1 00
"1 Blanket, ......................................... 1 00
"2 Hats or caps, ..................................... 75
——$11 51½

"Balance due the slave every year, .......................... $88 48½

The account stands unbalanced thus till the great day of reckoning comes.

Now, allow that one half of the slaves are capable of labor; that they can earn, on an average, one half the sum above named; that would give us $50 a year for 1,500,000 slaves, which would be *seventy-five millions* as *the sum robbed* from the slaves every year!! "Woe unto him that useth his neighbor's service without wages!"[24] Woe unto him that buildeth his house by iniquity, "for the stone shall cry out of the wall, and the beam out of the timber shall answer it!"[25] "Behold, the hire of the laborers, who have reaped down your fields, which is of you kept back by fraud, crieth; and the cries of them which have reaped are entered into the ears of the Lord of Sabaoth. Ye have lived in pleasure on the earth, and been wanton; ye have *nourished your hearts, as in a day of slaughter.*"[26]

*Have you ever known a slave mother to kill her own children?*—There was a slave mother near where I lived, who took her child into the cellar and killed it. She did it to prevent being separated from her child. Another slave mother took her three children and threw them into a well, and then jumped in with them, and they were all drowned. Other instances I have frequently heard of. At the death of many and many a slave child, I have seen the two feelings struggling in the bosom of a mother—joy, that it was beyond the reach of the slave monsters, and the natural grief of a mother over her child. In the presence of the master, grief seems to predominate; when away from them, they rejoice that there is one whom the slave-driver will never torment.

*How is it that masters* KILL *their slaves, when they are worth so much money?*—They do it to gratify passion; this must be done, cost what it may. Some say a man will not kill a horse worth a hundred dollars, much less a slave worth several hundred dollars. A horse has no such *will* of his own, as the slave has; he does not provoke the man, as a slave does. The master knows there is *contrivance* with the slave to outwit him; the horse has no such contrivance. This conflict of the *two* WILLS is what makes the master so much more passionate with his slave than with a horse. A slaveholder must be master on the plantation, or he knows the *example* would destroy all authority.

*What do they do with old slaves, who are past labor?*—Contrive all ways to keep them at work till the last hour of life. Make them shell corn and pack tobacco. They hunt and drive them as long as there is any life in them. Sometimes they turn them out to do the best they can, or die. One man, on moving to Missouri, sold an old slave for one dollar, to a man not worth a cent. The old slave was turned out to do the best he could; he fought with age and starvation a while, but was soon found, one morning, *starved* to death, out of doors, and half eaten up by animals. I have known several cases where slaves were left to starve to death in old age. Generally, they sell them south, and let them die there; send them, I mean, before they get very old.

*What makes them wash slaves in salt and water after they whip them?*—For two reasons; one is to make them smart, and another to prevent mortification in the lacerated flesh. I have seen men and women both washed after they had been cruelly beaten. *I have done it with my own hands.* It was the hardest work I ever did. The flesh would crawl, and creep, and quiver, under my hands. This slave's name was Tom. He had not started his team Sunday morning early enough. The neighbors *saw* that Mr. Banton had work done on the Sabbath. Dalton, the overseer, attempted to whip him. Tom knocked him down and trod on him, and then ran away. The patrols caught him, and he was whipped—*three hundred* lashes. Such a back I never saw; such work I pray that I may never do again.

*Do not slaves often say that they love their masters very much?*—Say so? yes, certainly. And this loving master and mistress is the hardest work that slaves have to do. When any stranger is present, we have to love them very much. When master is sick, we are in great trouble. Every night the slaves gather around the house, and send up one or two to see how master does. They creep up to the bed, and with a very soft voice, inquire, "How is dear massa? O massa, how we want to hear your voice out in the field again!" Well, this is what they say up in the sick room. They come down to their *anxious* companions. "How is the old man?" "Will he die?" "Yes, yes; he sure to go, this time; he never whip the slave no more." "Are you sure? Will he die?" "O yes! surely gone for it, now." Then they all look glad, and go to the cabin with a merry heart.

Two slaves were sent out to dig a grave for old master. They dug it very deep. As I passed by, I asked Jess and Bob what in the world they dug it so deep for. It was down six or seven feet. I told them there would be a fuss about it, and they had better fill it up some. Jess said it suited him exactly. Bob said he would not fill it up; he wanted to get the old man as near *home* as possible. When we got a stone to put on his grave, we hauled the largest we could find, so as to fasten him down as strong as possible.

Another story illustrates the feeling of the slaves on taking leave of their masters. I will not vouch for the truth of it; but it is a story slaves delight to tell each other. The master called the slave to his sick bed. "Good-by, Jack; I have a long journey to go; farewell." "Farewell, massa! pleasant journey: you soon be dere, massa—*all de way down hill!*"

*Who are the patrols?*—They are men appointed by the county courts to look after all slaves without a pass. They have almost unlimited power over the slaves. They are the sons of run-down families. The greatest scoundrel is always captain of the band of patrols. They are the offscouring of all things; the refuse, the fag end, the ears and tails of slavery; the scales and fins of fish; the tooth and tongues of serpents. They are the very fool's cap of baboons, the echo of parrots, the wallet and satchel of polecats, the scum of stagnant pools, the exuvial, the worn-out skins of slave-holders; they dress in their old clothes. They are, emphatically, the servants of servants, and slaves of the devil; they are the meanest, and lowest, and worst of all creation. Like starved wharf rats, they are out nights, creeping into slave cabins, to see if they have an old bone there; drive out husbands from their own beds, and then take their places. They get up all sorts of pretences, false as their lying tongues can make them, and then whip the slaves and carry a gory lash to the master, for a piece of bread.

The rascals run me with their dogs six miles, one night, and I was never nearer dead than when I reached home that night. I only escaped being half torn to pieces by the dogs, by turning their attention to some calves that were in the road. The dogs are so trained that they will seize a man as quick as any thing else. The dogs come very near being as mean as their masters.

Cyrus often suffered very much from these wretches. He was hired with a man named Baird. This man was reputed to be very good to his slaves. The patrols, therefore, had a special spite toward his slaves. They would seek for an opportunity to abuse them. Mr. Baird would generally give his slaves a pass to go to the neighbors, once or twice a week, if requested. He had been very good to Cyrus in this respect, and therefore Cyrus was unwilling to ask too often. Once he went out without his pass. The patrols found him and some other slaves on another plantation without any passes. The other slaves belonged to a plantation where they were often whipped; so they gave them a moderate punishment and sent them home. Cyrus, they said, they would take to the woods, and have a regular whipping spree. It was a cold winter night, the moon shining brightly. When they had got into the woods, they ordered him to take off his outside coat, then his jacket; then he said he had a new vest on; he did not want that whipped all to pieces. There were seven men standing in a ring around him. He looked for an opening, and started at full speed. They took after him, but he was too spry for them. He came to the cabin where I slept, and I lent him a hat and a pair of shoes. He was very much excited; said they were all around him, but couldn't whip him. He went over to Mr. Baird, and the patrols had got there before him, and had brought his clothes and told their story. It was now eight or nine o'clock in the evening. Mr. Baird, when a young man, had lived on the plantation of Mr. Logan, and had been treated very kindly by mother. He remembered this kindness to her children. When Cyrus came in, Mr. Baird took his clothes and handed them to him, and told him, "Well, boy, they came pretty near catching you." Cyrus put on his clothes, went into the room where the patrols were, and said, "Good evening, gentlemen. Why, I did not think the patrols would be out to-night. I was thinking of going over to Mr. Reed's; if I had, I should have gone without a pass. They would have caught me, sure enough. Mr. Baird, I wish you would be good enough to give me a pass, and then I won't be afraid of these fellows." Mr. Baird enjoyed the fun right well, and sat down and wrote him a pass; and the patrols started, and had to find the money for their peach brandy somewhere else.

There were several other times when he had but a hair-breadth escape for his skin. He was generally a little too shrewd for them. After he had outwitted them several times, they offered a premium to any one who would whip him.

*How do slaves get information of what is doing in the free states?*—In different ways. They get something from the waiters, that come out into the free states and then return with their masters. Persons from the free states tell them many things; the free blacks get something; and slaves learn most of all from hearing their masters talk.

*Don't slaves that run away return sometimes?*—Yes; there was one returned from Canada, very sorry he had run away. His master was delighted with him; thought he had him sure for life, and made much of him. He was sent round to tell how bad Canada was. He had a sermon for the public,—the ear of the masters,— and another for the slaves. How many he enlightened about the best way to get there, I don't know. His master, at last, was so sure of him, that he let him take his wife and children and go over to Ohio, to a camp-meeting, all fitted out in good style, with horse and wagon. They never stopped to hear any preaching, till they heard the waves of the lakes lift up their cheerful voices between them and the oppressor. George then wrote an affectionate note to his master, inviting him to take tea with him in Canada, beyond the waters, the barrier of freedom. Whether the old people ever went up to Canada, to see their affectionate children, I have not learned. I have heard of several instances very much like the above.

*If the slaves were set free, would they cut the throats of their masters?*—They are far more likely to kill them, if they don't set them free. Nothing but the hope of emancipation, and the fear they might not succeed, keeps them from rising to assert their rights. They are restrained, also, from affection for the children of those who so cruelly oppress them. If none would suffer but the masters themselves, the slaves would make many more efforts for freedom. And, sooner or later, unless the slaves are *given free,* they will take freedom, at all hazards. There are multitudes that chafe under the yoke, sorely enough. They could run away themselves, but they would hate to leave their families.

*Did the slaves in Kentucky hear of the emancipation in the West Indies?*—They did, in a very short time after it took place. It was the occasion of great joy. They expected they would be free next. This event has done much to keep up the hopes of the slave to the present hour.

*What do slaves think of the* PIETY *of their masters?*—They have very little confidence in them about any thing. As a specimen of their feelings on this subject, I will tell an anecdote of a slave.

A slave, named George, was the property of a man of high standing in the church. The old gentleman was taken sick, and the doctor told him he would die. He called George, and told him if he would wait upon him attentively, and do every thing for him possible, he would remember him in his will: he would do something handsome for him.

George was very much excited to know what it might be; hoped it might be in the heart of his master to give him his freedom. At last, the will was made. George was still more excited. The master noticed it, and asked what the matter was. "Massa, you promise do something for me in your will. Poor nigger! what massa done for George?" "O George, don't be concerned; I have done a very handsome thing for you—such as any slave would be proud to have done for him." This did not satisfy George. He was still very eager to know what it was. At length the master saw it necessary to tell George, to keep him quiet, and make him attend to his duty. "Well, George, I have made provision that, when you die, you shall have a good coffin, and be put into the same vault with me. Will not that satisfy you, George?" "Well, massa, one way I am satisfied, and one way I am not." "What, what," said the old master, "what is the matter with that?" "Why," says George, "I like to have good coffin when I die." "Well, don't you like to be in the same vault with me and other rich masters?" "Why, yes, massa, one way I like it, and one way I don't." "Well, what don't you like?" "Why, I fraid, massa, when de debbil come take you body, he make mistake, and get mine."

The slaves uniformly prefer to be buried at the greatest possible distance away from master. They are superstitious, and fear that the slave-driver, having whipped so much when alive, will, somehow, be beating them when dead. I was actually as much afraid of my old master when dead, as I was when he was alive. I often dreamed of him, too, after he was dead, and thought he had actually come back again, to torment me more.

*Do slaves have conscientious scruples about taking things from their masters?*—They think it wrong to take from a neighbor, but not from their masters. The only question with them is, "Can we keep it from master?" If they can keep their backs safe, conscience is quiet enough on this point. But a slave that will steal from a slave, is called *mean* as *master*. This is the lowest comparison slaves know how to use: "just as mean as white folks." "No right for to complain of white folks, who steal us all de days of our life; nigger dat what steal from nigger, he meaner nor all."

There is no standard of morality in the slave states. The master stands before the slave a robber and oppressor. His words count nothing with the slaves. The slaves are disrobed of the attributes of men, so that they cannot hold up the right standard, and there is none. The slaves frequently have discussions upon moral questions. Sol and Tom went, one night, to steal the chickens of a neighbor. Tom went up, to hand them down to Sol. While engaged in this operation, he paused a minute. "Sol, you tink dis right, to steal dese chicken from here?" "What dat you say, Tom?" "I say, you tink him right to steal dese chicken, Sol?" "What you come talk dat way, now, for? Dat question you ought settle 'fore you come here." "Me did tink about it, but want to hear what you say, Sol. Don't you tink it kind of wrong to take dese here chicken?" "I tell you, Sol, no time for 'scuss dat now. Dat is *de* great moral question. Make haste; hand me down anudder one; let us git away from here 'fore de daylight come."

*Do you think it was right for you to run away, and not pay any thing for yourself?*— I would be willing to pay, if I knew who to pay it to. But when I think it over, I can't find any body that has any better right to me than myself. I can't pay father and mother, for they are dead. I don't owe Mrs. Banton any thing for bringing me up the way she did. I worked five or six years, and earned more than one hundred dollars a year, for Mr. K. and family, and received about a dozen dollars a year in clothing. Who do I owe, then, in Kentucky? If I catch one of the administrators on here, I intend to sue him for wages, and interest, for six years' hard work. There will be a small bill of damages for abuse; old Kentucky is not rich enough to pay me for that.

*Soon after you came into Ohio, did you let yourself to work?*—I did.—*Was there any difference in your feelings while laboring there, and as a slave in Kentucky?*—I made a bargain to work for a man in Ohio. I took a job of digging a cellar. Before I began, the people told me he was bad pay; they would not do it for him. I told them I had agreed to do it. So at it I went, worked hard, and got it off as soon as possible, although I did not expect to get a cent for it; and yet I worked more readily, and with a better mind, than I ever did in Kentucky. If I worked for nothing then, I knew I had made my own bargain; and working with that thought made it easier than any day's work I ever did for a master in Kentucky. That *thought* was worth more than any pay I ever got in slavery. However, I was more fortunate than many thought I should be; through the exertions of a good friend, I got my pay soon after the work was done.

*Why do slaves dread so bad to go to the south—to Mississippi or Louisiana?*— Because they know that slaves are driven very hard there, and worked to death in a few years.

*Are those who have* GOOD *masters afraid of being sold south?*—They all suffer very much for fear master's circumstances will change, and that he may be compelled to sell them to the "SOUL-DRIVERS," a name given to the dealers by the slaves.

*What is the highest price you ever knew a slave to sell for?*—I have known a man sold for $1465. He was a waiter-man, very intelligent, very humble, and a good house servant. A good blacksmith, as I was told, was once sold in Kentucky for $3000. I have heard of handsome girls being sold in New Orleans for from $2000 to $3000. The common price of females is about from $500 to $700, when sold for plantation hands, for house hands, or for *breeders.*

*Why is a black slave-driver worse than a white one?*—He must be very strict and severe, or else he will be turned out. The master selects the hardest-hearted and most unprincipled slave upon the plantation. The overseers are usually a part of the patrols. Which is the worst of the two characters, or *officers,* is hard to tell.

*Are the masters afraid of insurrection?*—They live in constant and great fear upon this subject. The least unusual noise at night alarms them greatly. They cry out, "What is that?" "Are the boys all in?"

*What is the worst thing you ever saw in Kentucky?*—The worst thing I ever saw was a woman, stripped all naked, hung up by her hands, and then whipped till the blood ran down her back. Sometimes this is done by a young master, or mistress, to an aged mother, or even a grandmother. Nothing the slaves abhor as they do this.

*Which is the worst, a master or a mistress?*—A mistress is far worse. She is forever and ever tormenting. When the master whips it is done with; but a mistress will blackguard, scold, and tease, and whip the life out of a slave.

*How soon do the children begin to exercise their authority?*—From the very breast of the mother. I have seen a child, before he could talk a word, have a stick put into his hand, and he was permitted to whip a slave, in order to quiet him. And from the time they are born till they die, they live by whipping and abusing the slave.

*Do you suffer from cold in Kentucky?*—Many people think it so warm there that we are safe on this score. They are much mistaken. The weather is far too cold for our thin clothing; and in winter, from rain, sleet, and snow, to which we are exposed, we suffer very severely. Such a thing as a greatcoat the slave very seldom has.

*What do they raise in Kentucky?*—Corn and hemp, tobacco, oats, some wheat and rye; SLAVES, mules, hogs, and horses, for the southern market.

*Do the masters drink a great deal?*—They are nearly all *hard* drinkers—many of them drunkards; and you must not exclude mistress from the honor of drinking, as she is often *drunk,* too.

*Are you not afraid they will send up and catch you, and carry you back to Kentucky?*—They may make the *attempt;* but I made up my mind, when I left slavery, never to go back there and continue alive. I fancy I should be a load for one or two of them to carry back, any how. Besides, they well know that they could not take me out of any state this side of Pennsylvania. There are very few in New

England that would sell themselves to help a slaveholder; and if they should, they would have to run their country. They would be hooted at as they walked the streets.

Now, in conclusion, I just want to say, that all the abuses which I have here related are *necessary,* if slavery must continue to exist. It is impossible to cut off these abuses and keep slavery alive. Now, if you do not approve of these horrid sufferings, I entreat you to lift up your voice and your hand against the whole system, and, with one united effort, overturn the abominations of centuries, and restore scattered families to each other; pour light upon millions of dark minds, and make a thousand, yea, ten times ten thousand, abodes of wretchedness and woe to hail and bless you as angels of mercy sent for their deliverance.

---

## FACTS

## FROM THE PERSONAL KNOWLEDGE OF MILTON CLARKE.

General Leslie Coombs, of Lexington, owned a man named Ennis, a house carpenter. He had bargained with a slave-trader to take him and carry him down the river. Ennis was determined not to go. He took a broadaxe and cut one hand off; then contrived to lift the axe, with his arm pressing it to his body, and let it fall upon the other, cutting off the ends of his fingers. His master sold him for a nominal price, and down he went to Louisiana.

A slave named Jess, belonging to Deacon Logan, went out one Sabbath evening for the same purpose that many young men have for making calls on that evening. Jack White, a captain of the patrols, followed Jess, and took him out and whipped him, in the presence of the family where Jess was making his call. The indignation of poor Jess was roused. He sought his way by stealthy steps, at night, to the barn of Jack White, and touched it with the match. Jess was suspected, and his master told him, if guilty, he had better own it, and he would send him down the river to save him from being hung. Jess was put in jail on suspicion. Deacon Logan sent his slaves by night; they got Jess out of jail; he was concealed by his master for a few days, and then sold for $700, and sent down the river.

### HIRED SLAVES.—BAGGING FACTORIES.

In and around Lexington are numerous factories for spinning and weaving hemp bagging. Young slaves, from ten to fifteen years old, are employed in spinning. They are hired for $20 to $30 a year, and their condition is a very hard and cruel one. They have a weekly task. So much hemp is weighed out; so much filling must be returned, all of the right size, and at the proper time. Want of skill, mistakes of various kinds, subject them to frequent and unmerited stripes.

An overseer of one of these factories, Tom Monks, would tie up his poor boys, and give them from forty to fifty lashes. He kept them sometimes yoked with iron collars, with prongs sticking out, and the name of the owner written on them. Working in these factories takes all the life and spirit out of a young slave, and he soon becomes little better than an idiot. This is the worst kind of slavery in Kentucky. When the life is thus taken out of these poor lads, at the age of eighteen or twenty, they are sold for Louisiana. Here a short but bitter doom awaits them.

They are first carried to New Orleans, and put in pens. When a purchaser comes and inquires of the slave what he can do, he must make pretensions, of course, to great skill and ability, or the seller will abuse him. But what will be his condition with the purchaser, who finds that he cannot do half the things he promised? The sugar-planter blames the slave. He came from the bag factory, but said he was a good field hand; could hold plough, hoe corn, or any other kind of farming work in Kentucky. He has lied to his *present* master, for the benefit of his *former* one. He atones for it by many a cruel flogging. When they find one that is very awkward and ignorant, the master tells the overseer to "put him through for what he is worth;" "use him up as soon as you can;" "get what you can out of him in a short time, and let him die." In a few years, the poor fellow ends his labors and his sorrows.

The bell rings at four o'clock in the morning, and they have half an hour to get ready. Men and women start together, and the women must work as steadily as the men, and perform the same tasks as the men. If the plantation is far from the house, the sucking children are taken out and kept in the field all day. If the cabins are near, the women are permitted to go in two or three times a day to their infant children. The mother is driven out when the child is three to four weeks old. The dews of the morning are very heavy, and wet the slaves all through. Many, from the upper slave states, die from change of climate and diet. At the time of making sugar and molasses, the slaves are kept up half the night; and the worst-looking creatures I ever saw were the slaves that make the sugar for those sensitive ladies and gentlemen, who cannot bear the sight of a colored person, but who are compelled to use the sugar made by the filthiest class of slaves.

O, how would LIBERTY wash away the filth and the misery of millions! Then the slaves would be washed, and clothed, and fed, and instructed, and made happy!

There is another and very different class of slaves sent south. When a body servant refuses to be whipped, or his master breaks with him for any other reason, he is sold south. The purchaser questions him, and he tells the truth. "Can you farm?" "No, sir." "What can you do?" "Work in garden, drive horses, and work around the house." "Ay; gentleman nigger, are you? Well, you are gentleman nigger no longer." He is ordered upon the plantation, and soon acquires skill to perform his task. Always sure to perform all that is required, he does not intend to be beaten by any human being. The overseer soon discovers this spirit, and seeks occasion for a quarrel. The slave will not be whipped. A half a dozen overseers are called together, and the poor fellow is chained, and whipped to the border of his grave. In a week or two, the overseer tries his spirit again; comes into the field and strikes him, by way of insult, and the slave knocks him down, and perhaps kills him with his hoe, and flies for the woods. Then horses, dogs, overseers, planters, lawyers, doctors, ministers, are all summoned out on a grand nigger hunt, and poor Bill Turner is shot dead at the foot of a tree, and the trumpet sounds at once a triumph and a retreat.

I expect nothing but there may be an attempt made to carry me back to slavery: but I give fair warning to all concerned, that now, knowing the value of *liberty*, I prize it far above *life*; and no year of suns will ever shine upon my chains as a slave. I *can* die, but I *cannot* be made a slave again. Lewis says, "Amen! Brother Milton, give me your hand! You speak my mind exactly."

## CALLING ON THEIR MASTERS FOR HELP.

THE Frankfort (Ky.) "Commonwealth" publishes a rich letter from the Ohio justice of the peace, who assisted the kidnappers of Jerry Phinney.[27] It is addressed to the person who now has possession of Jerry, and calls lustily on him to save the wretched justice from the penitentiary. He, and the man who taught him that "that is property which the law declares to be property," ought both to go to the penitentiary till they can unlearn that diabolical sophism. The fellow really talks as though it made a vast difference in his crime, whether the victim had been entangled in a similar manner before. He writes,—

"I wish you, as a friend, to ascertain if the power of attorney, presented to me by said Forbes, is a lawful and true one, and if the said Jerry Phinney is a slave or not; for if he is not, it will go very hard with us, and is a perjury on the said Forbes, in consequence of the affidavit he filed with me.

"And to you, Kentuckians, I appeal for redress for the severe treatment we have received, in consequence of the seizure and conveying off of a slave, as I verily and solemnly believe Jerry; for I cannot for one moment believe that said power of attorney is a forgery, and that Forbes committed perjury.

"And we earnestly solicit your aid; for, without, the state prison is our doom; although I acted in good faith.

"The abolitionists are determined that we shall be convicted of kidnapping.

"We are very poor, but defy the world to bring a dishonorable act against us, except the one now against us, which they deem a great one; but I deny being guilty of any such charge.

"Unless you aid and assist us, you may rely on it that you never need expect an officer, in this section of the country, ever again to touch any thing of the kind, for fear of the penitentiary; for prejudice and abolitionism are bent to imprison any justice of the peace, who dare make an attempt to examine a fugitive from labor, and more particularly if he is poor, and has not money to carry him through a course of law.

"Prejudice is so great, that I am credibly informed the governor has issued his proclamation, offering a reward of one thousand dollars for the apprehension of said Forbes, and Jacob Armatage, the young man that went with Forbes; the citizens are to pay half of said reward.

"Please favor me with an immediate answer; and inform me what proof can be had that Jerry is a slave, and what relief can be rendered us in our distressing case. You may also look for a letter from our attorneys, F. J. Mathews and Colonel N. H. Swayne, as they will address all those whose signatures are in said power of attorney, which is in their hands at this time; and that is the reason I have not given their Christian names.

"WM. HENDERSON, J. P.
"H. D. HENDERSON.
"D. A. POTTER."

## PRESIDENT EDWARDS.—A TESTIMONY.

ON the 15th of September, 1791, the younger Edwards,[28] then pastor of a church in New Haven, preached a sermon before the Connecticut Society for the Promotion of Freedom, &c., in which he has the following remarks:—

"The arguments which have been urged against the slave-trade, are, with little variation, applicable to the holding of slaves. He who holds a slave, continues to deprive him of that liberty which was taken from him on the coast of Africa. And if it were wrong to deprive him of it in the first instance, why not in the second? If this be true, no man has a better right to retain his negro in slavery, than he had to take him from his native African shores. And every man who cannot show that his negro hath, by his voluntary conduct, forfeited his liberty, is obliged *immediately to manumit him.*

"I presume it will not be denied that to commit theft or robbery every day of a man's life, is as great a sin as to commit fornication in one instance. But to steal a MAN, or to rob him of his liberty, is a greater sin than to steal his property, or to take it by violence. And to hold a man in a state of slavery, who has a right to his liberty, is to be every day guilty of robbing him of his liberty, or of *man-stealing.* The consequence is inevitable, that, other things being the same, to hold a negro slave, unless he has forfeited his liberty, *is a greater sin than concubinage and fornication.*

"To convince yourselves that, your information being the same, to hold a negro slave is a greater sin than fornication, theft, or robbery, you need only bring the matter home to yourselves. I am willing to appeal to your own consciousness, whether you would not judge it to be a greater sin for a man to hold you or your children, during life, in such slavery as that of the negroes, than for him to indulge in one instance of licentious conduct, or in one instance to steal or rob. Let conscience speak, and I will submit to its decision."

If the above remarks were correct in 1791, can they be wrong in 1846? If our good divines were correct in calling slaveholders man-stealers, and slaveholding a greater sin in the sight of God than concubinage and fornication, what must we think of the moral state or the heart of those modern D. D.'s, who are willing to receive slaveholders into the church of God, and are ready to weave out of their own hearts a *theological fiction* to palliate the enormous evil? Alas! C. M. Clay[29] is right, when he says, "The *disease is of the heart, and not of the head.* We tell you, brothers, that the American people know well enough that the bloody stain is upon them—but they love its *taint!* If we can't arouse the conscience, and ennoble the heart, our labor is lost. A *seared conscience* and a *heart hardened by sin*—these are the grand supporters of slavery in and out of the church. How can these giants be subdued?"—*From the Charter Oak.*

# ORDER OF EXERCISES

## FOR A SLAVEHOLDERS' MEETING.

---

### I. PRAYER.

### By Cassius M. Clay.

#### Prayer and Slavery.

THERE are many men, professing the Christian religion, who also profess to believe slavery a divine institution! Now, we have lived thus long, and never yet have heard a prayer offered up to God in its behalf! *If it is of God, Christians, pray for it!* Try it; it will strengthen your faith and purify your souls.

O THOU omnipotent and benevolent God, who hast made all men of one flesh, thou Father of all nations, we do most devoutly beseech thee to defend and strengthen thy institution, American slavery! Do thou, O Lord, tighten the chains of our black brethren, and cause slavery to increase and multiply throughout the world! And whereas many nations of the earth have loved their neighbors as themselves, and have done unto others as they would that others should do unto them, and have broken every bond, and have let the oppressed go free, do thou, O God, turn their hearts from their evil ways, and let them seize once more upon the weak and defenceless, and subject them to eternal servitude!

And, O God, as thou hast commanded us not to muzzle even the poor ox that treadeth out the corn, let them labor unceasingly without reward, and let their own husbands, and wives, and children, be sold into distant lands without crime, that thy name may be glorified, and that unbelievers may be confounded, and forced to confess that indeed thou art a God of justice and mercy! Stop, stop, O God, the escape from the prison-house, by which thousands of these "*accursed*" men flee into foreign countries, where nothing but tyranny reigns; and compel them to enjoy the unequalled blessings of our own *free* land!

Whereas our rulers in the Alabama legislature have emancipated a black man, because of some eminent public service, thus bringing thy holy name into shame, do thou, O God, change their hearts, melt them into mercy, and into obedience to thy will, and cause them speedily to restore the chain to that unfortunate soul! And, O God, thou Searcher of all hearts, seeing that many of thine own professed followers, when they come to lie down on the bed of death, and enter upon that bourn whence no traveller returns,—where every one shall be called to account for the deeds done in the body, whether they be good or whether they be evil,—emancipate their fellow-men, failing in faith, and given over to hardness of heart and blindness of perception of the truth, do thou, O God, be merciful to them and the poor recipients of their deceitful philanthropy, *and let the chain enter into the flesh and the iron into the soul forever!*

## II. HYMN.

### PARODY.

COME, saints and sinners, hear me tell
How pious priests whip Jack and Nell,
And women buy, and children sell,
And preach all sinners down to hell,
    And *sing* of heavenly union.

They'll bleat and baa, dona like goats,
Gorge down black sheep, and strain at motes,
Array their backs in fine black coats,
And seize their negroes by their throats,
    And *choke*, for heavenly union.

They'll church you if you sip a dram,
And damn you if you steal a lamb;
Yet rob old Tony, Doll, and Sam,
Of human rights, and bread and ham—
    *Kidnapper's* heavenly union.

They'll talk of heaven and Christ's reward,
And bind his image with a cord,
And scold and swing the lash abhorred,
And sell their brother in the Lord
    To *handcuffed* heavenly union.

They'll read and sing a sacred song,
And make a prayer both loud and long,
And teach the right and do the wrong;
Hailing the brother, sister throng,
    With *words* of heavenly union.

We wonder how such saints can sing,
Or praise the Lord upon the wing,
Who roar and scold, and whip and sting,
And to their slaves and mammon cling,
    In guilty conscience union.

They'll raise tobacco, corn, and rye,
And drive and thieve, and cheat and lie,
And lay up treasures in the sky,
By making switch and cowskin fly,
    In *hope* of heavenly union.

They'll crack old Tony on the skull,
And preach and roar like Bashan bull,[30]
Or braying ass of mischief full;
Then seize old Jacob by the wool,
    And *pull* for heavenly union.

A roaring, ranting, sleek man-thief,
Who lived on mutton, veal, and beef,
And never would afford relief
To needy sable sons of grief,
    Was *big* with heavenly union.

Love not the world, the preacher said,
And winked his eye and shook his head;—
He seized on Tom, and Dick, and Ned,
Cut short their meat, and clothes, and bread,
    Yet still *loved* heavenly union.

Another preacher, whining, spoke
Of one whose heart for sinners broke;—
He tied old Nanny to an oak,
And drew the blood at every stroke,
    And *prayed* for heavenly union.

Two others oped their iron jaws,
And waved their children-stealing paws;
There sat their children in gewgaws;
By stinting negroes' backs and maws,
    They *keep up* heavenly union.

All good from Jack another takes,
And entertains their flirts and rakes,
Who dress as sleek as glossy snakes,
And cram their mouths with sweetened cakes;
    And *this* goes down for union.[31]

---

### III. SERMON.

#### BY OLD LORENZO.

Lord, what is wealth? It will not stay,
But ever flies away, away,
    As restless waters roll;
No sort of goods, beyond the grave,
Will ever meet its owner, save
    A faithful negro's soul.

Brethren, did you ever think of the importance of laying up treasures in heaven? What is gold, or houses, or land, or earthly honors? Will they purchase happiness here? Will they secure heaven hereafter? When you "shuffle off this mortal coil," all these things will become as dross, worthless as the sediments of a blacksmith's forge. You tell me, you are going to buy up a store of good works. But what will that avail you. Can you plead your good works at the bar of heaven? Will good works save you? Be not deceived with such a fatal delusion. How are you going to get your good works performed here on earth, to heaven? I tell you, you must have available funds there. They have got a bank up here in the moon. Suppose you could get one of their bills—what would it be worth here? It might be worth something as a curiosity, but as a medium of commerce, it would be worthless as a rag. So of good works; you can't get them to heaven. They are a sort of bank stock, valuable on earth, to be sure, and "nowhere else but there." A draft in heaven, on the Bank of Good Works, located here on earth, would not sell for its cost in white paper. This laying up good works, to purchase an inheritance in heaven, is like bottling jack-o'-lanterns to light up pandemonium.

My hearers, I see you look discouraged. Despair sits brooding on your hearts. "If good works will not save us," I seem to hear you ask, "what will?" Well, I'll tell you:—you must take something that you can get to heaven; that's plain. You must buy niggers. Niggers have souls, and when they die, if they are Orthodox niggers, they go right off to heaven. But, mind you, they must be Orthodox; if they are not, your fat will be in the fire. First, get them converted to the gospel of submission. Preach to them often, from the text "Servants, obey your masters." You will lose nothing by it. If you want to sell them, you can recommend them then, as Christians, and get your money back again; or, if you prefer, you can flog the souls out of them, and lay up a treasure in heaven. Just think of it, Deacon Ashley. Suppose yourself knocking at heaven's gate, and the old turnkey, St. Peter, demanding, "Who comes there?" "Deacon Ashley," you will reply. "What claim do you present to an entrance here?" inquires Peter. Well, now, you see, if you have no claim, you can't get in; so you up and say, "I have property here." "Property here?" asks Peter, in apparent surprise, though I warrant you he knows all about it; "what property?" You will say, "There was my man Caesar, a member of our church, whom I shot ten years ago, when he attempted to run away. I paid eight hundred dollars for him. I suppose he is here." "Yes," Peter says, "Caesar is here. Walk in, deacon; where a man's treasure is, there must he be also."

So you see the immense importance of owning slaves. Our hopes of everlasting salvation hang on the institution of slavery; and as McDuffie[32] said, (I think 'twas Mac,) it is the chief corner-stone of our republican edifice. When I look at it in this light, and think of the mad efforts that are now made to abolish this heaven-ordained institution, and thus secure the destruction of the only free government on earth, and the endless misery of all its inhabitants, my very blood boils with horror at sight of an abolitionist. To rob a man of his purse on earth, is inhuman enough; but to rob him of his treasure in heaven is absolutely diabolical. How many millions on millions of dollars have been paid for slaves, who have gone to heaven! So many millions of dollars, of course, laid up as a treasure there. And these fanatics would not only cheat us out of our just rights here, but would plunder us of our treasures in heaven. I am utterly alarmed at the supineness of our church. A few years ago, if an abolitionist attempted to inculcate his abominable doctrines, you stoned him, hissed at him, pelted him with bad eggs, poured water on him with fire engines, and even shot him dead. You then maintained your character as God's church militant. You have now settled down as God's church capitulated. May you buckle on your armor afresh, and, with brick-bats and unmerchantable eggs, go forth to defend your treasures in heaven. Amen.

## OUR COUNTRYMEN IN CHAINS.

OUR fellow-countrymen in chains,
    Slaves in a land of light and law!
Slaves crouching on the very plains
    Where rolled the storm of Freedom's war!
A groan from Eutaw's haunted wood—
    A wail where Camden's martyrs fell—
By every shrine of patriot blood,
    From Moultrie's wall and Jasper's well.

By storied hill and hallowed grot,
    By mossy wood and marshy glen,
Whence rang of old the rifle-shot,
    And hurrying shout of Marion's men!
The groan of breaking hearts is there—
    The falling lash—the fetter's clank!
Slaves—SLAVES are breathing in that air
    Which old De Kalb and Sumter drank![33]

What, ho!—our countrymen in chains!
    The whip on WOMAN's shrinking flesh!
Our soil yet reddening with the stains
    Caught from her scourging, warm and fresh!
What! mothers from their children riven!
    What! God's own image bought and sold!
AMERICANS to market driven,
    And bartered, as the brute, for gold!

Speak! shall their agony of prayer
    Come thrilling to our hearts in vain?
To us, whose fathers scorned to bear
    The paltry menace of a chain?
To us, whose boast is loud and long
    Of holy Liberty and Light—
Say, shall these writhing slaves of wrong
    Plead vainly for their plundered Right?

Shall every flap of England's flag
    Proclaim that all around are free,
From "farthest Ind" to each blue crag
    That beetles o'er the Western Sea?
And shall we scoff at Europe's kings,
    When Freedom's fire is dim with us,
And round our country's altar clings
    The damning shade of Slavery's curse?

Just God! and shall we calmly rest,
    The Christian's scorn—the Heathen's mirth—
Content to live the lingering jest
    And by-word of a mocking Earth?

Shall our own glorious land retain
 That curse which Europe scorns to bear?
Shall our own brethren drag the chain
 Which not e'en Russia's menials wear?

Down let the shrine of Moloch sink,
 And leave no traces where it stood;
No longer let its idol drink
 His daily cup of human blood:
But rear another altar there,
 To Truth, and Love, and Mercy given;
And Freedom's gift, and Freedom's prayer,
 Shall call an answer down from Heaven!

J. G. WHITTIER.[34]

1. Andrews, *Free Story,* 138–139; Starling, *Slave Narrative,* 129, 132.

2. Child, "Slave's Journal," 151–163.

3. Blassingame, *Slave Testimony,* xxi–xxii.

4. Volk, "Clarke, Lewis G.," 116; Jackson, *History,* 135.

5. Cassius M. Clay (1810–1903) was a Kentucky politician who founded an abolitionist paper, the *True American,* in 1845, and ran for governor in 1851.

6. William Cowper (1731–1800), "The Negro's Complaint."

7. Joseph C. Lovejoy (1805–71) was the brother of the well-known abolitionists Owen and Elijah P. Lovejoy. At the time he was minister of the church at Cambridgeport, Massachusetts, having been principal of Hallowell Academy and pastor of the Universalist church in Oldtown, Maine. His other books include biographies of his brother Elijah, who was murdered for his abolitionist activities, and of the Reverend Charles Torrey, a founder of the underground railroad. Merrill & Ruchames, *Letters of Garrison,* III:369; Blassingame, *Slave Testimony,* xxii.

8. Job cursed the day, not the place, of his birth: "Let the day perish wherein I was born, . . . Let darkness and the shadow of death stain it; let a cloud dwell upon it; let the blackness of the day terrify it." *Job* 3:3–5.

9. Edmund Burke (1729–97) was a British political writer and statesman who, while in Parliament, instigated the impeachment of Warren Hastings (1732–1818), the first governor general of British India. Hastings was prosecuted by Burke for extortion of money from provincial leaders, hiring out British troops to subdue Afghans, and the judicial murder of an Indian merchant; but was acquitted of all charges.

10. Cowper, "On the Receipt of My Mother's Picture out of Norfolk, the Gift of My Cousin, Ann Bodham."

11. *2 Corinthians* 7:5: "Without were fightings, within were fears."

12. Ontario.

13. As Moses had commanded, Joshua built an altar to God on Mount Ebal, and "wrote there upon the stones a copy of the law of Moses." *Deuteronomy* 17, *Joshua* 8:32.

14. Jerry Finney, a black man who had lived in Columbus, Ohio, for fifteen years with his wife and children, was kidnapped in March 1846 by Kentuckians, with the help of William Henderson, a justice of the peace in Franklinton, Ohio. Finney maintained that his master had granted him freedom years ago, but one of the abductors, Alexander C. Forbes, produced papers and swore to Finney's identity. After being pursued to Cincinnati, the kidnappers escaped to Kentucky. Justice Henderson and several others were arrested; several prominent Ohioans traveled to Frankfort, Kentucky, to try to obtain Finney's release; and Ohio governor Mordecai Bartley issued a requisition on the governor of Kentucky for the surrender of the

kidnappers. But all was for nought. Henderson was convicted, but his conviction was over-turned by the Supreme Court. Finney was legally purchased from his abductors by the citizens of Columbus, but died of consumption shortly after his return. Black, *Story of Ohio,* 221–222; Galbreath, *History of Ohio,* II:237–238.

15. *Proverbs* 17:12.

16. A treat.

17. He paid off his wife to induce her to refrain from further prosecution.

18. General James Harvey Paine (1791–1879) was a local abolitionist leader and chairman of the 1844 Ohio Liberty Party convention.

19. Salmon Portland Chase (1808–73) defended fugitives so often he became known as "at-torney general for runaway slaves." He was later elected governor of Ohio, served as Lincoln's secretary of the treasury, and became chief justice in 1864.

20. Gen. Leslie Coombs (1793–1881) was a hero of the War of 1812 and a member of the Kentucky House, becoming Speaker in 1846. John J. Crittenden (1787–1863) was then a U.S. senator from Kentucky; he served in the U.S. Senate for many years, and was also U.S. attor-ney general under presidents Harrison, Tyler, and Fillmore. Charles S. Morehead (1802–68) was then Speaker of the Kentucky House; he later became governor. Robert Perkins Letcher (1788–1861) served as Kentucky governor from 1840 to 1844. John Speed Smith (1792–1854) was a Kentucky legislator, for a time Speaker of the House; he was sent to the Ohio legislature in 1839 to influence it to pass laws against the assistance of fugitive slaves and to provide a more efficient method for recapturing them. Kentucky's Henry Clay (1777–1852) was the Whig candidate for U.S. president in 1844; he was among the most important politicians of the century.

21. *Jeremiah* 5:9.

22. Debtor.

23. Creditor.

24. *Jeremiah* 22:13.

25. *Habbakuk* 2:11.

26. *James* 5:4–5.

27. See note 14, above.

28. Jonathan Edwards the younger (1745–1801) was a famous American theologian, son of the immensely influential Jonathan Edwards (1703–58), and president of Union College at Schenectady, New York.

29. See note 5, above.

30. Bashan "was called the land of the giants." *Deut.* 3:13.

31. Attributed to Frederick Douglass (1818–95). The poem appears in his *Narrative,* and is a parody of a popular hymn.

32. George McDuffie (1790–1851), governor of South Carolina and later U.S. senator, was one of the most passionate and extravagant defenders of slavery. The laws he enacted in South Carolina while governor provided for the sale of any free black who returned to the state af-ter expulsion, and required officials to imprison free blacks aboard any ship during its stay in a South Carolina port.

33. Eutaw Springs, South Carolina, was the home of Lt. Col. Thomas Sumter (1734–1832); in 1781 it was the site of one of the major battles of the Revolutionary War, in which Major Francis Marion (1732–95), also known as "the Swamp Fox," helped save the Revolutionary Army from a severe defeat. Fort Moultrie, in Charleston harbor, was named after General William Moultrie (1730–1805), who defended it against the British in 1776. During the bat-tle, William Jasper (1750–79) climbed on the fortifications to recover a flag struck down by the British and remounted it. "Jasper's Well" refers to the redoubt at the fort named after him.

34. John Greenleaf Whittier (1807–92) was a well-known American Quaker poet, re-former, and abolitionist. He was the editor of the *Narrative of James Williams* (1838).

WILLIAM WELLS BROWN

WILLIAM WELLS BROWN (1814–84) was the first published African American novelist, playwright, travel writer, and military historian. "Brown's writings," as Paul Jefferson describes them, "exhibit the thematic richness and formal variety of nineteenth-century black literature at its best. As a pioneering architect of a black counter-discourse, an ambiguously subversive literary tradition whose complexity is now appreciated, his work warrants the close reading it is beginning at last to receive."[1] His career as the most versatile and prolific black writer of the century began with the Narrative of William W. Brown, a Fugitive Slave, which adheres so closely to the unwritten plot guidelines of the slave narrative that it exemplifies the genre perhaps better than any other book.[2] Yet it is no less "ambiguously subversive" than Brown's more openly pioneering efforts. By all accounts, it is a remarkably readable, original, and effective slave narrative, and its enduring popularity reflects these qualities.

Brown was one of the few slave narrators to spend most of his enslaved life west of the Mississippi—his master moved to the Missouri Territory in 1816, and Brown lived in the St. Louis area until his escape in 1834. Hired out as an assistant to a brutal slave trader, Brown shuttled up and down the Mississippi River between St. Louis and New Orleans, meeting hundreds of slaves, witnessing horrific abuses of power, and gaining an unparalleled education in the modus operandi of the peculiar institution.

Thirteen years elapsed between Brown's escape and his book's publication. During that time, as Brown states in his narrative, he worked on a steamboat, was active in the Underground Railroad, and helped bring dozens of fugitive slaves to Canada. But he also worked as a barber; got married, had three children, and separated from his wife; moved from Cleveland to Buffalo to Farmington, New York; helped rescue an ex-slave family from kidnappers; studied English, mathematics, history, and literature; visited Haiti and Cuba; met many of the most notable free blacks and abolitionists of his time; had numerous letters published in the National Anti-Slavery Standard; toured extensively, lecturing on slavery and radical politics; was elected general agent and corresponding secretary of the Western New York Anti-Slavery Society; and, in all, became one of New York's leading black citizens.[3]

In May 1847, due to his marital difficulties, Brown moved to Boston, where he worked on his narrative. In mid-June he submitted it to Edmund Quincy, secretary of the Massachusetts Anti-Slavery Society and an editor of the National Anti-Slavery Standard. Two weeks later, on the morning of July 1, Quincy began reading it. "I thought I would glance over a few pages," he explained, "to see what it was like. But it was so good that I could not lay it down until dinner-time." Since Brown's experience of slavery was more extensive than that of Frederick Douglass, whose own narrative had been published in Boston two years earlier with remarkable success, Quincy found Brown's narrative "a much more striking story than Douglass's & as well told." After meeting with Brown shortly thereafter, Quincy said, "He is the most valuable man we have got since Douglass— & in many respects he is more valuable. . . ." Quincy suggested "one or two alterations," corrected a few "clerical" errors, helped Brown come up with the title, and wrote a complimentary letter to Brown for inclusion in the *Narrative*.[4]

The book, numbering 110 widely spaced pages, was published in late July, and three thousand copies of it were sold by the end of the year. It went through four American editions totaling ten thousand copies in two years, each edition being longer than the last due to the inclusion of various appendices. Five British printings of a thousand copies each appeared between 1849 and 1853; an Irish edition was published in 1849; and it was translated into Dutch in 1850.[5] After Frederick Douglass's 1845 *Narrative*, Brown's was the bestselling slave narrative of the 1840s. According to the publisher's note to the third edition, "no anti-slavery work has met with a more rapid sale in the United States than this narrative."[6]

Quincy characterized the book as "a terrible picture of Slavery, told with great simplicity," and noted that there was "no attempt at fine writing, but only a minute account of scenes & things he saw & suffered, told with a good deal of skill & great propriety & delicacy."[7] What Quincy ignored, however, was the astonishing subtlety, compact energy, and hidden sophistication of Brown's prose. As Lucinda MacKethan notes:

> Brown dramatizes the power of the word by withholding all of the affective possibilities of words. The result, quite dramatically, is that the reader recognizes the need for strong emotion because of Brown's very lack of it. . . . Until [the] opening of his ninth chapter, Brown gives facts without conveying any expression of his feelings; the more brutal the facts, the more emotionless his way of presenting them.[8]

Similarly, Sidonie Smith has observed how

> In his rigid control of emotion through irony, [Brown] masters and gives artistic form to the turbulence of emotion lurking beneath the surface. This careful control through distancing, this rite of ordering, could be personally redemptive for those who escaped from a system as destructive of the personality as slavery. In other words, artistic distancing becomes a means of survival through which the narrator transcends the absurd incongruities of reality at the same time as those incongruities are fully confronted.[9]

Unlike Douglass's, Brown's style is one of *understatement;* each word is rhetorically poised to spring out upon careful reading rather than at first glance.

The first paragraph, for example, supplies us with a series of unexpected statements, each one quietly subverting the standard opening of a nineteenth-century autobiography. "I was born in Lexington, Ky. The man who stole me as soon as I was born, recorded the births of all the infants which he claimed to be born his property, in a book which he kept for that purpose." In seemingly straightforward prose, Brown implies that he was born *free*, while ironically contrasting his narrative to a record of property. He goes on to list, in imitation of "the man who stole him," the seven children of his mother, but without revealing his own name, thus foreshadowing its future complication. Rather than stating outright how slavery forces slave women to submit to sexual manipulation, he simply writes, "No two of us were children of the same father." And while a white autobiographer might take some pride in the fact that his father was "connected with some of the first families in Kentucky," coming from a slave the phrase takes on an ironic edge, especially since Brown had no real "family" himself.[10]

Brown here is essentially "signifying,"[11] playing ironically with the reader's expectations. This ironic play continues throughout the book—Brown even "signifies" to his master in several witty interchanges that implicitly deny the master's authority over his slave. As William Andrews writes, "Expropriating the white man's language, tricking it out in his own sly idiom, and then returning it dialogically, the signifying slave lays claim to the right to redefine terms like master and slave."[12]

Brown's prose—understated, mocking, subversive—goes hand in hand with his persona. Perhaps Andrews puts it best:

> Brown seems to have almost deliberately refused to identify himself according to Douglass's myth of the heroic resister. From the outset of Brown's *Narrative*, the reader encounters admirable black men who pit themselves physically and morally against ruthless slave-owners in an effort to attain human dignity. Yet invariably they fail. The slaves who succeed against these overwhelming odds are those who learn how to use guile and deception to protect and advance their interests. Brown makes it clear that he too was a slave trickster.[13]

While not as much of a trickster figure as J. D. Green (see pp. II:683–719), Brown engages in the sly behavior characteristic of the protagonists of African American folk tales.

The success of Brown's first book established him as an effective antislavery agent. He continued to lecture almost without pause until the end of the Civil War—it has been estimated that during his five-year stay in England alone, from 1849 to 1854, he delivered a thousand speeches.[14] He also continued to write: *The Anti-Slavery Harp: A Collection of Songs for Anti-Slavery Meetings* (1848); *Three Years in Europe, or Places I Have Seen and People I Have Met* (1852); *Clotel, or the President's Daughter, a novel* (1853, frequently revised thereafter); *The American Fugitive in Europe: Sketches of Places and People Abroad* (1855); *St. Domingo: Its Revolutions and Its Patriots* (1855); *Experience, or, How to Give a Northern Man a Backbone*, a play (unpublished, 1856); *The Escape, or A Leap for Freedom*, a play (1858); *Memoir of William Wells Brown, an American Bondman* (1859); *The Black Man: His Antecedents, His Genius, and His Achievements* (1863); *The Negro in the American Rebellion: His Heroism and His Fidelity* (1867); *The Rising Son; or, The Antecedents and Advancements of the Colored Race* (1867); and *My Southern Home, or The South and Its People* (1880). But despite the considerable merits of these works, none of them quite match the succinctness, clarity, and subversive power of the *Narrative of William W. Brown, a Fugitive Slave*.

Wm. W. Brown.

# NARRATIVE

## OF

# WILLIAM W. BROWN,

### A

# FUGITIVE SLAVE.

———

WRITTEN BY HIMSELF.

———

——— Is there not some chosen curse,
Some hidden thunder in the stores of heaven,
Red with uncommon wrath, to blast the man
Who gains his fortune from the blood of souls?
— COWPER.[15]

BOSTON:
PUBLISHED AT THE ANTI-SLAVERY OFFICE,
No. 25 CORNHILL.
1847.

## TO WELLS BROWN, OF OHIO.

THIRTEEN years ago, I came to your door, a weary fugitive from chains and stripes. I was a stranger, and you took me in. I was hungry, and you fed me. Naked was I, and you clothed me. Even a name by which to be known among men, slavery had denied me. You bestowed upon me your own. Base indeed should I be, if I ever forget what I owe to you, or do anything to disgrace that honored name!

As a slight testimony of my gratitude to my earliest benefactor, I take the liberty to inscribe to you this little Narrative of the sufferings from which I was fleeing when you had compassion upon me. In the multitude that you have succored, it is very possible that you may not remember me; but until I forget God and myself, I can never forget you.

Your grateful friend,
WILLIAM WELLS BROWN.

# LETTER

FROM

## EDMUND QUINCY, ESQ. [16]

DEDHAM, JULY 1, 1847.

TO WILLIAM W. BROWN.

MY DEAR FRIEND:—I heartily thank you for the privilege of reading the manuscript of your Narrative. I have read it with deep interest and strong emotion. I am much mistaken if it be not greatly successful and eminently useful. It presents a different phase of the infernal slave-system from that portrayed in the admirable story of Mr. Douglass,[17] and gives us a glimpse of its hideous cruelties in other portions of its domain.

Your opportunities of observing the workings of this accursed system have been singularly great. Your experiences in the Field, in the House, and especially on the River in the service of the slave-trader, Walker, have been such as few individuals have had;—no one, certainly, who has been competent to describe them. What I have admired, and marvelled at, in your Narrative, is the simplicity and calmness with which you describe scenes and actions which might well "move the very stones to rise and mutiny"[18] against the National Institution which makes them possible.

You will perceive that I have made very sparing use of your flattering permission to alter what you had written. To correct a few errors, which appeared to be merely clerical ones, committed in the hurry of composition, under unfavorable circumstances, and to suggest a few curtailments, is all that I have ventured to do. I should be a bold man, as well as a vain one, if I should attempt to improve your descriptions of what you have seen and suffered. Some of the scenes are not unworthy of De Foe[19] himself.

I trust and believe that your Narrative will have a wide circulation. I am sure it deserves it. At least, a man must be differently constituted from me, who can rise from the perusal of your Narrative without feeling that he understands slavery better, and hates it worse, than he ever did before.

I am, very faithfully and respectfully,

Your friend,
EDMUND QUINCY.

# PREFACE.

---

THE friends of freedom may well congratulate each other on the appearance of the following Narrative. It adds another volume to the rapidly increasing anti-slavery literature of the age. It has been remarked by a close observer of human nature, "Let me make the songs of a nation, and I care not who makes its laws;"[20] and it may with equal truth be said, that, among a reading people like our own, their books will at least give character to their laws. It is an influence which goes forth noiselessly upon its mission, but fails not to find its way to many a warm heart, to kindle on the altar thereof the fires of freedom, which will one day break forth in a living flame to consume oppression.

This little book is a voice from the prison-house, unfolding the deeds of darkness which are there perpetrated. Our cause has received efficient aid from this source. The names of those who have come from thence, and battled manfully for the right, need not to be recorded here. The works of some of them are an enduring monument of praise, and their perpetual record shall be found in the grateful hearts of the redeemed bondman.

Few persons have had greater facilities for becoming acquainted with slavery, in all its horrible aspects, than WILLIAM W. BROWN. He has been behind the curtain. He has visited its secret chambers. Its iron has entered his own soul. The dearest ties of nature have been riven in his own person. A mother has been cruelly scourged before his own eyes. A father,—alas! slaves have no father. A brother has been made the subject of its tender mercies. A sister has been given up to the irresponsible control of the pale-faced oppressor. This nation looks on approvingly. The American Union sanctions the deed. The Constitution shields the criminals. American religion sanctifies the crime. But the tide is turning. Already, a mighty undercurrent is sweeping onward. The voice of warning, of remonstrance, of rebuke, of entreaty, has gone forth. Hand is linked in hand, and heart mingles with heart, in this great work of the slave's deliverance.

The convulsive throes of the monster, even now, give evidence of deep wounds.

The writer of this Narrative was hired by his master to a "*soul-driver,*" and has witnessed all the horrors of the traffic, from the buying up of human cattle in the slave-breeding States, which produced a constant scene of separating the victims from all those whom they loved, to their final sale in the southern market, to be worked up in seven years, or given over to minister to the lust of southern *Christians*.

Many harrowing scenes are graphically portrayed; and yet with that simplicity and ingenuousness which carries with it a conviction of the truthfulness of the picture.

This book will do much to unmask those who have "clothed themselves in the livery of the court of heaven" to cover up the enormity of their deeds.

During the past three years, the author has devoted his entire energies to the anti-slavery cause. Laboring under all the disabilities and disadvantages growing out of his education in slavery—subjected, as he had been from his birth, to all the wrongs and deprivations incident to his condition—he yet went forth, impelled to the work by a love of liberty—stimulated by the remembrance of his own sufferings—urged on by the consideration that a mother, brothers, and sister, were still grinding in the prison-house of bondage, in common with three millions of our Father's children—sustained by an unfaltering faith in the omnipotence of truth and the final triumph of justice—to plead the cause of the slave, and by the eloquence of earnestness carried conviction to many minds, and enlisted the sympathy and secured the co-operation of many to the cause.

His labors have been chiefly confined to Western New York, where he has secured many warm friends, by his untiring zeal, persevering energy, continued fidelity, and universal kindness.

Reader, are you an Abolitionist? What have you done for the slave? What are you doing in his behalf? What do you purpose to do? There is a great work before us. Who will be an idler now? This is the great humanitary movement of the age, swallowing up, for the time being all other questions, comparatively speaking. The course of human events, in obedience to the unchangeable laws of our being, is fast hastening the final crisis, and

> "Have ye chosen, O my people, on whose party ye shall stand,
> Ere the Doom from its worn sandal shakes the dust against our land?"[21]

Are you a Christian? This is the carrying out of practical Christianity; and there is no other. Christianity is *practical* in its very nature and essence. It is a life, springing out of a soul imbued with its spirit. Are you a friend of the missionary cause? This is the greatest missionary enterprize of the day. Three millions of *Christian,* law-manufactured heathen are longing for the glad tidings of the Gospel of freedom. Are you a friend of the Bible? Come, then, and help us to restore to these millions, whose eyes have been bored out by slavery, their sight, that they may see to read the Bible. Do you love God whom you have not seen? Then manifest that love, by restoring to your brother whom you have seen, his rightful inheritance, of which he has been so long and so cruelly deprived.

It is not for a single generation alone, numbering three millions—sublime as would be that effort—that we are working. It is for HUMANITY, the wide world over, not only now, but for all coming time, and all future generations:—

> "For he who settles Freedom's principles,
> Writes the death-warrant of all tyranny."[22]

It is a vast work—a glorious enterprize—worthy the unswerving devotion of the entire life-time of the great and the good.

Slaveholding and slaveholders must be rendered disreputable and odious. They must be stripped of their respectability and Christian reputation. They must be treated as "MEN-STEALERS—guilty of tile highest kind of theft, and sinners of the first rank." Their more guilty accomplices in the persons of *northern apologists,* both in Church and State, must be placed in the same category. Honest men must be made to look upon their crimes with the same abhorrence and loathing, with which they regard the less guilty robber and assassin, until

> "The common damned shun their society,
> And look upon themselves as fiends less foul."[23]

When a just estimate is placed upon the crime of slaveholding, the work will have been accomplished, and the glorious day ushered in—

> "When man nor woman in all our wide domain,
> Shall buy, or sell, or hold, or be a slave."

J. C. HATHAWAY.[24]

Farmington, N.Y., 1847.

# NARRATIVE.

## CHAPTER I.

I WAS born in Lexington, Ky. The man who stole me as soon as I was born, recorded the births of all the infants which he claimed to be born his property, in a book which he kept for that purpose. My mother's name was Elizabeth. She had seven children, viz: Solomon, Leander, Benjamin, Joseph, Millford, Elizabeth, and myself. No two of us were children of the same father. My father's name, as I learned from my mother, was George Higgins. He was a white man, a relative of my master,[25] and connected with some of the first families in Kentucky.

My master owned about forty slaves, twenty-five of whom were field hands. He removed from Kentucky to Missouri, when I was quite young,[26] and settled thirty or forty miles above St. Charles, on the Missouri, where, in addition to his practice as a physician, he carried on milling, merchandizing and farming. He had a large farm, the principal productions of which were tobacco and hemp. The slave cabins were situated on the back part of the farm, with the house of the overseer, whose name was Grove Cook, in their midst. He had the entire charge of the farm, and having no family, was allowed a woman to keep house for him, whose business it was to deal out the provisions for the hands.

A woman was also kept at the quarters to do the cooking for the field hands, who were summoned to their unrequited toil every morning at four o'clock, by the ringing of a bell, hung on a post near the house of the overseer. They were allowed half an hour to eat their breakfast, and get to the field. At half past four, a horn was blown by the overseer, which was the signal to commence work; and every one that was not on the spot at the time, had to receive ten lashes from the negro-whip, with which the overseer always went armed. The handle was about three feet long, with the butt-end filled with lead, and the lash six or seven feet in length, made of cowhide, with platted wire on the end of it. This whip was put in requisition very frequently and freely, and a small offence on the part of a slave furnished an occasion for its use. During the time that Mr. Cook was overseer, I was a house servant—a situation preferable to that of a field hand, as I was better fed, better clothed, and not obliged to rise at the ringing of the bell, but about half an hour after. I have often laid and heard the crack of the whip, and the screams of the slave. My mother was a field hand, and one morning was ten or fifteen minutes behind the others in getting into the field. As soon as she reached the spot where they were at work, the overseer commenced whipping her. She cried, "Oh! pray—Oh! pray—Oh! pray"— these are generally the words of slaves, when imploring mercy at the hands of their oppressors. I heard her voice, and knew it, and jumped out of my bunk, and went to the door. Though the field was some distance from the house, I could hear every crack of the whip, and every groan and cry of my poor mother. I remained at the door, not daring to venture any further. The cold chills ran over me, and I wept aloud. After giving her ten lashes, the sound of the whip ceased, and I returned to my bed, and found no consolation but in my tears. It was not yet daylight.

## CHAPTER II.

MY master being a political demagogue, soon found those who were ready to put him into office, for the favors he could render them; and a few years after his arrival in Missouri, he was elected to a seat in the Legislature. In his absence from home, everything was left in charge of Mr. Cook, the overseer, and he soon became more tyrannical and cruel. Among the slaves on the plantation, was one by the name of Randall. He was a man about six feet high, and well-proportioned, and known as a man of great strength and power. He was considered the most valuable and able-bodied slave on the plantation; but no matter how good or useful a slave may be, he seldom escapes the lash. But it was not so with Randall. He had been on the plantation since my earliest recollection, and I had never known of his being flogged. No thanks were due to the master or overseer for this. I have often heard him declare, that no white man should ever whip him— that he would die first.

Cook, from the time that he came upon the plantation, had frequently declared, that he could and would flog any nigger that was put into the field to work under him. My master had repeatedly told him not to attempt to whip Randall, but he was determined to try it. As soon as he was left sole dictator, he thought the time had come to put his threats into execution. He soon began to find fault with Randall, and threatened to whip him, if he did not do better. One day he gave him a very hard task,—more than he could possibly do; and at night, the task not being performed, he told Randall that he should remember him the next morning. On the following morning, after the hands had taken breakfast, Cook called out to Randall, and told him that he intended to whip him, and ordered him to cross his hands and be tied. Randall asked why he wished to whip him. He answered, because he had not finished his task the day before. Randall said that the task was too great, or he should have done it. Cook said it made no difference,—he should whip him. Randall stood silent for a moment, and then said, "Mr. Cook, I have always tried to please you since you have been on the plantation, and I find you are determined not to be satisfied with my work, let me do as well as I may. No man has laid hands on me, to whip me, for the last ten years, and I have long since come to the conclusion not to be whipped by any man living." Cook, finding by Randall's determined look and gestures, that he would resist, called three of the hands from their work, and commanded them to seize Randall, and tie him. The hands stood still;—they knew Randall—and they also knew him to be a powerful man, and were afraid to grapple with him. As soon as Cook had ordered the men to seize him, Randall turned to them, and said—"Boys, you all know me; you know that I can handle any three of you, and the man that lays hands on me shall die. This white man can't whip me himself, and therefore he has called you to help him." The overseer was unable to prevail upon them to seize and secure Randall, and finally ordered them all to go to their work together.

Nothing was said to Randall by the overseer, for more than a week. One morning, however, while the hands were at work in the field, he came into it, accompanied by three friends of his, Thompson, Woodbridge and Jones. They came up to where Randall was at work, and Cook ordered him to leave his work, and go with them to the barn. He refused to go; whereupon he was attacked by the overseer and his companions, when he turned upon them, and laid them, one after another, prostrate on the ground. Woodbridge drew out his pistol, and fired at him, and brought him to the ground by a pistol ball. The others rushed upon him with their clubs, and beat him over the head and face, until they succeeded in tying, him. He was then taken to the barn, and tied to a beam. Cook gave him over one hundred lashes with a heavy cowhide, had him washed with salt and water, and left him tied during the day. The next day he was untied, and taken to a blacksmith's shop, and had a ball and chain attached to his leg. He was compelled to labor in the field, and perform the same amount of work that the other hands did. When his master returned home, he was much pleased to find that Randall had been subdued in his absence.

------

## CHAPTER III.

Soon afterwards, my master removed to the city of St. Louis, and purchased a farm four miles from there, which he placed under the charge of an overseer by the name of Friend Haskell. He was a regular Yankee from New England. The Yankees are noted for making the most cruel overseers.

My mother was hired out in the city, and I was also hired out there to Major Freeland, who kept a public house. He was formerly from Virginia, and was a horse-racer, cock-fighter, gambler, and withal an inveterate drunkard. There were ten or twelve servants in the house, and when he was present, it was cut and slash—knock down and drag out. In his fits of anger, he would take up a chair, and throw it at a servant; and in his more rational moments, when he wished to chastise one, he would tie them up in the smoke-house, and whip them; after which, he would cause a fire to be made of tobacco stems, and smoke them. This he called "*Virginia play.*"

I complained to my master of the treatment which I received from Major Freeland; but it made no difference. He cared nothing about it, so long as he received the money for my labor. After living with Major Freeland five or six months, I ran away, and went into the woods back of the city; and when night came on, I made my way to my master's farm, but was afraid to be seen, knowing that if Mr. Haskell, the overseer, should discover me, I should be again carried back to Major Freeland; so I kept in the woods. One day, while in the woods, I heard the barking and howling of dogs, and in a short time they came so near, that I knew them to be the bloodhounds of Major Benjamin O'Fallon. He kept five or six, to hunt runaway slaves with.

As soon as I was convinced that it was them, I knew there was no chance of escape. I took refuge in the top of a tree, and the hounds were soon at its base, and there remained until the hunters came up in a half or three quarters of an hour afterwards. There were two men with the dogs, who, as soon as they came up, ordered me to descend. I came down, was tied, and taken to St. Louis jail. Major Freeland soon made his appearance, and took me out, and ordered me to follow him, which I did. After we returned home, I was tied up in the smoke-house, and was very severely whipped. After the Major had flogged me to his satisfaction, he sent out his son Robert, a young man eighteen or twenty years of age, to see that I was well smoked. He made a fire of tobacco stems, which soon set me to coughing and sneezing. This, Robert told me, was the way his father used to do to his slaves in Virginia. After giving me what they conceived to be a decent smoking, I was untied and again set to work.

Robert Freeland was a "chip of the old block." Though quite young, it was not unfrequently that he came home in a state of intoxication. He is now, I believe, a popular commander of a steamboat on the Mississippi river. Major Freeland soon after failed in business, and I was put on board the steamboat Missouri, which plied between St. Louis and Galena. The commander of the boat was William B. Culver. I remained on her during the sailing season, which was the most pleasant time for me that I had ever experienced. At the close of navigation, I was hired to Mr. John Colburn, keeper of the Missouri Hotel. He was from one of the Free States; but a more inveterate hater of the negro, I do not believe ever walked on God's green earth. This hotel was at that time one of the largest in the city, and there were employed in it twenty or thirty servants, mostly slaves.

Mr. Colburn was very abusive, not only to the servants, but to his wife also, who was an excellent woman, and one from whom I never knew a servant to receive a harsh word; but never did I know a kind one to a servant from her husband. Among the slaves employed in the hotel, was one by the name of Aaron, who belonged to Mr. John F. Darby, a lawyer. Aaron was the knife-cleaner. One day, one of the knives was put on the table, not as clean as it might have been. Mr. Colburn, for this offense, tied Aaron up in the wood-house, and gave him over fifty lashes on the bare back with a cowhide, after which, he made me wash him down with rum. This seemed to put him into more agony than the whipping. After being untied, he went home to his master, and complained of the treatment which he had received. Mr. Darby would give no heed to anything he had to say, but sent him directly back. Colburn, learning that he had been to his master with complaints, tied him up again, and gave him a more severe whipping than before. The poor fellow's back was literally cut to pieces; so much so, that he was not able to work for ten or twelve days.

There was also, among the servants, a girl whose master resided in the country. Her name was Patsey. Mr. Colburn tied her up one evening, and whipped her until several of the boarders came out and begged him to desist. The reason for whipping her was this. She was engaged to be married to a man belonging to Major William Christie, who resided four or five miles north of the city. Mr. Colburn had forbid her to see John Christie. The reason of this was said to be the regard which he himself had for Patsey. She went to meeting that evening, and John returned home with her. Mr. Colburn had intended to flog John, if he came within the inclosure; but John knew too well the temper of his rival, and kept at a safe distance;—so he took vengeance on the poor girl. If all the slave-drivers had been called together, I do not think a more cruel man than John Colburn,—and he too a northern man,—could have been found among them.

While living at the Missouri Hotel, a circumstance occurred which caused me great unhappiness. My master sold my mother, and all her children, except myself. They were sold to different persons in the city of St. Louis.

---

## CHAPTER IV.

I WAS soon after taken from Mr. Colburn's, and hired to Elijah P. Lovejoy, who was at that time publisher and editor of the "St. Louis Times."[27] My work, while with him, was mainly in the printing office, waiting on the hands, working the press, &c. Mr. Lovejoy was a very good man, and decidedly the best master that I had ever had. I am chiefly indebted to him, and to my employment in the printing office, for what little learning I obtained while in slavery.

Though slavery is thought, by some, to be mild in Missouri, when compared with the cotton, sugar and rice growing States, yet no part of our slave-holding country, is more noted for the barbarity of its inhabitants, than St. Louis. It was here that Col. Harney, a United States officer, whipped a slave woman to death. It was here that Francis McIntosh, a free colored man from Pittsburgh, was taken from the steamboat Flora, and burned at the stake. During a residence of eight years in this city, numerous cases of extreme cruelty came under my own observation;—to record them all, would occupy more space than could possibly be allowed in this little volume. I shall, therefore, give but a few more, in addition to what I have already related.

Capt. J. B. Brunt, who resided near my master, had a slave named John. He was his body servant, carriage driver, &c. On one occasion, while driving his master through the city,—the streets being very muddy, and the horses going at a rapid rate,—some mud spattered upon a gentleman by the name of Robert More. More was determined to be revenged. Some three or four months after this occurrence, he purchased John, for the express purpose, as he said, "to tame the d——d nigger." After the purchase, he took him to a blacksmith's shop, and had a ball and chain fastened to his leg, and then put him to driving a yoke of oxen, and kept him at hard labor, until the iron around his leg was so worn into the flesh, that it was thought mortification would ensue. In addition to this, John told me that his master whipped him regularly three times a week for the first two months:—and all this to "tame him." A more noble looking man than he, was not to he found in all St. Louis, before he fell into the hands of More; and a more

degraded and spirit-crushed looking being was never seen on a southern plantation, after he had been subjected to this *"taming"* process for three months. The
last time that I saw him, he had nearly lost the entire use of his limbs.

While living with Mr. Lovejoy, I was often sent on errands to the office of
the "Missouri Republican," published by Mr. Edward Charles. Once, while returning to the office with type, I was attacked by several large boys, sons of slaveholders, who pelted me with snow-balls. Having the heavy form of type in my
hands, I could not make my escape by running; so I laid down the type and gave
them battle. They gathered around me, pelting me with stones and sticks, until
they overpowered me, and would have captured me, if I had not resorted to my
heels. Upon my retreat, they took possession of the type; and what to do to regain it I could not devise. Knowing Mr. Lovejoy to be a very humane man, I went
to the office, and laid the case before him. He told me to remain in the office. He
took one of the apprentices with him, and went after the type, and soon returned
with it; but on his return informed me that Samuel McKinney had told him that
he would whip me, because I had hurt his boy. Soon after, McKinney was seen
making his way to the office by one of the printers, who informed me of the fact,
and I made my escape through the back door.

McKinney not being able to find me on his arrival, left the office in a great
rage, swearing that he would whip me to death. A few days after, as I was walking along Main Street, he seized me by the collar, and struck me over the head
five or six times with a large cane, which caused the blood to gush from my nose
and ears in such a manner that my clothes were completely saturated with
blood. After beating me to his satisfaction, he let me go, and I returned to the
office so weak from the loss of blood, that Mr. Lovejoy sent me home to my
master. It was five weeks before I was able to walk again. During this time, it
was necessary to have some one to supply my place at the office, and I lost the
situation.

After my recovery, I was hired to Capt. Otis Reynolds, as a waiter on board
the steamboat Enterprize, owned by Messrs. John and Edward Walsh, commission merchants at St. Louis. This boat was then running on the upper Mississippi.
My employment on board was to wait on gentlemen, and the captain being a good
man, the situation was a pleasant one to me;—but in passing from place to place,
and seeing new faces every day, and knowing that they could go where they
pleased, I soon became unhappy, and several times thought of leaving the boat at
some landing place, and trying to make my escape to Canada, which I had heard
much about as a place where the slave might live, be free, and be protected.

But whenever such thoughts would come into my mind, my resolution
would soon be shaken by the remembrance that my dear mother was a slave in
St. Louis, and I could not bear the idea of leaving her in that condition. She had
often taken me upon her knee, and told me how she had carried me upon her
back to the field when I was an infant—how often she had been whipped for leaving her work to nurse me—and how happy I would appear when she would take
me into her arms. When these thoughts came over me, I would resolve never to
leave the land of slavery without my mother. I thought that to leave her in slavery, after she had undergone and suffered so much for me, would be proving

recreant to the duty which I owed to her. Besides this, I had three brothers and a sister there,—two of my brothers having died.

My mother, my brothers Joseph and Millford, and my sister Elizabeth, belonged to Mr. Isaac Mansfield, formerly from one of the Free States, (Massachusetts, I believe.) He was a tinner by trade, and carried on a large manufacturing establishment. Of all my relatives, mother was first, and sister next. One evening, while visiting them, I made some allusion to a proposed journey to Canada, and sister took her seat by my side, and taking my hand in hers, said, with tears in her eyes,—

"Brother, you are not going to leave mother and your dear sister here without a friend, are you?"

I looked into her face, as the tears coursed swiftly down her cheeks, and bursting into tears myself, said—

"No, I will never desert you and mother."

She clasped my hand in hers, and said—

"Brother, you have often declared that you would not end your days in slavery. I see no possible way in which you can escape with us; and now, brother, you are on a steamboat where there is some chance for you to escape to a land of liberty. I beseech you not to let us hinder you. If we cannot get our liberty, we do not wish to be the means of keeping you from a land of freedom."

I could restrain my feelings no longer, and an outburst of my own feelings, caused her to cease speaking upon that subject. In opposition to their wishes, I pledged myself not to leave them in the hand of the oppressor. I took leave of them, and returned to the boat, and laid down in my bunk; but "sleep departed from my eyes, and slumber from my eyelids."[28]

A few weeks after, on our downward passage, the boat took on board, at Hannibal, a drove of slaves, bound for the New Orleans market. They numbered from fifty to sixty, consisting of men and women from eighteen to forty years of age. A drove of slaves on a southern steamboat, bound for the cotton or sugar regions, is an occurrence so common, that no one, not even the passengers, appear to notice it, though they clank their chains at every step. There was, however, one in this gang that attracted the attention of the passengers and crew. It was a beautiful girl, apparently about twenty years of age, perfectly white, with straight light hair and blue eyes. But it was not the whiteness of her skin that created such a sensation among those who gazed upon her—it was her almost unparalleled beauty. She had been on the boat but a short time, before the attention of all the passengers, including the ladies, had been called to her, and the common topic of conversation was about the beautiful slave-girl. She was not in chains. The man who claimed this article of human merchandize was a Mr. Walker,—a well known slave-trader, residing in St. Louis. There was a general anxiety among the passengers and crew to learn the history of the girl. Her master kept close by her side, and it would have been considered impudent for any of the passengers to have spoken to her, and the crew were not allowed to have any conversation with them. When we reached St. Louis, the slaves were removed to a boat bound for New Orleans, and the history of the beautiful slave-girl remained a mystery.

I remained on the boat during the season, and it was not an unfrequent occurrence to have on board gangs of slaves on their way to the cotton, sugar and rice plantations of the South.

Toward the latter part of the summer, Captain Reynolds left the boat, and I was sent home. I was then placed on the farm under Mr. Haskell, the overseer. As I had been some time out of the field, and not accustomed to work in the burning sun, it was very hard; but I was compelled to keep up with the best of the hands.

I found a great difference between the work in a steamboat cabin and that in a corn-field.

My master, who was then living in the city, soon after removed to the farm, when I was taken out of the field to work in the house as a waiter.[29] Though his wife was very peevish, and hard to please, I much preferred to be under her control than the overseer's. They brought with them Mr. Sloane, a Presbyterian minister; Miss Martha Tulley, a neice of theirs from Kentucky; and their nephew William. The latter had been in the family a number of years, but the others were all new-comers.

Mr. Sloane was a young minister, who had been at the South but a short time, and it seemed as if his whole aim was to please the slaveholders, especially my master and mistress. He was intending to make a visit during the winter, and he not only tried to please them, but I think he succeeded admirably. When they wanted singing, he sung; when they wanted praying, he prayed; when they wanted a story told, he told a story. Instead of his teaching my master theology, my master taught theology to him. While I was with Captain Reynolds, my master "got religion," and new laws were made on the plantation. Formerly, we had the privilege of hunting, fishing, making splint brooms, baskets, &c. on Sunday; but this was all stopped. Every Sunday, we were all compelled to attend meeting. Master was so religious, that he induced some others to join him in hiring a preacher to preach to the slaves.

----

# CHAPTER V.

My master had family worship, night and morning. At night, the slaves were called in to attend; but in the mornings, they had to be at their work, and master did all the praying. My master and mistress were great lovers of mint julep, and every morning, a pitcher-full was made, of which they all partook freely, not excepting little master William. After drinking freely all round, they would have family worship, and then breakfast. I cannot say but I loved the julep as well as any of them, and during prayer was always careful to seat myself close to the table where it stood, so as to help myself when they were all busily engaged in their devotions. By the time prayer was over, I was about as happy as any of them. A sad accident happened one morning. In helping myself, and at the same time keeping an eye on my old mistress, I accidentally let the pitcher fall upon the floor, breaking it in pieces, and spilling the contents. This was a bad affair for me; for as soon as prayer was over, I was taken and severely chastised.

My master's family consisted of himself, his wife, and their nephew, William Moore. He was taken into the family, when only a few weeks of age. His name being that of my own, mine was changed, for the purpose of giving precedence to his, though I was his senior by ten or twelve years. The plantation being four miles from the city, I had to drive the family to church. I always dreaded the approach of the Sabbath; for, during service, I was obliged to stand by the horses in the hot broiling sun, or in the rain, just as it happened.

One Sabbath, as we were driving past the house of D. D. Page, a gentleman who owned a large baking establishment, as I was sitting upon the box of the carriage, which was very much elevated, I saw Mr. Page pursuing a slave around the yard, with a long whip, cutting him at every jump. The man soon escaped from the yard, and was followed by Mr. Page. They came running past us, and the slave perceiving that he would be overtaken, stopped suddenly, and Page stumbled over him, and falling on the stone pavement, fractured one of his legs, which crippled him for life. The same gentleman, but a short time previous, tied up a woman of his, by the name of Delphia, and whipped her nearly to death; yet he was a deacon in the Baptist church,[30] in good and regular standing. Poor Delphia! I was well acquainted with her, and called to see her while upon her sick bed; and I shall never forget her appearance. She was a member of the same church with her master.

Soon after this, I was hired out to Mr. Walker; the same man whom I have mentioned as having carried a gang of slaves down the river, on the steamboat Enterprize. Seeing me in the capacity of steward on the boat, and thinking that I would make a good hand to take care of slaves, he determined to have me for that purpose; and finding that my master would not sell me, he hired me for the term of one year.

When I learned the fact of my having been hired to a negro speculator, or a "soul-driver" as they are generally called among slaves, no one can tell my emotions. Mr. Walker had offered a high price for me, as I afterwards learned, but I suppose my master was restrained from selling me by the fact that I was a near relative of his. On entering the service of Mr. Walker, I found that my opportunity of getting to a land of liberty was gone, at least for the time being. He had a gang of slaves in readiness to start for New Orleans, and in a few days we were on our journey. I am at a loss for language to express my feelings on that occasion. Although my master had told me that he had not sold me, and Mr. Walker had told me that he had not purchased me, I did not believe them; and not until I had been to New Orleans, and was on my return, did I believe that I was not sold.

There was on the boat a large room on the lower deck, in which the slaves were kept, men and women, promiscuously—all chained two and two, and a strict watch kept that they did not get loose; for cases have occurred in which slaves have got off their chains, and made their escape at landing-places, while the boats were taking in wood;—and with all our care, we lost one woman who had been taken from her husband and children, and having no desire to live without them, in the agony of her soul jumped overboard, and drowned herself. She was not chained.

It was almost impossible to keep that part of the boat clean.

On landing at Natchez, the slaves were all carried to the slave-pen, and there kept one week, during which time, several of them were sold. Mr. Walker fed his slaves well. We took on board, at St. Louis, several hundred pounds of bacon (smoked meat) and corn-meal, and his slaves were better fed than slaves generally were in Natchez, so far as my observation extended.

At the end of a week, we left for New Orleans, the place of our final destination, which we reached in two days. Here the slaves were placed in a negro-pen, where those who wished to purchase could call and examine them. The negro-pen is a small yard, surrounded by buildings, from fifteen to twenty feet wide, with the exception of a large gate with iron bars. The slaves are kept in the buildings during the night, and turned out into the yard during the day. After the best of the stock was sold at private sale at the pen, the balance were taken to the Exchange Coffee House Auction Rooms, kept by Isaac L. McCoy, and sold at public auction. After the sale of this lot of slaves, we left New Orleans for St. Louis.

# CHAPTER VI.

ON our arrival at St. Louis, I went to Dr. Young. and told him that I did not wish to live with Mr. Walker any longer. I was heart-sick at seeing my fellow-creatures bought and sold. But the Dr. had hired me for the year, and stay I must. Mr. Walker again commenced purchasing another gang of slaves. He bought a man of Colonel John O'Fallon, who resided in the suburbs of the city. This man had a wife and three children. As soon as the purchase was made, he was put in jail for safe keeping, until we should be ready to start for New Orleans. His wife visited him while there, several times, and several times when she went for that purpose was refused admittance.

In the course of eight or nine weeks Mr. Walker had his cargo of human flesh made up. There was in this lot a number of old men and women, some of them with gray locks. We left St. Louis in the steamboat Carlton, Captain Swan, bound for New Orleans. On our way down, and before we reached Rodney,[31] the place where we made our first stop, I had to prepare the old slaves for market. I was ordered to have the old men's whiskers shaved off, and the grey hairs plucked out, where they were not too numerous, in which case he had a preparation of blacking to color it, and with a blacking-brush we would put it on. This was new business to me, and was performed in a room where the passengers could not see us. These slaves were also taught how old they were by Mr. Walker, and after going through the blacking process, they looked ten or fifteen years younger; and I am sure that some of those who purchased slaves of Mr. Walker, were dreadfully cheated, especially in the ages of the slaves which they bought.

We landed at Rodney, and the slaves were driven to the pen in the back part of the village. Several were sold at this place, during our stay of four or five days, when we proceeded to Natchez. There we landed at night, and the gang were put in the warehouse until morning, when they were driven to the pen. As soon as the slaves are put in these pens, swarms of planters may be seen in and about them. They knew when Walker was expected, as he always had the time advertised beforehand when he would be in Rodney, Natchez, and New Orleans. These were the principal places where he offered his slaves for sale.

When at Natchez the second time, I saw a slave very cruelly whipped. He belonged to a Mr. Broadwell, a merchant who kept a store on the wharf. The slave's name was Lewis. I had known him several years, as he was formerly from St. Louis. We were expecting a steamboat down the river, in which we were to take passage for New Orleans. Mr. Walker sent me to the landing to watch for the boat, ordering me to inform him on its arrival. While there, I went into the store to see Lewis. I saw a slave in the store, and asked him where Lewis was. Said he, "They have got Lewis hanging between the heavens and the earth." I asked him what he meant by that. He told me to go into the warehouse and see. I went in, and found Lewis there. He was tied up to a beam, with his toes just touching the floor. As there was no one in the warehouse but himself, I inquired the reason of his being in that situation. He said Mr. Broadwell had sold his wife to a planter six miles from the city, and that he had been to visit her,—that he went in the night, expecting to return before daylight, and went without his master's permission. The patrol had taken him up before he reached his wife. He was put in jail, and his master had to pay for his catching and keeping, and that was what he was tied up for.

Just as he finished his story, Mr. Broadwell came in, and inquired what I was doing there. I knew not what to say, and while I was thinking what reply to make, he struck me over the head with the cowhide, the end of which struck me over my right eye, sinking deep into the flesh, leaving a scar which I carry to this day. Before I visited Lewis, he had received fifty lashes. Mr. Broadwell gave him fifty lashes more after I came out, as I was afterwards informed by Lewis himself.

The next day we proceeded to New Orleans, and put the gang in the same negro-pen which we occupied before. In a short time, the planters came flocking to the pen to purchase slaves. Before the slaves were exhibited for sale, they were dressed and driven out into the yard. Some were set to dancing, some to jumping, some to singing, and some to playing cards. This was done to make them appear cheerful and happy. My business was to see that they were placed in those situations before the arrival of the purchasers, and I have often set them to dancing when their cheeks were wet with tears. As slaves were in good demand at that time, they were all soon disposed of, and we again set out for St. Louis.

On our arrival, Mr. Walker purchased a farm five or six miles from the city. He had no family, but made a housekeeper of one of his female slaves. Poor Cynthia! I knew her well. She was a quadroon, and one of the most beautiful women I ever saw. She was a native of St. Louis, and bore an irreproachable character for virtue and propriety of conduct. Mr. Walker bought her for the New Orleans market, and took her down with him on one of the trips that I made with him. Never shall I forget the circumstances of that voyage! On the first night that we were on board the steamboat, he directed me to put her into a state-room he had provided for her, apart from the other slaves. I had seen too much of the workings of slavery, not to know what this meant. I accordingly watched him into the state-room, and listened to hear what passed between them. I heard him make his base offers, and her reject them. He told her that if she would accept his vile proposals, he would take her back with him to St. Louis, and establish her as his housekeeper at his farm. But if she persisted in rejecting them, he would sell her as a field hand on the worst plantation on the river. Neither threats nor bribes prevailed, however, and he retired, disappointed of his prey.

The next morning, poor Cynthia told me what had past, and bewailed her sad fate with floods of tears. I comforted and encouraged her all I could; but I foresaw but too well what the result must be. Without entering into any farther particulars, suffice it to say that Walker performed his part of the contract, at that time. He took her back to St. Louis, established her as his mistress and housekeeper at his farm, and before I left, he had two children by her. But, mark the end! Since I have been at the North, I have been credibly informed that Walker has been married, and, as a previous measure, sold poor Cynthia and her four children (she having had two more since I came away) into hopeless bondage!

He soon commenced purchasing to make up the third gang. We took steamboat, and went to Jefferson City, a town on the Missouri river. Here we landed, and took stage for the interior of the State. He bought a number of slaves as he passed the different farms and villages. After getting twenty-two or twenty-three men and women, we arrived at St. Charles, a village on the banks of the Missouri. Here he purchased a woman who had a child in her arms, appearing to be four or five weeks old.

We had been travelling by land for some days, and were in hopes to have found a boat at this place for St. Louis, but were disappointed. As no boat was expected for some days, we started for St. Louis by land. Mr. Walker had purchased two horses. He rode one, and I the other. The slaves were chained together, and we took up our line to march, Mr. Walker taking the lead, and I bringing up the rear. Though the distance was not more than twenty miles, we did not reach it the first day. The road was worse than any that I have ever travelled.

Soon after we left St. Charles, the young child grew very cross, and kept up a noise during the greater part of the day. Mr. Walker complained of its crying several times, and told the mother to stop the child's d——d noise, or he would. The woman tried to keep the child from crying, but could not. We put up at night with an acquaintance of Mr. Walker, and in the morning, just as we were about to start, the child again commenced crying. Walker stepped up to her, and told her to give the child to him. The mother tremblingly obeyed. He took the child by one arm, as you would a cat by the leg, walked into the house, and said to the lady,

"Madam, I will make you a present of this little nigger; it keeps such a noise that I can't bear it."

"Thank you, sir," said the lady.

The mother, as soon as she saw that her child was to be left, ran up to Mr. Walker, and falling upon her knees begged him to let her have her child; she clung around his legs, and cried, "Oh, my child! my child! master, do let me have my child! oh, do, do, do. I will stop its crying, if you will only let me have it again." When I saw this woman crying for her child so piteously, a shudder,—a feeling akin to horror, shot through my frame. I have often since in imagination heard her crying for her child:—

> "O, master, let me stay to catch
>    My baby's sobbing breath,
> His little glassy eye to watch,
>    And smooth his limbs in death,
>
> And cover him with grass and leaf,
>    Beneath the large oak tree:
> It is not sullenness, but grief,—
>    O, master, pity me!
>
> The morn was chill—I spoke no word,
>    But feared my babe might die,
> And heard all day, or thought I heard,
>    My little baby cry.
>
> At noon, oh, how I ran and took
>    My baby to my breast!
> I lingered—and the long lash broke
>    My sleeping infant's rest.
>
> I worked till night—till darkest night,
>    In torture and disgrace;
> Went home and watched till morning light,
>    To see my baby's face.
>
> Then give me but one little hour—
>    O! do not lash me so!
> One little hour—one little hour—
>    And gratefully I'll go."[32]

Mr. Walker commanded her to return into the ranks with the other slaves. Women who had children were not chained, but those that had none were. As soon as her child was disposed of, she was chained in the gang.

The following song I have often heard the slaves sing, when about to be carried to the far south. It is said to have been composed by a slave.

> "See these poor souls from Africa
> Transported to America;
> We are stolen, and sold to Georgia,
> Will you go along with me?
> We are stolen, and sold to Georgia,
> Come sound the jubilee!
>
> See wives and husbands sold apart,
> Their children's screams will break my heart;—
> There 's a better day a coming,
> Will you go along with me?
> There 's a better day a coming,
> Go sound the jubilee!

O, gracious Lord! when shall it be,
That we poor souls shall all be free;
Lord, break them slavery powers—
Will you go along with me?
Lord break them slavery powers,
Go sound the jubilee!

Dear Lord, dear Lord, when slavery 'll cease,
Then we poor souls will have our peace;—
There 's a better day a coming,
Will you go along with me?
There 's a better day a coming,
Go sound the jubilee!"[33]

We finally arrived at Mr. Walker's farm. He had a house built during our absence to put slaves in. It was a kind of domestic jail. The slaves were put in the jail at night, and worked on the farm during the day. They were kept here until the gang was completed, when we again started for New Orleans, on board the steamboat North America, Capt. Alexander Scott. We had a large number of slaves in this gang. One, by the name of Joe, Mr. Walker was training up to take my place, as my time was nearly out, and glad was I. We made our first stop at Vicksburg, where we remained one week and sold several slaves.

Mr. Walker, though not a good master, had not flogged a slave since I had been with him, though he had threatened me. The slaves were kept in the pen, and he always put up at the best hotel, and kept his wines in his room, for the accommodation of those who called to negotiate with him for the purchase of slaves. One day while we were at Vicksburg, several gentlemen came to see him for this purpose, and as usual the wine was called for. I took the tray and started around with it, and having accidentally filled some of the glasses too full, the gentlemen spilled the wine on their clothes as they went to drink. Mr. Walker apologized to them for my carelessness, but looked at me as though he would see me again on this subject.

After the gentlemen had left the room, he asked me what I meant by my carelessness, and said that he would attend to me. The next morning, he gave me a note to carry to the jailer, and a dollar in money to give to him. I suspected that all was not right, so I went down near the landing where I met with a sailor, and walking up to him, asked him if he would be so kind as to read the note for me. He read it over, and then looked at me. I asked him to tell me what was in it. Said he,

"They are going to give you hell."

"Why?" said I.

He said, "This is a note to have you whipped, and says that you have a dollar to pay for it."

He handed me back the note, and off I started. I knew not what to do, but was determined not to be whipped. I went up to the jail—took a look at it, and walked off again. As Mr. Walker was acquainted with the jailer, I feared that I should be found out if I did not go, and be treated in consequence of it still worse.

While I was meditating on the subject, I saw a colored man about my size walk up, and the thought struck me in a moment to send him with my note. I walked up to him, and asked him who he belonged to. He said he was a free man, and had been in the city but a short time. I told him I had a note to go into the jail, and get a trunk to carry to one of the steamboats; but was so busily engaged that I could not do it, although I had a dollar to pay for it. He asked me if I would not give him the job. I handed him the note and the dollar, and off he started for the jail.

I watched to see that he went in, and as soon as I saw the door close behind him, I walked around the corner, and took my station, intending to see how my friend looked when he came out. I had been there but a short time, when a colored man came around the corner, and said to another colored man with whom he was acquainted—

"They are giving a nigger scissors in the jail."

"What for?" said the other. The man continued,

"A nigger came into the jail, and asked for the jailer. The jailer came out, and he handed him a note, and said he wanted to get a trunk. The jailer told him to go with him, and he would give him the trunk. So he took him into the room, and told the nigger to give up the dollar. He said a man had given him the dollar to pay for getting the trunk. But that lie would not answer. So they made him strip himself, and then they tied him down, and are now whipping him."

I stood by all the while listening to their talk, and soon found out that the person alluded to was my customer. I went into the street opposite the jail, and concealed myself in such a manner that I could not be seen by any one coming out. I had been there but a short time, when the young man made his appearance, and looked around for me. I, unobserved, came forth from my hiding-place, behind a pile of brick, and he pretty soon saw me and came up to me complaining bitterly, saying that I had played a trick upon him. I denied any knowledge of what the note contained, and asked him what they had done to him. He told me in substance what I heard the man tell who had come out of the jail.

"Yes," said he, "they whipped me and took my dollar, and gave me this note."

He showed me the note which the jailer had given him, telling him to give it to his master. I told him I would give him fifty cents for it,—that being all the money I had. He gave it to me, and took his money. He had received twenty lashes on his bare back, with the negro-whip.

I took the note and started for the hotel where I had left Mr. Walker. Upon reaching the hotel, I handed it to a stranger whom I had not seen before, and requested him to read it to me. As near as I can recollect, it was as follows:—

"Dear Sir:—By your direction, I have given your boy twenty lashes. He is a very saucy boy, and tried to make me believe that he did not belong to you, and I put it on to him well for lying to me.

I remain,

Your obedient servant."

It is true that in most of the slave-holding cities, when a gentleman wishes his servants whipped, he can send him to the jail and have it done. Before I went in where Mr. Walker was, I wet my cheeks a little, as though I had been crying. He looked at me, and inquired what was the matter. I told him that I had never had such a whipping in my life, and handed him the note. He looked at it and laughed;—"and so you told him that you did not belong to me." "Yes, sir," said I. "I did not know that there was any harm in that." He told me I must behave myself, if I did not want to be whipped again.

This incident shows how it is that slavery makes its victims lying and mean; for which vices it afterwards reproaches them, and uses them as arguments to prove that they deserve no better fate. I have often, since my escape, deeply regretted the deception I practised upon this poor fellow; and I heartily desire that it may be, at some time or other, in my power to make him amends for his vicarious sufferings in my behalf.

## CHAPTER VII.

IN a few days we reached New Orleans, and arriving there in the night, remained on board until morning. While at New Orleans this time,[34] I saw a slave killed; an account of which has been published by Theodore D. Weld, in his book entitled, "Slavery as it is."[35] The circumstances were as follows. In the evening, between seven and eight o'clock, a slave came running down the levee, followed by several men and boys. The whites were crying out, "Stop that nigger; stop that nigger;" while the poor panting slave, in almost breathless accents, was repeating, "I did not steal the meat—I did not steal the meat." The poor man at last took refuge in the river. The whites who were in pursuit of him, run on board of one of the boats to see if they could discover him. They finally espied him under the bow of the steamboat Trenton. They got a pike-pole, and tried to drive him from his hiding place. When they would strike at him, he would dive under the water. The water was so cold, that it soon became evident that he must come out or be drowned.

While they were trying to drive him from under the bow of the boat or drown him, he would in broken and imploring accents say, "I did not steal the meat; I did not steal the meat. My master lives up the river. I want to see my master. I did not steal the meat. Do let me go home to master." After punching him, and striking him over the head for some time, he at last sunk in the water, to rise no more alive.

On the end of the pike-pole with which they were striking him was a hook which caught in his clothing, and they hauled him up on the bow of the boat. Some said he was dead, others said he was "*playing possum*," while others kicked him to make him get up, but it was of no use—he was dead.

As soon as they became satisfied of this, they commenced leaving, one after another. One of the hands on the boat informed the captain that they had killed the man, and that the dead body was lying on the deck. The captain came on deck, and said to those who were remaining, "You have killed this nigger; now take him off of my boat." The captain's name was Hart. The dead body was dragged on shore and left there. I went on board of the boat where our gang of slaves were, and during the whole night my mind was occupied with what I had seen. Early in the morning, I went on shore to see if the dead body remained there. I found it in the same position that it was left the night before. I watched to see what they would do with it. It was left there until between eight and nine o'clock, when a cart, which takes up the trash out of the streets, came along, and the body was thrown in, and in a few minutes more was covered over with dirt which they were removing from the streets. During the whole time, I did not see more than six or seven persons around it, who, from their manner, evidently regarded it as no uncommon occurrence.

During our stay in the city, I met with a young white man with whom I was well acquainted in St. Louis. He had been sold into slavery, under the following circumstances. His father was a drunkard, and very poor, with a family of five or six children. The father died, and left the mother to take care of and provide for the children as best she might. The eldest was a boy, named Burrill, about thirteen years of age, who did chores in a store kept by Mr. Riley, to assist his mother in procuring a living for the family. After working with him two years, Mr. Riley took him to New Orleans to wait on him while in that city on a visit, and when he returned to St. Louis, he told the mother of the boy that he had died with the yellow fever. Nothing more was heard from him, no one supposing him to be alive. I was much astonished when Burrill told me his story. Though I sympathized with him, I could not assist him. We were both slaves. He was poor, uneducated, and without friends; and if living, is, I presume, still held as a slave.

After selling out this cargo of human flesh, we returned to St. Louis, and my time was up with Mr. Walker. I had served him one year, and it was the longest year I ever lived.

---

## CHAPTER VIII.

I WAS sent home, and was glad enough to leave the service of one who was tearing the husband from the wife, the child from the mother, and the sister from the brother,—but a trial more severe and heart-rending than any which I had yet met with awaited me. My dear sister had been sold to a man who was going to Natchez, and was lying in jail awaiting the hour of his departure. She had expressed her determination to die, rather than go to the far south, and she was put in jail for safe keeping. I went to the jail the same day that I arrived, but as the jailor was not in, I could not see her.

I went home to my master, in the country, and the first day after my return, he came where I was at work, and spoke to me very politely. I knew from his appearance that something was the matter. After talking about my several journeys to New Orleans with Mr. Walker, he told me that he was hard pressed for money, and as he had sold my mother and all her children except me, he thought it would be better to sell me than any other one, and that as I had been used to living in the city, he thought it probable that I would prefer it to a country life. I raised up my head, and looked him full in the face. When my eyes caught his, he immediately looked to the ground. After a short pause, I said,

"Master, mother has often told me that you are a near relative of mine, and I have often heard you admit the fact; and after you have hired me out, and received, as I once heard you say, nine hundred dollars for my services,—after receiving this large sum, will you sell me to be carried to New Orleans or some other place?"

"No," said he, "I do not intend to sell you to a negro trader. If I had wished to have done that, I might have sold you to Mr. Walker for a large sum, but I would not sell you to a negro trader. You may go to the city, and find you a good master."

"But," said I, "I cannot find a good master in the whole city of St. Louis."

"Why?" said he.

"Because there are no good masters in the State."

"Do you not call me a good master?"

"If you were, you would not sell me."

"Now I will give you one week to find a master in, and surely you can do it in that time."

The price set by my evangelical master upon my soul and body was the trifling sum of five hundred dollars. I tried to enter into some arrangement by which I might purchase my freedom; but he would enter into no such arrangement.

I set out for the city with the understanding that I was to return in a week with some one to become my new master. Soon after reaching the city, I went to the jail, to learn if I could once more see my sister; but could not gain admission. I then went to mother, and learned from her that the owner of my sister intended to start for Natchez in a few days.

I went to the jail again the next day, and Mr. Simonds, the keeper, allowed me to see my sister for the last time. I cannot give a just description of the scene at that parting interview. Never, never can be erased from my heart the occurrences of that day! When I entered the room where she was, she was seated in one corner, alone. There were four other women in the same room, belonging to the same man. He had purchased them, he said, for his own use. She was seated with her face towards the door where I entered, yet she did not look up until I walked up to her. As soon as she observed me, she sprung up, threw her arms around my neck, leaned her head upon my breast, and, without uttering a word, burst into tears. As soon as she recovered herself sufficiently to speak, she advised me to take mother, and try to get out of slavery. She said there was no hope for herself,—that she must live and die a slave. After giving her some advice, and taking from my finger a ring and placing it upon hers, I bade her farewell forever, and returned to my mother, and then and there made up my mind to leave for Canada as soon as possible.

I had been in the city nearly two days, and as I was to be absent only a week, I thought best to get on my journey as soon as possible. In conversing with mother, I found her unwilling to make the attempt to reach a land of liberty, but she counselled me to get my liberty if I could. She said, as all her children were in slavery, she did not wish to leave them. I could not bear the idea of leaving her among those pirates, when there was a prospect of being able to get away from them. After much persuasion, I succeeded in inducing her to make the attempt to get away.

The time fixed for our departure was the next night. I had with me a little money that I had received, from time to time, from gentlemen for whom I had done errands. I took my scanty means and purchased some dried beef, crackers and cheese, which I carried to mother, who had provided herself with a bag to carry it in. I occasionally thought of my old master, and of my mission to the city to find a new one. I waited with the most intense anxiety for the appointed time to leave the land of slavery, in search of a land of liberty.

The time at length arrived, and we left the city just as the clock struck nine. We proceeded to the upper part of the city, where I had been two or three times during the day, and selected a skiff to carry us across the river. The boat was not mine, nor did I know to whom it did belong; neither did I care. The boat was fastened with a small pole, which, with the aid of a rail, I soon loosened from its moorings. After hunting round and finding a board to use as an oar, I turned to the city, and bidding it a long farewell, pushed off my boat. The current running very swift, we had not reached the middle of the stream before we were directly opposite the city.

We were soon upon the Illinois shore, and, leaping from the boat, turned it adrift, and the last I saw of it, it was going down the river at good speed. We took the main road to Alton, and passed through just at daylight, when we made for the woods, where we remained during the day. Our reason for going into the woods was, that we expected that Mr. Mansfield (the man who owned my mother) would start in pursuit of her as soon as he discovered that she was missing. He also knew that I had been in the city looking for a new master, and we thought probably he would go out to my master's to see if he could find my mother, and in so doing, Dr. Young might be led to suspect that I had gone to Canada to find a purchaser.

We remained in the woods during the day, and as soon as darkness overshadowed the earth, we started again on our gloomy way, having no guide but the NORTH STAR. We continued to travel by night, and secrete ourselves in woods by day; and every night, before emerging from our hiding-place, we would anxiously look for our friend and leader,—the NORTH STAR.

---

## CHAPTER IX.

AS we travelled towards a land of liberty, my heart would at times leap for joy. At other times, being, as I was, almost constantly on my feet, I felt as though I could travel no further. But when I thought of slavery with its Democratic whips—its Republican chains—its evangelical blood-hounds, and its religious slave-holders—when I thought of all this paraphernalia of American Democracy and Religion behind me, and the prospect of liberty before me, I was encouraged to press forward, my heart was strengthened, and I forgot that I was tired or hungry.

On the eighth day of our journey, we had a very heavy rain, and in a few hours after it commenced, we had not a dry thread upon our bodies. This made our journey still more unpleasant. On the tenth day, we found ourselves entirely destitute of provisions, and how to obtain any we could not tell. We finally resolved to stop at some farmhouse, and try to get something to eat. We had no sooner determined to do this, than we went to a house, and asked them for some food. We were treated with great kindness, and they not only gave us something to eat, but gave us provisions to carry with us. They advised us to travel by day, and lye by at night. Finding ourselves about one hundred and fifty miles from St. Louis, we concluded that it would be safe to travel by daylight, and did not leave the house until the next morning. We travelled on that day through a thickly settled country, and through one small village. Though we were fleeing from a land of oppression, our hearts were still there. My dear sister and two beloved brothers were behind us, and the idea of giving them up, and leaving them forever, made us feel sad. But with all this depression of heart, the thought that I should one day be free, and call my body my own, buoyed me up, and made my heart leap for joy. I had just been telling mother how I should try to get employment as soon as we reached Canada, and how I intended to purchase us a little farm, and how I would earn money enough to buy sister and brothers, and how happy we would be in our own FREE HOME,—when three men came up on horseback, and ordered us to stop.

I turned to the one who appeared to be the principal man, and asked him what he wanted. He said he had a warrant to take us up. The three immediately dismounted, and one took from his pocket a handbill, advertising us as runaways, and offering a reward of two hundred dollars for our apprehension, and delivery in the city of St. Louis. The advertisement had been put out by Isaac Mansfield and John Young.

While they were reading the advertisement, mother looked me in the face, and burst into tears. A cold chill ran over me, and such a sensation I never experienced before, and I hope never to again. They took out a rope and tied me, and we were taken back about six miles, to the house of the individual who appeared to be the leader. We reached there about seven o'clock in the evening, had supper, and were separated for the night. Two men remained in the room during the night. Before the family retired to rest, they were all called together to attend prayers. The man who but a few hours before had bound my hands together with a strong cord, read a chapter from the Bible, and then offered up prayer, just as though God sanctioned the act he had just committed upon a poor panting, fugitive slave.

The next morning, a blacksmith came in, and put a pair of handcuffs on me, and we started on our journey back to the land of whips, chains and Bibles. Mother was not tied, but was closely watched at night. We were carried back in a wagon, and after four days travel, we came in sight of St. Louis. I cannot describe my feelings upon approaching the city.

As we were crossing the ferry, Mr. Wiggins, the owner of the ferry, came up to me, and inquired what I had been doing that I was in chains. He had not heard that I had run away. In a few minutes, we were on the Missouri side, and were taken directly to the jail. On the way thither, I saw several of my friends, who gave me a nod of recognition as I passed them. After reaching the jail, we were locked up in different apartments.

---

## CHAPTER X.

I HAD been in jail but a short time when I heard that my master was sick, and nothing brought more joy to my heart than that intelligence. I prayed fervently for him—not for his recovery, but for his death. I knew he would be exasperated at having to pay for my apprehension, and knowing his cruelty, I feared him. While in jail, I learned that my sister Elizabeth, who was in prison when we left the city, had been carried off four days before our arrival.

I had been in jail but a few hours when three negro-traders, learning that I was secured thus for running away, came to my prison-house and looked at me, expecting that I would be offered for sale. Mr. Mansfield, the man who owned mother, came into the jail as soon as Mr. Jones, the man who arrested us, informed him that he had brought her back. He told her that he would not whip her, but would sell her to a negro-trader, or take her to New Orleans himself. After being in jail about one week, master sent a man to take me out of jail, and send me home. I was taken out and carried home, and the old man was well enough to sit up. He had me brought into the room where he was, and as I entered, he asked me where I had been? I told I had acted according to his orders. He had told me to look for a master, and I had been to look for one. He answered that he did not tell me to go to Canada to look for a master. I told him that as I had served him faithfully, and had been the means of putting a number of hundreds of dollars into his pocket, I thought I had a right to my liberty. He said he had promised my father that I should not be sold to supply the New Orleans market, or he would sell me to a negro-trader.

I was ordered to go into the field to work, and was closely watched by the overseer during the day, and locked up at night. The overseer gave me a severe whipping on the second day that I was in the field. I had been at home but a short time, when master was able to ride to the city; and on his return, he informed me that he had sold me to Samuel Willi, a merchant tailor. I knew Mr. Willi. I had lived with him three or four months some years before, when he hired me of my master.

Mr. Willi was not considered by his servants as a very bad man, nor was he the best of masters. I went to my new home, and found my new mistress very glad to see me. Mr. Willi owned two servants before he purchased me,—Robert and Charlotte. Robert was an excellent white-washer, and hired his time from his master, paying him one dollar per day, besides taking care of himself. He was known in the city by the name of Bob Music. Charlotte was an old woman, who attended to the cooking, washing, &c. Mr. Willi was not a wealthy man, and did not feel able to keep many servants around his house; so he soon decided to hire me out, and as I had been accustomed to service in steamboats, he gave me the privilege of finding such employment.

I soon secured a situation on board the steamer Otto, Capt. J. B. Hill, which sailed from St. Louis to Independence, Missouri. My former master, Dr. Young, did not let Mr. Willi know that I had run away, or he would not have permitted me to go on board a steamboat. The boat was not quite ready to commence running, and therefore I had to remain with Mr. Willi. But during this time, I had to undergo a trial, for which I was entirely unprepared. My mother, who had been in jail since her return until the present time, was now about being carried to New Orleans, to die on a cotton, sugar, or rice plantation!

I had been several times to the jail, but could obtain no interview with her. I ascertained, however, the time the boat in which she was to embark would sail, and as I had not seen mother since her being thrown into prison, I felt anxious for the hour of sailing to come. At last, the day arrived when I was to see her for the first time after our painful separation, and, for aught that I knew, for the last time in this world!

At about ten o'clock in the morning I went on board of the boat, and found her there in company with fifty or sixty other slaves. She was chained to another woman. On seeing me, she immediately dropped her head upon her heaving bosom. She moved not, neither did she weep. Her emotions were too deep for tears. I approached, threw my arms around her neck, kissed her, and fell upon my knees, begging her forgiveness, for I thought myself to blame for her sad condition; for if I had not persuaded her to accompany me, she would not then have been in chains.

She finally raised her head, looked me in the face, (and such a look none but an angel can give!) and said, "*My dear son, you are not to blame for my being here. You have done nothing more nor less than your duty. Do not, I pray you, weep for me. I cannot last long upon a cotton plantation. I feel that my heavenly master will soon call me home, and then I shall be out of the hands of the slave-holders!*"

I could bear no more—my heart struggled to free itself from the human form. In a moment she saw Mr. Mansfield coming toward that part of the boat, and she whispered into my ear, "*My child, we must soon part to meet no more this side of the grave. You have ever said that you would not die a slave; that you would be a freeman. Now try to get your liberty! You will soon have no one to look after but yourself!*" and just as she whispered the last sentence into my ear, Mansfield came up to me, and with an oath, said, "Leave here this instant; you have been the means of my losing one hundred dollars to get this wench back,"— at the same time kicking me with a heavy pair of boots. As I left her, she gave one shriek, saying, "God be with you!" It was the last time that I saw her, and the last word I heard her utter.

I walked on shore. The bell was tolling. The boat was about to start. I stood with a heavy heart, waiting to see her leave the wharf. As I thought of my mother, I could but feel that I had lost

> "———— the glory of my life,
> My blessing and my pride!
> I half forgot the name of slave,
> When she was by my side."[36]

## CHAPTER XI.

THE love of liberty that had been burning in my bosom, had well nigh gone out. I felt as though I was ready to die. The boat moved gently from the wharf, and while she glided down the river, I realized that my mother was indeed

"Gone,—gone,—sold and gone,
To the rice swamp dank and lone!"[37]

After the boat was out of sight, I returned home; but my thoughts were so absorbed in what I had witnessed, that I knew not what I was about half of the time. Night came, but it brought no sleep to my eyes.

In a few days, the boat upon which I was to work being ready, I went on board to commence. This employment suited me better than living in the city, and I remained until the close of navigation; though it proved anything but pleasant. The captain was a drunken, profligate, hard-hearted creature, not knowing how to treat himself, or any other person.

The boat, on its second trip, brought down Mr. Walker, the man of whom I have spoken in a previous chapter, as hiring my time. He had between one and two hundred slaves, chained and manacled. Among them was a man that formerly belonged to my old master's brother, Aaron Young. His name was Solomon. He was a preacher, and belonged to the same church with his master. I was glad to see the old man. He wept like a child when he told me how he had been sold from his wife and children.

The boat carried down, while I remained on board, four or five gangs of slaves. Missouri, though a comparatively new State, is very much engaged in raising slaves to supply the southern market. In a former chapter, I have mentioned that I was once in the employ of a slave-trader, or driver, as he is called at the south. For fear that some may think that I have misrepresented a slave-driver, I will here give an extract from a paper published in a slaveholding State, Tennessee, called the "Millennial Trumpeter."

"Droves of negroes, chained together in dozens and scores, and handcuffed, have been driven through our country in numbers far surpassing any previous year, and these vile slave-drivers and dealers are swarming like buzzards around a carrion. Through this county, you cannot pass a few miles in the great roads without having every feeling of humanity insulted and lacerated by this spectacle, nor can you go into any county or any neighborhood, scarcely, without seeing or hearing of some of these despicable creatures, called negro-drivers.

"Who is a negro-driver? One whose eyes dwell with delight on lacerated bodies of helpless men, women and children; whose soul feels diabolical raptures at the chains, and handcuffs, and cart-whips, for inflicting tortures on weeping mothers torn from helpless babes, and on husbands and wives torn asunder forever!"

Dark and revolting as is the picture here drawn, it is from the pen of one living in the midst of slavery. But though these men may cant about negro-drivers, and tell what despicable creatures they are, who is it, I ask, that supplies them with the human beings that they are tearing asunder? I answer, as far as I have any knowledge of the State where I came from, that those who raise slaves for the market are to be found among all classes, from Thomas H. Benton[38] down to the lowest political demagogue, who may be able to purchase a woman for the purpose of raising stock, and from the Doctor of Divinity down to the most humble lay member in the church.

It was not uncommon in St. Louis to pass by an auction-stand, and behold a woman upon the auction-block, and hear the seller crying out, *"How much is offered for this woman? She is a good cook, good washer, a good obedient servant. She has got religion!"* Why should this man tell the purchasers that she has religion? I answer, because in Missouri, and as far as I have any knowledge of slavery in the other States, the religious teaching consists in teaching the slave that he must never strike a white man; that God made him for a slave; and that, when whipped, he must not find fault,—for the Bible says, "He that knoweth his master's will, and doeth it not, shall be beaten with many stripes!"[39] And slave-holders find such religion very profitable to them.

After leaving the steamer Otto, I resided at home, in Mr. Willi's family, and again began to lay my plans for making my escape from slavery. The anxiety to be a freeman would not let me rest day or night. I would think of the northern cities that I had heard so much about;—of Canada, where so many of my acquaintances had found refuge. I would dream at night that I was in Canada, a freeman, and on waking in the morning, weep to find myself so sadly mistaken.

> "I would think of Victoria's domain,
>     And in a moment I seemed to be there!
> But the fear of being taken again,
>     Soon hurried me back to despair."[40]

Mr. Willi treated me better than Dr. Young ever had; but instead of making me contented and happy, it only rendered me the more miserable, for it enabled me better to appreciate liberty. Mr. Willi was a man who loved money as most men do, and without looking for an opportunity to sell me, he found one in the offer of Captain Enoch Price, a steamboat owner and commission merchant, living in the city of St. Louis. Captain Price tendered seven hundred dollars, which was two hundred more than Mr. Willi had paid. He therefore thought best to accept the offer.[41] I was wanted for a carriage driver, and Mrs. Price was very much pleased with the captain's bargain. His family consisted besides of one child. He had three servants besides myself—one man and two women.

Mrs. Price was very proud of her servants, always keeping them well dressed, and as soon as I had been purchased, she resolved to have a new carriage. And soon one was procured, and all preparations were made for a turn-out in grand style, I being the driver.

One of the female servants was a girl some eighteen or twenty years of age, named Maria. Mrs. Price was very soon determined to have us united, if she could so arrange matters. She would often urge upon me the necessity of having a wife, saying that it would be so pleasant for me to take one in the same family! But getting married, while in slavery, was the last of my thoughts; and had I been ever so inclined, I should not have married Maria, as my love had already gone in another quarter. Mrs. Price soon found out that her efforts at this matchmaking between Maria and myself would not prove successful. She also discovered (or thought she had) that I was rather partial to a girl named Eliza, who was owned by Dr. Mills. This induced her at once to endeavor the purchase of Eliza, so great was her desire to get me a wife!

Before making the attempt, however, she deemed it best to talk to me a little upon the subject of love, courtship, and marriage. Accordingly one afternoon she called me into her room—telling me to take a chair and sit down. I did so, thinking it rather strange, for servants are not very often asked thus to sit down in the same room with the master or mistress. She said that she had found out that I did not care enough about Maria to marry her. I told her that was true. She then asked me if there was not a girl in the city that I loved. Well, now, this was coming into too close quarters with me! People, generally, don't like to tell their love stories to everybody that may think fit to ask about them, and it was so with me. But, after blushing awhile and recovering myself, I told her that I did not want a wife. She then asked me, if I did not think something of Eliza. I told her that I did. She then said that if I wished to marry Eliza, she would purchase her if she could.

I gave but little encouragement to this proposition, as I was determined to make another trial to get my liberty, and I knew that if I should have a wife, I should not be willing to leave her behind; and if I should attempt to bring her with me, the chances would be difficult for success. However, Eliza was purchased, and brought into the family.

## CHAPTER XII.

But the more I thought of the trap laid by Mrs. Price to make me satisfied with my new home, by getting me a wife, the more I determined never to marry any woman on earth until I should get my liberty. But this secret I was compelled to keep to myself, which placed me in a very critical position. I must keep upon good terms with Mrs. Price and Eliza. I therefore promised Mrs. Price that I would marry Eliza; but said that I was not then ready. And I had to keep upon good terms with Eliza, for fear that Mrs. Price would find out that I did not intend to get married.

I have here spoken of marriage, and it is very common among slaves themselves to talk of it. And it is common for slaves to be married; or at least have the marriage ceremony performed. But there is no such thing as slaves being lawfully married. There has never yet a case occurred where a slave has been tried for bigamy. The man may have as many women as he wishes, and the women as many men; and the law takes no cognizance of such acts among slaves. And in fact some masters, when they have sold the husband from the wife, compel her to take another.

There lived opposite Captain Price's, Doctor Farrar, well known in St. Louis.[42] He sold a man named Ben, to one of the traders. He also owned Ben's wife, and in a few days he compelled Sally (that was her name) to marry Peter, another man belonging to him. I asked Sally "why she married Peter so soon after Ben was sold." She said, "because master made her do it."

Mr. John Calvert, who resided near our place, had a woman named Lavinia. She was quite young, and a man to whom she was about to be married was sold, and carried into the country near St. Charles, about twenty miles from St. Louis. Mr. Calvert wanted her to get a husband; but she had resolved not to marry any other man, and she refused. Mr. Calvert whipped her in such a manner that it was thought she would die. Some of the citizens had him arrested, but it was soon hushed up. And that was the last of it. The woman did not die, but it would have been the same if she had.

Captain Price purchased me in the month of October, and I remained with him until December, when the family made a voyage to New Orleans, in a boat owned by himself, and named the "Chester." I served on board, as one of the stewards. On arriving at New Orleans, about the middle of the month,[43] the boat took in freight for Cincinnati; and it was decided that the family should go up the river in her, and what was of more interest to me, I was to accompany them.

The long looked for opportunity to make my escape from slavery was near at hand.

Captain Price had some fears as to the propriety of taking me near a free State, or a place where it was likely I could run away, with a prospect of liberty.[44] He asked me if I had ever been in a free State. "Oh yes," said I, "I have been in Ohio; my master carried me into that State once, but I never liked a free State."

It was soon decided that it would be safe to take me with them, and what made it more safe, Eliza was on the boat with us, and Mrs. Price, to try me, asked if I thought as much as ever of Eliza. I told her that Eliza was very dear to me indeed, and that nothing but death should part us. It was the same as if we were married. This had the desired effect. The boat left New Orleans, and proceeded up the river.

I had at different times obtained little sums of money, which I had reserved for a "rainy day." I procured some cotton cloth, and made me a bag to carry provisions in. The trials of the past were all lost in hopes for the future. The love of liberty, that had been burning in my bosom for years, and had been well nigh extinguished, was now resuscitated. At night, when all around was peaceful, I would walk the decks, meditating upon my happy prospects.

I should have stated, that before leaving St. Louis, I went to an old man named Frank, a slave, owned by a Mr. Sarpee. This old man was very distinguished (not only among the slave population, but also the whites) as a fortune-teller. He was about seventy years of age, something over six feet high, and very slender. Indeed, he was so small around his body that it looked as though it was not strong enough to hold up his head.

Uncle Frank was a very great favorite with the young ladies, who would go to him in great numbers to get their fortunes told. And it was generally believed that he could really penetrate into the mysteries of futurity. Whether true or not, he had the *name,* and that is about half of what one needs in this gullible age. I found Uncle Frank seated in the chimney corner, about ten o'clock at night. As soon as I entered, the old man left his seat. I watched his movement as well as I could by the dim light of the fire. He soon lit a lamp, and coming up, looked me full in the face, saying, "Well, my son, you have come to get uncle to tell your fortune, have you?" "Yes," said I. But how the old man should know what I had come for, I could not tell. However, I paid the fee of twenty-five cents, and he commenced by looking into a gourd, filled with water. Whether the old man was a prophet, or the son of a prophet, I cannot say; but there is one thing certain, many of his predictions were verified.

I am no believer in soothsaying; yet I am sometimes at a loss to know how Uncle Frank could tell so accurately what would occur in the future. Among the many things he told was one which was enough to pay me for all the trouble of hunting him up. It was that *I should be free!* He further said, that in trying to get my liberty, I would meet with many severe trials. I thought to myself, any fool could tell me that!

The first place in which we landed in a free State was Cairo, a small village at the mouth of the Ohio river. We remained here but a few hours, when we proceeded to Louisville. After unloading some of the cargo, the boat started on her upward trip. The next day was the first of January.[45] I had looked forward to New Year's day as the commencement of a new era in the history of my life. I had decided upon leaving the peculiar institution that day.

During the last night that I served in slavery, I did not close my eyes a single moment. When not thinking of the future, my mind dwelt on the past. The love of a dear mother, a dear sister, and three dear brothers, yet living, caused me to shed many tears. If I could only have been assured of their being dead, I should have felt satisfied; but I imagined I saw my dear mother in the cotton-field, followed by a merciless task-master, and no one to speak a consoling word to her! I beheld my dear sister in the hands of a slave-driver, and compelled to submit to his cruelty! None but one placed in such a situation can for a moment imagine the intense agony to which these reflections subjected me.

---

## CHAPTER XIII.

At last the time for action arrived. The boat landed at a point which appeared to me the place of all others to start from. I found that it would be impossible to carry anything with me, but what was upon my person. I had some provisions, and a single suit of clothes, about half worn. When the boat was discharging her cargo, and the passengers engaged carrying their baggage on and off shore, I improved the opportunity to convey myself with my little effects on land. Taking up a trunk, I went up the wharf, and was soon out of the crowd. I made directly for the woods, where I remained until night, knowing well that I could not travel, even in the State of Ohio, during the day, without danger of being arrested.

I had long since made up my mind that I would not trust myself in the hands of any man, white or colored. The slave is brought up to look upon every white man as an enemy to him and his race; and twenty-one years in slavery had taught me that there were traitors, even among colored people. After dark, I emerged from the woods into a narrow path, which led me into the main travelled road. But I knew not which way to go. I did not know North from South, East from West. I looked in vain for the North Star; a heavy cloud hid it from my view. I walked up and down the road until near midnight, when the clouds disappeared, and I welcomed the sight of my friend,—truly the slave's friend,—the North Star!

As soon as I saw it, I knew my course, and before daylight I travelled twenty or twenty-five miles.[46] It being in the winter, I suffered intensely from the cold; being without an overcoat, and my other clothes rather thin for the season. I was provided with a tinder-box, so that I could make up a fire when necessary. And but for this, I should certainly have frozen to death; for I was determined not to go to any house for shelter. I knew of a man belonging to Gen. Ashly, of St. Louis, who had run away near Cincinnati, on the way to Washington, but had been caught and carried back into slavery; and I felt that a similar fate awaited me, should I be seen by any one. I travelled at night, and lay by during the day.

On the fourth day, my provisions gave out, and then what to do I could not tell. Have something to eat, I must; but how to get it was the question! On the first night after my food was gone, I went to a barn on the road-side, and there found some ears of corn. I took ten or twelve of them, and kept on my journey. During the next day, while in the woods, I roasted my corn and feasted upon it, thanking God that I was so well provided for.

My escape to a land of freedom now appeared certain, and the prospects of the future occupied a great part of my thoughts. What should be my occupation, was a subject of much anxiety to me; and the next thing what should be my name? I have before stated that my old master, Dr. Young, had no children of his own, but had with him a nephew, the son of his brother, Benjamin Young. When this boy was brought to Doctor Young, his name being William, the same as mine, my mother was ordered to change mine to something else. This, at the time, I thought to be one of the most cruel acts that could be committed upon my rights; and I received several very severe whippings for telling people that my name was William, after orders were given to change it. Though young, I was old enough to place a high appreciation upon my name. It was decided, however, to call me "Sandford," and this name I was known by, not only upon my master's plantation, but up to the time that I made my escape. I was sold under the name of Sandford.

But as soon as the subject came to my mind, I resolved on adopting my old name of William, and let Sandford go by the board, for I always hated it. Not because there was anything peculiar in the name; but because it had been forced upon me. It is sometimes common at the south, for slaves to take the name of their masters. Some have a legitimate right to do so. But I always detested the idea of being called by the name of either of my masters. And as for my father,

I would rather have adopted the name of "Friday," and been known as the servant of some Robinson Crusoe,[47] than to have taken his name. So I was not only hunting for my liberty, but also hunting for a name; though I regarded the latter as of little consequence, if I could but gain the former. Travelling along the road, I would sometimes speak to myself, sounding my name over, by way of getting used to it, before I should arrive among civilized human beings. On the fifth or sixth day, it rained very fast, and it froze about as fast as it fell, so that my clothes were one glare of ice. I travelled on at night until I became so chilled and benumbed—the wind blowing into my face—that I found it impossible to go any further, and accordingly took shelter in a barn, where I was obliged to walk about to keep from freezing.

I have ever looked upon that night as the most eventful part of my escape from slavery. Nothing but the providence of God, and that old barn, saved me from freezing to death. I received a very severe cold, which settled upon my lungs, and from time to time my feet had been frost-bitten, so that it was with difficulty I could walk. In this situation I travelled two days, when I found that I must seek shelter somewhere, or die.

The thought of death was nothing frightful to me, compared with that of being caught, and again carried back into slavery. Nothing but the prospect of enjoying liberty could have induced me to undergo such trials, for

> "Behind I left the whips and chains,
> Before me were sweet Freedom's plains!"

This, and this alone, cheered me onward. But I at last resolved to seek protection from the inclemency of the weather, and therefore I secured myself behind some logs and brush, intending to wait there until some one should pass by; for I thought it probable that I might see some colored person, or, if not, some one who was not a slaveholder; for I had an idea that I should know a slaveholder as far as I could see him.

---

## CHAPTER XIV.

THE first person that passed was a man in a buggy-wagon. He looked too genteel for me to hail him. Very soon, another passed by on horseback. I attempted speaking to him, but fear made my voice fail me. As he passed, I left my hiding-place, and was approaching the road, when I observed an old man walking towards me, leading a white horse. He had on a broad-brimmed hat and a very long coat, and was evidently walking for exercise. As soon as I saw him, and observed his dress, I thought to myself, "You are the man that I have been looking for!" Nor was I mistaken. He was the very man!

On approaching me, he asked me, "if I was not a slave." I looked at him some time, and then asked him "if he knew of any one who would help me, as I was sick." He answered that he would; but again asked, if I was not a slave. I told him I was. He then said that I was in a very pro-slavery neighborhood, and if I would wait until he went home, he would get a covered wagon for me. I promised to remain. He mounted his horse, and was soon out of sight.

After he was gone, I meditated whether to wait or not; being apprehensive that he had gone for some one to arrest me. But I finally concluded to remain until he should return; removing some few rods to watch his movements. After a suspense of an hour and a half or more, he returned with a two horse covered-wagon, such as are usually seen under the shed of a Quaker meeting-house on Sundays and Thursdays; for the old man proved to be a Quaker of the George Fox[48] stamp.

He took me to his house, but it was some time before I could be induced to enter it; not until the old lady came out, did I venture into the house. I thought I saw something in the old lady's cap that told me I was not only safe, but welcome, in her house. I was not, however, prepared to receive their hospitalities. The only fault I found with them was their being too kind. I had never had a white man to treat me as an equal, and the idea of a white lady waiting on me at the table was still worse! Though the table was loaded with the good things of this life, I could not eat. I thought if I could only be allowed the privilege of eating in the kitchen, I should be more than satisfied!

Finding that I could not eat, the old lady, who was a "Thompsonian,"[49] made me a cup of "composition,"[50] or "number six;" but it was so strong and hot, that I called it *number seven!* However, I soon found myself at home in this family. On different occasions, when telling these facts, I have been asked how I felt upon finding myself regarded as a man by a white family; especially just having run away from one. I cannot say that I have ever answered the question yet.

The fact that I was in all probability a freeman, sounded in my ears like a charm. I am satisfied that none but a slave could place such an appreciation upon liberty as I did at that time. I wanted to see mother and sister, that I might tell them "I was free!" I wanted to see my fellow slaves in St. Louis, and let them know that the chains were no longer upon my limbs. I wanted to see Captain Price, and let him learn from my own lips that I was no more a chattel, but a man! I was anxious, too, thus to inform Mrs. Price that she must get another coachman. And I wanted to see Eliza more than I did either Mr. or Mrs. Price!

The fact that I was a freeman—could walk, talk, eat and sleep as a man, and no one to stand over me with the blood-clotted cowhide—all this made me feel that I was not myself.

The kind friend that had taken me in was named Wells Brown. He was a devoted friend of the slave; but was very old, and not in the enjoyment of good health. After being by the fire awhile, I found that my feet had been very much frozen. I was seized with a fever which threatened to confine me to my bed. But my Thompsonian friends soon raised me, treating me as kindly as if I had been one of their own children. I remained with them twelve or fifteen days, during which time they made me some clothing, and the old gentleman purchased me a pair of boots.

I found that I was about fifty or sixty miles from Dayton, in the State of

Ohio, and between one and two hundred miles from Cleaveland, on lake Erie, a place I was desirous of reaching on my way to Canada. This I know will sound strangely to the ears of people in foreign lands, but it is nevertheless true. An American citizen was fleeing from a Democratic, Republican, Christian government, to receive protection under the monarchy of Great Britain. While the people of the United States boast of their freedom, they at the same time keep three millions of their own citizens in chains; and while I am seated here in sight of Bunker Hill Monument, writing this narrative, I am a slave, and no law, not even in Massachusetts, can protect me from the hands of the slaveholder!

Before leaving this good Quaker friend, he inquired what my name was besides William. I told him that I had no other name. "Well," said he, "thee must have another name. Since thee has got out of slavery, thee has become a man, and men always have two names."

I told him that he was the first man to extend the hand of friendship to me, and I would give him the privilege of naming me.

"If I name thee," said he, "I shall call thee Wells Brown, after myself."

"But," said I, "I am not willing to lose my name of William. As it was taken from me once against my will, I am not willing to part with it again upon any terms."

"Then," said he, "I will call thee William Wells Brown."

"So be it," said I; and I have been known by that name ever since I left the house of my first white friend, Wells Brown.

After giving me some little change, I again started for Canada. In four days I reached a public house, and went in to warm myself. I there learned that some fugitive slaves had just passed through the place. The men in the bar-room were talking about it, and I thought that it must have been myself they referred to, and I was therefore afraid to start, fearing they would seize me; but I finally mustered courage enough, and took my leave. As soon as I was out of sight, I went into the woods, and remained there until night, when I again regained the road, and travelled on until the next day.

Not having had any food for nearly two days, I was faint with hunger, and was in a dilemma what to do, as the little cash supplied me by my adopted father, and which had contributed to my comfort, was now all gone. I however concluded to go to a farm-house, and ask for something to eat. On approaching the door of the first one presenting itself, I knocked, and was soon met by a man who asked me what I wanted. I told him that I would like something to eat. He asked where I was from, and where I was going. I replied that I had come some way, and was going to Cleaveland.

After hesitating a moment or two, he told me that he could give me nothing to eat, adding, "that if I would work, I could get something to eat."

I felt bad, being thus refused something to sustain nature, but did not dare tell him that I was a slave.

Just as I was leaving the door, with a heavy heart, a woman, who proved to be the wife of this gentleman, came to the door, and asked her husband what I wanted? He did not seem inclined to inform her. She therefore asked me herself. I told her that I had asked for something to eat. After a few other questions, she told me to come in, and that she would give me something to eat.

I walked up to the door, but the husband remained in the passage, as if unwilling to let me enter.

She asked him two or three times to get out of the way, and let me in. But as he did not move, she pushed him on one side, bidding me walk in! I was never before so glad to see a woman push a man aside! Ever since that act, I have been in favor of "woman's rights!"

After giving me as much food as I could eat, she presented me with ten cents, all the money then at her disposal, accompanied with a note to a friend, a few miles further on the road. Thinking this angel of mercy from an overflowing heart, I pushed on my way, and in three days arrived at Cleaveland, Ohio.

Being an entire stranger in this place, it was difficult for me to find where to stop. I had no money, and the lake being frozen, I saw that I must remain until the opening of navigation, or go to Canada by way of Buffalo. But believing myself to be somewhat out of danger, I secured an engagement at the Mansion House, as a table waiter, in payment for my board. The proprietor, however, whose name was E. M. Segur, in a short time, hired me for twelve dollars per month; on which terms I remained until spring, when I found good employment on board a lake steamboat.

I purchased some books, and at leisure moments perused them with considerable advantage to myself. While at Cleaveland, I saw, for the first time, an anti-slavery newspaper. It was the *"Genius of Universal Emancipation,"* published by Benjamin Lundy,[51] and though I had no home, I subscribed for the paper. It was my great desire, being out of slavery myself, to do what I could for the emancipation of my brethren yet in chains, and while on Lake Erie, I found many opportunities of "helping their cause along."

It is well known, that a great number of fugitives make their escape to Canada, by way of Cleaveland; and while on the lake, I always made arrangement to carry them on the boat to Buffalo or Detroit, and thus effect their escape to the "promised land." The friends of the slave, knowing that I would transport them without charge, never failed to have a delegation when the boat arrived at Cleaveland. I have sometimes had four or five on board, at one time.

In the year 1842, I conveyed, from the first of May to the first of December, sixty-nine fugitives over Lake Erie to Canada. In 1843, I visited Malden, in Upper Canada, and counted seventeen, in that small village, who owed their escape to my humble efforts.

Soon after coming North, I subscribed for the Liberator, edited by that champion of freedom, William Lloyd Garrison.[52] I labored a season to promote the temperance cause among the colored people, but for the last three years, have been pleading for the victims of American slavery.

WILLIAM WELLS BROWN.

Boston, Mass., June, 1847.

1. Jefferson, *Travels*, 1.

2. Andrews, *Fugitive Slave*, 1, 5.

3. Farrison, *William Wells Brown*, 60–108.

4. Ibid., 109–114.

5. Ibid., 114, 155–157; Andrews, *Free Story*, 336.

6. Starling, *Slave Narrative*, 138.

7. Farrison, *William Wells Brown*, 113.

8. MacKethan, "Metaphors of Mastery," 65.

9. Smith, *Where I'm Bound*, 12–13.

10. I am indebted for many of these observations to Andrews, *Free Story*, 27–28.

11. "One who signifies says without explicitly saying, criticizes without actually criticizing, insults without really insulting. . . . In its various forms, signifying substitutes verbal power for political or economic power." Mason, "Signifying," 665.

12. Andrews, *Free Story*, 274.

13. Andrews, *Fugitive Slave*, 6.

14. Redding, *Poet*, 24.

15. William Cowper (1731–1800) was a forerunner of the British romantic poets, and wrote a number of antislavery verses. The lines quoted, however, are not by Cowper; instead they are from Joseph Addison (1672–1719), *Cato: A Tragedy* (1713); Brown has substituted a new line for the last one, which originally read, "Who owes his Greatness to his Country's Ruin?"

16. Edmund Quincy (1808–77) was an ardent abolitionist, at this time corresponding secretary of the Massachusetts Anti-Slavery Society, and a prominent member of the American Anti-Slavery Society and the Non-Resistance Society. He was the editor of the *Abolitionist*, an editor of the *Anti-Slavery Standard*, and, in William Lloyd Garrison's absence, edited *The Liberator*.

17. Frederick Douglass (1818–95), *Narrative of the Life of Frederick Douglass, an American Slave*. See pp. I:523–599.

18. John Sheffield (1648–1721), *The Tragedy of Julius Caesar, Altered*. Shakespeare's own phrasing differs slightly.

19. Daniel Defoe (c. 1660–1731) was the British author of *Robinson Crusoe, Moll Flanders*, and other important novels.

20. Andrew Fletcher (1655–1716), *An Account of a Conversation Concerning the Right to Regulation of Governments* (1703).

21. James Russell Lowell (1819–91), "The Present Crisis."

22. Lowell, "L'Envoi."

23. Robert Blair (1699–1746), *The Grave* (1743).

24. Joseph Comstock Hathaway (1810–73) was president of the Western New York Anti-Slavery Society and a friend of Brown's.

25. Higgins was the cousin of Dr. John Young, Brown's master. Farrison, *William Wells Brown*, 4–6.

26. The move was made in 1816 to the Missouri territory (Ibid., 10); Missouri did not become a state until 1821, at which point it was the westernmost in the Union.

27. Elijah Parish Lovejoy (1802–37) was actually editor of the *St. Louis Observer*. He wrote in favor of the gradual abolition of slavery, and was forced by protesters to move to Alton, Illinois, in 1836, where he edited the *Alton Observer*. He soon became an important abolitionist leader, and was killed by an angry mob in November 1837, becoming a martyr to the cause.

28. See *Proverbs* 6:4, *Psalms* 132:4.

29. Brown worked as a house servant, and was made a part-time assistant to his master, preparing medicines, ministering to ailing slaves, running errands, and even pulling teeth. As William Farrison writes, "His experience in Dr. Young's office aroused in him a lifelong interest in medicine." Brown became a practicing physician himself in 1864 or 1865. Farrison, *William Wells Brown*, 24, 400.

30. Daniel D. Page (1790–1869) actually owned a pew in the First Presbyterian Church in St. Louis, and had no connection with the Baptists. Ibid., 26.

31. Mississippi.

32. Charlotte Elizabeth (1790–1846), "The Slave and her Babe."

33. This anonymous song was first published in *The Liberator* in 1844, under the title "The Plantation Song" (Eaklor, *American Antislavery Songs*, 326), and was republished in Brown's *Anti-Slavery Harp* under the title "Song of the Coffle-Gang" (29).

34. Brown actually witnessed this incident on his next, fourth trip to New Orleans, the one he made with Enoch Price, rather than on this one with Walker, since the incident occurred in December 1833. Farrison, *William Wells Brown*, 47.

35. Theodore Dwight Weld (1803–95), *American Slavery As It Is: Testimony of a Thousand Witnesses* (1839) was the most influential abolitionist book of its time.

36. Elizabeth Margaret Chandler (1807–34), "The Bereaved Father."

37. John Greenleaf Whittier (1807–92), "The Farewell of a Virginia Slave Mother to her Daughters, Sold into Southern Bondage" (1838).

38. Thomas Hart Benton (1782–1858) was a U.S. senator from Missouri from 1821 to 1850; he favored the gradual abolition of slavery.

39. *Luke* 12:47.

40. Anonymous, "I Am Monarch of Nought I Survey," published in several antislavery song collections. Eaklor, *American Antislavery Songs*, 351–352.

41. The sale was made on October 2, 1833. Farrison, *William Wells Brown*, 42.

42. Dr. Bernard Gaines Farrar, one of the most prominent physicians in town. Ibid., 44.

43. The trip was actually made in late November; the *Chester* arrived in New Orleans on November 29. Ibid., 46.

44. These fears were doubtless in no small part pecuniary. Price had apparently been offered two thousand dollars for Brown in New Orleans, and fifteen hundred in Louisville. Ibid., 48.

45. 1834.

46. This is unlikely. Not even slaves conducted by Underground Railroad conductors travelled this far in one night. Farrison, *William Wells Brown*, 53–54.

47. In Defoe's novel *Robinson Crusoe,* the shipwrecked hero lives alone on an island until he saves the life of a savage, whom he names Friday.

48. George Fox (1624–91) founded the Society of Friends.

49. A follower of Samuel Thompson (1769–1843), a popular medical herbalist who believed that health could be restored through the "vital heat" induced by cayenne and steam baths.

50. A potent mix of bayberry, ginger, cayenne, cinnamon, prickly ash, and hot water.

51. Benjamin Lundy (1789–1839) was a pioneering abolitionist who founded and started publishing the periodical *Genius of Universal Emancipation* in 1821. For a time William Lloyd Garrison was its associate editor.

52. William Lloyd Garrison (1805–79) published *The Liberator,* the most popular abolitionist newspaper, from 1831 to 1865. He helped organize the American Anti-Slavery Society, of which he was president from 1843 to 1865. He advocated Northern secession, publicly burned the Constitution, and was widely regarded as the foremost leader of the antislavery movement.

JOSIAH HENSON

JOSIAH HENSON (1789–1883), despite his later fame as the "original Uncle Tom," had little relationship either to the saintly title character of Harriet Beecher Stowe's wildly popular novel or to the popular stereotype that followed it. As Blyden Jackson puts it,

> Whatever Henson was in his many various guises from his birth to his death—local hero, accomplice of dishonest masters, sometimes himself a trickster, evangelist for Christ, first citizen of a free black Canadian community, and celebrity on two continents—he was never an epitome of weakness and self-effacement, and he was certainly not an instrument of accommodationism.[1]

During his life, however, Henson was regarded as little less than a saint. Ephraim Peabody, who heard him speak, wrote in 1849:

> He is a large-hearted, large-minded man, tolerant, calm, benevolent, and wise. . . . What Henson has done . . . shows a very unusual elevation of mind and moral feelings. . . . Under the slave's garb and this African skin there is no ordinary man. . . . Without noise or pretension, without bitterness towards the whites, without extravagant claims in behalf of the blacks, [he] has patiently, wisely, and devotedly given himself to the improvement of a large body of his wretched countrymen amongst whom his lot has been cast.[2]

Similarly, Harriet Beecher Stowe wrote in 1853, "It would be well for the most cultivated of us to ask, whether our ten talents in the way of religious knowledge have enabled us to bring forth as much fruit to the glory of God, to withstand temptation as patiently, to return good for evil as disinterestedly, as this poor, ignorant slave."[3]

But twentieth-century assessments have not been as kind. Robin Winks admits that "he was an unusual man, alert and intelligent," but calls him "vain behind his facade of humility, proud, possessive, and prone to seek out quick approbation rather than long-range solutions. . . . He rather enjoyed manipulating the lives of others, if always for what he conceived to be their benefit."[4] William Andrews calls him a "master of self-promotion"; Charles Nichols calls him "a specialist at charlatanry"; Jackson calls him vain, ebullient, and crafty; and John W. Blassingame claims that the later narratives present Henson as "an insufferable egotist [and] garrulous defender of his actions."[5]

There is no doubt, however, of his popularity. His first narrative, which is reprinted here, sold 6,000 copies in England and North America. His second narrative, retitled *Truth Stranger Than Fiction* and published in 1858 with a preface by Stowe, sold over 100,000 copies, according to a third narrative (1877), which was entitled *Uncle Tom's Story of His Life*. Also in 1877 a "Young People's Illustrated Edition" appeared, with a preface by the Earl of Shaftesbury, and sold a quarter of a million copies. Yet another version appeared in 1879, with a new preface by Stowe, notes by Wendell Phillips and John Greenleaf Whittier, and an appendix by Gilbert Haven; and in 1881 an even more "revised and enlarged" edition was published in Canada, entitled *An Autobiography of the Rev. Josiah Henson ("Uncle Tom") from 1789 to 1881*.[6] Translations appeared in Welsh, French, Swedish, German, and Dutch. As Winks puts it:

> Of the many narratives written for, and on occasion by, fugitive slaves who fled from the United States to [Canada] before the Civil War, no single book has been so widely read, so frequently revised, and so influential as the autobiography of Josiah Henson. . . . Henson became one of the best known of all fugitive slaves, the several editions of his narrative one of the most frequently consulted sources, his life thought to be the archetypal fugitive experience.[7]

The later versions read, for the most part, like novelized updates of the 1849 autobiography, which is straightforward yet dramatic, simple yet intelligent. Henson was an unusual slave narrator, for he suffered little ill-treatment at the hands of his owners, and never admits to having been whipped or severely punished. His master's confidence in him made him faithful—so much so that he deliberately ignored an opportunity to free himself and his fellow slaves. His narrative centers around the idea of *moral choice*—to such an extent that even slavery itself, which by definition involves compulsion, seems to become a matter of choice to the narrator. Henson was given the rare opportunity to repeatedly choose between *duty* (submission) and *freedom* (rebellion). The internal conflicts this choice entailed enabled his narrative to capture the imagination of a large audience who were facing a similar *political* choice.[8]

The narrative was dictated to Samuel A. Eliot (1798–1862), three-term mayor of Boston, treasurer of Harvard, congressman, and president of the Massachusetts Academy of Music. He seems to have been a faithful amanuensis, sticking as closely to the facts as possible. Unfortunately, the same cannot be said for later versions of Henson's story. For example, in 1858 Henson added a description of his trips back South, where he supposedly helped 118 other slaves escape to freedom—a feat which, if true, he would have certainly mentioned in his earlier narrative. Similarly, he claimed to have served as a captain in the second Essex Company of Colored Volunteers during the Canadian Rebellion (1837–38), which he did not. These statements fooled not only his readers, but later scholars, as did his equally false claims to have personally written his books, and to have met with Stowe prior to her completion of *Uncle Tom's Cabin*.[9]

To his credit, however, not until Henson was ninety-three years old and senile did he ever categorically state that he was the model for Uncle Tom; similarly, Stowe also denied more than once that the character of Uncle Tom was based on any one person.[10] In her 1853 *Key to Uncle Tom's Cabin*, Stowe had only briefly discussed Henson's *Life*, but said that it paralleled the history of Uncle Tom.[11] Out of this the legend quickly arose, and Henson's life was forever changed.

As early as 1851, Henson had been accused of being an impostor and carrying forged testimonials with him to England. But he successfully cleared his name, and his newfound fame as Uncle Tom eclipsed his woes. When his sawmill became indebted, he raised enough funds in England to cancel the debt. He exhibited his polished walnut lumber at the Crystal Palace Exhibition and was awarded a bronze medal and a picture of Queen Victoria. He was received by the Archbishop of Canterbury and by Lord John Russell, the Prime Minister, at the latter's home. His sawmill and the British-American Manual Labor Institute, a Canadian educational institution for ex-slaves that he had helped found, both failed due to gross mismanagement by those to whom he had entrusted their care. But near the end of his life, he was presented to Queen Victoria herself, and was received by President Rutherford B. Hayes. His cabin and grave in Dresden, Ontario, became tourist attractions and remained popular well into the twentieth century.[12]

THE

# LIFE OF JOSIAH HENSON,

FORMERLY A SLAVE,

NOW AN INHABITANT OF CANADA,

AS

NARRATED BY HIMSELF.

---

BOSTON:
ARTHUR D. PHELPS.
1849.

# ADVERTISEMENT.

THE following memoir was written from the dictation of JOSIAH HENSON. A portion of the story was told, which, when written, was read to him, that any errors of statement might be corrected. The substance of it, therefore, the facts, the reflections, and very often the words, are his; and little more than the structure of the sentences belongs to another.

The narrative, in this form, necessarily loses the attraction derived from the earnest manner, the natural eloquence of a man who tells a story in which he is deeply interested; but it is hoped that enough remains to repay perusal, and that the character of the man, and the striking nature of the events of his life will be thought to justify the endeavor to make them more extensively known. The story has this advantage, that it is not fiction, but fact; and it will be found fruitful in instruction by those who attentively consider its lessons.

# LIFE OF JOSIAH HENSON.

I WAS born, June 15, 1789, in Charles County, Maryland, on a farm belonging to Mr. Francis N.,[13] about a mile from Port Tobacco. My mother was the property of Dr. Josiah McP.,[14] but was hired by Mr. N., to whom my father belonged. The only incident I can remember, which occurred while my mother continued on N.'s farm, was the appearance of my father one day, with his head bloody and his back lacerated. He was in a state of great excitement, and though it was all a mystery to me at the age of three or four years, it was explained at a later period, and I understood that he had been suffering the cruel penalty of the Maryland law for beating a white man. His right ear had been cut off close to his head, and he had received a hundred lashes on his back. He had beaten the overseer for a brutal assault on my mother, and this was his punishment. Furious at such treatment, my father became a different man, and was so morose, disobedient, and intractable, that Mr. N. determined to sell him. He accordingly parted with him, not long after, to his son, who lived in Alabama; and neither my mother nor I, ever heard of him again. He was naturally, as I understood afterwards from my mother and other persons, a man of amiable temper, and of considerable energy of character; but it is not strange that he should be essentially changed by such cruelty and injustice under the sanction of law.

After the sale of my father by N., and his leaving Maryland for Alabama, Dr. McP. would no longer hire out my mother to N. She returned, therefore, to the estate of the doctor, who was very much kinder to his slaves than the generality of planters, never suffering them to be struck by any one. He was, indeed, a man of good natural impulses, kind-hearted, liberal, and jovial. The latter quality was so much developed as to be his great failing; and though his convivial excesses were not thought of as a fault by the community in which he lived, and did not even prevent his having a high reputation for goodness of heart, and an almost saint-like benevolence, yet they were, nevertheless, his ruin. My mother, and her young family of three girls and three boys, of which I was the youngest, resided on this estate for two or three years, during which my only recollections are of being rather a pet of the doctor's, who thought I was a bright child, and of being much impressed with what I afterwards recognized as the deep piety and devotional feeling and habits of my mother. I do not know how, or where she acquired her knowledge of God, or her acquaintance with the Lord's prayer, which she so frequently repeated and taught me to repeat. I remember seeing her often on her knees, endeavoring to arrange her thoughts in prayers appropriate to her situation, but which amounted to little more than constant ejaculation, and the repetition of short phrases, which were within my infant comprehension, and have remained in my memory to this hour.

After this brief period of comparative comfort, however, the death of Dr. McP. brought about a revolution in our condition, which, common as such things are in slave countries, can never be imagined by those not subject to them, nor recollected by those who have been, without emotions of grief and indignation deep and ineffaceable. The doctor was riding from one of his scenes of riotous excess, when, falling from his horse, in crossing a little run, not a foot deep, he was unable to save himself from drowning.

In consequence of his decease, it became necessary to sell the estate and the slaves, in order to divide the property among the heirs; and we were all put up at auction and sold to the highest bidder, and scattered over various parts of the country. My brothers and sisters were bid off one by one, while my mother, holding my hand, looked on in an agony of grief, the cause of which I but ill understood at first, but which dawned on my mind, with dreadful clearness, as the sale proceeded. My mother was then separated from me, and put up in her turn. She was bought by a man named Isaac R.,[15] residing in Montgomery county, and then I was offered to the assembled purchasers. My mother, half distracted with the parting forever from all her children, pushed through the crowd, while the bidding for me was going on, to the spot where R. was standing. She fell at his feet, and clung to his knees, entreating him in tones that a mother only could command, to buy her *baby* as well as herself, and spare to her one of her little ones at least. Will it, can it be believed that this man, thus appealed to, was capable not merely of turning a deaf ear to her supplication, but of disengaging himself from her with such violent blows and kicks, as to reduce her to the necessity of creeping out of his reach, and mingling the groan of bodily suffering with the sob of a breaking heart? Yet this was one of my earliest observations of men; an experience which has been common to me with thousands of my race, the bitterness of which its frequency cannot diminish to any individual who suffers it, while it is dark enough to overshadow the whole after-life with something blacker than a funeral pall.—I was bought by a stranger.[16]—Almost immediately, however, whether my childish strength, at five or six years of age, was overmastered by such scenes and experiences, or from some accidental cause, I fell sick, and seemed to my new master so little likely to recover, that he proposed to R., the purchaser of my mother, to take me too at such a trifling rate that it could not be refused. I was thus providentially restored to my mother; and under her care, destitute as she was of the proper means of nursing me, I recovered my health, and grew up to be an uncommonly vigorous and healthy boy and man.

The character of R., the master whom I faithfully served for many years, is by no means an uncommon one in any part of the world; but it is to be regretted that a domestic institution should anywhere put it in the power of such a one to tyrannize over his fellow beings, and inflict so much needless misery as is sure to be produced by such a man in such a position. Coarse and vulgar in his habits, unprincipled and cruel in his general deportment, and especially addicted to the vice of licentiousness, his slaves had little opportunity for relaxation from wearying labor, were supplied with the scantiest means of sustaining their toil by necessary food, and had no security for personal rights. The natural tendency of slavery is, to convert the master into a tyrant, and the slave into the cringing, treacherous, false, and thieving victim of tyranny. R. and his slaves were no exception to the general rule, but might be cited as apt illustrations of the nature of the case.

My earliest employments were, to carry buckets of water to the men at work, to hold a horse-plough, used for weeding between the rows of corn, and as I grew older and taller, to take care of master's saddle-horse. Then a hoe was put into my hands, and I was soon required to do the day's work of a man; and it was not long before I could do it, at least as well as my associates in misery.

The every-day life of a slave on one of our southern plantations, however frequently it may have been described, is generally little-known at the North; and must be mentioned as a necessary illustration of the character and habits of the slave and the slave-holder, created and perpetuated by their relative position. The principal food of those upon my master's plantation consisted of corn meal, and salt herrings; to which was added in summer a little buttermilk, and the few vegetables which each might raise for himself and his family, on the little piece of ground which was assigned to him for the purpose, called a truck patch. The meals were two, daily. The first, or breakfast, was taken at 12 o'clock, after laboring from daylight; and the other when the work of the remainder of the day was over. The only dress was of tow cloth, which for the young, and often even for those who had passed the period of childhood, consisted of a single garment, something like a shirt, but longer, reaching to the ancles; and for the older, a pair of pantaloons, or a gown, according to the sex; while some kind of round jacket, or overcoat, might be added in winter, a wool hat once in two or three years, for the males, and a pair of coarse shoes once a year. Our lodging was in log huts, of a single small room, with no other floor than the trodden earth, in which ten or a dozen persons—men, women, and children—might sleep, but which could not protect them from dampness and cold, nor permit the existence of the common decencies of life. There were neither beds, nor furniture of any description— a blanket being the only addition to the dress of the day for protection from the chillness of the air or the earth. In these hovels were we penned at night, and fed by day; here were the children born, and the sick—neglected. Such were the provisions for the daily toil of the slave.

Notwithstanding this system of management, however, I grew to be a robust and vigorous lad, and at fifteen years of age, there were few who could compete with me in work, or in sport—for not even the condition of the slave can altogether repress the animal spirits of the young negro. I was competent to all the work that was done upon the farm, and could run faster and farther, wrestle longer, and jump higher, than anybody about me. My master and my fellow slaves used to look upon me, and speak of me, as a wonderfully smart fellow, and prophecy great things I should do when I became a man. A casual word of this sort, sometimes overheard, would fill me with a pride and ambition which some would think impossible in a negro slave, degraded, starved, and abused as I was, and had been, from my earliest recollection. But the love of superiority is not confined to kings and emperors; and it is a positive fact, that pride and ambition were as active in my soul as probably they ever were in that of the greatest soldier or statesman. The objects I pursued, I must admit, were not just the same as theirs. Mine were to be first in the field, whether we were hoeing, mowing, or reaping; to surpass those of my own age, or indeed any age, in athletic exercises; and to obtain, if possible, the favorable regard of the petty despot who ruled over us. This last was an exercise of the understanding, rather than of the affections; and I was guided in it more by what I supposed would be effectual, than by a nice judgment of the propriety of the means I used.

I obtained great influence with my companions, as well by the superiority I showed in labor and in sport, as by the assistance I yielded them, and the favors I conferred upon them, from impulses which I cannot consider as wrong, though it was necessary for me to conceal sometimes the act as well as its motive. I have toiled, and induced others to toil, many an extra hour, in order to show my master what an excellent day's work had been accomplished, and to win a kind word, or a benevolent deed from his callous heart. In general, indifference, or a cool calculation of my value to him, were my reward, chilling those hopes of an improvement in my condition, which was the ultimate object of my efforts. I was much more easily moved to compassion and sympathy than he was; and one of the means I took to gain the good-will of my fellow sufferers, was by taking from him some things that he did not give, in part payment of my extra labor. The condition of the male slave is bad enough, Heaven knows; but that of the female, compelled to perform unfit labor, sick, suffering, and bearing the burdens of her own sex unpitied and unaided, as well as the toils which belong to the other, has often oppressed me with a load of sympathy. And sometimes, when I have seen them starved, and miserable, and unable to help themselves, I have helped them to some of the comforts which they were denied by him who owned them, and which my companions had not the wit or the daring to procure. Meat was not a part of our regular food; but my master had plenty of sheep and pigs, and sometimes I have picked out the best one I could find in the flock, or the drove, carried it a mile or two into the woods, slaughtered it, cut it up, and distributed it among the poor creatures, to whom it was at once food, luxury, and medicine. Was this wrong? I can only say that, at this distance of time, my conscience does not reproach me for it, and that then I esteemed it among the best of my deeds.

By means of the influence thus acquired, the increased amount of work done upon the farm, and by the detection of the knavery of the overseer, who plundered his employer for more selfish ends, and through my watchfulness was caught in the act and dismissed, I was promoted to be superintendent of the farm work, and managed to raise more than double the crops, with more cheerful and willing labor, than was ever seen on the estate before.

Previous to my attaining this important station, however, an incident occurred of so powerful an influence on my intellectual development, my prospect of improvement in character, as well as condition, my chance of religious culture, and in short, on my whole nature, body and soul, that it deserves especial notice and commemoration. There was a person living at Georgetown, a few miles only from R's plantation, whose business was that of a baker, and whose character was that of an upright, benevolent, Christian man.[17] He was noted especially for his detestation of slavery, and his resolute avoidance of the employment of slave labor in his business. He would not even hire a slave, the price of whose toil must be paid to his master, but contented himself with the work of his own hands, and with such free labor as he could procure. His reputation was high, not only for this almost singular abstinence from what no one about him thought wrong, but for his general probity and excellence. This man occasionally served as a minister of the Gospel, and preached in a neighborhood where preachers were somewhat rare at that period. One Sunday when he was to officiate in this way, at a place three or four miles distant, my mother persuaded me to ask master's leave to go and hear him; and although such permission was not given freely or often, yet his favor to me was shown for this once by allowing me to go, without much scolding, but not without a pretty distinct intimation of what would befall me, if I did not return immediately after the close of the service. I hurried off, pleased with the opportunity, but without any definite expectations of benefit or amusement; for up to this period of my life, and I was then eighteen years old, I had never heard a sermon, nor any discourse or conversation whatever, upon religious topics, except what had been impressed upon me by my mother, of the responsibility of all to a Supreme Being. When I arrived at the place of meeting, the services were so far advanced that the speaker was just beginning his discourse, from the text, Hebrews ii. 9; "That he, by the grace of God, should taste of death for every man." This was the first text of the Bible to which I had ever listened, knowing it to be such. I have never forgotten it, and scarce a day has passed since, in which I have not recalled it, and the sermon that was preached from it. The divine character of Jesus Christ, his life and teachings, his sacrifice of himself for others, his death and resurrection were all alluded to, and some of the points were dwelt upon with great power,—great, at least, to me, who heard of these things for the first time in my life. I was wonderfully impressed, too, with the use which the preacher made of the last words of the text, *"for every man."* He said the death of Christ was not designed for the benefit of a select few only, but for the salvation of the world, for the bond as well as the free; and he dwelt on the glad tidings of the Gospel to the poor, the persecuted, and the distressed, its deliverance to the captive, and the liberty wherewith Christ has made us free, till my heart burned within me, and I was in a state of the greatest excitement at the thought that such a being as Jesus Christ had been described should have died for me—for *me* among the rest, a poor, despised, abused slave, who was thought by his fellow creatures fit for nothing but unrequited toil and ignorance, for mental and bodily degradation. I immediately determined to find out something more about "Christ and him crucified;" and revolving the things which I had heard in my mind as I went home, I became so excited that I turned aside from the road into the woods, and prayed to God for light and for aid with an earnestness, which, however unenlightened, was at least sincere and heartfelt; and which the subsequent course of my life has led me to imagine might not have been unacceptable to Him who heareth prayer. At all events, I date my conversion, and my awakening to a new life—a consciousness of superior powers and destiny to any thing I had before conceived of—from this day, so memorable to me. I used every means and opportunity of inquiry into religious matters; and so deep was my conviction of their superior importance to every thing else, so clear my perception of my own faults, and so undoubting my observation of the darkness and sin that surrounded me, that I could not help talking much on these subjects with those about me; and it was not long before I began to pray with them, and exhort them, and to impart to the poor slaves those little glimmerings of light from another world, which had reached my own eye. In a few years I became quite an esteemed preacher among them, and I will not believe it is vanity which leads me to think I was useful to some.

I must return, however, for the present, to the course of my life in secular affairs, the facts of which it is my principal object to relate. The difference between the manner in which it was designed that all men should regard one another, as children of the same Father, and the manner in which men actually do treat each other, as if they were placed here for mutual annoyance and destruction, is well exemplified by an incident that happened to me within a year or two from this period, that is, when I was nineteen or twenty years old. My master's habits were such as were common enough among the dissipated planters of the neighborhood; and one of their frequent practices was, to assemble on Saturday or Sunday, which were their holidays, and gamble, run horses, or fight gamecocks, discuss politics, and drink whiskey, and brandy and water, all day long. Perfectly aware that they would not be able to find their own way home at night, each one ordered a slave, his particular attendant, to come after him and help him home. I was chosen for this confidential duty by my master; and many is the time I have held him on his horse, when he could not hold himself in the saddle, and walked by his side in darkness and mud from the tavern to his house. Of course, quarrels and brawls of the most violent description were frequent consequences of these meetings, and whenever they became especially dangerous, and glasses were thrown, dirks drawn, and pistols fired, it was the duty of the slaves to rush in, and each one was to drag his master from the fight, and carry him home. To tell the truth, this was a part of my business for which I felt no reluctance. I was young, remarkably athletic and self-relying, and in such affrays I carried it with a high hand, and would elbow my way among the whites, whom it would have been almost death for me to strike, seize my master, and drag him out, mount him on his horse, or crowd him into his buggy, with the ease with which I would handle a bag of corn, and at the same time with the pride of conscious superiority, and the kindness inspired by performing an act of benevolence. I knew I was doing for him what he could not do for himself, and showing my superiority to others, and acquiring their respect in some degree, at the same time.

On one of these occasions, my master got into a quarrel with his brother's overseer,[18] who was one of the party, and in rescuing the former, I suppose I was a little more rough with the latter than usual. I remember his falling upon the floor, and very likely it was from the effects of a push from me, or a movement of my elbow. He attributed his fall to me, rather than to the whiskey he had drunk, and treasured up his vengeance for the first favorable opportunity. About a week afterwards, I was sent by my master to a place a few miles distant, on horseback, with some letters. I took a short cut through a lane, separated by gates from the high road, and bounded by a fence on each side. This lane passed through some of the farm owned by my master's brother, and his overseer was in the adjoining field, with three negroes, when I went by. On my return, a half an hour afterwards, the overseer was sitting on the fence; but I could see nothing of the black fellows. I rode on, utterly unsuspicious of any trouble, but as I approached, he jumped off the fence, and at the same moment two of the negroes sprung up from under the bushes, where they had been concealed, and stood with him, immediately in front of me; while the third sprang over the fence just behind me. I was thus enclosed between what I could no longer doubt were hostile forces. The overseer seized my horse's bridle, and ordered me to alight, in the usual elegant phraseology used by such men to slaves. I asked what I was to alight for. "To take the cursedest flogging you ever had in your life, you d—d black scoundrel." "But what am I to be flogged for, Mr. L.," I asked. "Not a word," said he, "but 'light at once, and take off your jacket." I saw there was nothing else to be done, and slipped off the horse on the opposite side from him. "Now take off your shirt," cried he; and as I demurred at this, he lifted a stick he had in his hand to strike me, but so suddenly and violently, that he frightened the horse, which broke away from him, and ran home. I was thus left without means of escape, to sustain the attacks of four men, as well as I might. In avoiding Mr. L.'s blow, I had accidentally got into a corner of the fence, where I could not be approached except in front. The overseer called upon the negroes to seize me; but they, knowing something of my physical power, were rather slow to obey. At length they did their best, and as they brought themselves within my reach, I knocked them down successively; and one of them trying to trip up my feet when he was down, I gave him a kick with my heavy shoe, which knocked out several of his front teeth, and sent him groaning away. Meanwhile, the cowardly overseer was availing himself of every opportunity to hit me over the head with his stick, which was not heavy enough to knock me down, though it drew blood freely. At length, tired of the length of the affray, he seized a stake, six or seven feet long, from the fence, and struck at me with his whole strength. In attempting to ward off the blow, my right arm was broken, and I was brought to the ground; where repeated blows broke both my shoulder blades, and made the blood gush from my mouth copiously. The two blacks begged him not to murder me, and he just left me as I was, telling me to learn what it was to strike a white man. The alarm had been raised at the house, by seeing the horse come back without his rider, and it was not long before assistance arrived to convey me home. It may be supposed it was not done without some suffering on my part; as, besides my broken arm and the wounds on my head, I could feel and hear the pieces of my shoulder-blades grate against each other with every breath. No physician or surgeon was called to dress my wounds, and I never knew one to be called to a slave upon R.'s estate, on any occasion whatever, and have no knowledge of such a thing being done on any estate in the neighborhood. I was attended, if it may be called attendance, by my master's sister, who had some reputation in such affairs; and she splintered my arm, and bound up my back as well as she knew how, and nature did the rest. It was five months before I could work at all, and the first time I tried to plough, a hard knock of the colter[19] against a stone, shattered my shoulder-blades again, and gave me even greater agony than at first. I have been unable to raise my hands to my head from that day to this. My master prosecuted Mr. L. for abusing and maiming his slave; and when the case was tried before the magistrate, he made a statement of the facts as I have here related them. When Mr. L. was called upon to say why he should not be fined for the offence, he simply stated, without being put on oath, that he had acted in self-defence; that I had assaulted him; and that nothing had saved him from being killed on the spot by so stout a fellow, but the fortunate circumstance that his three negroes were within call. The result was, that my master paid all the costs of court. He had the satisfaction of calling Mr. L. a liar and scoundrel, and, afterwards, of beating him in a very thorough manner, for which he had also to pay a fine and costs.

My situation, as overseer, I retained, together with the especial favor of my master, who was not displeased either with saving the expense of a large salary for a white superintendent, or with the superior crops I was able to raise for him. I will not deny that I used his property more freely than he would have done himself, in supplying his people with better food; but if I cheated him in this way, in small matters, it was unequivocally for his own benefit in more important ones; and I accounted, with the strictest honesty, for every dollar I received in the sale of the property entrusted to me. Gradually the disposal of every thing raised on the farm, the wheat, oats, hay, fruit, butter, and whatever else there might be, was confided to me, as it was quite evident that I could, and did sell for better prices than any one else he could employ, and he was quite incompetent to attend to the business himself. For many years I was his factotum, and supplied him with all his means for all his purposes, whether they were good or bad. I had no reason to think highly of his moral character, but it was my duty to be faithful to him, in the position in which he placed me; and I can boldly declare, before God and man, that I was so. I forgave him the causeless blows and injuries he had inflicted on me in childhood and youth, and was proud of the favor he now showed me, and of the character and reputation I had earned by strenuous and persevering efforts.

When I was about twenty-two years of age, I married a very efficient, and, for a slave, a very well-taught girl, belonging to a neighboring family, reputed to be pious and kind, whom I first met at the chapel I attended; and during nearly forty years that have since elapsed, I have had no reason to regret the connection, but many, to rejoice in it, and be grateful for it. She has borne me twelve children, eight of whom survive, and promise to be the comfort of my declining years.

Things remained in this condition for a considerable period; my occupations being to superintend the farming operations, and to sell the produce in the neighboring markets of Washington and Georgetown. Many respectable people, yet living there, may possibly have some recollection of " 'Siah," or "Si," (as they used to call me,) as their market-man; but if they have forgotten me, I remember them with an honest satisfaction.

After passing his youth in the manner I have mentioned in a general way, and which I do not wish more particularly to describe, my master, at the age of forty-five, or upwards, married a young woman of eighteen, who had some little property, and more thrift. Her economy was remarkable, and was certainly no addition to the comfort of the establishment. She had a younger brother, Francis, to whom R. was appointed guardian, and who used to complain—not without reason, I am confident—of the meanness of the provision made for the household; and he would often come to me, with tears in his eyes, to tell me he could not get enough to eat. I made him my friend for life, by sympathizing in his emotions, and satisfying his appetite, sharing with him the food I took care to provide for my own family.

After a time, however, continual dissipation was more than a match for domestic saving. My master fell into difficulty, and from difficulty into a lawsuit with a brother-in-law, who charged him with dishonest mismanagement of property confided to him in trust. The lawsuit was protracted enough to cause his ruin, of itself. He used every resource to stave off the inevitable result, but at length saw no means of relief but removal to another State. He often came to my cabin to pass the evening in lamentations over his misfortune, in cursing his brother-in-law, and in asking my advice and assistance. The first time he ever intimated to me his ultimate project, he said he was ruined, that every thing was gone, that there was but one resource, and that depended upon me. "How can that be, master?" said I, in astonishment. Before he would explain himself, however, he begged me to promise to do what he should propose, well knowing, from his past experience of my character, that I should hold myself bound by such promise to do all that it implied, if it were within the limits of possibility. Solicited in this way, with urgency and tears, by the man whom I had so zealously served for twenty years, and who now seemed absolutely dependent upon his slave,—impelled, too, by the fear which he skilfully awakened, that the sheriff would seize every one who belonged to him, and that all would be separated, or perhaps sold to go to Georgia, or Louisiana—an object of perpetual dread to the slave of the more northern States—I consented, and promised faithfully to do all I could to save him from the fate impending over him. He then told me I must take his slaves to his brother, in Kentucky. In vain I represented to him that I had never travelled a day's journey from his plantation, and knew nothing of the way, or the means of getting to Kentucky. He insisted that such a smart fellow as I could travel anywhere, he promised to give me all necessary instructions, and urged that this was the only course by which he could be saved. The result was, that I agreed to undertake the enterprise—certainly no light one for me, as it could scarcely be considered for even an experienced manager. There were eighteen negroes, besides my wife, two children, and myself, to transport nearly a thousand miles, through a country I knew nothing about, and in winter time, for we started in the month of February, 1825. My master proposed to follow me in a few months, and establish himself in Kentucky. He furnished me with a small sum of money, and some provisions; and I bought a one-horse wagon, to carry them, and to give the women and children a lift now and then, and the rest of us were to trudge on foot. Fortunately for the success of the undertaking, these people had been long under my direction, and were devotedly attached to me for the many alleviations I had afforded to their miserable condition, the comforts I had procured them, and the consideration which I had always manifested for them.

Under these circumstances no difficulty arose from want of submission to my authority, and none of any sort, except that which I necessarily encountered from my ignorance of the country, and my inexperience in such business. On arriving at Wheeling, I sold the horse and wagon, and purchased a boat of sufficient size, and floated down the river without further trouble or fatigue, stopping every night to encamp.

I said I had no further trouble, but there was one source of anxiety which I was compelled to encounter, and a temptation I had to resist, the strength of which others can appreciate as well as myself. In passing along the State of Ohio, we were frequently told that we were free, if we chose to be so. At Cincinnati, especially, the colored people gathered round us, and urged us with much importunity to remain with them; told us it was folly to go on; and in short used all the arguments now so familiar to induce slaves to quit their masters. My companions probably had little perception of the nature of the boon that was offered to them, and were willing to do just as I told them, without a wish to judge for themselves. Not so with me. From my earliest recollection, freedom had been the object of my ambition, a constant motive to exertion, an ever-present stimulus to gain and to save. No other means of obtaining it, however, had occurred to me, but purchasing myself of my master. The idea of running away was not one that I had ever indulged. I had a sentiment of honor on the subject, or what I thought such, which I would not have violated even for freedom; and every cent which I had ever felt entitled to call my own, had been treasured up for this great purpose, till I had accumulated between thirty and forty dollars. Now was offered to me an opportunity I had not anticipated. I might liberate my family, my companions, and myself, without the smallest risk, and without injustice to any individual, except one whom we had none of us any reason to love, who had been guilty of cruelty and oppression to us all for many years, and who had never shown the smallest symptom of sympathy with us, or with any one in our condition. But I need not make the exception. There would have been no injustice to R. himself—it would have been a retribution which might be called righteous—if I had availed myself of the opportunity thus thrust suddenly upon me.

But it was a punishment which it was not for me to inflict. I had promised that man to take his property to Kentucky, and deposit it with his brother; and this, and this only, I resolved to do. I left Cincinnati before night, though I had intended to remain there, and encamped with my entire party a few miles below the city. What advantages I may have lost, by thus throwing away an opportunity of obtaining freedom, I know not; but the perception of my own strength of character, the feeling of integrity, the sentiment of high honor, I have experienced,—these advantages I do know, and prize; and would not lose them, nor the recollection of having attained them, for all that I can imagine to have resulted from an earlier release from bondage. I have often had painful doubts as to the propriety of my carrying so many other individuals into slavery again, and my consoling reflection has been, that I acted as I thought at the time was best.

I arrived at Daviess county, Kentucky, about the middle of April, 1825, and delivered myself and my companions to Mr. Amos R., the brother of my owner, who had a large plantation, with from eighty to one hundred negroes. His house was situated about five miles south of the Ohio River, and fifteen miles above the Yellow Banks, on Big Blackford's Creek. There I remained three years, expecting my master to follow; and employed meantime on the farm, of which I had the general management, in consequence of the recommendation for ability and honesty which I brought with me from Maryland. The situation was in many respects more comfortable than that I had left. The farm was larger, and more fertile, and there was a greater abundance of food, which is, of course, one of the principal sources of the comfort of a slave, debarred, as he is, from so many enjoyments which other men can obtain. Sufficiency of food is a pretty important item in any man's account of life; but is tenfold more so in that of the slave, whose appetite is always stimulated by as much labor as he can perform, and whose mind is little occupied by thought on subjects of deeper interest. My post of superintendent gave me some advantages, too, of which I did not fail to avail myself, particularly with regard to those religious privileges, which, since I first heard of Christ and Christianity, had greatly occupied my mind. In Kentucky, the opportunities of attending on the preaching of whites, as well as of blacks, were more numerous; and partly by attending them, and the camp-meetings which occurred from time to time, and partly from studying carefully my own heart, and observing the developments of character around me, in all the stations of life which I could watch, I became better acquainted with those religious feelings which are deeply implanted in the breast of every human being, and learnt by practice how best to arouse them, and keep them excited, how to stir up the callous and indifferent, and in general to produce some good religious impressions on the ignorant and thoughtless community by which I was surrounded.

No great amount of theological knowledge is requisite for the purpose. If it had been, it is manifest enough that preaching never could have been my vocation; but I am persuaded that, speaking from the fulness of a heart deeply impressed with its own sinfulness and imperfection, and with the mercy of God, in Christ Jesus, my humble ministrations have not been entirely useless to those who have had less opportunity than myself to reflect upon these all-important subjects. It is certain that I could not refrain from the endeavor to do what I saw others doing in this field; and I labored at once to improve myself and those about me in the cultivation of the harvests which ripen only in eternity. I cannot but derive some satisfaction, too, from the proofs I have had that my services have been acceptable to those to whom they have been rendered. In the course of the three years from 1825 to 1828, I availed myself of all the opportunities of improvement which occurred, and was admitted as a preacher by a Conference of the Methodist Episcopal Church.

In the spring of the year 1828, news arrived from my master that he was unable to induce his wife to accompany him to Kentucky, and he must therefore remain where he was. He sent out an agent to sell all his slaves but me and my family, and to carry back the proceeds to him. And now another of those heart-rending scenes was to be witnessed, which had impressed itself so deeply on my childish soul. Husbands and wives, parents and children were to be separated forever. Affections, which are as strong in the African as in the European were to be cruelly disregarded; and the iron selfishness generated by the hateful "institution" was to be exhibited in its most odious and naked deformity. I was exempted from a personal share in the dreadful calamity, but I could not see without the deepest grief the agony which I recollected in my own mother, and which was again brought before my eyes in the persons with whom I had been long associated; nor could I refrain from the bitterest feeling of hatred of the system and those who sustain it. What else, indeed, can be the feeling of the slave, liable at every moment of his life to these frightful and unnecessary calamities, which may be caused by the caprice of the abandoned, or the supposed necessities of the better part of the slaveholders, and inflicted upon him without sympathy or redress, under the sanction of the laws which uphold the institution? I lamented my agency in bringing the poor creatures hither, if such was to be the end of the expedition; but I could not reproach myself with having made their condition really worse, nor with any thing but complying with the commands of a heartless master.

In the course of the summer of 1828, a Methodist preacher, a white man of some reputation, visited our neighborhood, and I became acquainted with him. He was soon interested in me, and visited me frequently, and one day talked to me in a confidential manner about my position. He said I ought to be free; that I had too much capacity to be confined to the limited and comparatively useless sphere of a slave; "and though," said he, "I must not be known to have spoken to you on this subject, yet if you will obtain Mr. Amos's consent to go to see your old master in Maryland, I will try and put you in a way by which I think you may succeed in buying yourself." He said this to me more than once; and as it was in harmony with all my aspirations and wishes, was flattering to my self-esteem, and could be attended with no harm that I could foresee, I soon resolved to make the attempt to get the necessary leave. Somewhat to my surprise, Master Amos made no objection; but gave me a pass to go to Maryland and back, with some remarks which showed his sense of the value of my services to him, and his opinion that I had earned such a privilege if I desired it. Furnished with this, and with a letter of recommendation from my Methodist friend to a brother preacher in Cincinnati, I started about the middle of September, 1828, for the east. By the aid of the good man to whom I had a letter, I had an opportunity of preaching in two or three of the pulpits of Cincinnati, when I took the opportunity of stating my purpose, and was liberally aided in it by contributions made on the spot. My friend also procured some subscriptions in the city, so that in three or four days I left it with not less than one hundred and sixty dollars in my pocket. The annual Methodist Conference was about to be held at Chillicothe,[20] to which my kind friend accompanied me, and by his influence and exertions I succeeded well there also. By his advice I then purchased a suit of respectable clothes, and an excellent horse, and travelled leisurely from town to town, preaching as I went, and, wherever circumstances were favorable, soliciting aid in my great object. I succeeded so well, that when I arrived at Montgomery county, I was master of two hundred and seventy-five dollars, besides my horse and my clothes. My master was surprised to see me dressed and mounted in so respectable a style, and I must say my horse was a good one, and my clothes better than Mr. R.'s; and he was a little puzzled to understand why I was so long in reaching home, for it was now Christmas, and he had been informed that I had left Kentucky in September. I gave him such an account of my preaching and getting the assistance of friends, as, while it was consistent with the truth, and explained my appearance, did not betray to him my principal purpose. Amid expressions of an apparently cordial welcome, I could discern plainly enough the look of displeasure that a slave should have got possession of such luxuries; and he bantered me not a little, in his coarse way, upon my preaching, and my being so speedily converted into a "black gentleman." He asked for my pass, and saw that it was expressed so as to authorize my return to Kentucky. He then handed it to his wife, and desired her to put it into the desk. The manoeuvre was cool, but I resolved to manoeuvre too.

At night I was sent to such quarters as I had been accustomed to long enough,—the cabin used for a kitchen, with its earth floor, its filth, and its numerous occupants;—but it was so different from my accommodations in the free States for the last three months, and so incompatible with my nice wardrobe, that I looked round me with a sensation of disgust that was new to me; and instead of going to sleep, I sat down and deliberated upon the best plan to adopt for my next proceedings. I found my mother had died during my absence, and every tie which had ever connected me with this place was broken. Strangers were around me here, the slaves being those Mrs. R. had brought to her husband, and I had not a friend to consult but Master Frank, the brother of R.'s wife, before mentioned, who was now of age, and had established himself in business in Washington. To him I resolved to go, and as soon as I thought it time to start, I saddled my horse and rode up to the house. It was early in the morning, and my master had already gone to the tavern on his usual business, but Mrs. R. came out to look at my horse and equipments. "Where are you going, 'Siah?" was the natural question. I replied, "I am going to Washington, Mistress, to see Mr. Frank, and I must take my pass with me if you please." "O, everybody knows you here; you won't need your pass." "But I can't go to Washington without it. I may be met by some surly stranger, who will stop me and plague me, if he can't do any thing worse." "Well, I'll get it for you," she answered; and glad was I to see her return with it in her hand, and to have her give it to me, while she little imagined its importance to my plan.

My reception by Master Frank was all I expected, as kind and hearty as possible. He was delighted at my appearance, and I immediately told him all my plans and hopes. He entered cordially into them, with that sympathy which penetrates the heart of a slave, as little accustomed as I had been, to the exhibition of any such feeling on the part of a white man. I found he had a thorough detestation of Mr. R., whom he charged with having defrauded him of a large proportion of his property which he had held as guardian, though, as he was still on terms with him, he readily agreed to negotiate for my freedom; and bring him to the most favorable bargain. Accordingly, in a few days he rode over to the house, and had a long conversation with R. on the subject of my emancipation. He disclosed to him the facts that I had got some money, and *my pass,* and urged that I was a smart fellow, who was bent upon getting his freedom, and had served the family faithfully for many years; that I had really paid for myself a hundred times over, in the increased amount of produce I had raised by my skill and influence; and that if he did not take care, and accept a fair offer when I made it to him, he would find some day that I had the means to do without his help, and that he would see neither me nor my money; that with my horse and my pass I was pretty independent of him already, and he had better make up his mind to what was really inevitable, and do it with a good grace. By such arguments as these, Mr. Frank not only induced him to think of the thing, but before long brought him to an actual bargain, by which he agreed to give me my manumission papers for four hundred and fifty dollars, of which three hundred and fifty dollars were to be in cash, and the remainder in my note. My money and my horse enabled me to pay the cash at once, and thus my great hopes seemed in a fair way of being realized.

Some time was spent in the negotiations for this affair, and it was not till the 9th of March, 1829, that I received my manumission papers in due form of law. I was prepared to start immediately on my return to Kentucky, and on the 10th, as I was getting ready in the morning for my journey, my master accosted me in a very pleasant and friendly manner, and entered into conversation with me about my plans. He asked me what I was going to do with my freedom certificate; whether I was going to show it if I were questioned on the road. I told him yes, that I supposed it was given to me for that very purpose. "Ah," said he, "you do not understand the dangers to which you are exposed. You may meet with some ruffian slave-purchaser who will rob you of that piece of paper, and destroy it. You will then be thrown into prison, and sold for your jail fees, before any of your friends can know it. Why should you show it at all? You can go to Kentucky in perfect safety with your pass. Let me enclose that valuable document for you under cover to my brother, and nobody will dare to break a seal, for that is a State prison matter; and when you arrive in Kentucky you will have it all safe and sound." This seemed most friendly advice, and I felt very grateful for his kindness. I accordingly saw him enclose my precious piece of paper in two or three envelopes, seal it with three seals, and direct it to his brother in Daviess County, Kentucky, in my care. Leaving immediately for Wheeling, to which place I was obliged to travel on foot, I there took boat, and in due time reached my destination. I was arrested repeatedly on the way, but by insisting always upon being carried before a magistrate, I succeeded in escaping all serious impediments by means of my pass, which was quite regular, and could not be set aside by any responsible authority.

It so happened that the boat which took me down from Louisville, landed me about dark, and my walk of five miles brought me to the plantation at bedtime. I went directly to my own cabin, where I found my wife and little ones well; and of course, we had a good deal to communicate to each other. Letters had reached the "great house," as the master's was always called, long before I had arrived, telling them what I had been doing, and the children of the family had been eager to communicate the great news to my wife,—how I had been preaching, and raising money, and making a bargain for my freedom. It was not long before Charlotte began to tell me with much excitement what she had heard, and to question me about how I had raised the money I had paid, and how I expected to get the remainder of the *thousand dollars* I was to give for my freedom. I could scarcely believe my ears; but before telling her how the case exactly was, I questioned her again and again as to what she had heard. She persisted in repeating the same story as she had heard it from my master's letters, and I began to perceive the trick that had been played upon me, and to see the management by which Isaac R. had contrived that the only evidence of my freedom should be kept from every eye but that of his brother Amos, who was instructed to retain it till I had made up six hundred and fifty dollars, the balance I was reported to have agreed to pay. Indignation is a faint word to express my deep sense of such villainy. I was without the means of setting myself right. The only witness to the truth was my friend Frank, who was a thousand miles off; and I could neither write to him, nor get any one else to do it. Every man about me who could write was a slaveholder; and what chance had I to be believed, or to get evidence to the truth. In this dilemma I resolved not to deliver the paper to Amos, and told my wife I had not seen it since I was in Louisville. It might be in my bag, and perhaps it was lost; but at all events I did not wish to see it again at present; and if she should find it, and put it in some place which I did not know, it would be the best disposition of it. In a few minutes she went out, and I remained in ignorance where it was, till circumstances, presently to be mentioned, rendered it necessary for me to have it again.

The next morning I went up to the house, and showed myself to Mr. Amos, who welcomed me with apparent cordiality, and who, I have no doubt, was really glad to see me, as my time and labor were important to him. We had a long conversation, and after rallying me, as his brother had done, about my being turned fine gentleman, he entered upon the subject of my freedom, and told me what Isaac had written to him about the price I was to pay, how much I had already made up, &c. I found my wife was right. He then asked me if I had not a paper for him. I told him I certainly had received something for him, of which I had taken the greatest care; but that the last time I had seen it was at Louisville, and that now it was not in my bag, and I did not know what had become of it. I could not conceive how it could be lost, and yet I could not find it. He expressed great concern, and sent me back to the landing to see if it had been dropped on the way.

When the search proved in vain, he told me that, after all, it was of no consequence, for whenever I made up the money, his brother would renew the paper. "But," said he, "you have given too much for yourself. Isaac has been too hard upon you, and I don't see how you are going to get so much in Kentucky."

All this was very smooth and pleasant to a man who was in a frenzy of grief at the base and apparently irremediable trick that had been played upon him. I consoled myself as well as I could, and set about my work again, with as quiet a mind as I could command, resolved to trust in God, and never despair. Things went on as usual for about a year, when, one day, Mr. Amos told me that his brother kept writing to him about his want of money; and intimated that perhaps I might be ready to pay another instalment of my price. I told him I had nothing, as he knew very well, and that he never had said what he would allow me, or whether he would allow me anything for my labor in his service. That put an end to the conversation at the time, for he did not like the idea of paying for the labor I had bestowed on his farm, the care of his stock and of his people. It was not long, however, before the subject was brought up again, and he said Isaac was perpetually telling him he must have money, and added that I must get ready to go to New Orleans with his son Amos, a young man about twenty-one years of age, who was going down the river with a flat boat, and was nearly ready to start; in fact he was to leave the next day, and I must go and take care of him, and help him dispose of the cargo. The intimation was enough. Though it was not distinctly stated, yet I well knew what was intended, and my heart sunk within me at the near prospect of this fatal blight to all my long-cherished hopes. There was no alternative but death itself; and I thought that there was hope as long as there was life, and I would not despair even yet. The expectation of my fate, however, produced the degree of misery nearest to that of despair; and it is in vain for me to attempt to describe the wretchedness I experienced as I made ready to go on board the flat boat. I had little preparation to make, to be sure; and there was but one thing that seemed to me important. I asked my wife to sew up my manumission paper securely in a piece of cloth, and to sew that again round my person. I thought that having possession of it might be the means of saving me yet, and I would not neglect any thing that offered the smallest chance of escape from the frightful servitude that threatened me.

My wife and children accompanied me to the landing, where I bade them an adieu, which might be for life, and then stepped into the boat, which I found manned by three white men, who had been hired for the trip. Mr. Amos and myself were the only other persons on board. The load consisted of beef-cattle, pigs, poultry, corn, whiskey, and other articles from the farm, and from some of the neighboring estates, which were to be sold as we dropped down the river, wherever they could be disposed of to the greatest advantage. It was a common trading voyage to New Orleans, in which I was embarked, the interest of which consisted not in the incidents that occurred, not in storms, or shipwreck, or external disaster of any sort; but in the storm of passions contending within me, and the imminent risk of the shipwreck of my soul, which was impending over me nearly the whole period of the voyage. One circumstance, only, I will mention, illustrating, as other events of my life have often done, the counsel of the Saviour, "He that will be chief among you, let him be your servant."

We were, of course, all bound to take our trick at the helm in turn, sometimes under direction of the captain, and sometimes on our own responsibility, as he could not be always awake. In the daytime there was less difficulty than at night, when it required some one who knew the river, to avoid sand-bars and snags, and the captain was the only person on board who had this knowledge. But whether by day or by night, as I was the only negro on the boat, I was made to stand at least three tricks to any other person's one; so that from being much with the captain, and frequently thrown upon my own exertions, I learnt the art of steering and managing the boat far better than the rest. I watched the manoeuvres necessary to shoot by a sawyer,[21] to land on a bank, or avoid a snag, or a steamboat, in the rapid current of the Mississippi, till I could do it as well as the captain. After a while the captain had a disease of the eyes, by which they became very much inflamed and swollen. He was soon rendered totally blind, and unable to perform his share of duty. This disorder is not an infrequent consequence of exposure to the intense light of the sun, doubled as it is by the reflection from the river. I was the person who could best take his place, and I was, in fact, master of the boat from that time till our arrival at New Orleans.

After the captain became blind, we were obliged to lie by at night, as none of the rest of us had been down the river before; and it was necessary to keep watch all night, to prevent depredations by the negroes on shore, who used frequently to attack such boats as ours, for the sake of the provisions on board. As I paced backwards and forwards on the deck, during my watch, it may well be believed I revolved many a painful and passionate thought. After all that I had done for Isaac and Amos R., after all the regard they professed for me, and the value they could not but put upon me, such a return as this for my services, such an evidence of their utter inattention to my claims upon them, and the intense selfishness with which they were ready to sacrifice me, at any moment, to their supposed interest, turned my blood to gall and wormwood, and changed me from a lively, and I will say, a pleasant-tempered fellow, into a savage, morose, dangerous slave. I was going not at all as a lamb to the slaughter, but I felt myself becoming more ferocious every day; and as we approached the place where this iniquity was to be consummated, I became more and more agitated with an almost uncontrollable fury. I had met, on the passage, with some of my Maryland acquaintance who had been sold off to this region; and their haggard and wasted appearance told a piteous story of excessive labor and insufficient food. I said to myself, "If this is to be my lot, I cannot survive it long. I am not so young as these men, and if it has brought them to such a condition, it will soon kill me. I am to be taken by my masters and owners, who ought to be my grateful friends, to a place and a condition where my life is to be shortened, as well as made more wretched. Why should I not prevent this wrong, if I can, by shortening their lives, or those of their agents in accomplishing such detestable injustice? I can do the last easily enough. They have no suspicion of me, and they are at this moment under my control, and in my power. There are many ways in which I can despatch them and escape, and I feel that I should be justified in availing myself of the first good opportunity." These were not thoughts which just flitted across my mind's eye, and then disappeared. They fashioned themselves into shapes which grew larger, and seemed firmer, every time they presented themselves; and at length my mind was made up to convert the phantom shadow into a positive reality. I resolved to kill my four companions, take what money there was in the boat, then to scuttle the craft, and escape to the north. It was a poor plan, maybe, and would very likely have failed; but it was as well contrived, under the circumstances, as the plans of murderers usually are; and blinded by passion, and stung to madness as I was, I could not see any difficulty about it. One dark, rainy night, within a few days of New Orleans, my hour seemed to have come. I was alone on the deck; Mr. Amos and the hands were all asleep below, and I crept down noiselessly, got hold of an axe, entered the cabin, and looking by the aid of the dim light there for my victims, my eye fell upon Master Amos, who was nearest me; my hand slid along the axe-handle, I raised it to strike the fatal blow,—when suddenly the thought came to me, "What! commit *murder!* and you a Christian?" I had not called it murder before. It was self-defence,—it was preventing others from murdering me,—it was justifiable, it was even praise-worthy. But now, all at once, the truth burst upon me that it was a crime. I was going to kill a young man, who had done nothing to injure me, but obey com-mands which he could not resist; I was about to lose the fruit of all my efforts at self-improvement, the character I had acquired, and the peace of mind which had never deserted me. All this came upon me instantly, and with a distinctness which made me almost think I heard it whispered in my ear; and I believe I even turned my head to listen. I shrunk back, laid down the axe, crept up on deck again, and thanked God, as I have done every day since, that I had not committed murder.

My feelings were still agitated, but they were changed. I was filled with shame and remorse for the design I had entertained, and with the fear that my companions would detect it in my face, or that a careless word would betray my guilty thoughts. I remained on deck all night, instead of rousing one of the men to relieve me, and nothing brought composure to my mind, but the solemn reso-lution I then made to resign myself to the will of God, and take with thankful-ness, if I could, but with submission, at all events, whatever he might decide should be my lot. I reflected that if my life were reduced to a brief term, I should have less to suffer, and that it was better to die with a Christian's hope, and a quiet conscience, than to live with the incessant recollection of a crime that would destroy the value of life, and under the weight of a secret that would crush out the satisfaction that might be expected from freedom and every other blessing.

It was long before I recovered my self-control and serenity; but I believe no one but those to whom I have told the story myself, ever suspected me of having entertained such thoughts for a moment.

In a few days after this tremendous crisis we arrived in New Orleans, and the little that remained of our cargo was soon sold, the men were discharged, and nothing was left but to dispose of me, and break up the boat, and then Mr. Amos would take passage on a steamboat, and go home. There was no longer any dis-guise about the purpose of selling me. Mr. Amos acknowledged that such were his instructions, and he set about fulfilling them. Several planters came to the boat to look at me; and I was sent of some hasty errand, that they might see how I could run. My points were canvassed as those of a horse would have been; and doubtless some account of my human faculties was thrown into the discussion of the bargain, that my value as a domestic animal might be enhanced. Amos had talked, with apparent kindness, about getting me a good master, who would em-ploy me as a coachman, or as a house-servant; but as time passed on I could dis-cern no particular effort of the kind. At length every thing was wound up but this single affair. The boat was to be sold, and I was to be sold, the next day, and Amos was to set off on his return, at six o'clock in the afternoon. I could not sleep that night, which seemed long enough to me, though it was one of the short-est in the year. The slow way in which we had come down had brought us to the long days and the heat of June; and everybody knows what the climate of New Orleans is at that time of the year.

A little before daylight master Amos awoke indisposed. His stomach was disordered, but he lay down again, thinking it would pass off. In a little while he was up again, and felt more sick than before, and it was soon evident that the river fever[22] was upon him. He became rapidly worse, and by eight o'clock in the morning he was utterly prostrate; his head was on my lap, and he was begging me to help him, to do something for him, to save him. The tables were turned. He was now rather more dependent upon me than I had been upon him the day before. He entreated me to despatch matters, to sell the flat boat, in which we two had been living by ourselves for some days, and to get him and his trunk, containing the proceeds of the trip, on board the steamer as quick as possible, and especially not to desert him so long as he lived, nor to suffer his body, if he died, to be thrown into the river. I attended to all his requests, and by twelve o'-clock that day, he was in one of the cabins of the steamer appropriated to sick passengers.

All was done which could be done for the comfort and relief of any one in such a desperate condition. But he was reduced to extremity. He ceased to grow worse after a day or two, and he must speedily have died, if he had not; but his strength was so entirely gone, that he could neither speak, nor move a limb; and could only indicate his wish for a teaspoonful of gruel, or something to moisten his throat, by a feeble motion of his lips. I nursed him carefully and constantly. Nothing else could have saved his life. It hung by a thread for a long time. We were as much as twelve days in reaching home, for the water was low at that season, particularly in the Ohio river; and when we arrived at our landing he was still unable to speak, and could only be moved on a sheet, or a litter. Something of this sort was soon fixed up at the landing, on which he could be carried to the house, which was five miles off; and I got a party of the slaves belonging to the estate to form relays for the purpose. As we approached the house, the surprise at seeing me back again, and the perplexity to imagine what I was bringing along, with such a party, were extreme; but the discovery was soon made which explained the strange appearance; and the grief of father and mother, and brothers and sisters, made itself seen and heard. Loud and long were the lamentations over poor Amos; and when the family came a little to themselves, great were the commendations bestowed upon me, for my care of him and of the property.

We arrived home about the tenth of July, but it was not till the middle of August that Amos was well enough to move out of his chamber, though he had been convalescent all the while. As soon as he could speak, he told all I had done for him, and said, "If I had sold him, I should have died;" but it never seemed to occur to him or the rest of the family that they were under any, the slightest, obligation to me on that account. I had done well as a slave, and to have it acknowledged, and to be praised for it, was compensation enough for me. My merits, whatever they were, instead of exciting sympathy, or any feeling of attachment to me, seemed only to enhance my money value to them. This was not the view which I took of the case myself; and as soon as Amos began to recover, I began to meditate upon a plan of escape from the danger, in which I constantly stood, of a repetition of the attempt to sell me in the highest market. Providence seemed to have interfered once to defeat the scheme, but I could not expect such extraordinary circumstances to be repeated, and I was bound to do every thing in my power to secure myself and my family from the wicked conspiracy of Isaac and Amos R. against my life, as well as against my natural rights in my own person, and those which I had acquired, under even the barbarous laws of slavery, by the money I had paid for myself. If Isaac would only have been honest enough to adhere to his own bargain, I would have adhered to mine, and paid him all I had promised. But his attempt to kidnap me again, after having pocketed three-fourths of my market value, absolved me from all obligation, in my opinion, to pay him any more, or to continue in a position which exposed me to his machinations. I determined to make my escape to Canada, about which I had heard something, as beyond the limits of the United States; for, notwithstanding there were free States in the Union, I felt that I should be safer under an entirely foreign jurisdiction. The slave States had their emissaries in the others, and I feared that I might fall into their hands, and need a stronger protection than might be afforded me by public opinion in the northern States at that time.

It was not without long thought on the subject that I devised a plan of escape; but when I had fully made up my mind, I communicated my intention to my wife, who was too much terrified by the dangers of the attempt to do any thing, at first, but endeavor to dissuade me from it, and try to make me contented with my condition as it was. In vain I explained to her the liability we were in of being separated from our children as well as from each other; and presented every argument which had weighed with my own mind, and had at last decided me. She had not gone through my trials, and female timidity overcame her sense of the evils she had experienced. I argued the matter with her, at various times, till I was satisfied that argument alone would not prevail; and then I said to her, very deliberately, that though it was a cruel thing for me to part with her, yet I would do it, and take all the children with me but the youngest, rather than run the risk of forcible separation from them all, and of a much worse captivity besides, which we were constantly exposed to here. She wept and entreated, but found I was resolute, and after a whole night spent in talking over the matter, I left her to go to my work for the day. I had not gone far when I heard her voice calling me;—I waited till she came up to me, and then, finding me as determined as ever, she said, at last, she would go with me. It was an immense relief to my nerves, and my tears flowed as fast as her's had done before. I rode off with a heart a good deal lighter.

She was living, at the time, near the landing I have mentioned; for the plantation extended the whole five miles from the house to the river, and there were several different farms, all of which I was overseeing, and, therefore, riding about from one to another every day. The oldest boy was at the house with Master Amos, the rest were all with her. Her consent was given on Thursday morning, and on the night of the following Saturday, I had decided to set out, as it would then be several days before I should be missed, and I should get a good start. Some time previously I had got my wife to make me a large knapsack, big enough to hold the two smallest children; and I had arranged it that she should lead the second boy, while the oldest was stout enough to go by himself, and to help me carry the necessary food. I used to pack the little ones on my back, of an evening, after I had got through my day's work, and trot round the cabin with them, and go some little distance from it, in order to accustom both them and myself to the task before us.

At length the eventful night came. I went up to the house to ask leave to take Tom home with me that he might have his clothes mended. No objection was made, and I bade Master Amos "good night" for the last time. It was about the middle of September, and by nine o'clock in the evening all was ready. It was a dark, moonless night, and we got into the little skiff in which I had induced a fellow-slave to take us across the river. It was an agitating and solemn moment. The good fellow who was rowing us over, said this affair might end in his death; "but," said he, "you will not be brought back alive, will you?" "Not if I can help it," I answered. "And if you are overpowered and return," he asked, "will you conceal my part of the business?" "That I will, so help me God," I replied. "Then I am easy," he answered, "and wish you success." We landed on the Indiana shore, and I began to feel that I was my own master. But in what circumstances of fear and misery still! We were to travel by night, and rest by day, in the woods and bushes. We were thrown absolutely upon our own poor and small resources, and were to rely on our own strength alone. The population was not so numerous as now, nor so well disposed to the slave. We dared look to no one for help. But my courage was equal to the occasion, and we trudged on cautiously and steadily, and as fast as the darkness, and the feebleness of my wife and boys would allow.

It was nearly a fortnight before we reached Cincinnati; and a day or two previous to getting there, our provisions were used up, and I had the misery to hear the cry of hunger and exhaustion from those I loved so dearly. It was necessary to run the risk of exposure by day-light upon the road; so I sprung upon it boldly from our hiding place one morning, and turned towards the south, to prevent the suspicion of my going the other way. I approached the first house I saw, and asked if they would sell me a little bread and meat. No, they had nothing for black fellows. At the next I succeeded better, but had to make as good a bargain as I could, and that was not very successful, with a man who wanted to see how little he could give me for my quarter of a dollar. As soon as I had succeeded in making a purchase, I followed the road, still towards the south, till I got out of sight of the house, and then darted into the woods again, and returned northward, just out of sight of the road. The food which I bought, such as it was, put new life and strength into my wife and children when I got back to them again, and we at length arrived safe at Cincinnati. There we were kindly received and entertained for several days, my wife and little ones were refreshed, and then we were carried on our way thirty miles in a wagon.

We followed the same course as before, of travelling by night, and resting by day, till we arrived at the Scioto, where we had been told we should strike the military road of General Hull, in the last war with Great Britain, and might then safely travel by day.[23] We found the road, accordingly, by the large sycamore and elm which marked its beginning, and entered upon it with fresh spirits early in the day. Nobody had told us that it was cut through the wilderness, and I had neglected to provide any food, thinking we should soon come to some habitation, where we could be supplied. But we travelled on all day without seeing one, and laid down at night, hungry and weary enough. I thought I heard the howling of wolves, and the terror inspired by this, and the exertions I used to keep them off, by making as much noise as I could, took away all power of sleeping, till daylight, and rendered a little delay inevitable. In the morning we were as hungry as ever, but had nothing to relieve our appetites but a little piece of dried beef. I divided some of this all round, and then started for a second day's trip in the wilderness. It was a hard trial, and this day is a memorable one in my life. The road was rough, of course, being neglected, and the logs lying across it constantly; the underbrush was somewhat cleared away, and that was about all to mark the track. As we went wearily on, I was a little ahead of my wife and the boys, when I heard them call to me, and, turning round, saw that my wife had fallen over a log, and was prostrate on the ground. "Mother's dying," cried Tom; and when I reached her, it seemed really so. She had fainted. I did not know but it might be fatal, and was half distracted with the fear and the uncertainty. In a few minutes, however, she recovered sufficiently to take a few mouthfuls of the beef, and this, with a little rest, revived her so much that she bravely set out once more.

We had not gone far, and I suppose it was about three o'clock in the afternoon, when we discerned some persons approaching us at no great distance. We were instantly on the alert, as we could hardly expect them to be friends. The advance of a few paces showed me they were Indians, with packs on their shoulders; and they were so near that if they were hostile, it would be useless to try to escape. So I walked along boldly, till we came close upon them. They were bent down with their burdens, and had not raised their eyes till now; and when they did so, and saw me coming towards them, they looked at me in a frightened sort of way for a moment, and then, setting up a peculiar howl, turned round, and ran as fast as they could. There were three or four of them, and what they were afraid of I could not imagine, unless they supposed I was the devil, whom they had perhaps heard of as black. But even then one would have thought my wife and children might have reassured them. However, there was no doubt they were well frightened, and we heard their wild and prolonged howl, as they ran, for a mile or more. My wife was alarmed too, and thought they were merely running back to collect more of a party, and then to come and murder us, and she wanted to turn back. I told her they were numerous enough to do that, if they wanted to, without help; and that as for turning back, I had had quite too much of the road behind us, and that it would be a ridiculous thing that both parties should run away. If they were disposed to run, I would follow. We did follow on, and soon the noise was stopped; and, as we advanced, we could discover Indians peeping at us from behind the trees, and dodging out of our sight, if they thought we were looking at them. Presently we came upon their wigwams, and saw a fine looking, stately Indian, with his arms folded, waiting for us to approach. He was apparently the chief, and, saluting us civilly, he soon discovered that we were human beings, and spoke to his young men, who were scattered about, and made them come in, and give up their foolish fears. And now curiosity seemed to prevail. Each one wanted to touch the children, who were shy as partridges, with their long life in the woods; and as they shrunk away, and uttered a little cry of alarm, the Indian would jump back too, as if he thought they would bite him. However, a little while sufficed to make them understand what we were, and whither we were going, and what we needed; and as little, to set them about supplying our wants, feeding us bountifully, and giving us a comfortable wigwam for our night's rest. The next day we resumed our march, and found, from the Indians, that we were only about twenty-five miles from the lake. They sent some of their young men to point out the place where we were to turn off, and parted from us with as much kindness as possible.

In passing over the part of Ohio near the lake, where such an extensive plain is found, we came to a spot overflowed by a stream, across which the road passed. I forded it first, with the help of a sounding-pole, and then taking the children on my back, first, the two little ones, and then the others, one at a time, and, lastly, my wife, I succeeded in getting them all safely across, where the ford was one hundred to one hundred and fifty yards wide, and the deepest part perhaps four feet deep. At this time the skin was worn from my back to an extent almost equal to the size of my knapsack.

One night more was passed in the woods, and in the course of the next forenoon we came out upon the wide plain, without trees, which lies south and west of Sandusky city. We saw the houses of the village, and kept away from them for the present, till I should have an opportunity to reconnoitre a little. When about a mile from the lake, I hid my companions in the bushes, and pushed forward. Before I had gone far, I observed on the left, on the opposite side from the town, something which looked like a house, between which and a vessel, a number of men were passing and repassing with activity. I promptly decided to approach them; and, as I drew near, I was hailed by one of the number, who asked me if I wanted to work. I told him yes; and it was scarcely a minute before I had hold of a bag of corn, which, like the rest, I emptied into the hold of the vessel lying at anchor a few rods off. I got into the line of laborers hurrying along the plank next to the only colored man I saw engaged, and soon entered into conversation with him; in the course of which I inquired of him where they were going, the best route to Canada, who was the captain, and other particulars interesting to me, and communicated to him where I came from, and whither I wished to go. He told the captain, who called me one side, and by his frank look and manner soon induced me to acknowledge my condition and purpose. I found I had not mistaken him. He sympathized with me, at once, most heartily; and offered to take me and my family to Buffalo, whither they were bound, and where they might arrive the next evening, if the favorable wind continued, of which they were hurrying to take advantage. Never did men work with a better will, and soon two or three hundred bushels were thrown on board, the hatches were fastened down, the anchor raised, and the sails hoisted. The captain had agreed to send a boat for me, after sundown, rather than take me on board at the landing; as there were Kentucky spies, he said, on the watch for slaves, at Sandusky, who might get a glimpse of me, if I brought my party out of the bush by daylight. I watched the vessel, as she left her moorings, with intense interest, and began to fear that she would go without me, after all; she stretched off to so great a distance, as it seemed to me, before she rounded to. At length, however, I saw her come up to the wind, and lower a boat for the shore; and, in a few minutes, my black friend and two sailors jumped out upon the beach. They went with me, immediately, to bring my wife and children. But what was my alarm when I came back to the place where I had left them, to find they had gone! For a moment, my fears were overpowering; but I soon discerned them, in the fading twilight, at no great distance. My wife had been alarmed by my long absence, and thought I must have been discovered by some of our watchful enemies, and had given up all for lost. Her fears were not removed by seeing me returning with three other men; and she tried to hide herself. It was not without difficulty that I satisfied her all was right, for her agitation was so great that she could not, at once, understand what I said. However, this was soon over, and the kindness of my companions facilitated the matter very much. Before long, we were all on the way to the boat, and it did not require much time or labor to embark our luggage. A short row brought us to the vessel, and, to my astonishment, we were welcomed on board, with three hearty cheers; for the crew were as much pleased as the captain, with the help they were giving us to escape. A fine run brought us to Buffalo the next evening, but it was too late to cross the river that night. The next morning we dropped down to Black Rock,[24] and the friendly captain, whose name I have gratefully remembered as Captain Burnham, put us on board the ferry-boat to Waterloo, paid the passage money, and gave me a dollar at parting. He was a Scotchman, and had done enough to win my enduring gratitude, to prove himself a kind and generous man, and to give me a pleasant association with his dialect and his country.

When I got on the Canada side, on the morning of the 28th of October, 1830, my first impulse was to throw myself on the ground, and giving way to the riotous exultation of my feelings, to execute sundry antics which excited the astonishment of those who were looking on. A gentleman of the neighborhood, Colonel Warren, who happened to be present, thought I was in a fit, and as he inquired what was the matter with the poor fellow, I jumped up and told him *I was free.* "O," said he, with a hearty laugh, "is that it? I never knew freedom make a man roll in the sand before." It is not much to be wondered at, that my certainty of being free was not quite a sober one at the first moment; and I hugged and kissed my wife and children all round, with a vivacity which made them laugh as well as myself. There was not much time to be lost, though, in frolic, even at this extraordinary moment. I was a stranger, in a strange land, and had to look about me at once, for refuge and resource. I found a lodging for the night; and the next morning set about exploring the interior for the means of support. I knew nothing about the country, or the people; but kept my eyes and ears open, and made such inquiries as opportunity afforded. I heard, in the course of the day, of a Mr. Hibbard, who lived some six or seven miles off, and who was a rich man, as riches were counted there, with a large farm, and several small tenements on it, which he was in the habit of letting to his laborers. To him I went, immediately, though the character given him by his neighbors was not, by any means, unexceptionably good. But I thought he was not probably any worse than those I had been accustomed to serve, and that I could get along with him, if honest and faithful work would satisfy him. In the afternoon I found him, and soon struck a bargain with him for employment. I asked him if there was any house where he would let me live. He said yes, and led the way to an old two story sort of shanty, into the lower story of which the pigs had broken, and had apparently made it their resting-place for some time. Still, it was a house, and I forthwith expelled the pigs, and set about cleaning it for the occupancy of a better sort of tenants. With the aid of hoe and shovel, hot-water and a mop, I got the floor into a tolerable condition by midnight, and only then did I rest from my labor. The next day I brought the rest of the Hensons to *my house,* and though there was nothing there but bare walls and floors, we were all in a state of great delight, and my old woman laughed and acknowledged that it was worth while, and that it was better than a log-cabin with an earth-floor. I begged some straw of Mr. Hibbard, and confining it by logs in the corners of the room, I made beds of it three feet thick, upon which we reposed luxuriously after our long fatigues.

Another trial awaited me which I had not anticipated. In consequence of the great exposures we had gone through, my wife and all the children fell sick; and it was not without extreme peril that they escaped with their lives.

My employer soon found that my labor was of more value to him than that of those he was accustomed to hire; and as I consequently gained his favor, and his wife took quite a fancy to mine, we soon procured some of the comforts of life, while the necessaries of food and fuel were abundant. I remained with Mr. Hibbard three years, sometimes working on shares, and sometimes for wages; and I managed in that time to procure some pigs, a cow, and a horse. Thus my condition gradually improved, and I felt that my toils and sacrifices for freedom had not been in vain. Nor were my labors for the improvement of myself and others, in more important things than food and clothing, without effect. It so happened that one of my Maryland friends arrived in this neighborhood, and hearing of my being here, inquired if I ever preached now, and spread the reputation I had acquired elsewhere, for my gifts in the pulpit. I had said nothing myself, and had not intended to say any thing, of my having ever officiated in that way. I went to meeting with others, when I had an opportunity, and enjoyed the quiet of the Sabbath when there was no assembly. I would not refuse to labor in this field, however, when desired to do so; and I hope it is no violation of modesty to state the fact that I was frequently called upon, not by blacks alone, but by all classes in my vicinity, the comparatively educated, as well as the lamentably ignorant, to speak to them on their duty, responsibility, and immortality, on their obligations to their Maker, their Saviour, and themselves.

It may, nay, I am aware it must, seem strange to many that a man so ignorant as myself, unable to read, and having heard so little as I had of religion, natural or revealed, should be able to preach acceptably to persons who had enjoyed greater advantages than myself. I can explain it, only by reference to our Saviour's comparison of the kingdom of heaven to a plant which may spring from a seed no bigger than a mustard-seed, and may yet reach such a size, that the birds of the air may take shelter therein.[25] Religion is not so much knowledge, as wisdom;—and observation upon what passes without, and reflection upon what passes within a man's heart, will give him a larger growth in grace than is imagined by the devoted adherents of creeds, or the confident followers of Christ, who call him Lord, Lord, but do not the things which he says.

Mr. Hibbard was good enough to give my eldest boy, Tom, two quarters' schooling, to which the schoolmaster added more of his own kindness, so that my boy learned to read fluently and well. It was a great advantage, not only to him, but to me; for I used to get him to read much to me in the Bible, especially on Sunday mornings when I was going to preach; and I could easily commit to memory a few verses, or a chapter, from hearing him read it over. One beautiful summer-Sabbath I rose early, and called him to come and read to me. "Where shall I read, father?" "Anywhere, my son," I answered, for I knew not how to direct him. He opened upon Psalm ciii. "Bless the Lord, O my soul, and all that is within me bless his holy name;" and as he read this beautiful outpouring of gratitude which I now first heard, my heart melted within me. I recalled, with all the rapidity of which thought is capable, the whole current of my life; and as I remembered the dangers and afflictions from which the Lord had delivered me, and compared my present condition with what it had been, not only my heart but my eyes overflowed, and I could neither check nor conceal the emotion which overpowered me. The words "Bless the Lord, O my soul," with which the Psalm begins and ends, were all I needed, or could use, to express the fulness of my thankful heart. When he had finished, Tom turned to me and asked, "Father, who was David?" He had observed my excitement, and added, "He writes pretty, don't he?" and then repeated his question. It was a question I was utterly unable to answer. I had never heard of David, but could not bear to acknowledge my ignorance to my own child. So I answered evasively, "He was a man of God, my son." "I suppose so," said he; "but I want to know something more about him. Where did he live? What did he do?" As he went on questioning me, I saw it was in vain to attempt to escape, and so I told him frankly I did not know. "Why, father," said he, "can't you read?" This was a worse question than the other, and if I had any pride in me at the moment, it took it all out of me pretty quick. It was a direct question, and must have a direct answer; so I told him at once I could not. "Why not," said he. "Because I never had an opportunity to learn, nor anybody to teach me." "Well, you can learn now, father." "No, my son, I am too old, and have not time enough. I must work all day, or you would not have enough to eat." "Then you might do it at night." "But still there is nobody to teach me. I can't afford to pay anybody for it, and of course no one can do it for nothing." "Why, father, *I'll teach you*. I can do it, I know. And then you'll know so much more, that you can talk better, and preach better." The little fellow was so earnest, there was no resisting him; but it is hard to describe the conflicting feelings within me at such a proposition from such a quarter. I was delighted with the conviction that my children would have advantages I had never enjoyed; but it was no slight mortification to think of being instructed by a child of twelve years old. Yet ambition, and a true desire to learn, for the good it would do my own mind, conquered the shame, and I agreed to try. But I did not reach this state of mind instantly. I was greatly moved by the conversation I had had with Tom—so much so that I could not undertake to preach that day. The congregation were disappointed, and I passed the Sunday in solitary reflection in the woods. I was too much engrossed with the multitude of my thoughts within me to return home to dinner, and spent the whole day in secret meditation and prayer, trying to compose myself, and ascertain my true position. It was not difficult to see that my predicament was one of profound ignorance, and that I ought to use every opportunity of enlightening it. I began to take lessons of Tom, therefore, immediately, and followed it up, every evening, by the light of a pine knot, or some hickory bark, which was the only light I could afford. Weeks passed, and my progress was so slow, that poor Tom was almost discouraged, and used to drop asleep, sometimes, and whine a little over my dullness, and talk to me very much as a schoolmaster talks to a stupid boy, till I began to be afraid that my age, my want of practice in looking at such little scratches, the daily fatigue, and the dim light, would be effectual preventives of my ever acquiring the art of reading. But Tom's perseverance and mine conquered at last, and in the course of the winter I did really learn to read a little. It was, and has been ever since, a great comfort to me to have made this acquisition; though it has made me comprehend better the terrible abyss of ignorance in which I had been plunged all my previous life. It made me also feel more deeply and bitterly the oppression under which I had toiled and groaned; but the crushing and cruel nature of which I had not appreciated, till I found out, in some slight degree, from what I had been debarred. At the same time it made me more anxious than before to do something for the rescue and the elevation of those who were suffering the same evils I had endured, and who did not know how degraded and ignorant they really were.

After about three years had passed, I improved my condition again by taking service with a gentleman by the name of Riseley, whose residence was only a few miles distant, and who was a man of more elevation of mind than Mr. Hibbard, and of superior abilities. At his place I began to reflect, more and more, upon the circumstances of the blacks, who were already somewhat numerous in this region. I was not the only one who had escaped from the States, and had settled on the first spot in Canada which they had reached. Several hundreds of colored persons were in the neighborhood; and in the first joy of their deliverance, were going on in a way which, I could see, led to little or no progress in improvement. They were content to have the proceeds of their labor at their own command, and had not the ambition for, or the perception of what was within their easy reach, if they did but know it. They were generally working for hire upon the lands of others, and had not yet dreamed of becoming independent proprietors themselves. It soon became my great object to awaken them to a sense of the advantages which offered themselves to their grasp; and Mr. Riseley, seeing clearly the justness of my views, and willing to coöperate with me in the attempt to make them generally known among the blacks, permitted me to call meetings, at his house, of those who were known to be among the most intelligent and successful of our class. At these meetings we considered and discussed the subject, till we were all of one mind; and it was agreed, among the ten or twelve of us who assembled at them, that we would invest our earnings in land, and undertake the task, which, though no light one certainly, would yet soon reward us for our effort, of settling upon wild lands which we could call our own; and where every tree which we felled, and every bushel of corn we raised, would be for ourselves; in other words, where we could secure all the profits of our own labor.

The advantages of this course need not be dwelt upon in a country which is every day exemplifying it, and has done so for two hundred years and more; and has, by this very means, acquired an indestructible character for energy, enterprise, and self-reliance. It was precisely the Yankee spirit which I wished to instil into my fellow-slaves, if possible; and I was not deterred from the task by the perception of the immense contrast in all the habits and character generated by long ages of freedom and servitude, activity and sloth, independence and subjection. My associates agreed with me, and we resolved to select some spot among the many offered to our choice, where we would colonize and raise our own crops, eat our own bread, and be, in short, our own masters. I was deputed to explore the country, and find a place to which I would be willing to migrate myself; and they all said they would go with me whenever such a one should be found. I set out accordingly in the autumn of 1834, and travelled on foot all over the extensive region between lakes Ontario, Erie, and Huron. When I came to the territory east of Lake St. Clair and Detroit River, I was strongly impressed with its fertility, its convenience, and, indeed, its superiority, for our purposes, to any other spot I had seen. I determined this should be the place; and so reported, on my return, to my future companions. They were wisely cautious, however, and sent me off again in the summer, that I might see it at the opposite seasons of the year, and be better able to judge of its advantages. I found no reason to change my opinion, but upon going further towards the head of Lake Erie, I discovered an extensive tract of government land, which, for some years, had been granted to a Mr. McCormick upon certain conditions, and which he had rented out to settlers upon such terms as he could obtain. This land being already cleared, offered some advantages for the immediate raising of crops, which were not to be overlooked by persons whose resources were so limited as ours; and we determined to go there first, for a time, and with the proceeds of what we could earn there, to make our purchases in Dawn afterwards. This plan was followed, and some dozen or more of us settled upon these lands the following spring, and accumulated something by the crops of wheat and tobacco we were able to raise.

I discovered, before long, that McCormick had not complied with the conditions of his grant, and was not, therefore, entitled to the rent he exacted from settlers. I was advised by Sir John Cockburn, to whom I applied on the subject, to appeal to the legislature for relief. We did so; and though McCormick was able, by the aid of his friends, to defeat us for one year, yet we succeeded the next, upon a second appeal, and were freed from all rent, thereafter, so long as we remained. Still, this was not our own land. The government, though it demanded no rent, might set up the land for sale at any time, and then we should, probably, be driven off by wealthier purchasers, with the entire loss of all our improvements, and with no retreat provided. It was manifest that it was altogether better for us to purchase before competition was invited; and we kept this fully in mind during the time we staid here. We remained in this position six or seven years; and all this while the colored population was increasing rapidly around us, and spreading very fast into the interior settlements and the large towns. The immigration from the United States was incessant, and some, I am not unwilling to admit, were brought hither with my knowledge and connivance. I was glad to help such of my old friends as had the spirit to make the attempt to free themselves; and I made more than one trip, about this time, to Maryland and Kentucky, with the expectation, in which I was not disappointed, that some might be enabled to follow in my footsteps. I knew the route pretty well, and had much greater facilities for travelling than when I came out of that Egypt for the first time.

I did not find that our prosperity increased with our numbers. The mere delight the slave took in his freedom, rendered him, at first, contented with a lot far inferior to that which he might have attained. Then his ignorance led him to make unprofitable bargains, and he would often hire wild land on short terms, and bind himself to clear a certain number of acres; and by the time they were cleared and fitted for cultivation his lease was out, and his landlord would come in, and raise a splendid crop on the new land; and the tenant would, very likely, start again on just such another bargain, and be no better off at the end of ten years than he was at the beginning. Another way in which they lost the profits of their labor, was by raising nothing but tobacco, the high price of which was very tempting, and the cultivation of which was a monopoly in their hands, as no white man understood it, or could compete with them at all. The consequence was, however, that they had nothing but tobacco to sell; there was rather too much of it in the market, and the price of wheat rose, while their commodity was depressed; and they lost all they should have saved, in the profit they gave the trader for his corn and stores. I saw the effect of these things so clearly that I could not help trying to make my friends and neighbors see it too; and I set seriously about the business of lecturing upon the subject of crops, wages, and profits, as if I had been brought up to it. I insisted on the necessity of their raising their own crops, saving their own wages, and securing the profits of their own labor, with such plain arguments as occurred to me, and were as clear to their comprehension as to mine. I did this very openly; and, frequently, my audience consisted in part of the very traders whose inordinate profits upon individuals I was trying to diminish, but whose balance of profit would not be ultimately lessened, because they would have so many more persons to trade with who would be able to pay them a reasonable advance in cash, or its equivalent, on all their purchases. The purse is a tender part of the system; but I handled it so gently, that the sensible portion of my natural opponents were not, I believe, offended; while those whom I wished to benefit, saw, for the most part, the propriety of my advice, and took it. At least, there are now great numbers of settlers, in this region of Canada, who own their farms, and are training up their children in true independence, and giving them a good elementary education, who had not taken a single step towards such a result before I began to talk to them.

I said none of the respectable traders were offended with me; but one man had the folly to arrest me for a small debt, under the pretence that I was about to leave the country, when I was only going to Detroit for a few days, in the spring, leaving my crops on the ground, and all my family at home but one little girl, who was to go to school for a few weeks. It was so absurd, however, that I was soon released by some of my friends, of whom I had many among the whites as well as the blacks.

While I remained at Colchester, I became acquainted with a Congregational missionary from Massachusetts, by the name of Hiram Wilson, who took an interest in our people, and was disposed to do what he could to promote the cause of improvement which I had so much at heart. He coöperated with me in many efforts, and I have been associated with him from 1836 to the present time. He has been a faithful friend, and still continues his important labors of love in our behalf. Among other things which he did for us then, he wrote to a Quaker friend of his, an Englishman, by the name of James C. Fuller, residing at Skeneateles, New York, and endeavored to interest him in the welfare of our struggling population.

He succeeded so far, that Mr. Fuller, who was going on a visit to England, promised to do what he could among his friends there, to induce them to aid us. He came back with fifteen hundred dollars which had been subscribed for our benefit. It was a great question how this sum, which sounded vast to many of my brethren, should be appropriated. I had my own opinion pretty decidedly made up as to what it was best for us all to do with it. But, in order to come to a satisfactory conclusion, the first thing to be done was to call a convention of delegates from every settlement of blacks that was within reach; that all might see that whatever was decided on, was sanctioned by the disinterested votes of those who were thought by their companions best able to judge what was expedient. Mr. Wilson and myself called such a convention, therefore, to meet in London, Upper Canada, and it was held in June, 1838. I urged the appropriation of the money to the establishment of a manual-labor school, where our children could be taught those elements of knowledge which are usually the occupations of a grammar-school; and where the boys could be taught, in addition, the practice of some mechanic art, and the girls could be instructed in those domestic arts which are the proper occupation and ornament of their sex. Such an establishment would train up those who would afterwards instruct others; and we should thus gradually become independent of the white man for our intellectual progress, as we might be also for our physical prosperity. It was the more necessary, as in many districts, owing to the insurmountable prejudices of the inhabitants, the children of the blacks were not allowed to share the advantages of the common school. There was some opposition to this plan in the convention; but in the course of the discussion, which continued for three days, it appeared so obviously for the advantage of all to husband this donation, so as to preserve it for a purpose of permanent utility, that the proposal was, at last, unanimously adopted; and a committee of three was appointed to select and purchase a site for the establishment. Mr. Wilson and myself were the active members of this committee, and after traversing the country for several months, we could find no place more suitable than that upon which I had had my eye for three or four years, for a permanent settlement, in the town of Dawn. We therefore bought two hundred acres of fine, rich land, on the river Sydenham, covered with a heavy growth of black walnut and white wood, at four dollars the acre. I had made a bargain for two hundred acres adjoining this lot, on my own account; and circumstances favored me so that the man of whom I purchased was glad to let me have them at a large discount from the price I had agreed to pay, if I would give him cash for the balance I owed him. I transferred a portion of the advantage of this bargain to the institution, by selling to it one hundred acres more, at the low price at which I obtained them; and thus the school has three hundred acres of as fine land, and as well situated land, as Canada can show, at a very moderate cost. In 1842, I removed with my family to Dawn, and as a considerable number of my friends are there about me, and the school is permanently fixed there, the future importance of this settlement seems to be decided. There are many other settlements which are considerable; and, indeed, the colored population is scattered over a territory, which does not fall far short of three hundred miles in extent in each direction, and probably numbers not less than twenty thousand persons in all. We look to the school, and the possession of landed property by individuals, as two great means of the elevation of our oppressed and degraded race to a participation in the blessings, as they have hitherto been permitted to share only the miseries and vices, of civilization.

My efforts to aid them, in every way in my power, and to procure the aid of others for them, have been constant. I have made many journeys into New York, Connecticut, Massachusetts, and Maine, in all of which States I have found or made some friends to the cause, and, I hope, some personal friends. I have received many liberal gifts, and experienced much kindness of treatment; but I must be allowed to allude particularly to the donations received from Boston, by which we have been enabled to erect a sawmill, and thus to begin in good earnest, the clearing of our lands, and to secure a profitable return for the support of our school, as among those which have been most welcome and valuable to us.

I could give here a great many particulars, which would amuse and interest the reader, if they did not instruct him. But it is better not to indulge the inclination; and I will conclude my narrative by simply recording my gratitude, heartfelt and inexpressible, to God, and to many of my fellow-men, for the vast improvement in my condition, both physical and mental; for the great degree of comfort with which I am surrounded; for the good I have been enabled to effect; for the light which has risen upon me; for the religious privileges I enjoy, and the religious hopes I am permitted to cherish; for the prospects opening to my children, so different from what they might have been; and, finally, for the cheering expectation of benefiting not only the present, but many future generations of my race.

1. Jackson, *History*, 147.
2. Peabody, "Narratives," 26–28.
3. Stowe, *Key*, 27.
4. Winks, "Making," 120.
5. Andrews, *Free Story*, 122; Nichols, *Many Thousand Gone*, 2; Jackson, *History*, 145; Blassingame, *Slave Testimony*, xxxiii.
6. Winks, "Making," 127, 132–33; Nichols, *Many Thousand Gone*, xiv–xv.
7. Winks, "Making," 114–115.
8. William Andrews claims that Henson's narrative is "a kind of morality play" from which

Henson emerges victorious over his "dark side" (*Free Story*, 120–121). Yet Henson's *Life* is more far complex than Andrews's portrayal of it. After ignoring the opportunity to free himself, his wife and children, and eighteen other slaves in Cincinnati, Henson writes, "I have often had painful doubts as to the propriety of my carrying so many other individuals into slavery again, and my consoling reflection has been, that I acted as I thought at the time was right." This is hardly the good-vs.-evil language of a morality play.

9. Henson, *Autobiography*, 79–88, 128; Winks, "Making," 125. Even the estimable Rayford Logan was fooled—see "Henson, Josiah," 307.

10. Winks, "Making," 123, 130.

11. Stowe, *Key*, 26.

12. Henson, *Autobiography*, 96–161; Starling, *Slave Narrative*, 239–240; Nichols, *Many Thousand Gone*, 2, 83; Logan, "Henson, Josiah," 307; Winks, "Making," 114–115.

13. Francis Newman. This and the other names noted below are fully spelled out in Henson's later narratives.

14. Josiah McPherson. He gave Henson his own first name, and the surname of his uncle, who had served in the Revolutionary War. Henson, *Autobiography*, 16.

15. Isaac Riley.

16. A tavern-keeper named Robb.

17. John McKenny.

18. Bryce Litton.

19. The blade on the front of the plow that cuts through the soil.

20. A city of south-central Ohio.

21. A tree, or part thereof, that protrudes above the surface of the water.

22. Probably yellow fever.

23. The Scioto is a river south of Lake Erie. General William Hull (1753–1825) traveled along a route still known as Hull's Trail north to Detroit during the War of 1812.

24. A river crossing about a mile and a half from Buffalo.

25. *Luke* 13:18.

Part I: Ten highly recommended slave narratives not included in this collection (listed in chronological order)

Smith, Venture. *A Narrative of the Life and Adventures of Venture, a Native of Africa: But Resident Above Sixty Years in the United States of America.* New London: C. Holt, 1798. Reprinted in Porter, *Early Negro Writing*, 538–558, and Carretta, *Unchained Voices*, 369–387. Smith grew up in Africa, where he witnessed a tribal war in which his father, a king, was tortured and killed. A rebellious and combative slave, he purchased his own freedom for an exorbitant price. He then bought his wife and children, some land, and a slave of his own. Despite a condescending amanuensis, Smith's bitter pride and rebellious spirit come through intact.

Bayley, Solomon. *Incidents in the Life of Solomon Bayley.* Philadelphia: Tract Association of Friends, 1820. *A Narrative of Some Remarkable Incidents in the Life of Solomon Bayley, Formerly a Slave, in the State of Delaware, North America.* 2d ed., London: Harvey and Darton, 1825. Reprinted in Porter, *Early Negro Writing*, 587–613. The most remarkable passage of this intensely religious self-penned tract is Bayley's mystical account of how a circle of birds in the woods protected him from fugitive slave hunters.

Prince, Mary. *The History of Mary Prince, a West Indian Slave.* London: F. Westley and A. H. Davis, 1831. Reprinted in Gates, *Classic Slave Narratives*, 183–242. Prince was sold at a young age to an extraordinarily cruel master; her description of the salt works comes as close to hell on earth as any passage in the slave-narrative tradition. Although dictated to a British amanuensis, her *History* is the first West Indian autobiography, and the first narrative of a female slave.

Williams, James. *Narrative of James Williams, An American Slave.* New York: American Anti-slavery Society, 1838. On-line, <http://sunsite.unc.edu/docsouth/narratives.html>. After a mild childhood, Williams was separated from his wife and children, taken to Alabama, and made a slave driver. His overseer, Huckstep, was a brutal murderer, and Williams escaped by befriending his master's bloodhounds. His popular narrative, dictated to the abolitionist poet John Greenleaf Whittier, was widely discredited not long after its publication, because certain details, such as names of places and people, had been falsified.

Lane, Lunsford. *The Narrative of Lunsford Lane, Formerly of Raleigh, N. C.* Boston: J. G. Torry, 1842. Reprinted in Katz, *Flight from the Devil.* After making money as a tobacconist and buying his freedom, Lane was banished from North Carolina under a law that disallowed the residence of free blacks in the state. When he returned to Raleigh to purchase his wife and child, he was brought before a local court, accused of giving abolitionist lectures in Boston, and tarred and feathered.

Gilbert, Olive. *Narrative of Sojourner Truth, a Northern Slave.* Boston: the Author, 1850. Numerous reprints. Although entitled a slave narrative, this book is actually a biography largely drawn from the recollections of Truth, and was instrumental in bringing her to the world's attention. Its most unforgettable scene comes near the end, when Truth disperses a group of rioters at a revival meeting.

Douglass, Frederick. *My Bondage and My Freedom.* New York and Auburn: Miller, Orton and Mulligan, 1855. Numerous reprints. Three times as long as Douglass's earlier *Narrative,* his second autobiography not only updates and expands his first, but is less heroic and more sophisticated, complex, playful, nuanced, humorous, detached, and inclusive—all without sacrificing Douglass's militancy.

Steward, Austin. *Twenty-Two Years a Slave, and Forty Years a Freeman.* Rochester [N.Y.]: William Alling, 1857. On-line, <http://sunsite.unc.edu/docsouth/narratives.html>. Steward was an important abolitionist who spent most of his life in Canada. His lengthy and militant autobiography not only deals with the evils of slavery, but the "black codes" common in the free states and the difficulties of life in the black settlements of Canada.

Keckley, Elizabeth. *Behind the Scenes, or, Thirty Years a Slave, and Four Years in the White House.* New York: G. W. Carleton & Co., 1868. Reprint: New York, Oxford University Press, 1988. Keckley was dressmaker both to Virginia Davis, wife of Jefferson Davis, and to Mary Lincoln, wife of Abraham Lincoln. She had intimate knowledge of the entire Lincoln family, and her anecdotal account is priceless for its insider's view.

Hughes, Louis. *Thirty Years a Slave: From Bondage to Freedom.* Milwaukee: South Side Printing Company, 1897. Reprint, Detroit: Negro History Press, 1969. On-line, <http://sunsite.unc.edu/docsouth/narratives.html>. This narrative includes perhaps the longest, most interesting, and most exciting firsthand account of slave life during the Civil War.

## Part II: Other works cited

Andrews, William L. "*Narrative of the Life of Frederick Douglass.*" In Andrews et al., *Oxford Companion,* 526–527.

———. "The Representation of Slavery and the Rise of Afro-American Literary Realism, 1865–1920." In Andrews, *African American Autobiography.*

———. "Slave Narrative." In Andrews et al., *Oxford Companion,* 667–670.

———. *To Tell a Free Story: The First Century of Afro-American Autobiography, 1760–1865.* Urbana: University of Illinois Press, 1986.

———, ed. *African American Autobiography: A Collection of Critical Essays.* Englewood Cliffs, NJ: Prentice Hall, 1993.

————, ed. *From Fugitive Slave to Free Man: The Autobiographies of William Wells Brown.* New York: Mentor, 1993.

Andrews, William L., Frances Smith Foster, and Trudier Harris, eds. *The Oxford Companion to African American Literature.* New York: Oxford University Press, 1997.

Andrews, William L., and William S. McFeely, eds. *Narrative of the Life of Frederick Douglass, an American Slave, Written by Himself: A Norton Critical Edition.* New York: W. W. Norton, 1997.

Aptheker, Herbert. "Turner, Nat." In Logan and Winston, *Dictionary,* 611–613.

Bibb, Henry. *Narrative of the Life and Adventures of Henry Bibb, An American Slave.* 3d ed, New York: the author, 1850.

Black, Alexander. *The Story of Ohio.* Boston: D. Lothrop, 1888.

Blackett, R. J. M. *Beating Against the Barriers: Biographical Essays in Nineteenth-Century Afro-American History.* Baton Rouge: Louisiana State University Press, 1986.

Blassingame, John W. "Bibb, Henry Walton." In Logan and Winston, *Dictionary,* 44.

————. *The Slave Community: Plantation Life in the Antebellum South.* Rev. & enlarged ed. New York: Oxford University Press, 1979.

————, ed. *Slave Testimony: Two Centuries of Letters, Speeches, Interviews, and Autobiographies.* Baton Rouge: Louisiana State University Press, 1977.

Blight, David W. Introduction and notes to *Narrative of the Life of Frederick Douglass, An American Slave.* Boston: Bedford Books, 1993.

Bontemps, Arna, ed. *Great Slave Narratives.* Boston: Beacon Press, 1969.

Brown, Henry Box. *Narrative of the Life of Henry Box Brown.* Manchester [England]: Lee and Glynn, 1851.

Brown, William Wells. *The Anti-Slavery Harp; A Collection of Songs.* 4th ed., Boston: Bela Marsh, 1854.

Byrd, William. *The Correspondence of the Three William Byrds of Westover, Virginia, 1684–1776.* Ed. Marion Tinling. Charlottesville: University Press of Virginia, 1977.

Carby, Hazel V. " 'Hear My Voice, Ye Careless Daughters': Narratives of Slave and Free Women before Emancipation." In Andrews, *African American Autobiography,* 59–76.

Carretta, Vincent. Introduction and notes to *The Interesting Narrative and Other Writings* by Olaudah Equiano. New York: Penguin, 1995.

————, ed. *Unchained Voices: An Anthology of Black Authors in the English-Speaking World of the Eighteenth Century.* Lexington: University Press of Kentucky, 1996.

Chernow, Barbara A. and George A. Vallassi. *The Columbia Encyclopedia.* 5th ed., New York: Columbia University Press, 1993.

Child, Lydia Marie. "Leaves from a Slave's Journal of Life." *National Anti-Slavery Standard,* Oct. 20, 27, 1842. In Blassingame, *Slave Testimony,* 151–164.

Costanzo, Angelo. *Surprizing Narrative: Olaudah Equiano and the Beginnings of Black Autobiography.* Westport, CT: Greenwood Press, 1987.

Davis, Arthur P. "Hammon, Briton." In Logan and Winston, *Dictionary,* 281.

Davis, Charles T., and Henry Louis Gates, Jr., eds. *The Slave's Narrative.* New York: Oxford University Press, 1985.

Davis, David Brion. "A Big Business." *New York Review of Books* 45, no. 10 (June 11, 1998), 50–53.

Douglass, Frederick. *Autobiographies.* New York: The Library of America, 1994.

————. *My Bondage and My Freedom.* New York and Auburn: Miller, Orton & Mulligan, 1855.

Doyle, Mary Ellen. "The Slave Narratives as Rhetorical Art." In Sekora and Turner, *Art of Slave Narrative,* 83–95.

Drewry, William Sidney. *The Southampton Insurrection.* Washington: The Neale Company, 1900.

Dziwas, Doris. "Hammon, Briton." In Salzman et al., *Encyclopedia,* 1178–1179.

Eakin, Sue, and Joseph Logsdon. Introduction and notes to *Twelve Years a Slave,* by Solomon Northup. Reprint, Baton Rouge: Louisiana State University Press, 1968.

Eaklor, Vicki L. *American Antislavery Songs: A Collection and Analysis.* Westport, CT: Greenwood Press, 1988.

Edwards, Paul. Introduction to *The Life of Olaudah Equiano.* Reprint, London: Dawsons of Pall Mall, 1969.

————. "Three West African Writers of the 1780s." In Davis and Gates, *Slave's Narrative,* 175–198.

Fabricant, Daniel S. "Thomas R. Gray and William Styron: Finally, a Critical Look at the 1831 *Confessions of Nat Turner." The American Journal of Legal History* 37, no. 3 (July 1993), 332–361.

Farrison, William Edward. *William Wells Brown: Author & Reformer.* Chicago: University of Chicago Press, 1969.

Finkenbine, Roy E. "Christiana Revolt of 1851." In Salzman et al., *Encyclopedia,* 541.

Fisher[, Isaac]. *Slavery in the United States: A Narrative of the Life and Adventures of Charles Ball, a Black Man.* [2d ed.] New York: John S. Taylor, 1837. Reprint: New York: New American Library, 1969.

*Five Black Lives.* Middletown, CT: Wesleyan University Press, 1971.

Foner, Philip S. *The Life and Writings of Frederick Douglass.* New York: International Publishers, 1950–75.

Foster, Frances Smith. *Witnessing Slavery: The Development of Ante-Bellum Slave Narratives.* 2d ed. Madison: University of Wisconsin Press, 1994.

Franklin, John Hope, and Alfred A. Moss, Jr. *From Slavery to Freedom: A History of African Americans.* 7th ed. New York: Alfred A. Knopf, 1994.

Freedman, Florence B. Introduction to *Running a Thousand Miles for Freedom,* by William and Ellen Craft. Reprint, New York: Arno Press and The New York Times, 1969.

Galbreath, Charles B. *History of Ohio.* Chicago: American Historical Society, 1925.

Gara, Larry. "Craft, Ellen." In Logan and Winston, *Dictionary,* 139–140.

Garfield, Deborah M., and Rafia Zafar, eds. *Harriet Jacobs and* Incidents in the Life of a Slave Girl. Cambridge: Cambridge University Press, 1996.

*Garland of Freedom, The: A Collection of Poems, Chiefly Anti-Slavery.* London: W. and F. G. Cash & William Tweedie, 1853.

Gates, Henry Louis, Jr. "From Wheatley to Douglass: The Politics of Displacement." In Sundquist, *Frederick Douglass,* 47–65.

————. "James Gronniosaw and the Trope of the Talking Book." In Andrews, *African American Autobiography,* 8–25.

————, ed. *The Classic Slave Narratives.* New York: Mentor, 1987.

Goldsby, Jacqueline. "'I Disguised My Hand': Writing Versions of the Truth in Harriet Jacobs's *Incidents in the Life of a Slave Girl* and John Jacobs's 'A True Tale of Slavery.'" In Garfield and Zafar, *Harriet Jacobs*, 11–43.

Grandy, Moses. *Narrative of the Life of Moses Grandy, Late a Slave in the United States of America.* Boston: Oliver Johnson, 1844. 2d ed. reprinted in Katz, *Five Slave Narratives.*

Greenberg, Kenneth S., ed. *The Confessions of Nat Turner and Related Documents.* Boston: Bedford Books, 1996.

Grimes, William. *Life of William Grimes, the Runaway Slave, Brought Down to the Present Time.* [2d ed.] New Haven: the Author, 1855. Reprinted in *Five Black Lives*, 59–128.

Gross, Seymour L., and Eileen Bender. "History, Politics and Literature: The Myth of Nat Turner." *American Quarterly* 23, no. 4 (October 1971), 487–518.

Hammon, Briton. *A Narrative of the Uncommon Sufferings, and Surprising Deliverance of Briton Hammon, A Negro Man,—Servant to General Winslow, of Marshfield, in New England.* Boston: Green & Russell, 1760. Reprinted in Porter, *Early Negro Writing*, 522–528.

Hensel, W. U. *The Christiana Riot and the Treason Trials of 1851: An Historical Sketch.* Lancaster, PA: New Era, 1911.

Henson, Josiah. *An Autobiography of the Reverend Josiah Henson.* Reprint, Reading, MA: Addison-Wesley, 1969.

Higginson, Thomas Wentworth. *Black Rebellion.* Reprint, New York: Da Capo Press, 1998.

Hurd, John Codman. *The Law of Freedom and Bondage in the United States.* Boston: Little, Brown, 1862.

Jackson, Blyden. *A History of Afro-American Literature, Volume I: The Long Beginning, 1746–1895.* Baton Rouge: Louisiana State University Press, 1989.

Jefferson, Paul, ed. *The Travels of William Wells Brown.* New York: Markus Wiener, 1991.

Johnson, Charles, Patricia Smith, and the WGBH Series Research Team. *Africans in America: America's Journey Through Slavery.* New York: Harcourt Brace, 1998.

Jones, Thomas H. *The Experiences of Thomas H. Jones, Who Was a Slave for Forty-Three Years.* Boston: Daniel Lang, Jr., 1849.

Katz, Jonathan. *Resistance at Christiana: The Fugitive Slave Rebellion, Christiana, Pennsylvania, September 11, 1851; A Documentary Account.* New York: Thomas Y. Crowell, 1974.

Katz, William Loren, ed. *Flight from the Devil: Six Slave Narratives.* Lawrenceville, NJ: Red Sea Press, 1996.

Kolchin, Peter. *American Slavery 1619–1877.* New York: Hill and Wang, 1993.

"Life and Adventures of a Fugitive Slave, The." *Quarterly Anti-Slavery Magazine* 1, no. 4 (1836), 375–393. Excerpted in Davis and Gates, *Slave's Narrative*, 6–8.

"Life and Bondage of Frederick Douglass, The." *Putnam's Monthly Magazine* 6 (Nov. 1855), 547. Reprinted in Davis and Gates, *Slave's Narrative*, 30–31.

"Linda: Incidents in the Life of a Slave Girl: Written by Herself." *The Anti-Slavery Advocate* 53, vol. 2 (May 1, 1861), 1. Reprinted in Davis and Gates, *Slave's Narrative*, 32–34.

Logan, Rayford W. "Henson, Josiah." In Logan and Winston, *Dictionary*, 307–308.

Logan, Rayford W., and Michael R. Winston. *Dictionary of American Negro Biography*. New York: Norton, 1982.

Loggins, Vernon. *The Negro Author: His Development in America*. New York: Columbia University Press, 1931.

Logsdon, Joseph. "Northup, Solomon." In Logan and Winston, *Dictionary*, 473–474.

Low, W. Augustus, and Virgil A. Clift. *Encyclopedia of Black America*. New York: McGraw-Hill, 1981. Reprint, New York: Da Capo Press, 1984.

MacKethan, Lucinda H. "Metaphors of Mastery in the Slave Narratives." In Sekora and Turner, *Art of Slave Narrative*, 55–69.

Mars, James. *Life of James Mars, a Slave Born and Sold in Connecticut*. [1870 ed.] Reprinted in *Five Black Lives*, 35–58.

Mason, Theodore O., Jr. "Signifying." In Andrews et al., *Oxford Companion*, 665–666.

Merrill, Walter M., and Louis Ruchames, eds. *The Letters of William Lloyd Garrison*. Cambridge, MA: Harvard University Press, 1971–81.

Miller, James A. "Connecticut." In Salzman et al., *Encyclopedia*, 642–644.

Nash, Roderick W. "William Parker and the Christiana Riot." *Journal of Negro History* 96, no. 1 (1961): 24–31.

Nelson, John Herbert. *The Negro Character in American Literature*. Lawrence, KS: Department of Journalism Press, 1926.

Nichols, Charles H., Jr. "The Case of William Grimes, the Runaway Slave." *William and Mary Quarterly* 8, no. 4 (Oct. 1951), 552–560.

———. *Many Thousand Gone: The Ex-Slaves' Account of Their Bondage and Freedom*. Leiden: E. J. Brill, 1963.

Niemtzow, Annette. "The Problematic of Self in Autobiography: The Example of the Slave Narrative." In Sekora and Turner, *Art of Slave Narrative*, 96–109.

Oates, Stephen B. *The Fires of Jubilee: Nat Turner's Fierce Rebellion*. New York: Harper & Row, 1975. Reprint, New York: HarperPerennial, 1990.

Olmsted, Frederick Law. *A Journey in the Seaboard Slave States in the Years 1853–1854, with Remarks on Their Economy*. Reprint, New York: Putnam's, 1904.

Olney, James. "'I Was Born': Slave Narratives, Their Status as Autobiography and as Literature." In Davis and Gates, *Slave's Narrative*, 148–175.

Parker, William. "The Freedman's Story." *The Atlantic Monthly* 17, no. 100 (Feb. 1866): 152–166; no. 101 (March 1866): 276–295.

Parramore, Thomas C. *Southampton County, Virginia*. Charlottesville: University Press of Virginia, 1978.

Peabody, Ephraim. "Narratives of Fugitive Slaves." *Christian Examiner* 47, no. 1 (July–September, 1849), 61–93. Reprint: in Davis and Gates, *Slave's Narrative*, 19–28.

Porter, Dorothy, ed. *Early Negro Writing, 1750–1837*. Reprint, Baltimore: Black Classic Press, 1995.

Potkay, Adam, and Sandra Burr, eds. *Black Atlantic Writers of the Eighteenth Century: Living the New Exodus in England and the Americas*. New York: St. Martin's Press, 1995.

Quarles, Benjamin. *Black Abolitionists*. Reprint, New York: Da Capo Press, 1991.

———. Introduction to *Narrative of the Life of Frederick Douglass, an American Slave*. Cambridge: Belknap Press, 1960.

Redding, J. Saunders. *To Make a Poet Black*. Chapel Hill: University of North Carolina Press, 1939. Reprint, Ithaca: Cornell University Press, 1988.

Ripley, C. Peter, et al. *The Black Abolitionist Papers*. Chapel Hill: The University of North Carolina Press, 1985.

Ripley, Peter. "The Autobiographical Writings of Frederick Douglass." Excerpted in Andrews and McFeely, *Narrative*, 135–146.

Roper, Moses. "Moses Roper to the Committee of the British and Foreign Anti-Slavery Society." In Ripley, *Black Abolitionist Papers,* I:134–137.

———. "Moses Roper to Thomas Price." In Blassingame, *Slave Testimony*, 23–26.

———. *A Narrative of the Adventures and Escape of Moses Roper, from American Slavery*. 2d British ed. London: Darton, Harvey and Darton, 1838. Reprint, New York: Negro Universities Press, 1970.

Salzman, Jack, David Lionel Smith, and Cornel West. *Encyclopedia of African-American Culture and History*. New York: Macmillan, 1996.

Sartwell, Crispin. *Act Like You Know: African-American Autobiography and White Identity*. Chicago: University of Chicago Press, 1998.

Seager, Robert, II. *and Tyler too: A Biography of John & Julia Gardiner Tyler*. New York: McGraw-Hill, 1963.

Sekora, John, and Darwin T. Turner. *The Art of Slave Narrative: Original Essays in Criticism and Theory*. Macomb: Western Illinois University, 1982.

Slaughter, Thomas P. *Bloody Dawn: The Christiana Riot and Racial Violence in the Antebellum North*. New York: Oxford University Press, 1991.

Smith, Sidonie. *Where I'm Bound: Patterns of Slavery and Freedom in Black American Autobiography*. Westport, CT: Greenwood, 1974.

Starling, Marion Wilson. *The Slave Narrative: Its Place in American History*. Boston: G. K. Hall and Co., 1981.

Stearns, Charles. *Narrative of Henry Box Brown, Who Escaped from Slavery Enclosed in a Box 3 Feet Long and 2 Wide*. Boston: Brown and Stearns, 1849.

Stepto, Robert Burns. "I Rose and Found My Voice: Narration, Authentication, and Authorial Control in Four Slave Narratives." In Davis and Gates, *Slave's Narrative*, 225–241.

Stowe, Harriet Beecher. *A Key to Uncle Tom's Cabin, Presenting the Original Facts and Documents upon Which the Story Is Founded, Together with Corroborative Statements Verifying the Truth of the Work*. Boston: John P. Jewett & Co., 1853.

Stroud, George M. *A Sketch of the Laws Relating to Slavery in the Several States of the United States of America*. 2d ed. Philadelphia: the author, 1856.

Sundquist, Eric J. *To Wake the Nations: Race in the Making of American Literature*. Cambridge, MA: Harvard University Press, 1993.

———, ed. *Frederick Douglass: New Literary and Historical Essays*. Cambridge: Cambridge University Press, 1990.

Titus, Mary. "'This Poisonous System': Social Ills, Bodily Ills, and *Incidents in the Life of a Slave Girl*." In Garfield and Zafar, *Harriet Jacobs*, 199–215.

Tragle, Henry Irving. *The Southampton Slave Revolt of 1831: A Compilation of Source Material*. Reprint, New York: Vintage Books, 1973.

Volk, Betty. "Clarke, Lewis G." In Logan and Winston, *Dictionary*, 116–117.

Weiss, John McNish. *Free Black American Settlers in Trinidad 1815–16*. London: McNish & Weiss, 1995.

Williams, Kenny J. *They Also Spoke: An Essay on Negro Literature in America, 1787–1930.* Nashville: Townsend Press, 1970.

Winks, Robin W. "The Making of a Fugitive Slave Narrative: Josiah Henson and Uncle Tom—A Case Study." In Davis and Gates, *Slave's Narrative,* 112–146.

Wood, Peter H. "Nat Turner's Rebellion." In Salzman et al., *Encyclopedia,* 1970–1971.

Yellin, Jean Fagan. Introduction and notes in *Incidents in the Life of a Slave Girl* by Harriet A. Jacobs. Cambridge, MA: Harvard University Press, 1987.

———. "Jacobs, Harriet A." In Andrews et al., *Oxford Companion,* 394.

———. "Through Her Brother's Eyes: *Incidents* and 'A True Tale.'" In Garfield and Zafar, *Harriet Jacobs,* 44–56.

**The Library of Black America** publishes authoritative editions of important African American writing, much of it otherwise unavailable, ranging from the earliest slave narratives to the present day. Each volume includes a selection of works either by a single author or in a single genre and is introduced by an important black writer. The series makes accessible to all readers the impressive body of inventive, lucid, thoughtful, and passionate work that is the black contribution to American literature.

FORTHCOMING TITLES:

## FREDERICK DOUGLASS
*Selected Speeches and Writings*
Edited by Philip S. Foner
Abridged and with new material selected by Yuval Taylor
Foreword by Henry Louis Gates, Jr.

cloth: 1-55652-349-1
paper: 1-55652-352-1
July 1999

## THE FICTION OF LEROI JONES/ AMIRI BARAKA

cloth: 1-55652-346-7
paper: 1-55652-353-X
September 1999